ISC Exams 2026

AF819940

All in One®

Biology

Class 11

- Simplified Theory
- Topic & Chapter Exercises
- Exam Pattern Questions
- Sample Question Papers

ISC Exams 2026

All in One®

Biology

Class 11

- Simplified Theory
- Topic & Chapter Exercises
- Exam Pattern Questions
- Sample Question Papers

Authors
Kavita Thareja,
Dushyant Prajapati

arihant
SUCCESS AND NOTHING LESS

ARIHANT PRAKASHAN
(School Division Series)

ADMINISTRATIVE & PRODUCTION OFFICES
Regd. Office
'Ramchhaya' 4577/15, Agarwal Road, Darya Ganj, New Delhi -110002
Tele: 011- 47630600, 43518550; Fax: 011- 23280316
Head Office
Kalindi, TP Nagar, Meerut (UP) - 250002, Tel: 0121-7156203, 7156204

SALES & SUPPORT OFFICES
Agra, Ahmedabad, Bengaluru, Bareilly, Chennai, Delhi, Guwahati, Hyderabad, Jaipur, Jhansi, Kolkata, Lucknow, Nagpur & Pune.

PO No : TXT-XX-XXXXXXX-X-XX

Published By Arihant Publications (India) Ltd.

For further information about the books published by Arihant, log on to www.arihantbooks.com or e-mail at info@arihantbooks.com
Follow us on

PRICE ₹ 550.00

PRODUCTION TEAM

Publishing Managers	Cover Designer	Inner Designer
Mahendra Singh Rawat & Keshav Mohan	Salman Shaikh	Ankit Tyagi
Project Head	*Page Layouting*	*Proof Reader*
Yojna Sharma	Subhash Chaprana	Mansi Tomar, Ishan Khan

Index *cum* Study Planner

One Book- Endless Features

to Help you Succeed

In this Chapter

At the start of each chapter, all the topics of the chapter have been listed, so that students may know what they are going to study.

CHAPTER 02

Biological Classification, Monera and Viruses

Biological classification is the scientific procedure of arranging organisms in a hierarchical series of groups and sub-groups on the basis of their similarities and dissimilarities.

- Kingdom Classification System
- Types of Classification System
- Two Kingdom Classification System

TOPIC 01 **Kingdom Classification System**

There have been many attempts to classify living organisms since ancient times. **Aristotle** was the earliest to attempt a scientific basis of classification. He used simple morphological characters to classify plants as **trees, shrubs** and **herbs**. He also classified animals into two groups, i.e. **Enaima** (with red blood) and **Anaima** (without red blood). A need for proper system of classification was always felt.

Living organisms need to be classified because of the following reasons

(i) The study of one or two organisms is not sufficient to know the essential features of the group.

(ii) Classification helps in knowing the relationship amongst different groups of organisms.

(iii) It helps in studying of the evolutionary relationship between organisms.

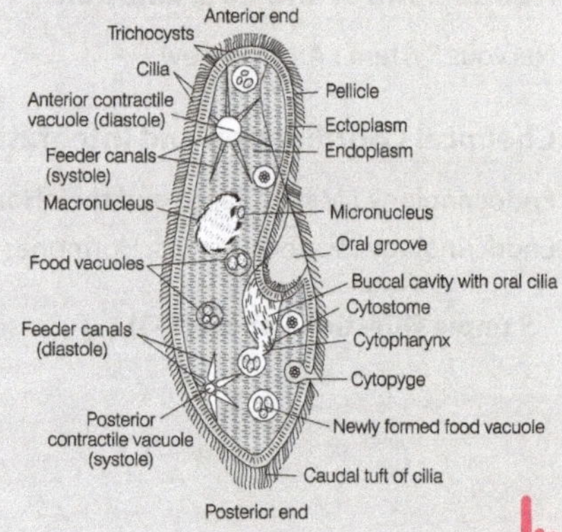

Complete Theory

To make the students understand the chapter completely, each chapter has been divided into Individual Topics and each such topic has been treated as a separate chapter. Each topic has detailed theory, supported by examples, well labelled diagrams, tables etc.

Illustrative Figures

To make the concepts completely visible, illustrative diagrams have been given at various place.

Topic Practice 1

Multiple Choice Questions

(1 Mark)

1. Aristotle classified the plants on the basis of their morphological characters and categorised them into
   (a) trees, shrubs and herbs
   (b) algae, bryophytes, pteridophytes, gymnosperms and angiosperms
   (c) embryophytes and tracheophytes
   (d) algae and embryophytes

Ans (a) Trees, shrubs and herbs. Aristotle divided plants into three groups those which have small soft and green stem called herbs, those which have comparably larger and stronger stem called shurbs and, those with huge woody and strong stem are called trees.

Topical Practices

To make students understand the chapter in a smooth part-by-part manner, Topical Exercises have been given in each chapter. These Exercises help students to assess the understanding of related concepts at regular interval.

One Book- Endless Features

to Help you Succeed

SUMMARY

- It is necessary to classify organisms to study them more easily.
- Aristotle was the earliest to attempt a more scientific basis for classification.
- Linnaeus (1758) proposed **two kingdom classification** on the basis of the presence or absence of cell wall.
- However, some organisms possessing characters of both plants and animals lead to **three kingdom classification** (Haeckel; 1866) organisms were classified into Plantae, Protista and Animalia on the basis of lack of tissue differentiation.
- Copeland (1956) proposed **four kingdom classification**. He divided living beings into four categories, namely–Monera, Protista, Plantae and Animalia.
- In 1969, RH Whittaker classified organisms into **five kingdom classification**. He classified them on the basis of complexity of cell structure and body structure, mode of nutrition, ecological life-style and phylogenetic relationships.
- **Kingdom–Monera** includes all prokaryotes, viz., mycoplasmas, bacteria, actinomycetes and cyanobacteria.
- All unicellular eukaryotic organisms like flagellates, diatoms, dinoflagellates, slime moulds, etc., were kept in the **kingdom–Protista**.
- **Kingdom–Fungi** contains achlorophyllous, thalloid plants. They are usually saprophytic, parasitic or occasionally symbiotic, e.g. *Penicillium notatum*, *Aspergillus niger*, yeast, etc.
- In the **kingdom–Plantae** all photoautotrophs were kept, e.g. mango, peepal, etc. However, it also includes thalloid algae.
- **Kingdom–Animalia** consists of heterotrophic holozoic organisms, e.g. tiger, cow, cat, etc.
- The most recent classification of living organisms is **six kingdom classification** proposed by Carl Woese, O Kandler and ML Wheelis (1990). These six kingdoms are Archaebacteria, Eubacteria, Protista, Fungi, Plantae and Animalia.
- **Kingdom–Monera** includes the smallest, simplest and most abundant microorganisms.
- Autotrophic bacteria are of two types on the basis of energy source, i.e. photoautotrophic and chemoautotrophic bacteria.
- Photoautotrophic bacteria contains chlorophyll-a, bacterio-purpurin and bacterio-viridin, which traps solar energy for food synthesis.
- Chemoautotrophic bacteria obtain energy from organic compounds made by other organisms. They oxidise substances like nitrates, nitrites and ammonia, e.g. *Nitrosomonas*, *Nitrobacter*.
- Heterotrophic bacteria (organotrophs) are dependent on external organic material for energy requirements, e.g. *Pseudomonas*, *E. coli*.
- Respiration in bacteria occur via aerobic and anaerobic modes.
- Reproduction in bacteria is asexual mainly.
- They rarely reproduce by sexual mode.
- **Asexual reproduction** takes place by two modes vegetative reproduction (fission and budding) and sporulation.
- **Sexual reproduction** takes place in form of genetic recombination where some genes are transferred from one bacterium to another. It is of three types
  - **Transformation** Genes transferred as naked DNA, does not involve contact between cells.
  - **Transduction** DNA transfer with the help of bacteriophage.
  - **Conjugation** Gene transfer involves cell to cell contact.
- **Mycoplasma** are the smallest free-living prokaryotes, lack cell wall, pleomorphic and can survive without oxygen.
- **Cyanobacteria** are Gram negative, photosynthetic prokaryotes, which are capable of fixing atmospheric nitrogen with the help of heterocyst.
- **Archaebacteria** differ from bacteria in terms of cell wall composition.
- Live in harsh habitats and categorised into
  - Methanogens (marsh areas)
  - Halophiles (salty areas)
  - Thermoacidophiles (hot springs)

Chaptera Summary

Summary of chapter given at the end helps to revise the chapter quickly at the time of examination or routine school tests.

Sample Question Papers

Chapterwise study is not the only feature of this book, after the Chapterwise Study it has a supplement of **3 Sample Question Papers.**

Chapter Practice

The students can check their understanding of the chapter through **Chapter Practice** given at the end of each chapter.

Chapter Practice

Multiple Choice Questions

(1 Mark)

1. The five kingdom classification was proposed by **NCERT Exemplar**
   (a) RH Whittaker (b) C Linnaeus
   (c) A Roxberg (d) Virchow
2. Organisms living in salty areas are called as **NCERT Exemplar**
   (a) methanogens (b) halophiles
   (c) heliophyles (d) thermoacidophiles

Reason (R) Two kingdom system of classification did not distinguish between the eukaryotes and prokaryotes, unicellular and multicellular organisms and green algae and fungi.

6. **Assertion** (A) Three domains system classifies organisms based on cellular characteristics.
   Reason (R) The three domains are, i.e. Archaea, Bacteria and Eukarya.
7. Observe the diagram of *Nostoc* and comment upon the appropriateness of the Assertion and the Reason.

SAMPLE QUESTION PAPER 1

A Highly Simulated Sample Question Paper for ISC Class XI

BIOLOGY (Unsolved)

Time : 3 hours Max. Marks : 70

GENERAL INSTRUCTIONS

1. This paper is divided into four sections-A, B, C and D. Answer all questions.
2. **Section-A** consists of one question having sub-parts of one mark/two marks each.
3. **Section-B** consists of seven questions of two marks each.
4. **Section-C** consists of seven questions of three marks each.
5. **Section-D** consists of three questions of five marks each.
6. Internal choices have been provided in one question each in Section-B, Section-C and Section-D.
7. The intended marks for questions or parts of questions are given in brackets[].

Section-A (20 Marks)

1. Answer the following questions briefly and to the point.
   (i) Give example of protistan having flagellar locomotion. • *Recall* [1]
   (ii) Name the point where two sister chromatids are held together. • *Recall* [1]
   (iii) In eukaryotes, where does TCA and ETS takes place? • *Recall* [1]
   (iv) The lawn grass needs to be mowed frequently to prevent its overgrowth. Which tissue is responsible for its rapid growth? • *Understanding* [1]
   (v) What does the symbols ⊕ and % indicate? • *Recall* [1]
   (vi) Define vital capacity. • *Recall* [1]
   (vii) Observe the diagram given below carefully and state one of its characteristic features. • *Analysis & Recall* [1]

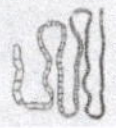

   (viii) Observe the relation between first two words and then fill the fourth word.
   Bolting: Gibberellins:: Stomata closure: .... • *Analysis* [1]
   (ix) The pyrimidines of DNA are represented by • *Recall* [1]
   (a) adenine and guanine
   (b) uracil and guanine
   (c) cytosine and adenine
   (d) thymine and cytosine
   (x) The hormone that initiate flowering and synchronism fruit set in pineapple. • *Recall* [1]
   (a) Cytokinin (b) Ethylene
   (c) ABA (d) Gibberellins
   (xi) **Assertion** (A) PS-I and PS-II names are given on the basis of activity in the photosynthesis.
   Reason (R) During non-cyclic photophosphorylation, PS-II works first and then PS-I. • *Analysis* [1]

Latest Course Structure

There will be two papers in the subject.

Paper I: Theory: 3 hours ...70 marks

Paper II: Practical: 3 hours ... 15 marks, Project Work ... 10 marks, Practical File ... 5 marks

PAPER 1 THEORY 70 Marks

S. No	Units	Total Weightage
1.	Diversity of Living Organisms	09 Marks
2.	Structural Organisation in Animals and Plants	11 Marks
3.	Cell: Structure and Function	15 Marks
4.	Plant Physiology	17 Marks
5.	Human Physiology	18 Marks
	Total	**70 Marks**

Note: All structures (internal and external) are required to be taught along with diagrams.

Diversity of Living Organisms

(i) The Living World

Need for classification; three domains of life; taxonomy and systematics; concept of species and taxonomical hierarchy; binomial nomenclature.

Need for classification should be discussed. Three domains of life – distinguishing features of (archaea, bacteria, eukarya), Definition and explanation of the terms taxonomy (numerical taxonomy, cytotaxonomy and chemotaxonomy) and systematics. Concept of species. Major taxonomical hierarchies (phylum, class, order, family, genus, species): definition and examples with reference to classification of man, housefly, mango and wheat.

Rules of binomial nomenclature and advantages of using scientific names.

Three systems of classification – artificial, natural and phylogenetic.

(ii) Biological Classification

Three domains of life; Five kingdom classification; salient features and classification of Monera, Protista, Fungi, Plantae and Animalia. Lichens, Viruses and Viroids.

(a) Three domains of life-distinguishing features of (Archae, bacteria, eukarya.) Five-kingdom system of classification and characteristics of different kingdoms with examples.

(b) Kingdom Monera: Bacteria-General structure of a typical bacterial cell; classification of bacteria according to shape, nutrition and mode of respiration; differences between gram +ve and gram –ve bacteria. Types of reproduction – definition of fission, conjugation, transduction and transformation (details not required).

A brief idea of the role of different types of archaebacteria (methanogens, halophiles and thermoacidophiles in their extreme environments). *Mycoplasma* – three distinctive features.

Economic importance with reference to role of bacteria in sewage treatment, antibiotics, energy production and household products (curd and cheese only).

(c) Kingdom Protista – only two general characteristics and two examples of subgroups:

(i) Chrysophytes (ii) Dinoflagellates,

(iii) Euglenoids, (iv) Slime moulds, (v) Protozoans (to be studied under rhizopods, flagellates, ciliates and sporozoans with two characteristics including modes of locomotion and two examples of each).

(d) Kingdom Fungi: general characteristics and mode of reproduction of each (including types of spores and sexual reproduction – definition of isogamy, anisogamy, oogamy, plasmogamy, karyogamy and dikaryophase). Zygomycetes, Ascomycetes, Basidiomycetes, Deuteromycetes - characteristics with examples. Role of fungi in the field of medicine, bakery and environmental decomposition. Definition of lichens and mycorrhiza (ecto and endo).

Life cycles not required.

(e) Virus (characteristic features – link between living and non-living, structure of TMV and bacteriophage and contribution of the following scientists: D.J. Ivanowsky, M.W. Beijerinck, W.M. Stanley) and Viroid (definition only).

(iii) Plant Kingdom

(a) Algae - characteristics (morphology, common name, major pigments, stored food, composition of cell wall, flagellar number and position of insertion, habitat, mode of sexual reproduction and examples of Chlorophyceae, Phaeophyceae, Rhodophyceae; Economic importance of algae –any five.

(b) Bryophyta – general characteristics, distinctive features of liverworts and mosses; graphic outline of life cycle of *Funaria* with reference to alternation of generations. Economic importance of bryophytes.

(c) Pteridophyta- characteristics; classification into classes: Psilopsida (*Psilotum*), Lycopsida (*Selaginella, Lycopodium*), Sphenopsida (*Equisetum*) and Pteropsida (*Dryopteris, Pteris* and *Adiantum*). Graphic outline of life cycle of a typical pteridophyte (fern). Definition of homospory and heterospory with relevant examples. Economic importance.

(d) Gymnosperms- general characteristics and graphic outline of life cycle of a typical gymnosperm (*Pinus*). Economic importance.

(iv) Animal Kingdom

Animal Kingdom: Levels of organisation (Cellular level, tissue level, organ level, organ system level); body plan (cell aggregate plan, blind-sac plan and tube-within-tube plan), symmetry (spherical, radial and bilateral symmetry), (diploblastic and triploblastic organisation in animals, acoelomate, pseudocoelomate, coelomate and haemocoelomate), coelom development segmentation.

Non-chordata - five distinguishing characters with two examples of Porifera, Cnidaria, Ctenophora, Platyhelminthes, Nematoda (Aschelminthes), Annelida, Mollusca, Arthropoda, Echinodermata, Hemichordata.

Chordata – sub-classification of Chordata with reference to notochord - subphyla Urochordata, Cephalochordata. Vertebrata (Classes – Cyclostomata, Chondrichthyes, Osteichthyes, Amphibia, Reptilia, Aves and Mammalia– three distinguishing characters with two examples of each).

Structural Organisation in Animals and Plants

(i) Morphology of Flowering Plants

(a) Morphology and modifications of root, stem, leaf.

Types of roots (tap, fibrous, adventitious), regions, modifications of roots for storage (Tuberous, e.g. *Mirabilis* and sweet potato; fusiform - e.g. radish; conical - e.g. carrot; napiform - e.g. turnip), respiration (pneumatophores) and support (stilt and prop).

Stems – features (nodes, internodes, buds), modifications – underground (tuber, rhizome, corm), aerial (tendril, thorn, phylloclade, cladode) and sub-aerial (runner, sucker, stolon, offset).

Leaves - parts of a simple leaf, venation, types of leaves (simple and compound – pinnate and palmate), phyllotaxy – alternate, opposite, whorled (with an example of each). Modifications for mechanical support (tendril), protection (spine), storage (bulb), reproduction (*Bryophyllum*); insectivorous plants (pitcher plant, Venus-fly-trap).

(b) Morphology of flower, Structure of a typical flower, types of inflorescence (racemose and cymose).

Structure of a typical flower, bracteates/ebracteate, [symmetry (actinomorphic, zygomorphic), trimerous/tetramerous/pentamerous complete/ incomplete, non-essential whorls (calyx: gamosepalous, polysepalous, corolla: gamopetalous, polysepalous, perianth, aestivation : valvate, twisted, imbricate, vexillary), essential whorls (androecium: cohesion - syngenesious, synandrous, monadelphous, diadelphous, polyadelphous; adhesion – epipetalous, epiphyllous; number of lobes – monothecous, dithecous; Gynoecium: position of ovary – epigynous, hypogynous, perigynous, cohesion – apocarpous, syncarpous, number of locules – unilocular, bilocular, multilocular], Placentation-axile, marginal Parietal, free central, basal; types of inflorescence (racemose and cymose – definition and differences; subtypes not required).

(ii) Anatomy of Flowering Plants

Plant Tissues: types of plant tissues: Meristematic tissues: classification of meristematic tissue. Permanent Tissues: structure and function of simple tissues (parenchyma, collenchyma and sclerenchyma) and complex tissues (xylem and phloem), tissue system. Internal structure of root, stem and leaf.

Characteristics of meristematic tissue; classification of meristems based on origin and location; structure, function and location of permanent tissues; simple and complex tissues; epidermal, ground and vascular tissue systems.

Cellular diagrams of T.S. of roots and stem and V.S. of monocot and dicot leaves are required.

(iii) Structural Organisation in Animals: Frog

Morphology, anatomy and functions of different systems (digestive, circulatory, respiratory, nervous and reproductive) of frog a brief account only.

Cell: Structure and Function

(i) Cell - The Unit of Life

Cell theory and cell as the basic unit of life: Structure of prokaryotic and eukaryotic cells; Plant cell and animal cell; cell envelope; cell membrane, cell wall: cell organelles – ultrastructure and function; endomembrane system, mitochondria, ribosomes, plastids, microbodies; cytoskeleton, cilia, flagella, centrioles; nucleus.

Historical aspects, cell theory, size and shape of cells.

General structure of eukaryotic cell, ultrastructure and function of cell wall (including definition of plasmodesmata), cell membrane (description of fluid mosaic model; functions of the plasma membrane: active and passive transport, brief explanation of facilitated diffusion (uniport, symport and antiport) with one example). Mitochondria, nucleus (nuclear membrane, chromatin, nucleolus, structure and types of chromosomes on the basis of the position of centromere, satellite), types of plastids, endomembrane system (endoplasmic reticulum, Golgi complex, lysosomes and vacuoles), ribosomes, microbodies cytoskeleton (microfilaments, microtubules and intermediate filaments), cilia, flagella and centrioles; differences between prokaryotic cell and eukaryotic cell, plant cell and animal cell.

(ii) Biomolecules

Proteins, carbohydrates, lipids, enzymes, secondary metabolites.

Carbohydrates: general classification and functions of: monosaccharides (glucose, ribose and deoxyribose), disaccharides (maltose, lactose and sucrose), polysaccharides (glycogen, starch, cellulose, inulin, and chitin).

Proteins: amino acids – (structure: glycine, alanine, serine); amino acids as zwitter-ion; examples of acidic, basic, neutral, sulphur containing amino acids; essential and non-essential amino acids; levels of protein structure (primary, secondary, tertiary and quaternary); functions of proteins.

Lipids: classification, structure and functions of fats and oils.

Enzymes: general properties, nomenclature and classification of enzymes according to type of reactions, co-factors (prosthetic groups, coenzymes and metal ions. Factors affecting enzyme activity - temperature, pH, substrate concentration. Competitive inhibitors.

(iii) Cell Cycle and Cell Division

Cell cycle, mitosis, meiosis and their significance. Definition of c-value, different stage of cell cycle (G_o, G_1, S, G_2 and M). Different stages of mitosis and meiosis (prophase - I) with diagrams. Significance of mitosis and meiosis. Differences between mitosis and meiosis.

Plant Physiology

(i) Photosynthesis in Higher Plants

Photosynthesis as a mean of autotrophic nutrition; site of photosynthesis, pigments involved in photosynthesis (elementary idea); photochemical and biosynthetic phases of photosynthesis; cyclic and non-cyclic photophosphorylation; chemiosmotic hypothesis; photorespiration; C_3 and C_4 pathways; factors affecting photosynthesis.

Differences between absorption and action spectra.

Brief idea of photosynthetic pigments (difference between chlorophyll '*a*'and '*b*', carotenoids and xanthophyll), photochemical phase - pigment systems, cyclic and non-cyclic photophosphorylation, chemiosmotic hypothesis; biosynthetic phase - C_3 and C_4 cycles – graphic representation in correct sequence (carboxylation, glycolytic reversal and regeneration of pentose); Kranz anatomy, graphic representation of C_4 cycle (Hatch and Slack Pathway) Differences between C_3 and C_4 plants, C_3 and C_4 cycles, Photosystems– I and II, Photorespiration pathway in brief - explanation of how RuBP carboxylase acts as RuBP oxygenase. Kranz anatomy. Blackman's Law of limiting factors, factors affecting photosynthesis (Light, C_2 temperature water).

(ii) Respiration in Plants

Exchange of gases; cellular respiration - glycolysis, fermentation (anaerobic), TCA cycle and electron transport system (aerobic); energy relations - number of ATP molecules generated; amphibolic pathways; respiratory quotient.

Types of respiration; mechanism of respiration: glycolysis, Krebs' cycle, ETS (only flowchart). Oxidative phosphorylation – definition; Brief idea of fermentation and amphibolic pathway. Definition of respiratory quotient and RQ values of carbohydrates, proteins and fats.

(iii) Plant Growth and Development

Seed germination; phases of plant growth; Plant growth rate; differentiation, dedifferentiation and redifferentiation; sequence of developmental processes in a plant cell; growth regulators - auxin, gibberellin, cytokinin, ethylene, ABA.

Definition of hypogeal, epigeal and viviparous germination with two examples of each. A brief idea about differentiation, dedifferentiation and redifferentiation. Phases of growth in meristems, growth rate – definition; measurement of growth by direct method and use of auxanometer, factors affecting growth.

Discovery and physiological role of growth regulators in plants (such as auxins, gibberellins, cytokinins, ethylene and abscisic acid – four effects of each); application of growth regulators.

Human Physiology

(i) **Breathing and Exchange of Gases**

Respiratory organs in animals (recall only); Respiratory system in humans; mechanism of breathing - exchange of gases, transport of gases and regulation of breathing, respiratory volumes; disorders related to respiration.

Organs involved in respiration; mechanism of pulmonary gas exchange; breathing process should be explained showing the action of diaphragm and intercostal muscles, regulation of breathing; transport of oxygen in the blood, oxyhaemoglobin dissociation curve; transport of CO_2; chloride shift, pulmonary air volumes and lung capacities; disorders of respiratory system such as - asthma, emphysema, occupational respiratory disorders.

(ii) **Body Fluids and Circulation**

Composition of blood, blood groups, coagulation of blood; composition of lymph and its function; human circulatory system - structure of human heart and blood vessels; cardiac cycle, cardiac output, ECG; double circulation; regulation of cardiac activity; disorders of circulatory system.

Composition of blood plasma, functions of plasma proteins, blood corpuscles. Importance of ABO groups in blood transfusion, Rh factor and its importance in transfusion and pregnancy; clotting of blood to be taught briefly; lymphatic system – a brief idea of lymph (composition and function), lymphatic capillaries and lymph nodes; Difference between closed and open vascular system; external and internal structure of heart; working of the heart and blood flow through the heart during different phases should be described under the following headings - auricular systole, auricular diastole, ventricular systole, ventricular diastole and joint diastole; definition of stroke volume and cardiac output, regulation of heartbeat, ECG; arterial blood pressure (systolic and diastolic), double circulation. The internal structure of artery, vein and capillary. Disorders of the circulatory system such as hypertension, coronary artery disease, angina pectoris and heart failure.

(iii) **Excretory Products and their Elimination**

Modes of excretion - ammonotelism, ureotelism, uricotelism; human excretory system - structure and function; urine formation, osmoregulation; regulation of kidney function, renin - angiotensin, atrial natriuretic factor, ADH and diabetes insipidus; role of erythropoietin; role of other organs in excretion; disorders of the excretory system - uraemia, renal failure, renal calculi, nephritis; dialysis and artificial kidney transplant.

Define, differentiate and explain the terms ammonotelism, ureotelism and uricotelism; external and internal structure of the kidney (L.S.); structure of nephron; physiology of urine formation - ultrafiltration, selective reabsorption and active (tubular) secretion. Counter current system, regulation of urine formation (definition of micturition), renin-angiotensin system role of atrial natriuretic factor, ADH and erythropoietin.

Role of skin, liver and lungs in excretion. Homeostasis – definition. Disorders of the excretory system - uraemia, renal failure, renal calculi, nephritis.
Haemodialysis and artificial. Kidney transplant.

(iv) Locomotion and Movement

Types of movement - ciliary, flagellar, muscular; skeletal muscles - contractile proteins and muscle contraction; skeletal system and its functions; joints; disorders of muscular and skeletal system.
Locomotion: Basic aspects of human skeleton (number and names of the bones of axial and appendicular skeleton).
Functions of human skeleton; different types of joints - their location and function; general properties of muscles; structure of skeletal muscle - sliding filament theory of muscle contraction; chemical events during muscle contraction; definition of summation, tetanus, rigor mortis, differences between red and white muscles.

Disorders of muscular and skeletal system:
(i) Myasthenia gravis, (ii) Tetany, (iii Muscular dystrophy, (iv) Arthritis, (v) Osteoporosis, (vi) Gout.

(v) Neural Control and Coordination

Neuron and nerves; nervous system in humans - central nervous system; peripheral nervous system and visceral nervous system; generation and conduction of nerve impulse.
Types of neurons-(unipolar, biopolar pseudounipolar and multipolar), Structure and functions of various parts of the brain and spinal cord; conduction of nerve impulses through nerve fibre (non-myelinated and myelinated) and through synapse.

(vi) Chemical Coordination and Integration

Human endocrine system - hypothalamus, pituitary, pineal, thyroid, parathyroid, adrenal, GI tract, pancreas, gonads; mechanism of hormone action (elementary idea); role of hormones as messengers and regulators, hypo and hyperactivity and related disorders; dwarfism, acromegaly, cretinism, goitre, exophthalmic goitre, diabetes mellitus and diabetes insipidus, Grave's disease, Addison's disease.

Brief idea of location of endocrine glands; role of hypothalamus; hormones secreted by different lobes of pituitary and their functions; feedback control of tropic hormones to be discussed giving examples; hormones of pineal, thymus, thyroid, parathyroid, pancreas, adrenal glands, GI tract (gastrin, secretin, GIP, CCK-PZ) and gonads; mechanism of hormone action (through cAMP and steroid hormones only); effects of hyposecretion and hypersecretion of various hormones of the above mentioned glands.

Note: Diseases related to all the human physiological systems to be taught in brief.

CHAPTER

01

The Living World

Planet earth is a habitat of diverse forms of life. Millions of plants and animals have been identified, but a large number still remains unknown. In this chapter, various means and ways of scientific methods have been discussed which help in identifying and naming of newly discovered organisms.

- Living World : Diversity and Taxonomic Categories
  - Systematics
  - Binomial Nomenclature
  - Taxonomy
  - Taxonomic Categories

Living World : Diversity and Taxonomic Categories

The earth hosts a vast variety of living organisms. According to a survey, the number of species that are known and described range between 1.7-1.8 million. This number refers to the known biodiversity on the earth. Although the actual biodiversity present on earth is far more than this number.

The term **Biodiversity** or **Biological diversity** refers to the entire number and types of organisms present on the earth. The living world includes all the living organisms, such as microorganisms, plants, animals and humans.

Biodiversity is not limited to the existing life forms. As we continue to explore new areas and even old ones, new organisms are continuously being added. This huge available variety cannot be studied and identified without having a proper system of **classification** and **nomenclature.**

Need for Classification

Classification is necessary for organisms due to the following reasons

(i) Convenience of study
(ii) Knowledge of adaptations
(iii) Knowledge of sequence of evolution
(iv) Knowledge of phylogenetic relationships
(v) Discovery of new organisms

Systematics

The word 'Systematics' is derived from the Latin word *Systema*, which means systematic arrangement of organisms. Linnaeus used *Systema Naturae* as the title of his book.

He coined the term **Systematics** in 1751. Systematics is the branch of science that deals with unique properties of species and groups to recognise, describe, name and arrange the diverse organisms according to an organised plan. In 1961, **Simpson** defined systematics as the study of diversity of organisms and all their comparative and evolutionary relationships based on comparative anatomy, physiology, biochemistry and ecology. In 1940, J Huxley developed the concept of new systematics.

The word 'Systematics' and 'Taxonomy' are often used interchangeably by the biologists, but they have different aspects of study.

Identification

It aims at finding the correct name and appropriate position of an organism. The **morphological** and **anatomical characters are examined for proper identification.**

Classification

The huge number and variety of living organisms make it difficult to study them. Therefore, there arises a need to classify all the organisms into different categories according to their specific features. Thus, classification is the process by which things are grouped into different categories based on some easily observable characters. **Biological classification** is the scientific arrangement of organisms in a hierarchy of groups and sub-groups on the basis of similarities and differences in their traits.

Advantages of Classification

Advantages of classification are as follows

(i) It helps to identify and study an organism easily.

(ii) New organisms easily get correct place in their respective groups.

(iii) It makes study of fossils easy.

(iv) It also helps in building evolutionary pathways.

(v) It becomes easy to know the features of whole group by studying one or two organisms of the group.

Nomenclature

It is the system of naming living organisms in a way that a particular organism is known by the same name all over the world.

1. Common Names

The common names or vernacular names are the local names given to an organism in a specific language in a particular region. There are different names of the same organism in different regions even within a country.

Common Names of Some Organisms in Different Parts of India

Organisms	Common Names
Rose	Gulab (Hindi), Golap (Bangla), Rajapo (Tamil)
Dog	Kukur (Bangla), Kutta (Hindi), Kutto (Gujarati), Svan (Sanskrit), Nay (Tamil)
Cat	Billi (Hindi), Biladi (Gujarati), Marjara (Sanskrit), Poonai (Tamil)
Cotton	Kapas (Hindi), Hatti (Kannada), Kapus (Marathi), Paruthi (Tamil), Karpus (Bengali)
Ginger	Adrakh (Hindi), Shunti (Kannada), Ale (Marathi), Ada (Bengali)

Advantages of Common Name

(i) Common names are easy to pronounce and are short, e.g. cat or billi.

(ii) People are familiar to these names since childhood.

(iii) They are based on some features of organisms, e.g. cowa (crow–caawn-caawn sound).

Disadvantages of Common Name

(i) All the organisms cannot be named by this method as there are organisms of different sizes and shapes, some of which are not directly perceived by man and thus remain unnamed, e.g. microbes.

(ii) An organism may have several names in a given language, e.g. there are 8 Hindi names of prickly poppy and water lily has 15 English names.

(iii) One common name may have different meanings in different countries, e.g. maize, means wheat and other grains in USA and it is called corn in common wealth countries.

2. Scientific Names

A scientific name is given by biologists based on world wide acceptible principles or criteria. Each name represents a particular organism in all parts of the world. The nomenclature system globoly accepted for providing scientific names is the **binomial nomenclature.**

The scientific names must be

(i) acceptable in every part of the world.

(ii) assigned on agreed principles and criteria.

(iii) different for each species and not have been used for other organisms earlier.

Binomial Nomenclature

Binomial nomenclature was first developed by **Carolus Linnaeus** in 1751 (*Philosophia Botanica*). All scientific names for animals under binomial nomenclature were given by Linnaeus in the tenth edition of his book *Systema Naturae* (1758). Linnaeus named plants according to binomial nomenclature in his book *Species Plantarum* (1753).

Binomial nomenclature is the system of providing distinct and appropriate names to organisms, each consisting of two words, first **generic name** (i.e. name of genus) and second **specific epithet** (i.e. name of species).
e.g. scientific name of mango is written as *Mangifera indica*. In this name, *Mangifera* represents the genus and *indica* is a particular species or specific epithet.

Scientific Names (asper Binomial Nomenclature) of Some Common Plants and Animals

Common Names	Binomial Nomenclature
Plants	
Pea	*Pisum sativum*
Onion	*Allium cepa*
Mango	*Mangifera indica*
Wheat	*Triticum aestivum*
Banyan	*Ficus benghalensis*
Soybean	*Glycine max*
Animals	
Indian frog	*Rana tigrina*
Cat	*Felis catus*
Dog	*Canis familiaris*
Housefly	*Musca domestica*
Cobra	*Naja naja*
Common carp (fish)	*Cyprinus carpio*
Humans	*Homo sapiens*
Western honeybee	*Apis mellifera*
Horse	*Equus ferus caballus*

Rules of Binomial Nomenclature

Rules of binomial nomenclature were initially framed by **Linnaeus** in his books, *Species Plantarum* and *Systema Naturae.*

The rules were revised again by the following nomenclature codes

(i) International Code for Botanical Nomenclature.
(ii) International Code of Zoological Nomenclature.
(iii) International Code of Bacteriological Nomenclature.
(iv) International Code of Viral Nomenclature.
(v) International Code of Nomenclature for Cultivated Plants.

The rules framed by Linnaeus and by these codes for nomenclating organisms are as follows

(i) The names are generally in **Latin** and written in **Italics.** They are Latinised or derived from Latin irrespective of their origin.
(ii) The **first word** in a biological name represents the genus while, the **second component** denotes the specific epithet.
(iii) Both the words in a biological name, when handwritten, are separately **underlined** or printed in **Italics** to indicate their Latin origin.
(iv) The first word denoting the **genus** starts with a capital letter while, the **specific epithet** starts with a small letter, e.g. *Mangifera indica.*
(v) Name of the author appears after the specific epithet, i.e. at the end of the biological name and is written in an abbreviated form, e.g. *Mangifera indica* **Linn.** Linn is for Linnaeus.
(vi) When name of a species is transferred or revised, then the name of the original worker is retained, but in parentheses, e.g. *Syzygium cumini* (L) Skeels.
(vii) No names are recognised prior to those used by Linnaeus in 1753 for plants in *Species Plantarum* and in 1758 for animals in the 10th edition of *Systema Naturae.*
(viii) Generic and common names may be same, e.g. *Gorilla gorilla.*
(ix) The name of categories higher than the rank of genus are not printed in Italics. Bold letters can, however be used.

Advantages of Binomial Nomenclature

(i) There is a single specific name for every species.
(ii) All the organisms, irrespective of their utility, have been provided scientific names.
(iii) The scientific names are universally accepted and used, irrespective of the local language of the people or a region.
(iv) The 'species' part of the scientific name of an organism indicates its relationship and common characteristics with other organisms placed in the same genus.

(v) The scientific names are usually descriptive, indicating some important characteristics of the organism.
(vi) A newly discovered organism can easily be described and named using binomial nomenclature.
(vii) An incorrect name can easily be corrected.
(viii) The scientific names are usually derived from Latin or Greek languages, therefore, there is no possibility of any change in meaning of their words.

Taxonomy

It is the science of identification, classification and nomenclature. Based on their special characteristics, all living organisms can be classified into different categories. The scientific term for these categories is **taxa**. This process of classification is called **taxonomy**. **Carolus Linnaeus** is known as **Father of Taxonomy**.

The basis of **modern taxonomic** studies are external and internal structures (comparative morphology), along with the structure of cells (cytology), development process (embryology) and ecological information of organisms (ecology). It provides information according to similarities, dissimilarities and evolutionary relationships of various organisms. Bentham and Hooker were the first to propose a systematic classification of plant kingdom.

The concept of **classical** or **old taxonomy** exists, since the time of Aristotle and Theophrastus till the time of Linnaeus. On the other hand, the concept of **modern taxonomy** was given by **Julian Huxley** (1940).

The basic processes for taxonomic studies are

(i) Organisms are described on the basis of morphology and other characteristics.
(ii) The description of characteristics helps in the placement of the organisms in various taxa.
(iii) A new taxon can be framed if the organism is different from the existing taxa.
(iv) The correct naming of an organism can be done after placing it in appropriate taxon. A new organism can be given a new name after following the standardised rules.

Comparison between Taxonomy and Systematics

Taxonomy	Systematics
It is related to identification, nomenclature and classification.	It is the science of identification, nomenclature, description and classification.
Taxonomic studies are based on rules and principles of classification.	Systematics is related to unique properties at every level of classification.

Types of Taxonomy

For the suitability in studies various categorisations has been done in taxonomy. The important taxonomies are as follows

1. Numerical Taxonomy

It is carried out by quantitative assessment of similarities and differences in order to make objective assessments. It is now easily carried out using computers based process on all observable characteristics.

Number and codes are assigned to all the characters and the data are then processed. In this way, each character is given equal importance and at the same time hundreds of characters can be considered.

2. Cytotaxonomy

It is based on cytological information like chromosome number, structure, behaviour and type of chromosome. For example,

(i) Chromosome number is constant for a species, e.g. 46 in man, 48 in apes and potato, 20 in maize, 16 in onion and 8 in *Drosophila*.
(ii) Behaviour of chromosomes was used by taxonomists during pairing and banding patterns to understand the relationships between species, e.g. origin of humans from apes, origin of wheat, etc.

3. Chemotaxonomy

It is the system based on the evidences from chemical constituents (enzymes, hormones, proteins, amino acids, etc.), some specific chemicals (usually secondary metabolites) and the chemical nature of proteins have been utilised to establish similarities and relationships. For example, the presence of raphides has been found to the common in 35 families of plants.

Taxonomic Categories

Classification is not a single step process. It involves hierarchy of steps in which each step represents a **rank** or **category**. Since, the category is a part of overall taxonomic arrangement, it is called the **taxonomic category** and all categories together constitute the taxonomic hierarchy.

Taxon

Each unit of classification, in fact, represents a rank and is commonly termed as **taxon** (Pl. taxa). The term Taxon was first introduced by **ICBN** during 1956.

According to **Mayr** (1964), taxon is a group of any rank that is sufficiently distinct to be worthy of being assigned a definite category. In simple words, taxon refers to a group of similar, genetically related individuals having certain characters distinct from those of other groups.

Taxonomic Hierarchy

The taxonomic hierarchy is the system of arranging taxonomic categories in a descending order. It was first introduced by Linnaeus (1751) and hence it is also known as **Linnaean hierarchy**.

Groups represent **category** and category further denotes **rank**. Each rank or taxon represents a unit of classification. These taxonomic groups/categories are distinct biological entities and not merely morphological aggregates.

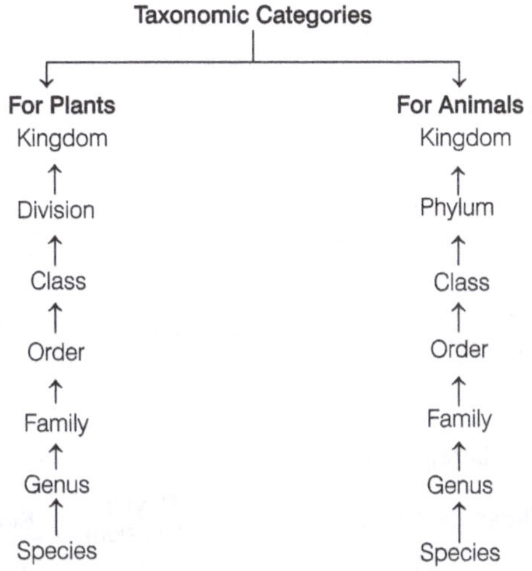

Fig 1.1 Taxonomic categories showing hierarchical arrangement in ascending order

Differences between Taxon and Category

Taxon	Category
A taxon deals with real biological objects.	A category is an abstract term that simply represents a rank or level in classification.
Taxon may belong to any ranking.	It belongs to one particular ranking.
e.g. the taxon of humans is mammalia.	e.g. the category of humans is class–Mammalia.

Obligate/Common Categories

The taxonomic categories which are always used in hierarchical classification of organisms are called **obligate** or **common categories**. They are seven in number. In descending order, these are– kingdom, phylum or division (for plants), class, order, family, genus and species.

All the members of taxonomic categories possess some similar characters, which are different from those of others. The maximum similarity occurs in species, which is also the **lowest category** in the hierarchy of categories. Similarity of characters decreases with the rise in hierarchy.

1. Species

Taxonomic studies consider a group of individual organisms with fundamental similarities as a species. Species is considered as the lowest or basic taxonomic category, which consists of one or more individuals of a population that resemble one another more closely than individuals of other species. The members of species interbreed freely and are reproductively isolated from others. e.g. *Mangifera indica* (mango), *Solanum tuberosum* (potato) and *Panthera leo* (lion). All the three names *indica*, *tuberosum* and *leo* represent the **specific epithets** while, the first words *Mangifera*, *Solanum* and *Panthera* are genera and represent another higher level of taxon or category. Each genus may have one or more than one specific epithets representing different organisms, but having morphological similarities. e.g. *Panthera* has another specific epithet called *tigris* and *Solanum* includes species like *nigrum* and *melongena*.

2. Genus

It comprises a group of related species, which have more characters in common in comparison to species of other genera. In other words, genera are aggregates of closely related species.

Some Genera and their Species

Genus	Species
Solanum	Potato (*Solanum tuberosum*) and Brinjal (*S. melongena*).
Panthera	Lion (*Panthera leo*), Leopard (*P. pardus*) and Tiger (*P. tigris*).
Felis	Common cat (*Felis catus*), Jungle cat (*F. chaus*) and Golden cat (*F. temminckii*).

3. Family

It is a group of related genera with less number of similarities as compared to genus and species. All the genera of a family have some common or correlated features. They are separable from genera of a related family by important differences in both vegetative and reproductive features.

Note A plant family ends in a suffix-aeae and sub-family has suffix-oideae. While, an animal family has a suffix -idae and sub-family-inae.

4. Order

An order is a group of one or more related families that possess some similar correlated characters, which are lesser in number as compared to a family or genera.

Plants and Animal Orders with their Respective Families

Order	Animals and Families
Carnivora	Canidae (dog, wolf and fox), Felidae (cat, leopard, tiger and lion), Ursidae (bear) and Hyaenidae (hyaena).
Polymoniales	Solanaceae (potato and tomato), Convolvucaceae (sweet potato and morning glory), Polymoniaceae (herbs, shrubs and small trees) and Hydrophyllaceae (water leaf).
Primates	Lemuridae (lemurs), Cebidae (new world monkeys), Pongidae (apes) and Hominidae (humans).

5. Class

It is a major category, which includes related orders, e.g. order–Primata comprises monkey, gorilla and gibbon and is placed in class–Mammalia along with order–Carnivora that includes animals like tiger, cat and dog.

6. Phylum or Division

Phylum or Division is a taxonomic category higher than class and lower in rank to kingdom. The term **phylum** is used for animals, while **division** is commonly used for plants. Both categories consist of more than one class having some similar correlated characters. e.g. phylum– Chordata of animals contains following classes– Pisces, Amphibia, Reptilia, Aves and Mammalia.

7. Kingdom

It is known to be the highest category in taxonomy. This includes all the organisms which share a set of distinguished characters, e.g. all the animals belonging to various phyla are assigned the highest category called **kingdom– Animalia.**

Similarly, all the plants are kept in **kingdom–Plantae.** RH Whittaker (1969) assigned five kingdom classification of organisms.

These are Monera, Protista, Fungi, Plantae and Animalia.

Taxonomic Categories Recognised by ICBN

Category	Standard Suffix	Category	Standard Suffix
Kingdom	-bionta	**Order**	-ales
		Suborder	-ineae
Phylum or **Division**	-phyta	Superfamily	-ariae
		Family	-aceae
Subphylum or subdivision	-phytina	subfamily	-oideae
		Tribe	-eae
Class	-opsida	Subtribe	-inae
Subclass	-idae	Genus	None
Superorder	-anae	Species	None

Some Organisms with their Taxonomic Categories

Common Name	Scientific Name	Species	Genus	Family	Order	Class	Phylum (Division)	Kingdom
Human	*Homo sapiens*	*sapiens*	*Homo*	Hominidae	Primata	Mammalia	Chordata	Animalia
Dog	*Canis familiaris*	*familiaris*	*Canis*	Canidae	Carnivora	Mammalia	Chordata	Animalia
Housefly	*Musca domestica*	*domestica*	*Musca*	Muscidae	Diptera	Insecta	Arthropoda	Animalia
Mango	*Mangifera indica*	*indica*	*Mangifera*	Anacardiaceae	Sapindales	Dicotyledonae	Angiospermae	Plantae
Tulsi	*Ocimum sanctum*	*sanctum*	*Ocimum*	Lamiaceae	Lamiales	Dicotyledonae	Angiospermae	Plantae
Wheat	*Triticum aestivum*	*aestivum*	*Triticum*	Poaceae	Poales	Monocotyledonae	Angiospermae	Plantae

Intermediate Categories

The taxonomic categories from species to kingdom are **broad categories** or **obligate categories.** However, taxonomists have also developed **sub-categories** in this hierarchy to facilitate more sound and scientific placement of various taxa.

These sub-categories are sub-species (or varieties), sub-genera, sub-families, sub-orders, sub-classes and sub-phyla. These sub-categories are referred to as **intermediate categories.**

Obligate Categories	Intermediate Categories
Kingdom	Subkingdom
Phylum or Division	Subphylum or Subdivision and superclass
Class	Infra class and subclass
Order	Superorder and suborder
Family	Subfamily and tribe
Genus	Subgenus
Species	Subspecies, variety or race

SUMMARY

- **Taxonomy** is the branch of science, that deals with principles and procedures of identification, nomenclature and classification of organisms.
- **Systematics** deals with identification, nomenclature, classification and evolutionary history of an organism.
- **Identification** is recognising and unknown specimen with already known taxon and giving a correct rank and position in an extant classification.
- **Nomenclature** deals with the determination of a scientific name of organisms using international code of nomenclature.
- **Binomial nomenclature** consists of two parts or epithets, i.e. generic epithet and specific epithet, e.g. *Homo sapiens*. First name, i.e. *Homo* is generic epithet and second name, i.e. *sapiens* is specific epithet.
- **Classification** is an arrangement of organisms into groups on the basis of similarities.
- Each category of taxonomic hierarchy referred to as unit of classification represents a rank and is commonly called taxon. The term 'Taxon' was first introduced by ICBN (1956).
- **Taxonomic hierarchy** is the sequence of taxonomic categories in an descending order of number of species as Kingdom → Phylum/Division → Class → Order → Family → Genus → Species

Chapter Practice

Multiple Choice Questions

1 Mark

1. The term systematics refers to
   (a) identification and classification of plants and animals
   (b) nomenclature and identification of plants and animals
   (c) diversity of kinds of organisms and their relationship
   (d) different kinds of organism and their classification **NCERT Exemplar**

Ans (c) Systematics refers to study of diversity of kinds of organisms and their relationship.

2. Standardising the naming of living organism is known as
   (a) classification (b) identification
   (c) nomenclature (d) Both (a) and (b)

Ans (c) Nomenclature is the process of standardising the name of living organisms so that a particular organism is known by same name all over the world.

3. In binomial nomenclature the name of author appears after the
   (a) genus (b) family
   (c) species (d) taxa

Ans (c) Name of the author appears after the specific epithet, i.e. at the end of the biological name and is written in an abbreviated form.

4. Scientific names are printed in ...... and are derived from...... .
   (a) Bold and English (b) Italics and Latin
   (c) Italics and German (d) Italics and French

Ans (b) Scientific names are printed in Italics and they are derived from Latin.

5. Ascending or descending arrangement of taxonomic categories is known as
   (a) classification (b) key
   (c) taxonomy (d) hierarchy

Ans (d) The arrangement of taxonomic categories is known as the taxonomical hierarchy, it could be in descending or in ascending order.

6. A 'taxa' differs from 'taxon' due to
   (a) being a higher taxonomic category than taxon
   (b) being a lower taxonomic category than taxon
   (c) being plural of taxon
   (d) being singular of taxon

Ans (c) Taxa is plural of taxon. A taxon represents a grouping in a systematic classification of organism (whatever its rank).

7. Which one is species?
   (a) *Cannis* (b) *Pisum*
   (c) *leo* (d) Carnivora

Ans (c) *Panthera leo* is the scientific name of lion. *Cannis* is a genus of cat. *Pisum* is the generic name of sweet pea, while Carnivora is order.

8. Genus represents
   (a) an individual plant or animal
   (b) a collection of plants or animals
   (c) a group of closely related species of plants or animals
   (d) None of the above **NCERT Exemplar**

Ans (c) Genus represents a group of closely related species of plants or animals.

9. In *Solanum tuberosum*, first and second words stand for, respectively
   (a) genus, generic name
   (b) specific epithet, species
   (c) specific name and generic name
   (d) generic name and specific name

Ans (d) In a scientific name, first name indicates the generic name of an organism, while second name stands for specific epithet or specific name.

10. Which one of the following features is shared by all living organisms at all hierarchical level?
    (a) Mode of nutrition
    (b) Cellular organisation
    (c) Nature of protoplasmic composition
    (d) Growth by cell division

Ans (c) Nature of protoplasmic composition is shared by all living organisms at all taxonomic categories. Mode of nutrition is an peculiar feature of five kingdom classification.

Assertion-Reason Type Questions

1 Mark

■ Direction (Q. Nos. 11-16) *In each of the following questions, a statement of Assertion (A) is given followed by corresponding statement of Reason (R). Of the statements, mark the correct answer as*

(a) If both A and R are true and R is the correct explanation of the A.
(b) If both A and R are true, but R is not the correct explanation of the A.
(c) If A is true, but R is false.
(d) If A is false, but R is true.

11. **Assertion** (A) Physical hierarchy includes organ system.

Reason (R) Biological hierarchy includes atoms, compounds and tissues.

Ans (d)

12. **Assertion** (A) Taxonomic studies require correct classification and identification of organisms.

Reason (R) Taxonomic studies are useful in knowing our bioresources and their diversity.

Ans (b)

13. **Assertion** (A) Linnaeus binomial system of animal classification is essentially an artificial system, yet it has become a natural system.

Reason (R) Similarities forming the basis of Linnaeus system are indicative of genetic relationship.

Ans (c)

14. **Assertion** (A) Species is a group of individuals with fundamental similarities.

Reason (R) *indica, leo, tuberosum* represent such group of individuals.

Ans (b)

15. **Assertion** (A) There are seven obligate categories in the hierarchy of taxonomy.

Reason (R) Other categories of similar type can be called as intermediate categories.

Ans (b)

16. Given below is the taxonomic category showing arrangement in descending order. Study this figure and comment upon the appropriateness of the Assertion and the Reason.

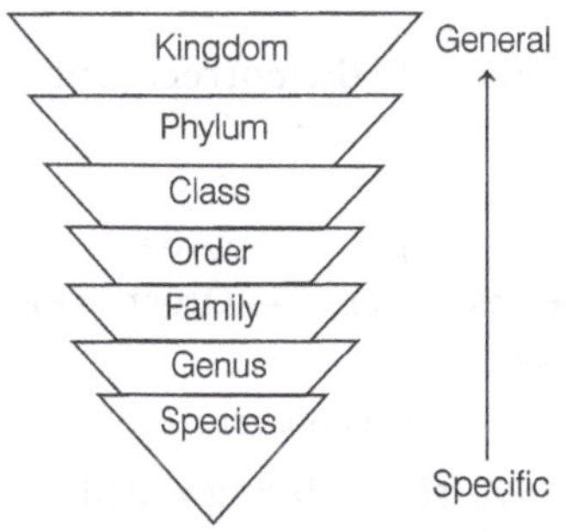

Assertion (A) As we go from species to kingdom in a taxonomic hierarchy, the number of common characteristic will decrease.

Reason (R) Any lower grade of classification (genus) has members with more similarities as compared to higher grade of classification (family).

Ans (a)

Very Short Answer Type Questions

1 Mark

17. In a given habitat we have 20 plant species and 20 animal species. Should we call it as 'diversity' or 'biodiversity'? Justify your answer.

NCERT Exemplar

Ans We should call it biodiversity or biological diversity as it shows diverse variety of living organisms.

18. Given below is the scientific name of mango. Identify the correctly written name.

(i) Mangifera Indica
(ii) *Mangifera indica* **NCERT**

Ans (ii) *Mangifera indica* (the name of species can never begin with a capital letter and scientific names are always printed in Italics).

19. The concept of new systematics was developed by which scientist?

Ans. Julian Huxley (1940).

20. Carolus Linnaeus is considered as father of taxonomy. Name two other botanists known for their contribution to the field of taxonomy.

NCERT Exemplar

Ans George Bentham and Joseph Dalton Hooker.

21. What does ICZN stand for? **NCERT Exemplar**

Ans ICZN stands for International Code of Zoological Nomenclature.

22. Can you identify the correct sequence of taxonomical categories?

(i) Species → Order → Phylum → Kingdom
(ii) Genus → Species → Order → Kingdom
(iii) Species → Genus → Order → Phylum **NCERT**

Ans The correct sequence is
(iii) Species → Genus→ Order → Phylum.

23. How is diversity in living world related to taxonomy?

Ans The spectrum of diversity in the living world can be known only through the study of taxonomy.

24. How correlated characters help in defining genus?

Ans Correlated characters are those common features, which are used in delimitation of a taxon above the rank of species.

Short Answer Type I Questions

(2 Marks)

25. Why are living organisms classified? **NCERT**

Ans Living organisms are classified because

(i) There are millions of organisms on the earth, which need a proper system of classification for their easy identification and methodical studies.
(ii) A number of new organisms are discovered each year. They require a particular system to be identified and to find out their correct position in a group. (2)

26. List out the scope of systematics. Whose publication is *Systema Naturae*?

Ans Scope of systematics are

(i) identification of organisms.
(ii) nomenclature of existing and new organisms.
(iii) classification of new organisms.
(iv) evolutionary relationships between different organisms. (1)

Systema Naturae is the publication of Linnaeus. (1)

27. Which are the basic processes in the taxonomy?

Ans The basic processes in taxonomy are

(i) characterisation(ii) identification
(iii) classification(iv) nomenclature ($\frac{1}{2}\times 4$)

28. Give the name of few nomenclature codes.

Ans Few nomenclature codes are

(i) International Code of Botanical Nomenclature (ICBN)
(ii) International Code of Zoological Nomenclature (ICZN)
(iii) International Code of Viral Nomenclature (ICVN)
(iv) International Code of Bacteriological Nomenclature (ICBN) ($\frac{1}{2}\times 4$)

29. How are living organisms divided into different taxa? What is the name given to this process?

Ans Living organisms can be divided into different taxa based on their characteristics. This process of classification is called taxonomy. (1+1)

30. International Code of Botanical Nomenclature (ICBN) has provided a code for classification of plants. Give hierarchy of units of classification botanists follow while classifying plants and mention different suffixes used for the unit. **NCERT Exemplar**

Ans Refer to table on page no. 5 (Taxonomic categories recognised by ICBN). (2)

31. What do we learn from identification of individual and populations? **NCERT**

Ans Identification of individuals and populations helps to categorise them into specific species. Each species has unique characteristic features. On the basis of these features, they can be distinguished from other closely related species, e.g.

Genus	Species	
Solanum	*tuberosum*	Both are two different species included in genus *Solanum*.
Solanum	*nigrum*	

(2)

32. Brinjal and potato belong to the same genus *Solanum*, but two different species. What defines them as separate species? **NCERT Exemplar**

Ans Brinjal and potato both belong to same genus as they share some common correlated characters.

They belong to different species because they have
(i) different morphological features.
(ii) reproductive isolation (inability to interbreed). (1+1)

33. Write examples of two species, each belonging to same genera.

Ans *Panthera leo* (lion), *P. pardus* (leopard). (1)
Solanum tuberosum (potato), *S. melanogena* (brinjal). (1)

34. A plant may have different names in different regions of the country or world. How do botanists solve this problem? **NCERT Exemplar**

Ans Botanists use binomial nomenclature to solve this problem. A scientific name is given to the plant based on certain principles and criteria. The scientific name of a particular plant is same all over the world and is not given to any other plant. (2)

35. All the organisms are not yet identified on the earth. Justify the statement.

Ans There are diverse habitats on earth hosting millions of living organisms. Due to limited number of taxonomists, absence of through survey of different areas and occurrence of several inaccessible regions, e.g. hot springs, underwater reefs, etc. it is difficult to identify all the organisms. (2)

36. **Why there is a need to standardise the system of naming of living organisms?**

Ans There are millions of living organisms in the world. Often, these organisms are known by their local names that vary from place to place, even within a country.

Hence, the naming process of living organism is standardised in a way that a particular organism is known by the same name all over the world in the scientific community. (2)

37. **On which criteria chemotaxonomy is based? Can it be used for classification?**

Ans Chemotaxonomy or Biochemical taxonomy is based on the protein and serum analysis and on the chemical constituents of the organsims.

This type of taxonomy is particularly utilised in the classification of plants, as chemical constituents of plant species are stable and do not change easily. (2)

38. **What makes species a basic taxonomic category?**

Ans Species is the lowest of a population or basic taxonomic category which consists of one or more individuals that resemble one another more closely than individuals of other species. The members of a species interbreed freely and are reproductively isolated from members of other species. These features make the species basic taxonomic category. (2)

39. **Differentiate between identification and classification.**

Ans Difference between identification and classification is

Identification	Classification
To identify an organism, its similarities and dissimilarities are compared with already known organism.	It is the method of arranging organisms into groups on the basis of their physical, cellular, morphological and other characteristics.

(2)

40. **Differentiate between cytotaxonomy and chemotaxonomy.**

Ans Differences between cytotaxonomy and chemotaxonomy are

Cytotaxonomy	Chemotaxonomy
It is based on cellular characteristics.	It is based on chemical constituents.
It is related to genetic similarities and changes.	It is related to expression of genetic similarities and changes.

(2)

Short Answer Type II Questions

(3 Marks)

41. **Why are classification systems changing every now and then?** **NCERT**

Ans Evolution is the major factor responsible for the change in classification systems. Since, evolution still continues, so many different species of plants and animals are added in the already existing biodiversity. These newly discovered plant and animal specimens are then identified classified and named according to the already existing classification systems.

Due to the evolution animal and plant species keep on changing, so necessary changes in the already existed classification systems are necessary to palce every newly discovered plant and animal in their respective ranks.

42. **What different criteria would you choose to classify people that you meet often?** **NCERT**

Ans We can recognise and classify the people we often meet on the basis of their

(i) language (ii) behaviour

(iii) geographical distribution

(iv) sex (v) weight

(vi) height, etc. (½ × 6)

43. **Define a taxon. Give some examples of taxa at different hierarchical levels.** **NCERT**

Ans The different taxonomical categories are–species, genus, family, order, class, phyla/division and kingdom. Some examples of taxa at different hierarchical levels are

(i) *Mangifera indica* is a taxon and species (*indica*) is its category. (1½)

(ii) The taxon of all the bacteria is Monera and the category is kingdom.

(iii) The taxon of fishes is Pisces and the category is class. (1½)

44. **Write the relation between taxonomic category and taxonomic hierarchy. Fill in the missing category in following hierarchical arrangement in ascending order.**

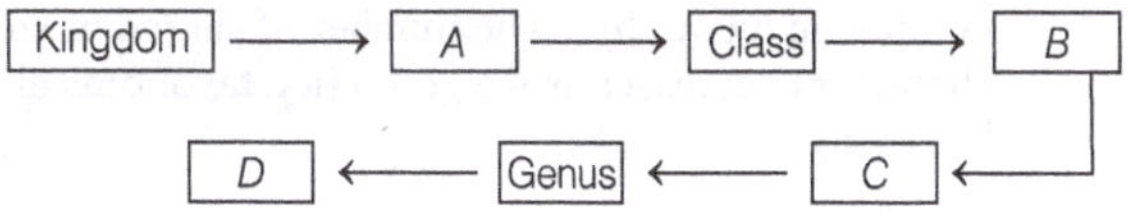

Ans The category is a part of overall taxonomic arrangement called taxonomic category in ascending or descending order. All the categories together constitute the taxonomic hierarchy. (2)

A – Phylum, *B* – Order, *C* – Family and *D* – Species (1)

45. **What are obligate categories? How these are different from intermediate categories. List out some intermediate categories.**

Ans The taxonomic categories which are always used in hierarchical classification of organisms are called obligate categories. (1)

The taxonomic categories from species to kingdom are broad categories or obligate categories. However, taxonomists have developed sub-categories in this hierarchy to facilitate more sound and scientific placement of various taxa. (1)

Intermediate categories are subphyla, subclasses, suborders, subfamilies, subgenera, varieties or subspecies (1)

Long Answer Type Questions

5 Marks

46. *Brassica campestris* **Linn. (i) Give the common name of the plant. (ii) What do the first two parts of the name denote? (iii) Why are they written in Italics? (iv) What is the meaning of Linn written at the end of the name?** **NCERT Exemplar**

Ans (i) **Common name** Mustard.

(ii) **Parts of the name** First part represents the genus or generic name, while the second part represents the specific name.

(iii) **Italics** In order to highlight their Latin origin.

(iv) **Linn** It is the abbreviation of the name of scientist Linnaeus, who gave the name to the plant. (5)

47. **Define a taxon. What is meant by taxonomic hierarchy? Give a flow diagram from the lowest to highest category for a plant and an animal. What happens to the number of individuals and number of shared characters as we go up the taxonomic hierarchy?** **NCERT Exemplar**

Ans Taxon is a group of organisms representing any level of category, e.g. sparrow, flatworm, lion, crocodile, etc.

Taxonomic hierarchy is the system of arranging taxonomic categories in a descending order with species at the base.

Refer to figure 1.1 on page no. 5 (Taxonomic categories)

The number of individuals increases as we go up in a taxonomic hierarchy. The number of shared or correlated characters decreases as we go up in a taxonomical hierarchy. (5)

48. **Define the following terms**

(i) Phylum

(ii) Class

(iii) Family

(iv) Order

(v) Genus **NCERT**

Ans (i) **Phylum** It is a taxonomic category ranked higher than class and lower than kingdom, which consists of more than one class having some similar correlated characters. e.g., classes–Aves, Amphibia, Pisces, Reptilia and Mammalia belong to the phylum–Chordata. Members of this phylum have notochord in their body plan.

(ii) **Class** The category class includes related orders. It is ranked higher than order and lower than phylum, e.g. class–Mammalia has orders–Carnivora, Primata, etc.

(iii) **Family** It is the category ranked higher than genus and lower than order, which has one or more related genera having some common features, e.g. Felidae, Canidae, etc.

(iv) **Order** It is a taxonomic category lower than class and higher than family. It consists of one or more related families possessing some similar correlated characters that differentiate them from families belonging to other orders, e.g. Carnivora, Primata, etc.

(v) **Genus** It comprises of a group of related species which has more characters common in comparison to species of other genera. In other words, genera are aggregates of closely related species, e.g. genus– *Panthera* has lion (*Panthera leo*), leopard (*P. pardus*) and tiger (*P. tigris*). (1 × 5)

49. **Try to collect all the currently accepted meanings for the word 'species'. Discuss with your teacher the meaning of species in case of higher plants and animals on one hand and bacteria on the other hand.** **NCERT**

Ans (i) Species is a basic unit of classification, where individuals share common characteristics.

(ii) It is a natural population or group of natural population of individuals having similar morphology, anatomy, physiology and cytology.

(iii) Species is an assemblage of structurally similar individuals, which can interbreed freely, but are reproductively isolated from members of other species.

Higher plants and animals These are sexually reproducing organisms. So, the third definition of species is applicable in case of higher plants and animals.

Bacteria The second definition of the species can be applied to bacteria. As bacteria do not reproduce sexually. Therefore, the criteria of free interbreeding and reproductive isolation cannot be applied to them(5)

Case Based Questions

4/5 Marks

50. Taxonomists refrain from using vernacular names of living organisms. They widely use binomial nomenclature as it has universal acceptance and explicitness. The scientific name of each organism is assigned by esteemed organisations, *viz*, ICBN and ICZN.

Consider the above given information and answer the following questions.

(i) What do the two components of binomial nomenclature represent?

(ii) Who proposed binomial nomenclature and what is the origin of biological names?

Or

There are universal rules for naming an organism. Comment.

(iii) How is the author's name mentioned in binomial nomenclature?

Ans (i) The two components of binomial nomenclature are generic name and specific epithet. (1)

(ii) Carl Linnaeus proposed binomial nomenclature.

Scientific names are based in Latin or Greek. (1)

Or

(ii) There are universal rules for naming an organism follows a system called binomial nomenclature, established by Carl Linnaeus. According to this system, each organism is given a two part name the genus and the species epithet. (1)

(iii) Name of the author appears after the specific epithet, i.e. at the end of the biological name. It is generally written in abbreviated form, e.g. *Mangifera indica* Linn. It indicates that this species was first described by Linnaeus. (2)

51. Consider the diagram given below showing a hierarchy of categories in which organisms are divided. **NCERT Exemplar**

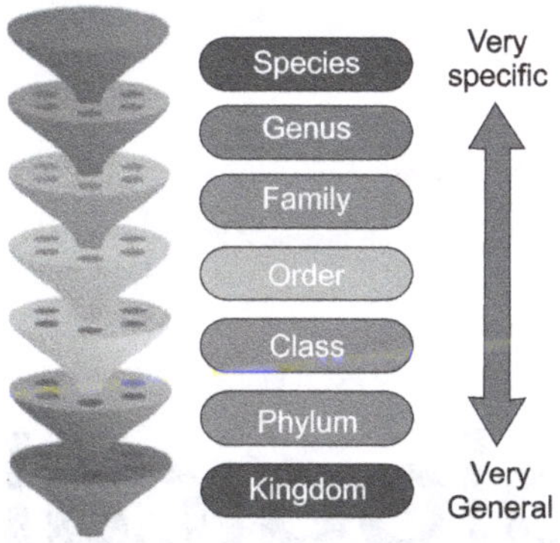

Study the diagram carefully and answer the following questions.

(i) How many obligate categories are used in hierarchical classification? Certain taxonomists have also developed sub categories why?

Or

(i) Demonstrate taxonomic category and hierarchy using an example.

(ii) What is the difference between taxon and category?

(iii) Mango belongs to which class of kingdom-Plantae?

Ans (i) There are typically seven obligate categories, i.e. kingdom, phylum, class, order, family, genus and species.

The creation of subcategories in taxonomy allows for a more nuanced understanding and organisation of the diversity of life on earth. (2)

Or

(i) To demonstrate taxonomic category and hierachy lets take an example of domestic dog, scientifically known as *Canis lupus*.

(a) Kingdom – Animalia

(b) Phylum – Chordata

(c) Class – Mammalia

(d) Order – Carnivora

(e) Family – Canidae

(f) Genus – *Canis*

(g) Species – *Canis lupus familiaris* (2)

(ii) Taxon refers to any group of organisms at any taxonomic level whereas category specifically refers to the hierarchical ranks within a taxonomic system. (1)

(iii) Mango belongs to class–Dicotyledonae of kingdom-Plantae. (1)

CHAPTER 02

Biological Classification, Monera and Viruses

Biological classification is the scientific procedure of arranging organisms in a hierarchical series of groups and sub-groups on the basis of their similarities and dissimilarities.

TOPIC 01 Kingdom Classification System

There have been many attempts to classify living organisms since ancient times. **Aristotle** was the earliest to attempt a scientific basis of classification. He used simple morphological characters to classify plants as **trees, shrubs** and **herbs**. He also classified animals into two groups, i.e. **Enaima** (with red blood) and **Anaima** (without red blood). A need for proper system of classification was always felt.

Living organisms need to be classified because of the following reasons

(i) The study of one or two organisms is not sufficient to know the essential features of the group.

(ii) Classification helps in knowing the relationship amongst different groups of organisms.

(iii) It helps in studying of the evolutionary relationship between organisms.

Types of Kingdom Classification System

Depending upon the types of system of classification, organisms are classified into following kingdoms

1. Two Kingdom Classification System

Linnaeus (the father of taxonomy system) divided all the living organisms into two kingdoms in 1758.

These are Plantae and Animalia.

Two Kingdom Classification System

↓

Plantae
- Algae
- Fungi
- Bacteria
- Bryophyta
- Pteridophyta
- Spermatophyta

Animalia
- Coelenterata
- Porifera
- Platyhelminthes
- Mollusca
- Nemathelminthes
- Annelida
- Echinodermata
- Chordata

Features of Kingdom–Plantae

The features of this kingdom are

(i) Cell wall is present.

(ii) A big central vacuole is present.

(iii) Absorb inorganic nutrients from outside.

(iv) Unlimited growth and well-defined growing points.

(v) Autotrophic mode of nutrition, reserve food is starch.

(vi) No locomotion (except in some lower algae).

(vii) Absence of excretory organs, nervous system, sense organs and muscular system.

(viii) Slow response to external stimuli.

Features of Kingdom–Animalia

The features of this kingdom are

(i) Absence of cell wall.

(ii) Inorganic crystals are not present in their cells.

(iii) Central vacuole is not present.

(iv) Heterotrophic mode of nutrition.

(v) Growth is limited and well-defined growing points are not present.

(vi) Reserve food as glycogen.

(vii) Excretory organs, nervous system and sense organs are present.

(viii) Locomotion is present.

(ix) Muscular system is present.

(x) Show quick response to external stimuli.

Shortcomings of Two Kingdom Classification System

The two kingdom system of classification was accepted for a long time. However, some difficulties arised from this classification as several new living organisms have been discovered.

Some of these difficulties are mentioned below

(i) The first formed organisms (bacteria) were not given proper place in the two kingdom classification system.

(ii) **Eukaryotes** have a well-defined nucleus, a double envelope organisation, spindle apparatus, meiosis and sexual reproduction. While prokaryotes do not possess above mentioned characteristics. On the other hand, **viruses** have no protoplasm and metabolic machinery of their own. Therefore, all of these cannot be kept in a single group.

(iii) It is not easy to recognise the lower organisms as plants or animals. For example, *Euglena* has chloroplast and follows mixotrophic (dual) mode of nutrition.

(iv) Fungi do not show structural, physiological and reproductive similarity with other plants under kingdom—Plantae.

(v) **Slime moulds**, a group of fungi are wall-less in vegetative phase. Slime moulds can neither be placed in animals, nor in plants.

(vi) **Lichens** are formed by the symbiotic association of an alga and a fungus. They neither resemble plants nor animals.

2. Three Kingdom Classification System

Ernst Haeckel in 1866, classified living organisms into three kingdoms–**Plantae**, **Protista** and **Animalia**. The new **kingdom–Protista** included all those organisms, which lack the capability of tissue differentiation. These are algae, fungi, protozoans, bacteria and slime moulds. Later, kingdom–Protista was reserved only for unicellular organisms.

Limitations of three kingdom classification are

(i) Prokaryotes and eukaryotes were not separated.

(ii) Both unicellular and multicellular organisms were kept together in Protista.

3. Four Kingdom Classification System

The four kingdom classification system included **Monera** in addition to Protista, Plantae and Animalia. Studies with electron microscope made it clear that bacteria and related organisms have a different nuclear structure as compared to others. They are prokaryotes, thus kingdom–Monera was created by **Copeland** (1956). Fungi continued to remain with Plantae in this system.

4. Five Kingdom Classification System

This classification was proposed by **RH Whittaker** in 1969. Before 1969, the classification systems for the living organisms had undergone several changes over time. Whittaker created **Fungi**, as separate kingdom.

The main criteria for classification used by Whittaker

(i) Cell structure (ii) Mode of nutrition (iii) Thallus organisation

(iv) Reproduction (v) Phylogenetic relationships

Characteristics of Different Kingdoms

Characters	Kingdom–Monera	Kingdom–Protista	Kingdom–Fungi	Kingdom–Plantae	Kingdom–Animalia
Cell type	Prokaryotic	Eukaryotic	Eukaryotic	Eukaryotic	Eukaryotic
Complexity of body	Unicellular to multicellular	Unicellular	Unicellular to multicellular	Multicellular	Multicellular
Ecological role	Producers/ Decomposers	Producers/ Decomposers/ Consumers	Decomposers	Producers	Consumers
Cell wall	Non-cellulosic and peptidoglycan	Present or Absent	Chitin	Cellulose	Absent
Nutrition	Autotrophic or Heterotrophic	Autotrophic or Heterotrophic	Heterotrophic (saprophytic)/ Parasitic	Autotrophic (photosynthetic)	Heterotrophic (holozoic or parasitic)
Motility	Present (flagella) or absent	Present (flagella 9 + 9)	Present (flagella 9 + 2)	Present (flagella 9 + 2)	Present (flagella 9 + 2)
Reproduction	Asexual (fission) or Conjugation	Asexual and sexual (gametic or zygotic)	Asexual and sexual (zygotic)	Asexual, by vegetative means and sexual (spore or zygotic)	Asexual and sexual (gametic)
Examples	• Archaebacteria (methanogens, halophiles and thermoacidophiles) • Eubacteria (Cyanobacteria, mycoplasmas, etc.)	• Chrysophytes (diatoms and desmids) • Dinoflagellates (*Gonyaulax*) • Slime moulds • Euglenoids (*Euglena*) • Protozoans (*Amoeba*)	• Phycomycetes (*Mucor, Rhizopus* and *Albugo*) • Ascomycetes (*Penicillium, Saccharomyces, Aspergillus*, etc.) • Basidiomycetes (*Agaricus*) • Deuteromycetes (*Alternaria* and *Trichoderma*)	• Algae • Bryophytes (liverworts) • Pteridophytes (ferns) • Gymnosperms (*Cycas, Pinus*, etc.) • Angiosperms (*Helianthus* and *Zea*)	• Porifera (sponges) • Coelenterata (jellyfish) • Platyhelminthes (tapeworm) • Aschelminthes (roundworm) • Annelida (earthworm) • Arthropoda (cockroach) • Mollusca (snail) • Echinodermata (starfish) • Chordata (vertebrates)

Merits of Five Kingdom Classification System

Merits of five kingdom classification system are

(i) *Euglena* and other transition types which had been included both amongst plants and animals are given proper place under kingdom–Protista.

(ii) Fungi have their own biochemical, physiological and structural organisation. They have never been related to plants. In this system of classification, fungi are separately placed.

(iii) A separate kingdom–Monera including prokaryotes has been created. Monerans differ from all other organisms in their cellular, reproductive and physiological organisations.

(iv) The five kingdom classification system is based on cellular organisation, the mode of nutrition and complexity of structure. These were the basic factors used in earliest two kingdom system of classification.

(v) The system shows the gradual evolution of early organisms into plants and animals.

(vi) The plant and animal kingdoms become more homogenous than they were in the two kingdom system of classification.

Demerits of Five Kingdom Classification System

Demerits of five kingdom classification system are

(i) Animal protozoans have been included in kingdom–Protista, which also includes unicellular plants. They show different modes of nutrition.

(ii) *Chlorella* and *Chlamydomonas*, though unicellular are included under the kingdom–Plantae. They should be kept in Protista.

(iii) *Euglena* like organisms and slime moulds with flexible life style may need the creation of an intermediate kingdom other than Protista.

(iv) Viruses and viroids are not kept in proper place in this system.

(v) Lichens have also not been placed in this system.

5. Six Kingdom Classification System

It was introduced by **Carl Woese**, a Professor in the department of Microbiology, University of Illinois in 1990. This system is also named as **three domain system** as in it organisms are classified into three domains, i.e. **Archaea**, **Bacteria** and **Eukarya**.

It mainly used basic principles of five kingdom system, but divides **Monera** into two domains Archaebacteria, Eubacteria and other eukaryotes in third kingdom.

Differences between Three Domains

Characters	Archaea	Bacteria	Eukarya
Cell type	Prokaryotic	Prokaryotic	Eukaryotic
Histones	Have proteins similar to histones	No histones	Have histones
Introns	Some introns	No introns	Most contain introns
Ribosome size	70 S ribosomes	70 S ribosomes	80 S ribosomes
Cell wall composition	Made of protein (but lack peptidoglycan)	Made of peptidoglycan	Not always present; Plants: Cellulose, Fungi: Chitin
Cell membrane composition	Ester linked lipids with L-glycerol (branched chain)	Ester linked lipids with D-glycerol (straight chain)	Ester linked lipids with proteins (straight chain)

Topic Practice 1

Multiple Choice Questions

(1 Mark)

1. Aristotle classified the plants on the basis of their morphological characters and categorised them into
   (a) trees, shrubs and herbs
   (b) algae, bryophytes, pteridophytes, gymnosperms and angiosperms
   (c) embryophytes and tracheophytes
   (d) algae and embryophytes

Ans (a) Trees, shrubs and herbs. Aristotle divided plants into three groups those which have small soft and green stem called herbs, those which have comparably larger and stronger stem called shurbs and, those with huge woody and strong stem are called trees.

2. Who proposed two kingdom system of classification and named kingdoms as Plantae and Animalia?
   (a) Carolus Linnaeus (b) RH Whittaker
   (c) Carl Woese (d) Herbert Copeland

Ans (a) Earlier, all the organisms of the world had been divided into two kingdoms, i.e. plant kingdom and animal kingdom.
This system was given by Carolus Linnaeus in the book *Systema Naturae* (1735).

3. Two kingdoms constantly figured in all biological classifications are
(a) Plantae and Animalia
(b) Monera and Animalia
(c) Protista and Animalia
(d) Protista and Plantae

Ans (a) Plantae and Animalia kingdoms were constantly used in all the biological classification systems.

4. Which of the following characters served as the criteria for five kingdom system of classification proposed by Whittaker?
(a) Cell structure
(b) Body organisation and mode of nutrition
(c) Reproduction and phylogenetic relationships
(d) All of the above

Ans (d) All of the above characters were used by Whittaker as criteria to propose five kingdom system.

5. In Whittaker's system of classification, prokaryotes are placed in the kingdom
(a) Plantae (b) Protista
(c) Monera (d) Animalia

Ans (c) All the prokaryotes were classified in kingdom–Monera in the five kingdom classification system.

6. In the five kingdom classification, *Chlamydomonas* and *Chlorella* are included in
(a) Plantae (b) Algae
(c) Protista (d) Monera

Ans (a) In the five kingdom classification, *Chlamydomonas* and *Chlorella* have been included in kingdom–Plantae as they are photosynthetic algae and algae are included in kingdom–Plantae.

7. Consider the following statement with respect to characteristic features of the kingdom.
I. In Animalia, the mode of nutrition is autotrophic.
II. In Monera, the nuclear membrane is present.
III. In Protista, the cell type is prokaryotic.
IV. In Plantae, the cell wall is present.
Which of the above statements is/are correct?
(a) Only I (b) Only II
(c) Only III (d) Only IV

Ans (d) Mode of nutrition of kingdom–Animalia is heterotrophic.
Nuclear envelope is absent in kingdom–Monera.
Protists are eukaryotic. The only prokaryotic kingdom is Monera.

Very Short Answer Type Questions

1 Mark

8. How the Aristotle divided animals into two groups?

Ans Aristotle divided animals in two groups. These are Enaima (with red blood) and Anaima (without red blood).

9. Who proposed the two kingdom classification?

Ans Linnaeus proposed the two kingdom classification in 1758.

10. Why two kingdom classification continued to be used for a long time ?

Ans Classification of organisms into plants and animals was easily done and was easy to understand.

11. Who coined the term 'Protista' ?

Ans Ernst Haeckel (1866).

12. Give the names of the kingdoms in three kingdom classification.

Ans Plantae, Protista and Animalia.

13. Which biologist proposed the kingdom–Monera?

Ans Copeland (1956).

14. The five kingdom classification was proposed by **NCERT Exemplar**

Ans RH Whittaker proposed five kingdom system classification in 1969.

15. In which group all prokaryotes were kept in five kingdom system ?

Ans Monera.

16. In which kingdom of five kingdom classification, nuclear membrane is not present?

Ans Bacteria are prokaryotes which belong to kingdom–Monera. Monerans do not have nuclear membrane enclosing the nucleus of the cell.

17. In the five kingdom system of Whittaker, how many kingdoms are eukaryotes? **NCERT Exemplar**

Ans In the five kingdom classification system given by Whittaker, four kingdoms belong to eukaryotes, i.e. Protista, Fungi, Plantae and Animalia. Only kingdom- Monera belongs to prokaryotes.

18. Mention any two cellular structures that are absent in kingdom–Animalia but present in kingdom–Protista of four kingdom classification system of organisms.

Ans Cell wall and chloroplasts are absent in cells of members of kingdom–Animalia.

19. In the five kingdom classification of Whittaker, some acellular organisms are not included. What are these organisms?

Ans Viruses and viroids are not included in the five kingdom classification.

Short Answer Type I Questions

(2 Marks)

20. What is two kingdom system of classification?

Ans The two kingdom system of classification of living organisms was proposed by Linnaeus. He divided organisms into two kingdoms–Animalia (including all animals) and Plantae (including all plants). (2)

21. Who proposed three kingdom system of classification? Give the name of new kingdom included in this.

Ans Ernst Haeckel in 1866 proposed three kingdom system of classification, i.e. Plantae, Protista and Animalia. The new kingdom was Protista which included the organisms that lack the capability of tissue differentiation. (2)

22. How was three kingdom system different than four kingdom system ?

Ans The three kingdom classification system was proposed by Ernst Haeckel in 1866. He did not distinguish bacteria from other living beings. They were incorrectly placed under kingdom–Protista.

This shortcoming was removed by Copeland in 1956 when he placed all the bacteria and related organisms into another kingdom—Monera. Copeland's system of classification was able to separate prokaryotic organisms from eukaryotic organisms which was a major drawback of Haeckel's system of classification. (2)

23. What are the main criteria used for five kingdom system of classification?

Ans The main criteria used for five kingdom system of classification are

(i) Complexity of cell structure.

(ii) Complexity of organism's body.

(iii) Mode of obtaining nutrition.

(iv) Life cycle and phylogenetic relationship. (½ × 4)

24. How is the five kingdom classification advantageous over the two kingdom classification? **NCERT Exemplar**

Ans The two kingdom system is divided into Plantae and Animalia solely on the basis of their gross morphology. On the other hand, the five kingdom classification is based upon more specific characters like cell structure, body structure, nutrition, evolutionary relationships, etc. and it separates prokaryotic and eukaryotic life forms. (2)

Short Answer Type II Questions

(3 Marks)

25. The two kingdom classification system placed bacteria, algae, blue-green algae, fungi, mosses, ferns, gymnosperm, and angiosperms, together under one single kingdom–Plantae. According to you, what could have been the basis of such classification ?

Ans The two kingdom classification system was given by Linnaeus in 1758. Lesser number of organisms were known then in comparison to what the world knows today.

He classified all the known living beings into two categories–Animalia and Plantae on the basis of the presence or absence of cell wall in their cells. As bacteria, blue-green algae, fungi, algae, mosses, ferns, gymnosperms and angiosperms have their cells surrounded by cell walls, unlike animals, therefore, they were placed together under kingdom–Plantae. (3)

26. List atleast three demerits of two kingdom classification system proposed by Linnaeus.

Ans Refer to text on page no. 15.

27. How Ernst Haeckel classified the organisms ? Write down the limitations of his proposition.

Ans Refer to text on page no. 15.

28. Describe the three domains of Carl Woese.

Ans Refer to text on page no. 17.

29. Justify at what extent the phylogenetic relationship is useful as a criterion for classification.

Ans Phylogeny is the evolutionary history of an organism. It shows the true kinship of organism. Such relationships are not clear in all cases. Only fossil record can provide such relationships, but complete records are not available for such studies. Hence, the phylogenetic relationships are ascertained from morphology, cytology, genetics, physiology and biochemistry for the correct classification of the organisms. (3)

30. **Discuss how classification system have undergone several changes over a period of time.** **NCERT**

Ans Changes in classification system over a period of time

(i) Biological classification of living organisms was first done by Aristotle. On the morphological basis, he gave the broad classification of plants and animals. He further divided plants into trees, shrubs and herbs. The animal classification was done on the basis of the presence or absence of red blood into Enaima and Anaima. However, the first proper classification system was proposed by Linnaeus who divided living beings in two kingdoms– Plantae (all plants) and Animalia (all animals). Although this system of classification had been accepted, but eventually it was rejected due to its inadequacies.

(ii) Later, more criteria for classification were implemented based on observable morphological features.

These criteria were habitat, cell structure, nature of cell wall when present, mode of nutrition and reproduction, evolutionary relationships.

(iii) Classification on the basis of these criteria led to the creation of three more kingdoms which are now part of the five kingdom system of classification given by Whittaker in 1969. The five kingdoms are—Monera (prokaryotes), Protista (single-celled eukaryotes), Fungi, Plantae and Animalia.

(iv) The six kingdom classification system is the latest system introduced by Carl Woese in 1990. It divides Monera into two kingdoms–Archaebacteria and Eubacteria. **(3)**

Long Answer Type Questions

5 Marks

31. **Distinguish between kingdom-Plantae and Animalia on the following basis**

(i) Motility (ii) Nutrition
(iii) Reproduction (iv) Cell type
(v) Cell wall

Ans Refer to text on page no. 16. **(5)**

32. **What is three domain system? Who introduced it? Name these domains and their salient features.**

Ans Three domains system or six kingdom classification is a biological classification system, in which living organisms were divided based on cellular characteristics. **Carl Woese** in **1990** introduced it.

The three domains are

(i) **Archaea** It contains prokaryotic organisms, which have a monolayer core of lipids in the cell membrane and distinct nucleotides in their 16 S RNA.

(ii) **Bacteria** It contains typical prokaryotes, which lack membrane covered cell organelles, but do not have a type of microchambers for separating various activities.

(iii) **Eukarya** This domain contains eukaryotic organisms, originated by endosymbiotic association between some archaebacteria and eubacteria. It have four kingdoms–Protista, Fungi, Plantae and Animalia. **(5)**

33. **List out the merits of the five kingdom system of classification.**

Ans Refer to text on page no. 17. **(5)**

34. **Describe how five kingdom system is meritorious over two kingdom and three kingdom classification system ?**

Ans Refer to text on page no. 17.

35. **Biological classification is a dynamic and ever evolving phenomenon which keeps changing with our understanding of life forms. Justify the statement by taking any two examples.** **NCERT Exemplar**

Ans Biological classification keeps changing with our understanding of life forms. Initially, new characters were taken by Aristotle, Theophrastus, John Ray and Linnaeus. Linnaeus divided plants on the basis of sex organs only. **(1)**

As more and more knowledge was gathered about the diverse organisms with the advancement in technology to study them, the ways for natural system of classification kept changing.

This can be understood by following examples

(i) Two kingdom classification was replaced by three kingdom classification when Haeckel (1866) proposed the kingdom–Protista.

(ii) It was converted into four kingdom classification by Copeland when he proposed the kingdom–Monera.

(iii) Whittaker in 1969 proposed five kingdom classification.

(iv) As the information about biochemistry of archa2ebacteria gathered, Carl Woese in 1990 raised another kingdom–Archaea. **(4)**

TOPIC 02

Kingdom–Monera

Kingdom–Monera was created by **Copeland** in **1956**. It contains all the prokaryotic organisms including bacteria, archaebacteria, mycoplasma, actinomycetes, cyanobacteria and rickettsia. **Prokaryotes** (Gr. *Pro*–primitive, *karyos*–nucleus) are organisms containing primitive nucleus. The word primitive nucleus here implies to an unorganised nucleus, which does not have associated proteins and membranes.

This nucleus is usually seen in the form of a double-stranded DNA coil. All of these organisms are microscopic and contribute a major part in **microbiology**, i.e. the biology of microorganisms.

General Characteristics

The characteristic features of kingdom–Monera are given below

(i) They are simplest, most primitive and unicellular prokaryotes.

(ii) The cell wall contains peptidoglycan or murein (no cellulose), but the membrane bound cell organelles are not present.

(iii) They have various types of modes of nutrition like saprophytic, parasitic, chemoautotrophic, photoautotrophic and symbiotic.

(iv) DNA is naked. It lies inside the cytoplasm in coiled form. This is called **nucleoid** or false nucleus.

(v) The flagella, if present, are single-stranded instead of being multi stranded as in eukaryotes. These contain a protein called **flagellin**.

(vi) Reproduction is by asexual methods. Gametes are not present.

(vii) Mitotic spindle is absent.

(viii) Some of the monerans have the ability to fix nitrogen into useful nitrates.

Classification

In 1977, Carl Woese and George Fox reported two quite distinct groups in this kingdom. These groups are archaebacteria and eubacteria.

Archaebacteria (Gr. *Archae*–primitive; bacteria) includes methanogens, halophiles and thermoacidophiles.
Eubacteria (Gr. *Eu*—true; bacteria) are true bacteria that includes cyanobacteria, mycoplasma, actinomycetes, rickettsia and spirochaetes. In this chapter, we will focus on characteristics of different true bacteria and their comparison with archaebacteria.

I. Archaebacteria

Archaebacteria (*Archae*–ancient; *bact*–rod) are special since, they live in some of the most harsh habitats such as extreme salty areas (halophiles), hot springs (thermoacidophiles) and marshy areas (methanogens).

The characteristics of members of this domain are

(i) They are most primitive prokaryotes.

(ii) They are found in stressed environment conditions, such as high salt content (Great Salt Lake, The Dead Sea), edge of the ocean, hot sulphur springs, volcanic walls, gut of animals, etc.

(iii) Their cell walls lack peptidoglycan. In most cases, the cell wall is composed of non-cellulosic polysaccharides and some proteins. In some members, cell wall may even be absent. This feature of having different kinds of cell walls is responsible for their survival in extreme conditions.

(iv) Most of the archaebacteria are chemoautotrophs.

Types of Archaebacteria

Archaebacteria are of following three types

1. Methanogens

These are strictly anaerobes. They live anaerobically in gut of several ruminants such as cows, buffaloes, goats, etc. These bacteria have been exploited for the production of methane (gobar gas) from the dung of these animals. These bacteria also help in fermentation of cellulose. They produce almost 65% of atmospheric methane. Examples are *Methanobacterium, Methanobacillus, Methanosarcina* and *Methanococcus.*

Knowledge Plus

- Methane is a pollutant that contributes to greenhouse effect and global warming.
- The fermentation of cattle dung by methanogens is done in specially designed **gobar gas plants** to produce cooking gas.

2. Halophiles

These are found in extremely saline environments like salt lakes, salt marshes, salt pans, salt solutions, etc. They are mostly anaerobes. They contain a chemical called **halorhodopsin** to pump in chlorides into the cell to prevent cellular dehydration.

Halobacterium develops purple membrane having photoreceptor pigment **bacteriorhodopsin**. In light, it acts as a proton pump and helps in synthesis of ATP. The formation of ATP is a survival mechanism under anaerobic conditions. Examples include *Halobacterium* and *Halococcus*.

3. Thermoacidophiles

These archaebacteria can live in both extreme heat and acidic pH (around 2) environment conditions. Under anaerobic conditions, these organisms oxidise sulphur to sulphuric acid.

$$2S + 2H_2O + 3O_2 \longrightarrow 2H_2SO_4 + \text{Energy}$$

Thermoacidophiles can survive in high temperature and low pH conditions because of the following special features

(i) Special branched chain lipids in cell membranes that reduce cell fluidity.
(ii) Enzymes that can work at low pH.
(iii) Enzymes that are resistant to high temperature coagulation. Examples are *Sulfobolus, Thermoplasma* and *Thermoproteus.*

Importance of Archaebacteria

Archaebacteria can live in extreme environments, so they are useful in

(i) Modern biotechnology (ii) Generation of biogas
(iii) Thermophilic enzymes (iv) Biosensors
(v) Restriction enzymes, etc.

II. Eubacteria

They are called '**true bacteria**' and are characterised by the presence of a rigid cell wall and if motile, have flagellum.

Bacteria

The term bacteria was proposed by **Ehrenberg** in 1829. They have widespread distribution in air, water and soil. They can even survive in extreme range of temperatures like upto 78°C and −190°C.

Important characteristics of bacteria are

(i) They are found in all kinds of habitats.
(ii) They are prokaryotic microorganisms.
(iii) They are unicellular.
(iv) Cell wall contains peptidoglycan.
(v) An organised nucleus is absent.
(vi) Extrachromosomal self-replicating DNA segments called **plasmids** occur in most of the bacteria.
(vii) Mitochondria, plastids, Golgi apparatus, endoplasmic reticulum and other membrane bound cell organelles are absent.

Size

The size of bacterial cell ranges from 1-10 μm in length and from 0.7-1.5 μm in width.

Classification of Bacteria

Bacteria classified on the following basis

On the Basis of Shape

Depending upon the shape, bacteria possess the following forms

(i) **Coccus** (Pl. cocci) bacteria are oval or spherical cells without flagella. The spheres occur as single cells (*Monococcus*), a pair of cells (*Diplococcus*), in groups of four cells (*Tetracoccus*), as chain of cells (*Streptococcus*) or in sheets (*Staphylococcus*).

A few cocci may also occur in cube-like arrangements of 8 or more cells (*Sarcina*).

(ii) **Bacillus** (Pl. bacilli) bacteria are rod-shaped cells which may occur singly (*Monobacillus*), in pairs (*Diplobacillus*), in chains (*Streptobacillus*) or as a layer (stack) with many cells called ***Palisade bacillus.***

(iii) **Spirillum** (Pl. spirilla) bacteria are cells, which are twisted, like a screw. They occur as free single cells, e.g. *Spirillum, Spirochaete,* etc.

(iv) **Vibrio** are cells, which are curved, C-shaped or comma-shaped, e.g. *Vibrio cholerae.*

Apart from these shapes of bacteria, some other shapes are also found such as mycelial, stalked, budding bacteria.

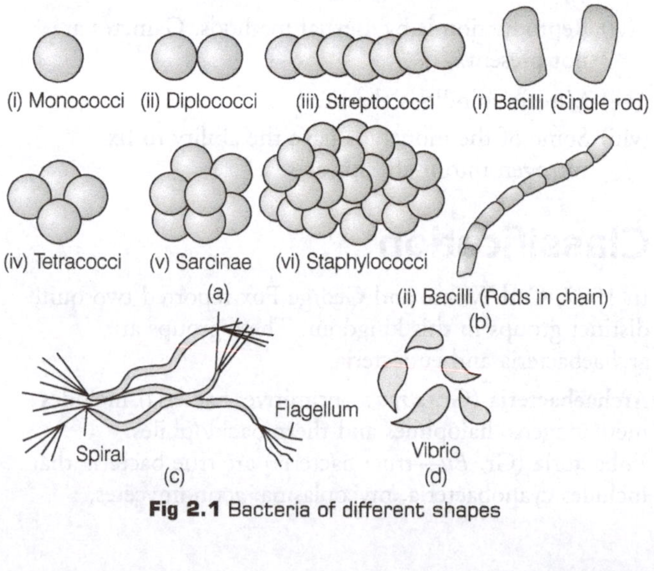

Fig 2.1 Bacteria of different shapes

On the Basis of Nutrition

Depending upon the mode of nutrition, bacteria are of two types

(i) **Autotrophic Bacteria** These are of following two types

(a) **Photosynthetic Bacteria** These bacteria have green sunlight trapping pigment called **bacteriochlorophyll**. These are found at the bottom of ponds and lakes. Bacterial photosynthesis does not release oxygen.

(b) **Chemosynthetic Bacteria** These bacteria are able to synthesise organic food from inorganic raw materials with the help of energy derived from exergonic chemical reactions. Examples include nitrifying bacteria (*Nitrosomonas*), iron bacteria (*Ferrobacillus ferroxidants*) and sulphur oxidising bacteria (*Beggiatoa*).

(ii) **Heterotrophic Bacteria** These bacteria are not capable of synthesising their own food. Instead, they obtain food from different sources. These may be of following types

(a) **Saprophytic Bacteria** These obtain food by decomposing dead bodies, excreta of animals, dead plants and their parts. These are also called **decomposers**, detrivores or transformers.

(b) **Parasitic Bacteria** These are disease causing bacteria called as **pathogens**, e.g. *Salmonella typhimurium*, which causes typhoid in humans.

(c) **Symbiotic Bacteria** These bacteria live in mutually beneficial associations with other organisms, e.g. *Rhizobium* and *Bacillus* species form nodules in roots of leguminous plants. They obtain nutrition from the plant and in turn, help the plant in nitrogen-fixation.

On the Basis of Respiration

Depending upon the mode of respiration bacteria can be of following types

(i) **Aerobic Respiration** (In the presence of oxygen)

Those bacteria, which perform aerobic respiration are called **aerobes**. These are of following two types

(a) **Obligate Aerobes** These bacteria grow exclusively in the presence of molecular oxygen and fail to survive in its absence, e.g. *Bacillus subtilis*.

(b) **Facultative Anaerobes** The aerobic bacteria that can also survive when oxygen is absent are called facultative anaerobes, e.g. *Enterobacter*, *Klebsiella*.

(ii) **Anaerobic Respiration** (In the absence of oxygen)

Those bacteria, which perform anaerobic respiration are called **anaerobes**. These are of following two types

(a) **Obligate Anaerobes** These bacteria grow and multiply in the absence of free oxygen. They fail to survive under aerobic conditions, e.g. *Clostridium botulinum*.

(b) **Facultative Aerobes** The anaerobic bacteria, which can also survive in the presence of oxygen are called facultative aerobes, e.g. *Chlorobium limicola*.

Structure of Bacteria

A bacterial cell is covered by mucilage. It is differentiated into cell wall, plasma membrane, cytoplasm, nucleoid, plasmids, inclusion bodies, flagella, pilli and fimbriae. Membrane bound organelles are absent.

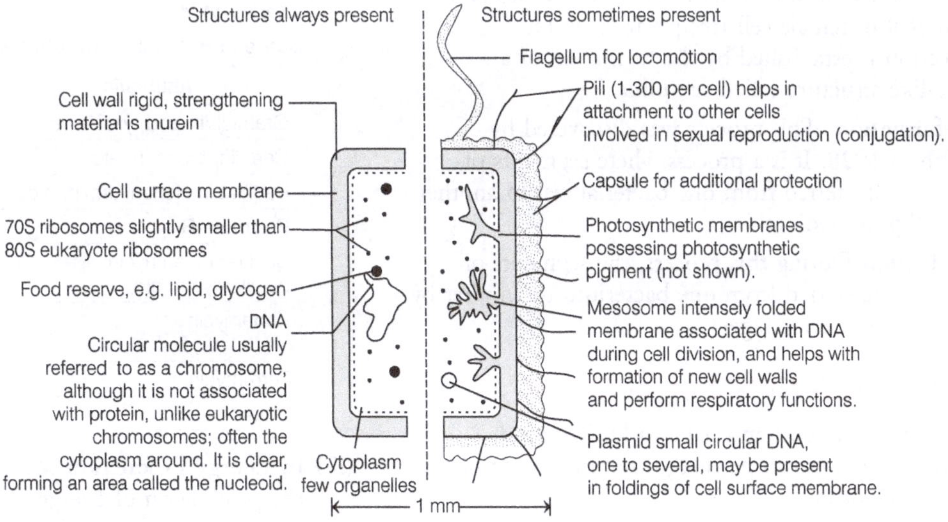

Fig 2.2 A bacterial cell

Details about the structure of bacteria (prokaryotes) will be studied later in chapter 10th of this book.

NOTE Bacteria were discovered by **Antony van Leeuwenhoek** (1632-1723). He observed bacteria in 1675.

Louis Pasteur laid the foundation of **Bacteriology** by developing culture techniques.

Reproduction

Bacteria reproduce by asexual and sexual (parasexual) processes.

1. Asexual Reproduction

Asexual reproduction occurs by binary fission and endospore formation.

(i) **Binary Fission** It is a simple cell division, in which bacterial cell divides into two daughters. A constriction appears at the equator of the cell that, deepens further by growing from margin to centre, and finally two new cells are produced.

(ii) **Endospore Formation** Endospores are perennial structures, which help in survival even during unfavourable environmental conditions, e.g. in *Clostridium* and *Bacillus*, the endospore has many wall layers containing heat resistant chemicals such as **sialic acid** and **dipicolinic acid.**

2. Sexual Reproduction

Sexual reproduction in bacteria occurs by a parasexual process actually called **genetic recombination.**

The three methods involved are as follows

(i) **Conjugation** The exchange of genetic material by direct cell to cell contact in bacteria is known as conjugation. The male cell (donor cell) has fertility factor or **F-factor**, on its plasmid, which connects itself to cell wall of female cell (recipient cell). The connection is established by the formation of a bridge-like structure called **sex pilus.**

(ii) **Transformation** This process was discovered by **Griffith** in 1928. It is a process where segments of DNA are transferred from one bacterial cell to another *via* the liquid medium.

(iii) **Transduction** During this process, the segments of DNA are transferred from one bacterium to another by the viruses (bacteriophages).

Economic Importance of Bacteria

Bacteria serve as both boon and bane to human kind. Therefore, their activites can be categorised into harmful as well as useful categories.

Useful Activities of Bacteria

Bacteria are useful in the following ways

(i) **In Sewage Treatment** Municipal waste water is called sewage, which contains large amount of organic matter and microbes. Treatment of waste water is done by the heterotrophic microbes, which are naturally present in the sewage. The treatment of sewage is carried out in Sewage Treatment Plants (STPs).

In this process, primary effluent is aerated in large tanks and constantly agitated mechanically, so that vigorous growth of useful aerobic microbes into **flocs** (masses of bacteria associated with fungal filaments to form mesh-like structures) takes place. This decreases Biological Oxygen Demand (BOD) of the effluent. When BOD of the effluent is reduced significantly, it is passed into settling tank where the bacterial flocs settle and sediment, then effluent is released into water bodies. This sediment is called **activated sludge.**

A small part of activated sludge is pumped back to serve as inoculum in the aeration tank and the remaining is pumped in large tanks called anaerobic sludge digesters.

Here, heterotrophic microbes *(Methanobacterium)* anaerobically digest bacteria and fungi and produces **biogas.**

(ii) **In Antibiotic Production** Antibiotics are the drugs, which work against microbial pathogens. About 2100 antibiotics have been reported, so far from Actinomycetes alone. Of these, maximum antibiotics have been reported from *Streptomyces.*

Some Important Antibiotics and Their Sources

Antibiotic	Source
Gramicidin and tyrocidine	*Bacillus brevis*
Cerexin, biocerin, etc.	*B. cereus*
Bacitracin, licheniformin, etc.	*B. licheniformis*
Polymixin-B	*B. polymyxa*
Bacitracin, eumycin, bacillomycin, etc.	*B. subtilis*
Kanamycin	*Streptomyces kanomyceticus*
Terramycin	*S. rimosus*
Chloromycetin	*S. venezuelae*

(iii) **In Energy Production** Microbes also helpful in the production of energy like biofuels. Biofuels are the fuels of biological origin and are used for the production of heat and other forms of energy. The energy derived from biofuels is called **bioenergy**. Biofuels are renewable energy resources that release low greenhouse gases than fossil fuels. They are produced from waste and thus, help in controlling pollution.

Biofuels and Related Microorganisms

Biofuels and their Substrate	Microorganisms
Bioethanol Starch and sugar crops	*Bacillus licheniformis* (amylase activity)
Biogas (methane) Farm and human wastes, municipal solid wastes, effluents from food and dairy industries, etc.	Archaebacteria (Methanobacterium) and Bacillus, etc.
Butanol Soluble carbohydrates	*Clostridium acetobutylicum, C. beijernickii*
Hydrogen Sunlight, water, sugars and fatty acids (from starch, cellulose)	*Chlamydomonas reinhardtii, C. moewusii*, anerobic bacteria like *Clostridium*

(iv) **In Household Products** For thousands of years, the microorganisms have been used to make products such as curd, cheese, butter, vinegar and alcohol, etc. Some important products produced by microorganisms are given below

(a) **Curd** It is prepared by the action of *Lactobacillus*, commonly called **Lactic Acid Bacteria** (LAB), which grow in milk and convert it into curd. LAB produces some enzymes (e.g. lactase) that coagulate and partially digest the milk proteins improving the nutritional quality of curd by increasing vitamin-B_{12} and organic acid content. LAB also plays a beneficial role in checking the growth of disease causing microbes in our stomach.

(b) **Cheese** It is one of the oldest food items, in which microbes are used. This is formed by coagulation of the milk protein **casein**. The large holes in 'Swiss cheese' are due to the production of a large amount of CO_2 by a bacterium named *Propionibacterium shermani*.

(c) **Other Foods** Dosa and idli are also fermented by bacteria. A number of traditional drinks and foods are also made by fermentation by the microbes. For example, 'toddy', a traditional drink in some parts of Southern India is made by fermenting sap from unopened spadices of *Caryota urens* (palms).

Harmful Activities of Bacteria

Harmful bacterial activities are as follows

(i) **Water Pollution** Several bacterial forms cause water pollution, by spoiling drinking water, e.g. *Vibrio cholerae, Salmonella typhi*. Another hazard caused by bacteria is the conversion of mercury compounds released by industries into methyl mercury. The famous '**minamata disease**' is due to methyl mercury poisoning in water resources.

(ii) **Food Spoilage** The bacteria like *Micrococcus, Salmonella, Staphylococcus, Clostridium*, etc., spoil the food stuffs. They can cause **botulism** (*Clostridium botulinum*) and **food poisoning** (*Clostridium perfringens, E. coli, Staphylococcus aurens*) by producing endotoxins and exotoxins. Marine foods such as sea weeds, oysters, crabs and fishes are destroyed by *Spirillum rectiphysetaris.*

(iii) **Plant Diseases** Bacteria causes several diseases in plants, few of which are given in the table below

Some Common Plant Diseases Caused by Bacteria

Disease	Causal bacterial species
Angular leaf spot of cotton	*Xanthomonas malvacearum*
Black rot of cabbage	*Xanthomonas campestris*
Blight of paddy	*Xanthomonas oryzae*
Brown rot/wilt of potato	*Pseudomonas solanacearum*
Canker of citrus	*Xanthomonas citri*
Crown gall of apple	*Agrobacterium tumefaciens*

(iv) **Animal Diseases** Bacteria can also cause various diseases in human and other animals, few of which are given in the table below

Important Human Diseases Caused by Bacteria

Diseases	Pathogen
Anthrax	*Bacillus anthracis*
Chlamydia	*Chlamydia trachomatis*
Cholera	*Vibrio cholerae*
Dental caries	*Streptococcus*
Hansen's disease (leprosy)	*Mycobacterium leprae*
Peptic ulcers	*Helicobacter pylori*
Plague	*Yersinia pestis*
Pneumonia	*Streptococcus, Mycoplasma, Chlamydia*
Tuberculosis	*Mycobacterium tuberculosis*
Typhoid fever	*Salmonella typhi*

Cyanobacteria

The members of this group have many characters similar to bacteria. These are also known as **blue-green algae**. The examples of cyanobacteria are *Nostoc, Oscillatoria, Spirulina, Rivularia, Anabaena,* etc. They can survive in a wide variety of habitats, such as hot springs, seawater, polluted water, etc.

They are predominantly aquatic, but many species are known to be terrestrial also.

These can grow even in minimal moisture conditions

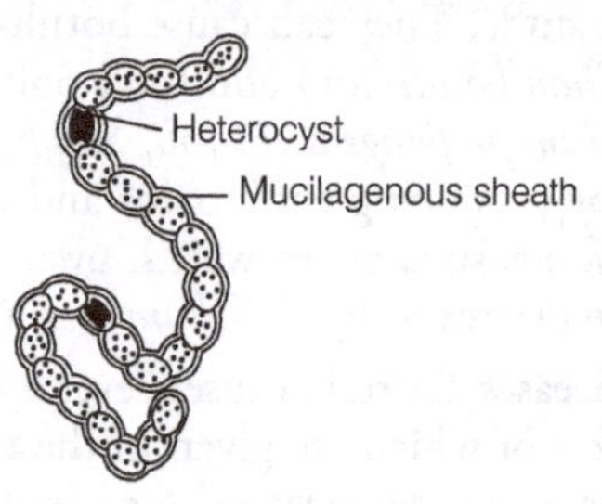

Fig. 2.3 Filamentous blue-green algae (*Nostoc*)

Cyanobacteria have following three forms

(i) Unicellular as in *Chrococcus* and *Synechococcus.*

(ii) Colonial as in *Microcystis* and *Gloeocapsa.*

(iii) Filamentous as in *Nostoc, Oscillatoria* and *Anabaena.*

Cell Structure

Cells of Eubacteria have a definite firm and rigid cell wall surrounded by mucilaginous sheath. It is bilayered. The inner layer is made up of peptidoglycan. The cell wall is followed by plasma membrane made up of **lipid** and **proteins.** The membrane bound structures like true mitochondria, endoplasmic reticulum, Golgi bodies, etc., are absent.

The photosynthetic pigments presents in the cell are located in membranous extension called chromatophores. The pigments are chlorophyll-*a*, β-carotene, myxoxanthophyll, myxoxanthin, C-phycocyanin and C-phycoerythrin. The C-phycocyanin is blue in colour, while C-phycoerythrin is red. The former is present in more amount than later, this gives the cyanobacteria its characteristic blue-green colour. The nucleolus is absent and the nucleoid is not bound by nuclear membrane.

Some cyanobacteria (*Nostoc, Anabaena, Scytonema,* etc.) possess special type of cells called **heterocysts** to perform special functions. These are large cells with walls so thick that they are impermeable to oxygen. Heterocysts are the sites of nitrogen-fixation.

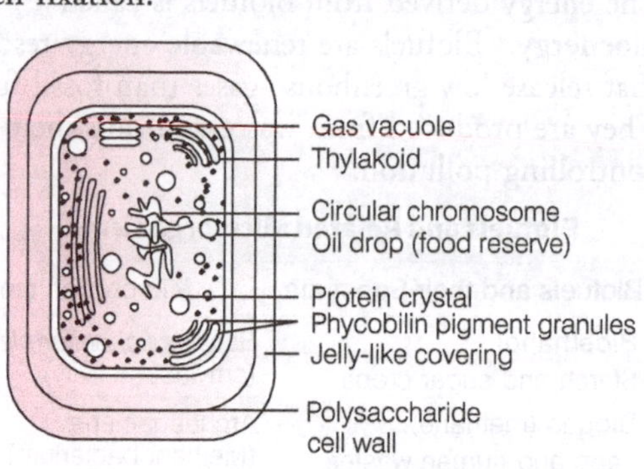

Fig 2.4 Ultrastructure of a cyanobacterial cell

Nutrition

Cyanobacteria are mostly photoautotrophs. They contain chlorophyll-*a* and other photosynthetic pigments.

Reproduction

Cyanobacteria multiply asexually and vegetatively. Sexual reproduction does not occur.

The types of multiplication are

(i) **Binary fission** occurs in unicellular forms.

(ii) **Fragmentation** occurs in colonial and filamentous forms. The small segments formed are called **hormogonia.**

(iii) **Asexual reproduction** involves formation of following structures

- **Endospores** These are the spores produced endogenously within a vegetative cell.
- **Exospores** These are the exogenously produced spores.
- **Akinetes** These are thick-walled spores that also have food material stored in them.

Economic Importance of Cyanobacteria

Economic importance of cyanobacteria are as follows

(i) Some cyanobacteria have the ability to fix atmospheric nitrogen. The green manuring by farmers is done on this basis to enrich the soil with nitrogenous fertilisers.

(ii) Cyanobacteria like *Anabaena, Tolypothrix,* etc., help in prevention of soil erosion and its conservation.

(iii) *Spirulina* is a protein rich supplement for humans. It is a fast growing cyanobacteria. It is also known as **Single Cell Protein** (SCP).

(iv) Bacteria like *Pseudomonas* fluorosceus are used for the retting of fibres (separation of fibres from soft tissue).

Note *Oscillatoria* causes asthma and gastrointestinal problems by releasing its toxins.

Excessive growth of cyanobacteria causes **water blooms** (or algal blooms), which decreases oxygen level in water causing death of aquatic animals.

Differences between Bacteria and Cyanobacteria

Bacteria	Cyanobacteria
Cells are smaller.	Cells are comparatively larger.
They may possess flagella.	They usually lack flagella.
They are both autotrophic and heterotrophic.	They are autotrophic.
Autotrophic bacteria contain bacteriochlorophyll.	They possess chlorophyll-*a* phycocyanin and phycoerythrin as found in eukaryotic autotrophs.
Photosynthesis is anoxygenic.	Photosynthesis is oxygenic.
They may be aerobic or anaerobic.	They are aerobic.
The reserve food is glycogen.	The reserve food is cyanophycean starch.
They does not possess the heterocysts.	They possess heterocysts.

Differences between Eubacteria and Archaebacteria

Eubacteria	Archaebacteria
Cell wall is made up of peptidoglycans.	Peptidoglycan is absent in cell wall. It is made up of cellulosic carbohydrate.
Plasma membrane consists of phospholipids.	It is a single layer of branched chain lipids.
Genes are not interrupted by non-coding zones or introns.	Genes are interrupted by introns like eukaryotes.

Mycoplasma

Mycoplasma are organisms that completely lack a cell wall. They were discovered by **Roux** (1898) in pleural fluid of cattle suffering from pleuropneumonia. The organisms are often called **PPLOs** (Pleuropneumonia Like Organisms).

The characteristic features of mycoplasma are

(i) Mycoplasmas are the smallest (0.1-0.5 μm) free-living microorganisms. They are so small that they can easily pass through bacteria-proof filters. These occur saprotrophically in soil, sewage water and in dead and decaying organic matter. Some of them also parasiticise plants, animals and human beings. Pathogenic mycoplasmas cause diseases in their hosts.

(ii) They are unicellular with plasma membrane as the outermost boundary. The cell membrane is made up of protein, lipids and cholesterol.

(iii) DNA is naked (because of the absence of histones) and ribosomes of 70 S type are present.

(iv) Mycoplasmas possess heterotrophic nutrition. Examples are *Mycoplasma gallisepticum, M. laidlawii*. They cause pleuropneumonia in domestic animals, mycoplasmal urethritis in humans.

(v) They can survive without oxygen.

Topic Practice 2

Multiple Choice Questions

(1 Mark)

1. **Some bacteria thrive in extreme environmental conditions such as the absence of oxygen, high salt concentration, high temperature and acidic pH. Identify the type of bacteria.**

(a) Cyanobacteria (b) Eubacteria
(c) Archaebacteria (d) Mycobacteria

Ans (c) The three main groups of Archaebacteria, methanogens (can live in the absence of O_2), halophiles (can live at high temperature) and thermoacidophiles (can live at high temperature and low pH) can survive in external environmental conditions due to their specialised cell walls.

2. **In the light of recent classification of living organisms into three domains of life (bacteria, Archaea and Eukarya), which one of the following statements is true about Archaea?**

(a) Archaea resemble Eukarya in all respects
(b) Archaea have some noble features that are absent in other prokaryotes and eukaryotes
(c) Archaea completely differ from both prokaryotes and eukaryotes
(d) Archaea completely differ from prokaryotes

Ans (b) All Archaebacteria share certain key characteristics like

(i) Their cell wall lacks peptidoglycans (important component of cell wall of Eubacteria).

(ii) Archaebacteria have distinct ribosomal RNA sequence.

(iii) Some genes of Archaebacteria possess introns, unlike other bacteria.

3. **The primitive prokaryotes responsible for the production of biogas from the dung of ruminant animals, include the**
(a) thermoacidophiles (b) methanogens
(c) eubacteria (d) halophiles

Ans (b) Methanogens are group of obligate anaerobic ancient and primitive bacteria. They are involved in methanogenesis and produce methane gas in gut of ruminant of cattles.

4. **Which of the following conditions would be favoured by thermoacidophiles?**
(a) Hot and alkaline
(b) Snow and acidic
(c) Hot and sulphur spring
(d) Gut of cows

Ans (c) Thermoacidophiles have dual ability to tolerate high temperature as well as high acidity. They often live in hot sulphur springs where the temperature may be as high as 80°C and pH as low as 2.

5. **Select the wrong statement.**
(a) Bacterial cell wall is made up of peptidoglycan
(b) Pili and fimbriae are mainly involved in motility of bacterial cells
(c) Cyanobacteria lack flagellated cells
(d) Mycoplasma is a wall-less microorganism

Ans (b) Fimbriae or Pili are fine hair-like appendages used by bacteria for attachment rather than motility. These are formed of protein called pilin.
Pili are longer than fimbriae and are one or two per cell. Some special type of pili called sex pili are present in certain strains of bacteria, which help the bacterium for forming conjugation canal during sexual reproduction by conjugation method. Fimbriae also help bacterium for cell to cell adhering and colonisation.

6. **Which of the following bacteria play an important role in the recycling of nutrients like nitrogen, phosphorus, iron and sulphur?**
(a) Chemoheterotrophic bacteria
(b) Chemosynthetic autotrophic bacteria
(c) Parasitic bacteria
(d) Saprophytic bacteria

Ans (b) Chemosynthetic autotrophic bacteria oxidise various inorganic substances such as nitrates, nitrites and ammonia and use the released energy for their ATP production. They play an important role in the recycling of nutrients like nitrogen, phosphorus, iron and sulphur.

7. **Pigment containing membranous extensions in some cyanobacteria are**
(a) heterocysts (b) basal bodies
(c) pneumatophores (d) chromatophores

Ans (d) Cyanobacteria contain photosynthetic pigments found in chromatophores, in folding of the plasma membrane, where photosynthesis is carried out.
Heterocysts are specialised nitrogen-fixing cells formed by some filamentous cyanobacteria such as *Nostoc*.
A basal body is an organelle formed from a centriole and a short cylindrical array of microtubules. Pneumatophores are lateral roots *Rhizophora* that grow upward for varying distance and function as the site of oxygen intake for the submerged primary roots.

8. **...... include blue-green algae, which have chlorophyll-*a* similar to green plants. Complete the given sentence with an appropriate option.**
(a) Chemosynthetic autotrophic bacteria
(b) Photosynthetic autotrophic bacteria
(c) Protista
(d) Saprophytic

Ans (b) Photosynthetic autotrophic bacteria include blue-green algae, which have chlorophyll-*a* similar to the green plants.

9. **Some of the cyanobacteria can fix atmospheric nitrogen in their specialised cells called**
(a) akinetes
(b) heterocyst
(c) endospores
(d) homocyst

Ans (b) Some of the cyanobacteria can fix atmospheric nitrogen in their specialised cells called heterocysts, e.g. *Nostoc* and *Anabaena*.

10. **Mycoplasmas are classified under which of the following kingdoms?**
(a) Animalia (b) Protista
(c) Monera (d) Fungi

Ans (c) There are two major groups of monerans, archaebacteria and eubacteria. Some other groups of monerans are mycoplasma, rickettsiae and actinomycetes. Mycoplasma are the simplest and the smallest free-living prokaryotes.

Very Short Answer Type Questions

(1 Mark)

11. **Give the scientific term used for organisms that produce gobar gas.**

Ans Methanogens

12. **Name the organisms living in salty areas.** **NCERT Exemplar**

Ans Halophiles live in habitats having high salinity, e.g. *Halobacterium* and *Halococcus*.

13. How do halophiles prevent cellular dehydration?

Ans Halophiles contain a chemical called halorhodopsin that pumps chlorides into the cells and prevents cellular dehydration.

14. What kind of nutrition occurs in a parasite?

Ans Parasites have phagotrophic and absorptive type of nutrition.

15. Are chemosynthetic bacteria autotrophic or heterotrophic? **NCERT Exemplar**

Ans Chemosynthetic bacteria are autotrophs because they are able to synthesise their food from inorganic raw material with the help of energy obtained from chemical reaction.

16. Gamete formation and fusion are absent in bacteria. How do then bacteria undergo sexual reproduction?

Ans It occurs by conjugation. It involves transfer of genetic material from one bacterium to another through cell to cell contact.

17. Name any two antibiotics prepared from bacteria, besides penicillin.

Ans Neomycin and streptomycin.

18. What is retting of fibres? Name a bacterium involved in it.

Ans. The separation of fibres from soft tissue is called retting of fibres, e.g. jute, flax. Bacterium used for this is *Pseudomonas fluoroscens.*

19. Which organism causes food poisoning?

Ans Food poisoning is caused by *Streptomyces aureus.*

20. Give the name of causative agents of these diseases.
(i) Cholera (ii) Typhoid

Ans (i) **Cholera** *Vibrio cholerae*
(ii) **Typhoid** *Salmonella typhii.* (½ + ½)

21. Which bacteria live inside human body without causing any harm?

Ans *Treponema denticola, T. orale, Staphylococcus aureus* and *Escherichia coli.* They are called coliforms.

22. Name the kingdom under which cyanobacteria have been classified.

Ans Cyanobacteria are prokaryotic organisms belonging to kingdom–Monera.

23. What is the principle underlying the use of cyanobacteria in agricultural fields for crop improvement? **NCERT Exemplar**

Ans Some cyanobacteria live in mutually beneficial relationship with plants, obtaining food and shelter and fixing nitrogen for the plant. They also reduce soil alkalinity and improve soil texture.

Short Answer Type I Questions

(2 Marks)

24. State two economically important uses of
(i) Heterotrophic bacteria
(ii) Archaebacteria **NCERT**

Ans (i) **Heterotrophic Bacteria** They decompose dead bodies of plants and animals. So, they are nature's scavengers, the organic content of sewage is broken down by these bacteria. They also generate humus which is used in agriculture.

(ii) **Archaebacteria** They are used in gobar gas (biogas) production and are helpful causing fermentation of cellulose in ruminants. (1+1)

25. Draw a labelled diagram of bacterial cell.

Ans Refer to fig. no. 2.2. on page no. 23.

26. What are mesosomes and what its use in bacterial cell?

Ans Mesosomes are intensely folded invagination of the membranes. Large septal mesosomes occur near centre of the cell associated with DNA during cell division, while smaller lateral mesosomes away from the centre. Mesosome are the site of respiration in bacterial cells they also help in the formation of new cell wall. (2)

27. Give the name of causative agents of following diseases. Tuberculosis, Leprosy, Diphtheria, Pneumonia.

Ans Causative agents of the following diseases are

Tuberculosis	*Mycobacterium tuberculosis*
Leprosy	*Mycobacterium leprae*
Diphtheria	*Corynebacterium diphtheriae*
Pneumonia	*Diplococcus pneumoniae.*

(½ × 4)

28. Polluted water bodies have usually high abundance of plants like *Nostoc* and *Oscillatoria*. Give reasons. **NCERT Exemplar**

Ans Polluted water bodies possess high algal growth due to the presence of nutrients. These nutrients increase the rapid growth of water plants, i.e. algae especially *Nostoc* and *Oscillitoria*, etc., and result in colonies. These colonies are generally surrounded by a gelatinous sheath and furtherleads to the formation of blooms in waterbodies. (2)

29. When did cyanobacteria evolved? Why are they referred as the earliest colonisers of barren areas?

Ans Cyanobacteria evolved more than three million years back. They are the self-contained photosynthetic organisms. They can live under any type of environment and on any of substrate with the help of their specialised cell wall. Because of this, they are one of the earliest colonisers of barren areas. (2)

Short Answer Type II Questions
3 Marks

30. **List out the characteristics of Archaebacteria.**

Ans Refer to text on page no. 21.

31. **What is the special feature of Archaebacteria? How do these obtain food? How are they able to tolerate high temperature as well as acidity?**

Ans Archaebacteria are able to tolerate high temperature as well as high acidity. (1)

These bacteria are chemoautotrophic, which obtain energy for synthesis of food by oxidising sulphur. Under anaerobic conditions they oxidise sulphur to sulphuric acid.

$$2S + 2H_2O + 3O_2 \longrightarrow 2H_2SO_4$$

Thermoacidophiles are able to tolerate high temperature as well as acidity, due to the presence of

(i) branched chain lipids in the cell membranes.

(ii) special resistant enzymes capable of operating under aerobic conditions. (2)

32. **Differentiate between pili and fimbriae.**

Ans Differences between pili and fimbriae are

Pili	Fimbriae
They are tube-like outgrowths of bacterial cells.	They are solid outgrowths of bacterial cells.
Their length is about 18-20 μm.	Their length is about 0.15-1.5 μm.
Only 1-4 pili occur per cell.	About 300-400 fimbriae occur per cell.
They help in conjugation.	They help in clinging to various objects.

(3)

33. **Give the name of the bacteria for following activities**

(i) Food poisoning

(ii) Denitrification of soil

(iii) Dairy industry

(iv) Vinegar production

(v) Retting of fibres

(vi) Genetic engineering

Ans (i) *Staphylococcus aureus* and *Clostridium botulinum.*

(ii) *Thiobacillus denitrificans* and *Micrococcus denitrificans.*

(iii) *Lactobacillus acidophyllus.*

(iv) *Acetobacter acetic.*

(v) *Pseudomonas fluorescens* and *Clostridium* sp.

(vi) *Escherichia coli* and *Agrobacterium tumefaciens.*

(½ × 6)

34. **Cyanobacteria and heterotrophic bacteria have been clubbed together in Eubacteria of Kingdom–Monera as per the five kingdom classification even though the two are vastly different from each other. Is this grouping of the two types of taxa in the same kingdom justified? If so, why?** **NCERT Exemplar**

Ans Although the two are vastly different from each other. They still bear some common characters, on the basis of which they are introduced in Eubacteria of kingdom–Monera. (1)

These characters are as follows

(i) Both the groups do not possess well-defined nucleus.

(ii) Nucleus lacks nucleous and nuclear membrane.

(iii) DNA (genetic material) lies freely in the cytoplasm.

(iv) They possess 70 S type of ribosomes. (2)

35. **List out the differences between bacteria and cyanobacteria.**

Ans Refer to text on page no. 27.

36. **Mention two harmful effects of cyanobacteria.**

Ans Cyanobacteria have the following harmful effects

(i) *Oscillatoria* causes asthama and gastrointestinal problems.

(ii) Excessive growth in waterbodies decreases oxygen levels, thereby killing aquatic animals. (3)

Long Answer Type Questions
5 Marks

37. **List out the important characteristics of bacteria.**

Ans Refer to text on page no. 22.

38. **Breifly describe the components of a typical bacterial cell.**

Ans A bacterial cell consists of following components

(i) **Cell envelope** It is the outer covering of protoplasm of bacterial cell. It contains mucilage sheath, cell wall and plasma membrane.

(ii) **Cytoplasm** It is a crystallo colloidal complex that forms the protoplasm excluding its nucleoid. Membrane bound cell organelles are absent. Cytoplasm along with nucleoid are together called as protoplasm.

(iii) **Nucleoid** It represents the genetic material of prokaryotes. Nucleoid consists of a single circular strand of DNA.

(iv) **Plasmids** These are self-replicating, extrachromosomal segments of double-stranded, circular, naked DNA.

(v) **Flagella** These are unstranded, equivalent to a single microtubular fibre. These help in movement and locomotion.

(vi) **Pili and Fimbriae** Pili are longer, fewer and thicker tubular outgrowths made up of protein pilin. Fimbriae are small bristle-like fibres sprouting from cell surface in large number.

Pili are helpful in attaching to recipient cell and forming conjugation tube. Fimbriae cause agglutination of RBC. They also help in mutual clinging of bacteria. (5)

39. Why does the interior of bacterial cell appear simple and granular? Which components make cell envelope of bacterial cell? What gives gummy or sticky trait to bacterial cells and if it is not essential for survival, what are its functions?

Ans (i) The interior of bacterial cell seems simple and granular because the membrane bound organelles are not present in it.

(ii) Mucilage, cell wall and plasma membrane are together called cell envelope.

(iii) Mucilage or Glycocalyx gives gummy or sticky trait to cells. (3)

Though it is not essential for bacterial survival, glycocalyx has several functions such as

(a) Protection from dessication and toxins.

(b) Preventing host phagocytes to get attached to the bacterium.

(c) Holding cells together.

(d) Storing chemicals for virulence. (2)

40. In which organisms heterocyst is present? Mention two features of heterocysts. Which features make it suitable for nitrogen-fixation?

Ans (i) Heterocysts are present in some cyanobacteria. It is a large-sized, pale coloured, thick-walled cell which occurs in terminal, intercalary or lateral position in filamentous cyanobacteria, e.g. *Nostoc*. (2)

(ii) Heterocyst is dependent for its nourishment on adjacent vegetative cells.

The thick wall is impermeable to oxygen, but permeable to nitrogen. It has enzyme nitrogenase which is specialised to perform nitrogen-fixation. (3)

TOPIC 03 Viruses

Five kingdom classification of **RH Whittaker** has not classified viruses, viroids and lichens in any group.

The viruses did not find a place in any classification system since they are not truly living, as living organisms are those that have a cellular structure.

Viruses are small, submicroscopic, acellular, obligate parasite. Despite simple physical and chemical composition, attributes of life such as multiplication, variation and transmission of genetic information are inherent in viruses. Their characteristic features are

- These cannot be separated by bacterial filters.
- These cannot be grown in artificial medium.
- These can be inactivated by chemotherapy and thermotherapy and show response to change in temperature and humidity.
- They are obligate intracellular parasites.
- They lack functional autonomy but develop independently and have their own nucleic acid.
- Possess only one type of nucleic acid and protein coat.
- Lack division but show replication of nucleic acid using host cell machinery.

Living Properties of Virus

- Genetic material replicates.
- Mutant forms of viruses are reported.
- Show sensitivity to stimulants such as temperature, humidity, chemicals, radiations, etc.
- Possess antigenic properties.
- Host specific and multiply inside host cell.

Non-living Properties of Virus

- Can be crystallised.
- Are inert outside host cell.
- Do not possess functional autonomy.
- Devoid of cell membrane and wall.
- Do not respire.
- Their properties are similar to biomolecules.

Since, viruses possess properties of both living and non-living they are considered link between living and non-living forms.

Discoveries Related to Virus

(i) The name virus was given by **Pasteur** (virus means venom or poisonous fluid). **DJ Ivanowsky** (1892) recognised certain microbes as causative organism of the mosaic disease of tobacco.

(ii) **MW Beijerinck** (1898) demonstrated that the extract of the infected plants of tobacco could cause infection in healthy plants. He called the fluid as *Contagium vivum fluidum* (infectious living fluid).

(iii) **WM Stanley** (1935) showed that viruses could be crystallised and crystals consist largely of proteins.

Size

Virus is a ultramicroscopic nucleoprotein entity. Size of virus ranges from about 10 nm (foot and mouth virus of cattle), 17 nm (alfalfa mosaic virus) to 1250×40 nm (beet yellow virus), TMV (Tobacco Mosaic Virus) is 300×15 nm, 400 nm (parrot fever virus), 1300×15 nm (*Pseudomonas*).

Shape

The architecture of viruses is mainly of following types

(i) **Spherical**, e.g. Alfalfa mosaic virus.

(ii) **Cubical**, e.g. *Vaccinia*.

(iii) **Helical** (elongate body) e.g. TMV.

(iv) **Polyhedral** (short, broad body, rounded, polyhedral shape), e.g. Poliomyelitis virus.

(v) **Binal** (cuboidal and helical parts both), e.g. many bacteriophages like T_2 and T_4.

Structure

A virus structure has mainly four parts

1. Envelope

It is the outer covering present in certain viruses. It is made of protein of viral origin, lipid and carbohydrate of host. Spikes or Outgrowths may or may not be present. Some common enveloped viruses are HIV, Herpes virus, *Vaccinia* virus.

2. Capsid

It is a protein covering around the genetic material. Capsid has protein subunits called **capsomeres**. TMV has 2130 capsomeres.

The capsomeres are arranged helically or in geometric forms.

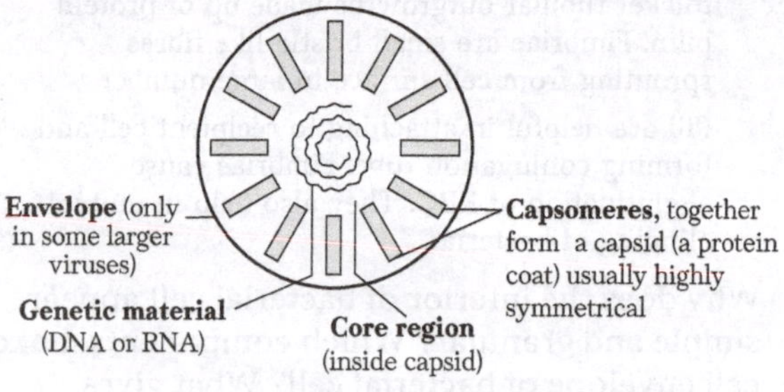

Fig. 2.5 Structure of a generalised virus

3. Core or Nucleoid

It contains genetic material which is either DNA or RNA but never both. Most of the animal viruses have double-stranded DNA as genetic material, while majority of plant viruses have single-stranded RNA as genetic material. Some animal viruses may even have single or double-stranded RNA.

4. Enzymes

They are rarely present. Lysozyme is found in bacteriophages. In some RNA viruses called **retroviruses**, RNA polymerase, reverse transcriptase enzymes are present.

Classification

Based on the presence of DNA or RNA, viruses are divided in two main groups

1. Deoxyvira or DNA Viruses

These are generally animal viruses with a few important ones having RNA as genetic material, e.g. rabies virus, polio virus, retroviruses including HIV or AIDS virus. The structural form of deoxyvira are deoxyhelica, deoxycubica and deoxybinala.

2. Ribovira or RNA Viruses

These are generally plant viruses with a few containing DNA as material e.g. cauliflower mosaic virus. The structural form of ribovira are ribohelica and ribocubica.

Types of Viruses

Viruses are classified by **Holmes** (1948) into three groups based on their host types

1. Plants Viruses (Phytophagineae)

These viruses cause disease in plants. Examples of plant viruses are Tobacco Mosaic Virus (TMV), Potato Mosaic Virus (PMV), tomato leaf curl virus, etc.

Structure of Tobacco Mosaic Virus

It is rod-shaped, about 3000Å long and 170Å in diameter. The capsomeres of TMV are elliptical and arranged helically around the central nucleic acid core.

Hans Fraenkel Conrat *et. al.* demonstrated that the RNA is the genetic material in TMV. Its complete structure is shown below

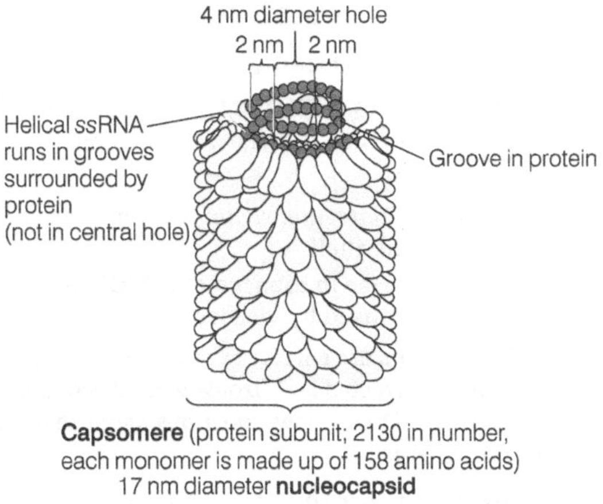

Fig. 2.6 Structure of TMV

2. Animal Viruses (Zoophagineae)

These viruses cause disease in humans, e.g. influenza virus, smallpox virus, poliomyelitis virus, hepatitis virus, mumps virus, rhino viruses.

3. Bacterial Viruses (Phagineae)

These are also known as **bacteriophages** and mainly infect lower organisms (phagineae bacteria). Bacteriophages were discovered by **Edward Twort** (1915) and **d' Herelle** (1917) independently.

For example, T_2, T_4, lambda, coliphages (bacteriophages of *E. coli*), cyanophages (blue-green algal viruses, e.g. LPP-1, SM-1, N-1), phycophages (algal viruses), mycophages (fungal viruses), zymophages (mycophages of yeast).

Structure of Bacteriophage

The shape of bacteriophages is tadpole-like consisting of a head (icosahadral) and a tail. **Head** has a protein cover or capsid. Internally, the head encloses a highly folded double-stranded DNA (approximately 50 μ in length).

A **connector** is present in between the head and the tail. The connector contains a neck and a collar. **Collar** possesses several whiskers. The **tail** is the narrow cylindrical part. It has central hollow core or tube through which viral DNA is injected into the host.

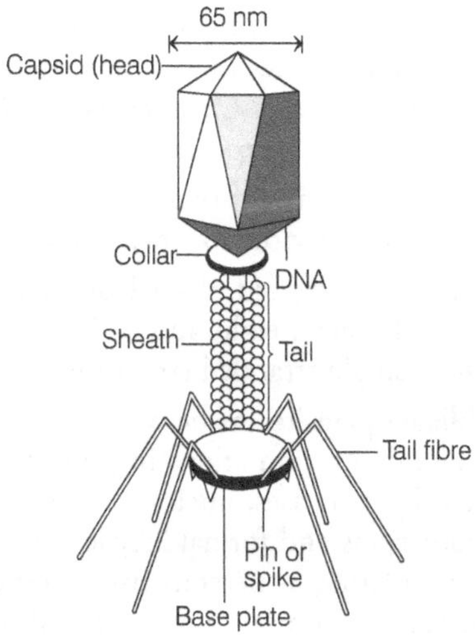

Fig 2.7 Structure of T_4-bacteriophage

The core contains enzymes like lysozyme, etc., and is surrounded by sheath proteins (formed of 2000 capsomeres). The tail ends in a **basal plate** or end plate. The basal plate includes tail pins and tail fibres (spikes) that are generally involved in attachment to the host cell.

Some Common Viral Diseases

Plant Viral Diseases	Animal Viral Diseases	Human Viral Diseases
Tobacco Mosaic	Foot and mouth disease	Poliomyelitis
Potato Mosaic	Equine encephalitis Rinderpest	Rabies
Pumpkin Mosaic	Kysanur Forest Disease (KFD) of monkeys	Mumps
Apple Mosaic		Measles
Wheat Mosaic Streak	Ranikhet disease of fowl	Chickenpox
Potato Leaf Roll		Dengue
Tobacco Leaf Curl		Encephalitis
Banana Bunchy Top		Common flu
		Yellow fever
		Hepatitis
		AIDS
		Herpes

Sub-Viral Pathogens

Viroids (satellite RNA) and prions belong to this category. TO Diener (1971) discovered a new infectious agent viroid that was smaller than viruses and caused potato spindle tuber disease, *Citrus* exocortis disease.

Virusoids are small circular RNAs similar to viroids, but are located inside protein coat of a true virus. Virusoids require the assistance of virus for their replication.

Viroids are free RNAs devoid of nucleoprotein coat. The RNA has low molecular weight and is tightly folded into circular or linear single-stranded structure.

Prions are obligate parasites made of glycoproteins only. They are formed due to mutations in gene PRNP. Prions are not affected by proteases, nucleases, temperature upto 800°C, UV radiations and formaldehyde. These cause disease by accumulating in nervous tissue and cause its degeneration. Some common diseases caused by them are scrapie of sheep, mad cow disease, etc.

Topic Practice 3

Multiple Choice Questions

1 Mark

1. Viruses are non-cellular organisms, but replicate themselves once they infect the host cell. To which of the following kindgom viruses belong to? **NCERT Exemplar**
   (a) Monera (b) Protista
   (c) Fungi (d) None of these

Ans (d) Viruses and viroids are the non-cellular organisms, which are not characterised in the classification of Whittaker.

2. Which of the following phenomenon proves that viruses are living?
   (a) They carry metabolic activity
   (b) They carry anaerobic respiration
   (c) They multiply in host cells
   (d) They cause infection

Ans (c) They multiply in host cells. It proves that they are living.

3. Viruses are also known as
   (a) nucleoprotein particles
   (b) virion
   (c) lipoprotein particles
   (d) core

Ans (a) Viruses are also known as nucleoprotein particles. The nucleic acid of virus is surrounded by a protein shell called capsid.

4. The non-living characteristic of viruses is
   (a) ability to multiply only inside the host
   (b) ability to cause diseases in the host
   (c) ability to undergo mutation
   (d) ability of crystallisation

Ans (d) Viruses are known as a connecting link between non-living and living beings. They are thought to be non-living as they do not show any sign of life outside the host and can be crystallised in laboratory.

5. Select the wrong statement.
   (a) The viroids were discovered by DJ Ivanowski
   (b) WM Stanley showed that viruses could be crystallised
   (c) The term *'Contagium vivum fluidum'* was coined by MW Beijerinck
   (d) Mosaic disease in tobacco and AIDS in human being are caused by viruses

Ans (a) All statements are correct except the statement (a), which can be corrected as–Viroids were discovered by TO Diener in 1971 as a new infectious agent that was smaller than virus.

6. The latest view for the origin of viruses is
   (a) they have arisen from nucleic acid and proteins found in primitive soup
   (b) they arose from bacteria as a result of the loss of cell wall, ribosome, etc.
   (c) they arose from some bacteria, which had developed a nucleus only
   (d) they are modified plasmids, which are infact the fragments of the nucleic acids of the host

Ans (d) Many scientists believe that viruses are modified plasmids, which are the fragments of the nucleic acids of the host.
Their genome fractions escaped and got inducted into new host cells.

7. The genetic material of viruses consists of
   (a) Only *ds* or *ss* DNA
   (b) Only *ds* or *ss* RNA
   (c) DNA or RNA (Both *ds* and *ss*)
   (d) *ss*DNA or *ss*RNA

Ans (c) Viruses are nucleoproteins having one or more nucleic acid molecules, either double-stranded or single-stranded DNA or RNA, encased in a protective coat of protein or lipoprotein.

8. Which of the following plant viruses has DNA?
   (a) Tobacco mosaic virus
   (b) Potato mosaic virus
   (c) Tomato mosaic virus
   (d) Cauliflower mosaic virus

Ans (d) Cauliflower mosaic virus is one of a few double-stranded DNA plant viruses.

9. A new infectious agent that is smaller than virus is
(a) prion (b) viroid
(c) bacteria (d) mycoplasma

Ans (b) Viroids were discovered by TO Diener in 1971 as a new infectious agent that were smaller than viruses. Viroids lack capsid and have not proteins associated with them.

10. Which of the following groups of diseases is caused by viruses?
(a) Mumps, smallpox, herpes, influenza
(b) AIDS, diabetes, herpes, tuberculosis
(c) Anthrax, cholera, tetanus, tuberculosis
(d) Cholera, tetanus, smallpox, influenza

Ans (a) In human, virus causes various diseases like AIDS (HIV virus), mumps (paramyxovirus), smallpox (variola virus), herpes (HSVI) and influenza (RNA viruses of the family–Orthomyxoviridae).

Very Short Answer Type Questions

(1 Mark)

11. Name the scientist who describes viruses as *Contagium vivum fluidum.*

Ans **MW Beijerinck** (1898) demonstrated that the extract of infected plants of tobacco could cause disease in healthy plants. He called the fluid as *Contagium vivum fluidum* (infectious living fluid).

12. Name the scientist who first crystalise viruses.

Ans **WM Stanley** (1935) showed that viruses could be crystallised and crystals consist of proteins.

13. What is capsid and how is it useful for viruses?

Ans Capsid is a proteinaceous covering around the virus. It protects the nucleoid from damage from physical and chemical agents.

14. Name the type of viruses that possess enzymes like reverse transcriptase, RNA polymerase, etc.

Ans Retroviruses

15. Give two examples of DNA viruses.

Ans (i) Rabies virus (ii) Polio virus

16. Give name of any two animal viral disease.

Ans (i) Foot and mouth disease
(ii) Ranikhet disease of fowl

17. Name the scientist who discovered bacteriophage.

Ans Bacteriophages were discovered by Edward Twort (1915) and d' Herelle (1917) independently.

18. Which enzyme is present in bacteriophages?

Ans Lysozyme is present in the bacteriophages is released when comes in contact with host cell.

19. Name the infection agent that causes potato spindle tuber.

Ans Viroids.

Short Answer Type I Questions

(2 Marks)

20. Why virus cannot grow on non-living culture medium?

Ans A virus cannot grow on non-living culture medium because it needs living cells for its metabolism and multiplication. (2)

21. A virus is considered as a living organism and an obligate parasite when inside a host cell. But virus is not classified along with bacteria or fungi. What are the characters of virus that are similar to non-living objects?

Ans Viruses are considered as living when they are inside a host, but outside any host they are referred to as non-living due to their
(a) inert nature
(b) can be crystallised
(c) lack of cell membrane and cell wall
(d) inability for respiration
(e) do not exhibit functional anatomy

These characters potraited by viruses make them identical to non-living organisms. Viruses are considered a connecting link between living and non-living organisms. (2)

22. Why viruses are called obligate parasites?

Ans All viruses are considered as obligate parasites because they lack metabolic machinery of their own to generate energy or to synthesise proteins. Thus, they depend on their host to carry out these vital functions. (2)

23. Give a brief account of different types of shape found in viruses along with examples.

Ans The architecture of viruses is mainly of following types
(i) **Spherical**, e.g. Alfalfa mosaic virus.
(ii) **Cubical**, e.g. *Vaccinia.*
(iii) **Helical** (elongate body), e.g. TMV.
(iv) **Polyhedral** (short, broad body, rounded, polyhedral shape), e.g. Poliomyelitis virus.
(v) **Binal** (cuboidal and helical parts both), e.g. many bacteriophages like T_2 and T_4. (2)

24. In which virus two single RNA strands are present? What is the role of reverse transcriptase?

Ans HIV has two single RNA strands in its nucleoid. Reverse transcriptase enzyme catalyses the formation of DNA from RNA. It is found in some RNA viruses called retroviruses, e.g. HIV. (2)

25. What are bacteriophages and their types? Identify their shape.

Ans Bacteriophages are viruses which infect bacteria. They are numbered T_1 to T_7 as their types. The shape of bacteriophages is tadpole-like with a head and a tail. (2)

26. How are viroids different from viruses? NCERT

Ans Differences between viroids and viruses are

Viroids	Viruses
Protein coat is not present.	Protein coat is present.
These are short segments of free RNA which are infectious.	The genetic/infectious material is RNA or DNA enclose in protein coat.
RNA is small.	RNA is comparatively larger in size.

(2)

27. Name the scientist who discovered viroids?

Ans Viroids were first discovered and named by TO Diener (1971).

28. Define viroids.

Ans Viroids are small circular RNAs which mainly infects plants.

Short Answer Type II Questions

3 Marks

29. List out some living features of viruses.

Ans Viruses have the following features that make them similar to living things

(i) They have DNA or RNA.
(ii) Their nucleic acid can undergo mutation.
(iii) They can reproduce only in living host cells.
(iv) They infect different types of host cells.
(v) The nucleic acids of viruses are identical in composition to those of other organisms.
(vi) They respond against temperature and other stimulus. (3)

30. Explain the structure of bacteriophage with the help of well-labelled diagram.

Ans A bacteriophage consists of two main parts, i.e. head and tail.

Head The head is in the form of bipyramidal hexagonal prism. It consists of proteinaceous membrane enclosing a core of viral DNA. The DNA is double-stranded.

Tail It is cylindrical. It has four components are

(i) a central core.
(ii) a protein sheath surrounding the core.
(iii) a sheath connected to head by a collar and at distal end to a hexagonal basal plate.
(iv) pins at the corners of basal plate. Basal plate also bears six long tail fibres which are the organs of attachment to the bacterial surface.

For diagram Refer to fig no. 2.7 on page no 33. [3]

31. Give a comparision between viruses and prions.

Ans Refer to text on page on. 34.

32. What are prions? Describe briefly.

Ans Prions are obligate parasites made of glycoproteins only. They are formed due to mutations in gene PRNP. Prions are not affected by proteases, nucleases, temperature upto 800°C, UV radiations and formaldehyde.

These cause disease by accumulating in nervous tissue and cause its degeneration. Some common diseases caused by them are scrapie of sheep, mad cow disease, etc. (3)

Long Answer Type Questions

5 Marks

33. How do viruses resemble non-living things?

Or Organise a discussion in your class on the topic. 'Are viruses living or non-living'? NCERT

Ans Viruses are intermediate between living and non-living objects. (1)

They resemble non-living objects in

(i) Lacking protoplast.
(ii) Ability to get crystallised.
(iii) High specific gravity which is found only in non-living objects.
(iv) Absence of respiration and energy storing system.
(v) Absence of growth and division.
(vi) Cannot live independent of a living cell.

They resemble living objects in (2)

(i) Presence of genetic material (DNA or RNA).
(ii) Capable of mutation.
(iii) Irritability.
(iv) Can grow and multiply inside the host cell. (2)

34. Describe the basic structure of virus.

Ans Refer to text on page on. 31, 32 and 33.

35. Give a brief account of viruses with respect to their structure and nature of genetic material. Also name four common viral diseases. NCERT

Ans Viruses are nucleoproteins. The genetic material is protected within a protein coat, called **capsid**. The capsid consists of a number of subunits called capsomeres. The capsids are arranged in helical, polyhedral or geometric form.

The genetic material, i.e. DNA or RNA may be single-stranded or double-stranded.

The four common viral diseases are poliomyelitis, rinderpest, dengue, potato mosaic. (5)

SUMMARY

- It is necessary to classify organisms to study them more easily.
- Aristotle was the earliest to attempt a more scientific basis for classification.
- Linnaeus (1758) proposed **two kingdom classification** on the basis of the presence or absence of cell wall.
- However, some organisms possessing characters of both plants and animals lead to **three kingdom classification** (Haeckel; 1866) organisms were classified into Plantae, Protista and Animalia on the basis of lack of tissue differentiation.
- Copeland (1956) proposed **four kingdom classification**. He divided living beings into four categories, namely–Monera, Protista, Plantae and Animalia.
- In 1969, RH Whittaker classified organisms into **five kingdom classification**. He classified them on the basis of complexity of cell structure and body structure, mode of nutrition, ecological life-style and phylogenetic relationships.
- **Kingdom–Monera** includes all prokaryotes, *viz.*, mycoplasmas, bacteria, actinomycetes and cyanobacteria.
- All unicellular eukaryotic organisms like flagellates, diatoms, dinoflagellates, slime moulds, etc., were kept in the **kingdom–Protista**.
- **Kingdom–Fungi** contains achlorophyllous, thalloid plants. They are usually saprophytic, parasitic or occasionally symbiotic, e.g. *Penicillium notatum*, *Aspergillus niger*, yeast, etc.
- In the **kingdom–Plantae** all photoautotrophs were kept, e.g. mango, peepal, etc. However, it also includes thalloid algae.
- **Kingdom–Animalia** consists of heterotrophic holozoic organisms, e.g. tiger, cow, cat, etc.
- The most recent classification of living organisms is **six kingdom classification** proposed by Carl Woese, O Kandler and ML Wheelis (1990). These six kingdoms are Archaebacteria, Eubacteria, Protista, Fungi, Plantae and Animalia.
- **Kingdom–Monera** includes the smallest, simplest and most abundant microorganisms.
- All the members of monera are prokaryotes, characterised by the presence of nucleoid, 70 S ribosomes and lacks double membrane bond organelles.
- All the members of monera are placed in two groups–Archaebacteria and Eubacteria.
- **Bacteria** were first reported by Av Leeuwenhoek (Father of Bacteriology) in 1683. F. Cohn (Father of Modern Bacteriology) gave the term 'Bacteria' in 1872.
- Bacterial cell contains glycocalyx, flagella, fimbriae, pili, cell wall, plasma membrane, mesosomes, 70 S ribosomes and inclusions in cytoplasm.
- Bacteria greatly varies in shape, grouped under four categories; spherical coccus, rod-shaped bacillus; spiral, spirillum and comma-shaped vibrium.
- On the basis of Gram staining technique bacteria are classified into Gram positive and Gram negative bacteria.
- Bacterial flagella is single stranded microtubular fibre that helps in locomotion.
- Nutrition in bacteria can be autotrophic or heterotrophic.
- Autotrophic bacteria are of two types on the basis of energy source, i.e. photoautotrophic and chemoautotrophic bacteria.
- Photoautotrophic bacteria contains chlorophyll-*a*, bacterio-purpurin and bacterio-viridin, which traps solar energy for food synthesis.
- Chemoautotrophic bacteria obtain energy from organic compounds made by other organisms. They oxidise substances like nitrates, nitrites and ammonia, e.g. *Nitrosomonas, Nitrobacter*.
- Heterotrophic bacteria (organotrophs) are dependent on external organic material for energy requirements, e.g. *Pseudomonas*, *E. coli*.
- Respiration in bacteria occur *via* aerobic and anaerobic modes.
- Reproduction in bacteria is asexual mainly.
- They rarely reproduce by sexual mode.
- **Asexual reproduction** takes place by two modes vegetative reproduction (fission and budding) and sporulation.
- **Sexual reproduction** takes place in form of genetic recombination where some genes are transferred from one bacterium to another. It is of three types
  - **Transformation** Genes transferred as naked DNA, does not involve contact between cells.
  - **Transduction** DNA transfer with the help of bacteriophage.
  - **Conjugation** Gene transfer involves cell to cell contact.
- **Mycoplasma** are the smallest free-living prokaryotes, lack cell wall, pleomorphic and can survive without oxygen.
- **Cyanobacteria** are Gram negative, photosynthetic prokaryotes, which are capable of fixing atmospheric nitrogen with the help of heterocyst.
- **Archaebacteria** differ from bacteria in terms of cell wall composition.
- Live in harsh habitats and categorised into
  - Methanogens (marsh areas)
  - Halophiles (salty areas)
  - Thermoacidophiles (hot springs).
- **Viruses** are very small infective obligate intracellular parasites, made up of nucleic acids and proteins.
- Viruses do not have a proper cellular organisation and their own metabolic machinery. They multiply within the host cell by utilising its reproductive mechinery.
- The core of a virus contains the nucleic acid, i.e. either DNA or RNA or both.
- Viruses are classified on the basis of phenotypic morphology, nucleic acid type, mode of replication, host organisms and the type of disease they cause.
- **Viroids** are circular, *ss*RNA molecules containing pathogen. These lack viroin like dormant phase.
- **Prions** are proteinaceous infectious particles that cause a number of fatal degenerative disorders of central nervous system of humans and other animals.
- **Virusoids** are small circular RNA particles found in plants. They are located inside the protein coat of a true virus.

Chapter Practice

Multiple Choice Questions

1 Mark

1. The five kingdom classification was proposed by **NCERT Exemplar**
   (a) RH Whittaker (b) C Linnaeus
   (c) A Roxberg (d) Virchow
2. Organisms living in salty areas are called as **NCERT Exemplar**
   (a) methanogens (b) halophiles
   (c) heliophyles (d) thermoacidophiles
3. *Contagium vivum fluidum* was proposed by **NCERT Exemplar**
   (a) DJ Ivanowsky (b) MW Beijerinck
   (c) Stanley Miller (d) Robert Hook
4. Difference between virus and viroid is **NCERT Exemplar**
   (a) the absence of protein coat in viroid, but present in virus
   (b) the presence of low molecular weight RNA in virus, but absent in viroid
   (c) Both (a) and (b)
   (d) None of the above

Assertion-Reason Type Questions

1 Mark

■ Direction (Q. Nos. 5-8) *In each of the following questions, a statement of Assertion (A) is given followed by corresponding statement of Reason (R). Of the statements, mark the correct answer as*

(a) If both A and R are true and R is the correct explanation of A
(b) If both A and R are true, but R is not the correct explanation of A
(c) If A is true, but R is false
(d) If A is false, but R is true

5. **Assertion** (A) The two kingdom classification, used for a long time, was found to be inadequate.
   Reason (R) Two kingdom system of classification did not distinguish between the eukaryotes and prokaryotes, unicellular and multicellular organisms and green algae and fungi.
6. **Assertion** (A) Three domains system classifies organisms based on cellular characteristics.
   Reason (R) The three domains are, i.e. Archaea, Bacteria and Eukarya.
7. Observe the diagram of *Nostoc* and comment upon the appropriateness of the Assertion and the Reason.

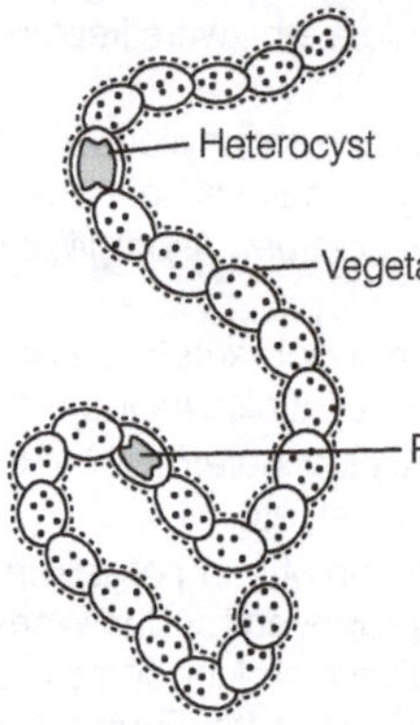

   Assertion (A) *Nostoc* are prokaryotic and are often grouped with bacteria. They are kept in cyanobacteria since, they are able to photosynthesise.
   Reason (R) These blue-green bacteria can tolerate adverse conditions very well as compared to other aquatic plants.
8. **Assertion** (A) Viruses cause diseases and replicate when they are in the host cell.
   Reason (R) Viruses do not replicate outside the host, but they survive in environment.

Answers

1. (a) **2.** (b) **3.** (b) **4.** (a) **5.** (a)
6. (b) **7.** (b) **8.** (b)

Very Short Answer Type Questions

(1 Mark)

9. Which kingdoms were created by RH Whittaker?
10. Given the names of the types of nutrition on which the five kingdom system of classification is based.
11. Kingdom–Monera was added to the classification system by whom and why?
12. Which bacteria are called the true becteria? Give reason.

Short Answer Type I Questions

(2 Marks)

13. Mention any two differences between prokaryotes and eukaryotes.
14. Why Whittaker left viruses in his system of classification?
15. Archaebacteria are called as primitive prokaryotes.
    Why? Identify the name of any two Archaebacteria based on the environment they are found in.
16. Give the name of any two plant and animal viral diseases.

Short Answer Type II Questions

(3 Marks)

17. Write a brief account of three kingdom classification system.
18. Discuss the modes of sexual reproduction occurring in the becteria.
19. Which are called viroids and also give their harmful effects ?

Long Answer Type Questions

(5 Marks)

20. Explain the need of biological classification.
21. Classify viruses on the basis of host cell they infect.
22. Explain the structure of bacteriophage.

Case Based Questions

(4/5 Marks)

23. The histogram given below shows the use of bacteria in different fields of our lives.

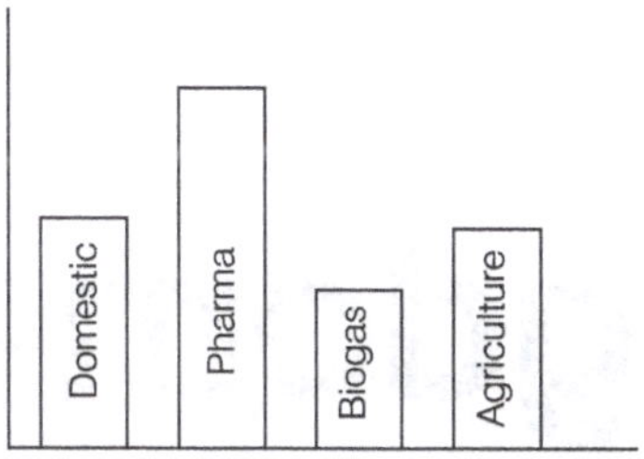

Study the graph and answer the following questions.
   (i) Give one example where bacteria can be used in household purposes.
   (ii) Bacteria are species with both harm and benefits. Comment.
   (iii) Why is bar 'C' the least when compared to others ?
   (iv) Write the importance of cyanobacteria in agriculture.

24. A student observed polluted water bodies. He found green gelatinous organisms which spread the all over the water. He studied some of these organisms under microscope and discussed with his teacher.
   (i) What are these green gelatinous organisms?
   (ii) What is heterocysts?
   (iii) Write any two features of the cyanobacteria.
   (iv) Write any one similarity between cyanobacteria and plants.
   (v) What is the other name of cyanobacteria?

25. *Read the following passage and answer the questions that follow*

Viruses are non-cellular organisms that are characterised by an inert crystalline structure surrounding the genetic material. These are obligate parasites and do not have a biosynthetic machinery. Therefore, they use host machinery to replicate themselves.

Viruses are ultramicroscopic nucleoprotein entities having variable size and shape. The basic structure of virus is composed of envelope, capsid and nucleoid. Based on the type of genetic mateial, viruses are classified as Deoxyvira and Ribovira.
   (i) Name the viruses which do not contain DNA.
   (ii) What is the features of virus capsid?
   (iii) Name a polyhedral-shaped virus.
   (iv) Name a virus that affects plants.

CHAPTER

03

Kingdom–Protista

The term 'Protisa' was given by **Ernst Haeckel** (1866). This kingdom includes eukaryotic unicellular organisms that cannot be classified as plants, animals or fungus. Besides their relatively simple levels of organisation, protistans do not necessarily have much in common. Protistans were the first eukaryotes to evolve, about 1000 million years ago. These are the most primitive living organisms and are found wherever life exists.

- General Characteristics and Classification of Protists
  - General Characteristics of Protists
  - Classification of Kingdom-Protista
  - Photosynthetic Protists
- Non-Photosynthetic Protists
  - Fungus-like Protists or Slime Moulds
  - Animal-like Protists or Protozoan

TOPIC 01 General Characteristics and Classification of Protists

Kingdom–Protista includes diverse forms of all **single-celled predominantly water dwelling eukaryotes** but the boundries of this kingdom are not well-defined. This kingdom was first proposed by **Ernst Haeckel** (1866). Physiologically, kingdom–Protista acts as a connecting link between the kingdom–Monera and the complex multicellular kingdoms–Fungi, Plantae and Animalia.

Kingdom–Protista includes the following categories such as dinoflagellates, chrysophytes, euglenoids, slime moulds and protozoans.

General Characteristics of Protists

The main characteristics of protists are as follows

(i) These are mostly aquatic organisms. Some protists also live in the bodies of animals as parasites.

(ii) The cells are eukaryotic. These contain membrane bound cell organelles like mitochondria, Golgi complex, endoplasmic reticulum, 80 S ribosomes, double layered nuclear membrane, etc.

(iii) Locomotion may either occur by **pseudopodia** (*Amoeba, Euglypha*), **cilia** (*Paramecium*), **wriggling** (sporozoans, non-flagellates), **flagellar** (*Euglena*) and **mucilage propulsion** (some protists like diatoms).

Diatoms do not have any organelles for locomotion.

(iv) Protists show various modes of nutrition such as

(a) **Photosynthetic** (Holophytic) Dinoflagellates, diatoms and euglenoids.

(b) **Holozoic** (Zootrophic) Protozoans like *Amoeba* and *Paramecium.*

(c) **Saprobic** (Saprotrophic) In slime moulds.

(d) **Parasitic** *Trypanosoma, Giardia, Plasmodium, Entamoeba.*

(e) **Mixotrophic** In *Euglena.*

(f) **Symbiotic** In zooflagellates like *Trichonympha* and *Lophomonas.*

(g) **Pinocytosis** In *Amoeba* to absorb soluble organic substances.

(v) Most of the protists are aerobic. However, some protists that live at the bottom of aquatic habitats can respire anaerobically.

(vi) Protists reproduce asexually by fission after acquiring maturity and divides into two or more parts and sexually by a process involving cell fusion and zygote formation, i.e. syngamy which may be isogamous or anisogamous. Conjugation and autogamy are also observed in certain protist organisms.

Classification of Kingdom–Protista

They are classified into three groups, i.e. photosynthetic protists, fungi-like protists (slime mould) and animal-like protists.

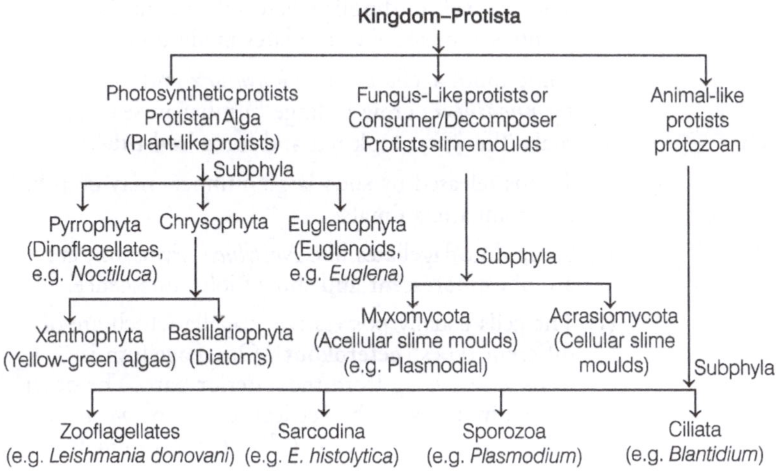

Phyla of Kingdom–Protista

Phylum	Features of Some Characteristics	Example
Euglenophyta (euglenoids)	One-celled, make or take in food, most have one flagellum.	*Euglena*
Chrysophyta (golden algae) diatoms	Most are one-celled, make their own food, yellow-brown in colour.	*Navicula*
Pyrrophyta (dinoflagellates)	One-celled, make their own food, have two flagella.	*Gonyaulax*
Sarcodina (sarcodines)	One-celled, take in food, have pseudopods.	*Amoeba*
Ciliophora (ciliates)	One-celled, take in food, have cilia.	*Paramecium*
Mastigophora (flagellates)	One-celled, take in food, have two or more flagella.	*Leishmania*
Sporozoa (sporozoans)	One-celled, take in food, no means of movement.	*Monocystis*
Myxomycetes (slime molds)	Many or one-celled, absorb food, change form during life cycle.	*Plasmodium*

Photosynthetic Protists

These are plant-like protists or phytoplanktons. Their common habitats are lakes and oceans.

They are responsible for about 70% photosynthesis of the biosphere that occurs in marine habitat. Hence, they are the major productive factors of the aquatic ecosystem.

These include chrysophytes, dinoflagellates and euglenoids.

1. Chrysophytes

The members of this phylum store food as oil. Some forms give unpleasant odours to the freshwater lakes where they inhabit. Reproduction is usually asexual type, but occasionally sexual type also occurs.

This group includes diatoms and golden algae (desmids).

i. Diatoms

(a) Diatoms occur in all aquatic and moist terrestrial habitats and are also known as **chief producer** in the ocean.

(b) They pile up at the bottom of water reservoirs and form big hips called **diatomaceous earth.**

(c) They are microscopic, unicellular organisms having different shapes, such as circles, semicircles, triangular, spindle-shaped, boat-shaped or filamentous.

(d) The cells of diatoms are called **frustules.** The body wall of the diatoms is made up of cellulose impregnated with glass-like silica. This makes these cells simply indestructible.

The cell wall has two overlapping halves like a soapbox. The upper half is called **epitheca** and the lower half is called **hypotheca.**

(e) Diatoms are variously coloured, do not possess flagella except in the reproductive state.

(f) Each cell has a large central vacuole.

(g) Chloroplasts are yellowish brown to greenish brown. They contain chlorophyll-*a* and *c*. Chlorophyll-*b* is absent. They contain fucoxanthin that provides brownish tint.

(h) Food is reserved in the form of oils and leucosin (polysaccharide).

(i) The diatoms mostly reproduce asexually by binary fission. Sexual reproduction varies from isogamy to oogamy, e.g. *Navicula, Amphipleura, Triceratium* and *Cymbella.*

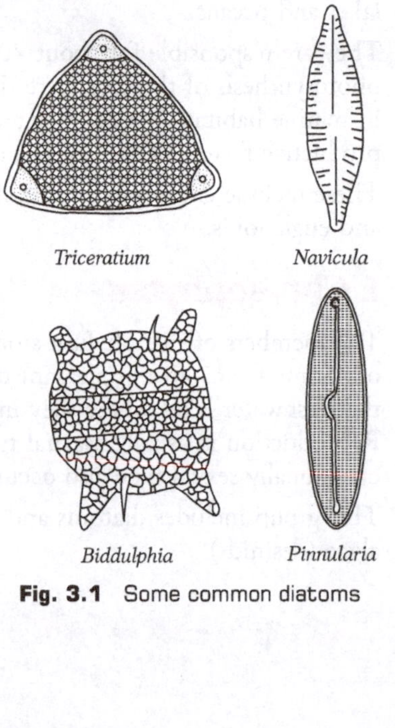

Fig. 3.1 Some common diatoms

Economic Importance of Diatoms

Diatoms are economically important in the following ways

- Diatoms are very important photosynthesisers.
- Diatomite deposits are often accompanied by petroleum fields.
- These are used as a cleaning agent in toothpastes and metal polishes and are used in filtration of oil and syrups. They are also used to enhance night visibility of sign boards.
- Diatoms are used as insulation material in refrigerators boilers and furnaces. These are also used to make sound-proof rooms.

ii. Golden Algae (Desmids)

These are unicellular green algae. Their cell walls have distinct halves. Sexual reproduction occurs by 'conjugation' (similar to *Spirogyra*). They are usually found in freshwater and act as an indicators of polluted water.

2. Dinoflagellates

These are mainly marine and photosynthetic organisms of **division-Pyrrophyta.** There are about 1000 species of photosynthetic protists known to mankind.

The general characteristic features of dinoflagellates are listed below

(i) These are important phytoplanktons. Most of them are marine but some also occur in freshwater.

(ii) They appear yellow, green, brown, blue or red depending on the main pigments present in their cells.

(iii) The cell wall in dinoflagellates, if present, is composed of number of plates made up of cellulose.

Some dinoflagellates like *Gonyaulax* and *Gymnodinium* grow in large number in sea and make the water look red and form '**red tide**'.

Toxins released by such large numbers may even kill other aquatic animals.

(iv) Some dinoflagellates like *Noctiluca*, *Pyrocystis*, etc. are phosphorescent and show bioluminescence.

(v) The cells usually possess two flagella which are of different types (**heterokont**). One flagellum is transverse arising from the anterior part. The other flagellum arises in the vertical furrow between the wall plates. Both these flagella beat in different directions.

(vi) The nucleus is enlarged and is named as mesokaryon. Chromosomes do not have histones and RNA.

(vii) The cells possess an osmoregulatory organelle called **pusule,** which superficially looks like contractile vacuoles.

(viii) Dinoflagellates reproduce asexually through cell division or by the formation of zoospores and cysts.

(ix) Reserve food is stored in the form of starch and oils. e.g. *Gonyaulax, Ceratium, Noctiluca, Peridinium* and *Gymnodinium*, etc.

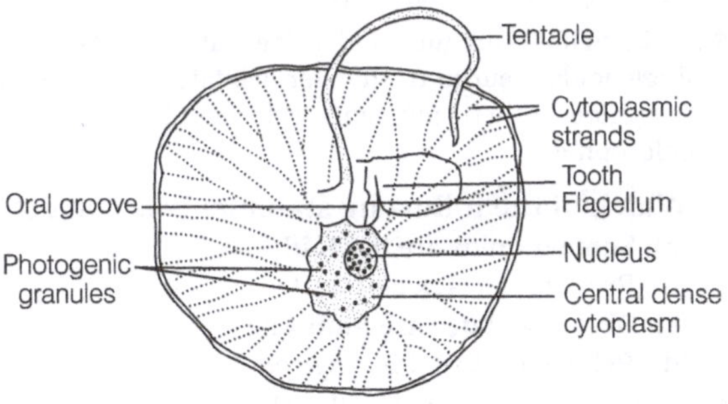

Fig. 3.2 *Noctiluca*

3. Euglenoids

Euglenoids live in fresh aquatic habitats and damp soils. They occur mostly in stagnant waters.

The characteristic features of euglenoids are described below

(i) They are unicellular flagellate protists.

(ii) Body is covered by a thin protein rich layer called **pellicle** which makes their body flexible. It lacks cellulosic cell wall.

(iii) Euglenoids have two flagella, usually one long and one short.

(iv) They perform creeping movements by expansion and contraction of their body. This phenomenon is called **metaboly.**

(v) Each cell possesses a mouth (**cytostome**) at the anterior end.

(vi) Euglenoids are autotrophic in the presence of sunlight. If deprived of sunlight, they behave like heterotrophs by predating on other smaller organisms. This mode of nutrition is **mixotrophic.**

(vii) The photosynthetic pigments include chlorophyll-*a* and *b*.

(viii) Reserve food is carbohydrate in the form of **paramylon** or **paramylum** bodies.

(ix) Euglenoids reproduce by longitudinal binary fission starting at the flagellar end under favourable conditions. The **palmella stage** is found during unfavourable conditions, e.g. *Euglena, Peranema, Eutreptia, Phacus,* etc.

Sexual reproduction is very rarely seen in euglenoids.

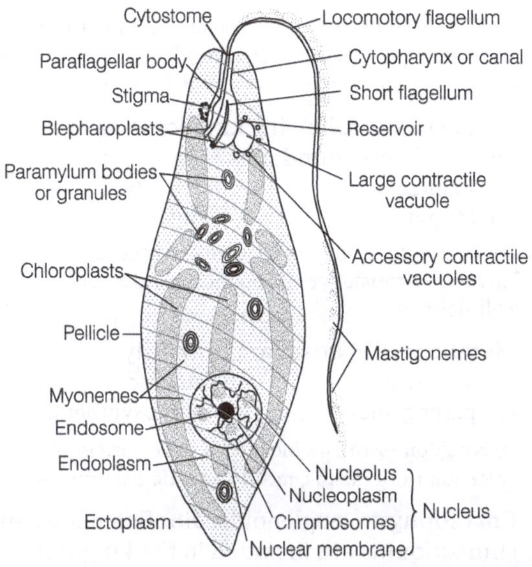

Fig 3.3 *Euglena*

Euglena is considered as plant as well as animal. It is also called as **plant animal.** Therefore it act as connecting link between plant and animal. Plant and animal features are

- **Plant Features** Chloroplasts and chlorophyll are present. It has autotrophic nutrition.
- **Animal Features** Presence of pellicle which is not made of cellulose. A contractile vacuole for performing osmoregulatory function is present. Heterotrophic nutrition and flagella for locomotion.

Note

- Euglenozoa is a diverse clade that includes predatory heterotrophs, photosynthetic autotrophs and pathogenic parasites.
- The main feature that distinguishes protists in this clade is the presence of a spiral or crystalline rod with unknown function inside the flagella.

Topic Practice 1

Multiple Choice Questions

1 Mark

1. **Which of the following is not a character of Protista?**
(a) Protists are prokaryotic
(b) Some protists have cell walls
(c) Mode of nutrition is both autotrophic and heterotrophic
(d) Body organisation is cellular

Ans (a) Kingdom–Protista includes all unicellular eukaryotic organisms (like diatoms, dinoflagellates, slime moulds, sarcodines, etc.) possessing well-defined nucleus.

2. **Which of the following kingdoms have not well- defined boundaries?**
(a) Plantae (b) Protista
(c) Monera (d) Algae

Ans (b) Although all single-celled eukaryotes are placed in kingdom–Protista, yet its boundaries are not well-defined.

3. **Members of Protista are primarily**
(a) terrestrial (b) aquatic
(c) pathogenic (d) photosynthetic

Ans (b) Kingdom–Protista includes a wide variety of unicellular organisms, mostly aquatic eukaryotes.

4. **Chrysophytes, euglenoids, dinoflagellates and slime moulds are included in the kingdom**
(a) Protista (b) Fungi
(c) Animalia (d) Monera

Ans (a) All single-celled eukaryotic organisms like chrysophytes (diatoms and desmids), euglenoids (*Euglena*), dinoflagellates and slime moulds are included in kingdom–Protista.

5. **Which of the following groups of organisms is/are placed under the group–Chrysophyta?**
(a) Diatoms only
(b) Desmids only
(c) Diatoms and golden algae
(d) Desmids and *Paramecium*

Ans (c) Chrysophytes include diatoms and desmids (golden algae). They belong to the division–Chrysophyta/ Bacillariophyta.

6. **Which of the following protists releases toxins that may even kill fishes and other marine animals?**
(a) *Euglena* (b) *Gonyaulax*
(c) *Paramecium* (d) *Plasmodium*

Ans (b) Some dinoflagellates (e.g. *Gonyaulax catenella*) are poisonous to vertebrates. When they are in large number, they forms red tides and produce the toxin called saxitoxin into the sea water, which kills fishes and other marine animals.

7. **Which of the following statement about *Euglena* is true?**
(a) Euglenoids bear flagella
(b) *Euglena* when placed in continuous darkness, loose their photosynthetic activity and die
(c) The pigments of *Euglena* are quite different from those of green plants
(d) *Euglena* is a marine protist

Ans (a) Euglenoids are unicellular flagellate protists. Euglenoids occur in freshwater habitats. They contain the photosynthetic pigments, chlorophyll-*a* and chlorophyll-*b*.

8. **Which of the following statements is correct?**
(a) Slime moulds are haploid
(b) Protozoans lack cell wall
(c) Dinoflagellates are immotile
(d) Pellicle is absent in *Euglena*

Ans (b) Protozoans lack cell wall. Cell wall is the characteristic feature of plant cells. Slime moulds are diploid, e.g. *Physarum*. Dinoflagellates are motile, e.g. *Noctiluca*, *Peridinium*, etc. The body of *Euglena* is covered with pellicle.

9. ***Paramecium* is an aquatic and actively moving organism due to the presence of**
(a) pseudopodia (b) false feet
(c) thousands of cilia (d) flagella

Ans (c) The most characteristic feature of *Paramecium* is the presence of large number of cilia on the whole body surface. *Paramecium* uses cilia for locomotion and capturing food.

10. ***Plasmodium* is a**
(a) ciliated protozoan
(b) sporozoan
(c) flagellated protozoan
(d) amoeboid protozoan

Ans (b) *Plasmodium* is a sporozoan protists.

Very Short Answer Type Questions

1 Mark

11. **Why there is large population of protists?**

Ans Because they rapidly reproduce by asexual mode reproduction.

12. **Fusion of two gametes which are dissimilar in size is termed as** **NCERT Exemplar**

Ans Anisogamy, it occurs in *Ceratium*, a dinoflagellate.

13. Why are cysts formed in protistans?

Ans Cysts formation helps to overcome unfavourable condition for reproduction.

14. What is the nature of cell wall in diatoms? **NCERT**

Ans Cell wall in diatoms is made up of cellulose and pectin compounds. It is a two-valved layer called frustule.

15. Flagellar locomotion can be observed in which protistans?

Ans *Euglena*, dinoflagellates and zooflagellates.

Short Answer Type I Questions

2 Marks

16. What is the cellular nature and body organisation of members of kingdom–Protista?

Ans **Unicellular Nature** These are unicellular eukaryotic organisms. Some of them also form colonies. Here, the individual cells do not lose their independent identity.

Body Organisation Cellular differentiation is absent. Organisation is protoplasmic or acellular. (1+1)

17. Define chrysophytes. Why are they considered as the chief producers in the ocean?

Ans Organisms like diatoms and desmids are called chrysophytes. They are found in both marine and freshwater and constitute the primary producers of aquatic ecosystem i.e. phytoplanktons. Therefore, they are the chief producers in the ocean. (1+1)

18. Diatoms are called as pearls of ocean. Why? What is diatomaceous earth? **NCERT Exemplar**

Ans **Pearl of Ocean** Diatoms have a shinning silicified two valved covering or frustule. Because of their distinctive cell walls these are sometimes called the pearls of ocean.

Diatomaceous Earth It is a pile of siliceous skeletons of diatoms which accumulates at the bottom of sea or oceans, being resistant to decay. (2)

19. Which of the organisms are called jewels of the plant world? Elaborate about them.

Ans Diatoms are called the jewels of the plant kingdom because of cell wall ornamentation and the presence of golden brown chromatophores. There are two types of diatoms, i.e. the pennate diatom and centric diatom. Pennate diatoms are like small rectangular soap boxes. Centric diatoms are circular. (2)

20. Suppose you accidently find an old preserved permanent slide without a lable. In your effort to identify it, you place the slide under microscope and observe the following features.

(i) Unicellular
(ii) Well-defined nucleus
(iii) Biflagellate, one flagellum lying longitudinally and other transversely.

What would you identify it as? Can you name the kingdom it belongs to? **NCERT Exemplar**

Ans Dinoflagellate, kingdom–Protista. (2)

21. List two important features of *Gonyaulax*.

Ans Important features of *Gonyaulax* are

(i) They have red coloured pigments present in their cells make the sea glow red and when present in abundance they form red tides.
(ii) They produce toxins such as saxitoxin that can kill other aquatic life forms. (1+1)

22. Name three organs that assist locomotion in protists. Give an example each of protists showing these locomotions.

Ans Locomotion in protists occurs by flagella, cilia, pseudopodia, wriggling of cells and by mucilage secretion.

Flagella In euglenoids, dinoflagellates and zooflagellates.

Cilia In *Paramecium*.

Pseudopodia In *Amoeba* and slime moulds.

Wriggling In Sporozoans

Mucilage propulsion In diatoms. (1+1)

23. Justify the statement *Euglena* is a taxonomic puzzle.

Ans *Euglena* is a taxonomic puzzle since, it shows both plant and animal characters. Absence of cell wall is an animal feature and presence of chloroplast is a plant character of *Euglena*.

It has mixotrophic nutrition. In the presence of sunlight, it can photosynthesise its food and in the absence of sunlight, it behaves like a heterotroph by predating on other smaller organisms. (2)

Short Answer Type II Questions

3 Marks

24. List out the differences between Monera and Protista.

Ans Differences between Monera and Protista are

Monera	Protista
Cell wall is made up of peptidoglycan.	It is made up of cellulose.
Respiratory apparatus is present in respiratory membrane.	It is present in mitochondria.
Ribosomes are 70S type.	Ribosomes are 80S type.
These are prokaryotic and have naked circular DNA.	Eukaryotic, linear DNA is present in nucleus.
Extrachromosomal DNA is present in the form of plasmids.	Extrachromosomal DNA is present in organelles like mitochondria and chloroplast.

(3)

25. **Briefly describe the locomotion of protists by different structures.**

Ans Refer to text on page no. 40 and 41

26. **How do following activities take place in dinoflagellates?**
(i) Nutrition (ii) Locomotion
(iii) Reproduction

Ans (i) **Nutrition** It is photosynthetic or autotrophic. They prepare their food using sunlight, CO_2 and water.
(ii) **Locomotion** Dinoflagellates show rolling and spinning type of locomotion due to the presence of two flagella. Hence, they are also called whirling whips.
(iii) **Reproduction** It occurs by asexual and sexual methods. Asexual reproduction occurs by cell division, spores and cysts. Sexual reproduction occurs by conjugation. (1×3)

27. **How do dinoflagellates differ from euglenoids?** NCERT

Ans Differences between dinoflagellates and euglenoids are

Dinoflagellates	Euglenoids
They are mostly marine.	They are freshwater forms found in stagnant water.
They have a cell wall with stiff cellulose plates on the outer surface.	They have no cell wall, but pellicle which gives shape and flexibility to body.
They are always photoautotrophic.	They may be photoautotrophic or heterotrophic.
They have two flagella, one transverse and one longitudinal.	They have two flagella and both are anterior.

(3)

28. **What are the characteristic features of euglenoids?** NCERT

Ans Refer to text on page no. 43.

29. **How do some protozoans maintain osmotic pressure?**

Ans. Protozoans take in water in bulk. As they mostly live in aquatic environments. They are likely to burst due to excessive intake of water. Therefore, protozoans need to osmoregulate continuously to keep only the required amount of water in their cells.

They get rid of excess water through contractile vacuoles. (3)

Long Answer Type Questions

5 Marks

30. **Describe kingdom–Protista with suitable examples in detail.**

Ans Refer to text on page no. 40 and 41.

31. **Define chrysophytes and mention their general characteristics along with their importance.**

Ans Refer to text on page no. 41 and 42.

32. **Describe the division-Pyrrophyta in detail.**

Ans Refer to text on page no. 42 and 43.

33. **Write a brief discription of euglenoids. Also write the significance of *Euglena* as connecting link.**

Ans Refer to text on page no. 43.

TOPIC 02 Non-Photosynthetic Protists

Fungus-like Protists or Slime Moulds

These organisms share characters with both animals and fungi. Due to this, they are commonly called as **fungal animal** protists.

Slime moulds are **saprophytic protists. Anton de Bary** (1887) related them to animals and called them as **Mycetozoa**. These are also named as **fungus animals** because they share the common characters of both animals and fungi and are known as **protistian fungi**, due to their protistian nature. The general features of slime moulds are discussed here

(i) They are found in moist terrestrial places rich in decaying organic food.
(ii) The body of slime moulds is covered with mucilage having gelatinous consistency. That is why they are called **slime moulds.**
(iii) The vegetative parts lack cell wall. They are surrounded by plasma membrane. However, the spores have the cellulosic cell walls.

(iv) Locomotion in slime moulds mainly occurs with the help of pseudopodia. They generally move towards moisture and avoid light.

(v) They show phagotropic or saprotrophic nutrition; they do not have chlorophyll.

(vi) Both sexual and asexual modes of reproduction occur.

(vii) They are like protozoan in their amoeboid plasmodial stage and similar to true fungi in spore formation.

(viii) The **cellular slime moulds** occur in all humus-containing upper layer of damp soil. When the food supply is short or conditions are not favourable the amoeboid cells form aggregate without any fusion. This aggregated mass is called **pseudoplasmodium.** The examples of cellular slime moulds are *Dictyostelium* and *Polysphondylium.*

(ix) **Acellular slime moulds** (plasmodial slime moulds) are commonly found on dead and decaying plant matter. *Plasmodium* is the free-living thalloid body of the acellular slime moulds. It is wall-less mass of multinucleate protoplasm covered by slime layer. During unfavourable conditions, the *Plasmodium* differentiates and forms fruiting bodies bearing spores at their tips.

During favourable conditions, *Plasmodium* can spread over several feet.

(x) Slime moulds are beneficial as they cause the decomposition of organic matter in the soil.

Animal-like Protists or Protozoan

Include unicellular protists with animal-like behaviour. They were first studied by **Leeuwenhoek** (1677). Protozoan protists may be aquatic, terrestrial or parasites. They can cause several diseases in humans and animals. General characteristics of protozoans are described below

(i) They are microscopic, unicellular and colourless organisms with different shapes.

(ii) Locomotion occurs with the help of finger-like pseudopodia, flagella or hairy cilia.

(iii) All protozoans are heterotrophs and live as predators or parasites.

(iv) Respiration occurs through the general surface of the body.

(v) Asexual reproduction occurs by binary fission, multiple fission or budding. Sexual reproduction occurs by syngamy and conjugation.

There are four major groups of protozoans

1. Rhizopod/Amoeboid Protozoans

These organisms live in freshwater, seawater or moist soil, some of like *Entamoeba* are parasite.

General features of this group are following

(i) They move and capture their prey by putting out pseudopodia (false feet) as in *Amoeba* (as mouth is absent).

(ii) The body is without periplast. It may be naked or have a calcareous shell (marine).

(iii) Flagella are present in some developmental stages. They also develop when food becomes scarce.

(iv) Nutrition is holozoic.

(v) Asexual reproduction occurs by binary fission, multiple fission, spores and budding and sexual reproduction occurs by syngamy.

(vi) Examples include *Amoeba, Entamoeba, Radiolaria, Pelomyxa, Foraminifera* and *Heliozoa.*

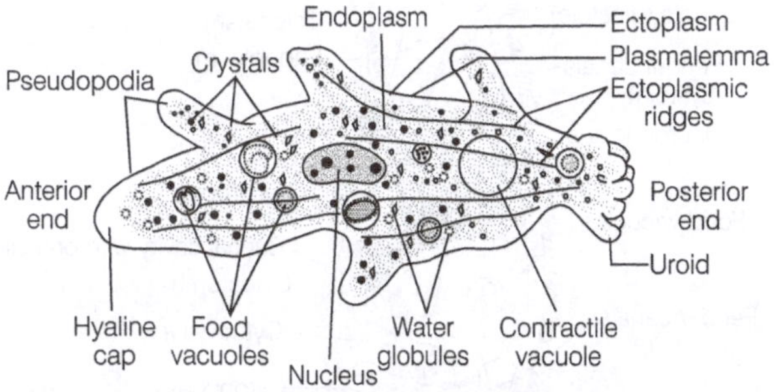

Fig. 3.4 Microscopic view of *Amoeba proteus*

2. Flagellated Protozoans

The members of this group are either free-living or parasitic. General features of this group are following

(i) They have flagella for locomotion as their name suggests.

(ii) They may be aquatic, free-living, parasitic, commensals or symbiotic. They are generally uninucleate (occasionally multinucleate).

(iii) The body is enclosed by a firm pellicle.

(iv) Nutrition is holozoic, saprobic and parasitic.

(v) Asexual reproduction is by binary fission and cyst formation.

(vi) Sexual reproduction is observed in some forms only.

(vii) Examples include *Giardia, Trypanosoma, Leishmania, Trichonympha* and *Trichomonas.* Various species of these protozoans causes diseases in humans.

For example
- *Trypanosoma* (sleeping sickness)
- *Leishmania* (kala-azar, dum-dum fever)
- *Giardia* (giardiasis)
- *Trichomonas* (leucorrhoea).

3. Ciliated Protozoans

These are aquatic, actively moving organisms because of the presence of thousands of cilia. They are considered as the highly evolved protozoan organisms with over 7000 species. General features of this group are following

(i) Many ciliates live as free-living individual in fresh and marine water (*Paramecium*).

(ii) A large number of cilia present on whole body surface. Cilia are used to capture food and for locomotion.

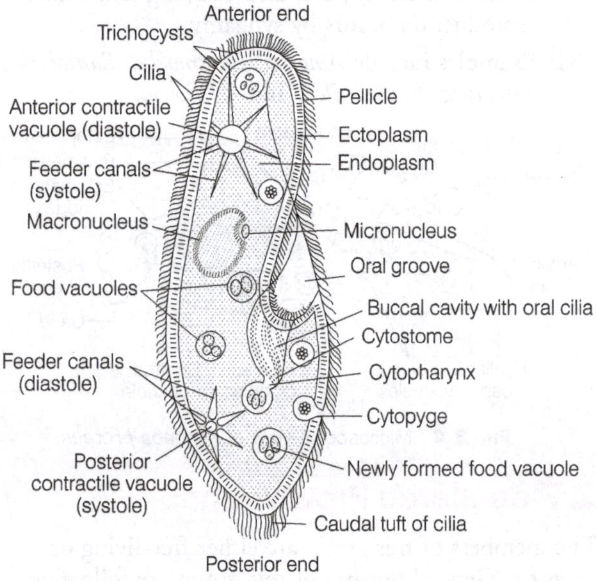

Fig 3.5 Structure of *Paramecium caudatum*

(iii) Ciliated protozoans have a cavity (gullet) that opens to the outside of the cell surface. The coordinated movement of rows of cilia causes the water laden with food to be steered into the gullet. Nutrition is holozoic except in some parasitic forms where it is absorptive.

(iv) The body is covered with flexible pellicle.

(v) Ciliates have a larger **macronucleus** and smaller **micronucleus** for sexual reproduction.

(vi) They have small ejectable **trichocysts** for defence.

(vii) **Osmoregulation** occurs by contractile vacuoles.

(viii) Asexual reproduction occurs by transverse binary fission or budding. Cyst formation also occurs during unfavourable condition.

(ix) Sexual reproduction by means of conjugation.

(x) Examples include *Paramecium, Opalina, Vorticella, Podophyra, Balantidium*, etc.

4. Sporozoan Protozoans

This group includes organisms that have an infectious spore-like stage in their life cycle.

General features of this group are following

(i) All sporozoans are endoparasites and pathogenic.

(ii) Locomotory organs and contractile vacuoles are absent.

(iii) Nutrition is parasitic (absorptive).

(iv) Body is covered with an elastic pellicle or cuticle.

(v) Asexual reproduction occurs through multiple fission and sexual reproduction by syngamy.

(vi) Life cycle may include two different hosts (digenetic), e.g. *Plasmodium* requires two hosts female *Anopheles* mosquito and human beings.

(vii) Examples include *Plasmodium* (malarial parasite), *Monocystis, Eimeria.*

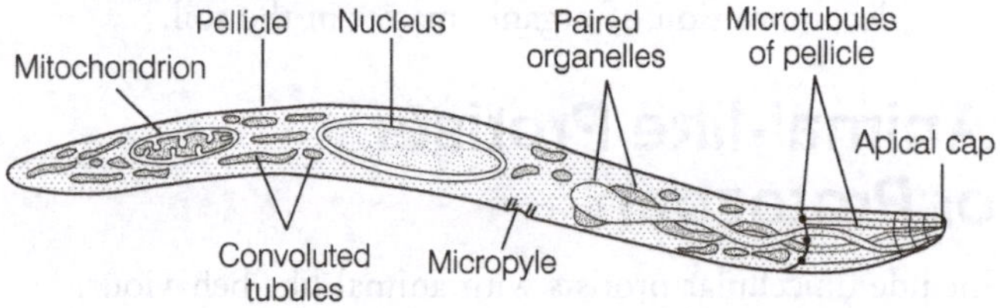

Fig. 3.6 *Plasmodium* structure of a sporozoite as revealed by electron microscope

Knowledge Plus

- The search for malarial vaccines has been hampered by the fact that *Plasmodium* spends most of its time inside human cells, hidden from host's immune system. It also continuously changes its surface proteins.
- By 2003, researchers had tracked the expression of most of the parasitic genes at numerous points in its life cycle. This research could help to identify the potential new targets for vaccines.

Topic Practice 2

Multiple Choice Questions

1 Mark

1. Slime moulds are
   (a) pathogenic (b) parasite
   (c) saprophytic protists (d) autotrophic

Ans (c) Slime moulds lack chlorophyll and are heterotrophic. They generally, live as saprotrophs except a few, which are parasites on algae, other fungi and flowering plants.

2. The free-living thalloid body of the slime mould is known as
   (a) protonema (b) *Plasmodium*
   (c) fruiting body (d) mycelium

Ans (b) A free-living thalloid body of the acellular slime moulds is called *Plasmodium*.

The *Plasmodium* is a wall less mass of multinucleate protoplasm, covered by slime.

3. Under favourable conditions slime moulds form
   (a) protonema (b) *Plasmodium*
   (c) mycelium (d) fruiting bodies

Ans (b) Slime moulds form an aggregation called *Plasmodium*, which may grow and spread over several feets.

During unfavourable conditions, the *Plasmodium* differentiates and forms fruiting bodies bearing spores at their tips. Spores are extremely resistant and survive for many years.

4. During unfavourable conditions, slime moulds form ...*A*..., which are ...*B*... and survive for many years. Identify *A* and *B* to complete the given statement.
   (a) *A*–zoospores; *B*–round in shape
   (b) *A*–endospores; *B*–hexagonal in shape
   (c) *A*–akinetes; *B*–highly resistant
   (d) *A*–spores; *B*–highly resistant

Ans (d) During unfavourable conditions, the slime moulds form spores, which are highly resistant and survive for many years.

5. Protozoans are
   (a) heterotrophs (b) autotrophs
   (c) producer (d) saprophytes

Ans (a) Protozoans are heterotrophic protists.

6. Which of the following group is considered as primitive relatives of animals?
   (a) Chrysophytes (b) Protozoans
   (c) Euglenoids (d) Slime moulds

Ans (b) Protozoans acts as connecting link between heterotropic unicellular eukaryotes (protists) and multicellular heterotrophic eukaryotes (animals).

7. Protozoans are divided into .... groups.
   Most suitable word to fill the blank is
   (a) three (b) four
   (c) two (d) eight

Ans (b) On the basis of locomotory organelles, the protozoans are divided into four groups.

Flagellated protozoans, amoeboid protozoans, sporozoans and ciliated protozoans.

8. Which of the following is a flagellated protozoan?
   (a) *Amoeba* (b) *Entamoeba*
   (c) *Plasmodium* (d) *Trypanosoma*

Ans (d) *Trypanosoma* exhibits locomotion due to the presence of flagella.

9. *Trypanosoma* causes
   (a) sleeping sickness (b) cholera
   (c) malaria (d) food poisoning

Ans (a) *Trypanosoma gambiense* causes gambian sleeping sickness. It was first observed by Forde in 1901. Bruce discovered that the parasite of sleeping sickness is transmitted by tse-tse fly.

10. Which of the following groups always produce an infectious spore-like stage in their life cycle?
    (a) Amoeboid protozoans
    (b) Ciliated protozoans
    (c) Flagellated protozoans
    (d) Sporozoans

Ans (d) Sporozoans include diverse organisms that have an infectious spore-like stage in their life cycle.

Very Short Answer Type Questions

1 Mark

11. Naked cytoplasm, multinucleated and saprophytic are the characteristics of which protist group? **NCERT Exemplar**

Ans Slime moulds are saprophytic protists that possess all these characteristics.

12. Which protists are called protistian fungi?

Ans Slime moulds.

13. Why slime moulds are named so?

Ans Due to the presence of gelatinous mucilage covering on their body and their saprophytic mode of nutrition.

14. What kind of nutrition occurs in a parasite?

Ans Parasites have phagotrophic and absorptive type of nutrition.

15. What is common in *Entamoeba* and radiolarians?

Ans Both are amoeboid protozoans.

Short Answer Type I Questions

2 Marks

16. What are acellular slime moulds ?

Ans Acellular slime moulds are consumer-decomposer protists which have a free-living thalloid body called *Plasmodium*. It is wall less mass of multinucleate protoplasm covered with slime layer. (2)

17. Why slime moulds are called fungus animals? Name some slime moulds.

Ans Slime moulds possess the characters of both animals and fungi. Therefore, they are commonly called fungus animals. Modern biologists called them protistan fungi. They are like Protozoa in their amoeboid plasmodial stage and similar to true fungi in spore formation, e.g. *Physarum, Physarella, Fuligo, Lycogala* and *Tubifera*. (2)

18. What observable features in *Trypanosoma* would make you classify it under kingdom–Protista? **NCERT Exemplar**

Ans Observable features in *Trypanosoma* are

(i) Unicellular, flagellum with basal granules.
(ii) Well-developed nucleus like eukaryotes.
(iii) Reproduces asexually.
(iv) Reserved food material is in the form of granules. (1/2 × 4)

19. Which protists show symbiotic relationships? How is this relation carried out?

Ans Zooflagellates like *Trichonympha* and *Lophomonas* live as a symbiont in the intestine of termites and wood roaches, respectively. They secrete cellulose digesting enzymes which convert cellulose into glucose. The digested food (glucose) is shared by both zooflagellates and the hosts. (2)

20. Give the name of the hosts of malarial parasite *Plasmodium*.

Ans Malarial parasite *Plasmodium* has following two hosts

(i) **Female *Anopheles* Mosquito** It is a primary host of malarial parasite. The sexual phase of parasite occurs in mosquito.
(ii) **Human Beings** These are intermediate or secondary host of *Plasmodium*. The asexual phase of parasite occurs in humans. (2)

21. Why do mosquito bites cause itching?

Ans When female mosquitoes like *Anopheles*, suck human blood, it simultaneously injects an enzyme containing the protozoan cells into our blood. This enzyme prevents coagulation of blood and causes the itching and swelling of the area. (2)

Short Answer Type II Questions

3 Marks

22. Give three characteristics of slime moulds.

Ans Refer to text on page no. 46.

23. In which organism pseudoplasmodia is found and what is its role? Also mention its kingdom.

Ans **Pseudoplasmodia** These are found in slime moulds. Which are members of kingdom-Protista. Pseudoplasmodia are formed when the food supply of the medium is exhausted. (1×3)

24. Give three characteristics of amoebied protozoans.

Ans Refer to text on page no. 47.

25. Give one example of each of the four major group of protozoans.

Ans

Rhizopods protists	–	*Entamoeba*
Fllagellated protists	–	*Giardia*
Cilliated protists	–	*Paramecium*
Sporozoan protists	–	*Plasmodium vivax*

(3)

26. Differentiate between slime moulds and protozoans.

Ans Differences between slime moulds and protozoans are

Slime moulds	Protozoans
Saprophytic protists.	Parasitic protists.
Acts as decomposer in ecosystem.	Acts as consumers in ecosystem.
Link between fungi and protists.	Link between animals and protists.

(3)

Long Answer Type Questions

5 Marks

27. Describe the characteristic of non-photosynthetic protists.

Ans Refer to text on page no. 46, 47 and 48.

28. Describe briefly the four major groups of Protozoa. **NCERT**

Ans Refer to text on page no. 47 and 48.

29. Sporozoans are parasitic protozoan protists which lack locomotory organelles atleast in trophozoite stage.

(i) Where are they found?
(ii) What kind of nutrition they have?
(iii) Do they have nucleus?
(iv) What is the mode of reproduction ?
(v) List any four examples of sporozoans.

Ans (i) Sporozoans are intracellular endoparasites of invertebrates and vertebrates.
(ii) They have heterotrophic mode nutrition which is mostly absorptive type and rarely digestive.
(iii) Sporozoans are commonly uninucleate.
(iv) Asexual reproduction occurs by multiple fission and sexual reproduction involves fusion of gametes.
(v) Examples *Plasmodium, Toxoplasma, Monocystis* and *Eimeria*. (1 × 5)

SUMMARY

- **Kingdom–Protista** includes all single-celled eukaryotes that cannot be classified under plant, animals and fungi. These include photosynthetic protists, slime moulds and protozoan protists.
- **Protistans are primarily aquatic**. They may or may not possess cell wall. These cell body contains a well-defined nucleus and other membrane bound organelles. They can adopt autotrophic as well as heterotrophic mode of nutrition.
- **Photosynthetic protists** These constitute the primary produces of aquatic ecosystem, i.e. phytoplankton. These are plant-like protists as they perform autotrophic nutrition. They include chrysophytes (diatoms), dinoflagellates, euglenoids.
- **Chrysophyte** These include diatoms and desmids. There cell wall is called frustule/shell which has silica, and consists of epitheca (upper half) and hyphotheca (lower half). There siliceous shell is indestructible this pile up at sea bottom thereby forming diatomaceous earth or kieselguhr. They reproduce by binary fission (asexual) or by forming rejuvenescent cell called auxospore (sexual).
- **Dinoflagellates** These include unicellular protists with thick cell wall (theca or lorica) having one vertical (sulcus) and one horizontal (cingulum/annulus/girdle) groove. They possess eyespots, trichocysts and chromosomes without histones. There are two different types of flagella on their body (heterokont). Reserve food is oil or starch. Some forms show bioluminiscence like *Noctiluca* and *Gonyaulax*. Presence of theca gives them the name armoured dinoflagellates.
- ***Euglena*** These are freshwater inhabitant possessing characters of both plants and animals. They do not have cell wall instead have flexible proteinaceous pellicle on their body. They have eyespot with astaxanthin, gullet and paraflagellar body. There flagella show metaboly. They can perform photosynthesis due to the presence of chlorophyll-*a* and *b* in them. But in the absence of light they perform saprobic nutrition. Thus, are also called mixtrophs.
- **Slime moulds** These are fungi-like protists. They perform saprophytic mode of nutrition under favourable conditions. During scarcity of food, they form an aggregation called *Plasmodium*, which grows and spreads over several feet. During unfavourable conditions, the *Plasmodium* differentiates and forms spores bearing fruiting bodies. These are classified into acellular slime moulds and cellular slime moulds.
- **Acellular slime moulds** Their vegetative thallus is free-living *Plasmodium*, i.e. naked, multinucleated mass of protoplasm (protoplasmodium), with or without branched veins. They show amoeboid movement by pseudopodia thus asymmetric in shape. They reproduce asexually by spores, cyst, sclerotium, plasmotomy and binary fission. Their spores form non-motile myxamoebae or biflagellate swarm cells that fuse to form zygote (isogamy). Zygote through repeated mitosis forms *Plasmodium*. Their sporangium is covered by peridium that forms internal branched capillitium.
- **Cellular slime moulds** Their vegetative thallus is uninucleate, haploid amoeboid cell called myxamoeba. Flagella is completely absent in their life cycle. Their sporangium lacks peridium and capillitium. Their myxamoebae show anisogamous sexual reproduction, which forms pseudoplasmodium.
- **Protozoan** These are animal-like protists. They are heterotrophs, who are free-living or lives as predators or parasites. These are without cell wall and have one to many nucleus. These are divided into
  - **Mastigophora** or flagellated protozons, e.g. *Trypanosoma*.
  - **Sporozoans,** e.g. *Plasmodium*.
  - **Sarcodina** or Amoeboid protozoans, e.g. *Amoeba* and *Entamoeba*.
  - **Ciliophora** or ciliated protozoans, e.g. *Paramecium*.
- ***Trypanosoma gambiense*** It is parasitic protozoan causing African sleeping sickness. Its body possesses a nucleus, a flagellum, undulating membrane, basal granule and kinetoplast.
- ***Plasmodium*** These species are spore forming parasitic protists, which lack locomotary structure and contractile vacuoles. The body is covered by pellicle or cuticle. They are known to cause malaria.
- ***Amoeba*** It is a protozoan with body covered by plasmalemma. Their body bears a number of pseudopodia, which help in capturing food.
- ***Paramecium*** It is a ciliate protozoan. It is of free-living and aquatic forms. Its body is distinguished into an oral and aboral surface. It is heterokaryotic, i.e. with macronucleus and micronucleus.

Chapter Practice

Multiple Choice Questions

1 Mark

1. Protozoan protists perform respiration through
(a) mitochondria
(b) pseudopodia
(c) contractile vacoule
(d) general surface

2. Which of the following is a red dinoflagellate?
(a) *Euglena* (b) Diatoms
(c) *Gonyaulax* (d) *Plasmodium*

3. Red tides in warm coastal water develop due to the presence of
(a) dinoflagellates
(b) euglenoid forms
(c) diatoms and desmids
(d) slime moulds

4. Plant-like nutrition is present in
(a) *Amoeba* (b) *Paramecium*
(c) *Euglena* (d) *Plasmodium*

5. Slime moulds are
(a) pathogenic (b) parasite
(c) saprophytic protists (d) autotrophic

6. Microcyst formation is a means of perennation observed in
(a) acellular slime moulds
(b) cellular slime moulds
(c) protozoan protists
(d) *Euglena*

Assertion-Reason Type Questions

1 Mark

■ **Direction** (Q. Nos. 7-10) *In each of the following questions, a statement of Assertion (A) is given followed by corresponding statement of Reason (R). Of the statements, mark the correct answer as*

(a) If both A and R are true and R is the correct explanation of A
(b) If both A and R are true, but R is not the correct explanation of A
(c) If A is true, but R is false
(d) If A is false, but R is true

7. **Assertion** (A) *Euglena* is a plant due to the presence of chlorophyll.
Reason (R) *Euglena* cannot be classified on the basis of two kingdom system.

8. **Assertion** (A) *Euglena* has protein rich cell wall pellicle.
Reason (R) Pellicle makes the body of *Euglena* flexible.

9. **Assertion** (A) Diatoms are microscopic and float passively in water currents.
Reason (R) Diatoms are found only in marine environment.

10. **Assertion** (A) *Entamoeba* are flagellated protozoans.
Reason (R) *Entamoeba* have silica shells on their surface.

Answers

1. (d) 2. (c) 3. (a) 4. (c) 5. (c) 6. (b)
7. (d) 8. (d) 9. (c) 10. (d)

Very Short Answer Type Questions

1 Mark

11. What features distinguish protists of Euglenophyta from others?

12. Define mixotrophic nutrition.

13. What is the use of trichocysts in *Paramecium*?

14. Contractile vacuoles present in ciliated protozoans are present for what purpose?

Short Answer Type I Questions

2 Marks

15. Name the photosynthetic phyla of kingdom–Protista?

16. Give two example of photosynthetic protists?

17. What are rhizopods, give an example?

18. Name any two ciliated protists.

Short Answer Type II Questions

3 Marks

19. Describe the cell structure of a typical protist.
20. What are the modes of locomotion found in protists ?
21. Write short note on the economic importance of diatoms.
22. Give the general characteristics of dinoflagellates.
23. Various species of flagellated protozoans cause diseases in humans. Give any three examples of diseases caused and the causative agent for the same.

Long Answer Type Questions

5 Marks

24. Kingdom–Protista was introduced by whom in classification system? Discuss its major characteristics and organisms classified in it.
25. Make an outline classification of kingdom–Protista.
26. Explain the important characters of kingdom–Protista.
27. How are photosynthetic protists different from slime moulds ?

Case Based Question

4/5 Marks

28. Recognise the figure and answer the questions that follows.

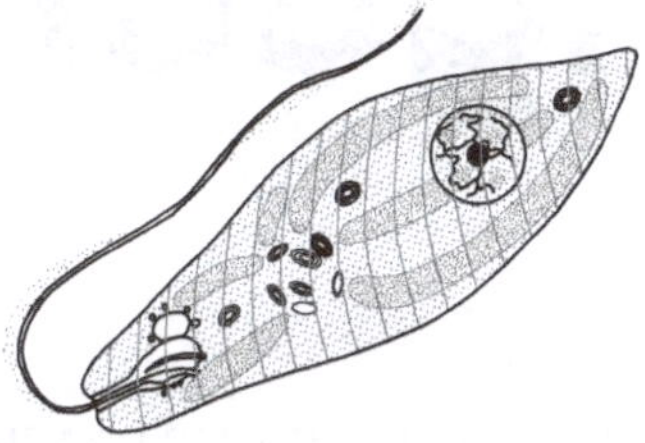

(i) Identify the organism and mention its kingdom.

(ii) The body of the given organism is flexible and contractible. What enables this organism an exceptional flexibility?

(iii) Name the locomotory organ which is found in this type organism.

CHAPTER

04

Kingdom-Fungi

After the evolution of **monerans** and **protistans** (already studied in previous chapter), it was assumed that fungi were the first to be evolved from the protists. And after that about millions years later some protists got evolved into Animalia and others evolved into Plantae.

TOPIC 01 General Characteristics and Classification of Fungi

The kingdom–Fungi or Mycota constitute a unique kingdom of heterotrophic organisms. They show a great diversity in morphology and habitat. There are about 100000 species in this kingdom. The characteristic features of kingdom fungi are discussed here.

Mycology is the branch of science that deals with the study of various fungi. A scientist having specialisation in the study of fungi is called **mycologist**. PA Micheli is known as the Father of Mycology.

General Characteristics of Fungi

General characteristics of fungi are as follows

1. Fungi are cosmopolitan in distribution, i.e. they can be found everywhere. These are mostly terrestrial but a few forms are aquatic also. These mostly grow in warm and humid places, e.g. tree barks (corticolous), dung (coprophilous), wood (epixylic) and on hairs or horns of animals (keratinophilous).
2. **Nutrition** Fungi are heterotrophic but they cannot ingest food materials like animals. Instead, they directly absorb nutrients from the substratum through their cell membranes. This process is known as osmotrophy and related fungus are called osmotrophs. Depending upon the mode of nutrition fungi can be **saprophytic** or **parasitic**. The saprophytic fungi grows on dead, decaying organic matter. They derives nutrition by secreting some special enzymes for the purpose. Parasites live inside or on the body of a host organisms, e.g. plants and animals.

They derive their nutrition by means of a haustorium. It is a peg-like outgrowth that penetrates the host tissue.

3. On the basis of nutrition, the fungi can be categorised into
   (i) **Obligate parasites** live strictly as parasites, e.g. *Peronospora* causing downy mildews in cucurbits.
   (ii) **Facultative parasites** are normally saprophytic, but under forced conditions (like starvation) may become parasites, e.g. *Fusarium* and *Botrytis cinerea.*
   (iii) **Obligate saprophytes** live strictly as saprophytes, e.g. *Mucor,* toadstools, mushrooms and most of the species of *Penicillium.*
   (iv) **Facultative saprophytes** normally live as parasites, but they may become saprophytes under emergent circumstances, e.g. *Phytophthora infestans* that causes late blight of potato.
4. The vegetative phase of a fungus is called **thallus,** i.e. a plant body which is not differentiated into distinct roots, stem and leaves.

   This thallus may be unicellular, e.g. *Chytrids* or filamentous in most of the fungi.
5. Thallus consists of large number of fine, tubular, thread-like filaments called **hyphae.** These hyphae are interwoven loosely to form mycelium.
6. The hyphae may be aseptate (without walls) or septate (with walls). The aseptate hyphae are multinucleated (coenocytic).

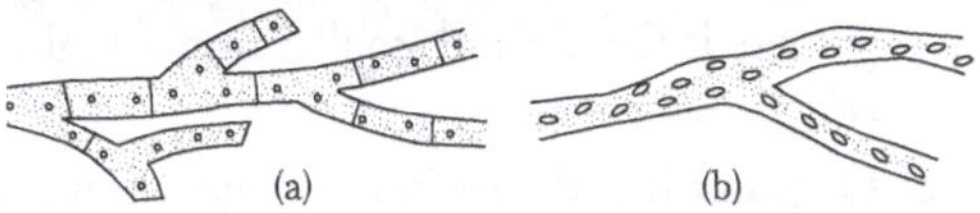

Fig 4.1 Mycelium of a fungus with (a) Septate hyphae, (b) Aseptate hyphae

7. The cells of hyphae have cell wall that is made up of chitin. The reserved food material in fungi is glycogen or animal starch.
8. Fungal mycelium may be of following types
   (i) **Plectenchyma** A false tissue formed by the loose aggregation of hyphae. It is further of two types
      (a) **Pseudoparenchyma** The hyphae mass consists of isodiametric cells. These cells are similar to parenchyma of higher plants in appearances, e.g. In the fungal part of lichens and mycorrhiza.
      (b) **Prosenchyma** hyphae are composed of elongated cells. These cells run parallel to each other.
   (ii) **Rhizomorph** It is a thick strand or root-like aggregation of somatic hyphae, e.g. *Armillaria mellea.*
   (iii) **Sclerotia** It is compact and globose or elongated structure. It can survive for many years in unfavourable conditions, e.g. *Claviceps purpurea* and *Rhizoctonia solani.*

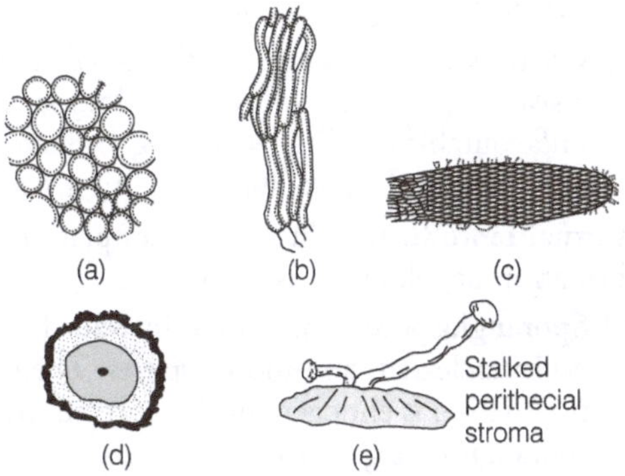

Fig. 4.2 (a) Pseudoparenchyma, (b) Prosenchyma, (c) and (d) Rhizomorph (e) Sclerotia

9. The vegetative body of a fungus can be
   (i) **Holocarpic**, i.e. the entire fungal body transforms into reproductive body, e.g. *Synchytrium.*
   (ii) **Eucarpic**, i.e. only a part of body transforms into reproductive structures, e.g. *Phytophthora.*
10. **Reproduction** in fungi may take place by vegetative, asexual or sexual means.
11. **Vegetative reproduction** in fungi may occur through following methods
    (i) **Fragmentation**, e.g. In *Rhizopus.*
    (ii) **Fission**, e.g. In *Schizosaccharomyces.*

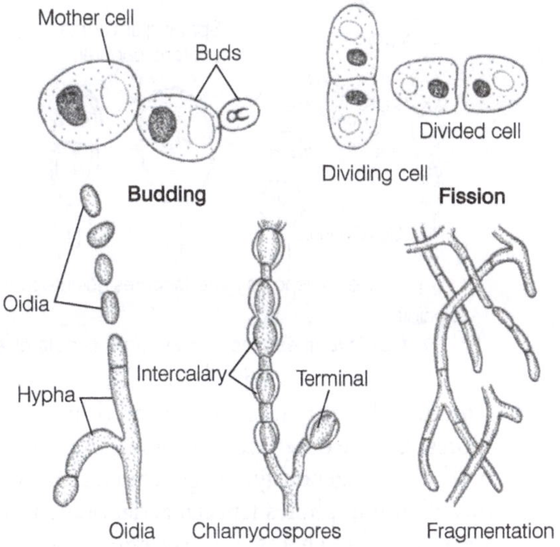

Fig 4.3 Different types of vegetative reproduction in fungi

(iii) **Budding** In few fungi small buds arise on the parent cells. Upon considerable enlargement these buds cut-off from parent cell and develop into a new organism.

(iv) **Oidium Formation** In some fungi, the hyphae breaks up into numerous small fragments known as **oidia**. These oidia grow and later on give rise to new hyphae, e.g. *Rhizopus*.

(v) **Chlamydospores** These are thick-walled, highly resistant spores. These are formed under unfavourable conditions. They germinate to form mycelium under favourable condition, e.g. *Rhizopus.*

12. **Asexual reproduction** in fungi takes place by the formation of following asexual spores

(i) **Sporangiospores** These are thin-walled, uni or multinucleated, non-motile spores. Their production is endogenous, i.e. formed inside the sporangium, e.g. *Rhizopus* and *Mucor*.

(ii) **Zoospores** These are formed by the lower group of fungi-like phycomycetes. These are thin-walled and uninucleated structures. Their production is endogenous. These possess a flagellum with 9+2 microtubule arrangement, e.g. *Synchytrium.*

(iii) **Aplanospores** These are thin-walled, non-motile structures. They are produced inside the sporangium, e.g. *Rhizopus.*

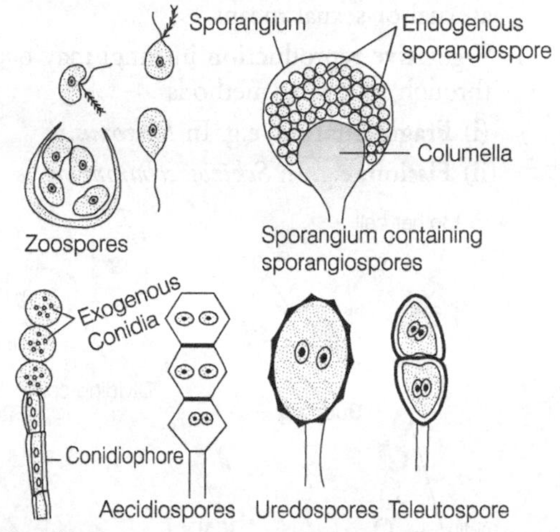

Fig. 4.4 Different spores formed as a result of asexual reproduction

(iv) **Conidia** These are non-motile and thin-walled spores. Unlike other asexual spores, they are produced exogenously, i.e. generated freely on the tips of conidiophores (special aerial branches) and are arranged in chains, e.g. *Aspergillus* and *Penicillium.*

(v) **Binucleate spores** These are binucleated spores, e.g. aecidiospores, uredospores and teleutospores of Basidiomycetes.

13. **Sexual reproduction** all fungi reproduce asexually except the artificial group, i.e. fungi imperfecti (Deuteromycetes). The sex organs that produce gametes are called **gametangia** (sing. gametangium). The sexual reproduction in fungi occurs by oospores, ascospores and basidiospores. The various spores produced in distinct structures are called **fruiting bodies.**

The sexual cycle involves the following three stages

I. Plasmogamy

It is the first stage in which the cytoplasm of two sex cells come close together but do not fuse with each other.

Only the protoplasm of both cells fuse together. The resulting cell is **dikaryon** or **binucleate.**

Plasmogamy occurs in following five ways

(i) **Planogametic Copulation** In this method Flagellated gametes or planogametes of opposite strains fuse with each other. This leads to formation of a diploid zygote. Fusion of planogametes can occur by either of following three ways

(a) **Isogamy** It is the fusion of motile gametes that are similar in appearance, e.g. *Synchytrium.*

(b) **Anisogamy** It is the fusion of motile gametes that differ in size and structure. The larger gamete is female and smaller one is male, e.g. *Allomyces.*

(c) **Oogamy** It is the fusion of larger, non-motile female gamete with smaller, motile male gamete. The male gamete is formed inside the antheridium. The female gamete is formed inside the oogonium.

(ii) **Gametangial Contact** It is the fusion of two gametangia. These are the structures in which gametes are formed.

The male gametangia is called **antheridium** and the female one is called **oogonium** (in oomycetes) or **ascogonium** (in ascomycetes). A fertilisation tube is formed first at gametangial contact followed by karyogamy to form zygote (2*n*) or zygospore.

(iii) **Gametangial Copulation** It is the direct fusion of male and female gametangia forming diploid zygospore, e.g. *Rhizopus.*

(iv) **Spermatisation** It is a sexual fusion between spermatia and a female receptive hyphae. Spermatia are conidia like, uninucleated, small male sex cells.

These are formed on reproductive hyphae called the **spermatiophores.** Upon maturation spermatia get detached from spermatiophores and are carried to female receptive hyphae. The karyogamy is delayed and a dikaryotic stage ($n+n$) begins, e.g. *Neurospora.*

(v) **Somatogamy** In some fungi distinct sex organs are absent. In these, two vegetative hyphae from mycelia of opposite strains (+ and −) come in contact and fuse. The nuclei of one migrate to the other. Thus, dikaryons are formed, e.g. *Ustilago*, *Agaricus* and some ascomycetes.

Different Types of Sexual Reproduction in Fungi

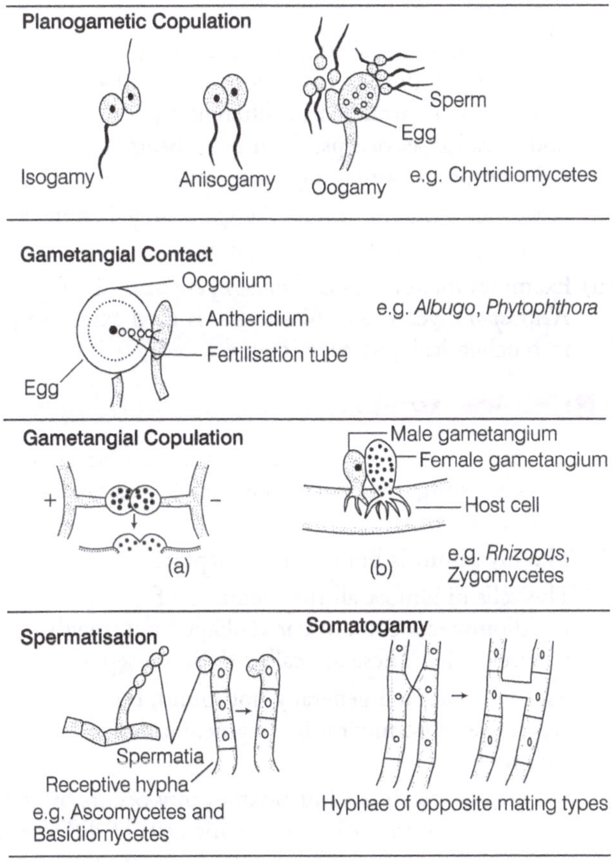

II. Karyogamy

It is the stage in which two compatible nuclei fuse together resulting into a diploid nucleus is called **synkaryon.**

III. Meiosis

It is the stage in which the diploid nucleus divides resulting in the formation of haploid nucleus (reduction division).

Dikaryophase

In most of the lower fungi, the fungus reproduces sexually by compatible mating of two haploid hyphae (they come together and fuse), i.e. plasmogamy is immediately followed by karyogamy and meiosis, and in some fungi, the fusion of two haploid cells immediately results in diploid cells ($2n$).

However, in some higher forms (Ascomycetes and Basidiomycetes), karyogamy is delayed and an intervening dikaryotic stage ($n+n$, i.e. two nuclei per cell) occurs. Such a condition is called a **dikaryon and the phase is called dikaryotic phase** of fungus. After that the parental nuclei fuse and the cell becomes diploid.

The fungi form fruiting bodies in which reduction division occurs, leading to the formation of haploid spores.

Sexual reproduction leads to the formation of following haploid sexual spores

(i) **Ascospores** These are formed endogenously in sac-like structures called **ascus.** Each ascus contain two haploid nuclei. These nuclei fuse during sexual reproduction. The zygote undergo meiosis to form four or eight ascospores, e.g. Ascomycetes.

(ii) **Basidiospores** They are formed exogenously on specialised structures called **basidium.** Inside basidium, two nuclei fuse to form zygote.

This zygote undergo meiosis later on to form four basidiospores. Basidiospores are attached on a peg-like outgrowth basidium through sterigmata, e.g. Basidiomycetes.

(iii) **Zygospores** These are thick-walled spores. They are produced by the fusion of entire gametangia, e.g. Zygomycetes.

(iv) **Oospores** These are formed within females structures called **oogonium,** e.g. Oomycetes. All these haploid sexual spores form haploid hyphae after germination.

Classification of Fungi

Kingdom–Fungi can be divided into various classes on the basis of morphology of mycelium, mode of spore formation and fruiting bodies.

1. Phycomycetes

The members of Phycomycetes are found in aquatic habitats and on decaying wood in moist and damp places or as obligate parasites on plants.

General characteristics of this class are as follows

(i) Mycelium is aseptate and coenocytic.

(ii) Hyphal wall contains microfibrils of cellulose, chitin or both.

(iii) Asexual reproduction involves the endogenous formation of sporangia. The sporangia function as conidia in dry habitats and as zoosporangia under wet conditions.

(iv) Zoospores may be uniflagellate or biflagellate with flagella being anterior, lateral or posterior. A zoospore is formed by the fusion of two gametes.

(v) The gametes are similar in morphology (isogamous) or dissimilar (anisogamous or oogamous).

(vi) Disease caused by the members of Phycomycetes are white rust (*Albugo*), late blight of potato (*Phytophthora infestans*), downy mildew (*Peronospora parasitica*), etc.

Examples include *Albugo* (parasitic fungi on mustard), *Rhizopus* (the bread mould), *Pythium, Plasmospara, Phytophthora.*

It is divided into two groups as follows

(i) Oomycetes or Algal Fungi

Most of them are parasites. Unlike true fungi, cell wall of hyphae cells are made up of cellulose and not chitin. Asexual reproduction takes place by means of pear-shaped, biflagellate zoospores. These zoospores require water for their movement. Sexual reproduction is oogamous and occurs through gametangial contact resulting into the formation of oospores, e.g. *Phytophthora, Albugo candida, Pythium debaryanum*, etc.

(ii) Zygomycetes or Conjugation Fungi

These are terrestrial and saprophytic fungi. Unlike oomycetes their cell wall contains chitin. There is complete absence of any motile cell in the life cycle. Asexual reproduction takes place by the formation of sporangiospores.

Sexual reproduction occurs through gametangial conjugation. That is why, zygomycetes are also called as **conjugation fungi**. The gametes are multinucleated and are called as **coenogametes**. These are basically the hyphae, that directly act as gametes. As a result of sexual reproduction, thick-walled zygospores ($2n$) are formed. These zygospores do not germinate directly rather they produce germ spores inside the germ sporangium *via* meiosis. Germ spores give rise to mycelia.

Few common members are *Pilobolus crystallinus* (dung mould/squirting fungus), *Rhizopus stolonifer*, etc.

2. Ascomycetes

The members of Ascomycetes are commonly called as **sac fungi**. They are mostly multicellular (*Penicillium*) and rarely unicellular (yeast).

The common features of Ascomycetes are described below

(i) They are mostly terrestrial, some are aquatic. A number of Ascomycetes are parasites on plants, animals and humans.

(ii) Mycelium is branched and septate. It may consist of distinct hyphae or the same may aggregate to produce prosenchyma and pseudoparenchyma.

(iii) They are saprophytic, decomposers parasitic or coprophilous (growing on dung).

(iv) The asexual spores are conidia produced exogenously on the special mycelium called **conidiophores**. Conidia on germination produce mycelium.

(v) Sexual spores are called **ascospores** (sing. ascus) which are produced endogenously in sac-like asci. These asci are arranged in different types of fruiting bodies called **ascocarps**. Each ascus bears 4-8 ascospores, sometimes numerous.

(vi) Sexual reproduction occurs by gametangial contact resulting in formation of oospores.

(vii) Examples include *Penicillium, Aspergillus, Claviceps, Neurospora,* yeast, etc. *Neurospora* is used extensively in biochemical and genetic work.

3. Basidiomycetes

These are terrestrial, saprotrophic and parasitic forms, also known as **club fungi**. Many of them attack trees. A few species form mycorrhizal association.

(i) The mycelium is branched and septate.

(ii) The cells of almost all the members of Basidiomycetes contain barrel-shaped outgrowths between cells. These are called **dolipore** septa.

(iii) Asexual spores are generally not found, but vegetative reproduction by fragmentation is common.

(iv) Sex organs are absent but plasmogamy occurs by the fusion of two vegetative or somatic cells of different strains or genotypes. The resultant structure is a dikaryon which ultimately gives rise to basidium.

(v) Karyogamy and meiosis take place in basidium producing four basidiospores. The basidiospores are exogenously produced on the basidium (Pl. basidia). The basidia are arranged in fruiting bodies called **basidiocarps**.

(vi) Examples include *Agaricus compestris* (edible mushroom), *Puccinia* (cause rust), *Ustilago* (cause smut diseases), *Amanita* (toad stools), bracket fungi, *Lycoperdon* (puffballs), *Armillaria* (honey mushroom).

NOTE
Mushrooms are found in moist humus rich soil, open fields and grasslands. They develop in rings called **fairy rings**.

4. Deuteromycetes

These are commonly known as imperfect fungi because only the asexual or vegetative phases of these fungi are known. These are mostly terrestrial, only few of them are aquatic, e.g. *Tricladium, Pyricularia.*

The characteristics of Deuteromycetes are

(i) The mycelium is septate and branched. Cells are usually multinucleate and septa possess simple pores. The clamp connections are absent.

(ii) Asexual reproduction occurs by the formation of conidia or sometimes by **oidia** and **chlamydospores.**

(iii) Sexual reproduction is not certain.

(iv) Mycelium structure and conidia indicate that most of the Deuteromycetes belong to Ascomycetes whose sexual reproduction is not known.

Examples of these fungi and diseases caused by them are

(a)	*Trichoderma*	(soil fungus) leucopenia called alimentary **aleukia**.
(b)	*Gibberella fujikuroi*	bakane or foolish disease of rice
(c)	*Colletotrichum falcatum*	red rot of sugarcane.
(d)	*Helminthosporium oryzae*	leaf spot disease of rice.
(e)	*Alternaria solani*	early blight of potato and tomato.
(f)	*Cercospora personata*	tikka disease of groundnut.
(g)	*Fusarium oxysporum*	wilts in potato, cotton, banana, flax, etc.

Knowledge Plus

Animals are much less susceptible to parasitic fungi than plants. Only about 50 species of fungus are known to parasitise human and other animals, but these few species cause considerable damage. The general term for such a fungal infection is **mycosis.**

Topic Practice 1

Multiple Choice Questions

1 Mark

1. Fungi that absorb soluble organic matter from dead substrates are called

(a) saprophytes (b) parasites
(c) obligate parasite (d) lichens

Ans (a) Fungi that absorb soluble organic matter from dead substrates are called saprophytes.

2. Fungi that absorb nutrients directly from the cytoplasm of living host are called

(a) saprophytes (b) parasites
(c) symbionts (d) mycorrhiza

Ans (b) Fungi that absorb nutrients directly from the cytoplasm of living host are called parasites.

3. Which of the following options describes the coenocytic condition in fungus?

(a) Uninucleate hypha without septum
(b) Multinucleate hypha without septum
(c) Multicellular hypha
(d) Multiciliate hypha

Ans (b) Continued nuclear division makes the hyphae multinucleate. If the whole mycelium is without septum, the same is called coenocytic.

4. Fungi show vegetative reproduction by all of the following methods except

(a) by fragmentation
(b) by fission
(c) by budding
(d) by protonema

Ans (d) In fungi, vegetative reproduction occurs by fragmentation, budding, fission, sclerotia and rhizomorphs.

5. Fungi show asexual reproduction by all of the following kinds of spores except

(a) conidia
(b) oospores
(c) sporangiospores
(d) zoospores

Ans (b) In fungi, asexual reproduction occurs through the formation of spores, e.g. zoospores, sporangiospores, chlamydospores, oidia, conidia, etc. Oospore is a sexual structure.

6. In fungi, the various types of spores are produced in distinct structures known as
   (a) fruiting body (b) spore sac
   (c) peristome (d) pollen sac

Ans (a) In fungi, the various types of spores are produced in distinct structures called fruiting bodies.

7. In fungi, the fusion of protoplasms between two motile or non-motile gametes is called
   (a) plasmogamy (b) plasmokinesis
   (c) karyogamy (d) cytokinesis

Ans (a) Plasmogamy is the first stage of sexual reproduction in which the cytoplasms of two sex cells fuse with each other.

8. With respect to fungal sexual cycle, choose the correct sequence of events. **NCERT Exemplar**
   (a) Karyogamy, plasmogamy and meiosis
   (b) Meiosis, plasmogamy and karyogamy
   (c) Plasmogamy, karyogamy and meiosis
   (d) Meiosis, karyogamy and plasmogamy

Ans (c) Plasmogamy means fusion of protoplasm and karyogamy means fusion of nucleus. These two events lead to the formation of zygote ($2n$) which is diploid structure where meiosis takes place.

9. Fungi show sexual reproduction by all of the following processes except
   (a) oospores (b) ascospores
   (c) basidiospores (d) zoospores

Ans (d) Fungi show sexual reproduction by oospores, ascospores and basidiospores. Zoospores are the asexual spores.

10. Which of the following is a non-hyphal unicellular fungus?
    (a) Yeast (b) *Puccinia*
    (c) *Ustilago* (d) *Alternaria*

Ans (a) Yeasts are unicellular, degenerated, non-mycelial, saprophytic fungi possessing no hyphae. But sometimes, chain of buds is formed during rapid growth, which may give false appearance of a mycelium and called as pseudomycelium.

11. In Basidiomycetes, the mycelium is
    (a) branched and aseptate
    (b) branched and septate
    (c) unbranched and septate
    (d) coenocytic

Ans (b) The class–Basidiomycetes include those members that produce their basidia and basidiospores on or in a basidiocarp. In Basidiomycetes, the mycelium is branched and septate.

Very Short Answer Type Questions

(1 Mark)

12. Name the scientist named as Father of Mycology.

Ans PA Micheli.

13. Why the pseudoparenchyma fungal tissue is called false parenchyma?

Ans This is because pseudoparenchyma is formed by close packing and fusion of hyphae. Individual hyphae are not distinguishable.

14. The two gametangia come in contact and fuse to form a zygote in which event? Give two examples.

Ans Gametangial copulation, e.g. *Rhizopus, Mucor,* etc.

15. A dikaryon is formed when. **NCERT Exemplar**

Ans Plasmogamy produces a dikaryotic cell or a cell with a pair of nuclei called dikaryon, when karyogamy is delayed.

16. Which are the most advanced group of fungi?

Ans Basidiomycetes (the club fungi) are the most advanced and most commonly seen fungi.

17. What are dolipores? In which class of fungi are these present ?

Ans Dolipores or Central pores are barrel-shaped outgrowths present in septa of class–Basidiomycetes (club fungi).

18. How the saprotrophic Basidiomycetes are able to decompose plant matter ?

Ans The saprotrophic Basidiomycetes can decompose plant matter because they have enzymes for metabolising both cellulose and lignin.

Short Answer Type I Questions

(2 Marks)

19. What are the most common habitats of fungi?

Ans Fungi are known to grow well in moist, dark and warm places, so they can be commonly seen in any habitat where organic matter and moisture are available. (2)

20. What are the criteria used to classify fungi?

Ans Criteria used to classify fungi are
(i) Morphology and appearance of fungus
(ii) Life cycle
(iii) Types of spores and their dispersal
(iv) Physiology and biochemistry. (2)

21. **Write any two differences between Phycomycetes and Ascomycetes.**

Ans Differences between Phycomycetes and Ascomycetes are

Phycomycetes	Ascomycetes
Hyphae are aseptate and coenocytic.	Hyphae are septate and branched.
Asexual spores are zoospores.	Asexual spores are conidia.

(2)

22. **What is the characteristic feature of class–Ascomycetes?**

Ans Ascospore formation is the characteristic of class–Ascomycetes. Ascospores are a type of non-motile meiospores which are produced inside special sacs called asci (sing. ascus). An ascus often contains 8 ascospores because meiosis is accompanied by one mitotic division. (2)

23. **Which type of fungi are also called bracket fungi?**

Ans Basidiomycetes are also called bracket or shelf fungi. They are lignocolous fungi which produce bracket or shelf-shaped, hard, leathery basidiocarps that are found to come out from the tree trunk on loss of wood, e.g. *Fomes tomentarius*, etc. (2)

Short Answer Type II Questions

3 Marks

24. **Briefly describe the life cycle phases of fungi.**

Ans All fungi pass through two phases or stages in their life cycle. These phases are vegetative or assimilative phase and reproductive phase.

Vegetative phase In this phase, they go speedily in the food giving substratum. The food substratum may be bread, cheese, wood, etc. Coprophilous fungi grow well on cow dung, dead parts of plants like fallen leaves.

Reproductive phase In this phase, erect hyphae develop and produce reproductive structure. In unicellular yeasts, the entire cell becomes a reproductive structure. This is the holocarpic condition. In other fungi, reproductive structures develop from a part of the vegetative body and the condition is called eucarpic. (3)

25. **Write a brief account of reproduction in fungi.**

Ans Reproduction in fungi occurs by asexual and sexual methods. Asexually, it takes place either by formation of motile spores (zoospores) or by formation of non-motile spores (aplanospores) or conidia.

In lower fungi like Phycomycetes, sex organs like the unicellular antheridia (male) and unicellular oogonia (female) are produced. In higher fungi like Basidiomycetes, sex organs are absent but sexual process is present. Ascomycetes and Basidiomycetes fungi produce fruiting bodies by sexual process called ascospores and basidiospores, respectively. (3)

26. **Explain the following terms in relation to Phycomycetes.**

(i) Mycelium (ii) Eucarpy and holocarpy
(iii) Asexual reproduction

Ans (i) **Mycelium** It is coenocytic and non-septate or aseptate. Septa are formed only in connection with separation of old senescent parts and delimitation of reproductive structures.

(ii) **Eucarpy and holocarpy** In eucarpy, only a portion of somatic body is transformed into reproductive body. In holocarpy, transformation of the whole somatic body into reproductive structure is found in only some primitive forms.

(iii) **Asexual reproduction** It involves the formation of sporangia. The sporangia function as conidia in dry habitats as zoosporangia under wet conditions. (1×3)

27. **At a stage of their cycle, Ascomycetes fungi produce the fruiting bodies like apothecium, perithecium and cleistothecium. How are these three types of fruiting bodies different from each other?** **NCERT Exemplar**

Ans The fruiting bodies of Ascomycetes are called ascocarps. A fertile layer called hymenium bears asci. These fruiting bodies are different from each other in following ways

(i) **Cleistothecium** Closed ascocarp, i.e. ascocarp with no opening.

(ii) **Perithecium** Flask-shaped ascocarp with an apical pore called ostiole.

(iii) **Apothecium** Cup-shaped open ascocarp. (1× 3)

28. **Explain the terms**

(i) Basidiocarp (ii) Basidia
(iii) Basidiospores

Ans (i) **Basidiocarp** It may be minute or very large structure which bears basidia, e.g. bracket fungi, puffballs.

(ii) **Basidia** These are special reproductive bodies of Basidiomycetes where karyogamy, meiosis and basidiospore formation occurs.

(iii) **Basidiospores** These are meiospores of Basidiomycetes. Basidiospores are borne at the tips of sterigmata or outgrowths of basidia. (1× 3)

29. **There is a myth that immediately after heavy rains in forest, mushrooms appear in large number and make a very large ring or circle, which may be several metres in diameter. These are called 'fairy rings'. Can you explain the myth of fairy rings in biological terms?** **NCERT Exemplar**

Ans The fairy rings form as the mycelium of the mushroom fungus spreads in the soil from a central point. It grows peripherally, so that the younger hyphae will appear almost in a circle. The forest cover contains sufficient organic matter and favourable conditions that cause young fungal hyphae to form compact masses that grow into mushrooms. This is the reason, the mushrooms appear growing in a circle or ring. (3)

30. **Why the members of class–Deuteromycetes are considered the fungi imperfecti?**

Ans Deuteromycetes is an artificial class of fungi which has been created to include all those fungi (fungi imperfecti) in which sexual stage is either absent or not known. Their mycelium is usually septate. Coenocytic forms are not known. Clamp connections, typical character of Basidiomycetes are absent. It is believed that most members of Deuteromycetes are actually Ascomycetes in which sexual reproduction is either absent or yet to be discovered. (3)

Long Answer Type Questions

5 Marks

31. **Describe the cell structure of fungus in detail.**

Ans Fungus cells are eukaryotic. These cells contain all the eukaryotic organelles except plastids. Some of these organelles are nucleus, ribosomes, endoplasmic reticulum, mitochondria, Golgi bodies, etc. A fungal cell wall contains mostly chitin. Plasmalemma bears coiled membranous outgrowths called lomasomes. Nuclei are small and connected to endoplasmic reticulum. Nuclear division involves formation of internal spindle. Vacuoles are small. Near the hyphal tips, the cytoplasm contains small vesicles called chitosomes. Food reserve is in the form of glycogen and oil. (5)

32. **Give a comparative account of the classes of kingdom–Fungi under the following**
(i) Mode of nutrition
(ii) Mode of reproduction **NCERT**

Ans Classes of kingdom–Fungi are

(i) **Mode of Nutrition**

- **Phycomycetes** Saprotrophic and parasitic
- **Ascomycetes** Saprotrophic and parasitic
- **Basidiomycetes** Saprotrophic, parasitic and predaceous
- **Deuteromycetes** Parasitic and saprotrophic.

(ii) **Mode of Reproduction**

- **Phycomycetes** Asexual reproduction occurs by zoospores (motile) or by aplanospores (non-motile). Sexual reproduction is by gametangial fusion and gametic fusion.
- **Ascomycetes** Asexual reproduction is by conidia and sexual reproduction is by gametangial contact, spermatisation and somatogamy.
- **Basidiomycetes** Asexual spores are generally not found but vegetative reproduction by fragmentation is common. Sexual reproduction is by somatogamy.
- **Deuteromycetes** Reproduce only by asexual spores called conidia. Sexual reproduction is not reported.

(2½×2)

33. **Write differences between ascocarp and basidiocarp.**

Ans Differences between ascocarp and basidiocarp are as follows

Ascocarp	Basidiocarp
It is a fructification found in Ascomycetes.	It is a fructification found in Basidiomycetes.
It is simpler in construction.	It is more elaborate in construction.
Ascocarp contains numerous asci.	Basidiocarp contains several basidia.
Ascus is generally aseptate.	Basidium may be septate or aseptate.
An ascus forms eight ascocarps.	A basidium produces four basidiospores.
These are formed endogenously.	These are formed exogenously.

(5)

34. **Name the following**
(i) A poisonous mushroom having white spores
(ii) Edible Basidiomycetes
(iii) Fungus used in brewing industry
(iv) It is searched by trained pets
(v) Root-like, cards-like hyphal masses having a distinct growing point.
(vi) Non-motile meiospores develop in Basidiomycetes
(vii) Compact groups of hyphae produced to overcome unfavourable conditions.

Ans (i) Toadstools
(ii) Mushrooms and young puffballs
(iii) Brewer's yeast (*Saccharomyces cerevisiae*)
(iv) Truffles (tuber-like underground fungus)
(v) Rhizomorphs perennate during periods of scarcity of food and water.
(vi) Basidiospores (develop exogenously)
(vii) Sclerotia under favourable conditions each one forms a new mycelium. (5)

35. **List any six diseases caused by different classes of fungi.**

Ans Diseases caused by different classes of fungi are given below

Phycomycetes	Ascomycetes	Basidiomycetes	Deuteromycetes
Club rot of crucifers	Stem galls of coriander	Loose smut of wheat	Red rot of sugarcane
Wart disease of potato	Leaf curl of peach	Smut of corn	Blast of rice
Rhizome rot of ginger	Powdery mildew of grapes	Black rust of wheat	Wilt of potato, tomato, cotton and banana
White rust of crucifers	Powdery mildew of peas	Yellow rust of wheat	Tikka disease
Downy mildew of grapes	Ergot rye and grasses	Rust of peas	Early blight of potato
Late blight of potato	Brown rot of pear	Leaf rust of coffee	Die back of chillies

(5)

TOPIC 02 Economic Importance of Fungi, Lichens and Mycorrhiza

Fungi are directly or indirectly associated to mankind and play a significant role. Some fungi are awarded for their usefulness whereas others are very harmful.

Useful Activities of Fungi

Fungi play many important roles in the ecosystem and several fungi are used commonly due to their economic significance. Some beneficial roles of fungi in nature and to the mankind are

1. Fungi as Food

(i) The fructifications of certain fungi are used as nutritious and delicious foods, e.g. *Agaricus campestris* (common field mushroom) and *Morchella* (used in Himachal Pradesh and Jammu and Kashmir) possess an edible basidiocarp.

(ii) Mushrooms are rich source of vegetable protein (21-30% protein on dry weight basis), vitamins (B, C, D and K) and minerals (Ca, Na, K, P, Fe), hence mushroom cultivation is done in different parts of our country. *Agaricus bisporus* also known as **white button mushroom.** It is a saprophyte.

(iii) Some yeasts are an important source of vitamin-B and some Deuteromycetes like *Endomyces, Rhodotorula, Torulopsis* are rich in proteins. A food called sufu is produced from *Mucor.*

2. Fungi as Medicine

Several fungi are used in the production of medicines.

(i) **Ergot** It is prepared from the sclerotia of *Claviceps purpurea.* It contains some alkaloids which are **used to induce uterine contraction** for abortion, in the treatment of menstrual disorders and to check haemorrhages.

(ii) **Ephedrine** It is synthesised from benzaldehyde by the action of yeast and is used in the treatment of asthama and nasal troubles.

(iii) **Steroids** These are complex organic compounds, effective against rheumatoid arthritis, allergic, dermatologic and other diseases. They are also used as anaesthetic and antifertility agents.
A wide variety of fungi have the capacity of synthesizing many steroids; for instance, cortisone is prepared by fermentation of plant glycosides by *Rhizopus nigricans* and *Aspergillus niger.*

(iv) Fungi are used in the production of different **antibiotics.** These are the substances of microbial origin and have antimicrobial activities.

Some Important Antibiotics and their Sources

Antibiotic	Source
Penicillin	*Penicillium notatum* and *P. chrysogenum*
Ergotine	*Claviceps purpurea* (sclerotia). Given after childbirth
Citrinine	*P. citrinum*
Campestrin	*Psaliotta campestris* (*Agaricus campestris*)
Glyotoxin	*Trichoderma* species
Proliferin	*Aspergillus proliferans*
Clavicin (anti-cancerous)	*Aspergillus clavatus*
Flavicin	*Aspergillus flavus* and *A. fumigatus*

3. Fungi in Industry

Fungi are responsible for the production of several useful products in industries. These are

(i) Yeast (*Saccharomyces* also called **Baker's yeast**) perform fermentation hence, it is used in the production of ethyl alcohol. Ethyl alcohol is the basis of brewing industry.

(ii) In **baking industry**, yeast produces CO_2, which is used to raise dough while making bread.

(iii) Digestive enzymes like diastase, digestin and polyzyme are produced from *Aspergillus flavus-oryzae*.

(iv) *Penicillium camemberti* and *P. roqueforti* are used for flavouring cheese.

(v) Organic acids, production, e.g.

- **Citric acid** by *Aspergillus niger* and *Aspergillus wentii, Mucor,* etc.
- **Gluconic acid** by *Aspergillus niger* and *Penicillium purpurogenum.*
- **Gallic acid** by *Penicillium glacum* and *Aspergillus gallomyces.*
- **Kojic acid** by *Aspergillus oryzae.*
- **Fumaric acid** by *Rhizopus stolonifer.*

4. Fungi in Agriculture

Fungi play an important role in agriculture in various ways

(i) Fungi is used to increase soil fertility and as biological control, e.g. *Trichoderma* and *Rhizoctonia.*

(ii) Predacious fungi like *Dactylella, Dactylaria, Zoophagus* and *Arthrobotrys,* etc., destroy certain nematodes, eelworms and thus act as good biological control agents.

(iii) Fungi plays the role of **decomposers** in detritus food chain and carries out the decomposition of complex molecules. The enzyme secreted by these fungi decompose complex organic substance into their inorganic components and thus increase soil fertility. Thus, they also help in cycling of nutrients like carbon, nitrogen, etc., in ecosystem.

Harmful Activities of Fungi

Some harmful fungi are as follows

1. Fungi are causal organisms of many diseases in living beings.

Some harmful fungal diseases in plants, humans and animals are as follows

Fungi Cause Several Diseases in Plants

Diseases	Fungus responsible
Black wart disease of potato	*Synchytrium endobioticum*
White rust of crucifers	*Albugo candida* or *Cystopus candidus*
Late blight of potato	*Phytophthora infestans* (famous famine of Ireland in 1845 is caused due to this fungi).
Early blight of potato	*Alternaria solani*
Powdery mildews	*Erysiphe* sp.
Damping of disease and seedlings of cereals and vegetable	*Pythium debaryanum*
Loose smut of wheat	*Ustilago tritici*
Downy mildew in cereals	*Sclerospora graminicola*
Downy mildew of cucurbits	*Peronospora parasitica*
Red rot of sugarcane	*Colletotrichum falcatum*

Some Important Fungal Diseases in Humans and Animals

Diseases	Fungus
Athlete foot	*Tinea rubrum*
Ringworm	*Trichophyton, Microsporum* and *Epidermophyton*
Mucomycosis	*Mucor* and *Rhizopus*
Aspergillosis (lung disease)	*Aspergillus niger*
Penicillosis	*Penicillium* sp.
Salmon disease of gills in fishes	*Saprolegnia*
Ear infection (Automycosis)	*Aspergillus flavus* and *Aspergillus nidulans*
Thrush disease of throat	*Monilia* species
Candidiasis	*Candida albicans*

Lichens

These are symbiotic associations between algae and fungi. The algal component (autotrophic) is called **phycobiont** and fungal component (heterotrophic) is **mycobiont.** Lichens are found in least polluted habitats like walls, window panes, barren rocks, cooled volcanic lava, tree bark, soil and aquatic habitats.

Morphology

Lichens vary in colour like orange, brown, dark brown, grey, yellowish green, etc.

Based on their morphology, lichens can be of various types

(i) **Crustose** These lichens are crust-like, closely attached to the substratum, e.g. *Graphis, Lecanora.*

(ii) **Leprose** These are like minute scales attached superficially to the substratum, e.g. *Lepraria.*

(iii) **Foliose** These are like twisted and wrinkled leaf, e.g. *Parmelia, Physcia.*

(iv) **Fruticose** These are branched, erect with bushy appearance, e.g. *Evernia, Ramalina, Usnea.*

(v) **Filamentous** These lichens consist of chains of algal cells wrapped around by fungal hyphae, e.g. *Racodium.*

Internal Structure

The major part of lichen body constitutes fungus and only 5% part is algal component. The body is divided as upper cortex, algal zone (gonidial layer), middle medulla, lower cortex and rhizines.

Only the algal zone contains photosynthetic partner. In about 98% lichens, the fungal partner belongs to Ascomycetes. In the rest, the fungal partner belongs to Basidiomycetes and Deuteromycetes.

Reproduction

Lichens may reproduce vegetatively or sexually. They reproduce vegetatively by the following ways such as fragmentation, death and decay, etc.

Lichens reproduce sexually by following ways

(i) Formation of ascomycetous fruiting body.

(ii) Formation of basidiocarp.

Sexual reproduction is not considered to be a common means of reproduction to form a new lichen.

Economic Importance of Lichens

Lichens have widespread importance for the mankind. Some of the important uses of lichens are as follows

(i) Lichens contain a complex carbohydrate called **lichenin**. It is used as food for many animals. *Cladonia* is used as fodder.

(ii) Many lichens are useful in producing medicines.
Usnea and *Cladonia* (antibiotics and usnic acid).
Cetraria islandica (laxative mucilage).
Parmelia (curing epilepsy).
Lobaria (treating lung diseases).

(iii) Lichens like *Roccella tinctoria, Parmelia omphalodes* are used in making different types of dyes. **Litmus** was also previously obtained from *Roccella montaingne.*

(iv) Extracts of *Lobaria pulmonaria* and *Cetraria islandica* are used in tanning leather.

(v) Some lichens like *Usnea* are used in brewing industry.

(vi) Lichens are best indicators of pollution. They do not grow in polluted environments.

(vii) Lichens help in understanding the process of **biological succession** by the ecologists. Lichens are the pioneer of succession in xerosere.

Mycorrhiza

It is a symbiotic association between a fungus and the root of a plant. Mycorrhizal roots often show wooly covering of fungal hyphae on the surface and remain in the upper layers of the soil where organic matter is abundant. A fungus can form association with roots of many plants and the roots of a plant in turn can form association with many fungi.

Mycorrhizae are of the following two types

1. Ectomycorrhizae

In this type, the bulk of the fungus grows over the surface as a mantle and only a part of it lives in the intercellular spaces of the cortex of the root.

2. Endomycorrhizae

In this type, the fungus grows inside the cortex of the root with some intercellular hyphae tips. In some forms of endomycorrhizae, the fungal hyphae develop some special organs called **vesicles** with the root cortical cells. This kind of mycorrhizae are called **Vesicular Arbuscular Mycorrhizae** (VAM).

The VAM occur in large number of crop plants. Vesicles and arbuscules help fungi in absorption of nourishment from cortical cells. A single endomycorrhizal fungus can form association with the roots of a number of plants.

Economic Importance of Mycorrhiza

(i) Mycorrhiza help in absorption of minerals from the soil and provide to the root.

(ii) These help in increased absorption of water.

(iii) These produce growth inducing hormones. In the absence of fungus, *Pinus* and *Betula* show stunted growth despite providing all types of nutrients.

(iv) Mycorrhiza enable the plants to grow in mineral deficient soil, saline soil and unfavourable pH and temperature.

(v) In case of orchids, the fungus absorbs nourishment from outside and deliver to the germinating seed as the same is devoid of stored food.

(vi) Mycorrhiza have antimicrobial substances which protect the root from parasitic fungi and harmful bacteria by secreting antimicrobial substances.

Topic Practice 2

Multiple Choice Questions

(1 Mark)

1. Lichens are composites consisting of algae and
   (a) mosses (b) fungi
   (c) bacteria (d) mycoplasma

Ans (b) Lichens are composites consisting of algae and fungi.

2. Association between mycobiont and phycobiont are found in
   (a) mycorrhiza (b) root
   (c) lichens (d) BGA

Ans (c) **Lichens** are composite organisms which has a permanent symbiotic association of fungus and an alga. The fungal partner is called mycobiont an the algal partner is called phycobiont.

3. The role of fungus in lichen is
   (a) food (b) anchoring
   (c) mineral absorption (d) Both (b) and (c)

Ans (d) The fungal partner protects the alga by retaining water. It provides a large surface area for the absorption of mineral nutrients. It helps in the anchorage also.

4. The benefit given by algae in lichen is
   (a) food for fungi (b) shelter
   (c) mineral absorption (d) protection

Ans (a) The algal or cyanobacterial cells are photosynthetic and make their own food from water and CO_2 in presence of photosynthetic pigment and sunlight through photosynthesis. They also provide vitamins to the fungus.

5. Lichens, which grow on the barks of trees are called
   (a) saxicolous (b) corticolous
   (c) terricolous (d) None of these

Ans (b) Lichens, which grow on the bark of trees are termed as corticolous, e.g. *Usnea*.

6. A terricolous lichen is
   (a) *Cladonia*
   (b) *Usnea*
   (c) *Dermatocarpon*
   (d) *Cyphelium*

Ans (a) The lichens growing on soil are termed as terricolous, e.g. *Cladonia* and *Lecidea*.

7. Which of the following are most suitable indicators of SO_2 pollution in the environment?
   (a) Lichens (b) Conifers
   (c) Algae (d) Fungi

Ans (a) Lichens are useful bioindicators for air pollution, especially sulphur dioxide pollution, since they derive their water and essential nutrients mainly from the atmosphere rather than from soil.

8. Which of the following would appear as the pioneer organisms on bare rocks?
   (a) Liverworts (b) Mosses
   (c) Green algae (d) Lichens

Ans (d) In primary succession on rocks, lichens secrete acids to dissolve rock, help in weathering and soil formation. So, lichens are pioneer species to colonise the bare rock.

9. Mycorrhiza is
   (a) symbiotic (b) parasitic
   (c) saprophyte (d) Both (a) and (b)

Ans (a) Mycorrhiza is a symbiotic association between fungus and roots of higher plants.

Very Short Answer Type Questions

(1 Mark)

10. Name a fungi useful for bakery industry.

Ans Baker's yeast (*Saccharomyces cerevisiae*)

11. How fungi play a vital role in ecosystem.

Ans Fungi carries out the crucial process of decomposition which is essential for nutrient cycling.

12. Name a fungi which is utilised in health and medicine industry.

Ans Fungi are used to produce antibiotics. *Penicillium notatum* is used to produce antibiotic called penicillin.

13. Give the name of a fungus which causes rust diseases.

Ans *Puccinia graminis tritici* causes black stem rust of wheat.

14. List the types of lichens.

Ans Types of lichens are
(i) Crustose (crust-like)
(ii) Foliose (flat and lobed -like a leaf)
(iii) Fruticose (branched-like a bush).

15. Why lichens are called dual organisms?

Ans Lichens are dual organisms which contain a fungus or mycobiont and an alga or phycobiont in symbiotic association.

16. How are lichens related to air pollution?

Ans The decrease in lichen population of an area is an indicative of air pollution particularly SO_2 pollution.

17. An association between roots of higher plants and fungi is called. **NCERT Exemplar**

Ans Mycorrhiza is a symbiotic association between a fungus and the root of higher plant.

18. What are the types of mycorrhiza?

Ans Mycorrhiza can be of two types

(i) Ectomycorrhiza (ii) Endomycorrhiza

19. How mycorrhizae are beneficial for plants?

Ans They help in absorption of minerals from soil and protect them from other parasitic fungi and bacteria.

Short Answer Type I Questions

(2 Marks)

20. Give the name of a fungus used in biological control of other fungi. How is it harmful to humans?

Ans *Trichoderma,* is a soil fungus used in biological control of other fungi as it produces allelochemicals against them. If this fungus happens to pass into human alimentary canal, it causes leukopenia called alimentary canal aleukia. (2)

21. *Neurospora,* an Ascomycetes fungus has been used as a biological tool to understand the mechanism of plant genetics much in the same way as *Drosophila* has been used to study animal genetics. What makes *Neurospora* as a genetic tool? **NCERT Exemplar**

Ans *Neurospora* (pink bread mould) is often called *Drosophila* of plant kingdom. It is haploid in nature which helps in immediate expression of every mutation. Beadle and Tatum used it as an experimental tool to find out that genes express their effect through synthesis of specific enzymes. (2)

22. Give the name of the causative agents of

(i) red rot (ii) early blight

(iii) wilts (iv) brown leaf spot of rice

Ans (i) **Red rot** *Colletotrichum falcatum*

(ii) **Early blight** *Alternaria solani*

(iii) **Wilts** *Fusarium oxysporum*

(iv) **Brown leaf spot of rice** *Helminthosporium oryzae.* (½ × 4)

23. What do the terms phycobiont and mycobiont signify? **NCERT**

Ans Phycobiont and mycobiont are parts of lichens. The phycobiont is the algal partner in lichens and mycobiont is the fungal partner in lichens. (2)

24. Mention four industrial importance of lichens.

Ans Lichens are industrially important in the following ways

(i) They are used to make perfumes and soaps.

(ii) They are used to obtain alcohol after brewing and distillation.

(iii) Their absence in the environment indicates air pollution.

(iv) They are used to create medicines for various diseases like epilepsy and lung diseases. (½ × 4)

25. Lichens play important role in biological succession and soil formation. Justify.

Ans Lichens growing on rocks secrete organic acids like oxalic acid. The acids enter the rock and produce a number of honey comb-like small crevices. Dust and organic matter collect in the crevices. Moss spores are able to grow over such crevices and start the process of succession and soil formation. (2)

26. How do fungi form partnership with most plants?

Ans Some fungi have evolved essential relationships with the roots of many living plants. These fungi grow around and into the roots, such that both partners benefit and in case of orchids neither would thrive without the other. This partnership is called mycorrhizal symbiosis. (2)

Short Answer Type II Questions

(3 Marks)

27. Give a brief description about applications of fungi in healthcare industry.

Ans Refer to text on page no. 63.

28. Write atleast three beneficial applications of fungi.

Ans Refer to text on page no. 63-64.

29. What are lichens? Give an example. Also write their importance.

Ans Refer to text on page no. 64 and 65.

30. Justify that lichens are the pioneer organisms.

Ans Lichens are the pioneer organisms in the new terrains which colonise bare rocks, mountains and cliffs. They corrode the rocks and accumulate a certain amount of minerals and organic matter.

The plants like mossess and grasses appear later in succession, utilising the soil initially formed by lichens.

Lichens thus, can convert a barren area into one that can support vegetation. (3)

31. **Define the term mycorrhiza. How are these associations affect a plant? Explain with examples.**

Ans Mycorrhiza is a mutually beneficial or symbiotic association of fungi with roots of higher plants. Orchids grow as epiphyte on plants, have their roots associated with fungi right from the seedling stage.

Many orchids cannot survive without mycorrhizae associations. Many forest trees such as pines appear stunted if mycorrhizal associations are absent. In the presence of these associations, these plants absorb 2-3 times more nitrogen, potassium and phosphorus compared to without them. (3)

32. **How mycorrhizae are ecologically beneficial for plants describe?**

Ans Refer to text on page no. 65-66.

Long Answer Type Questions

5 Marks

33. **Discuss in detail about beneficial acitivites of fungi.**

Ans Refer to text on page no. 63 and 64.

34. **State and describe two ecological and economical importance of fungi.**

Ans Refer to text on page no. 64.

35. **How lichens are beneficial, explain their importance?**

Ans Refer to text on page no. 65.

36. **Explain the types of mycorrhizae and their significance.**

Ans Refer to text on page no. 65-66.

37. **Explain the following in terms of mycorrhizal association.**

(i) Growth promotion
(ii) Antimicrobial substance
(iii) Nourishment
(iv) Adverse environment
(v) Absorption of water

Ans (i) **Growth promotion** Fungus produces growth promoting hormones. In the absence of this association, *Pinus* and *Betula* show stunted growth despite providing all types of nutrients.

(ii) **Antimicrobial substance** Fungus protects the root from parasitic fungi and harmful bacteria by secreting antimicrobial substances.

(iii) **Nourishment** In orchids, the fungus absorbs nourishment from outside and provide it to the germinating seed.

(iv) **Adverse environment** Mycorrhiza enable plants to grow in mineral deficient soil, saline soil, unfavourable pH and temperature.

(v) **Absorption of water** Fungal association increases water availability to the root of plants. (1×5)

SUMMARY

- **Fungi** constitute a unique kingdom of nucleated, spore-bearing, achlorophyllous thallophytes. These includes the yeasts, molds, mushrooms, puffballs, rusts and smuts, morels, etc.
- These are saprophytic and ingestive in their mode of nutrition. They do not synthesise their own food.
- **Plant body** of fungi is multicellular and thalloid, i.e. distinct roots, stems, leaves or any other parts are absent.
- **Thallus** consists of tubular filaments called **hyphae,** which are aggregated to form mycelium. The hyphae may be coenocytic or uninucleated, septate or aseptate, primary or secondary or tertiary.
- Fungi may reproduce vegetatively, asexually or sexually.
- **Vegetatively fungi** may reproduce by fragmentation, fission, budding, oidium formation or chlamydospore formation.
- **Fungi reproduce asexually** by sporangiospores, zoospores, aplanospores, conidiospores or binucleated spores.
- **Sexual reproduction in fungi** involves plasmogamy, i.e. fusion of protoplasts, karyogamy, i.e. fusion of nuclei to form zygote and zygotic meiosis, i.e. division of zygote to form haploid spores. It also involves dikaryon stage.
- **Plasmogamy** may occur *via* planogametic copulation, i.e. fusion of motile gametes, gametangial contact, i.e. fusion of hyphae acting as gametangium, gametangial copulation, i.e. direct fusion of male and female gametangia, spermatisation, i.e. sexual fusion between spermatia and female receptive hyphae, somatogamy, i.e. fusion of two vegetative cells.
- The **sexual spores** in fungi can be basidiospores (e.g. Basidiomycetes), ascospores, (e.g. Ascomycetes), zygospores (e.g. Zygomycetes) and oospore (e.g. Oomycetes).
- **Classification of fungi** is based on their morphology of the mycelium, mode of spore formation and type of fruiting bodies. This divides the kingdom-Fungi into Phycomycetes, Ascomycetes, Basidiomycetes and Deuteromycetes. Phycomycetes is further divided into Oomycetes and Zygomycetes.
- **Oomycetes** (The algal fungi) Most of them are parasites. Their thallus may be unicellular of filamentous. The filamentous forms are coenocytic and aseptate. They derive their nutrition from host with the help of haustoria. Asexual reproduction takes place by biflagellated zoospores. The members of this group shows oogamous type of sexual reproduction, e.g. *Phytophthora infestans* (cause late blight of potato) and *Albugo candida* (causes white rust of crucifers), etc.
- **Zygomycetes** (The conjugation fungi) the members of this group are terrestrial. They live in soil, dung or on decaying plant and animal matter. Their thallus is coenocytic and filamentous and aseptate. Their sexual or asexual cells do not have flagella, thus are completely non-motile. They reproduce asexually with the help of sporangiospores and sexually by gametangial copulation or conjugation, e.g. *Rhizopus, Mucor*, etc.
- **Ascomycetes** (The sac fungi) Their thallus is unicellular in yeast. While other fungi of this group are filamentous having septate uninucleate mycelium.
- These fungi have a sac-like structure termed as **ascus**. Thus called sac-fungi. This ascus is the product of **sexual reproduction**.
- **Asexual reproduction** occurs with the help of conidiospores.
- **Basidiomycetes** (The club fungi) These fungi possess septate primary mycelia. Sexual reproduction leads to formation of dikaryotic mycelia having binucleated hyphae. Motile cells are absent in them. They forms clamp connections during cell division.
- Sexual reproduction leads to exogenous production of spores termed as basidiospores. These are produced on club-shaped structures called **basidium.**
- **Deuteromycetes** (The fungi imperfecti) These fungi only possess asexual and vegetative phase in their life cycle. Sexual reproduction is absent in them. The mycelium is septate and branched in these fungi, e.g. *Alternaria, Colletotrichum* and *Trichoderma*.
- Fungi can used for industrial products, antibiotics, household products, as biocontrol and biofertilisers.
- Fungi can cause severe diseases in humans, animals and plants such as ringworm in humans caused by *Candida albicans*, black wart disease of potato is caused by *Synchytrium*, etc.
- **Lichens** are composite organisms having an algal and a fungal component, e.g *Cladonia*. The algal component is known as phycobiont and fungi component as mycobiont, which are autotrophic and heterotrophic, respectively. The fungal partner provide shelter to phycobiont, while phycobiont provide food to mycobiont.
- **Mycorrhiza** is a symbiotic associations of roots of higher plants and fungi. In this fungi being heterotrophic derive nutrition from plant roots and in return fix phosphorus for the plants, e.g. *Glomus*.

Chapter Practice

Multiple Choice Questions

1 Mark

1. Dikaryophase of fungus occurs in
(a) Ascomycetes and Basidiomycetes
(b) Phycomycetes and Ascomycetes
(c) Phycomycetes and Basidiomycetes
(d) Basidiomycetes and Deuteromycetes

2. Fungi are divided into four classes on the basis of
(a) morphology of the mycelium
(b) mode of spore formation
(c) fruiting bodies
(d) All of the above

3. *Mucor* and *Rhizopus* are included in the class
(a) Ascomycetes (b) Phycomycetes
(c) Basidiomycetes (d) Deuteromycetes

4. Lichens are pioneer of vegetation in a
(a) xerosere (b) hydroponics
(c) marine life (d) hydrosere

5. Which of the following is an example of crustose lichen ?
(a) *Parmelia* (b) *Cladonia*
(c) *Usnea* (d) *Graphis*

Assertion-Reason Type Questions

1 Mark

■ Direction (Q. Nos. 6-9) *In each of the following questions, a statement of Assertion (A) is given followed by corresponding statement of Reason (R). Of the statements, mark the correct answer as*

(a) If both A and R are true and R is the correct explanation of A
(b) If both A and R are true, but R is not the correct explanation of A
(c) If A is true, but R is false
(d) If A is false, but R is true

6. Fungi are one of the most important groups of organism on the plantlet as they play a vital role in biosphere. They also play important role in recycling dead and decayed matter.

Observe the diagram of fungi below and comment upon the appropriateness of the Assertion and the Reason.

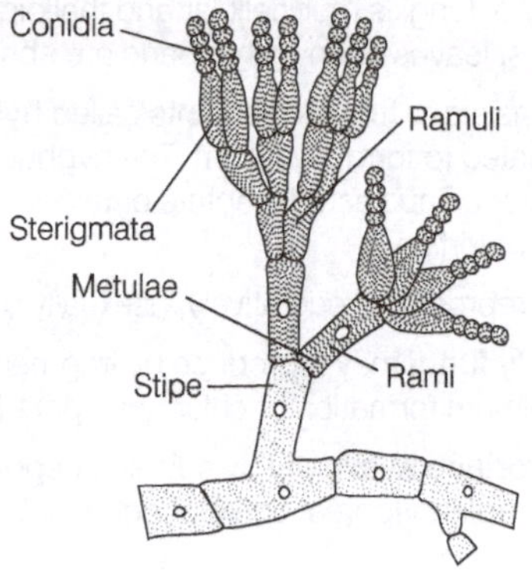

Assertion (A) In fungi, sexual apparatus decreases in complexity from lower to higher forms.
Reason (R) In algae, sexual apparatus increases in complexity from simple to higher forms.

7. **Assertion** (A) Fungi are wide spread in distribution and they can even live on or inside other plants and animals.
Reason (R) Fungi are able to grow anywhere on land, water or on other organisms because they have variety of pigments including chlorophyll, carotenoids, fucoxanthin and phycoerythrin.

8. **Assertion** (A) Slime moulds are called as fungus like animals.
Reason (R) These do not have cell wall.

9. **Assertion** (A) Mycelium in Deuteromycetes is aseptate.
Reason (R) Phycomycetes possess septate and branched mycelium.

Answers

1. (a) 2. (d) 3. (b) 4. (a) 5. (d)
6. (b) 7. (c) 8. (c) 9. (d)

Very Short Answer Type Questions

(1 Mark)

10. Which microorganisms are called sac fungi?
11. Name the group of fungi which is commonly called the club fungi.
12. Which yeast is used in baking industry ?

Short Answer Type I Questions

(2 Marks)

13. On what basis were the fungi earlier included in the plant kingdom ?
14. Explain the tissue structure of fungal cell.
15. Which class includes club fungi? List its two features.
16. Explain the physiological relationships between the algal and fungal components of lichen.
17. 'Differentiate between ecto and endo mycorrhizae.

Short Answer Type II Questions

(3 Marks)

18. Draw the labelled diagram of budding in yeast cell.
19. What are the main differences between Ascomycetes and Basidiomycetes ?
20. Explain the phycobiont and mycobiont relation in lichens.
21. Explain mycorrhizal association and its importance.

Long Answer Type Questions

(5 Marks)

22. Enlist five differences between Ascomycetes and Deuteromycetes.
23. List five important uses of fungi to mankind.
24. How lichens and mycorrhizae are different structurally and functinally? Explain.

Case Based Question

(4/5 Marks)

25. Given below is a graphical representation of abundance of lichens in a given area for a period of 10 Years.

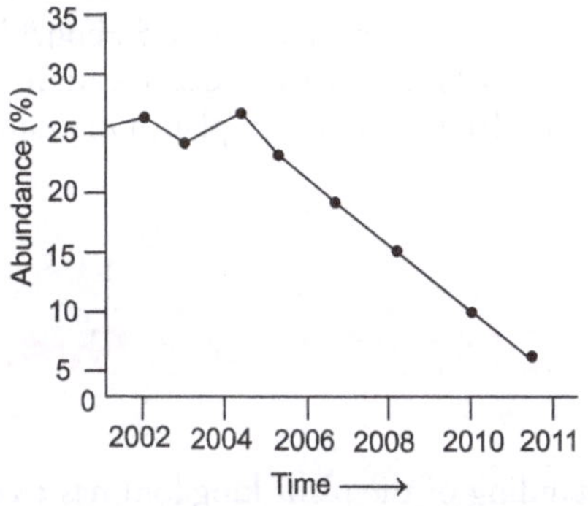

Study the graph carefully and answer the following questions

(i) What conclusion can be drawn from the graph?

(ii) Give reason for your answer in (i).

(iii) Comment upon the components that make up lichens.

Or (iii) Write two economic importance of lichens that makes it valuable for industry purpose.

CHAPTER

05

Plant Kingdom

In the previous chapter, we have studied about the classification of organisms under various kingdom systems of classifications. Now, in this chapter we will study more details about the plant kingdom.

- Classification System and Algae
  - Types of Classification Systems
  - Algae
- Bryophytes and Pteridophytes
- Gymnosperms

TOPIC 01 Classification System and Algae

Our understanding of the plant kingdom has changed over time. Fungi and members of the Monera and Protista having cell walls have been included in Plantae in the earlier classifications. The kingdom–Plantae now includes algae, bryophytes, pteridophytes, gymnosperms and angiosperms and fungi, monera, protista have been excluded from this.

Types of Classification Systems

The various systems used in classification of plants are being discussed here

1. Artificial System of Classification

This system is based on the comparison of one or a few gross superficial morphological characteristics, which are helpful in easy identification of organisms. This system remained in use for about two thousand years.

Advantages

Advantages of artificial system are given below

(i) Artificial system is easy to remember as only one or a few characters are used.

(ii) The traits used are of interest to humans.

Disadvantages

Disadvantages of artificial system are given below

(i) This system uses only few superficial characters (like habits, numbers, colours and shape of leaves, etc.) which may be very common in many organisms grouped together.

(ii) This system considers mainly the vegetative characters or the androecium characters as given by **Linnaeus.**

(iii) It does not demonstrate natural and phylogenetic relationships.

(iv) This gave equal weightage to vegetative and reproductive/sexual characters which is not acceptable, as vegetative characters get more easily influenced by the environmental factors.

(v) It separated the closely related species.

2. Natural System of Classification

It is also known as **phenetic system** of classification. The natural system of classification is based on natural affinities among the organisms. It considers both external and internal features like structure, anatomy, embryology and phytochemistry.

This type of classification was first given by **George Bentham** and **Joseph Dalton Hooker.**

Advantages

Advantages of natural system are given below

(i) Only related organisms are kept in a group.

(ii) Unrelated organisms are kept in separate groups.

(iii) It shows natural relationships among the organisms.

(iv) It shows possible origin of different taxa.

Disadvantages

Disadvantages of natural system are given below

(i) There is more emphasis given on natural characters.

(ii) In this system, several related families are separated and unrelated families are put together.

(iii) Evolutionary characteristics of organisms were neglected for their classification.

3. Phylogenetic System of Classification

The phylogenetic system of classification indicates the evolutionary as well as genetic relationships among organisms. This system is based on fossil records of biochemical, anatomical, morphological, physiological, embryological and genetical studies.

The system was initiated by **Engler** and **Prantl** (1887-1899) in *Die Naturalichen Pflanzefamilien.* In phylogenetic system, flowering plants are placed in ascending series related to complexity of floral morphology.

The phylogenetic system of classification is mainly the rearrangement of taxonomic characters in the light of phylogenetic information of plants.

Advantages

Advantages of phylogenetic system are given below

(i) Families and order in this system are of small size.

(ii) This system is in conformation with the modern views of phylogeny.

(iii) They use information from various resources to solve the problems of classification. Such informations become more important in the absence of supporting fossil evidences.

Disadvantages

Disadvantages of phylogenetic system is that, this is not helpful in plant identification as plants are identified mainly on morphological characters.

The outline of present classification is given below

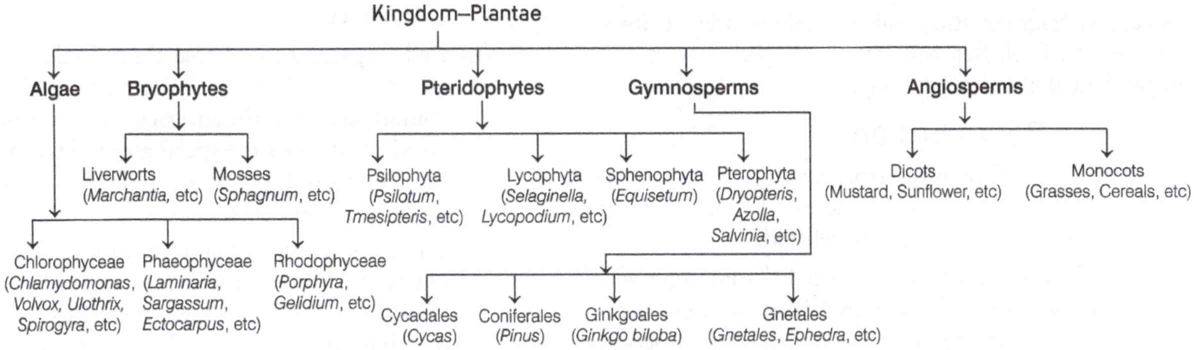

Fig. 5.1 Classification of Plantae

Algae

Algae are chlorophyll containing , simple, thalloid, autotrophic and largely aquatic (both freshwater and marine) organisms.

The important salient features of algae are given below

Habitat

These are found in both freshwater and marine habitats. Some algal forms are also found in moist habitats like wet rocks and soil, tree trunks, etc. Some of them are also found in close association with fungi (lichen) and animals (e.g., on sloth bear). Few algae species are parasites.

Thallus Organisation

The plant body (thallus) is without differentiation. The basic form and size of algae are highly variable, and ranges from unicellular forms (e.g. *Chlamydomonas*), filamentous (e.g. *Ulothrix* and *Spirogyra*) to colonial forms (e.g. *Volvox*). Filamentous forms are attached on the substratum with the help of holdfast.

Structure of Algal Cell

It has a eukaryotic plant cell structure. The cytoplasm contains membrane bound chloroplast, mitochondria, ER, Golgi bodies and other cell organelles. The cell wall contains cellulose. The nucleus contains nuclear membrane.

Food Material

Algae have main food reserve as starch. In brown algae, **mannitol** and **laminarin** are the main reserve food material, whereas in red algae **floridean** starch is the reserve food material.

Reproduction

The algae reproduce vegetatively, asexually and sexually.

1. Vegetative Reproduction

It occurs by fragmentation, tubers, stolons, adventitious branches, etc. Each fragment gets developed into an independent thalloid plant body.

2. Asexual Reproduction

It occurs by a number of accessory spores, such as zoospores aplanospores, akinetes, carpospores, etc. The most common being the zoospores, which are flagellated.

The cells which produce spores are called **sporangia** which may be the vegetative cells (e.g. in *Chlamydomonas* and *Ulothrix*) or modified vegetative cells (e.g. in *Vaucheria*).

3. Sexual Reproduction

It occurs by fusion of two gametes.

On the basis of morphology of reproductive cells, sexual reproduction is of three types

(i) **Isogamous** In this method, two morphologically similar gametes fuse to form a zygote, e.g. *Spirogyra.*

(ii) **Anisogamous** It is the fusion of structurally dissimilar gametes, which differ in size and behaviour. Male gamete is more active and bigger in size than female gamete, e.g. some species of *Chlamydomonas.*

(iii) **Oogamous** In this process, the male gamete is motile, active, small and without reserve food. The female gamete is bigger, passive, non-motile and laden with food, e.g. *Volvox, Fucus.*

Life Cycle

Life cycle in algae can be haplontic, diplontic, diplohaplontic, haplohaplontic, etc. An alternation of generation occurs in diplohaplontic life cycle.

Classification of Algae

Algae are divided into various classes based on pigmentation, type of stored food materials and kind of flagellation. The three main classes are Chlorophyceae, Phaeophyceae and Rhodophyceae.

1. Class–Chlorophyceae (Green Algae)

The members of Chlorophyceae are commonly called **green algae**. There are about 7000 species in this class. The reserve food material is starch. The characteristic features of Chlorophyceae are discussed below

(i) **Habitat** These are mostly marine forms, only some are freshwater. *Chlorella* can tolerate moderately warm waters. Snow dwelling forms are called **cryophytes,** e.g. *Chlamydomonas nivalis, Scotiella,* etc.

(ii) **Cell Organisation** These are unicellular, colonial, coenocytic and multicellular forms. Cell walls contain cellulose (inner layer) and pectose (outer layer) in most of the green algae. The chloroplasts may be discoid, plate-like, reticulate, cup-shaped, spiral or ribbon-shaped.

The chloroplasts contain photosynthetic pigments. Most of the members have one or more storage bodies called **pyrenoids** located in the chloroplasts. Pyrenoids contain protein besides starch.

Some algae may store food in the form of oil droplets also.

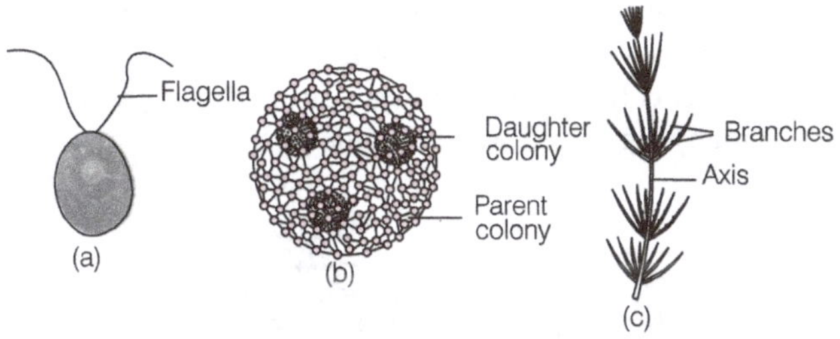

Fig 5.2 Green algae (a) *Chlamydomonas*, (b) *Volvox*, (c) *Chara*

(iii) **Thallus** Unicellular green algae can be flagellate, (*Chlamydomonas*) or non-flagellate (*Chlorella*). *Acetabularia* (umbrella plant) has an unicell upto 10 cm long with distinction of nucleus containing rhizoid, elongated stalk and umbrella-like cap.

A colony for fixed number of individual unicells (*Volvox*) is called **coenobium**. Coenocytic or siphonaceaus thallus occurs in *Caulerpa*. Unbranched filamentous thallus is found in *Ulothrix, Spirogyra, Cladophora,* heterotrichous in *Stigeoclonium* and parenchymatous in *Ulva*.

(iv) **Reproduction** The members of Chlorophyceae reproduce vegetatively, asexually and sexually by various methods. Vegetative reproduction occurs through cell division (unicellular forms), fragmentation, tubers, storage cells, etc.

Asexual reproduction occurs by zoospores, aplanospores, hypnospores, akinetes and daughters colonies. Sexual reproduction may be isogamous, anisogamous or oogamous.

(v) **Life Cycle** It can be haplontic, diplontic and diplohaplontic. In haplontic life cycle, there is a single somatic phase, which is haploid. Diploid stage is represented by a single cell or zygote, e.g. in *Spirogyra*.

Economic Importance of Green Algae

(i) Algae are responsible for carrying out about a half of the total carbon dioxide fixation on earth by the process of photosynthesis.

(ii) Some protein rich algae, like *Chlorella* are used as food supplements by sailors and space travellers.

(iii) Green algae are involved in sewage oxidation.

(iv) Antibiotics can also be extracted from *Chlorella*.

2. Class–Phaeophyceae (Brown Algae)

The members of Phaeophyceae contain **fucoxanthin** pigment and include phycocolloid rich multicellular eukaryotic algae. Its common members are seaweeds called **kelps**. This class is comprised of about 2000 species.

(i) **Habitat** Brown algae are mostly marine. These are found mostly in colder seas or during cold seasons in tropical regions.

(ii) **Size** They range from simple branched, filamentous forms (*Ectocarpus*) to profusely branched forms as represented by kelps. These represent the largest algae. The largest kelps are *Macrocystis* (40-100 m) and *Nereocystis* (20-30 m).

(iii) **Cell Organisation** All members are multicellular. Cell wall is composed of cellulose, pectose and phycocolloids. The cellulosic wall of vegetative cells is usually enclosed by a gelatinous coating of algin.

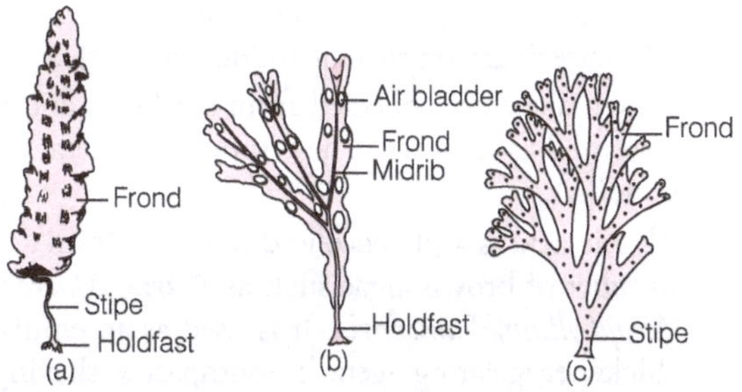

Fig 5.3 Brown algae (a) *Laminaria*, (b) *Fucus*, (c) *Dictyota*

(iv) **Thallus** It is heterotrichous filament with both prostrate and upright branches (*Ectocarpus*). The parenchymatous structure is found in higher forms. The plant body of large forms is often differentiated into **holdfast** (with which it usually attaches to the substratum), a stalk called the **stipe** and **lamina** (frond), which is photosynthetic. Conducting tubes or **trumpet hyphae** are present in larger brown algae or kelps. They help in conduction of food materials.

(v) **Photosynthetic Pigments and Colour** These include chlorophyll-*a*, *c* and carotenoids. They range in colour from olive green to various shades of brown depending upon the amount of the xanthophyll and fucoxanthin present in them.

(vi) **Food Reserve** It remains in the form of complex carbohydrates such as laminarin or mannitol.

(vii) **Flagellation** These contain heterokont flagellation with one smooth (whiplash) and one tinsel flagella.

(viii) **Reproduction** Vegetative reproduction occurs through fragmentation (e.g. *Sargassum*), adventitious branches and stolons (e.g. *Dictyota*).

Asexual reproduction occurs by biflagellate zoospores, which are pear-shaped having two unequal laterally attached flagella.

Sexual reproduction is performed by isogamy, anisogamy and oogamy. Union of gametes may take place in water or within the oogonium (oogamous species). The gametes are pyriform (pear-shaped) and have two laterally attached flagella.

(ix) **Life Cycle** Isomorphic alternation of generation is found in some brown algae, e.g. *Ectocarpus*, *Dictyota*. In many brown algae, the diploid generation or phase is dominant. The haploid phase is either microscopic or represented by gametes only (e.g. *Fucus*).

Economic Importance of Brown Algae

(i) The brown algae that are used as food are *Laminaria, Nerocystis, Macrocystis, Alaria*, etc.

(ii) Some brown algae like *Fucus, Sargassam, Laminaria, Macrocystis* are important fodder for cattle.

(iii) Brown algae are collected from seashores and are also used as manure. They improve mineral content of soils.

(iv) Alginic acid is a phycocolloid obtained from a number of brown algae such as *Alaria, Macrocystis, Ascophyllum, Laminaria*. It is used as an emulsifier, thickener, gelating agent in toothpastes, shaving creams, ice-creams, emulsion paints, shampoo, cosmetics, etc.

(v) *Fucus* and *Laminaria* are rich in iodine.

3. Class–Rhodophyceae (Red Algae)

The members of Rhodophyceae are commonly called **red algae** because of the predominance of the red pigment, i.e. *r*-**phycoerythrin** in their body.

(i) **Habitat** Most of the red algae are marine with greater concentrations found in the warmer areas. They are found in both well-lighted regions close to the surface of water and also at great depths in oceans where relatively little light penetrates.

(ii) **Thallus** The red thalli of most of the algae is multicellular. Some of them have complex body organisation like *Asterocystis* which is pseudofilamentous, *Porphyridium* is unicellular, *Porphyra* has parenchymatous sheets, *Chondrus* is ribbon-like, *Gelidium* is a multicellular sea weed.

(iii) **Cell Wall** The cell wall contains cellulose, pectic compounds and certain mucopolysaccharides called **phycocolloids**, such as agar, carrageenan, etc. In many algae, cell wall contains pits.

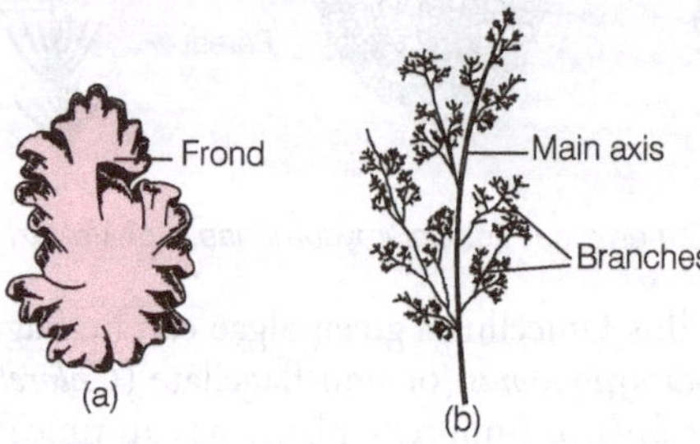

Fig 5.4 Red algae (a) *Porphyra* (b) *Polysiphonia*

(iv) **Photosynthetic Pigments** These include chlorophyll-*a* and d, carotenes, xanthophylls and phycobilins. Phycobilins are water soluble and are of two types, i.e. red-coloured **phycoerythrin** and blue-coloured **phycocyanin**.

(v) **Reserve Food** They store food as floridean starch which is similar in constitution to glycogen and amylopectin.

(vi) **Reproduction** Vegetative reproduction occurs by fragmentation, regeneration of hold fast and gemmae. Asexual reproduction occurs by non-motile spores (carpospores, monospores, tetraspores and neutral spores). Sexual reproduction occurs by non-motile gametes and is **oogamous type.** The male sex organ is called **spermatogonium** or **antheridium**. The male gamete produced is non-flagellated and is called **spermatium.**

The female sex organ is called **carpogonium**. After fertilisation, a new structure called **carposporophyte** is produced. It remains attached to the parent alga.

(vii) **Life Cycle** It has two or more phases such as haplohaplontic, haplohaplohaplontic, diplodiplohaplontic, etc.

Table 5.1 Divisions of Algae and their Main Characteristics

Classes	Common Name	Major pigments	Stored Food	Cell Wall	Flagellar Number and Position of Insertions	Habitat
Chlorophyceae	Green algae	Chlorophyll-*a*, *b*	Starch	Cellulose	2-8, equal, apical	Freshwater, (some) brackish water, salt water (most)
Phaeophyceae	Brown algae	Chlorophyll-*a*, *c*, fucoxanthin	Mannitol, Laminarin	Cellulose and algin	2, unequal, lateral	Freshwater (rare), brackish water, salt water (most)
Rhodophyceae	Red algae	Chlorophyll-*a*, *d*, phycoerythrin	Floridean starch	Cellulose, pectin and poly sulphate esters	Absent	Freshwater (some), brackish water, salt water (most)

Economic Importance of Red Algae

(i) The red algae like *Porphyra, Chondrus, Rhodymenia, Centerella* and *Bostrychia* are used as food in various parts of the world.

(ii) Agar yielding algae are called **agarophytes,** such as *Gelidium, Gracilaria, Ceramium, Gelidiella*, etc.

(iii) Algae like *Rhodymenia* are used as fodder for cattle.

(iv) Carrageenin, a phycocolloid obtained from red algae like *Chondrus* and *Gigartina*, is used in the preparations of emulsions for ice-cream, chocolates, sauces, toothpastes, cosmetics, etc. It is also used in clearing liquors and finishing leather, etc.

(v) Funori an adhesive phycocolloid is obtained from red alga, *Gloiopeltis*. It is used in sizing textiles, paper and as glue. Some algae like *Corallina, Polysiphonia* have medicinal properties.

Harmful Effects of Algae

(i) The luxuriant growth of algae in water reservoirs make the water unfit for drinking by imparting bad taste, odour and colouration.

(ii) **Water blooms** are formed by the growth of some microscopic or semi-microscopic algae such as *Anabaena, Aphanizomenon, Anabaenopsis, Arthrospira, Coelosphaerium, Gloeotrichia, Lyngbya, Nodularia, Nostoc, Microcystis*, etc. Water blooms may be harmful, because they are indirectly responsible for fish mortality due to depletion of oxygen.

(iii) The green algae *Cephaleuros virescens* is parasitic on tea leaves and cause a disease called red rust of tea, while *Cephaleuros coffea* is parasitic on coffee plants.

Topic Practice 1

Multiple Choice Questions

(1 Mark)

1. Identify the correct statement for artificial system of classification.
   (a) Artificial system was based on natural affinities present among the organisms.
   (b) It was proposed by Engler and Prantl.
   (c) The artificial system gave equal weightage to the vegetative and sexual characteristics.
   (d) It considers both the external features and internal features like anatomy, embryology, etc.

Ans (c) Artificial system of classification used only gross superficial morphological characters. As Linnaeus gave equal weightage to vegetative and sexual characters to classify plants.

2. Select the correct match from those given below.
   (a) Artificial system of classification – Englar and Prantl
   (b) Natural system of classification – Bentham and Hooker
   (c) Phylogenetic system of classification – Linnaeus
   (d) Phylogenetic classification – Aristotle

Ans (b) Natural classification system was based on natural affinities among the organisms.

It considered external and internal features of the organisms. This classification was proposed by George Bentham and Joseph Dalton Hooker.

3. Phylogenetic system of classification was given by
   (a) Engler and Prantl (b) Aristotle
   (c) Linnaeus (d) Bentham and Hooker

Ans (a) Phylogenetic system of classification was given by Engler and Prantl. It was based on the evolutionary relationships of the organisms.

4. In algae, asexual reproduction occurs by the production of different types of spores. The most common type of spore is
   (a) aplanospore (b) endospore
   (c) zoospore (d) oospore

Ans (c) Algae produce different types of spores, the most common being the zoospores. These are motile, flagellated spores and give rise to new plants on germination.

5. Anisogamous means both gametes are
   (a) similar in size and non-motile
   (b) dissimilar in size
   (c) similar in size and motile
   (d) dissimilar in morphology

Ans (d) Anisogamous means fusion of morphologically dissimilar gametes, which may be motile or non-motile, small or big, etc.

6. How many pyrenoids are present in the members of class–Chlorophyceae?
   (a) One
   (b) Two
   (c) One to many
   (d) Pyrenoids are absent

Ans (c) Most of the members of Chlorophyceae have one to many storage bodies called pyrenoids located in the chloroplasts. Pyrenoids contain proteins besides starch.

7. Holdfast, stipe and frond constitute the plant body in case of **NCERT Exemplar**

(a) Rhodophyceae (b) Chlorophyceae
(c) Phaeophyceae (d) All of these

Ans (c) The Phaeophyceae members have large sized body which is differentiated into holdfast, stipe and lamina.

Very Short Answer Type Questions

1 Mark

8. Name the different types of classification systems of plants.

Ans Artificial, natural and phylogenetic.

9. Why the artificial system of classification was not considered reliable by the taxonomists?

Ans The artificial system of classification was based only on gross morphological characters like habit, colour, number, shape of leaves, etc.

10. What does the natural system of classification indicate?

Ans It indicates the natural relationship between different organisms.

11. Name the characters used in natural system of classification.

Ans Natural system of classification is based on characters from morphology, anatomy, cytology, embryology, molecular biology and genetics of organisms.

12. How does the natural system of classification provide detailed information about the groups?

Ans This system is based on common characters shared by the group of organisms, so it can give more or detailed information about the groups of organisms.

13. How are algae classified in Whittaker's classification?

Ans In Whittaker's classification algae are grouped into the kingdom–Plantae, within the phylum–Thallophyta. They are classified into three classes *viz.*, Chlorophyceae (green algae), Phaeophyceae (brown algae) and Rhodophyceae (red algae).

14. Which system indicates evolutionary as well as genetic relationships among organisms?

Ans Phylogenetic system of classification.

15. How are plants placed in phylogenetic system of classification?

Ans Flowering plants are placed in ascending series related to their complexity of floral morphology.

16. Which unicellular plants are included in kingdom–Plantae?

Ans Kingdom–Plantae includes unicellular members of green algae, e.g. *Chlamydomonas, Chlorella.*

17. What is the basis of classification of algae?

Ans Basis of classification of algae **NCERT**

(i) The type of photosynthetic pigments
(ii) Nature of reserve food materials.

18. Why does green algae looks green?

Ans It is due to pigments chlorophyll-*a* and *b*.

19. Food is stored as floridean starch in Rhodophyceae. Similarly Mannitol is the reserve food material of which group of algae?

Ans Phaeophyceae. **NCERT Exemplar**

20. Give one example each of Chlorophyceae, Phaeophyceae and Rhodophyceae.

Ans **Chlorophyceae** *Spirogyra*, **Phaeophyceae** *Sargassum* and **Rhodophyceae** *Porphyra.*

21. Which green algae is used by space travellers as protein rich food?

Ans *Chlorella.*

22. Which substance covers the cell wall of Phaeophyceae?

Ans Algin.

23. In which algae reserve food is in the form of laminarin?

Ans Brown algae (Phaeophyceae).

Short Answer Type I Questions

2 Marks

24. List any two advantages of artificial system of classification.

Ans Two advantages of artificial system of classification are

(i) Artificial system is very easy to remember as it uses only one or a few characters for comparison.
(ii) It is practical and the traits useful for mankind are used for the identification of various taxa. (1×2)

25. What was the drawback of artificial system of classification?

Ans The artificial system of classification was mainly based on vegetative characters or on the androecium structure (system given by Linnaeus). Such system separated the closely related species since they were based on a few characteristics.

The artificial system gives equal weightage to vegetative and sexual characteristics. This is not convincing because the vegetative characters are more easily affected by the environment. (2)

26. Natural system of classification is considered better than artificial system of classification. Explain.

Ans The following reasons explain this

(i) Only related organisms occur in a group, in natural system of classification as it prevents grouping of unrelated organisms.

(ii) it shows natural relationship among organisms. (2)

27. What is kingdom–Plantae?

Ans Kingdom–Plantae includes multicellular eukaryotic organisms with photosynthetic mode of nutrition, cell wall with cellulose and plastids containing certain structures as the reserve food. (2)

28. Write a brief account of reproduction in algae.

Ans Refer to text on page no. 76. (2)

29. Write the types of thallus found in members of Rhodophyceae.

Ans The thallus structure in Rhodophyceae varies from unicellular to pseudoparenchymatous.

(i) Unicellular thallus (*Porphyridium*).

(ii) Filamentous thallus (*Polysiphonia*).

(iii) Pseudoparenchymatous thallus (*Gelidium*). (2)

30. Differentiate between red algae and brown algae. **NCERT**

Ans Refer to table on page no. 76. (2)

31. Give one word answer for the following.

(i) In brown algae, what is the function of frond?

(ii) Name the constituents of cell wall in green algae.

Ans (i) Frond is a leaf-like organ meant for performing the photosynthesis process. (1)

(ii) The cell wall in green algae is made up of cellulose (inner layer) and pectose (outer layer). (1)

Short Answer Type II Questions

3 Marks

32. Describe the salient features of artificial classification system.

Ans Salient features of artificial classification system are

(i) They use only gross superficial morphological characters such as habits, colours, numbers and shapes of leaves, etc.

(ii) These consider mainly the vegetative characters or the androecium characters as given by Linnaeus.

(iii) They separated closely related species. (3)

33. Which characters are used in natural system of classification? Explain with examples.

Ans The characters used in natural system of classification are morphology, anatomy, reproduction, cell structure, behaviour and biochemistry of the organism. The similarity in large number of characters show kinship. (1)

Examples

(i) Monocotyledons have one cotyledon in their seeds and their leaves have parallel venation.

(ii) Dicotyledons have two cotyledons in their seeds and their leaves have reticulate venation. (2)

34. Describe the type of photosynthetic pigments in red algae, green algae and brown algae.

Ans **Red algae** The photosynthetic pigments are located in the chromatophores. These are chlorophyll-*a*, *d* and α, β-carotenes, xanthophyll and biliproteins.

Green algae Chromoplasts contain chlorophyll-*a*, *b*, carotene and xanthophyll.

Brown algae The chromatophores contain chlorophyll-*a*, *c* and β, α-carotenes and xanthophyll. (1×3)

35. Write a note of economic importance of algae. **NCERT**

Ans Refer to text on page no. 75, 76 and 77. (3)

Long Answer Type Questions

5 Marks

36. How is natural system different from artificial system of classification? List some features.

Ans Differences between natural and artificial systems are

Natural System	Artificial System
It is based on the large number of characters.	It is based on only one or a few characters.
The characters are stable.	The characters are liable to change with change in the environment.
It avoids analogy.	It accepts analogy for grouping.
It is based on morphology, anatomy, cytology, embryology, molecular biology and genetics.	It is based on morphological or reproductive traits. Others are not used.
Natural system brings out homology.	Artificial system does not study homology.
It explains natural and some phylogenetic relationships.	It does not give any idea about natural and phylogenetic relationships.

(5)

37. Algae are known to reproduce asexually by a variety of spores under different environmental conditions. Name these spores and the conditions under which they are produced.

Ans **Zoospores** Flagellate spores, under favourable conditions.

Aplanospores Non-flagellate, thin-walled spores under approaching unfavourable conditions.

Hypnospores Thick-walled, resting spores in unfavourable conditions.

Akinetes Thin-walled and thick-walled spores formed from whole cells in unfavourable conditions.

Autospores Spores which look exactly like parent cell formed under favourable conditions. (1×5)

TOPIC 02 Bryophytes and Pteridophytes

Bryophytes

Bryophytes include the various mosses and liverworts. These are non-vascular embryophytes, characterised by the presence of an independent gametophyte and parasitic sporophyte.

Habitat

Bryophytes commonly grow in moist, shaded areas in hills. These are also called as **amphibians of the plant kingdom** because, these can live in soil, but are dependent on water for sexual reproduction.

Some bryophytes grow in diverse habitats, such as

(i) **Aquatic**, e.g. *Riccia, Ricciocarpus, Riella*

(ii) **Epiphyte**, e.g. *Radula, Dendroceros*

(iii) **Saprophyte**, e.g. *Buxbaumia, Cryptothallus*

(iv) **Dry habitats**, e.g. *Polytrichum*

(v) **Deserts**, e.g. *Tortula desertorum*

(vi) **Dry rocks**, e.g. *Porella*

Thallus Organisation

The plant body of bryophytes is more differentiated than that of algae. It is thallus-like and prostrate erect and attached to the substratum by unicellular or multicellular rhizoids. Root, stem and leaves are not present on thallus.

Sex Organs

The main plant body is haploid that produces gametes, hence it is called **gametophyte**. The sex organs in bryophytes are multicellular, the male sex organ in bryophytes is called **antheridium** (which produces biflagellate antherozoids) and the flask-shaped female sex organ is called **archegonium** (produces a single egg).

Reproduction

It is a sexual type of reproduction. The antherozoids are released into water where they come in contact with archegonium.

Fertilisation

It occurs inside the archegonium. The egg secretes a chemical which attracts spermatozoids. Sperms require a thin film of water for swimming and reaching the dehisced archegonium. One sperm fuses with an egg and produces a **diploid zygote.** Zygotes do not undergo reduction division immediately instead, they produce a multicellular body called **sporophyte.**

Dependent Sporophyte

The sporophyte is not free-living, but remain attached to the photosynthetic gametophyte deriving nourishment from it. Some cells of the sporophyte undergo reduction division (meiosis) to produce **haploid spores** (which germinate to produce gametophyte).

Sporogonium

The sporophyte of bryophytes is called **sporogonium** because it is mainly dependent on gametophyte and is meant for producing spores.

Life Cycle

Bryophytes have heteromorphic alternation of generation.

In bryophytes, a **haploid gametophytic** generation and a **diploid sporophytic** generation alternate in the life cycle. The haploid generation (gametophytic) undergoes sexual reproduction to produce gametes. The gametes fuse to form a diploid zygote which gives rise to the diploid sporophyte generation. It produces asexual spores. Meiosis takes place during the formation of spores thus, there is return of haploid condition. The haploid spores give rise to the gametophytic generation.

The gametophyte may be produced directly or first a juvenile stage is formed, called **protonema.**

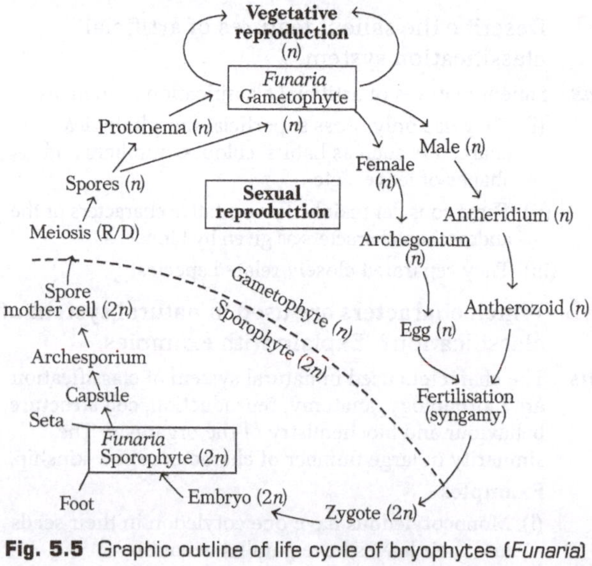

Fig. 5.5 Graphic outline of life cycle of bryophytes (*Funaria*)

Bryophytes do not attain great heights. They may range from 0.4-70 cm in height and have thalloid plant body.

The reasons may be following

(i) Root is absent.
(ii) Vascular tissues are not present.
(iii) Cuticle is not present on the plant body.
(iv) Mechanical tissues are absent.
(v) Male gametes need to swim upto the interior of dehisced archegonia (female organ containing egg cell).

Classification

According to the most accepted classification system, bryophytes are classified into three main classes, i.e. Hepaticopsida, Anthocerotopsida and Bryopsida.

Bryophyta

Classes

- **Hepaticopsida** (Hepaticae) (Liverworts), *Riccia, Marchantia* and *Pellia*
- **Anthocerotopsida** (Anthocerotae) (Hornworts) *Anthoceros*
- **Bryopsida** (Musci) Mosses, *Funaria, Sphagnum Polytrichum* and *Tokakia*

Types of Bryophytes

The bryophytes are generally classified into two main groups

1. Liverworts

Liverworts (Hepaticopsida) usually grow in moist, shady places such as banks of streams, marshy ground, damp soil, bark of trees and deep in the woods.

(i) **Thallus** The plant body of a liverwort is thalloid, e.g. *Marchantia*,. The thallus is dorsoventral and closely appressed to the substrate. The leafy members have tiny leaf-like appendages in two rows on the stem-like structure.

(ii) **Rhizoids** These are unicellular. These may be of two types in some liverworts, i.e. smooth-walled and tuberculate.

(iii) **Reproduction** It occurs both by asexual and sexual means.

- **Asexual Reproduction** It occurs by fragmentation of thalli or by the formation of specialised structures called **gemmae** (sing. gemma). Gemmae are green, multicellular, asexual buds which develop in small receptacles called **gemma cups** located on the thalli. The gemmae detach from the parent body and germinate to form new individuals.
- **Sexual Reproduction** It is accomplished by the formation of male and female sex organs either on the same or on different thalli. The sporophyte develops from zygote which continues to grow on gametophyte. It is differentiated into a foot, seta and capsule. After meiosis, spores (n) are produced within the capsule.
- These spores germinate to form free-living gametophytes, e.g. *Riccia, Marchantia, Pellia, Porella,* etc.

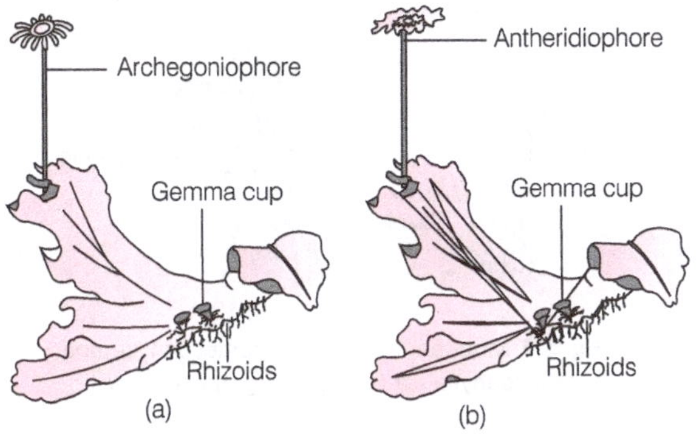

Fig 5.6 A liverwort (*Marchantia*) : (a) Female thallus, (b) Male thallus

2. Mosses

Mosses (**Bryopsida**) grow in dense mats over moist shady places, especially during rainy seasons. Some mosses grow in desert bogs and streams.

(i) **Plant Body** The predominant stage of life cycle of a moss is the gametophyte which consists of two stages. The first stage is the **protonema stage** which develops directly from a spore. It is a creeping, green, branched and frequently filamentous stage. The second stage is the **leafy stage** which develops from the secondary protonema as a lateral bud.

They consist of upright, slender axes bearing spirally arranged leaves. This stage bears sex cells.

(ii) **Rhizoids** These are long, multicellular branched structures with oblique septa. They take part in fixation and absorption of water. However, surface conduction through capillarity is an important mechanism of water supply to aerial parts.

(iii) **Reproduction** This can occur both by vegetative and sexual means.

Vegetative Reproduction It occurs by fragmentation and by budding in the secondary protonema from exposed rhizoids and other parts (like gemmae, buds and tubers) of the plant body.

Sexual Reproduction Sex organs, **antheridia** (male) and **archegonia** (female) are produced at the apex of the leafy surface. Male organs appear cup-shaped, while female organs are bud-like. After fertilisation, the zygote develops into a sporophyte, consisting of foot, seta and capsule (containing spores).

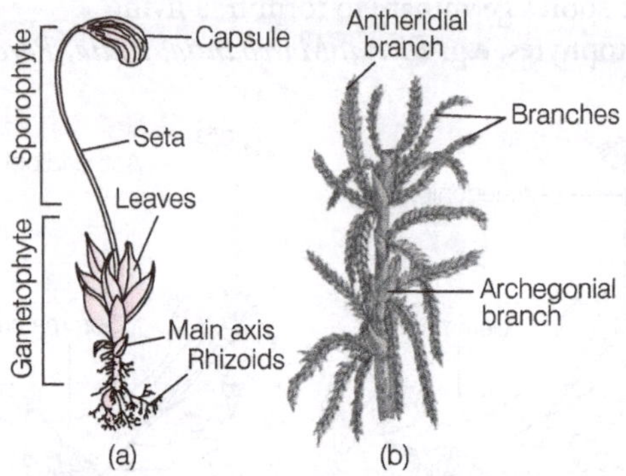

Fig 5.7 Mosses (a) *Funaria*, gametophyte and sporophyte (b) *Sphagnum* gametophyte

(iv) **Sporophyte** The sporophyte in mosses is more elaborate than that in liverworts. It derives its nutrition from gametophyte for its development. Spores are formed after meiosis in sporophyte.

The mosses have an elaborate mechanism of spore dispersal, e.g., *Funaria, Polytrichum* and *Sphagnum*.

Differences between Liverworts and Mosses

Liverworts	Mosses
They are dorsiventral.	They have radial symmetry.
Plants are thalloid or foliose.	Mosses are foliose.
Midribs are not present in leaves.	Leaves have unbranched midrib.
Rhizoids are unicellular and unbranched.	Rhizoids are multicellular and branched.
Plants bear scales.	Scales are absent in plants.
A conducting strand is absent.	A conducting strand is commonly present.
Sporophyte is differentiated in foot, seta and capsule.	It is not differentiated in foot, seta and capsule.
Capsule often possesses elaters.	Elaters are absent.
Dehiscence occurs through elaters.	Peristome performs this function.
A protonema stage is absent.	A juvenile protonemal stage is present.

Note

Anthocerose is a hornwort. It belongs to Anthocerotopsida.

Economic Importance of Bryophytes

Bryophytes in general are of little economic importance. But, several species have some uses.

(i) Some mosses provide food for herbaceous mammals, birds and other animals.

(ii) Species of *Sphagnum* (a moss), provides peat that have long been used as fuel. It has the capacity to hold water as packing material for trans-shipment of living materials.

(iii) Mosses along with lichens are the first organisms to colonise rocks. Hence, these help in biological succession. They decompose rocks making the substrate suitable for the growth of higher plants.

(iv) Mosses form dense mats on the soil. They reduce the impact of falling raindrops and thus prevent soil erosion.

(v) *Marchantia* has medicinal properties to cure lungs and liver infections. It also has anti-tumour properties.

Pteridophytes

Pteridophytes are primitive seedless vascular plants also called **cryptogams**. These have conspicuous sporophytic plant body, inconspicuous independent gametophytes with antheridia and partially embedded archegonia having 4-rowed necks.

The term Pteridophyte was coined by **Haeckel** (1866). About 13000 species of pteridophytes have been reported. They were perhaps the first land plants evolved during ordovician (450-500 million years ago) period.

The characteristic features of pteridophytes are as follows

Habitat

The pteridophytes are found in cool, damp shady places though some may flourish well in sandy-soil conditions.

Some members like *Azolla, Salvinia, Marsilea* species are aquatic pteridophytes.

Plant Body

The size varies from a fraction of centimeter (e.g. *Azolla*) to 20 m in tree ferns (e.g. *Angiopteris*). The main plant body is a sporophyte which is differentiated into true root, stem and leaves.

These organs possess well-differentiated vascular tissues. The leaves are small (microphyllus) as in *Selaginella* or large (macrophylls) as in *Dryopteris* (ferns).

Vascular Tissues

These plants evolved as first terrestrial plants to possess xylem and phloem throughout their body. Xylem consists of tracheids and phloem is made up of sieve cells and albuminous cells.

Sporophylls

The sporophytes bear sporangia that are subtended by leaf like appendages called **sporophylls.** In some cases sporophylls may form distinct compact structures called **strobili** or **cones** (*Selaginella* and *Equisetum*). The sporangia produce spores by meiosis in spore mother cells.

Spores

The spores germinate to give rise to inconspicuous, small but multicellular, free-living, mostly photosynthetic thalloid gametophytes called **prothallus.** In majority of the pteridophytes, all the spores are of similar kind; such plants are called **homosporous** and production of these kinds of spore called **homospory**. Genera like *Selaginella* and *Salvinia* produce two kinds of spores, macro (large) and micro (small) spores; thus, are called **heterosporous** and production of these kinds of spore called **heterospory.**

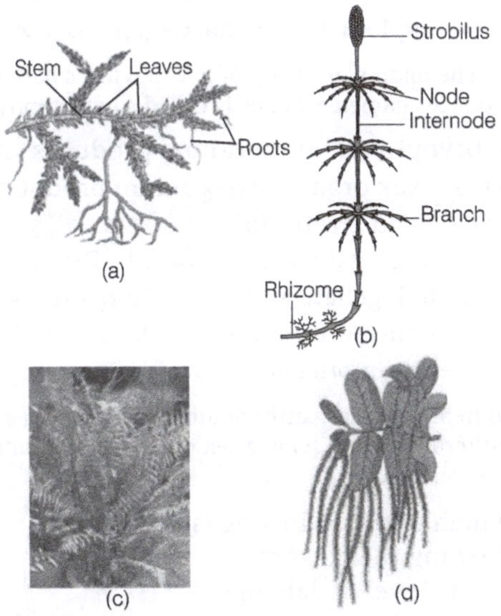

Fig 5.8 (a) *Selaginella* (b) *Equisetum* (c) Fern (d) *Salvinia*

Gametophyte

The thalloid gametophyte or prothallus requires cool, damp, shady places to grow. The megaspores and microspores germinate and give rise to female and male gametophytes, respectively. The female gametophyte in these plants is retained on the parent sporophytes for viable periods. In most ferns, **prothallus** is green and autotrophic. In heterosporous ferns, the female gametophyte depends on food stored by the megaspore.

Sex Organs

The gametophytes bear male sex organs called **antheridia** and female sex organs called **archegonia.** Antheridium is sessile and surrounded by a single layered jacket. Archegonium is flask-shaped. It is partially embedded.

Fertilisation

Water is required for the transfer of antherozoids (male gametes). These are released from the antheridia and reach to the mouth of archegonium through a film of water only. Fusion of male gamete with the egg present in the archegonium results in the formation of zygote.

This zygote develops into multicellular, well-differentiated **sporophyte**(2*n*) which is the dominant phase of the pteridophytes.

Embryo

Fertilisation produces a zygote that undergoes division to produce embryo. The development of the zygote into young embryo takes place within the female gametophyte. This event is a precursor of the **seed habit** and considered as an important step in evolution, e.g., *Dryopteris, Selaginella, Adiantum, Equisetum* and *Salvinia.*

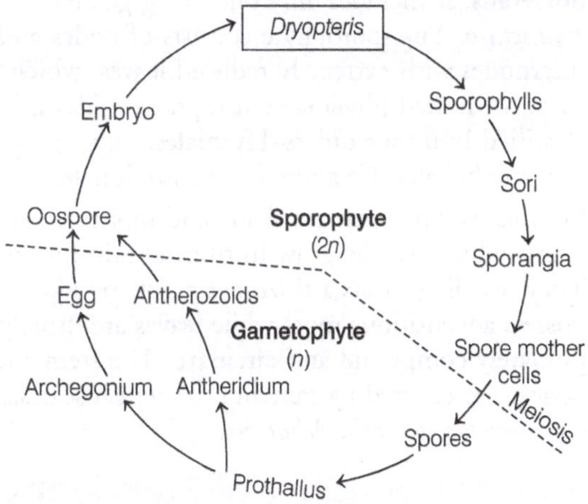

Fig. 5.9 Life cycle of *Dryopteris* (fern)

Differences between Bryophytes and Pteridophytes

Bryophytes	Pteridophytes
The main plant body is gametophyte.	It is sporophyte.
These are non-vascular plants.	These are vascular plants.
Sporophyte is parasitic over gametophyte.	Sporophyte is independent of gametophyte.
Plant body can be thallus or foliose.	It is differentiated into stem, leaves and roots.

Bryophytes	Pteridophytes
True stems and leaves are not present.	It has true stems and leaves.
Roots are absent, rhizoids are present.	Roots are present.
Sex organs are stalked.	Sex organs are sessile.
The wall of archegonial neck is 5-6 rowed.	The wall of archegonial neck is 4-rowed.

Classification of Pteridophytes

The pteridophytes are further classified into four classes

(i) **Psilopsida** The sporophyte is rootless with dichotomous rhizomes and aerial branches. The scale like or leaf like lateral appandages are arranged spirally. These are homosporous with multiflagellated antherozoids, e.g. *Psilotum*.

(ii) **Lycopsida** Group-Eligulate includes only two genera-*Lycopodium* and *Phylloglossum*. Their leaves are microphyllous and lack ligules. They are homosporous. The gametophyte is usually dependent on a symbiotic fungus for the nutrition.
The group ligulate has microphyllous, ligulate leaves. The sporophyte is heterosporous and forms a definite strobili at the apices of branches, e.g. *Selaginella*.

(iii) **Sphenopsida** Its members are commonly called as **horsetails**. It includes only one living genus- *Equisetum*. The sporophyte consists of nodes and internodes with extremely reduced leaves, which show a whorled phyllotaxy. It (Sphenopsida) is classified into four orders–Hyeniales. Sphenophyllales, Calamitales and Equisetales.

(iv) **Pteropsida** The ferns are shade and moisture loving plants which usually grow in tropical rain forests. They usually possess a rhizomatous stem. They possess adventitious roots while leaves are usually pinnately compound and **circinate**. The stem and petiole are covered by **ramenta**, brownish scales, e.g. *Dryopteris Pteris, Adiantum*.

Economic Importance of Pteridophytes

(i) Pteridophytes are a good source of food for animals. For example, sporocarps of *Marsilea* are edible. *Angiopteris* and *Alsophila* have starchy pith which is eaten by natives of Australia.

(ii) Ferns protect soil from erosion by providing a good cover on the hill slopes and other fragile places.

(iii) *Equisetum* stems have rough surfaces. They are used in scrubbing and polishing.

(iv) *Azolla*, a water fern, has a symbiotic association with nitrogen-fixing cyanobacterium *Anabaena azollae*. It is cultured in paddy fields to harbour nitrogen-fixing bacterium. Thus, it is used as a **biofertiliser.**

(v) Rhizomes and petioles of *Dryopteris* are used to produce anti-helmintic drug. Roots of *Adiantum* can cure throat infections. *Lycopodium* is used in the treatment of rheumatism and disorders of lungs and kidneys.

(vi) Ferns are also grown as ornamental plants for their graceful plant body.

Topic Practice 2

Multiple Choice Questions

1 Mark

1. **The main plant body of bryophytes is ...*A*.... It produces ...*B*..., hence is called a ...*C*.... Fill in the blanks by choosing the correct option for *A, B* and *C*.**

(a) A–diploid, B–spores, C–sporophyte
(b) A–haploid, B–gametes, C–gametophyte
(c) A–diploid, B–endospores, C–sporophyte
(d) A–haploid, B–conidia, C–gametophyte

Ans (b) The main plant body of bryophytes is haploid. It produces gametes, hence is called a gametophyte.

2. **In bryophytes, antheridium produces ...*A*... and female sex organ archegonium produces ...*B*.... Here *A* and *B* refer to**

(a) A–uniflagellate antherozoids; B–two eggs
(b) A–biflagellate antherozoids; B–one egg
(c) A–non-motile antherozoids; B–one egg
(d) A–non-motile antherozoids; B–two eggs

Ans (b) In bryophytes, antheridium produces biflagellate antherozoids and female sex organ, archegonium produces one egg.

3. **Which of the following is showing the correct ploidy level of labelled organs of plant in the given figure?**

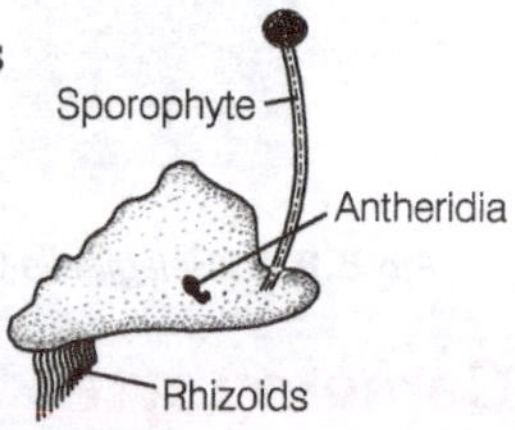

(a) Sporophyte – Diploid (2*n*)
(b) Antheridia – Haploid (*n*)
(c) Rhizoids – Haploid (*n*)
(d) All of the above

Ans (d) In liverworts, the sporophyte is diploid (2*n*), antheridia is haploid (*n*) and rhizoids are haploid (*n*)

4. The archegonia of *Funaria* are surrounded by
(a) perigonial leaves
(b) perichaetial leaves
(c) needles
(d) None of these

Ans (b) Perichaetial leaves.

5. The leaves in pteridophytes are small as in
(a) *Volvox* (b) *Marsilea*
(c) *Selaginela* (d) *Azolla*

Ans (c) The leaves in pteridophytes are small (microphylls) as in *Selaginella* or large (macrophylls) as in fern.

6. In pteridophyte, the sporophytes consist of leaf-like appendages called
(a) megaphylls
(b) sporophylls
(c) thalli
(d) sporangia

Ans (b) In pteridophytes, the sporophyte consists of leaf-like appendages called sporophylls. The sporophylls in cluster form distinct compact structures called strobili or cones, e.g. *Selaginella* and *Equisetum*.

7. In bryophytes and pteridophytes, transport of male gametes requires
(a) insects (b) birds
(c) water (d) wind

Ans (c) In several primitive and simple plants–like algae, bryophytes and pteridophytes, water is the medium through which male gametes are transferred to the female reproductive organ or gamete to bring about fertilisation.

8. In pteridophytes, spore germinates and give rise to
(a) thalloid gametophyte called prothallus
(b) thalloid sporophyte called prothallus
(c) thalloid sporocarp
(d) thalloid, photosynthetic sporophyte

Ans (a) In pteridophytes Haploid spore germinates to form a prothallus (gametophyte), which is monoecious, i.e. has both antheridia (♂) and archegonia (♀).

9. A prothallus is
(a) a structure in pteridophyte formed before the development of thallus
(b) a sporophytic free-living structure formed in pteridophytes
(c) a gametophytic free-living structure formed in pteridophytes
(d) a primitive structure formed after fertilisation in pteridophytes **NCERT Exemplar**

Ans (c) In pteridophytes, gametophyte is a free-living, small, thalloid structure called prothallus. In most ferns, the prothallus is green and autotrophic.

Very Short Answer Type Questions

(1 Mark)

10. State the ploidy of gametophyte and sporophyte of a bryophytic plant.

Ans Cells of gametophyte have (n) number of chromosomes, whereas sporophytic cells have ($2n$) number of chromosomes.

11. Which specialised structures are present in liverworts for asexual reproduction?

Ans Gemma cup.

12. Name the filamentous structure produced early in mosses.

Ans The filamentous structure produced early in mosses is protonema.

13. Write the names of capsular regions of *Funaria*.

Ans The capsule of *Funaria* consists of three regions; apophysis, theca proper and an apical region.

14. How are mosses considered ecologically important?

Ans Mosses, along with lichens are the first organism to colonise rocks, hence are ecologically important to develop an ecosystem in bare places.

15. Which is the dominate phase in pteridophyte?

Ans Sporophyte.

16. How are pteridophytes similar to bryophytes?

Ans Pteridophytes also need water for fertilisation like bryophytes.

17. Which event in pteridophytes is considered an important step in the evolution of seed habit in plants?

Ans The event of development of the zygote into young embryo within the female gametophyte is considered as precursor of seed habit.

18. Give the common name of members of Sphenopsida.

Ans The members of sphenopsida are commonly called as horsetails.

Short Answer Type I Questions

(2 Marks)

19. Write one feature each of liverworts and mosses.

Ans In liverworts, the plant body is thalloid, e.g. *Marchantia*. The thallus is dorsiventral and closely appressed to the substrate. (1)

In mosses, the predominant stage is the gametophyte. It has two phases

(i) **Protonema stage** which develops directly from a spore.

(ii) **Leafy stage** which develops from the secondary protonema as a leaf bud. (1)

20. **Write few important features of mosses.**

Ans **Features of Mosses**

(i) Erect, radially symmetrical leafy body produced from filamentous or thalloid juvenile stage, called protonema.
(ii) They bear multicellular branched rhizoids.
(iii) Sporophyte contains large amount of green tissue and is partially dependent upon the gametophyte. (2)

21. **To which class of Bryophyta *Anthoceros* belongs? Why is it called a hornwort?**

Ans The bryophyte *Anthoceros* belongs to the class–Anthocerotopsida. (1)

The sporophyte of *Anthoceros* is partially dependent on the gametophyte which is cylindrical like a horn hence it is called as hornwort. (1)

22. **Vascular tissues are not present in bryophytes, then how does the conduction of water and food take place?**

Ans Vascular tissues, i.e. xylem and phloem are absent in bryophytes. The conduction of water and food takes place from cell to cell by diffusion and capilarity (in mosses). (2)

23. **Why are bryophytes called as amphibians of plant kingdom?**

Ans Bryophytes are terrestrial plants. But, they need water for completion of their life cycle. The external water is required for dehiscence of antheridia, liberation of antherozoids, transfer of antherozoids from antheridia to archegonia, etc.

Rest other stages of life cycle are terrestrial, so they are called amphibians of the plant kingdom. (2)

24. **On the basis of which three features, *Selaginella* shows traits of seed habit?**

Ans *Selaginella* shows seed habit because of

(i) heterospory
(ii) Archegonium remains attached to sporophyte after fertilisation until meiotic development of zygote.
(iii) Development of zygote into embryo within female gametophyte. (2)

25. **Which pteridophytes are useful in nitrogen-fixation and how?**

Ans *Azolla* is a water fern, having a symbiotic association with nitrogen-fixing cyanobacterium (*Anabaena*). It is introduced into paddy fields to function as biofertiliser. (2)

26. **Differentiate between homosporous and heterosporous pteridophytes.** **NCERT**

Ans Differences between homosporous and heterosporous pteridophytes are

Homosporous Pteridophytes	Heterosporous Pteridophytes
These produce only one kind of spores.	These pteridophytes produce microspores and megaspores.
Each spore germinates into a monoecious prothallus, that bears both antheridia and archegonia, e.g. *Dryopteris*.	Microspores germinate into male gametophyte and megaspores germinate into female gamete, e.g. *Selaginella*, *Salvinia*.

(1×2)

27. **How do gametophytes of pteridophytes germinate?**

Ans The megaspores and microspores are produced mitotically from the archegonium and antheridium and by the help of water male gametes (antherozoids) are transfered to the female gamete (archegonium) thus they germinate and give rise to gametophytes. (2)

28. **Write some examples of**

(i) mosses (ii) liverworts
(iii) pteridophytes.

Ans (i) **Mosses** *Funaria, Polytrichum, Sphagnum.*
(ii) **Liverworts** *Riccia, Marchantia, Porella, Pellia.*
(iii) **Pteridophytes** *Selaginella, Adiantum, Dryopteris, Equisetum.* (2)

Short Answer Type II Questions

3 Marks

29. **Bryophytes are found in which diverse habitats. Describe briefly.**

Ans Refer to text on page no. 80. (3)

30. **What is the most common liverwort? Draw its well-labelled diagram. What is the nature of its thallus?**

Ans The most common example of liverworts is *Marchantia*. (1)

For diagram Refer to fig 5.6 on page no. 81. (1)

The vegetative plant body of *Marchantia* is a dorsoventral lobed thallus, appressed to substratum. (1)

31. **Write a brief account on mosses.**

Ans Mosses are widely distributed and grow in dense mats over moist shady places during rainy seasons. The gametophytic plant body is with leafy axis and shows a radial symmetry. The rhizoid are multicellular, branched and have oblique septa. Sex organs, i.e. antheridia and archegonia are usually borne in groups at the apices of reproductive branches. The sporophyte is usually differentiated into foot, seta and capsule. (3)

32. **Differentiate between liverworts and mosses.** NCERT

Ans Refer to table on page no. 82. (3)

33. **Write about the sex organs of bryophytes.**

Ans In bryophytes the male sex organ is antheridium and female sex organ is archegonium. The gametophyte (*n*) in bryophytes bears the premature sex organs in the form of **antheridium** (male) which produces flagellate antherozoids which are male gamete and need a thin film of water to swim and reach female reproductive organ (archegonium). **Archegonia** are female sex organs which possess a single egg cell.

Both these reproductive parts are born on male and female, antheridiophore and archegoniophores present on haploid gametophyte.

34. **What is the habitat of ferns? Describe their plant body. Explain the nature of spores ferns have. List out some common ferns.**

Ans Ferns are widely distributed all over the world in warm, moist and shady places. The main plant body of ferns is sporophyte, which is differentiated into underground stem called rhizome, roots and aerial shoots with leaves. Ferns are homosporous (e.g. *Dryopteris*, etc.) or heterosporous (e.g. *Marsilea*). Spores are born in the sporangia which are grouped in sori. Some common ferns are *Dryopteris, Pteridium, Pteris*, etc. (1 × 3)

35. **Heterospory, i.e. formation of two types of spores–microspores and megaspores is a characteristic feature in the life cycle of a few members of pteridophytes and all spermatophytes. Do you think heterospory has some evolutionary significance in plant kingdom?**

Ans Heterospory is the production of spores of two different sizes and sexes by the sporophytes of land plants.Two types of spores are produced by heterosporic plants.

Small spores are microspores which germinate into male gametophyte and large spores are macrospores which develop into female gametophyte.

In evolution of plants, pteridophytes are intermediate between bryophytes and gymnosperms. All bryophytes are homosporous and all gymnosperms are heterosporous.

This condition is advanced as sexual dimorphism result in cross fertilisation.

Primitive or earlier pteridophytes are homosporous, later pteriodophytes are heterosporous, e.g. *Dryopteris, Pteris* (homosporous), *Selaginella, salvinia* (heterosporous). (3)

36. **Why did the vascular plants dominate land?**

Ans The vascular plants dominated land due to the following features

(i) Presence of deep, penetrating and widespread roots which anchor the plants and also absorb water and minerals from the soil. (1)

(ii) Covering of aerial parts with waterproof material like cutin that prevented water loss. (1)

(iii) Mechanical tissues are present to allow them to rise to great heights. (1)

Long Answer Type Questions

5 Marks

37. **Give the life cycle of *Funaria*.**

Ans Refer to the text on page no. 80.

38. **Describe the economic importance of seedless vascular plants as**
(i) Food source
(ii) Soil erosion
(iii) Biofertiliser
(iv) Drugs
(v) Ornamental plants.

Ans Seedless vascular plants are pteridophytes. Economic importance of pteridophytes are

(i) Pteridophytes are a good source of food for animals. For example, sporocarps of *Marsilea* are edible. *Angiopteris* and *Alsophila* have starchy pith eaten by natives of Australia.

(ii) Ferns protect soil from erosion by providing a good cover on the hill slopes to prevent runoff.

(iii) *Azolla*, a water fern has a symbiotic association with nitrogen-fixing cyanobacterium, *Anabaena azollae*. It is cultured in paddy fields to harbour nitrogen-fixing bacterium. Thus, acts as a biofertiliser.

(iv) Rhizomes and petioles of *Dryopteris* are used to produce anthelmintic drug. Roots of *Adiantum* can cure throat infections. *Lycopodium* is used in the treatment of rheumatism and disorders of lungs and kidneys.

(v) Ferns are grown as ornamental plants for their graceful plant body. (1×5)

39. **What role vascular plants play in keeping the earth green? Which features help them to dominate the earth?**

Ans The vascular plants dominate earth and make the planet green everywhere. They act as producers in the terrestrial ecosystem by photosynthesising food and releasing oxygen for survival of other living beings. (1)

The features which enable this quality to happen are

(i) Strong roots capable of penetrating deep into the soil.

(ii) Development of waterproof layer on aerial surfaces especially the leaves to reduce transpiration.

(iii) Presence of strong, woody mechanical tissue to provide mechanical support to aerial parts and allow them to rise to a great height.

(iv) Vascular tissues are present for long distance transport of substances. (1×4)

TOPIC 03 Gymnosperms

Gymnosperms

The gymnosperms (*Gymnos* = naked; *sperma* = seeds) are plants in which the ovules are not enclosed by any ovary wall and remain exposed, both before and after fertilisation. These are a small group of seed plants which are represented by only 900 living species. Unlike bryophytes and pteridophytes, in gymnosperms the male and the female gametophytes do not have an independent free-living existence. They remain within the sporangia retained on the sporophytes.

Habitat

These plants are mostly found in colder parts of northern hemisphere, where they form extensive forests. A number of gymnosperms are now known as ornamentals, e.g. *Cycas, Ginkgo, Thuja, Araucaria*, etc.

Morphology

Gymnosperms include, medium-sized trees or tall trees and shrubs. The giant red wood tree, *Sequoia* is one of the tallest trees (upto 100 m). The species of *Gnetum* are woody climbers. The smallest gymnosperm is *Zamia pygmaea* which reaches a height of 25 cm. Many of the gymnosperms live for more than 4000 years, e.g. pine (*Pinus*), redwood (*Sequoia*) trees.

External Features

The plant body is sporophyte and very well-differentiated into root, stem and leaves.

Plant Body

Tap roots is present, it serves the function of proper anchorage of heavy plants to the soil. Roots in some genera have fungal association in the form of **mycorrhiza** (*Pinus*), while in some others (*Cycas*) small specialised roots called **coralloid** roots, are associated with N_2-fixing cyanobacteria such as *Anabaena, Nostoc*, etc.

The stems are branched (*Pinus, Cedrus*) or unbranched (*Cycas*). The leaves may be simple or compound.

In *Cycas*, the pinnate leaves persist for few years. The leaves in gymnosperms are well-adapted to withstand the extremes of temperature, humidity and wind.

While, in conifers, the needle-like leaves reduce the surface area to withstand the extremes of cold temperatures and snowfall. Their thick cuticle and sunken stomata also help to reduce water loss.

Internal Features

Plants possess vascular tissues, i.e. xylem and phloem. They are arranged in vascular bundles.

Vascular Tissues

The conducting part of xylem consists of tracheid. Vessels occur in *Gnetum* and its relatives. Phloem has sieve cells, but are arranged in rows in *Gnetum*.

Reproduction

The gymnosperms are heterosporous, i.e. they produce haploid microspores and megaspores.

Cones

The two kinds of spores are produced within the sporangia that are born on sporophylls, which are arranged spirally along an axis to form compact strobili or cones. The microspore and megaspore are produced in different types of sporangia called microsporangia or microsporophylls and ovules or megasporangia, respectively.

The strobili bearing microsporangia are called **microsporangiate** or **male strobili** and the strobili, bearing megasporophylls with ovules or megasporangia are called **macrosporangiate** or **female strobili.**

The plant may be **monoecious** in *Pinus* (i.e. male and female cones or strobili may be borne on the same tree) or may be **dioecious** as in *Cycas* (i.e. they are present on different trees).

Pollen Grains

The microspores develop into a male gametophytic generation which is highly reduced and is confined only to a limited number of cells, known as pollen grain. The development of pollen grains occurs within the microsporangia.

Ovules

The megaspore mother cell differentiates from one of the cells of the nucellus, which is protected by envelopes and the composite structure called **ovule.** The ovules are borne on the megasporophylls which may be clustered together forming female cones.

Archegonia

The megaspore mother cell, undergoes meiotic division forming four megaspores. Out of which one is enclosed within the megasporangium (nucellus) and develops into a multicellular female gametophyte, bearing two or more **archegonia** of female sex organs.

The multicellular female gametophyte is also retained within the megasporangium.

Fertilisation

Air current is required for the transport of male gametes. The male gametes are carried to the archegonia (i.e. gamete in the ovule) by means of a tube called **pollen tube.** It discharges its contents near the mouth of the archegonia. This is called **siphonogamy**.

Seeds

Following fertilisation, zygote develops into an embryo and the ovules into seeds. The seeds contain food laden tissue called **endosperm**. It lies naked or exposed. Endosperm provides nourishment for growth of seedling at the time of seed germination, e.g. *Cycas, Pinus, Ginkgo, Ephedra, Gnetum, Cedrus, Abies,* etc.

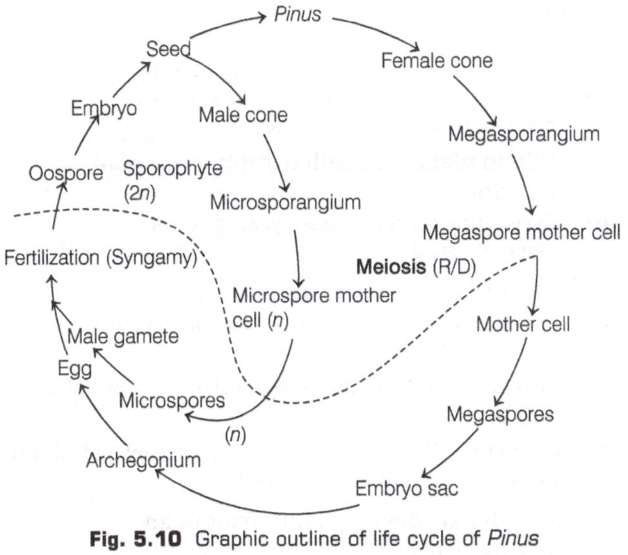

Fig. 5.10 Graphic outline of life cycle of *Pinus*

Differences between Microsporophyll and Megasporophyll

Microsporophyll	Megasporophyll
It bears microsporangia.	It bears megasporangia.
It contains numerous microspores.	It usually contains one megaspore.
Microspores are released.	Megaspores are retained inside the megasporangium.

Fig. 5.11 Gymnosperms : (a) *Cycas* (b) *Pinus* (c) *Ginkgo*

Differences between Male Gametophyte of Pteridophytes and Gymnosperms

Male Gametophyte of Pteridophytes	Male Gametophyte of Gymnosperms
A distinct male gametophyte may not be present.	A distinct male gametophyte is present.
It contains an antheridium.	Antheridium is not present.
Male gametes are flagellate.	Male gametes can be flagellate or non-flagellate.
Male gametes reach female gametes by swimming in water.	Male gametes reach the female gametes through a pollen tube.

Classification of Gymnosperms

Gymnosperms further include three main classes Cycadopsida (cycads), Coniferopsida (conifers) and Gnetopsida (*Gnetum*).

Economic Importance of Gymnosperms

(i) Seeds of *Pinus gerardiana* (chilgoza) are used as food after roasting. Some other edible gymnosperms plant parts are endosperm of *Ginkgo*, seed kernel of some *Cycas* and *Gnetum*, sago grains from stems of *Cycas*, etc.

(ii) Gymnosperms provide softwood for construction, plywood and paper industry.

(iii) Branches of gymnosperm trees are used as fuel.

(iv) Saw dust of conifers is used in making **plastics** and linoleum.

(v) Resin is a semifluid secreted by special tubes of a number of conifers. It helps in sealing female cones after pollination, scale leaves around leaf bases and apical buds. Resin is distilled to obtain **turpentine** and **resin**. Turpentine is used for thinning paints, varnishes, etc., and resin is used for sealing joints of wheel, preparation of writing paper, oil, clothes, etc.

(vi) **Ephedrine**, an antibiotic, is obtained from *Ephedra*. It is used for curing respiratory problems and asthma. **Taxol** is an anti-cancer drug, obtained from *Taxus*.

Topic Practice 3

Multiple Choice Questions

1 Mark

1. The giant redwood tree (*Sequoia sempervirens*) is a/an

(a) angiosperm (b) free fern
(c) pteridophyte (d) gymnosperm

NCERT Exemplar

Ans (d) It is a gymnosperm belonging to conifers. It lives for several years (4-5 thousand years).

2. In gymnosperms, the leaves are well-adapted to withstand extremes of temperature, humidity and wind. Which is/are the xeric character(s) of conifers?

(a) Needle-like leaves
(b) Thick cuticle
(c) Sunken stomata
(d) All of these

Ans (d) The leaves, in case of gymnosperms, are well-adapted to withstand extremes of temperature, humidity and wind.

These xeromorphic adaptations, include a thick cuticle, needle like leaves sclerified epidermal cells, sunken stomata, a sclerotic hypodermis, tightly packed mesophyll, an endodermis, leaf with few or no lateral veins and centrally located vascular tissue. These are xeromorphic adaptations because they reduce the amount of surface area available for evaporation.

3. In gymnosperms, the pollen chamber represents

(a) a cell in the pollen grain in which the sperms are formed.
(b) a cavity in the ovule in which pollen grains are stored after pollination.
(c) an opening in the megagametophyte through which the pollen tube approaches the egg.
(d) the microsporangium in which pollen grains develop.

Ans (b) In gymnosperms, the pollen chamber is a cavity in the ovule in which pollen grains are stored after pollination.

4. In gymnosperms, the nucellus is protected by envelops and this composite structure is known as

(a) ovule (b) ovary
(c) anther (d) strobili

Ans (a) In gymnosperms, the nucellus is protected by envelops and this composite structure is called ovule. Each ovule is actually the female spore-producing organ surrounded by a protective envelope called integuments.

5. In gymnosperms, pollination takes place by

(a) water (b) air
(c) insects (d) animals

Ans (b) In gymnosperms, pollen grains are released from microsporangium and carried with the help of air current. It comes in contact with the opening of ovule.

6. The ovules of *Pinus* are present at the base of

(a) bract scales (b) ovuliferous scales
(c) pollen scales (d) Both (a) and (b)

Ans (b) Ovuliferous scales

Very Short Answer Type Questions

1 Mark

7. Where are seeds located in gymnosperms?

Ans Seeds lie naked or exposed on the surface of megasporophyll in gymnosperms.

8. Which plants are called 'reptiles of plant kingdom'?

Ans Cycads (members of class–Cycadopsida of gymnosperms).

9. In which plant coralloid roots are present?

Ans *Cycas* have coralloid roots in which nitrogen-fixing cyanobacteria are present.

10. How are conifer needles helpful in preventing soil erosion?

Ans Conifer needles fall down and cover the soil and absorb rainwater that present soil runoff.

11. Which part develops into fruit in an angiosperm?

Ans Fruit develops from the whole ovary of a pistil.

12. Write the parts of female gametophyte of angiosperm.

Ans Female gametophyte (embryo sac) has one oospore or egg and two helping cells or synergids for guiding the pollen tube. It has three antipodal cells and one central cell.

13. Why *Cycas* is called a living fossil?

Ans *Cycas* is a living representative of one of the large group of gymnosperms which has now became extinct.

14. **Why seeds remain exposed in gymnosperms?**

Ans Seeds in gymnosperms remain exposed over the surface of the megasporophylls. This is because megasporophylls are not folded to form pistils like in angiosperms.

15. **How does pollination occur in gymnosperms and how the pollen grains approach ovules?**

Ans Pollination (by wind) in gymnosperms is direct and mediated by air currents. As stigma is absent, the pollen grains reach the micropylar ends of ovules directly.

16. **The plant body in higher plants is well developed. Roots are the organs used for the purpose of absorption. What is the equivalent of roots in the less developed lower plants?** **NCERT Exemplar**

Ans Roots are represented by root like structure called rhizoids in less developed lower plants (bryophytes and pteridophytes).

The plant tissue system in these is not differentiated into true leaf, stem and roots as it is found in higher plants (gymnosperms and angiosperms).

17. **From where ephedrine is obtained? What is its use?**

Ans Ephedrine is obtained from *Ephedra*, a gymnosperm. It is used in curing respiratory diseases in humans.

Short Answer Type I Questions

2 Marks

18. **Which is the most highly evolved gymnosperm? What are its features?**

Ans The most highly evolved gymnosperm is *Gnetum*. It belongs to Gnetopsida. The *Gnetum* looks like an angiosperm tree with reticulate venation in leaves and branching pattern, vessels in xylem and presence of archegonia in female gametophyte. (1+1)

19. **How does fertilisation occur in gymnosperms?**

Ans Fertilisation is of siphonogamous type, i.e. the male gametes are carried to the archegonia through pollen tube in gymnosperms. In *Cycas* only, pollen tube functions as haustorium and fertilisation occurs by zoodiogamy. (2)

20. **What is the economic importance of gymnosperms?**

Ans Economic importance of gymnosperms are

(i) Resins obtained from conifers have commercial importance.
(ii) The seeds of *Pinus* are edible.
(iii) Many gymnosperms yield medicinal compounds.
(iv) Some gymnosperms are ornamental plants. ($\frac{1}{2}\times 4$)

21. **How does *Cycas* resemble bryophytes and pteridophytes?**

Ans Cycas resembles bryophytes and pteridophytes in following ways

(i) In its female gametophyte, archegonia are differentiated which contain the female gametes.
(ii) It has ciliated antherozoids. (2)

22. **In which plant will you look for mycorrhiza and corolloid roots? Also explain what these terms mean.**

Ans Mycorrhiza (*Myco's* = fungus, *rize* = roots) is a symbiotic association between fungus and the roots of vascular plants. The fungus colonizes the roots of the host either intra or inter cellularly. It helps in the nutrient absorption from soil for the plant. Mycorrhizal associations are present in conifers, i.e. *Pinus, Cedrus, Abies* and *Picea.*

Coralloid roots are found in *Cycas.* They are produced in clusters at the base of the stem and protrude out over the ground. They are dichotomously branched and greenish in colour. They contain algal zone in cortex. (2)

23. **Which gymnosperms provide these items?**

(i) Taxol (ii) Canada balsam
(iii) Tannins (iv) Copal

Ans (i) **Taxol** *Taxus*
(ii) **Canada balsam** *Abies balsamea*
(iii) **Tannins** *Tsuga canadensis*
(iv) **Copal** *Agathis australis.* ($\frac{1}{2}\times 4$)

Short Answer Type II Questions

3 Marks

24. **Each plant or group of plants has some phylogenetic significance in relation to evolution. *Cycas*, one of the few living members of gymnosperms is called as 'relic of the past'. Can you establish a phylogenetic relationship of *Cycas* with any other group of plants that justifies the above statement.** **NCERT Exemplar**

Ans Cycas is called the 'relic of the past.' It has following properties to justify this

(i) Monoxylic wood through secondary growth.
(ii) Shedding of seed when embryo is still immature.
(iii) Arrangement of microsporangia in well defined sori.

Phylogenetically, *Cycas* is related to pteridosperms (seed ferns) and through them, it seems to have get evolved. It can be ascertained by the presence of

(i) leaf-like megasporophyll
(ii) persistence of leaf bases. (3)

25. What is the advantage of development of seed habits in seed plants?

Ans Seed habit developed in extinct pteridosperms or Cycadofilicales. It is a group intermediate between cycads and ferns.

The seed habit made the seed plants independent of the requirement of external sources of water at the time of fertilisation.

In seedless vascular plants, the gametophyte must develop on moist soil with a thin sheet of water.

The latter is required for the swimming of sperms to reach the female sex organs.

As a result, seedless vascular plants could never become true land plants. They were popularly called as amphibians of plant kingdom. (3)

On its contrary the seed plants could have established themselves very well only because of their seed habit.

Long Answer Type Questions

5 Marks

26. Describe the important characteristics of gymnosperms. NCERT

Ans Characteristics of gymnosperms are as follows

(i) Naked-seeded plants, i.e. their ovules are exposed and not enclosed in ovaries. Hence, the seeds are naked without fruits.

(ii) Tap root system is present. They show symbiotic association with fungi to form mycorrhizae or with N_2-fixing cyanobacteria to form coralloid roots as in *Cycas*.

(iii) Leaves are large and needle-shaped.

(iv) Vascular tissues are well-developed.

(v) Gymnosperms are heterosporous.

(vi) Pollination by wind and pollens get deposited in ovules.

(vii) Fertilisation occurs in archegonia.

(viii) Retention of female gametophyte inside the ovule and the ovules on the sporophytic plant for complete development. It is responsible for the development of seed habit. (5)

27. What is heterospory? Briefly comment on its significance. Give two examples. NCERT

Ans Heterospory is the phenomenon in which a plant produces two types of spores, namely microspores and megaspores. (1)

Heterospory is significant in the following ways

(i) Microspores give rise to male gametophyte and megaspores give rise to female gametophyte.

(ii) Female gametophyte is retained on the parent plant. So, that the development of zygote takes place within the female gametophyte.

(iii) This leads to the formation of seeds. (1 × 3)

Examples All gymnosperms and all angiosperm, *Pinus, Gnetum*, neem, peepal, etc. (1)

28. Mention the ploidy of the following. Protonemal cell of a moss, primary endosperm nucleus in dicot, leaf cell of a moss, prothallus of a fern, gemma cell in *Marchantia*, meristem cell of monocot, ovum of a liverwort and zygote of a fern. NCERT

Ans Protonemal cell of moss – Haploid

Primary endosperm nucleus in dicots– Triploid

Leaf cell of moss– Haploid

Prothallus cells of ferns– Haploid

Gemma cell in *Marchantia*– Haploid

Meristem cell of monocots– Diploid

Ovum of liverworts– Haploid

Zygote of ferns– Diploid (5)

29. Why *Ginkgo biloba* is called living fossil? Explain how is it useful for horticulturists. What are its important features? Why horticulturists prefer to grow only male plants?

Ans *Ginkgo biloba* has not changed for last several millions of years, since its appearance in triassic period. So, it is called as living fossil.

Horticulturists are interested in *Ginkgo* as it has natural immunity to several plant diseases. (2)

Its important features are as follows

(i) The plant is a tall tree of upto 30 m height.

(ii) Leaves are fan-shaped.

(iii) Leaves have furcate venation.

(iv) Dwarf shoots of female plant bear distinct megasporangiate structures.

(v) Endosperm of roasted seed is edible. (2)

Horticulturists prefer to grow only male plants, as female plants give unpleasant smell. (1)

SUMMARY

- **Kingdom–Plantae** includes all those organisms that are unicellular or multicellular, eukaryotic, phototrophic and have cellulosic cell wall.
- Kingdom–Plantae is divided into two subkingdoms, i.e. **Cryptogamae** (having conspicious reproductive structures) and **Phanerogamae** (having visible reproductive structures). Cryptogamae includes algal, bryophytes and pteridophytes and Phanerogamae includes gymnosperms and angiosperms.
- **Algae** includes all chlorophyllous, photosynthetic, thalloid (no differentiation into roots, stems and leaves) plants. These are mostly aquatic plants.
- These plants can reproduce vegetatively by fragmentation, asexually by means of zoospores (flagellated, motile), aplanospores, hypnospores, etc. and sexually by isogamy (fusion between gametes of similar size), anisogamy, (i.e. fusion between gametes that are dissimilar in size) and oogamy, (i.e. fusion between large non-motile female gamete and small, motile male gamete.)
- Based on the presence of different pigments algae can be divided into Chlorophyceae, Phaeophyceae and Rhodophyceae.
- **Chlorophyceae** (green alga) These are green due to the presence of chlorophyll-*a* and *b* pigments localised in chloroplast and have starch as reserved food material, e.g. *Spirogyra, Ulothrix, Volvox*, etc.
- **Phaeophyceae** (Brown algae) These appear brown in colour due to the presence of pigments chlorophyll-*a, c*, carotenoids and fucoxanthin. Their plant body is differentiated into holdfast stipe and frond. Their reserved food materials is laminarin and mannitol, e.g. *Sargassum, Fucus, Ectocarpus*, etc.
- **Rhodophyceae** (Red algae) These appear red in colour due to the presence of red pigment phycoerythrin. Their reserved food material is floridean starch, e.g. *Polysiphonia, Gelidium*, etc. Members of red algae yield carrageenan which is commercially used.
- **Bryophytes** are the terrestrial plants, which require moisture or water for fertilisation. These are non-vascular, non-seeded plants in which gametophyte dominates the life cycle and sporophyte is dependent upon the gametophyte.
- Embryo formation is seen in them. They can reproduce vegetatively and sexually. Sexual reproduction is strictly oogamous. The female sex organ in them is archegonia while the male sex organ is antheridia. Bryophytes are of two types, i.e. liverworts and mosses.
- ***Funaria*** is a moss with a leafy plant body that remain attached to the substratum by rhizoids (root like structures). The sex organs are jacketed multicellular and stalked. Antheridia bears antherozoids and archegonia bear egg cell. Their fusion requires presence of water. After fusion, zygote form embryo that develops into sporophyte which meiotically divide to form spores that germinate into **protonema** which develop into gametophyte.
- **Pteridophytes** are non-seeded plants having vascular tissue. These are dependent on water for fertilisation. Their main plant body is sporophyte, which is well differentiated into roots, stems and leaves. The gametophyte is reduced and some of these show advances towards seed habit.
- ***Dryopteris*** is commonly called as fern. It's main plant body is sporophytic (2*n*). The stem is underground (rhizome) and shoot system is well-developed. The leaves show characteristic circinate vernation (young leaves are folded).
- Sporophytes bear sporophylls that are leaf-like appendages with sporangia. Sporangia produces haploid spores that germinate into gametophyte.
- Prothallus is a transitory stage. The gametophyte possess antheridia and archegonia. The male gametes swim in water to reach archegonia. After fusion zygote is formed that develop into sporophyte.
- Asexual reproduction is through spores produced in sporangia, which develop on the ventral surface of leaves. Male and female gametes are produces on gametophyte in special structures called anthridia and archegonia.
- **Gymnosperms** are naked-seeded plants that possess exposed ovules on megasporophylls. These plants do not contain their sex organs in flowers.
- Sporophytic plant body dominates the life while the gametophyte is of reduced type.
- These are vascular plants. The plants are heterosporous, i.e. producing microspores (male gametophyte) and megaspores (female gametophyte).
- The male gametes released from microsporangia are carried by pollen tube towards archegonia. Male gamete fuse with egg that give rise to zygote which develops into embryo and forms naked seeds. This group includes some of the largest plants on the earth.

Chapter Practice

Multiple Choice Questions

1 Mark

1. Phylogenetic system of classification is based upon
   (a) evolutionary relationship of organisms
   (b) economically essential characters
   (c) superficial characters
   (d) anatomical and morphological characters only
2. Kingdom–Plantae includes
   (a) algae, bryophytes and pteridophytes
   (b) algae, bryophytes, pteridophytes, gymnosperms and angiosperms
   (c) algae, fungi, pteridophytes, gymnosperms and angiosperms
   (d) algae, pteridophytes, gymnosperms and angiosperms
3. Algae include unicellular forms like ...*A*..., filamentous forms like ...*B*... and colonial forms like ...*C*... . Here *A*, *B* and *C* refer to
   (a) A–*Chlamydomonas*, B–*Volvox*, C–*Ulothrix*
   (b) A–*Ulothrix*, B–*Volvox*, C–*Chlamydomonas*
   (c) A–*Volvox*, B–*Ulothrix*, C–*Chlamydomonas*
   (d) A–*Chlamydomonas*, B–*Ulothrix*, C–*Volvox*
4. Bryophytes are also called 'amphibians of the plant kingdom' because
   (a) water is essential for reproduction
   (b) they occur only in water
   (c) these plants can live in soil, but are dependent on water for sexual reproduction
   (d) water is essential for spore formation
5. Select the correct sequential arrangement of reproductive structures in pteridophytes.
   (a) Sporophyll → Strobili → Sporangia → Spore mother cell → Spores
   (b) Strobili → Sporophyll → Sporangia → Spores
   (c) Spores → Sporophyll → Sporangia → Strobili
   (d) Spores → Sporangia → Sporophyll → Strobili
6. Which of the following pteridophytes is heterosporous in nature?
   (a) *Selaginella* and *Salvinia*
   (b) *Adiantum* and *Equisetum*
   (c) *Psilotum* and *Lycopodium*
   (d) *Adiantum* and *Psilotum*
7. Megasporophyll is the term used in gymnosperm to denote
   (a) carpel (b) leaves
   (c) female cone (d) stamens

Assertion-Reason Type Questions

1 Mark

■ Direction (Q. Nos. 8-14) *In each of the following questions, a statement of Assertion (A) is given followed by corresponding statement of Reason (R). Of the statements, mark the correct answer as*

(a) If both A and R are true and R is the correct explanation of A
(b) If both A and R are true, but R is not the correct explanation of A
(c) If A is true, but R is false
(d) If A is false, but R is true

8. **Assertion** (A) Algae are the primary producers of many food cycles.
   Reason (R) Half of the total carbon dioxide-fixation on earth is carried out by algae.
9. **Assertion** (A) Red algae contribute in the development of coral reefs.
   Reason (R) Red algae secrete and deposit calcium carbonate over their walls.
10. **Assertion** (A) Bryophytes are the amphibians of plant kingdom.
    Reason (R) They are found in swamps and the areas, where water and land meet.
11. **Assertion** (A) Bryophytes are a class of kingdom–Plantae.

Reason (R) Algae, fungi, lichens and mosses are included in bryophytes.

12. **Assertion** (A) *Lycopodium* and *Selaginella* are heterosporous.
Reason (R) In heterosporous condition, two kinds of spores are produced by the plant.

13. **Assertion** (A) Production of two types of spores is a pre-requisite of seed habit.
Reason (R) In pteridophytes, *Lycopodium* is precursor of seed habit.

14. Gymnosperms include conifers, cycads, *Ginkgo*, etc. These plants have naked seeds. The fossil evidence as surveyed, suggests that they originated during the Paleozoic era some 400 million years ago. Considering the above information, comment upon the appropriateness of the Assertion and the Reason.

Assertion (A) The leaves in gymnosperms are well-adapted to withstand extremes of temperature, humidity and wind.
Reason (R) Unlike bryophytes and pteridophytes, in gymnosperms, the male and female gametophytes do not have an independent free-living existence.

Answers

1. (a) 2. (b) 3. (d) 4. (c) 5. (a) 6. (a) 7. (a)
8. (b) 9. (a) 10. (a) 11. (c) 12. (d) 13. (c) 14. (b)

Very Short Answer Type Questions

(1 Mark)

15. Name the gelatinous substance that covers the cell wall of Phaeophyceae.
16. Give the name of pigment which imparts colour to red algae.
17. Name two mosses other than fern.
18. Which plant provides us resin?
19. Which gymnosperm is called maiden hair tree?
20. Name any three ornamental gymnosperms?
21. Which plants have diplontic life cycle?

Short Answer Type I Questions

(2 Marks)

22. Fern prothallus is monoecious. Justify.
23. Write any two important features of gymnosperms.

Short Answer Type II Questions

(3 Marks)

24. Why phylogenetic system is difficult to achieve?
25. Classify kingdom-Plantae into various groups.
26. Why do we call bryophytes as amphibians of plant kingdom?
27. How are bryophytes different from pteridophytes?
28. Write the external morphology of gymnosperms.
29. What are the features of vascular plants?

Long Answer Type Questions

(5 Marks)

30. Explain about two advantages of phylogenetic system of classification.
31. According to your observation, which classification system is least effective and which is most accurate? Give reasons for both the choices.
32. List out the similarities and differences in sexual reproduction between mosses and fern.
33. Describe briefly the life cycle of pteridophytes.
34. Describe some salient features of conifers.
35. How are gymnosperms useful to us?
36. Write the salient features of monocots and dicots.

Case Based Questions

(4/5 Marks)

37. The pie chart given below shows a representation of various areas where algae can be used and are being used in Ireland. Analyse the given pie chart and answer the following questions.

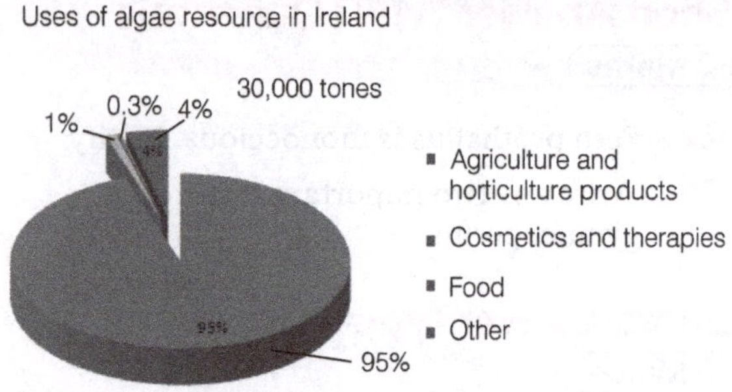

(i) *Chlorella* a green algae, has marked its use in the field of agriculture and horticulture. Name another algae that can replace *Chlorella* in the field of agriculture.

(ii) A farmer noticed deficiency of potassium in the soil due to which he faced a decline in the crop productivity. He opted for biological methods. Name the algae that can make the soil rich in potassium content. Will this provide any benefit to the farmer otherwise?

(iii) Algae provide valuable nutrients to human diet. Comment.

Or

(iii) Comment upon the use of agar-agar in food preparation.

38. The graph given below is a linear representation of the use of an effective gymnosperm *Ephedra* in the Traditional Chinese Medicine (TCM) in drug industry with growing years.

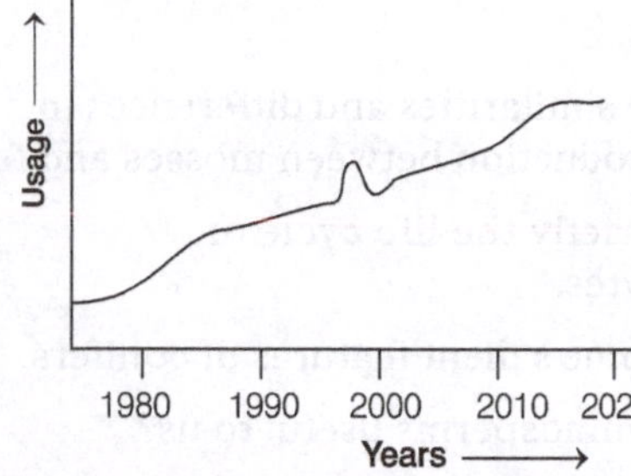

Consider the above graph, answer the following questions.

(i) Why do you think is *Ephedra* so much in use in the TCM? Which part of it yields the raw material for drug manufacture?

(ii) The drug ephedrine is used to treat what types of ailments?

(iii) Mention other products of therapeautic use obtained from gymnosperms.

(iv) Write two economic importance of gymnsoperm other than in the field of medicine.

39. In pteridophytes, the main plant body is a sporophyte which is differentiated into true root, stem and leaves. These organs possess well differentiated vascular tissues.

(i) What are sporophylls?

(ii) Name any two species of pteridophytes which show heterospory.

(iii) Name the male and female sex organ of pteridophytes.

(iv) Can pteridophytes surpass the advantages of gymnosperms?

(v) What is the economic importance of *Azolla*?

40. Recognise the figure of the given pteridophyte species and answer the questions that follows.

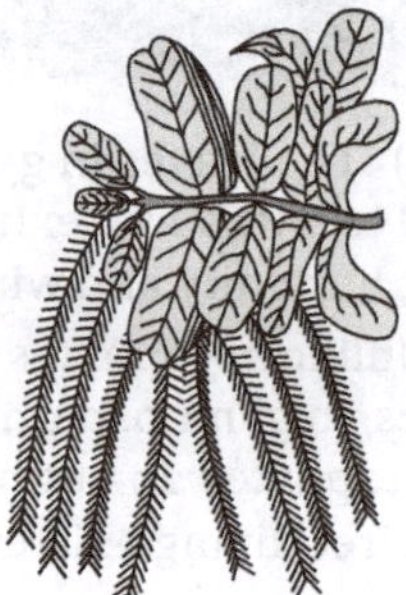

(i) Identify the pteridophyte and name the kind of spores formed in them.

(ii) What do you call the leaf-like appendages in the sporophyte of this plant that bear sporangia?

(iii) Heterosporous pteridophyte show characteristics that are considered as precursor to seed habit. Comment.

Or

(iii) Comment upon the fertilisation pattern of pteridophytes.

CHAPTER

06

Animal Kingdom

Biologist have described and named approximately 1.4 million living organisms present on the Earth. Out of these, approximately 1 million are animals. These animals differ from each other in their body plan. Few animals have been described in this chapter based on their similarities and dissimilarities with each other.

TOPIC 01 Animal Construction

The classification helps in easy identification and also in assigning a systematic position to newly described species.

Inspite of differences in structure and form of different animals, there are certain fundamental features common in various individuals in relation to the body plan, body symmetry, nature of coelom and segmentation. These features are used as the basis of animal classification.

Body Plan

Animals have three types of body plans. These are as follows

(i) **Cell Aggregate Plan** A cluster of cells with a limited division of labour, in which tissues or organs are absent, e.g. sponges.

(iii) **Blind Sac Body Plan** Cells are organised into tissues. There is division of labour and each tissue performs a specific task. Single opening of the body for ingestion and egestion, e.g. coelenterates, flatworms, ctenophores.

(iii) **Tube within Tube Plan** Level of organisation is organ system, proper digestive canal is present, having two openings, i.e. one for ingestion and other for egestion, e.g. Aschelminthes.

The tube within tube body plans of all higher invertebrates and vertebrates cannot be described due to increase in their body complexity. However, on the basis of their development from blastopore, these can be classified as

(a) **Protostomes** Mouth develops from blastopore region and anus develops later, e.g. annelids, molluscs, arthropods and roundworms.

(b) **Deuterostomes** Anus develops first from blastopore region and mouth develops later, e.g. echinoderms and chordates.

Symmetry

The symmetry refers to the arrangement of parts on the opposite sides (or halves) of the body of a three dimensional animal. On the basis of symmetry, animals can be of following types

(i) **Asymmetrical** Animals in which, any plane passes through the centre does not divide them into equal halves are called asymmetrical, e.g. sponges.

(ii) **Symmetrical** The body of some animals can be divided into two similar equal halves by one or more planes. Such animals are called symmetrical.

The symmetry can be further divided as

(a) **Spherical Symmetry** Found very rarely in animals. It occurs in organisms, which can be cut into two identical halves through any plane. Their body is more or less of spherical shape, e.g. *Volvox* and *Heliozoa*.

(b) **Radial Symmetry** When any plane passing through the central axis of the body divides the organism into two identical halves, it is called radial symmetry, e.g. coelenterates, ctenophores and echinoderms.

When the body can be divided into two similar halves by one or two vertical planes only, the radial symmetry is called **biradial symmetry**, e.g. sea anemones. Adult sponges are asymmetrical, however they start their life form as a radial symmetrical larvae.

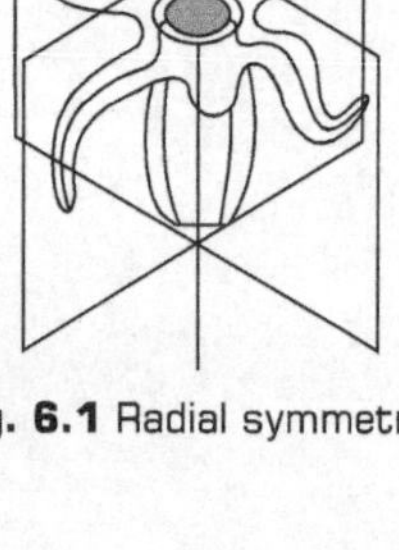

Fig. 6.1 Radial symmetry

(c) **Bilateral Symmetry** In some animals, body can be divided into identical left and right halves in only one plane. This is called bilateral symmetry, e.g. annelids, arthropods, etc.

Adult echinoderm are radially symmetrical but their larvae are bilaterally symmetrical.

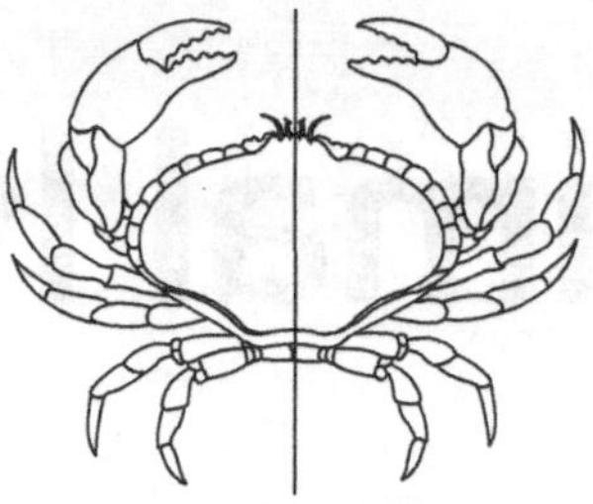

Fig. 6.2 Bilateral symmetry

Diploblastic and Triploblastic Organisation

Germ layers are group of cells behaving as a unit during early stages of embryonic development. These germ layers differentiate to give rise to all the tissues/organs of the fully formed body of individuals.

On the basis of germ layers, animals are classified as follows

(i) **Diploblastic** The animals, in which the cells are arranged in two embryonic layers—an external ectoderm and an internal endoderm, are called **diploblastic animals.** In addition, an undifferentiated layer, mesoglea is also present in between the ectoderm and the endoderm, e.g. coelenterates.

(ii) **Triploblastic** The animals, in which the developing embryo has a third germinal layer mesoderm, in between the ectoderm and endoderm are called **triploblastic animals**, e.g. all animals from phylum–Platyhelminthes to phylum– Chordata.

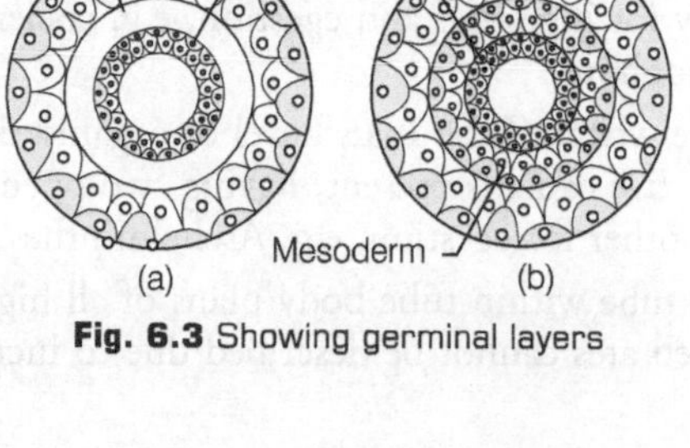

Fig. 6.3 Showing germinal layers

Coelom

The body cavity (between the body wall and gut wall), which is lined by mesoderm is called coelom. The presence or absence of coelom is very important in classifying animals.

The coelom acts as shock absorber to protect internal organs; as hydrostatic skeleton and plays important role in osmoregulation.

On the basis of coelom, animals can be classified in four different groups

(i) **Acoelomates** The animals, in which the body cavity is absent are called acoelomates, e.g. poriferans, platyhelminthes, coelenterates, ctenophore and flatworms.

(ii) **Pseudocoelomates** In some animals, the body cavity is not lined by mesoderm. Instead, the mesoderm is present as scattered pouches in between the ectoderm and endoderm. Such a body cavity is called **pseudocoelom** and the animals possessing them are called pseudocoelomates, e.g. aschelminthes, rotifera.

(iii) **Coelomates** The animals having true coelom are called coelomates. A **true coelom** or **eucoelomate** arises within mesoderm and is therefore, lined by mesodermal tissues, i.e. externally by **parietal peritoneum** and internally by **visceral peritoneum.**

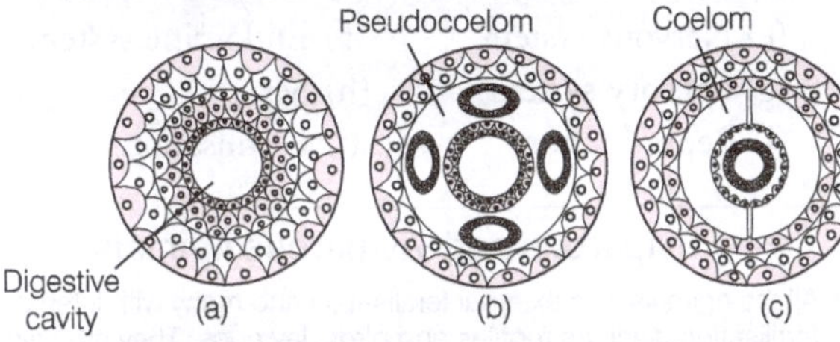

Fig. 6.4 Sectional view of (a) Acoelomates (b) Pseudocoelomate and (c) Eucoelomate

(iv) **Haemocoelomates** In some animals, the actual or true coelom is reduced, but spaces between viscera grow and form a large cavity with blood called **haemocoel** and the animals possessing them are called haemocoelomates. Haemocoel is found in Arthropoda and Mollusca.

Notochord

It is a mesodermally derived rod-like structure formed on the dorsal side during embryonic development in some animals. Animals with notochord are called **chordates** and those animals which lacks notochord are called **non-chordates**, e.g. Porifera to Echinodermata.

Segmentation

In some animals, the body is externally and internally divided into **segments** or **somites** with a serial repetition of atleast some organs. Segmentation can be of following two types

(i) **Metameric Segmentation** A segmentation that simultaneously divides body both externally and internally is called metamerism or metameric segmentation. This kind of segmentation is found in annelids, arthropods and chordates.

(ii) **Pseudometamerism** It is found in tapeworm, the body is divisible into parts or segments called **proglottides.** They develop from the neck but are not embryonic in origin. Such a repetition, which appears due to repeated budding is known as **false segmentation** or **pseudometamerism.**

Levels of Organisation

All members of kingdom– **Animalia** are multicellular, heterotrophic eukaryotes. But, all of them do not exhibit the same pattern of organisation of cells. The cells in their body are of several types. These are organised into many functional units of progressively increasing complexity.

The animal body shows four basic plan of structural organisation as given below

(i) **Cellular Level** In this level, the body shows some division of labour among cells. They are remarkably independent and can change their form and function. It is found in **sponges.** The body consists of many cells arranged as loose cell aggregates but, the cells do not form tissues rather each cell is independent and functionally active, e.g. *Hydra.*

(ii) **Tissue Level** The cells performing the same function are arranged into tissues, hence is called **tissue level** of organisation, e.g. in coelenterates, the arrangement of cells is more complex.

(iii) **Organ Level** In Platyhelminthes and other higher phyla, tissues are grouped together to form organs, each specialised for a particular function, i.e. organ level organisation is present.

(iv) **Organ System Level** In animals like annelids, arthropods, molluscs, echinoderms and chordates, organs have associated to form functional systems, each system concerned with a specific physiological function. This is called **organ system level of organisation.** Organ systems in different groups of animals exhibit various patterns of complexities.

For instance, the digestive system in Platyhelminthes has only a single opening in body that serves as both mouth and anus and is thus, called **incomplete**. Whereas a complete digestive system has two openings, i.e. mouth and anus.

Another example is the two types of circulatory systems. Open type circulatory system, in which blood is pumped out of the heart and cells and tissues are directly bath in blood. In closed type system, the blood is circulated through a network of blood vessels of varying diameters (arteries, veins and capillaries) where tissues remain in contact with it.

Body Temperature

In animals body temperature varies according to the surrounding environment for normal vital activities. On the basis of this, animals are classified as follows

(i) **Warm-Blooded Animals** These animals are also called **endotherms** (Gr. *Endon*–within or internal) or **homoeothermic** animals. They have constant body temperature, which is independent of their external environment.

Body temperature is derived from the heat produced by the oxidative metabolism of their food. The presence of insulating hair, feathers and blubbers (fat layer) prevent this internally generated heat from free diffusion to the external environment, e.g. few fishes, mammals and birds.

(ii) **Cold-Blooded Animals** These animals are also called as **ectotherms** (Gr. *Ektos*–outside or external) or **poikilothermic** animals. Their body temperature varies with the change in environmental temperature, e.g. invertebrates, fishes, amphibians and reptiles.

These animals undergo hibernation and aestivation to prevent their body from the ill effects of temperature variations.

Other Important Features

Apart from the basic features of body, size and shape of animals also possess some other important features as given below

1. Cephalisation

It is the differentiation of head in anterior part of the body. It involves the concentration of nervous tissue and sense organs and feeding structures in the head.

2. Appendages

The projecting structures of the body that perform specific functions like locomotion, capturing of food, sensation, etc., are called **appendages**, e.g. wings, fins, limbs, tentacles, parapodia, setae, etc.

3. Body Support and Protection

Skeletal system is a hard, internal or external framework that provides support and shape to the body. Some animals which are devoid of a skeleton have soft body, e.g. platyhelminthes, aschelminthes, annelids.

Skeleton system can be of following types

(i) **Exoskeleton** It is the hard supporting and protective framework present on exterior of the body. It is made of non-living matter, e.g. external shells of molluscs, cuticle of arthropods, scales of fishes and reptiles, feathers of birds, hair, hoofs, nails, horns and claws of mammals.

(ii) **Endoskeleton** It is a hard supporting framework present in the interior of the body. In invertebrates such as sponges, it is made up of calcareous or siliceous spicules. In vertebrates, it is composed of hard living tissues called **cartilages** and **bones**. Endoskeleton supports whole body of an organism.

Some of other features are given below

(a) Digestive system
(b) Respiratory system
(c) Circulatory system
(d) Excretory system
(e) Nervous system
(f) Endocrine system
(g) Sensory system
(h) Sex
(i) Reproduction
(j) Fertilisation

Oviparous and Viviparous Animals

- All the animals with external fertilisation and many with internal fertilisation, such as reptiles and birds, lay eggs. They are called **oviparous animals.**
- Some animals with internal fertilisation give birth to young ones. Such animals are of two types
- **Ovoviviparous animals** produce large, heavily yolked eggs that develop in the reproductive tract of the mother without deriving nourishment from her, e.g. rattle snake, sharks, etc.
- **Viviparous animals** produce minute eggs and the embryos are nourished during development in the mother's genital tract, e.g. mammals.
- In oviparous animals, the newly hatched young one, may resemble the adult. This kind of development is called **direct development**. In some animals, the young hatching from eggs do not resemble the adult. These are called **larvae** or **nymph**.
- The larvae lead independent life for some time and later undergo important changes to become adults. These changes from larvae to adults are called **metamorphosis.** This kind of development is called **indirect development.**

Outline Classification of Kingdom-Animalia

Animal kingdom is broadly classified as follows

Animal kingdom

Subkingdoms

- **Protozoa** Unicellular, heterotrophic, eukaryotes
- **Metazoa** Multicellular eukaryotes
  - Infra kingdoms or branches
    - **Mesozoa** (Extinct) Worm-like small, bilaterally symmetrical animals, parasitic on cephalopods and other invertebrates, e.g. phylum-Mesozoa.
    - **Parazoa** Animals with loosely organised cells, no organs, diploblastic and no digestive cavity, e.g. phylum-Porifera.
    - **Enterozoa** True tissues or organs are found, a digestive cavity present. Entero word in itself signifies digestive cavity.
      - Divisions
        - **Radiata** Radial or biradial symmetry, no organs, diploblastic, e.g. phylum-Coelenterata
        - **Bilateria** Bilateral symmetry, organ systems present, triploblastic, digestive tract complete.
          - Subdivisions
            - **Protostomia** Blastopore forms mouth; cleavage is spiral and determinate.
              - Sections
                - **Acoelomata** No coelom, mesoderm as parenchyma, e.g. phylum-Platyhelminthes.
                - **Pseudocoelomata** Pseudocoelom present, e.g. phylum-Nematoda.
                - **Eucoelomata** (schizocoela) True coelom which is schizocoelous, e.g. phylum-Annelida, Arthropoda and Mollusca.
            - *** Deuterostomia** Mouth do not form blastopore, mesoderm develops from archenteron.

*** Subdivision-Deuterostomia** contains one section, i.e. **Eucoelomata**

(In which coelom is enterocoelous thus also called Enterocoela) with following **three phyla**

- Echinodermata
- Hemichordata
- Chordata
  - **Urochordata** Notochord and nerve cord only in tadpole larva, adult form is encased in the protective tunic.
  - **Cephalochordata** Notochord and nerve cord is present throughout the life all along the entire body and is persistent.
  - **Vertebrata** Notochord is replaced with vertebral column, body divided into head, neck, trunk and tail.

Topic Practice 1

Multiple Choice Questions

(1 Mark)

1. Tube-within-tube body plan is found in which animal?

(a) *Euspongia* (b) *Fasciola*

(c) *Hydra* (d) None of these

Ans (d) Tube-within-tube is a body plan in which two tubes are present, an outer body wall and an inner digestive tract.

All animals from phylum–Aschelminthes to Chordata have tube-within-tube body plan and may be either protostomous or deuterostomous.

2. The term 'bilateral symmetry' refers

(a) when the body can be divided into two unequal halves on passing central axis through it

(b) to any plane passing through centre, which does not divide the body into equal halves

(c) when the body can be divided into identical left and right halves only in one plane

(d) any plane passing through the central axis of the body dividing the organism into two equal halves

Ans (c) In bilateral symmetry, the animal body can be divided into identical left and right equal halves in only one plane.

3. The response to external stimulus is maximally quicker and more precise in which of the following symmetry?
   (a) Radial (b) Bilateral
   (c) Spherical (d) Biradial

Ans (b) In bilaterally symmetrical animals, the response to external stimulus is quicker and more precise.

4. Diploblastic animals belong to the phylum
   (a) Protista (b) Protozoa
   (c) Coelenterata (d) Platyhelminthes

Ans (c) Poriferans and coelenterates are diploblastic animals, while all animals in and after Platyhelminthes are triploblastic animals. Protozoans are the protists (single-celled animals) that do not form any germ layer.

5. A coelom is a
   (a) cavity between body wall and cell wall
   (b) body cavity lined by mesoderm
   (c) body cavity not lined by mesoderm
   (d) body cavity lined by endoderm

Ans (b) Body cavity lined by mesoderm is called a coelomic cavity. Coelom is absent in acoelomate animals. When the mesoderm is present as scattered pouches in between ectoderm and endoderm, the animals are called pseudocoelomates.

6. The pseudocoelomate among these is
   (a) Porifera (b) Annelida
   (c) Aschelminthes (d) Mollusca

Ans (c) Aschelminthes are triploblastic, bilaterally symmetrical, pseudocoelomate (false coelom derived from embryonic blastocoel) and unsegmented organisms.

7. The notochord is derived from which of the following layers?
   (a) Ectoderm (b) Mesoderm
   (c) Endoderm (d) Placoderm

Ans (b) Notochord is derived from mesoderm and formed on the dorsal side in the chordate animals during their embryonic development.

8. In some animal groups, the body is divided into compartments with at least some organs. This characteristic feature is called. **NCERT Exemplar**
   (a) Cephalisation (b) Metamerism
   (c) Metagenesis (d) Metamorphosis

Ans (b) Metamerism is the division of animal body, externally and internally into segments with a serial repetition of at least some organs, e.g. annelids (earthworm).

9. In tissue level of organisation, the
   (a) cells are arranged as loose cell aggregate
   (b) tissues are grouped to form organs
   (c) cells performing the same function are arranged into groups
   (d) tissues are grouped to form systems

Ans (c) The cells performing the same function are arranged in tissues and forms the tissue level of organisation. Molluscs show this organisation in their body plan.

Very Short Answer Type Questions

1 Mark

10. Identify the phylum, in which adults exhibit radial symmetry and larva exhibit bilateral symmetry.

Ans Symmetry is an attribute of an organism showing regularity in body parts on a plane or around an axis.
In phylum–Echinodermata, the adult echinoderms are radially symmetrical, but the larvae are bilaterally symmetrical.

11. Name two non-chordate phyla, where animals are radially symmetrical.

Ans Cnidaria and Echinodermata.

12. Whose embryos have two germ layers ?

Ans Coelenterates.

13. Differentiate between a diploblastic and a triploblastic animal.

Ans Animals, in which the cells are arranged in two embryonic layers, an external ectoderm and an internal endoderm are called diploblastic animals (e.g. coelentrates).
While, those animals, in which the developing embryo has a third germinal layer, i.e. mesoderm lying between the ectoderm and endoderm are called triploblastic animals (e.g. chordates).

14. Body cavity is the cavity present between body wall and gut wall. In some animals, the body cavity is not lined by mesoderm. Such animals are called **NCERT Exemplar**

Ans Pseudocoelomates.

15. What are coelomates? Give two examples.

Ans Animals possessing coelom lined with mesoderm are called coelomates, e.g. annelids, molluscs, arthropods, etc.

16. Which animals have notochord?

Ans Chordates.

17. In some animal groups, the body is found to be divided into compartments with atleast some organs/organ repeated. Name this characteristic feature. **NCERT Exemplar**

Ans The type of the segmentation that simultaneously divides body both externally and internally is called metamerism.

18. Pseudometamerism is found in ....

Ans tapeworms.

19. What is pseudosegmentation?

Ans In tapeworms, the body is divided into number of segments called **proglottids** that are budded off from the neck. Each segment is able to perform all the vital functions of body. This type of segmentation is called pseudometamerism or pseudosegmentation.

Short Answer Type I Questions

2 Marks

20. Sort out the animals on the basis of their symmetry (radial or bilateral) coelenterates, ctenophores, annelids, arthropods and echinoderms.

Ans Body symmetry is the similarity of body parts in different region and directions of the body plan.

In radial symmetry, body of an individual can be divided into equal halves by any plane passing through the longitudinal axis (e.g. coelentrates, ctenophores, echinoderms).

In bilateral symmetry, body can be divided into two equal halves when the plane passes through the median longitudinal or saggital axis (e.g. annelids, arthropods). (1+1)

21. Which animals are called diploblastic animals?

Ans The diploblastic animals are those animals, in which the cells are arranged in two embryonic layers - an external ectoderm and an internal endoderm. Also, an undifferentiated layer (mesoglea) is present in between the ectoderm and the endoderm, e.g. coelenterates. (2)

22. Distinguish between coelomates and haemocoelomates.

Ans Differences between coelomates and haemocoelomates are

Coelomates	Haemocoelomates
The animals having true coelom are called coelomates.	The animals having reduced true coelom are called haemocoelomates.
The true coelom is lined by mesodermal tissue, i.e. externally by parietal peritoneum and internally by visceral peritoneum.	The space between viscera grow and form a large cavity with blood called haemocoel.
Examples : Chordates	Examples : Molluscs

(2)

23. How the body segmentation in annelids is different from those in a platyhelminth like tapeworm?

Ans The annelids exhibit metameric body segmentation, in which the metameres divide body externally by grooves and internally by septa.

In tapeworms, the body segmentation is called pseudometamerism or pseudosegmentation, in which the body is divided into number of segments called proglottids that are budded off from neck. (2)

24. What is a notochord and in which animals it is found?

Ans Notochord is a flexible rod-like material similar to cartilage present on dorsal side between alimentary canal and nervous system in some animals. It is derived from mesoderm. (1)

Notochord is found in chordates (atleast in some stages of their life cycle, e.g. vertebrates). (1)

25. Which characteristics differentiate members of kingdom–Animalia from other kingdoms?

Ans Animal kingdom has a high degree of variation and specialisation as compared to the other kingdoms.

There are several features which distinguish animals from the members of other kingdoms.

These are as follows

(i) Multicellularity without possessing chlorophyll.
(ii) Presence of eukaryotic cells.
(iii) Absence of cell wall (most striking feature).
(iv) Heterotrophic mode of nutrition.
(v) Capability to contract and relax body parts due to the presence of muscle cells.
(vi) Presence of nerve cells which help to transmit impulses in response to external stimuli.
(vii) Sexual reproduction, lower forms have asexual reproduction also.
(viii) A multicellular embryo is formed during development from the zygote.
(ix) Animals require oxygen for aerobic respiration. (2)

26. Match the following list of animals with their level of organisation. **NCERT Exemplar**

	Division of Level		Animals
A.	Organ level	1.	*Pheretima*
B.	Cellular aggregate level	2.	*Fasciola*
C.	Tissue level	3.	*Spongilla*
D.	Organ system level	4.	*Obelia*

Ans A–4, B–1, C–2, D–3. Refer to text on page no. 99. (½ × 4)

27. **Differentiate between complete and incomplete digestive systems.**

Ans Digestive system having only a single opening to the outside of the body that serves as both mouth and anus is called incomplete digestive system while a complete digestive system has two separate openings, i.e. mouth and anus. (2)

28. **Distinguish between intracellular and extracellular digestion.** NCERT

Ans Differences between intracellular and extracellular digestion are

(i) **Intracellular digestion** occurs inside the living cells with the help of lysosomal enzymes. Food particle is taken in through endocytosis. It forms a phagosome, which fuses with a lysosome.

The digested material passes into the cytoplasm. The undigested matter is thrown out by exocytosis. It occurs in *Amoeba, Paramecium*, etc.

(ii) **Extracellular digestion** In case of coelenterates, digestion occurs in gastrovascular cavity. This cavity has gland cells which secrete digestive enzymes over the food.

The nutrients from partially digested and fragmented food particles are absorbed by nutritive cells. It occurs in *Hydra, Aurelia* and higher animals, etc. (1+1)

29. **In which groups of animals, closed circulatory system is found? Why blood flows with faster speed and high pressure in these animals?**

Ans Closed circulatory system is found in most annelids and all vertebrates. In these groups, blood flows at faster speed and high pressure due to force provided by the rythmic contraction and relaxation of heart muscles. (1+1)

30. **List out the different exoskeletal structures present in different animals.**

Ans Different exoskeletal structures present in different animals are

Arthropods	Chitinous plates called sclerites
Molluscs	Calcareous shell
Reptiles	Epidermal scales
Birds	Epidermal feathers
Mammals	Epidermal hair, nails, claws, horns and hoofs.

(½ × 4)

31. **What is the difference between direct and indirect development?** NCERT

Ans Differences between direct and indirect development are as follows

(i) **Direct development** In case of direct development, the life cycle of an adult individual lacks any larval stage in its life cycle. The adults give rise to young ones which directly matures into the adult, e.g., mammals.

(ii) **Indirect development** It is present mostly in case of lower animals, the adult individual gives rise to eggs mostly which develop into the adult after being passing through several larval stages, e.g. echinoderms, *Ascaris*, cockroach have prolonged larval stages in their life cycle. (1+1)

Short Answer Type II Questions

(3 Marks)

32. **What are the difficulties that you would face in classification of animals, if common fundamental features are not taken into account?** NCERT

Ans The difficulties that will be faced if common fundamental features are not taken into account are as follows

(i) The interrelationship among different animals cannot be traced.

(ii) The picture of all animals at a glance cannot be projected.

(iii) The development of other animal species cannot be made.

(iv) There are numerous animal species which show great variety of life. The various common fundamental characters are taken into account for the classification of these animals. If this has not been done, it is not possible to deal with every living form separately at individual level. Therefore, a classification has to be based on the common fundamental characters for the sake of study of diversity in living forms. (3)

33. **If you are given a specimen, what are the steps that you would follow to classify it?** NCERT

Ans One has to follow the following steps to classify a specimen

(i) Body plan.

(ii) Body symmetry.

(iii) Segmentation pattern.

(iv) Presence or absence of vertebral column.

(v) Locomotory organelles limbs/fins/wings.

(vi) Patterns of organ systems like digestive, circulatory or reproductive systems. (½ × 6)

34. **How useful is the study of the nature of body cavity and coelom in the classification of animals?** NCERT

Ans Presence or absence of a cavity between the body wall and the gut wall is very important in classification. The body cavity which is lined by mesoderm is called coelom.

(i) Animals possessing coelom are called coelomate, e.g. annelids, molluscs, arthropods, echinoderms, hemichordates and chordates.

(ii) In some animals, the body cavity is not mesoderm, instead the mesoderm is present as scattered pouches in between the ectoderm and endoderm. Such a body cavity is called pseudocoelom and the animals possessing them are called pseudocoelomates, e.g. Aschelminthes.

(iii) The animals in which the body cavity is absent are known as acoelomates, e.g. Platyhelminthes.

Body coelom helps, in assigning the exact taxonomic position of the animal on the basis of its presence or absence in the animals's body. (2)

35. **Draw the sectional view of coelomate, pseudocoelomate and acoelomate.**

Ans Refer to fig. no. 6.4. on page no. 99.

36. **What is a pseudocoelom ? What are the advantages of having a coelom ? What two groups of animals have a pseudocoelom?**

Ans Refer to text on page no. 99. (3)

37. **Organ systems in different groups of animals exhibit various patterns of complexities. Explain.**

Ans In animals like annelids, arthropods, molluscs, echinoderms and chordates, organs have associated to form functional systems, where each system is concerned with a specific physiological function.

This pattern is called organ system level of organisation. Organ systems in different groups of animals exhibit various patterns of complexities. For example, the digestive system in platyhelminthes has only a single opening to the outside of the body that serves as both mouth and anus and is hence called incomplete.

Whereas a complete digestive system has two separate openings, mouth and anus as in vertebrates. (3)

38. **How is cephalisation considered as an asset in an adjustment with the environment?**

Ans The animals having bilateral symmetry move with their anterior end forward.

This has led to cephalisation, i.e. differentiation of a definite head at the anterior end. Cephalisation involves the concentration of nervous tissue (brain) and sense organs in the head.

This arrangement is an asset in an adjustment with the environment, as the anterior end of a moving animal is the first to encounter changes in the area it is entering. (3)

39. **Write an account on modes of respiration in animals with examples.**

Ans Different modes of respiration in animals are given in the table below

Respiratory Organ	Mode of Respiration	Examples
Body surface	Body surface respiration	Sponges and coelenterate
Gills	Branchial respiration	Fishes
Book gills	Book gill respiration	Limulus (king crab)
Skin	Cutaneous respiration	Annelids and amphibians
Trachea	Tracheal respiration	Insects
Lungs	Pulmonary respiration	Most of the tetrapods
Book lungs	Book lungs respiration	Arachnids (spiders and scorpion)

(3)

40. **Differentiate between** **NCERT Exemplar**

(a) Open circulatory system and closed circulatary system.

(b) Oviparous and viviparous characteristic .

(c) Direct development and Indirect development.

Ans Differentiation between these are as follows

	Open Circulatory System	Closed Circulatory System
(a)	**Open Circulatory System**	**Closed Circulatory System**
	In this type of circulation, blood flows in spaces called sinuses and the cells and tissues are directly bathed in it. e.g. arthropods (grasshopper, cockroach), gastropods (snail).	In this type of circulation, blood is circulated *via* a series of vessels (arteries, veins and capillaries). e.g. annelids (earthworm) and vertebrates (birds, primates etc).
(b)	**Oviparous Characteristics Animals**	**Viviparous Characteristic Animals**
	Oviparity is expulsion of undeveloped eggs rather than live young ones. Animals that lay eggs. are called oviparous. e.g. fishes, reptiles, amphibians, birds, insects and monotremes (mammals that lay eggs).	Viviparity is retention and growth of fertilised egg within the maternal body until the young one is capable of independent existence. Animals which give birth to their young ones and are called viviparous animals. e.g. mammals.

(c)	Direct Development	Indirect Development
	It is usually observed in higher animals.	Indirect development is mostly observed in lower animals.
	Direct development is the type of development in which there is no larval/nymphal or other intermediate stages in life, cycle between the egg (or birth) and the adult (e.g. mammals).	The adult individuals lay eggs, which develop into the adult after passing through few to several larval nymphal stages (e.g. echinoderms, arthropods).

(1 × 3)

Long Answer Type Questions

5 Marks

41. Describe the different body plans of animals, with an example of each.

Or

What is the basic body plan of animals?

Ans Animals have three basic body plan as given below

(i) **Cell aggregate body plan** Cells are loosely arranged and do not organise to form tissues, e.g. sponges.

(ii) **Blind sac body plan** Body has a cavity that helps in digestion with a single opening, the mouth, e.g. coelenterates.

(iii) **Tube within tube body plan** It is found in higher animal groups from nematodes to chordates. The body consists of two openings, i.e. one for ingestion and one for egestion.
It is further divided into two types

(a) **Protostomous plan** (*Proto*-first; *stoma*–mouth) found in non-chordates like flatworms, roundworms, annelids, molluscs and arthropods. In this, mouth is derived from the blastopore of the embryo and anus is formed later.

(b) **Deuterostomous plan** It is found in echinoderms, hemichordates and chordates. In this, anus is derived from the blastopore and mouth arises at the opposite end. (5)

42. Contrast the development of protostomes and deuterostomes, along with the three body plans. Also mention the example of each. (5)

Ans Refer to text on page no. 98.

43. Diagrammatically show the types of symmetry in animals.

Ans Types of symmetry in animals

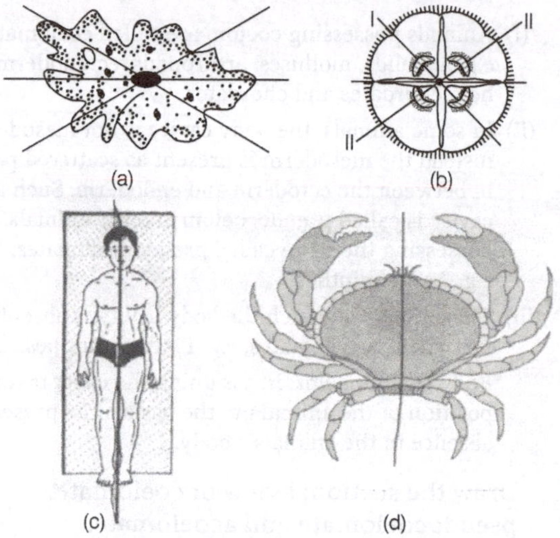

Symmetry in animals, (a) Asymmetry (b) Radial symmetry, (c) and (d) Bilateral symmetry

(5)

44. What is the relationship between germinal layers and the formation of body cavity in case of coelomate, acoelomates and pseudocoelomates?

Ans All adult multicellular organisms typically possess a concentric arrangement of tissues in the body. These tissues are derived from the three embryonic cell layers called **germinal layers**.

(i) The outer layer is the **ectoderm**, the middle layer is the **mesoderm** and the innermost layer is the **endoderm**.

(ii) Endoderm layer is associated with the formation of the stomach, colon, liver, pancreas, urinary bladder and other vital organs in an organism.

(iii) Mesoderm forms the main structural components of the body like the skeletal muscles, the skeleton, the dermis of the skin connective tissue, etc.

(iv) Ectoderm is associated with the formation of CNS, eye lens, ganglia, nerves and glands.

(v) The body cavity that is lined by mesoderm is called coelom, and the animals possessing coelom are called as **coelomates**, e.g. phylum–Annelida, Mollusca, Arthropoda, Echinodermata, Hemichordata and Chordata.

(vi) In some organisms, body cavity is not lined by mesoderm, instead mesoderm is present in the form of scattered pouches in between ectoderm and endoderm. Such body cavity is called **pseudocoelom** and animals possessing these structures are refered to as **pseudocoelomates**, e.g. *Ascaris*.

(vii) The animals in which there is complete the absence of body cavity are called **acoelomates**, e.g. Platyhelminthes. (5)

TOPIC 02 Non-Chordata

The animal kingdom includes about **35 phyla**, out of which 11 are considered as **major phyla.** Animals can be classified in two major groups on the basis of presence or absence of notochord. They are

(i) Non-chordata (absence of notochord)

(ii) Chordata (presence of notochord)

Chordotes can also be classified on the basis of presence or absence of vertebral column (backbone) into

(i) Invertebrates (without backbone)

(ii) Vertebrates (with backbone)

The non-chordata includes the following phyla

Phylum–Porifera

Phylum–Porifera (*Porous* – pore; *ferre* – to bear) includes the first and the most primitive group of multicellular animals, referred to as poriferans, i.e. pore bearing animals (sponges).

The study of poriferans is called **Parazoology.** Even though they are multicellular, they do not have tissue grade of organisation.

General Features

Some general features of phylum–Porifera are discussed below

1. **Habitat** They are mostly marine and some are freshwater habitat, found in ponds and lakes, e.g. *Spongilla.*
2. **Shape and Size** The size of sponges ranges from 1 cm to 1m in length. Some of them have vase-like cylindrical shape and majority have irregular shape.
3. **Symmetry** The cylindrical form (e.g. *Sycon*) show radial symmetry, while others show irregular shape and have no symmetry.
4. **Body Wall** The body wall contains outer dermal layer or **pinacoderm** and inner gastral layer or **choanoderm.**
   - The pinacoderm contains flat cells called **pinacocytes.**
   - The choanoderm consists of spherical cells with collar from which a flagellum emerges out. Hence, they are also called **flagellated cells** or **collar cells.**
5. **Body Organisation** Sponges show cellular level of organisation. The cells are almost independent, i.e. cooperating very little with one another in function.
6. **Germ Layers** These are diploblastic, i.e. having ectoderm and endoderm in between them a third layer mesenchyme is also found.
7. **Body Cavity** The sponges have a large cavity called **spongocoel** or **paragastric cavity.** It opens to the outside by a terminal opening called **osculum.**
8. **Skeleton** It is internal and includes inorganic **spicules** and organic **spongin fibres.**
9. **Canal System** It is one of the most important feature of sponges. Canal system is the network of channels called **canals,** which connect the spongocoel to the outside through **ostia.**

   The canals are lined by **choanocytes.** It maintains a constant flow of water from ostia to osculum through **spongocoel.** It helps in nutrition, respiration, reproduction and excretion.
10. **Digestion** Digestion in animals of this phylum is intracellular (inside collar cells) in nature. The amoeboid cells transport food from ingesting cells to other cells.
11. **Circulation** The flagellated collar cells regulates the flow of water throughout the canals and body cavity.
12. **Respiration** It occurs through the body surface by diffusion.
13. **Excretion** It also occurs through the body surface by diffusion in the form of ammonia.
14. **Sensory System** Sponges lack sensory and nerve cells, so they are poor in response to stimuli.
15. **Reproduction** Sponges reproduce both asexually and sexually. Asexual reproduction occurs by budding or gemmules or internal buds. Sexual reproduction involves the fusion of ova and spermatozoa.
16. **Fertilisation and Development** Fertilisation is internal, i.e. sperms of one sponge are carried by water current to the ova of another sponge for *in situ* fertilisation.

Development is mostly indirect with larval stages called **parenchymula** (*Leucosolenia*) or **amphiblastula** (*Sycon*).

Common Name of Some Sponges

Biological Name	Common Name
Sycon	Crown sponge
Spongilla	Freshwater sponge
Euplectella	Venus flower basket
Euspongia	Bath sponge
Cliona	Boring sponge
Pheronema	Bowl sponge
Haliclona	Finger sponge

Important Members of Porifera

Sycon

It is commonly called as **urn sponge** or **crown sponge.** *Sycon* is a marine sponge, which possesses a vase-like shape and radially symmetrical body. It measures 1-3 cm in height and 5-6 mm in diameter and canal system is of *Sycon* type. The larval stage is called **amphiblastula** with one-half of the larva have flagella. It is a freely swimming stage until the larva settles down and undergoes gastrulation.

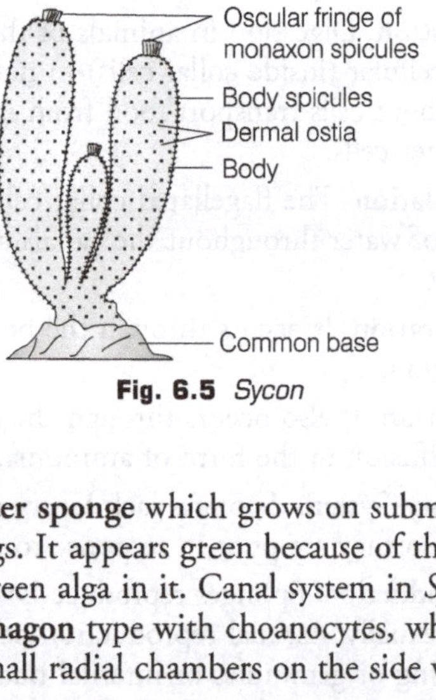

Fig. 6.5 *Sycon*

Spongilla

It is a **freshwater sponge** which grows on submerged plants and twigs. It appears green because of the presence of symbiotic green alga in it. Canal system in *Spongilla* is essentially of **rhagon** type with choanocytes, which are restricted to small radial chambers on the side walls.

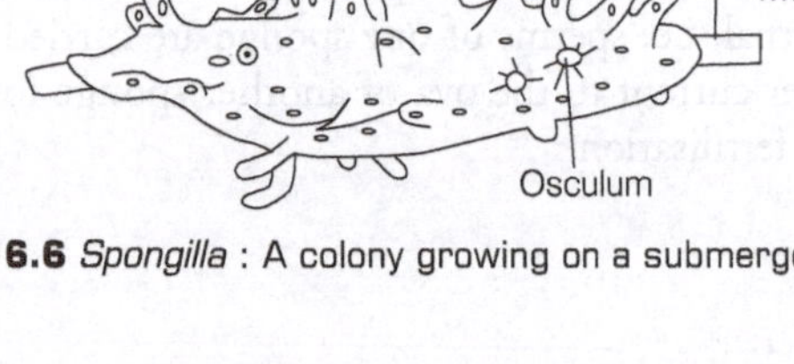

Fig. 6.6 *Spongilla* : A colony growing on a submerged twig

Spicules are of monaxon type, with larger ones called **megasceleres** (held by spongin fibres and provide support to the colony) and smaller ones called **microsceleres** (embedded in the cells of sponges).

Phylum–Coelenterata (Cnidaria)

There are about 9000 species of cnidarians. The name Cnidaria (*Knide* – nettle or sting cells) is derived from the **stinging cell** or **cnidoblasts** or **cnidocytes** or **nematocytes** present on the ectoderm of tentacles and body of these animals.

General Features

Some important general features of phylum–Coelenterata are discussed below

1. **Habit and Habitat** Cnidarians are exclusively of marine forms (*Obelia, Aurelia, Physalia, Metridium*), but few of them are freshwater form (e.g., *Hydra*). They are either sedentary (fixed) or free-swimming forms.
2. **Body Organisation and Body Wall** They have **tissue grade** organisation. Coelenterates are diploblastic and radially symmetric. The layers of body wall contain several types of cells, such as interestitial cells, sensory cells, nerve cells, epitheliomuscular cells, stinging cells (cnidoblasts), etc.
3. **Coelentric Cavity** A coelenteron or gastrovascular cavity is present, which is blind at one end and opens as **mouth** or **hypostome** at other end. Mouth is used both for ingestion and egestion.
4. **Tentacles** The mouth is surrounded by many thin, long, slender hollow structures called **tentacles.** Their function is to paralyse and capture the prey, attachment, defence and offence. Nematocytes (Cnidoblasts) or stinging cells acts as organs of predation and defence.

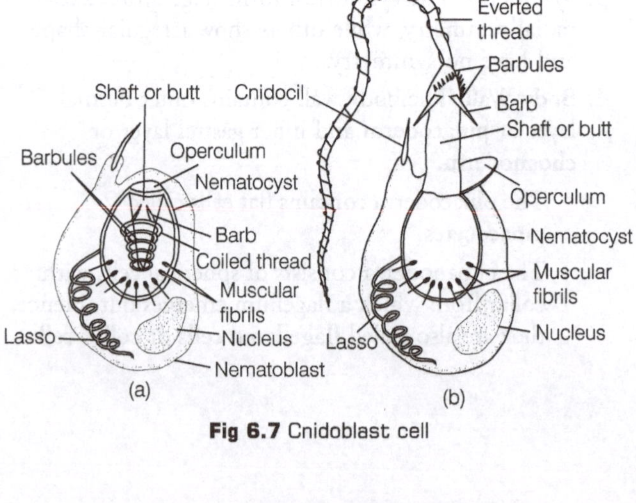

Fig 6.7 Cnidoblast cell

5. **Skeleton** A horny or calcareous exoskeleton as well as endoskeleton is present in many cases. The coelenterates with exoskeleton of calcium carbonate are called **corals.**
6. **Digestion** In coelenteron or gastrovascular cavity, both intracellular and extracellular digestion occur.
7. **Respiration and Excretion** Exchange of gases and excretion occur directly as all the cells that are in direct contact with water.
8. **Sensation** Sensory cells occur in the body wall such as **statocyst** for balancing and **ocelli** for photosensitivity.
9. **Nervous System** It is in the form of a nerve net, i.e. the unipolar neurons are loosely arranged in the body wall.
10. **Polymorphism** in cnidarians, there are mainly two types of individuals, i.e. **polyp** (cup-shaped) and **medusa** (umbrella-shaped).

    Polyp is sessile, cylindrical structure with mouth and tentacles facing upwards, e.g. *Hydra, Adamsia,* etc. Medusa is free-swimming zooid with mouth and tentacles facing downwards, e.g. *Aurelia* (jelly fish).

    Medusae may form polyps after sexual reproduction, while polyps form medusae through vegetative budding. Many variations occur in zooid forms. This phenomenon is called **polymorphism** which helps in alternation of generations.
11. **Reproduction** Coelenterates reproduce both by asexual and sexual methods. In many cnidarians, the polyps usually reproduce asexually by budding to give rise to medusae.

    The medusae bear gonads or sex organs and reproduce sexually to form polyps.
12. **Fertilisation** It may be external or internal.
13. **Alternation of Generations** The cnidarians complete their life cycle through two phases, i.e. asexually reproducing polyp phase and sexually reproducing medusa phase.

    Those cnidarians, which exist in both forms exhibit alternation of generations (metagenesis).

Advancement Over Sponges

The cnidarians or coelenterates exhibit advancement over sponges, as they possess a tissue level of organisation of the body with well-defined layers of cells and a digestive cavity.

Zoological Names and Common Names of Some Coelenterates

Zoological Name	Common Name
Velella	Sail by the wind
Aurelia	Jellyfish
Fungia	Mushroom coral
Adamsia	Sea anemone
Gorgonia	Sea fan
Tubipora	Organ pipe coral
Madrepora	Stag horn coral
Physalia	Portuguese man of war
Obelia	Sea fur
Alcyonium	Dead man's finger

Important Members of Coelenterata

Hydra vulgaris (Freshwater polyp)

- *Hydra* is commonly called as **freshwater solitary polyp**. It is negatively chemotrophic, i.e. remains away from chemicals hence, avoids chlorinated water. It is found attached to solid objects in water such as leaves, stones, weeds, etc.
- The body of *Hydra* has mouth over hypostome. It is the most sensitive region of *Hydra's* body. The basal part of the body has a pedal or basal disc. It has glandular zone, which secretes adhesive that are helpful in attachment.

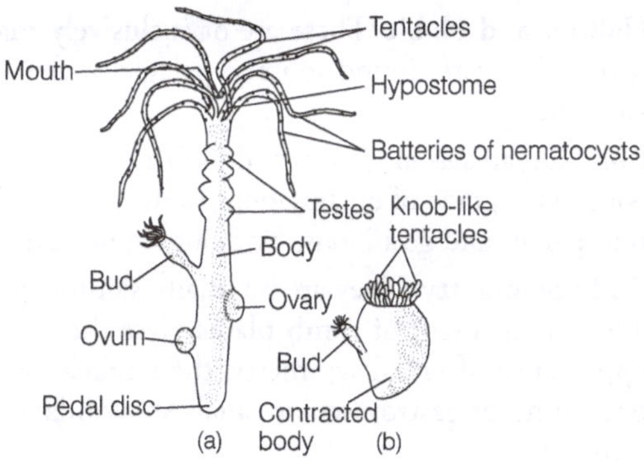

Fig. 6.8 External morphology; (a) Expanded body with bud and gonads, (b) Contracted body bearing bud

Physalia (Portugese Man of War)

- This animal is considered as one of the best example of polymorphism in Coelenterata.
- The animal body is a well-defined colony. It has a large (upto 30 cm), semitransparent and gas-filled, bladder-like bright blue float or pneumatophore, which always keeps the colony at water surface. The up and

down movements of body in water occur due to the secretion and absorption of gases like N_2 and CO.

- These gases are secreted by gas glands located in inner lining of the float.

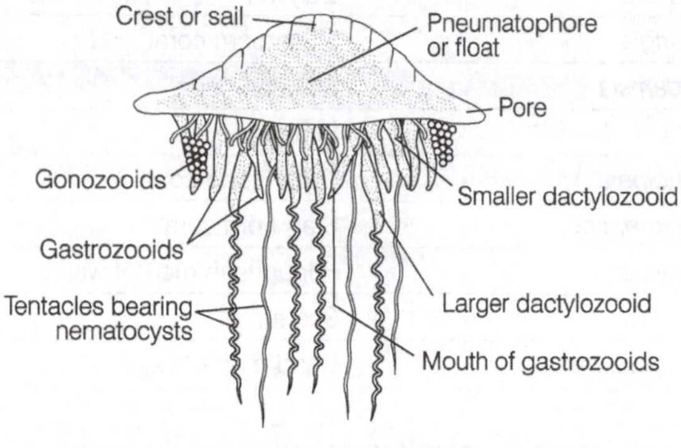

Fig. 6.9 *Physalia* : A colony

Phylum–Ctenophora

Phylum–Ctenophora (*Ktene*–comb; *phors*–bearing) Acnidaria or **comb jellies** or **sea walnuts** are exclusively marine forms. The term 'Ctenophora' was coined by **Georges Cuvier**. It includes about 50 species.

General Features

Some important general features of phylum–Ctenophora are discussed below

1. **Habitat and Habit** These are of exclusively marine forms. They are found solitary, pelagic or free-swimming.
2. **Body Organisation** They are diploblastic, acoelomate with tissue grade of organisation. Body is soft, delicate, transparent and gelatinous, without segmentation.
3. **Body Symmetry** They are biradially symmetrical. The arrangement of **comb plates** gives the appearance of radial symmetry, the tentacles and branching of gastrovascular canals show bilateral symmetry.
4. **Digestive System** Digestion is both extracellular and intracellular. Skeletal, circulatory, respiratory and excretory systems are absent.
5. **Respiration and Excretion** These processes occur through general body surface, no specific organs are found.
6. **Nervous System** It consists of subepidermal plexus with an aboral sense organ called **statocyst for balance.**
7. **Reproduction and Development** They are hermaphrodite or monoecious. Gonads are endodermal. Fertilisation is generally external. Development is indirect, e.g. *Ctenoplana, Pleurobrachia, Beroe, Velamen*, etc.

Note Bioluminescence (the property of a living organism to emit light) is well-marked in ctenophores.

Important Members of Ctenophora

Pleurobrachia

These are common marine pelagic forms, found all over the world. Their body is transparent and pear or walnut-shaped. These are commonly called as **sea walnuts.**

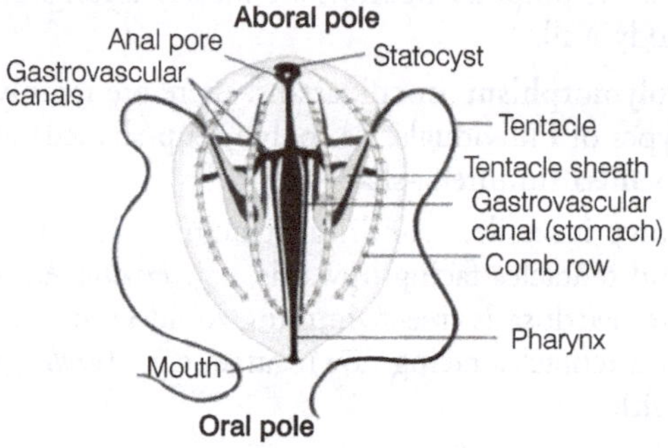

Fig. 6.10 *Pleurobrachia sp.*

Beroe

It has a thimble-shaped body, which is somewhat compressed along the sagittal axis. It is commonly called as **swimming eye of cat.**

Phylum–Platyhelminthes

Phylum–Platyhelminthes (*Platy* – flat; *helminth* – worm) includes **flatworms**. The group includes the first simplest triploblastic group of animals. **Gegenbaur** coined the term 'Platyhelminthes'. It includes about 12,000 species of animals. They have leaf-like or ribbon-like body.

General Features

Some important general features of phylum–Platyhelminthes are discussed below

1. **Habit and Habitat** Majority of forms are parasitic (tapeworms, liver flukes, blood flukes), etc., and free-living forms (planarians). Hooks and suckers are present in parasitic forms.
2. **Symmetry** The body is bilaterally symmetrical with definite orientation like anterior and posterior end.

3. **Cephalisation** Primitive form of cephalisation is present in free-living flatworms.
4. **Germ Layers** They are triploblastic.
5. **Body Cavity** They are **acoelomate**. The space between the body wall and body organ is filled by characteristic connective tissue called **parenchyme** or **mesenchyme**.
6. **Body Organisation** They show organ system grade of organisation, with pseudosegmentation in few.
7. **Digestive System** It is simple and incomplete with only one opening called **mouth**. The anus is absent.
8. **Respiration** It occurs through general body surface.
9. No specific organ for circulation is present and also lacks skeleton.
10. **Excretory System** It consists of peculiar flame cells that can help in osmoregulation and excretion. Circulatory and skeletal systems are absent in Platyhelminthes.
11. **Nervous System** It is ladder-like and poorly, developed, consisting of a brain and two main longitudinal nerve cords jointed at intervals by the transverse commissures.
12. **Reproduction** Flatworms are hermaphrodite, monoecious or bisexual, having both male and female reproductive system. Fertilisation is internal and development often includes one or more larval stages. Some also can regenerate, e.g. *Planaria*, *Taenia* (tapeworm) and *Echinococcus* (dog tapeworm).
13. Some examples of this phylum, are *Fasciola* (liver fluke), *Schistosoma* (blood fluke), *Polystomum*, etc.

Important Members of Platyhelminthes

Fasciola hepatica (Liver fluke)

- It is a digenetic endoparasite. Body is soft, oval, flat, leaf-like with dull pink-ground colour and brown border.
- The broad anterior portion of animal bears a distinct triangular projection called the **head lobe** or **oral cone**. This structure bears mouth and two suckers, i.e. oral sucker (anterior sucker) and acetabulum (ventral sucker).
- Life cycle of *Fasciola* is complex. Primary host in which adult fluke lives is sheep, while the intermediate or secondary host in which numerous stages are passed is a snail.
- The liver fluke causes liver rot (acute fascioliasis) in sheep.
- The symptoms appear about one month after the infection.

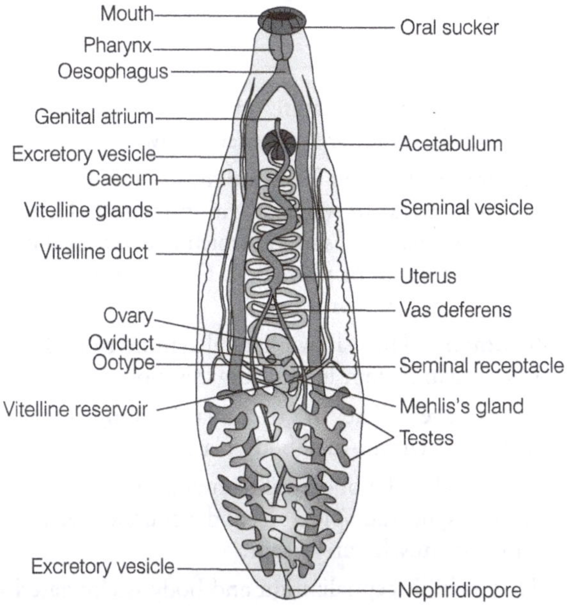

Fig. 6.11 Structure of liver fluke

Taenia solium (Pork tapeworm)

- It is commonly called as **pork tapeworm** due to its ribbon-like flat appearance. It is a digenetic parasite.
- It lacks a mouth and digestive tract in all their life stages. Thus, absorption of food occurs through their general body surface.

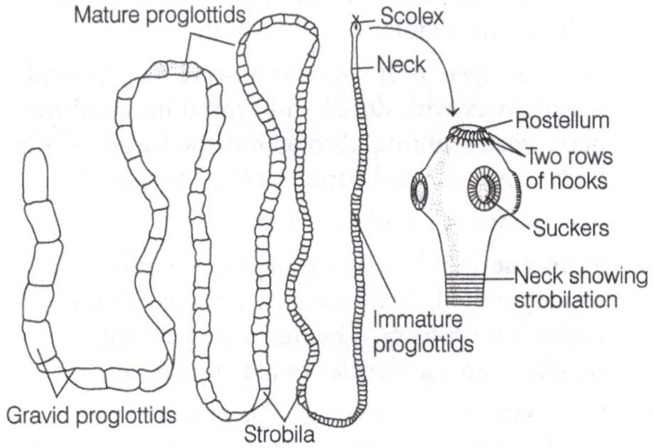

Fig. 6.12 Morphology of *Taenia solium*

- Humans are considered as the primary host of this parasite, while the animals like pig (or dog and sheep) are considered as the secondary or intermediate hosts of this parasite.

Phylum–Aschelminthes

Phylum–Aschelminthes or Nemathelminthes or Nematoda (*Nema* – thread; *helminth* – worms) includes roundworms. They are commonly called as **nematodes.**

General Features

Some important general features of phylum–Aschelminthes are discussed below

1. **Habitat and Habit** They are mostly free-living and may occur in water or within the soil. There are several parasitic species, which live within the body of animals or plants, e.g. Guineaworms, whipworms, eyeworms, etc.
2. **Symmetry** They show bilateral symmetry and have organ system level of organisation.
3. **Germ Layers** They are triploblastic animals and have tube-within-tube body plan.
4. **Body Wall** The body wall contains an outer cuticle, syncytial epidermis and a muscle layer. Circular muscles are absent.

   They exhibit cephalization and body is elongated and cylindrical with tapering ends. They do not show metamerisation.
5. **Body Cavity** Aschelminthes are **pseudocoelomates** as the cavity present between the body wall and gut is not lined by mesodermal epithelium.
6. **Digestive System** Alimentary canal is complete with a well-developed muscular pharynx and anus.
7. **Excretory System** It consists of a pair of gland cells or intracellular canals or both.
8. **Nervous System** It contains a nerve ring around the pharynx with dorsal and ventral longitudinal nerve cords running throughout the length of the body. Amphids and papillae are sensory organs.
9. Cutaneous respiration is found.
10. **Reproduction** Nematodes reproduce only by sexual method. Sexes are separate and exhibit sexual dimorphism. The males are generally smaller than the females to aid copulation.
11. **Fertilisation** It is internal. The fertilised eggs develop directly or indirectly through larvae that undergo moulting and finally grow into adults.
12. *Dracunculus, Ancylostoma* (hookworm), *Ascaris* (round worm), *Heterodera, Desmoscolex, Enterobius*, etc., are some members of this phylum.

Advancement Over Flatworms

Aschelminthes show advancement over flatworms as they contain complete alimentary canal and sexes are separate in them.

Important Members of Aschelminthes

Ascaris lumbricoides (Round worms)

- It is found in small intestine of man and some other vertebrates like pigs, cattles, sheep, squirrels, etc.
- In man, it is more frequently seen in children than in adults.

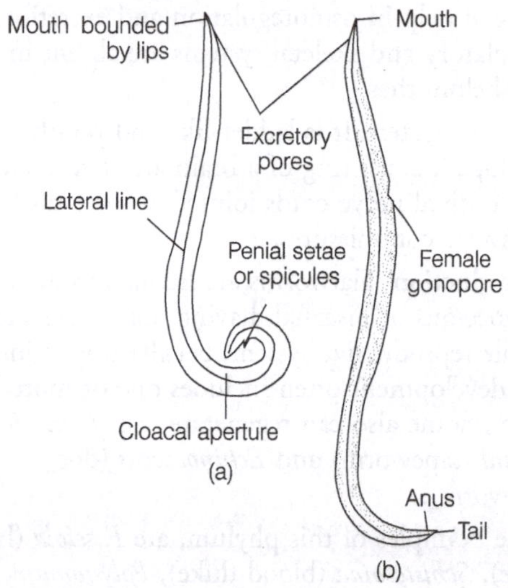

Fig. 6.13 *Ascaris lumbricoides* : (a) Adult male (b) Adult female

- A clear sexual dimorphism is seen, **female** is 20-40 cm in length, 4-6 mm in diameter and male is smaller with 15-30 cm in length, 2- 4 mm in diameter.

Ancylostoma duodenale

- The common hookworms or *Ancylostoma duodenale* are the most dangerous roundworms. The name hookworm is given, because of the fact that the male have a hook-shaped body. These worms live as endoparasites of human small intestine and possess a monogenetic life cycle.
- They differ from roundworms like *Ascaris* in the absence of lips and in possessing a copulatory bursa in male.

- The mode of infection to the host is specific. The larva of animal enters into the host body after boring through the skin. Generally, they penetrate the soft skin of sides of feet and hands.

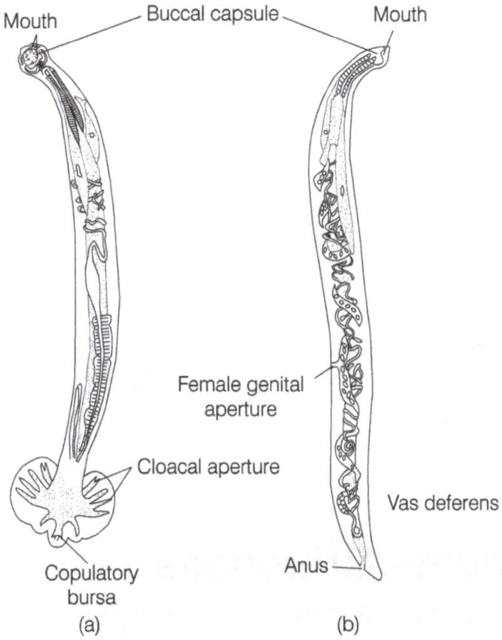

Fig 6.14 *Ancylostoma* : (a) Male, (b) Female

Phylum–Annelida

Phylum–Annelida (*Annulus* – ring; *lidos* – form) includes segmented worms. The term 'Annelida' was first coined by **Lamarck** (1809). It includes about 12,000 species of animals.

General Features

Some important general features of phylum–Annelida are discussed below

1. **Habit and Habitat** They may be aquatic, terrestrial and free-living or parasitic.
2. **Body Wall** The outermost covering of body is thin and moist cuticle secreted by the epidermis.
3. **Metamerism** The body is divided into segments or metameres by ring-like grooves–called annuli. It is called **metameric segmentation.** The segmentation is external as well as internal.
4. **Symmetry** Annelids are bilaterally symmetrical.
5. **Germ Layers** They are triploblastic and protostomial animals.
6. **Organisation and Body Plan** They show organ system level of organisation and tube within a tube body plan.
7. **Cephalisation** These show true cephalisation.
8. **Body Cavity** Annelids have true coelom. It is formed by splitting of mesodermal epithelium and such a coelom is called as **schizocoelom.**
9. **Skeleton** The coelomic fluid in the body cavity acts as **hydrostatic skeleton** for the animal.
10. **Locomotion** Annelids move by paired, lateral, hollow, fleshy, appendages in each segment called **chitinous setae.** Aquatic annelids like *Nereis* possess lateral appendages (parapodia) that help in swimming and have longitudinal and circular muscle for locomotion.
11. **Digestive System** The digestive tract is straight and complete, starting from mouth and ending at anus.
12. **Respiration** It occurs through skin, gills or parapodia.
13. **Circulatory System** They are first animals that have a closed circulatory system, i.e. the blood flows through a system of blood vessels. The respiratory pigment haemoglobin or erythrocruorin are dissolved in blood plasma.
14. **Excretory System** The excretory organs are **nephridia** in each segment, which helps in excretion and osmoregulation.
15. **Nervous System** It contains a nerve ring around the pharynx and a double ventral nerve cord with ganglion. Sensory receptors like taste buds, photoreceptor cells eyes and statocyst bodies are also present.
16. **Reproduction** Annelids reproduce sexually. They are unisexual, e.g. *Nereis,* and bisexual (hermaphrodite), e.g., leech, earthworm (*Pheretima*).
17. *Polygordius, Aphrodite, Chaetopterus, Arenicola, Tubifex, Birudinaria, Lumbricus* and *Pheretima*, etc., are several members.

Important Members of Annelida

Nereis or *Neanthes*

- It is commonly called **clamworm** or **sandworm.** It is a marine, nocturnal and carnivorous animal. The animal lives in burrows on tidal areas of sea shores.
  The body of animal is divisible into head, trunk and pygidium.

- Peristomium has four pairs of long tentacular processes called **cirrus.**
- The trunk region have about 80-200 segments. Each segment bears a pair of parapodia.
  The pygidium is the last or anal segment. It bears anus along with one pair of anal cirri (sensory) and several minute sensory papillae.
- The sexual form of Nereis is called Heteronereis. The phenomenon of formation of Heteronereis is called **epitoky.**
- Fertilisation occurs in sea water.

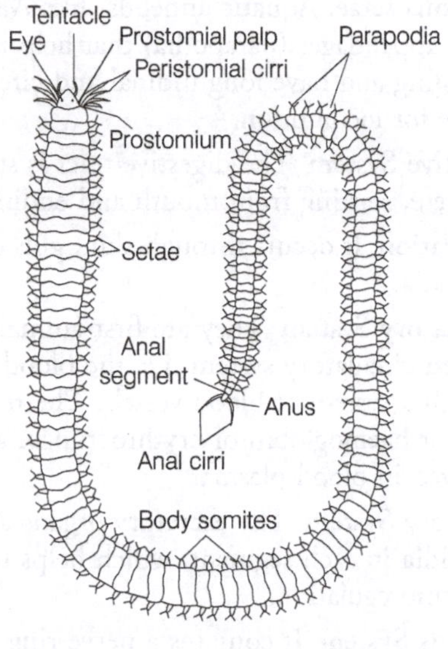

Fig. 6.15 *Nereis* : External morphology

Hirudinaria granulosa

- It is commonly called common Indian cattle leech.
- The mouth of leeches is triradiate, which is guarded by a structure called **velum.**
- The salivary secretion of animal contains an anticoagulant called **hirudin** or **anticoagulin.** It prevents the clotting of blood during ingestion.
- The alimentary canal in leeches is complete.
- The animal contains anterior and posterior suckers meant for adhesion and locomotion, respectively.
- It is a hermaphrodite, but cross-fertilisation is a common.
- Principal male organs are eleven pairs of testes sacs in segments 12-20th and accessory organs in 10th segment. Female organs are a pair of ovisacs, oviducts and vagina located in 11th segment.

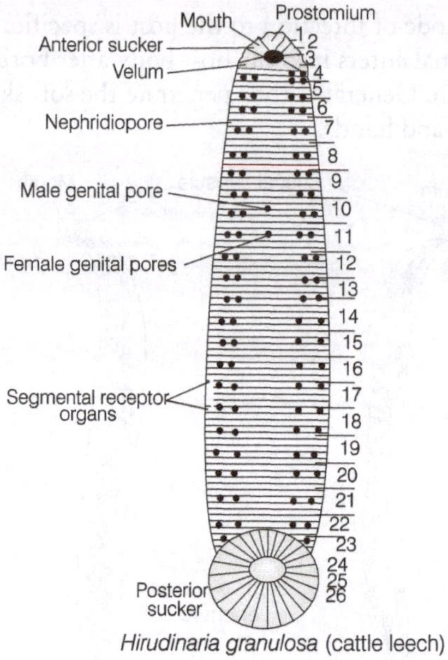

Fig 6.16 *Hirudinaria granulosa* (cattle leech)

Phylum–Arthropoda

Phylum–Arthropoda (*Arthron* – jointed; *podos* – foot) includes the first and simplest segmented animals. These are commonly called as **jointed legged animals.**

It is the largest group of animal that includes about 1000000 insect species, 102248 spiders and scorpion species, 103248 arachnoid species and 47000 crustacean species representing about 80% of total known animal species.

General Features

Some important general features of phylum–Arthropoda are discussed below

1. **Habitat and Habit** They may be aquatic or terrestrial. They may occur as free-living or parasitic forms e.g. bed bugs, ticks, mosquitoes, etc.
2. **Body Parts** Body is segmented externally. It has distinct head, thorax and abdomen. Head bears many fused segments and sense organs.
3. **Symmetry and Body Organisation** Arthropods are bilaterally symmetrical and protostomial. They are triploblastic with organ system level of organisation.
4. **Appendages** They have jointed, paired appendages, which are present in some or all somites or segments. These perform various functions like walking, clinging, jumping, feeding, etc.

5. **Exoskeleton** The exoskeleton is formed of thick, tough and non-living **chitinous cuticle** in which periodic moulting (ecdysis) occurs.

   Exoskeleton protects animal from mechanical and chemical injuries, prevents desiccation and also helps in attachment.
6. **Locomotion** Jointed appendages help in locomotion. Cilia are found to be absent in arthropod.
7. **Digestive System** Alimentary canal is complete and well-developed, i.e. divided into foregut, midgut and hindgut.
8. **Respiration** It occurs through general body surface, gills (e.g. prawn), book lungs (e.g. scorpion and spider), trachea (e.g. cockroach) and book gills (e.g. king crab).
9. **Circulation** The circulatory system is open type, i.e. blood flows in the **haemocoel** instead of blood vessels.
10. **Excretion** The excretory organs are **Malpighian tubules** (opening into duct) or **green glands** opening directly to the exterior.
11. **Nervous System** The nervous system consists of a nerve ring and a **double ganglionated ventral** nerve cord.
12. **Sense Organs** Arthropods have simple eyes called **ocelli** and compound eyes. Aquatic forms have **statocysts** for balancing.
13. **Reproduction** Arthropods reproduce by sexual methods. Fertilisation is usually internal type. They are generally oviparous but few are viviparous, i.e., scorpion. Development may be direct or indirect involving metamorphosis.

Advancement Over Annelids

They have distinct head, jointed appendages for different functions, exoskeleton, special respiratory organ, secrete pheromones and have well-developed sense organs. These features are not present in annelids.

14. *Limulus* (king crab; a living fossil), *Palamnaeus* (scorpion), *Peripates* (walking worm), Cancer (crab), *Palaemon* (prawn), *Schistocera* (locust), *Periplaneta* (cockroach), *Bombyx* (silkworm), *Musca* (housefly), *Apis* (honeybee), *Anopheles*, *Aedes* and *Culex* mosquitoes, etc., are some examples of this phylum.

Important Members of Arthropoda

Limulus

It is a large sized marine animal. It is living member of very ancient (200 million years) primitive chelicerates and hence called a '**living fossil**'. Its prosoma is covered by a large horseshoe-shaped carapace, thus also called **horseshoe crab**. It bears a median simple eyes (ocelli) and two lateral compound eyes.

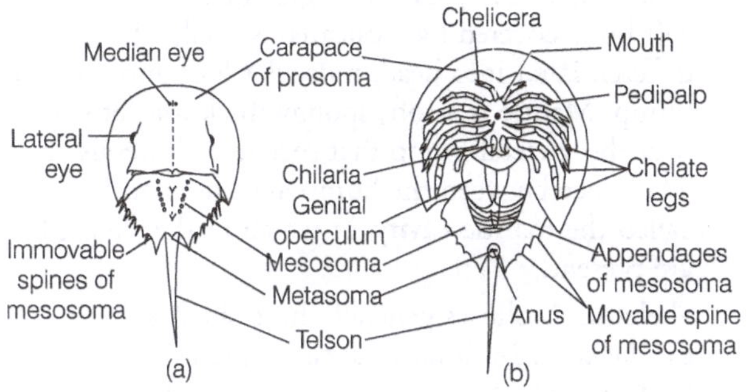

Fig. 6.17 *Limulus* : (a) Dorsal view, (b) Ventral view

Peripatus (Walking worm)

It is a connecting link between arthropods and annelids. These bear nephridia, unjointed legs (like parapodia of polychaeta) as annelidan characters. The presence of antennae, haemocoel, trachaeal respiration are their arthropodian characters.

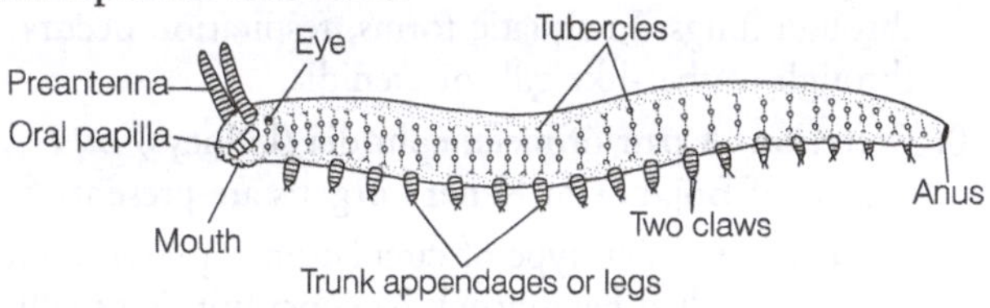

Fig. 6.18 *Peripatus* : External view

Phylum–Mollusca

The phylum–Mollusca (*Molluscs* – soft bodied) includes the soft bodied, unsegmented, eu-coelomate animals. These are called **molluscs** or **shelled animals. Johnston** (1650) coined the term 'Mollusca'. Mollusca is the **second largest** animal phylum and includes about 85,000 species. The study of molluscs is called '**Malacology**'.

General Features

Some important general features of phylum–Mollusca are discussed below

1. **Habit and Habitat** Molluscs are mostly of marine forms (*Sepia*, *Octopus*, *Chiton*, etc.). Some are freshwater (e.g. *Unio* and *Pila*).

These are generally bilaterally symmetrical and some are asymmetrical due to **torsion**. Terrestrial form include land snails. Few molluscs are parasites also, e.g. *Glochidium* larva, etc.

2. Animals show symmor twisting during growth.
3. **Germ Layers and Organisation** They are triploblastic and possess organ system level of organisation.
4. **Body Form** They have unsegmented, protostomial, soft body covered by a calcareous shell, which is differentiated into head, muscular foot and visceral hump. Mantle is a soft, spongy thick fold of skin over the visceral hump that secretes calcareous shell. The space between the hump and the mantle is called the **mantle cavity**, in which feather-like gills are present.
5. **Skeleton** Molluscs generally have shell as exoskeleton. In *Octopus*, shell is absent.
6. **Body Cavity** The coelom is greatly reduced although they are **eucoelomate**.
7. **Locomotion** The locomotory organ is muscular foot.
8. **Digestion** The digestive tract is complete. The mouth contains a rasping organ called **radula** with file-like transverse row of chitinous teeth. Anus opens into the mantle cavity.
9. **Respiration** In terrestrial forms, respiration occurs through lungs. In aquatic forms, respiration occurs through feather-like gills or ctenidia.
10. **Excretion** A pair of metanephridia (kidneys) or **organs of Bojanus** or **Keber's organs** are present.
11. **Circulation** Open type of circulation is present. The coelom is called **haemocoel**, haemocyanin is usually the circulatory pigment.
12. **Sense Organs** These have eyes, statocyst, tentacles for equilibrium and receptors for touch, smell and taste.
13. **Nervous System** Few pairs of ganglia like cerebral, visceral and pedal with nerves are present.
14. **Reproduction** Molluscs reproduce sexually. Sexes are separate and mostly oviparous. Fertilisation is external or internal.
15. Development is either direct or indirect with larval stages like **trochophore, glochidium** and **veliger**.
16. For example, include *Chaetopleura* (chiton), *Dentalium* (elephant tusk shell), *Pila* (apple snail), *Pinctada* (pearl oyster), *Aplysia* (sea hare), *Sepia* (cuttlefish), *Loligo* (squid), *Octopus* (devil fish).

Important Members of Mollusca

Chiton

It is nocturnal and herbivorous animal. It has a very long and wide foot which helps in clinging to coastal rocks. It has boat-shaped shell composed of overlapping eight symmetrical plates. Sexes are separate.

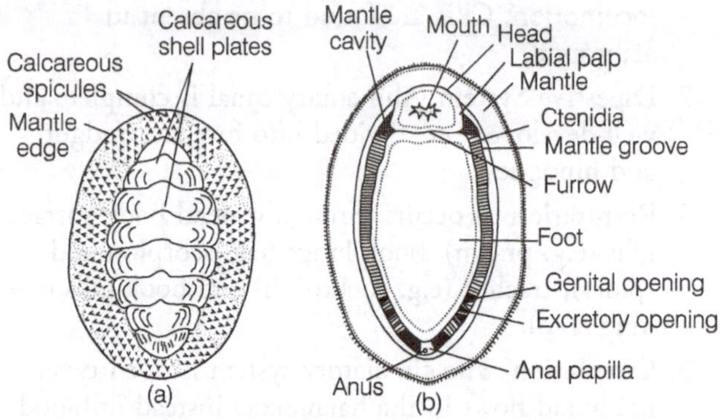

Fig. 6.19 *Chiton* : (a) Dorsal view, (b) Ventral view

Pila

It is a herbivorous animal, which inhabits pond, lakes and streams. Asymmetrical body is covered by a spiral shell. The coils of the shell round the axis are called **whorls**. The digestive system is complete. It leads an amphibious life.

Gaseous exchange occurs by means of gills or ctenidia (in water) and by lungs (when on land). It has osphradium (for testing nature of water) and radula (rasping organ). *Pila* bears 8-shaped nervous system.

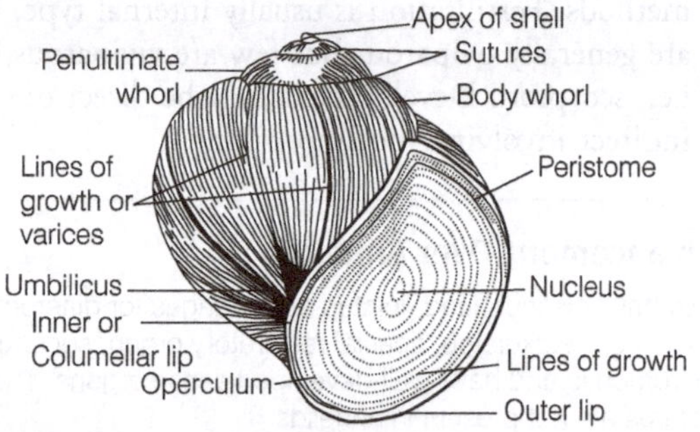

Fig. 6.20 *Pila* (apple snail) : The shell with operculum (ventral view)

Knowledge Plus

- They have distinct head, much better sense organs and gills or lungs for respiration as compared to annelids.
- *Neopilina* is a connecting link between Annelida and Mollusca.
- *Nautilus* is commonly called as pearly *Nautilus*. It is used extensively for ornamental purposes.

Phylum–Echinodermata

Phylum–Echinodermata (Echinos–spines; *derma*–skin) includes the spiny skinned animals, which are exclusively marine. **Jacob Klein** (1734) coined the term 'Echinodermata'. It includes about 6,000 living species.

General Features

Some important general features of phylum–Echinodermata are discussed below

1. **Habit and Habitat** These are marine forms (except *Synapta similis*) and are bottom dwellers. They are sedentary or pelagic.
2. **Symmetry** The adults have radial (pentamerous) symmetry, but the larval forms have bilateral symmetry.
3. **Germ Layers and Organisation** They are triploblastic, deuterostomial and exhibit organ system grade of organisation and regeneration.
4. **Head** It is absent in echinoderm and body also lacks segmentation.
5. **Body Cavity** They have true coelom, which is lined by a **ciliated peritoneum.** The most distinctive feature is the presence of water vascular system or ambulacral (oral surface) system with tube feet that help in locomotion, capture of food and respiration.
6. **Endoskeleton** It contains numerous calcareous plates called **ossicles** beneath the skin.
7. **Locomotion** The locomotion is carried out by tube feet.
8. **Digestion** The digestive tract is simple and complete type. The mouth is present on the lower side (oral surface) and the anus is on the upper side (aboral surface).
9. **Respiration** Through occurs minute peristomial gills, protruding from tube feet, which help in respiration.
10. **Circulation** It is reduced and open type called as **haemal system** having a lacunate tissue with vessels embedded into coelomic channels.
11. **Excretion** The excretory organs are absent. The waste products are removed by diffusion through **branchiae** or **amoebocytes.**
12. **Nervous System** It contains circum-oral nerve ring, transverse and radial nerves.
13. **Reproduction** Echinoderms reproduce sexually. Sexes are separate and show no sexual dimorphism. Fertilisation is external and development is indirect, e.g. *Asterias,* (seastar or starfish), *Ophiura* (brittle star), *Echinus* (sea urchin).
14. Examples include *Cucumaria* (sea cucumber), *Asterias* (Star fish), *Antedon* (feather star or sea lily), holothuria, etc.

Important Members of Echinodermata

Cucumaria

This animal is very common in shallow tropical water. It has fifteen sets of feeding arms that fan out into bushy tentacles. Respiration occurs through system of tubules called **respiratory tree.** It feeds upon detritus and planktons.

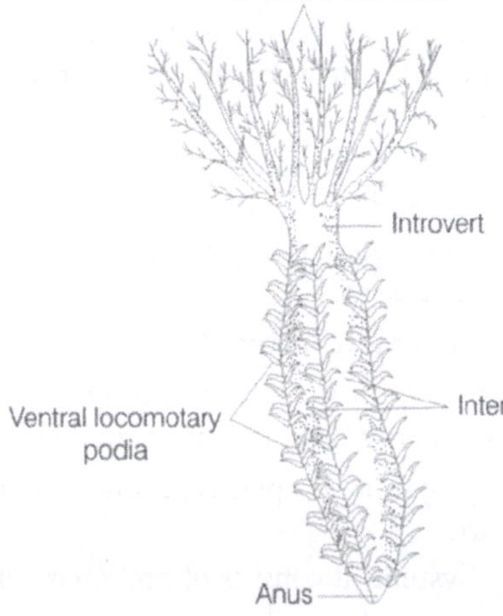

Fig. 6.21 *Cucumaria*

Asterias

It is a benthonic (bottom dwelling), nocturnal and carnivorous animal. The stomach is protrusible in nature, i.e. it comes out of the body. It shows autotomy and regeneration. Dried and powdered starfishes form a calcium rich fertiliser. Starfish feeds on molluscs and destroys pearl oyster.

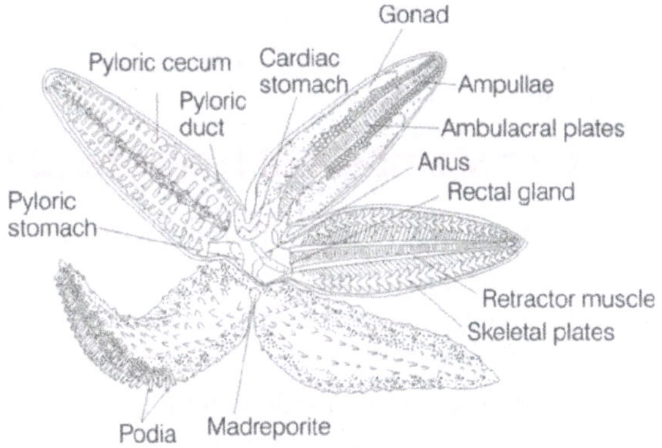

Fig. 6.22 *Asterias*

Phylum–Hemichordata

Hemichordata (*Hemi* – half; *chordata* – notochord) was earlier placed as a subphylum under phylum–Chordata. But, now it is considered as a separate phylum under Non-chordata. These are also called **half chordates.** This phylum consists of a small group of **worm-like** animal.

General Features

Some important general features of phylum–Hemichordata are discussed below

1. **Habit and Habitat** They are exclusively marine and mostly live in **burrows.**
2. **Symmetry and Body Organisation** They are deuterostomial bilaterally symmetrical and triploblastic. They have organ system level of organisation.
3. **Body Form** They are soft bodied, cylindrical and unsegmented body is divisible into proboscis, collar and trunk. The body cavity is true coelom. A true notochord is absent.
4. **Digestive System** It is complete.
5. **Respiraton** Respiration occurs through several pairs of **gill slits** or through the general body surface.
6. **Circulatory System** is open type and contains a dorsal heart.
7. **Excretory System** It consists of proboscis gland.
8. **Nervous System** It is primitive, consists mainly of an intraepidermal nerve plexus.
9. **Sensation** Sensory cells of the epidermis act as sense organs.
10. **Reproduction** It is mostly sexual. Sexes are separate. Development is indirect with tornaria larva.
11. Examples include *Balanoglossus* (acorn or tongue worm), *Saccoglossus, Cephalodiscus,* etc.

Note

Subphylum–Hemichordata is the connecting link between echinoderms and chordates.

Important Members of Hemichordata

Balanoglossus (The acorn or Tongue worm)

A sluggish marine animal, which moves slowly with the help of cilia present all over its body and feeds on organic matter ingested along with sand.

Unisexual with external fertilisation and life cycle includes a **tornaria larva.** The power of regeneration is well marked. The body is cylindrical, bilaterally symmetrical, elongated and uniformly ciliated without exoskeleton or external appendages.

The body is divisible into three regions, i.e.

(i) **Proboscis** A tongue-like projection, hence, the name **tongue worm.**

(ii) **Collar** The muscular region, which bears mouth ventrally below the proboscis stalk.

(iii) **Trunk** Trunk is further divisible into three regions, as follows

- The anterior branchiogenital region.
- The middle hepatic region.
- The posterior abdominal region.

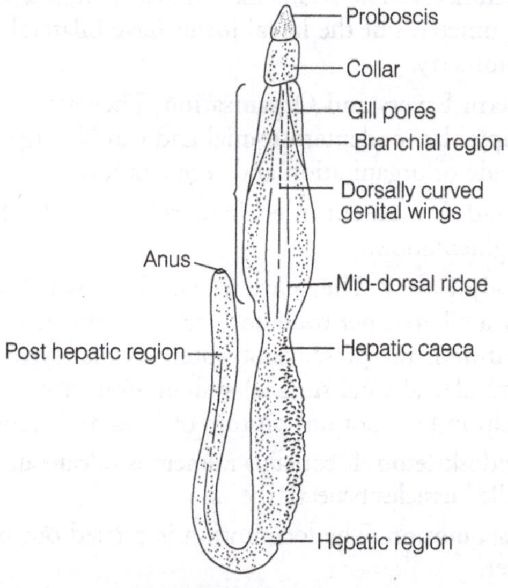

Fig.6.23 *Balanoglossus*

Topic Practice 2

Multiple Choice Questions

(1 Mark)

1. In phylum–Porifera opening, through which water leaves the spongocoel is called

(a) ostia
(b) ommatidia
(c) osculum
(d) choanocytes

Ans (c) Ostia are the minute pores on the body, through which water enters the central cavity (called the spongocoel) and water exits the spongocoel through the osculum.

2. Given below are types of cells present in some animals each one is specialised to perform a single function except **NCERT Exemplar**
(a) choanocytes (b) interstitial cells
(c) gastrodermal cells (d) nematocytes

Ans (b) Interstitial cells are reserve cells in coelenterates. They are also called as totipotent cells and can be converted into any type of cells or into a full organism.

3. Reproduction in *Ctenoplana* takes place by
(a) budding (b) sexual reproduction
(c) binary fission (d) multiple fission

Ans (b) *Ctenoplana* belongs to phylum–Ctenophora. Reproduction in all the animals belonging to phylum–Ctenophora takes place by sexual reproduction only.

4. Aschelminthes are usually
(a) dioecious (b) hermaphrodites
(c) metagenic (d) coelomates

Ans (a) Aschelminthes are dioecious with separate sexes and females are usually longer than males.

5. Earliest occurrence of metamerism is witnessed in phylum
(a) Platyhelminthes (b) Coelenterata
(c) Arthropoda (d) Annelida

Ans (d) A condition in which body is segmented both internaly and externaly by septa and setae respectively is called true segmentation or metamerism.
It first appeared in the members of phylum–Annelida.

6. Which of the following statements is incorrect?
(a) In cockroaches and prawns excretion of waste material occurs through Malpighian tubules.
(b) In Ctenophora, locomotion is mediated by comb plates.
(c) In *Fasciola*, flame cells take part in excretion.
(d) Earthworms are hermaphrodite and yet cross fertilisation takes place among them.
NCERT Exemplar

Ans (a) In cockroaches, excretion occurs through Malpighian cells and in prawns it occurs through green glands.

7. What is true about Mollusca?
(a) The presence of metameric segmentation
(b) The presence of mantle cavity and coelom cavity
(c) The presence of tissue level of organisation
(d) The presence of chitinous exoskeleton

Ans (b) Phylum–Mollusca do not have metameric segmentation, they have a calcareous exoskeleton with organ system level of organisation, mantle cavity and also shows the presence of coelomic cavity during development.

8. Choose the animals that belong to phylum–Echinodermata from the options.
(a) Sea urchin, cuttlefish and sea lily
(b) *Echinus*, sea hare and sea cucumber
(c) *Antedon*, *Ophiura* and *Echinus*
(d) *Ophiura*, *Chaetopleura* and *Echinus*

Ans (c) Cuttlefish or *Sepia*, *Chaetopleura* or chiton and *Aplysea* or sea hare belong to phylum–Mollusca. *Antedon* or sea lily, *Cucumaria* or sea cucumber, *Echinus* or sea urchins and *Ophiura* or brittle star belong to phylum– Echinodermata.

9. Which one of the following statements is incorrect? **NCERT Exemplar**
(a) Mesoglea is present in between ectoderm and endoderm in *Obelia*.
(b) Radial symmetry is found in *Asterias*.
(c) *Fasciola* is a pseudocoelomate animal.
(d) *Taenia* is a triploblastic animal.

Ans (c) *Fasciola* (liver fluke) is an acoelomate, i.e. without coelom or body cavity.

10. Excretory organ in phylum–Hemichordata is
(a) proboscis gland (b) gills
(c) collar cells (d) None of these

Ans (a) Excretory organ in animals belonging to phylum–Hemichordata is the proboscis gland.

Very Short Answer Type Questions

1 Mark

11. The commonly known 'venus flower basket' belongs to which phylum ?

Ans It is a sponge that belongs to phylum–Porifera. Its scientific name is *Euplectella*.

12. Name an animal having canal system and spicules. **NCERT Exemplar**

Ans *Scypha* (sycon)/*Leucosolenia*.

13. Name the phylum characterised by collar cells.

Ans Porifera

14. Which common feature is used to classify sponges?

Ans The nature of skeleton.

15. Name the cells that line the spongocoel in *Sycon*.

Ans Choanocytes (collar cells).

16. What is the skeleton of poriferans made of?

Ans Spicules or spongin fibres.

17. **Name the group which lacks digestive tract.**

Ans Porifera.

18. **Why is Coelenterata called Cnidaria?**

Ans Coelenterata is called Cnidaria because of the presence of stinging cells called cnidoblasts or nematoblasts.

19. **Name a Coelenterate found in freshwater habitat.**

Ans *Hydra*

20. **Nematoblasts are characteristic feature of which phylum ?**

Ans Coelenterata

21. **The term 'polyp' and 'medusa' refers to which phylum?**

Ans Cnidaria.

22. **Provide appropriate technical term**
(a) free-floating form of Cnidaria
(b) Stinging organ of jellyfishes **NCERT Exemplar**

Ans (a) Medusa (b) Cnidoblast

23. **Give an example of animal which exhibits alternation of generation.** **NCERT Exemplar**

Ans *Obelia*, shows alternation of asexual and sexual phases in its life cycle.

24. **Which coral is used to make precious jewellery?**

Ans *Corallium nobile* (red coral).

25. **How is mesoglea different in ctenophores than in cnidarians?**

Ans The mesoglea in ctenophores also contains amoebocytes, elastic fibres and muscle cells.

26. **Segmentation in the body is first observed in.**

Ans In Platyhelminthes, true segmentation is absent, instead pseudosegmentation is found. However, true segmentation is first observed in Annelida.

27. **In which group pseudosegmentation occurs? What is it?**

Ans It is found in Platyhelminthes. Pseudosegmentation is the formation of new segments through budding or strobilation.

28. **Why digestive tract of flatworms and coelenterates is called incomplete?**

Ans Because they have single opening both for ingestion and egestion.

29. **Write the scientific name of roundworm.**

Ans *Ascaris lumbricoides.* **NCERT Exemplar**

30. **Name the Aschelminthes in which rhabditiform larva is present.**

Ans *Ascaris* and *Enterobius* (pinworm).

31. **Skeleton is absent in annelids. How their body shape is maintained?**

Ans Skeleton in annelids is absent. Coelomic fluid acts as hydrostatic skeleton, which maintains their body shape.

32. **Provide appropriate technical term for lateral appendages in aquatic annelids.** **NCERT Exemplar**

Ans Parapodia are lateral, unjointed and paired appendages.

33. **What is the difference in blood of annelids and of vertebrates?**

Ans In annelids, haemoglobin is present in plasma, while in vertebrates it is present in RBCs.

34. **What is ecdysis?**

Ans The periodic moulting of chitinous exoskeleton in arthropods is termed as ecdysis.

35. **What is the role of radula in Mollusca?** **NCERT Exemplar**

Ans It is the rasping organ that helps in feeding.

36. **Name a mollusca in which respiration occurs through mantle cavity.**

Ans In *Limax* (slug) and *Helix* (land snail).

37. **Identify the animal in which adults exhibit radial symmetry and larvae exhibit bilateral symmetry.** **NCERT Exemplar**

Ans In Echinodermata, the adults are radially symmetrical and larvae are bilaterally symmetrical.

38. **The presence of proboscis gland is the feature of which phylum?**

Ans Proboscis gland is a excretory organ in hemichordates.

Short Answer Type I Questions

2 Marks

39. **Sponges are filter feeders. How does it take place?**

Ans The tiny food particles are strained out of the water current by the choanocytes which pass them on to the other cells.

These cells ingest food particles and digestion is intracellular. Planktons are the important food source for the filter feeders such as sponges. (2)

40. **How are canals in canal system connect spongocoel to the outside? What is the role of choanocytes in maintaining water flow?**

Ans The canals connect the spongocoel to the outside through ostia and osculum The canals are generally lined by choanocytes. The continuous beating of flagella of choanocytes maintain a steady current of water through the canals. (1+1)

41. Name the types of zooids present in coelenterates. What is this phenomenon called?

Ans Cnidarians have basically two types of zooids, i.e. polyp (cup-shaped) and medusa (umbrella-shaped). This phenomenon is called polymorphism (metagenesis). (1×2)

42. Name the animal, which exhibits the phenomenon of bioluminescence. Mention the phylum to which it belongs? **NCERT Exemplar**

Ans The phenomenon of production and emission of light by an organism as a result of chemical reaction during which chemical energy is converted to light energy is called **bioluminescence**.

Ctenoplana from phylum–Ctenophora, exhibits the phenomenon of bioluminescence. (2)

43. What are the peculiar features that you find in parasitic helminthes? **NCERT**

Ans Parasitic platyhelminthes have a thick cuticle. They lack alimentary canal and absorb the nutrients directly through their body surface. Some parasites are provided with hooks and suckers. (2)

44. What is hydrostatic skeleton?

Ans Hydrostatic skeleton is a system of water-filled spaces that act as turgor operated chambers or valve for movements and pressure points in aschelminths. (2)

45. Define the terms amphids and phasmids found in Aschelminthes.

Ans Amphids are pits commonly having olfactory chemoreceptors.

Phasmids are glandulo-secretory porous sensory structures. (1+1)

46. Correctly match the column I and II. Also give the correct reason **NCERT**

Column I		Column II	
A.	Parapodia	1.	Porifera
B.	Choanocytes	2.	Mollusca
		3.	Annelida

Ans A–3, B–1. Choanocytes or collar cells are characteristic features of Porifera. They take part in ingestion of food, formation and differentiation of sex cells, while parapodia in annelids like *Nereis*, are used for locomotion. (2)

47. Why *Peripatus* is called a connecting link between annelids and arthropods?

Ans **Annelid Characters** *Peripatus* have jointed parapodia (legs) nephridia for excretion and simple gut.

Arthropod Characters *Peripatus* have claws on the legs, haemocoel, trachae for respiration and head with a pair of compound eyes and antennae. (1+1)

48. Provide the appropriate technical term for blood-filled cavity in arthropods and lateral appendages in aquatic annelids.

Ans Blood-filled cavity in arthropods is **haemocoel** and lateral appendages in aquatic annelids are **parapodia**. (1×2)

49. What are the reasons that you could think of for the arthropods to constitute the largest group of animal kingdom? **NCERT**

Ans Arthropods constitute the longest group of animal kingdom due to following reasons

(i) Arthropods have a tough chitinous exoskeleton that gives protection.

(ii) A single ootheca contains a huge number of developing eggs inside it. (1 + 1)

50. Which is the first group of animals that have endocrine system? How pheromones work in insects?

Ans Arthropods are the first animals evolved the endocrine system. Some insects release pheromones that act as sex attractants by which males can locate females even if it is present far away from them. (1+1)

51. Name the respiratory organs of these arthropods.

(i) Prawn
(ii) Cockroach
(iii) Scorpion and spider
(iv) King crab

Ans (i) Prawn–gills
(ii) Cockroach–trachea
(iii) Scorpion and spider–book lungs
(iv) King crab–book gills ($\frac{1}{2}$ × 4)

52. Name a molluscs which has an internal shell and which does not have a shell?

Ans Internal shell– In *Sepia* (cuttle fish), *Loligo* (squid)

Shell absent– *Octopus* (devil fish). (1+1)

53. Mention one example each for animals with chitinous exoskeleton and those covered by a calcareous shell. **NCERT Exemplar**

Ans Every living form maintain a proper shape, size and structure. In multicellular lower organisms the shape of body is maintained by certain biological materials like **chitin** and **calcium substances. Chitinous exoskeleton** is the characteristic feature of arthropods. (e.g. cockroach, termite, wasp), whereas **calcareous shell** is present in molluscs (gastropods, e.g. snail and slugs). (2)

54. Match the column I with column II and choose the correct option **NCERT Exemplar**

	Column I	Column II
A.	Porifera	Canal system
B.	Aschelminthes	Complete alimentary canal and pseudcoelomates.
C.	Annelida	Jointed appendages
D.	Arthropoda	Metameres

Ans A–Canal system, B–Muscular, pharynx, comb plates C– Metameres, D– Jointed appendages

Canal system is a characteristic feature of poriferans; Annelides have metamerically segmented body; Arthropods are characterised by jointed appendaged and Aschelminthes have complete alimantary canal and are pseudocelomates. ($\frac{1}{2} \times 4$)

55. Name the phylum with endoskeleton of calcareous plates, and also mention its one specific feature.

Ans Echinoderms have a endosketeton of calcareous plates called ossicles. Presence of water vascular system is one of their peculiar feature. (2)

56. How the hemichordates differ from echinoderms?

Ans The hemichordates differ from echinoderms in the following ways

(i) They are soft bodied.

(ii) They lack endoskeleton of calcareous plates.

(iii) They have proboscis gland as excretory organ.

(iv) Body is segmented into trunk, collar and proboscis. (2)

Short Answer Type II Questions

3 Marks

57. Write an account on skeleton of sponges.

Ans The body of sponges contains a supporting exoskeleton. It is made up of either spicules or spongin fibres proteinaceous or both.

They are either highly branched or show anastomosis. Spicules are calcareous or siliceous with hard spine-like structures. Depending on the branching, the spicules are

(i) monoaxons (single axis).

(ii) triaxons (three axis forming six rays of hexactinal spicules).

(iii) tetraxons (four rays or tetra actinal).

(iv) polyaxons (several rays). (1+2)

58. What do you understand by alternation of generation in cnidarians?

Ans The cnidarians complete their life cycle through two phases, i.e. asexually reproducing polyp phase sessile and sexually reproducing medusa phase free-living. Those cnidarians which exist in both forms exhibit alternation of generation (metagenesis). (1×3)

59. What are the general characteristics of members of Ctenophora?

Ans Refer to text on page no. 110.

60. Provide appropriate technical term in the space provided. **NCERT Exemplar**

(i) Blood-filled cavity in arthropods ....

(ii) Free-floating form of cnidaria ....

(iii) Stinging organ of jelly fishes ....

Ans (i) **Haemocoel** is the blood-filled cavity in arthropods containing haemolymph.

(ii) **Medusa** is a form in cnidarians in which the body is shaped **like an umbrella** which can float freely in sea water.

(iii) **Nematocytes** are capsules of specialised cells **in cnidarians** which act as a paralysing sting. (1×3)

61. Why the blood vascular system of leeches is also called haemocoelomic system? Write its details.

Ans In leeches, there is no true blood vascular system, the coelomic space and fluid have been modified to form the circulatory system. Hence, it is called haemocoelomic system and the coelomic fluid is called haemocoelomic fluid.

Blood is red due to the presence of respiratory pigment haemoglobin or erythrocyanin found dissolved in the plasma. Free amoeboid blood corpuscles are present, but there are no red blood corpuscles. (3)

62. Why *Limulus* is called living fossil? How does excretion and respiration occur in it? Give its well-labelled diagram.

Ans *Limulus* (the king crab or horse-shoe crab) continues to remain unchanged for past 190 million years. It is therefore, also called living fossil. Excretion occurs through four pairs of coxal glands. Respiration occurs through book gills. For diagram refer to fig. no. 6.17 on page no. 115. (1+1+1)

63. What are the different habitats of molluscs? Give with examples.

Ans Molluscs have diverse habitats

(i) **Marine** *Chiton, Sepia, Octopus.*

(ii) **Freshwater** *Unio* and *Pila.*

(iii) **Terrestrial** Land snails.

(iv) **Parasites** *Glochidium* larva. (3)

64. (i) Why molluscs are considered advanced over annelids?
(ii) Justify that annelids are evolutionary precursors of molluscs.

Ans (i) The molluscs have advancement over annelids, as they have distinct head, better sense organs and gills or lungs for respiration.

(ii) Annelids are considered evolutionary precursors of molluscs as they do not have metameric segmentation.

However, *Neopilina* mollusca a living fossil shows metameric segmentation. Besides, its trochophore larva, it has structural similarities to annelid trochophore larva. These two evidences suggest that molluscs have descended from annelids. (1+2)

65. How arthropods are different from molluscs and animals?

Ans The following characteristic features of arthropods differentiate them from molluscs and annelids
(i) They have a chitinous exoskeleton.
(ii) They have jointed appendages.
(iii) Their body is segmented into head, thorax and abdomen. (1×3)

66. Draw a well-labelled diagram of *Balanoglossus*.

Ans Refer to fig no. 6.23 on page no. 118.

Long Answer Type Questions

5 Marks

67. Describe briefly the body wall of sponges.

Ans The body wall of a common sponge consists of three layers which are
(i) **Pinacoderm** (dermal layer) It is an outer cellular layer which consists of
(a) flattened pinacocytes (b) oval porocytes
(ii) **Choanoderm** (gastral layer) It is inner cellular layer consisting of highly specialised flagellated cells called choanocytes or collar cells.
(iii) **Mesoglial layer** (mesenchyme) It is a non-cellular layer found in between pinacoderm and choanoderm. It has fine dispersed spongin fibres and numerous spicules.
It also contains amoebocytes of both pinacoderm and choanoderm. (1×3)

Amoebocytes are modified into following cells
(a) Archaeocytes (totipotent cells)
(b) Trophocytes (nurse cells)
(c) Thesocytes
(d) Gland cells
(e) Collencytes
(f) Myocytes
(g) Germ cells
(h) Chromocytes
(i) Phagocytes. (2)

68. Differentiate between polyp and medusa.
NCERT Exemplar

Ans Differences between polyp and medusa are

Polyp	Medusa
It is a fixed zooid.	It is free-swimming.
It reproduces asexually.	It reproduces sexually.
It is cylindrical in outline.	Medusa is umbrella-shaped.
Tentacles found at upper end of manubrium.	Tentacles occur along the margin of umbrella.
Mouth is circular and terminal over upright manubrium.	Mouth is four sided, lies at the lower end of hanging manubrium.
Velum and sense organs are absent.	Medusa have a circular velum and eight sense organs or statocysts.

(5)

69. Write an account of general features of roundworms.

Ans General features of roundworms are
(i) The body is cylindrical and tapering at both ends.
(ii) No segmentation.
(iii) Bilateral symmetry.
(iv) They have organ system level of organisation.
(v) The anterior end does not form a distinct head.
(vi) There are no locomotory appendages in roundworms.
(vii) The body wall consists of firm, non-living, resistant cuticle, epidermis and muscle layer.
(viii) These are pseudocoelomates.
(ix) Hydroskeleton is present.
(x) Digestive tract is complete. Respiration occurs by body surface.
(xi) Circulatory system is undeveloped. Excretion occurs through gland cells.
(xii) Sexes are separate. Sexual dimorphism is present. Fertilisation is internal. There is no asexual reproduction.
(xiii) Development is direct. (5)

70. *Pheretima* belongs to which animal phylum? Give some important characteristic features of that phylum.

Ans *Pheretima* belongs to Annelida phylum. For important characteristics of Annelida phylum refer to text on page no. 113.

71. Endoparasites are found inside the host body. Mention the special structure, possessed by these and which enables them to survive in those conditions. **NCERT Exemplar**

Ans The endoparasites such as *Taenia solium* and *Fasciola hepatica* (liver fluke), etc., are found inside the host body, and survive due to the presence of certain characters.

Special characters present in by endoparasites are as folows

(i) The show anaerobic respiration and the gaseous exchange is through general body surface.

(ii) These organisms bear additional organ for the attachment to the host. *Fasciola hepatica* possesses acetabulum or posterior sucker for the attachment. *Taenia solium* posses hooks and suckers for the attachment with the host.

(iii) Reproductive organs are well developed. They are generally, hermaphrodite and self fertilisation is common in them.

(iv) The thick tegument (body covering) is present which is resistant to the host's digestive enzymes and antitoxins.

(v) Absence of locomotary organs.

(vi) Tapeworms lack digestive organs because digested and semidigested food of the host is directly absorbed through their body surface. (5)

72. Enlist the major invertibrate phyla and their respective characteristic feature.

Ans

Porifera	Pinacocytes, choanocytes (collar cells), spongocoel, canal system.
Cnideria	Nematocysts or cnidoblasts and polymorphism.
Ctenophora	Comb plates and bioluminescence.
Platyhelminthes	Acoelomates, flame cells.
Aschelminthes	Pseudocoelomates, sensory Amphids and papillae.
Annelida	True metameric segmentation, hydrostatic skeleton. Respiratory pigment in plasma.
Arthropoda	Jointed appendages and body segmented into head, thorax and abdomen, chitinous exoskeleton.
Mollusca	Calcareous shell on hump, radula, head, muscular foot and visceral hump.
Echinodermata	Water vascular system, endoskeleton of calcareous ossicles.
Hemichordata	Body in divided into proboscis, collar and trunk. Proboscis gland.

(5)

TOPIC 03 Chordata

Animals belonging to phylum–Chordata are fundamentally characterised by the presence of a **notochord**, a **dorsal hollow nerve cord** and **paired pharyngeal gill slits**. These are bilaterally symmetrical, triploblastic, coelomate animals with organ system level of organisation. They possess a post-anal tail and a closed circulatory system.

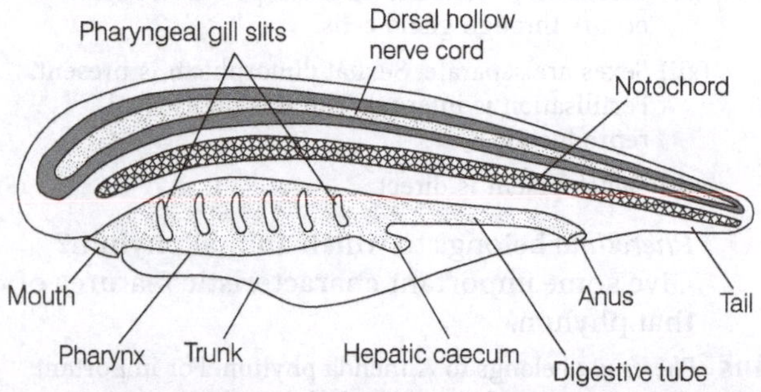

Fig. 6.24. Internal organisation of a chordate

Characteristic Features of Chordata

The following unique features help to distinguish chordates from all other animals of the animal kingdom

(i) **Notochord** It is a solid, rod-like structure present on the dorsal side of the body. It is derived from the mesoderm. Its function is to support and provide surface for attachment of muscles.

(ii) **Nerve Cord** It is a hollow tube-like structure present on the dorsal side of the body. The anterior end becomes brain, while the posterior end forms the spinal cord. It coordinates all the functions of body.

(iii) **Pharyngeal Gill Slits** These are like paired openings formed on the lateral sides of the pharynx that communicate to the exterior.

They are derived from **endoderm.** They help in respiration. These are retained throughout the life in lower chordates and aquatic vertebrates and only during embryonic stage in all other chordates.

(iv) **Post-Anal Tail** It is reduced in some adults and found in majority of chordates. It is a solid, slender structure formed at the posterior end of the body after the anus.

Some Other Important Features of Chordata

Apart from the above mentioned features chordates also possess some other features as given below

(a) A ventral heart and closed circulatory system is present.
(b) Haemoglobin is present in red blood corpuscles.
(c) Hepatic portal system is present.
(d) Digestive system is well-developed.
(e) Excretion occurs through kidney.

Differences between Chordates and Non-Chordates

Chordates	Non-chordates
Notochord is present.	Notochord is not present.
Central nervous system is dorsal, hollow and single.	Central nervous system is ventral, solid and double.
Pharynx perforated by gill slits.	Gill slits are absent.
Heart is ventral.	Heart is dorsal (if present).
Post- anal part (tail) is present.	Post-anal tail is absent.

Classification of Phylum–Chordata

The classification of phylum–Chordata is divided into three subphyla, i.e., Urochordata (Tunicata), Cephalochordata and Vertebrata. Subphyla–Urochordata and Cephalochordata are often referred to as **protochordates** and are exclusively marine. Details of each subphyla and its numerous classes are given below

SubPhylum–Urochordata

The body is covered by a testa (tunic) composed largely of **tunicine**. So, they are commonly called as **tunicates.** The notochord is present only in the tail of the larva and disappears in the adult.

Coelom is absent, digestive tract is complete, respiratory system has two to numerous gill slits in the pharyngeal wall.

Circulatory system is open and has a simple tubular heart. Larva undergoes **retrogressive metamorphosis**, e.g. *Ascidia, Herdmania* (sea squirt), *Salpa, Doliolum.*

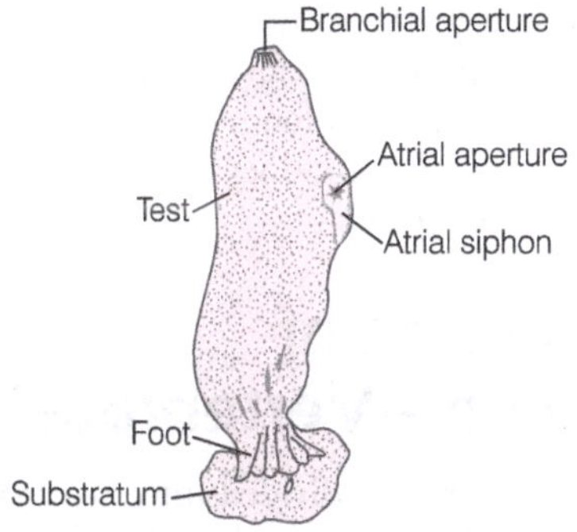

Fig. 6.25 *Ascidia*

Subphylum-Cephalochordata

These are the only protochordates with all four basic chordate characteristics. Their name in itself signifies the presence of notochord in head region.

These are marine animals found in shallow water. They have lance-like pointed body form both ends, so commonly called **sea lancelets.** Body is fish-like, transparent and lacks a head. It is only divisible into trunk and a tail. Paired appendages absent, but fins are present. Notochord is rod-like, extending from head to tail. It persists throughout the life. Digestive tract is complete. Pharyngeal gill slits are more numerous and better developed. No specialised respiratory organs are present. Gaseous exchange is through general body surface. Circulatory system is well-developed and closed. It is without heart and respiratory pigment. Excretion occurs by protonephridia with solenocytes. Sexes are separate (dioecious). Asexual reproduction is absent.

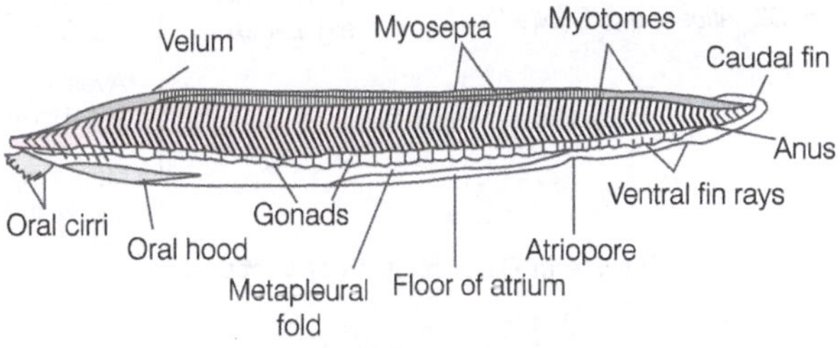

Fig. 6.26 *Amphiouxus*

SubPhylum–Vertebrata

The subphylum–Vertebrata represents **advanced or higher chordates** which include vertebrates or craniates. Notochord is present only in the embryonic stage. In adults, it is replaced by **a vertebral column** consisting of ring-like bones called **vertebrae.**

The anterior part of the notochord is however, replaced by **skull** or **cranium** to protect brain, hence named **Craniata**. Pharyngeal gill slits persist only in adults of lower forms.

Circulatory system is closed type with ventrally situated heart and hepatic portal system. Respiratory pigment haemoglobin is present in blood corpuscles. Excretory organs consist of a pair of kidneys. They are unisexual and lack asexual reproduction.

Classification of SubPhylum–Vertebrata

Subphylum–Vertebrata is divided into two main divisions, i.e. Agnatha (called jawless vertebrata) and Gnathostomata, which is further subdivided into two main superclasses (i.e. Pisces and Tetrapoda). Further, these super class, has 6 main classes. This can be easily predicted by the flowchart given below

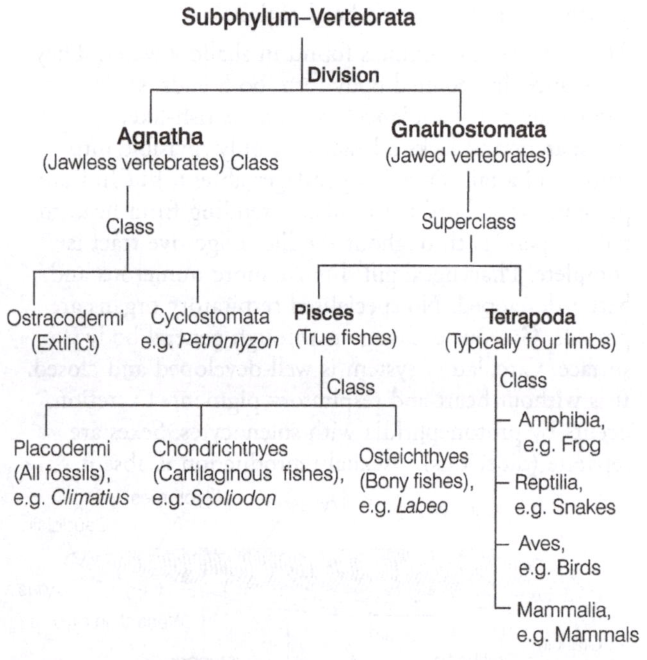

Outline of Classification of Vertabrata

Agnatha (The Jawless Vertebrates)

Agnatha is a paraphyletic super-class of jawless fish. It is the most primitive of all craniates. Mouth is without jaws hence, named as Agnatha. They lack paired appandages, organised pancreas and spleen and bears a single median nostril.

Notochord persists throughout life. Vertebral column is small and imperfectly developed. Animals are without exoskeleton and paired appendages. They are cold blooded (poikilotherms). It includes the extinct class–Ostracodermi and living class–Cyclostomata.

Class–Cyclostomata

Class–Cyclostomata(*Cyklos* – circular; *stome* – mouth) includes the round mouthed fishes. They are also called **jawless fishes** as they have sucking mouth without jaws. They are marine, but show migration to freshwater for spawning. Adult die within few days after spawning but their larvae return to the ocean.

The body of cyclostomes is elongated, smooth has paired fins and are without scales. The cranium and vertebral column are **cartilaginous**. Circulation is of closed type. They have 6-15 pairs of gill slits for respiration, e.g. *Petromyzon* (lamprey), *Myxine* (hagfish).

Note *Petromyzon* is sanguivorous as it sucks blood of fishes, is an ectoparasite. *Myxine* feeds on flesh of dead animals, so it is necrophagous.

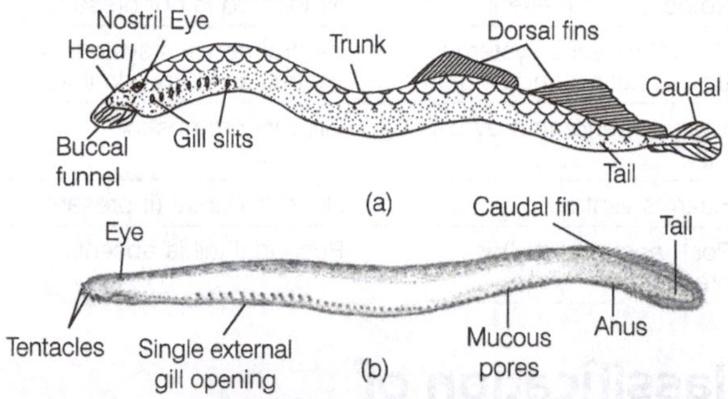

Fig 6.27 Examples of Cyclostomata (a) *Petromyzon* (b) *Myxine* (jawless vertebrate)

Gnathostomata (Jawed Vertebrates)

Gnathostomata includes advanced vertebrates. The notochord is usually replaced by vertebral column. They possess jaws, paired appendages, exoskeleton, paired nares and distinct pancreas and spleen. There are 10-12 pairs of cranial nerves. Olfactory sac is double, internal ear has 3 semicircular ducts.

The gonads are paired and have gonoducts. They appeared in silurian, flourished in carboniferous and became extinct in permean period of Paleozoic era. The Gnathostomata are divided into two superclass–Pisces and Tetrapoda.

Super-Class–Pisces

Super-class–Pisces is considered as true fishes and includes two main classes

1. Class–Chondrichthyes (Cartilaginous Fishes)

Class–Chondrichthyes (*Chondros*-cartilage; *ichthys*– fish) have over 600 species including sharks, rays and skates. They are called **cartilaginous fishes** due to the presence of cartilaginous skeleton.

The distinguishing features of Chondrichthyes are as follows

(i) They are mostly marine called **poikilothermic animals.** They do not have the capacity to regulate their body temperature.

(ii) The body is laterally compressed and **spindle-shaped.**

(iii) **Notochord** is persistent throughout the life.

(iv) Mouth is ventral in position, skin is tough containing minute **placoid scales** and teeth are modified placoid scales. They have strong jaw and are predaceous by nature.

(v) Gill slits are generally five pairs. The gill covering **operculum** are absent.

(vi) Heart is two-chambered with one auricle and one ventricle.

(vii) Air bladders are absent, so they swim constantly to avoid sinking.

(viii) Some of them possess **electric organs** (e.g. *Torpedo*) and some possess **poison sting** (e.g. Trygon).

(ix) Paired and unpaired fins are present, which are not supported by fin rays. The tail fin is always heterocercal (unequal lobes).

(x) They are called **ureotelic animals** as they secrete urea.

(xi) Sexes are separate and fertilisation is internal.

(xii) Males usually have **claspers** on pelvic fins, which help in copulation.

(xiii) Many of them are viviparous, e.g. *Scoliodon* (shark or dog fish), *Carcharodon* (great white shark), *Pristis* (saw fish), *Trygon* (sting ray), *Sphyrna* (hammer-headed shark).

Important Members of Chondrichthyes

Scoliodon

Scoliodon (*Scoliodon dumerili*) is seen in the Bay of Bengal. It is also known as dog fish due to its great sense of smell. It is carnivorous normally found as feeding upon Indian shark, other fishes, crabs, etc. The male can be distinguished from the female, with the help of a pair of hard elongated **claspers** attached to the pelvic fins.

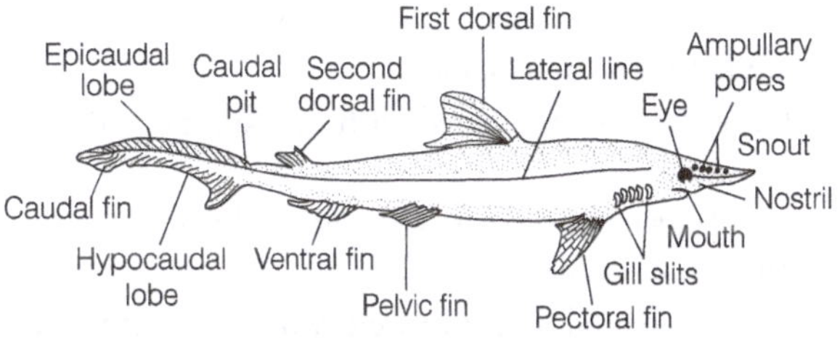

Fig 6.28 *Scoliodon*

Torpedo

Torpedo (electric ray) is a bottom-living marine fish, famous for discharging electricity, which is sufficient enough to stun preys such as small fishes, etc. It is a carnivorous fish with smooth skin (without scales).

The **spiracles** are situated behind the eyes and are used for taking in water for gaseous exchange. Both pectoral fins are fused with the trunk and a pair of **electric organs** (modified bronchial muscle) are situated on the dorsal side of the trunk region.

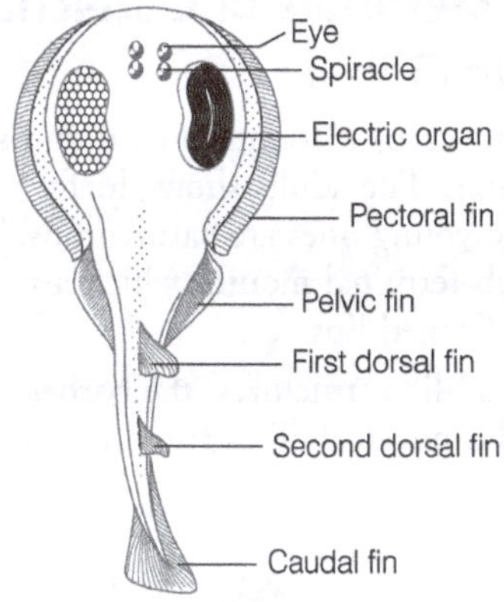

Fig 6.29 *Torpedo* (dorsal view)

2. Class–Osteichthyes (Bony Fishes)

Class–Osteichthyes (*Osteon* – bone; *ichthys* – fish) includes bony fishes such as carps, catfishes, sardines, mackerels, seahorse, etc.

There are about 25000 species of bony fishes found all over the world. They have a bony endoskeleton.

The distinguished features of Osteichthyes are as follows

(i) They are found in marine water as well as in freshwater. They are cold-blooded animals.

(ii) The body is **streamlined** to facilitate swimming easily through water.

(iii) Exoskeleton contains dermal scales like **cycloid** or **ctenoid scales.**

(iv) Gills are covered with **operculum** (gill cover) and are generally four pairs.

(v) Heart is two-chambered with one auricle and one ventricle.

(vi) Air bladders are present. They are the hydrostatic organs and avoids sinking.

(vii) Fins are paired and unpaired, which are supported by fin rays.

(viii) Tail fin is always **homocercal** (equal lobes) or **diphycercal** type.

(ix) These are ammonotelic animals that excrete ammonia.

(x) Sexes are separate. Fertilisation is usually external, mostly viviparous and development is direct. e.g. *Labeo* (rohu), *Mrigal* (carps), *Catla* (catla), *Hippocampus* (seahorse), *Exocoetus* (flying fish), *Remora* (suckerfish), *Anabas* (climbing perch), *Protopterus* (African lung fish).

Important Members of Osteichthyes

Labeo rohita (Rohu)

Labeo rohita (the carp) is found in clear and sluggish rivers and streams. The adults show chiefly herbivorous habit, while the young ones are carnivorous. The scaleless head bears a sub-terminal mouth, which also contains very thick and fringed lips.

Two short thread-like structures, the barbels, are present and the tail is homocercal. This fish serves as a popular edible fish.

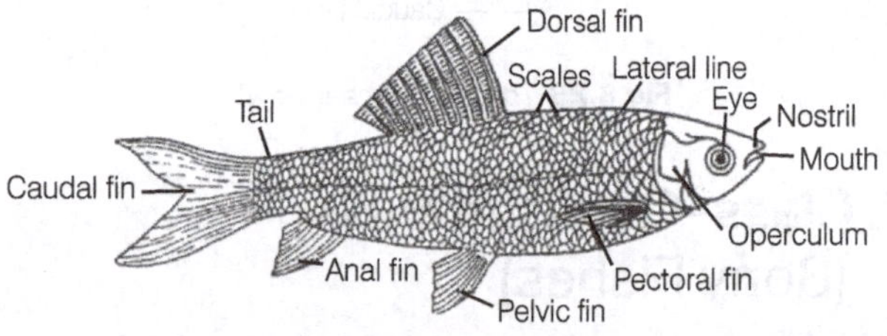

Fig 6.30 *Labeo rohita*

Anabas (Climbing Perch)

It is a common freshwater fish, which can also live out of water for sometime. Outside water, it respires through the accessory respiratory organs lying in front of the gills. It is a carnivorous predatory fish, which is very fond of eating earthworms and often comes out of the ponds in search of them.

Dorsal and anal fins of fish are long and are supported by stiff rays. The climbing perch is a good food fish.

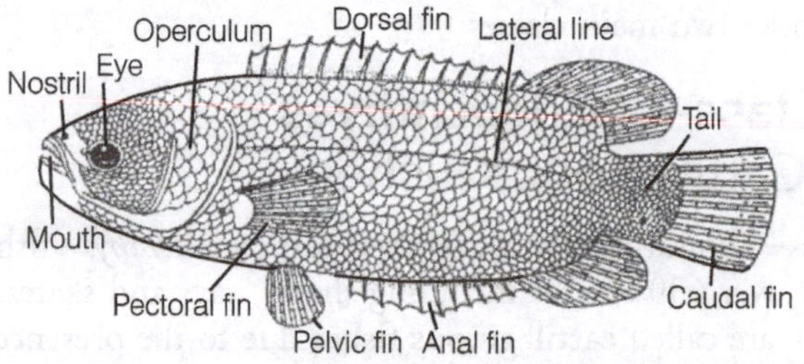

Fig 6.31 *Anabas*

Differences between Chondrichthyes and Osteichthyes

Chondrichthyes (Cartilaginous fishes)	Osteichthyes (Bony fishes)
They are always marine.	They may be marine or fresh water.
Skin is covered by small placoid scales.	Skin is covered with large cycloid or gonoid or ctenoid scales.
Endoskeleton is cartilaginous.	Endoskeleton is partly or wholly bony.
Gill slits are not covered by gill covers.	Gill slits are covered by gill covers.
Mouth is ventral and intestine has scroll valve.	Mouth is anterior and intestine lacks scroll valve.
Swim bladder is absent.	Swim bladder is present.
Tail fin is asymmetrical (heterocercal).	Tail fin is symmetrical (homocercal).
Excretory matter is urea.	Excretory matter is ammonia.
They exhibit sexual dimorphism.	Sexual dimorphism is usually absent.
Mostly viviparous, e.g., sharks, rays, skates.	Usually oviparous, e.g., *Labeo*, *catla*, sea horse.

Super-class–Tetrapoda

Super-class–Tetrapoda is subdivided into four main classes, i.e. Amphibia, Reptilia, Aves and Mammalia. These are given below as

1. Class–Amphibia

The class–Amphibia (*Amphi*–double; *bios*–life) includes about 6771 species. These animals are frogs, toads, salamanders and caecilians. They are the first cold-blooded vertebrates, which ventured to live on land from water. 8The common features of amphibians are

(i) They live in freshwater and on moist land.

(ii) Body is compressed and cylindrical and differentiated into **head** and **trunk.**

(iii) **Nostrils** are connected to the buccal cavity. A pair of external nares for olfaction, a pair of eyes with movable eyelids are present. **Tympanum** represents the ear.

(iv) Skin is mostly smooth, moist, highly vascular and rich in gland. Scales are generally absent. It helps in **cutaneous respiration**.

(v) Amphibians mostly have two pairs of **pentadactyl limbs**. They are used for locomotion.

(vi) Skeleton is bony. Notochord does not persist. Skull is **dicondylic** (i.e., it has two occipital condyles). Most vertebrae are **procoelous**.

(vii) Digestive system is well-developed. Mouth is large and armed with teeth in upper or lower jaw or both the jaws. **Vomarine teeth** also found. Amphibians are first vertebrates, in which **true tongue** is found (a true tongue contains muscles and is protrusible). Alimentary canal leads into **cloaca**.

(viii) Respiration occurs by gills, lungs, lining of **buccopharyngeal cavity** and skin either separately or in combination. Gills are always present in the larvae that may or may not persist in adult stage.

(ix) Heart is three-chambered, with two auricles and one ventricle. **Aortic arches** occur in three pairs. RBCs are oval, biconvex and nucleated.

(x) Kidneys are **mesonephric**. Amphibians are mostly ureotelic.

(xi) Larvae and adult aquatic amphibian show lateral line sensory system.

(xii) Cranial nerves are ten in pairs.

(xiii) Fertilisation is usually external, but sometimes internal as seen in *Salamendra* and *Ichthyophis*.

(xiv) Development is indirect and larval stage called **tadpole.**

(xv) They are oviparous. Adult female lays eggs and the embryo develops inside the eggs.

(xvi) Amphibians undergo **hibernation** in winter and **aestivation** in summer to avoid extremes of temperature, e.g. tail less amphibians are *Rana* (frog), *Bufo* (toad), *Hyla* (tree frog), *Rhacophorus* (flying frog), etc.

Tailed and limbed amphibians are *Salamandra* (salamander), *Amblystoma* (tiger salamander), *Ichthyophis* (limbless amphibian).

Important Members of Amphibia

Salamandra

It is semiterrestrial and oviparous lizard. The male discharges sperms in sperm packet (spermatophore), which is picked up by the female with cloacal lip to fertilise her eggs internally. Egg hatches into tadpole which metamorphose into adults. *S. atra* is **ovaviviparous** (animals produce eggs inside their body, but then give birth to live young). Tail is laterally compressed.

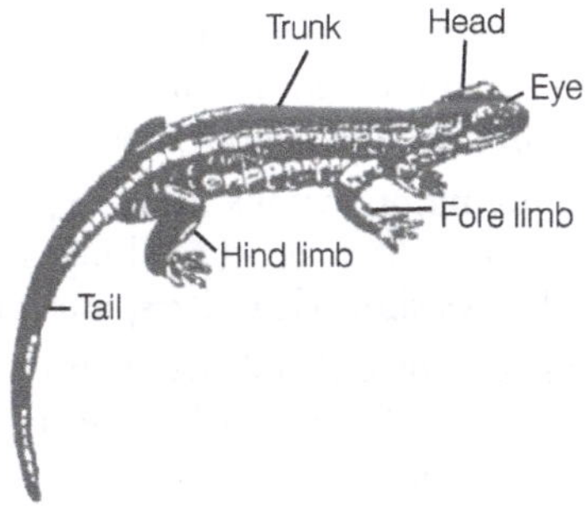

Fig 6.32 *Salamandra*

Ichthyophis

It is a limbless amphibian and feeds underground on worms and insects. It lays eggs in wet burrows and the eggs are guarded by the female.

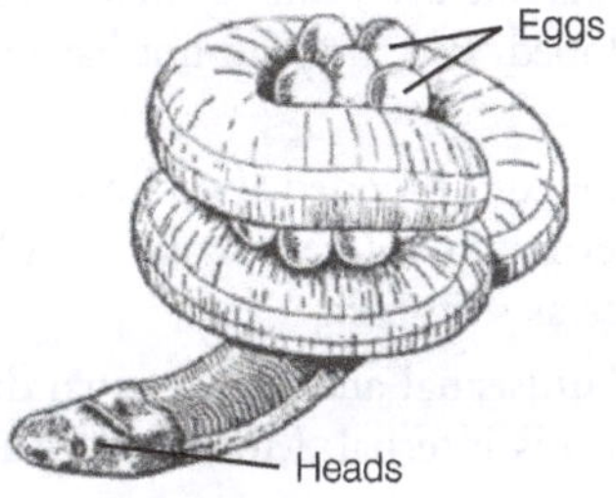

Fig 6.33 *Ichthyophis*

2. Class–Reptilia

The class–Reptilia (*Reptare*, repere or reptum – to creep) includes about 9500 species that include animals like lizards, snakes, turtles, tortoises, crocodiles, etc. Reptiles are the first fully adapted terrestrial animals.

They dominated the earth about 200 millions year ago in the Jurassic period of Mesozoic era, called the **golden age** of reptiles. During this period many huge sized reptiles lived on earth, swarm on water and flew in the air. These fossil reptiles are known as dinosaurs. The largest reptiles of today are **pythons** (10m), **crocodiles** (7m) and **komodo dragon** (3m).

The general features of reptiles are given below

(i) They are terrestrial, a few of them live in water, such as tortoise, crocodile, etc.

(ii) The body may be long, cylindrical or short and broad. It is divisible as head, neck, trunk and tail.

(iii) They have dry, rough and non-glandular skin. It is provided with horny, epidermal **scales** or **scutes**.

(iv) Appendages are of two pairs of pentadactyl limbs with powerful horny claws. Limbs are locomotory organs.

(v) Endoskeleton is bony. Skull is monocondylic for articulation with the vertebral column.

(vi) Digestive system is well-developed. The mouth is large with acrodont teeth in both the jaws. Jaw bones are movable to swallow large prey.

(vii) Lungs are respiratory organs. Ribs help expand and contract body cavity making the lungs more efficient. Turtles show **cloacal respiration**.

(viii) Heart is usually three-chambered with two auricles and one ventricle. The ventricle is incompletely divided by a septum.

The heart is **four-chambered** in **crocodiles**. RBCs are oval, biconvex and nucleated.

(ix) Excretion occurs through kidneys. The land forms release uric acid, while aquatic forms excrete urea.

(x) Nervous system contains 12 pairs of cranial nerves.

(xi) Sense organs like eyes, ears (tympanum) and nose are well-developed. But, they do not have external ear openings.

(xii) Reptiles are cold-blooded (poikilothermic) animals. They hibernate in winter. Snakes and lizards shed their scales as skin cast.

(xiii) These are unisexual and show sexual dimorphism. Fertilisation is internal. Most reptiles are oviparous and some are ovoviviparous, such as vipers, sea snakes, etc.

(xiv) The eggs are retained inside the body of the mother and growing embryos derive shelter and nourishment from the mother.

Development is direct. e.g. *Calotes* (garden lizard), *Draco* (flying lizard), *Chameleon* (arboreal lizard), *Hemidactylus* (wall lizard), *Crocodilus* (crocodile), *Alligator* (alligator), *Sphenodon* (tuatara-the living fossil), *Naja* (cobra), *Bungarus* (krait), *Vipera* (viper).

Important Members of Reptiles

Snakes

The study of snakes is called as **Serpentology**. Sternum, pectoral girdle, tympanum and urinary bladder are absent in snakes. The eyelids are absent but, if present are immovable.

3Nictitating membrane is absent. The tympanic membrane and tympanic cavity are absent. The tongue is long, slender, forked protrusible and sensitive to both odours and vibrations. Post end tail is found is snakes. They produce hissing sound by the forceful expulsion of air from nares.

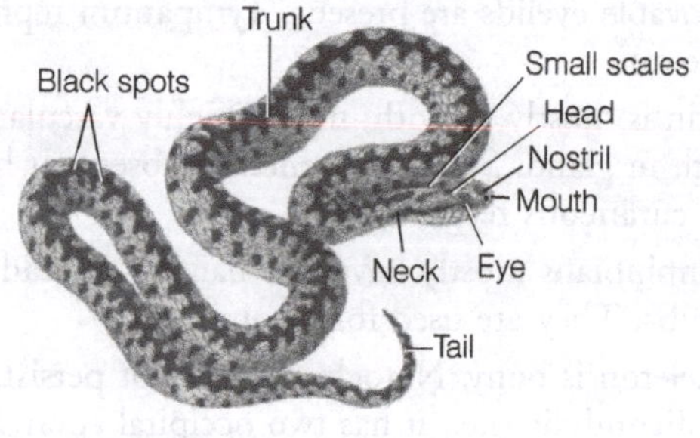

Fig 6.34 *Vipera russelli* (Russel's viper)

Lizard

Lizards are the most typical of the modern reptiles, possessing an elongate body, a long tail and 4 well-developed clawed pentadactyl limbs adapted for running, climbing and digging. The skin is usually covered with small scales. When threatened, they can break off their tail and escape. They are mostly carnivorous, feeding largely on insects, worms and other small animals.

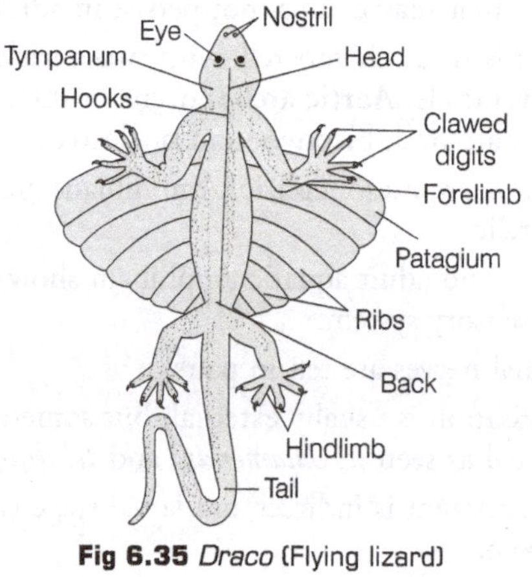

Fig 6.35 *Draco* (Flying lizard)

3. Class–Aves

The class–Aves *(avis* – bird) or flying vertebrates include about 10052 species. An immense variety in birds is found such as parrots, pigeons, crows, ostrich, penguins, ducks, sparrows, kingfishers, etc.

The general features of class–Aves are listed below

(i) Birds have aerial mode of life. They spend most of the time in air (arborrhael). Characteristic feature of aves is the presence of feathers.

(ii) The body is usually streamlined. It is divided into head, neck, trunk and tail.

(iii) Exoskeleton consists of light feathers. It acts as **insulator** and helps in flight. Most of them fly except the flightless birds (e.g. ostrich). The skin is dry without glands except the oil gland, at the base of the tail.

(iv) Endoskeleton is fully ossified (i.e. bony) and is made up of delicate and light bones with air cavities (pneumatic).

(v) Locomotion occurs through wings. They have modified forelimbs into wings. Hindlimbs generally have scales and are modified for walking, swimming or clasping the tree branches.

(vi) The digestive system of birds has additional chambers, the crop and gizzard. Alimentary canal leads into three-chambered cloaca.

(vii) Lungs are respiratory organs, which are spongy, inelastic and are connected to large air sacs. The pharynx is without voice box and voice is produced by special organs called **syrinx** present at the base of trachea.

(viii) Excretory organs are kidneys that are metanephric in adults. Excretory matter is mainly uric acid and urine is semisolid.

(ix) Heart is four-chambered with two auricles and two ventricles. Only right aortic arch persists. Red Blood Corpuscles (RBCs) are oval, biconvex and nucleated.

(x) Birds are warm-blooded or **homeothermal animals**, i.e. they maintain the constant body temperature.

(xi) Nervous system contains 12 pairs of cranial nerves.

(xii) Sexes are separate with sexual dimorphism. Left ovary is present in females, while the right one is absent. Fertilisation is internal.

(xiii) Birds are oviparous. Eggs possess extraembryonic membrane and development is direct.

(xiv) **Cleidoic eggs** are present and are covered by calcareous shell. e.g. **Flight birds**, *Corvus* (crow), *Passer* (sparrow), *Columba* (pigeon), *Psittacula* (parrot), *Anas* (duck), *Pavo* (peacock), *Milvus* (kite), *Neophron* (vulture), etc.

Flightless Birds Emu, Kiwi, Rhea, *Struthio* (ostrich), *Aptenodytes* (penguin), etc.

Note Birds are well-known for their attractive body colours and interesting habits like singing, nest building, parental care and migration.

Knowledge Plus

- Largest bird is *Struthio camelus* (8 feet).
- Smallest bird is *Mellisugo helenae* (5.5 cm long).
- Largest egg laying bird is ostrich (1.5 lit.).
- Fastest runner bird is *Struthio* (ostrich) (30 km/hour).
- Fastest swimmer bird is *Pygoscelis papua* (penguin).

Important Members of Aves

Pigeon

Pigeons occur all over the world except (coldest regions and remote islands). About 250 species are known. All pigeon parents feed their young "pigeon's milk". *Columba livia* have a cluster of neurons used for changing the intensity, direction and polarity of magnetic fields around them.

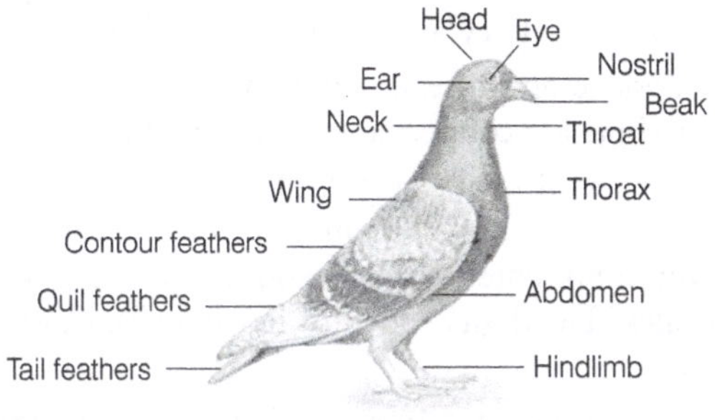

Fig 6.36 *Columba livia* (Pigeon)

Archaeopteryx

It is connecting link between **reptiles** and **birds**.

Some reptilian characters of *Archaeopteryx* are given below

- Jaws are provided with homodont teeth.
- Long lizard like tail with 20 free caudal vertebrae.
- Bones are not pneumatic.
- Cervical vertebrae are fewer 9-19.
- Amphicoelus vertebrae.
- Cervical and abdominal rib are present.
- Scales are present.

Some Avian characters of *Archaeopteryx* are given below

- Presence of feathers.
- Forelimbs are modified as wings.
- Rounded brain case.
- Beaks are present.
- Bones in the skull are intimately fused.
- Bones of limb and girdle are bird like.

4. Class–Mammalia

The class–Mammalia (*Mamma* – breast) includes about 5499 species. The examples of Mammalia are bats, tigers, lions, elephants, whale, rat, rabbits, horses, sheeps, monkeys, etc. The term Mammalia was introduced by **Linnaeus** in 1758.

The general features of class– Mammalia are as follows

(i) Mammals are found in a variety of habitats, such as forests, grasslands, mountains, deserts, polar ice caps, caves, etc. Some of them have adapted to fly or live in water.

(ii) The body is divided into head, neck, trunk and tail.

(iii) The presence of **mammary glands** is the most characteristic feature of mammals. Their number varies from two to many. Mammary glands are well-developed in females.

(iv) Skin in mammals is unique in possessing hair and is covered with **sweat glands** and **sebaceous glands.**

(v) Exoskeleton contains feathers, hairs, fur, nails, claws, horns, hooves, etc. External ear called **pinnae** are present. They are the skin derivatives.

(vi) Endoskeleton possesses skull and vertebrae. Vertebrae are connected by intervertebral discs.

(vii) Two pairs of pentadactyl limbs are present for walking, running, climbing, burrowing, flying and swimming. Forelimbs are modified as flippers in whales. The digits end with horny nails, claws or hoofs.

(viii) Digestive system comprises of complete digestive system. Different types of teeth are present in the jaw.

(ix) Lungs are spongy and elastic. A sound producing organ called **larynx** is also present in mammals.

(x) Heart is four-chambered with two auricles and two ventricles. RBCs are oval, biconcave and enucleated.

(xi) Excretory organs are kidneys. They excrete urea.

(xii) Brain is well-developed with large convoluted cerebrum and cerebellum. 12 pairs of cranial nerves are present.

(xiii) Sense organs are well-developed. Ear comprises of three regions, i.e. internal, middle and external. External opening is protected by a **large fleshy pinna.** Eyes are protected by lids of which upper one is movable.

(xiv) Mammals are unisexual and show prominent sexual dimorphism. Gonads are paired. The testes present in males descend into scrotal sacs. Most of them are viviparous except prototherians.

(xv) Fertilisation is internal. Embryo develops in the uterus.

The foetus is connected to uterine wall through placenta and gets nutrition and respiration. Placenta formation is not found in **prototherians.**

(xvi) Development is direct. Larval stage is not present. They are amniotes, i.e. the embryo develops four embryonic layers during development.

(xvii) They are viviparous generally. Exeption is *Ornithorhynchus* (platypus), which is oviparous. Parental care is highly developed. They feed their young ones on their milk and protect them from enemies, e.g. *Macropus* (kangaroo), *Pteropus* (flying fox), *Camelus* (camel), *Macaca* (monkey), *Rattus* (rat), *Canis* (dog), *Felis* (cat), *Elephas* (elephant), *Equus* (horse), *Delphinus* (common dolphin). *Balaenoptera* (blue whale), *Panthera tigris* (tiger), *Panthera leo* (lion).

Important Members of Mammalia

Blue Whale (*Balaenoptera indica*)

A gregarious marine mammal of large size, which feeds on small fishes, molluscs, crustaceans, etc., including plankton. Whale swims with the help of tail and flippers. It can remain submerged for several minutes. Echolocation sends out a thick cloud of air mixed with water drops to several metres in height. The upper jaw bears a whale bone, consisting of two rows of 600-800 plates. This bone acts as a strainer. It is hunted for its blubber.

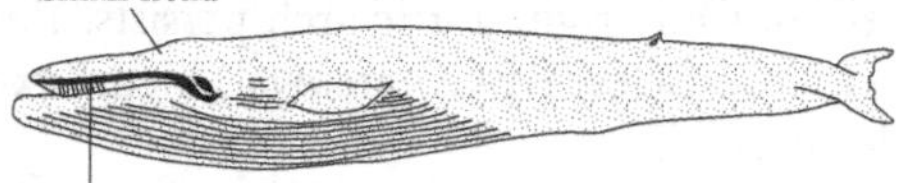

Fig 6.37 Blue whale

Duck-Billed Platypus (*Ornithorhynchus anatinus*)

It is a semi-aquatic prototherian found in Tasmania, Australia, lives in burrows on the banks of river and streams. The animal has a broad bill or beak, teeth only in the young stage, flat tail, webbed and clawed digits. Females possess mammary glands, but teats or nipples are absent. It is connecting link between reptiles and mammals.

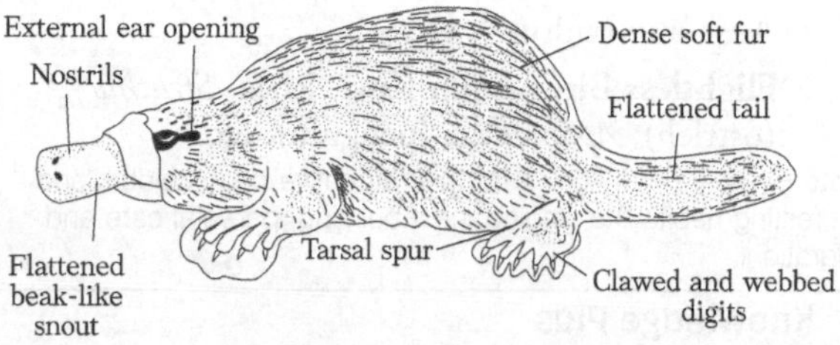

Fig 6.38 Duck-billed platypus

Salient Features of Different Phyla in the Animal Kingdom

Phylum	Level of Organisation	Symmetry	Coelom	Segmentation	Digestive System	Circulatory System	Respiratory System	Distinctive Features
Porifera	Cellular	Various	Absent	Absent	Absent	Absent	Absent	Body with pores and canals in walls.
Coelenterata (Cnidaria)	Tissue	Radial	Absent	Absent	Incomplete	Absent	Absent	Cnidoblasts present.
Ctenophora	Tissue	Radial	Absent	Absent	Incomplete	Absent	Absent	Comb plates for locomotion.
Platyhelminthes	Organ and Organ system	Bilateral	Absent	Absent	Incomplete	Absent	Absent	Flat body suckers.
Aschelminthes	Organ system	Bilateral	Pseudo coelomate	Absent	Complete	Absent	Absent	Often worm-shaped, elongated.
Annelida	Organ system	Bilateral	Coelomate	Present	Complete	Present	Absent	Body segmentation like rings.
Arthropoda	Organ system	Bilateral	Coelomate	Present	Complete	Present	Present	Exoskeleton of cuticle, jointed appendages.
Mollusca	Organ system	Bilateral	Coelomate	Absent	Complete	Present	Present	External skeleton of shell is usually present.
Echinodermata	Organ system	Radial	Coelomate	Absent	Complete	Present	Present	Water vascular system, radial symmetry.
Hemichordata	Organ system	Bilateral	Coelomate	Absent	Complete	Present	Present	Worm-like with proboscis, collar and trunk.
Chordata	Organ system	Bilateral	Coelomate	Present	Complete	Present	Present	Notochord, dor-sal hollow nerve cord, gill slits with limbs or fins.

Topic Practice 3

Multiple Choice Questions

(1 Mark)

1. A jawless fish, which lays eggs in freshwater and whose ammocoetes larvae after metamorphosis return to the ocean is
   (a) *Eptatratus* (b) *Myxine*
   (c) *Neomyxine* (d) *Petromyzon*

Ans. (d) *Petromyzon* (the lamprey) belongs to the section Agnatha of the subphylum–Vertebrata. They lay eggs in freshwater, but their ammocoete larvae (lower) after metamorphosis return to the ocean.

2. Which statement is incorrect for animals belonging to class of Chondrichthyes?
   (a) The presence of placoid scales
   (b) The absence of air bladder
   (c) The presence of cartilaginous endoskeleton
   (d) Notochord is persistent only at larval stage, after that it disappears

Ans. (d) Animals belonging to class–Chondrichthyes are named, so because of the presence of cartilaginous endoskeleton. They lack air bladder thus, swim constantly and have placoid scales. Notochord is persistent throughout their life.

3. Which one of the following animals have both exoskeletal and endoskeletal structures?
   (a) Freshwater mussel (b) Tortoise
   (c) Frog (d) Jellyfish

Ans. (b) In tortoise (*Testudo*), member of class–Reptilia and phylum–Chordata, both exoskeleton and endoskeleton are found.

4. Which of the following sets of derivatives of integumentary structures characterise birds, as glorified reptiles?
(a) Scales and claws
(b) Syrinx and uropygial gland
(c) Claws and uropygial gland
(d) Syrinx and scales

Ans. (a) The presence of scales and claws are important characters of reptiles.

5. Which features are common to the animals belonging to class–Amphibia and class–Reptilia?
(a) the presence of scales with internal fertilisation and usually four-chambered heart
(b) the presence of tympanum, poikilotherms and usually three-chambered heart
(c) the presence of cloaca, oviparous and external fertilisation
(d) skin is moist

Ans. (b) Class–Amphibia and Reptilia share the following features. The presence of tympanum is seen in both classes, which represents the ear. Animals of both classes are cold-blooded or poikilotherms and usually have a three-chambered heart with the exception of a crocodile.

6. The unique character of animals belonging to class–Mammalia is
(a) bipedal locomotion
(b) completely four-chambered heart
(c) the presence of mammary glands
(d) fertilisation is internal

Ans. (c) Mammalia is the only class, which bears mammary glands. It is a unique characteristic among the members of this class, but four-chambered heart and internal fertilisation found in the members of class–Mammalia is also observed in Aves.

7. Select the correct set of animals of true mammals.
(a) Lion, *Hippopotamus*, penguin, bat
(b) Lion, bat, whale, ostrich
(c) *Hippopotamus*, penguin, whale, chelone
(d) Whale, flying fox, kangaroo, *Hippopotamus*

Ans. (d) Penguin and ostrich are not mammals, while whale, flying fox, bat, kangaroo, *Hippopotamus* are mammals.

8. Which one of the following is not a mammalian character without exception?
(a) The presence of milk producing gland
(b) They have two pairs of limbs
(c) Skin is unique in possessing hairs
(d) Heterodent type of dentition

Ans. (a) The presence of milk poducing gland-mammary glands is characteristic feature of mammals without and exception.

9. Vivipary is characteristically found in
(a) Coelenterata (b) Protozoa
(c) Rabbit (d) Pisces

Ans. (c) An animal, whose female gives birth to young one is called viviparous and this phenomenon as vivipary, e.g. rabbit, dog, humans, etc.

10. Choose the correct statement.
(a) All mammals are viviparous
(b) All cyclostomes do not possess jaw and paired fins
(c) All reptiles have a three-chambered heart
(d) All pisces have gills covered by an operculum

Ans. (b) Cyclostomata is a class belonging to section Agnatha of subphylum–Vertebrata. It is a paraphytelic superclass of jawless fishes. They lack paired fins too. Thus, option (b) is correct.

Very Short Answer Type Questions

1 Mark

11. Which organism acts as connecting link between the non-chordates and chordates?

Ans. *Balanoglossus* of phylum-Hemichordata.

12. Write the example of urochordates.

Ans. *Herdmania, Salpa, Doliolum, Ascidia, Oikopleura,* etc.

13. Why are urochordates called tunicates?

Ans. This is because the soft body of urochordates is surrounded by a thick test or tunic, often transparent or translucent.

14. Which structure replaces notochord in vertebrates?

Ans. Vertebral column.

15. Write few common features of all the vertebrates.

Ans. Few common features of all vertebrates are
(i) Organ system organisation.
(ii) Bilateral symmetry.
(iii) Triploblastic germ layers. (Any two)

16. What kind of body scales are present in bony fishes?

Ans. Ctenoid or cycloid scales.

17. How important is the presence of air bladder in Pisces? **NCERT**

Ans. In fishes, air bladder regulates buoyancy and helps them in floating in water. If it is absent, animals need to swim constantly to avoid sinking.

18. Why the heart of fishes is commonly called 'the venous heart'?

Ans. This is because it supplies deoxygenated blood to gills for oxygenation and lacks double circulation also there is mixing of oxygenated and deoxygenated blood in heart.

19. Why the caudal fin in bony fishes is called as homocercal type?

Ans. This is because caudal fin has equal lobes.

20. Why is lateral line sensory system present in Pisces?

Ans. It is used by fishes to note the changes in surrounding water.

21. In which fishes cartilaginous skeleton is present?

Ans. Chondrichthyes.

22. Give an example of

(i) limbless reptile/amphibian

(ii) an oviparous mammal

Ans. (i) Limbless reptile—Snake
Limbless amphibian—*Ichthyophis*

(ii) Oviparous mammal—Duck-billed platypus

23. Which amphibians show branchial (gills) respiration?

Ans. Young ones of most of the amphibians which are aquatic show branchial respiration.

24. Which amphibian carries its young on its back?

Ans. Surinam toad (*Pipa*)

25. How many living species are present in class – Reptilia?

Ans. About 6000.

26. Why pneumatic bones are present in birds?

Ans. The empty space in pneumatic bones helps in weight reduction of skeleton in birds. It is a kind of flight adaptation in birds.

27. What is the importance of pneumatic bones and air sacs in Aves? **NCERT Exemplar**

Ans. (i) Pneumatic bones are light, but strong. This feature helps birds in flight.

(ii) Air sacs increase the efficiency of respiration and provide sufficient oxygen to the animal.

28. Birds have no teeth, then how do they grind the grains they eat as food?

Ans. Birds have food storing crop and food masticating gizzard, which helps them to grind the food.

29. Write the scientific name of a flightless bird and an oviparous mammal.

Ans. ***Struthio*** (ostrich-a flightless bird) and ***Ornithorhynchus*** (platypus-an egg laying mammal).

30. Homeothermy is common feature of which of the class of chordates?

Ans. Homeothermy is common feature of Aves and mammals.

31. Which mammals are oviparous?

Ans. *Tachyglossus* (spiny anteater) and *Ornithorhynchus* (duck platypus).

32. Write two unique features of mammals.

Ans. Mammals are unique due to following features

(i) Presence of milk producing mammary glands in females.

(ii) Hairs present on the whole body.

33. Give example of two unisexual animals.

Ans. Frog and birds.

Short Answer Type I Questions

(2 Marks)

34. All vertebrates are chordates, but all chordates are not vertebrates. Justify the statement.

Ans. All chordates have a notochord, but only in vertebrate the vertebral column develops from notochord, so all chordates are not vertebrates.

All vertebrates are chordates as they have notochord in embryonic stage. **(2)**

35. Which group of chordates possess sucking and circular mouth without jaws? **NCERT Exemplar**

Ans. Class–Cyclostomata is comprised of, the living jawless fishes. Their mouth is circular and lack jaws, hence they are also called agnathans.

It works like a sucker and is surrounded by tentacles (e.g. lampreys and hagfish). These also prosses rectroctable horny teeth. (2)

36. List out some freshwater and some marine bony fishes.

Ans. **Freshwater bony fishes** *Labeo rohita, Catla catla, Cirrhina mrigala, Cyprio corpio.*

Marine bony fishes *Hilsa, Harpodon, Stromateus.* (1+1)

37. What kind of exoskeleton is present in the members of class–Osteichthyes?

Ans. In the members of Osteichthyes (bony fishes) skin is covered by exoskeleton made up of large cycloid scales impermeable to water.

They reduce osmotic water loss in marine environment and entry of water in fresh environment. (2)

38. Which special features help fishes to sense their environment?

Ans. Fishes have following sense organs to sense their external environment.

(i) Ear is formed of only one internal ear having three semicircular canals.

(ii) Olfactory sacs (nasal chambers) do not open in buccal cavity as internal nares are absent.

(iii) Lateral line sensory system is present to note the thermal changes in surrounding water. (2)

39. Give one example each for an animal possessing placoid scales and that with cycloid scales. **NCERT Exemplar**

Ans. Fishes possess dermal scales, each scale made of dentine that is secreted by dermal papilla.

Placoid scales are hard and microscopic in size, their body is made up of dentine and exposed surface is covered with enamel. Cycloid scales are strong and extremely flexible.

They are large, oval and made up of isopectine (layer of collagenous fibre). Placoid scales are the characteristic features of cartilaginous fishes. (e.g. *Scoliodon*). Whereas, cycloid scale are found in bony fishes (e.g. *Catla catla*). (2)

40. How will you differentiate between the heart of an amphibian and a reptile?

Ans. In both amphibians and reptiles, heart is three-chambered with two auricles and one ventricle. Ventricle is unpartitioned in the amphibians, while it is incompletely partitioned in the reptiles. (2)

41. Mention two modifications in reptiles required for terrestrial mode of life. **NCERT Exemplar**

Ans. There are certain characters acquired by reptiles for the terrestrial adaptations.

Two of then are

(i) Their body is covered by dry and cornified skin and epidermal scales or scutes.

(ii) Fertilisation is internal. (1+1)

42. List two terrestrial adaptations of reptiles.

Ans. Terrestrial adaptations of reptiles are mentioned below

(i) Epidermal scales forming exoskeleton.

(ii) Shelled and cledoic egg. (1×2)

43. Justify 'snakes have strong sense of smell'.

Ans. Snakes have strong sense of smell because, their forked tongue is frequently linked to pick up smell bearing molecules from the air or ground and are inserted with special sense organs called Jacobson's organs in the roof of the mouth to identify the smell. (2)

44. How do the appendages support the bird's body?

Ans. Birds have two pairs of limbs, forelimbs are modified into wings for flight. The wings are powered by the powerful flight or breast muscles attached to the large sternum of breast bone.

Hindlimbs support the body and used for grasping, perching, wading and swimming. (2)

45. Why birds are called warm-blooded animals? How does this help them?

Ans. Birds are warm-blooded or homeothermal animals as they are able to maintain constant body temperature. This helps them to maintain high metabolic rate for quick energy supply required for flight. (1+1)

46. Describe the respiratory system of birds.

Ans. Birds respire through lungs (pulmonary respiration). The lungs have air sacs which help in respiration and act as an internal cooling agents. Sound producing organ is syrinx (at the base of trachea) and larynx has no vocal cords. (2)

47. What is the role of feathers? **NCERT Exemplar**

Ans. Feathers are the epidermal growth that forms distinctive outer covering or plumage in birds.

Feathers play a variety of roles like

(i) They help in creating airfoil shape for wings so, as to provide lift and help in flight.

(ii) Feathers helps in maintaining body temperature.

(iii) Feathers play a vital role in mating by providing secondary sex characters in both the sexes the colour and markings determine the attractiveness of mate. (2)

48. Why mammals are considered more intelligent as compared to other animals?

Ans. In mammals, brain is well-developed with large sized cerebrum, four optic lobes and a neural band called corpus callosum. Grey matter is more developed which makes them more intelligent among all other animals. (2)

49. Name the following

(i) Limbless animal

(ii) Cold-blooded animal

(iii) Warm-blooded animal

(iv) Dry cornified skin. **NCERT Exemplar**

Ans.

(i)	Limbless animal	Snake (reptile), *Ichthyophis* (amphibian)
(ii)	Cold-blooded animal	Frog, wall lizard
(iii)	Warm-blooded animal	Pigeon
(iv)	Dry cornified skin	*Chameleon*

(½ × 4)

50. Match the following columns.

	Column-I		Column-II
A.	Amphibia	1.	Air bladder
B.	Mammals	2.	Cartilaginous notochord
C.	Chondrichthyes	3.	Mammary gland
D.	Osteichthyes	4.	Dual habitat

NCERT Exemplar

Ans. A–4, B–3, C–2, D–1, Amphibians can survive on land as well as in water, mammals bear mammary glands; Chondrichthyes are characterised by cartilagenous notochord; Osteichthyes are characterised by air bladder. (½ × 4)

51. There has been an increase in the number of chambers in heart during evolution of vertebrates. Give the name of the class of vertebrates having two, three or four-chambered heart. **NCERT Exemplar**

Ans. (i) **Two-chambered heart**—Pisces

(ii) **Three-chambered heart**—Amphibians and reptiles except crocodiles

(iii) **Four-chambered heart**—Crocodiles, Aves and Mammalia. (2)

Short Answer Type II Questions

(3 Marks)

52. Differentiate between notochord and nerve cord. **NCERT Exemplar**

Ans. Differences between notochord and nerve cord are as follows

Notochord	Nerve cord
It is a solid ensheathed dorsal rod of large cartilaginous tissue.	It is a bundle of nerve fibres with chains of ganglia, generally running ventrally.
It occurs in chordates.	It occurs in invertebrates.
It provides support and point of attachment to muscles.	It gives rise to peripheral nerves.
In vertebrates, it forms the axial skeleton.	It forms a major part of nervous system.

(3)

53. List out any six general features of cartilaginous fishes.

Ans. Features of cartilaginous fishes

(i) Cartilaginous endoskeleton is present.

(ii) These are mostly marine, poikilothermic animals.

(iii) Notochord is persistent throughout the life.

(iv) Placoid scales are present.

(v) Heart is two-chambered with one auricle and one ventrical.

(vi) Tail fin is always heterocercal. (½ × 6)

54. How many species are present in class Amphibia? Make a list of its members. What may be the reason that they are partially successful although they can also live on land?

Ans. The class Amphibia includes about 6771 species. It includes animals like frogs, toads, salamanders and caecilians.

They were the first group of vertebrates that have ventured to live on land from water. They were partially successful as the adults have to return back to water for reproduction. (3)

55. Distinguish between lizards and snakes.

Ans. Differences between lizard and snakes are

Lizards	Snakes
Two pairs of limbs are present.	Limbs are absent.
Scales are of uniform size.	Scales are differentiated into plates and shields.
Eyelids are movable.	Eyelids are immovable.
Nictitating membrane is present.	Absent.
Tongue is not bifid.	It is protrusible and bifid.
Urinary bladder is present.	It is absent.
Jaw bones are fixed.	These are movable.

(3)

56. What flight adaptations are present in birds?

Or

What are the modifications observed in birds that help them to fly? **NCERT**

Ans. Flight adaptations found in birds

(i) Body is streamlined to reduce air resistance during flight.

(ii) Forelimbs are modified into wings.

(iii) Wings have long quill feathers to increase the efficiency of beating of wings.

(iv) Pneumatic bones are present to reduce the body weight.

(v) High metabolic rate to provide energy for flight.

(vi) Air sacs present in lungs help in respiration. (½ × 6)

57. Could the number of eggs or young ones produced by an oviparous and viviparous mother be equal. Why? **NCERT**

Ans. An oviparous animal always produces more number of eggs than the young ones produced by a viviparous animal. This is because their eggs are exposed to external environment and predators and they have to pass through a large number of developmental stages before becoming an adult. Hence, they face less chances of survival than the foetus developing inside the mother's body. The large number of eggs compensates the inevitable loss and ensures the continuation of race. (3)

58. Mention two similarities between
(i) Aves and mammals (ii) A frog and crocodile
(iii) A turtle and *Pila* **NCERT Exemplar**

Ans. (i) Aves and mammals are homeothermal and have extra embryonic membranes.

(ii) Frog and crocodile are cold-blooded and are tetrapods.

(iii) A turtle and *Pila* have hard covering over the body and are cold-blooded animals. (1×3)

59. Write the types of following structures in mammals
(i) Kidneys (ii) Fertilisation
(iii) RBCs (iv) Brain
(v) Parental care (vi) Sexual dimorphism

Ans.

(i) Kidneys	Metanephric
(ii) Fertilisation	Internal
(iii) RBCs	Small, circular and non-nucleated
(iv) Brain	Highly developed
(v) Parental care	Well-developed
(vi) Sexual dimorphism	Well-marked

(1½ × 6)

60. Give an example for each of the following **NCERT Exemplar**
(a) A viviparous animal
(b) A fish possessing a poison sting
(c) A fish possessing an electric organ
(d) An organ, which regulates buoyancy
(e) Animal, which exhibits alternation of generation
(f) Oviparous animal with mammary gland

Ans. (a) A viviparous animal is the one in which development of young ones is direct, later they provides nutrition to their offspring. It includes all mammals, except Platypus.

(b) A fish possessing a poison sting is *Trygon* (sting-ray). It is found on its tail. The poison released is strong enough to stun an animal.

(c) A fish possessing an electric organ *Torpedo* (electric ray). Electric organ in *Torpedo* is located in its big round pectoral fin which is just behind the *Torpedo* can generate a fish killing current of up to 200 volts.

(d) An organ, which regulates buoyancy is air bladder present in class–Osteichthyes (e.g. *Exocoetus, Catla*).

(e) Animal exhibiting alteration of generation is *Aurelia* or jelly fish of phylum–Cnidaria. It has two basic body forms called polyp and medusa are present. Polyp is sessile and cylindrical whereas medusa is umbrella-shaped and free-swimming form. Polyp produces medusa asexually and medusa forms polyps sexually (e.g., *Obelia).*

(f) Oviparous animal with mammary gland is *Ornithorhynchus* (duck-billed platypes). Duck bill platypus is the only mammal which lays egg and also bear mammary gland, which is a characteristic feature of mammals. (½ × 6)

Long Answer Type Questions

5 Marks

61. Give the characteristic features of the following citing one example of each **NCERT Exemplar**
(a) Chondrichthyes and ostichthyes
(b) Urochordata and cephalochordata

Ans. Characteristic features of different classes mentioned are as follows

(a) **Chondrichthyes**

(i) These are marine animals with a streamlined body.
(ii) Body is has cartilaginous exoskeleton and the skin is tough due to the presence of minute placoid scales.
(iii) These animals are predaceous.
(iv) Due to the absence of air bladder they have to swim constantly to avoid sinking.
(v) They are cold-blooded animals, e.g. *Scoliodon* (dog fish), *Pristis* (saw fish).
(vi) Some of them possess electric organs and poison sting, e.g. *Torpedo* and *Trygon.*

Osteichthyes

(i) These animals are found in both habitats, i.e. marine and freshwater. They bear bony endoskeleton.
(ii) Body is streamlined, posseses four pairs of gills covered by an operculum, on each side.
(iii) Skin is covered by cycloid or ctenoid scales.
(iv) Presence of air bladder is an additional feature providing buoyancy to animal.
(v) Heart is two chambered.
(vi) Sexes are seperate, fertilisation usually external, oviparous animal with direct development.

e.g. marine- *Exocoetus* (flying fish), *Hippocampus* (sea horse); freshwater- *Labeo* (rohu). (2½)

(b) **Urochordata**

(i) In urochordates, notochord is only present in larval tail.
(ii) They contain a tough outer covering called tunic.
(iii) Persence of pharyngeal slits during some stage of the life cycle and a muscular, post anal tail is the characteristic features in urochordates.

e.g. *Salpa, Ascidia, Doliolum.*

Cephalochordata

(i) Cephalochordates are exclusively marine animals.

(ii) The notochord in cephalochordates extends, from the heart to tail region and is persistent throughout the life.

(iii) Body-wall shows one cell thick, non-ciliated epidermis, connective tissue, striated muscle and parietal peritonium.

(iv) Fertilisation is external. e.g. *Branchiostoma* (*Amphioxus* or *Lancelet*). (2½)

62. (i) List out some flightless birds.

(ii) Describe briefly any four with their important features.

(iii) Write the name of any two extinct flightless birds.

Ans. (i) The flightless birds are ostrich, rhea, kiwi, penguin, cassowary, emu and Island rail. (1)

(ii) (a) **Ostrich** (*Struthio*) is the largest living flightless bird also called as Shutarmurg (in Hindi). It has largest eyes of any land animal.

It swallows small stones to aid their digestion of vegetable matter.

It can run at the speed to 60 km/hr. Ostrich lays the largest egg produced by any living bird. It is commonly found in deserts of Africa and Arabia.

(b) **Rhea** is smaller than ostrich but similar to it in many habits. Its head and neck are feathered not naked as in ostrich. It is found in South America.

(c) **Emu** (*Dromaius*) is the second largest living bird. It is confined to Australia.

(d) **Kiwi** (*Apteryx*) has most sensitive beak among birds. It can detect worms in the ground. It lays largest egg in proportion to its own size. It is the New Zealand's Emblem bird. (3)

(iii) Extinct flightless birds are

(a) Dodo of Mauritius became extinct in 1681.

(b) Moais of New Zealand. (1)

63. Which features make mammals as most successful and dominant animals?

Ans. Features which make mammals as dominant and successful animals are

(i) The presence of an insulating and protective hairy exoskeleton.

(ii) They are warm-blooded, so have high rate of metabolism.

(iii) They are viviparous animals and show placentation and intrauterine development which increases the chances for survival of young ones.

(iv) They show high degree of parental care.

(v) They have more developed hearing efficiency due to the presence of pinna, three ear-ossicles and coiled cochlea in the ear.

(vi) They are able to speak through indicative/verbal language.

(vii) They have good power of learning due to the presence of more developed brain. (5)

SUMMARY

- The **kingdom–Animalia** is characterised by heterotrophic eukaryotic organisms that are multicellular and their cell lack cell wall.
- In animals certain fundamental features are common to various individuals, which forms the basis of their classification.
- **Level of organisation** also called grades of arrangement cellular level (poriferans), tissue level (coelenterates and ctenophores), tissue organ level (Platyhelminthes) and organ system level (Aschelminthes to chordates).
- **Body symmetry** asymmetric (sponges), radially symmetric (some sponges, coelenterates, ctenophorans and adult echinoderms), bilaterally symmetric (Platyhelminthes to chordates).
- **Germ layers** diploblastic (sponges and coelentrates) and triploblastic (Platyhelminthes to chordates).
- **Body plan** cell aggregate (sponges), blind sac (coelenterates to Platyhelminthes) and tube within a tube (Aschelminthes onwards).
- **Body cavity or Coelom** refers to a large fluid filled space lined by mesoderm. On the basis of the presence or absence of this coelom animals are acoelomates (sponges to Platyhelminthes), pseudocoelomates (Aschelminthes) and eucoelomates (with true coelom like in annelides to chordates).
- **Segmentation** is the serial repetition of similar parts along the length of an animal. According to this animals can be unsegmented (poriferans to roundworms Echinodermata and Mollusca) and metamerically segmented (annelids segmented arthropods to chordates).
- **Notochord** is mesodermally derived rod-like structure formed during embryonic development in some animals, which are thus called chordates. Animals without notochord, i.e. poriferans to hemichordates are called non-chordates.
- **Phylum–Porifera** is a group of animals commonly called as sponges. They are generally marine and mostly asymmetrical animals, having cellular level of body organisation.
- These have a water transport system or canal system.
- The body of sponges is supported by a skeleton made up of **spicules** or **spongin fibres**. These are **hermaphrodite**, i.e. sexes are not separate in them. Fertilisation is internal and development is indirect through larval stages, like amphiblastula (in *Sycon*) and parenchymula (in *Leucosolenia*).
- **Phylum–Coelenterata** or **Cnidaria** consists of diploblastic, aquatic and radially symmetrical animals with cellular tissue level of body organisation.
- They have characteristic cells called **cnidoblasts** or **cnidocytes** (which contain stinging capsules or nematocytes) present on the tentacles and the body.
- Cnidarians exhibit two basic body forms called **polyp** and **medusa**.
- Those cnidarians which exist in both forms exhibit alternation of generations (metagenesis), i.e. polyp produces. medusae asexually and medusae form the polyps sexually (e.g. *Obelia*). Some of cnidarians, namely **corals** have a skeleton composed of calcium carbonate.
- **Phylum–Ctenophora** are marine, radially symmetrical, diploblastic organisms with tissue level of organisation. There body bears eight external rows of ciliated **comb plates**, which help in locomotion. They are also called **comb-jellies** and **sea walnuts**.
- The presence of a special sense organ 'statocyst' at the opposite end of the mouth is the characteristic feature of this phylum. These are hermaphrodite and reproduction takes place only by sexual means. The property of bioluminescence is well-marked in ctenophores, e.g. *Pleurobrachia, Beroe*, etc.
- **Phylum–Platyhelminthes** includes animals having dorsoventrally flattened bodies, hence commonly known as **flatworms**. These are primitive, bilaterally symmetrical, triploblastic and acoelomate animals with organ level of organisation.
- These are mostly endoparasites found in animals including humans, with hooks and suckers is the characteristic feature in the parasitic form like *Taenia* (tapeworm), *Fasciola* (liver fluke), etc.
- Platyhelminthes have specialised cells which help in excretion as well as osmoregulation in them. These are called **flame cells** or **solenocytes** or **protonephridia**.
- The life cycle of parasitic form involves more than one larval forms within the life cycle of one individual and paedogenesis, i.e. larval forms with the power of reproduction.
- *Fasciola hepatica* is a digenetic parasite. It completes its life cycle in two hosts, i.e primary (liver of sheep) and intermediate host (snail). In primary host it causes liver rot. The eggs of *Fasciola* are released from the sheep body through its faeces.
- **Phylum–Aschelminthes** includes bilaterally symmetrical, triploblastic and pseudocoelomate animals. Their body is circular in cross section, hence also referred to as roundworms.
- Their alimentary canal is complete with a well-developed muscular pharynx. These animals are dioecious, i.e. male and female are distinct, as male is usually smaller than female. Fertilisation is internal and development is direct or indirect when direct, have many **juvenile stages** or **larval forms**, e.g. filariform larva in *Ancylostoma* (hookworm), microfilaria larva in *Wuchereria* (filariasi worm) and rhabditiform larva in *Ascaris* and *Enterobius* (pinworm).
- **Phylum–Annelida** includes metamerically segmented animals with true schizocoelous coelom. They may be aquatic (marine and freshwater) or terrestrial, free-living and sometimes parasitic.
- They exhibit organ-system level of body organisation and bilateral symmetry. Their body surface is distinctly marked into segments or metameres.
- Animal can be monoecious (earthworn) or dioecious (*Nereis*).
- Reproduction can be direct or indirect with a trochophore larva.
- **Phylum–Arthropoda** is the largest phylum of animal kingdom which includes insects.
- They are triploblastic, coelomate and bilaterally symmetrical animals. The body of arthropods is coverd by sclerites (chitinous exoskeleton) which are shed at regular intervals during growth and development by a process called **ecdysis** or **moulting**.

- These animals are metamerically segmented with regionalisation of segments called **tagmatisation**. Their body is divisible into head, thorax and abdomen.
- They are mostly dioecious and have internal fertilisation.
- Development is direct or indirect with one to several larval stages. In some, like honeybees parthenogenesis is also seen.
- **Phylum–Mollusca** includes soft bodies animals. These are terrestrial or aquatic (marine or freshwater) having an organ-system level of organisation.
- They are bilaterally symmetrical, triploblastic, coelomate animals.
- Body is covered by calcareous shell and is unsegmented with a distinct head, muscular foot and visceral hump. A soft and spongy layer of skin forms a delicate covering over the visceral hump called the **mantle**. The space between the hump and the mantle is called the amntte **mantle cavity** in which feather-like gills are present.
- Molluscs are dioecious and oviparous with indirect development with veliger (in *Pila*), trochophore or glochidium larva (in *Unio*). Examples are *Pila* (apple snail), *Neopilina* (living fossil), *Chiton* (sea mouse), *Octopus* (devil fish), *Loligo* (squid), etc.
- **Phylum–Echinodermata** includes spiny skinned animals. Their endoskeleton is of calcareous ossicles and hence named Echinodermata.
- All of the species are marine with organ level of organisation.
- The adult echinoderms are radially symmetrical but larvae are bilaterally symmetrical. They are triploblastic and coelomate animals. Digestive system is complete with mouth on the lower (ventral) side and anus on the upper (dorsal) side.
- Sexes are separate, but lack sexual dimorphism. Reproduction is sexual, fertilisation is external with indirect development. The larval forms in echinoderms are dipleural, brachiolaria, bipinnaria, pluteus, ophipluteus, echinopluteus, aericularia and doliolaria. Examples are *Asterias* (star fish), *Echinus* (sea urchin), *Antedon* (feather star), etc.
- **Phylum–Chordata** includes the animals which are characterised by the presence of a notochord, a dorsal tubular nerve cord, paired pharyngeal gill slits and post-anal tail at some stages in their life. This phylum is divided into two groups, i.e. Acraniates and Craniates.
- **Phylum– Hemichordata** are worm-like marine animals which are commonly called half chordates. This is because they lack two major characteristics of chordates, i.e. notochord and post-anal tail.
- Sexes are separate, fertilisation is external and development is indirect with a free-swimming tornaria larva, e.g. *Balanoglossus* (Acorn or tongue worm), *Saccoglossus,* etc.
- **Subphylum–Urochordates** and **Subphylum–Cephalochordates** along with phylum–Hemichordata they are often referred to as protochordates or primitive chordates. These are considered as the connecting link between true invertebrates and vertebrates. **Urochordates** are also called tunicates, as there body is covered with test or tunic. While cepalochordates have notochord persistant throughout life and it extends, anteriorly upto the tip of the snout, e.g. *Amphioxus*.
- **Subphylum–Vetebrata** possess notochord during their embryonic period which is replaced by cartilaginous or bony vertebral column in adult.
- Vertebrata is further divided into two groups, i.e. Agnatha (without jaws) and Gnathostomata (with true jaws).
- **Agnatha** comprises of an extinct class–Ostracodermi (e.g. *Pterspis*) and a living Class–Cyclostomata (e.g lamprey and hagfish). Cyclostomes are marine fishes, which migrates to freshwater for spawning. These are ectoparasites on some fishes and have gill slits for respiration. They have sucking type circular mouth without jaws. Their endoskeleton is cartilaginous.
- **Superclass–Pisces** contains true fishes, which are divided into class–Chondrichthyes (cartilagenous fishes), class–Osteichthyes (bony fishes) and an extinct class–Placodermi.
- **Class–Chondrichthyes** are fishes with ventral mouth, heterocercal tail, placoid scales, 5-7 pair of naked gills, cloacal apertures present, exhibit sexual dimorphism, e.g. *Scoliodon* (dogfish and shark), *Torpedo* (electric ray), *Pristis* (sawfish), etc.
- **Class–Osteichthyes** are fishes with terminal mouth, homocercal tail with ctenoid, ganoid or cycloid scales, bladders with four pairs of gills covered with operculum. Anus and genital apertures separate, sexual dimorphism is rare, e.g. *Labeo* (rohu), *Catla, Hippocampus* (sea horse), *Exocoetus* (flying fish), *Anabas* (climbing perch), etc.
- **Superclass–Tetrapoda** are animals with limbs. They respire by gills, lungs and skin. These are further categorised into four classes, i.e. Amphibia, Reptilia, Aves and Mammalia.
- **Class–Amphibia** are the first animals to attempt transition from aquatic to terrestrial life. Most of them have two pairs of limbs. Their body is divisible into head and trunk, while tail may be present in some.
- These are cold-blooded animals and perform respiration by gills, lungs and through skin. Their heart is three-chambered.
- **Class–Reptilia** includes mostly terrestrial animals and their body is covered by dry and cornified skin, epidermal scales or scutes.
- Heart is three-chambered but it is four-chambered in crocodiles. Reptiles are poikilotherms. Their sexes are separate and they show internal fertilisation. They are oviparous with direct development.
- **Class–Aves** includes birds having a unique feature, i.e. having feathers on their body. They are warm-blooded animals with their forelimbs modified into wings and hindlimbs have scales, modified for walking, swimming or clasping the tree branches. Bone marrow is absent.
- Their heart is completely four-chambered. Birds exhibit double respiration by lungs. They also produce different sounds through syrinx (sound box) present in them. Reproduction in them is similar to that of reptiles.
- **Class–Mammalia** are the most advanced group of chordates having unique features like mammary glands, hairs on their body, external pinna, jaw with teeth and exhibit vivipary. They are warm-blooded land vertebrates.
- Heart is completely four-chambered. They have quadrated limbs but few species like whales and dolphins are without limbs. Sexes are separate and fertilisation is internal.

Chapter Practice

Multiple Choice Questions

1 Mark

1. Radial symmetry is seen in
   (a) Echinodermata, Ctenophora and Cnidaria
   (b) Mollusca, Porifera and Echinodermata
   (c) Porifera, Annelida and Arthropoda
   (d) None of the above

2. Body having meshwork of cells, internal cavities lined with food filtering flagellated cells and indirect development are the characteristics of phylum
   (a) Coelenterata (b) Porifera
   (c) Mollusca (d) Protozoa

3. Medusa is the sexually reproductive structure of
   (a) *Hydra* (b) *Obelia*
   (c) Sea anemone (d) None of these

4. Alternation of generation is also called
   (a) metamorphosis
   (b) metastasis
   (c) metazoan
   (d) metagenesis

5. Mark what is incorrect regarding to the phylum–Arthropoda.
   (a) Open type of circulatory system
   (b) Bilaterally symmetrical, coelomate animals
   (c) Diploblastic with head, thorax and abdomen
   (d) The presence of Malpighian tubules and antennae

6. When the circulatory system lacks arteries, veins and capillaries, it is called as
   (a) closed type
   (b) mixed type
   (c) inappropriate information
   (d) open type

7. Which of the following groups is formed of only the hermaphrodite organisms?
   (a) Earthworm, tapeworm, housefly, frog
   (b) Earthworm, tapeworm, sea horse, housefly
   (c) Earthworm, leech, sponge, roundworm
   (d) Earthworm, tapeworm, leech, sponge

8. Chondrichthyes is characterised by
   (a) placoid scale
   (b) ventral mouth
   (c) ctenoid scale and ventral mouth
   (d) placoid scale and ventral mouth

9. Which one of the following is incorrect for Aves?
   (a) Heart is four-chambered and animals are oviparous
   (b) The presence of air cavities in bones and the presence of feathers on the body
   (c) Digestive tract has additional chambers and animals are homeothermous
   (d) The forelimbs are not modified into wings

10. Which one of the following categories of animals, is correctly described with no single exception in it?
    (a) All reptiles possess scales, have a three-chambered heart and are cold-blooded (poikilothermal)
    (b) All bony fishes have four pairs of gills and an operculum on each side
    (c) All sponges are marine and have collared cells
    (d) All mammals are viviparous and possess diaphragm for breathing

11. Reptiles are different from amphibians in
    (a) the skin
    (b) structure of the heart
    (c) development stages
    (d) All of the above

Assertion-Reason Type Questions

1 Mark

■ **Direction** (Q. Nos. 12-18) *In each of the following questions, a statement of Assertion (A) is given followed by corresponding statement of Reason (R). Of the statements, mark the correct answer as*

(a) If both A and R are true and R is the correct explanation of A
(b) If both A and R are true, but R is not the correct explanation of A
(c) If A is true, but R is false
(d) If A is false, but R is true

12. **Assertion** (A) In many gastropods, the anus and the mantle cavity are placed anteriorly above the head.
Reason (R) During embryonic development in many gastropods, one side of the visceral mass grows faster than the other side. This uneven growth rotates the visceral organs upto 180° in many gastropods.

13. **Assertion** (A) Radial symmetry in animals is advantageous in detecting food and danger.
Reason (R) It allows the animal to be able to respond to stimulus from any direction.

14. **Assertion** (A) Tapeworm, roundworm and pinworm are endoparasites of human intestine.
Reason (R) Contaminated food is the main cause of intestinal infections by Aschelminthes.

15. **Assertion** (A) Amphibians cannot survive in sea water.
Reason (R) Amphibians have lungs for breathing on land which would collapse under the water pressure of the sea.

16. **Assertion** (A) Duck-bill platypus is not a true mammal.
Reason (R) True mammals are all viviparous, while platypus lays eggs.

17. Given below is the representative animal of phylum having an endoskeleton of calcareous ossicles. Study the animal and comment upon the appropriateness of the Assertion and the Reason.

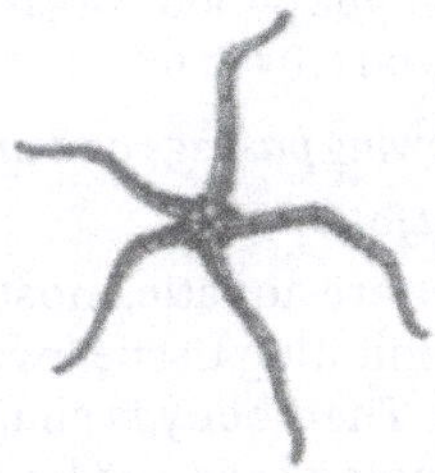

Assertion (A) Presence of water vascular system is the characteristic of this animal.
Reason (R) Main function of water vascular system is locomotion.

18. Given below is the diagrammatic sectional view of a cavity between the body wall and the gut wall which is very important in classification. Study the animal and comment upon the appropriateness of the Assertion and the Reason.

Assertion (A) It is a sectional view of pseudocoelom.
Reason (R) It has the body cavity not lined by mesoderm, instead, the mesoderm is present as scattered pouches in between the ectoderm and endoderm.

Answers

1. (a)	2. (b)	3. (b)	4. (d)	5. (c)	6. (d)
7. (d)	8. (d)	9. (d)	10. (b)	11. (d)	12. (a)
13. (a)	14. (b)	15. (c)	16. (a)	17. (b)	18. (a)

Very short answer Type Questions

(1 Mark)

19. Name some diseases caused by roundworms.
20. Which animals have nephridia?
21. Which animal shows the presence of tornarica larvae?
22. Give three examples of exoskeletal structures.
23. Which animals have branchial respiration?
24. State two differences between *Petromyzon* and *Myxine*.

Short Answer Type I Questions

(2 Marks)

25. Distinguish between radial symmetry and bilateral symmetry.
26. Which animals are called triploblastic animals?
27. What is the role of flame cells in Platyhelminthes?
28. What is organ of Bojanus? What is its function?
29. Which animals have compound eyes? What other sense organs are present in these animals?

30. Distinguish between Urochordata and Cephalochordata.
31. State four characteristics of Cyclostomata.
32. How does a frog respire?
33. Bat and whale are mammals. Comment.

Short Answer Type II Questions

3 Marks

34. Which system is involved in living organisms to guide and inform them about environment?
35. What are the sense organs present in class – Mollusca? How do respiration and excretion occurs in these?
36. Give features of bony fishes.
37. Give salient features of class–Amphibia.
38. Draw a labelled diagram of *Amphioxus.*
39. Write the name of one animal which show these kind of respiration.
    (i) Through body surface
    (ii) Branchial respiration
    (iii) Tracheal respiration
    (iv) Cutaneous respiration
40. Why some animals are oviparous, viviparous and ovoviviparous ? What value lies in this vividness?

Long Answer Type Questions

5 Marks

41. How will you classify animal kingdom on the basis of common fundamental features?
42. Write an account on polymorphism in cnidarians.
43. Distinguish between male *Ascaris* and female *Ascaris.*
44. Why Arthropoda is the largest phylum among non-chordates? Justify.
45. Give five distinguished features of Echinodermata.
46. List any six features of cartilaginous fishes. Give four examples of these.
47. Differentiate between Agnatha and Gnathostomata.
48. Explain, how birds adapt themselves for aerial mode of life?
49. How do birds and mammals resemble?

Case Based Questions

4/5 Marks

50. *Read the following passage and answer the questions that follows*
    Prakhar, a class XI student went out after rains in the garden. He saw earthworms on the ground and wondered how they are able to move, eat and perform various function of life Next day, he went to his biology teacher and asked her about the same. Her biology teacher politely explained him about how different animals have various levels of organisation of cells. She also told her that except sponges and coelenterates, all the animals of the kingdom–Animalia have either organ level or organ- system level of organisation.
    (i) What kind of body organisation are present in sponges and coelenterates?
    (ii) Write about the organisation type in lower animals, like protozoans.
    (iii) In which phylums organ system level organisation is found?
    (iv) Why does the digestive system of Platyhelminthes is called incomplete?
    (v) What the type of body organisation seen in starfish and jelly fish?
51. *Read the following passage and answer the questions that follows*
    Coelenterates are aquatic, mostly marine organisms exhibiting tissue level of organisation. Their body is characterised by tentacles, stinging cells and horny or calcareous exoskeleton. They possess well-defined gastrovascular cavity having single opening, polymorphism is one of the major characteristic of coelenterates.
    In this, the organism exists in different forms out of which one is sessile, while the other is free-swimming. These forms exhibit division of

labour and alternation of generation. Major representative animals of this group are *Adamsia, Physalia, Gorgonia*, etc.

(i) Name a freshwater coelenterate.
(ii) The exoskeleton of corals is composed of
(iii) In which coelenterates medusae form is seen?
(iv) What is the common name of *Adamsia*?
(v) What is the special character of Coelenterata?

52. Study the chart of evolutionary classification of vertebrates given below and answer the questions that follows

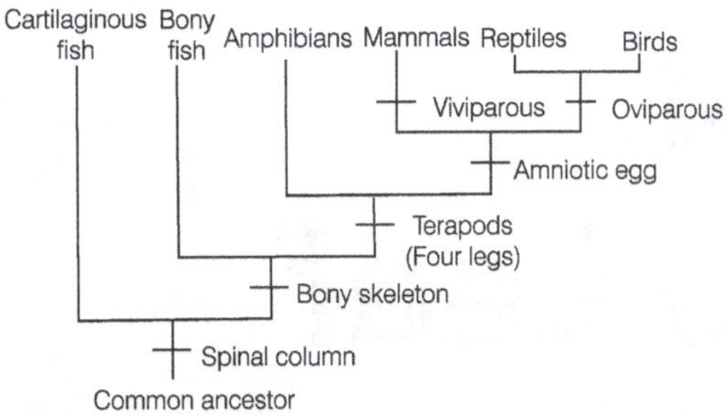

(i) On the basis of the classification pattern exhibited in this chart, why are mammals-viviparous and reptiles-oviparous?
(ii) There has been an increase in the number of chambers in heart during evolution of vertebrates. Give the names of the class of vertebrates having two, three or four-chambered heart.
(iii) To which class cartilaginous and bony fishes belong. Also, write about the scales present in them.
(iv) Write one feature common to all vertebrates.

53. Study the graph of hagfish species in freshwater given below and answer the questions that follows

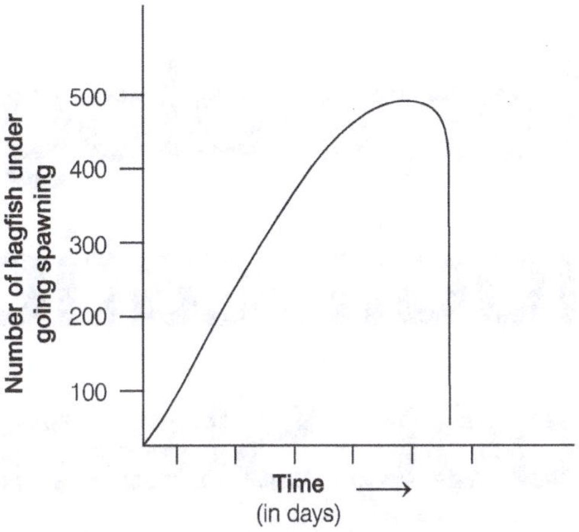

(i) With reference to the above graph explain why there is seen sudden decline in hagfish population in freshwater?
(ii) To which animal class does hagfish belong?
(iii) What happens to the larval population of hagfish after metamorphosis ?
(iv) Given one difference between hagfish and flying fish.

CHAPTER

07

Morphology and Modification of Root, Stem and Leaf

- Morphology and Modification of Root and Stem
  - The Root
  - The Stem
- Morphology and Modification of Leaf

The angiosperms or flowering plants show a large diversity in their external structures. Their study is called as **morphology** (Gk. *Morphe*–form; *logos*–study). However, they all are characterised by the presence of roots, stems, leaves, flowers and fruits. A general morphology of root, stem and leaf of flowering plants is given in this chapter.

The plant body consists of a main axis, which may be branched or unbranched bearing lateral appendages. The main axis is divided into two parts

(i) **Root System** The underground root system develops from the radicle of embryo and helps in fixation of the plant as well as absorption of water and minerals.

(ii) **Shoot System** The aerial shoot system develops from the plumule of embryo.

Plant contains root, stem, leaves as vegetative parts and flowers, fruits and seeds as reproductive parts. The vegetative parts are involved in various vegetative functions like structural organisation, fixation, absorption, nourishment, growth and maintenance of various components. The reproductive parts are for sexual reproduction and germination of seeds to make new plants.

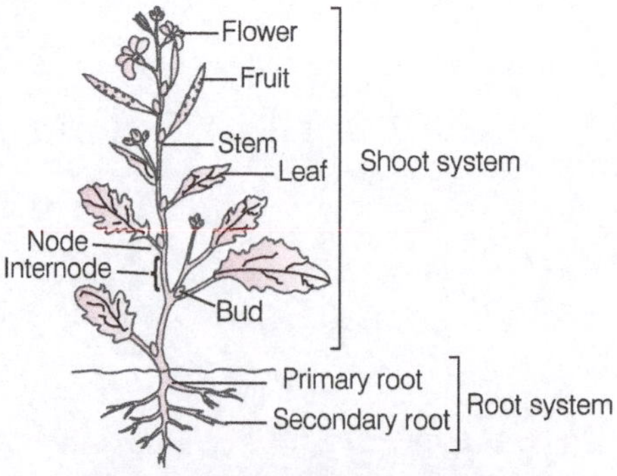

Fig. 7.1 Parts of a flowering plant

TOPIC 01 Morphology and Modification of Root and Stem

The Root

In plants, root is the non-green (due to the absence of chlorophyll), cylindrical and descending part that normally grows downwards into the soil. It does not bear leaves, buds and is not distinguished into nodes and internodes.

Regions of the Root

A typical root contains following five regions. However, there is no clear line of distinction between these regions.

1. Root Cap (Calyptra)

The root is covered at the apex by a thimble or cap-like structure called the **root cap**. It protects the root meristem from friction of the soil particles and also protects tender apex which allows the passage of root through the soil, e.g. *Lemna, Eichhornia*. Roots of parasitic plants lack root caps.

2. Growing Point (Meristematic) Zone

It is a small (about 1 mm in length) thin-walled region having dense protoplasm. It lies partly within and partly beyond the root cap. Its cells divide regularly and repeatedly for elongation. It is responsible for the growth of the root.

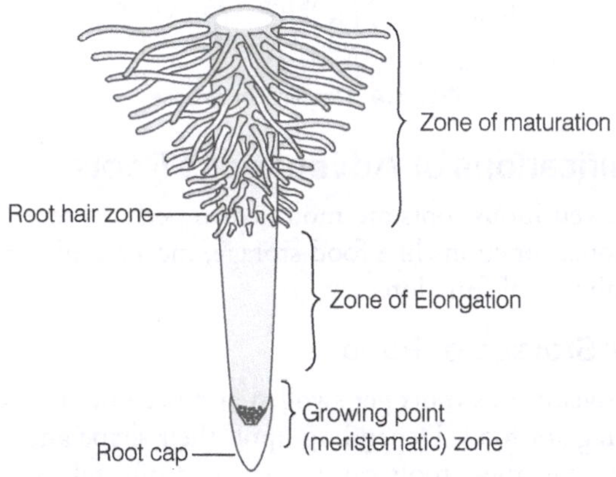

Fig. 7.2 The regions of the root tip

3. Zone of Elongation

It is situated behind the meristematic region (growing point). The cells elongate speedily and increase the length of the root. The cells of this region can absorb water and minerals from the soil.

4. Root Hair Zone

It is the region where primary tissues differentiate into the root. The vascular tissues like xylem and phloem are formed. Root hair zone is the most important part of the root for absorption of water (most of the water) from the soil.

The root hairs increase the exposed surface of the root for absorption. In aquatic plants, root hairs are usually absent and the roots are not well-developed.

5. Zone of Maturation

This zone contains mature cells. It forms the permanent zone of the root and also gives out lateral roots from the interior part of this region, e.g. dicots and gymnosperms.

Types of Root System

The root system can be of two types on the basis of place of origin

1. Tap Root System

The tap root develops from the radicle of embryo of a seed. In most of the plants, primary root persists and becomes stronger to form tap root. The first root formed by the elongation of radicle, is called **primary root.** It continuously grows and produces lateral roots called **secondary roots.**

The further branches of the secondary roots are called **tertiary roots** and so on. These types of roots are present in dicots, e.g. pea, gram, groundnut, etc.

2. Adventitious Root System

The roots developing from any part of the plant other than the radicle are known as adventitious roots (*L. adventitious*-extraordinary). These are usually found in monocots.

The adventitious roots can be further classified as following on the basis of nature of development

(i) **Fibrous Roots** The primary roots soon gets replaced by a cluster of slender, thread-like roots originating from the base of the stem in monocotyledonous plants, e.g. *Triticum vulgare* (wheat), *Oryza sativa* (rice), *Allium cepa* (onion).

(ii) **Foliar Roots** These roots develop from the leaf, i.e. from the petiole of the leaf, e.g. *Pogostemon*, rubber plant.

(iii) **True Adventitious Roots** These roots develop from the nodes and internodes of the stem, e.g. prop roots of banyan (*Ficus*), climbing roots of money plant (*Pothos*), roots from the stem that remain partially immersed in water (*Coleus*), roots from nodes (*Oxalis repens*), etc.

Modification of Roots

The modifications are the changes in shape, form or structure in an organ to carry out special functions such as support, storage of food and respiration other than or in addition to the normal functions. Modifications of roots are found in both tap roots and adventitious roots.

Modifications of Tap Roots

The tap roots are modified for the function like storage, nitrogen-fixation and respiration.

1. For Storage of Food

These roots modify to store food materials. The primary root becomes swollen due to the presence of stored food. Depending upon the shape, the storage tap roots can be classified into following types

(i) **Conical Roots** These are fleshy tap roots that resemble a cone (broad at the base and gradually tapering towards the apex), e.g. carrot (*Daucus carota*).

(ii) **Fusiform Roots** The primary root is spindle-shaped. It is swollen in the middle and gradually tapers at both the ends, e.g. radish (*Raphanus sativus*).

(iii) **Napiform Roots** The primary root is almost spherical (pitcher-shaped) at the base and tapers abruptly at the lower end, e.g. beetroot (*Beta vulgaris*), turnip (*Brassica rapa*), etc.

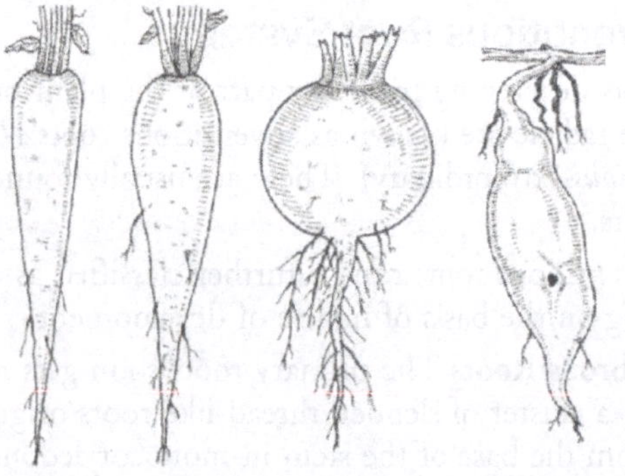

Fig. 7.3 Modifications of tap roots for storage
(a) Conical root (carrot), (b) Fusiform root, (radish)
(c) Napiform root (turnip), (d) Tuberous root (4 'O'clock plant)

(iv) **Tuberous Roots** The primary root becomes thick and fleshy, but do not attain any definite shape (irregularly-shaped), e.g. 4 O'clock plant (*Mirabilis jalapa*), *Echinocystis lobata*.

2. For N_2-fixation

In this the secondary, tertiary and sometimes primary roots bear many small irregular swellings called **root nodules** which contain countless, minute nitrogen-fixing bacteria of the genus *Rhizobium*, e.g. groundnut (*Arachis hypogea*), clover (*Medicago falcata*), pea (*Pisum sativum*), etc.

3. For Respiration

Pneumatophores These are special roots that develop in mangrove plants (grow in marshy areas). The pneumatophores or aerophores or respiratory roots grow vertically upward and are negatively geotropic. They have minute breathing pores called **pneumatophores** present on the tips of vertical roots that help in getting oxygen for respiration.

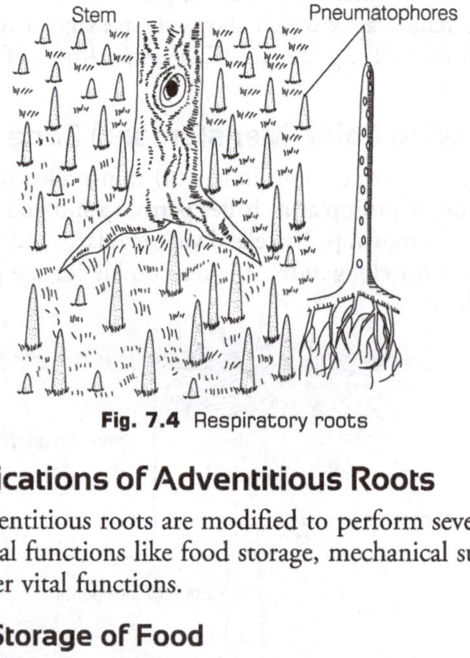

Fig. 7.4 Respiratory roots

Modifications of Adventitious Roots

The adventitious roots are modified to perform several additional functions like food storage, mechanical support and other vital functions.

1. For Storage of Food

The adventitious roots get swollen and become thick due to storage of food. Depending upon their shape and place of swellings, these roots can be classified into following categories

(i) **Fasiculated Roots** These arise in clusters from the base of the stem, e.g. *Dahlia*, *Asparagus*.

(ii) **Nodulous Roots** These roots have swellings that occur only near the tips, e.g. arrow root (*Maranta*), amia haldi (*Curcuma amada*).

(iii) **Tuberous Roots** (Single Root Tubers) These are swollen without any definite shape, e.g. *Ipomoea batatas* (sweet potato).

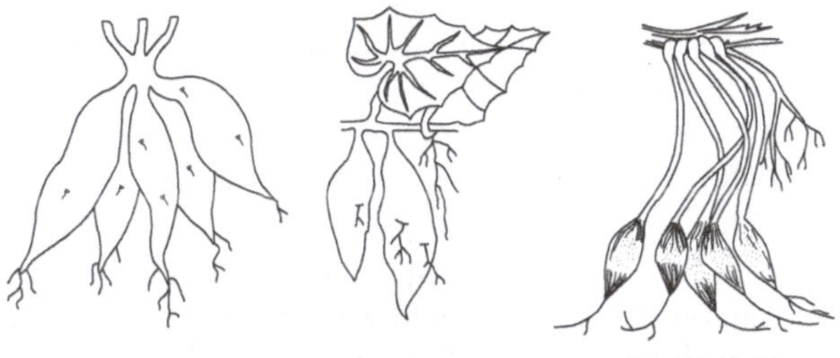

(a) Fasciculated roots of *Dahlia* (b) Tuberous roots of *Ipomoea batata* (sweet potato) (d) Nodulose roots of *Curcuma amada*

Fig. 7.5 Modification of adventitious root (storage)

2. For Mechanical Support

The adventitious roots modify into following types to provide mechanical support.

(i) **Prop** (Pillar) **Roots** The prop roots grow from the horizontal branches of the stem and hang vertically downward. They become thick, pillar-like and provide mechanical support to the giant trees, e.g. banyan tree (*Ficus benghalensis*).

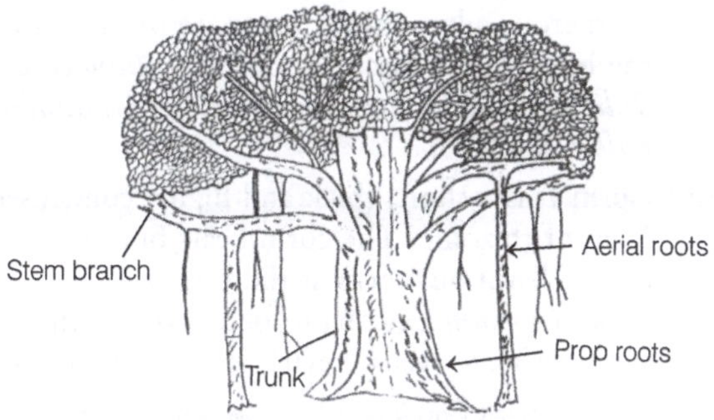

Fig. 7.6 Banyan tree

(ii) **Stilt Roots** These are small, thick and supporting roots growing obliquely from the basal nodes of the main stem. These provide mechanical support, e.g. *Saccharum officinarum* (sugarcane), *Zea mays* (maize).

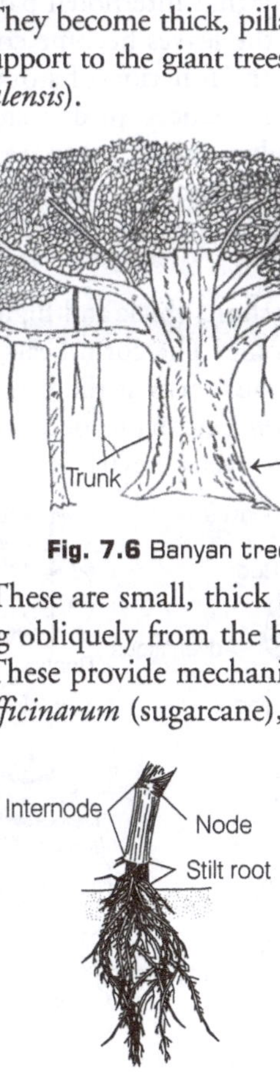

Fig. 7.7 Stilt roots of sugarcane

(iii) **Climbing** (Clinging) **Roots** These roots are found in climbers. They may arise from the nodes, e.g. *Ivy, Pothos* (money plant).

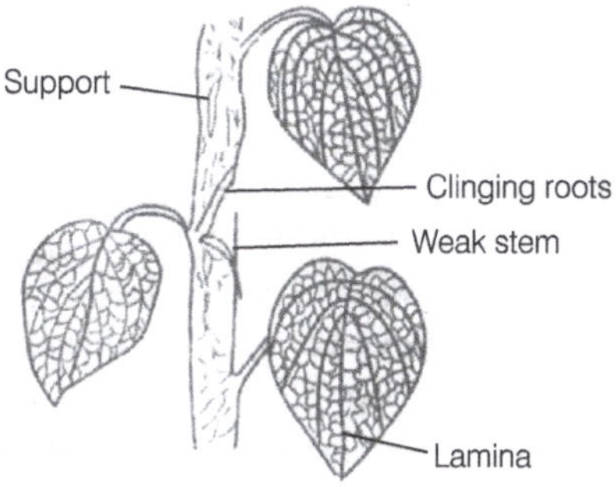

Fig. 7.8 Betel (*Piper betel*)

3. For Vital or Physiological Functions

Roots modify into following types to perform vital functions

(i) **Assimilatory** (Photosynthetic) **Roots** These roots have chlorophyll and can synthesise food, e.g. aerial or hanging roots of some orchids.

(ii) **Parasitic** (Sucking) **Roots** These roots occur in parasitic plant for absorbing nourishment from their host. These roots function as haustoria, e.g. *Cuscuta* (dodder plants or amarbel).

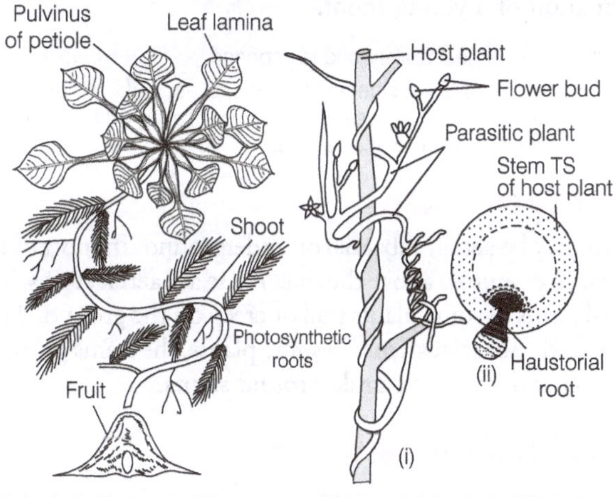

(a) Assimilatory root of *Trapa* (b) Haustorial root of *Cuscuta*

Fig. 7.9 Showing different types of root according to their vital functions

Note

Epiphytic roots The roots of the epiphytes hang in the air. These absorb hygroscopic water present in the atmosphere by special tissue called velaman, e.g. *Vanda, Dendrobium*, orchids.

Functions of Roots

The major functions of roots are as follows

(i) **Fixation** Root provides fixation to the plants with soil.

(ii) **Absorption** Roots absorb water and minerals from the soil and provide it to all parts of the body.

(iii) **Storage** Roots of many plants store food for the use of other plant parts and for animals.

(iv) **Aeration** Plants growing in waterlogged soil or marshy areas have special roots, i.e. pneumatophores for respiration.

(v) **Conduction** Roots transport water and minerals in upward direction for the use of stems and leaves.

The Stem

The stem is the ascending part of the axis bearing branches, leaves, flowers and fruits. It develops from the plumule of the embryo of a germinating seed.

It shows distinction into **nodes** and **internodes,** where node is the regions from where leaves are born and internodes are the regions between two nodes. It bears bud, which may be terminal or axillary.

A **bud** can be defined as a condensed embryonic shoot that has a growing point surrounded by closely packed immature leaves. When bud grows, the internodes become longer and the leaves spread out, resulting in the formation of a young shoot.

Note
- The largest axillary bud is cabbage.
- Bamboo is considered to be the tallest herb, tallest shrub or arborescent grass. Bamboos are called **culms**, after the jointed nature of their stems.

Forms of Stem

Stem may be aerial, subaerial or underground. In most of the plants, stems grow above the soil. These are **aerial stems.** The aerial stems of some plants trail or creep on the ground. They are called **subaerial stems.** In some plants, the stems grow in the soil and are called **underground stems.**

Modification of Stems

Like roots, stems also modify into various forms to perform different functions. These modifications are classified into following categories

1. Underground Stem Modifications

Certain plants have stems that develop under the soil. These are called as underground stems. They store food material and become thick and fleshy. This type of underground stem is divided into following categories

(i) **Rhizome** This underground stem grows horizontally.
It is fleshy, dorsiventral and perennial. Rhizomes possess nodes and internodes. These nodes bear scale leaves in the axil of which axillary buds are born, e.g. *Dryopteris,* banana—*Musa paradisiaca,* lotus—*Nelumbo,* ginger—*Zingiber officinale, Canna indica* and turmeric—*Curcuma domestica.*

(ii) **Tuber** In plants like potato, the lower branches of stem become positively geotropic and get buried in the soil. The food (starch) get accumulated in the tip of such underground branches. Thus, they swelled up and become oval/spherical in shape.
These possess a number of spirally arranged depressions called **eyes** or **buds.** Each eye represents a node and bears a small scale leaf having a bud in its axil. The food reserve is starch in potato (*Solanum tuberosum*) and inulin in Jerusalem artichoke (*Helianthus tuberosus*). Tubers are used for the vegetative propagation.

(iii) **Bulb** In this type of stem, modification takes place in such a way that internodal part becomes highly reduced. So the leaves become condensed (rosette) and take up the function of storage and become fleshy. Stem is reduced to disc-shaped structure. Numerous adventitious roots are produced from the base of this disc, e.g. onion (*Allium cepa*), *Tulipa,* garlic (*Allium sativum*), lily (*Lilium bulbiferum*).

(iv) **Corm** It is a short, thick and highly condensed form of rhizome. The corm bears buds at nodes and adventitious roots at the base, e.g. *Amorphophallus* (elephant foot, vern. zamikand, suran), *Crocus* (vern. kesar), *Alocasia, Colocasia.*

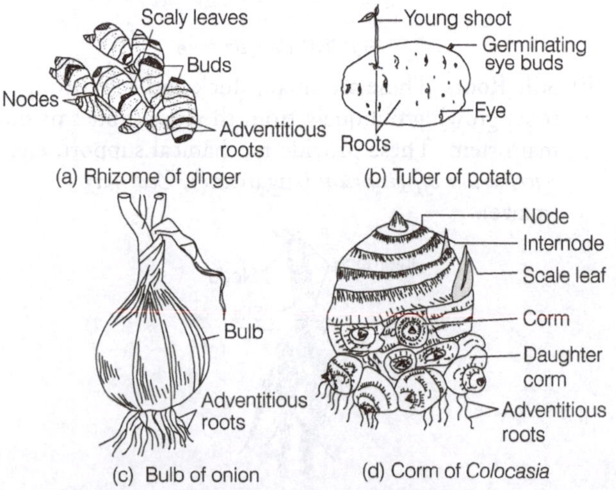

Fig. 7.10 Underground stem modification

2. Subaerial Stem Modifications

In these modifications, a part of stem remains underground and the remaining part becomes aerial. The dormant bud present on the stem becomes active and develops lateral branches for vegetative reproduction. This type of subaerial stems are modified into the following types

(i) **Runners** These stems have weak, long and thin internodes. These creep over the surface of soil, e.g. doob grass or lawn grass (*Cynodon dactylon*), brahmi booti (*Centella asiatica*), wood sorrel (*Oxalis*).

(ii) **Suckers** Some axillary branches that arise from the node of underground stem grow horizontally for some time. These branches then become obliquely upward and give rise to a new plant, e.g. *Chrysanthemum,* banana.

(iii) **Stolons** These are long, lateral branches that arise from base of the stem. They grow aerially for some time and then arch downwards to touch the ground and give rise to daughter plant, e.g. wild strawberry (*Fragaria*), jasmine (*Jasminum*), peppermint (*Mentha piperita*).

(iv) **Offsets** These are lateral branches that bear short internodes. Each node bears a rosette of leaves upwards (aerial) and cluster of roots downwards, e.g. water lettuce (*Pistia*), water hyacinth (*Eichhornia crassipes*).

Note Stolons and runners are quite similar to each other. The only difference between them is that stolons grow below the surface of soil, while runners grow above the surface of soil.

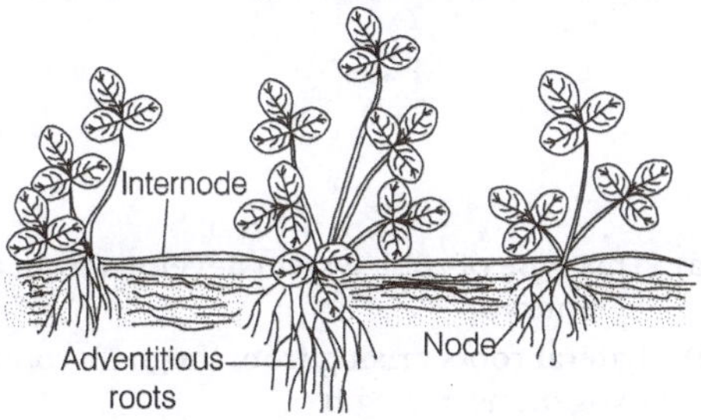

(a) Runner

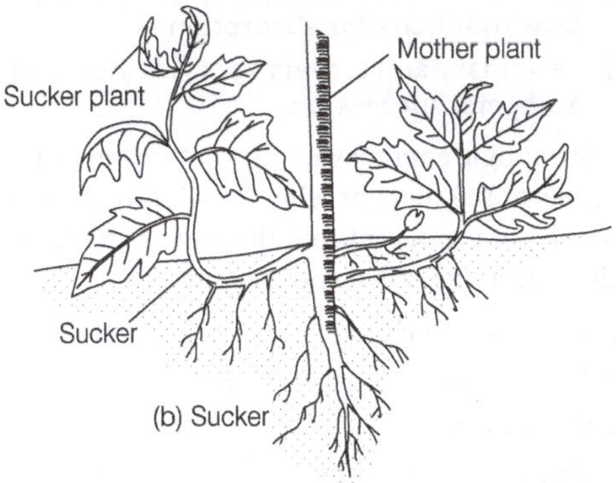

(b) Sucker

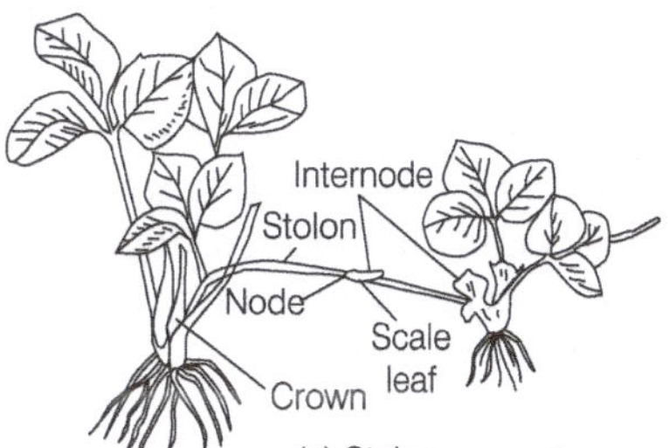

(c) Stolon

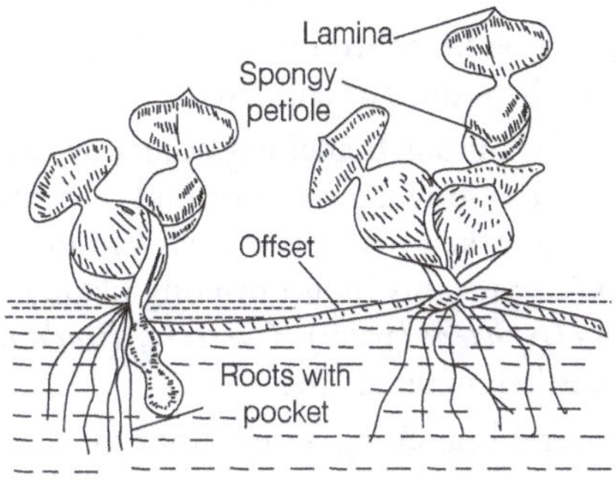

(d) Offset

Fig. 7.11 Subaerial stem modifications

3. Aerial Stem Modifications

In this, the real stem gets so much modified that it is difficult to identify it as a stem. Aerial stem modifications are of following types

(i) **Stem tendrils** When stem is weak, the axillary or terminal bud gets modified into tendril. These tendrils perform the function of climbing, e.g. *Vitis* (modified apical bud), *Passiflora* (modified axillary bud), etc.

Note In cucurbits, the lower portion of tendril is modified stem, while the upper portion of tendril is modified leaf.

(ii) **Stem thorns** The axillary bud gets modified into thorn. They are formed in the axil of a leaf or apex of stem. These perform the function of either climbing or defense, e.g. *Duranta*, climbing rose (with curved prickles), *Asparagus* (with leaf spines), *Bougainvillea* (with extra axillary thorns), *Calamus* (with leaf sheath spines). Thorns are modified stems while spikes are modified leaves.

(iii) **Phylloclades** The stems become flattened, thick, succulent, green and photosynthetic. They help the plants to grow in dry and xerophytic habitats. The phylloclades can be flattened, e.g. *Opuntia*, *Muchlenbeckia* = *Coccoloba, Epiphyllum* or cylindrical, e.g. *Casuarina, Euphorbia royleana, E. tirucalli*.

(iv) **Cladodes** (Cladophylls) The axillary bud develops into green one internode long stem. They are photosynthetic. Hence, they perform the function of leaves. The true leaves of such plants are usually reduced to scales or spines, e.g. *Asparagus* and *Ruscus*.

(v) **Bulbil** It is a modified stem developed either from a vegetative bud or a flower bud. It gets swollen because of accumulation of food. It gives rise to a new plant after being detached from the parent plant, e.g. *Dioscorea bulbifera*.

Branching Patterns of Stems

The stems may be branched or unbranched. Branching in stems may be dichotomous and lateral.

(i) The **dichotomous branching** occurs by the division of the apical growing point or bud into two equal parts in a forked manner. It occurs in lower plants–cryptogams (non-flowering plants), higher plants–*Hyphaene* (palm), *Canscora, Pandanus tectorius* (screw pine), etc.

(ii) The **lateral branching** occurs from the axillary buds of the nodes, e.g. *Pinus*, grapevine, etc.

Functions of Stem

Stems perform various primary and secondary functions.

Primary Functions

(i) It bears leaves, fruits, flowers and seeds in position.

(ii) It conducts water and minerals to roots, leaves, flowers, fruits, etc.

(iii) It holds flowers in suitable position, so that pollination and fertilistaion can take place.

Secondary Functions

(i) Many stems store food as reserve food materials.

(ii) Some stems also help in photosynthesis and vegetative propagation.

(iii) The underground stems help in perennation.

(iv) Stem branches provide support to its various parts.

Topic Practice 1

Multiple Choice Questions

1 Mark

1. The aerial shoot system of flowering plants develops from

(a) radicle (b) plumule
(c) cotyledone (d) None of these

Ans (b) The aerial shoot system of flowering plants develops from the plumule of embryo.

2. Which of the following statements is correct with respect to the given figure showing different zones of a typical root?

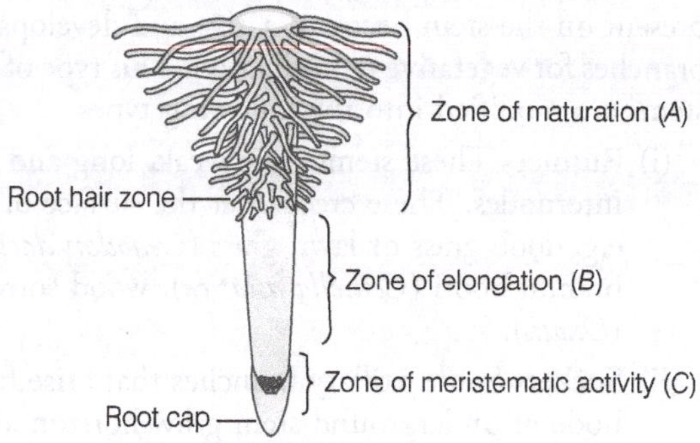

(a) Part *B* mainly helps in absorption of water
(b) Quiescent centre is present in part *B*
(c) Part *A* is most suitable for anatomical studies of root
(d) Differentiation of cells can be observed in part *C*

Ans (c) Part *A* is the root hair zone which represents the zone of differentiation or maturation. This is the most suitable part for anatomical studies of root, because different types of primary tissues differentiate or mature in this region. Xylem, phloem, pericycle, endodermis, cortex and epiblema are clearly visible in this region.

3. Refer to the given figure and select the incorrect statement regarding this.

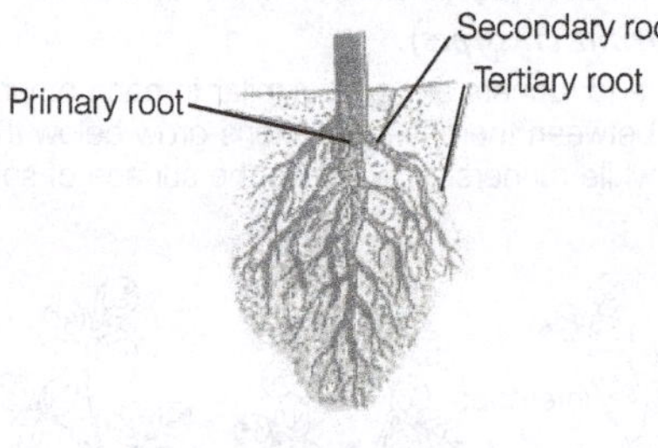

(a) This type of root system develops from radicle of embryo
(b) Lateral roots arising from the main roots are exogenous in origin
(c) Rootlets are the ultimate root branches that bear root hairs for absorption
(d) Secondary and tertiary roots are borne in acropetal succession

Ans (b) Given figure represents tap root system. Lateral branches of the roots develop from interior (usually pericycle) of the parent root that bear vascular bundle. Such an origin is called endogenous.

4. Fibrous roots are found in

(a) *Pogostemon* (b) *Ficus*
(c) *Oryza sativa* (d) *Oxalis repens*

Ans (c) Fibrous roots are found in *Oryza sativa.*

5. Select the group of plants that possess stilt roots.
(a) *Zea mays, Saccharum officinarum*
(b) *Pandanus odoratissimus, Ficus benghalensis*
(c) *Rhizophora mangal, Hedera helix*
(d) *Ficus benghalensis, Pisum sativum*

Ans (a) Stilt roots are supporting roots coming out of the lower nodes of the stem. They can be seen in *Zea mays*, sugarcane *(Saccharum officinarum)*, etc.

6. Nodes are the regions of stem where
(a) food is stored by plants
(b) leaves are borne
(c) xylem and phloem are present
(d) axillary buds develop

Ans (b) The stem bears nodes and internodes. The region of the stem where leaves are borne are called nodes, while internodes are the portions between two nodes. Axillary buds develop in the axil of a leaf.

7. In plants like mint and jasmine, a slender lateral branch arises from the base of the main axis and after growing aerially for some time, arch downwards to touch the ground. This slender branch is called
(a) sucker (b) stolon
(c) offset (d) scramblers

Ans (b) They are elongated, horizontal or arched runners, which can cross over small obstacles. Each stolon has one or more nodes possessing scale leaves and axillary buds.

8. Which of the following statements is not correct?
(a) Underground stems of turmeric, zamikand and *Colocasia* modify to store food
(b) Stem tendrils develop from the internodes of stem
(c) Thorns in *Citrus* and *Bougainvillea* are modified axillary buds
(d) Stem tendrils help cucumber and watermelon plants to climb

Ans (b) The statement (b) is incorrect. Stem tendrils develop from axillary buds of stem. They are slender and spirally coiled and help the plant to climb such as in gourds (cucumber, pumpkins, watermelon) and grapevines.

9. A modified stem developed from a vegetative bud or a flower bud that gets swollen due to the accumulation of food is
(a) cladode (b) bulbil (c) bulb (d) corm

Ans (b) Bulbil is a modified stem developed from a vegetative bud or a floral bud that swellup to store food.

10. Some stems help in
(a) photosyntheis
(b) vegetative propagation
(c) storage of food material
(d) All of the above

Ans (d) Some stems help in photosynthesis (e.g. *Opuntia*) and vegetative propagation (e.g. jasmine). Many stems store food as reserve food materials (e.g. potato).

Very Short Answer Type Questions

1 Mark

11. Where are root hairs present in root?

Ans The root bears unicellular root hairs in the zone of maturation.

12. Why development of root branches is endogenous?

Ans Root branches develop from the interior (usually pericycle) of the parent root. This type of origin is called endogenous, as it bears supply of vascular bundles.

13. Why some tap roots become swollen and fleshy?

Ans Tap roots become swollen as these roots store food in them.

14. In swampy areas like Sunderbans in West Bengal, plants bear special kind of roots called **NCERT Exemplar**

Ans Pneumatophores. These are respiratory roots present in mangrove plants which grow in marshy and saline soils.

15. In aquatic plants like *Pistia* and *Eichhornia*, leaves and roots are found near **NCERT Exemplar**

Ans In aquatic plants like *Pistia* and *Eichhornia* leaves and roots are found near water surface. This helps in balancing the plants over water surface.

16. Roots obtain oxygen from air present in the soil for respiration. In the absence or deficiency of O_2, root growth is constricted or completely stopped. How do these plants growing in marshlands or swamps obtain their oxygen required for root respiration? **NCERT Exemplar**

Ans Plants growing in marshlands obtain oxygen by pneumatophores, from dissolved part in water and intercellular diffusion from aerial parts.

17. Why are velamen tissues present in epiphytic roots?

Ans The velamens are spongy tissues, which help epiphytic roots in absorbing **atmospheric** water vapours.

18. In cucurbits which portion of plant gets modified into tendril ?

Ans In cucurbits, the lower portion of tendril is modified stem, while the upper portion of tendril is modified leaf.

19. How stolons are different from runners ?

Ans Stolons and runners are quite similar to each other. The only difference between then is that stolons grow below the surface of soil, while runners grow above the surface of soil.

20. How the runners of grasses can serve as means of vegetative propagation?

Ans Runners are the weak, thin and long stem that creep over surface and give rise to a new plant wherever the mode touches the ground.

Short Answer Type I Questions

2 Marks

21. What is root cap? Which any two variations are found in this?

Ans The apex of each root is covered by a cushion of thin-walled cells known as root cap.

Variations

(i) Multiple root caps are present in *Pandanus* (screw pine).

(ii) In aquatic plants, the root apex is enclosed within a sac-like structure called root packet, e.g. *Pistia, Eichhornia*, etc. (1 × 2)

22. Give two examples of roots that develop from different parts of the angiospermic plants other than the radicle. **NCERT Exemplar**

Ans (i) Prop roots in banyan tree from horizontal stem branches.

(ii) Stilt roots in maize form lower stem nodes. (2)

23. Which part of root is responsible for the absorption of water from the soil ? Why do aquatic plants lack a well-developed root system ?

Ans The root hair zone of root is the region where primary tissues differentiate into the root. The vascular tissues like xylem and phloem are formed. Root hair zone is the most important part of the root for absorption of water from the soil. The root hairs increase the exposed surface of the root for absorption. In aquatic plants, roots hairs are usually absent and the roots are not well-developed. They absorb water from their whole body. (2)

24. What are adventitious roots ? On the basis of their nature of development, how can they be classified ?

Ans The roots developing from any part of the plant other than the radicle are known as adventitious roots. These roots can be classified on the basis of nature of development. This classification is given below

(i) **Fibrous Roots** When the primary roots soon gets replaced by a cluster of slender, thread-like roots originating from the base of stem as in monocots are called fibrous roots e.g. *Triticum vulgare, Oryza sativa*, etc.

(ii) **Foliar Roots** These roots develop from the petiole of the leaf, e.g. *Pogostemon*.

(iii) **True Adventitious Roots** These roots develop from the nodes and internodes of the stem, e.g. prop roots of money plant (*Pothos*), roots from nodes (*Oxalis repens*), etc. (1+1)

25. Identify the following diagram and write important features.

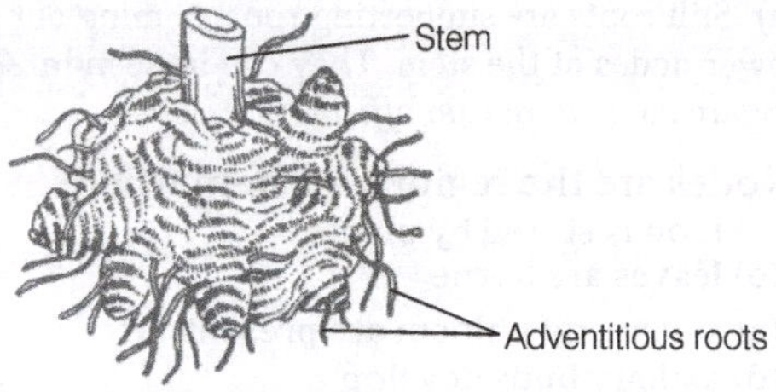

Ans The given diagram is of a corm. It is a condensed, fleshy, solid and vertically growing stock with large apical buds. The shape of corm is spherical, flattened on top and bottom.

It has number of circular nodes with scales and one or more axillary buds, e.g. *Colocasia, Amorphophallus, Gladiolus*, etc. (2)

26. Which parts in ginger and onion are edible?

Ans The edible part of ginger is the modified stem, called rhizome, which stores food material, whereas in onion the edible part is fleshy leaves. In this case, the internode becomes shortened, leaves get condensed to form a tunic and store food material. (1 + 1)

27. In *Opuntia* the stem is modified into a flattened green structure to perform the function of leaves (i.e. photosynthesis). Write some other examples of modification of plant parts for the purpose of photosynthesis. **NCERT Exemplar**

Ans For the purpose of photosynthesis there are

(i) Photosynthetic roots, e.g. *Trapa, Tinospora.*

(ii) Phyllode (flattened petiole), e.g. *Acacia longifolia.*

(iii) Foliaceous stipules, e.g. *Lathyrus aphaca.* (2)

28. Name the type of stem tendrils found in these plants.

(i) *Passiflora* (ii) *Luffa*

(iii) *Vitis* (iv) *Antigonon*

Ans (i) *Passiflora* – Axillary

(ii) *Luffa* – Extra-axillary

(iii) *Vitis* – Apical

(iv) *Antigonon* – Floral (½ × 4)

29. Tendrils of grapevine are homologous to tendrils of pumpkin, but analogous to those of pea. Justify the above statement. **NCERT Exemplar**

Ans Tendrils of grapevine and pumpkin are stem structures, while those of pea are foliar in nature. Hence, the tendrils of grapevine and pea are analogous structures. (2)

Short Answer Type II Questions

(3 Marks)

30. Differentiate between fibrous roots and adventitious roots. **NCERT**

Ans Differences between fibrous and adventitious roots are

Fibrous Roots	Adventitious Roots
They arise from the radicle.	These develop from any part of the plant other than radicle.
They help in anchorage and absorption.	They help in different functions like storage, climbing, respiration, etc.
They are found in grasses.	They are found in a variety of plants.
They are usually below the soil.	They may be underground or aerial.

(3)

31. The essential functions of roots are anchorage and absorption of water and minerals in the terrestrial plants. What functions are associated with the roots of aquatic plants? How are the roots of aquatic plants and terrestrial plants different?

Ans Functions of roots in aquatic plants are

(i) Buoyancy in floating plants.

(ii) Anchorage in submerged fixed plants. (1½)

Differences in roots of aquatic and terrestrial plants are

Roots of Aquatic Plants	Roots of Terrestrial Plants
Poorly developed	Profusely developed
Root hair absent	Root hair present
Xylem atrophied (poorly developed)	Xylem well-developed
Aerenchyma occurs	Aerenchyma is absent

(1½)

32. Justify the following statements on the basis of external features.

(i) Underground parts of a plant are not always roots.

(ii) Flower is a modified shoot.

Ans (i) Underground parts of a plant are not always roots. Sometimes stem or stem branches occur underground to perform some special functions. For example, potato tuber is a modified stem which is underground.

A potato tuber shows nodes and internodes, scale leaves and buds at the nodes. It also has an apical bud at the tip of potato tuber which confirms it as a stem. (1½)

(ii) Flower is a modified shoot consisting of a highly reduced stem branch to form thalamus in which the nodes are borne concentrically only towards the tip.

The floral parts, i.e. sepals, petals, stamens and carpels are arranged in their respective whorls and arise from nodes. The growing point of floral bud is used up in the production of floral organs. (1½)

33. Tendrils are found in the following plants. Identify whether they are stem tendrils or leaf tendrils.

(i) Cucumber

(ii) Pea

(iii) Pumpkin

(iv) Grapevine

Ans (i) Cucumber — Stem tendril

(ii) Pea — Leaf or leaflet tendril

(iii) Pumpkin — Stem tendril

(iv) Grapevine — Stem tendrils (3)

Long Answer Type Questions

(5 Marks)

34. Which type of modifications are found in tap roots for the storage of food ?

Ans Refer to text on page no. 148.

35. What is meant by modifications of root? What type of modification of the root is found in the

(i) Banyan tree (ii) Turnip

(iii) Mangrove tree **NCERT**

Ans Modification of root is the change in the (morphology) shape, size, structure and normal functioning of the root to perform some secondary functions. (2)

(i) **Banyan Tree** It has huge, pillar-like prop roots, hanging from the aerial branches. They support the expanding canopy of the trees.

(ii) **Turnip** In this root, the tap root becomes swollen with reserve food material.

(iii) **Mangrove Tree** They have pneumatophores. These are the roots which grow vertically upwards and come above the ground level.

They bear openings called pneumatophores, which help in taking oxygen from the air. (3)

36. Describe modifications of stems with suitable examples. **NCERT**

Ans Modifications of stems are as follows

(i) **Tendrils** help plants to climb on the support, e.g. cucumber.

(ii) **Thorns** are woody, pointed, straight structures to protect plants from browsing animals, e.g. *Baugainvillea.*

(iii) **Fleshy Stems** In arid regions plants have modified their stems into flattened (*Opuntia*) or fleshy cylindrical (*Euphorbia*) structures. They contain chlorophyll and carry out photosynthesis.
(iv) Underground stems of some plants such as grass and strawberry, etc. spread to new areas and when older parts die, new plants are formed.
(v) In *Pistia* and *Eichhornia*, a lateral branch with short internodes and each node bearing a rosette of leaves and a tuft of roots is found.
(vi) Stolons or runners help in vegetative propagation in jasmine and grass, respectively. (5)

37. **Stolon, offset and rhizome are different forms of stem modification. How can these modified forms of stem be distinguished from each other?** **NCERT Exemplar**

Ans These can be distinguished as follows

Stolon	Offset	Rhizome
It is more than one internode long arched horizontal stem branch.	It is one internode long horizontal stem branch.	It represents the main axis.
It is subaerial.	It is subaerial.	It is underground.
It does not store food.	It does not store food.	It stores food for growth.
It is generally green.	It is green.	It is non-green.
e.g. strawberry	e.g. *Pistia*	e.g. ginger

(5)

38. **Discuss about the branching patterns of stems as well as write their primary functions.**

Ans Refer to the text on page no. 152.

TOPIC 02 Morphology and Modification of Leaf

The leaf is a lateral, generally flattened structure borne on the stem. It develops at the node and bears a bud in its axil. The bud later develops into a branch. Leaves originate from shoot apical meristems and are arranged in an acropetal order. They are the most important vegetative organs for photosynthesis.

Parts of a Leaf

A typical leaf has following three main parts

1. Leaf Base (Hypopodium)

The leaf is attached to the stem by the leaf base. In monocots, the leaf base is said to be sheathing as it expands and surrounds the stem partially and wholly. In dicots, the leaf base bears two lateral outgrowths called **stipules.**

In some leguminous plants, the leaf base may become swollen which is called the **pulvinus**. Leaves with stipules are called **stipulate** and those without them are termed as **exstipulate.**

2. Petiole (Mesopodium)

It is the stalk of a leaf. Petiole helps to hold the leaf blade towards light. Petiole raises the lamina high to the level of stem so, as to provide maximum required exposure to light and air.

3. Lamina (Epipodium)

The lamina or leaf blade is the green, expanded part of the leaf with veins and veinlets. It has a prominent median vein called the **midrib.** It produces thinner lateral veins which in turn branch to form veinlets. The lamina is the site of photosynthesis, gaseous exchange, transpiration and other metabolic activities. The shape, margin, apex, surface and extent of **incision** of lamina varies in different leaves.

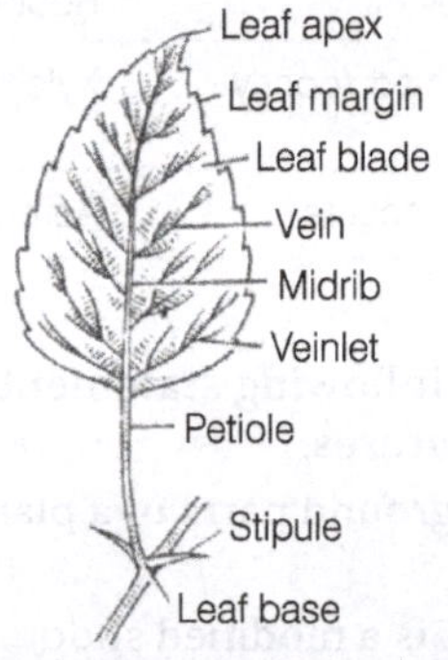

Fig. 7.12 Various parts of a leaf

Venation

The arrangement of veins and veinlets in the lamina of leaf is called **venation.** The midrib, veins and veinlets contain vascular tissues, i.e. xylem and phloem for conduction of water, mineral salts and food. Leaves have mainly two types of venation

1. Reticulate Venation

When the veinlets form a network, the venation is called **reticulate.** It is found in dicot leaves. However, some monocot leaves like *Smilax*, *Dioscorea* and *Alocasia* also show reticulate venation.

2. Parallel Venation

When the veins run parallel to each other within a lamina, the venation is termed as parallel, e.g. *Calophyllum*, *Zingiber officinale,* etc. It can be of the following types as shown in the figure below

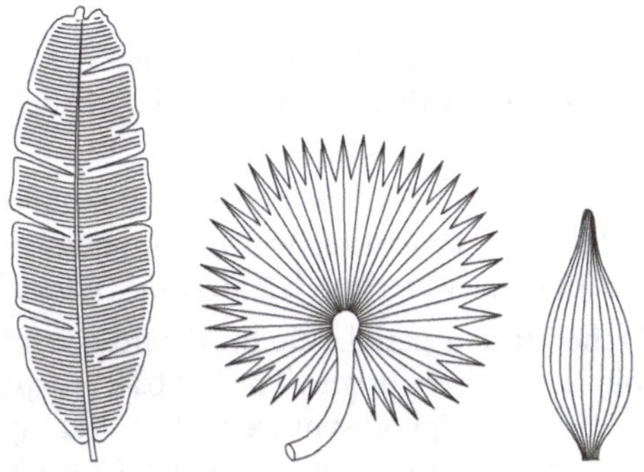

Fig. 7.13 Types of parallel venation

Types of Leaves

Leaves can be of following types

1. Simple Leaves

A leaf having a single or undivided lamina is called **simple leaf.** The lamina of a simple leaf may be incised, but the incisions do not touch the midrib. An axillary bud is always present in the axil of leaf petiole and stem. The lamina can have various types of incisions which may reach upto half (fid), more than half (partite) or near the base or midrib (sect).

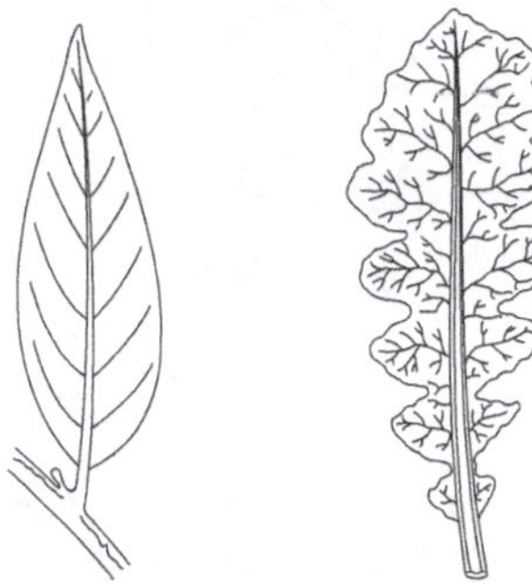

Fig. 7.14 Simple leaves

2. Compound Leaves

A leaf is called compound when the incision of the leaf blade goes down to the midrib (rachis) or to the petiole so that the leaf is broken up into a number of segments called **leaflets.**

A bud is present in the axil of petiole in both **simple** and **compound** leaves, but not in the axil of leaflets of the compound leaf. A compound leaf can be of following two types

(i) **Pinnately Compound Leaves** In these leaves, the incision of lamina is directed towards the midrib, which is known as **rachis.** Leaflets are arranged on both side, of the rachis, e.g. neem, rose, etc.

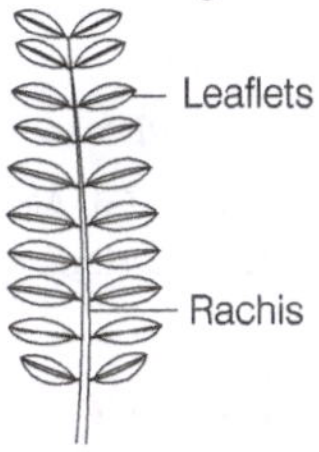

Fig. 7.15 Pinnately compound leaf

(ii) **Palmate Compound Leaves** The leaflets are attached at a common point, i.e. at the tip of petiole as in silk cotton.

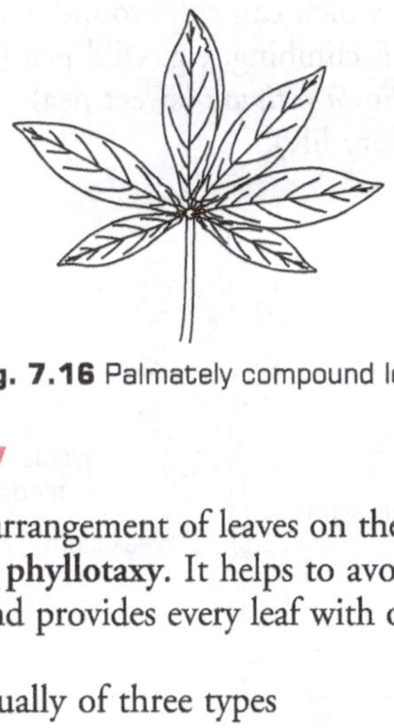

Fig. 7.16 Palmately compound leaf

Phyllotaxy

The pattern of arrangement of leaves on the stem or branch is called **phyllotaxy.** It helps to avoid overcrowding and provides every leaf with optimum sunshine.

Phyllotaxy is usually of three types

1. Alternate (Spiral) Phyllotaxy

In this type, a single leaf arises at each node in alternate manner, e.g. China rose, mustard and sunflower plants.

2. Opposite Phyllotaxy

In this type, a pair of leaves arises at each node and opposite to each other, e.g. *Calotropis* and *Psidium guajava* (guava plants).

3. Whorled (Verticillate) Phyllotaxy

If more than two leaves arise at a node and form a whorl, it is called **whorled**. The leaves of one whorl generally alternate with those of the adjacent whorls in order to provide maximum exposure, e.g. *Nerium* (kaner), *Alstonia*.

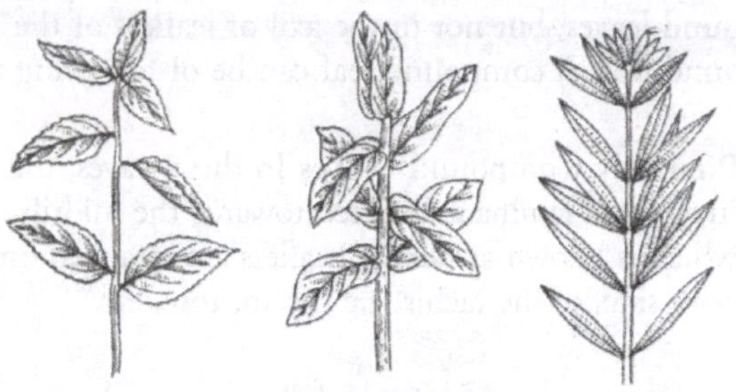

Fig. 7.17 Types of phyllotaxy (a) Alternate (b) Opposite (c) Whorled

Modifications of Leaves

Leaves of plants are modified to perform different additional functions in addition to their main function, i.e. photosynthesis.

(i) **Leaf Tendrils** These are thread-like sensitive structures, which can coil around a support to help the plant in climbing, e.g. wild pea (*Lathyrus aphaca*), *Pisum sativum* (sweet pea) and *Gloriosa superba* (glory lily).

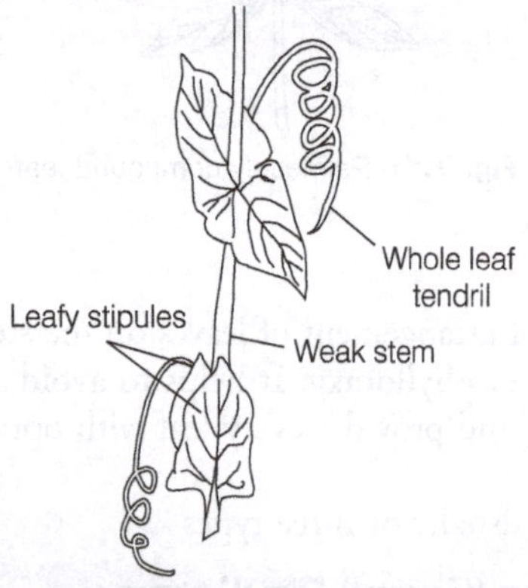

Fig. 7.18 Whole leaf tendril of *L. aphaca*

(ii) **Phyllode** It is a green, short-lived and flattened petiole or rachis of a leaf, which performs the function of photosynthesis, e.g. Australian *Acacia*. Phyllodes develop usually vertically and possess fewer stomata hence, reduce transpiration.

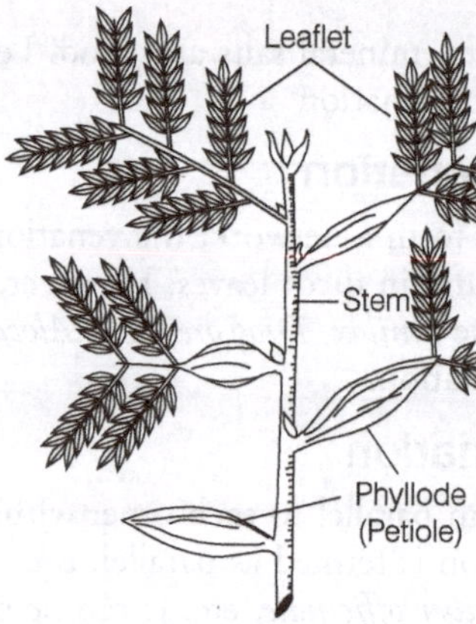

Fig. 7.19 Phyllode of *Acacia*

(iii) **Insectivorous Plants** These are those that capture insects to obtain nutrients (nitrogenous compounds) from them. The examples of such plants are as follows

(a) **Bladder** The segments of the leaf modify into bladder-like structures, which trap small insects present in the water, e.g. bladderwort (*Utricularia*).

(b) **Pitcher** It is a petiole modified into a tendril to hold the pitcher upright. The leaf base is expanded to carry out photosynthesis. The leaf apex is modified into a lid, e.g. *Nepenthes, Dischidia* and *Sarracenia*.

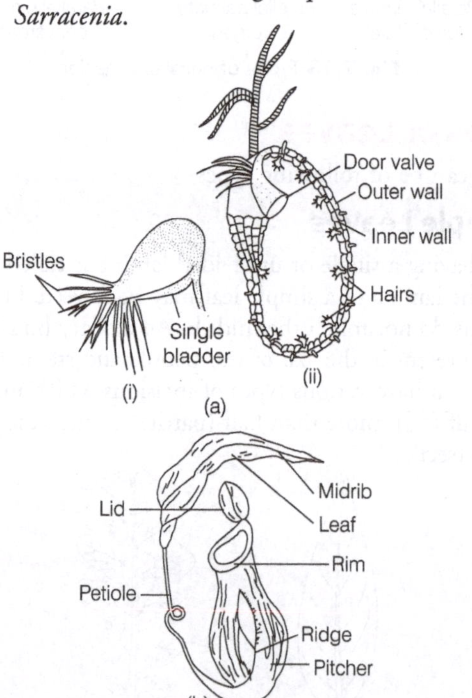

Fig. 7.20 (a)-(i) Single leaf bladder of *Utricularia*, (ii) LS of bladder (b) Leaf pitcher of *Nepenthes*

Note

Venus fly trap (*Dionaea muscipula*) is an insectivorous plant. It has snap trap mechanism for capturing insects. The petiole is winged. The lamina is bilobed. Each lobe possesses blades which are hinged at the midline. These leaves with spiny teeth can fold together to capture an insect that arrives on the leaf.

(iv) **Protection** Some leaves are modified for protection of plant. These are

(a) **Leaf Spines** The entire leaf or a part of a leaf may be modified into a pointed structure called **spine**, as in *Opuntia*. They protect the plant from grazing animals and also help to check transpiration by reducing the leaf area.

(b) **Scale Leaves** These are thin, membranous leaves found at the nodal region. Each scaly leaf contains an axillary bud in its axil. They protect axillary buds, e.g. *Zingiber officinale* (ginger).

(v) **Storage of Food Scaly Storage Leaf** In onion, leaves become scaly and store food.

(vi) **Reproduction** In *Bryophyllum*, vegetative propagation takes place by leaves as they possess marginal buds which form plantlets while they remain attached to the plant.

Functions of Leaves

The leaves have many primary and secondary functions.

Primary Functions

(i) The most important function of leaves is photosynthesis to prepare food with the help of sunlight and carbon dioxide.

(ii) Leaves contain stomata through which gaseous exchange occurs.

(iii) Leaves are the site of transpiration.

(iv) They protect axillary, floral and terminal buds from mechanical injury and desiccation.

Secondary Functions

(i) Leaves store food as in the leaf base, e.g. onion.

(ii) Leaves change into phyllodes to protect against transpiration.

(iii) Storage of water in the cells of some succulent plants, e.g. *Aloe*.

(iv) In *Salvinia*, one leaf of each node is changed into roots that acts as balancer for floating.

(v) In some plants like *Euphorbia*, the young leaves are brightly coloured to attract insects for pollination.

Topic Practice 2

Multiple Choice Questions

(1 Mark)

1. The leaf remain attached to the stem through

(a) hypopodium (b) mesopodium
(c) epipodium (d) None of these

Ans (a) The leaf remain attached to the stem through hypopodium.

2. Given below is the diagram of a typical leaf. In which of the following all the four parts labelled as *A, B, C* and *D* are correctly identified?

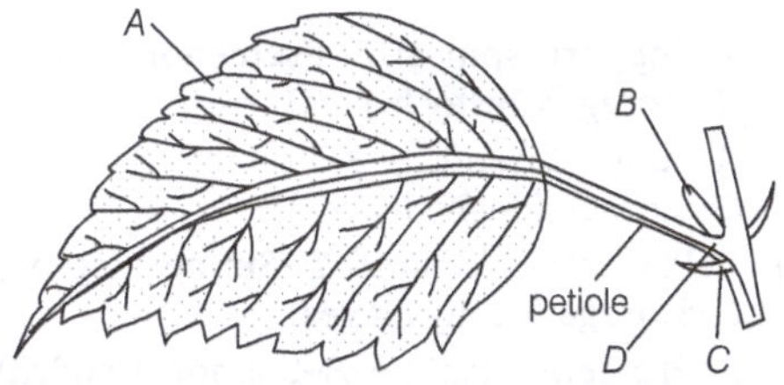

	A	B	C	D
(a)	Lamina	Axillary bud	Stipule	Leaf base
(b)	Lamina	Stipule	Axillary bud	Leaf base
(c)	Lamina	Axillary bud	Stipule	Pedicel
(d)	Leaflet	Axillary bud	Stipule	Leaf base

Ans (a)

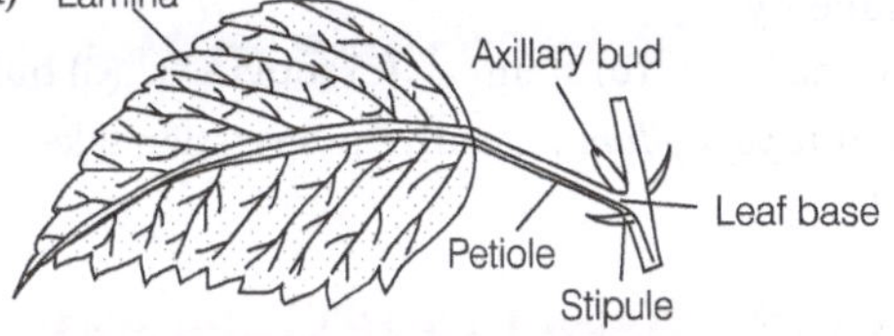

Structure of a leaf showing different parts

3. Which of the following statements is not correct?

(a) Arrangement of veins in leaf lamina is called venation.
(b) In reticulate venation, veinlets form a network
(c) In parallel venation, veins run parallel to each other.
(d) Leaves of dicotyledonous plants possesses parallel venation.

Ans (d) The statement (d) is incorrect. Leaves of dicotyledonous plants, generally possess reticulate venation, while parallel venation is the characteristic feature of most monocotyledons.

4. Whorled phyllotaxy is found in

(a) *Nerium* (b) *Alstonia*
(c) *Calotropis* (d) Both (a) and (b)

Ans (d) Whorled phyllotaxy is found in *Nerium* and *Alstonia*

5. Identify the type of leaf modification in the given diagram (*A* to *C*).

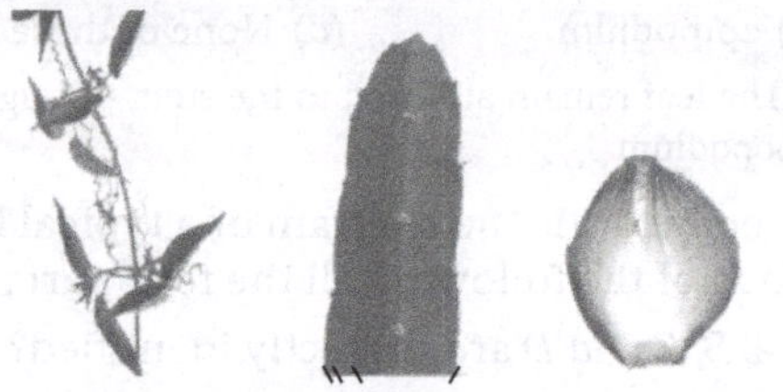

A B C

(a) *A*–Support (spines), *B*–Protection (tendril), *C*–Storage (fleshy leaves)
(b) *A*–Support (tendril), *B*–Protection (spine), *C*–Storage (fleshy leaves)
(c) *A*–Protection (tendril), *B*–Support (spine), *C*–Storage (fleshy leaves)
(d) *A*–Protection (spine), *B*–Support (tendril), *C*–Storage (fleshy leaves)

Ans (b) Figure *A* represents leaf tendrils, which help the plant in supporting around other plants for climbing. Figure *B* represents leaves modified into spines, which protect the plant and figure *C* is showing fleshy leaves, which store the food.

6. In *Bryophyllum*, vegetative propagation takes place by

(a) leaf (b) stem (c) roots (d) bulbil

Ans (a) In *Bryophyllum* vegetative propagation takes place by leaf.

Very Short Answer Type Questions

1 Mark

7. What is the expanded, green part of leaf called ?

Ans The expanded, green part of leaf is called lamina or epipodium.

8. Reticulate and parallel venations are characteristics of .... and ...., respectively. **NCERT Exemplar**

Ans Reticulate venation–Dicot plants
Parallel venation–Monocot plants.

9. Give any two examples of parallel venation.

Ans (i) *Calophyllum*
(ii) *Zingiber officinale.*

10. In *Alstonia*, the phyllotaxy is called whorled. Why?

Ans A number of leaves arise radially from a single node in *Alstonia*, so it is called whorled.

11. Why the leaves of *Aloe* and *Agave* store water?

Ans In *Aloe* and *Agave*, the leaves store water to resist drought conditions.

12. Why do insects get attract towards pitcher plants?

Ans In pitcher plants, the leaf apex gives rise to a coloured lid for attracting the insects.

13. Why do leaves modify into bladder-like structure in *Utricularia*?

Ans In *Utricularia*, leaves modify into bladder-like structure to trap small insect. They obtain nitrogenous compounds from them.

Short Answer Type I Questions

2 Marks

14. What is pulvinus? Give an example of a plant that has pulvinus.

Ans Pulvinus is the swollen leaf base. It is found in some leguminous plants, e.g. pea, bean, etc. (2)

15. Differentiate between reticulate venation and parallel venation.

Ans Differences between reticulate and parallel venation are

Reticulate Venation	Parallel Venation
Veins are not oriented parallel to one another.	Veins are oriented parallel to one another.
Smaller veins produce a network or reticulum.	A reticulum is not produced.
It is the characteristic feature of dicotyledons.	It is the characteristic feature of monocotyledons.

(2)

16. Reticulate venation is found in dicot leaves, while in monocot leaves venation is of parallel type. Biology being a science of exceptions, find out any exception to this generalisation. **NCERT Exemplar**

Ans Some dicot leaves have parallel venation, e.g. *Corymbium, Calophyllum, Eryngium.*
Some monocot leaves have reticulate venation, e.g. *Smilax, Colocasia, Dioscorea.* (2)

17. How is pinnately compound leaf different from a palmately compound leaf? **NCERT**

Ans Differences between pinnately and palmately compound leaves are

Pinnately Compound Leaf	Palmately Compound Leaf
The leaflets arise lateral to the rachis all along its length.	Leaflets arise radially from the tip of the rachis as the fingers of a palm.
The rachis may branched.	The rachis does not get branched.
e.g. rose, neem.	e.g. silk, cotton. (2)

18. You have heard about several insectivorous plants that feed on insects. *Nepenthes* or the pitcher plant is one such example which usually grows in shallow water or in marsh lands. Which part of the plant is modified into a 'pitcher'. How does this modification help the plant for food even though it can photosynthesise like any other green plant? **NCERT Exemplar**

Ans Part modified into pitcher—Lamina of leaf.

Uses This modification helps plant to obtain nitrogen which is deficient in marshy areas. (2)

Short Answer Type II Questions

3 Marks

19. What are the different parts of a leaf ?

Ans Refer to the text on page no. 156.

20. What do you understand venation? Leaves show how many types of venation ?

Ans Refer to the text on page no. 156 and 157.

21. How are pinnately compound leaves different from palmate compound leaves ?

Ans Refer to Answer no. 17

22. Discuss the different functions of leaves.

Ans Refer to the text on page no. 159.

Long Answer Type Questions

5 Marks

23. How do various leaf modifications help plants? **NCERT**

Ans Various leaf modifications help plants in the following ways

(i) Leaf tendrils help in climbing up for support, e.g. pea.

(ii) Spines provide protection from browsing animals, e.g. *Opuntia*.

(iii) Leaves modified into pitcher help in trapping insects to fulfill nitrogen requirements, e.g. insectivorous plants.

(iv) Storage of food materials, e.g. onion.

(v) Petiole expands and carry out photosynthesis, e.g. Australian *Acacia*. (1× 5)

24. Explain with suitable examples the different types of phyllotaxy. **NCERT**

Ans The mode of arrangement of leaves on the stem and its branches is called phyllotaxy (*Phyllon*–leaf; *taxis*–arrangement).

They are arranged most systematically, regularly and mathematically, so as to get proper sunlight and avoid overcrowding.

Phyllotaxy in leaves is of following three types

(i) **Alternate** A single leaf arises at a node, e.g. China rose, mango, mustard, sunflower, etc.

(ii) **Opposite** Two leaves arise at a node, opposite to each other, e.g. guava, *Calotropis*, tulsi, etc.

(iii) **Whorled** More than two leaves arise at each node forming a circle or whorl, e.g. *Alstonia scholaris*, etc. (5)

SUMMARY

- Plant morphology deals with the study of external forms and features of different plant organs.
- Angiosperms exhibit enormous variety in their forms, habits, habitats, mode of nutrition and the whole lifespan.
- **Angiosperms** consists of various organ systems, i.e. a descending, positively geotropic **root system** and an ascending, negatively geotropic **shoot system**.
- Roots mainly consist of four zones, i.e. **root cap, meristematic zone**, **elongation zone** and **maturation zone**. Every part of the root perform specific function. Root hairs absorb water and minerals and are numerous in the region of maturation. Root cap protects the growing tip of the roots.
- **Root system** consists of either **tap root** (i.e. originate from radicle) or **adventitious root** (i.e. originate from any other part of the plant except the radicle).
- Tap roots sometimes modify to perform secondary functions, i.e. fleshy storage tap root, e.g. **conical, fusiform, napiform, tuberous** roots, nodulated tap root and respiratory roots.
- Adventitious root also modify fo perform various functions, i.e storage of food, e.g, **tuberous fasciculated, moniliform, annulated, palmate** roots, etc. mechanical support, e.g. **buttress, stilt, prop**, contractile roots, etc. and vital roots, e.g. assimilatory, parasitic, epiphytic, floating roots, etc.
- **Shoot system** consists of aerial part of plant, which includes stem, branches, leaves, flowers, fruits, bud, etc. Stem is differentiated into nodes and internodes.
- **Buds** are young, immature, under developed and compact shoots. It mainly arises from stem, but sometimes roots and leaf also bear bud.
- **Stem** gets modified to various forms so as to perform different specialised functions in many plants, e.g. underground stem, subaerial and aerial stem.
- **Underground stem** modifies to store food, e.g. Rhizome (e.g *Zingiber officinale*), Tuber (e.g. potato), Bulb (e.g onion) and corm (e.g. *Alocasia*)
- **Subaerial stem** modifies into Runner (e.g. *Cynodon dactylon*), sucker (e.g. banana), stolons (e.g. jasmine), and offsets (e.g. *Pistia*).
- **Aerial stem** modifies into **stem tendrils** (e.g. *Passiflora*), stem thorns (e.g. *Asparagus*), phylloclades (e.g. *Opuntia*), **cladodes** (e.g. *Ruscus*) and bulbil (e.g. *Dioscorea bulbifera*).
- **Leaf** of angiosperms are flattened, green, lateral appendages meant for performing photosynthesis. These arise from nodes of stems and its branches. It consists of three parts–leaf lamina, petiole and leaf base.
- **Venation** is the arrangement of veins and veinlets in the leaf lamina. It is of two types, i.e. reticulate venation and parallel venation.
- In **reticulate venation** main vein divides into few veinlets to form network in the lamina, e.g. *Ficus religiosa* . In **Parallel** venation veins are arranged in paralleled fashion, e.g. banana.
- There are two types of leaves, i.e simple and compound.
- **Simple** leaf lamina is entire, and it bears an auxilliary bud at the axil of petiole, e.g mango. In **compound** leaf lamina is completely incised up to the midrib or petiole, e.g. rose, *oxalis*. In **palmately compound** leaves incisions of lamina are directed towards the petiole.
- **Phyllotaxy** is the arrangement of leaves on the stem. In **alternate phyllotaxy** a single leaf is present at each node in alternate manner, e.g. China rose. In **opposite phyllotaxy** leaves are borne on each node opposite to each other, e.g. *Ocimum*.
- Leaves are modified into various structures to perform various functions, e.g. **tendrils, hooks, pitcher, phyllode**, etc.

Chapter Practice

Multiple Choice Questions

(1 Mark)

1. Which amongst the following options contains mismatched pair?
   (a) Direct elongation of radicle – Primary roots
   (b) Root system originating from the stem's base – Fibrous roots
   (c) Roots not arising from the radicle – Tap roots
   (d) Constitution of primary root and its branches – Tap root system
2. Which of the following is the smallest region of the root?
   (a) Root cap
   (b) Region of elongation
   (c) Region of meristematic activity
   (d) Region of maturation
3. Identify the mismatched pair.
   (a) Prop roots – Provide support
   (b) Stilt roots – Originate from stem's nodal part
   (c) Pneumatophores – Help in storing food
   (d) Edible roots – Sweet potato
4. In which plant underground stem spread to new niches and when older parts die new plants are formed?
   (a) grasses (b) strawberry
   (c) *Pistia* (d) Both (a) and (b)
5. Leaf base expands into sheath covering the stem partially or wholly.
   This is the characteristic of
   (a) dicot (b) monocot
   (c) pteridophytes (d) gymnosperm

Assertion-Reason Type Questions

(1 Mark)

■ **Direction** (Q. Nos. 6-9) *In each of the following questions, a statement of Assertion (A) is given followed by corresponding statement of Reason (R). Of the statements, mark the correct answer as*

(a) If both A and R are true and R is the correct explanation of A
(b) If both A and R are true, but R is not the correct explanation of A
(c) If A is true, but R is false
(d) If A is false, but R is true

6. **Assertion** (A) Root hairs are not present on whole root surface.
   Reason (R) Root hairs absorb water.
7. **Assertion** (A) Adventitious roots develop from any part of plant.
   Reason (R) In such plants, tap root is not developed.
8. **Assertion** (A) Stem develops from hypocotyl of embryo.
   Reason (R) Nodes bear axillary buds.
9. **Assertion** (A) The underground root system develop from the radicle of embryo.
   Reason (R) Roots helps in fixation of the plant as wall as absorption of water and minerals.

Answers

1. (c) 2. (c) 3. (c) 4. (d) 5. (b)
6. (b) 7. (c) 8. (d) 9. (d)

Very Short Answer Type Questions

(1 Mark)

10. Why type of roots are found in *Dahlia* ?
11. Which special tissue is found in epiphytic roots for the absorption of hygroscopic water ?
12. Which is the largest axillary bud ?
13. Rhizome is an underground stem Why ?
14. Which type of venation is found in *Dioscorea* ?
15. Which plants show alternate phyllotaxy?

Short Answer Type I Questions

(2 Marks)

16. Why do roots of *Pisum sativum* become nodulated ?
17. Why in *Dueanata* axillary bud develops into thorns ?

18. In which plants phyllodes present? Give examples.
19. Draw a labelled diagram of a typical leaf.
20. Diagrammatically show the reticulate and parallel venation.

Short Answer Type II Questions

3 Marks

21. What is tap root system ? Explain with examples.
22. How are prop roots different from stilt roots ?
23. Differentiate between phylloclades and cladodes.
24. What are compound leaves ? Explain with examples.
25. List out the four primary functions of leaves.

Long Answer Type Questions

5 Marks

26. Differentiate between tap root and adventitious root.
27. Discuss the different modifications of tap root for the storage of food N_2 fixation and respiration.
28. What are different modifications of subaerial stems ?

Case Based Question

4/5 Marks

29. *Read the following passage and answer the questions that follows*

During his field trip to a botanical garden, Raju observed diffrent patterns of leaves arranged on the stem/branch of different plants. He collected three samples or given below as *A*, *B* and *C*. Study the figure and answer the following question.

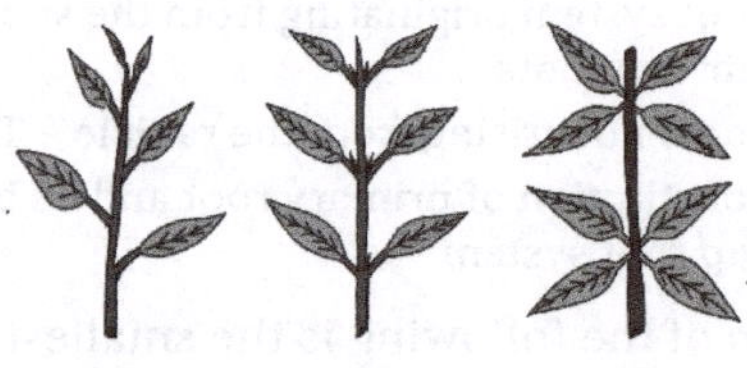

(i) What term is used for this arrangement in the samples?

(ii) Identify the type of arrangement in *B*.

(iii) Describe the type of leaf arrangement as observed in *C*. Give an example of a plant with this arrangement.

Or (iii) Which of the given plant denotes alternate phyllotaxy? Out of the three cases given above, which one do you think is advantageous and why?

CHAPTER

08

Morphology of Flower, Fruit and Seed

In the previous chapter, we have learnt about the morphology and modifications of root, stem and leaf. In this chapter, we will discuss about the inflorescence, flower, fruit, seed and some important angiospermic families.

TOPIC 01 The Flower and Inflorescence

The Flower

A flower is the reproductive unit in the angiosperms. It is meant for sexual reproduction. Morphologically, it is considered as a shoot bearing nodes and modified floral leaves. **Flower** is called **modified shoot** because the position of the buds in both flower and shoot is same and can be in terminal or axillary in position.

Structure of a Flower

A flower arises at the axil of a leaf-like structure called **bract.** Flowers with bracts are called **bracteate** and those without bracts are called **ebracteate.**

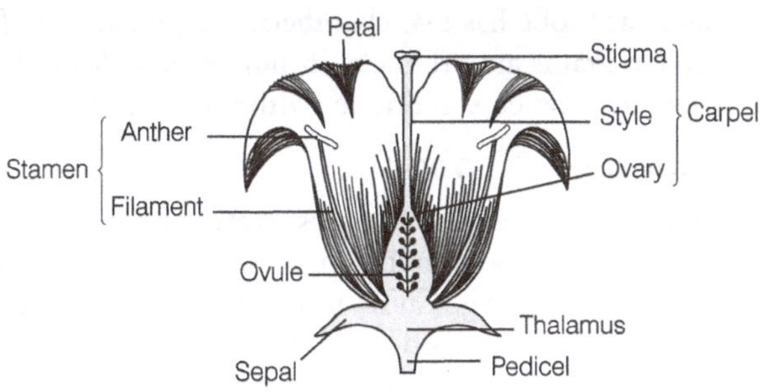

Fig 8.1 Structure of a typical flower

The terminal and swollen part of the axis of the flower is the **receptacle** or **thalamus.** The receptacle contains four different types of whorls arranged in successive mode of sepals, petals, stamens and carpels. If the leaves are present on the pedicel, they are called **bracteoles**.

Parts of a Flower

A typical flower consists of four distinct parts; the calyx, the corolla, the androecium and the gynoecium. The calyx and corolla are **accessory parts** while the androecium and gynoecium are **essential parts**. Hence, sepals and petals are the sterile parts of a flower and are called **non-essential whorls**. The gynoecium and androecium are the fertile parts of a flower and are called **essential whorls**.

These essential parts consist of two kinds of sporophylls, the microsporophyll (male) and the megasporophyll (female). A flower can be **unisexual** or **bisexual**. It is borne on short or long axis.

The axis contains two regions the pedicel and the thalamus or receptacle. The pedicel may be short, long or even absent. The thalamus is the swollen end of the axis on which the floral whorls are arranged.

A flower is called **complete** when it contains all the floral whorls, i.e. calyx, corolla, androecium and gynoecium, e.g. *Solanum*. While the flower in the absence of any one of these four floral whorls, is called **incomplete flower**, e.g. *Cucurbita*.

Different whorls present on flower are given below

1. Calyx

It is the outermost whorl of a flower. It is made up of units like sepals. The sepals are generally green, leaf-like and protect the flower in the bud stage. They have veins and stomata like ordinary leaves, but are thicker in nature. The sepals may be **gamosepalous** (sepals united), e.g. *Caesalpinia* or **polysepalous** (sepals free), e.g. *Crotalaria*.

The sepals also prevent transpiration from inner parts of the flower. Coloured sepals attract insects for pollination.

2. Corolla

It is composed of petals. The petals are usually brightly coloured to attract insects for pollination. Like calyx, corolla may also be **gamopetalous** (petals united) or **polypetalous** (petals free).

The shape and colour of corolla may vary greatly in shape. Corolla may be tubular, bell-shaped or funnel-shaped.

Perianth

It is a collective term given to the group of undifferentiated sepals and petals. The unit of perianth is called **tepal. Sepaloid** is when tepal resembles with sepal. **Petaloid** is when tepal resembles with petal.

Aestivation

The mode of arrangement of sepals or petals in floral bud with respect to the other members of the same whorl is known as aestivation. The aestivation pattern is important in classification of plants. It is of following types

(i) **Valvate** Petals are close to each other, but do not overlap, e.g. mustard (*Brassica*).

(ii) **Twisted** Regular overlapping of petals occurs in which margin of one petal overlaps with the next one petal, e.g. China rose (*Hibiscus rosa-sinensis*).

(iii) **Imbricate** There are five petals, arranged in such a way that one petal is completely external and another petal is completely internal, while three petals are partially external and partially internal, e.g. *Cassia, Cullistemon, Caesalpinia*.

(iv) **Vexillary** When the largest petal overlaps the two lateral petals which in turn overlap the two smallest anterior petals (keel), the aestivation is called as vexillary or papilionaceous.

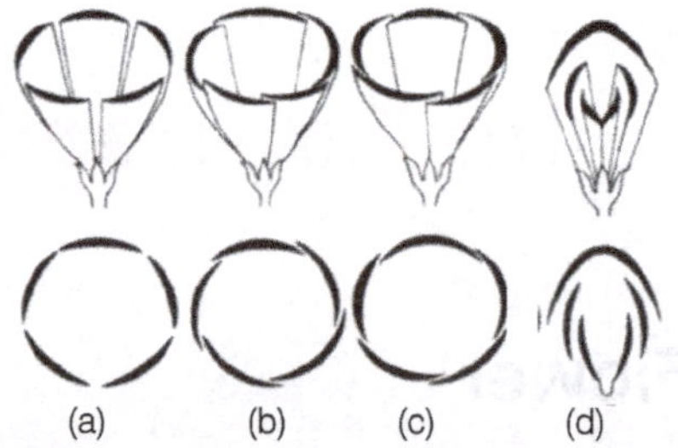

Fig 8.2 Different types of aestivation of calyx and corolla (a) Valvate, (b) Twisted, (c) Imbricate, (d) Vexillary

3. Androecium

It is the third whorl of flower composed of stamens or **microsporangium.** Each stamen, which represents the male reproductive organ consists of a stalk or a filament and an **anther.** Each anther is usually bilobed which are attached at the back by a sterile band called **connective** and each lobe has two chambers, the pollen sacs. The pollen grains are produced in **pollen sacs.** A sterile stamen is called **staminode** (without anther).

Number of Lobes

Most of the anthers of angiospermic plants are **dithecous**, i.e. have two lobes, but some also have only one lobe, i.e. **monothecous**, e.g. China rose (Malvaceae). Stamens can be of different types depending on their union with other members such as petals or among themselves.

Adhesion of Stamens

It is the fusion of stamens with other whorls of flowers. It is of following types

(i) When stamens are attached to the petals, they are **epipetalous,** e.g. brinjal.

(ii) When stamens are attached to the perianth, the condition is called **epiphyllous,** e.g. lily.

Cohesion of Stamens

It is the fusion of stamens or their parts, which is of following types

(i) The stamens in a flower may either remain free, i.e. **polyandrous** or may be united in varying degrees.

(ii) The stamens may be united into one bunch or one bundle, i.e. **monoadelphous** as in China rose. They may be in two bundles, i.e. **diadelphous** as in pea or into more than two bundles, i.e. **polyadelphous** as in citrus.

(iii) In **synandrous,** the stamens are united throughout their whole length by both filaments and lengths, e.g. members of family–Cucurbitaceae.

(iv) In **syngenesious,** all anthers are united, but their filaments remain free, e.g. members of family–Compositae.

(v) There may be a variation in the length of filament as in *Salvia* and mustard.

4. Gynoecium

It is the female reproductive part of a flower. It is made up of one or more carpels or megasporangium. Megaspores are produced within the megasporangium. A carpel consists of three parts, i.e. stigma, style and ovary.

The **stigma** is usually present at the tip of style and is the receptive surface for pollen grains.

Ovary is the enlarged basal part on which lies the elongated tube, the **style.** The style connects the ovary to the stigma. Each ovary bears one or more ovules attached to a flattened, cushion-like **placenta.**

Cohesion of Carpels

It is the interaction between the members of gynoecium. It is of following two types

(i) **Apocarpous** When more than one carpel is present, they may be free called as **apocarpous,** e.g. lotus and rose.

(ii) **Syncarpous** When carpels are fused together, the gynoecium is called **syncarpous,** e.g. brinjal and *Hibiscus.*

Number of Locules in the Ovary

The cavity enclosed by the ovary wall is called **locule.** The number of locules in the ovary correspond to the **number of carpels in the gynoecium,** i.e. **unilocular** (only one locule, e.g. pea), **bilocular** (two locules, e.g. tomato), **trilocular** (three locules, e.g. *Ricinus*), **multilocular** (many locules, e.g. orange and lemon).

Placentation

The arrangement of ovules within the ovary is known as **placentation.** The placenta is a tissue, which develops along the inner wall of the ovary. The ovule or ovules remain attached to the placenta.

The placentation can be of different types

(a) **Marginal** The placenta forms a ridge along the ventral suture of the ovary and the ovules are borne on this ridge forming two rows which is called **marginal** placentation, e.g. pea.

(b) **Axile** When the placenta is axial and the ovules are attached to it in a multilocular ovary, the placentation is called **axile,** e.g. China rose, tomato and lemon.

(c) **Parietal** When the ovules develop on the inner wall of the ovary or on peripheral part, it is called **parietal placentation.** Ovary is one-chambered, but it becomes two-chambered due to the formation of false septum, e.g. mustard and *Argemone.*

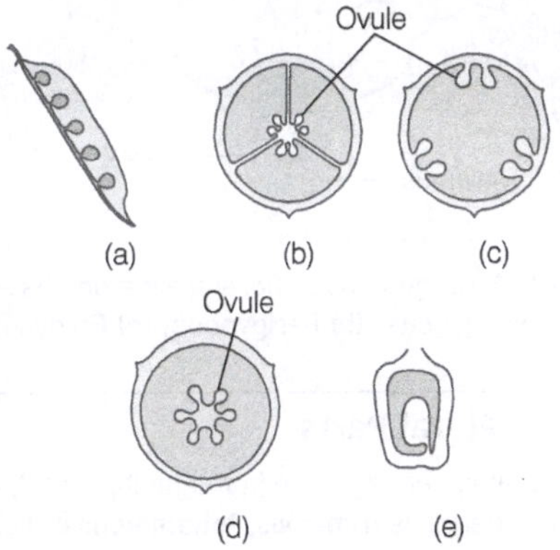

Fig 8.3 Types of placentation (a) Marginal, (b) Axile, (c) Parietal, (d) Free central, (e) Basal

(d) **Free-Central** When the ovules are borne on central axis and septa are absent, the placentation is called **free central,** e.g. *Dianthus* and primrose.

(e) **Basal** In this type, of placentation, the placenta develops at the base of ovary and a single ovule is attached to it as in sunflower, marigold. The placenta develops directly on the thalamus.

Insertion of Floral Parts (Forms of Thalamus)

The positions of different whorls of flowers are different. This is due to the position of ovary. These positions may be of three types

1. Hypogynous Flower

The thalamus is conical, dome-shaped or flat. The ovary is present at the top of thalamus. The stamen, petals and sepals are separate and successively inserted below the ovary. Ovary is superior, whereas rest of the structures are inferior, e.g. *Brassica*, *Hibiscus*, *Petunia*.

2. Perigynous Flower

The margin of thalamus grows upwards forming a cup-like structure called **calyx tube**. The calyx tube encloses ovary, but remains free from it and the sepals, petals and stamens are present in it. The ovary is **half inferior**, e.g. rose, plum, peach, etc.

3. Epigynous Flower

The thalamus grows upwards to completely **cover** the ovary and also fused inseparably with the latter. The other floral parts are borne at the top of the fused thalamus and ovary. The ovary is called **inferior**, e.g. *Helianthus* (sunflower), *Cucurbita* (pumpkin), *Pyrus* (apple).

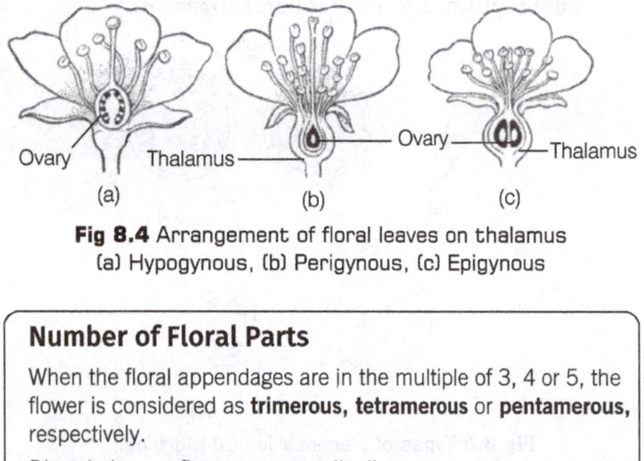

Fig 8.4 Arrangement of floral leaves on thalamus (a) Hypogynous, (b) Perigynous, (c) Epigynous

> **Number of Floral Parts**
>
> When the floral appendages are in the multiple of 3, 4 or 5, the flower is considered as **trimerous, tetramerous** or **pentamerous**, respectively.
>
> Dicotyledonous flowers are usually di, tetra or pentamerous, while, monocotyledonous flowers are trimerous.

Symmetry of a Flower

The symmetry of a flower depends upon the shape, size and arrangement of floral parts, e.g. calyx, corolla, androecium and gynoecium.

Flowers can be actinomorphic and zygomorphic on the basis of symmetry.

1. Actinomorphic

In this type, a flower can be divided into exactly equal halves by any vertical section passing through the centre of a flower, e.g. mustard, *Datura*.

2. Zygomorphic

In this type, flower can be divided into two identical halves through only one particular vertical plane, e.g. *Ocimum*, *Cassia*.

The Inflorescence

The arrangement and distribution of flowers over a plant is called **inflorescence**. The main axis that bears flowers is known as **peduncle**. The inflorescence can be of following three types

1. Racemose Inflorescence

In racemose type of inflorescence, the main axis continues to grow and the flowers are borne laterally in an **acropetal succession** (the older flowers are found towards the base and younger ones at the apex) or **centripetal** (older towards periphery and younger towards centre).

Fig 8.5 Racemose inflorescence

2. Cymose Inflorescence

In cymose inflorescence, the tip of the main axis terminates in a flower and further growth continues by one or more lateral branches, which also behave like the main axis. The arrangement of flowers is either basipetal (younger flowers occupy basal position, while older flowers towards the apex) or centrifugal (older towards centre and younger towards periphery).

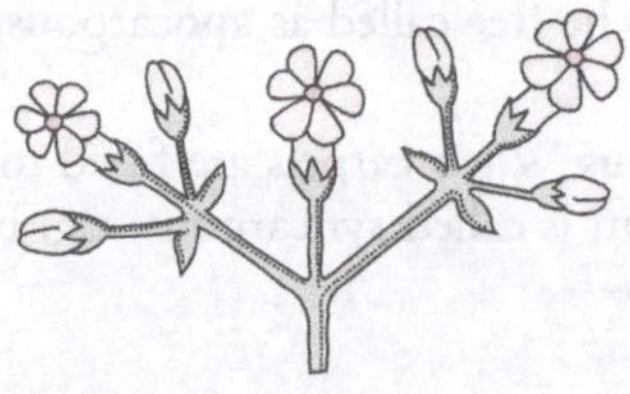

Fig 8.6 Cymose inflorescence

Differences between Racemose and Cymose Inflorescence

Racemose	Cymose
Indefinite growth of flower bearing shoot.	The apex terminates into flower so growth of flower bearning shoot is definite.
Flowers borne in acropetal mannar (older flower at base).	Flowers arranged in basipetal manner (older flower at apical position).

3. Special Inflorescence

It mainly involves highly modified and densely crowded inflorescences. The special type of inflorescences can be divided into following types

(i) **Cyathium** It is highly reduced and is a cup-shaped involucre of five bracts having nectariferous glands. A single large female flower is present in the centre of the cup and scorpioid male flowers surround this female flower. Every male flower is represented by a single stalked stamen borne in the axil of a scaly bract, e.g. *Euphorbia.*

(ii) **Verticillaster** It is a modified condensed dichasial cyme like inflorescence. There are two clusters each having 3-9 flowers that develop on a node in the axils of opposite leaves, e.g. *Ocimum sanctum* (basil).

(iii) **Hypanthodium** In this type, the main axis is condensed into a cup or flask-shaped, fleshy receptacle. It bears three kinds of flowers, i.e. **male flowers** (towards the pore), **female flowers** (towards the base) and **neutral flowers** occur in between male and female flowers, e.g. peepal (*Ficus relegiosa*) and banyan (*Ficus benghalensis*).

Topic Practice 1

Multiple Choice Questions

1 Mark

1. Find the incorrect statement.

(a) A flower is a modified shoot wherein the shoot apical meristem changes into floral meristem.

(b) Flower is always solitary when shoot bud transforms into flower.

(c) The arrangement of flowers on the floral axis is called inflorescence.

(d) The apex produces different floral appendages horizontally and internodes elongates.

Ans (d) The statement (d) is incorrect. A flower is a modified shoot wherein the shoot apical meristem changes to floral meristem. Internodes do not elongate and the axis gets condensed.

The apex produces different kinds of floral appendages laterally at successive nodes instead of leaves.

2. Identify flower parts *A* to *D* in the given diagrams correctly.

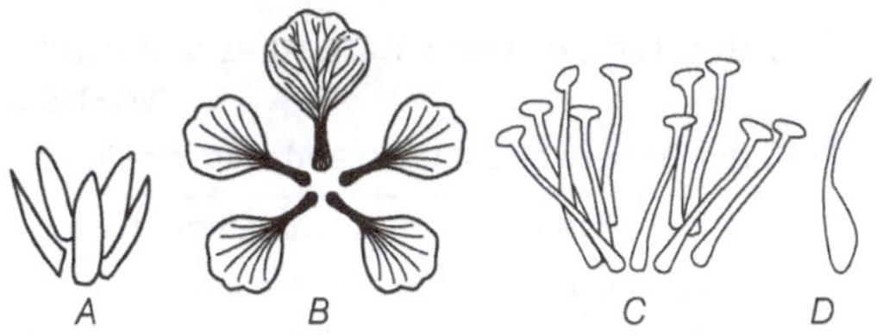

(a) *A*–Corolla, *B*–Calyx, *C*–Androecium, *D*–Gynoecium

(b) *A*–Calyx, *B*–Corolla, *C*–Androecium, *D*–Gynoecium

(c) *A*–Calyx, *B*–Corolla, *C*–Gynoecium, *D*–Androecium

(d) *A*–Corolla, *B*–Calyx, *C*–Gynoecium, *D*–Androecium

Ans (b) Parts of a flower

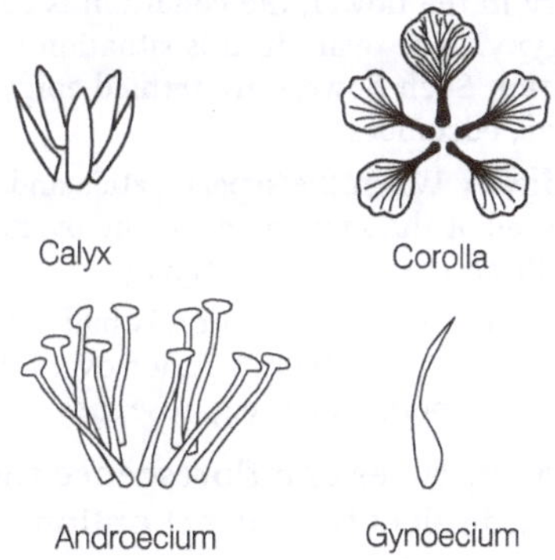

3. Choose the incorrect pair.

(a) Aestivation–Arrangement of sepals or petals in a floral bud

(b) Valvate–No overlapping of sepals or petals; *Calotropis*

(c) Imbricate aestivation–Overlapping margins, but in a particular direction; Cotton

(d) Vexillary aestivation – Also called papilionaceous aestivation; Pea

Ans (c) When the margins of sepals or petals overlap one another, but not in any particular direction as in *Cassia* and gulmohur, the aestivation is called imbricate.

4. On the basis of relative positions of different floral parts on the thalamus, a flower can be hypogynous, perigynous or epigynous. With respect to the given figures (*A*, *B*, *C* and *D*), select the correct option.

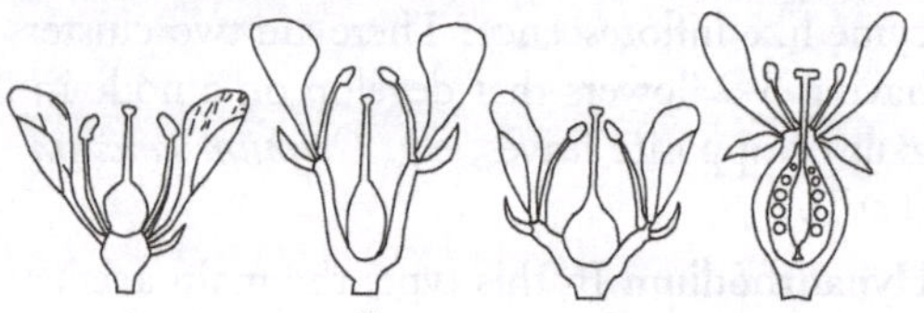

	A	*B*	*C*	*D*
(a)	Hypogynous	Perigynous	Perigynous	Epigynous
(b)	Hypogynous	Epigynous	Epigynous	Perigynous
(c)	Epigynous	Hypogynous	Hypogynous	Perigynous
(d)	Hypogynous	Hypogynous	Hypogynous	Epigynous

Ans (a) There are three forms of thalamus in regard to the relative positions of pistil and other whorls.

(i) **Hypogyny** When the sepals, petals and stamens are successively and separately inserted below the ovary in the flowers, the condition is known to be hypogyny and the ovary is said to be superior. Such flowers are called hypogynous as in mustard, China rose and brinjal.

(ii) **Epigyny** When the sepals, petals and stamens are successively and separately inserted above the ovary in the flower, the condition is described as epigyny. The ovary in this situation is said to be inferior. Such flowers are termed epigynous, e.g. guava, cucumber.

(iii) **Perigyny** When the sepals, petals and stamens are inserted at the same plane as the ovary, the condition is known as perigyny.

The ovary in such condition is half superior, subinferior or partially inferior ovary. Such flowers are called perigynous, e.g. rose, pea.

5. Identify the types of inflorescence shown in figure and select the correct option for *A* and *B*.

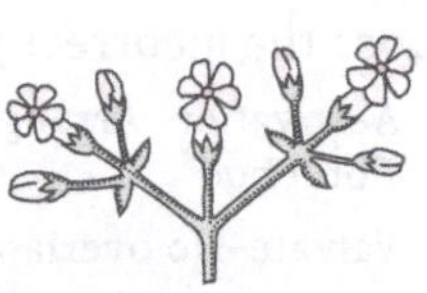

	A	*B*
(a)	Cymose	Racemose
(b)	Racemose	Cymose
(c)	Racemose	Racemose
(d)	Cymose	Cymose

Ans (b) The figures *A* and *B* show racemose and cymose inflorescence, respectively. Racemose inflorescence is an indeterminate inflorescence due to the presence of active growing point.

The axis of flowers, show indefinite growth and bears a number of flowers in either acropetal (older towards base and younger towards apex) or centripetal (older towards periphery and younger towards centre). In cymose inflorescence the main axis terminates in a flower, arranged in basipetal order.

Very Short Answer Type Questions

1 Mark

6. '*X*' is the female reproductive part of the flower, which consists of three parts *A*, *B*, and *C*. '*A*' is the swollen bottom part *B* is the long cylindrical part and *C* is the sticky part. Name all *X*, *A*, *B*, and *C*.

Ans *X* is a carpel; *A* is ovary; *B* is style and *C* is stigma.

7. Which is the technical term used for the androecium in a flower of China rose?

Ans Monadelphous.

Short Answer Type I Questions

2 Marks

8. Differentiate between pedicel and peduncle.

NCERT Exemplar

Ans Differences between pedicel and peduncle are

Pedicel	Peduncle
It is the stalk of a flower.	It is the axis of an inflorescence.
Pedicel bears a single flower.	It generally bears a number of flowers.

(2)

9. Write the name of units of these flower parts.
(i) Calyx (ii) Corolla
(iii) Androecium (iv) Gynoecium

Ans (i) Calyx–Sepals (ii) Corolla–Petals
(iii) Androecium–Stamens (iv) Gynoecium–Carpels

(1/2 × 4)

10. Distinguish between stamen and staminoide.

NCERT Exemplar

Ans Differences between stamen and staminoide are

Stamen	Staminoide
It is a complete functional male reproductive part of a flower.	It is a rudimentary, sterile or non-functional male reproductive part of a flower.
In produces pollen grains.	It does not produce pollen grains

(2)

11. Differentiate between apocarpous and syncarpous ovary. **NCERT**

Ans Difference between apocarpous and syncarpous ovary is

Apocarpous Ovary	Syncarpous Ovary
It has more than one and free carpels, e.g. lotus, rose.	It has more than one and fused carpels, e.g. *Hibiscus* (shoe flower), *Petunia*.

(2)

Short Answer Type II Questions
(3 Marks)

12. Sunflower is not a flower. Explain. **NCERT Exemplar**

Ans Sunflower is an inflorescence called capitulum or racemose head. It has a flat disc-shaped peduncle called receptacle. It bears an involucre of bracts on the periphery and two types of small sessile flowers called florets. The flower is arranged centripetally with youngest towards the periphery. There are ray florets which are sterile female flowers of ligulate type on the outside. The rest of the flower structure contains disc florets which are fertile bisexual flowers of tubular type. (3)

13. A typical angiospermic flower consists of four floral parts. Give the names of the floral parts and their arrangement sequentially. **NCERT Exemplar**

Ans (i) **Sepals** It is the green leaf-like outermost whorl (calyx).

(ii) **Petals** It is the second whorl (corolla) from below, often brightly coloured floral parts.

(iii) **Stamens** Third whorl (androecium) of knobbed thread-like male reproductive floral parts.

(iv) **Carpels** Central single whorl (gynoecium) of female reproductive floral parts. (3)

14. Differentiate between bract and bracteole.

Ans Differences between bract and bracteole are

Bract	Bracteole
It is a small leaf-like structure borne on the mother axis from where a flower develops.	It is a small leaf-like structure present on the pedicel of a flower.
It bears a flower in its axil.	It is borne over the stalk of the flower.
A single bract occurs at one place.	Generally two bracteoles occur over the pedicel of a flower.

(3)

15. Which structures form gynoecium? How is placenta related to gynoecium? What are its types?

Ans Gynoecium is the female reproductive whorl of the flower. It is composed of one or more carpels. Each carpel is differentiated into three parts, i.e. the ovary, style and stigma. (1)

Placenta is the tissue on which ovule(s) develops in the ovary. The placentation in the ovary may be

(i) marginal
(ii) axile
(iii) parietal
(iv) basal
(v) free-central. (2)

16. Represent all types of placentation diagrammatically only.

Ans Refer to fig. no. 8.3. (3)

17. How can you differentiate between free central and axile placentation?

Ans **Placentation** is the arrangement of ovules on the walls of ovary with the help of special kind of tissue called placenta. Plants show different types of placentation, central and axile are among them. (1)

They have the following differences

Free Central Placentation	Axile Placentation
Ovary contains only one chamber.	Ovary is syncarpous and multi-carpellary, i.e. contains many chambers.
The ovules are borne on the central axis and less free inside the ovary. The septa are absent.	Placenta arise from the central axis where the septa fuse to form axile column to which ovules are attached.

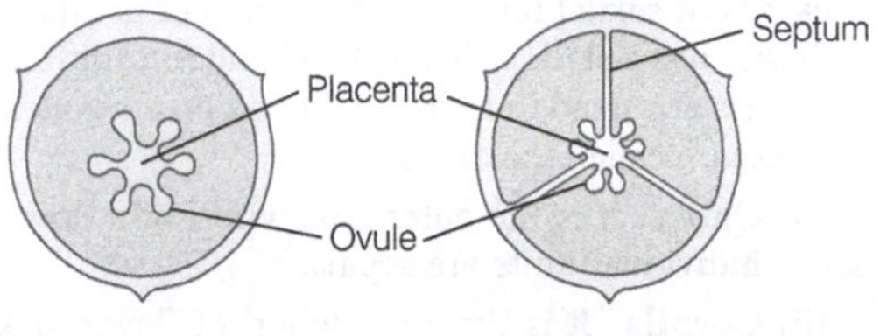

e.g. *Dianthus, Silensa*, etc. | e.g. *Citrus*, tomato, etc.

(2)

18. Define the term inflorescence. Explain the basis for the different types of inflorescence in flowering plants. **NCERT**

Ans Inflorescence is the arrangement and distribution of flowers on the floral axis. (1)

Basis for the different types of inflorescence in flowering plants is given below

Growth Indefinite (racemose) and definite.

Number of branches Cymose, uniparous, biparous, multiparous.
Pedicel Presence or absence of pedicel in inflorescence.
Branching of peduncle Unbranched and branched.
Sex of flowers Certain types have unisexual flowers, e.g. catkin. (2)

19. **Differentiate between racemose inflorescence and cymose inflorescence.** **NCERT**

Ans Differences between racemose and cymose inflorescence are

Racemose	Cymose
Flowers are borne laterally.	Flowers are actually terminal.
Growing point does not end in a flower.	Growing point or terminal bud always ends in a flower.
Flowers develop from all sides.	Flowers develop from one or two sides.
Opening of flowers occurs at short intervals.	Opening of successive flowers takes longer intervals.
Young fruits are not protected by flowers.	Young fruits are protected by flowers.

(3)

Long Answer Type Questions

5 Marks

20. **What is a flower? Describe the parts of a typical angiospermic flower.** **NCERT**

Ans A flower is a modified, condensed shoot specialised to carry out sexual reproduction in higher plants. A typical flower has a stalk, called pedicel and four different whorls arranged in a ring and fixed on a swollen structure called thalamus.

(i) **Calyx** It is the outermost whorl of a flower. Its individual units are sepals.

(ii) **Corolla** It is the inner whorl of flower next to calyx. The individual units are petals.

(iii) **Androecium** It is the third whorl of flower whose individual units are stamens.

(iv) **Gynoecium or Pistil** It is the fourth and last whorl. The individual units are carpels. (5)

21. **The mode of arrangement of sepals or petals in the floral bud is known as aestivation. Draw the various types of aestivation possible for a typical pentamerous flower.** **NCERT Exemplar**

Ans Refer to fig. no. 8.2.

22. **Define the following terms**

(i) Aestivation (ii) Placentation
(iii) Actinomorphic (iv) Zygomorphic
(v) Superior ovary
(vi) Perigynous ovary
(vii) Epipetalous stamen **NCERT**

Ans (i) **Aestivation** The mode of arrangement of sepals or petals in relation to one another in a flower bud is called aestivation.

(ii) **Placentation** The pattern by which the ovules are attached in an ovary is called placentation.

(iii) **Actinomorphic** A flower having radial symmetry. The parts of each whorl are similar in size and shape. The flower can be divided in two equal halves along more than one median longitudinal plane.

(iv) **Zygomorphic** A flower having bilateral symmetry. The parts of one or more whorls are dissimilar. The flower can be divided into two equal halves in only one vertical plane.

(v) **Superior Ovary** The ovary is called superior when it is borne above the point of attachment of perianth and stamens on the thalamus.

(vi) **Perigynous Ovary** It is the condition in which gynoecium of a flower is situated in the centre and other parts of the flower are located on the rim of the thalamus almost at the same level.

(vii) **Epipetalous Stamen** Stamens adhere to the petals by their filaments so, appear to arise from them. (5)

23. **Describe the arrangement of floral members in relation to their insertion on thalamus.** **NCERT**

Ans Refer to text on page no. 168.

24. **Describe the various types of placentations found in flowering plants.** **NCERT**

Ans Refer to text on page no. 167.

TOPIC 02 Fruit and Seed

The Fruit

The characteristic feature of flowering plants is fruit. Fruit is a mature or ripened ovary, developed after fertilisation.

During fertilisation, the important changes taking place in the ovary are

(i) The ovules present in it develop into seeds.

(ii) The wall of the ovary thickens and ripens into pericarp (fruit wall).

The ovary after these changes is known as the **fruit**. If a fruit is formed without fertilisation, it is called **parthenocarpic fruit**, e.g. banana, grapes, pineapple, etc. The parthenocarpic fruits do not have seeds.

The fruit consists of a wall or **pericarp** and seeds. The pericarp may be dry or fleshy.

When pericarp is thick and fleshy, it is differentiated into outer **epicarp**, the middle **mesocarp** and the inner **endocarp**.

Classification of Fruits

Fruits can be classified as follows

(i) **True Fruits** Fruit developed from the fertilised ovary is called **true fruit**. A true fruit has two parts; pericarp and the seeds.

(ii) **False Fruits** Fruit developed from any part of the flower along with ovary is called **false fruit**. The thalamus grows along with the ovary to form a false fruit, i.e. in *Pyrus malus* (apple).

Structure of Typical Fruit

The fruits of mango and coconut are also known as **drupe**, as they develop from monocarpellary superior ovaries and have only one seed. In mango, pericarp is well-differentiated into an outer thin epicarp, a middle fleshy edible mesocarp and an inner stony hard endocarp. In coconut, the mesocarp is fibrous.

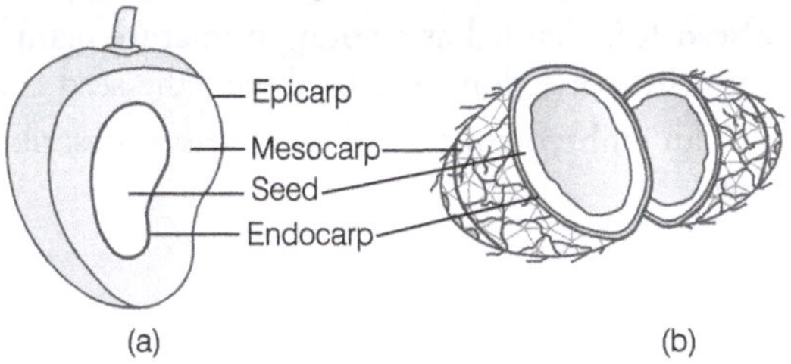

Fig 8.7 Parts of a fruit (a) Mango, (b) Coconut

Types of Fruits

Fruits can be broadly classified into following three types

(i) **Simple Fruits** A simple fruit develops from the single simple or compound ovary of a flower. These can be dry fruits (pericarp dry) or succulent fruits (pericarp fleshy).

(ii) **Aggregate** (Etaerio) **Fruits** An aggregate fruit is a group of fruitlets which develops from a flower having polycarpellary apocarpous (free) gynoecium. The aggregate fruit is also called **etaerio.**

(iii) **Multiple** (Composite) **Fruits** A composite (multiple) fruit develops from an entire inflorescence. The multiple fruit is composed of a number of closely associated fruits (which may or may not get fused) along with its peduncle. Hence, these fruits are called **pseudocarpic fruits.**

Pomology is the branch of horticulture that deals with the study of fruits and their cultivation.

Edible Parts of Some Common Fruits

Simple Fruits	Scientific Name	Type	Edible Parts
Wheat	*Triticum aestivum*	Caryopsis	Endosperm and embryo
Maize	*Zea mays*	Caryopsis	Endosperm and embryo
Rice	*Oryza sativa*	Caryopsis	Endosperm and embryo
Tomato	*Lycopersicum esculentum*	Berry	Pericarp and placenta
Litchi	Litchi *(Nephalium chinensis)*	Nut	Fleshy aril
Banana	*Musa paradisiaca*	Berry	Mesocarp and endocarp
Brinjal	*Solanum melongena*	Berry	Pericarp and placenta
Coconut	*Cocos nuccifera*	Drupe	Endosperm, testa, cotyledon and embryo
Almond	*Prunus amygdalus*	Drupe	Seeds
Cucumber	*Cucumis melo*	Pepo	Mesocarp and endocarp
Aggregate Fruits			
Strawberry	*Fragaria vesco*	Etaerio of achenes	Fleshy thalamus and seeds

Simple Fruits	Scientific Name	Type	Edible Parts
Lotus	*Nelumbo nucifera*	Etaerio of achenes	Fleshy thalamus and seeds
Multiple Fruits			
Jack fruit	*Artocarpus heterophyllus*	Sorosis	Fleshy axis, bracts, perianth and seeds
Fig	*Ficus carica*	Syconus	Peduncle and seeds
Mulberry	*Morus alba*	Sorosis	Fleshy axis and succulent perianth

Importance of Fruits

(i) Fruits are a source of vitamins, organic acids, minerals, pectin and sugars and some of them are used as vegetables, e.g. Okra (lady's finger), tomato, pumpkin, cucumber, gourd, etc.

(ii) Cereals are one seeded dry fruits, form the staple food of humans.

(iii) Fruits are important foods for fruit eating birds (frugivorous) and some animals.

(iv) Some fruits are also used as medicines, e.g. *Emblica officinalis* (amla), *Datura stramonium* (datura), *Papaver somniferum* (poppy), etc.

(v) They protect immature seeds against climatic conditions till their maturity.

(vi) The unripe fruits are bitter due to the presence of tannins, bitter alkaloids, astringents, sour acids, etc. This way they keep the animals away from eating them.

The Seed

Seed is a ripened ovule which contains an embryo or tiny plant with sufficient reserve food for the development of embryo. The ovules after fertilisation develop into seeds. A seed is made up of **seed coats** and **an embryo.** The embryo is made up of a radicle, an embryonal axis and one (wheat and maize) or two cotyledons (gram and pea).

Endosperm acts as the food storage tissue of a seed. The seeds with endosperm are called **endospermic** or **albuminous** (e.g. *Zea mays*), while those without endosperm are called **non-endospermic** or **exalbuminous seeds** (e.g. *Brassica campestris*).

Types of Seed

The seeds can be classified on the basis of number of cotyledons and the presence or absence of endosperm (nutritive tissue), as given below

Seeds

- **Dicotyledonous** (seeds with two cotyledons)
  - **Exalbuminous seed** or **Non-endospermic seed** (Seeds without endosperm, e.g. bean, gram and pea)
  - **Albuminous seed** or **Endospermic seed** (Seeds with endosperm, e.g. castor, cotton, etc)
- **Monocotyledonous** (seeds with one cotyledon)
  - **Exalbuminous seed** (Seeds without endosperm, e.g. orchids)
  - **Albuminous seed** (Seeds with endosperm, e.g. maize, wheat and rice)

Structure of Dicotyledonous Seed (Bean)

Bean seeds are kidney-shaped being convex on one side and concave on the other. Bean seed contains two cotyledons so, called **dicotyledon.**

The detailed structure of dicot seed (bean) is as follows

(i) **Seed coat** Each seed is covered by a protective covering called seed coat. It develops from the integuments of ovule. The seed coat is differentiated into an outer testa and inner tegmen. These functions as

(a) **Testa** It is the outer, thick, protective layer. It protects the seed from pathogens-like bacteria, fungi, insects, etc.

(b) **Tegmen** It is inner, thin membranous covering which protects the inner part of the seed.

(ii) **Hilum** It shows the point of attachment of ovule to the ovary. It is just a mark (scar) on the concave side of the seed.

(iii) **Micropyle** It is a small pore near the hilum, through which oxygen, water, etc. enters into the seed.

(iv) **Raphe** It is a ridge-like structure present around the median groove. It represents the portion of the stalk which remains fused with the testa.

(v) **Embryo** It is defined as a young miniature plant along with cotyledons, enclosed with the seed coat.

Thus, an embryo consists of two parts as described below

(a) **Cotyledons** These are seed leaves. These vary in numbers in both dicot and monocot. Beans have two cotyledons. They are food laden, fleshy structures attached to the embryonal axis. They provide nourishment to the embryo in the early stages of development.

(b) **Embryonal axis** A young miniature plant is present between the two cotyledons. It is called the embryonal axis. It consist of the following parts
- **Plumule** This is a leafy part of the embryo giving rise to shoot.
- **Radicle** This is the lower end of the embryo, giving rise to roots.
- **Epicotyl** It is the part of the embryo over the plumule.
- **Hypocotyl** It is the part of the embryo just above the radicle.
- **Mesocotyl** The part of the embryo axis, where cotyledons are attached.

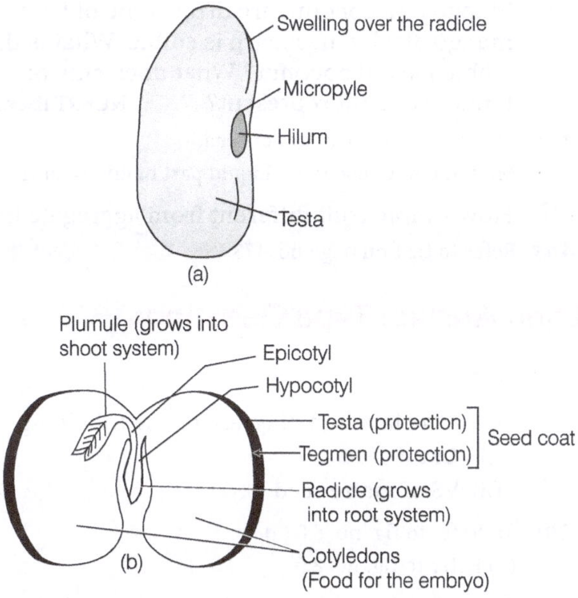

Fig. 8.8 (a) External structure of bean seed, (b) Internal structure of bean seed

Structure of Monocotyledonous Seed (Maize)

The maize seed contains only one cotyledon so called, monocotyledonous. It is a single seeded fruit. The maize grain is a flat, almost triangular structure. Externally it is differentiated into a large, upper area, which marks the position of endosperm and a small lower area that contains the embryo. These are separated by a prominent epithelial layer. Its detailed structure is as follows

(i) **Seed coat** The seed coat in maize seed is not separable. It is fused with pericarp (fruit wall).

(ii) **Hilum and micropyle** These are not clearly visible in maize seed and are not distinguishable.

(iii) **Endosperm** It is the nutritive tissue of the seed. It contains starch as reserve food material which is surrounded by one cell thick aleurone layer. It is rich in protein and enzymes.

(iv) **Embryo** The embryo of maize seed consists of the following parts

(a) **Cotyledon** The maize grain contains a thin, papery, single cotyledon called **scutellum.** It does not contain food. It is present near the endosperm.

(b) **Plumule** It represent growing tip of the shoot along with embryonic leaves. It is covered with a sheath called **coleoptile.**

(c) **Radicle** It is present at the lower base part of a seed and is covered by root cap.

The protective membranous covering of radicle is called **coleorhiza.**

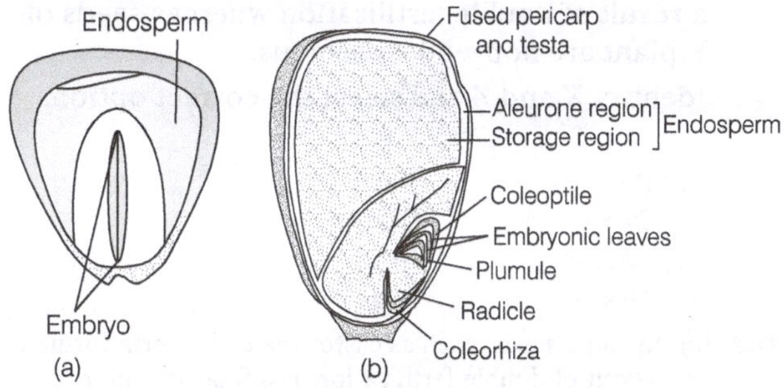

Fig. 8.9 (a) External structure and (b) Internal structure of maize seed

Note
- The fruits dispersed by bat are called **ornithochorous.** The seeds/fruits dispersed by ants are called **myrmecochorous.**
- Mostly nucellus (central part of ovule) is consumed after fertilisation due of absorption of food by the endosperm and embryo. Sometimes when the nucellus remains persistent in the seed, such seeds are called **perispermic seeds**.

Topic Practice 2

Multiple Choice Questions

(1 Mark)

1. An aggregate fruit is one which develops from
   (a) multicarpellary syncarpous gynoecium
   (b) multicarpellary apocarpous gynoecium
   (c) complete inflorescence
   (d) multicarpellary superior ovary

Ans (b) Aggregate fruits or etario are those fruits that develop from the multicarpellary apocarpous gynoecium (ovary). Aggregate fruit may also be called accessory fruit in which part of the flower other than the ovary becomes fleshy and forms part of the fruit.

2. Cotyledon of maize grain is called
   (a) coleorhiza
   (b) coleoptile
   (c) scutellum
   (d) plumule

Ans (c) Large, shield-shaped cotyledon of grass family is called scutellum. Coleorhiza is a sheath protecting the root of germinating grass.

Coleoptile is a sheath covering emerging shoot. Plumule is rudimentary shoot of an embryo plant.

3. In the seed of *X* plant, the endosperm formed as a result of double fertilisation whereas seeds of *Y* plant are non-endospermous.

   Identify *X* and *Y* and select the correct option.

	X	*Y*
(a)	Pea	Bean
(b)	Bean	Castor
(c)	Castor	Gram
(d)	Gram	Pea

Ans (c) In some seeds, such as castor the endosperm formed as a result of double fertilisation, is a food storing tissue. In plants, such as bean, gram and pea, the endosperm is not present in mature seeds and such seeds are called non-endospermic.

Very Short Answer Type Questions

(1 Mark)

4. The scutellum observed in a grain of wheat or maize is comparable to which part of the seed in other monocots?

Ans Cotyledons.

5. Name the sheath covering the plumule in maize grain.

Ans The sheath covering the plumule in maize grain is coleoptile.

6. A maize grain is not a seed. Explain.

Ans A maize grain is a single-seeded fruit called caryopsis or grain, in which the pericarp (fruit wall) is inseparably fused with testa.

Short Answer Type I Questions

(2 Marks)

7. Mango and coconut are drupe type of fruits. In mango, fleshy mesocarp is edible. What is the edible part of coconut? What does milk of tender coconut represent? **NCERT Exemplar**

Ans Edible part—Endosperm of seed.

Milk of tender coconut—Liquid part of endosperm. (2)

8. How simple fruit different from aggregate fruit?

Ans Refer to text on page no. 173.

Long Answer Type Questions

(5 Marks)

9. Draw the labelled diagram of the following
   (i) Gram seed
   (ii) VS of maize seed

Ans (i) Refer to fig. no. 8.8 (a)

(ii) Refer to fig. no. 8.9

10. Describe the structure of monocotyledon seed.

Ans Refer to text on page no. 175.

SUMMARY

- A **flower** is a modified shoot that contains four floral whorls, i.e. calyx, corolla, androecium and gynoecium. Androecium is the male reproductive unit that consists of stamens (anthers and filaments). Gynoecium is the female reproductive unit that consists of carpels (stigma, style and ovary).
- **Perianth** is when the sepals and petals are not differentiated. The unit of perianth is called tepal.
- **Aestivation** is the mode of arrangement of sepals and petals on the thalamus, i.e. valvate, twisted, imbricate, quincuncial and vexillary.
- **Androecium** is male part of the flower. It **epipetalous**, stamens are fused with the petals, e.g. *Solanum* . In **synandrous**, stamens are united throughout their whole length, e.g. *Cucurbita*, In **diadelphous** two separate bundles of united filaments are formed, e.g. *Pisum*.
- **Gynoecium** is female part of the flower. The basic unit of gynoecium is **carpel**. Each carpel consists of **ovary**, **style** and **stigma**.
- **Stigma** is terminally situated. It can be capitate, plumose, bifid, discoid lamellate, sticky, etc.
- **Style** is cylindrical. It can be terminal, lateral and gynobasic.
- **Ovary** is the basal, swollen part of the gynoecium. It can be superior, semi-inferior or inferior.
- In **apocarpous** carpels are free from each other, e.g. *Aconitum* and in **syncarpous** carpels are fused, e.g. China rose.
- **Placentation** is the arrangement of ovules inside the ovary. It can be marginal, axile, parietal, free-central, basal and superficial.
- In **marginal placentation** placenta arises from the margin of the unilocular ovary, e.g. pea.
- In **axile placentation** placenta a rises from the central axis, e.g. *Citrus*.
- In **parietal placentation** placenta arises from the inner side of fused margins of two carpels, e.g. *Cucurbita*.
- In **free-central placentation** placenta arises from the central axis in unilocular ovary, e.g. *Dianthus*.
- **Basal placentation** bears the placenta at the base and contains a single large ovule, e.g. sunflower.
- In **superficial placentation** ovule bearing placenta arises all over the inner partition of the ovary, e.g. *Nymphaea*.
- **Inflorescence** is the arrangement of flowers on shoot. These are two types, i.e. **racemose** and **cymose**.
- **Racemose inflorescence** grows in acropetal manner. It is divided into simple racemose and compound racemose. Simple racemose have unbranched, long peduncle. It is categorised into raceme, spike, catkin, spadix, corymb, umbel, capitulum, etc.
- **Cymose inflorescence** grows in basipetal manner. It is categorised into monochasial cyme, dichasial cyme, polychasial cyme, cymose head, and scapigerous head.
- **Cyathium** inflorescence is a cup-shaped structure. It encloses a large, achlamydous pedicellate, female flower and numerous male flower.
- **Verticillaster** is a condensed dichasial cyme-like inflorescence, this dichasial cyme changes into monochasial scorpioid cyme later, e.g. *Ocimum*.
- In **hypanthodium** peduncle becomes a cup-shaped. It bears many male flowers, female flowers and sterile flowers, e.g. *Ficus*.
- **Fruits** are developed from ripened ovary after fertilisation, seeds are ripened ovules. True fruits develop from ovary while false fruit from any other part of flower except ovary. **The fruits which develop from unfertilised ovule are called parthenocarpic fruits.**
- Fruits are of different fypes, i.e. **simple**, **aggregate** and **composite** fruits.
- **Caryopsis** is simple, dry, indehiscent fruits, e.g. *Zea mays*. **Pome** is a false fruit, it is developed from thalamus, e.g. *Pyrus malus*.
- **Seed** is a product of sexual reproduction in angiospermic plants. Embryo of seed is covered with seed coat. It consists of radicle, embryonal axis and cotyledons.
- Based on the number of cotyledons in the seeds angiosperms could be **dicotyledonous seed** with two cotyledons and **monocotyledonous seed** with one cotyledons.
- Angiospermic plants show great diversity in their flower morphology. On the basis of flower structure dicots and monocots are further grouped into many classes, orders and families.

Chapter Practice

Multiple Choice Questions

1 Mark

1. Choose the incorrect match.
   (a) Zygomorphic flowers (bilateral symmetry)–pea, gulmohur, bean, *Cassia*
   (b) Asymmetric (irregular flower) – *Canna*
   (c) Actinomorphic flower (radial symmetry) – mustard, *Datura*, chilli
   (d) Pentamerous flower – 5 calyx

2. Perianth is the condition in which
   (a) calyx and corolla are not distinct
   (b) calyx is present, but corolla is absent
   (c) corolla is present, but calyx is absent
   (d) calyx and corolla are not present

3. Complete the paragraph given below by replacing *A*, *B* and *C* with correct terms.
   Androecium is composed of *A*, which represents the male reproductive organ. It consists of a stalk and *B*, which is usually bilobed and each lobe has two chambers, the pollen sacs. The pollen grains are produced in pollen sacs. A sterile stamen is called *C*.
   (a) *A* – Stamens; *B* – Anther; *C* – Staminode
   (b) *A* – Stigma; *B* – Filament; *C* – Epiphyllous
   (c) *A* – Axile; *B* – Anther; *C* – Monoadelphous
   (d) *A* – Stamens; *B* – Filament; *C* – Adelphous.

4. Which of the following is an incorrect pair?
   (a) Superior ovary – Mustard, China rose
   (b) Half-inferior ovary – Plum, rose
   (c) Inferior ovary – Guava, cucumber
   (d) None of the above

5. Identify *A* to *D* in the given diagram.

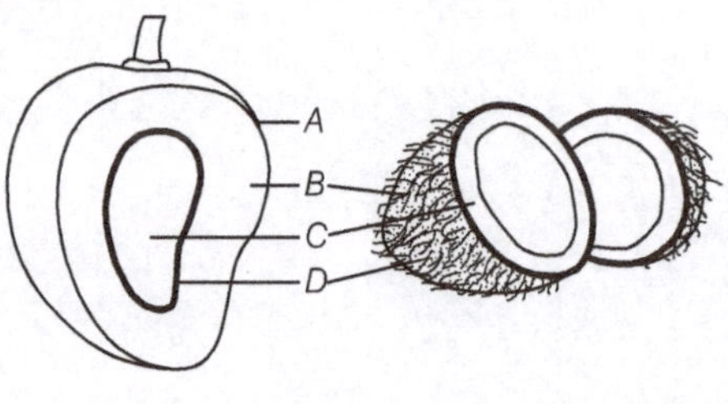

   (a) *A*–Epicarp, *B*–Mesocarp, *C*–Seed, *D*–Endocrap
   (b) *A*–Mesocarp, *B*–Epicarp, *C*–Seed, *D*–Endocarp
   (c) *A*–Mesocarp, *B*–Epicarp, *C*–Endocarp, *D*–Seed
   (d) *A*–Epicarp, *B*–Mesocarp, *C*–Endocarp, *D*–Seed

6. Choose the incorrect pair.
   (a) Seed – Contains an embryo
   (b) Monocotyledonous seed – Wheat
   (c) Dicotyledonous seed – Maize
   (d) Seed coat – Outermost covering

Assertion-Reason Type Questions

1 Mark

■ **Direction** (Q. Nos. 7-12) *In each of the following questions, a statement of Assertion (A) is given followed by corresponding statement of Reason (R). Of the statements, mark the correct answer as*

(a) If both A and R are true and R is the correct explanation of A
(b) If both A and R are true, but R is not the correct explanation of A
(c) If A is true, but R is false
(d) If A is false, but R is true

7. **Assertion** (A) In some flowers like lily, perianth is a term used when calyx and corolla are not distinct.
   Reason (R) Calyx and corolla are the reproductive organs.

8. Figure given below represents monoadelphous condition of stamens. Study the figure given below and comment upon the appropriateness of the Assertion and the Reason.

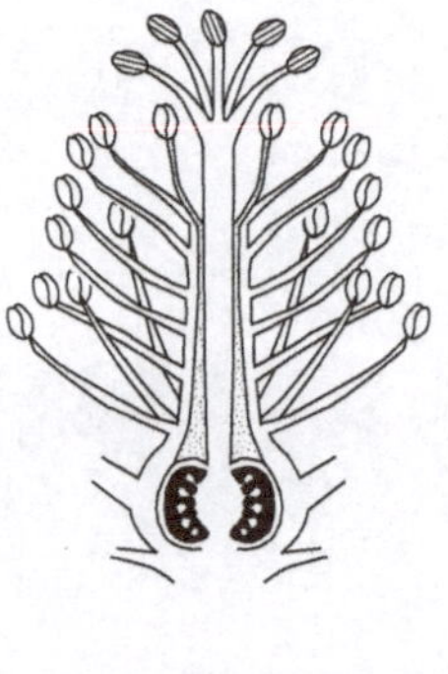

Assertion (A) Monoadelphous stamens are found in China rose.

Reason (R) When the stamens are united into one bunch or bundle, the condition is said to be monoadelphous.

9. **Assertion** (A) $\underline{G}_2$ is the symbol for inferior ovary.

Reason (R) Fusion is indicated by enclosing the figure within bracket.

10. **Assertion** (A) Type of inflorescence in *Sphaeranthus* is cyathium.

Reason (R) In cyathium type inflorescence, the flowers are achlamydeous.

11. **Assertion** (A) In racemose type of inflorescence, the main axis grows indefinitely.

Reason (R) Main axis is not terminated by flower.

12. Given below is the diagram showing uniparous cyme inflorescence. In this type of inflorescence, the peduncle ends up in a flower producing new single floral lateral axis at the base of older flower. Observe the figure carefully and comment upon the appropriateness of the Assertion and the Reason.

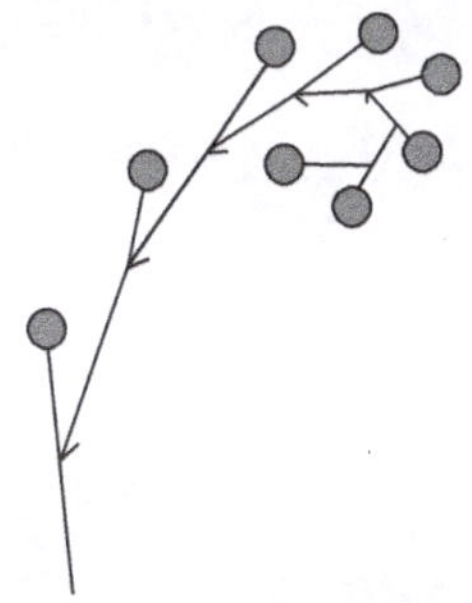

Assertion (A) In cymose inflorescence, growth of terminal bud stops after sometime.

Reason (R) The growth of the main stem is definite.

Answers

1. (c) 2. (a) 3. (a) 4. (d) 5. (a) 6. (c)
7. (c) 8. (a) 9. (d) 10. (d) 11. (a) 12. (a)

Very Short Answer Type Questions

1 Mark

13. Name the accessory organs of a flower.
14. What is a staminode?
15. Name any two plants whose ovary shows free-central placentation.

Short Answer Type I Questions

2 Marks

16. When the corolla is described as gamopetalous?
17. Draw the androecium of *Solanum nigram*.
18. What is the position of ovary in epigynous flower?

Short Answer Type II Questions

3 Marks

19. Explain the different kinds of gynoecium based on the number of carpels.
20. How can you differentiate between aggregate fruit and multiple fruit?

Long Answer Type Questions

5 Marks

21. Explain the different kinds of special inflorescences found in flowering plants.
22. Describe the structure of monocotyledonous seed with labelled diagram.

Case Based Questions

(4/5 Marks)

23. Sonali, a 7 years old girl was roaming in the garden, when she saw a butterfly hovering over a flower. She was attracted to the flower and plucked it. On coming back home, she showed it to her brother (a biology graduate student) who scolded her for her action. He explained the importance of flowers for the plants and insects like butterflies, honeybees, etc. Sonali realised her mistake and immediately promised not to repeat it.
    (i) What is the importance of flower?
    (ii) Name the different parts of a flower.
    (iii) Name the condition of flower where stamens remain free.
    (iv) Define zygomorphic symmetry.

24. Rekha was reading a topic position of floral parts on thalamus. Her mother pointed out the flower of China rose, rose and guava and asked about their ovary position. Rekha explained the all queries of her mother.
    (i) What is hypogynous flower?
    (ii) Which type of ovary is found in guava and rose, respectively?
    (iii) What is epigynous situation?
    (iv) What is the difference between the position of ovary in cucumber and China rose?
    (v) Give an example of half inferior ovary.

CHAPTER

09

Anatomy of Flowering Plants

The study of internal structure of plant is called **plant anatomy**. The study of internal structures shows plant adaptations to diverse environmental conditions. In this chapter, we will study the plant tissue systems and internal structure of dicot and monocot plants.

TOPIC 01 Tissues and Tissue Systems

A tissue is a group of cells having a common origin and usually performing a common function. The plant body is made up of different kinds of tissues. Generally, the cells of a tissue share the same origin in the embryonic stage. The tissues help in body function by allowing division of labour. For example in leaf, various cells commonly perform the function of photosynthesis.

The plant tissues can be divided into two main types

I. Meristematic tissues II. Permanent tissues

I. Meristematic Tissues

The growth in plants is mainly restricted to specialised regions of active cell division called **meristems** (Gk. *Meristos*–divided). A meristematic tissue is an undifferentiated mass of cells that is in a continuous state of rapid divisions and have retained their power of division.

These tissues divide to form new cells, which differentiate to give rise to permanent tissues.

Characteristics of Meristematic Tissue

The characteristics of meristematic tissue are listed below

(i) They are living and contain undifferentiated mass of rapidly dividing cells.
(ii) The shape of cells is spherical, polygonal or rectangular.
(iii) The cells are compactly arranged without intercellular spaces and are interconnected by plasmodesmata.
(iv) Nucleus is large and present either in interphase or in subphases of divisions.
(v) Cell wall is thin with only a primary wall made up of cellulose. Secondary wall is absent.

Classification of Meristematic Tissue

Meristem can be classified based on their position in the plant origin, position and functions.

Classification Based on Origin

The meristems are grouped on the basis of origin as

(i) **Primary Meristems** These meristems are derived during the early embryonic stages. They divide rapidly and differentiate into primary permanent tissues, which make the fundamental structure of the plant body.

They are mainly found in the growing apical regions of the root and shoot.

(ii) **Secondary Meristems** These meristems appear in later stage of development in the plant body. They lie lateral in position in both the stem and root. Some primary permanent tissues acquire the power of division and become meristematic.

These tissues can get dedifferentiated to form secondary meristems as per need of the plant. Some examples of secondary meristems are **cork cambium** and **interfascicular cambium**. They allow secondary growth in tissues.

Classification Based on Position

Meristems can be divided into three types, based on their position in the plant body. These are as given below

(i) **Apical Meristems** The meristems, which occur at the tips of root and shoot produce primary tissues are called apical meristems.

The **Root Apical Meristem** (RAM) occupies the tip of a root, while the **Shoot Apical Meristem** (SAM) occupies the most distinct region of the stem axis.

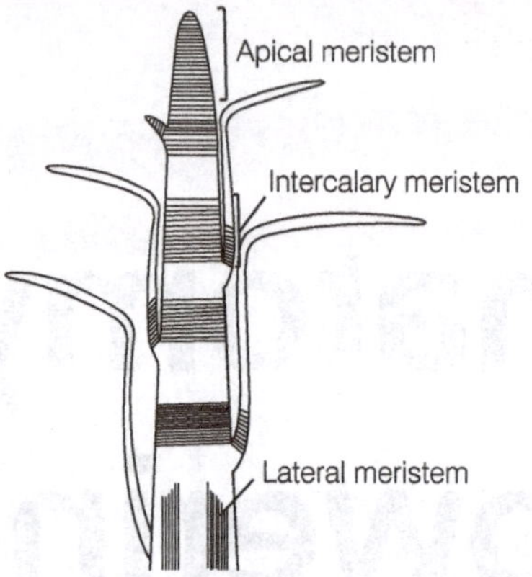

Fig. 9.1 Position of meristems in LS of a shoot

During the formation of leaves and elongation of stem, some cells left behind from shoot apical meristem, constitute the **axillary bud**. These buds are present in the axil of leaves and are capable of forming a branch or a flower. Specific regions of the apical meristem produce dermal tissues, ground tissues and vascular tissues.

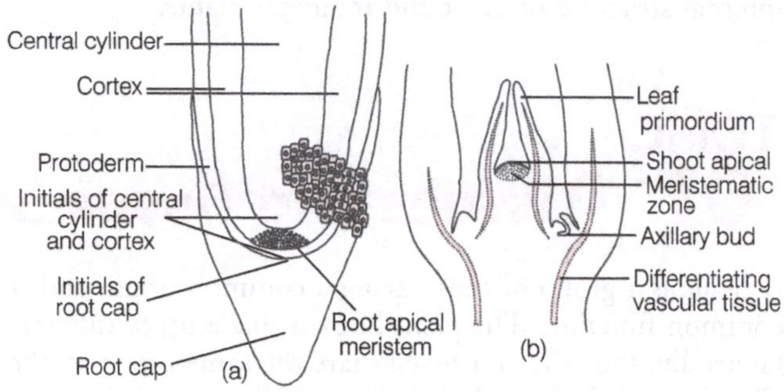

Fig. 9.2 Apical meristem (a) Root, (b) Shoot

(ii) **Intercalary Meristems** The meristem, which occurs between mature tissues is known as intercalary meristem. They occur in grasses and regenerate their parts removed by the grazing herbivores.

Both apical and intercalary meristems are **primary meristems** because they appear early in life of a plant and contribute to the formation of the primary plant body. These meristems are usually responsible for growth in length and present mostly at the base of **node** (e.g. mint), base of **internode** (e.g. stem of wheat and grasses) or at the base of **leaf** (e.g. *Pinus*).

(iii) **Lateral Meristems** The meristems that occur in the mature regions of roots and shoots of many plants is known as lateral meristems. These meristems produce woody axis. These appear later than **primary meristem**, so are called the **secondary meristem**.

They are cylindrical meristems. Some examples of lateral meristems are fascicular vascular cambium, interfascicular cambium and cork cambium. These are responsible for producing the secondary tissues.

Classification Based on Functions

The meristems are also classified on the basis of their functions as

(i) **Protoderm** It is the outermost portion of the primary meristem found at the apex of the stem and root. It develops into epidermis.

(ii) **Procambium** It develops into primary vascular tissues. It forms the isolated strands of elongated cells, very near to the central region.

(iii) **Ground Meristem** It develops into the ground tissue. The cells are thin-walled, living and isodiametric.

In the later stages of growth, they become differentiated into hypodermis, cortex, endodermis, pericycle, medullary rays and pith.

II. Permanent Tissues

The meristematic cells gradually differentiate and loose the ability to divide. Such cells are termed as **mature** or **permanent cells.** The permanent tissues actually composed of cells, in which the growth has stopped.

Permanent tissues can be divided into two types

Simple Permanent Tissues

The permanent tissues having all cells similar in structure and function are called **simple tissues.** These are groups of homogenous cells, which perform the same function.

1. Parenchyma

It is a living, simple permanent tissue composed of thin-walled cells. Parenchyma (*Para*–beside; *enchein* – to pour) is also called primary tissue or ground tissue. It is present in cortex, pith, palisade, mesophyll and some other parts of flower. It is mostly produced by the ground tissue. The parenchyma forms the major part of the plant organs.

The characteristic features of parenchyma are as follows

(i) The cells are thin-walled, less spherical and polyhedral in shape. These are generally isodiametric.

(ii) The cell wall composed of cellulose, hemicellulose and pectin.

(iii) Cells have a large central vacuole, peripheral cytoplasm with a conspicuous big nucleus.

(iv) The cells may be either closely packed or have small intercellular spaces.

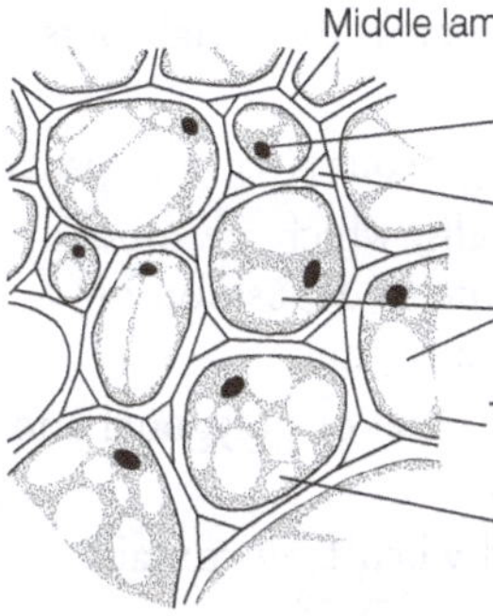

Fig. 9.3 Parenchyma

The parenchyma can be further classified as

- **Chlorenchyma** specialised for photosynthesis.
- **Aerenchyma** forms a connected air system throughout the entire plant.
- **Storage parenchyma** stores sugars, protein granules, oil drops, etc.
- **Xylem parenchyma** helps in the conduction of water.
- **Phloem parenchyma** helps in the translocation of food.
- **Stellate parenchyma** is star-shaped parenchymatous tissue with large air spaces.

Different functions performed by parenchyma are

(i) These help in storage of food, water and air.

(ii) The vital activities like photosynthesis, respiration and conduction are carried out inside parenchyma tissue.

(iii) It helps in wound healing, grafting, etc. and also provides buoyancy in aquatic plants.

(iv) Parenchyma cells associated with xylem and phloem help in conduction of water and food materials.

(v) These cells can dedifferentiate, acquire the power of division to form secondary meristem which produce secondary tissues.

2. Collenchyma

Collenchyma (Gr. *Colla* – glue; *enchyma*–an infusion) is a simple, living mechanical tissue. Its cells are composed of more or less elongated cells with thick, primary non-lignified walls. Intercellular spaces are found to be absent.

The characteristic features of collenchymatous tissues are listed below

(i) It is present in layer below the epidermis in dicotyledonous plants. Collenchyma is commonly found in stems, leaves, floral parts and fruits and not found in the roots except in the aerial roots of some plants, e.g. *Monstera*.

(ii) It is found either as a homogeneous layer or in patches.

(iii) Collenchyma consists of cells, which are much thickened at the corners due to deposition of cellulose, hemicellulose and pectin.

(iv) The cells may be oval, spherical or polygonal and often contain chloroplasts.

(v) These cells assimilate food when they contain chloroplasts.

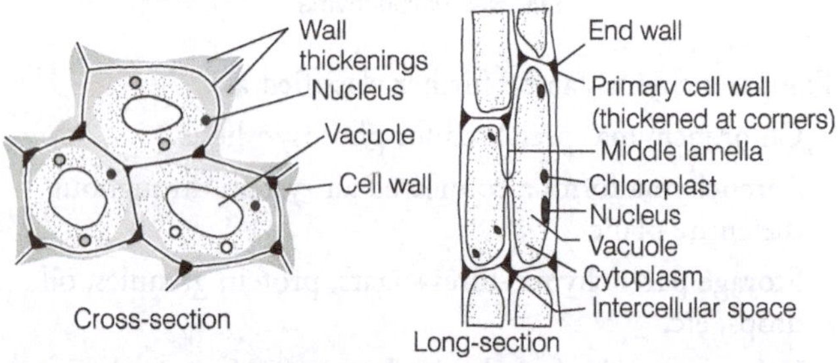

Fig. 9.4 Collenchyma

Based on pectinisation of the cell wall, there are three types of collenchyma

(a) Angular collenchyma (b) Lamellar collenchyma

(c) Lacunar collenchyma

Different functions performed by collenchyma are

(i) It provides mechanical support to the growing parts of the plant, such as young stem and petiole of a leaf.

(ii) Collenchyma cells are capable of photosynthesis, as they contain chloroplasts.

3. Sclerenchyma

The sclerenchyma (Gr. *Sclerous*–hard; *enchyma*–an infusion) consists of long, narrow cells with thick and lignified cell walls having a few or numerous pits.

The characteristic features of sclerenchymatous cells are

(i) These are dead cells and do not perform any metabolic function.

(ii) They possess hard and extremely thick secondary walls due to uniform deposition of lignin.

(iii) Cells are long or short, narrow, thick-walled and lignified.

(iv) They show different types of lignin depositions and also have pits.

The sclerenchymatous cells are of two types

(i) **Xylary fibres** These are thick-walled, elongated and pointed cells, generally occurring in groups, in various parts of the plant. It is found in pericycle of stems, outer regions of cortex, etc.

(ii) **Sclereids** These are short or irregular, spherical, oval or cylindrical sclerenchymatous cells. The walls are very thick, irregular and the lumen is very narrow. The walls show simple pits. These are commonly found in the fruit wall of nuts, pulp of the fruits, like guava, pear and sapota, seed coats of legumes and leaves of tea.

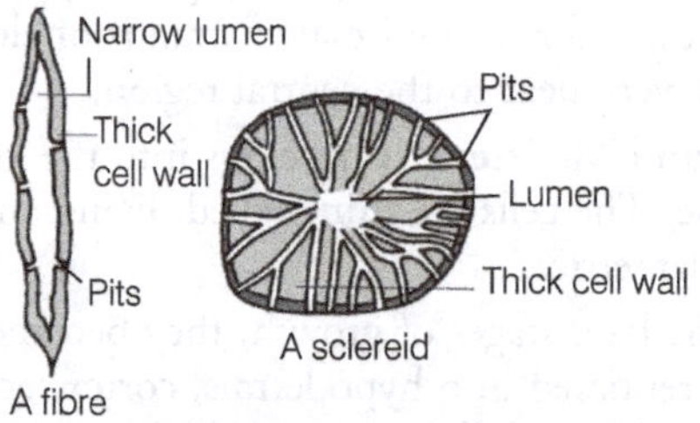

Fig. 9.5 Sclerenchyma

Different functions performed by sclerenchyma are

(i) It provides mechanical strength and support.

(ii) Surface fibres help in dispersal of seeds.

Differences between Parenchyma, Collenchyma and Sclerenchyma

Parenchyma	Collenchyma	Sclerenchyma
Cells are living and filled with protoplasm.	Cells are living and filled with protoplasm.	Cells are dead and empty.
No wall thickening.	Wall thickenings not uniform and consist of cellulose.	Wall thickening uniform and consist of cellulose, lignin or both.
Found in both the outer and inner parts of plant organs.	Found restricted to the outer parts of plant organs.	Found in both the outer and inner parts restricted to the areas, which have stopped elongation.
Provide mechanical strength only, when they are fully turgid.	Provide mechanical strength as well as elasticity.	Provide only mechanical strength.
Have ability to dedifferentiate and produce secondary meristem.	Ability to dedifferentiate is almost absent.	No dedifferentiation at all.

Complex Permanent Tissues

Complex permanent tissues are a group of more than one type of cells having common origin and working together as a unit. The main complex tissues in vascular plants are xylem and phloem.

1. Xylem

Xylem (Gr. *Xylos* – wood) is a complex permanent tissue which conducts water and mineral nutrients upwards from the root to the all aerial parts of the plant.

Components of Xylem

The xylem tissues are composed of four components

(i) **Tracheids** These are elongated, tubular and primitive cells with tapering end walls. They are dead cells and do not contain protoplasts. The inner layers of the cell walls have thickenings which vary in form. The end of the tracheids are tapering, blunt or chisel-like. These are constituents of xylem of primitive plants.

Note These are found in pteridophytes and gymnosperm, tracheids may be classified as annular or helical, spiral and scalariform or pitted depending on type of cell wall depositions.

The tracheids conduct water and dissolved mineral elements from roots to leaves. They also provide mechanical support.

(ii) **Vessels** These are long, cylindrical, tube-like structures made up of many cells called **vessel members,** each with lignified walls and a large central cavity. The vessel cells are also devoid of protoplasm.

The vessel members are interconnected through perforations in their common walls. The presence of vessels is a characteristic feature of **angiosperms.** Gymnosperms lack vessels in their xylem.

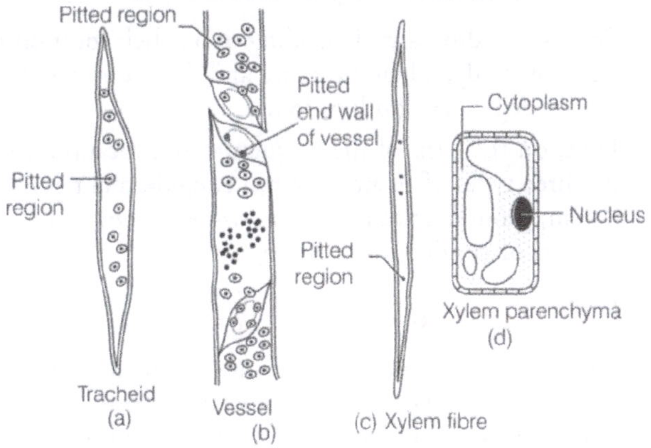

Fig. 9.6 Components of xylem

Differences between Vessel and Tracheid

Vessel	Tracheid
Longer	Comparatively quite short.
Usually upto 10 cm long.	Usually upto 1 mm long.
Exceptionally, upto 2m long (e.g. *Quercus*) or even 3-6 m long (*Wistaria* and *Eucalyptus*).	Exceptionally upto 12 cm or more long as in some conifers.
A vessel composed of a row of cells placed one above the other.	A tracheid is a single cell.
Intervening walls of the cells of the row absent hence, composed of pipes.	Nothing like this.
Since, formed by the fusion of row of cells, it is called a syncyte.	No fusion of any cells. Cross–walls of the tracheids placed on above the other are separated by cross-walls.
Bordered pits absent.	Bordered pits present in cross-walls.

(iii) **Xylem Fibres** The sclerenchymatous fibres associated with the xylem are called **xylem fibres.** These fibres have lignified cell walls. The thickness of the walls varies considerably, but these are usually thicker than the walls of the tracheids in the same wood. These are found in both primary and secondary xylem. The xylem fibres provide mechanical strength.

(iv) **Xylem Parenchyma** These cells form the only living component of the xylem. Xylem parenchyma cells are thin-walled and their cell walls are made up of cellulose. Xylem parenchyma stores food in the form of starch or fat and other substances like tannins. These cells assist directly or indirectly in the conduction of water upward through the vessels and tracheids.

The xylem parenchyma can be subdivided into two types

(a) **Primary Xylem** The xylem which appears first in the plant body is the primary xylem. The primary source of this xylem is the procambium. The primary xylem is of two types, i.e. protoxylem and metaxylem. The first formed primary xylem elements are called **protoxylem.** The latter formed primary xylem is called **metaxylem.**

In stems, the protoxylem lies towards the centre (pith) and the metaxylem lies towards the periphery of the organ. This type of primary xylem is called **endarch.**

In roots, the protoxylem lies towards periphery and metaxylem lies towards the centre. Such arrangement of primary xylem is called **exarch.**

(b) **Secondary Xylem** is composed of tracheary elements, rays, fibres and interspersed axial parenchyma cells. The cell formed towards inside of cambium tissue are called secondary xylem or **wood**. The primary function of secondary xylem is to provide mechanical support to plants.

2. Phloem

Phloem (Gk. *Phlois*–bark) is a food conducting complex permanent tissue. The term 'phloem' was coined by **Nageli** (1958). In angiosperms, it is also called **bast**. In gymnosperms, albuminous cells and sieve cells are present.

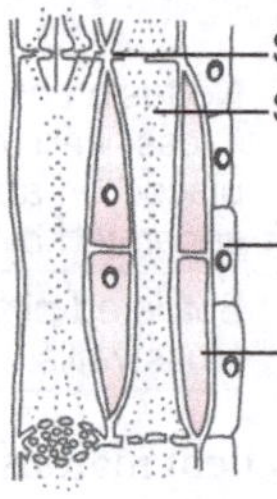

Fig. 9.7 Phloem

Components of Phloem

Phloem consists of four types of cellular components

(i) **Sieve Elements** The sieve tube elements are long, tube-like structures arranged longitudinally and are associated with the companion cells. Their end walls are perforated in a sieve-like manner to form the sieve plates. A mature sieve element possesses a **peripheral cytoplasm** and a **large vacuole**, but lacks a nucleus, Golgi body and most cytosol.

Sieve elements are of following two types

- **Sieve Cell** It is a special kind of cell which posseses sieve areas in its lateral walls. There is no specialised plate in it. Sieve cells are usually found in pteridophytes and gymnosperms.
- **Sieve Tube Members** In this type, the sieve areas are localised on its end walls. Sieve tube members are placed one above the other forming a tube called **sieve tube.** The end walls are perforated (sieve pores) like a sieve. These are found in angiosperms. The uniqueness of the sieve tube is that even without nucleus, it is living and the nucleus of the companion cell controls its cellular functions.

The main function of sieve element is **translocation of organic solutes.**

(ii) **Companion Cells** These are specialised parenchymatous cells, which are closely associated with the sieve tube elements, by a thin cytoplasmic strands called **plasmodesmata,**

Companion cells are absent in the phloem of pteridophytes and gymnosperms. They have albuminous cells in abundance which contain stored food materials.

The companion cells functions in maintenance of a pressure gradient in sieve tubes during food transport.

They form a link between sieve tube cells and other cells and regulate the passage of materials.

(iii) **Phloem Parenchyma** The phloem parenchyma is made up of elongated, tapering cylindrical cells which have dense cytoplasm and nucleus.

The cell wall is composed of cellulose and has pits through the **plasmodesmatal connections,** which exist between the cells. The phloem parenchyma is absent in most of the monocotyledons.

Phloem parenchyma stores food materials and other substances like resins, latex and mucilage.

(iv) **Phloem Fibres** The phloem fibres (bast fibres) are made up of sclerenchymatous cells. These are generally absent in the primary phloem, but are found in secondary phloem. The cell wall of phloem fibres is very thick.

These are much elongated, unbranched, have pointed apices. At maturity, these fibres lose their protoplasm and become dead. The phloem fibres of jute, flax and hemp have important economic uses.

The first formed primary phloem consists of narrow sieve tubes and is referred to as protophloem and later formed phloem has bigger sieve tubes and is referred to as metaphloem.

The Tissue System

The tissues also vary, depending upon their location in the plant body. Their structure and function would also be dependent on location.

Thus, on the basis of their structure and location, there are three types of tissue system, i.e. epidermal tissue system, ground or fundamental tissue system and vascular or conducting tissue system.

1. Epidermal Tissue System

The epidermal tissue system forms the outermost covering of the whole plant body. Its various components are epidermal cells, stomata and the epidermal appendages, i.e. trichomes and emergences.

i. Epidermis

The epidermis (Gr. *Epi*–upon; *derma*–skin) is the outermost layer of the main plant body. The epidermal cells are elongated and compactly arranged to form a continuous layer. This layer is interrupted by stomata. Sometimes, they are separated by intercellular spaces.

It is usually single-layered, but is also multilayered in the aerial roots of orchids and leaves of *Nerium* and *Ficus elastica*.

The cells are parenchymatous and living. Each cell has a large central vacuole and a peripheral thin cytoplasm.

It is thicker in xerophytic plants. In roots, epidermis has tubular, unicellular projections called **root hairs**. The other substances deposited on cuticle surface may be oil, resin, silicon and salts (calcium oxalate or calcium carbonate).

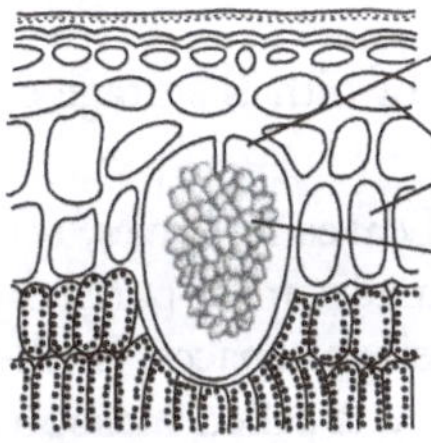

Fig. 9.8 Epidermis with a layer of cuticle and multiple epidermis

ii. Stomata

The stomata (sing. stoma) are openings in the epidermis of most of the aerial parts of the plants, especially the leaves. Each stomata is composed of two bean-shaped cells called as **guard cells**, which enclose stomatal pore. The guard cells are generally much smaller in size as compared to other epidermal cells.

They are sensitive to even a small change in turgor pressure. The dimension of stomatal pore varies from species to species, but it measures about 20 μm long and about 10-20 μm wide when fully open.

In some species, the guard cells are surrounded by **subsidiary cells** or **accessory cells**, which differ morphologically from the other epidermal cells. The guard cell walls have special elastic properties. The adjoining cell walls of two guard cells around pore are free and not attached with each other. These properties help them to stretch laterally during stomatal opening. The stomatal aperture, guard cells and the surrounding subsidiary cells are together called **stomatal apparatus.**

In most monocots, the guard cells are dumb-bell-shaped. The stomata are mostly found on the **upper epidermis** of the leaves. In some hydrophytes, the stomata occur on the upper surface to avoid water contact.

Based on their distribution, stomata are of following types

(a) **Apple Type** Present on the underside of a leaf, e.g. apple, mulberry.

(b) **Oat Type** Stomata are almost equal on the two surfaces, e.g. maize, oat.

(c) **Potato Type** These are more on the under surface, e.g. cabbage, potato, bean.

(d) **Water-lily Type** These stomata are more on the upper surface, e.g. many aquatic plants.

(e) **Potamogeton Type** Stomata vestigial or absent, e.g. *Potamogeton*.

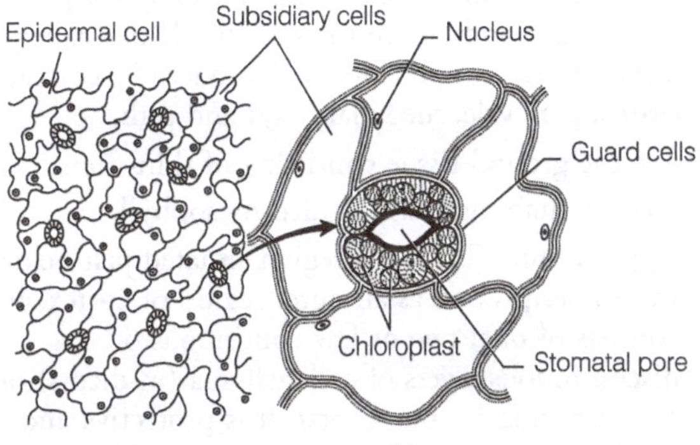

Fig. 9.9 Structure of stomata in dicot plant

iii. Epidermal Appendages (Outgrowths)

The epidermis of most plants often bears outgrowth known as **epidermal appendages** or **epidermal outgrowths**. They protect the plant against excessive loss of water and grazing. They also help in climbing in some plants, e.g. rose. They are of following two types

(a) **Trichomes** The epidermal hairs present on the stem are called trichomes. These are epidermal outgrowths present temporarily or permanently on almost all plant parts. They are multicellular structures, which may be branched or unbranched. They may be secretory in nature.

They also help in checking the rate of transpiration from aerial plant surfaces.

(b) **Emergences** (Prickles) They are multicellular, stiff and sharp epidermal outgrowths containing some inner tissues.

Functions of Epidermal Tissue System

Epidermal tissue system serves the following important functions

(a) It provides a protective covering all over the plant parts.

(b) It helps in gaseous exchange through stomata and lenticles present on the surface.

(c) The presence of cuticle helps in the reduction of evaporation of water (epidermis).

(d) The glandular trichomes excrete various useful plant products for the plant function.

(e) In some monocot leaves, the **bulliform cells** help in the rolling and unrolling of leaves. The rolling of leaves in peak summer mid-day helps to reduce transpiration in plants.

2. Ground Tissue System

All tissues, except epidermis and vascular bundles constitute the ground tissue system. It mainly forms the bulk of the plant body. It consists of simple permanent tissues. Its various components are hypodermis, cortex, endodermis, pericycle, medullary rays and pith.

In leaves, the ground tissue consisting of thin-walled chloroplast containing cells is called **mesophyll.**

(i) **Hypodermis** This is the region situated just below the epidermis and as an outer region of cortex. It consists of one, two or few continuous or discontinuous layers of collenchyma (in dicots) or sclerenchyma (in monocots). It is protective and mechanical in function.

(ii) **Cortex** The cortex lies between epidermis and endodermis. It consists of parenchyma, collenchyma and sclerenchyma tissues. The cortex is very distinct layer in dicotyledons, but not in monocotyledons. The cells of cortex contain starch grains, oil, tannins and crystals. Sometimes, cortical cells may develop chloroplasts, thus becoming photosynthetic and are called **chlorenchyma.**

In hydrophytes, the cortex may be **aerenchymatous** (spongy tissue with large air spaces found between the cells of the stems and leaves of aquatic plants). The special types of cells like sclereids, resin ducts, oil glands, laticifers are found in this region. The cortex helps in performing vital functions, such as storage, etc.

(iii) **Endodermis** This is the innermost layer of the cortex. It is single-layered, barrel-shaped and arranged without intercellular spaces. The cells are parenchymatous. The presence of bands of suberin on the radial and transverse wall is the characteristic feature. These bands are called **Casparian strips.**

The endodermis helps to control the outward movement of water and air between the cortex and xylem. It also helps to maintain the root pressure and conducts water to the protoxylem.

(iv) **Pericycle** It is made up of a single layer or many layers of cells present between endodermis and vascular tissue. In roots, pericycle comprises cells of parenchyma. Initiation of lateral roots and vascular cambium during the secondary growth takes place in these cells. The pericycle is absent in roots and stems of some aquatic plants.

(v) **Medullary Rays** The medullary rays are non-vascular areas which occur between vascular bundles in dicot stems for lateral conduction. These are made up of parenchyma cells. These originate from the apical meristem. They serve the function of lateral transport.

(vi) **Pith** The central portion of root and stem is occupied by pith. It contains parenchymatous cells and also sclerenchymatous cells, laticifers, medullary vascular bundles, in some cases. In leaves, the ground tissue is parenchymatous and possesses chloroplast.

The main function of pith is storage of water and food materials.

(vii) **Ground Tissue of Leaves** In leaves, the ground tissue of petiole is made up of parenchymatous cells with distinct intercellular spaces. In the lamina, the bulk of ground tissue is called **mesophyll,** which is usually differentiated into palisade and spongy parenchyma.

These cells are thin-walled and possess chloroplasts. The main function of mesophyll is **photosynthesis.**

3. Vascular Tissue System

A **vascular bundle** is a strand of conducting tissue, which is generally composed of xylem and phloem in monocots and xylem, phloem and cambium in dicots. These tissues originate from the procambium and apical meristems.

The arrangement of xylem and phloem is the characteristic to particular plant organs. However, a few exceptions are also there.

On the basis of arrangement of xylem and phloem in the vascular bundles, there are three types of bundles, i.e. **radial, conjoint** and **concentric.**

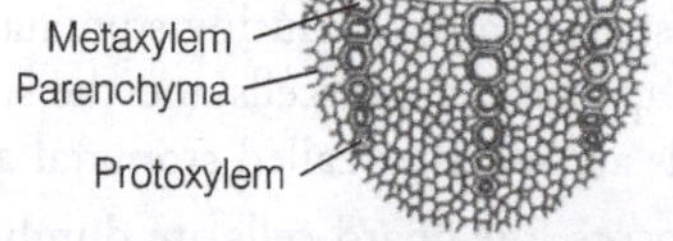

Fig. 9.10 Parts of a vascular bundle

(i) **Radial** The xylem and phloem alternate with each other separated by parenchymatous cells. This type of vascular bundles are called **radial** and is found mainly in roots.

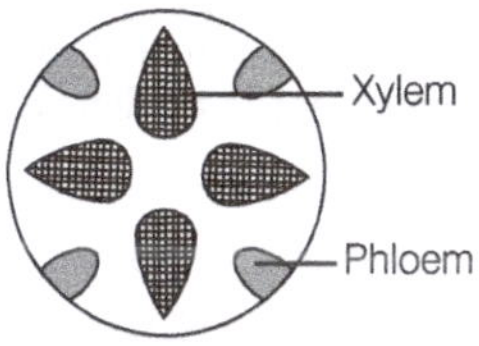

Fig. 9.11 Radial

(ii) **Conjoint** The xylem and phloem are present together in the same bundle on the same radius. Conjoint bundles are of two types, i.e. collateral and bicollateral.

(a) **Collateral** The xylem and phloem lie together on the same radius. The xylem lies inwards and the phloem outwards.

They are of two types

- In a dicot stem, the cambium is found to be present in between the xylem and phloem, such bundles are called **open**, e.g. *Helianthus* (sunflower).
- In monocots, the cambium is absent, the vascular bundle is called as a **closed** bundle, e.g. *Zea mays* (maize).

(b) **Bicollateral** This is the conjoint vascular bundle with two groups or patches of phloem, one on each side of the centrally located xylem.

The various components are arranged in sequence of outer phloem, outer cambium, xylem, inner cambium and inner phloem. Such bundles are commonly found in the members of Cucurbitaceae. Such bundles are always open.

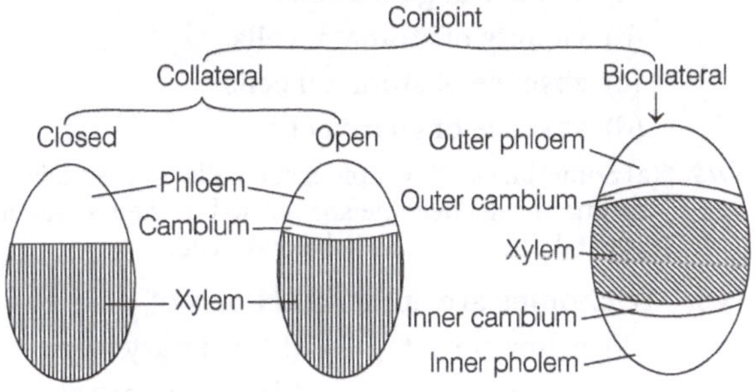

Fig. 9.12 Types of conjoint vascular bundles

(iii) **Concentric** A vascular bundle in which one tissue is completely surrounded by the other is called concentric.

The concentric bundles are of two types, i.e. **amphivasal** (phloem lies in the centre and remains completely surrounded by xylem) and **amphicribal** (xylem lies in the centre and remains completely surrounded by phloem).

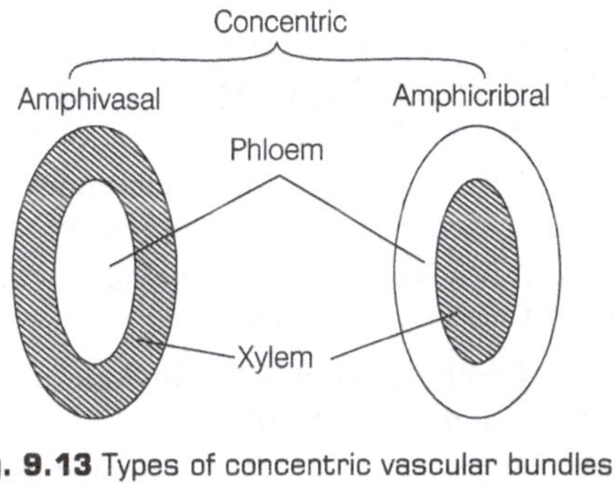

Fig. 9.13 Types of concentric vascular bundles

Topic Practice 1

Multiple Choice Questions

(1 Mark)

1. Choose the correct statement.
   (a) A group of cells having common origin generally performs common function
   (b) All the cells in a plant body are capable of dividing
   (c) Permanent tissues have all cells same in function, but different in structure
   (d) None of the above

Ans (a) A group of cells having common origin generally perform same function, e.g. meristematic tissue either primary or secondary in origin, divide repeatitively to increase the number of cells.

2. Apical meristem and intercalary meristem are called primary meristem because
   (a) they appear early in plant and contribute to the formation of primary plant body
   (b) they make secondary tissue
   (c) they make whole plant body
   (d) All of the above

Ans (a) Both apical meristem and intercalary meristem are called primary meristem because they appear early in life of a plant and contribute to the formation of primary plant body.

3. Simple tissue, which constitute few layers below the epidermis in dicotyledonous plants are
   (a) simple parenchyma
   (b) complex parenchyma
   (c) collenchyma
   (d) simple tissue

Ans (c) Collenchyma occurs in layers below the epidermis in dicotyledonous plants. It is found either as a homogenous layer or in patches.

4. The cells of this tissue are living and show angular wall thickenings. They also provide mechanical support. The tissue is **NCERT Exemplar**
(a) xylem (b) sclerenchyma
(c) collenchyma (d) epidermis

Ans (c) The collenchyma is a simple permanent tissue, which provides mechanical support.

5. Cells of collenchyma have thickened corners due to the deposition of
(a) cellulose (b) hemicellulose
(c) pectin (d) All of these

Ans (d) Collenchyma consists of cells, which are much thickened at the corners due to the deposition of cellulose, hemicellulose and pectin.

6. Sclerenchyma mainly provides
(a) storage tissue to the plants
(b) mechanical support to the organs of plant
(c) secretory tissue to the plants
(d) strength to monocot plants, specially their abundance in the layers below the epidermis

Ans (b) Sclerenchymatous cells are commonly found in fruit wall of nuts; pulp of fruits like guava, pear and sapota; seed coat of legumes and leaves of tea. Sclerenchyma provides mechanical support to plant organs.

7. Choose the incorrect pair.

(a)	Main water transporting elements in flowering plants	–	Tracheids and vessels
(b)	Characteristic feature of angiosperms	–	Xylem fibre
(c)	First formed xylem elements	–	Protoxylem
(d)	Later formed primary xylem elements	–	Metaxylem

Ans (b) Vessel is a long cylindrical tube-like structure made up of many cells called vessel members. Vessel cells are devoid of protoplasm. Presence of vessels in xylem is a characteristic feature of angiosperms.

8. Mark the incorrect statement.
(a) Phloem transports the food materials usually from the leaves to other plant parts.
(b) Phloem in the angiosperm is composed of sieve tube elements, companion cells, phloem parenchyma and phloem fibres.
(c) The function of sieve tubes are controlled by cytoplasm of sieve tube cells.
(d) Companion cells lies adjacent to sieve tube cells.

Ans (c) Sieve tube elements are long, tube-like structures, arranged longitudinally and are associated with the companion cells. Their end walls are perforated in a sieve-like manner to form the sieve plates. A mature sieve element possesses a peripheral cytoplasm and a large vacuole, but lacks a nucleus. Functions of sieve tube are controlled by the nucleus of companion cells.

9. Companion cells are closely associated with
(a) sieve elements (b) vessel elements
(c) trichomes (d) guard cells

Ans (a) Companion cells are characteristic elements of phloem tissue associated with the sieve tubes (sieve elements) in the angiosperms. The sieve tubes and companion cells are related ontogenically as they develop from the same mother cell.
The companion cells and sieve tubes maintain close cytoplasmic connections through plasmodesmata.

10. Which of the statements given below is not correct?
(a) Tissues are of three types on the basis of their structure and location
(b) Epidermal tissue gives rise to root hairs, trichomes and stomata
(c) Epidermis is parenchymatous and possesses a large vacuole
(d) Waxy thick layer over epidermis is suberin

Ans (d) The outside of the epidermis is often covered with waxy thick layer called cuticle, which prevents the loss of water. Cuticle is absent in roots.

11. Identify the tissue system from the following. **NCERT Exemplar**
(a) Parenchyma (b) Xylem
(c) Epidermis (d) Phloem

Ans (c) Epidermis forms epidermal tissue system.

12. Subsidiary cells are the specialised cell in the
(a) vicinity of guard cells
(b) vicinity of stomatal cells
(c) absence of stomatal cells
(d) absence of guard cells

Ans (a) Sometimes, a few epidermal cells, in the vicinity of the guard cells become specialised in their shape and size and are known as subsidiary cells.

13. Trichomes are epidermal hairs of
(a) primary root (b) primary stem
(c) primary leaves (d) secondary root

Ans (b) The cells of epidermis bear a number of hairs. On the primary stem, the epidermal hairs are called trichomes. The trichomes in the shoot system are usually multicellular.

14. In leaves, the ground tissues consist of
(a) epidermis (b) vascular tissue
(c) mesophyll cells (d) medullary rays

Ans (c) Ground tissue system occupies the whole of the interior of plant organs with the exclusion of vascular system. Ground tissue system of leaves is called mesophyll. Mesophyll is made up of two types of photosynthetic cells, palisade and spongy.

15. Choose the incorrrect pair.
    (a) Vascular bundle without cambium – Closed
    (b) Vascular bundle with cambium in between xylem and phloem – Open
    (c) Xylem and phloem are arranged in an alternate manner – Radial
    (d) Xylem and phloem are situated at different radius – Conjoint

Ans (d) In conjoint type of vascular bundles, the xylem and phloem are situated at the same radius of vascular cylinder. Such vascular bundles are common in stems and leaves. The conjoint vascular bundles usually have the phloem located only on the outer side of xylem.

Very Short Answer Type Questions

(1 Mark)

16. Write the location of root apical meristem and shoot apical meristem.

Ans Root apical meristem — Root tip
Shoot apical meristem — Topmost regions of stem axis

17. Give two examples of lateral meristem in plants.

Ans The two examples of lateral meristem in plants is fascicular combium and phellogen (cork cambium).

18. Why root's apical meristem is subterminal?

Ans The presence of root cap makes the root's apical meristem subterminal.

19. Why is cambium called as lateral meristem?

Ans The cambium lies parallel to the circumference and helps to increase in girth, hence is called as lateral meristem.

20. The lawn grass (*Cynodon dactylon*) needs to be mowed frequently to prevent its overgrowth. Which tissue is responsible for its rapid growth?

Ans The meristematic tissue is responsible for the rapid growth of such mowed lawn grass. When the apex of grass is cut frequently, it leads to the growth of the lateral branches, that makes it more bushy.

21. The product of photosynthesis is transported from the leaves to various parts of the plant and stored in some cells before being utilised. What are the cells/tissues that store them? **NCERT Exemplar**

Ans Parenchyma.

22. How are the adjacent parenchyma cells are connected to each other?

Ans By plasmodesmata or cytoplasmic bridges.

23. What is the composition of collenchyma cells?

Ans Collenchyma is made up of cellulose, hemicellulose and pectin.

24. Wall thickenings are uneven in which tissues?

Ans Wall thickenings are uneven in collenchyma tissue. The thickenings are present only at corners of cells.

25. Give two examples of fruits having sclereids?

Ans Two examples of fruits having sclereids is pulp of the guava and pear.

26. How vascular tissue system originate?

Ans Vascular tissue system develops from part of pleurome or procambium.

27. Name the only living component of xylem.

Ans Xylem parenchyma is the only living component of xylem.

28. How the vessel members in xylems are interconnected?

Ans The vessel members in xylems are interconnected through perforations in their end/common walls.

29. Protoxylem is the first formed xylem. If the protoxylem lies next to phloem, what kind of arrangement of xylem would you call it?

Ans Exarch.

30. What is the function of phloem parenchyma? **NCERT Exemplar**

Ans Phloem parenchyma takes part in lateral conduction of food and supply of water from xylem.

31. Why xylem vessels are called syncytes?

Ans The xylem vessels are formed from a number of cells, so they are called syncytes.

32. What is the epidermal cell modification in plants that prevent water loss? **NCERT Exemplar**

Ans Cuticularised trichoblasts or epidermal hair which produce a stationary layer of air over the surface that reduces isolation and rate of transpiration.

33. What is the common name of root epidermis?

Ans Epiblema.

34. A separate layer of cuticle covers the epidermis. What is its use?

Ans Cuticle and cutinised outer walls of epidermal cells reduce the rate of water loss through transpiration.

35. How do the bulliform cells present in the epidermis help grasses?

Ans The bulliform cells present in the epidermis of grasses help in folding of leaves during hot summer day and prevent transpiration.

36. **Name certain adaxial epidermal cells in grasses, along the midrib modify themselves to large, empty, colourless cells.**

Ans The large, empty, colourless cells are called bulliform cells.

37. **In how many zones, the ground tissue system is differentiated?**

Ans The ground tissue system is differentiated in three major zones, i.e. cortex, pericycle and pith with medullary rays.

38. **In which vascular bundles, phloem lies on the outerside and xylem towards the inner side or central axis?**

Ans Collateral vascular bundles.

39. **Name the term used to describe the vascular bundles, in which phloem lies at the centre and is surrounded by the xylem?**

Ans Amphivasal

Short Answer Type I Questions

(2 Marks)

40. **How the study of anatomy is useful to us?**

Ans The study of anatomy helps us in **NCERT**

(i) solving taxonomic problems.

(ii) analysing the microstructure, adulteration of spices, tea, tobacco, etc.

(iii) extraction of compounds for use as medicine.

(iv) differentiation of inferior quality wood from the superior quality. ($\frac{1}{2}\times 4$)

41. **Which kind of tissue stores starch in potato and makes the shells of the nuts?**

Ans Parenchymatous tissue stores starch (food) in potato and sclerenchymatous tissues make the shells of the nuts. (1+1)

42. **While eating peach or pear, it is usually seen that some stone-like structures get entangled in the teeth. What are these stone-like structures called?** **NCERT Exemplar**

Ans The fruits like pear and peach, have stone-like structures present in the pith. These are small groups of short, isodiametric sclereids. (2)

43. **What are the characteristic differences found in vascular tissue of gymnosperms and angiosperms?** **NCERT Exemplar**

Ans In gymnosperms, vessel elements are not present in xylem, whereas these are main constituents in angiosperms.

In the phloem of gymnosperms, companion cells are not associated with the sieve elements. In angiosperms, companion cells are associated with the sieve elements of phloem. (2)

44. **Why are xylem and phloem called complex tissues?** **NCERT**

Ans A group of more than one type of cells having common origin and working together as a unit, is called complex tissue.

Since, both xylem and phloem are made up of several kinds of cells, they are called complex tissues. (1+1)

45. **Name those parenchymatous cells which are associated with sieve tubes in angiosperms. Mention their role also.**

Ans Companion cells are associated with sieve tubes in angiosperms. They help sieve tubes in the translocation of solutes. (2)

46. **Below is a list of plant fibres. From which part of the plant these are obtained (i) coir (ii) hemp (iii) cotton (iv) jute?**

Ans (i) **Coir** Mesocarp from the fruit (drupe) of coconut.

(ii) **Hemp** Phloem or bast fibres.

(iii) **Cotton** Trichomes or hair from seed surface of *Gossypium* (cotton).

(iv) **Jute** Phloem or bast fibres. ($\frac{1}{2}\times 4$)

47. **Differentiate between vascular tissues of gymnosperms and angiosperms.**

Ans Differences between vascular tissues of gymnosperms and angiosperms are

Vascular Tissues of Gymnosperms	Vascular Tissues of Angiosperms
Xylem is devoid of vessels.	Xylem possesses vessels.
Phloem does not contain sieve tubes.	Sieve tubes are present.
Phloem does not contain companion cells.	Phloem possesses companion cells.

(2)

48. **List out the functions of ground tissue system.**

Ans Functions of ground tissue systems are

(i) It provides mechanical strength, while bending.

(ii) It has spaces to allow gaseous exchange between cortex and atmosphere.

(iii) It carries out photosynthesis. (2)

49. **(i) Name the tissue that live between epidermis and pericycle.**

(ii) In which parts it is divided?

Ans (i) The tissue between epidermis and pericycle is called cortex.

(ii) Cortex has three parts, i.e. hypodermis, general cortex and endodermis. (1+1)

Short Answer Type II Questions

(3 Marks)

50. List out the important characteristics of meristematic tissue.

Ans Characteristics of meristematic tissues are

(i) Cells are usually rectangular with a thin cell wall made up of cellulose.

(ii) They are closely arranged without any intercellular space.

(iii) They show a prominent nucleus and are full of cytoplasm.

(iv) They are always capable of division. (3)

51. Classify vascular bundles on the basis of position of the protoxylem.

Ans Vascular bundles on the basis of position of protoxylem are

(i) **Endarch** Protoxylem faces the centre of the plant organ.

(ii) **Exarch** Protoxylem faces periphery of the plant. (3)

52. (i) Define the term vascular strand.

(ii) Name the type of vascular bundles in case of

(a) root

(b) stems and leaves

Ans (i) The vascular tissue system forms a strand of vascular tissues known as vascular strand or vascular cylinder. (1)

(ii) (a) In case of root vascular bundles are radial.

(b) In case of stems and leaves, these are conjoint. (1+1)

Long Answer Type Questions

(5 Marks)

53. State the location and function of different types of meristems. **NCERT**

Ans Meristems are divided into three types on the basis of position in the plant body (1)

(i) **Apical meristem** The apical meristem is located at the apices/tips of roots and shoots.

It has following functions

(a) Forms the primary tissues of the plant and helps in growth in length.

(b) Certain cells of apical meristem constitute the axillary buds present in the axils of leaves. (2)

(ii) **Intercalary meristem** It occurs in between mature tissues, at the bases of internodes and leaf sheaths of grasses and other monocots. They help to regenerate the parts of grasses, eaten by herbivores and help in primary growth of plants. (1)

(iii) **Lateral meristem** It is arranged parallel to the sides of the organs of plants. The lateral meristem is responsible for increase in the diameter of an organ. (1)

54. Name the three basic tissue systems in the flowering plants. Give the tissue names under each system. **NCERT**

Ans Refer to text on page no. 186, 187 and 188.

55. What is stomatal apparatus? Explain the structure of stomata with a labelled diagram. **NCERT**

Ans **Stomata** are structures present in the epidermis of leaves. Each stoma is composed of two bean-shaped cells called **guard cells**, which enclose stomatal pore. In grasses, guard cells are dumb-bell-shaped. The guard cells possess chloroplasts and regulate the opening and closing of stomata.

Sometimes, a few epidermal cells in the vicinity of the guard cells become specialised in their shape and size known as **subsidiary cells**.

The stomatal aperture, guard cells and the surrounding subsidiary cells are together called stomatal apparatus(3)

For diagram Refer to fig. no. 9.9. (2)

56. Epidermal cells are often modified to perform specialised functions in plants. Name some of them and functions they perform. **NCERT Exemplar**

Ans The following epidermal cells are found in plants

(i) **Cuticle** They reduce surface transpiration.

(ii) **Stomata** Exchange of gases and transpiration.

(iii) **Stem hair** For reducing temperature changes and rate of transpiration.

(iv) **Glandular hair** Various secretions.

(v) **Prickles** Protect from grazing animals.

(vi) **Root hair** Absorb water. (5)

57. Which tissues are called complex permanent tissues? Describe in detail.

Ans The complex permanent tissues are made of more than one type of cells. They are of two types

(i) Xylem

(ii) Phloem (2)

Refer to text on page no. 185 and 186.

58. (i) How will you classify vascular bundles in different types?

(ii) Describe the open and closed type of vascular bundles.

Ans (i) According to the arrangement of xylem and pholem in the vascular bundles, there are three types of bundles. These are radial, conjoint and concentric. (2)

(ii) Refer to text on page no. 189. (3)

59. Distinguish between following
(i) Exarch and endarch condition of protoxylem
(ii) Stele and vascular bundles
(iii) Protoxylem and metaxylem
(iv) Open and closed vascular bundles
(v) Stem hairs and root hairs **NCERT Exemplar**

Ans (i) In **exarch condition** Protoxylem is towards the periphery.
In **endarch condition** Protoxylem is towards the centre. (1)
(ii) Stele is the arrangement of vascular tissues and vascular bundle in groups of xylem and phloem. (1)
(iii) Protoxylem is an early formed xylem and metaxylem is lately formed xylem. (1)
(iv) Open vascular bundles have intrafascicular cambium and show secondary growth. Closed vascular bundles do not have intrafascicular cambium. (1)
(v) Stem hairs are multicellular, whereas root hairs are unicellular. (1)

TOPIC 02 Anatomy of Dicotyledonous And Monocotyledonous Plants

The tissue organisation of roots, stems and leaves can be studied better and conveniently by the **transverse sections** of the mature zones of the following mentioned plant parts.

Dicotyledonous Root

The primary internal structure of dicot root can be studied from the Transverse Section (TS) of a young root of sunflower, pea or gram.

The primary root is the one, which has only primary permanent tissues that are formed from vegetative shoot apex. Secondary tissues are absent. The following structures can be seen from periphery towards the centre

1. Epidermis

It forms the outermost layer in young root. It is equivalent to epidermis of stem. The stomata and cuticle are not present in it. The cells are thin-walled and tubular.

Some of the epidermis cells are prolonged to form thin-walled tubular structures called **root hairs.**

The cells, which produce root hair are called **root hair cells** or **trichoblasts.** Due to the presence of root hairs, epiblema is also called **piliferous layer** (*Pilus* – hair; *ferre* – to carry) and **rhizodermis** (*Rhiza* – root; *derma* – skin).

Root hairs have pectose layer on the outside, this is to help them to pass into the soil spaces for absorption of water and mineral salts.

The active lifespan of root hairs is upto 7 days and die off in older parts of the root.

The cells of older epidermis shrivel afterwards and become cutinised and suberised.

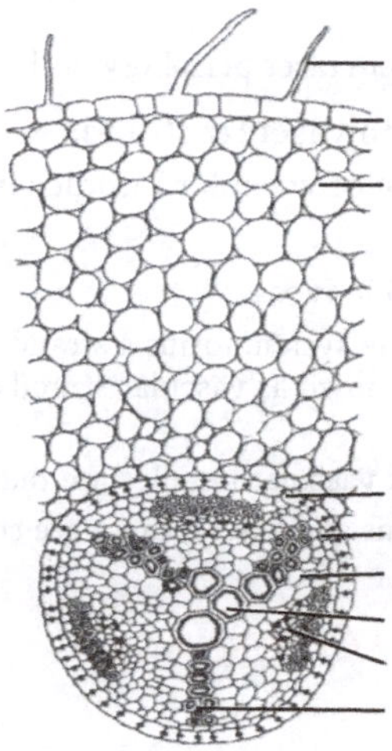

Fig. 9.14 Structure of a portion of TS of dicotyledonous root

2. Cortex

It lies beneath the epiblema. It consists of several layers of thin-walled parenchymatous cells with conspicuous intercellular spaces. The cells of cortex store food. It also conducts water from the epiblema to the inner tissues.

3. Endodermis

The innermost layer of the cortex is endodermis. It comprises of a single layer of barrel-shaped cells without any intercellular spaces. The endodermal cells are living and are rich in starch grains.

They have characteristic bands of thickenings along their radial and tangential walls. These are called **Casparian bands** or **Casparian strips.**

The Casparian strips are made up of suberin and lignin. These strips prevent plasmolysis of endodermal cells and do not allow wall to wall movement of substances between cortex and pericycle. The cells of endodermis lying opposite to the protoxylem are thin-walled to permit free passage of water and minerals from cortex into the xylem. These are called **passage cells**.

4. Stele

All tissues on the innerside of the endodermis such as pericycle, vascular strand and pith constitute the stele.

(i) **Pericycle** The next to endodermis lies a layer of thick-walled parenchymatous cells referred to as pericycle. The initiation of lateral roots and vascular cambium during the secondary growth takes place in these cells.

(ii) **Vascular Strand** The vascular strand consists of separate bundles of xylem and phloem arranged alternately inner to the pericycle. Hence, the xylem and phloem bundles are equal in number and lie on different radii. Such vascular bundles are called **radial bundles.**

On the basis of number of xylem bundles, the root may be **diarch** (with two xylem bundles), **triarch**, **tetrarch**, **pentarch** and **polyarch** (with more than five xylem bundles).

When the protoxylem is towards the periphery and the later formed xylem (metaxylem) is towards the centre of the root, the kind of xylem condition is called **exarch** and is characteristic of root.

The phloem and xylem bundles are separated from each other by one or more layers of small thin-walled cells called **conjuctive tissue.**

Later, it becomes meristematic and forms vascular cambium. The phloem tissues conducts organic food from leaf to the other parts of the plant. Secondary growth occurs in dicot roots.

(iii) **Pith** It is generally absent in dicot roots. If present, it is small and consists of **parenchyma** cells. These function to store food and waste products.

Features for Identification of Dicotyledonous Root

Dicotyledonous root can be easily identified with the following features

(i) Presence of root hairs.

(ii) Endodermis with Casparian strips.

(iii) Absence of pith.

(iv) Radial bundles less than eight.

(v) Presence of exarch xylem.

Monocotyledonous Root

This can be inferred from the following structures given below

1. Epidermis

It is the outermost, thin-walled, compactly arranged layer of cells. Some of the cells give rise to root hair. The root hairs are unicellular and lie in contact with soil water. Both epidermis and root hair are devoid of cuticle. These help in absorption of water and minerals. In older parts, the epidermis is shed or impervious.

2. Cortex

It is a broad zone of parenchyma cells. The cells are thin-walled and enclose intercellular spaces. They normally store food. The cortex provides for radial movement of water and minerals from epiblema to the root interior.

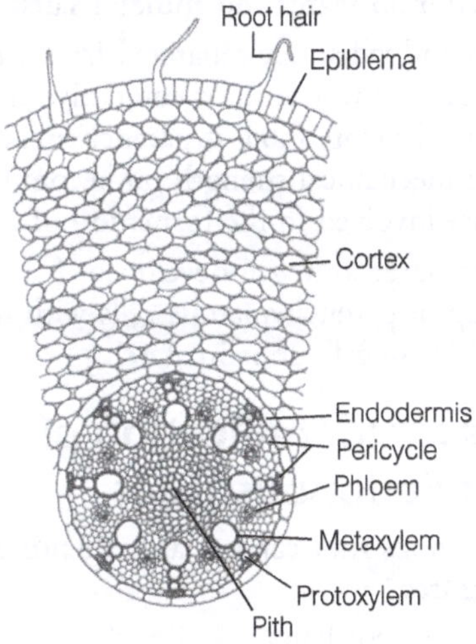

Fig. 9.15 Structure of TS of monocot root

3. Endodermis

It is single-layered and made up of barrel-shaped cells which do not enclose intercellular spaces. The young endodermal cells possess an internal strip of suberin and lignin, which is known as **Casparian strip.**

Endodermal cells lying opposite the protoxylem groups however, remain in the primary stage with usual Casparian strip.

These unthickened cells are called **passage** or **transfusion cells.** These cells help in conduction of fluids and minerals from cortex into the xylem.

4. Stele

All tissues inside the endodermis, i.e. pericycle, vascular bundles and pith form the stele.

(i) **Pericycle** It forms the outer boundary of stele. Pericycle may be **uniseriate** (single-layered) or **multiseriate** (multilayered). The pericycle does not form cambium. It only produces lateral roots. The pericycle is composed of thin-walled parenchymatous cells in a young root. Later, it becomes thick-walled in many monocot roots.

(ii) **Vascular Strand** It is in the form of several alternate and radial xylem and phloem bundles. The vascular bundles are arranged in the form of a ring around a central pith.
The xylem bundles are **exarch**, i.e. protoxylem lies towards the outside, while the metaxylem faces inwards. Due to the pressure of numerous xylem bundles and exarch condition, the xylem of monocot root is **polyarch. Protoxylem vessels are narrow, while the metaxylem vessels are broad. Xylem provides mechanical strength and helps in conduction of water and mineral salts.**

Phloem and xylem are separated from each other by means of a narrow strip of conjuctive tissue. The phloem cells store food, if parenchymatous. They provide mechanical strength on becoming sclerified. They are involved in the formation of cambium.

(iii) **Pith** It is large and well-developed. It is large and made up of parenchymatous cells with intercellular spaces. These cells contain starch.

Features for Identification of Monocotyledonous Root

Monocotyledonous root can be easily identified with the following features

(i) Presence of root hairs.
(ii) Endodermis with passage cells.
(iii) Presence of pith.
(iv) Radial bundles are more than eight.
(v) Xylem exarch.
(vi) Presence of an exodermis.

Differences between Dicot Root and Monocot Root

Dicot Root	Monocot Root
The cortex is simple homogeneous and made up of parenchymatous cells.	Cortex is well-developed. It develops from one or more layers of thick-walled cells towards outside, called exodermis. Rest of the cells are parenchymatous.
The endodermis is prominent with casparian thickenings.	Endodermis is more prominent showing casparian thickenings.
Secondary growth occurs.	No secondary growth occurs (except in some plants).
Conjunctive tissue is parenchymatous.	Conjunctive tissue around metaxylem vessels is sclerenchymatous.
Pith is very small or absent.	Pith is large.

Dicotyledonous Stem

The transverse section (TS) of a typical young dicotyledonous stem shows the following areas

1. Epidermis

The outermost protective layer of the stem is called **epidermis**. It is covered with a thin-layer of cuticle and may bear trichomes and a few **stomata**. The cuticle protects the tissues from injury as well as diseases caused from the entry of fungal spores and bacteria. It also helps to prevent loss of water.

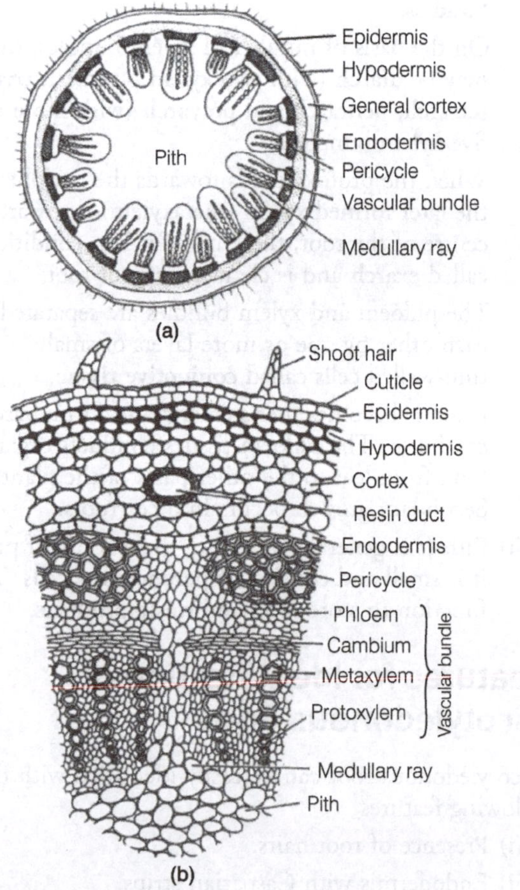

Fig. 9.16 Dicot stem : (a) TS of dicot stem, (b) Magnified structure of a portion of TS of dicot stem

2. Cortex

This layer lies just below the epidermis and extends till endodermis. Its various parts are hypodermis, general cortex and endodermis.

(i) **Hypodermis** It is just below the epidermis consisting of collenchymatous cells. The cells contain chloroplasts. It provides mechanical strength to the stem.

(ii) **General Cortex** It is located just below the hypodermis and consists of a few layers of parenchymatous cells. These cells are thin-walled have big intercellular spaces and may contain chloroplasts.

(iii) **Endodermis** It lies just beneath the general cortex in the form of single layer of barrel-shaped cells surrounding the stele. It is the innermost layer of cortex. In sunflower, it contains starch, hence is called **starch sheath**.

3. Pericycle

It exists between the endodermis and the vascular bundles. The cells are sclerenchymatous with lignified cell walls and a few parenchymatous cells dispersed in between. Each patch is associated with phloem of the vascular bundle and is called the **hard bast**.

4. Vascular Strand

The vascular strand consists of many vascular bundles, arranged in the form of a ring around a central pith and inner to pericycle. Each vascular bundle consists of **phloem** (on the outside), **xylem** (towards the inner side) with a strip of **cambium**, in between the two.

The vascular bundles are thus, **conjoint** (i.e. consists of both xylem and phloem), **collateral** (i.e. phloem and xylem are on the same radius), **open** (i.e. a strip of cambium present between the two) and with endarch protoxylem.

5. Medullary or Pith Rays

These are non-vascular areas present in between the vascular bundles. The medullary rays connect pith with pericycle and cortex. Cells are larger than those of cortex. The medullary rays take part in radial conduction of materials, i.e. food, water, gases, etc.

6. Pith or Medulla

It consists of the central part of the stem. It consists of rounded, oval or polygonal parenchymatous cells. Intercellular spaces are absent. The cells store food materials and waste products.

Features for Identification of Dicotyledonous Stem

Dicotyledonous stem can be easily identified with the following features

(i) Occurrence of multicellular hair over epidermis.

(ii) Collenchymatous hypodermis.

(iii) Presence of bundle caps or sclerenchymatous pericycle over vascular bundles.

(iv) Endarch xylem.

Monocotyledonous Stem

The monocot stem possesses only primary structure. The different monocot stems from outside towards inside consist of epidermis, hypodermis, ground tissue and vascular system.

1. Epidermis

It is single-layered, having stomata in it. The cells have a thick cuticle layer on the outside.

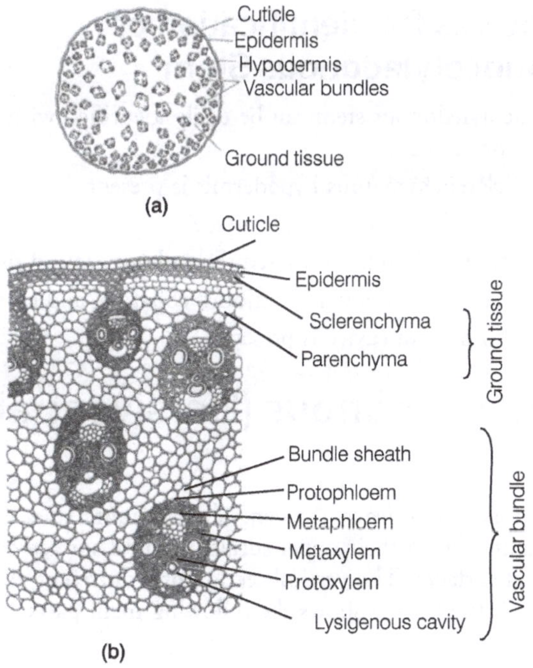

Fig. 9.17 Monocot stem : (a) TS of young monocot stem, (b) Magnified structure of a portion of TS of monocot stem

2. Hypodermis

It is 2-3 layered having lignified sclerenchymatous cells present just below the epidermis.

3. Ground Tissue

It fills the whole interior of the stem containing parenchymatous cells. A number of vascular bundles are scattered in it.

4. Vascular System

Monocot stems has scattered vascular bundles. Each vascular bundle in vascular strand is surrounded by a sheath of sclerenchyma known as **bundle sheath cells**. The vascular bundles possess both phloem (phloem parenchyma is absent) and xylem so, these are conjoint type.

The bundles are **endarch** with the protoxylem and metaxylem arranged in the form of a 'Y'. The divergent ends are occupied by two pitted vessels and convergent end by two smaller spiral vessels lying radially in the centre. A water containing cavity called **lysigenous cavity** is present in association with the protoxylem.

It is formed by the breakdown of inner protoxylem vessels and parenchyma during the earlier stages of growth. The cavity is absent or reduced in the smaller vascular bundles that occur in contact with sclerenchymatous hypodermis.

Features for Identification of Monocotyledonous Stem

Monocotyledonous stem can be easily identified with the following features

(i) Sclerenchymatous hypodermis is present.
(ii) Undifferentiated ground tissue.
(iii) Vascular bundles scattered throughout ground tissue.
(iv) Vascular bundles are conjoint, collateral and closed.
(v) Protoxylem cavity is present.

Dicotyledonous (Dorsiventral) Leaf

The dorsiventral leaves are generally horizontal and sunlight falls on their upper surface (ventral surface or adaxial surface). The vertical section of a dorsiventral leaf through the lamina shows the following main parts

1. Epidermis

The epidermis covers both the upper (adaxial) and the lower (abaxial) surfaces of the leaf.

(i) **Upper Epidermis** It is the uppermost, single-layered, made up of parenchymatous cell, but sometimes, multilayered, e.g. *Ficus, Piper, Nerium, Begonia.* Also there is cuticle, which covers the upper epidermis. The outgrowths called **papillae** (e.g. *Gladiolus*) are sometimes present in epidermal cells. The stomata are usually less present in the upper surface. Chloroplasts are not present in this layer.

(ii) **Lower Epidermis** The stomata and chloroplasts are more in number in the lower epidermis. There are substomatal cavities present below the stomata for the gaseous exchange.

2. Mesophyll

It is differentiated in two parts in dorsiventral leaves, i.e. **upper palisade** and **lower spongy parenchyma.** The palisade cells contain abundant chloroplasts. Hence, they are the major seat of photosynthetic activity.

The spongy parenchyma lies below the palisade parenchyma and above the lower epidermis. This spongy parenchyma cells contain several chloroplasts, but less than the number present in palisade cells.

3. Vascular System

The vascular bundles are conjoint, collateral, endarch and closed. Each bundle is surrounded by a bundle sheath of parenchymatous cells. The xylem is present towards upper epidermis (adaxial surface) and phloem towards lower epidermis (abaxial surface).

The xylem consists of vessels or trachae, tracheids, xylem parenchyma and xylem fibres. It is meant for the conduction of water and minerals. The phloem is made up of sieve tubes, companion cells, phloem parenchyma and phloem fibres. Each vascular bundle is surrounded by a layer of thick-walled cells arranged compactly and known as **bundle sheath cell** (in C_4-plants only).

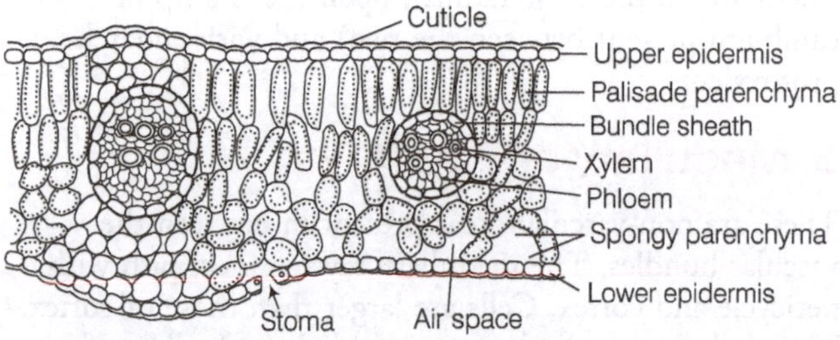

Fig. 9.18 TS of dicot leaf

The vascular bundles can be seen in the veins and the midrib. The size of vascular bundles varies according to the size of the veins.

The veins vary in thickness in the reticulate venation.

4. Midrib

Mesophyll is absent in the region of midrib and other larger veins. Collenchyma or sclerenchyma occurs towards the two epidermal layers for providing mechanical strength. The centre contains a number of vascular bundles, which are embedded in a parenchymatous ground tissue.

Features for Identification of Dicotyledonous Leaf

Dicotyledonous leaf can be easily identified with the following features

(i) Dorsiventrally flattened with stomata mostly on upper surface.
(ii) Mesophyll differentiated into palisade and spongy parenchyma.
(iii) Vascular bundles with colourless bundle sheath (in C_4-plants).
(iv) Vascular bundle with xylem towards upper side and phloem towards lower side.

Monocotyledonous (Isobilateral) Leaf

Monocot leaves are generally isobilateral (*Isos* – equal; *bis* – twice; *latris* – side), but in some plants (*Musa*, *Canna*, etc.), these are dorsiventral. The leaves usually show parallel venation (veins running parallel to each other). The various components of a monocot leaf are

1. Epidermis

The leaf composes of upper and lower epidermis made up of single-layered, compactly arranged cells. The upper layer is covered with cuticle. In some grasses, the epidermal cells are impregnated with silica. The stomata are generally found in both the upper and lower layers of epidermis. At some places, the epidermis possesses large sized, thin-walled, colourless protruding cells called **bulliform** or **motor cells**. These become placcid when water is not sufficient. The leaves again become flat when water is available and bulliform cells become turgid. The bulliform cells may be distributed irregularly or arranged in regular pattern.

2. Mesophyll

It is made up of chlorenchymatous ground tissue of leaves. It is undifferentiated (i.e. not differentiated between palisade and spongy parenchyma) in monocot leaves. All the cells are similar. The intercellular spaces are connected with the two substomatal cavities. Mesophyll cells contain abundant chloroplasts. Hence, they are the seat of photosynthesis.

3. Vascular Bundle

A large number of vascular bundles are present, some of them are small and some are big. Each vascular bundle is surrounded by a bundle sheath of parenchymatous cells. Above and below the larger bundle, the patches of sclerenchymatous cells are present.

The vascular bundles are **conjoint**, **collateral**, **endarch** and **closed**. In some grasses, these are surrounded by a distinct parenchymatous bundle sheath. The xylem is present towards the upper epidermis and phloem towards the lower epidermis. The xylem and phloem elements of monocot leaves are similar to those of dicot leaves.

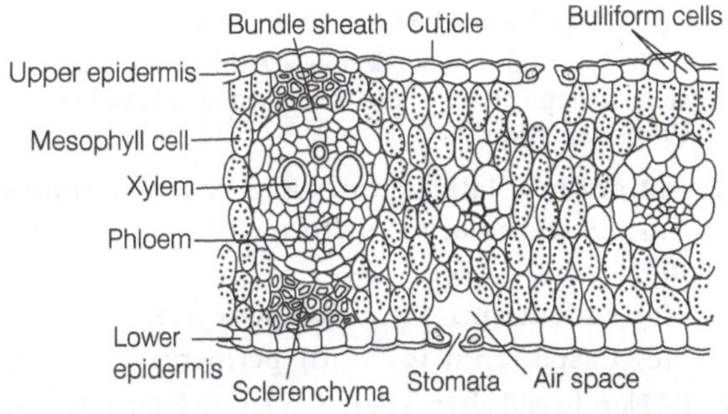

Fig. 9.19 Detailed structure of a part of TS of monocot leaf

4. Midrib

It is the widest part of monocot leaf. A shallow groove is present in the upper or adaxial surface, while a broad ridge is present on the abaxial surface.

Features for Identification of Monocotyledonous Leaf

Monocotyledonous leaf can be easily identified with the following features

(i) Undifferentiated mesophyll.
(ii) Presence of bundle sheath with chloroplasts.
(iii) Vascular bundle with xylem towards upper side and phloem towards lower side.
(iv) Xylem vessels are rounded.
(v) Presence of few large sized bulliform cells on upper surface.

☑ Topic Practice 2

Multiple Choice Questions

1 Mark

1. Cortex is the region found between
(a) epidermis and stele
(b) pericycle and endodermis
(c) endodermis and pith
(d) endodermis and vascular bundle

Ans (a) Cortex tissue is found in between the epidermis and stele. It is multilayered and is made up of parenchymatous cells with big intercellular spaces.

2. Water impermeable, waxy material secreted by endodermal cells in the form of Casparian strip is
(a) lignin (b) suberin
(c) conjunctive tissue (d) pectin

Ans (b) Radial walls of endodermis are thickened due to suberin deposition. These thickened areas are known as Casparian strips.

3. Initiation of lateral roots and vascular cambium during secondary growth occurs due to activity of
(a) endodermis (b) pericycle
(c) Casparian strip (d) periderm

Ans (b) Next to endodermis lies a few layered thin thick-walled parenchymatous cells referred to as pericycle. Initiation of lateral roots and vascular cambium during secondary growth takes place in these cells.

4. Central part of root occupied by parenchymatous (thin or thick-walled) cells is called
(a) pith (b) endodermis
(c) pericycle (d) meristem

Ans (a) The centre of monocot or dicot root is occupied by pith. It consists of parenchymatous (thin-walled or thick-walled) cells, which may be rounded or angular. Intercellular spaces are present. The pith cells store food. Pith is small and inconspicuous in dicots and large and conspicuous in monocots.

5. Vascular bundles in monocotyledons are considered closed because
(a) a bundle sheath surrounds each bundle
(b) cambium is absent
(c) there are no vessels with perforations
(d) xylem is surrounded all around by phloem

Ans (b) The vascular bundles of monocots do not contain a layer of meristematic tissue (cambium). Due to the absence of meristematic tissue in vascular bundles, they are termed closed in monocots. Hence, secondary growth is not seen in them.

6. Water containing cavities in vascular bundles are found in
(a) sunflower (b) maize
(c) *Cycas* (d) *Pinus*

Ans (b) In monocot stem like *Zea mays*, vascular bundles are conjoint, collateral and closed. In vascular bundles, the lowermost protoxylem vessels and xylem parenchyma cells dissolve forming a water containing cavity called protoxylem cavity or lacuna or lysigenous cavity.

7. A conjoint and open vascular bundle will be observed in the transverse section of
(a) monocot root (b) monocot stem
(c) dicot root (d) dicot stem

Ans (d) Each vascular bundle is conjoint open and with endarch protoxylem in the stem of dicot plant.

8. The growth of root and stem in length with the help of apical meristem is called ...*A*.... Apart from primary growth, most dicotyledonous plants exhibit an increase in girth called ...*B*....
Choose the correct option of *A* and *B* in respect to the above paragraph.
(a) *A*–primary growth; *B*–secondary growth
(b) *A*–secondary growth; *B*–primary growth
(c) *A*–secondary growth; *B*–tertiary growth
(d) *A*–primary growth; *B*–tertiary growth

Ans (a) The primary growth in plants occur as a result of activity of the root and shoot apical meristems, which helps in elongation of roots and shoot, respectively. Secondary growth is exhibited due to the presence of vascular cambium.

9. The meristematic tissue responsible for the cutting of vascular tissue (xylem and phloem) is called
(a) cork cambium (b) vascular cambium
(c) lateral meristem (d) endodermis

Ans (b) The meristematic layer that is responsible for cutting off vascular tissues (xylem and phloem) is called vascular cambium. In the young stem, it is present in patches as a single layer between the xylem and phloem. Later, it forms a complete ring.

10. Identify the incorrect statement about dicot root.
(a) In dicot root, 2-4 xylem and phloem patches are found
(b) Cambium develops inside xylem
(c) All tissues on innerside of endodermis constitute to form stele
(d) They have less xylem bundles as compared to monocot root

Ans (b) The initiation of vascular cambium during secondary growth phase takes place in pericycle, which is present in between xylem and phloem.

Very Short Answer Type Questions

1 Mark

11. **What is present on the surface of the leaves which helps the plant to prevent loss of water, but is absent in roots?** **NCERT Exemplar**

Ans Waxy cuticle layer.

12. **The cross-section of a plant material showed the following features when viewed under the microscope**
   (a) Vascular bundles were radially arranged
   (b) Four xylem strands with exarch condition of protoxylem. To which organ should it be assigned? **NCERT Exemplar**

Ans Dicot root.

13. **Name the characteristic bands that are found in endodermis of dicot root.**

Ans Casparian strips or Casparian bands.

14. **Which part of the plant would show the following?**
   (i) Radial vascular bundle
   (ii) Polyarch xylem
   (iii) Well-developed pith

Ans (i) Root (ii) Monocot root
(iii) Monocot root

15. **What is the difference between hypodermis of dicot and monocot stems?**

Ans In dicot stems, hypodermis consists of a few layers of collenchyma cells, whereas in case of monocot stems, hypodermis consists of 2-3 layers of sclerenchyma cells.

16. **Describe the features of pith in dicot stems.**

Ans The pith consists of a large number of rounded, parenchymatous cells with big intercellular spaces. It occupies the central portion of the stem.

17. **Why the endodermis of a dicot stem is called starch sheath?**

Ans The endodermis of a dicot stem is rich in starch grains, so it is called starch sheath.

18. **Name the tissues related to mesophyll.**

Ans Palisade and spongy parenchyma are the two tissues related to mesophyll.

19. **Name the epidermis which covers both the upper surface and lower surface of the leaf.**

Ans **Upper surface** is covered by adaxial epidermis.
Lower surface is covered by abaxial epidermis.

20. **In dicot leaves, how the vascular bundles are related to size of the veins?**

Ans The size of the vascular bundles is dependent on the size of veins present in leaves.

Short Answer Type I Questions

2 Marks

21. **Describe the cortex region of dicot root.**

Ans The cortex consists of several layers of thin-walled parenchyma cells. Intercellular spaces are small but abundant. The cortical cells can be rounded, oval or angular. They store food. The major function of the cortex in the root hair zone is conduction of water and minerals from epiblema to the interior of the root. (2)

22. **(i) Which kind of cells form pericycle?**
   (ii) What is its function?

Ans (i) Pericycle is formed of parenchymatous cells.
(ii) It gives rise to lateral roots. (1+1)

23. **Differentiate between pith in monocot root and dicot root.**

Ans Differences in pith in monocot and dicot root are

Pith in Monocot Root	Pith in Dicot Root
The centre of root is occupied by the pith.	It is often absent. When present, it is very small.
Intercellular spaces are present in between pith cells.	Intercellular spaces are absent.
The pith cells store food.	The pith cells store food as well as waste materials.

(2)

24. **Mention the functions of cortex region of monocot root.**

Ans The cortex of a monocot root has following three functions
(i) Conduction of water from the root hairs to the inner tissues.
(ii) Storage of food.
(iii) Outermost layer of the cortex produce protective exodermis in the older roots. (2)

25. **Write one difference between mesophyll of dicot leaf and a monocot leaf.**

Ans In dicot leaves, mesophyll is differentiated into palisade and spongy parenchyma. In case of monocot leaves, mesophyll is not differentiated and all cells are like spongy parenchyma. (2)

26. **Mention the features of isobilateral leaves.**

Ans Isobilateral (equifacial) leaves are placed in a plant in such a way that both its surfaces receive equal amount of sunlight. It does not have distinct upper and lower surfaces. Mesophyll is usually indistinguishable. Most of the monocot plants have isobilateral leaves. (2)

27. How does the periderm formation take place in the dicot stems? What are its components?

Ans Cork cambium develops in cortex and cuts off cells on both outer and inner sides of stem. The outer cells differentiate into cork or phellem and inner cells form the secondary cortex or phelloderm. The various components of periderm are phellogen, phellem and phelloderm. (1+1)

Short Answer Type II Questions

3 Marks

28. Draw the diagram of a dicot root and a monocot root. Write two points difference between them.

Ans Refer to fig. no. 9.14 and 9.15. (2)

Differences In dicot roots, cortex region is narrow and in monocot roots, it is wider. The older roots of dicot plants have a covering of cork, while in monocots, it is covered by exodermis. (1)

29. Cut a transverse section of young stem of a plant from your school garden and observe it under the microscope. How would you ascertain whether it is a monocot stem or a dicot stem? Give reasons. **NCERT**

Ans If you see scattered, several vascular bundles with sclerenchymatous bundle sheath, undifferentiated ground tissue and no pith is there, then it is the transverse section is of a monocot stem.

If the section has vascular bundles arranged in a ring, differentiated ground tissue into cortex, endodermis, pericycle and pith, then the section is of dicot stem. (3)

30. Point out the differences in the anatomy of leaf of peepal (*Ficus religiosa*) and maize (*Zea mays*).

NCERT Exemplar

Ans Differences between dicot and monocot leaves are

Dicot Leaf (Dorsiventral)	Monocot Leaf (Isobilateral)
The upper surface is darker green as compared to lower surface.	The two surfaces have shade of green colour.
The upper surface has larger and thick-walled cells as compared to those of lower epidermis.	The epidermal cells are similar on the two surfaces of the leaf.
Silica does not occur on the outer wall of epidermal cells.	Silica deposition is common on the outer wall of epidermal cells.

(1×3)

Long Answer Type Questions

5 Marks

31. Describe briefly the anatomy of a dicot root.

Ans In a dicot root, the outermost layer is epidermis. The cortex consists of several layers of thin-walled parenchyma cells with intercellular spaces. The innermost layer of cortex is called endodermis.

The walls of endodermal cells have a deposition of water impermeable waxy material suberin in the form of Casparian strips.

Next layer to the endodermis is thick-walled parenchymatous cells called pericycle. The pith is small and inconspicuous. There are usually two to four xylem and phloem patches. Later, a cambium ring develops between the xylem and phloem. All tissues on the innerside of the endodermis such as pericycle, vascular bundles and pith form the stele. (3)

For diagram Refer to fig. no. 9.14. (2)

32. Draw illustrations to bring out the anatomical difference between.

(i) Monocot root and dicot root.

(ii) Monocot stem and dicot stem.

Ans (i) Refer to text on page no. 196. (2½)

(ii) Differences between monocot and dicot stem are

Monocot Stem	Dicot Stem
Internally, the stem is not differentiated into cortex, endodermis, etc.	Internally, the stem is differentiated into epidermis, cortex, endodermis, pericycle, stelar system and pith.
Hypodermis is sclerenchymatous.	Hypodermis is collenchymatous.
Vascular bundles are scattered in the parenchymatous ground tissue.	Vascular bundles are arranged in a ring.
Medullary rays are absent.	Medullay rays occur in between vascular bundles.
Vascular bundles are surrounded by bundle sheath.	Vascular bundles are not surrounded by bundle sheath.
Secondary growth does not occur, since cambium is absent.	Secondary growth takes place due to the presence of cambium.

(2½)

33. Describe the internal structure of a dorsiventral leaf with the help of labelled diagram. **NCERT**

Ans The adaxial (upper) epidermis and abaxial (lower) epidermis, both have a layer of conspicuous cuticle. The abaxial epidermis generally bears more stomata than the adaxial epidermis. The latter may even lack stomata. The tissue between the upper and lower epidermis is called mesophyll. It contains palisade and spongy parenchyma. The vascular bundles represent the midrib and other veins. The xylem is adaxial and phloem is abaxial. The vascular bundles are surrounded by a layer of thin-walled bundle sheath cells. (3)

For diagram Refer to fig. no. 9.18 on page no. 198. (2)

SUMMARY

- **Plant anatomy** deals with study of internal structure of various organs of plants.
- **Plant tissue** is a group of similar or dissimilar cells of common origin that perform or help to common function. It is classified into meristematic tissues, permanent tissues and secretory tissues.
- **Meristematic tissues** consist of actively dividing cells. These cells are densely cytoplasmic and possess a large nucleus.
- **Apical meristems** are found at the apices of shoots and roots. This tissue is responsible for the growth in length of roots and shoots.
- **Permanent tissues** consist of cells that have lost their ability to divide. These cells are structurally and functionally specialised to perform particular functions.
- **Parenchyma tissues** are most abundant and common tissues of plants. These are thin-walled with large intercellular spaces. These cells, store food material and secrete some enzymes, resins, nectar, etc. Chlorenchyma, aerenchyma and prosenchyma are parenchymatous cells that are modified to perform specialised task.
- **Collenchyma cells** are elastic, living and mechanical tissue. Cell wall of these cells possesses thickenings of cellulose, hemicellulose and pectin at the corner.
- **Sclerenchyma** is a mechanical and dead tissue. These cells are elongated with narrow ends. Sclerenchyma provides grittiness in the pulp of the fruits and provides mechanical strength to the plant.
- **Xylem** is the main water conduting tissue of the plants. It consists of four types of elements, i.e. tracheids, vessels, xylem fibre and xylem parenchyma. Tracheids and vessels are dead element.
- In **exarch** condition protoxylem (first formed primary xylem) lies towards the periphery and metaxylem (i.e. formed after protoxylem) lies towards the centre.
- In **endarch** situation protoxylem lies towards the centre and metaxylem towards the periphery.
- **Phloem** transports organic food in plants. It consists of four types of elements, i.e. sieve tube, companion cell, phloem fibre and phloem parenchyma.
- Companion cells and sieve tubes are absent in gymnosperms. In gymnosperms, albuminous cells are present instead of companion cells. Sieve tube elements lack nucleus and possess a large vacuole with peripheral cytoplasm.
- Secretory tissues are group of cells that secrete some products in plants such as nectaries, gum, resin, toxins, etc. These are mainly of two types, i.e. laticiferous and glandular tissues.
- **Epidermal tissue system** forms the outer covering of plant and is made up of **epidermal cells**, **epidermal outgrowths** and **stomata**.
- Stomata are minute openings found in the epidermis of green aerial parts of plant. Pore of each stomata is surrounded by pair of kidney-shaped guard cells. These are dumb-bell- shaped in some monocots, e.g. maize.
- **Ground tissue system** constitutes main bulk of plant body and is differentiated into **cortex**, **pericycle** and **pith**.
- **Vascular tissue system** is made up of **xylem** and **phloem**. It also contains **cambium** in dicots. Depending upon the relative position of xylem and phloem, presence of cambium, vascular bundles are classified into radial, conjoint collateral open and closed vascular bundles.
- **Radial vascular bundles** are mainly found in roots. In these, xylem and phloem are arranged alternately. Conjoint vascular bundles are commonly found in stems and leaves. In them, xylem and phloem are situated at the same radius. These are of two types, i.e. collateral and bicollateral. In concentric vascular bundles, either phloem surrounds the xylem or xylem surrounds the phloem completely.
- **A dicot root** is characterised by narrow cortex, endodermis with prominent Casparian strips radial, diarch to hexarch and exarch vascular bundles.
- **Monocot root** contains a wide cortex, outer cortex differentiated into exodermis and polyarch, exarch, radial vascular, bundles.
- The **stem in dicots** has a collenchymatous hypodermis. The epidermis bears kidney-shaped guard cells in stomata. Ground tissue differentiated into cortex, endodermis, pericycle and pith. Vascular bundles are conjoint and open, arranged in a ring.
- The **monocot stem** contains a sclerenchymatons hypodermis and dumb- bell-shaped guard cells. Ground tissue undifferentiated. Vascular bundles scattered in ground tissue. Vascular bundles are conjoint and closed.
- A **dorsiventral leaf** present in dicot plants is marked by presence of numerous stomata in lower epidermis which have kidney-shaped guard cells. The mesophyll is differentiated into palisade and spongy parenchyma vascular bundles arranged irregularly. Bundle sheath cells are colourless.
- The **isobilateral** leaf found in monocot plants shows the presence of equally distributed stomata, on upper and lower epidermis dumb-bell-shaped guard cells and bulliform cells are found.

Chapter Practice

Multiple Choice Quetions

1 Mark

1. Specialised regions of plant having active cell division are called
   (a) tissues (b) organs
   (c) meristems (d) All of these

2. Apical meristems are present at the
   (a) tips of roots
   (b) tips of shoots
   (c) lateral sides of roots and shoots
   (d) Both (a) and (b)

3. Intercalary meristem is found between the
   (a) mature tissue (b) apical root meristem
   (c) shoot meristem (d) two nodes

4. Primary meristem is
   (a) apical meristem (b) intercalary meristem
   (c) lateral meristem (d) Both (a) and (b)

5. Grass elongates after cutting (moving) due to
   (a) primary meristem
   (b) secondary meristem
   (c) apical meristem
   (d) intercalary meristem

6. Conjunctive tissue is made up of
   (a) parenchymatous cells that lies between the xylem and phloem
   (b) sclerenchymatous cells that lies between the xylem and phloem
   (c) collenchymatous cells that lies between the xylem and phloem
   (d) meristematic cells that lies between the xylem and phloem

7. Which of the following statement is true for stem (dicot/monocot)?
   (a) Ring arrangement of vascular bundle is found in dicot stem
   (b) Vascular bundles are conjoint and open in monocot stem
   (c) Hypodermis is parenchymatous in monocot stem
   (d) None of the above

8. Medullary rays are formed by the
   (a) radially placed parenchymatous cells between vascular bundles
   (b) longitudinally placed parenchymatous cells between vascular bundles
   (c) laterally placed parenchymatous cells between vascular bundles
   (d) obliquely placed parenchymatous cells between vascular bundles

9. Trichomes are epidermal hairs of
   (a) primary root
   (b) primary stem
   (c) primary leaves
   (d) secondary root

10. Cambium activity is
    (a) more active towards periphery of stem
    (b) more active towards lateral sides of stem
    (c) more active towards innerside of stem
    (d) Same on both sides

11. Cells having no power of cell division are formed by
    (a) primary meristem (b) fascicular cambium
    (c) cork cambium (d) All of these

Assertion-Reason Type Questions

1 Mark

■ **Direction** (Q. Nos. 12-19) *In each of the following questions, a statement of Assertion (A) is given followed by corresponding statement of Reason (R). Of the statements, mark the correct answer as*

(a) If both A and R are true and R is the correct explanation of A
(b) If both A and R are true, but R is not the correct explanation of A
(c) If A is true, but R is false
(d) If A is false, but R is true

12. **Assertion** (A) All the endodermal cells of root do not contain Casparian thickening on their radial and transverse walls.
    Reason (R) Passage cells are formed in the root endodermis.

13. **Assertion** (A) Vascular bundles in monocots are considered closed.
    Reason (R) A bundle sheath surrounds each vascular bundle in monocots.
14. **Assertion** (A) Root hairs are unicellular and trichomes are usually multicellular.
    Reason (R) Root hairs are found in root epidermis and trichomes are found in stem epidermis.
15. **Assertion** (A) Vascular bundles are conjoint, collateral and closed in monocot stem.
    Reason (R) Vascular bundles are conjoint, collateral and open in dicot stem.
16. Given below is the TS structure of a monocot root whose outer most thin walled covering is called epiblema and the inner to it is cortex that contains parenchyma cells. Study the structure and comment upon the appropriateness of the Assertion and Reason.

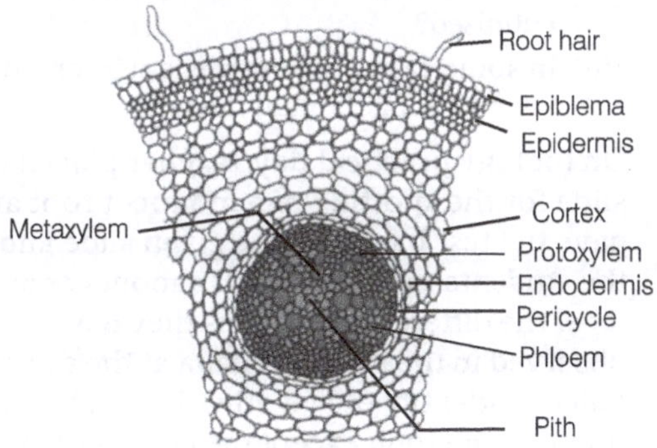

Assertion (A) The young endodermal cells possess an internal strip of suberin and lignin.
Reason (R) This strip is called Casparian strip which is water impermeable in nature.

17. **Assertion** (A) The quiescent centre acts as a reservoir of relatively resistant cells, which constitute a permanent source of active initials.
    Reason (R) The cells of the inactive region of quiescent centre become active when the previous active initials get damaged.
18. **Assertion** (A) Mesophyll consists of two types of cells palisade and spongy parenchyma.
    Reason (R) Mesophyll tissue is rich in chlorophyll and carries out photosynthesis.
19. Given below is the TS of a dicot leaf. It is generally horizontal in orientation and has distinct upper and lower surfaces. Study the structure and comment upon the appropriateness of Assertion and Reason

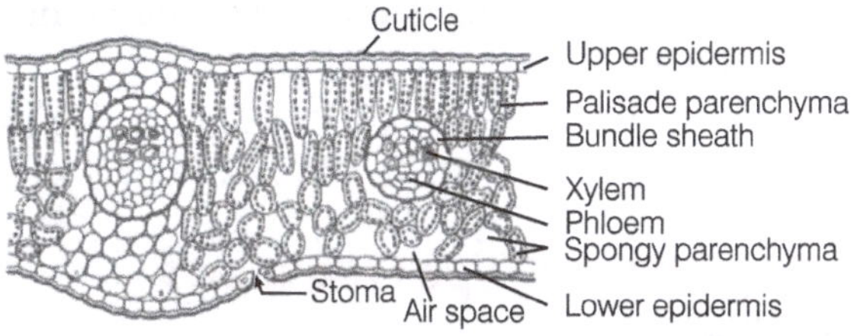

TS of dicot leaf

Assertion (A) In dicot leaf, mesophyll is absent in the region of midrib and other larger veins.
Reason (R) Midrib is found at the back part of the leaf.

Answers

1. (c)	2. (d)	3. (a)	4. (d)	5. (d)	6. (a)
7. (a)	8. (a)	9. (b)	10. (c)	11. (d)	12. (a)
13. (b)	14. (b)	15. (b)	16. (a)	17. (a)	18. (b)
19. (b)					

Very Short Answer Type Questions

1 Mark

20. Which type of cells/tissue constitute(s) the pith?
21. Explain the polyarch condition of vascular bundles.

Short Answer Type I Questions

2 Marks

22. How does the apical meristem differ from lateral meristem?
23. How does protoxylem differ from mataxylem?
24. (i) Mention the types of tissue systems in plants.
    (ii) Elaborate one of the briefly.
25. What are guard cells and their significance?
26. Trace the location of hypodermis and the tissue it comprises of. Also write its main function.
27. Mention the two important features of dorsiventral leaves.

Short Answer Type II Questions

3 Marks

28. What are vessels? How they are different than tracheids?

29. Write the types of vascular bundles and describe briefly.

Long Answer Type Questions

5 Marks

30. Write a note on medullary rays.

31. Name the epidermal surrounding of the guard cells. How does a guard cell differ from an epidermal cell?

32. Explain the anatomy of monocot root.

33. Which major structure can be observed in the TS of a dicot stem?

Case Based Questions

4/5 Marks

34. While explaining the internal structure in plants stem, teacher makes a statement about vascular strand in plants. After lecture, Arun asked about the reason and significance of such arrangements.
    (i) What are vascular strands?
    (ii) What functions they perform in plants?
    (iii) What is conjunctive tissue?
    (iv) Define exarch.

35. *Read the following passage and answer the questions that follows*

    A student observed a slide of root under microscope. He saw four xylem and phloem patches in radial arrangement in the root. He also observed thick-walled cells of endodermis. He discuss with his teacher about the anatomy of the given root.
    (i) Identify the root and give one example.
    (ii) What is Casparian strip?
    (iii) Write the features of pith of this root.
    (iv) What is epiblema?
    (v) Write characteristic features of the cells which originate lateral roots.

36. Rani was amazed to read about the layers and coverings in the plant. As her teacher taught her that like mammals, plants are also formed by various layers of tissues. Thus, forming the different plant system. As the epidermal tissue system forms the outermost covering of the body. She felt curious and asked her elder sister about the same, that how come this is possible. Her sister cleared all her doubts patiently.
    (i) From where it is derived?
    (ii) Why are outer wall of some plants is cutinised?
    (iii) In some cases, the cuticle is reinforced by a layer of wax. Explain the reason.

37. On biology practical day, teacher placed the slide for the spotting of a monocot root and gave the test based on the given slide and told the students to draw a TS of a monocot and label the different structures they have observed in the slide. Archana at the same time failed to identify the all other internal structure found in the root, except the endodermis. She got sad and asked her teacher to guide her after the test.
    (i) What according to you, is the endodermis in monocot root? Write its cellular structure.
    (ii) Where are Casparian strips located?
    (iii) What is the role of passage cells in endodermis? Also write their location.

CHAPTER

10

Structural Organisation in Animals

In unicellular organisms, all vital cellular functions like digestion, respiration, excretion, etc., are performed by a single cell. The multicellular animals have complex body organisation. In these organisms, the body functions are carried out by different groups of cells in a well-organised and coordinated manner.

For example, the body of a simple organism like *Hydra* is made up of different types of cells and the number of cells in each type can be in thousands. In human body, there are tribillions of cells to perform various functions in an coordinated manner.

Morphology and Anatomy of Animal

In this, we will discuss morphology and anatomy of frog representing vertebrate at different evolutionary levels to show their structural body organisation and functioning.

Frog

Frog can live both on land and in water. The most common species of frog found in India is *Rana tigrina.*

Systematic Position

Kingdom – Animalia
Phylum – Chordata (notochord in the embryonic stage).
Class – Amphibia (can live in water as well as on land and lacks exoskeleton).
Order – Phaneroglossa (has tongue and tympanum and separate Eustachian tubes).
Family – Ranidae (lacks cartilaginous discs, teeth only on upper jaw).
Genus – *Rana* (sternum is largely bony).
Species – *tigrina* (upper surface is olive-green, mottled with dark spots, under surface is white, fifth toe externally).

Distribution

Frogs are widespread in tropical and temperate regions. There are about 2600 species of frogs all over the world. In India, four species of frogs are mainly found.

These are as follows

(i) *Rana tigrina* Most widely distributed found all over the world except in countries like Australia, New Zealand and South America.
(ii) *Rana cyanophlyctis* Found in Rajasthan, UP and MP.
(iii) *Rana malabarica* Common in Maharashtra.
(iv) *Rana temporaria* Common British frog.

The most common species of frog found in India is *Rana tigrina.*

Habitat and Habit

Rana tigrina also called **bull frog** because of its large size and loud call. It is found in or near freshwater, marshes, ditches, ponds and shallow waterbodies. It has various reasons to lead amphibious (*Amphi* – two; *bios* – life) life, such as

(i) It can respire both through skin and lungs.
(ii) Frog breeds in water and spends its early life in water.
(iii) It is unable to drink water and absorbs it through the skin. Hence, it lives near the water.

The important habits of frog are described below

(i) **Feeding** Adult frog is carnivores as gets its food, from live insects, worms and spiders mostly near the water, whereas the tadpole of frog is herbivores.
The prey is captured with the help of tongue.
(ii) **Locomotion** The body of frog is boat-shaped due to the absence of neck. This helps the frog in swimming. Frog is also well adopted for leaping and walking.
(iii) **Breeding** Frogs breed in rainy season. They show sexual dimorphism. The male frog can be differentiated from the female by **vocal sacs** and **nuptial pad**. Male frog possesses vocal sacs, which are most developed during breeding season.
The male frog lacks **copulatory organs** and produces a high pitched croaking sound to attract the female. The sexual embrace in which the eggs and sperms are discharged in water is called **amplexus** or **false copulation.**
(iv) **Hibernation and Aestivation** Frog is a cold-blooded (poikilothermic) animal. Its body temperature fluctuates according to its surrounding temperature. To avoid the adverse conditions of environment, frog burrows inside the soil and lies in a state of rest or sleep during summers and winters.
The resting condition in winter is called **hibernation** or **winter sleep** and the condition of rest in summer is called **aestivation** or **summer sleep.**
(v) **Defence** Frogs escape from their enemies by several ways. If chased, they leap away to safe places or jump into water. They can also darken or lighten their green shade to blend with the background and thus, prevent easy detection (camouflage). This protective colouration is called **mimicry.**

Morphology

The frog has an ovoid, streamlined and slightly flattened body. It is about 10-15 cm long and shows bilateral symmetry, i.e. its right and left halves are mirror images of each other.

The skin of frog is naked, smooth, moist and slippery. A thin film of mucus is secreted by the cutaneous glands present in the skin. The skin of frog consists of an outer epidermis and inner dermis.

Epidermis is the outermost, non-vascular layer made up of stratified epithelium. The innermost layer of epidermis consists of **Malpighian layer or stratum germinativum.**

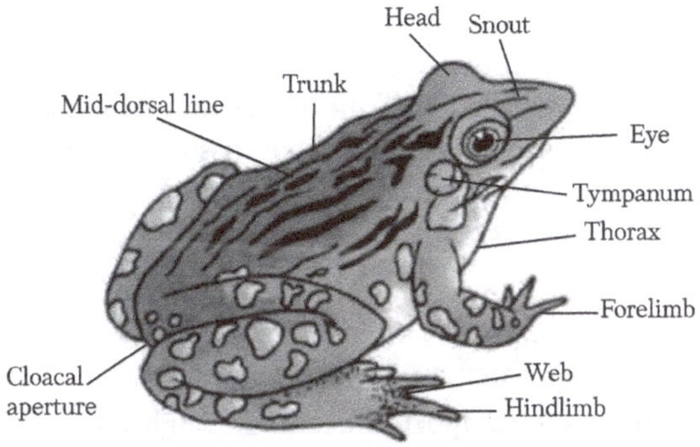

Fig. 10.1 External features of frog

Dermis layer contains **mucous glands** and **poison glands.** The poison glands secrete poisonous fluid which protects the frogs from their enemies. Frog never drinks water, but absorbs it through the skin. Dorsal side of body is generally olive green with dark irregular spots. Ventral side of the body is pale yellow.

The body of frog is divisible into head and trunk. It is to be noted that neck tail in frogs seem to be absent.

1. Head

The head is triangular in shape with a blunt snout. It bears mouth, external nares, eyes, brown spots and ear drums on the upper side and throat on the lower side.

(i) **Mouth** The mouth extends along the entire border of the head. It is bounded by upper and lower jaws. (the lower jaw is toothless in frogs). The mouth gets open only during feeding.

(ii) **External Nares** At the top of anterior end, the head bears two small apertures called **external nares.** Air enters and leaves the body through the nares.

(iii) **Eyes** A little behind the nostrils, two large eyes are present, situated along the sides. The eyes are spherical and protruded laterally.

Each eye has a thick upper and a thin lower eyelid. The upper part of the lower eyelid is modified into a transparent fold called **nictitating membrane.** This membrane protects the eye and is pulled over the eyeball when the frog is in water or under the mud and frog can see through it.

(iv) **Eardrums** A little behind and below the eye on each side of head, a circular patch of tightly stretched, dark skin is present. This is called **tympanic membrane** or **tympanum** or **eardrum.** It receives sound waves.

(v) **Throat** The floor of the head is occupied by a soft throat. In a male frog, there is a pair of bluish-wrinkled patches of skin called **vocal sacs.** They help in intensifying the croaking sounds.

2. Trunk

It contains an anterior portion called **thorax** and a posterior larger portion called **abdomen.** A pair of forelimb and hindlimb is attached to the trunk. Each forelimb has an upper arm, a forearm and a hand. The hand has a wrist, a palm and four digits.

Each hindlimb consists of an upper thigh, a middle shank and a lower foot. The foot has an ankle, a **sole** and **five** digits. The digits are joined together by a fold of skin called **web.**

At the end of the trunk, between the hindlegs, there is a circular aperture called **cloacal aperture** through which faeces, urine and gametes passes out.

Anatomy

The description of frog's anatomy is given below

Coelom

The body cavity is a true coelom and large having two parts, a very small **pericardial** cavity around the heart which contains pericardial fluid and a very large **pleuroperitoneal cavity** around the other viscera that have coelomic fluid except the kidneys. The body cavity of frogs accommodate different organ systems such as digestive, circulatory, respiratory, nervous, excretory and reproductive systems with well-developed structures and functions.

Both the fluids are watery, colourless and secreted by peritoneum.

Digestive System

The digestive system of frog consists of alimentary canal and associated digestive glands.

1. Alimentary Canal

The alimentary canal of frog is short because frogs are carnivores and hence, the length of intestine is reduced. It contains, mouth, buccopharyngeal cavity, oesophagus, stomach, small intestine, rectum and cloaca.

(i) **Mouth** It is present as a wide opening which opens into buccopharyngeal cavity. In frog, teeth are not used for chewing but they prevent the escape of live food.

Mouth opens into the buccal cavity that leads to oesophagus through pharynx.

(ii) **Oesophagus** It is a narrow, short tube, which continues in large and distended stomach.

(iii) **Stomach** It helps in converting the food into **chyme** and secretes gastric juice containing HCl and proteolytic enzymes.

(iv) **Intestine** It is a coiled structure continued with the stomach. The intestinal wall has several finger-like folds called **villi** and **microvilli**, projecting into its lumen to enhance the surface area for absorption of digested food. The first part of small intestine lying parallel to stomach is called **duodenum.** The duodenum is followed by **ileum.** Small intestine continues into a wider **rectum** which opens into a **cloaca** through an aperture called anus.

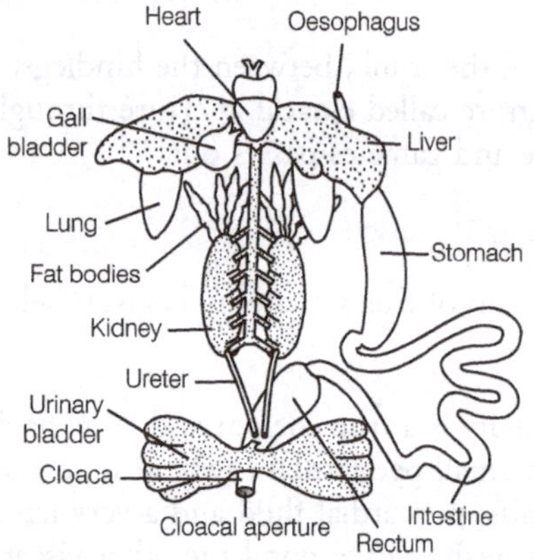

Fig. 10.2 Diagrammatic representation of internal organs of frog showing complete digestive system

2. Digestive Glands

These glands include gastric glands, intestinal glands, liver and pancreas.

(i) **The gastric glands** secrete **gastric juice.**

(ii) The intestinal glands secrete **intestinal juice**, which contains a number of digestive enzymes.

(iii) The **liver** produces bile which is temporarily stored in the gall bladder before being released into duodenum.

(iv) **Pancreas** is an irregular, elongated gland that produces pancreatic juice containing several digestive enzymes.

Digestion of Food

The digestion of food takes place by the action of HCl and gastric juices secreted from the walls of stomach. The partially digested food called **chyme** is passed from stomach to the first part of the intestine, the duodenum.

The duodenum receives bile from gall bladder and pancreatic juice from the pancreas through a common bile duct. Bile emulsifies fat and pancreatic juices digest carbohydrates and proteins.

Final digestion occurs in the intestine. Digested food is absorbed by the numerous finger-like folds in the inner wall of intestine called **villi** and **microvilli.** The digested food is distributed to different body tissues and cell through blood to release energy. The undigested solid waste moves into rectum and passes out through cloaca.

Respiratory System

Frogs respire by three modes of respiration

(i) **Cutaneous respiration** occurs through moist skin of the frog. Frogs respire only by the skin when under water or deep under the mud.

(ii) **Buccopharyngeal respiration** occurs when the animal is on land or partially immersed in water. It occurs by thin, vascular, moist lining of buccopharyngeal cavity.

(iii) **Pulmonary respiration** occurs by the lungs and is less frequent than the cutaneous and buccopharyngeal respiration. It occurs when more oxygen is required.

The lungs are a pair of elongated, pink coloured sac-like structures present in the upper part of the trunk region (thorax). Air enters through the nostrils into the buccal cavity and then to lungs.

Circulatory System

The circulatory system of frog is well-developed and is of **closed type.** It also has a **lymphatic system.** The blood vascular system includes the heart, blood and blood vessels.

1. Heart

It is a muscular structure situated in the upper part of the body cavity. It has three chambers, i.e. two atria (sing. atrium) and one ventricle. The heart is covered by a membrane called **pericardium.**

There are two accessory chambers in the frog's heart, a tubular **truncus arteriosus** placed on the ventral side of the right auricle and a triangular **sinus venosus** present on the dorsal side of the heart.

Sinus venosus receives blood through the major veins called **vena cava** and opens into right auricle.

The left auricle receives oxygenated blood from the lungs by a **common pulmonary vein.** The auricles send their blood into ventricle where the blood gets mixed up. The ventricle opens into a sac-like **conus arteriosus** on the ventral side of the heart.

Special venous connection between liver and intestine as well as the kidney and lower parts of the body are present in frogs. The former is called **hepatic portal system** and the latter is called **renal portal system.**

2. Blood

The blood is composed of **plasma** and **blood cells.** The blood cells are RBCs (Red Blood Cells) or erythrocytes, WBCs (White Blood Cells) or leucocytes and platelets. RBCs are nucleated and contain red coloured pigment namely **haemoglobin.** The blood carries nutrients, gases and water to the respective sites during circulations.

3. Blood Vessels

The blood vessels found in frogs are arteries, arterioles, veins, venules and blood capillaries.

Arteries carry blood from the heart to different body parts. Veins bring blood from different body parts to the heart. Arteries further divide to form arterioles. The **arterioles** branch out to form **capillaries,** which further unite to form **venules.** The venules thus, join to form veins (which have valves to prevent backflow of the blood).

Lymphatic System

The lymphatic system comprises of lymph vessels, lymphatic channels and lymph. **Lymph** is a mobile connective tissue filtered out from the blood through capillaries. It contains plasma and white corpuscles and lacks red blood cells.

Lymph in the body always flows in following direction

Lymph capillaries → Lymph sinus → Lymph hearts → Veins

Nervous System

The system for control and coordination is highly evolved in the frog. It includes both nervous system and endocrine system. The nervous system of frogs consists of a central nervous system, a peripheral nervous system and an autonomic nervous system.

Central Nervous System

It includes **brain** and **spinal cord.** The brain is enclosed in a bony structure called **cranium** or **brain box** and the spinal cord lies inside the vertebral column. The brain is surrounded by two meninges-outer **duramater** and inner **pia- arachnoid** and classified as forebrain, midbrain and hindbrain.

(i) The forebrain consists of olfactory lobes, paired cerebral hemispheres and unpaired diencephalon.

(ii) The midbrain comprises paired optic lobes.

(iii) The hindbrain comprises cerebellum and medulla oblongata. The medulla oblongata thus, passes out through the **foramen magnum** and continues into spinal cord present in the vertebral column.

Peripheral Nervous System

It contains nerves arising from the central nervous system and extending into the organs of the body. Ten pairs of **cranial nerves** arise from the brain and nine pairs of **spinal nerves** supply the trunk and limb regions.

Autonomic Nervous System

It consists of sympathetic nervous system of two ganglionic chains and parasympathetic nervous system of isolated ganglia in the viscera. The autonomic nervous system controls the functions of organs that are not under the voluntary control.

Endocrine System

The chemical coordination of various organs of the body is carried out by **hormones,** which are secreted by the endocrine glands. The prominent endocrine glands found in the frog are pituitary, thyroid, parathyroid, thymus, pineal body, pancreatic islets, adrenals and gonads.

Sensory System

Frog has different types of sensory organs for different functions

(i) **Sensory papillae** organ for touch.

(ii) **Taste buds** for taste.

(iii) **Nasal epithelium** for smell.

(iv) **Eyes for vision** are two large simple eyes seen in frog. Each eyeball is spherical in structure and lodged inside the orbit.

(v) Tympanum with internal ears for hearing and balancing captive to external ear absent in frogs. Out of these, eyes and ears are well organised structures and the rest are cellular aggregations around the nerve endings.

Excretory System

The elimination of nitrogenous wastes is carried out by a well-developed excretory system.

The excretory system consists of a pair of kidneys, ureters, cloaca and urinary bladder. The kidneys are compact, dark red and bean-like structure, situated little posterior in the body cavity on both sides of vertebral column.

Each kidney is composed of several structural and functional units called **uriniferous tubules** or **nephrons.** Each nephron is the structural and functional unit of kidney. The **Bowman's capsule** leads into a coiled, urinary tubule. The urinary tubule opens into transverse collecting tubules, which ultimately communicate with the ureter or urinogenital duct.

In females, the ureters and oviduct open separately into the cloaca. The thin-walled urinary bladder is present ventral to the rectum which also opens in the cloaca.

The frog excretes urea and thus is a **ureotelic animal.** The excretory wastes are carried by blood into the kidney where these are separated and excreted.

Reproductive System

Frogs have well-organised male and female reproductive system. It shows **sexual dimorphism.**

Male Reproductive System

It includes a pair of yellowish, ovoid testes which are found adhered to the upper part of the kidneys by a double fold of peritoneum called **mesorchium.**

Each testis consists of coiled structures called seminiferous tubules. The epithelium lining of the tubule contains germinal cells, which produce spermatozoa. From testes, 10-12 **vasa efferentia** arise. They enter the kidneys on their side and open into **Bidder's canal.** The urinogenital duct comes out of the kidneys and opens into the **cloaca.** The cloaca is a small, median chamber that is used to pass faecal matter, urine and sperm to the exterior.

Note Ureter in male frog and vas deferens together called **urogenital duct.**

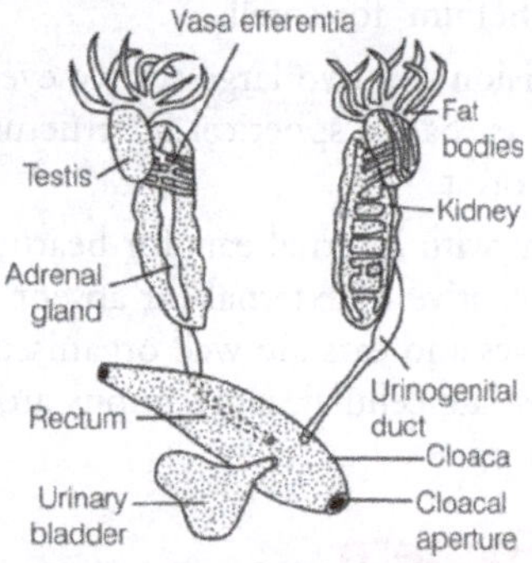

Fig. 10.3 Reproductive system of male frog

Female Reproductive System

It consists of a pair of ovaries covered by a membrane of peritoneum called mesovarium ovary is situated near the kidneys and there is no functional connection with kidneys. A pair of long **oviducts** from ovaries opens into the cloaca. A mature female frog ovaries release about 2500-3000 eggs at a time.

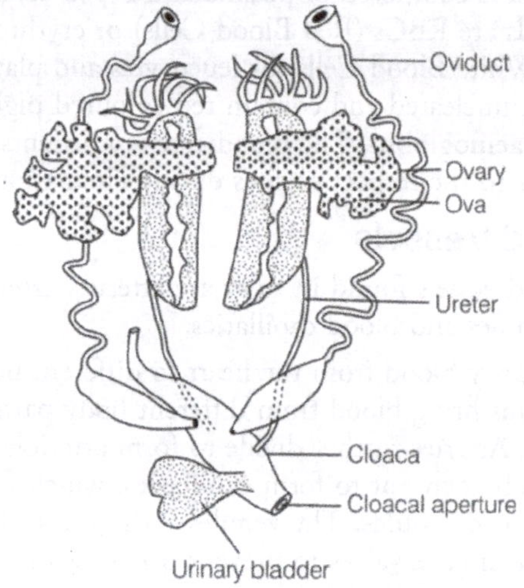

Fig. 10.4 Reproductive system of female frog

Fertilisation

The eggs are released in water. The fertilisation is **external.** Development is **indirect.** A fish-like tailed larva called **tadpole** is formed. The tadpole undergoes **metamorphosis** to form an adult in about three months by the help of thyroxine hormone.

Economic Importance of Frogs

Frog is a useful animal for humans in the following ways

(i) It feeds on insects which destroy crops and frogs, and eat up mosquitoes, which are the carriers of various diseases.

(ii) They help to maintain ecological balance by forming an important part of food chain.

(iii) The muscles of legs of frogs are used as food in some parts of India and many other countries.

(iv) Baby frogs are used as fish baits (any substance which is used to attract or catch fish).

(v) Frogs are used for researches in medical science and pharmacology.

SUMMARY

- *Rana tigrina* (Indian bullfrog) is a cold-blooded animal, which is found in or near freshwater.
- Body of frog consists of a head and a trunk without neck and tail.
- Head bears bulged eyes covered by a nictitating membrane that protect them while in water.
- On either sides of eyes a membranous tympanum (ear) is present, which receives sound signals as external ears are absent. Frog have smooth, moist and scaleless skin consisting of mucous and poison glands.
- The **alimentary canal** consists of buccal cavity, pharynx, oesophagus, stomach, intestine and rectum, which open into the cloaca.
- The buccal cavity bears teeth and a tongue. Stomach secretes gastric juices containing HCl and proteolytic enzymes. The main digestive glands are liver and pancreas.
- **Respiration** in frog can be cutaneous, buccopharyngeal and pulmonary types. The exchange of gases occurs by diffusion in all three modes.
- **Circulatory system** in frog is of closed type. It comprises of heart, blood vessels and blood (containing haemoglobin). There is an incomplete double circulation in frog because of the presence of three chambered heart (two atria + one ventricle).
- There are two accessory chambers in the frog's heart, a tubular truncus arteriosus (on ventral side) and a triangular sinus venosus (on dorsal side).
- Both hepatic and renal portal systems are present in frog. RBCs in frog are nucleated and contain haemoglobin.
- Frog is ureotelic, i.e. secrete urea. Its excretory system consists of a pair of kidney, a pair of ureters, a urinary bladder and cloaca. The ureters are also called urinogenital ducts in male frog, since they pass out sperms as well as urine.
- **Nervous system** is well defined in frog and is divided in CNS (brain and spinal cord), PNS (cranial and spinal nerves) and ANS (sympathetic and parasympathetic). Brain is enclosed in a bony structure called **brain box**. Ten pairs of cranial nerves arise from the brain.
- **Reproductive system** in frog is well organised. Testes and ovaries are found attached to kidneys. A female lays 2500-3000 ova at a time.
- **Fertilisation** is external (in water) and development is indirect through metamorphosis of tadpole larva into an adult frog.

Chapter Practice

Multiple Choice Questions

1 Mark

1. Which of the following statements are correct with reference to the frog?
   I. Eyes are bulged and covered by nictitating membrane.
   II. Membranous tympanum receives the sound signal.
   III. The frog never drinks water.
   IV. A pair of nostrils is present above the mouth.

   Codes
   (a) I and II (b) III and IV
   (c) I and IV (d) I, II, III and IV

Ans (d)

2. Which of the following statements are correct about the respiration in frog?
   I. In frog, cutaneous and pulmonary respirations are found.
   II. A pair of elongated pink hollow lungs are found in thorax.
   III. During aestivation and hibernation, gaseous exchange takes place through skin.

   Codes
   (a) I, II and III (b) I and II
   (c) II and III (d) I and II

Ans (a)

3. Which of the following is present in the skin of frog?
   (a) Mucous gland (b) Poison gland
   (c) Chromatophores (d) All of these

Ans (d)

4. Read the following statements for frog and answer accordingly.
   I. Duodenum receives bile and pancreatic juice through hepatopancreatic duct.
   II. Salivary glands are absent in frog, so digestion starts in stomach.
   (a) Both the statements I and II are correct and II is the correct explanation of I
   (b) Both the statements I and II are correct, but II is not the correct explanation of I
   (c) Statement I is correct, but II is incorrect
   (d) Statements I incorrect and II are correct

Ans (b)

5. Which of the following statement is incorrect about circulatory system of frog.
   (a) It is of closed type
   (b) There is incomplete double circulation present
   (c) It comprises of heart, blood vessels and blood
   (d) None of the above

Ans (d)

6. Frog's heart when taken out of the body continues to beat for the some time because the heart is
   (a) neurogenic and autoexcitable
   (b) myogenic and autoexcitable
   (c) myogenic and hyperexcitable
   (d) neurogenic and hyperexcitable

Ans (a)

7. Match the following columns.

	Column I		Column II
A.	Forebrain	1.	A pair of optic lobes
B.	Midbrain	2.	Cerebellum and medulla oblongata
C.	Hindbrain	3.	Olfactory lobe, paired cerebral hemispheres, unpaired diencephalon

Codes

	A	B	C		A	B	C
(a)	1	3	2	(b)	2	1	3
(c)	3	1	2	(d)	1	2	3

Ans (c)

8. Which of the following statement is incorrect regarding frog?
   (a) Renal portal vein in frog carries blood from lower part of the body to kidney
   (b) Arterial system of frog begins with conus arteriosus or truncus arteriosus
   (c) External ears are absent and only tympanum can be seen
   (d) Four pairs of lymph are found in frog

Ans (d)

9. Consider the following four statements (I-IV) related to the common frog *Rana tigrina* and select the correct option stating which ones are True (T) and which ones are False (F).

I. On dry land, it would die due to lack of O_2 if its mouth is forcibly kept closed for a few days.

II. It has four-chambered heart.

III. On dry land, it turns uricotelic from ureotelic.

IV. Its life history is carried out in pond water.

Codes

	I	II	III	IV
(a)	F	F	T	T
(b)	F	T	T	F
(c)	T	F	F	T
(d)	T	T	F	F

Ans (c)

10. Observe the following figure indicating the male reproductive system of frog. Identify *A, B, C* and *D*.

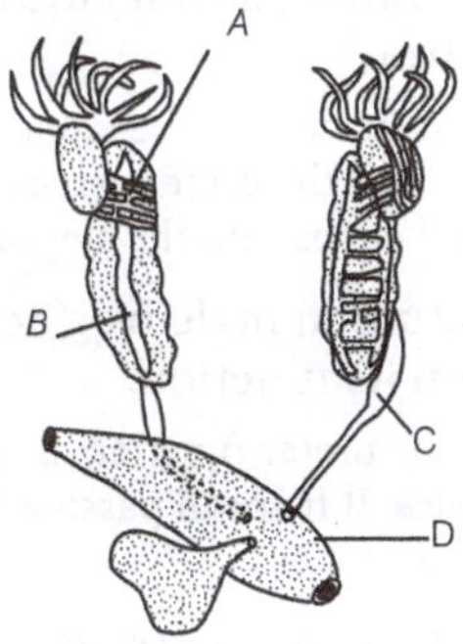

Which of the labeling (*A, B, C, D*) is representing urogenital duct.

(a) *A* (b) *C*
(c) *B* (d) *D*

Ans (b)

11. Select the correct route for the passage of sperms in male frog.

(a) Testes → Bidder's canal → Kidney → Vasa efferentia → Urinogenital duct → Cloaca

(b) Testes → Vasa efferentia → Kidney → Seminal vesicle → Urinogenital duct → Cloaca

(c) Testes → Vasa efferentia → Bidder's canal →→ Ureter → Cloaca

(d) Testes → Vasa efferentia → Kidney → Bidder's canal → Urinogenital duct → Cloaca

Ans (d)

Assertion-Reason Type Questions

1 Mark

Direction (Q. Nos. 12-15) *In each of the following questions, a statement of Assertion (A) is given followed by corresponding statement of Reason (R). Of the statements, mark the correct answer as*

(a) If both A and R are true and R is the correct explanation of A

(b) If both A and R are true, but R is not the correct explanation of A

(c) If A is true, but R is false

(d) If A is false, but R is true

12. **Assertion** (A) Frog have webbed feets.

Reason (R) Degree of webbing is directly proportional to the amount of time they spend in water.

Ans (b)

13. **Assertion** (A) The alimentary canal of the frog is short.

Reason (R) Frogs are carnivores.

Ans (a)

14. **Assertion** (A) In frog's vascular system, the composition of lymph is same as that of blood.

Reason (R) In frog, lymph lacks RBCs and few proteins.

Ans (d)

15. **Assertion** (A) Excretory and reproductive systems in frog are collectively referred to as urinogenital system.

Reason (R) In female frog, ureters and oviduct open separately into cloaca.

Ans (b)

Very Short Answer Type Questions

1 Mark

16. Name the phylum and class to which frog belongs.

Ans Phylum - Chordata
Class - Amphibia

17. State the appearance of dorsal side of frog's body.

Ans Dorsal side of body is generally olive green with dark irregular spots.

18. In frog the upper part of lower eyelid is modified into which membrane? Mention its function.

Ans The upper part of lower eyelid is modified into nictitating membrane. This membrane protects the eye when frog is in water or under the mud.

19. State the significance of webbed digits in frogs.

Ans Refer to text on page no. 209.

20. Where is bile stored in the body of frog?

Ans The liver produces bile which is temporarily stored in the gall bladder before being released into duodenum.

21. When does buccopharyngeal respiration occurs in frog?

Ans When the frog is on land or partially immersed in water

Short Answer Type I Questions

2 Marks

22. Comment upon the distribution of frogs.

Ans Refer to text on page no. 207-208.

23. What are the reasons that makes frog suitable in both land and water ?

Ans Refer to text on page no. 208.

24. As we know frogs are poikilothermic animals. What are the adaptations that frogs have to maintain its body temperature ?

Ans Refer to text on page no. 208.

25. Which finger of the male frog develops into nuptial pad?

Ans Inner side of the first finger.

26. How does the skin of the frog is suitable for respiration?

Ans The skin in frog is richly supplied with blood and provides extensive surface for respiration.

27. Where does final digestion take place in frogs?

Ans Final digestion in frogs takes place in the intestine where pancreatic juices breakdown proteins and carbohydrates, the undigested food moves to the rectum and exits through the cloaca.

28. Why the alimentary canal of frog is short?

Ans Because the frog is a carnivorous animal.

29. What is the difference between cutaneous and pulmonary respiration?

Ans Cutaneous respiration refers to the exchange of gases through skin whereas pulmonary respiration refers to the exchange of gases through lungs.

30. Write the steps involved the process of digestion of frog?

Ans Refer to text on page no. 210.

31. State the significance of cloaca aperture in frogs?

Ans Cloaca is the chamber which is used to pass urine, sperms and faecal matter outside the body. Hence, it is a common chamber for urinary tract, reproductive tract and alimentary canal.

32. Which blood vessel is responsible for sending blood to the left auricle in frog?

Ans The left auricle receives oxygenated blood from the lungs by common pulmonary vein.

33. In frog, these are special connections between same parts of the body comment.

Ans Special venous connection between liver and intestine as well as the kidney and lower parts of the body are present in frogs. The former is called hepatic portal system and latter is renal portal system.

34. Where is the Bidder's canal located and how is it useful in frog?

Ans Bidder's canal is present in the kidney of frog. It communicates with the ureter, which leaves the kidney near its end and opens into the cloaca.

35. Which structure in male frog act as urogenital tract mention its function.

Ans In male frogs, the ureter function as urogenital duct that opens into cloaca. It helps in passing the urine as well as sperm to the exterior.

36. Write the correct route for the passage of sperms in male frog.

Ans The correct route for the passage of sperms in male frog is

Testes → Vasa efferentia → Kidney → Bidder's canal → Urogenital tract → Cloaca.

37. Why breeding in frogs is termed as false copulation?

Ans Refer to text on page no. 208.

38. How the central nervous system differ from peripheral nervous system in frog ?

Ans Refer to the text on page no. 211.

Long Answer Type Questions

5 Marks

39. Describe the external characters of frog.

Ans Refer to the text on page no. 208-209.

40. Write the function of the following in case of frog.

(i) Tongue
(ii) Pigment cells
(iii) Vocal sacs
(iv) Mucous glands
(v) Tympanic membrane

Ans (i) Tongue is used to capture the prey.
(ii) Pigment cells impart colour to the skin.
(iii) Vocal sacs raise pitch of the sound during croaking.
(iv) Mucous glands discharge their slimy mucus onto the surface of ducts passing through the epidermis.
(v) Tympanic membrane serves to receive the sound waves.

41. Distinguish between male frog and female frog.

Ans Differences between male and female frog are as follows

Male Frog	Female Frog
Vocal cords are present on ventrolateral side of throat.	Vocal sacs are absent.
Croaking is more louder.	Croaking is less louder.
Forelimbs are stouter and more muscular.	Forelimbs are less muscular.
Amplexusory pads are present on ventral side of index fingers.	Amplexusory pads are absent.
During breeding season, abdomen does not change much.	Abdomen gets swollen during breeding season as it is full of ova released from mature ovaries.

(1×5)

42. Describe the circulatory system of frog.

Ans Refer to text on page no. 210-211.

Case Based Question

4/5 Marks

43. Given below is a pie chart showing various importance of frog.

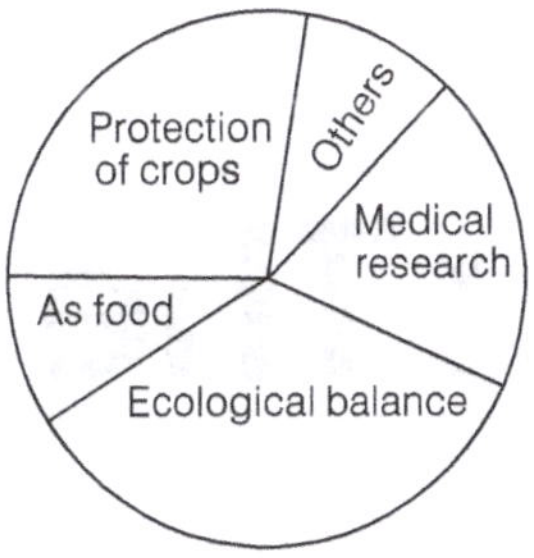

Observe the above chart and answer the questions that follows.

(i) How does frog help in maintaining balance in an ecosystem?
(ii) Mention the use of frog in medical science.
(iii) Frogs are know to prevent mosquito borne diseases, how?
(iv) Frogs are beneficial for mankind. Justify the statement.

Ans (i) Frogs play a vital role in ecosystem worldwide, as they form an integral part of the food chain, prevent disease transmission by feeding on potential carriers, and keep waterways clean. (1)
(ii) Secretions from the skin of frog and from their glands can be used as remedies for infections, allergies, inflammation, etc. (1)
(iii) Refer to text on page no. 212. (1)
(iv) Frogs are beneficial in the following ways
(a) **Bioindicators** They are sensitive to environmental changes.
(b) Component of food chain
(c) Biocontrol agent (2)

CHAPTER

11

Cell : The Unit of Life

Cell is known to be the fundamental, structural and functional unit of all living organisms. It is well-known fact that life is based on specialised units called **cells**. In 17th century, an Englishman **Robert Hooke** (1665) saw the honeycomb-like structure in dead cork sections and called them cell. **Antony van Leeuwenhoek** first saw and described a living cell. The term 'Cell' was introduced by an English scientist **Robert Hooke**.

TOPIC 01 Cell : An Overview

An organism consists of one or more cells, accordingly there are two types of organisms, i.e. **unicellular** (composed of single cell) and **multicellular** (composed of many cells). Unicellular organisms are capable of independent existence and performing the essential functions of life.

Cell Theory

This theroy was formulated by a German botanist **Matthias Jakob Schleiden** (5 April, 1804-23 June, 1881) and a German physiologist **Theodor Schwann** (7 December, 1810-11 January, 1882) in the year 1838-39.

Their original theory contained following two statements

1. All living beings are made up of cells and their products.
2. Cells are the structural and functional units of life.

Objections to Cell Theory

Cell theory failed to explain how and from where the new cells were formed. All these observations lead to a major expansion of cell theory that was expressed by **Rudolf Virchow** in 1855. He modified the hypothesis of Schleiden and Schwann and explained in his statement that cells divide and new cells are formed from pre-existing cells, i.e. *Omnis cellula-e-cellula*, this statement is known as cell lineage theory.

Thus, the cell theory states that

(i) All living organisms are composed of cells and their products.

(ii) Cells are the structural and functional unit of living organism.

(iii) All cells arise from pre-existing cells.

(iv) Cells show similarity in chemical composition and metabolic activities.

Structural Outline of a Cell

The basic structural organisation of a typical cell is as follows

(i) **Nucleus,** the central part and brain of the cell, which is spherical in shape. Its number can be one or more per cell. It is denser than the surrounding cytoplasm.

The nucleus is composed of chromosomes (i.e. genetic material or DNA), nuclear membrane and centrioles (only in animal cells).

(ii) **Cytoplasm** is a semi-fluid matrix that occupies the volume of the cell. It is mainly composed of water with free-floating molecules. Inside the cytoplasm all cellular activities occur like gaseous exchange, elimination of wastes, hereditary mechanisms, etc.

Eukaryotic cells also contain other cell membrane bound distinct structures called **cell organelles,** like mitochondria, vacuoles, Endoplasmic Reticulum (ER), Golgi complex, etc.

The prokaryotic cells lack all these **membrane bound organelles.** It is to be noted that as ribosomes are not **bounded** by membrane and are found in all cells. Ribosomes are also found in chloroplasts (in plants) and mitochondria and on rough ER other than cytoplasm. Animal cells contain another non-membrane bound organelle called **centrioles,** which helps in cell division.

(iii) **Outer membrane,** the **boundary** of the cell, which provides protection to the cell and controls the exchange of ions, molecules and other components in and out of the cell. The outer membrane of a cell contains cell wall (only in plant cells) and **plasma membrane.**

Knowledge Plus

Microscopes allow us to study the structure of cells, two types are commonly used, i.e. light microscope and electron microscope.

Size of a Cell

The cells exhibit an endless variation in size, lifespan and cellular activities, e.g. mycoplasmas (smallest cell) or PPLOs (Pleuro-Pneumonia Like Organisms) is only 0.3 μm in length and bacteria are approximately 3-5 μm in size. An ostrich egg, which is known to be the largest isolated single cell measures is about 170×135 mm. Human Red Blood Cells (RBCs) are about 7 μm in diameter and the nerve cell of human being is the longest cell having length of 90-100 cm.

The factors affecting the cell size are

(i) The nucleoplasmic index, i.e. the ratio between the volume of nucleus and the cytoplasm.

(ii) The ratio of cell surface to the cell volume.

(iii) Metabolism.

Shape of a Cell

The cells also vary in their shapes. They may be polygonal, disc-like amoeboid, thread-like, cuboid or irregular. The cell shape is always related and vary with the function they perform.

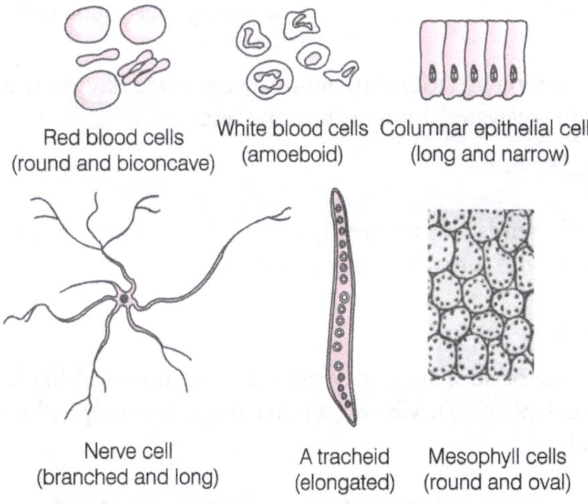

Fig 11.1 Diagram showing different shapes of the cels

Types of Cell

Broadly all living cells are classified into two groups namely **prokaryotic** (Gr. *Pro*-primitive or pre or before; *karyon*-nucleus) and **eukaryotic** (Gr. *Eu*-true; *karyon*-nucleus). Prokaryotic cells contain a primitive type of nucleus which is not bounded by a membrane. It is also called as **nucleoid** or **genophore.** On the other hand, eukaryotic cells contain a true double membrane bound nucleus. Both kind of cells possess cytoplasm as a semi-fluid matrix.

Prokaryotic Cell

Cell which does not have a nuclear membrane and other membrane bound organelles, is called prokaryotic cell.

Occurrence

Prokaryotic cells are placed in **kingdom–Monera**. These cells are represented by bacteria, cyanobacteria (blue-green algae), mycoplasma or PPLO.

Bacteria are the simplest and most common type of organism amongst prokaryotes. They are generally smaller and multiply more rapidly than the eukaryotic cell.

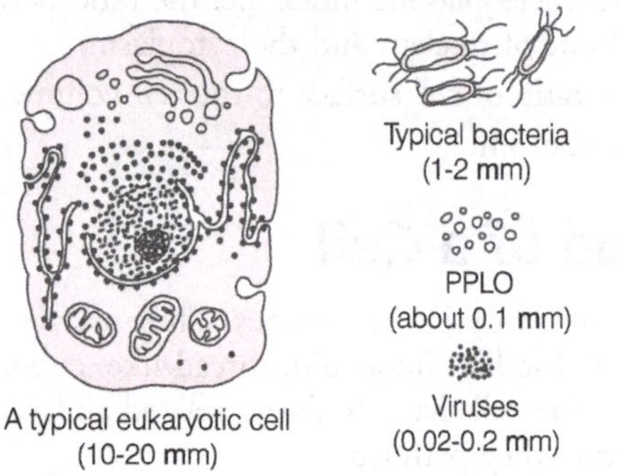

Fig 11.2 Diagram showing comparison of eukaryotic cell with other organisms

The bacteria are found in almost every place like deep in the soil, seawater, human intestine, etc.

Size

Bacteria tends to vary greatly in size. It normally ranges from 0.3-1.5 μm with some exceptions.

Shape

The four basic shapes of bacteria are **bacillus** (rod-like), **coccus** (spherical), **vibrio** (comma-shaped) and **spirillum** (spiral).

General Structure of a Prokaryotic (Bacterial) Cell

All prokaryotic cells are similar in their organisation although they exhibit a wide variety of shapes and functions. A bacterial cell is composed of various components as genetic material, cell envelope, cytoplasm, nucleoid, inclusion bodies, ribosomes, flagella, pili, fimbriae, etc.

1. Cell Envelope and Its Modifications

It is the outermost covering of protoplasm of the bacterial cell. It is known to protect the cell from mechanical shocks and injuries. It is composed of following three layers, which perform specialised function

(i) **Glycocalyx** (Mucilage Sheath) It is the outermost layer, made up of macromolecules that gives sticky character to the cell. Glycocalyx differs in composition and thickness among different bacteria. It could be in the form of loose mucilaginous sheath called **slime layer** or thick and tough covering called **capsule. Function** It helps in resisting phagocytosis.

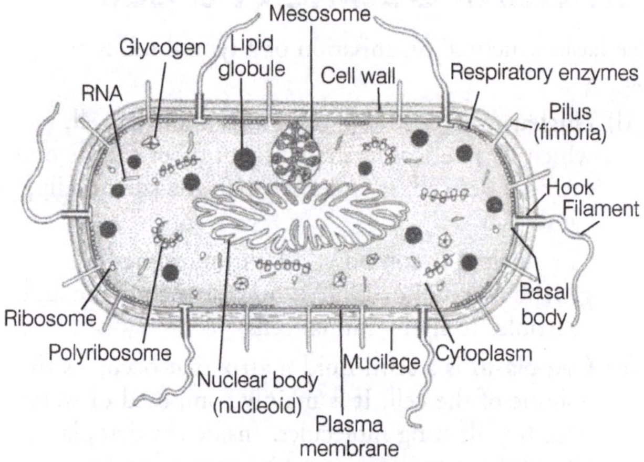

Fig 11.3 Diagrammatic representation of a typical bacterial cell

(ii) **Cell Wall** It is present just below the glycocalyx made up of **peptidoglycan** or **murein** in all eubacteria and cyanobacteria. It is a rigid and solid covering that gives shape and strong structural support to the cell.

Cell wall performs the following functions

(a) It helps in preventing cell from bursting or collapsing.

(b) It allows the material to pass in and out of the cell.

(c) It wards off the attack of pathogens like viruses, bacteria, fungi, protozoans.

(d) Provides mechanical support to the cell against gravity.

According to Christian Gram (1884) various types of reactions are shown by the **cell walls** of different bacteria.

Thus, on the basis of differences in the cell wall and the response to the staining procedures developed by Gram bacteria are classified as Gram positive and Gram negative.

The major differences between Gram positive and Gram negative bacteria are as follows

Gram Positive	Gram Negative
Retain Gram stain.	Does not retain Gram stain.
Rigid cell wall due to the presence of high proportion of peptidoglycan ~80%.	Less rigid and more elastic cell wall. Peptidoglycans account for only about 3-12%.
Single layered thick cell wall (100-200 Å) containing teichoic acid. Lipopolysaccharide is absent.	Triple layered thin cell wall (70-120 Å) with absence of teichoic acid. The outer layer that surrounds the cell wall is made up of Lipopolysaccharide (LPS).
Basal body of flagellum has two rings of swellings.	Four rings of swellings occur in basal body of flagellum.
Lipid content is very low (2-4%) due to the absence of outer membrane.	Lipid content is high (20-30%) due to the presence of outer membrane.
Phospholipids are absent.	Phospholipids are present.
L-lysine is present.	L-lysine is absent.
Cell wall is sensitive to antibiotics such as penicillin and cephalosporin.	Cell wall is insensitive to penicillin and cephalosporin.
They produce exotoxins.	They produce endotoxins.
e.g. *Streptomyces*, *Actinomyces* and *Clostridium*.	e.g. *E. coli*, *Salmonella*, *Nostoc* and *Rhizobium*.

(iii) **Plasma Membrane** It is the innermost layer of the cell envelope. It is semipermeable in nature and is responsible for the interaction of the cell with the outside environment.

Plasma membrane performs the following functions

(a) It helps in the regulation of the exchange of specific materials between the cytoplasm and extracellular medium.

(b) Selectively permits particular molecules to pass and prevents others.

(c) Prevents loss of components from the cells through leakage.

(d) The plasma membrane is vital to cellular homeostasis and therefore, the health and welfare of all living organisms.

Knowledge Plus

- Molecules move through membranes either passively, flowing down concentration gradients or actively, being pumped in or out of cells.
- Membrane in prokaryotes is structurally similar to eukaryotes.

2. Genetic Material

Nucleoid represents the genetic material in case of prokaryotes that is naked, not enveloped by a nuclear membrane. Many bacteria contain a small circular DNA known as **plasmid** other than the chromosomal or genomic DNA. These plasmids confer certain unique characters to the bacteria like antibiotic resistance, sex factor, etc.

3. Membranous Structures

Prokaryotic cells lack the complex membrane bound organelles (such as chloroplast, mitochondria, etc). However, some other special membranous structures are found in them (i.e. mesosomes and chromatophores).

(i) **Mesosomes** These are formed by the extensions of the plasma membrane into the cell in the form of **vesicles, tubules** and **lamellae.** Mesosomes are equal to mitochondria in eukaryotes, as these structures participate in aerobic cellular respiration in prokaryotes. Mesosomes perform the following functions in bacterium

(a) Helps in respiration, cellular secretion, etc.

(b) Helps in increasing the enzymatic content and surface area of the plasma membrane.

(c) Helps in the formation of a cell wall.

(d) Helps in the replication of DNA and distribution of genetic material to daughter cells during fission.

(ii) **Chromatophores** They are another membranous structures present in some prokaryotes like cyanobacteria, etc.

They are internal membrane systems of photosynthetic forms, which possess photosynthetic pigments. These pigments are light reflecting.

4. Flagella

Bacteria can be motile or non-motile. Thus, motile bacteria possess one or more thread-like appendages extending from their cell wall called flagella (sing. flagellum). Bacteria are also classified according to the number and arrangement of flagellum in them.

Each flagellum is about 1-7 µm long covered by a protein coat. The bacterial flagellum is differentiated into the following three parts

(i) **Filament**, the longest portion, extending from the cell surface to the outside. It is made up of protein called **flagellin.**

(ii) **Hook**, a curved and tubular structure made up of protein subunits.

(iii) **Basal body**, the most complex part of flagellum.

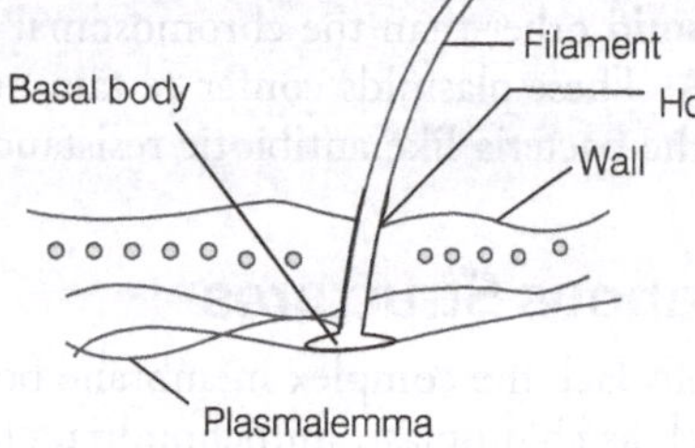

Fig 11.4 Bacterial flagellum showing different parts

They help in locomotion, i.e. movement from one place to another.

5. Pili and Fimbriae

These are also surface structures, but do not play any role in locomotion of bacteria. The pili are the elongated, tubular structures made up of a special protein called **pilin** and fimbriae are the small bristle-like fibres coming out of the cell.

The **pili** helps in forming conjugation tube during transfer of genetic material between donor and recipient cell. While, the **fimbriae** helps the bacteria to attach to solid surfaces.

Differences between Pili and Fimbriae

Pili	Fimbriae
They occur only in Gram negative bacteria.	They occur in both Gram positive and Gram negative bacteria.
They are longer and broader.	They are shorter and narrower.
They are responsible for sexduction (conjugation) in bacteria.	They are specialised for attachment of bacteria to its host (e.g. bacteria, *Salmonella typhimurium, Neisseria gonorrhoeae*, etc).
They are tubular structures.	They are bristle-like solid structures.

6. Ribosomes and Inclusion Bodies

Cytoplasm in prokaryotes appears granular, due to the presence of following structures

(i) **Ribosomes** Like eukaryotes, ribosomes are also found in prokaryotes and serves a common function, i.e. acts as a site of protein synthesis. Ribosomes are small, but are complex both in structure and chemical composition. They are about 15-20 nm in size.

In prokaryotes, ribosomes are found in association with the plasma membrane of the cell (as it lacks the endoplasmic reticulum) in the cytoplasmic matrix. The prokaryotic ribosomes are of 70S type. It has following two subunits

(a) Smaller subunit (30S)

(b) Larger subunit (50S)

Ribosomes generally occur in helical groups called **polysome** or **polyribosomes**. In each polysome 4-8 ribosomes are attached to a single strand of *m*RNA.

The ribosomes of a polysome help in the translation (mechanisms to synthesise several copies of the same protein) of *m*RNA into protein.

(ii) **Inclusion Bodies** They are non-living structures present in the cytoplasm and not bounded by any membrane system. They may either lie free in the cytoplasm (e.g. cyanophycean granules, glycogen granules) or may be covered by 2-4 nm thick, non-protein membrane (e.g. gas vacuoles, sulphur granules, etc).

Knowledge Plus

- Gas vacuoles are gas storing vacuoles that do not have any covering of their own. They are found in cyanobacteria (blue-green algae), purple and green photosynthetic bacteria.
- These are named so, because they are permeable to atmospheric gases, but not to water.

Topic Practice 1

Multiple Choice Questions

1 Mark

1. Schwann proposed cell theory according to which
   (a) each cell of the body possesses the same genetic information
   (b) all life activities of the organisms are present in miniature form in each and every cell of its body
   (c) bodies of animals and plants are made up of cells and their products
   (d) a new cell always develops by the division of pre-existing cells

Ans (c) Schwann defined a cell as a membrane bound, nucleus containing structure. He also proposed a hypothesis (Schwann; 1838) that bodies of animals and plants are made up of cells and their products.

2. Cell theory was formulated by
(a) Schleiden and Schwann
(b) Rudolf Virchow
(c) Robert Brown
(d) Robert Hooke

Ans (a) Cell theory was formulated by Schleiden and Schwann in 1839 in their proper microscope investigations on the similarity of structure and growth in animals and plants.

3. Schleiden and Schwann's cell theory could not explain
(a) cell formed from pre-existing cell
(b) how new cells were formed
(c) body of animals are composed of cells
(d) None of the above

Ans (b) Schleiden and Schwann cell theory did not explain as to how new cells were formed.

4. *'Omnis cellula-e-cellula* (all cells arise from pre-existing cells). Who gave this concept and modified the cell theory?
(a) Schleiden and Schwann
(b) Virchow
(c) Robert Brown
(d) Leeuwenhoek

Ans (b) Rudolf Virchow modified the cell theory and gave the theory *'Omnis cellula-e-cellula'* means new cells develop by division of the pre-existing cell. This is called theory of cell lineage or common ancestry.

5. The genetic material is naked in
(a) prokaryotic cells (b) eukaryotic cells
(c) multicellular cell (d) Both (a) and (b)

Ans (a) The genetic material is not membrane bound or is naked in prokaryotic cells.

6. The largest isolated single cell is
(a) egg of ostrich (b) egg of peacock
(c) egg of duck (d) None of these

Ans (a) Largest isolated single cell is the egg of ostrich.

7. Which of the following represents prokaryotic cells?
(a) PPLO (b) Mycoplasma
(c) Bacteria (d) All of these

Ans (d) The prokaryotic cells are represented by bacteria, blue-green algae, mycoplasma and PPLO.

8. Which one of the following is not an inclusion body found in prokaryotes?
(a) Cyanophycean granules
(b) Glycogen granules
(c) Polysomes
(d) Phosphate granules

Ans (c) Polysomes are formed in eukaryotes and are defined as a cluster of ribosomes attached to *m*RNA.

9. A specialised differentiated form of cell membrane of prokaryotes is
(a) ribosomes (b) mesosomes
(c) microvilli (d) vacuoles

Ans (b) A specialised differentiated form of cell membrane called mesosome is the characteristic feature of prokaryotes.

10. Select the incorrect statement.
(a) Bacterial cell wall is made up of peptidoglycan
(b) Pili and fimbriae are mainly involved in motility of bacterial cells
(c) Cyanobacteria lack flagellated cells
(d) Mycoplasma is a walless microorganism

Ans (b) Fimbriae and pili are fine hair-like appendages used by bacteria for attachment rather than motility. These are formed of protein called pilin.

Very Short Answer Type Questions

(1 Mark)

11. How new cells generate according to cell theory? **NCERT**

Ans New cells generate from pre-existing cells.

12. Which is known to be the longest cell in human body?

Ans Nerve cell is the longest cell in human body.

13. What is the shape of WBCs and tracheid?

Ans WBCs are amoeboid and tracheids are elongated in shape.

14. Where is glycocalyx found?

Ans Glycocalyx is found as a thick outer most covering of cell either as a capsule or a slime layer.

15. Which layer of cell envelope is sticky in nature? Also give another name for this layer.

Ans The sticky layer of cell envelope is called glycocalyx. It is also known as mucilage sheath.

16. Give one difference between the characteristic feature of Gram positive and Gram negative bacteria.

Ans Gram positive bacteria retain crystal violet dye and stain blue in colour, while Gram negative bacteria loose colour on washing.

17. What is the name given to the infoldings of plasmalemma in prokaryotic cell below the wall?

Ans Mesosomes.

18. Why are mesosomes present in bacterial cell, known to be equivalent to mitochondrion in eukaryotic cell?

Ans This is because mesosomes also participates in aerobic cellular respiration in prokaryotes as mitochondrion does in eukaryotes.

19. Give the name of the protein, which pili is composed of.

Ans Pilin.

20. Name the only organelle found in prokaryotic cell.

Ans Ribosomes.

21. What is the function of a polysome? (Gk. *Poly* = many, *soma* = body)

Ans A polysome consists of a cluster of ribosomes that are held, simultaneously by a strand of messenger RNA (*m*RNA). They are involved in formation of multiple copies of same polypeptide.

22. Why are gas vacuoles named so ?

Ans Gas vacuoles are named so, because these are permeable to atmospheric gases and not to water.

Short Answer Type I Questions

2 Marks

23. 'Cell is the basic unit of life'. Discuss in brief. **NCERT**

Ans All organisms begin their life as a single cell. Certain organisms complete their life cycle as a single cell. They are called unicellular or acellular organisms, e.g. *Amoeba, Chlamydomonas,* bacteria and yeast.

In other organisms, single cell undergoes divisions to form multicellular body. Body of human being is made up of trillion of cells.

All the cells of an organism carry the same genetic material, developed from same pre-existing cells and possess several organelles to perform various life activities. The cells are therefore, basic unit of life and structural unit of an organism. (2)

24. Briefly give the contributions of the following scientists in formulating the cell theory

(i) Rudolf Virchow

(ii) Schleiden and Schwann **NCERT Exemplar**

Ans (i) **Rudolf Virchow** (1855) first explained that the cells divide and new cells are formed from the pre-existing cells.

(ii) **Schleiden** and **Schwann** observed the cells and cell membranes for the first time. They proposed that animal and plant cells are composed of cells and products of cells. (1+1)

25. Write about cellular autonomy in unicellular organisms.

Ans Unicellular organisms possess the following cellular autonomy

(i) The cell has complete independent existence.

(ii) All life activities are carried out by the same cell.

(iii) Division of labour is absent.

(iv) The cell depends upon its own internal and intrinsic information. (½ × 4)

26. What is the difference between cell walls of Gram positive and Gram negative bacteria?

Ans The cell wall of Gram positive bacteria is single-layered (outer membrane is absent) and contains 70-80% peptidoglycan, teichoic acid and little amount of lipids.

The light cell wall of Gram negative bacteria on the other hand is two-layered, outer membrane is present, i.e. thin layer of peptidoglycan and plasma membrane is present and teichoic acid is absent. (2)

27. Give significance of glycocalyx.

Ans Glycocalyx is significant in the following ways

(i) It protects the cell from loss of water and nutrients.

(ii) Serves as a protective layer against attack by phagocytosis and viruses.

(iii) Helps in attachment to a surface.

(iv) Provides virulence. (½ × 4)

28. What is a mesosome in a prokaryotic cell? Mention the functions that it performs. **NCERT**

Ans Mesosome is a special membrane structure, formed by the extension of the plasma membrane into the cell in a prokaryotic cell. It helps in cell wall formation, DNA replication and its distribution to daughter cells. It also helps in respiration, secretion process, to increase the surface area of the plasma membrane and enzymatic content. (2)

29. (i) Name two surface extensions that are not concerned with motility in bacterial cells.

(ii) Give the name of the structure that helps in motility of bacterial cells.

Ans (i) Pili and fimbriae are the two surface extensions that are not concerned with motility.

(ii) Structure that helps in motility of bacterial cell is flagella. (1+1)

30. (i) Do bacterial cells have nucleus like eukaryotic cell? Explain.
(ii) Are there any form of bacteria present that are made up of more than one cell?

Ans (i) No, bacterial cells do not have well-defined nucleus instead, the genetic material in them is dispersed in the cytosol, also there is no internal membrane that delimits a nucleus.
(ii) No, there is no multicellular bacteria, i.e. made up of more than one cell. All bacterial cells are unicellular prokaryotes. (1+1)

31. What are gas vacuoles? State their functions. **NCERT**

Ans Gas vacuoles are also known as pseudovacuoles or air vacuoles. Gas vacuoles are the characteristic feature of prokaryotes reported only in prokaryotes.
Each gas vesicles is made up of sub-microscopic hexagonal vesicles and are surrounded by a thin protein membrane. Gas vacuoles store metabolic gases and take part in buoyancy regulation. (2)

32. What are inclusion bodies in prokaryotic cell?

Ans Inclusion bodies are the non-living structures present in cytoplasm not bounded by, the membrane system. They may either lie free in cytoplasm or may be covered by 2-4 nm- thick, non-protein membrane, e.g. vacuoles, sulphur granules, etc. (2)

Short Answer Type II Questions

3 Marks

33. Briefly describe the cell theory. **NCERT Exemplar**

Ans Refer to text on page no. 218-219.

34. What are the characteristics of prokaryotic cells? **NCERT**

Ans Characteristics of prokaryotic cells are as follows
(i) A prokaryotic cell, i.e. of bacteria is surrounded by a cell membrane.
The cell wall in turn is surrounded by a slimy layer.
(ii) Absence of well-organised chloroplast, mitochondria and nucleus.
(iii) Nucleolus is absent. It is known as nucleoid. The DNA of a prokaryotic cell is circular and not associated with basic proteins.
(iv) The cytoplasm is filled with dense granules. Most of these granules are ribosomes.
(v) A prokaryotic cell possesses single chromosome (not paired) that exists as circular loops of DNA without histone proteins. (3)

35. What are plasmids? Describe their role in bacteria. **NCERT Exemplar**

Ans A plasmid is usually a circular (sometimes linear) piece of double-stranded DNA found in bacteria that is different from bacterium's chromosome. It carries non-essential genes that can augment a bacterium's ability to survive in certain circumstances.
For example, plasmids carry genes that enable a bacterium to metabolise a certain type of nutrient otherwise they cannot conjugate. Plasmids are used for a vast variety of experiments from expressing human genes in bacterial cells to DNA sequencing. (1½ × 2)

36. Match the items listed in column I with the appropriate items from column II.

Column I	Column II
A. Spherical bacteria	1. Contractile vacuoles
B. A double membrane system	2. 70S ribosomes
C. Rod-shaped bacteria	3. Cocci
D. A single membrane system	4. Prokaryotic cell
E. Animal cell	5. Bacilli
F. Prokaryotic cell	6. Eukaryotic cell

Ans A–3; B–6; C–5; D–4; E–1; F–2 (½ × 6)

37. Describe briefly the difference between pili and fimbriae.

Ans Refer to text on page no. 222.

Long Answer Type Questions

5 Marks

38. Discuss the basic structural organisation of a typical cell.

Ans Refer to text on page no. 220-222.

39. Discuss in detail about the outermost covering of bacterial cell and the three layers.

Ans Refer to text on page no. 220 and 221.

TOPIC 02 Eukaryotic Cell

A cell which has a well-organised nucleus with a nuclear envelope and several membrane bound organelles is called **eukaryotic cell.** Internal organisation of eukaryotic cells is more advanced and elaborate, than the prokaryotic cells. All eukaryotic cells are not identical. Except **monerans**, eukaryotic organisation is seen in all the **protists, plants, fungi** and **animals.** Eukaryotic cell is larger than the prokaryotic cell (i.e. around 10-100 µm in size).

Generalised Structure

An extensive compartmentalisation of cytoplasm is seen through the presence of membrane bound organelles. Eukaryotic cells also possess a variety of **locomotory** and **cytoskeletal** structures. All eukaryotic cells are not identical, instead they differ from each other on the basis of structure and function.

Cell wall is a special membrane, being present in plants, fungi and some protists. **Plants cells** also contain a large vacuole and plastids, which are absent in animal cells, while animal cells possess centrioles, which are absent in plant cells.

Components of an Eukaryotic Cell

An eukaryotic cell is composed of various cell components such as cell membrane, cell wall (only in plants), mitochondria, chloroplast, Golgi bodies, ribosomes, centrioles (only in animals), etc. All these are described here in detail

Cell Wall

It was first discovered by **Robert Hooke** (1665). It is a rigid and a non-living structure which forms an outer covering of the plasma membrane in plants and fungi. It is absent in animal cells.

Structure of Cell Wall

On the basis of the structure, cell wall is differentiated into the following three parts

(i) **Middle Lamella** It is the layer mainly made up of calcium and magnesium pectates. It cements the cell walls of two adjoining cells together. It is absent on the outer side of surface cells middle lamella along with a cell wall transversed by plasmodesmata which connects cytoplasm of neighbouring cells.

(ii) **Primary Cell Wall** It is produced inner to the middle lamella in a young and growing cell. It is capable of growth and extension. It tends to diminish gradually as the cell attains maturity.

(iii) **Secondary Cell Wall** The thick secondary wall is formed inner towards membrane to the primary wall. As the cell gets fully matured. Its composition is similar to the primary wall.

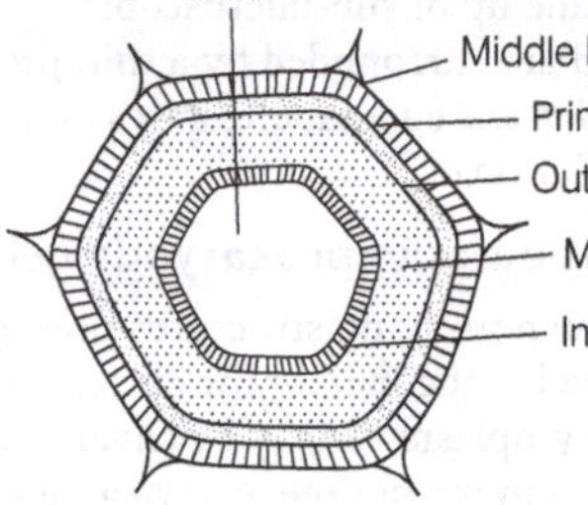

Fig 11.5 Layers of the cell wall

Cell wall consists of cellulose microfibrils. The microfibrils are long, thin and oval or circular in cross-section. The cellulose molecules in microfibrils form chains, which are arranged into 3-dimensional crystalline lattices termed micelles.

The microfibrils are grouped in cluster to form macrofibrils. These macrofibrils are about 0.4 µm wide.

Structures Associated with Cell Wall

Structures associated with cell wall are as follows

(i) **Pits** In the cell wall, there are some areas that lack secondary wall.

These unthickened regions are called pits. Pits of two neighbouring cells are complementary. Together these constitute a pit pair.

(ii) **Plasmodesmata** These are the cytoplasmic strands found in the cell wall of plants. They constitute the only living component of the dead cell walls. These are made up of a fine tubules called **desmo tubule** which are considered as extensions of SER (Smooth Endoplasmic Reticulum).

Plasmodesmata connects the cytoplasm of one cell to that of the other.

Functions of Cell Wall

Cell wall performs the following functions

(i) It helps in providing a definite shape to the cell and also protects protoplasm against any mechanical injury, i.e. damage and infection.

(ii) It also helps in cell-to-cell interaction.

(iii) It provides barrier to undesirable macromolecules and attack of pathogens.

Cell Membrane

Every living cell is covered by a thin, elastic, transparent, semi-permeable and regenerative membrane called **cell membrane** also called **plasma membrane** or **plasmalemma.** The plasma membrane separates the internal environment of the cell from external environment.

This membrane helps in regulating the entrance and exit of molecules into and out of the cell. In 1950s, with the advancement of electron microscope, the detailed structure of the membrane was studied. Studies on cell membrane structure, i.e. especially on the human **Red Blood Cells** (RBCs), enabled the scientists to deduce the possible structure of plasma membrane.

Note

Human RBCs are considered to be the best material for the study of biochemical composition of the cell membrane because they lack **nucleus** as well as **cytoplasmic organelles.**

Structure

Studies on human RBCs concluded that the cell membrane is composed of lipids which forms a bilayer with protein molecules embedded in it at places. Later it was revealed that cell membranes also possess protein and carbohydrates.

(i) **Lipid** The lipid molecules are amphipathic in nature and are arranged within the membrane by the help of two types of ends. These are as follows

(a) **Polar Hydrophilic End** This region is in the form of (water loving) head, which faces towards the outer sides of the cell membrane to interact with the aqueous environments on both sides.

(b) **Non-polar Hydrophobic End** This region is in the form of (water repelling) tail, both ends of which face each other and occur towards the centre of the cell membrane. The proportion of lipid molecules varies in plasma membrane of different cell types.

These are formed of cholesterol (25-32%) and mainly of phosphoglycerides or phospholipids (55-75%).

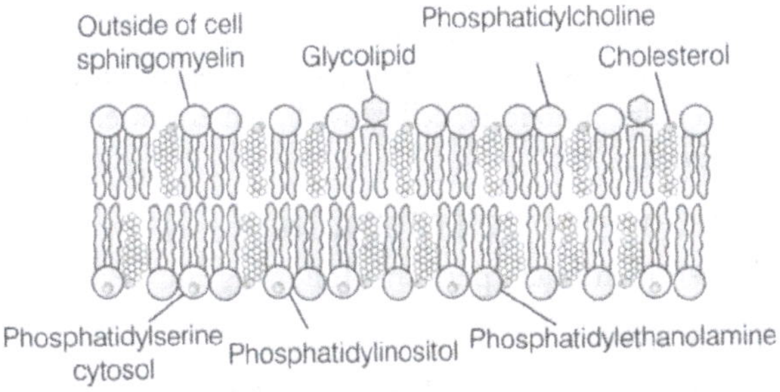

Fig 11.6 Generalised view of plasma membrane

(ii) **Proteins** Depending upon the ease of extraction, the ratio of protein and lipid varies considerably in different cell types. In human beings, the membrane of the erythrocytes (RBCs) has approximately 52% protein and 40% lipid. The membrane proteins can be classified as

(a) **Integral Proteins** (Intrinsic Protein) They have stronger association and are bound firmly to the membrane. These proteins are buried partially or totally in the phospholipid bilayer.

(b) **Peripheral Proteins** (Extrinsic Protein) They have weaker association and are bound to lipids of membrane by electrostatic interactions.

(iii) **Carbohydrates** These constitute about 1-5% of chemical composition of plasma membrane. These are associated with the phospholipids or with the peripheral proteins to form glycolipids and glycoproteins, respectively. To understand the structure of plasma membrane various models are given, out of which the most accepted model is **Fluid Mosaic Model.**

Fluid Mosaic Model

This model was given by **Singer** and **Nicolson** (1972). According to this model, the lipid bilayer and integral proteins appear like a mosaic arrangement and the **quasi-fluid** nature of lipid enables the lateral movement of the proteins within the overall bilayer. This ability of proteins to move within the membrane indicates the fluidity of the lipid part.

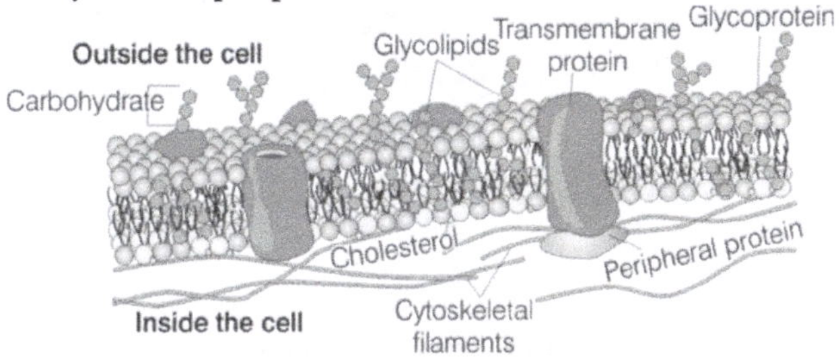

Fig 11.7 Fluid mosaic model of plasma membrane

Fluidity of Membrane

The fluid nature of the membrane is important from the point of view of interactions of molecules within the membrane as well as other functions like formation of intercellular junctions, cell growth, secretion, endocytosis, cell division, etc.

Functions of Cell Membrane

The cell membrane performs following important functions

(i) Transport

The transport of metabolites across the plasma membrane takes place in the following two ways

(a) **Passive Transport** It is the transport of molecules that occurs along the concentration gradient, i.e. from a high concentration region to a low concentration region. This transport does not require any energy. This transport may occur in the following ways

- **Simple Diffusion** It is the movement of non-polar substances from region of higher concentration to their region of lower concentration.
- **Facilitated Diffusion** This is a special kind of diffusion. In this, movement of polar molecules across plasma membrane is facilitated. Some carrier proteins are involved in this prosses. The process is carried out with the formation of a metabolites carrier complex, e.g. entry of glucose in erythrocytes. In relation to facilitated diffusion, some carrier or transport proteins allow the movement of molecules only if two molecules move together. This type of movement is known as **cotransport.**
  It can be of following three types
  - **Symport** In this, both molecules cross the membrane in the same direction.
  - **Antiport** In this both molecules cross membrane in opposite directions.
  - **Uniport** In this type, the molecules moves across a membrane independent of any other molecules

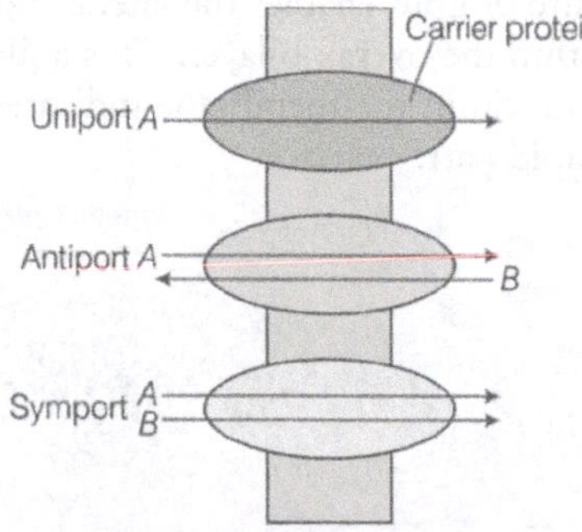

Fig. 11.8 Facilitated diffusion

(b) **Active Transport** In this transport, molecules move against the concentration gradient, i.e. from the region of their low concentration to the region of their high concentration. This type of transport requires energy in the form of ATP. Active transport is of following two types

- **Primary active transport,** e.g. transport of Na^+/K^+ with the help of ATPase complex.
- **Secondary active transport,** e.g. glucose transport in *E. coli.*

(ii) Transportation at Cellular Level

Membranes of cell organelles by the process of blebbing (formation of vesicles or blebs), carry out transportation of various substances. This process involves repeated fusion and detachment of these vesicles. This fusion and detachment help in the maintenance of membrane flow.

(iii) Bulk Transport

Transport of materials from outside the cell to inside and *vice versa* is carried out by bulk transport system. This may occur through following ways

(a) **Endocytosis** It is the process through which materials are transported into cells. The term includes two essentially similar processes, namely

- **Phagocytosis,** i.e. cell eating, means intake of solid particles by the cell.
- **Pinocytosis,** i.e. cell drinking, means intake of liquid particles by the cell.

(b) **Exocytosis** It is a process through which materials are transported out of the cells.

Differences between Active and Passive Transport

Active Transport	Passive Transport
In this process, energy is required.	Energy is not required.
It is a rapid process.	It is comparatively slower process.
It occurs usually against the concentration gradient.	It occurs along the concentration gradient.
It is highly selective.	It is non-selective.
It requires carrier proteins.	It occurs without carrier proteins.

Mitochondria

These are membrane bound cell organelles, essential for aerobic respiration of eukaryotic cells. These are also known as **powerhouse of the cell.** Thus, they produces cellular energy in the form of ATP.

Occurrence

Mitochondria are present in all living cells except, prokaryotic cell and certain specialised eukaryotic cell such as anaerobic cells and mature RBCs. It is revealed from the studies that mitochondria is not easily visible, unless it is specifically stained.

Shape and Size

Mitochondria vary considerably according to the shape and size. They have varying shape such as granular fibrillar, spherical, oval, discoidal, etc. Average size of mitochondria is 2-6 μm in length and 0.5 μm in diameter (typical cylindrical or sausage-shaped mitochondria has diameter of 0.2-1.0 μm).

Ultrastructure

A mitochondrion contains two membranes, i.e. outer and inner. Out of which **outer membrane** is smooth and forms the continuous boundary of the organelle. The **inner membrane** is semi-permeable to some metabolities. It is infolded into the matrix as incomplete partitions called **cristae**. The cristae are responsible for increasing the physiological active area or surface area. The density of cristae determines the intensity of respiration.

The outer and the inner membranes divide its lumen into two aqueous compartments separately, i.e. the outer and the inner compartment. Inner compartment is also called **matrix**, which forms the inner core of the mitochondrion. The matrix also possesses single circular DNA molecule, a few RNA molecules, ribosomes (70S) and the components required for the synthesis of proteins. The mitochondria divide by fission. The two membranes of mitochondria have their own specific enzymes associated with mitochondrial function.

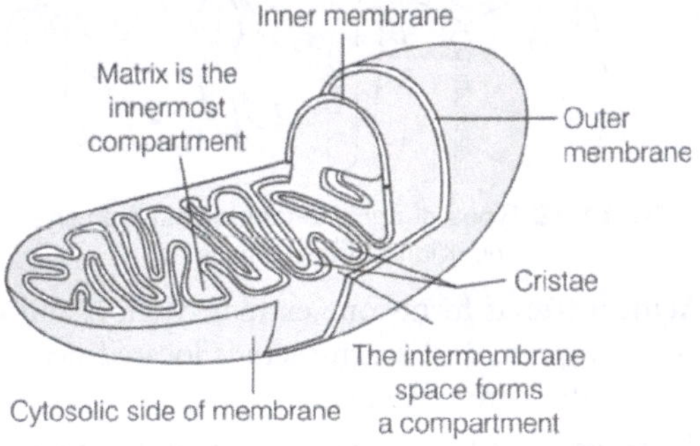

Fig 11.9 Structure of mitochondria (LS)

Functions

Mitochondria performs the following functions

(i) Mitochondria provide important intermediates for the synthesis of several biochemicals like pyrimidines, alkaloids, etc.

(ii) The inner chamber matrix of the mitochondria has enzyme for the synthesis of fatty acids.

(iii) Helps in regulation of cellular metabolism.

(iv) Helps in apoptosis (programmed cell death).

Note

Mitochondrion is the second largest cell organelle and are more in animal cells than in plant cells.

Nucleus

It is a double membrane bound dense body, which controls all cellular metabolism and encloses the genetic information of the cell. Nucleus was first described by **Robert Brown** as early as 1831. Later the name **chromatin** was given by **Flemming** when the material of the nucleus was stained by the basic dyes. Nucleus is known to be the largest cell organelle also known as brain of the cell.

Occurrence

A nucleus is known to be present in all eukaryotic cells except a few cell types such as RBCs of humans, sieve cells of vascular plants, etc.

Structure

In an electron microscopic view following components are seen in nucleus

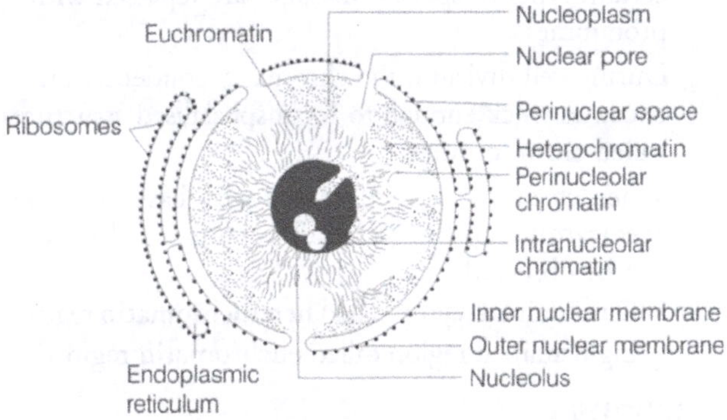

Fig 11.10 Structure of nucleus

(i) **Nuclear Membrane** It is also called as **nuclear envelope or karyotheca**. It is composed of two membranes, i.e. the outer and the inner membrane. These are separated by means of a perinuclear space. The outer membrane of nucleus is continuous with ER (Endoplasmic Reticulum) and it may bear ribosomes also.

Nuclear membrane contains octagonal nuclear pores formed by the fusion of outer and inner membranes.

These pores control the inward and outward movement of different materials such as *m*RNA, nucleoproteins, etc. from the nucleus.

(ii) **Nucleoplasm** Nuclear sap or Nucleoplasm is the fluid part of a nucleus. It majorly contains DNA and associated proteins along with water, ions, enzymes, soluble molecules and nucleotides.

It is considered as the main site for the synthesis of DNA. The DNA and associated proteins are visible either as chromatin or as chromosomes.

(iii) **Nucleolus** The nucleolus was first recognised by **Fontana** in 1874. It is a spherical membraneless body within the nucleus. Its constituents are RNA, DNA and proteins. The nucleoli are formed from specific sites on chromosomes. These sites are called **nucleolar organiser regions.** A nucleolus can be best visualised at interphase.

Nucleolus is the most important site of ribosomal RNA synthesis, which comprises about 80% of total RNA content of the cell. Thus, it is the site of ribosome synthesis.

(iv) **Chromatin** The chromatin (meaning coloured fibres) are fine fibres composed of DNA, some proteins and transcribing RNA. The proteins associated with chromatin are mainly histone proteins.

These are positively charged basic proteins mainly composed of lysine and arginine. However, in certain types of sperms, histones are replaced with protamines.

During cell division, the chromatin condenses and becomes thick enough to form specialised structures called **chromosomes.**

When chromosomes are stained with basic dyes like acetocarmine or fuelgen strain, two types of regions can be observed

- Dark stained region called **heterochromatin** region.
- Light stained region called **euchromatin region.**

Functions

Nucleus performs the following functions

(i) It stores information that controls cellular functions.
(ii) It controls the synthesis of structural proteins.
(iii) It also stores the genetic information for development reproduction and behaviour.
(iv) It also induces genetic variations.

Chromosomes

It has been already studied in the chapter that the nucleus in the interphase has a loose and indistinct network of nucleoprotein fibres called **chromatin.** But during different stages of cell division cells show structured chromosomes in place of the nucleus.

The chromosomes are meant for the equal distribution of genetic material. Their number is fixed and is same in all individuals of a species. A single human cell has approximately two metre long thread of DNA distributed among its 46 (23 pairs) chromosomes.

Chromatin is composed of DNA and some basic proteins called **histones.** Some **non-histone** proteins and RNA are also present in the chromatin. Each and every chromosome is composed of a **primary constriction** or the **centromere.** On the sides of which the disc-shaped structures are present known as **kinetochores.**

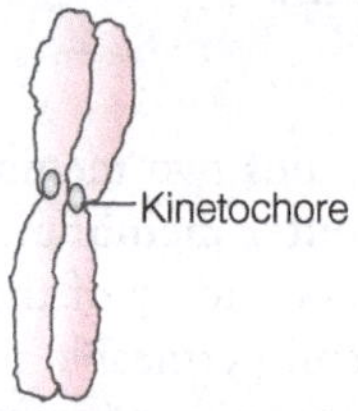

Fig 11.11 Chromosome with kinetochore

On the basis of the position of the centromere, the chromosomes can be classified into four following types

(i) **Metacentric** It has chromosome with equal arms and centromere lies in the centre.
(ii) **Submetacentric** It has one shorter arm and one longer arm with centromere slightly away from the middle of the chromosome.

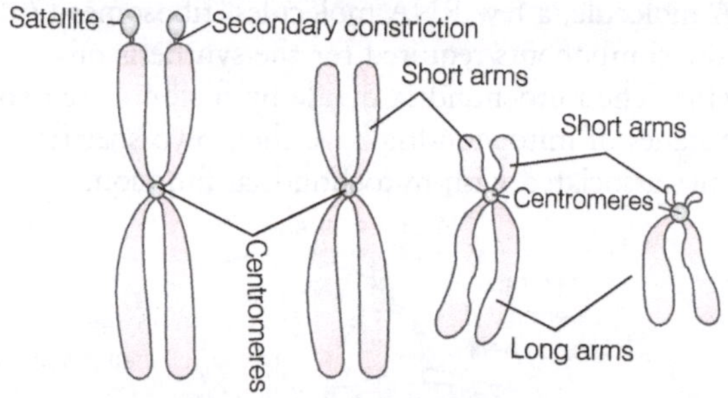

Fig 11.12 Types of chromosomes based on the position of centromere

(iii) **Acrocentric** It forms one extremely short and one very long arm and centromere is located near the end of the chromosome.
(iv) **Telocentric** It has the terminal centromere, i.e. centromere is placed at an extreme end. Telocentric chromosomes are not present in humans.

Few chromosomes have a non-staining **secondary constrictions** being present at a constant location at some or the other time which gives the appearance of a small fragment known a **satellite.**

Functions

Chromosomes performs the following functions

(i) Control cellular differentiation.

(ii) Contains all hereditary information located in the genes.

(iii) Forms a link between the offspring and the parents.

(iv) Introduce variations, through the process of crossing over.

(v) Control cell metabolism.

Plastids

These are semiautonomous organelles that have double membrane envelope. Plastids have their own genetic material (i.e. DNA). Due to their large size, they are easily seen under the microscope.

Occurrence

Plastids are found in all plant cells and euglenoides except in some protistans (e.g. *Euglena,* Dinophyceae, etc).

Types of Plastids

Plastids are differentiated into three different types on the basis of the colour, i.e. type of pigments found in them.

(i) **Leucoplasts** These are the colourless plastids of varied shapes and sizes with stored nutrients in the form of carbohydrates, lipids and proteins. These are of following three types

(a) **Amyloplasts** are the carbohydrates (starch) containing leucoplast, e.g. rice, wheat, potato, etc. Amyloplasts are larger than the normal/original size of leucoplast.

(b) **Elaioplasts** are the leucoplast which stores oils and fats, e.g. tuberose endosperm of castor seeds, etc.

(c) **Aleuroplasts** are the protein storing leucoplast. e.g. maize (aleurone cells).

(ii) **Chromoplasts** These are the plastids, which are yellow or reddish in appearance because of the presence of fat soluble carotenoid pigment **carotene.** Xanthophyll and some other pigments are also present as the fat soluble carotenoid pigment other than carotene, e.g. orange colour of carrot, etc.

(iii) **Chloroplasts** These are the plastids which are greenish in colour containing photosynthetic pigments **chlorophyll** and **carotenoids.**

These pigments are responsible for trapping the light energy, essential for the photosynthesis, i.e. the synthesis of organic food from an inorganic raw materials in the presence of sunlight.

(a) **Occurrence** Chloroplasts occur in major number in the photosynthetic mesophyll cells of leaves and green stem of plants.

(b) **Shape and Size** They may be lens-shaped, oval, spherical, discoid or even ribbon-like organelles. They also have variable length (5-10 mm) and width (2-4 mm).

(c) **Number** Their number also varies from 1per cell of the *Chlamydomonas* (a green alga) to 2-40 per cell in mesophyll.

(d) **Ultrastructure** Chloroplasts are also bounded by double membrane envelope like mitochondria, the two membranes are smooth and are thick of about 90-100 Å. The inner membrane of chloroplast is less permeable than the other one.

The inner membrane is grounded by a space known as **stroma** or **matrix,** a dense, colourless and a granular substance mainly formed of soluble proteins. It also contains enzymes which are essential for the synthesis of carbohydrates, lipids and proteins.

Thylakoids are number of membranous-like flattened structures that run throughout the matrix or stroma.

When several thylakoids are arranged or organised in the stack (like the piles of coins), called **grana** or the **intergranal thylakoids.** Many flat membranous tubules interconnect the thylakoids of different grana known as **stroma lamellae.**

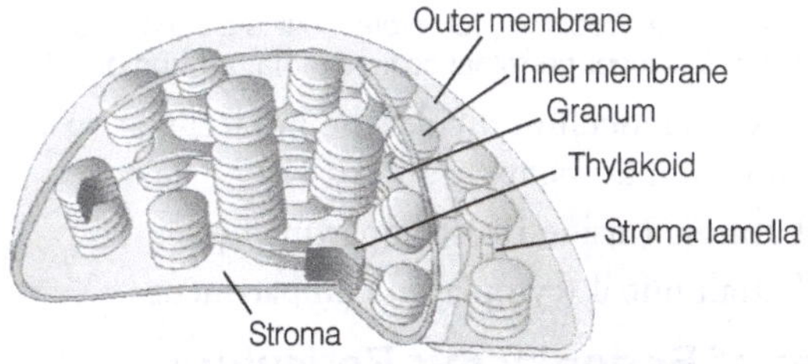

Fig 11.13 Sectional view of chloroplast

Chloroplasts perform the following functions

(i) Help in photosynthesis, i.e. formation of organic compounds.

(ii) In consumption of CO_2 and release of O_2 in photosynthesis.

(iii) May also change into chromoplast in order to provide colour to many flowers and fruits.

(iv) Help in storing fat and lipids.

(v) Function in transduction of energy.

Knowledge Plus

- The sum total of all plastids in a cell is called plastidome.
- The chloroplast with nitrogen-fixing genes are called nitroplast.
- The space between the two membrane is called intermembrane space, which separates the two membrane. This space contains a narrow fluid. Stroma also contains small, double-stranded circular DNA, molecules and ribosomes.
- Ribosomes of chloroplasts are smaller (70S) than the ribosomes of cytoplasm (80S).

Endomembrane System

The endomembrane system consists of nuclear envelope, Endoplasmic Reticulum (ER), Golgi complex, lysosomes and vacuoles suspended in the cytoplasm.

These are considered together as an **endomembrane system** because their functions are coordinated with each other, inspite of this, each membranous organelle is distinct in terms of its structure and functioning.

1. Endoplasmic Reticulum (ER)

The endoplasmic reticulum is a complicated system of membranous channels and flattened vesicles. It is physically continuous with the outer membrane of the nuclear envelope. It is revealed from the electron microscopic studies of eukaryotic cells that there is a presence of a network or reticulum of tiny tubular structures that are being scattered in the cytoplasm.

Note

ER is known to be absent in prokaryotes, but is present in all eukaryotic cells except **germinal cells** and **mature human RBCs**.

Endoplasmic reticulum divides the intracellular space into two main compartments

(i) Luminal (inside ER) compartment

(ii) Extraluminal (cytoplasm) compartment

Types of Endoplasmic Reticulum

Endoplasmic reticulum is mainly of two types, depending upon the nature of its membranes

(i) **Smooth Endoplasmic Reticulum** (SER) These are smooth because they do not bear ribosomes in the form of granules on their surfaces. It is present in cells where they act as a major site for the synthesis of **lipid** and also help in synthesis of steroidal hormone in animal cells.

(ii) **Rough Endoplasmic Reticulum** (RER) They are found extensive and continuous with the outer membrane of nucleus. These have rough membrane because they bear ribosomes being attached to their surfaces.

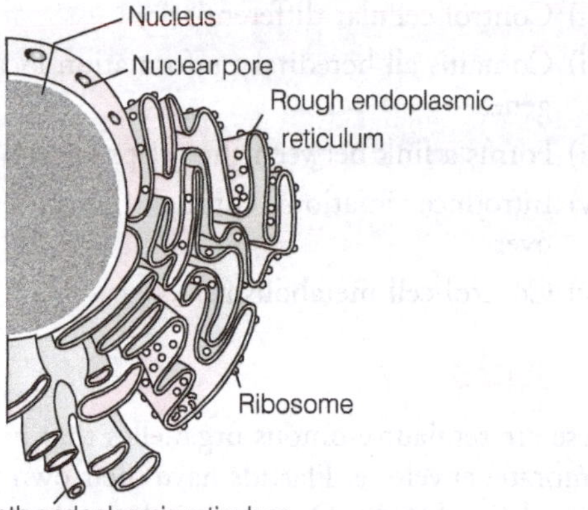

Fig 11.14 Structure of an endoplasmic reticulum

They are actively seen in the cells which have their involvement in the synthesis and secretion of proteins.

Functions

Endoplasmic reticulum performs the following functions

(i) It provides support to the colloidal cytoplasmic matrix.

(ii) Helps in the rapid intracellular transport of the material.

(iii) ER membrane contains a variety of enzymes for various metabolic processes, e.g. ATPase, phosphatases, etc.

Differences between SER and RER

SER	RER
It is not associated with ribosomes, but generally associated with plasma membrane.	It is associated with ribosomes and nuclear membrane.
Its main function is synthesis of lipids.	Its main function is synthesis of proteins.
Formed of vesicles and tubules.	Formed of cisternae and few tubules.
It is usually found in periphery.	It is found deep inside the cytoplasm.

2. Golgi Apparatus

It was first discovered by **Camillo Golgi** (1898), when he was observing the densly stained reticular structures being present near the nucleus of the cell. These structures were named Golgi bodies after his discovery.

Golgi complex or **Golgi apparatus** is a major complex protoplasmic structure being made up of many flat, disc-shaped sacs or **cisternae** (0.5-1.0 μm) in diameter.

Occurrence

Golgi complex, occurs in all cells except prokaryotes (i.e. PPLO, bacteria, cyanobacteria) and some eukaryotes such as human RBCs, sieve tubes of plants, etc.

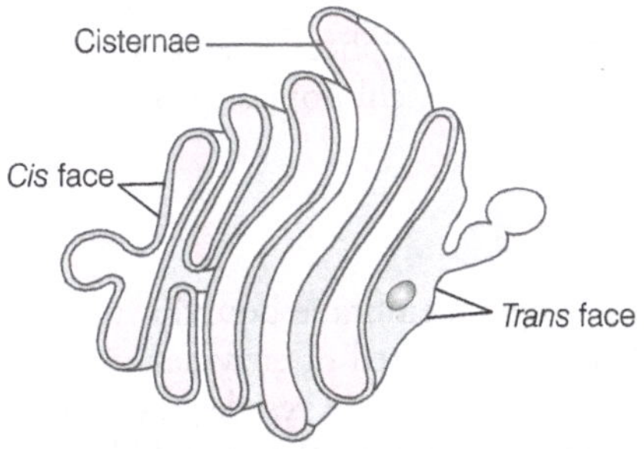

Fig 11.15 Golgi apparatus

Cisternae of Golgi apparatus are found stacked parallel to each other. They vary in number in a cell. They are often curved like a shallow bowl to give Golgi complex a definite polarity.

They are concentrically arranged near the nucleus with two distinct faces

(i) ***Cis* face** (forming face) This is convex in shape that lies towards the cell membrane and is responsible for receiving secretory materials through the transitional vesicles, which are pinched off from the SER.

(ii) ***Trans* face** (maturing face) This is concave in shape that lies towards the nucleus and is responsible for releasing the material, which is being secreted by *cis* face and modified in the cisternae.

Knowledge Plus

- Although, the *cis* and the *trans* faces of the organelle are entirely different in origin, but they inter connect each other.
- Proteins that are synthesised by ribosomes on ER are first modified in cisternae before they released from its *trans* face.

The Golgi apparatus acts as a site where the material to be released is being packaged in the form of vesicles delivered either to the intracellular targets or secreted outside the cell.

Functions

Golgi apparatus performs the following functions

(i) The Golgi apparatus is involved in the formation of lysosomes, vesicles that contain proteins and remains within the cell.

(ii) It performs the function of packaging material.

(iii) It acts as an important site for the formation of glycoproteins and glycolipids.

(iv) It helps in the production of complex carbohydrates other than glycogen and starch.

(v) It helps in the formation of cell wall.

3. Lysosomes

These are membrane bound vesicles that are produced by the **Golgi apparatus.** They are rich in several hydrolytic digestive enzymes (hydrolases-lipases, proteases, carbohy-drases, etc). As these are optimally active at the acidic pH (less than 7). Therefore, are also called **acid hydrolases** and are capable of digesting macromolecules from various sources like carbohydrates, lipids and nucleic acids.

Functions

Lysosomes performs the following functions

(i) They digest the food contents (intracellular digestion).

(ii) They also perform extracellular digestion.

(iii) They also digest the old and useless organelles of the cells.

(iv) They also have functioning in cell division.

Note

- These are called **suicidal bags** due to the presence of hydrolytic enzymes.
- **C de Duve** observed the rounded bodies in liver cells and called them **pericanalicular dense bodies** (1949).

4. Vacuoles

These are large membranous sacs found in the cytoplasm. These store substances that are not essentially useful for the cell (like water, sap, excretory product and other materials).

Plant vacuoles contain not only water, sugars and salts, but also contain pigments and toxic molecules and also occupy upto 90% of the volume of the cell. The vacuole is bounded by a single membrane structure known as **tonoplast** which in plant cells, facilitates the transport of materials and some ions against the concentration gradient inside the vacuole.

Thus, the concentration of materials tend to be the higher in vacuole, than to be in the cytoplasm. Animal cells also have vacuole, but they are much more prominent in case of plant cells. Thus, plant cells have typically large central vacuole filled with a watery fluid that gives added support to the cell.

Following types of vacuoles are being found in different organisms

(i) **Contractile Vacuoles** They play an important part in osmoregulation and excretion in *Amoeba*, etc. It occurs mostly in protistan and algal cells that are found mainly in water.

(ii) **Food Vacuoles** They occur in the cells of mainly protozoan protists. These are formed by engulfing the food particles, i.e. by the fusion of lysosome and phagosome. The digested material thus, passes out into the surrounding cytoplasm.

Functions

Vacuoles performs the following functions

(i) Storage of various substances including waste products.

(ii) Important contribution to the osmotic properties of the cell

(iii) Sometimes function as lysosomes.

Ribosomes

These are the small subspherical granular organelles, not bounded by any membrane. Ribosomes were first observed by **George Palade** (1953), as the dense particles under the electron microscope. Hence, are also called **Palade** particles.

Ribosomes are mainly composed of ribonucleoproteins (i.e. RNA + proteins) and are also known as **protein factories**, as they are primarily involved in the synthesis of proteins or polypeptides.

As studied earlier, the prokaryotic ribosomes are 70S type, while the eukaryotic ribosomes are 80S type. Here, 'S' (Svedberg's unit) stands for sedimentation coefficient (measure of density and size). Both 70S and 80S ribosomes contain two subunits, i.e. the smaller and the larger subunit.

Differences between 70S and 80S Ribosomes

70S Ribosomes	80S Ribosomes
They are found in prokaryotes (bacteria, cyanobacteria and viruses).	They are found in eukaryotes (algae, fungi, higher plants and animals).
Larger subunit (50S)	Larger subunit (60S)
Small subunit (30S)	Smaller subunit (40S)
Comparatively smaller	Larger than 70S
Synthesised in cytoplasm	Synthesised inside the nucleolus
RNA: Protein = 60:40	RNA: Protein = 50:50

Functions

The ribosomes are the **protein factories** of the cell. The proteins formed through the membrane bound ribosomes are secreted proteins, integral membrane proteins and lysosomal proteins while free ribosomes synthesise soluble cytoplasmic proteins, peripheral membrane proteins, mitochondrial proteins, chloroplast proteins, peroxisomal and nuclear proteins.

Microbodies

These are the single membrane bound cytoplasmic elements that are composed of enzymes and other substances. These are minute vesicles found in both plant cells and animal cells, e.g. in the liver, kidney, protozoan, yeast and many other types of cells. Their shape can be ovoid, spherical, granular, etc.

Glyoxysomes These are microbodies usually found in fat rich plants. These were first reparted by Beevers in 1969 from the endosperm of germinating seeds.

Peroxisomes These are small, round to oval bodies discovered by Tolbert and Yamazerki in 1969 in liver cells. These organelles are named sebaceous these are the sites of H_2O_2 formed by a number of enzymes, e.g. glycolate oxidase.

Sphaerosomes These microbodies were discovered by Hanstein in 1880 who called them microsomes. The term sphaerosomes was given later in 1919 by Dangeard.

Note Peroxisomes and glyoxysomes are the types of microbodies being found in plant cell and animal cell, respectively.

Cytoskeleton

The network of interconnected proteinaceous filaments and tubules, which extends from the nucleus to the plasma membrane in eukaryotic cells.

It consists of following different types of elements

(i) **Microtubules** These are hollow and unbranched cylinders. They are about 25 nm in size. Microtubules are made up of 13 parallel protofilaments of tubulin proteins. These are the constituents of spindle fibres, centrioles, cilia and flagella.

(ii) **Microfilaments** These are solid, unbranched, rod-like fibres. They are about 7 nm in size. Microfilaments consist of actin and some amount of myosin protein.

(iii) **Intermediate Filaments** They are filaments of intermediate size, i.e. 10 nm. These are composed of acidic proteins.

Differences between Microfilaments and Microtubule

Microfilaments	Microtubule
Contain solid protein actin which is assembled at one end and disassembled at the other.	Contain a globular protein, tubulin which make up hollow tubes.
Brings about directed movement of particles and organelles.	Maintain cells shape, allow movement of organelles.
Cause cleavage of animal cell.	Form spindle.
Support fluid matrix.	Serve as track for motor proteins such as kinesin.

Functions

Cytoskeleton performs the following functions

(i) The cytoskeletal structure maintains the shape of the cell and its extensions.

(ii) It is also involved in many functions in a cell as mechanical support, motility, etc.

Cilia and Flagella

These are hair-like projections of cell membrane. Both cilia and flagella are almost identical in structure, but differ somewhat in length. As **cilia** are small structures, working as oars (causing the movement of either the cell or the surrounding fluid), while **flagella** are comparatively longer in size than cilia and are responsible for the movement of cell. Flagella are also present in prokaryotic bacteria, but these are structurally different from that of eukaryotic flagella.

According to the electron microscopic studies it is predicted that the cilium or the flagellum are covered with plasma membrane. Their core called the **axoneme**, contains a number of microtubules, running parallel to the long axis. Usually, the axoneme has nine pairs of doublets of peripheral microtubules that are radially arranged and a pair of centrally located microtubules. This arrangement of axonemal microtubules is referred to as the **(9 + 2) array.**

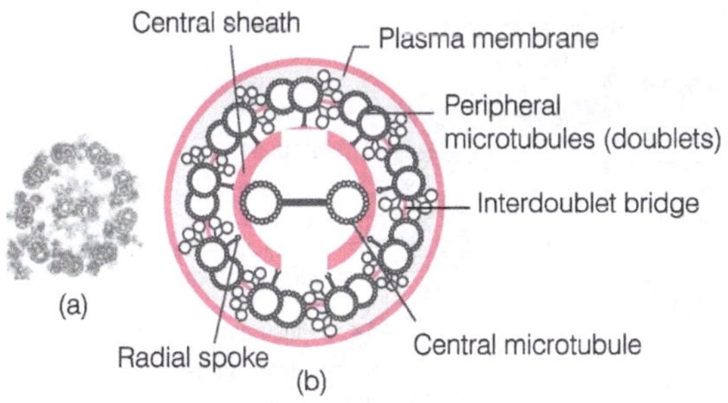

Fig 11.16 Section of cilia/flagella showing different parts (a) Electron micrograph, (b) Diagram representation of internal structure

The central tubules are connected by bridges and is also enclosed by a **central sheath**, which is connected to one of the tubules of each peripheral doublets by a **radial spoke.** Thus, it has been estimated that there are nine radial spokes.

The peripheral doublets are also interconnected by **linkers.** Both the cilium and flagellum emerge from centriole-like structure called the **basal bodies.**

Differences between Cilia and Flagella

Cilia	Flagella
Cilia are short, hair-like organelles, 2-20 μm in length.	Flagella are long, whip-like organelles that may be 10-200 μm long.
They occur relatively in large numbers per cell.	They are usually fewer per cell.
They often cover the entire cell or the entire exposed surface of a cell.	They are often at one end of a cell.
They show sweeping or rowing motion.	They show undulatory motion.

Centrosomes and Centrioles

Centrosome is an organelle that generally have two cylindrical structures known as **centrioles.** They are basically surrounded by an amorphous pericentriolar materials.

Both the centrioles in a centrosome lie perpendicular to each other in which each has an organisation like the cartwheel and together they are called diplosomes.

They are usually made up of nine evenly spaced **peripheral fibrils** (triplet in nature) of tubulin protein. Fibrils are absent in the centre. The arrangement is, therefore, called 9 + 0. Fibrils run parallel to one another but at an angle of 40°. Each fibril is made up of three sub-fibres.

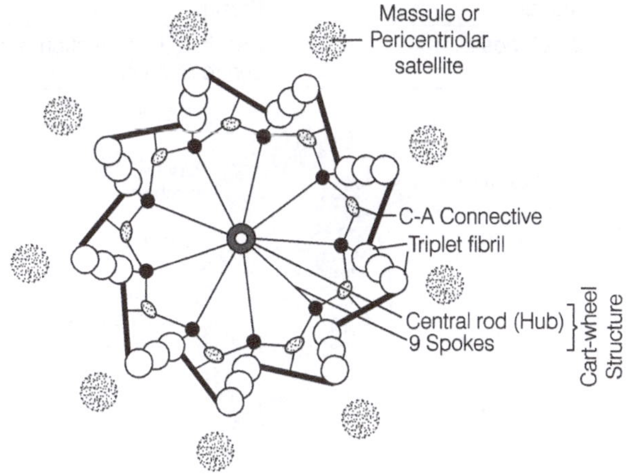

Fig 11.17 Ultrastructure of centriole as seen in TS

Each sub-fibre has a diameter of 25 nm. From outside to inside, the three sub-fibres of a triplet fibrils are named as *C*, *B* and *A*.

Sub-fibre *A* is complete with 13 protofilaments while *B* and *C* sub-fibres are incomplete due to sharing of some microfilaments.

The centre part of the proximal region of the centriole posseses rod-shaped proteinaceous mass known as hub, which is connected with tubules of the peripheral triplets fibrils known as **radial spokes** (made up of protein).

From the basal body of cilia or flagella the centrioles and spindle fibres give rise to spindle apparatus during cell division in animal cells.

Functions

Centrosomes and centrioles perform the following functions

(i) These form spindle fibres and move to the poles, at the time of cell division, which thus help in the movement of chromatids in daughter cells.

(ii) Help in the formation of cilia and flagella of the cells.

Differences between Plant and Animal Cell

Characters	Animal Cells	Plant Cells
Cell wall	Absent	Present (formed of cellulose)
Shape	Round (irregular shape)	Rectangular (fixed shape)
Centrioles	Present in all animal cells.	Only present in lower plant forms.
Vacuole	One or more small vacuoles (much smaller than plant cells).	One, large central vacuole taking up 90% of cell volume.
Cytoplasm	Present	Present
Ribosomes	Present	Present
Plastids	Absent	Present
Plasma membrane	Only cell membrane	Cell wall and a cell membrane.
Golgi apparatus	Present	Present
Mitochondria	Present	Present
Endoplasmic reticulum (smooth and rough)	Present	Present
Chloroplast	Animal cells do not have chloroplasts because they do not have the ability to prepare their food.	Plant cells have chloroplasts because they make their own food (autotrophs).
Flagella	May be found in some cells.	May be found in some cells.
Microtubules	Present	Present
Microfilaments	Present	Present
Cilia	Present	It is very rare
Lysosomes	Lysosomes occur in cytoplasm.	Lysosomes are usually not evident.
Nucleus	Present	Present
Cytokinesis	Result in the formation of a furrow in the centre of a cell.	Occurs due to the formation of a cell plate.

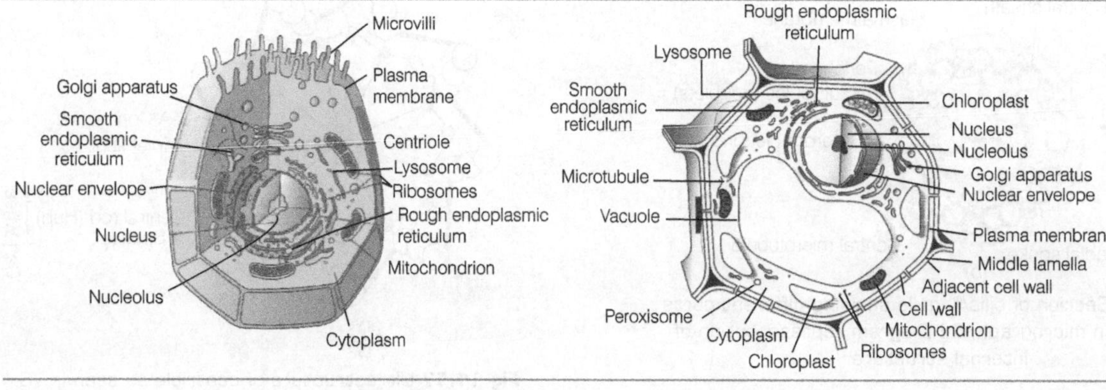

Differences between Prokaryotic and Eukaryotic Cells

Prokaryotic Cell	Eukaryotic Cell
The cell size is usually small (0.1 - 5.0 μm) in diameter.	The cell size is comparatively larger (10-100 μm) in diameter.
An organised nucleus is absent, instead a nucleoid is found.	An organised nucleus is found. It is differentiated into nuclear envelope, chromatin, one or more nucleoli and nucleoplasm.
DNA is naked or without an association with histones. DNA is usually circular.	Nuclear DNA is associated with histone proteins. Nuclear DNA is linear while extranuclear DNA is circular.
DNA lies freely in the cytoplasm. It is not associated with any organelle.	Most of the cell DNA lies in the nucleus. A small quantity is also found in the plastids and mitochondria.
Additional small circular DNA segments or plasmids may occur.	Plasmids are usually absent.
ER, mitochondria, Golgi apparatus, lysosomes and centrioles (centrosome, central apparatus) are absent.	ER, mitochondria, Golgi apparatus and lysosomes or their equivalents are present in all the eukaryotic cells. Centrioles are usually present in animal cells.
Cell wall contains muramic acid.	Cell wall, if present, does not contain muramic acid.
Cell membrane may be infolded to form a complex structure called **mesosome**.	Mesosome like structures are absent.
Ribosomes are of 70S type.	Ribosomes are of 80S type. 70S ribosomes, however occur in plastids and mitochondria.
Transcription occurs in the cytoplasm.	Transcription occurs in the nucleus.
The flagella are single-stranded and without differentiation of axoneme and sheath.	The flagella, if present are 11-stranded, (9 + 2 arrangement). They show differentiation of axoneme and sheath.

Topic Practice 2

Multiple Choice Questions

(1 Mark)

1. Which of the following differentiate plant cells from animal cells ?
   (a) Large vacuole, plastid and cell wall
   (b) Cell wall, plastid and centriole
   (c) Cell wall, plastid and mitochondria
   (d) Cell membrane, plastid and cell wall

Ans (a) All eukaryotic cells are not identical. Plant and animal cells are different as plant cells possess cell wall, plastids and a large vacuole, which are absent in animal cells. On the other hand, animal cells have centrioles, which are absent in almost all plant cells.

2. Lipids are arranged within the membrane with
   (a) polar heads towards innerside and the hydrophobic tails towards outerside
   (b) Both heads and tails towards outerside
   (c) heads towards outerside and tail towards inside
   (d) Both heads and tails towards innerside

Ans (c) The lipids are arranged within the membrane with the polar head towards the outerside and the hydrophobic tails towards the inner part.

3. Which of the following statement is incorrect about the plasma membrane?
   (a) The ratio of proteins and lipid varies considerably in different cell types
   (b) 52% protein and 40% lipids are in the membrane of human RBC
   (c) Integral proteins are found on the intracellular surface of cell membrane
   (d) Head of lipid is hydrophilic

Ans (c) Depending on the ease of extraction, membrane proteins can be classified as integral or peripheral. Peripheral proteins lie on the surface of membrane while the integral proteins are partially or totally buried in the membrane.

4. Which of the following statement is not true for plasma membrane? **NCERT Exemplar**
   (a) It is present in both plant and animal cell
   (b) Lipid is present as a bilayer in it
   (c) Proteins are present integrated as well as loosely associated with the lipid bilayer
   (d) Carbohydrate is never found in it

Ans (d) **Statement is false.**
The biochemical investigation done on cell membrane clearly demonstrate that the cell membrane possess protein and carbohydrates as biochemical components.

5. Cell membrane is selectively permeable. This means that it
   (a) allows all materials to pass through
   (b) allows only water to pass through
   (c) allows only certain materials to pass through
   (d) allows only ions to pass through

Ans (c) One of the most important functions of the plasma membrane is the transport of the molecules across it. The membrane is selectively permeable to some molecules present on either sides of it.

6. Choose the incorrect statement regarding cell membrane.
   (a) Generally smaller molecules pass easily without energy requirement by passive transport
   (b) Water soluble substances pass through it less rapidly than lipid soluble substances
   (c) Neutral solutes move across it by simple diffusion
   (d) None of the above

Ans (d) Many molecules can move across the membrane without any requirement of energy and this is called the passive transport.

Neutral solutes may move across the membrane by the process of simple diffusion along the concentration gradient, i.e. from higher concentration to the lower. Water may also move across this membrane from higher to lower concentration.

7. Which one is false about osmosis ?

(a) It is a specific form of diffusion
(b) It refers to the movement of water along its concentration gradient
(c) It is a passive movement of water
(d) It occurs through a carrier protein and needs ATP

Ans (d) Movement of water by diffusion is called osmosis. As the polar molecules cannot pass through the non-polar lipid bilayer, they require a carrier protein of the membrane to facilitate their transport across the membrane.

8. Na^+/K^+ pump represents

(a) active transport (b) passive transport
(c) osmosis (d) simple diffusion

Ans (a) Few ions or molecules are transported across the membrane against their concentration gradient, i.e. from lower to the higher concentration.

This is an energy dependent process, in which ATP is utilised and is called active transport, e.g. Na^+/K^+ pump.

9. Plastid differs from mitochondria on the basis of one of the following features. Mark the right answer. **NCERT Exemplar**

(a) Presence of two layers of membrane
(b) Presence of ribosome
(c) Presence of thylakoids
(d) Presence of DNA

Ans (c) Presence of thylakoids, the structural elements of chloroplast, differs then (plastids) from mitochondria. Thylakoids are flattened sacs stocked one above the other to form grana. They help in photosynthesis Rest of the features mentioned are common to both plastids and mitochondria.

10. Important site for the formation of glycoprotein and glycolipid is

(a) lysosomes
(b) Golgi apparatus
(c) vacuoles
(d) plastids

Ans (b) Golgi apparatus is primarily involved in protein trafficking. It packages materials and delivers it to various cell targets. It is also involved in the glycosylation of proteins and lipids.

11. Which of these is not a function of Golgi apparatus?

(a) Material packaging
(b) Secretion
(c) Membrane transformation
(d) Site of protein synthesis

Ans (d) A number of proteins synthesised by ribosomes on the endoplasmic reticulum are modified in the cisternae of the Golgi apparatus before they are released from its *trans* face.

12. Which one of the following cell organelles is enclosed by a single membrane?

(a) Chloroplasts (b) Lysosomes
(c) Nuclei (d) Mitochondria

Ans (b) Lysosomes are enclosed by a single membrane and store the hydrolysing enzymes of the cell.

13. Which of the following is not a function of cytoskeleton in a cell? **NCERT Exemplar**

(a) Intracellular transport
(b) Maintenance of cell shape and structure
(c) Support of the organelle
(d) Cell motility

Ans (a) Cytoskeleton is not associated with the intracellular transport. The microtubules and microfilaments, are the components of cytoskeleton and are responsible for cellular and intercellular movements Rest of the options are functions of cytoskeleton is a cell.

Very Short Answer Type Questions

1 Mark

14. Which layer is referred to as cementing layer and why?

Ans Middle lamellae is referred to as cementing layer because it holds the primary cell wall of adjacent cells together.

15. Where are extrinsic proteins found in the cell membrane?

Ans On the outer and inner surface of phospholipid matrix.

16. In which organelle the proteins required for functioning of nucleus are formed?

Ans Proteins required are formed in cytoplasm.

17. Name two type of cells which lack nucleus.

Ans RBCs of humans and sieve cells of vascular plants.

18. What is the feature of metacentric chromosome? **NCERT Exemplar**

Ans The metacentric chromosome has the centromere near the centre forming two equal arms and thus, appears V-shaped.

19. What is referred to as satellite chromosome? **NCERT Exemplar**

Ans Sometimes, few chromosomes have non-staining secondary constrictions at a constant location. This gives appearance of a small fragment called satellite. The chromosome having satellite are known as satellite chromosomes.

20. What is the major difference between leucoplasts and chromoplasts?

Ans Leucoplasts are colourless plastids while, chromoplast are coloured plastids.

21. Why are the mitochondria and plastids called semi-autonomous particles?

Ans These are called so, because they are not dependent upon nuclear DNA and cytoplasmic ribosomes for the synthesis of proteins, while other organelles are dependent.

22. Match the following columns.

	Column I		Column II
A.	Cristae	1.	Fat membranous sacs in stroma.
B.	Cisternae	2.	Infoldings in mitochondria.
C.	Thylakoids	3.	Disc-shaped sacs in Golgi apparatus.

Ans A-2, B-3, C-1

23. Which pigment is mainly responsible for the colour of the carrot? **NCERT**

Ans Carotene pigment is responsible for the colour of the carrot.

24. What is the term given to the 70S ribosomes found in the matrix of chloroplast?

Ans The term given is plastido ribosomes.

25. Which type of endoplasmic reticulum has its main functioning in the synthesis of lipid?

Ans Smooth Endoplasmic Reticulum (SER), helps in synthesis of lipid.

26. Which cells have well-developed SER and which cell contain abundant RER?

Ans Muscle cells have a well-developed SER and cells which synthesise proteins, i.e. liver and pancreatic cell has abundant RER.

27. What is the significance of vacuole in a plant cell? **NCERT Exemplar**

Ans The vacuole in a plant cell helps to maintain osmotic pressure for turgidity and osmosis. It also stores useful as well as waste substances.

28. Why mitochondrion and chloroplast are not considered in the endomembrane system?

Ans They are not considered in the endomembrane system as their functions are not coordinated by other components of the cells as ER, lysosomes, Golgi complex, etc.

29. Mention a single membrane bound organelle, which is rich in hydrolytic enzymes. **NCERT Exemplar**

Ans Lysosome.

30. What does 'S' refers in a 70S and 80S ribosome? **NCERT Exemplar**

Ans. The 'S' refers to Svedberg units of sedimentation coefficient. The sedimentation coefficient is a measure of the speed of the sedimentation for a particular cell organelle in ultracentrifuge.

31. What do you meant by 9 +2 pattern of organisation?

Ans It means that 9 microtubule doublets surround two single microtubules.

Short Answer Type I Questions

(2 Marks)

32. What are the disadvantages of multicellularity?

Ans The disadvantages of multicellularity are (any two)

(i) Specialised cells often loose the power of division, so that injury is not repaired, e.g. nerve cells.

(ii) Regeneration ability of multicellular organisms decrease with specialisation.

(iii) Specialised cells may loose vital functions in order to carry out specific activity, e.g. RBCs, sieve tube cells. (2)

33. Multicellular organisms have division of labour. Explain. **NCERT Exemplar**

Ans The body of a multicellular organism has cell as a basic structural unit. The cells are organised to form tissues such as blood, bone, etc. The tissues are organised to form organs such as heart, kidney, etc.

The organs are then organised to form organ systems such as digestive system, reproductive system, respiratory system, etc. The various organ systems of organism get arranged to form a complete individual. (2)

34. What is the benefit of cell wall in plant cells?

Ans Cell wall is stronger and less impervious than plasma membrane. It tends to provide greater mechanical strength to plants. Since, plants have to withstand vagaries of nature and they cannot run for safety, so they need a stronger structure.

Cell wall also prevents entry of undesirable matters in cell and facilitates exchange of materials among cells. (2)

35. How do neutral solutes move across the plasma membrane? Can the polar molecules also move across it in the same way? If not, then how are these transported across the membrane? NCERT

Ans Neutral solutes may move across the membrane by the process of simple diffusion along the concentration gradient.

The polar molecules cannot pass through the non-polar lipid bilayer, they require a carrier protein to facilitate their transport across the membrane. A few ions or molecules are transported across the membrane against their concentration gradient, i.e. from lower to the higher concentration.

Such a transport is an energy dependent process, in which ATP is utilised and is called active transport, e.g. Na^+/K^+pump. (2)

36. Differentiate between active and passive transport.

Ans Refer to text on page no. 228.

37. Draw a neat diagram of mitochondria and label all the parts.

Ans Refer to fig no. 11.9.

38. Describe in brief the structure of brain of cell.

Ans Refer to text on page no. 229 and 230.

39. What are histones? What are their functions? NCERT Exemplar

Ans Histones are basic proteins, which are soluble in water or dilute acids but are insoluble in dilute ammonia (NH_3). They are rich in basic amino acids like histidine and arginine.

Histones are readily hydrolysed by trypsin and pepsin and are considered as 'gene repressors'. The histone proteins are not coagulated by heat and are also found to be associated with DNA of nucleus forming the chromatin material. (1+1)

40. What is the difference between animal and bacterial cells with respect to the presence of nucleus?

Ans Animal cells have an interior membrane that delimits a cell nucleus thus, they are eukaryotic cells. In these cells, the genetic material is located within the nucleus whereas, the bacterial cells do not have an organised cellular nuclei so, are called prokaryotic cells. Their genetic material is found freely dispersed in the cytosol of the cell. (2)

41. Differentiate between Rough Endoplasmic Reticulum (RER) and Smooth Endoplasmic Reticulum (SER). NCERT Exemplar

Ans Refer to text page no. 232.

42. Which cell organelles are referred to as suicidal bags? Why are they given this name?

Ans Lysosomes are the organelle known as suicidal bags. They consist of a single membrane surrounding powerful digestive enzymes. If the membrane of a lysosome breaks, the enzymes released may also destroy the cell itself, giving lysosomes the name suicidal bags. (2)

43. On which organelle of the cell structure does intracellular digestion depend? What is the chemical content of those organelles?

Ans Intracellular digestion takes place by the action of lysosomes. The lysosomes possess the digestive enzymes (hydrolases) which are produced in the rough endoplasmic reticulum and stored in the Golgi apparatus. (2)

44. Which four different sites in plant cells have ribosomes?

Ans Ribosomes are found in plant cell at following different sites

(i) Freely in the cytoplasm

(ii) Attached to ER in the cytoplasm.

(iii) Inside mitochondria.

(iv) Inside plastids (chloroplasts). (½ × 4)

45. How do the ribosomes of prokaryotic cells differ from the ribosomes of eukaryotic cells? Also tell what is similar about them?

Ans Ribosomes in the cytoplasm of prokaryotic and eukaryotic cells slightly differ. Prokaryotes have 70S ribosomes, each consisting of a (small) 30S and a (large) 50S subunit whereas eukaryotes have 80S ribosomes, each consisting of (small) 40S and a bound (large) 60S subunit.

Both prokaryotic and eukaryotic ribosomes are composed of ribosomal RNA and ribosomal proteins. Their basic functioning is protein synthesis. (1+1)

46. Describe the differences between cilia and flagella. (any four)

Ans Refer to text on page no. 235.

47. Mention two functions of the centrioles.

Ans Functions of centrioles are

(i) The centrioles play a vital role in cell division by forming spindle fibres, which act as guides for the alignment of the chromosomes as they separate later during the process of cell division.

(ii) The centrioles are also responsible for formation of basal bodies, cilia and flagella. (1×2)

48. What are the facts which prove that all cells are autonomous?

Ans All cells are autonomous because of the following facts

(i) Each and every cell converts non-living materials into components of living matter.

(ii) Each cell builds up its own macromolecules from micromolecules.

(iii) All cells obtain or manufacture food.

(iv) A cell always builds up new structure to replace the worn out ones. (½ × 4)

49. Differentiate between animal cell and plant cell.

Ans Differences between animal cell and plant cell are as fallows

Animal Cell	Plant Cell
Cell wall absent	Cell wall present
Chloroplast absent	Chloroplast present in green parts
Centriole present	Centriole absent
Vacuoles are smaller	Comparatively vacuoles are larger

(½ × 4)

Short Answer Type II Questions

(3 Marks)

50. Differentiate between primary cell wall and secondary cell wall (any three).

Ans Refer to text on page no. 226.

51. Give the biochemical composition of plasma membrane. How are lipid molecules arranged in the membrane? **NCERT Exemplar**

Ans Chemically the plasma membrane consists of proteins (20-70%), lipids (20-79%), carbohydrates (1-5%) and water (20%). Nucleic acids (DNA and RNA) are absent in the plasma membrane. The lipids present in the plasma membrane are phospholipids, glycolipids (sugar lipids) and sterols. (1½)

Each lipid molecule consists of a three carbon glycerol poles (head) which is hydrophilic (water loving) in nature and two long tails of fatty acids which are hydrophobic (water-fearing) in nature.

The hydrophilic glycerol poles of lipids are located towards the outside of the lipid bilayer whereas, the hydrophobic fatty acid tails are repelled by water and face towards the inner side of the membrane.

The hydrophilic and hydrophobic forces in lipid molecules cause the membrane to become a bilayer. (1½)

52. The diagram shows a section of cell membrane. Identify the components labelled *A–F*

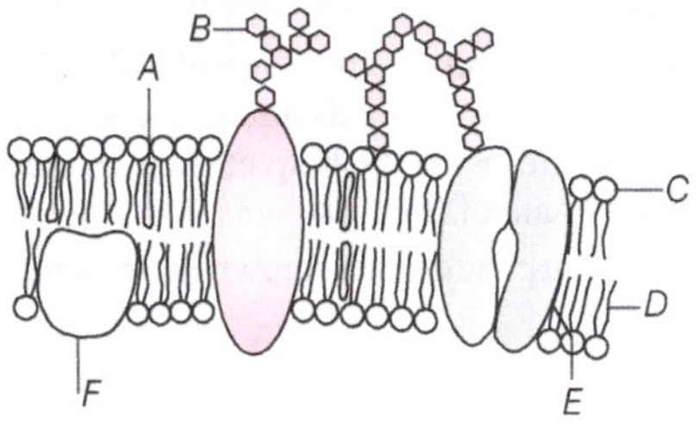

Ans Following are the labelled sections of cell membrane

A – Cholesterol, *B* – Glycolipid

C – Hydrophilic head of phospholipid

D – Hydrophobic tail of phospholipid

E – Transmembrane protein

F – Intrinsic protein (1/2×6)

53. Explain the association of carbohydrate to the plasma membrane and its significance.

Ans The plasma membrane also known as cell membrane, which surrounds the cell. It consists of lipids, proteins and carbohydrates that are imperative in both structure and function of the cell.

Sugar residues or carbohydrates attaches either with proteins or lipids, usually making up less than 10% of the membrane weight. They can give rise to a wide variety of structures in relatively short chains.

They give individual cell types a distinguishing features. Therefore, they may be involved in.

Cell Recognition, e.g. surface of RBC have carbohydrates arranged in branched chains differences in the arrangement give rise to different blood group antigens (i.e. AB and O).

Cell surface differences are also responsible for the specificity of action of cells with hormones, drugs, viruses or bacteria. The cause of cell surface differences is related to characteristic surface due to carbohydrate component. (3)

54. Distinguish between cell membrane and cell wall.

Ans Differences between cell membrane and cell wall are

Cell Membrane	Cell Wall
It is found in both prokaryotes and eukaryotes.	It is found in only plant cells as well as bacteria, fungi, algae and some archaea, i.e. absent in animal cells and protozoans.
Its function is to separate the components inside the cell from outside.	Its function is to provide barrier to undesirable substance and attack of pathogen.
It provides support to the cytoskeleton of the cell, give shape to the cell.	It provides strength and rigidity to the cell.

(1×3)

55. What are mitochondria? What is the basic morphology of these organelles and in which cell can they be found?

Ans Mitochondria are the organelles in which the most important part of the cellular respiration occurs, i.e. the ATP production.

Mitochondria are organelles bounded by two lipid membranes. The inner membrane is infolded to the interior of the organelle forming cristae that defines the internal space known as mitochondrial matrix and where mitochondrial DNA (*mt*DNA), mitochondrial RNA (*mt*RNA), mitochondrial ribosomes and respiratory enzymes can be found.

Mitochondria are found in eukaryotic cells in high number and are also more abundant in those cells that use more energy, like muscle cells. Because mitochondrion have their own DNA, RNA and ribosomes. They can even has the ability to self-replicate. (1+2)

56. Fill in the blanks at *A*, *B* and *C* as shown in diagram

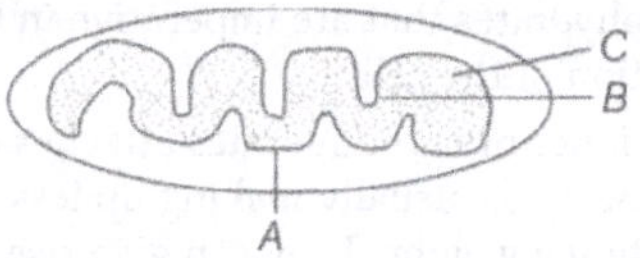

Ans *A* – Inner membrane, *B* – Crista, *C* – Matrix. (1×3)

57. State the chief functions of mitochondria.

Ans Mitochondria perform the following major functions

(i) Mitochondria are the main site of aerobic respiration, where respiratory substrates are completely oxidised to carbon dioxide and water. The energy liberated in the process is utilised in the synthesis of energy rich molecules ATP.

(ii) They have a group of enzymes that carry out elongation of fatty acids by adding acetyl Co-A and subsequently reducing the keto-acid produced.

(iii) The matrix of mitochondria has enzymes for the synthesis of fatty acids. (1×3)

58. Justify the statement, 'Mitochondria is the powerhouse of the cell'. **NCERT Exemplar**

Ans Mitochondria are known as powerhouse of the cell because they generate ATP, the energy currency of the cell. Terminal oxidation takes place through oxidative phosphorylation.

This produces ATP. Even the reduced coenzymes produced in cytosol through glycolysis, transfer their reducing power to mitochondria for ATP synthesis. ATP synthesised inside mitochondria provides energy for all cellular activities including over coming tendencey for entropy. Hence, known as power house of the cell. (3)

59. The genomic content of the nucleus is constant for a given species whereas, the extra chromosomal DNA is found to be variable among the members of a population. Explain. **NCERT Exemplar**

Ans The DNA content of the nucleus is constant for a given species. The haploid organisms have half the content of DNA than that of their diploid parents. The amount of DNA remains constant in all the members of a given species.

On the other hand, the extrachomosomal DNA which occur either in the mitochondria or in chloroplast is found to be variable among the members of a population. In case of highly active organisms, the DNA (extrachromosomal) is found to be more as compared to less active ones. (3)

60. Discuss briefly the role of nucleolus in the cells actively involved in protein synthesis.

Ans **Nucleolus** is the round, naked and a slightly irregular structure, which is attached to the chromatin at a specific region called as **Nucleolar Organizer Region** (NOR).

Nucleolus was first discovered by **Fontana** (1781).

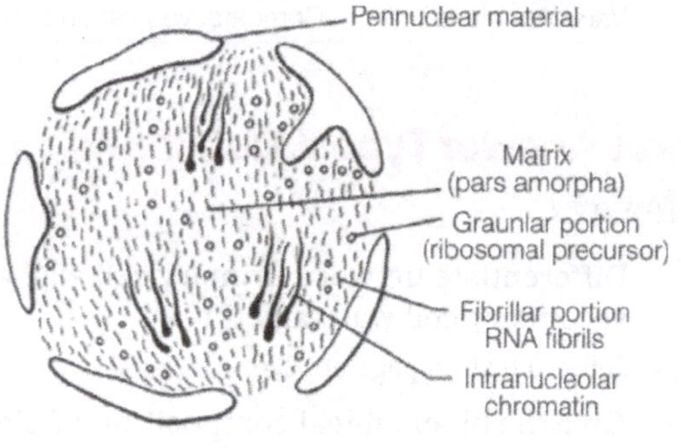

Ultrastructure of nucleolus

(i) Nucleolus is the chief site for the ribosomal RNA synthesis.

(ii) It is the centre for formation of ribosome components.

(iii) It is the colloidal complex that fills the nucleus.

(iv) It combines *r*RNA with proteins to produce ribosomal sub-units. After their formation, the ribosomes sub-units pass out and get established in the cytoplasm.

(v) It also receive and store ribosomal proteins formed in the cytoplasm.

(vi) These ribosomal proteins formed are the sites for protein synthesis in the cell.

(vii) Nucleolus is essential for spindle formation during nuclear division. (3)

61. Is extra genomic DNA present in prokaryotes and eukaryotes? If yes, locate their position in both types of organisms. **NCERT Exemplar**

Ans Yes, extra genomic DNA is present in both prokaryotes and eukaryotes.

In case of eukaryotes, extra genomic DNA is present in two organelles, e.g. plastids and mitochondria. Both these organelles with the help of their own DNA, synthesise some of their proteins.

Thus, these organelles are known as semiautonomous organelles.

In case of prokaryotic cells, the extragenomic DNA is present in the form of plasmids. The plasmids are circular DNA molecules, which confer certain unique phenotypic characters to such bacteria. One such character is resistance to bacteria. This plasmid DNA is also used to monitor bacteria transformation with foreign DNA. (1+2)

62. Distinguish between chloroplast and chromoplast (any three).

Ans Differences between chloroplast and chromoplast are

Chloroplasts	Chromoplasts
They contain mainly chlorophylls and some amount of carotene and xanthophyll.	They contain mainly carotene and xanthophyll.
They are present in the mesophyll of leaves.	They are present in the petals of flowers, skin of fruits, etc.
Their main role is to prepare food by the process of photosynthesis.	Their main role is to impart colouration to plants.

(1×3)

63. Give a brief account on leucoplasts.

Ans Refer to text on page no. 231.

64. Are the different types of plastids interchangeable? If yes, give examples where they are getting converted from one type to another. **NCERT Exemplar**

Ans The different types of plastids leucoplasts (colourless), chromoplasts (coloured), chloroplasts (green coloured) such as are interchangeable.

The transformation from chloroplasts is observed during ripening of fruits (e.g. tomato, chilli) when they change their colour from green to reddish orange. It takes place through loss of chlorophylls and degeneration of lamellae.

The most common carotenoid of the fruit is lycopene. Petals of *Calendula* develop orange yellow colour due to the formation of chromoplasts from proplastids. Carrot root develops it characteristic colour because of the conversion of leucoplasts into chromoplasts. It is rich in carotene. (3)

65. The lysosomal enzyme does not destroy the cell's own cytoplasm. Why?

Ans The lysosomal enzyme does not destroy its own cytoplasm, because of the following reasons

(i) The enzymes are separated from the cytoplasm by the lysosomal membrane.

(ii) The enzymes have the capability of recognising and digest only foreign matter.

(iii) The lysosomal enzymes usually works in acidic medium of pH less than 7 and the medium is more than 7, i.e. around 7.4 or more. (1×3)

66. Give differences between 70S and 80S ribosomes.

Ans Refer to text on page no. 234.

67. What do you mean by (9+2) array? Describe it with reference to cilia and flagella.

Ans Refer to text on page no. 235 and 236.

68. Comment on the cartwheel structure of centriole.

Ans Refer to text on page no. 235 and 236.

69. Eukaryotic cells have organelles which may **NCERT Exemplar**

(i) not be bounded by a membrane.

(ii) be bounded by a single membrane.

(iii) be bounded by a double membrane.

Group the various sub-cellular organelles into these categories.

Ans (i) Ribosomes are membraneless organelle.

(ii) Lysosomes are single membrane bounded organelle. Sphaerosomes and microbodies are also have single membranes.

(iii) Mitochondria and plastids are double membrane bounded organelles. (1×3)

Long Answer Type Questions

5 Marks

70. Structure and function are correlatable in living organisms. Can you justify this by taking plasma membrane as an example?

Ans In animals and plants, plasma membrane structure and function are correlated. A cell membrane consists of protein, lipid and carbohydrates.

The protein component present in membrane acts as a solute channels allowing the flow of minerals, hormones and cellular information from one organelle to another or from one cell to another. In case of plants where minerals are absorbed actively from the soil. The plasma membrane possess proteinaceous carrier.

The oligosaccharides attached to membrane serve as recognition centres and help in recognising foreign entities before allowing them entry into the cell.

The lipid content of plasma membrane in plant and animal cells are arranged with their hydrophilic polar head directed outwards and non-polar hydrophobic tails directed inwards providing fluidity to the membrane. Glycocalyx present in cell membrane also helps in cellular attachment. (5)

71. Name two cell organelles that are double membrane bound. What are the characteristics of these two organelles? State their functions and draw labelled diagrams of both. **NCERT**

Ans Refer to text 'Nucleus and Plastid' on page no. 229-231.

72. Describe the structure of the following with the help of labelled diagram **NCERT**

(i) Nucleus (ii) Centrosome

Ans (i) Refer to text on page no. 229 and 230.

(ii)

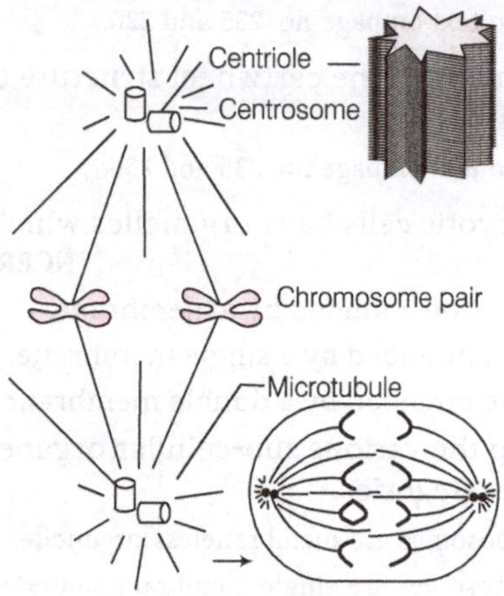

Structure of centrosome

73. What is a centromere? How does the position of the centromere form the basis of classification of chromosomes? Support your answer with a diagram showing the position of centromere on different types of chromosomes. **NCERT**

Ans Centromere is a narrow non-stainable area, which join two similar threads or chromatids of a late prophase or metaphase chromosome.

The two parts of the chromosome on either side of the centromere are known as arm.

They may be **isobranchial** (equal) or **heterobranchial** (unequal in length).

Depending upon the position of the centromere, the chromosomes are classified as follows

Refer to text on page no. 235-236.

Depending upon the number of centromeres a chromosome possess, it may be monocentric, dicentric (two centromeres), polycentric (many centromeres), acentric chromosome (having no centromere).

Refer to fig no. 11.12. (5)

74. Is there a species or region specific type of plastids? How does one distinguish one from the other? **NCERT Exemplar**

Ans Plastids are both region or species specific. These are as follows

(i) **Proplastids** These are colourless, rounded but amoeboid plastid precursors, found in meristematic and newly formed cells of plants. It has a double membrane envelope that surrounds a colourless matrix, containing DNA, ribosomes and reserve food. A few vesicles and lamellae also occur in the matrix.

(ii) **Leucoplasts** These are colourless plastids that occur in non-green plant cells commonly near the nucleus. They are as follows

(a) **Amyloplasts** These leucoplasts store starch, e.g. tuber of potato, grain of rice and wheat.

(b) **Elaioplasts** These store fats, e.g. rose.

(c) **Aleuroplasts** They are protein storing plastids, e.g. castor endosperm.

(iii) **Chromoplasts** These are non-photosynthetic coloured plastids which synthesise and store carotenoid pigments.

They appear, orange, red or yellow in colour. These mostly occur in ripe fruits (tomato and chillies) carrot roots, etc.

(iv) **Chloroplasts** These are photosynthetic plastids, which are green in colour and found in the leaves of all green plants. They have lamellae organised in the form of grana. (5)

75. Write the functions of the following **NCERT Exemplar**

(i) Centromere (ii) Cell wall

(iii) Smooth ER (iv) Golgi apparatus

(v) Centrioles

Ans (i) **Functions of Centromere**

(a) It is a narrow non-stainable area which join chromatids together to form a chromosome.

(b) The centromere thus, keep the two chromatids of a chromosome in an intact stage.

(c) This is an essential step for chromosomes of a cell during cell division whether it may be mitosis or meiosis.

(ii) **Functions of Cell Wall** Refer to text on page no. 228.

(iii) **Functions of Smooth Endoplasmic Reticulum**

(a) It provides mechanical support to colloidal complex of cytoplasmic matrix.

(b) It holds various cell organelles in position.

(c) It conducts information from outside to inside of cell.

(iv) **Functions of Golgi Apparatus** Refer to text on page no. 233.

(v) **Functions of Centrioles**

(a) Formation of new centrioles from pre-existing one's during cell division.

(b) They form basal bodies, which in turn form cilia and flagella. (1×5)

SUMMARY

- **Cell** is the basic structural and functional unit of life.
- **Cell Theory** Schleiden and Schwann formulated cell theory which includes three statements, i.e.
  - (i) All organisms are composed of one or more cell and cell products.
  - (ii) Cells are the structural and functional unit of living organisms.
  - (iii) Cells arise from pre-existing cells (*Omnis-cellula-e-cellula*) (given by Virchow).
- **Types of Cells** Cells are of two basic types
  - (i) **Prokaryotic Cell** These cells have incipient nucleus that is devoid of membrane. They do not have membrane bound cell organelles.
  - (ii) **Eukaryotic Cell** These cells consist of outer cell wall (only in plants and fungi), plasma membrane, cytoplasm, membrane bound nucleus within cytoplasm cell organelles are suspended.
- **Cell Wall** It is the outermost, rigid protective covering present in plants and fungi. It is composed of structural polysaccharides such as cellulose, hemicellulose or pectin.
- **Plasma Membrane** It is the selectively permeable outer covering that limits the cytoplasm of cell.
- **Mitochondria** These are semiautonomous organelles involved in ATP generation in cell. They contain double membranes, i.e. an outer and inner membrane. The inner membrane is folded to form cristae that increase the surface area of mitochondria.
- **Nucleus** It is the main controller of cell activities that is bounded by a nuclear envelope. It also consists of nucleoplasm, chromatin and nucleolus.
- **Nucleolus** It is a spherical membraneless body within nucleus. It acts as a site of synthesis of ribosomes and *r*RNA.
- **Chromatin** These are fine fibres composed of DNA and histone proteins.
- **Chromosome** During cell division, chromatin condense into thick chromosomes.In the centre of chromosome, centromere is present at which chromatids, arms of chromosome meet.
- **Plastids** These are double membrane-bound organelles used for trapping radiations and storage.
- **Chloroplast** A plastid containing chlolorophyll. It is involved in photosynthesis. It contains an outer and inner membrane. The matrix inside the membrane is stroma in which membranous sacs, i.e thylakoids are present. In these thylakoids chlorophyll is found. Chloroplasts are semiautonomous.
- **Ribosomes** These organelles are smallest non-membranous RNA-protein complexes. These are involved in protein synthesis.
- **Endomembrane System** It consists of organelles such as Golgi apparatus, Endoplasmic Reticulum and Lysosome (GERL).
- **Endoplasmic Reticulum** It consists of interconnected membranes in the form of cisternae, vesicles and tubules. It is of two types
- **Golgi Apparatus** It is also a membranous organelle consisting of flattened sac-like structures cisternae. These are concerned with modifying, sorting and packaging of cell products into secretory vesicles.
- **Lysosomes** These are single-membrane bound small-spherical organelles that contain hydrolytic enzymes in them. Due to their function of digesting cell products these are also called as suicidal bags of cell.
- **Vacuoles** These are single membrane bound organelles limited by a membrane called tonoplast.
- **Cytoskeleton** It is a network of interconnected, proteinaceous filaments and tubules. It maintains the shape of the cell.
- **Cilia and Flagella** These are filamentous outgrowths extending from the cell surface. Cilia are smaller in size. They show 9+2 microtubular arrangement in which there are 9 peripheral doublets of microtubules and 2 central singlet microtubules.

Chapter Practice

Multiple Choice Questions

1 Mark

1. Name the scientist, who saw a live cell first time.
   (a) Robert Brown
   (b) Antony van Leeuwenhoek
   (c) Robert White
   (d) Schleiden

2. What is true about the genetic material of prokaryotic cell?
   (a) Possess small circular DNA called plasmids
   (b) Not enveloped by nuclear membrane
   (c) Composed of a single circular DNA molecule
   (d) All of the above

3. Choose the incorrect pair.
   (a) Gram-positive bacteria–Take up the Gram stain
   (b) Cell wall–Prevents bacterium from collapsing
   (c) Capsule–Thick and tough glycocalyx
   (d) Pili– Locomotory structure in bacteria

4. The fluid mosaic model explains
   (a) Only structural aspects of cell membrane
   (b) Only functional aspects of cell membrane
   (c) Both structural and functional aspects of cell membrane
   (d) Only fluidity of membrane

5. Fluid nature of membrane is able to explain
   (a) cell growth, cell division
   (b) formation of intercellular junctions
   (c) secretion and permeation of various substances across membrane
   (d) All of the above

6. Which of the following statements is incorrect?
   (a) Unicellular oganisms are capable of independent existence
   (b) Any structure less than a complete structure of a cell does not ensure independent living
   (c) Matthias Schleiden, a German Zoologist discovered the nucleus
   (d) Leeuwenhoek first saw and described a live cell

7. The cell organelle that is present in cytoplasm as well as other organelle
   (a) mitochondria (b) ribosome
   (c) chloroplast (d) endoplasmic reticulum

8. Who discovered ribosomes as dense particles under the electron microscope?
   (a) George Palade (b) Kolliker
   (c) Boveri (d) Strasburger

9. The sedimentation coefficient of ribosome is a measure of
   (a) density (b) number
   (c) structure (d) None of these

10. Which of the following statements is false?
    (a) Both the centrioles in a centrosome lie perpendicular to each other
    (b) Centrioles form the basal body of spindle fibres only
    (c) Each centriole has an organisation like that of a cartwheel
    (d) Centrosome usually contains two cylindrical centrioles

Assertion-Reason Type Questions

1 Mark

■ Direction (Q. Nos. 11-18) *In each of the following questions, a statement of Assertion (A) is given followed by corresponding statement of Reason (R). Of the statements, mark the correct answer as*

(a) If both A and R are true and R is the correct explanation of A
(b) If both A and R are true, but R is not the correct explanation of A
(c) If A is true, but R is false
(d) If A is false, but R is true

11. **Assertion** (A) Smaller cells are usually metabolically active cells.
    Reason (R) Smaller cells have higher nucleocytoplasmic ratio and higher surface volume ratio.

12. **Assertion** (A) The cisternae in Golgi complex have *cis* face and *trans* face.

Reason (R) The *cis* face is also called forming face and *trans* face is also called maturing face.

13. Given below is the structure of a mitochondria found in the cytoplasm of every cell. It is often known as the powerhouse of the cell. Study its internal structure and comment upon the appropriateness of the Assertion and the Reason.

Assertion (A) The inner membrane forms the number of infolding called the cristae.

Reason (R) The matrix of the mitochondria increase the surface area.

14. **Assertion** (A) The chromoplasts contain fat soluble carotenoid pigments.

Reason (R) These pigments provide colour to plant parts other than green.

15. Given below is the structure that is responsible for providing the mechanical support to the colloidal cytoplasmic matrix and helps to keep the various organelles in their position. Study the diagram below and comment upon the appropriateness of the Assertion and Reason.

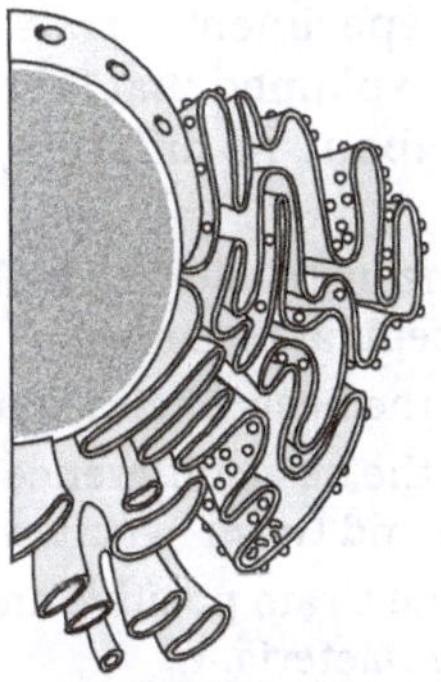

Assertion (A) This cell organelle acts as a means of quick intracellular transport.

Reason (R) In cells, it conducts information from one part of the cell to another.

16. **Assertion** (A) The vacuole is bounded by a single membrane structure known as tonoplast. In plants it facilitates the transport of materials against the concentration gradient inside the vacuole.

Reason (R) The concentration of material is tend to be the lower in vacuole, than to be in the cytoplasm.

17. **Assertion** (A) Mesosomes are equal to mitochondria in eukaryotes.

Reason (R) These structures participate in aerobic cellular respiration in prokaryotes.

18. **Assertion** (A) The prokaryotic ribosomes are 70S while the eukaryotic ribosomes are 80S.

Reason (R) Here 'S' stands for the sedimentation coefficient which is indirectly measure of density and size.

Answers

1. (b)	2. (d)	3. (d)	4. (c)	5. (d)
6. (c)	7. (b)	8. (a)	9. (a)	10. (b)
11. (a)	12. (b)	13. (c)	14. (b)	15. (a)
16. (c)	17. (a)	18. (b)		

Very Short Answer Type Questions

1 Mark

19. What was the drawback of cell theory proposed by Schleiden and Schwann ?

20. What is the size of human erythrocyte on the basis of diameter?

21. Which type of cell came first in evolution, the eukaryotic cell or the prokaryotic cell?

22. What is the name given to the glycocalyx if it is hard, thick and tough?

23. Is cell wall permeable, semipermeable or impermeable?

24. ER divides the intracellular space of the cell into two distinct compartments. Name them.

25. Give the term used for the stacks of thylakoids.

26. What is the approximate length of DNA that the human cell possess?

27. What do you mean by axoneme?

Short Answer Type I Questions

(2 Marks)

28. On the basis of the type of membrane, highlight one characteristic difference between prokaryotic cell and eukaryotic cell.
29. Why cytoplasm is known as main arena of cell, give its one function?
30. What are the major functions of plant cell vacuoles? What is the covering membrane of the vacuoles called?
31. What are chloroplasts? Mention their main functions.

Short Answer Type II Questions

(3 Marks)

32. Unicellular counterparts does not have better survival chances than multicellular organisms. Why?
33. Give a brief difference between prokaryotic and eukaryotic ribosomes.
34. (i) What are the two subunits of ribosomes in bacteria?
    (ii) Give two functions of ribosomes in prokaryotic cells.
35. What is polysome? Explain its role in bacterial cell.
36. Describe briefly the structure of chromosomes.
37. Give a detailed description of chloroplast.
38. Why do not the lysosomal enzymes destroy the cell's own cytoplasm? Explain.
39. Which organelle functions as cytoskeleton? Explain one of them in short.
40. Describe the ultrastructure of cilia and flagella diagrammatically.

Long Answer Type Questions

(5 Marks)

41. Give any five functions of plasma membrane found in prokaryotic cells.
42. Distinguish between Gram positive and Gram negative bacteria with example of each.
43. What are the different types of membranous structures found in bacterial cell? Discuss.
44. Explain the basic structure of flagella with labelled diagram.
45. Discuss the structure of cell wall in plant with all three layers.
46. With the help of suitable diagram explain the detailed ultrastructure of mitochondrion. How would you justify that mitochondria are genetically autonomous or semi-autonomous organelle?
47. Write short note on
    (i) Grana
    (ii) Glyoxysomes
    (iii) Centriole
48. Draw a generalised plant cell as seen under electron microscope.

Case Based Questions

(4/5 Marks)

49. *Read the following passage and answer the questions that follows.*
    Manish while performing a practical in laboratory on Grams stain observed that one type of bacteria stained dark blue or purple in colour, while the other type of bacteria did not retain the crystal violet dye even after staining again and again. Instead it keeps on loosing the dye on washing. He rushed to his teacher for showing the specimen.
    His teacher explained that there is nothing to get worried about. As different kinds of bacteria are found.
    (i) Name the instrument that allows us to study the unicellular organism.
    (ii) What is the basis of classifying bacteria?
    (iii) What is the basic difference between Gram positive and Gram negative bacteria?
    (iv) Name one Gram positive and one Gram negative bacteria.
50. Amrita's biology teacher taught in biology class that food helps in building the body and also provides us energy to work. However, she was not able to understand the mechanisms involved.

So, she discussed it with his father who is a professor of biology in a college. He answered that in living organisms certain structures, present in the cells and known as power houses of cells, which are responsible for the conversion of food into energy.

(i) Which cell organelles are known as powerhouse of the cell? Why?
(ii) List major components of mitochondrion.
(iii) What is the role of cristae in mitochondria?
(iv) Write two functions of mitochondria other than providing energy.

51. Mahima after returning from biology class asked his father why do only green plants manufacture their food using sunlight and not the animals?
Father replied that green plants have this ability due to the presence of green pigment called chlorophyll (present in the chloroplasts) in their cells?

(i) Why chloroplast are only present in plant cells?
(ii) Name the various types of plastids found in plants.
(iii) What is the function of chloroplast in plant cells?
(iv) Which plastids are known as kitchen of the cell?
(v) Which plastids are found in flowers and fruits?

CHAPTER 12

Biomolecules

A cell is composed of variety of atoms (like carbon, hydrogen, oxygen), which are the components of many biologically important molecules.

Other than these basic elements, some metals and non-metals are also present as cellular materials. Hence, all these materials combine in different ways in order to form various biomolecules, which are found in cells of organisms.

These molecules are not living, but perform various living functions. Thus, **biomolecules** are the organic substances (e.g. carbohydrates, proteins, lipids, etc.) that play a major role in the structure and function of the living organism.

TOPIC 01 Analysis of Basic Units of Biomolecules

Chemical Analysis of Organic Compounds

To analyse the chemical composition of any organic compound of a living organism, the chemical analysis of living tissue is done. As organic compounds play a major role, it is essential to have knowledge of their molecular formula and structure.

This can be easily done by performing following steps

(i) Weight of a living tissue (like a piece of a liver, fruit, vegetable or any other body tissue) is taken.

(ii) The tissue is then grinded in a solvent called trichloroacetic acid (Cl_3CCOOH) with the help of mortar and pestle.

(iii) The thick slurry obtained is then filtered through a cheese-cloth or cotton. This will generate two fractions of solution

  (a) Filtrate or the acid-soluble fraction.

  (b) Retentate or the acid-insoluble fraction.

(iv) The extract can then be subjected to numerous separation techniques, in order to obtain the desirable compound from all other components. By successfully performing all the above steps, we can get an idea of the molecular formula and the probable structure of the compound.

(v) All the carbon compounds that we get from living tissues are called **biomolecules**.

Ash Analysis for Inorganic Compound and Elements

After the analysis of chemical composition of an organic compound in a tissue, it is necessary to do the analysis of inorganic elements and compounds. It can be done easily by performing a destructive experiment that separates inorganic compounds from organic compounds in the form of ash (contains inorganic compounds and elements). **Ash** is the remaining part of any living tissue, which remains after burning of any organic compound.

Ash analysis is done in order to analyse the chemical composition of different inorganic compounds and elements present in the organic materials after burning.

It is done in the following way

(i) For analysis, a small amount of a living tissue is taken, which is oven dried till all the water evaporates.

(ii) This gives the dry weight.

(iii) After that tissue is burnt completely, which results in the formation of ash. All the carbon compounds are oxidised to gaseous form (CO_2, water vapour) and are removed.

Thus, ash formed contains inorganic elements like potassium, sodium, calcium, magnesium, etc., (inorganic compounds are also seen in the acid soluble fraction).

The table given below compares the human body composition and the Earth crust

* Adapted from CNR Rao, Understanding Chemistry, Universities Press, Hyderabad.

Cellular Pool

The sum total of different types of biomolecules, compounds and ions present in the cell is called **cellular pool**. It contains more than 5000 chemicals.

List of Few Main Representative Inorganic Constituents of Living Tissues

Components	Formula
Sodium	Na^+
Potassium	K^+
Calcium	Ca^{2+}
Magnesium	Mg^{2+}
Water	H_2O
Compounds	$NaCl$, $CaCO_3$, PO_4^{3-}, SO_4^{2-}

Primary and Secondary Metabolites

A large number of organic biomolecules are present in the cells, which are used in various metabolic reactions of cell. Hence, these compounds are called **metabolites**.

These are divided into two types

1. Primary Metabolites

These are metabolites, which are found in animal tissues. Their functions are easily identifiable. They play specific known roles in the normal physiological processes, e.g. amino acids, carbohydrates, proteins, nitrogen bases, nucleic acids, etc.

2. Secondary Metabolites

These are metabolites, which are generally found in plant, fungal and microbial cells as a byproduct of main metabolic reactions. Their functions are not identifiable in host organism and are not yet understood, e.g. alkaloids, flavonoids, rubber, essential oils, antibiotics, coloured pigments, scents, gums, spices.

Some Secondary Metabolites

Alkaloids	Morphine, codeine, etc.
Terpenoids	Monoterpenes, diterpenes, etc.
Essential oils	Lemon grass oil, etc.
Toxins	Abrin and ricin
Lectins	Concanavalin A
Drugs	Vinblastin, curcumin, etc.
Polymeric substances	Rubber, gums and cellulose

Functions

Both primary and secondary metabolites serve the following functions

(i) Many of them are used for welfare of human beings, e.g. rubber, drugs, spices, scents, pigments.

(ii) Some have ecological importance.

Carbohydrates

These are the organic compounds mainly made up of C, H and O. They are defined as polyhydroxy aldehydes and ketones. These are produced directly by the plants during photosynthesis. Carbohydrates are also known as **saccharides** because their major constituents are **sugars**.

- On the basis of their reducing properties carbohydrates can be of two types, i.e. reducing and non-reducing sugar.
- On the basis of hydrolysis, products of carbohydrates can be monosaccharides, oligosaccharides and polysaccharides.

1. Monosaccharides

These are simplest carbohydrates, which cannot be hydrolysed further into smaller components. These are generally composed of three to seven carbon atoms per molecule.

Monosaccharides are also known as reducing sugars, because they have a free aldehydic (—CHO) or ketonic ($>C=O$) group and can also reduce Cu^{2+} (cupric ions) of **Benedict's** or **Fehling's solution** to Cu^{+} (cuprous ions), e.g. ribose, glucose, erythrose, etc.

Classification of Monosaccharides

1. Based on the functional group attached to them they are of two types
   (i) **Aldoses** When the functional group in monosaccharide is aldehyde $\left[-\overset{\overset{\displaystyle O}{\|}}{C}-H\right]$, they are known as aldoses, e.g. glyceraldehyde, glucose, ribose, erythrose, etc. Among these, glucose is called **universal sugar** and is also known as **grape sugar** or **corn sugar** or **dextrose.**
   (ii) **Ketoses** When the functional group in the monosaccharide is keto group $(-\overset{|}{C}=O)$, they are referred as ketones, e.g. ribulose, fructose, etc. Among these, fructose (6C) is most common. It is also called as **fruit sugar** or **levulose.** It is naturally occurring sweetest sugar.
2. Based on the number of carbon atom, the monosaccharides are regarded as
   (i) **Trioses** having 3C atoms, e.g. glyceraldehyde and dihydroxyacetone.
   (ii) **Tetroses** having 4C atoms, e.g. thriose and erythrose.
   (iii) **Pentoses** having 5C atoms, e.g. ribose, ribulose, xylose, arabinose and deoxyribose.
   (iv) **Hexoses** having 6C atoms, e.g. glucose, galactose and mannose. They are white, sweet-tasting, crystalline and soluble in water.

Pentoses and hexoses of monosaccharide can occur in two forms, e.g. open chain and ring form. This ring form can be of two types

(a) **Pyranose Ring** which has hexagonal shape with 5C and 1 oxygen atom.

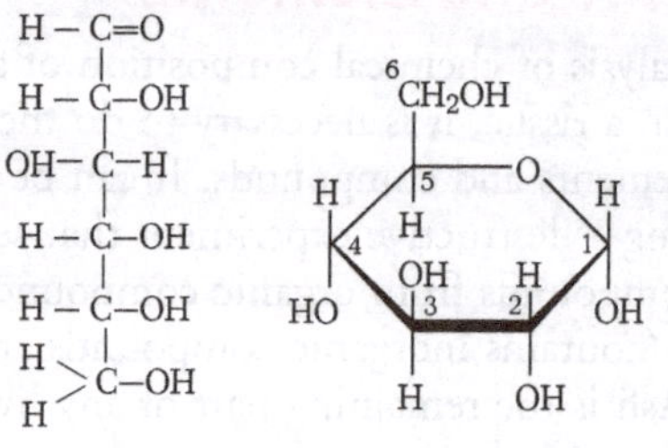

Open chain **Ring form**

Fig. 12.1 Open and ring form of glucose

(b) **Furanose Ring** which has pentagonal shape with 4C atom and 1 oxygen atom.

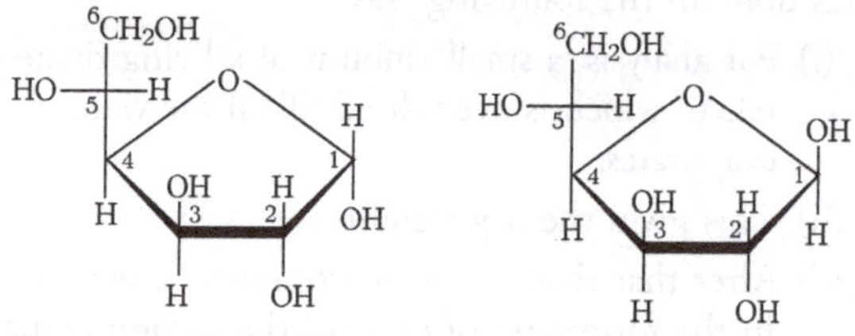

α-D glucofuranose β-D glucofuranose

Fig 12.2 Furanose ring

Some Important Monosaccharides

Some important monosaccharides are

Glucose

It is an aldohexose and occurs freely as well as in combined form in the nature. It is present in sweet fruits and honey. It is also present in large quantities in ripe grapes. It is also known as **grape sugar** or **dextrose.**

As glucose is an aldohexose, it consists of six C-atoms and an aldehyde group. It is the monomer of many of the larger carbohydrates such as starch, cellulose, etc. It is the most abundant organic compound on the earth and used as an immediate source of energy for all metabolic reactions in the animals.

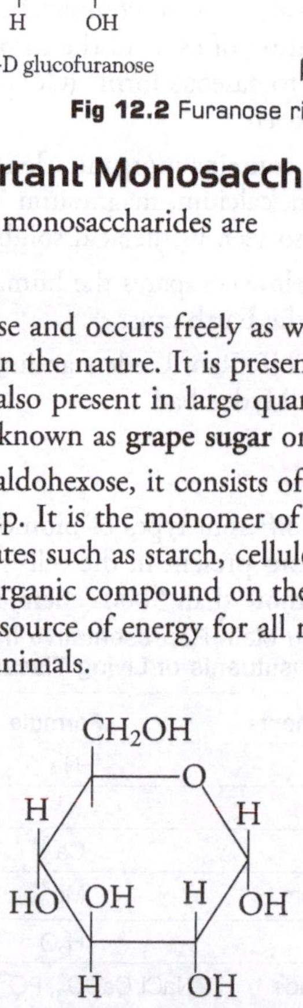

Fig. 12.3 $C_6H_{12}O_6$ z(glucose)

Ribose and Deoxyribose Sugar

The 5-carbon sugars ribose and deoxyribose are important components of nucleotides and are found in RNA and DNA, respectively.

The sugars found in nucleic acids are pentose sugars; a pentose sugar has five carbon atoms.

A combination of a base and a sugar is called nucleoside. Ribose, found in RNA, is a 'normal' sugar, with one oxygen atom attached to each carbon atom.

Deoxyribose, found in DNA, is a modified sugar, lacking one oxygen atom (hence the name 'deoxy').

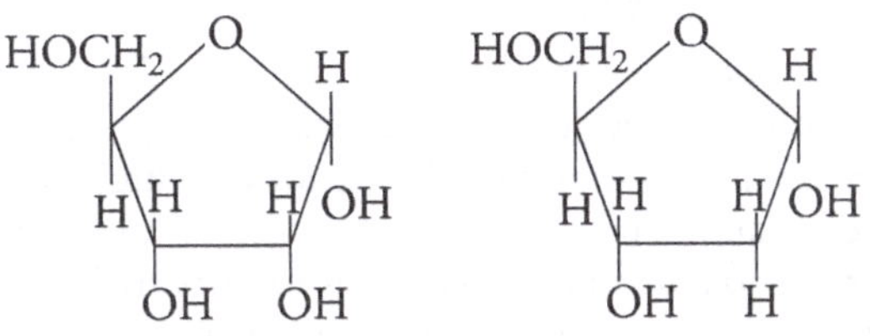

$C_5H_{10}O_5$ (Ribose) $C_5H_{10}O_4$ (Deoxyribose)

Fig. 12.4 Ribose and deoxyribose sugar

Functions of Monosaccharides

(i) Trioses are involved in respiratory and photosynthesis processes.

(ii) Ribose and deoxyribose are structural components of RNA and DNA, respectively.

(iii) Glucose is an important energy source.

2. Oligosaccharides

These are formed by the condensation of 2-9 monosaccharide units. In oligosaccharides these units are held together by glycosidic bonds.

A **glycosidic bond** is formed between >C=O group of one monosaccharide and the alcoholic group of another along with the liberation of one H_2O molecule. On hydrolysis they produce two or more molecules of same or different monosaccharides.

Oligosaccharides are crystalline, water soluble and sweet in taste. On the basis of number of monosaccharide units given by them on hydrolysis. These can be of following types

1. **Disaccharide**, e.g. sucrose, maltose, lactose, trehalose, etc.
2. **Trisaccharide**, e.g. raffinose.
3. **Tetrasaccharide**, e.g. stachyose.

Some Important Disaccharides

Some important disaccharides are

Lactose or Milk Sugar

It is a disaccharide present in the milk of mammals. On hydrolysis it gives one glucose and one β-D galactose unit. The glycosidic linkage of lactose is β-1,4 type.

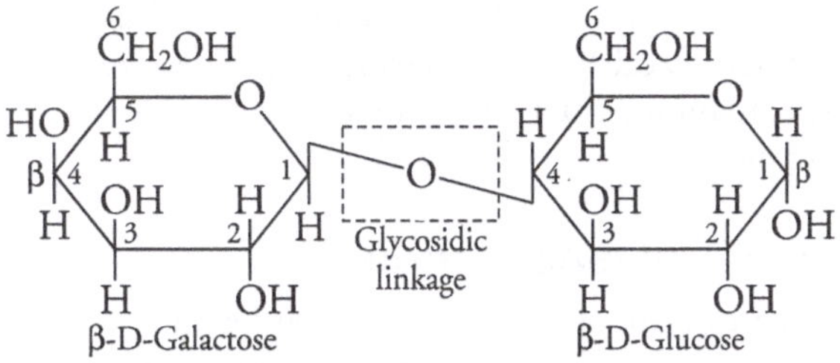

β-D-Galactose β-D-Glucose

Fig. 12.5 Haworth structure of lactose

Maltose or Malt Sugar

It is also a disaccharide. This sugar is found in germinating seeds. It is also produced during the digestion of starch by an enzyme α-amylase. On hydrolysis it gives 2-α-D glucose units. The glycosidic linkage of maltose is α-1, 4 type.

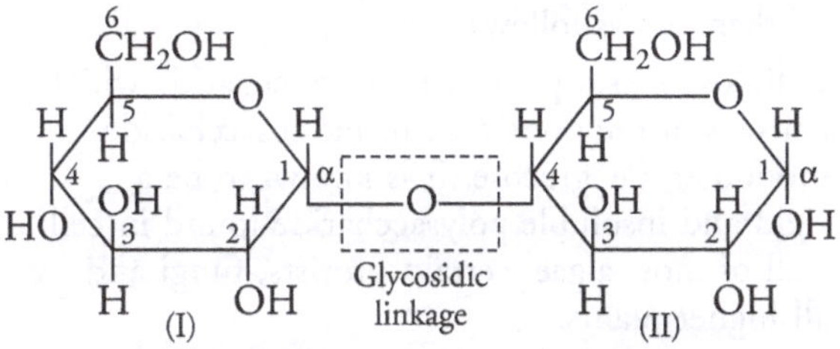

α-D-Glucose α-D-Glucose

Fig. 12.6 Haworth structure of maltose

- **Cellobiose** is a disaccharide formed during the hydrolysis of cellulose. It is identical to maltose except the fact that, here linkage is β-1, 4-glycosidic linkage.
- **Isomaltose** also resembles maltose except that here linkage is α-1, 6-glycosidic linkage.

Sucrose or Cane Sugar

This disaccharide is widely distributed among higher plants. On commercial scale it is obtained from sugarcane and sugarbeet. On hydrolysis it produces one α-D glucose and one β-D fructose unit. The glycosidic linkage in sucrose is α-1,2 type.

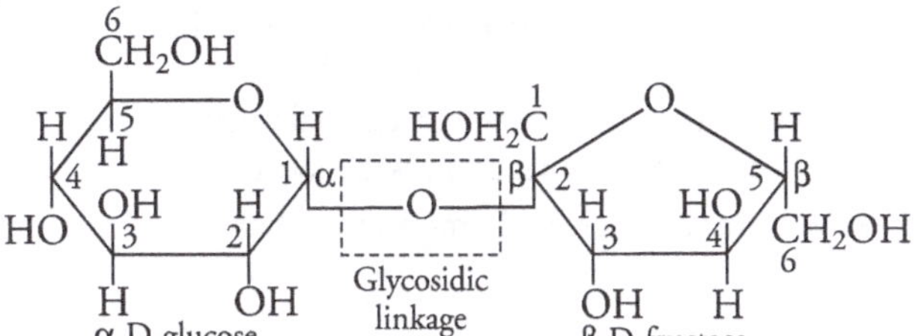

α-D-glucose β-D-fructose

Fig. 12.7 Haworth structure of sucrose

3. Polysaccharides

These are another class of macromolecules that are present in the acid insoluble fraction. Polysaccharides are long chains of sugars.

They are not sweet and are insoluble in water. Polysaccharide chain (like glycogen) is made up of two end, whose right end is called **reducing end** and the other left end is called **non-reducing end.** They are threads containing different monosaccharides as building blocks.

Types of Polysaccharides

Polysaccharides are of two types as given below

i. Homopolysaccharides

These are those complex carbohydrates which are formed by polymerisation of only one type of monosaccharide monomers, e.g. starch, glycogen and cellulose (these all are composed of single type of monosaccharide unit namely glucose).

Some of them are as follows

(a) **Cellulose** It is a polymeric polysaccharide which consists of only one type of monosaccharide monomer, i.e. glucose. It is known to be a rigid and insoluble polysaccharide found in cell wall of most algae, certain protists, fungi and all higher plants.

For example, Paper made from pulp of plant and cotton fibres are also made up of cellulose. As cellulose is not composed of complex helices so, it cannot hold iodine (I_2) and cannot give colour with iodine.

(b) **Starch** It is a storage polysaccharide because it helps in storing energy in plant tissues.

Chemically, the starch is formed of two components, i.e. α-amylose and amylopectin. Starch forms helical secondary structures. Thus, it can hold iodine (I_2) molecules in its helical portions. Therefore, gives blue-black colour with iodine solution.

(c) **Glycogen** It is also a storage polysaccharide found in animals only (in liver cells and muscles). It is also known as **animal starch.** It gives red colour on reaction with iodine.

It is a branched chain homopolysaccharide.

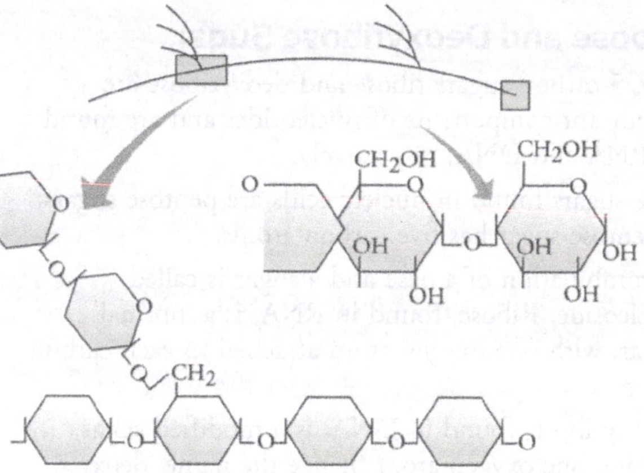

Fig. 12.8 Diagrammatic representation of a portion of glycogen

(d) **Inulin** It is a polymer of fructose. It is a naturally occurring polysaccharide produced by many types of plants. Some plants store food in the form of inulin, e.g. sweet potato. These plants that synthesise and store inulin are unable to store other forms of carbohydrates like starch, etc. Agar, xylan, araban, etc., are some other types of homopolysaccharides synthesised by algae and some plants.

ii. Heteropolysaccharides

These are complex carbohydrates formed by the polymerisation of two or more than two types of monosaccharide monomers, e.g. chitin, pectin, peptidoglycans (murein), hyaluronic acid.

One of them is explained below

Chitin

It is the second most abundant natural polymer found in exoskeleton of arthropods (e.g. prawns, crabs, etc.) and in cell wall of fungi. It has building blocks of amino sugars and chemically modified sugar. It is made up of N-acetylglucosamine units interlinked by glycosidic bond.

Functions of Polysaccharides

Polysaccharides play multiple functions as described below

(i) Acts as structural compounds in cell wall of plants, certain fungi and protists, e.g. cellulose, chitin.

(ii) Helps in anticoagulation and prevents blood clotting inside the vessels, e.g. heparin.

(iii) Helps in lubrication of joints between bones, e.g. hyaluronic acid.

(iv) Also used in tissue culture, e.g. agar.

(v) Acts as a reserve food materials in plants, e.g. starch.

Topic Practice 1

Multiple Choice Questions

1 Mark

1. After doing the chemical analysis of organic compounds found in living organisms, two fractions were observed namely
   (a) acid soluble pool and acid insoluble pool
   (b) carbon pool and hydrogen pool
   (c) inorganic pool and organic pool
   (d) aqueous pool and non-aqueous pool

Ans (a) After doing the chemical analysis of organic compounds found in living organisms, two types of organic compounds were observed. They were filtrate (acid soluble pool) and the retentate (acid insoluble pool).

2. Identify the term 'Ash' in terms of living tissue sample analysis from the statements given below.
   (a) Organic compounds oxidised to gaseous form (CO_2 and water vapour) after burning of the tissue
   (b) The material left after burning the tissue, which contains inorganic elements (e.g. calcium, magnesium, etc.)
   (c) Compounds removed in the form of gases
   (d) Compounds which may be soluble in intracellular fluid

Ans (b) After burning the dry tissue, all the organic compounds are oxidised to gaseous form (CO_2 and water vapour) and are removed. The material left is termed 'Ash', which contains inorganic elements (e.g. calcium, magnesium, etc.).

3. Primary metabolites play known roles in
   (a) ecology
   (b) chemical process
   (c) human welfare
   (d) physiological process

Ans (d) Primary metabolites include amino acids, sugars, etc. They play a major role in physiological processes.

4. Which of the following secondary metabolites are used as drugs?
   (a) Vinblastin and curcumin
   (b) Anthocyanin
   (c) Gums and cellulose
   (d) Abrin and ricin

Ans (a) Vinblastin treats cancer and curcumin (haldi) has several medicinal properties.

5. Which of the following is/are secondary metabolites?
   (a) Rubber (b) Morphine
   (c) Curcumin (d) All of these

Ans (d) Secondary metabolites are organic compounds that are indirectly involved in normal growth of an organism.

6. Name the term given to the left and right ends of a polysaccharide.

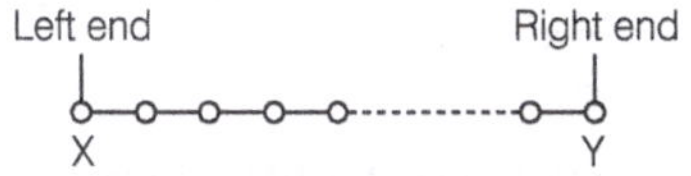

   (a) Left end–N-terminal end, Right end–C-terminal end
   (b) Left end–reducing end, Right end–non-reducing end
   (c) Left end–non-reducing end, Right end–reducing end
   (d) Left end–C-terminal end, Right end–N-terminal end

Ans (c) In a polysaccharide chain (say glycogen), the right end is called the reducing end and the left end is called the non-reducing end.

7. Select the correct option, which represents the homopolysaccharides made up of glucose monomers.
   (a) Sucrose, lactose, maltose
   (b) Chitin, glycogen, starch
   (c) Starch, inulin, peptidoglycan
   (d) Starch, glycogen, cellulose

Ans (d) Homopolysaccharides are composed of monosaccharide molecules of a single type. They include three biologically important substances, i.e. glycogen, starch and cellulose.

Very Short Answer Type Questions

1 Mark

8. A chemical is used for grinding the animal tissue for chemical analysis of organic compounds. Can you name it?

Ans Trichloroacetic acid is used for grinding animal tissue for chemical analysis of organic compounds.

9. **Can you attempt building models of biomolecules using commercially available atomic models (ball and stick models).** [NCERT]

Ans Yes, we can make models of biomolecules using commercially available atomic models.

10. **Mention four essential major elements of life.**

Ans Oxygen, carbon, hydrogen and nitrogen are the four basic essential elements of life.

11. **Why is cellulose considered as a homopolymer?**

Ans Since, cellulose is made up of only one type of monomer (glucose), it is considered as a homopolymer.

12. **Why does starch turn blue-black with iodine?**

Ans Appearance of blue colour with the addition of iodine is due to its reaction with amylose of starch.

13. **The polymer of fructose is known as ....**

Ans Inulin is the polymer of fructose.

14. **What is the name given to a polysaccharide composed of two different monomers? Also give example for this.**

Ans The name given is heteropolysaccharide to the type of polysaccharide, which is composed of different types of monomers, e.g. pectin.

15. **Name one homopolysaccharide and one heteropolysaccharide.**

Ans **Homopolysaccharide**–Starch
Heteropolysaccharide–Chitin

16. **Name the polysaccharide which constitutes the exoskeleton of arthropods.**

Ans Chitin

17. **Name the basic unit of chitin.**

Ans N-acetyl glucosamine is the basic unit of chitin.

Short Answer Type I Questions

2 Marks

18. **Arrange the following carbohydrates in the order of increasing complexity of chemical structures- fructose, starch, oligosaccharide, maltose, triose.**

Ans Triose, fructose, maltose, oligosaccharides and starch. (2)

19. **Bring out the differences between primary and secondary metabolites. Write an example for each of them.**

Ans Differences between primary and secondary metabolites are as follows

Primary Metabolites	Secondary Metabolites
These are the metabolites, which have identifiable functions and play a specific role in the metabolism.	These are the metabolites formed during metabolism whose role or exact functions in the tissue are not known.
These are important in human metabolic processes, e.g. amino acids, sugars.	These are useful to human welfare, e.g. alkaloids, flavonoids, essential oils.

(2)

20. **Write the cyclic structural formula of**

(i) glucose (ii) ribose

Ans Refer to fig. no. 12.3 and 12.4 on page no. 252 and 253. (1+1)

21. **Why are starch and glycogen more suitable than glucose as storage product?**

Ans Starch and glycogen are branched polysaccharides made up of glucose units. Therefore, they occupy lesser space and are less bulky.

Moreover, they can be hydrolysed to glucose whenever required. (2)

22. **Starch is not a single material, but is regarded as a homopolysaccharide. Explain.**

Ans Starch consists of two components, i.e. unbranched spirally coiled amylose molecules and branched amylopectin molecules.

Both are glucose polymers, hence it is called as homopolysaccharide. (2)

23. **What are gums made of? Is fevicol different?** [NCERT]

Ans Gums are sticky breakdown products of plant cell walls consisting of polysaccharides and pectins which exude from the wounds in the bark. They are generally water soluble. (1)

Fevicol is a synthetic sticky substance called resin. Resins are insoluble in water. (1)

24. **Starch, cellulose, glycogen, chitin are polysaccharides. From the options below, choose the one appropriate and write against each.**

Cotton fibre..........
Exoskeleton of cockroach.............
Liver....................
Peeled potato....................

Ans **Cotton fibre**–Cellulose
Exoskeleton of cockroach–Chitin
Liver–Glycogen
Peeled potato–Starch ($\frac{1}{2} \times 4$)

Short Answer Type II Questions

(3 Marks)

25. **Is rubber a primary metabolite or a secondary metabolite? Write four sentences about rubber.** **[NCERT Exemplar]**

Ans (i) Yes, natural rubber (*cis*-1, 4-polyisoprene) is a secondary metabolite. It is extracted from the rubber tree *(Hevea brasiliensis)*.

(ii) In the rubber tree, latex is produced in the highly specialised cells, called laticifers in phloem.

(iii) Rubber is a terpenoid and due to its high tensile strength, elasticity and plasticity properties, it is widely used in industries.

(iv) It is a polymeric substance. **(3)**

26. **Differentiate between homopolysaccharides and heteropolysaccharides.**

Ans Difference between homopolysaccharides and heteropolysaccharides is as follows

Homopolysaccharides	Heteropolysaccharides
They are the complex carbohydrates formed by the polymerisation of one type of monosaccharide units, e.g. starch, glycogen and cellulose.	They are the complex carbohydrates formed by the polymerisation of more than one type of monosaccharide units, e.g. chitin and agar. (3)

Long Answer Type Question

|5 Marks|

27. **(i) Differentiate between aldoses and ketoses.**

(ii) Write a note on oligosaccharides

Ans. (i) Refer to text on page no. 252.

(ii) Refer to text on page no. 253.

TOPIC 02 Proteins, Lipids and Nucleic Acids

Amino Acids

These are small molecules made up of carbon, hydrogen, nitrogen, oxygen and in some cases sulphur also. They are considered to be the first molecule formed in the atmosphere of the Earth. They serve as monomers of proteins.

Structure

Amino acids are organic compounds containing an amino group and an acidic group as substituent on the same carbon, i.e. the α-carbon. Hence, they are called **α-amino acids.** These are substituted methanes.

α-carbon also bears a hydrogen and a variable group designated as *R* group. Thus, there are four substituent groups present on α-carbon, which occupy the four different valency position. These are hydrogen, carboxyl, amino and *R* group. Based on the nature of *R* group, there are many amino acids. However, those which occur in proteins are only of twenty types.

General formula of α-amino acid is given below as

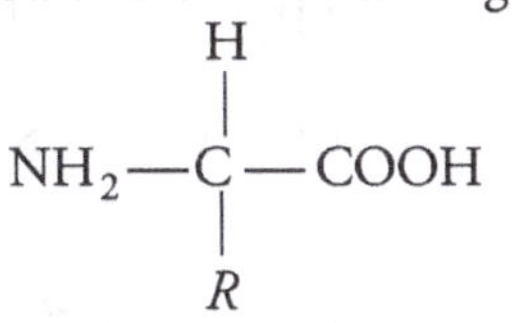

where, R = side chain of amino acids

The amino group accepts a proton, whereas the carboxyl group donates a proton. So, an amino acid can act as both acid and base. Hence, it is **amphoteric** in nature.

The *R* group in these proteinaceous amino acids could be a hydrogen (glycine), a methyl group (alanine), hydroxyl methyl (serine), etc. For example,

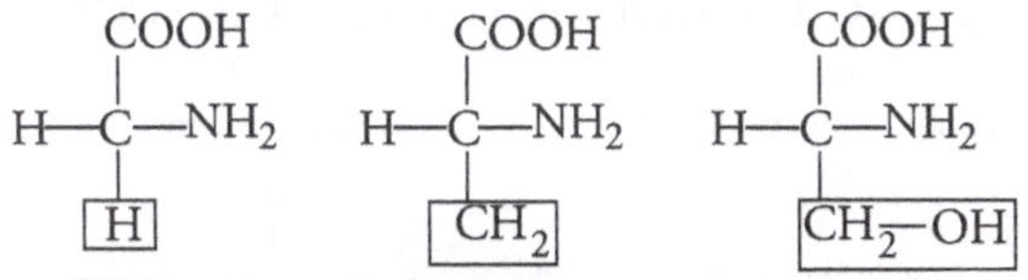

Glycine Alanine Serine

The chemical and physical properties of amino acids are essentially due to the amino, carboxyl and *R*-functional groups present.

Classification of Amino Acids

1. The amino acids are divided into two main types on the basis of their utility

(i) **Essential Amino Acids** These are those amino acids that are essential for our health so, are needed to be supplied through our diet. The dietary proteins are the source of essential amino acids, e.g. leucine, isoleucine, etc.

(ii) **Non-Essential Amino Acids** These are those amino acids, which our body can synthesise, e.g. proline, serine.

2. Based on the number of amino and carboxyl group present, amino acids are categorised into following types
   (i) **Acidic Amino Acids** These contain one amino group and two carboxyl groups per molecule, e.g. glutamic acid and aspartic acid.
   (ii) **Basic Amino Acids** These contain two amino groups and one carboxyl group per molecule, e.g. arginine, lysine and histidine.
   (iii) **Neutral Amino Acids** These contain one amino group and one carboxyl group per molecule, e.g. methionine, isoleucine, serine, threonine, cysteine, glycine, alanine, valine, leucine, aspargine, glutamine and proline.
   (iv) **Aromatic Amino Acids** These contain aromatic rings in their side chain, e.g. phenylalanine, tyrosine and tryptophan.
   (v) **Sulphur Containing Amino Acids** These contain sulphahydryl (—SH) group in their structure, e.g. cystine and cysteine.

Amino Acids as Zwitter Ion

Zwitter ion formation is another particular property of an amino acid. It is a neutral molecule (with positive and negative charge), having the ionisable nature of $—NH_2$ and —COOH groups. Hence, in solutions of different pHs, the structure of amino acid changes variably.

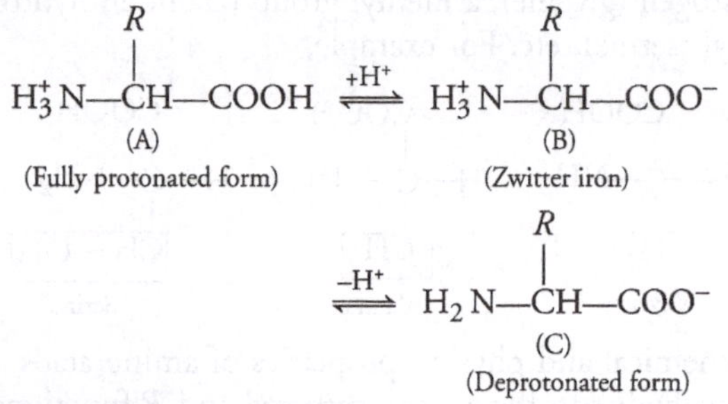

Fig. 12.9 Representations of a Zwitter ion formation

Proteins

These are the most important and abundant intracellular organic biomolecules. These are polypeptides having chains of amino acid arranged linearly that are linked by **peptide bonds.**

Thus, each protein is a polymer of amino acids (as studied earlier in the chapter), there are 20 types of amino acids, e.g. alanine, valine, arginine, leucine, histidine, etc. So, proteins are considered as heteropolymer not homopolymer.

Peptide Bond

In a polypeptide or a protein, amino acids are linked by a peptide bond, formed when the carboxyl group (—COOH) of one amino acid reacts with the amino group $(—NH_2)$ of the next amino acid with elimination of water.

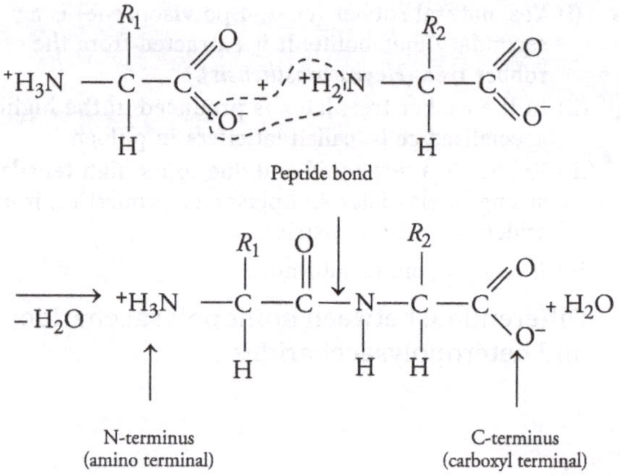

Fig. 12.10 Formation of a peptide bond

Structure Level in Proteins

Proteins are heteropolymers containing strings of amino acids. Biologists describe the protein structure at four different levels, i.e. primary, secondary, tertiary and quaternary.

1. Primary Structure

It is the description of basic structure of a protein. This includes number and sequence of amino acids in each polypeptide. The distance between two adjacent peptide bonds is about 0.35 nm. A protein is imagined as a line whose left end is represented by the first amino acid, also called as the **N-terminal amino acid** and the right end is represented by the last amino acid called the **C-terminal amino acid,** e.g. insulin, ribonuclease.

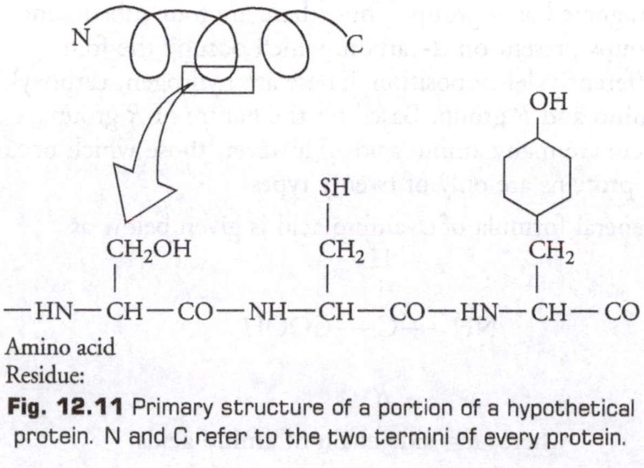

Fig. 12.11 Primary structure of a portion of a hypothetical protein. N and C refer to the two termini of every protein.

2. Secondary Structure

The thread of the primary protein is folded in the form of α-**helix**. The α-helix is stabilised by hydrogen bonds between oxygen of the carboxylic group of one amino acid residue and —NH group of the next fourth amino acid residue, e.g. keratin. In β -pleated **secondary structure**, two or more polypeptide chains get interconnected by hydrogen bonds. Adjacent strands of polypeptide may run in the same direction or in opposite direction, e.g. silk fibre.

Note In proteins, only right-handed helices are observed.

Differences between α-Helix and β-Pleated Structure of Proteins

α-Helix Structure	β-Pleated Structure
The polypeptide chain curls longitudinally by the action of hydrogen bonds forming a spiral or helix.	The protein is more distended and the hydrogen bond forms a *zig-zag*-shaped protein structure called β-strand (which combines and forms β-sheet).
It is highly compact and rigid.	It is less compact and rigid.
It is always antiparallel.	It can either be parallel or antiparallel.

3. Tertiary Structure of Polypeptide Chain

There is bending and folding of various types to form a hollow wollen ball-like spheres, rods or fibres. Tertiary structure is stabilised by several types of bonds–hydrogen bonds, ionic bonds, Van der Waals interactions, covalent bonds and hydrophobic bonds.

It gives information about a 3-dimensional (3D) configuration to the protein molecule, e.g. myoglobin.

Note Tertiary structure is helpful for many biological activities of proteins.

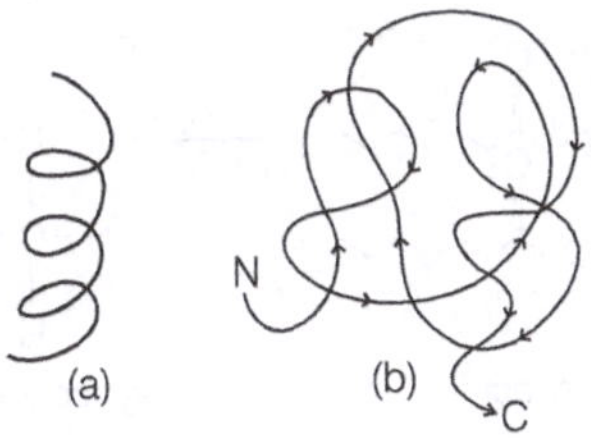

Fig. 12.12 Diagram showing (a) A secondary structure, (b) A tertiary structure of proteins

4. Quaternary Structure

Certain proteins consist of an assembly of more than one polypeptide or subunits. Thus, the individual polypeptide or subunit are arranged with respect to one another (linear strings of spheres, spheres arranged one upon each other in the form of a cube or plate, etc.), e.g. haemoglobin, lactic acid dehydrogenase enzyme.

Structure of Haemoglobin (Hb)

An adult human haemoglobin is a iron containing pigment that acts as an oxygen carrier. It has a quaternary structure because it is made up of four monomeric protein subunits each about the size of many normal individual proteins.

Every subunit has its own tertiary structure and is identical to each other. Hence, two subunits of α-type and two subunits of β-type together constitute the human haemoglobin (Hb). Insulin is an another example of protein having quaternary structure.

Types of Proteins

Proteins are classified on the basis of shape, chemical composition and function. Accordingly on the basis of structural function in animal's body, these are of two main types

1. Fibrous Proteins

The proteins have spiral secondary polypeptide chains wound around each other in order to form fibres. These are insoluble in water generally, but soluble in concentrated acids, alkalis and salts, e.g. collagen of connective tissue, keratin of hair, etc.

2. Globular Proteins

They are rounded in shape and are generally soluble in water and in dilute acids, alkalis, salts, e.g. egg albumin, serum globulins.

Some Proteins and their Functions

Protein	Functions
Collagen	Intercellular ground substance
Trypsin	Enzyme
Insulin	Hormone
Antibody	Fights infectious agents
Receptro	Sensory reception (smell, taste, hormone, etc.)
GLUT-4	Enables glucose transport into cells

Knowledge Plus

Collagen, the most abundant protein of animal world and Ribulose Bisphosphate Carboxylase Oxygenase (RuBisCO) is the most abundant protein in plants and the whole of the biosphere.

Denaturation of Proteins

When proteins are exposed to extreme change in pH, acids or temperature (or bases or high salt concentrations) the weak bonds holding the tertiary and the quaternary structure get disrupted so that the protein unfold (into primary structure). This unfolding is known as **denaturation of proteins** or loss of its functioning. Denaturation is not strong enough to break peptide bonds thus, primary structure remains unaffected.

A denatured protein may spontaneously refold into its original structure when suitable conditions are given. This is called **renaturation**.

Functions of Proteins

Proteins have various basic functions in living organism as given below

(i) Helps in transportation of nutrients across the cell membrane by acting as protein transporter.
(ii) Helps in fighting with infectious organisms.
(iii) These are helpful in movement of muscles, e.g. myosin and actin.
(iv) Helps in maintenance of pH and regulation of the volume of body fluids.
(v) Helps at the time of injury in blood clotting and acts as antibodies and provides immunity.
(vi) Helps in growth and repair of body tissues.
(vii) Some proteins function as hormones and some function as enzymes and catalyse the reactions.

Lipids

These are the esters of **fatty acids** and **alcohol**. These are generally insoluble in water. They could be simply fatty acids.

Fatty Acids

Fatty acids are the organic acids having hydrocarbon chains that end in a carboxylic group (— COOH). The carboxylic group is attached to an *R* group that could be a methyl ($-CH_3$) or ethyl ($-C_2H_5$) or higher number of $-CH_2$ groups (1 carbon to 19 carbons), e.g. palmitic acid has 16 carbons including carboxyl carbon.

Arachidonic acid has 20 carbon atoms including the carboxyl carbon.

Depending upon the types of bonds present, fatty acids are of following two types

(i) **Saturated Fatty Acids** Fatty acids which do not have double bonds (C — C). These are generally solid at room temperature.
(ii) **Unsaturated Fatty Acids** Fatty acids which contain one or more than one double bonds (C$=$C). These are generally liquid at room temperature.

$$CH_3-(CH_2)_{14}-COOH$$
(Palmitic acid)
(a)

$$CH_3(CH_2)_7\ CH{=}CH\ (CH_2)_7\ COOH$$
(Oleic acid)
(b)

Fig. 12.13 Fatty acids (a) Saturated, (b) Unsaturated

Differences between Saturated and Unsaturated Fatty Acids

Saturated Fatty Acids	Unsaturated Fatty Acids
Do not possess any double bond in their carbon chains.	Possess one or more double bonds in their carbon chains.
Solid at room temperature.	Liquid at room temperature.
Occur in most animal fats.	Occur in most plant fats.
Relatively higher melting point.	Relatively lower melting point.
e.g. palmitic acid, stearic acid.	e.g. oleic acid, linoleic acid.

Classification of Lipids

Lipids are classified into the following subgroups

1. Simple Lipids

These are esters of fatty acids and various alcohol.

They are of further two types

(i) **Neutral or True Fats** These are esters of fatty acids with glycerol (glycerine). They are also called **glycerides**.

Glycerol is a simple lipid which is known as trihydroxypropane as it is an alcohol with a backbone of three carbon atoms, each carrying an —OH group.

When glycerol is esterified with fatty acid it is known as triglyceride.

The ester is called **monoglyceride, diglyceride** and **triglyceride** depending on the number of fatty acids attached to a glycerol molecule.

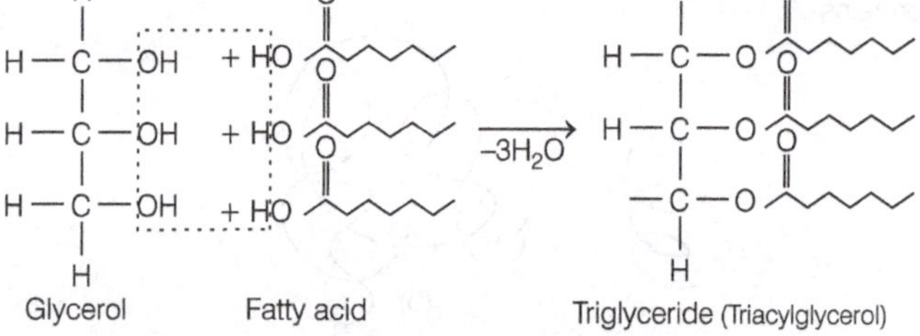

Fig. 12.14 Triglyceride

(ii) **Waxes** These are esters of fatty acids with alcohols other than glycerol.

2. Compound or Conjugated Lipids

These are the esters of fatty acids and alcohol but contain other substances also, e.g. phospholipids, glycolipids, cutin, suberin, etc.

Phospholipids are lipids which have phosphorus and phosphorylated organic compound in them. One of the common example of phospholipid is **lecithin.**

Note
Some tissues have complex structure of lipids, e.g. neural tissues.

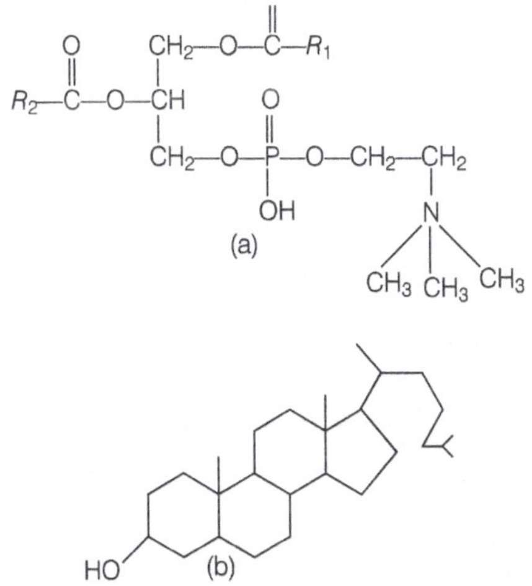

Fig. 12.15 Compound lipids (a) Phospholipid (lecithin) (b) Cholesterol

3. Derived Lipids

These are lipid-like substances such as sterol or derivatives of lipids, e.g. steroids, prostaglandins and terpenes.

Fats are also differentiated into two main types, on the basis of their melting points at room temperature as follows

(i) **Hard fats** are solid at room temperature and contain long chains of fatty acids, e.g. animal fat.

(ii) **Oils** are usually liquid at room temperature because they have low melting point, e.g. groundnut (peanut) oil, cotton seed oil, mustard oil, etc. Oil is non-polar and is not attracted to water. So, oil does not dissolve in water.

Note Vegetative oils have low melting points. They remain liquid even at low temperatures in winters, e.g. gingelly oil.

Functions of Fats and Oils

Fats act as reserve food material, insulation coats in mammals and shock absorbing cushions in eyeballs and kidneys. Edible oils from many seeds are used in cooking. Plant oils are used as low cholesterol fat.

They are also hydrogenated to form vegetable ghee. Fragrance of many plant products is because of many fat-like substances called **terpenes.**

Carotenoids are found in carrots and other plant species. The are of isoprene origin. Carotenoids metabolise into vitamin-A in our body.

Nucleic Acids

They constitute the genetic material of all living organism. The two most important nucleic acid present in living cell are deoxyribonucleic acids (DNA) and ribonucleic acid (RNA). DNA and RNA were discovered by Friedrich Miescher in 1969.

These are macromolecules, made up of polymeric units called as **nucleotides.** A nucleotide is composed of following three molecules

1. **Phosphoric acid,** i.e. H_3PO_4 with 3 reactive —OH groups. Out of these 2 are involved in forming sugar phosphate backbone with the help of phosphodiester linkages (— C— O—P— O— C—).
2. **Pentose sugar,** i.e. the carbohydrate (monosaccharide) with 5 C atoms. This may be deoxyribose in DNA or ribose in RNA. Both of these sugars differ as shown

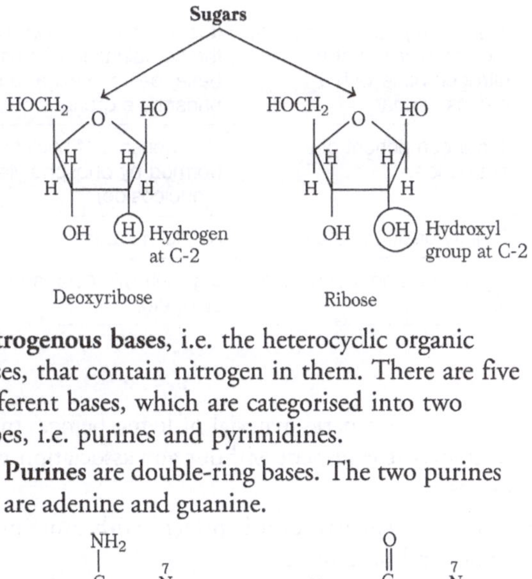

3. **Nitrogenous bases,** i.e. the heterocyclic organic bases, that contain nitrogen in them. There are five different bases, which are categorised into two types, i.e. purines and pyrimidines.
   (a) **Purines** are double-ring bases. The two purines are adenine and guanine.

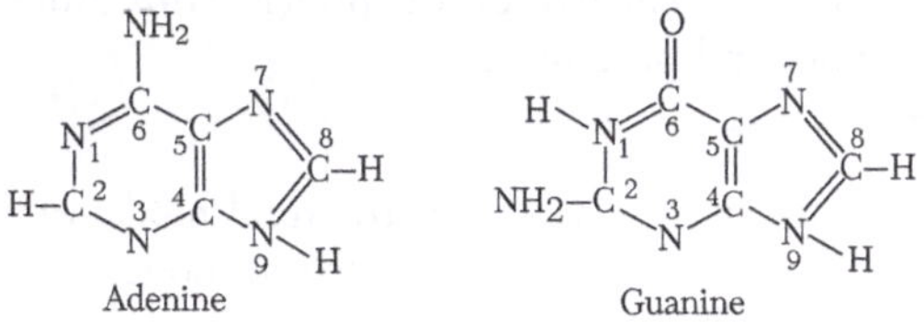

   (b) **Pyrimidines** are single ring bases, which include cytosine, thymine and uracil. Of these nitrogenous bases, DNA consists of adenine, guanine, cytosine and thymine, whereas RNA contains adenine, guanine, cytosine and uracil.

Among the above written contituents the sugar molecule and nitrogenous base together form the nucleoside.
Nucleoside + Phosphate group = Nucleotide.

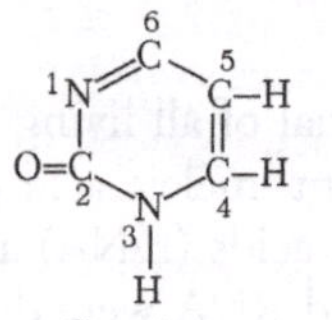

Cytosine

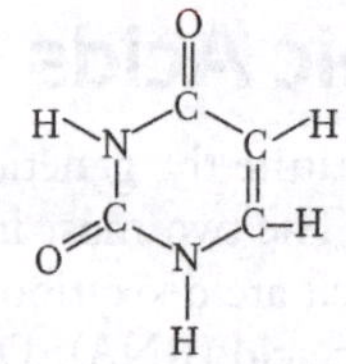

Uracil (only in RNA)

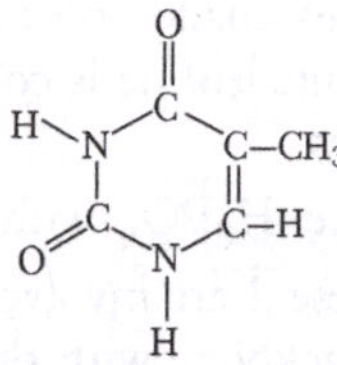

Thymine (only in DNA)

Thus, these nucleosides are considered as smaller possible frame work forming units of nucleic acids.

Differences between Nucleoside and Nucleotide

Nucleoside	Nucleotide
It is a compound formed by the combination of a nitrogen base with a pentose sugar.	It is a compound formed by the combination of a nitrogen base, pentose sugar and a phosphate group.
It is a component of a nucleotide.	Components of nucleic acids (formed by phosphorylation of a nucleoside).
Slightly basic in nature.	Acidic in nature.
e.g. guanosine, adenosine, etc.	e.g. guanylic acid, adenylic acid, etc.

DNA

It is the main genetic material of living beings. In prokaryotes it is present without any association with proteins.
However, in eukaryotes it is present with proteins like histones and protamines.

Structure

The most widely accepted structural model of DNA is the double- stranded double helical model of Watson, Crick and Wilkins (1953).
According to the model proposed by Watson and Crick

(i) The DNA molecule consists of two helically twisted antiparallel strands connected together *via* base pairs.

(ii) The twisting or coiling of strands results into formation of deep (major) and shallow (minor) grooves as shown in the figure below

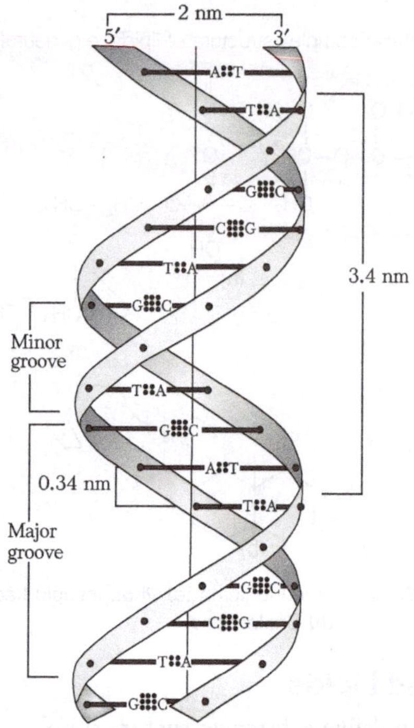

Fig. 12. 16 According to Watson and Crick, double helical model of DNA

(iii) Each strand of DNA consists of alternating molecules of deoxyribose sugar and phosphate groups. The linkage between the sugar and phosphate molecule is called **phosphodiester linkage.** In this linkage the phosphate group is attached to 3rd C-atom of one sugar molecule and 5th C-atom of other molecule as shown below

(iv) The two strands are interwined in a clockwise direction, i.e. in the form of a right-handed helix and have antiparallel arrangement. This right-handed form of DNA is called as **B-DNA** and left-handed form is called **A-DNA.**

(v) DNA has a uniform thickness of 2nm (20 Å). Its pitch or 1 turn is about 0.34 nm. Thus, 2 successive bases in DNA are 3.4 nm apart as each turn consists of 10 nucleotides.

Ribonucleic Acid (RNA)

The other nucleic acid present in the cell is RNA, i.e. ribose nucleic acid. It is found predominantly in cytoplasm. It is mostly present in single-stranded form though some viruses like retrovirus and wound tumour virus have double-stranded RNA.

The single RNA strand is folded upon itself either entirely or in certain regions. All normal RNA chains begin with adenine or guanine.

The RNA can be of following three types

(i) Messenger RNA or *m*RNA or template RNA

(ii) Ribosomal RNA or *r*RNA

(iii) Soluble RNA or transfer RNA (*s* or *t*RNA)

The transfer and messenger RNAs are synthesised on chromosomal DNA. On the other hand, ribosomal RNA is synthesised on ribosomal DNA of nucleolus. The three types of RNA are synthesised during different stages of embryonic development. The *m*RNA is synthesised during cleavage, *t*RNA is synthesised at the end of cleavage, while *r*RNA is synthesised during gastrulation.

Differences between DNA and RNA

Deoxyribonucleic Acid (DNA)	**Ribonucleic Acid** (RNA)
Found in chromosomes of the nucleus.	Found in the cytoplasm, in nucleolus and nucleoplasm and associated with chromosomes.
Double-stranded structure; two strands coiled spirally in opposite direction.	Single-stranded polynucleotide chains; strand in RNA is coiled on itself and may be united by hydrogen (H) bonds.
The sugar is deoxyribose.	The sugar is ribose.
Four nitrogenous bases in it are (i) Adenine, (ii) Guanine } Purine (iii) Cytosine, (iv) Thymine } Pyrimidine	Four nitrogenous bases in it are (i) Adenine, (ii) Guanine } Purine (iii) Cytosine, (iv) Uracil } Pyrimidine i.e., in RNA, thymine is replaced by uracil.
Purines and pyrimidines occur in equal proportion.	Do not occur in equal proportion/ratio.
DNA is the hereditary material.	It is hereditary material only in few viruses.
Controls structure, metabolism, differentiation and inheritance.	Helps in protein synthesis; functions as a messenger and translates messages coded in DNA into protein.
Long molecule with high molecular weight.	Relatively short molecule with low molecular weight.
Genetic material in all prokaryotic and eukaryotic cells.	Genetic material only in some viruses.
It occur in three different types. (i) *A*-DNA (ii) *B*-DNA (iii) *Z*-DNA	It occurs in three different types (i) *m*RNA (ii) *t*RNA (iii) *r*RNA

Functions of Nucleic Acids

Nucleic acids play multiple role in living organisms, these are given as follows

(i) It enables cell to grow, maintain and divide by directing the synthesis of structural proteins.

(ii) Acts as a genetic material, i.e. transfers hereditary characters from one generation to the next.

Topic Practice 2

Multiple Choice Questions

(1 Mark)

1. Amino acids are substituted methanes. Name the four substituent groups occupying the four valency positions.

(a) Hydrogen, carboxyl group, amino group and a variable group (*R*)

(b) Two carboxyl groups, amino group and OH

(c) Two hydrogen, one carboxyl group, amino group and a variable group (*R*)

(d) Two amino groups, one hydrogen and one carboxyl group

Ans (a) There are four substituent groups occupying the four valency positions.

These are hydrogen, carboxyl group, amino group and a variable group designated as *R* group.

2. Acidic amino acids carry two —COOH and one —NH_2 groups per molecule. Keeping this in mind, select the correct pair of acidic amino acid.

(a) Lysine and arginine

(b) Aspartic acid and glutamic acid

(c) Glycine and alanine

(d) Both (a) and (b)

Ans (b) Acidic amino acids have two carboxyl groups and one amino group per molecule. They include aspartic acid and glutamic acid.

3. Which of the following is/are essential amino acids?

(a) Valine

(b) Leucine

(c) Tryptophan

(d) All of the above

Ans (d) Essential amino acids are those that are essential for our health and are supplied through diet.

4. Types of amino acids found in proteins are
   (a) 21 (b) 19
   (c) 20 (d) 23

Ans (c) Amino acids, which occur in proteins are mainly of 20 types.

5. In a protein structure, the first amino acid and the last amino acid are respectively called as
   (a) N-terminal amino acid, C-terminal amino acid
   (b) C-terminal amino acid, N-terminal amino acid
   (c) α-amino acid, β-amino acid
   (d) β-amino acid, α-amino acid

Ans (a) In protein, the left end is represented by first amino acid (N-terminal amino acid) and the right end by last amino acid (C-terminal amino acid) because at left side amino group is free and at right side carboxy group is free.

6. Fatty acids contain
   (a) greater proportion of oxygen than in carbohydrates
   (b) no oxygen
   (c) equal oxygen in comparison to carbohydrates
   (d) less oxygen than in carbohydrates

Ans (d) Carbohydrates are polyhydroxy aldehydes and ketones. This implies that they have hydroxyl groups, i.e. glucose has six oxygen atoms.
However, fatty acids are organic acids ending with a carboxylic group. So, they have two oxygen atoms.

7. Which of the following is a saturated fatty acid?
   (a) Stearic acid (b) Oleic acid
   (c) Linoleic acid (d) Linolenic acid

Ans (a) Stearic acid is a saturated fatty acid, while oleic acid, linoleic acid and linolenic acid are unsaturated fatty acids.

8. Nitrogen bases are
   (a) homocyclic
   (b) heterocyclic
   (c) open chain hydrocarbons
   (d) All of the above

Ans (b) Nitrogenous bases are the flat heterocyclic compounds having nitrogen and carbon in a ring structure.

9. Which are purines amongst the following?
   (a) Cytosine and Thymine
   (b) Adenine and Thymine
   (c) Adenine and Guanine
   (d) Cytosine and Guanine

Ans (c) Adenine and guanine are purines, while uracil, cytosine and thymine are pyrimidines.

10. Number of pyrimidines found in nucleotides is
    (a) three (b) two
    (c) one (d) numerous

Ans (a) These are three pyrimidines found in nucleotides, i.e. uracil, cytosine and thymine.

11. Which pyrimidine base is not the part of RNA structure?
    (a) Thymine (b) Uracil
    (c) Cytosine (d) Guanine

Ans (a) Out of three pyrimidines (uracil, cytosine and thymine), uracil is only found in RNA, thymine is only found in DNA and cytosine is found in both DNA and RNA.

12. Nucleoside is composed of
    (a) ribose as pentose sugar
    (b) phosphoric acid
    (c) nitrogenous base
    (d) Both (a) and (c)

Ans (d) Nucleoside is made up of a pentose sugar (e.g. ribose) attached to a nitrogen base by a glycosidic bond.

Very Short Answer Type Questions

1 Mark

13. Name one element invariably found in proteins, but not in all carbohydrates and lipids.

Ans Nitrogen is found invariably in proteins, but not in all carbohydrates and lipids.

14. Write the name of any one amino acid.
NCERT Exemplar

Ans Alanine is an amino acid.

15. Give one example each of
    (i) an acidic amino acid
    (ii) a basic amino acid

Ans (i) An acidic amino acid–Aspartic acid.
(ii) A basic amino acid–Arginine.

16. Name any two aromatic amino acids.

Ans Tyrosine and tryptophan are the two aromatic amino acids.

17. Name two amino sugars.

Ans N-acetyl glucosamine and glucosamine.

18. Name the protein which forms the intercellular ground substance.

Ans Collagen forms the intercellular ground substance.

19. Name the protein that is most abundant in the
(i) animal world (ii) plant world

Ans (i) Collagen
(ii) Ribulose-1, 5-bisphosphate carboxylase oxygenase.

20. Give the another name of the glycerol.

Ans Trihydroxy propane.

21. Name the macromolecules that form the hereditary determinants of the living organism.

Ans Nucleic acid.

22. A nitrogenous base is present in RNA, but absent in DNA. Name it. Also, give example in which it exists.

Ans Uracil (U) is the nitrogenous base present only in RNA, e.g. viruses like hepatitis-C.

23. The backbone of DNA molecule is formed of two different molecules. Name them.

Ans Backbone of DNA molecule is formed of sugar and phosphates.

24. How many hydrogen bonds are formed between
(i) guanine and cytosine
(ii) adenine and thymine, respectively?

Ans (i) Three hydrogen bonds are formed between guanine and cytosine.
(ii) Two hydrogen bonds are formed between adenine and thymine.

Short Answer Type I Questions

2 Marks

25. Amino acids are substituted methanes. Justify why are they called α-amino acids ?

Ans Amino acids are substituted methanes because they contain four substituent groups, hydrogen, carboxyl group, amino group and a variable group (*R*), these substituents are present on the α-carbon and hence are called α-amino acids. (2)

26. Draw the structure of amino acid alanine. **NCERT**

Ans Refer to text on page no. 257.

27. Glycine and alanine are different with respect to one substituent on the α-carbon. What are the other common substituent groups? **NCERT Exemplar**

Ans There are four substituent groups occupying the four valency positions in an amino acid. These are hydrogen, carboxyl group, amino group and a variable group designated as *R* group.

The *R* group in amino acid glycine is a hydrogen and a methyl group in case of amino acid alanine, etc. (2)

28. Name the amino acid whose *R*-group is
(i) hydrogen (ii) hydroxy methyl

Ans (i) Glycine (ii) Serine (1 + 1)

29. Different forms of the amino acids also has acidic amino acids. Write about it. Also, give structure of any one acidic amino acid.

Ans Acidic amino acids are those which contain one amino group and two carboxylic groups, e.g.

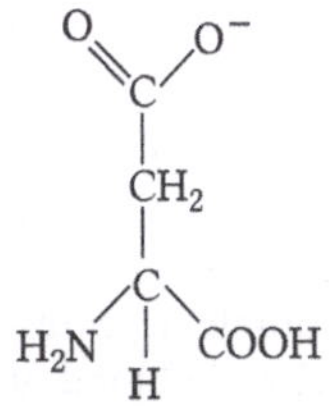

Aspartic acid

(1+1)

30. Attempt titrating an amino acid against a weak base and discover the number of dissociating (ionisable) functional groups in the amino acid. **NCERT**

Ans When an amino acid is titrated against a weak base, it dissociates and gives two functional groups.
(i) —COOH group (carboxylic group)
(ii) Amino group (NH_2). (2)

31. Do amino acids exist as Zwitter ion. Give its structure. Why is it formed?

Ans Yes, amino acids exist as Zwitter ion.
Refer to text on page no. 258. (2)

32. How do proteins act as carrier proteins?

Ans Proteins act as a carrier protein in the following ways
(i) Some proteins act as carrier which bind and transport specific molecules across a membrane or in a body fluid.
(ii) Haemoglobin of RBCs transports oxygen in the body.
(iii) Myoglobin of muscles stores oxygen.
(iv) Serum albumin carries fatty acids and lipids in the blood. (½ × 4)

33. What is trihydroxy propane commonly called? Write its structural formula. **NCERT**

Ans Trihydroxy propane is commonly known as glycerol.
Its general formula is $CH_2OH—CH(OH)—CH_2OH$. (1+1)

34. Account for the following.
Phospholipids form a thin layer on the surface of an aqueous medium.

Ans The hydrocarbon chains of the two fatty acids function as hydrophobic non-polar tails of the phospholipid molecule.

The phosphate and the additional group behave as hydrophilic polar head of the molecule. In the aqueous medium, the phospholipid molecules arrange themselves to form a thin double layer.

The polar hydrophilic heads of the molecules form the two surfaces which are in contact with water. The hydrophobic or non-polar tails of the phospholipid molecules are towards the centre of the bilayer. (2)

35. Identify the lipid molecule that is crystallisable in nature. Also, give the name of the disorder produced by it in the human body.

Ans Cholesterol is a crystallisable lipid of high molecular weight which possesses 17 carbon nuclei of four fused hydrocarbon rings (cyclopentano-perhydrophenanthrene) and a long side chain. Cholesterol is insoluble in water and therefore, when cholesterol level rises in blood, it tends to get deposited in the wall of arteries. This causes arteriosclerosis. (2)

36. Why do doctors recommend vegetable oils with polyunsaturated fatty acids for persons suffering from cardiovascular disease?

Ans Polyunsaturated oils contain fatty acids having one or more double bonds, the clotting property of blood decreases due to high proportions of PUFA. Thus, the possibility of blockage is reduced. (2)

37. Give any two examples of derived lipids.

Ans Steroids and terpenes. (2)

38. Nucleotides are phosphorylated nucleosides. Justify.

Ans A nucleoside consists of a nitrogen base and a pentose sugar, but when a phosphate is added to the nucleoside, it is called nucleotide, hence a nucleotide is a phosphorylated nucleoside. (2)

39. The double helical model of DNA was proposed by two famous scientists. Name them and discuss that why are the two strands of DNA described as antiparallel?

Ans Watson and Crick proposed the double helical model of DNA structure.

The two strands are antiparallel because they run in opposite directions, one in the 5′ → 3′ direction and the other in 3′ → 5′ direction. (1+1)

40. Select an appropriate chemical bond among ester bond, glycosidic bond, peptide bond and hydrogen bond and write against each of the following. **[NCERT Exemplar]**

(i) Polysaccharide..........
(ii) Protein...........
(iii) Fat................
(iv) Water.............

Ans (i) **Polysaccharide**–Glycosidic bond
(ii) **Protein**–Peptide bond
(iii) **Fat**–Ester bond
(iv) **Water**–Hydrogen bond ($\frac{1}{2} \times 4$)

Short Answer Type II Questions

3 Marks

41. Schematically represent primary, secondary and tertiary structures of a protein.

Ans Refer to text on page no. 258 and 259.

42. Find out and make a list of proteins used as therapeutic agents. Find other applications of proteins, e.g. cosmetics, etc. **NCERT**

Ans Refer to text on page no. 259.

43. Proteins have been called 'biological polymers'. Explain.

Ans All the cells are basically made up of proteins. Enzymes which carry out biological reactions are also proteinaceous in nature.

Antibodies, haemoglobin and even adrenaline receptors are all proteins. Therefore, they are called as biological polymers. (3)

44. Proteins have primary structure. If you are given a method to know which amino acid is at either of the two termini (ends) of a protein, can you connect this information to purity or homogeneity of a protein? **NCERT**

Ans The sequence of amino acids, i.e. the positional configuration in a protein which is the first amino acid, which is second and so on is called the primary structure of a protein. The first amino acid is also called as N-terminal amino acid.

The last amino acid is called the C-terminal amino acid. Yes, we can connect this information to purity or homogeneity of a protein.

Based on number of amino and carboxyl groups, these can be acidic (e.g. glutamic acid), basic (lysine) and neutral (valine) amino acids. (1+2)

45. Explain the composition of triglyceride. **NCERT**

Ans Triglycerides are composed of two types of molecules, i.e. glycerol (3 carbon molecules) and fatty acids which is attached to the glycerol at the alcohol unit.

The following is a structural representation of a triglyceride at the molecular level. Fatty acids are chains of hydrocarbons composed of 4-22 (or more) carbons along with a carboxyl group at one end.

If each carbon has two hydrogen atoms, the fatty acid is saturated. If two carbon atoms are double-bonded, so, that there is less hydrogen in the fatty acid, it is unsaturated (monounsaturated). If more than two carbon atoms are unsaturated, the fatty acid is polyunsaturated. (3)

46. (i) Name the category to which fats belong?
(ii) What is cholesterol?
(iii) What are the two forms of cholesterol?

Ans (i) Lipids
(ii) It is a common sterol and also the parent compound for steroid hormones.
(iii) Cholesterol exists in two forms, i.e. low density cholesterol which is harmful and high density cholesterol, which is essential for various physiological processes. **(1×3)**

47. Illustrate a glycosidic, peptide and a phosphodiester bond. **NCERT**

Ans Refer to text on page no. 253, 258 and 262.

48. Distinguish between
(i) Reducing sugars and non-reducing sugars
(ii) Purine and pyrimidine

Ans (i) Differences between reducing sugars and non-reducing sugars are

Reducing Sugars	Non-Reducing Sugars
The sugars have a free aldehyde or ketone group. The sugars can reduce cupric ions of Benedict's or Fehling's solution to cuprous ions.	A free aldehyde or ketone group is absent. They do not reduce cupric ions of Benedict's or Fehling's solution to cuprous ions.
e.g. ribose, glucose, erythrose, maltose and lactose.	e.g. sucrose.

(1½)

(ii) Differences between purine and pyrimidine are

Purine	Pyrimidine
These are large sized nitrogen containing biomolecules.	These are smaller sized nitrogen containing biomolecules.
It is nine membered and has a double ring. A purine contains four nitrogen atoms at 1′, 3′, 7′ and 9′.	It is 6 membered and has a single ring. A pyrimidine has nitrogen atoms at two places 1′ and 3′.
e.g. adenine and guanine.	e.g. cytosine, thymine and uracil.

(1½)

49. Differentiate between nucleosides and nucleotides. Give one example for each.

Ans Refer to text on page no. 262.

50. Nucleic acids exhibit secondary structure, justify with example. **NCERT Exemplar**

Ans For nucleic acids, the building block is a nucleotide. A nucleotide has three chemically distinct components. One is a heterocyclic compound, the second is a monosaccharide and the third is a phosphoric acid or phosphate.

The heterocyclic compounds in nucleic acids are the nitrogenous bases named adenine, guanine, uracil, cytosine and thymine. Adenine and guanine are substituted purines while, the rest are substituted pyrimidines.

The skeletal heterocyclic ring is called as purine and pyrimidine, respectively. The sugar found in polynucleotides is either ribose (a monosaccharide pentose) or 2′ deoxyribose.

A nucleic acid containing deoxyribose is called Deoxyribonucleic Acid (DNA), while that which contains ribose is called Ribonucleic Acid (RNA). (3)

Long Answer Type Questions

5 Marks

51. Explain briefly the structural levels of proteins.

Ans Refer to text on page no. 258 and 259.

52. Find and write down structures of 10 interesting small molecular weight biomolecules. Find if there is any industry which manufactures the compounds by isolation. Find out who are the buyers. **NCERT**

Ans (i) Sugars (carbohydrates) (ii) Amino acids

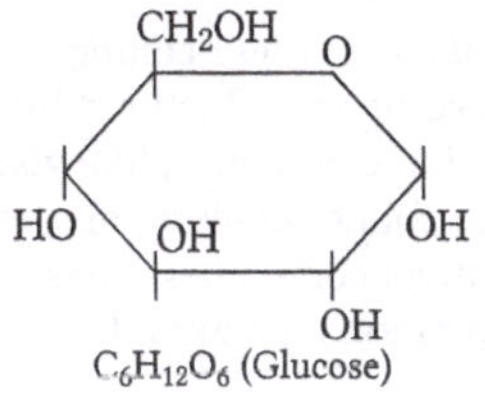

$C_6H_{12}O_6$ (Glucose)

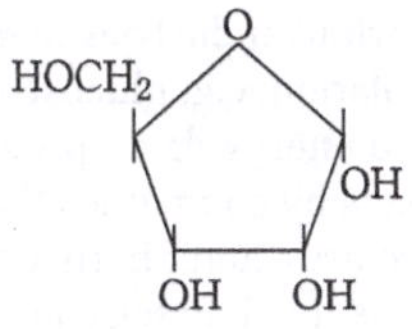

$C_5H_{10}O_5$ (Ribose)

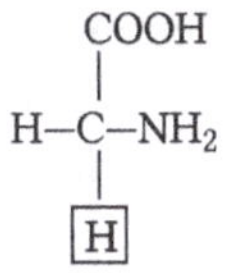

Glycine

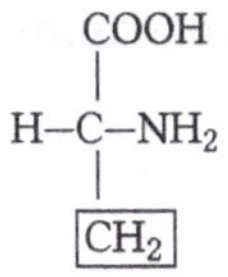

Alanine

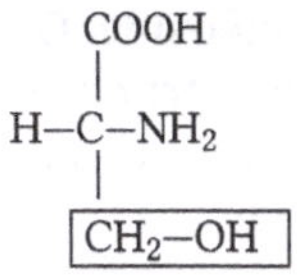

Serine

(iii) Fats and Oils (lipids)

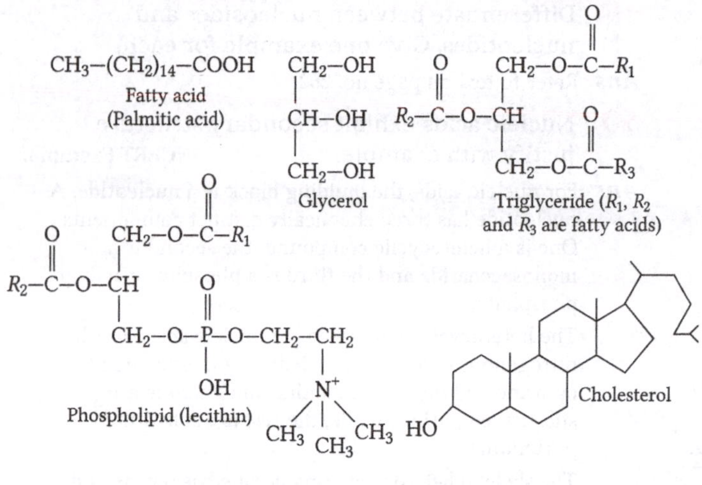

(iv) Nitrogen bases (v) Nucleosides (vi) Nucleotide

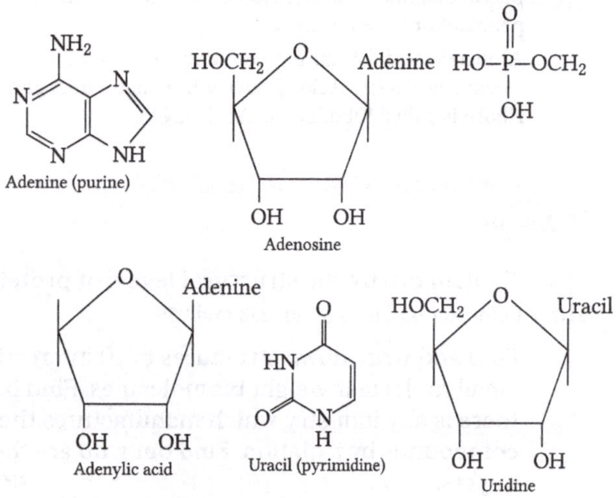

Diagrammatic representation of small molecular weight biomolecules of living tissues

Various industries manufacture these compounds by isolation, e.g. glucose is being manufactured by health and energy drink producing companies, likewise fatty acids by companies that produce cooking oils, etc. The buyers are drug and pharmaceutical companies. These products are consumed directly by common man as well. (5)

53. Enumerate the difference between a nucleotide and nucleoside. Give two examples of each with their structures. **NCERT Exemplar**

Ans Differences between nucleotide and nucleoside are given below

Nucleotide	Nucleoside
It consists of a nitrogenous base, a sugar (ribose or deoxyribose) and one to three phosphate groups, i.e. sugar + base + phosphate.	It consists of a nitrogenous base covalently attached to a sugar (ribose or deoxyribose), but without the phosphate group, i.e. sugar + base.
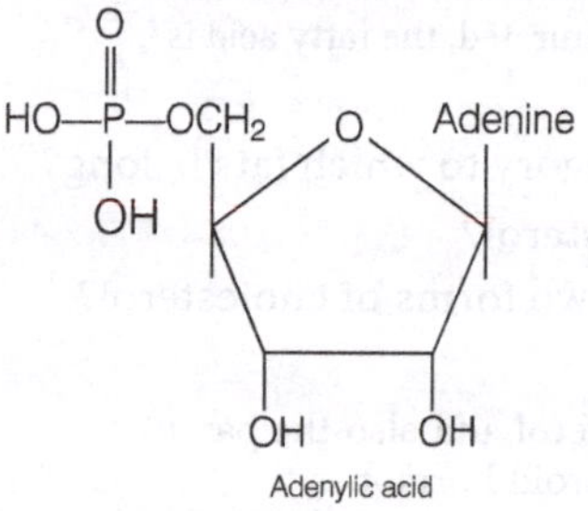 Adenylic acid	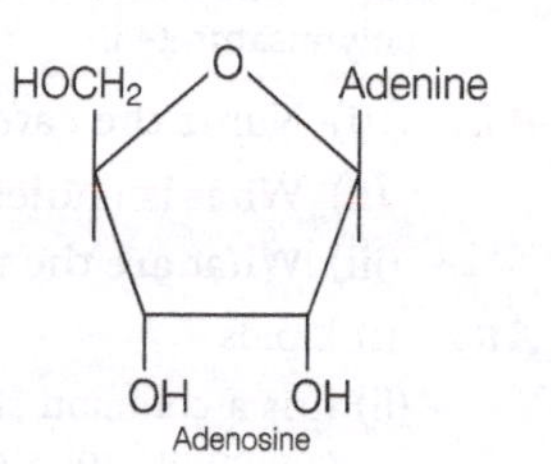 Adenosine
e.g. adenine, guanine, cytosine, uracil and thymine.	e.g. cytidine, uridine, adenosine, guanosine, thymidine and inosine.

(5)

54. Describe Watson and Crick model of DNA.

Ans Refer to text on page no. 262.

55. (i) Identify the structure shown in figure.

(ii) Write the measurement (distance) of the parts marked (*A*), (*B*), (*C*).

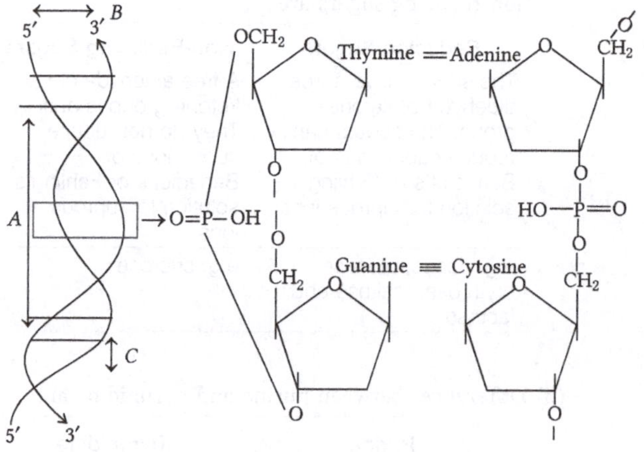

(iii) How many H-bonds are there at the place marked as (6)?

(iv) Which form of DNA is shown in the figure?

(v) Whether B type DNA has left-handed spiral structure or right-handed?

Ans (i) Double helix model of DNA (Waston-Crick model of DNA).

(ii) (*A*) 2 nm (*B*) 3.4 nm (*C*) 0.34 nm.

(iii) The bonds between C and G are three.

(iv) This is B-form of DNA.

(v) B-DNA is right-handed spiral structure. (1×5)

56. Differentiate between DNA and RNA.

Ans Refer to text on page no. 263.

TOPIC 03 Enzymes

The term 'Enzyme' was coined by **Kuhne**. Enzymes are colloidal organic macromolecules, which are mostly proteinaceous in nature, except ribozyme (catalytically active RNA).

These are essential for normal metabolism in the cells. Enzymes are **water soluble** in nature. These are useful for catalysing biochemical reactions in living cells. Hence, also known as **biocatalysts.**

Each and every enzyme catalyses the reaction of a specific substrate because of the configuration of the active site of that protein. An enzyme like any protein have primary, secondary and tertiary structure.

General Properties of Enzymes

Enzymes show the various important properties. These are as follows

(i) They enhance the rate of a chemical reaction without themselves being changed or used.

(ii) Enzymes are efficient in very small amounts.

(iii) Enzymes are highly specific, as each of them catalyses only a specific reaction, e.g. maltase acts only on maltose.

(iv) Enzymes can be denatured by heat (thermolabile or heat sensitive) human enzymes are active at 35-40°C, denature at 50-55°C. The enzymes of bacteria living in hot springs have optimal temperature of 70°C.

Active Site

It is a crevice or pocket of an enzyme into which a particular substrate fits. Thus, enzymes catalyse reactions at a higher rate through their active sites. Each enzyme functions at specific pH and temperature.

Differences between Enzyme Catalysts and Inorganic Catalysts

Enzyme Catalysts	Inorganic Catalysts
These get damaged at high temperature and pressure (above 40°C).	These do not get affected by high temperature and pressure.
Catalyses only specific reactions.	Can catalyse a number of reactions. Thus, are not specific.
Sensitive to changes of the medium like pH, etc.	Do not have any effect of the changes in pH, etc.
These can be regulated by specific molecules.	These cannot be regulated by any other molecules.

Classification and Nomenclature of Enzymes

According to the International Union of Biochemistry (1961), the enzymes have been classified into different groups on the basis of the type of reaction they catalyse. They are divided into six main classes each with 4-13 subclasses and named accordingly by a four digit number.

International System of Enzyme Classification

Class No.	Enzyme	Types of Reaction Catalysed and Example
1	Oxidoreductases	Removing or adding electrons (or H^+), i.e. oxidation reduction reactions, e.g. cytochrome oxidase, succinate dehydrogenase. $\text{Ethanol} + \text{NAD} \underset{\text{DNase}}{\overset{\text{Alcohol}}{\rightleftharpoons}} \text{Acetaldehyde} + \text{NADH}_2$
2	Transferases	Transfer of functional group, carbon group, phosphate group and sulphur containing group, e.g. glutamate pyruvate transaminase, hexokinase, etc. $\text{Glucose} + \text{ATP} \overset{\text{Hexokinase}}{\rightleftharpoons} \text{Glucose}-6-\text{P} + \text{ADP}$
3	Hydrolases	Hydrolysis reactions, i.e. breakdown by introduction of water and also breakdown of covalent bonds, e.g. digestive enzymes (amylase, cellulase, sucrase, maltose, etc.). $\underset{\text{Maltose}}{C_{12}H_{22}O_{11}} + H_2O \xrightarrow{\text{Maltase}} \underset{\text{Glucose}}{2\,C_6H_{12}O_6}$

4	Lyases	Catalyse the cleavage of specific covalent bonds and removal of groups without hydrolysis. They act on C—C, C—O, C—N,C—S and C – halide bonds, e.g. histidine decarboxylase (acts on C—C bond in histidine to form CO_2 and histamine), aldolase. Fructose 1, 6 diphosphate $\xrightarrow{\text{Aldolase}}$ Dihydroxy acetone phospate + glyceraldehyde phosphate
5	Isomerases	Isomerisation reactions catalyse the rearrangement of molecular structure forms of isomers, e.g. phosphohexoisomerase, epimerase, maltase, etc. Xylulose 5 phosphate $\xrightarrow{\text{Epimerase}}$ Ribulose 5 phosphate
6	Ligases	Formation of bonds with ATP cleavage, e.g. pyruvate and CO_2 combine to form oxaloacetic acid in the presence of enzyme pyruvate carboxylase. Pyruvic acid $+ CO_2 \xrightarrow[\text{ATP}]{\text{Pyruvate carboxylase}}$ Oxaloacetic acid + ADP + Pi

Functioning of Enzyme

For a chemical reaction to proceed, the substrate (S) must bind to enzyme at the active site within a cleft or pocket.

During conversion of substrate into a product, formation of an enzyme-substrate complex takes place.

$$\text{E (Enzyme)} + \text{S (Substrate)} \longrightarrow \text{ES complex}$$

This complex formation is a **transient phenomenon.** Thus, during the state, when substrate is bound to the enzyme active site, a new structure of the substrate, called **transition state** structure is formed. After the expected reaction of breaking and making of bond is completed, the product is released from the active site and the substrate gets transformed into the structure of product.

Stability is related to energy status of the molecule or the structure. It is pictorially represented through a graph as given below. In the graph, Y-axis represents the potential energy content and the X-axis represents the progression of the structural transformation (states through the transition state). Following levels are noticed between the energy levels of S and P

(i) When P is at a lower level than S, reaction is exothermic or spontaneous, i.e. no need for external supply of energy.

(ii) When P is at higher level than S, reaction is endothermic or energy requiring reaction, i.e. external supply of energy is needed.

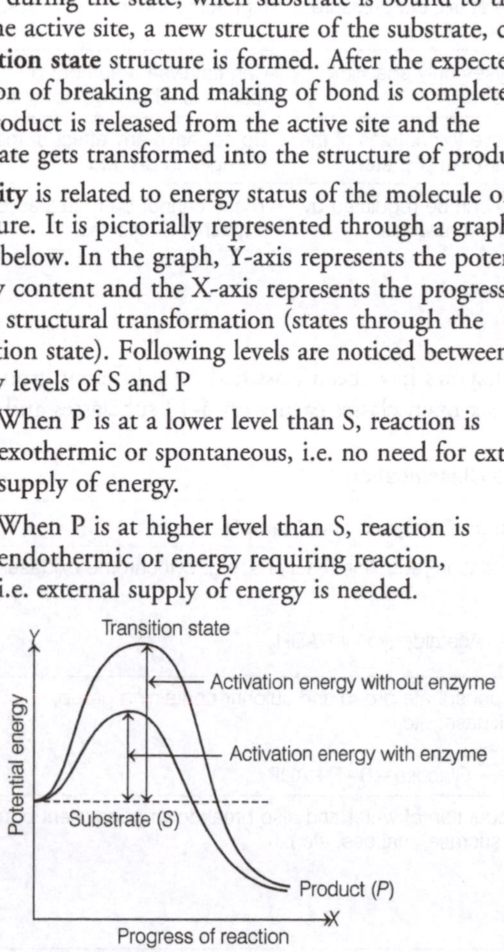

Fig. 12.17 Concept of activation energy

It proves that whether it is an exothermic or an endothermic state, the 'S' has to go through a much higher energy state (transition state).

This difference between the average energy content of S from that of its transition state is called **activation energy**.

Note

Enzymes help in bringing this energy barrier down, thus making the transition of substrate to product more easy.

Nature of Enzyme Action

Each enzyme (E) has a substrate (S) binding site in its molecule in order to form a highly reactive Enzyme **Substrate** (ES) complex.

This complex is short lived and dissociates into its product (P) and unchanged enzyme with an intermediate formation of the Enzyme Product (EP) complex.

This hypothesis is also known as **lock and key mechanism.** It was given by **Emil Fischer** in 1894.

The catalytic cycle of an enzyme action can be described in the following steps

(i) First, the substrate binds to its active site of the enzyme, fitting into the active site.

(ii) The binding of the substrate induces the enzyme to alter its shape, so that it can fit more tightly around the substrate.

(iii) The active site of the enzyme now in close proximity of the substrate breaks the chemical bonds of the substrate, due to which the new enzyme product complex is formed.

(iv) The enzyme releases the products of the reaction and the free enzyme is ready to bind to another molecule of the substrate, so that it can run through the catalytic cycle once again.

$$E + S \rightarrow ES \ldots \rightarrow EP \rightarrow E + P$$

Note

Another hypothesis that explains the mode of enzyme activity is the Induced fit hypothesis, proposed by **Koshland** (1960). It states that the active site of enzyme does not initially exist in a shape that is complementary to the substrate, but is induced to assume the complementary shape as the substrate becomes bound to the enzyme.

Factors Affecting Enzyme Activity

Enzyme activity is altered or affected by the change in the conditions that can alter the tertiary structure of the protein. The factors include temperature, pH, change in substrate concentration or binding of specific chemicals that regulate its activity.

Some of the factors responsible are given below

1. Temperature and pH

Enzymes generally work at narrow range of temperature and pH. Each enzyme shows highest activity at a specific temperature and pH known as **optimum temperature** and **optimum pH**, e.g. amylase functions at 37°C. During low temperature, the enzyme is preserved temporarily in an inactive state, whereas at high temperature its activity gets destroyed (because proteins denature at high temperature). If we talk about pH, change in pH of the medium alters the physical structure of the enzyme molecule(or denaturation) and decreases enzyme activity. The peaks in the graphs show maximum (optimum) enzymatic activity.

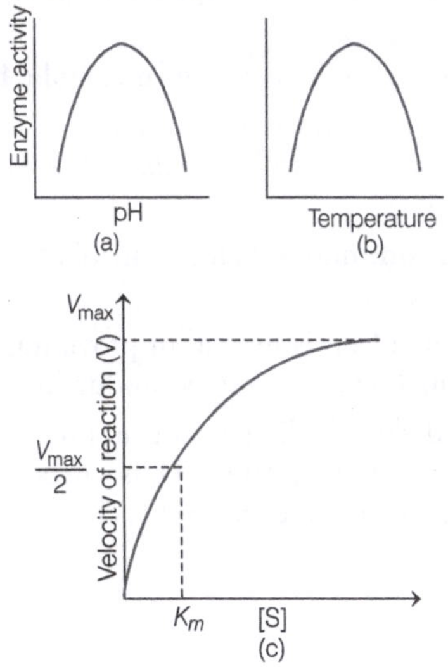

Fig. 12.18 Effect of change in (a) pH, (b) Temperature, (c) Concentration of substrate on enzyme activity

The enzyme activity decreases with decrease in temperature. Therefore, organs are kept in low temperature during transport for transplantation in human beings.

2. Concentration of Substrate

With the increase in the concentration of substrate, the velocity of the enzymatic reaction rises at first. Thus, the reaction finally reaches a maximum velocity, i.e. V_{max}.

V_{max} is the maximum velocity, which does not exceed by any further rise in concentration of the substrate. This is because at this stage, the enzyme molecules (fewer than substrate molecules) become fully saturated and no active site is left free to bind to additional substrate molecules.

3. Enzyme Inhibition

The enzyme activity is also sensitive to the presence of specific chemicals that shuts off the enzyme, the moment they bind to the enzyme. This process is known as **inhibition** and the chemical responsible is known as **inhibitor**, e.g. cyanides, heavy metal, salts, etc. The factors that activate the activity of enzymes are known as activators, e.g. Mg^{2+}, Ca^{2+}, HCl, etc.

Competitive Inhibitor

When the inhibitor closely resembles the molecular structure of the substrate and inhibits the activity of the enzyme, it is known as competitive inhibitor. The inhibitor competes with the substrate for binding to the enzyme (binding site).

Consequently, the substrate is unable to bind and inhibitor binds to it. Thus, the overall activity of the enzyme declines, e.g. inhibition of succinic dehydrogenase by malonate which closely resembles the substrate succinate in structure. These type of competitive inhibitors are used in controlling bacterial pathogens.

Cofactors

These are the non-protein constituents of conjugated or compound enzymes associated with the apoenzyme of the enzyme (protein portion). As it is already studied that simple enzyme are composed of one or several polypeptide chains. However, there are a number of cases in which non-protein constituents called **cofactors** bound to the enzyme in order to make it catalytically active.

Categories of Cofactors

Cofactor Type	Properties	Examples
Prosthetic groups	Tightly bound to the apoenzyme and are always organic in nature.	**Haem** is the prosthetic group and is part of the active site of **catalase enzyme,** which hydrolyses H_2O_2 into water and oxygen is evolved. $2H_2O_2 \longrightarrow 2H_2O + O_2$

Cofactor Type	Properties	Examples
Coenzymes	Associate with apoenzyme only during the course of catalysis. Also they are always organic in nature. Generally derived from the vitamins. Act as carriers of chemical groups or atoms or electrons.	**FAD** (from Riboflavin–B_2) for Succinate DNase. **NAD** (from Niacin–B_5) for Malate DNase. **TPP** (from Thiamine–B_1) for Decarboxylases.
Metal ions	Form bond with the side chains (of enzyme) and substrate	Zinc is a cofactor for carboxypeptidase.

Dynamic State of Body Constituents

Concept of Metabolism

Each cell contains thousands of organic compounds. These compounds or biomolecules are present in living organisms in various concentrations. Turn over of biomolecules is one of the greatest discoveries. It is the phenomenon, in which biomolecules change constantly into some other biomolecules or made from some other biomolecules.

All these transfers of one biomolecule into other occur due to chemical reaction, which continuously take place in an organism. The chemical reactions together are called **metabolism.**

Each metabolic reaction results in the process of transformation. For example,

- Removal of CO_2 from amino acids into an amine.
- Removal of amino group in a nucleotide base.
- Hydrolysis of a glycosidic bond in a disaccharide.

Majority of these metabolic reactions do not occur in isolation, instead they take place in a series of linked reaction known as **metabolic pathways.** These pathways are either linear or circular and *criss-cross* with each other.

Flow of metabolites through metabolic pathway has a definite rate and direction and this metabolic flow is called the **dynamic state** of body constituents. Also, these metabolic reactions are always **catalysed reaction,** i.e. no uncatalysed metabolic conversion is present in living systems. The catalysts, which hasten the rate of a given metabolic conversion are also proteins. These proteins with catalytic power are called **enzymes.**

Metabolic Basis for Living

Metabolic pathways in living organisms are divided into two main types

(i) **Anabolic Pathways** These include the formation of complex structure from simple ones, e.g. formation of cholesterol from acetic acid, protein synthesis, etc. These are energy consuming pathways.

(ii) **Catabolic Pathways** These include the formation of simpler structures, i.e. the breakage of complex structures into simpler ones, e.g. conversion of glucose into lactic acid in skeletal muscles. These are energy releasing pathways.

Adenosine Triphosphate (ATP)

The most important form of energy currency present in living systems is the bond energy in a chemical compound of ATP.

The Living State

Various chemical compounds (metabolites or biomolecules) are present at a concentration characteristic of each of them, i.e. all living organisms exist in a steady state characterised by concentrations of each of these biomolecules. It is the most important fact of biological systems.

These metabolites are in a state of **metabolic flux.**

Hence, the living system is kept in a non-equilibrium state by metabolic flux, which enables it to perform work as living organism.

It has to work continuously and is unable to reach equilibrium.

Therefore, metabolism is helpful in providing a mechanism which enables energy production.

It can be stated that the living state and metabolism are synonymous and are correlated. Thus, metabolism and living state are incomplete without each other.

Topic Practice 3

Multiple Choice Questions

1 Mark

1. Enzyme catalysts are different from inorganic catalysts in which way?
   (a) Enzyme catalysts are smaller in size and lesser in weight in comparison to that of inorganic catalysts
   (b) Inorganic catalysts can work efficiently at high temperature, but enzyme catalysts cannot (except few enzymes)
   (c) Inorganic catalysts can work efficiently at high pressure, but enzyme catalysts cannot
   (d) Both (b) and (c)

Ans (d) Inorganic catalysts work at high temperature and pressure whereas organic catalysts do not.

2. Enzymes that catalyse the removal of groups from substrates by mechanism other than hydrolysis, addition of groups to double bonds are called
   (a) lyases
   (b) ligases
   (c) hydrolases
   (d) dehydrogenases

Ans (a) Lyases catalyse the breakage of specific covalent bonds and removal of groups without hydrolysis, e.g. histidine decarboxylase splits C—C bonds of histidine forming CO_2 and histamine.

3. Choose the correct option.
   (a) $E + S \longrightarrow ES \longrightarrow E + P \longrightarrow EP$
   (b) $E + S \rightleftharpoons ES \longrightarrow E - P \longrightarrow E + P$
   (c) $E + S \longrightarrow ES \rightleftharpoons E - P \longrightarrow E + P$
   (d) $E + S \rightleftharpoons ES \rightleftharpoons E - P \rightleftharpoons E + P$

Ans (b) Each enzyme [E] has a substrate [S] binding site in its molecule, so that a highly reactive Enzyme Substrate [ES] complex is produced.

This complex is short lived and dissociates into its product and the unchanged enzyme with an intermediate formation of the enzyme product complex [EP].

The formation of the ES complex is essential for catalysis.

$$E + S \rightleftharpoons ES \longrightarrow E - P \longrightarrow E + P$$

4. Choose the correct graph, showing the effect of pH on the velocity (V) of a typical enzymatic reaction?

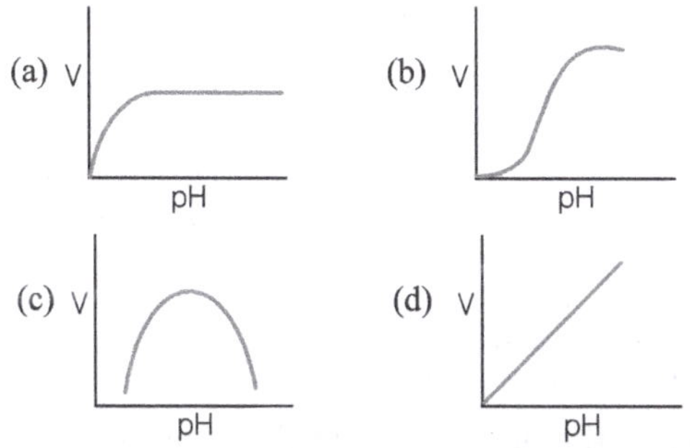

Ans (c) Some enzymes act best in an acidic medium and others in an alkaline medium. For every enzyme, there is an optimum pH where its action is maximum. Most enzymes show activity in a pH range of about 6.0-7.5, i.e. neutral pH. A shift towards the alkaline or acid side rapidly decreases the enzyme activity and finally stops it altogether.

5. Select the correct graph, which shows the effect of temperature on the velocity (V) of a typical enzymatic reaction.

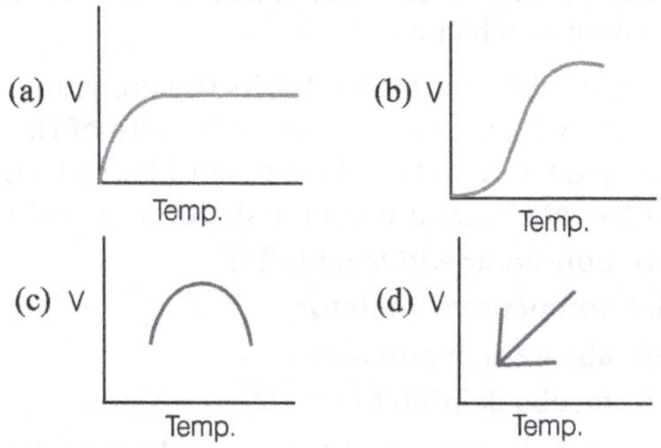

Ans (c) Enzymes generally function in a narrow range of temperature. Each enzyme shows its highest activity at a particular temperature, called the optimum value.

Low temperature preserves the enzyme in a temporarily inactive state, whereas high temperature destroys enzymatic activity because proteins are denatured by heat.

6. Select the correct graph, which shows the relationship between the rate of an enzymatic activity and substrate concentration.

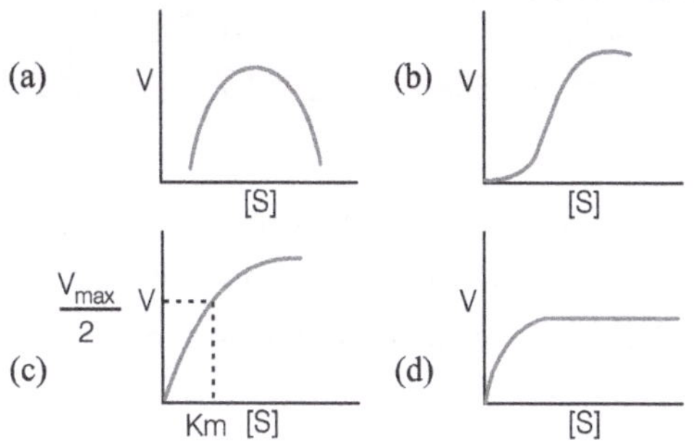

Ans (c) When enzyme molecules are more than substrate molecules, a progressive increase in the substrate molecules (S), increases the velocity (V) of their conversion to products.
However, eventually the rate of reaction reaches a maximum. At this stage, the active sites of all the available enzyme molecules are occupied by the substrate molecules. Therefore, the substrate molecules occupy the active sites vacated by the products and cannot increase the rate of reaction further.

7. **When the binding of the chemical shuts off enzyme activity, the process and the chemical are respectively called as**
(a) inhibition; inhibitor
(b) competition; substrate
(c) initiation; promoter
(d) None of the above

Ans (a) The activity of an enzyme is also sensitive to the presence of specific chemicals that bind to the enzyme. When the binding of the chemical shuts off enzyme activity, the process is called inhibition and the chemical is called an inhibitor.

8. **The inhibitor, which inhibits the enzyme activity by binding to the active site of the enzyme, due to the close resemblance to the substrate in its molecular structure is called**
(a) non-competitive inhibitor
(b) competitive inhibitor
(c) allosteric modulator
(d) feedback inhibitor

Ans (b) When the inhibitor closely resembles the substrate in its molecular structure and inhibits the activity of the enzyme, it is known as competitive inhibitor.

9. **The cofactors that associate with the apoenzyme only during course of catalysis are called as**
(a) cofactors (b) coenzymes
(c) metal ions (d) prosthetic group

Ans (b) Coenzymes are organic compounds and they associate with apoenzyme temporarily, i.e. during the course of catalysis.

Very Short Answer Type Questions
(1 Mark)

10. **Mention the chemical nature of enzymes.**

Ans Enzymes are proteinaceous in nature, except ribozyme.

11. **What is the term given to ribonucleic acid with catalytic power?**

Ans Ribozymes.

12. **What is the name given to that part of the enzyme where catalytic work is carried out?**

Ans Active or Catalytic site is that part of an enzyme where catalytic work is carried out.

13. **Reaction given below is catalysed by oxidoreductase between two substrates *A* and *A'*. Complete the reaction.** **NCERT Exemplar**

A reduced + *A'* oxidised $\longrightarrow$

Ans *A* reduced + *A'* oxidised $\longrightarrow$ *A* oxidised + *A'* reduced

14. **Name the principle on which the enzymes work.**

Ans Enzymes work on the principle of lock and key model.

15. **Lock and key hypothesis was proposed by which scientist?**

Ans Emil Fischer (1894) proposed lock and key hypothesis.

16. **Name two physical factors which can affect the enzyme activity.**

Ans Temperature and pH are the two physical factors that affect activity of an enzyme.

17. **The enzyme that works only in the presence of a cofactor or coenzyme is called.**

Ans Apoenzyme works only in the presence of a cofactor or coenzyme.

18. **The enzymes activity gets destroyed on increasing high temperature. What happens during that state that enzyme looses its activity?**

Ans The enzyme becomes inactive on increasing temperature because the proteins denature at high temperature due to which its tertiary structure gets disrupted.

Short Answer Type I Questions
(2 Marks)

19. **Name the six classes of enzymes.**

Ans Six classes of enzymes are
(i) Oxidoreductases (ii) Transferases
(iii) Hydrolases (iv) Lyases
(v) Isomerases (vi) Ligases (2)

20. **According to the classification of enzymes ligases are one of the important class of enzymes. Explain it by giving example.**

Ans Ligases are the class of enzymes that function in the formation of bond with ATP cleavage, e.g. pyruvic acid and CO_2 combines to form oxaloacetic acid in the presence of enzyme pyruvate carboxylase.

$$\text{Pyruvic acid} + CO_2 \xrightleftharpoons[\text{ATP}]{\text{Pyruvate carboxylase}} \text{Oxaloacetic acid} + \text{ADP} + \text{Pi}$$ (2)

21. Bring out the difference between ligases and lyases.

Ans Difference between ligases and lyases is given below

Ligases	Lyases
These are the enzymes, which catalyse the covalent bonding between two substrates to form a large molecule.	These are the enzymes, which catalyse the cleavage of specific covalent bonds in a large molecule to form smaller molecules without the addition of water.

(2)

22. How does temperature and pH affect activity of enzyme?

Ans The activity of enzyme is affected by the following

(i) **Temperature** Enzyme becomes temporarily inactive at lower temperature and its activity gets completely destroyed at high temperature.

(ii) **pH** Any change in pH of the medium alter the tertiary structure of protein. Thus, decreasing the enzyme activity. (1 × 2)

23. Draw graphs for the following

(i) Effect of change in pH

(ii) Effect of change in temperature

Ans Refer to text on page no. 271.

24. How does temperature affect an enzyme catalysed reaction?

Ans The temperature affects the velocity of enzyme action. When the temperature is high, there is a sudden decrease in enzyme action due to denaturation. Most enzymatic reactions occur below 45°C. (1 + 1)

25. What would happen when salivary amylase that acts specifically on starch enters the stomach and mixes with gastric juice ?

Ans In mouth, salivary amylase changes starch to maltose. Action of amylase stops in stomach as it cannot act in acidic medium. (2)

26. Discuss about competitive inhibition of enzymes? How is it different from non-competitive inhibition?

Ans When the enzyme inhibitor closely resemble the molecular structure of the substrate, the enzyme action is inhibited.

This is called competitive inhibition. When the active site is blocked by the inhibitor, the inhibition is said to be non-competitive and no enzyme substrate complex is formed. (1+1)

27. How are prosthetic groups different from cofactors?

Ans Differences between prosthetic groups and cofactors are

Prosthetic group	Cofactor
It is the non-protein part or the group which gets permanently attached to the enzyme.	It is the non-protein substance or group which gets attached to the enzyme, temporarily or permanently.
Prosthetic groups are organic factors, but some are metallic also like Iron, prophyrin of the cytochromes.	These can be organic, inorganic or metallic factors.

(2)

Short Answer Type II Questions

3 Marks

28. Describe the important properties of enzymes. **NCERT**

Ans Refer to text on page no. 269.

29. Observe the given figure related to enzyme action and answer the following questions.

(i) What is the figure showing?

(ii) Name the substances marked as (*A*) and (*B*).

(iii) What does the arrows marked (*C*) to (*E*) indicate?

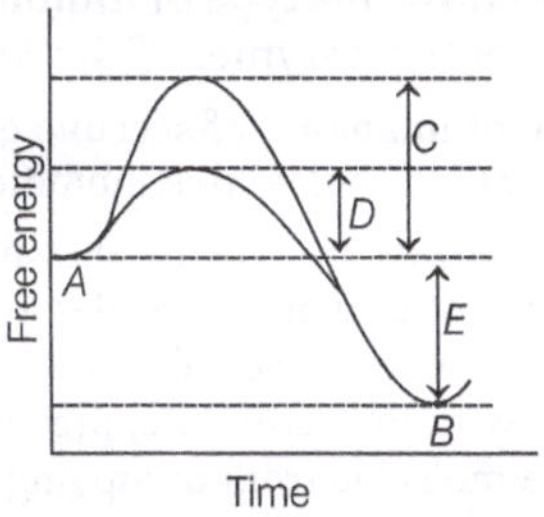

Ans (i) Figure is showing the activation energy requirement for non-catalysed and enzyme catalysed reactions.

(ii) Substances marked on arrows *A* and *B* are

A–Substrate *B*–End products

(iii) Arrows marked shows

C–Energy of activaton without enzyme.

D–Energy of activation with enzymes.

E–Free energy difference between the substrate and the end product. (1×3)

30. Nature of enzyme action is best explained by lock and key hypothesis. What were the basis of that model? Explain.

Ans Refer to text on page no. 270.

31. **Describe the influence of temperature on enzyme action.**

Ans Enzymes generally function at a narrow range of temperature. The temperature at which the enzyme shows its maximum activity, is called its optimum temperature. The enzyme activity decreases at temperatures below and above the optimum temperature.

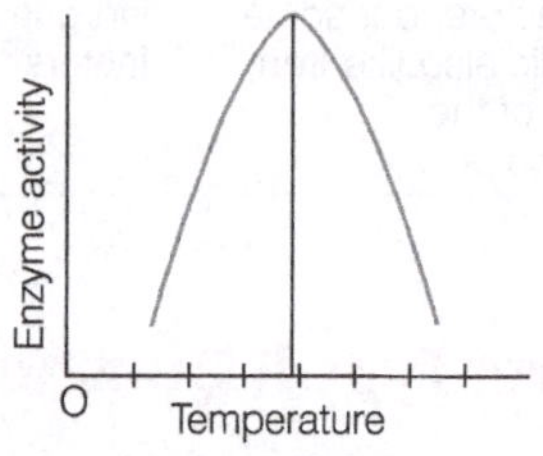

At low temperatures, the enzyme is inactive, while at high temperature, the enzyme is denatured and so it loses its activity. (3)

32. **Succinic dehydrogenase is an enzyme that causes the substrate, succinate, to breakdown into fumarate.**
Malonate is a substance that resembles succinate and inhibits the activity of succinic dehydrogenase.

(i) State the type of inhibition of succinic dehydrogenase by malonate.

(ii) Explain how this type of inhibition affects the activity of the enzyme.

Ans (i) The type of inhibition of succinic dehydrogenase by malonate is competitive inhibition.

(ii) The inhibitor competes with the substrate for the active sites of enzyme molecules as it has a structure similar to the substrate that allows it to combine with the active site, preventing any substrate molecule from occupying that site.

This reduces the rate of the reaction since, the substrate can only use the enzyme molecules that are not occupied by the inhibitor, resulting in the same quantity of product being formed at a slower rate. (1+2)

Long Answer Type Questions

5 Marks

33. **Explain different classes of enzymes. Explain any two with the type of reaction they catalyse.** **NCERT Exemplar**

Ans Refer to text on page no. 269 and 270.

34. **Formation of Enzyme-Substrate (ES) complex is the first step in catalysed reactions. Describe the other steps till the formation of product.**

Ans **Mechanism of Enzymatic Action** Refer to text on page no. 270.

35. **What are factors which affect action of enzyme?**

Ans Refer to text on page no. 271.

36. **Discuss the types of enzyme cofactors that are required for the efficient activity of enzymes.**

Ans Cofactors are non-protein molecules that are relatively stable at high temperatures, consisting of three main types, i.e. inorganic ions, coenzymes and prosthetic groups.

(i) Examples of inorganic ions are calcium ions (activates the enzyme thrombokinase to convert prothrombin into thrombin during the blood clotting process) and chloride ions (activates salivary amylase to convert starch into maltose).

(ii) Examples of coenzymes are NAD, acetyl coenzyme-A, ATP and NADP.

(iii) Prosthetic groups are molecules that are permanently attached to the enzyme. Examples of prosthetic groups are haem and FAD. (5)

37. **Differentiate between anabolism and catabolism, along with an example for each.**

Ans Differences between anabolism and catabolism are as follows

Anabolism	Catabolism
The metabolic pathways that lead to the synthesis of complex molecules from simpler ones, constitute anabolism.	The metabolic pathways that lead to the formation of simpler molecules from a larger molecule by its breakdown, constitute catabolism.
These are the biosynthetic pathways.	These are the degradative pathways.
Energy is stored in the form of chemical bonds.	Chemical bonds are broken and energy is released.
They consume energy, e.g. protein synthesis from amino acids.	They release energy, e.g. breakdown of glucose into pyruvic acid in glycolysis.

(5)

38. **What is the concept of metabolism? What are the metabolic basis for living?**

Ans Refer to text on page no. 272.

SUMMARY

- **Biomolecules** are organic molecules present in living organism made up of H, O, C and N in different proportions. They are further classified into biomacromolecules (proteins, nucleic acids, lipids and polysaccharides) and biomicromolecules (amino acids and fatty acids).
- **Living tissue** is composed of two pools-acid soluble pool, which represents cytoplasmic composition and acid insoluble pool, which represents cytoplasmic and organelle composition.
- **Carbohydrates** are represented by molecular formula $C_nH_{2n}O_n$ and defined as polyhydroxy aldehydes or ketone compounds, which on hydrolysis give aldehydes or ketones. Broadly, they are classified into-monosaccharides, oligosaccharides and polysaccharides.
- **Amino acids** are made up of C, H, N, O and sometimes sulphur too and they serve as monomers of proteins. Each amino acid has a free carboxyl group, amino group and a side chain Broadly amino acids are classified into–alcoholic, aromatic, heterocyclic and sulphur containing.
- **Zwitter ion** is a molecule containing positive and negative ionic groups. Amino acid can act as acid and base as it contains one amino and one carboxylic group. When put in a neutral solution amino acid exists as dipolar ion or Zwitter ion.
- **Isoelectric point** is the pH at which amino acid is electrically neutral or exists as Zwitter ion.
- **Proteins** are the linear, unbranched polymers of amino acids which are linked together *via* peptide bond. They can be simple (albumins, globulins and prolamins) or conjugated (glycoproteins and diploproteins), structurally, they are classified into primary, secondary, tertiary and quaternary.
- **Lipids** are hydrophobic compounds made up of long chain of fatty acids with carboxyl group. They can be simple (fats and waxes), compound (phospholipids, glycolipids and chromolipids) or derived (sterols and prostaglandins).
- **Nucleic acids** constitute the genetic material. DNA and RNA are present in all living cells. The basic unit that forms them is nucleotides, which is made up of phosphoric acid, pentose sugar and a nitrogenous base. Structure of DNA was given by Watson and Crick.
- **ATP** or **Adenosine Triphosphate** forms the energy currency of the cell. It was discovered by Karl Lehmann in 1929.
- **Enzymes** are proteinaceous substances capable of altering the rate of chemical reactions without undergoing any changes in themselves. They are also known as biological catalyst. They work by lock and key mechanism or induced fit mechanism.
- **Activation energy** is defined as the amount of energy required by substrate molecules to form the product.
- **Active site** is a distinct cavity in which substrate is bound and active centre of enzyme is present. Here, the amino acids are grouped together to combine with the substrate.
- **Lock and key hypothesis** proposed that geometry of active sites of enzyme and shape of substrate molecule are complementary to each other. This theory explains the specificity of enzyme action.
- **Activity of enzyme** is affected by many factors such as temperature, pH, ionic concentration, E-S concentration and product concentration.
- **Inhibitors** are specific chemicals which when binds to an enzyme shuts off the enzymic activity and this process is called inhibition. It can be competitive or non-competitive.
- **Proenzymes** are the precursor of a proteolytic enzyme. They are cleaved to form an active enzyme. Other name for proenzymes is zymogen.
- **Induced fit hypothesis** proposed that active site of enzyme does not initially exist in a shape complimentary to the substrate. Rather, it is induced to assume the complementary shape as the substrate become bound to enzyme.

Chapter Practice

Multiple Choice Questions

1 Mark

1. Secondary metabolites can be observed in
   (a) plant cells
   (b) fungal cells
   (c) microbial cells
   (d) All of the above

2. Identify the correct statement from those given below.
   (a) Lipids with molecular weight not exceeding 800 Da, comes under acid soluble fraction
   (b) The acid soluble fraction have four types of organic compounds, i.e. proteins, nucleic acid, polysaccharides and lipids
   (c) The macromolecules from cytoplasm and organelles become the acid insoluble fraction
   (d) The acid insoluble pool represents roughly the cytoplasmic composition of cells

3. Identify the given structure and name the compound.

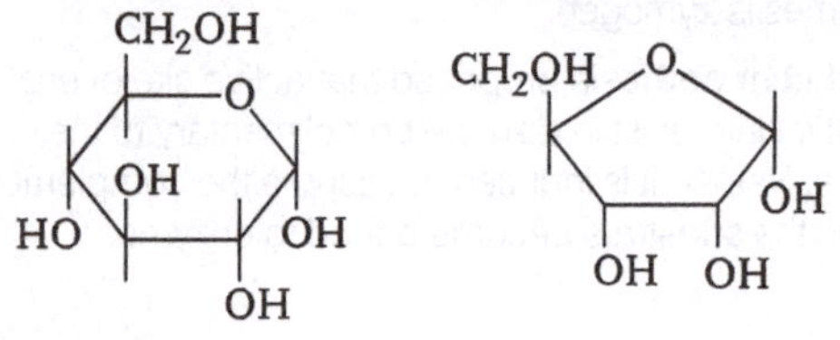

A B

   (a) Ribose, Glucose
   (b) Deoxyribose, Ribose
   (c) Glucose, Ribose
   (d) Ribose, Deoxyribose

4. A fatty acid has a carboxyl group attached to *R* group. The *R* group could be a/an
   (a) methyl
   (b) ethyl
   (c) higher number of —CH_2groups (1 to 19 carbons)
   (d) All of the above

5. Identify *A* and *B*.

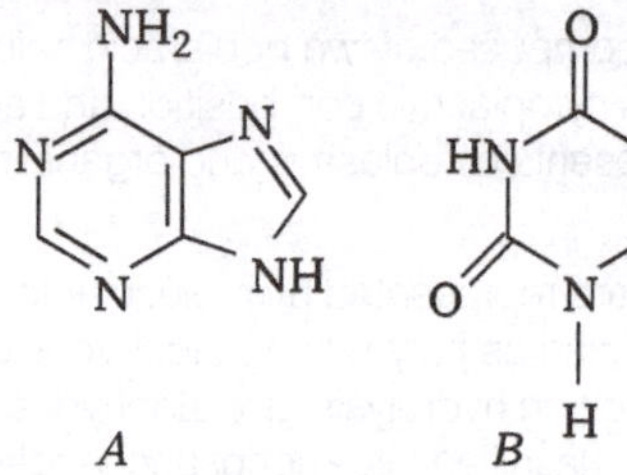

A *B*

	A	*B*
(a)	Cytosine	Uracil
(b)	Adenine	Thymine
(c)	Adenine	Uracil
(d)	Guanine	Thymine

6. Which of the following is incorrect?
   (a) In cellular organisms, DNA is genetic material
   (b) Adenylic acid is nucleoside
   (c) Cytidine is nucleoside
   (d) N-bases (A, G, C, T, U) have heterocyclic rings

7. Which of the following statements is/are correct?
   (a) Living steady state has a self-regulatory mechanism called homeostasis
   (b) Energy flow and energy transformation of living system follow law of thermodynamics
   (c) Metabolism is the release and gain of energy
   (d) All of the above

8. Choose the correct statements.
   (a) The living state is a non-equilibrium steady state to be able to perform work
   (b) The constant flow of materials for energy in and out of cell prevent the cell from reaching equilibrium
   (c) Living state and metabolism are synonyms
   (d) All are correct

9. Pick the odd statement out.
   (a) Removal of CO_2 from amino acids converts an amino acid into an amine
   (b) All the biomolecules have a turnover
   (c) Metabolic pathways are termed as transformation reactions
   (d) Metabolic pathways always follow a linear route

Assertion-Reason Type Questions

(1 Mark)

Direction (Q. Nos. 10-17) *In each of the following questions, a statement of Assertion (A) is given followed by corresponding statement of Reason (R). Of the statements, mark the correct answer as*

(a) If both A and R are true and R is the correct explanation of A

(b) If both A and R are true, but R is not the correct explanation of A

(c) If A is true, but R is false

(d) If A is false, but R is true

10. **Assertion** (A) Secondary metabolites are produced in small quantities and their extraction from the plant is difficult and expensive.

Reason (R) Secondary metabolites can be commercially produced by using tissue culture technique.

11. Given below is the structure of an animal steroid. Which is insoluble in water and chemically unreactive. Study the structure and comment upon the appropriateness of Assertion and the Reason.

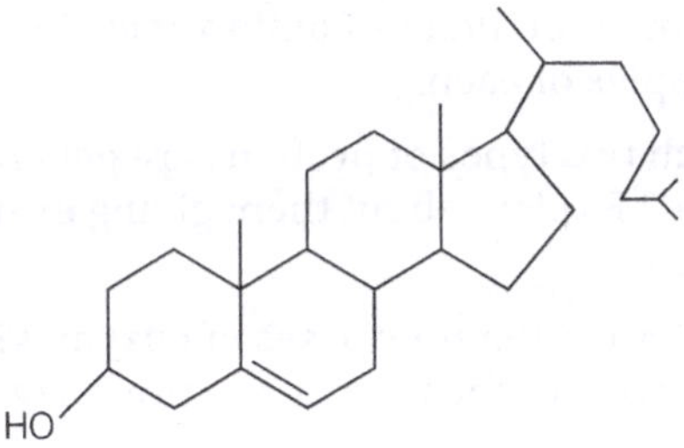

Assertion (A) It is an important component of the membranes of cells providing stability.

Reason (R) It is important because it can be found in large concentrations in liver, brain etc.

12. **Assertion** (A) Nine amino acid are reffered to as essential amino acids for humans.

Reason (R) These are synthesised in the human body.

13. **Assertion** (A) An example of non-competitive inhibitor is cyanide.

Reason (R) Cyanide kills animals by inhibiting cytochrome oxidase.

14. **Assertion** (A) Zinc is an apoenzyme for carboxypeptidase.

Reason (R) A complete catalytically active enzyme together with its bound prosthetic group is called apoenzyme.

15. **Assertion** (A) Enzymes are not divided into different classes.

Reason (R) All enzymes catalyse the different reactions.

16. Given below is the graph showing the concept of activation energy related to the functioning of an enzyme. Study the graph and comment upon the appropriateness of the Assertion and Reason.

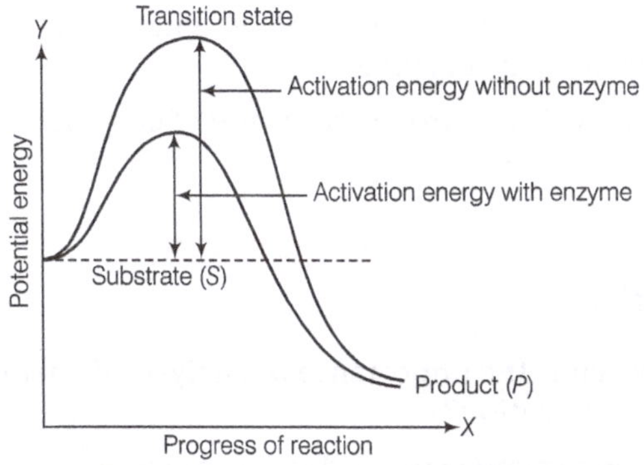

Assertion (A) Enzymes lower down the activation energy of the reactant molecule to make its transition into product easier.

Reason (R) Enzyme are highly substrate specific catalysts.

17. **Assertion** (A) Coenzyme is a non-protein group without which certain enzymes are inactive or incomplete.

Reason (R) Coenzymes not only provide a point of attachment of the chemical group being transformed, but also influence the properties of the group.

Answers

1. (d)	2. (a)	3. (c)	4. (d)	5. (c)
6. (b)	7. (d)	8. (d)	9. (a)	10. (b)
11. (b)	12. (c)	13. (b)	14. (d)	15. (d)
16. (b)	17. (a)			

Very Short Answer Type Questions

(1 Mark)

18. What are the simplest sugars having 3-7 carbon atoms known as?

19. What is the common sugar found in animals?

20. Write the name of simplest amino acid.
21. Give one example each of saturated and unsaturated fatty acids.
22. Which nitrogen base is present in RNA, but not in DNA?
23. Name the two categories of nitrogenous bases.
24. Give any two functions of nucleic acids.
25. How does enzyme isomerase function?
26. Name the enzyme present in saliva.
27. What role does competitive inhibitor play?
28. Name a cofactor of carboxypeptidase, a proteolytic enzyme.
29. Name is the prosthetic group of enzyme peroxidase.

Short Answer Type I Questions

(2 Marks)

30. What is the importance of analysis of chemical composition?
31. Why amino acids said to be amphoteric in nature?
32. Explain how amino acids can be basic.
33. Although all proteins are made of the same amino acids, explain how your proteins may be different from those of a dog.
34. How do metal ions influence the action of enzymes? Give an example.
35. What are cofactors for enzymes? Name any two types of cofactors.
36. (i) In which case, a cofactor becomes a prosthetic group?
    (ii) Why are enzymes referred as biocatalysts?
37. Differentiate between apoenzyme and coenzyme.
38. What is the difference between anabolic and catabolic pathways?

Short Answer Type II Questions

(3 Marks)

39. Give general chemical formulae for monosaccharides, disaccharides and amino acids.
40. What are oligosaccharides? How are these different from polysaccharides?
41. Biological activity of proteins depends on their specific tertiary structure. Explain with the help of a neat and well-labelled diagram.
42. Mention about structure of glycerol and also give the equation for the formation of a triglyceride from glycerol.
43. Why do phospholipids produce bilayer in contact with water?
44. What does an enzyme do in term of energy requirement of a reaction? What would happen if the enzyme did not play this role?
45. Illustrate the concept of activation energy in the mechanism of enzyme action.
46. How does inhibition of an enzyme occur? How is such inhibition useful?

Long Answer Type Questions

(5 Marks)

47. Discuss the chemical analysis of organic compounds in detail.
48. Explain cellulose in detail with the help of a neat and well-labelled diagram.
49. Enumerate the role of amino acids in body and also mention types of amino acids in detail with examples of each.
50. Which two types of proteins are generally found? Explain about them giving examples of each.
51. What are different classes of enzymes? Explain any two with the type of reaction they catalyse.
52. Describe the steps in the formation of product during enzymatic reactions.

Case Based Questions

(4/5 Marks)

53. *Read the following passage and answer the questions that follows.*
    Class XI biology students attended a seminar where the speaker explained the students about the basic macromolecule found in the body, i.e. protein. He started with the monomer unit of protein and explained about different amino acids found. As amino acids are organic compounds containing an amino group and an acidic group as substituents on the same carbon; they are also considered as substituted methane. Suddenly, Ajay stood up and asked

about his queries based on the topic. The guest of seminar patiently explained him all the things. Ajay became satisfied and returned home happily from the seminar.

(i) What are the four substituent groups in an amino acid?

(ii) Why are there so many different types of amino acids?

(iii) Give the general formula of α-amino acids.

(iv) What are acidic amino acids? Give examples.

54. *Read the following passage and answer the questions that follows.*

The zwitter ion formation is particular property of amino acid. It is a neutral molecule (with positive and negative charge), having the ionisable nature of $—NH_2$ and $—COOH$ groups. Hence, in solutions of different pH, the structure of amino acid changes variably.

$$\underset{\text{(Fully protonated form)}}{\underset{(A)}{H_3\overset{+}{N}-\overset{\displaystyle R \atop |}{C}H-COOH}} \underset{}{\overset{+H^+}{\rightleftharpoons}} \underset{\text{(Zwitter ion)}}{\underset{(B)}{H_3\overset{+}{N}-\overset{\displaystyle R \atop |}{C}H-COO^-}}$$

$$\overset{-H^+}{\rightleftharpoons} \underset{\text{(Deprotonated form)}}{\underset{(C)}{H_2N-\overset{\displaystyle R \atop |}{C}H-COO^-}}$$

Representations of a zwitter ion formation

(i) Describe amphoteric nature of amino acids.

(ii) What are α-amino acids ?

(iii) State the importance of zwitter ion formation in biological system.

55. *Read the following passage and answer the questions that follows.*

Nutan's grandfather read in the newspaper that, for predicting the identity of criminals or for deciding the controversies regarding biological parents of the child, court always asks for DNA test. He wanted to know the procedure behind it. So, asked Nutan about DNA as she was studying biology in class XI. She replied that it is a substance present in the cells of living organisms which store the information about an individual.

(i) According to you, what is DNA? And what percentage of DNA varies from one individual to the other?

(ii) What are the main constituents of DNA?

(iii) Why are biologists interested in studying human genome?

(iv) Compare the DNA found in prokaryotes and eukaryotes.

56. *Read the following passage and answer the questions that follows.*

Ankita prepared hard for the test at home. All text based question and one practical based question on lock and key hypothesis was given to check whether the students had understood the phenomenon or not. Ankita who was a topper of class was the only student who was able to solve the problem. All others were unable to attempt the same. Teacher felt happy and asked Ankita to explain the process in the class.

(i) Who proposed the lock and key hypothesis?

(ii) What is the nature of enzyme action?

(iii) Why are enzymes also called biocatalyst?

(iv) Write any two properties of enzymes.

(v) Name the factors which affect enzyme activity.

CHAPTER 13

Cell Cycle and Cell Division

The growth and reproduction are the most important vital characteristics of all living beings. Reproduction produces a new individual of a species which eventually grows into an adult, so these processes go hand in hands. It involves the process of cell division. In this chapter, cell cycle and cell division are discussed in detail.

TOPIC 01 Cell Cycle and Mitosis

Cell Cycle

Cell division is an essential process in all living organisms. The mode of cell division is fundamentally similar in all organisms. During the process of division of a cell, the processes like DNA replication and cell growth must take place in a sequential and coordinated manner to ensure the correct division and formation of progeny cells with intact genomes.

Cell cycle is an orderly sequence of events or a set of stages by which a cell duplicates its genome, synthesises the other constituents (important for the cell) of the cell and eventually divides into two daughter cells.

In terms of cytoplasmic increase, **cell growth** is a continuous process, while DNA synthesis occurs during a specific stage of the cell cycle only. The DNA (chromosomes) are further distributed to daughter nuclei by a series of events. All these events are well-coordinated and under genetic control.

Phases of Cell Cycle

A typical eukaryotic cell (human cell) divides once in every 24 hrs. This duration of cell cycle can vary from an organism to other organism and also from one cell type to another, e.g. yeast cell progresses through the cell cycle and divides in only about 90 minutes.

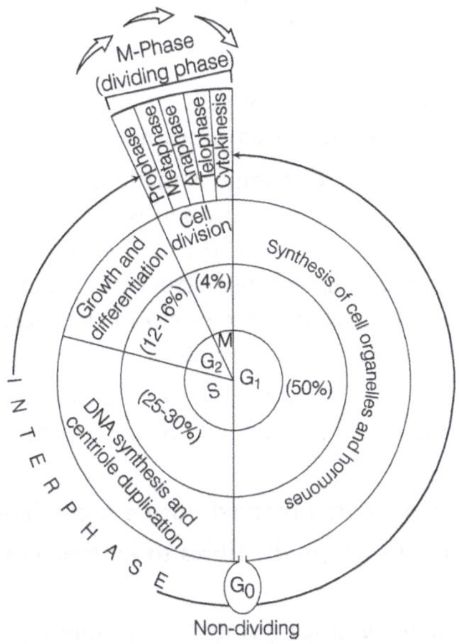

Fig. 13.1 The eukaryotic cell cycle

The cell cycle is divided into two phases

1. Interphase

It is the intense period of cytogenic activities between the end of one cell division to the beginning of the next cell division, i.e. between two successive M-phase.

During this phase, cell prepares itself for both cell growth and DNA replication in an orderly manner. So, it is also known as **preparation phase.** It lasts for about 90-96%, i.e. more than 95% of the total duration of cell cycle. In a cell cycle of human cell, only about one hour is taken by the dividing phase out of 24 hours duration of one cell cycle.

Interphase is further divided into following three substages on the basis of various synthetic activities

(i) **G_1(Gap-1)-Phase** It corresponds to the duration between the mitosis (M-phase) and initiation of replication of DNA. The cell becomes metabolically very active during this period. It grows continuously and prepares itself for DNA replication. Thus, synthesis of enzymes and proteins are needed for this process.

(ii) S **(Synthesis)-Phase** It is known to be the phase in which actual synthesis or replication of DNA takes place. The overall amount of DNA doubles per cell, but no increase in chromosome number takes place during this phase. If the initial amount of DNA is 2C, it will become 4C. In case of animal cell, during S-phase DNA replication begins inside the nucleus while, the duplication of centrioles takes place in the cytoplasm.

(iii) **G_2** (Gap-2)-**Phase** This phase is also called **post-synthetic** or **pre-mitotic phase.** During this stage, the synthesis of DNA stops and proteins required for mitosis are being synthesised while, the growth of cell continues. It prepares the cell to undergo division.

G_0-Phase (Quiescent Stage)

This phase is an extension of G_1-phase and is known as the stage of inactivation of cell cycle. Cells in G_0-phase remain metabolically active, but do not proliferate. This means these cells do not grow or differentiate till the time they do not get instruction to do so depending upon the requirement of an organism.

In adult animals, some cells like heart cells or nerve cells do not undergo division and many other cells divide only occasionally, to replace cells that have already been lost (because of some injury or cell death).

After completing G_2-phase, a cell may enter either into the G_0-phase or into the M-phase directly. The duration of G_0-phase may vary from indefinitely long to very short, except the nerve, bone and heart cells of chordates that are in permanent G_0-phase.

2. M-phase

Following the interphase, the cell enters the **M-phase** or **mitotic phase.**

Mitosis

In this type of division, the chromosomes replicate themselves and get equally distributed into daughter nuclei, i.e. the chromosome number in the parental and progeny cell (diploid) becomes the same. Therefore, it is also known as **equational division.**

Mitosis is also known as **somatic cell division** because it always occurs in somatic cells. Mitotic cell division is seen in the diploid somatic cells in animals, whereas, in plants, mitotic division is seen in both haploid and diploid cells.

It is known to be the phase of actual cell division, which starts with the division of nucleus, followed by the separation of daughter chromosomes, i.e. **karyokinesis** and terminates with the cytoplasmic division, i.e. **cytokinesis.**

Karyokinesis

It is further divided into four main substages, i.e. prophase, metaphase, anaphase and telophase.

1. Prophase

This phase is known for the initiation of condensation of chromosomal material, which during the process of chromatin condensation becomes untangled, and finally the **centriole** (already duplicated during S-phase of interphase) begins to move towards the opposite poles of the animal cell. For the suitability in study we can categorise prophase as

(i) **Early Prophase** During this phase, condensation of chromosomal material takes place in order to form compact mitotic chromosomes composed of two chromatids which are attached together at centromere. The most conspicuous change that takes place during prophase is the **formation of mitotic spindle.** The initiation of mitotic spindle assembly, the microtubules and the proteinaceous components of the cell cytoplasm helps in the completion of the process.

The mitotic spindle is formed between the two pairs of centrioles (duplicated during S-phase) that migrate towards the opposite poles of the cell.

(ii) **Late Prophase** At the end of the prophase, i.e. during late prophase the **nucleolus disintegrates** gradually and the nuclear envelope disappears. This disappearance marks the end of the prophase.

2. Metaphase

It is the phase that starts after the **disintegration of nuclear envelope** in the late prophase. The chromosomes spreadout through the cytoplasm of the cell and are seem to be shortest and thickest. The chromosome can be easily observed under the microscope.

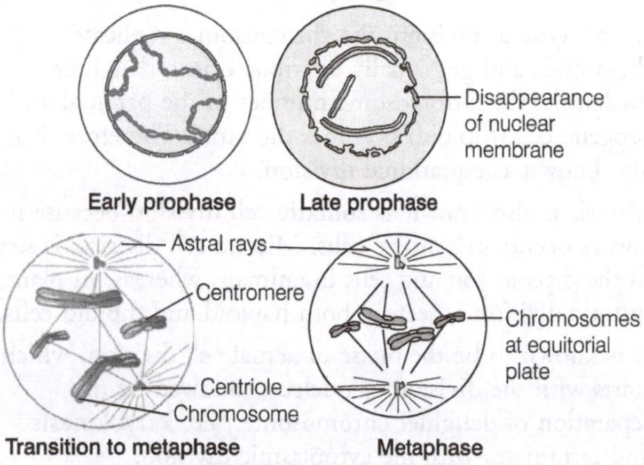

Fig. 13.2 A diagrammatic view of stages in mitosis (prophase and metaphase)

> **Knowledge Plus**
>
> **Mitotic Poison : Colchicine** Colchicine, an alkaloids is extracted from the corms of autumn crocus (*Colchicum autumnale*). It acts as a poison for mitosis as it does not allow the formation of mitotic spindle to take place by preventing the assembly of microtubules. It does not affect replication of chromosomes. Thus, meristematic cells treated with this chemical show doubling of chromosomes. It usually causes arrest of cell division at metaphase of mitosis.

Amitosis is direct division of cellular and nuclear content without the appearance of chromosomes.

Each chromosome at this stage is made up of two longitudinal threads (sister chromatids) and are held together by the centromere in the centre. At the surface of each centromere disc-shaped structures called **kinetochores** are present, which help in the attachment of spindle fibres to the chromosomes.

The chromosomes finally arrange themselves at the equator in one equitorial plane known as **metaphase plate.**

Following changes are observed during metaphase

(i) Attachment of spindle fibres to kinetochores of chromosomes.

(ii) Movement of chromosomes to spindle equator and its alignment along the **metaphase plate** through spindle fibres to both poles.

3. Anaphase

It is known to be the shortest duration phase, i.e. only of 2-3 min and is also very simple stage. At the beginning of this phase, splitting of chromosomes (that are already arranged at metaphase plate) takes place.

The two daughter chromatids now become the chromosomes of future daughter nuclei and start migrating towards the opposite poles along the path of their chromosome fibres.

Thus, following changes are observed during anaphase

(i) Splitting of centromeres and separation of chromatids.

(ii) Movement of chromatids towards the opposite poles.

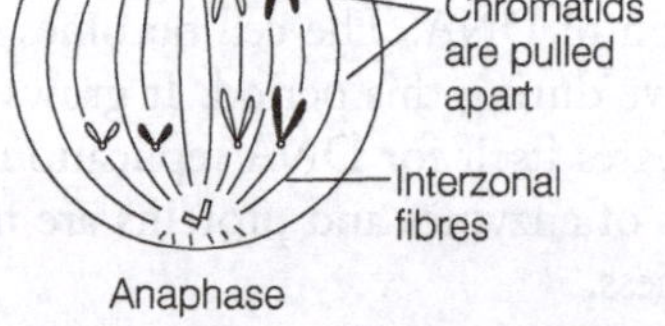

Fig. 13.3 Diagrammatic view of a stage in mitosis (anaphase)

4. Telophase

This is considered to be long and complex phase like prophase. It is the final stage of mitosis. At the onset of this stage, the spindle fibres disappear (absorbed in cytoplasm).

The chromosomes decondense and further lose their individuality after reaching their respective poles.

In general terms, the events of prophase occur just in reverse sequence during this phase. Now, the individual chromosome cannot be seen and the chromatin material gets collected in the form of mass at both opposite poles.

Thus, following changes are observed during telophase

(i) The chromosomes gradually uncoil and cluster at opposite spindle poles. Thus, their individual identity as discrete elements is lost.

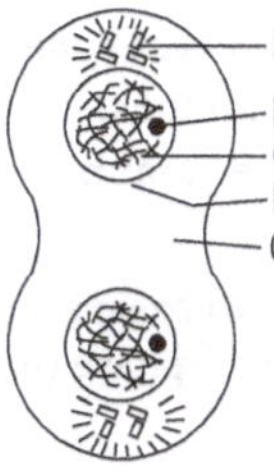

Fig. 13.4 Diagrammatic view of a stage in mitosis (telophase)

(ii) Nuclear envelope slowly reformes around the chromosomes.

(iii) Reappearance of nucleolus, Golgi complex and ER also takes place.

Cytokinesis

It is commonly known as the **division of cytoplasm** of the parent cell into two daughter cells after the **division of nucleus** or **karyokinesis.**

Mitosis is not only the segregation of nucleus into two daughter nuclei, infact, the cell also divides itself into two daughter cells.

Differences between Karyokinesis and Cytokinesis

Karyokinesis	Cytokinesis
It is known as division of daughter chromosomes (M-phase).	It is known as division of cytoplasm.
Occurs or starts with karyokinesis itself.	Occurs at the end of M-phase.
It can occur independent of cytokinesis.	It cannot occur without karyokinesis.

Cytokinesis in Animal Cells

In animal cells, cytokinesis starts at metaphase. They typically divide by furrowing or by the appearance of furrow in the plasma membrane. This is also known as **cleavage.**

Due to the contraction and development of micro-filaments, a constriction develops which further deepens in a centripetal way known as **cell furrow.**

The furrow starts deepening gradually during telophase and finally gets joined in the centre by dividing the cytoplasm into two.

Cytokinesis in Plant Cells

Due to the presence of a solid, rigid and inextensible cell wall on the outside of the cell, the plant cell cannot undergo cytokinesis by the furrowing method. Therefore, plant cell divides by the **cell-plate method.**

The formation of cell-plate usually begins during the late anaphase or early telophase. The formation of a new wall in plant cells takes place in the centre of the cell and starts growing outward towards the opposite sides in order to reach the already existed lateral walls.

Note Cell plate represents the middle lamella between the walls of two adjacent cells along with which actual cell wall formation takes place.

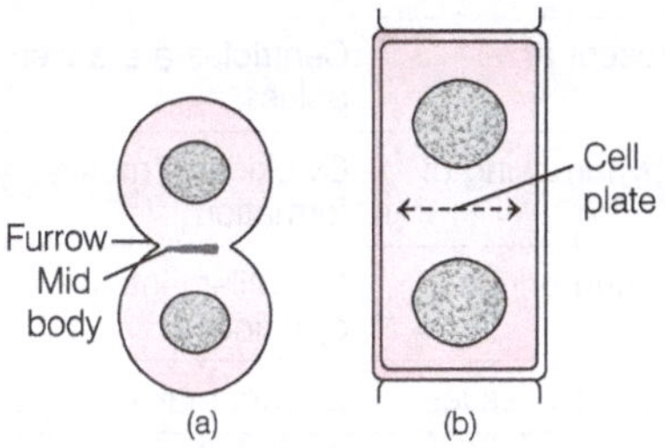

Fig. 13.5 Cytokinesis : (a) Furrowing in animal cells, (b) Cell-plate formation in plant cells

Once cell plate has divided the cell into two cells, it will continue to grow and develop new cell organelles. The mitochondria and plastids also gets distributed among two daughter cells during the cytoplasmic division or cytokinesis.

Syncytium Cells

In some organisms karyokinesis is not followed by cytokinesis. Therefore, only nuclear division takes place and the whole cell does not divide.

As a result, multinucleated condition arises leading to the formation of syncytium, e.g. liquid endosperm in coconut as well as in coenocytic hyphae of lower fungi.

Significance of Mitosis

Mitosis has following significance

(i) It helps in the production of diploid daughter cells with equal and identical genetic complement.

(ii) Mitosis helps in growth of multicellular organisms.

(iii) It also helps in maintaining a proper cell size by dividing an overgrown somatic cell.

(iv) It is helpful in cell repair mechanism, e.g. continuous replacement of the cells like of the upper layer of the epidermis, cells of the lining of the gut and blood cells.

(v) It regulates the growth of multicellular organism by maintaining a certain ratio between the nucleus and the cytoplasm. After reaching the particular size, the cell divides in order to restore the nucleocytoplasmic ratio.

(vi) It is also helpful in producing new cells for healing wounds and for regeneration.

(vii) Mitosis plays an important role in continuous growth of plants throughout their life by meristematic tissues like the apical and the lateral cambium.

Differences between Mitosis in Animal and Plant Cells

Animal Cells	Plant Cells
Centrioles present at spindle poles.	Centrioles are absent at spindle poles.
Cytokinesis by furrowing of cytoplasm.	Cytokinesis mostly by cell plate formation.
Microfilament ring brings about cleavage.	Microfilaments have no role in cytokinesis.
Occurs nearly in all tissues.	Occurs mainly at meristems.
Cell becomes rounded and its cytoplasm becomes more viscous during mitosis.	Cell does not change its form or nature at the time of mitosis.
Animal mitosis is controlled by certain mitogens.	Plant mitosis is usually controlled by a hormone cytokinin.
Midbody is formed at the equator of the spindle.	Equator of the spindle changes into phragmoplast.
Furrow extends centripetally.	Cell plate grows centrifugally.
Asters are formed (amphiastral).	No asters are formed (anastral).
New cell membrane is derived from ER.	New cell membrane is derived from vesicles of Golgi apparatus.
Spindles degenerate after anaphase.	Spindles persists during cytokinesis.

Topic Practice 1

Multiple Choice Questions

1 Mark

1. What is the approximate duration of cell cycle for a mammalian cell?

(a) 90 min (b) 24 hrs
(c) 24 days (d) 12 hrs

Ans (b) Duration of the cell cycle, i.e. period between two successive cell divisions is called generation time. It depends on the type of cell and external factors such as temperature, food and oxygen supplies. Mammalian (e.g. human) cell divides once in approximate every 24 hrs.

2. Two basic stages of cell cycle are

(a) interphase and M-phase/divisional phase
(b) karyokinesis and cytokinesi
(c) prophase, metaphase, anaphase and telophase
(d) G_1, S and G_2-phases

Ans (a) Cell cycle consists of two basic stages. There is a long undividing stage called I-phase (interphase) and a short dividing M-phase.

3. During the G_1-phase of cell division

(a) RNA and proteins are synthesised for cell growth and subsequent DNA replication
(b) DNA and proteins are synthesised
(c) centriole duplicates in the cytoplasm
(d) cell undergoes duplication

Ans (a) G_1 is the longest phase of cell cycle in which cell synthesises RNAs, proteins and other biochemicals for cell growth and subsequent replication of DNA. While in G_2-phase, synthesis of RNAs, protein and other biochemicals for spindle formation takes place.

4. The phase of cell cycle in which the centriole duplicates in the cytoplasm is

(a) S- phase (b) G_1- phase
(c) G_2- phase (d) G_0- phase

Ans (a) During S-phase, DNA replication begins in the nucleus and the centriole duplicates in the cytoplasm.

5. Which of the following statements is true for cells in G_0-stage of cell cycle?

(a) Cells in G_0-stage are metabolically more active
(b) Cells are metabolically inactive
(c) Cells are metabolically active, but no longer proliferate in normal condition
(d) None of the above

Ans (c) During the G_0-phase, cells are metabolically active, but no longer proliferate in normal condition.

6. This is the best stage to count the number and study the morphology of chromosomes.
(a) Prophase (b) Metaphase
(c) Anaphase (d) Telophase

Ans (b) Metaphase is the best phase to count total number of chromosomes in any species and detailed study of morphology of chromosome. Idiogram (arrangement of chromosomes in a series of decreasing length) can be drawn in this stage as chromosome is maximally condensed here.

7. At which stage of mitosis, the two daughter chromatids separate from each other, migrate towards the opposite poles and are now referred to as chromosomes of the future daughter nuclei?
(a) Prophase (b) Metaphase
(c) Anaphase (d) Telophase

Ans (c) In anaphase, the centromeres of chromosomes start to divide into two, forming daughter chromosomes with centromere in each.

Daughter chromosomes are repulsive, so they migrate towards opposite poles. Spindle fibres attached to the centromeres, shorten and pull the chromosomes to the poles.

8. When karyokinesis is not followed by cytokinesis, it results in formation of
(a) uninucleate cells
(b) multinucleate cells
(c) undifferentiated cells
(d) two cells

Ans (b) In some organisms, karyokinesis is not followed by cytokinesis as a result of which multinucleate condition arises.

9. Mitosis usually results in the
(a) production of diploid daughter cells
(b) growth of multicellular organisms
(c) cell repair
(d) All of the above

Ans (d) Mitosis usually results in the production of diploid daughter cells with identical genetic complement. The growth of multicellular organisms is due to mitosis.

Cell growth results in disturbing the ratio between the nucleus and the cytoplasm.

It therefore, becomes essential for the cell to divide to restore the nucleocytoplasmic ratio. A very significant contribution of mitosis is cell repair.

Very Short Answer Type Questions
(1 Mark)

10. Between a prokaryote and an eukaryote, which cell has a shorter cell division time? **NCERT Exemplar**

Ans Prokaryotic cell has shorter cell cycle than the eukaryotic cell.

11. Mention the duration of cell cycle in yeast.

Ans The duration of cell cycle in yeast is 90 minutes approximately.

12. What is the average cell cycle span for a mammalian cell? **NCERT**

Ans The average cell cycle span for a mammalian cell is 24 hours.

13. Given that, average duplication time of *E. coli* is 20 minutes. How much time will two *E. coli* cells take to become 32 cells? **NCERT Exemplar**

Ans 1 hour -20 minutes

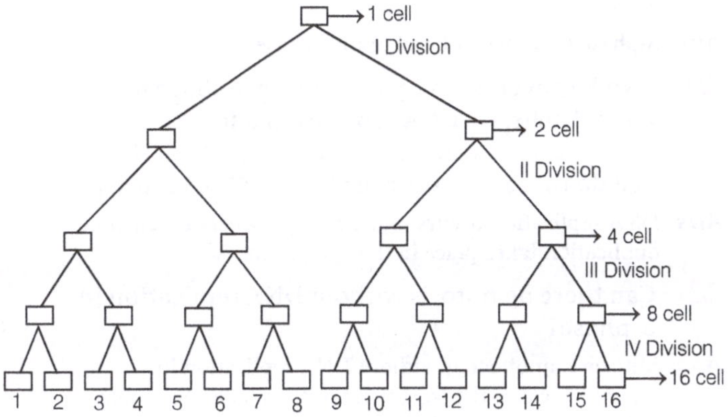

These are the 4 subsequent cell divisions to produce 16 cells and each division takes = 20 min; Total time = 20 × 4 = 80 minutes or 1 hr 20 minutes. So, 1 cell produces 16 cells in 1 hour 20 minutes and 2 cells produces 32 cells in 1 hour 20 minutes.

14. If a tissue has 1024 cells at a given time, how many cycles of mitosis had the original parental single cell undergone? **NCERT Exemplar**

Ans 10 (2^n, where $n = 10$ generations). Thus, 10 cycles of mitosis are required for 1024 cells original parental single cell.

15. Give the name of the phase between the two successive mitotic divisions.

Ans Interphase is the period between the two successive mitotic cell divisions.

16. Does mitosis occur before or after the interphase?

Ans Yes, mitosis can occur before or after the interphase, as dividing phase (meiosis or mitosis) and interphase is the only major phase of a cell cycle.

17. **It is said that one cell cycle of cell division in human cells (eukaryotic cells) takes 24 hrs. Which phase of the cycle, do you think occupies the maximum part of the cell cycle.** **NCERT Exemplar**

Ans Interphase occupies the maximum part of the cell cycle.

18. **What percentage of duration of cell cycle does interphase take?**

Ans About 90-96% of total time duration of cell cycle is taken by interphase.

19. **What is the terminology used for the period between mitotic division and initiation of DNA replication?**

Ans G_1 (Gap-1) phase is the period between mitotic division and initiation of DNA replication.

20. **At which stage during mitosis and meiosis the replication of DNA and chromosomes takes place?**

Ans S-phase (Synthetic phase) of interphase.

21. **Two key events take place during S-phase in animal cells, i.e. DNA replication and duplication of centriole. In which parts of the cell do these events occur?** **NCERT Exemplar**

Ans DNA replication occurs in the nucleus whereas centriole duplication takes place in the cytoplasm.

22. **Can there be mitosis without DNA replication in S-phase?**

Ans Mitosis cannot occur without DNA replication in S-phase because the trigger for mitosis takes place due to the disturbance in nucleocytoplasmic ratio caused by DNA replication in S-phase.

23. **Can there be DNA replication without cell division?** **NCERT**

Ans Yes, DNA replication takes place during the synthetic stage of interphase in the cell cycle. It is totally independent of cell division. After G_2-phase a cell may or may not enter into the M-phase.

24. **Name a drug that has an inhibitory effect on cell cycle in mitotic stage.**

Ans Colchicine drug shows an inhibitory effect on cell cycle in mitotic stage.

25. **What is the term used for point of attachment of two sister chromatids?**

Ans Centromere is the point of attachment of two sister chromatids.

26. **State the role of centrioles other than spindle formation.** **NCERT Exemplar**

Ans The two centrioles in the centrosome lie perpendicular to each other. These form the basal body of cilia and flagella of plant/animal cells besides forming spindle fibre in animal cell division. It also helps in the formation of microtubules and sperm tail.

27. **Name the chemical compound used for visualing chromosomes.** **NCERT Exemplar**

Ans Acetocarmine and Giemsa stain.

28. **During which phase of mitotic cell division, chromosomes get separated?**

Ans During anaphase chromosomes get separated.

29. **Distinguish cytokinesis from karyokinesis?** **NCERT**

Ans Cytokinesis is the division of cytoplasm, whereas karyokinesis is the division of nucleus of the cell.

30. **Mitosis cell division helps in regeneration process. How?**

Ans Mitosis helps in regeneration by keeping all the somatic cells of an organism genetically similar, so that they are able to regenerate part or whole of the organism.

31. **Which part of the human body should one use to demonstrate stages in mitosis?** **NCERT Exemplar**

Ans All the cells in the human body are somatic cells except germinal cells in the male and female reproductive organs. The somatic cells divide by mitotic cell division for growth and regeneration. These can be used to demonstrate mitosis.

Short Answer Type I Questions

2 Marks

32. **Supply a specific scientific term for each of the following**

(i) The period between two successive mitotic divisions.

(ii) Point at which two sister chromatids are held together.

(iii) Phase in the cell cycle when protein and RNA are synthesised.

(iv) Nuclear division.

Ans (i) Interphase (ii) Kinetochore
(iii) G_1-phase (iv) Mitotic or M-phase ($\frac{1}{2} \times 4$)

33. **What is quiescent stage of cell cycle?** **NCERT**

Ans G_0 is the quiescent stage of the cell cycle. Also known as inactive stage of the cell cycle. Cells in this stage remain metabolically active, but no longer proliferate unless they do not get instruction to do so, depending on the requirement of the organisms. (2)

34. **A cell having 32 chromosomes, undergoes mitotic divisions. What will be the chromosome number (*n*) during metaphase? What would be the DNA content (C) during anaphase?** **NCERT Exemplar**

Ans The number of chromosome during metaphase will be 32. Also the DNA content during anaphase will be same as in the parent cell. (1+1)

35. **There occurs a process in which division of nucleus takes place. Identify the process and also write about its different phases.**

Ans Karyokinesis is a series of uninterrupted changes before forming two daughter nuclei.

Though karyokinesis is a continuous process, it has been divided into four phases. They are prophase, metaphase, anaphase and telophase. (2)

36. **Why do the chromosomes become short and thick in prophase?**

Ans It happens so because it is physically easier for short and compact chromosomes to move through the cytoplasm than the very long and twisted interphase chromosomes. (2)

37. **The following events occur during the various phases of the cell cycle. Name the phase against each of the events;**

(i) Disintegration of nuclear membrane ....
(ii) Appearance of nucleolus ....
(iii) Division of centromere ....
(iv) Replication of DNA .... **NCERT Exemplar**

Ans (i) prophase
(ii) telophase
(iii) anaphase
(iv) S-phase ($\frac{1}{2} \times 4$)

38. **The following statements describe the four main stages in the process of mitosis.**

I. The spindle fibres breakdown and the nuclear membrane forms.
II. The chromosomes arrange themselves on the equator of the cell.
III. The spindle forms and the nuclear membrane disintegrates.
IV. The centromere splits and the sister chromatids migrate to the opposite poles of the cell.
Write the correct sequence of the stages in mitosis and also name the each stage.

Ans III (prophase) $\rightarrow$ II (metaphase) $\rightarrow$ IV (anaphase) $\rightarrow$ I (telophase) (2)

39. **Colchicine is known to be the mitotic poison. How?**

Ans Colchicine is considered to be the mitotic poison because

(i) This alkaloid inhibits the formation of spindle by preventing assembly of microtubules. It is an alkaloid obtained from the corms of Autumn crocus.

(ii) The chromosomes duplicate, but they remain within the same cell, increasing the number of chromosomes. As a result, the colchicine treated meristematic cells show doubling of chromosome. (1×2)

40. **What is the term given to multinucleated condition? Explain briefly.**

Ans Syncytium is the term given to multinucleated condition of the cell. This condition occurs when karyokinesis is not followed by cytokinesis. (2)

41. **While examining the mitotic stage in a tissue. One finds some cells with 16 chromosomes and some with 32 chromosomes. What possible reasons could you assign to this difference in chromosome number? Do you think that cells with 16 chromosomes number could have arisen from cells with 32 chromosomes or *Vice-versa*?** **NCERT Exemplar**

Ans This shows that the cells with 16 chromosomes are parent cells that had undergone mitotic divisions, whereas, cells with 32 chromosomes are the cells that had not undergone the process of segregation. (2)

42. **What is metaphasic plate?**

Ans Metaphasic plate is the equatorial plane at the centre of cell on which chromosomes arrange during metaphase. (2)

43. **Distinguish cytokinesis from karyokinesis.**

Ans Differences between cytokinesis and karyokinesis are

Cytokinesis	Karyokinesis
It is the division of cytoplasm.	It is the division of nucleus.
It occurs at the end of M-phase.	M-phase starts with karyokinesis.

(1× 2)

44. **Cell '*X*' contains 24 chromosomes. It is divided by mitosis to produce cells '*Y*' and '*Z*'. Deduce how many chromosomes, cell *Z* will contain after division?**

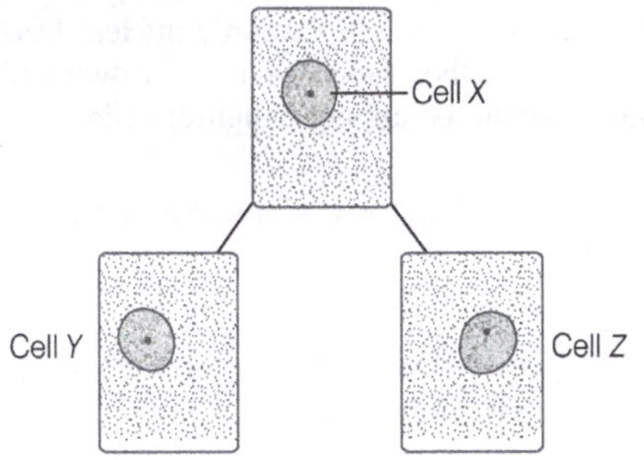

Ans The cell *Z* will also contain 24 chromosomes after mitotic division. Since, mitosis is a division in which daughter cells have same number of chromosomes as the parent has. (2)

45. **Why is mitosis called equational division?** **NCERT**

Ans Mitosis is called an equational division because it divides the mother cell into two daughter cells, which are identical to the original mother cell in every respect. In mitosis, the chromosomes of the mother cell are duplicated and distributed equally to the two daughter cells and these daughter cells have same number of chromosome as mother cell has. (2)

46. **How would you analyse that the cell's entire energy is devoted to the process of division in the M-phase?**

Ans Gene expression, protein synthesis, secretion, motility etc., do not happen during M-phase. (2)

47. **Discuss the significance of mitosis. Give any four points.**

Ans Refer to text on page no. 286.

48. **Name the pathological condition when uncontrolled cell division occurs.** **NCERT Exemplar**

Ans Cancer is the pathological condition in which the cells loose control over cell division and this results into malformation of the organ in which such cell division occurs.

Underlying tissue (2)

49. **Mitochondria and plastids have their own DNA (genetic material). What is known about their fate during nuclear division like mitosis?** **NCERT Exemplar**

Ans The DNA present in mitochondria and chloroplast is extrachromosomal DNA. It has nothing to do with the nuclear divisions. In mitosis, only nuclear DNA takes part. However they replicate on their own and gets equally distributed among daughter cells. (2)

Short Answer Type II Questions

(3 Marks)

50. **Name three phases of interphase. Give one major event of each phase.**

Ans Three main events that occur in interphase are G_1-phase (post-mitotic or pre-synthetic phase), S-phase (synthesising phase) and G_2-phase (post-synthetic or pre-mitotic phase).

Major events of each phase are

(i) **G_1-phase** is the longest phase during which synthesis of RNA and DNA takes place.

(ii) **S-phase** is the phase during which chromosomes replicates and prepare themselves for equal distribution.

(iii) **G_2-phase**, is the phase in which synthesis of DNA gets stopped. However, formation of RNA takes place. (3)

51. **Describe the events taking place during interphase.** **NCERT**

Ans The interphase, though called the resting phase, is the time during which the cell is preparing for division by undergoing cell growth and DNA replication.

The interphase is divided into three further phases

(i) G_1-phase (Gap-1)

(ii) S-phase (Synthesis)

(iii) G_2-phase (Gap-2) (1½)

G_1-phase corresponds to the interval between mitosis and initiation of DNA replication. During G_1-phase the cell is metabolically active and continuously grows but does not replicate its DNA. S or Synthesis phase marks the period during which, DNA synthesis or replication takes place and also the amount of DNA per cell gets doubled.

During the G_2-phase, proteins are synthesised in preparation for mitosis, while cell growth continues. Cell in this stage remains metabolically active, but no longer proliferate unless called on to do so, depending on the requirement of the organism. (1½)

52. **Differentiate between S-phase and G_2-phase.**

Ans Differences between S-phase and G_2- phase are

S-phase	G_2-phase
It is called synthetic phase.	It is called pre-mitotic phase.
Replication of DNA occurs.	RNA of all three types and proteins precursors of asters and spindle are synthesised in it.
It lasts for 6-8 hours.	It lasts for 2-5 years.

(1 × 3)

53. **Differentiate between G_1 and G_2-phase.**

Ans Differences between G_1 and G_2-phase are

G_1-phase	G_2-phase
It is called first growth period.	It is post-synthetic phase.
Its duration is variable.	It lasts for 2-5 years.
Cells grow in size.	Cell prepares to go into mitotic phase.

(3)

54. **Analyse the events during every stage of cell cycle and notice how the following two parameters change?**
(i) Number of chromosomes (*n*) per cell.
(ii) Amount of DNA content (*c*) per cell. **NCERT**

Ans (i) During the complete cell cycle, the number of chromosomes (*n*) per cell remains same. It does not show any changes if the division is of mitosis type.
(ii) The overall DNA content will remain same however it doubles up during the S-phase and afterwards becomes half during the dividing phase. (3)

55. **Root tip cells of a plant have 12 chromosomes in each cell. Determine the number of chromosomes in a cell at G_1-phase, after S-phase and after M-phase. Also mention the amount of DNA content of the cell at G_1 after S and at G_2-phase if the content after M-phase is 2C.**

Ans The root tip cells repeatedly undergo mitotic divisions for the elongation of root.

Therefore the number of chromosomes in the cell at G_1-phase after S-phase and after M-phase will be 12. However, the amount of DNA content of cell at G_1phase will be 2C, but after the S (synthetic) phase, and at G_2-phase it will be 4C, because cell doubles the DNA content at S-phase to prepare for karyokinesis. (3)

56. **Describe cell division. List various types of cell division. Also mention about the need of cell division?**

Ans Cell division, cell reproduction or cell multiplication is the process of formation of new daughter cells from the pre-existing cell or parent cell. It is of three types
(i) Amitosis (ii) Mitosis
(iii) Meiosis.

A cell divides when it attains the size and the nucleocytoplasmic ratio is disturbed. The DNA duplication also causes a cell to divide. (1 + 1 + 1)

57. **Describe the prophase and metaphase of mitosis with neat and labelled diagrams.**

Ans Refer to text on page no. 284. (3)

58. **State the role of centrioles in cell division.**

Ans Centrioles play an important role in formation of spindle during cell division. They organise the mitotic spindle and thus, help in the completion of cytokinesis. They generate the cell's cytoskeleton and help in the formation of the mitotic spindles. In organisms with flagella and cilia, the position of these organelles is determined by the mother centriole, which becomes the basal body. (3)

59. **Give the sequence of events occurring during anaphase of mitosis, diagrammatically.**

Ans Refer to text on page no. 284.

60. **What are kinetochores? Give their functions also.**

Ans Refer to text on page no. 284.

61. **Comment on the statement 'telophase is reverse of prophase'.** **NCERT Exemplar**

Ans In prophase, the chromatin network begins to coil and appears as a long thread-like structures called chromosomes.

Each chromosome consists of two chromatids that disappears from early prophase to late prophase. The nuclear membrane also starts disappearing in late prophase.

In telophase opposite poles of the chromosomes lose their identity and nuclear membrane is formed around the daughter nuclei. Nucleolus also reappears. So, it is reverse of prophase. (3)

62. **How does cytokinesis in plant cells differ from that in animal cells?** **NCERT Exemplar**

Ans Differences between cytokinesis in plant cell and animal cell is as follows

Cytokinesis in Plant Cell	Cytokinesis in Animal Cell
The division of cytoplasm takes place by cell plate formation.	The division of cytoplasm takes place by cleavage.
The cell plate formation starts at the centre of the cell and grow outward, toward the lateral walls.	Cleavage starts at the periphery and then moves inward, dividing the cell into two parts.

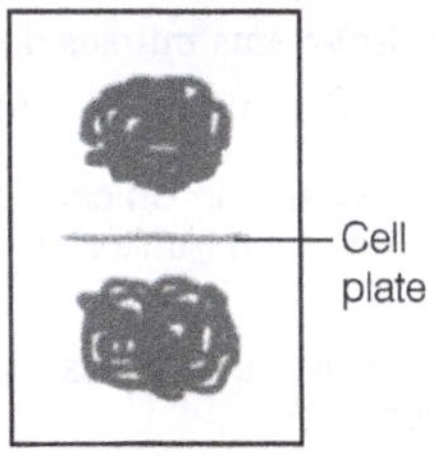

Plant cell

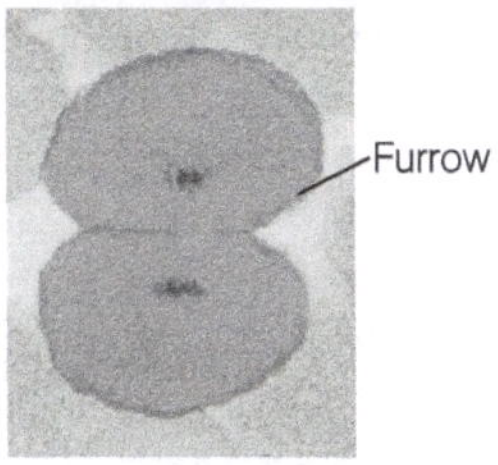

Animal cell

(3)

Long Answer Type Questions
(5 Marks)

63. **What is cell cycle? Explain cell cycle and interphase in detail.**

Ans Refer to text on page no. 282 and 283.

64. **Describe the process of mitosis and give a short account of its various stages.**

Ans Refer to text on page no. 283, 284-285.

65. Briefly describe the significance of cell division. **NCERT**

Ans Cell division is significant in the following ways

(i) **Cell multiplication** Cell division is a means of cell multiplication or formation of new cells from pre-existing cells.

(ii) **Continuity** It maintains continuity of living matter generation after generation.

(iii) **Multicellular organisms** The body of a multicellular organism is formed of innumerable cells. They are formed by repeated divisions of a single cell or zygote. As the number of cells increases, many of them begin to differentiate, form tissues and organisms.

(iv) **Cell size** Cell division helps in maintenance of a particular cell size which is essential for efficiency and control of cell activities.

(v) **Genetic similarity** The common type of cell division or mitosis maintains genetic similarity of all the cells in an individual despite being different, i.e. structurally and functionally. (1 × 5)

66. Mitosis results in producing two cells which are similar to each other. What would be the consequence if each of the following irregularities occur during mitosis? **NCERT Exemplar**

(i) Nuclear membrane fails to disintegrate
(ii) Duplication of DNA does not occur
(iii) Centromeres do not divide
(iv) Cytokinesis does not occur

Ans Cell division is under genetic control and is highly precised phenomenon. However, some mistake occur sometimes at genetic and molecular level in cell cycle which may lead to certain abnormalities.

(i) If nuclear membrane fails to disintegrate, the spindle fibres would not be able to reach chromosomes and they would not move towards opposite poles of the cell. In certain protozoans, such as *Amoeba*, the spindle is formed within the nucleus and this is called intranuclear mitosis or pre-mitosis.

(ii) If DNA duplication does not occur than cell might not be able to surpass S-phase of cell cycle as no chromosome formation will take place, and will not be able to enter M-(mitotic) phase or if in case it enters mitosis the cycle will cease.

(iii) If the centromeres do not divide,one of the daughter cell will receive a complete pair of chromosomes and other cell would not get any of them. This may result in trisomy.

(iv) If cytokinesis does not occur, then multinucleate condition called coenocyte, syncytium is produced, as in *Rhizopus* and *Vaucheria*, etc. (5)

67. Both unicellular and multicellular organisms undergo mitosis. What are the differences, if any, observed in the process between the two? **NCERT Exemplar**

Ans In unicellular organisms, the type of cell division is known as amitosis in which somatic cell is divided into two parts directly. In multicellular organisms mitosis division occurs which is an indirect process. (2½)

Both cell division in unicellular and multicellular organisms undergo mitosis which have differences as below

Cell Division in Unicellular Organism (Amitosis)	Cell Division in Multicellular Organism (Mitosis)
It is direct division of cellular and nuclear content without the appearance of chromosomes. Different phases of cell division are not seen. 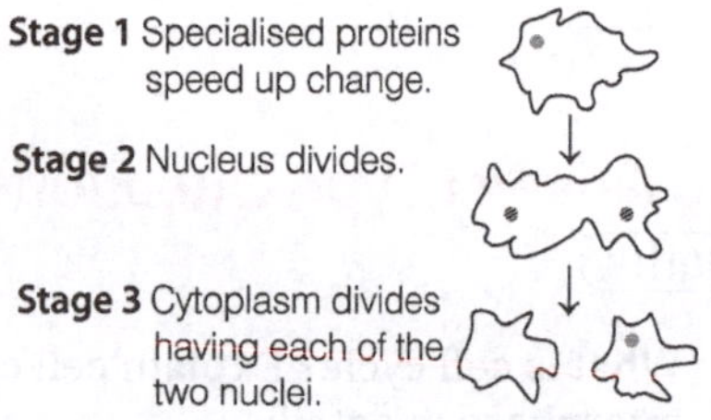 Division of acellular organism by amitosis	Nucleus and cellular content do not divide directly and involves formation of chromosomes. It involves different phases of cell division. 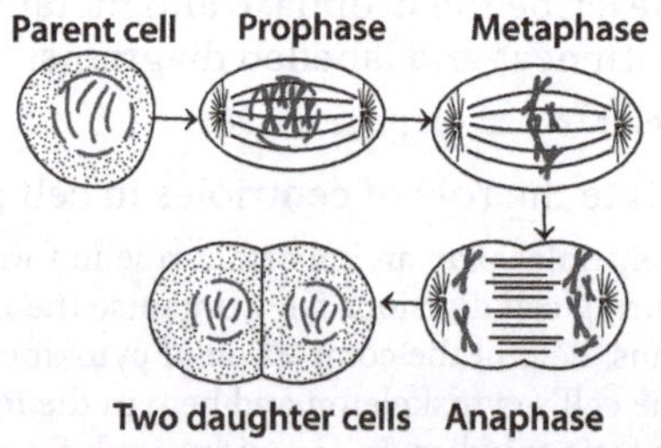 Division of cell in muiticellular organism by mitosis

(2½)

TOPIC 02 Meiosis

Meiosis is the phenomenon which occurs in every life cycle that involves the process of sexual reproduction. The gametes during sexual reproduction are formed in male and female reproductive organs by meiotic cell division.

Thus, meiosis is known to be the specialised form of cell division which reduces the chromosome number in such a way that each daughter nuclei receives only one set of each kind of chromosome (i.e. maternal and paternal). In meiosis, the nucleus divides twice, but the replication of chromosome takes place only once, i.e. interphase of meiosis-I.

Thus, it is also known as the **reductional division.** In case of diploid organisms, meiosis takes place during the formation of spores or gametes whereas, in haploid organisms it takes place during germination of zygote.

The essential features of meiosis are as follows

(i) Meiosis undergoes two successive cycles of nuclear and cytoplasm division, i.e. meiosis-I and II.

(ii) Meiosis-I and II occur one after the another with a very short or no interphase.

(iii) After the replication of parental chromosomes, initiation of meiosis-I takes place in order to produce identical sister chromatids at S-phase.

(iv) Meiosis takes about days to get completed instead of hours or minutes that are needed for mitosis.

(v) Pairing of homologous chromosomes and recombination takes place during meiosis.

(vi) Finally, after the second meiotic division four haploid cells are formed.

Meiosis-I

During this division, the homologous chromosomes of each pair separate from each other and reaches to separate daughter cells. This reduces the number of chromosomes from diploid to haploid, i.e. from $2n$ to n. Thus, it is known as **heterotypic division.**
It is further divided into four phases, i.e. prophase-I, metaphase-I, anaphase-I and telophase-I.

Prophase-I

This phase is further subdivided into five subphases on the basis of chromosomal behaviour, i.e. leptotene, zygotene, pachytene, diplotene and diakinesis.

1. Leptotene

It is known to be the very first stage of meiotic division following the interphase. Following features are seen during this phase

- Chromosomes become gradually visible under light microscope.
- Centrioles start moving towards opposite ends or poles and each centriole develops astral rays.
- Each chromosome is attached to the nuclear envelope through the attachment plate at both of its ends.

Homologous Chromosomes

There are two sets of chromosomes in a diploid cell which undergo meiosis. One set of chromosomes is contributed by the male parent and the other by the female parent. There are always two similar chromosomes, having the same size, shape and position of centromere. In some organisms, the chromosomes give beaded appearance due to the presence of chromomeres (swollen area).

2. Zygotene

This is the next short lived substage that involves following changes

- Homologous chromosomes pair up. This pairing is done in such a way that the genes of the same character present on the two chromosomes lie at the same loci. This process of association is known as **synapsis.**
- It is revealed from the electron micrographic studies that the formation of **synaptonemal complex** takes place by a pair of homologous chromosomes that show synapsis. The complex so formed, on account of synapsis forms a **bivalent** or a **tetrad.**

3. Pachytene

In this stage, the pair of chromosomes become twisted spirally around each other and cannot be distinguished separately. This stage is comparatively long lived as compared to the previous two stages.
Following changes are seen during this stage

(i) Bivalent chromosomes clearly seen as tetrads.

(ii) In this stage, sometimes exchange of genes (or crossing over) between the two non-sister chromatids of homologous chromosomes occurs at the points called **recombination nodules**, which appear at intervals, on synaptonemal complex.

(iii) By the end of pachytene, recombination gets completed leaving the chromosomes linked at the sites of crossing over.

Crossing Over

In this process, exchange of genetic material takes place between the non-sister chromatids of two homologous chromosomes. It finally leads to recombination of genetic material on the two chromosomes.

4. Diplotene

It is the longest duration stage. Following changes are observed during this stage

(i) In this, the **synaptonemal complex** appears to get dissolved while, the chromatids of each tetrad remain clearly visible.

(ii) Recombined homologous chromosomes of the bivalents get separated and form **chiasmata** (X-shaped structures).

(iii) Chiasmata formation is necessary for the separation of homologous chromosome which have undergone the process of crossing over.

5. Diakinesis

This is known to be the final stage of meiotic prophase-I. Also known as **terminalisation**, due to the shifting of chiasmata towards the end of the chromosomes.

Following changes are observed during this stage

(i) Chromosomes become fully condensed.

(ii) Nucleolus degenerates.

(iii) Breakdown of nuclear envelope into vesicles occurs.

(iv) Formation of meiotic spindle (as in mitosis) in order to prepare the homologous chromosomes for separation also occurs.

(v) Diakinesis phase represents the transition from prophase to metaphase of meiosis-I.

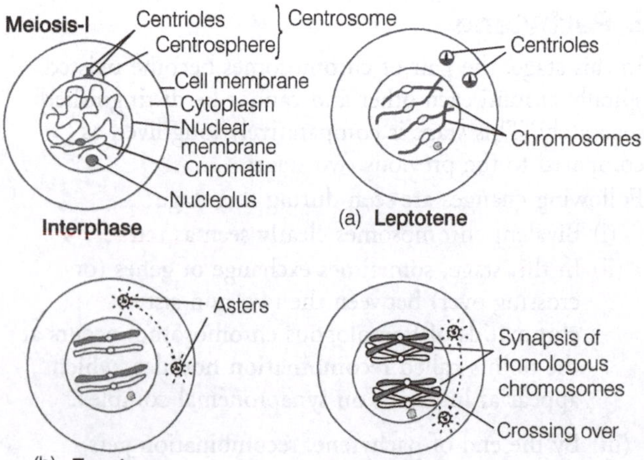

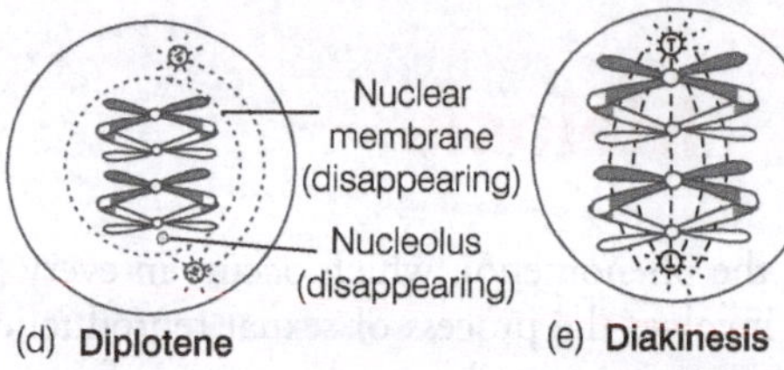

Fig. 13.6 Different stages of prophase-I (meiosis-I) in an animal cell

Metaphase-I

It is the stage followed by prophase (same as mitosis). Following changes are observed during this stage

(i) The bivalents during this phase arrange themselves on the two parallel **equatorial plates**.

(ii) The centromeres project little bit towards periphery. Since, there are two centromeres in each bivalent. Thus, each centromere is joined by chromosomal fibres.

(iii) The fibres of the homologous chromosomes are always in the opposite directions.

Anaphase-I

In this phase homologous chromosomes break their connection with each other and get separated. This process of separation of homologous chromosomes is known as **disjunction**. The separated chromosomes are univalents and are also called **dyads**. On reaching at the end of the anaphase, the two groups of chromosomes are produced (with each having half number of chromosomes).

Note The sister chromatid remains attached at their centromeres on the separation of the homologous pairs of chromosomes.

Telophase-I

This is the last stage of meiosis-I in which the chromatids at each pole of the spindle usually remain uncoiled and get elongated.

Following changes are seen during this stage

(i) Homologous chromosomes reach at their respective poles.

(ii) Reappearance of nuclear membrane and nucleolus takes place.

Cytokinesis

It is the stage during which the cytoplasm and other organelles divide into two equal halves of cells.

Interkinesis

This is the stage between the two meiotic divisions, i.e. the meiosis-I and II. It is generally short lived.

During this process, no replication of DNA occurs. It is necessary for bringing true haploidy DNA in daughter cells. It is a fact considered as incipient interphase.

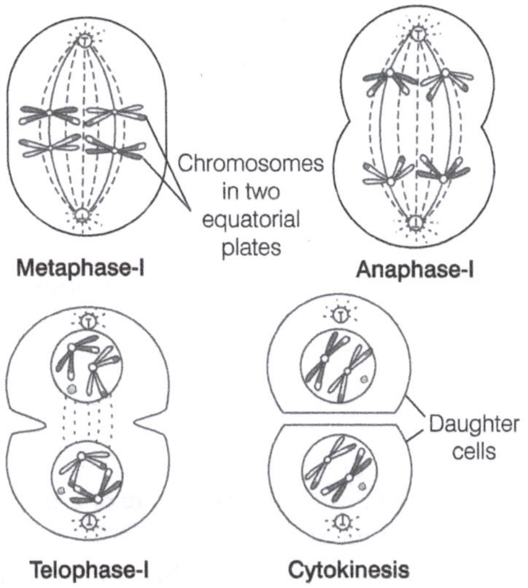

Fig. 13.7 Stages of meiosis-I

Meiosis-II

Meiosis-II is known by another term, i.e. **homotypic division**, because in this division chromosome number remains same, as in meiosis-I. It is initiated immediately after cytokinesis. It is often known an **equational division**. Meiosis-II distributes chromatids to daughter cells.

Prophase-II

This is known to be the very short stage out of the all stages. During this process the chromosomes again become compact in organisation. Following changes are seen during this process

(i) The centrioles duplicate themselves by the separation of the two members of the pair.

(ii) Each chromosome comprising two chromatids becomes visible in the nucleus. These chromosomes further become thick and short in size.

(iii) Nuclear envelope breaks down and the formation of spindle apparatus takes place and nucleoli disappears.

Metaphase-II

This is the next phase followed immediately after prophase-II. Following changes are seen during this process

(i) The chromosomes align at the equator or the metaphase plate, in the similar way as in mitosis.

(ii) **Chromosomes** get attached to the fully formed spindle apparatus and the kinetochores of sister chromatids for each chromosome face the opposite poles and each is attached to the kinetochore microtubule coming from the pole of that side.

Anaphase-II

This is the phase followed immediately after metaphase-II.

Following changes are seen during this process

(i) The centromere of each chromosome splits, that was holding the sister chromatids together.

(ii) The shortening of chromosomal microtubules takes place. The two chromatids of each chromosome start moving away from each other and finally reach the opposite poles of the spindle (now called chromosomes).

Telophase-II

This is known to be the last stage of second meiotic division and shows changes equally opposite to that of the prophase-II. Meiosis ends up with the progress of this particular phase, i.e. telophase-II.

Following changes are seen during this process

(i) Formation of a nuclear envelope (from ER) around each set of chromosomes.

(ii) Nucleoli reappears due to the synthesis of ribosomal RNA (*r*RNA) and ribosomal DNA (*r*DNA).

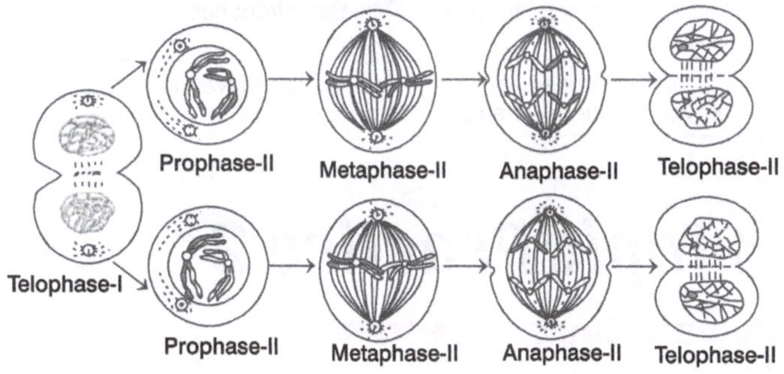

Fig. 13.8 Stages in meiosis-II (progressing from telophase-I of meiosis-I) thus producing four haploid (*n*) cells

Cytokinesis

This occurs after every nuclear division. It includes separation of cytoplasm and organelles in the two halves of the cell. Thus, the two daughter cells formed have half the number of chromosomes and the amount of nuclear DNA. Both the cells undergo divisions and give rise to four cells. These haploid cells are arranged tetrahedrally and are collectively called **tetrahedral tetrad**.

Significance of Meiosis

(i) It maintains the same chromosome number in the sexually reproducing organisms.
(ii) It restricts the multiplication of chromosome number and maintains the stability of the species.
(iii) Maternal and paternal genes get exchanged during crossing over. It results in variations among the offsprings.
(iv) All the four chromatids of a homologous pair of chromosomes segregate and go over separately to four different daughter cells. This leads to variation in the daughter cells genetically.
(v) Paternal and maternal chromosomes assort independently. This causes reshuffling of chromosomes and changes traits controlled by them.

Differences between Mitosis and Meiosis

Mitosis	Meiosis
This division occurs in somatic cells.	It occurs in reproductive cells.
It is a single division.	It is a double division.
The daughter cells resemble each other as well as their mother cell.	The daughter cells neither resemble one another nor their mother cell.
Replication of chromosomes occurs before every mitotic division.	Replication of chromosomes occurs only once though meiosis which is a double division.
Mitosis does not introduce variations.	Meiosis introduces variations.
Mitosis is required for growth, repair and healing.	Meiosis is involved in sexual reproduction.

Topic Practice 2

Multiple Choice Questions

1 Mark

1. At the end of meiosis-II, number of haploid cells formed are
(a) two (b) four
(c) eight (d) None of these

Ans (b) Meiosis starts with one diploid cell containing copies of chromosomes, one from mother and one from father. The cell divides twice, producing upto four haploid cells containing one copy of each chromosome.

2. In a cell cycle, crossing over occurs at
(a) single-stranded stage (b) two-stranded stage
(c) four-stranded stage (d) eight-stranded stage

Ans (c) Crossing over occurs during prophase-I at four-stranded stage, which involves the exchange of segments between the non-sister chromatids of homologous chromosomes.

3. In diploid organism, phenomenon of crossing over is responsible for
(a) linkages between genes
(b) recombination between homologous genes
(c) segregation between genes
(d) dominance of gene

Ans (b) Recombination of genes on the same chromosome is accomplished by crossing over, a process by which parts of homologous chromosomes are interchanged.

4. Which of the following shows diplotene stage of cell cycle?
(a) Separation of synapsed homologous chromosomes except at the site of cross overs
(b) Degeneration of nucleolus
(c) Chiasmata shifts towards chromosome ends
(d) All of the above

Ans (a) The beginning of diplotene stage is marked by chiasma formation. The chiasma formation is the indication of crossing over and the beginning of separation of chromosomes. The chiasma formation is associated with the process of terminalisation.

5. Diakinesis is marked by
(a) terminalisation of chiasmata
(b) degeneration of nucleolus
(c) fully condensed chromosomes
(d) All of the above

Ans (d) Diakinesis is the final stage of the prophase in meiosis. It is characterised by shortening and thickening of the paired chromosomes, formation of the spindle fibres, disappearance of the nucleolus and degeneration of the nuclear membrane.

6. When paternal and maternal chromosomes exchange their genetic material with each other in cell division, this event is called
(a) bivalent forming (b) crossing over
(c) synapsis (d) dyad forming

Ans (b) Chromosomal crossing over is the exchange of genetic material between homologous chromosomes that results in the recombinant chromosomes. It occurs during prophase-I of meiosis.

7. During anaphase-I of meiosis
(a) homologous chromosomes separate
(b) non-homologous autosomes separate
(c) sister chromatids separate
(d) non-sister chromatids separate

Ans (a) During anaphase-I of meiosis homologous chromosomes separate, while sister chromatids remain associated at their centromeres.

8. Splitting of centromere and hence separation of chromatids occurs during
(a) prophase-II (b) anaphase-I
(c) anaphase-II (d) metaphase-II

Ans (c) During anaphase of mitosis, each chromosome arranged at metaphase plate is split and two daughter chromatids are formed. Centromeres split and chromatids move to opposite poles. During anaphase-II of meiosis sister chromatids separate.

9. Which of the events listed below is not observed during mitosis?
(a) Chromatin condensation
(b) Movement of centrioles to opposite poles
(c) Appearance of chromosomes with two chromosomes joined together at the centromere
(d) Crossing over

Ans (d) Crossing over is the phenomenon of genetic exchange between homologous pair of chromosomes and is a characteristic feature of meiotic cell division. It does not occur in mitosis. Rest of the options represents stages in mitosis.

10. Significance of meiosis lies in
(a) reduction of chromosome number to one-half
(b) maintaining consistency of chromosome number during sexual reproduction
(c) production of genetic variability
(d) All of the above

Ans (d) Meiosis is a reductional division, in which chromosome number is reduced to half. It is observed in sex cells only, i.e. male and female gametes. Crossing over during meiosis is responsible for producing genetic variability.

11. The type of division that ensures the production of haploid phase in the life cycle of sexually reproducing organisms is
(a) mitosis (b) meiosis
(c) cytokinesis (d) interphase

Ans (b) During meiosis, four haploid cells are produced by reductional division from a single diploid cell in sexually reproducing organisms. Parent cell contains replicated chromosomes, but the daughter cells contain unreplicated chromosomes.

Very Short Answer Type Questions

(1 Mark)

12. Which cells of our body do not divide?

Ans Neuron stops dividing soon after the birth of a child.

13. Why dose the cell under going meiotic division, at the G_2-phase is characterised by an increase in nuclear volume?

Ans G_2-phase is a pre-divisional phase, which is followed by the synthetic phase (S-phase) during which a cell doubles is nuclear content as a pre-requisite for the cellular division. Thus, here is an increase in nuclear volume.

14. Meiosis occurs in plants and animal cells in similar locations. Identify.

Ans Meiosis occurs in sex cells of plants and in germ cells of animals.

15. Why several tissues of animals and plants exhibit meiosis?

Ans Meiosis or reduction division, occurs in the germ cells or sex cells of male and female reproductive organs of plants and animals. They produce male (♂) and female (♀) gametes that take part in sexual reproduction.

16. Meiosis is essential in sexually reproducing organisms. Why?

Ans Meiosis is essential in sexually reproducing organisms because it keeps the chromosome number constant.

17. At the following stage of meiosis, the chromosomes appear to be beaded. Can you find out the stage?

Ans Chromosomes seem to be beaded during leptotene (prophase-I) of meiosis.

18. Name the substages of prophase of meiosis.

Ans The various substages of prophase occurring in meiosis are leptotene, zygotene, pachytene, diplotene and diakinesis.

19. These are the pair of chromosomes one from each parent, which are similar in length, gene position and also location of a centromere, identify the type of chromosomes.

Ans Homologous chromosomes.

20. What does a bivalent of meiosis-I consist of ?

Ans Bivalent of meiosis-I consists of four chromatids and two centromeres.

21. At what stage of meiosis, formation of tetrads occurs. Name it?

Ans Tetrads are formed during pachytene of prophase-I (meiosis-I). At this stage crossing over occurs.

22. What indicates on the beginning of diplotene stage of prophase-I?

Ans On the beginning of diplotene stage, synaptonemal complex dissolutes and recombined homologous chromosomes separate from each other.

23. The diagram shows a bivalent at prophase-I of meiosis. Which of the four chromatids can cross over? **NCERT Exemplar**

Ans The non-sister chromatids of homologous pair of chromosomes undergo crossing over in pachytene stage of meiosis.

24. In a healing wound does the event of crossing over could be observed? Why?

Ans No, because a wound mainly heals by the mitotic division of epithelial cells and mitosis does not involve the event of crossing over.

25. During anaphase-I, i.e. a stage of meiosis, the homologous chromosomes separate, but sister chromatids remain associated. State whether true or false.

Ans True.

26. An anther has 1200 pollen grains. How many pollen mother cells must have been there to produce them? **NCERT Exemplar**

Ans The pollen mother cell ($2n$) undergoes meiotic cell divisions. Each such cell produced four daughter cells with haploid (n) number of chromosomes.

300 pollen mother cells have to be there to produce 1200 pollen grains because one pollen mother cell will produce four pollen grains.

Short Answer Type I Questions

(2 Mark)

27. How many chromosomes in daughter cells are formed by mitosis from diploid parent cells? And what is the chromosome number in daughter cells formed by meiosis from diploid parent cells?

Ans Mitosis–$2n$ (diploid); Meiosis–n (haploid). (1 × 2)

28. List the differences between metaphase of mitosis and metaphase-I of meiosis.

Ans Differences between metaphase of mitosis and metaphase-I of meiosis are

Mitotic Metaphase	Meiotic Metaphase
The chromosomes at the metaphase are arranged in such a way that the centromeres lie at the metaphase plate and the arms of chromosomes are free.	The chromosomes at the metaphase (meiosis-I) are arranged in such a way that the centromeres of homologous chromosomes lie on either side of the metaphase plate, pointing towards the opposite poles.
A chromosome is connected to both the spindle poles due to the presence of two tractile fibrils.	In metaphase-I, a chromosome is connected to only one spindle pole of its side due to the presence of a single tractile fibril.

(1×2)

29. Complete the following sentences with suitable words.

(i) Chromosome condensation occurs during ......

(ii) .... is marked by the alignment of chromosomes at the equatorial plate.

(iii) .... is the equational division in which the chromosome number of the parent is conserved in the daughter cell.

(iv) Each parent cell has pairs of .... chromosomes, one homologous from the father and one from the mother.

Ans (i) Prophase (ii) Metaphase (iii) Meiosis-II (iv) Homologous. (½ × 4)

30. Name the stage of cell cycle at which one of the following events occur? **NCERT**

(i) Chromosomes move to spindle equator.

(ii) Centromere splits and chromatids separate.

(iii) Pairing between homologous chromosomes takes place.

(iv) Crossing over between homologous chromosomes takes place.

Ans (i) Metaphase (ii) Anaphase (iii) Zygotene stage of meiosis-I (iv) Pachytene stage. (½ × 4)

31. Match the words in column I with those in column II.

Column I	Column II
A. Cell plate	1. Anaphase-I
B. Disjunction	2. Zygotene
C. Synapsis	3. Pachytene
D. Crossing over	4. Telophase-II

Ans A–4; B–1; C–2; D–3. (½ × 4)

32. Answer the following questions based upon the given figure.

(i) What type of division is this? Whether meiotic or/and mitotic and which stage?

(ii) What is A and B?

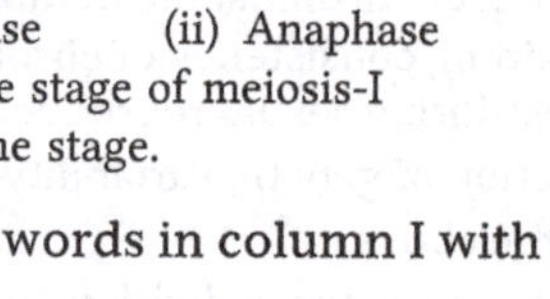

Ans (i) It is a meiotic division showing synapsis and it is in the zygotene stage of prophase-I of meiosis-I.

(ii) A–centromere, B–chromatid. (1×2)

33. Discuss about the synaptonemal complex?

Ans Synaptonemal complex is a protein complex, visible with the electron microscope, that is the physical basis of the pairing of homologous chromosomes (synapsis) during meiosis.

It is assembled during zygotene as homologous chromosomes pair up, and it is unpaired during diplotene as homologous chromosomes separate. (2)

34. Discuss about the attributes. Does a chromatid require to be classified as a chromosome? **NCERT**

Ans In telophase-I of meiosis-I, chromosome number becomes half, but the chromosomes are still composed of two chromatids.

If crossing over occurred, these chromatids are not genetically identical. They divide in IInd meiotic division. Hence, crossing over is an attribute, which classifies chromatids as chromosome. (2)

35. Substance W is a chemical that inhibits spindle formation during cell division. If a meristematic plant cell were exposed to substance W, which process will not be able to occur in that plant cell?

Ans When a meristematic plant cell were exposed to the substance W, the separation of sister chromatids will be inhibited. (2)

36. The second meiotic division is similar to mitosis as it results in the separation of the sister chromatids. However, it also differs from mitosis. Explain how?

Ans The main reason for the difference between the two is that the separating sister chromatids during the meiosis-II differ genetically due to crossing over that had occurred during prophase-I. (2)

37. Mention the significance of meiosis. **NCERT**

Ans Refer to text on page no 296. (2)

38. Comment on the statement-meiosis enables the conservation of specific chromosome number of each species even through the process results in reduction of chromosome number. **NCERT Exemplar**

Ans Meiosis is the mechanism by which conservation of specific chromosome number of each species is achieved across generations in sexually reproducing organisms. Even though the process results in reduction of chromosome number by half, it is gradually conserved by union of male gamete (*n*) and female gamete (*n*) in next generation.

Meiosis also increases the genetic variability in the population of organisms from one generation to the next. (2)

Short Answer Type II Questions

3 Marks

39. The diagram below represents the changes in the number of chromosomes during several processes that occur in an animal cell.

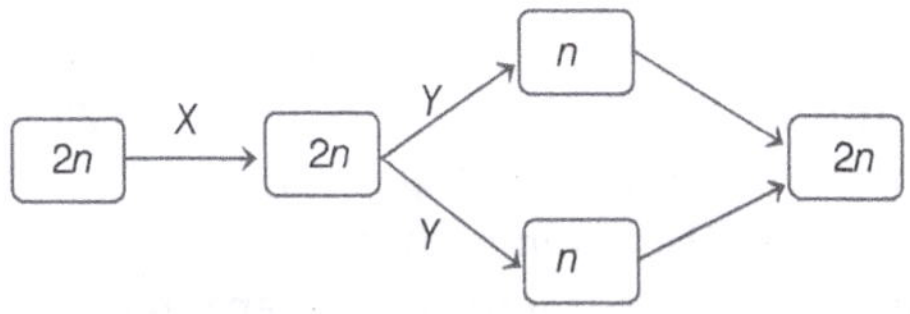

(i) Name the process of cell division occurring at *X* and *Y*.

(ii) State two differences in the behaviour of chromosomes between *X* and *Y*.

Ans (i) *X*–Mitosis. *Y*–Meiosis (1)

(ii) (a) In *X*, there is no association of homologous chromosomes, but in *Y*, homologous chromosomes pair up together to form bivalents during prophase-I.

(b) In *X*, there is no crossing over as there is no formation of chiasmata, but in *Y*, crossing over occurs at the chiasmata whereby some genes are swapped between homologous chromosomes. (2)

40. Identify the following structures labelled as *A*-*F* in the diagram.

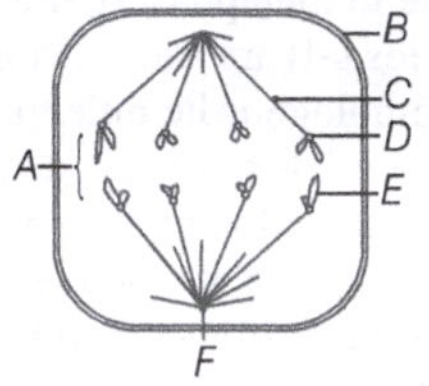

Ans *A*– Chromosomes *B*– Cell membrane

C– Spindle fibre *D*– Centromere

E– Chromatid *F*– Spindle organiser (½ × 6)

41. Name a cell that is found arrested in diplotene stage for months and years. Comment in 2-3 lines how it completes cell cycle? **NCERT**

Ans The cells found arrested in diplotene stage for months and years are oocyte cells of vertebrates such as tailed and tailless amphibians, birds and insects.

The chromosomes of these cells transform into the lampbrush form during the diplotene stage of meiotic prophase due to an active transcription of many genes.

These chromosomes produce large amounts of RNA for the oocyte and most of the genes present in the DNA loops are being expressed actively. (3)

42. **What is chiasmata? Mention its significance also.**

Ans Chiasmata is X-shaped structure of separated bivalents of recombined homologous chromosomes. Chiasmata formation is necessary for the separation of homologous chromosomes which have undergone the process of crossing over. (3)

43. **In which phase of meiosis are the following formed?** **NCERT Exemplar**

(i) Synaptonemal complex ....
(ii) Recombination nodules ....
(iii) Appearance/activation of enzyme recombinase ...
(iv) Termination of chiasmata ....
(v) Interkinesis
(vi) Formation of dyad of cells ....

Ans (i) Synaptonemal complex–zygotene.
(ii) Recombination nodules–pachytene.
(iii) Appearance/activation of enzyme recombinase–pachytene.
(iv) Termination of chiasmata–diakinesis.
(v) Interkinesis–after telophase-I/before meiosis-II.
(vi) Formation of dyad of cells–anaphase-I. (½ × 6)

44. **During meiosis, why sister chromatids do not separate and migrate to opposite poles?**

Ans During interphase-I of meiosis, sister chromatids do not separate and migrate to opposite poles, as observed in mitosis, because in metaphase-I, the chromosomes at the metaphase (meiosis-I) are arranged in a manner that the centromeres homologous lie on either side of metaphase plate pointing towards the opposite pole. As a result, a chromosome is connected only to one spindle pole, of its side due to the presence of a single tractile fibril. Hence, instead of sister chromatids, the homologous chromosomes separate apart during meiosis. (3)

45. **(i) Name the stages and type of cell division represented in A and B, respectively.**

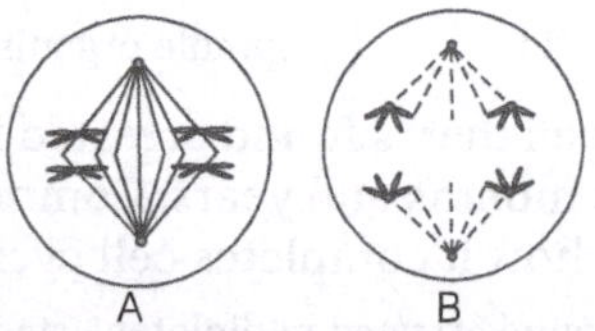

(ii) Also explain any one of them.

Ans (i) Stages and type of cell division are
(A) Metaphase-I-meiosis (B) Anaphase-I-meiosis (1)

(ii) **For metaphase-I** Refer to text on page no. 294. (2)

46. **Distinguish anaphase of mitosis from anaphase-I of meiosis.** **NCERT**

Ans Differences between anaphase of mitosis and anaphase-I of meiosis are

Anaphase of Mitosis	Anaphase-I of Meiosis
Each chromosome arranged at the metaphase plate, splits simultaneously and the two daughter chromatids migrate towards the two opposite poles.	The spindle fibres contract and pull the centromeres of homologous chromosomes towards the opposite poles. So, each chromosome goes to opposite pole.
The centromere of each chromosome is towards the pole with arms of chromosome trailing behind.	The centromere is not divided, so half set of the chromosomes of parent nucleus go to one pole and the remaining half set in the opposite pole.
During this stage (i) Centromeres split and chromatids separate. (ii) Chromatids move to opposite poles.	During this stage (i) Homologous chromosomes separate. (ii) Sister chromatids remain associated at their centromere.

(1 × 3)

47. **Draw a neat and labelled diagram of the following.**

(i) Metaphase-I (ii) Prophase-II
(iii) Telophase-II

Ans Refer to fig. no. 13.7 and 13.8.

48. **Meiosis is advantageous than mitosis as it produces variations, so plays important role in evolution. What are the stages during which chances of recombination of genes are increased during meiosis? Explain these events.**

Ans Stages during which recombination of genes occurs in meiosis are

(i) Crossing over is exchange of genes between the non-sister chromatids of homologous chromosomes.
It occurs at recombination nodules during pachytene stage of prophase-I of meiosis-I and is regulated by recombinase enzyme.

(ii) Arrangement of bivalents at the equator of the spindle during metaphase-I of meiosis. (3)

49. **What is the need of meiosis in cell division?**

Ans There is a need of meiosis in cell division as

(i) Meiosis is essential for all sexually reproducing organisms.
(ii) It occurs in reproductive cells, so that gametes formed are haploid or have half the number of chromosomes of those cells which are directly derived from zygote.
(iii) Two types of gametes fuse during zygote formation. As a result, zygote comes to have double the number of chromosomes contained in gametes.

Meiosis maintains a fixed number of chromosomes of a species by reducing the number by half. (1 × 3)

50. List the main differences between mitosis and meiosis. NCERT

Ans Refer to text on page no. 296.

Long Answer Type Questions

(5 Marks)

51. What are the various stages of meiotic prophase-I? Enumerate the chromosome events during each stage. NCERT

Ans Refer to text on page no. 293-294.

52. Describe the following words

(i) Synapsis (ii) Bivalent

(iii) Chiasmata

Draw a diagram to illustrate your answer. NCERT

Ans (i) **Synapsis** During meiosis-I, the process of pairing of two homologous chromosomes is known as synapsis.

It is so exact that pairing is not merely between corresponding chromosomes, but between corresponding individual units.

(ii) **Bivalent** The complex formed by a pair of synapsed homologous chromosomes is called a bivalent or a tetrad. It consists of four chromatids.

(iii) **Chiasmata** The chiasmata formation is the indication of completion of crossing over and beginning of separation of chromosomes.

The chiasmata is formed when the chromosomal parts begin to repel each other except in the region where these are in contact. Thus, chiasmata formation is necessary for the separation of homologous chromosomes. (3)

See fig no. 13.6 on page no. 294. (2)

53. Write brief note on the following NCERT Exemplar

(i) Synaptonemal complex (ii) Metaphase plate

Ans (i) **Synaptonemal complex** It is formed, when corresponding chromosome becomes intimately associated. The process of pairing is known as synapsis. It is so exact that pairing is not merely occurs between corresponding chromosomes, but between corresponding individual units.

(ii) **Metaphase plate** The bivalents arrange themselves on the equator of the bipolar spindle. The centromeres slightly project towards the periphery. The distribution of bivalents is at random, so that the individual paternal and maternal chromosomes can face either of two poles of the spindle. (2½ × 2)

54. Explain, why a pair of homologous chromosomes is genetically different, but a pair of sister chromatids is genetically identical before crossing over in meiosis?

Ans A pair of homologous chromosomes is genetically different because in a set of homologous chromosomes, one of the chromosome belongs to the male parent and the other comes from the female parent. Therefore, one of a pair will contain paternal genes and the other will contain maternal genes.

However, a pair of sister chromatids is genetically identical before crossing over as the chromatids are formed from the replication of DNA during the S-phase of interphase. DNA replication ensures that the DNA content is doubled with identical genes being copied from the original DNA. Therefore, there is no genetic variation because there is no exchange of genetic material between sister chromatids.

If crossing over occurs, then it would be possible for some genes to be exchanged between the chromatids of homologous chromosomes that have chiasmata, thus leading to genetic variation. (5)

55. Explain meiosis-II in an animal cell.

Ans All these stages happen in the two haploid nuclei simultaneously.

(i) **Prophase-II**, takes short time. Spindle formation begins and the chromosomes become short. Two chromatids are joined to a single centromere. Nuclear membrane and nucleolus disintegrate.

(ii) **Metaphase-II** At the equator, the chromosomes align at the equator and spindle is formed. The centromere of every chromosome is joined to the spindle fibre and centromere also divides.

(iii) **Anaphase-II** The daughter chromosomes are formed. Chromatids move towards their poles with the spindle fibres.

(iv) **Telophase-II** Reaching at the poles, chromosomes form nuclei which are haploid (n) daughter nuclei. Again nuclear membrane is constructed. Nucleolus now becomes clearly visible. (1×4)

Cytokinesis Four daughter cells are formed which are haploid (n). Cytokinesis may occur once or twice (i.e. in meiosis-I and II) or only after the meiosis-II cell division. (1)

56. Describe briefly the phases of meiotic cell division.

Ans Meiotic division takes place in germ cells. The number of chromosomes is reduced to half in daughter cells.

Meiotic cell division is divided into two phases, i.e. meiosis-I and II.

In the meiotic-I division, the homologous chromosomes pair to form bivalents. Exchange of genetic material takes place. The chromosomes now separate and get distributed into daughter cells. (2½ × 2)

For further detail refer to text on page no. 293-296.

SUMMARY

- All multicellular organisms start life as a single cell, formed after fertilisation and further grow to give rise to new population. The phenomenon of production of daughter cells from parent cell is known as cell **division**.
- **Cell cycle** is the sequence of events through which a cell duplicates its content and divides into daughter cell. It is comprised of two main stages, i.e. interphase and M-phase or dividing phase.
- The interphase is the longest phase (about 96%) of the cell cycle during which cell prepares itself for both cell growth and DNA replication. It consists of four phases, i.e. G_1-phase, G_0-phase, S-phase and G_2-phase.
- In **G_1-phase** cell remains metabolically active and acquires nutrients. Synthesis of cell organelles, RNA, ribosomes, protein, etc., takes place.
- **G_0-phase** known as **quiescent stage** during this phase, cell neither divides nor synthesises organelles. Some cells such as nerve cells and erythrocytes that do not divide further during cell cycle exit from G_1-phase to enter into an inactive phase called G_0-phase.
- **S-phase** also called as **synthesis phase**. DNA replication occur in this phase.
- In **G_2-phase** preparations are made for genomic separation. Mitochondria and other organelles replicate, chromosomes condense, etc.
- **M-phase** is the phase of actual division. It consists of major events, karyokinesis (division of nucleus) and cytokinesis (division of cell cytoplasm).
- The karyokinesis of cell division occurs *via* two processes known as **mitosis** and **meiosis**.
- **Mitosis** is an equational division in which parent cell ($2n$) divides into two daughter cells ($2n$).
- The various stages of mitosis are prophase, metaphase, anaphase and telophase.
- During **prophase** the chromatin fibres become shorten and thicken. Each chromosome consist of two chromatids. Nucleoli and nuclear envelope are no longer visible.
- During **metaphase** the chromosomes line up at the equator of the spindle to form metaphase plate. The **kinetochores** of sister chromatids get joined to spindle fibres from opposite poles.
- During **anaphase** the sister chromatids of each chromosome starts moving to the opposite poles of the spindle. Splitting of chromosome takes place due to the division of centromere which attaches two chromatids.
- During **telophase** nuclear envelope is reformed around the chromatids, nucleolus reforms in each nucleus, chromosomes decondense into long fine filaments and mitotic spindle disappears.
- **Amitosis** is also called direct cell division. It occurs without formation of spindle and appearance of chromosomes.
- **Meiosis** is reductional division in which the parent cell ($2n$) divides into four daughter cells (n). Meiosis comprises of two substages meiosis-I and meiosis-II.
- **Meiosis-I** is further divided into prophase-I (with stage like leptotene, zygotene, pachytene, diplotene and diakinesis), metaphase-I, anaphase-I and telophase-I.
- At **leptotene** stage, chromosomes shorten and become visible as single structures and appear as beaded structure.
- At **zygotene** stage, homologous chromosomes pair up. This pairing is called **synapsis**.
- At **pachytene** stage, non-sister chromatids of homologous chromosomes exchange segments between themselves. This exchange of segments is called crossing over.
- At **diplotene** stage, chiasma formation occur. Chiasmata formation is necessary for the separation of homologous chromosomes which have undergone crossing over.
- At **diakinesis** chiasmata shifts towards the terminals of the chromosomes. It is known as terminalisation of chiasmata.
- **Meiosis-II** is similar to mitosis but only difference lies in the fact that after completion of meiosis-II four haploid (n) daughter cells are formed.
- **Cytokinesis** is the process of division of cytoplasm. It occurs in plant cell by cell plate fomation while in animal cell by cell furrowing method.

Chapter Practice

Multiple Choice Questions

1 Mark

1. The interphase is divided into three main phases. Three phases are
   (a) G_1-phase, M-phase and G_2-phase
   (b) M-phase, S-phase and divisional phase
   (c) G_1-phase, synthesis phase and G_2-phase
   (d) M-phase, G_2-phase and divisional phase
2. In G_1-phase of cell cycle, what would be the change in DNA content of the cell?
   (a) DNA content increases to double
   (b) DNA content gets reduced
   (c) Four fold increase of DNA content
   (d) No change in DNA content
3. During cell growth, DNA synthesis takes place in
   (a) S-phase (b) G_1-phase
   (c) G_2-phase (d) M-phase
4. When cell has stalled DNA replication fork, which checkpoint should be predominantly activated?
   (a) G_1/S (b) G_2/M
   (c) M (d) Both (b) and (c)
5. Which of the following is not a characteristic feature during mitosis in somatic cells?
   (a) Disappearance of nucleolus
   (b) Chromosome movement
   (c) Synapsis
   (d) Spindle fibres
6. The centriole moves to opposite poles of the cell in which stage?
   (a) Prophase (b) Metaphase
   (c) Anaphase (d) Telophase
7. The complete disintegration of nuclear envelope in a cell cycle marks the
   (a) start of prophase of mitosis
   (b) start of metaphase of mitosis
   (c) end of anaphase of mitosis
   (d) start of telophase of mitosis
8. Zygotene of prophase-I is characterised by
   (a) chromomeres
   (b) synaptonemal complex
   (c) crossing over
   (d) terminalisation of chiasmata
9. Synaptonemal complex is formed during
   (a) pachytene (b) zygotene
   (c) leptotene (d) diplotene
10. Which of the following events does not occur during zygotene?
    (a) Formation of synaptonemal complex
    (b) Pairing of chromosomes
    (c) Appearance of bivalents
    (d) Involvement of recombinase

Assertion-Reason Type Questions

1 Mark

■ **Direction** (Q. Nos. 11-18) *In each of the following questions, a statement of Assertion (A) is given followed by corresponding statement of Reason (R). Of the statements, mark the correct answer as*

(a) If both A and R are true and R is the correct explanation of A
(b) If both A and R are true, but R is not the correct explanation of A
(c) If A is true, but R is false
(d) If A is false, but R is true

11. **Assertion** (A) Cell normally proceeds to mitosis without interruption, once it enters the G_2-phase.
    Reason (R) Replicated chromosomes (DNA) are distributed to daughter nuclei by a complex series of events under genetic control.
12. **Assertion** (A) Some cells undergo G_0-phase due to inactivation of cell cycle.
    Reason (R) Cells at this stage remain metabolically active, but no longer proliferate.
13. **Assertion** (A) In mitosis, two identical cells are produced from a single cell and karyokinesis is followed by cytokinesis.
    Reason (R) Cytokinesis is of two types, i.e. by cell-furrow method and cell-plate method.

14. **Assertion** (A) In animal cells, cytokinesis is achieved by the appearance of a furrow in plasma membrane.

Reason (R) In plant cells, the formation of the new cell wall begins with the formation of simple precursor called cell-plate.

15. The following graph shows the total amount of DNA present in a cell during various stages of the cell cycle.

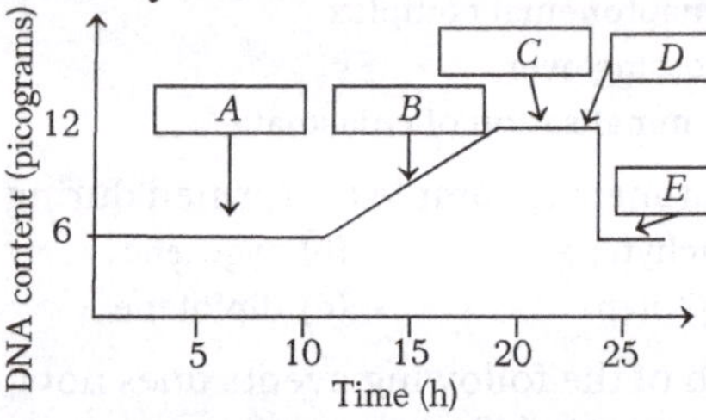

Assertion (A) The stage E in the above graph is showing the division of protoplast.

Reason (R) Cytokinesis is the physical splitting of parent cell into two identical daughter cells.

16. **Assertion** (A) Small disc-shaped structures at the surface of the centromeres are called kinetochores .

Reason (R) Kinetochores are proteinaceous structures.

17. **Assertion** (A) Gametes formed as a result of meiosis are haploid in nature.

Reason (R) Meiotic division occurs in reproductive cells.

18. **Assertion** (A) Diakinesis is the final stage of prophase-I.

Reason (R) Terminalisation of chiasmata occurs in diakinesis.

Answers

1. (c)	2. (d)	3. (a)	4. (a)	5. (c)	6. (a)
7. (b)	8. (b)	9. (b)	10. (d)	11. (d)	12. (b)
13. (b)	14. (b)	15. (b)	16. (b)	17. (a)	18. (b)

Very Short Answer Type Questions

1 Mark

19. Interphase stage is called resting stage, but it is in fact a period of great activity. State whether true or false.

20. What is kinetochore?

21. The shortest phase of mitosis is anaphase. State whether this statement is true or false.

22. In which mitotic phase do paired chromosomes (sister chromatids) separate and begin moving to opposite ends (poles) of the cell?

23. Name the components of a mitotic apparatus in an animal cell, that lacks in a plant cell.

24. The centriole forms spindle during cell division in .... cells.

25. Name the stage of meiosis in which the paired homologous chromosomes get shortened and thickened.

26. What do you mean by sister and non-sister chromatids?

Short Answer Type I Questions

2 Marks

27. It is observed that heart cells do not exhibit cell division. Such cells do not divide further and exit .... phase to enter an inactive stage called .... of cell cycle.

28. Match the words listed in column I with suitable words from the column II.

Column I		Column II	
A.	Karyokinesis	1.	Meiocytes
B.	Cytokinesis	2.	Plant cells
C.	Meiosis	3.	Nuclear division
D.	Cell plate	4.	Cytoplasmic division

(½ × 4)

29. (i) During cell division in apical meristem, the nuclear membrane appears in which phase?

(ii) At which point the polytene chromosomes appear to be attached?

30. Describe the arrangement of chromosomes and their attachment to spindle fibres during mitotic metaphase.

31. Differentiate between pachytene and diakinesis. Also support your answer with suitable diagrams.

32. Draw the stage of meiosis when synapsis takes place.

33. Describe the following in brief.

(i) Leptotene (ii) Zygotene

(iii) Diakinesis (iv) Metaphase-I

34. Give difference in the attachment of chromosomes to the spindle fibres in mitosis and meiosis-I.

Short Answer Type II Questions

(3 Marks)

35. Why do the chromosomes change into long fine chromatin fibres in the interphase?

36. Why does a multicellular organism require two types of cell division? Which of two produces the greater number of cells?

37. (i) Why is mitosis also known as an equational division?

(ii) You are viewing a dividing cell under a microscope. How can you determine whether it is an animal cell or a plant cell?

38. (i) How many division take place in meiosis? How many times, the chromosomes replicate during meiotic cell division?

(ii) How many daughter cells are produced during mitotic cell division and a meiotic cell division?

(iii) What is the status of chromosomes and DNA content in each daughter cell?

39. With the help of diagrams, only depict the events that occur during prophase-I of meiotic division.

40. What marked the transition between

(i) Zygotene and pachytene

(ii) Pachytene and early diplotene

(iii) Mitotic metaphase and anaphase.

Long Answer Type Questions

(5 Marks)

41. Explain the various stages of mitosis with the alignment of how chromosomes change their pattern from prophase to the end of the telophase?

42. Explain cytokinesis. Also with the help of diagram write about cytokinesis in plant cell and animal cell.

43. Draw labelled sketches to depict different phases of mitosis in plant cells.

44. What are homologous chromosomes? What happens to homologous chromosomes during meiosis?

45. How does meiosis differ from mitosis? Give any five differences.

46. Anaphase-I of meiosis differs from anaphase of mitosis in one essential way. Describe the difference and explain, how does it affect the daughter cells?

Case Based Questions

(4/5 Marks)

47. *Read the following passage and answer the questions that follows.*

In a lecture on cell cycle and cell division, the teacher taught the two basic stages of cell cycle *viz*, Interphase and M-phase. She also taught about the substages of each basic stage and their significance.

(i) What is an average duration of cell cycle in humans and yeast ?

(ii) Mention the name of three substages of interphase.

(iii) What would be the amount of DNA and chromosome in each substage of interphase, if the initial amount is 2 C and $2n$, respectively?

(iv) Define the terms karyokinesis and cytokinesis and when does these processes occur in cell cycle?

(v) What do you understand by the quiescent stage of cell cycle?

48. The cytokinesis in plant cell and animal cell during mitotic cell division is depicted in the figure given below.

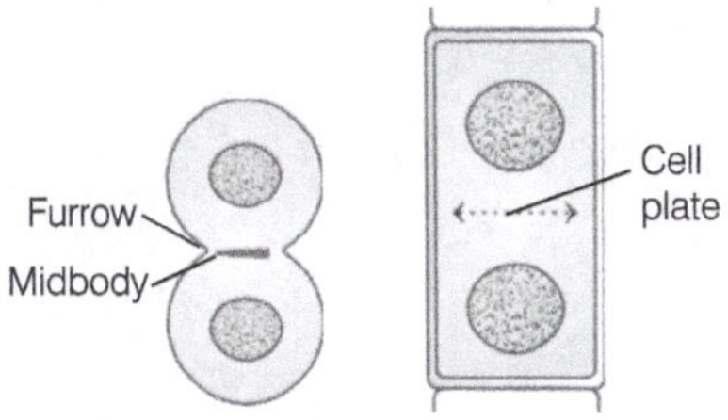

Answer the questions given below.

(i) State the stage of mitosis at which the cytokinesis begins in the animal cells.

(ii) Can a cell undergo cytokinesis before it has divided its nuclear content?

(iii) How is formation of phragmoplast related to cytokinesis?

(iv) In which type of cell, karyokinesis is not followed by cytokinesis?

49. The graph below shows the two cycles of mitotic cell division. Read it carefully and answer the questions given below.

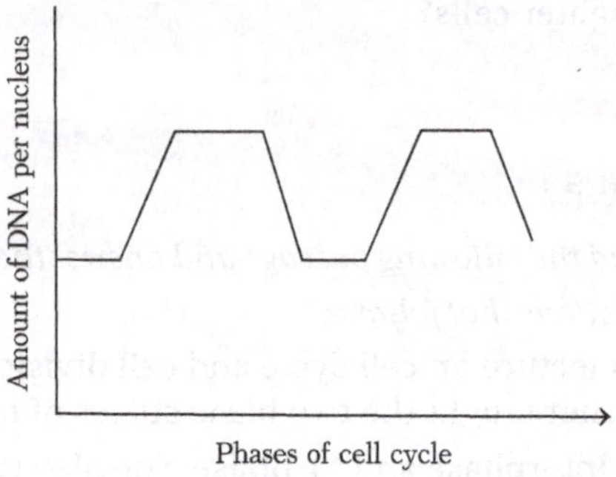

(i) Label G_1, G_2 and S phase on this graph.
(ii) What the hardest phase to identify in mitosis?
(iii) If you started with one cell at the beginning (left) how much total DNA would you have at the end of the phases?

Or (iii) Consider a somatic cell haring 38 chromosomes fill in the table below

Per cell	G_1 phase	G_2 phase
No. of chromosomes		
No. of sister chromatids		

50. A biology student asked his teacher that why two individuals of same population does not look similar. The teacher told him the concept of meiosis and crossing over. The teacher also mentioned that meiosis occurs in two stages which differ significantly.
(i) When does the crossing over occur in humans. Name the type of cells involved in it.
(ii) Is crossing over important? What would happen if crossing over does not take place during meiosis?
(iii) Name the site at which the crossing over occur between homologous chromosomes.

Or (iii) How many daughter cells are produced at the end of meiosis-I and II, respectively?

CHAPTER

14

Photosynthesis in Higher Plants

All animals including human beings depend on plants for their requirement of food. Green plants can synthesise the food they need, but all other organisms depend on them for their needs. Green plants carry out **photosynthesis.** It is a physio-chemical process by which they use the light energy to manufacture organic compounds.

- Introduction to Photosynthesis
  - Landmarks in Discovery of Photosynthesis
  - Raw Materials for Photosynthesis
  - Chloroplast: The Site of Photosynthesis
- Mechanism of Photosynthesis
  - Light Reaction
  - Electron Transport
  - Dark Reaction (Biosynthetic Phase)
  - Calvin Cycle (C_3 Pathway)
- Photorespiration and Factors Affecting Photosynthesis
  - C_4 Pathway
  - Photorespiration
  - Factors Affecting Photosynthesis

TOPIC 01 Introduction to Photosynthesis

The energy required by all living organisms comes directly or indirectly from the sunlight.

Thus, sunlight plays an important role in fixation of CO_2 through which, conversion of solar energy into chemical energy takes place. Water plays a significant role during this process. Hence, photosynthesis is the process by which all green plants, some bacteria and some protists *(Euglena)* use the energy from sunlight to produce sugar, which through cellular respiration produce ATP, the fuel used by all living organisms. Photosynthesis is an important phenomenon due to the following two reasons

(i) It is the primary source of all food on the earth.

(ii) It is also responsible for the release of oxygen into the atmosphere by green plants.

Landmarks in Discovery of Photosynthesis

Study of photosynthesis started about hundreds of years ago. Prior to that, researchers used to believe that plants get all of their nourishment from soil only by the means of roots. Thus, several simple experiments led to the development of understanding of the process involved.

Some early experiments performed by different scholars proved the following facts regarding photosynthesis

Contribution of Joseph Priestley

Joseph Priestley performed a series of experiments in 1770s that revealed about the **essentiality of air** in the growth of green plants. He observed that a burning candle or a respiring mouse in a closed space (i.e. bell jar) soon gets extinguished and died due to suffocation respectively, because burning candle and animal that breathe the air soon get damaged. On the other hand after placing a mint plant in the bell jar along with the burning candle and mouse, he observed that the mouse stayed alive and also the candle continued to burn for a longer time.

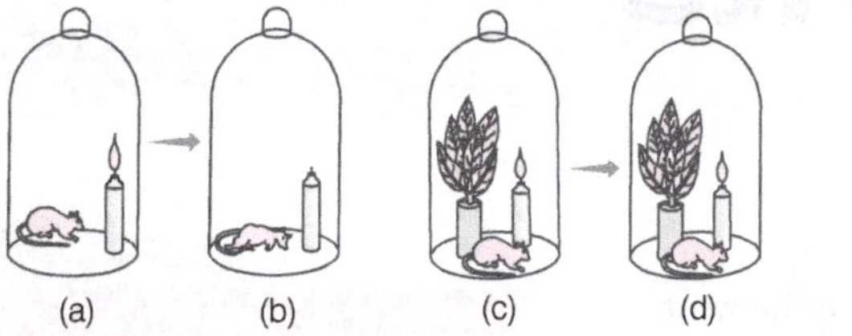

Fig.14.1 Priestley's experiment (a),(b) Mouse dies in foul air (c), (d) Mouse survives in air purified by mint plant.

Conclusion

He hypothesised that the **foul air** produced by the burning of candle and mouse respiration could be converted into **pure air** by plant (mint plant in this case).

Contribution of Julius von Sachs

Julius von Sachs with his experiments in 1854 provided evidence that glucose is produced when plants grow, which is usually stored as starch. He later showed that a green substance, i.e. chlorophyll is found to be located in special bodies called **chloroplast** in plant cells.

Conclusion

He came to the conclusion that green parts are the place in the plants where **production of glucose** takes place and the same gets converted in the form of starch for storage.

Contribution of TW Engelmann

TW Engelmann performed an interesting experiment with green alga, *Cladophora*. He splitted light into its **spectral components** by using prism. He then illuminated the alga placed in a suspension of aerobic bacteria *Rhodospirillum*.

He noticed that the accumulation of bacteria was mainly in the region of the blue and red light of the split spectrum.

Conclusion

By the work done by him at first, action spectrum of photosynthesis was thus described, which roughly resembles the **absorption spectra** of chlorophyll-*a* and *b*.

Therefore, the key features of the process of photosynthesis were known by the middle of the nineteenth century, which detailed that plants acquire light energy harvested from sunlight for the formation of carbohydrates (food) from CO_2 and water.

The empirical equation thus, determined the total process of photosynthesis for organisms that evolve oxygen is understood as

$$nCO_2 + nH_2O \xrightarrow{\text{Light}} [CH_2O]_n + O_2$$

$[CH_2O]_n$ is a carbohydrate here, like glucose (six carbon sugar).

Contribution of Cornelius van Neil

Cornelius van Neil was a microbiologist, who made a significant contribution on the basis of his studies of **purple** and **green** sulphur bacteria (photosynthetic bacteria) in understanding the photosynthesis.

He demonstrated that during the process of photosynthesis, the hydrogen from a suitable oxidisable compound transferred, which reduces CO_2 to carbohydrates in the presence of sunlight.

$$2H_2A + CO_2 \xrightarrow{\text{Light}} 2A + CH_2O + H_2O$$

With the help of this, he concluded that, photosynthesis is a **light dependent** phenomenon.

Further, he stated that in photosynthetic bacteria H_2S acts as a **hydrogen donor,** which gets oxidised to sulphur, so this bacterium does not evolve O_2 during the process of photosynthesis.

While in case of green plants, H_2O acts as a hydrogen donor, which evolves O_2 as a product.

Thus, he inferred that O_2, which is evolved by the green plants comes from the water (H_2O) not from the CO_2 (later proved by the use of radioisotopic techniques).

Thus, the overall reaction of the photosynthesis is represented as

$$6CO_2 + 12H_2O \xrightarrow{\text{Light}} C_6H_{12}O_6 + 6H_2O + 6O_2$$

Conclusion

He concluded that the light is necessary to oxidise the photosynthetic substrate (H_2S in photosynthetic bacteria and H_2O in green plants) and release byproduct sulphur and O_2 in bacteria and green plants, respectively.

In the absence of sunlight, this process does not occur.

The experiments conducted by van Neil has revealed that there exist two types of photosynthesis

(i) **Oxygenic photosynthesis occurs** in cyanobacterium *Oscillatoria*. In this, water is the electron donor and O_2 is evolved.

(ii) **Non-oxygenic photosynthesis** *Rhodospirillum* (purple non-sulphur bacteria), *Chlorobium* (green sulphur bacterium) and *Chromatium* (purple sulphur bacterium) carry out photosynthesis by use of H_2S. It is electron donor for them. Here, O_2 is not evolved. Instead sulphur is the byproduct. This bacterium photosynthesis is called **anoxygenic** or **non-oxygenic photosynthesis.**

Raw Materials for Photosynthesis

On the basis of outline knowledge about the role of light, green plants, CO_2, etc., in the process of photosynthesis, several simple experiments might be performed indicating that light, carbon dioxide, chlorophyll and water are essential raw materials for photosynthesis to take place.

1. Light

The rate of photosynthesis is directly proportional to the intensity of light. The necessity of light for photosynthesis can be shown by fixing a dark paper on leaf of well-watered, but destarched plant (plant can be destarched, by placing it in dark for 48 hours).

After fixing paper, the setup is exposed to sunlight for 2-6 hours. After removing paper, the test for starch is performed over leaf. Starch is produced only in area that received light, showing that light is necessary for photosynthesis.

2. Carbon Dioxide

To initiate the **half leaf experiment** (given by Moll), a part of leaf is enclosed in a test tube. The test tube contains some cotton soaked in KOH (KOH is used because it absorbs carbon dioxide) and the another half of leaf is exposed to light. The setup is then allowed to stand in light for about few hours. When starch test was done, it was observed that the exposed part of leaf was tested positive for starch while, the portion that was enclosed in the tube tested negative. This indicates that, the CO_2 is also essential for photosynthesis to take place.

Note

The difference between the two parts of the leaves in the Moll's half leaf experiment was due to the difference in the availability of CO_2 outside and its absence inside the bottle.

3. Chlorophyll (Green Pigment of Leaf)

To start with this experiment two leaves are taken, one is a **variegated leaf** or a leaf that must be partially covered with black paper and another leaf that must be exposed to light.

When these leaves are tested for **presence of starch,** it was observed that photosynthesis had occurred only in the green part of the leaves in the presence of light, which ensures that **chlorophyll** is essential for photosynthesis.

4. Water

Through **radiolabeling** of oxygen in water molecule, by **Ruben** and **Kamen** (1941), it is confirmed that the O_2 released during photosynthesis comes from H_2O, not from CO_2.

Chloroplast : The Site of Photosynthesis

These are the green plastids that function as the site of photosynthesis, i.e. help in the synthesis of organic food. The process of photosynthesis takes place in the green leaves of the plants because chloroplasts are abundantly present in the mesophyll cell of the leaves.

Chloroplast is double membrane bound, DNA and ribosome containing semiautonomous cell organalle.

Internally, a chloroplast contains a proteinaceous matrix or fluid called **stroma,** the membrane system called **lamellae** or **thylakoids**. At some places, the thylakoid gets aggregated to form stacks of discs, called **grana.**

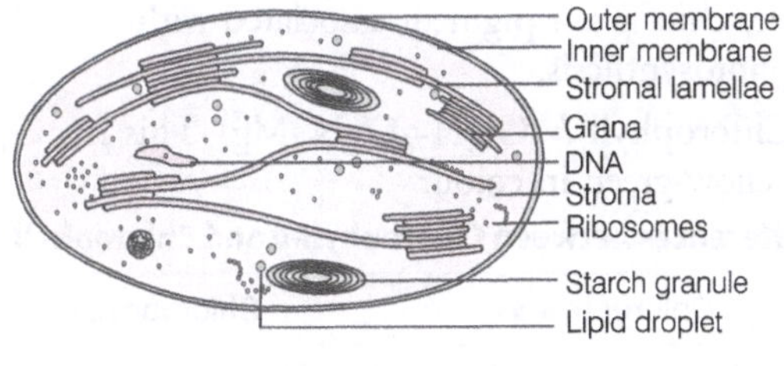

Fig. 14.2 Diagrammatic representation of an electron micrograph of a section of chloroplast

The clear division of labour occurs within the chloroplasts, i.e. the membrane system is responsible for trapping of solar energy and the synthesis of ATP and NADPH (photochemical phase), whereas the stroma has enzymes, which are responsible for the reduction of carbon dioxide into carbohydrates and formation of sugars.

As the former set of reactions is dependent on light so are called **light reactions** while, the latter is dependent on the products of light reactions, i.e. ATP and NADPH (and independent from direct sunlight), thus are called **dark reactions.**

Pigments Involved in Photosynthesis

The pigments involved in the process of photosynthesis are called **photosynthetic pigments.** These pigments provide different shades of green in the leaves in different plants or in the leaves of same plant.

These pigments can easily be separated out by chromatographic technique (paper chromatography). On the basis of their significance, the photosynthetic pigments are of two types

(i) **Primary Pigments** The pigment forms the main molecule of photosystem, e.g. chlorophyll- *a, b.*

(ii) **Accessory Pigments** These support the function of primary pigments, e.g. xanthophylls and carotenoids.

A chromatographic separation of the leaf pigments shows that it is not only the single pigment, which is responsible for the colour in the leaves. Instead the different shades in leaf are due to four different pigments that have different ability to absorb **light at specific** wavelength.

Different pigments present in leaf are described below

(a) **Chlorophyll-*a*** ($C_{55}H_{72}O_5N_4Mg$) This is bright or blue-green in the chromatogram. It is known to be the chief plant pigment associated with photosynthesis.

(b) **Chlorophyll-*b*** ($C_{55}H_{70}O_6N_4Mg$) This is yellow-green in colour.

Differences between Chlorophyll-*a* and Chlorophyll-*b*

Chlorophyll-*a*	Chlorophyll-*b*
It is blue-green in colour.	It is yellow-green in colour.
It is the primary pigment.	It is the accessory pigment.
It has methyl group attached to third carbon.	It has aldehyde group attached to third carbon.
It is soluble in ether.	It is soluble in methyl alcohol.

(c) **Xanthophylls** This is yellow in colour. These pigments are oxidised carotenoids.

(d) **Carotenoids** This is yellow to yellow-orange in colour. They are also known as 'antenna pigment'.

Differences between Xanthophylls and Carotenoids

Xanthophylls	Carotenoids
These are yellow photosynthetic pigments found in plants.	These are orange photosynthetic pigments in plants.
There are three kinds of xanthophylls–canthaxanthin, zeaxanthin and lutein.	These are of four types– α -carotene, β -carotene lycopene and rhodopsin.
They provide protection against excessive amount of light to chlorophyll.	They protect plant by absorbing the energy of nascent oxygen produced during photosynthesis.

Chlorophyll is the most abundant plant pigment found in plants in the world. It contains magnesium (Mg^{2+}) metal as its constituent. Chlorophyll-*a* is found in all photosynthesising cells.

Absorption Spectrum

It is the curve that shows the amount of different wavelength of lights absorbed by a substance (photosynthetic pigment). The graph given below shows the ability of chlorophyll-*a* to absorb lights of different wavelengths.

Chlorophyll-*a* shows the maximum absorption peak at 450 nm and also shows another peak at 650 nm.

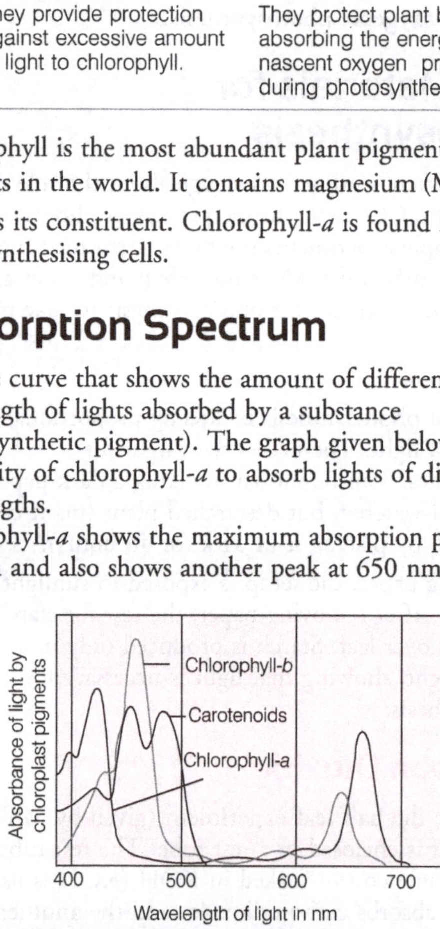

Fig. 14.3 Graph showing the absorption spectrum of chlorophyll-*a*, *b* and the carotenoids

Absorption spectrum is constituted by the pigments like violet, blue, orange and red (400-500 and 600-700 nm) lights. The emission spectrum is constituted by yellow and yellow-green pigment (500-550 nm).

Action Spectrum

It is the curve that depicts the **relative rates** of photosynthesis at different wavelengths of light. Now, another graph given below, shows the wavelength at which maximum photosynthesis occurs at blue, violet and red wavelength in a plant (which is shown by chlorophyll-*a*).

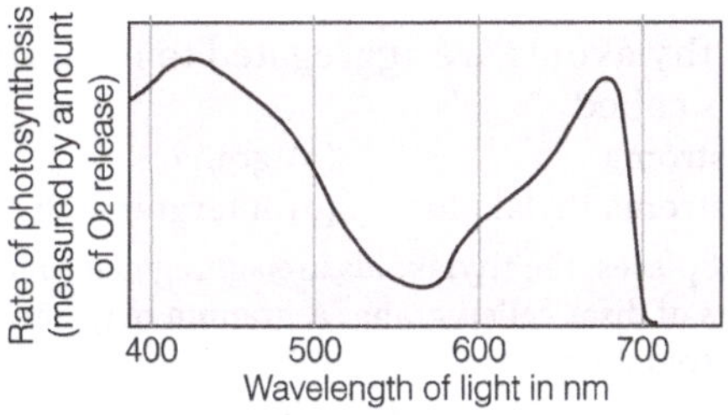

Fig. 14.4 Graph showing action spectrum of photosynthesis

Hence, this concludes that chlorophyll-*a* is the chief pigment, which is majorly responsible for the photosynthesis. The another graph given below shows the action spectrum of photosynthesis, which coincide closely to the absorption spectrum of chlorophyll.

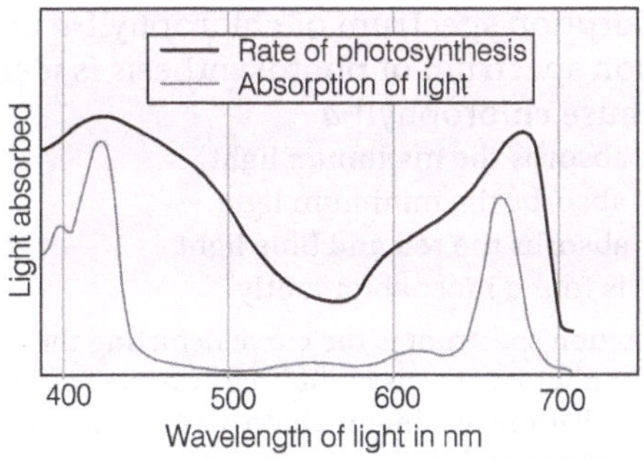

Fig. 14.5 Superimposed absorption spectrum of chlorophyll-*a*

Hence, all three graphs together show that the major part of the photosynthesis takes place in the blue and red regions, while some of the photosynthesis takes place at other wavelengths also in the **visible spectrum.**

Apart from chlorophyll-*a* (the major pigment,) which is mainly responsible for trapping of light, other thylakoid pigments such as chlorophyll-*b*, xanthophylls and carotenoids also absorb light, transferring energy to chlorophyll-*a*. These pigments are called **accessory pigments.**

These pigments enable a wider range of wavelength of incoming light to be utilised for photosynthesis and also provide protection to chlorophyll-*a* from photo-oxidation.

Note **Photosynthetically Active Radiation** (PAR) It is the region of wavelength in which photosynthesis takes place normally. It ranges from 400-700 nm.

Differences between Absorption Spectrum and Action Spectrum

Absorption Spectrum	Action Spectrum
It is the graphical representation of wavelengths of light absorbed by different pigments during photosynthesis.	It is the graphical representation of rate of photosynthesis due to different wavelengths of light during photosynthesis.
It exhibits intensity of light absorbed relative to its wavelengths.	It exhibits relative efficiency of photosynthesis by different wavelengths.
It shows relation between wavelengths of light and the absorbing potential of pigments.	It shows relation between photosynthetic activity with wavelengths of light.

Topic Practice 1

Multiple Choice Questions

(1 Mark)

1. Julius von Sachs in 1854 stated that
   (a) green parts of plant release O_2
   (b) green parts of plant synthesise glucose
   (c) glucose in green parts is stored as starch
   (d) Both (b) and (c)

Ans (d) Julius von Sachs stated that the green parts in plant is where glucose is synthesised and the same gets converted in the form of starch for storage.

2. The first action spectrum of photosynthesis was related to
   (a) algae (b) mint plant
   (c) bacteria (d) bryophytes

Ans (a) TW Engelmann (1843-1909) performed an interesting experiment using a prism. He splitted light into its spectral components and then illuminated a green alga, *Cladophora* (Algae), placed in a suspension of aerobic bacteria. The bacteria were used to detect the sites of O_2 evolution. He observed that the bacteria accumulated mainly in the region of blue and red light of the split spectrum. The first action spectrum of photosynthesis was thus described.

3. Neil concluded that O_2 evolved by the green plant comes from water and not from CO_2. This was proved by
   (a) radioisotope technique
   (b) X-ray crystallography
   (c) X-ray diffraction
   (d) Both (b) and (c)

Ans (a) The O_2 is released from water, was proved using radioisotope technique.

4. Which one is the correct reaction of photosynthesis?

(a) $6CO_2 + 6H_2O \xrightarrow[\text{Chlorophyll}]{\text{Light}} 6O_2 + C_6H_{12}O_6$

(b) $6CO_2 + 12H_2O \xrightarrow[\text{Chlorophyll}]{\text{Light}} C_6H_{12}O_6 + 6O_2 + 6H_2O$

(c) $C_6H_{12}O_6 + 6O_2 + 6H_2O \xrightarrow[\text{Chlorophyll}]{\text{Light}} 6CO_2 + 12H_2O + \text{Energy}$

(d) $C_6H_{12}O_6 + 6O_2 \xrightarrow[\text{Chlorophyll}]{\text{Light}} 6CO_2 + 6H_2O + \text{Energy}$

Ans (b) In green plants, H_2O is the hydrogen donor and is oxidised to O_2 in photosynthesis. Some organisms do not release O_2 during photosynthesis.

When H_2S, instead of H_2O is the hydrogen donor for purple and sulphur bacteria.

The oxidation product is sulphur or sulphate depending on the organism and not O_2. Hence, it was inferred that O_2 evolved by green plant comes from H_2O and not from carbon dioxide.

5. Which equation is correct to prove that O_2 comes from water during photosynthesis?

(a) $6CO_2{}^{18} + 12H_2O \longrightarrow 6O_2{}^{18} + C_6H_{12}O_6 + 6H_2O$

(b) $6CO_2 + 12H_2O^{18} \longrightarrow 6O_2 + C_6H_{12}O_6 + 6H_2O^{18}$

(c) $6CO_2{}^{18} + 12H_2O \longrightarrow 6CO_2{}^{18} + C_6H_{12}O_6$

(d) $6CO_2 + 12H_2O^{18} \longrightarrow 6O_2{}^{18} + C_6H_{12}O_6 + 6H_2O$

Ans (d) Ruben and Kamen (1941) and Ruben, *et. al.* (1941) suspended *Chlorella* in water having non-radioactive heavy isotope of oxygen ^{18}O, instead of natural oxygen (^{16}O).

The suspension was illuminated. Oxygen evolved was tested by means of mass spectrometer. It was found to be having isotope, O^{18}. This is possible only if, oxygen evolved during photosynthesis comes from splitting of water.

$$6CO_2 + 12H_2O^{18} \xrightarrow[\text{Chlorophyll}]{\text{Light}} C_6H_{12}O_6 + 6H_2O + 6\,O_2$$

6. Which metal ion is a constituent of chlorophyll? **NCERT Exemplar**

(a) Iron (b) Copper
(c) Magnesium (d) Zinc

Ans (c) **Magnesium** (Mg) is present in the centre of porphyrin ring of the chlorophyll molecule. Other ions, i.e. iron, copper and zinc participate in other metabolic processes which are

Fe (Iron) is an important part of **cytochrome** and **ferredoxin.**

Cu (Copper) plays an important role in enzyme catalysing redox reactions.

Zn (Zine) is associated with auxin (a phytohormone) synthesis.

7. Which pigment acts directly to convert light energy to chemical energy ? **NCERT Exemplar**

(a) Chlorophyll-*a* (b) Chlorophyll-*b*
(c) Xanthophyll (d) Carotenoid

Ans (a) **Chlorophyll-*a*** acts directly to convert light energy to chemical energy. The other pigments chlorophyll-*b*, xanthophyll and carotenoids are accessory pigments associated with the pigment, i.e. chlorophyll-*a* to harvest the light energy.

8. The thylakoids are aggregated to form stalks of discs called

(a) stroma (b) grana
(c) stroma thylakoids (d) intergranal thylakoids

Ans (b) At places, the thylakoids are aggregated to form stocks of discs called grana. A granum may have 20-50 thylakoid discs.

9. The function(s) of chloroplast's membrane system is/are

(a) trapping of light energy (b) synthesis of ATP
(c) synthesis of NADPH (d) All of these

Ans (d) The membranous system is responsible for trapping the light energy that makes ATP and NADPH necessary for the starch synthesis.

10. Absorption spectrum of chlorophyll-*a* and the action spectrum of photosynthesis is identical because chlorophyll-*a*

(a) absorbs the maximum light
(b) absorbs the minimum light
(c) absorbs the red and blue light
(d) is found most abundantly

Ans (c) Action spectrum is the curve depicting the relative rate of photosynthesis at different wavelength of light. It shows that the maximum photosynthesis occurs at the blue and red region.

11. Correct sequence of rate of photosynthesis in different light is

(a) Red > Blue > Green (b) Blue > Red > Green
(c) Green > Blue > Red (d) Green > Red > Blue

Ans (a) Maximum photosynthesis rate has been observed in the full spectrum. Regarding the effect of different wavelengths, maximum photosynthesis occurs in red light (660 nm), second maximum in blue (440 nm) and minimum in green.

Very Short Answer Type Questions

(1 Mark)

12. Whose hypothesis revealed that plant purifies air while breathing animals and burning candles fouls it?

Ans The plant purifies air while breathing animals and burning candles fouls it was revealed by Priestley's hypothesis.

13. **Oxygen evolved during photosynthesis comes from H_2O or CO_2?**

Ans Oxygen in photosynthesis evolves from H_2O (i.e. by splitting of water) during light reaction.

14. **Photosynthetic pigments are located in which part of the chloroplast?**

Ans Photosynthetic pigments are located in the lipid part of the thylakoid membrane.

15. **Enumerate the type of chlorophyll known as universal photosynthetic pigment.**

Ans Chlorophyll-*a* is known as the universal photosynthetic pigment present in almost all photosynthetic organisms.

16. **Which range of wavelength (in nm) is called Photosynthetically Active Radiation (PAR)?** **NCERT Exemplar**

Ans The light range between 400-700 nm of wavelength is called PAR.

17. **Tomatoes, carrots and chillies are red in colour due to the presence of one pigment. Name the pigment. Is it a photosynthetic pigment?** **NCERT Exemplar**

Ans Lycopene pigment, which is a chromoplast is present in tomatoes, carrots and chillies. It is a non-photosynthetic pigment.

18. **Does moonlight support photosynthesis? Find out.** **NCERT Exemplar**

Ans The intensity of moonlight is several thousands times less than that of direct sunlight, which is insufficient for the light dependent phase of photosynthesis. So, photosynthesis does not occur in moonlight.

19. **Look at leaves of the same plant on the shady side and compare it with the leaves on the sunny side. Or, compare the potted plants kept in the sunlight with those in the shade. Which of them has leaves that are darker green ? Why ?** **NCERT**

Ans The leaves of the same plant on the shady side are dark green as compare it with the leaves on the sunny side.

Short Answer Type I Questions

(2 Marks)

20. **Mention any two reasons, which prove that photosynthesis is essential for sustaining life on the earth?**

Ans Two reasons which prove that photosynthesis is essential for sustaining life on the earth are as follows

(i) It is the process by which food is manufactured for all living organisms.

(ii) It is the only natural process by which oxygen is liberated into the atmosphere. This O_2 is used by all living organisms respiring aerobically. (1×2)

21. **How are photosynthesis and respiration related to each other?**

Ans **Photosynthesis and respiration** are related, as in both mechanisms, the plants gain energy.

In photosynthesis, plants gain energy from solar radiations whereas, in respiration, they breakdown glucose molecule to get energy in the form of ATP molecules.

They are related also because they are dependent on each other. The product of photosynthesis, i.e. glucose (food) is utilised in respiration to yield energy (ATP).

While doing so, it releases many other simple molecules ($CO_2 + H_2O$) which are utilised in photosynthesis to produce more sugars. (2)

22. **Why is the colour of a leaf kept in the dark frequently becomes yellow or pale green? Which pigment do you think is more stable?** **NCERT**

Ans The colour of a leaf kept in the dark frequently becomes yellow or pale green due to the disintegration of chlorophyll pigment in continuous absence of light. The carotene pigment is more stable, so leaves become pale. (2)

23. **If a green plant is kept in dark with proper ventilation, can this plant carryout photosynthesis? Can anything be given as supplement to maintain its growth or survival?** **NCERT Exemplar**

Ans Plants need sunlight for photosynthesis. The sun is the only thing that will help plants make their own food. If there is a small opening in the room that let in sunlight, the plant would grow towards the opening or the light to carry out photosynthesis and will survive. (2)

24. **Discuss the contribution of Cornelius van Neil.**

Ans Refer to text on page no. 308.

25. **Differentiate between stroma and grana of chloroplasts.**

Ans Differences between stroma and grana of chloroplasts are

Stroma	Grana
It is the jelly-like matrix of the chloroplast.	These are formed of stacks of thylakoids.
Dark reaction takes place here.	Light reaction takes place here.

(1+1)

26. **Cyanobacteria and some other photosynthetic bacteria do not have chloroplasts. How do they conduct photosynthesis?** **NCERT Exemplar**

Ans Cyanobacteria and some other photosynthetic bacteria have photosynthetic lamellae (membranes) suspended freely in the cytoplasm. These carry bacteriochlorophyll to conduct photosynthesis. (1+1)

27. **Which property of the pigment is responsible for its ability to initiate the process of photosynthesis? Why is the rate of photosynthesis higher in the red and blue regions of the spectrum of light?**

Ans The chlorophyll pigments are present in the thylakoid membranes. They have the property of excitability and emits e^- in the excited stage, though this e^- is replaced and transferred by the e^- generated from splitting of water molecules. (1)

Red and blue light have maximum energy which a chlorophyll pigment absorbs and get excited and initiate the process of photosynthesis.

Also, its wavelength are 400-700 nm, i.e. between the Photosynthetic Active Radiation (PAR). Thus, the rate of photosynthesis is higher in blue and red light. (1)

28. **In tropical rainforests, the canopy is thick and shorter plants growing below it, receive filtered light. How are they able to carry out photosynthesis?** **NCERT Exemplar**

Ans The light transmitted through the tree canopy is of low intensity light. Therefore, plants growing under the canopy of others have adapted themselves to carry out photosynthesis in low light intensities. (2)

Short Answer Type II Questions

3 Marks

29. **Describe how Engelmann arrived at the first action spectrum of photosynthesis.**

Ans Refer to text on page no. 308.

30. **Give reasons for the following**

(i) Plants are the lungs of nature

(ii) Chlorophyll-*b* and other accessory pigments are necessary for photosynthesis.

(iii) In the highlight intensities, the chlorophyll-*a* gets damaged.

Ans (i) Plants are also called lungs of the nature because, they perform the exact function as lungs do in mammals. They produce oxygen, which is necessary for all forms of life. So, in essence since our lungs keep us alive, in the same way the trees keep our lungs alive. Thus, they are considered to be the part of our lung existence.

(ii) Chlorophyll-*b* and other accessory pigments are necessary as these are light absorbing compounds found in photosynthetic organisms. These pigments enable a wider range of wavelength of incoming light to be utilised for photosynthesis.

(iii) Chlorophyll-*a* structure is such that it gets damaged by bright/high light intensities. It is protected by carotenoid pigments. (1×3)

31. **Chlorophyll-*a* is the primary pigment for the light reaction. What are accessory pigments? What is their role in photosynthesis?**

Ans Accessory pigments are also photosynthetic pigments. These are chlorophyll-*b*, xanthophyll and carotenoids. These are not directly involved in emission of excited electrons, but they help in harvesting solar radiation and pass it on to chlorophyll-*a*.

This pigment itself absorbs maximum radiation at blue and red region. So, chlorophyll-*a* is the chief pigment of photosynthesis and others (i.e. chlorophyll-*b*, xanthophyll and carotenoids) are accessory pigment. (3)

32. **Suppose there were plants that had a high concentration of chlorophyll-*b*, but lacked chlorophyll-*a*, would it carry out photosynthesis? Also mention why do plants have chlorophyll-*b* and other accessory pigments?** **NCERT**

Ans Though chlorophyll-*a* is the major pigment responsible for trapping light, other photosynthetic pigments like chlorophyll-*b*, xanthophylls and carotenoids, which are called accessory pigments, also absorb light of different energy wavelengths and transfer their energy to chlorophyll-*a*.

Indeed, they not only enable a wider range of wavelength of incoming light to be utilised for photosynthesis, but carotene also protects chlorophyll-*a* from photo-oxidation. (2+1)

33. **What can we conclude from the statement that the action and absorption spectra of photosynthesis overlap? At which wavelength, do they show peaks?** **NCERT Exemplar**

Ans The absorption spectrum is the graph plotted, with the amount of light absorbed as a function of wavelength. The action spectrum is the graph plotted with the rate of photosynthesis as a function of wavelength.

Since, the amount of light absorbed and the rate of photosynthesis have a direct relationship, the two curves overlap. They show peaks around wavelengths 450 nm (blue region) and 650-680 nm (red region). (3)

34. **Two groups (*A* and *B*) of bean plants of similar size and same leaf area were placed in identical conditions. Group *A* was exposed to light of wavelength 400-450 nm and Group *B* to the light of wavelength of 500-550 nm. Compare the photosynthetic rate of the two groups by giving reason.**

Ans Group *A* will show more photosynthesis. Chlorophyll absorbs maximum light in the blue region of the spectrum, i.e. 400-450 nm and hence photosynthetic rate will also be high. Group *B* will show negligible amount of photosynthesis or no photosynthesis. Chlorophyll does not absorb any light in the green region, i.e. 500-550 nm, but reflects green, so plants appear green. (1½ × 2)

35. **Photosynthetic organisms occur at different depths in the ocean. Do they receive the light? How do they adapt to carry out photosynthesis under these conditions?** **NCERT Exemplar**

Ans Photosynthetic organisms at different depths in the ocean do not receive the same light qualitatively and quantitatively. The plants growing at the banks of water bodies get good quality of light. Algae which can tolerate more dilutions of light penetrate deeper inside water. Green algae remain in the shore line, brown algae descend to intermediate depths, while red algae form the limit below where no other autotrophic plants can grow. (3)

36. **Explain the reasons of following.**

(i) Photosynthesis can occur in the absence of light.

(ii) Even non-green leaves can make the food.

(iii) Photosynthesis can occur under water.

Ans (i) Photosynthesis cannot occur in the absence of sunlight. The sunlight originally supplies the energy for conversion of CO_2 to carbohydrate.

(ii) Yes, the chlorophyll is the most prominent plant pigment, but not in all plants. Some other accessory pigments such as xanthophylls and carotenoids can also perform photosynthesis separately (in some algae).

(iii) Photosynthesis can occur under water only when the water is clear and shallow. Some alga (Rhodophyta) can synthesise food at deep water layers as they can absorb the light of blue wavelength, efficiently. (1+1+1)

Long Answer Type Questions

5 Marks

37. **Is it correct to say that photosynthesis occurs only in leaves of a plant? Besides leaves, what are the other parts that may be capable of carrying out photosynthesis? Justify.** **NCERT Exemplar**

Ans Although all cells in the green part of a plant have chloroplasts, most of the energy is captured in the leaves. The cells in the interior tissues of a leaf, called the mesophyll, can contain between 450000 and 800000 chloroplasts for every square millimetre of leaf (nearly 60-70 chloroplasts/cell).

The surface of the leaf is uniformly coated with a water-resistant waxy cuticle that protects the leaf from excessive evaporation of water and decreases the absorption of ultraviolet or blue light to reduce heating. The transparent epidermal layer allows light to pass through to the palisade mesophyll cells, where most of the photosynthesis takes place. (4)

The green stems are also capable of performing photosynthesis. (1)

38. **In the figure given below, the black line (upper) indicates action spectrum for photosynthesis and the lighter line (lower) indicates the absorption spectrum of chlorophyll-*a*, answer the following.**

(i) What does the action spectrum indicate? How can we plot an action spectrum? Explain with an example.

(ii) How can we derive an absorption spectrum for any substance?

(iii) If chlorophyll-*a* is responsible for light reaction of photosynthesis, why do the action spectrum and absorption spectrum not overlap? **NCERT Exemplar**

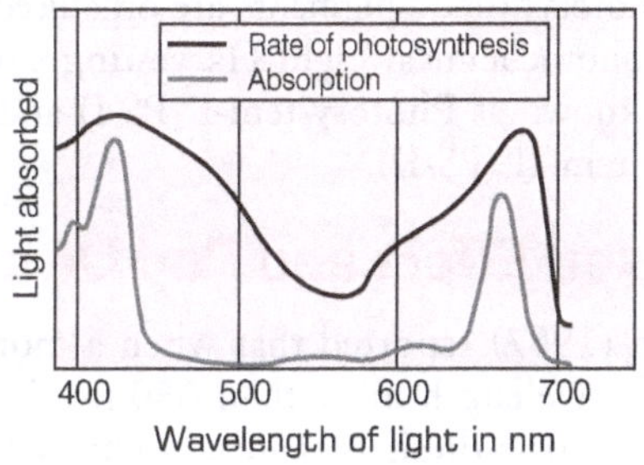

Ans (i) Action spectrum is the relative rates of photosynthesis at different wavelengths of light. Refer to text for details on page no. 405. (1½)

(ii) Absorption of different wavelengths of light by a particular pigment is plotted and is called the absorption spectrum of that pigment. (1½)

(iii) Chlorophyll-*a* is responsible for light reaction of photosynthesis, but the action spectrum and absorption spectrum do not overlap because, though chlorophyll is the main pigment responsible for absorption of light, other thylakoid pigments like chlorophyll-*b*, xanthophylls and carotenoids, which are called accessory pigments, also absorb and transfer the energy to chlorophyll-*a*.

Indeed they not only enable a wider range of wavelength of incoming light to be utilised for photosynthesis, but also protect chlorophyll-*a* from photo-oxidation. (2)

TOPIC 02 Mechanism of Photosynthesis

It is a complicated oxidation-reduction process. In this, process oxidation of water and reduction of CO_2 takes place.

Photosynthesis consists of two phases, i.e. photochemical phase or light reaction and biosynthetic phase or dark reaction.

Light Reaction

(The Photochemical Phase or Hill Reaction)

Light reaction includes the following steps, i.e. absorption of light, splitting of water, release of oxygen and finally the formation of high energy chemical intermediates, i.e. ATP and NADPH. During the course of light reaction, light is trapped by photosynthetic pigments present in the **quantasomes** of grana thylakoids.

These photosynthetic pigments are organised into two discrete photochemical **Light Harvesting Complexes** (LHCs) known as **Photosystem-I** (PS-I) and **Photosystem-II** (PS-II).

Emerson Effect and Red Drop

Emerson (1957) reported that when a monochromatic beam of wavelength more than 680 nm is used, the rate of photosynthesis is reduced. This fall in quantum yield above 680 nm is called red drop.

He later on found that if two monochromatic beams of wavelength 650-680 nm and 700-720 nm are used, the rates of photosynthesis increases. This is know as **Emerson's enhancement effect.**

Emerson's effect suggests the role of two different photosynthetic units. One that is driven by longer wavelength and the other by shorter wavelength.

Photosystems or Pigment Systems

The light harvesting complexes or photosystems are made up of hundreds of pigment molecules bounded by proteins. Each photosystem has a **photocentre** or **reaction centre**, where actual reaction takes place.

This reaction centre contains a special chlorophyll-*a* molecule. It is fed by hundred other pigment molecules and it forms the light harvesting system called **antennae.**

These antennae molecule absorb light of different wavelength, but shorter than reaction centre in order to make photosynthesis more efficient.

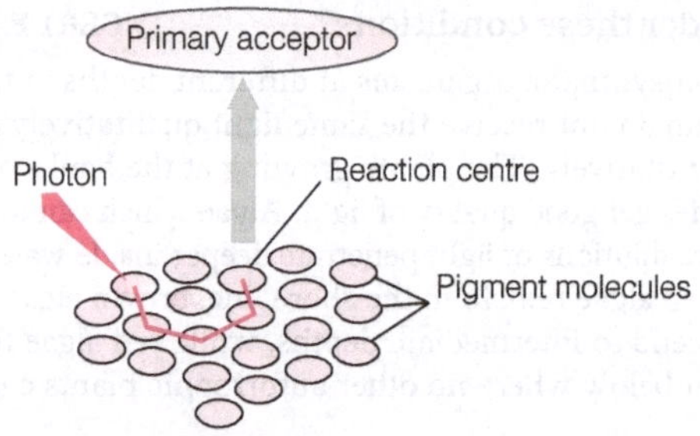

Fig. 14.6 The light harvesting complex

The reaction centre is different in both the photosystem as given below

(i) In PS-I, the reaction centre or chlorophyll-*a* has peak of absorption at 700 nm, known as P_{700}.

(ii) In PS-II, the reaction centre has absorption peak at 680 nm hence called P_{680}.

Note

These photosystems are named according to the sequence of their discoveries not in the sequence in which they function during the light reaction.

Differences between PS-I and PS-II

Photosystem-I	Photosystem-II
Reaction centre is P_{700}, i.e. it absorbs 700 nm wavelength.	Reaction centre is P_{680}, i.e. it absorbs 680 nm wavelength of light.
It is situated on the outer surface of thylakoid membrane. It is found on stroma lamellae also.	It is situated on the inner surface of thylakoid membrane.
It is involved in both cyclic and non-cyclic photo-phosphorylation.	It is involved in non-cyclic photophosphorylation only.
It is basically concerned with $NADP^+$ reduction.	It is concerned with water splitting.

Electron Transport

The photosynthetic electron transport chain initiates with the absorption of light energy by the **photosystem-II.** The light of wavelength 680 nm is absorbed by the reaction centre of photosystem-II due to which a pair of electrons becomes excited and jump into an orbit away from the atomic nucleus.

These electrons are then picked up by an **electron acceptor**, which passes them further to electron transport system consisting of cytochromes.

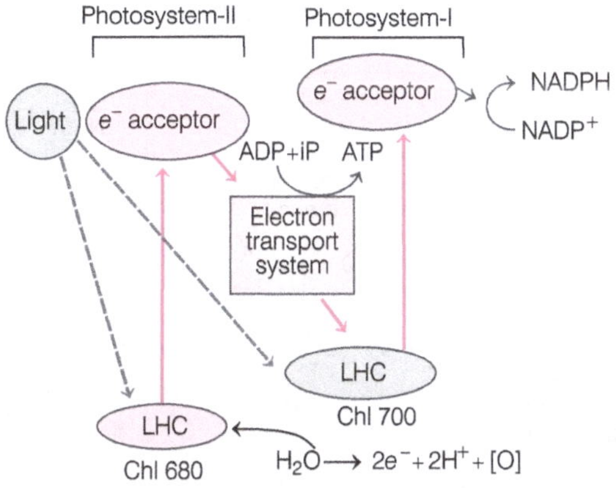

Fig. 14.7 Z-scheme of light reaction

It is to be noted that this movement of electrons is **downhill** according to the **redox potential scale** (oxidation-reduction scale). The electrons of the electron transport chain are not used up in the chain instead they are further passed on to the pigments of PS-I.

Now, like the PS-II, the electrons in the reaction centre of PS-I also get excited on **receiving red light** of wavelength 700 nm and get transferred to the another electron acceptor with **higher redox potential.**

But this time the electron does not move to a reaction centre or chlorophyll-*a*. Instead, it moves to a molecule **rich in energy** and $NADP^+$. On addition of these electrons the $NADP^+$ gets reduced to NADPH + H^+.

In 1960, **Bendall** and **Hill** discovered the **Z-scheme** of electron transport. It is a series of reactions that we have just studied above from the whole scheme of electron transfer initiating from PS-II, uphill to the acceptor molecule, down the electron transport chain to PS-I, excitation of electrons and then their transfer to another acceptor and finally downhill to $NADP^+$ in order to get reduced to NADPH and H^+.

Knowledge Plus

Cytochrome, plastoquinone and plastocyanin are the important electron carriers.

(i) **Cytochromes** These are small proteins that contain a cofactor, haem, having an Fe-atom. Cytochromes are intrinsic membrane proteins of thylakoid membranes.

(ii) **Plastoquinones** These transport electrons over short distance within a membrane. Their long hydrocarbon tail is hydrophobic Thus, they dissolve easily into the lipid component of the chloroplast membrane.

(iii) **Plastocyanin** It is a small protein that carries electrons with the help of copper.

Splitting of Water

The electrons are continuously supplied to the photosystem-II by the available electrons, which get replaced due to the splitting of water. In this process, the water splits into protons, electrons and oxygen. The complex for water splitting is associated with the photosystem-II that is located on the inner side of the thylakoid membrane. Mn^+ and Cl^- ions also play important role in the photolysis of water molecule.

These electrons thus, obtained by the splitting of water are needed to replace those electrons which are removed from the photosytem-I The electrons needed to replace those removed from photosystem-I are provided by photosystem-II.

$$2H_2O \rightarrow 4H^+ + O_2 \uparrow + 4e^-$$

While all the electrons formed, are replaced, the protons get accumulated in the lumen of the thylakoid and the oxygen is evolved into the atmosphere.

Photophosphorylation

Phosphorylation is the process through which, ATP is synthesised from ADP and inorganic phosphate (P) by the cell organelles (like mitochondria and chloroplast). When it occurs in the presence of sunlight in chloroplast, it is called photophosphorylation. Phosphorylation in mitochondria is not light dependent, but it uses the energy by oxidation of nutrients to produce ATP, hence it is called **oxidative phosphorylation.**

The process of photophosphorylation is of two types

1. Non-cyclic Photophosphorylation

It is a type of photophosphorylation in which both the photosystems (PS-I and PS-II) cooperate in light driven synthesis of ATP. During this cycle, the electron released from PS-II does not return back to it hence, it is known as non-cyclic photophosphorylation. Both NADPH and ATP are formed during this reaction These are used in light independent reaction and are called **reducing power.**

2. Cyclic Photophosphorylation

It is the type of photophosphorylation in which only PS-I is taking part and the electron released from the reaction centre P_{700} returns back to it after passing through a series of carrier, i.e. circulation takes within the photosystem and the phosphorylation occurs due to the cyclic flow of electrons.

Note

When non-cyclic form of photophosphorylation gets stopped under certain conditions, the cyclic photophosphorylation keeps operating and photosynthesis continues for some time.

The cyclic photophosphorylation takes place in the **stromal lamellae** of the chloroplast. This happens because the stromal lamellae does not possess enzyme NADP reductase (essential for reducing $NADP^+$ to NADPH) and PS-II.

Thus, the excited electrons in the cyclic photophosphorylation does not pass on to $NADP^+$ instead it gets cycled back to the PS-I complex.

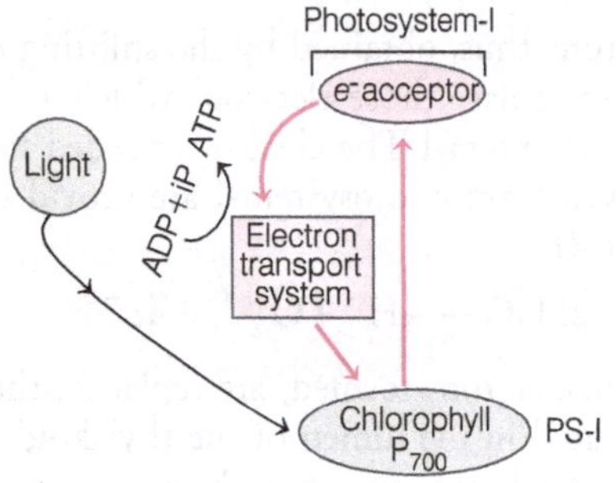

Fig. 14.8 Cyclic photophosphorylation

Hence, in the cyclic photophosphorylation only the synthesis of ATP takes place.

Chemiosmotic Hypothesis

This hypothesis was given by **Peter Mitchell** (1961) in order to explain the ATP synthesis in photosynthesis (also in respiration).

The synthesis of ATP is directly linked to the development of a proton gradient across the thylakoid membranes of a chloroplast. The main difference that lies between the photosynthesis and respiration is the location where the accumulation of protons takes place.

In chloroplast (photosynthesis), it occurs in thylakoid lumen, while in mitochondria (respiration), it occurs in intermembrane space.

The development of proton gradient results due to the reasons given below

(i) As the water molecule splits into the inner side of the membrane the protons or hydrogen ions that are produced by the water splitting get accumulated within the thylakoid lumen.

(ii) Transportation of protons takes place across the membrane when the electron moves through the photosystems.

The **primary acceptor** of electron is located towards the outer side of the membrane, which transfers electron to the proton (H^+) carrier and not to the electron carrier.

So, this molecule, while transporting an electron removes a proton from the stroma thus release of proton takes place into the inner side of thylakoid, i.e. on the lumen of the membrane.

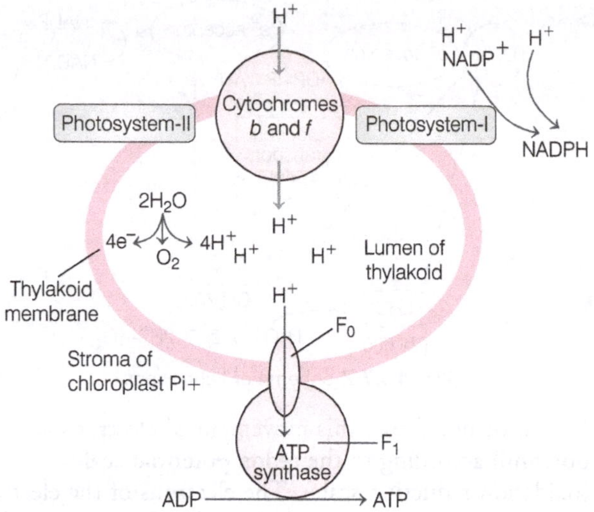

Fig. 14.9 ATP synthesis through chemiosmosis

(iii) The enzyme **NADP reductase** is present on the stromal side of the membrane. Thus, alongwith the electrons that come from the acceptor of electrons of PS-I, protons are also necessary to reduce $NADP^+$ to $NADPH + H^+$.

Hence, protons in the stroma within the chloroplasts decrease in number, while accumulation of protons takes place in the lumen. Due to which the proton gradient is created across thylakoid membrane, which lead to decrease in the pH at the side of the lumen.

The gradient is broken down due to the movement of protons across the membrane to the stroma through the transmembrane channel of the F_0 portion of the ATPase enzyme. Therefore, the proton gradient is important as it is the gradient whose breakdown leads to the release of energy (ATP).

ATPase Enzyme

The enzyme ATPase consists of the following two parts

(i) **F_0-Particle** This portion remains embedded in the membrane and forms a transmembrane channel, which carries out facilitated diffusion of protons (H^+) across the membrane.

(ii) **F_1-Particle** This portion protrudes towards the outer surface of the thylakoid membrane which faces the stroma. Conformational change occurs in F_1-particle of ATPase, which is caused due to the breakdown of the gradient.

This allows the enzyme ATP synthase to synthesise several molecules of ADP from ADP and inorganic phosphate.

Thus, the chemiosmosis, for its functioning, requires a membrane, a proton pump, a proton gradient and ATPase enzyme. The ATP thus, produced will be used simultaneously in the **biosynthetic reaction** (in stroma), responsible for the fixing of CO_2 and synthesis of sugar.

Dark Reaction (Biosynthetic Phase)

This phase does not require direct sunlight, but it depends on the products of the light reaction, i.e. ATP and NADPH beside CO_2 and water that drive the processes leading to the synthesis of food more accurately, the sugars (glucose is first product of photosynthesis).

As soon as the light becomes unavailable, the biosynthetic process continues for some time and then eventually stops and starts again if the light is made available.

Originally, this process is known as carbon-fixation or Photosynthetic Carbon Reduction (PCR) cycle.

These reactions are sensitive to temperature change, but are independent of light, hence called **dark reaction**. This takes place in the stroma of chloroplast.

Thus, assimilation of CO_2 during photosynthesis is of two main types

(i) **C_3 Pathway** This pathway is followed by the plants when first product of CO_2-fixation is a C_3 acid, i.e. PGA.

(ii) **C_4 Pathway** This pathway is followed or shown by the plants in which first product of CO_2-fixation is a C_4 acid, i.e. OAA.

Note

The O_2 produced in the light reaction of photosynthesis diffuses out of the chloroplast and is released in atmosphere.

Calvin Cycle (C_3 Pathway)

This is a cycle of biochemical pathway of reduction of CO_2 or photosynthetic carbon cycle which was discovered by **Calvin**.

The Calvin cycle runs in all **photosynthetic plants**, no matter they show C_3, C_4 or any other pathway. It occurs in stroma of the chloroplast.

Primary Acceptor of CO_2 in C_3 Pathway

After a long research and conducting many experiments it was concluded by the scientists that in C_3 pathway, the acceptor molecule is a 5-carbon ketose sugar, i.e. Ribulose 5-Bisphosphate (5 RuBP).

Calvin or C_3-cycle has many steps which are known as glycolytic reversal or formation of sugar and takes place between reduction and regeneration. There are three major steps which are as follows

1. Carboxylation

It is the most crucial step of the Calvin cycle. In this fixation of CO_2 molecule takes place in the form of carboxylation of RuBP(5C). This reaction is catalysed by the enzyme **RuBP carboxylase**. This finally leads to the formation of two molecules of 3 Phosphoglyceric Acid (3PGA). As the RuBP carboxylase enzyme also has an activity of oxygenation.

Thus, it is more commonly known as **RuBP carboxylase - oxygenase** or **RuBisCO**.

$$CO_2 + RuBP + H_2O \xrightarrow[Mg^{2+}]{RuBisCO} 2\ (3\text{-PGA})$$

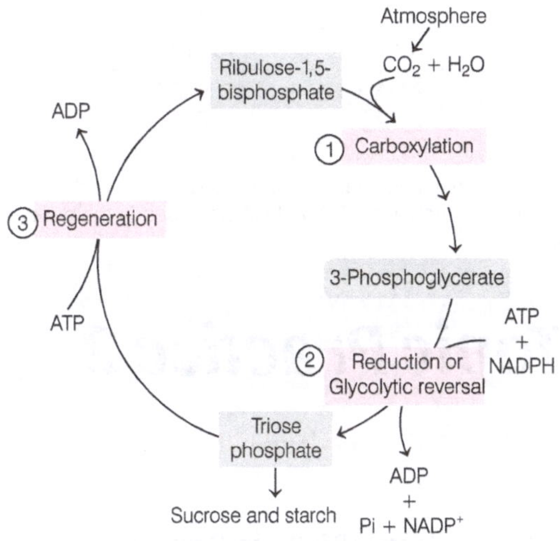

Fig. 14.10 Calvin cycle (C_3 pathway)

2. Reduction or Glycolytic Reversal

After the carboxylation reaction, reduction of PGA takes place through a series of reactions leading to the formation of glucose. In this step, the ATP (as energy source) and NADPH (hydrogen atom carrier) are utilised. It is to be noted that 2 molecules of ATP and 2 molecules of NADPH are utilised in this step for phosphorylation and for the reduction of CO_2, respectively.

Hence, the fixation of 6 molecules of CO_2 and 6 turns of the cycle are required in order to release one molecule of glucose from the pathway. Since, these reactions are opposite of glycolysis, they are known as **glycolytic reversal**.

3. Regeneration of RuBP

For the continuous and uninterrupted functioning of the Calvin cycle, there must be a regular supply of ATP, NADPH and also sufficient amount of RuBP is required. The regeneration of RuBP (CO_2 acceptor) is a complex process and involves many types of sugar starting from triose (3C) to heptose (7C).

The regeneration step requires one ATP molecule for phosphorylation. Hence, for every CO_2 molecule that enters the Calvin cycle, are required 3 molecules of ATP and 2 molecules of NADPH.

Thus, in order to produce one molecule of glucose through the Calvin pathway, 18 ATPs and 12 NADPHs are required. This can be easily understood by the following table given below

In	Out
6 CO_2	1 glucose
18 ATP	18 ADP
12 NADPH	12 NADP

Note

The cyclic phosphorylation takes place in order to meet the difference in the number of ATP and NADPH used in the dark reaction.

Topic Practice 2

Multiple Choice Questions

1 Mark

1. Photosystem-I (PS-I) and Photosystem-II (PS-II) are named
   (a) in the sequence they work in light reaction
   (b) according to their molecular weight
   (c) in sequence of their discovery
   (d) in the sequence of their constituents

Ans (c) The pigments are organised into two discrete photochemical Light Harvesting Complexe (LHC) within the Photosystem-I (PS-I) and Photosystem-II (PS-II). These are named in the sequence of their discovery and not in the sequence in which they function during the light reaction.

2. PS-I is located on the
   (a) non-appressed part of grana thylakoids
   (b) stroma thylakoids
   (c) appressed part of grana thylakoids
   (d) Both (a) and (b)

Ans (d) PS-I is present on both the non-appressed part of grana thylakoids as well as on stroma thylakoids.

3. Light Harvesting Complex (LHC) is
   (a) one molecule of chlorophyll-*a*
   (b) very few molecule of chlorophyll-*a*
   (c) hundreds of pigment molecules bound to proteins
   (d) chlorophyll-*a* + chlorophyll-*c* + protein + DNA

Ans (c) The light harvesting complex is made up of hundreds of pigment molecules bounded to proteins.

4. Emerson's enhancement effect and red drop have been instrumental in the discovery of
   (a) two photosystems operating simultaneously
   (b) photophosphorylation and cyclic electron transport
   (c) photophosphorylation
   (d) photophosphorylation and non-cyclic electron transport

Ans (a) Emerson performed photosynthetic experiment on *Chlorella*. He provided monochromatic light of more than 680 nm and observed decrease in rate of photosynthesis known as red drop.
Later, he provided synchronised light of 680 nm and 700 nm and observed increase in rate of photosynthesis, known as enhancement effect. This experiment led to discovery of two photosystems, i.e. PS-I and PS-II operating in photosynthesis.

5. pH of thylakoid lumen during photosynthesis is
   (a) basic
   (b) neutral
   (c) acidic
   (d) depends on H^+ concentration

Ans (c) During the photosynthesis within chloroplast protons in the stroma decrease in number, while in lumen there is accumulation of protons.
Thus, pH of thylakoid lumen during photosynthesis is acidic.

6. What is the advantage of light reactions producing ATP and $NADPH_2$ on stromal side of thylakoid membrane?
   (a) Calvin cycle consumes ATP and $NADPH_2$ from stroma
   (b) Light reaction occurs in stroma
   (c) Dark reaction occurring in grana need ATP + $NADPH_2$
   (d) CO_2 is produced in stroma

Ans (a) Energy formed on the stroma side of thylakoids membrane during light reaction, i.e. NADPH + H^+ and ATP, is used by the Calvin cycle or dark reaction and form the starch or carbohydrates.

7. **In terms of the spatial organisation of photosynthesis within the chloroplast, what is the advantage of light reactions producing ATP and $NADPH_2$ on the stromal side of the thylakoid membrane?**

(a) Water is more in thylakoid
(b) Light reaction occurs in stroma
(c) Dark reaction/Calvin cycle occurs in grana and needs ATP + $NADPH_2$
(d) The Calvin cycle, which consumes ATP and $NADPH_2$ occurs in stroma

Ans (d) Calvin cycle occurs in stroma that is why ATP and $NADPH_2$ are produced on stromal side of thylakoid membrane.

8. **Splitting of water is associated with**

NCERT Exemplar

(a) photosystem I
(b) lumen of thylakoid
(c) both photosystem I and II
(d) inner surface of thylakoid membrane

Ans (d) The thylakoid is a photosynthetic unit in the chloroplast. It is a membrane bound structure. The membrane has photosystems I and II embedded in it, in the form of chemicals and molecules. Splitting of water is associated with PS-II, which occurs in presence of Mn^{2+} and Cl^- ions on the inner surface of thylakoid membrane.

$$2H_2O \xrightarrow[Cl^-]{Mn^+} 4H^+ + O_2 + 4e^-$$

Photosystem I and II are associated with reactions.

9. **Why are dark reaction called so?**

(a) They occur in darkness
(b) They are not light dependent
(c) They are not directly light driven
(d) Both (a) and (b)

Ans (c) Dark reaction is not directly light driven, but are dependent on the products of light reaction.

10. **In dark reaction, regeneration of RuBP needs**

(a) 2 molecules of ATP (b) 1 molecule of ATP
(c) 3 molecules of ATP (d) 4 molecules of ATP

Ans (b) The Calvin cycle proceeds in three stages–RuBP is crucial if the cycle is to continue uninterrupted. The regeneration steps require one ATP for phosphorylation to form RuBP.

11. **Every CO_2 molecule entering the Calvin cycle needs**

(a) 2 molecules of NADPH and 3 molecules of ATP for its fixation
(b) 2 molecules of NADPH and 2 molecules of ATP for its fixation
(c) variable amount of ATP
(d) only NADPH

Ans (a) For every CO_2 molecule entering the Calvin cycle, 3 molecules of ATP and 2 molecules of NADPH are required.

The difference in the number of ATP and NADPH used in dark reaction is overcome by cyclic phosphorylation.

12. **In Calvin cycle, if one molecule of RuBP is carboxylated than how many PGA molecule will be formed?**

(a) 2 (b) 3
(c) 4 (d) 5

Ans (a) Carboxylation of one molecule of RuBP leads to the formation of 2 molecules of PGA.

$$RuBP + CO_2 \xrightarrow[\text{carboxylase}]{\text{RuBP}} \text{2-carboxyl 3-keto}$$
$$\text{1-5-bisphosphoribotol} + H_2O \longrightarrow 2PGA.$$

Very Short Answer Type Questions

1 Mark

13. **Which mechanism of photosynthesis is responsible for trapping of light energy, splitting of water, oxygen release and formation of ATP and NADPH?**

Ans Light reaction is responsible for all the above mentioned conditions.

14. **Mention any condition under which PS-I functions.**

Ans Conditions necessary under which PS-I functions are

(i) When the wavelength of light is higher than 680 nm.
(ii) When NADPH accumulates and CO_2-fixation is retarded.

15. **In which photosystem, you find O_2 evolving complex?**

Ans Oxygen evolving complex is observed associated with PS-II.

16. **Where do the electrons move from the electron acceptor of PS-II in the Z-scheme?**

Ans The electrons move to PS-I from the electron acceptor of the PS-II in the Z-scheme.

17. **Mention the possible location in the chloroplast, where cyclic flow of electrons (cyclic photophosphorylation) occurs.**

Ans Cyclic flow of electrons occur in the stromal lamellae of chloroplast.

18. **Indicate the source of electrons for non-cyclic photophosphorylation.**

Ans Photolysis of water molecule acts as a source of electrons for non-cyclic photophosphorylation.

19. Why is proton gradient important in photosynthesis?

Ans Proton gradient is important in photosynthesis as it makes energy available for ATP synthesis.

20. (i) NADP reductase enzyme is located on
(ii) Breakdown of proton gradient leads to release of **NCERT Exemplar**

Ans (i) Grana-lamellae. (ii) Energy in form of ATP.

21. Which products formed during the light reaction of photosynthesis are used to drive the dark reaction?

Ans ATP and NADPH formed during light reaction of photosynthesis are used in dark reaction for fixing CO_2 and to form glucose molecule.

22. How many molecules of carbon dioxide, ATP and NADPH are required to make one molecule of glucose?

Ans 6 molecules of carbon dioxide, 18 molecules of ATP, 12 molecules of NADPH are required to make 1 glucose molecule.

23. List the main steps of the Calvin cycle.

Ans The main steps of Calvin cycle are carboxylation, reduction and regeneration.

24. Give the name of the first stable intermediate compound formed after CO_2 absorption during C_3 pathway.

Ans The name of the first stable intermediate compound formed after CO_2 absorption during C_3 pathway is 3-Phosphoglyceric Acid (3PGA).

25. Which compound is meant for donating hydrogen to carbohydrate in Calvin cycle?

Ans NADPH is responsible for donating hydrogen to reduce CO_2 in Calvin cycle.

Short Answer Type I Questions

2 Marks

26. $2H_2O \longrightarrow 2H^+ + 4e^- + O_2\uparrow$

Based on the above equation, answer the following questions **NCERT Exemplar**

(i) Where does this reaction take place in plants?
(ii) What is the significance of this reaction?

Ans (i) The reaction takes place in lumen of the thylakoids.
(ii) O_2 is evolved during this reaction, moreover electrons are made available to PS-II continuously. (1+1)

27. Mention the four basic requirements for chemiosmosis to occur.

Ans Four basic requirements are as follows
(i) A unit membrane (ii) A proton pump
(iii) A proton gradient (iv) ATP synthase enzyme. (½ × 4)

28. Why is the lumen of thylakoids acidic while, the stroma is alkaline in nature?

Ans The acidic nature of lumen of thylakoids is due to the accumulation of protons by the photolysis of water. The same reaction does not occur in stroma, so it is basic in nature. (2)

29. ATPase enzyme consists of two parts. What are those parts? How are they arranged in the thylakoid membrane?
The conformational changes occur in which part of the enzyme? **NCERT Exemplar**

Ans ATPase enzyme consists of two parts, i.e. a stalk (F_0) and a headpiece (F_1). These two parts are located completely across the membrane of thylakoid membrane. The conformational changes occur in the headpiece (F_1) of this enzyme. (½ + 1 + ½)

30. $3\ CO_2 + 9\ ATP + 6\ NADPH + Water \rightarrow$ Glyceraldehyde 3–phosphate + 9ADP + 6 NADP + 6 Pi. Analyse the above reaction and answer the following questions.
(i) How many molecules of ATP and NADPH are required to fix one molecule of CO_2?
(ii) Where in the chloroplast does this process occur? **NCERT Exemplar**

Ans (i) 3 molecules of ATP and 2 molecules of NADPH are required of fix one molecule of CO_2.
(ii) The process occurs in the stroma of chloroplast. (1+1)

31. Expand RuBP and also mention the role of RuBP in photosynthesis.

Ans RuBP is known as Ribulose 1, 5-bisphosphate. It is the primary acceptor of carbon dioxide in Calvin cycle of C_3-plants. It forms the first stable compound of photosynthesis known as PGA. (1+1)

32. Dark reactions are dependent on light yet are called dark reactions. Justify.

Ans Dark reactions are dependent on the products of light reaction that are ATP and NADPH to carryout reduction of CO_2 to form glucose. This does not need light, so they are called dark reactions. (2)

33. Do reactions of photosynthesis called, as 'Dark Reaction' need light? Why?

Ans Dark reactions are actually light independent reactions. CO_2 is reduced through various biochemical reactions to produce $C_6H_{12}O_6$ (glucose) which does not need light. But they depend on the products formed during light reactions, i.e. $NADPH_2$ and ATP. (2)

Short Answer Type II Questions

(3 Marks)

34. Examine the figure

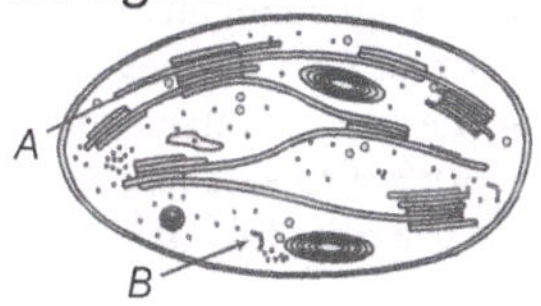

(i) This structure is present in animal cell or plant cell?

(ii) Can these be passed on to the progeny? How?

(iii) Name the metabolic processes taking place in the places marked (*A*) and (*B*).

NCERT Exemplar

Ans (i) Plant cell.

(ii) Yes, these can be passed on to the progeny through female gametes.

(iii) In part (*A*) photophosphorylation and in part (*B*) Calvin cycle. (1×3)

35. Name the end products of light reaction of photosynthesis. Mention the fate of each of them.

Ans ATP, NADPH and oxygen are the products of light reaction. ATP and NADPH are used in the reduction step of biosynthetic phase of photosynthesis. Oxygen is liberated into the atmosphere. (3)

36. What are the important events and end products of the light reaction? NCERT Exemplar

Ans The important events of light reactions are

(i) Excitation of chlorophyll molecule to emit a pair of electrons and use of their energy in the formation of ATP from ADP + Pi. This process is called photophosphorylation.

(ii) Splitting of water molecule

(a) $2H_2O \longrightarrow 4H^+ + 4e^- + O_2 \uparrow$

(b) $NADP + 2H^+ \longrightarrow NADPH_2$

End products of light reaction are NADPH and ATP. Reducing power is produced in the light reaction, i.e. ATP and $NADPH_2$ molecules which are used up in dark reaction. O_2 is evolved as a byproduct by the splitting of water. (3)

37. Cyclic photophosphorylation results in the production of ATPs and not NADPH. Give reasons.

Ans Cyclic phosphorylation occurs when only 700 nm light is available and PS-I is functional. It occurs in the stroma lamellae where enzyme NADP reductase is absent and PS-II is also absent. Hence, electrons are passed on back to PS-I and not to $NADP^+$. So, the cyclic flow results in the formation of ATP, but not NADPH. (3)

38. Explain how during light reaction of photosynthesis, ATP synthesis as a chemiosmotic phenomenon takes place?

NCERT Exemplar

Ans Chemiosmosis requires a membrane, a proton pump, a proton gradient and ATP synthase enzyme. Energy is used to pump protons across a membrane, to create a gradient or a high concentration of protons within the thylakoid lumen. ATP synthase enzyme catalyses the formation of ATP, along with the NADPH produced by the movement of electrons. The energy carried by ATP molecules will be used immediately in the biosynthetic reaction taking place in the stroma for fixing CO_2 and synthesis of sugars. (3)

39. Where is NADP reductase enzyme located in the chloroplasts? What is the role of this enzyme in proton gradient development?

NCERT Exemplar

Ans NADP reductase enzyme is located on the outer/stroma side of the thylakoid membrane. Along with the electrons from the primary acceptor of PS-I, it uses the protons of stroma for the reduction of $NADP^+$ to NADPH, this removal of protons from the stroma causes a proton gradient between the lumen of thylakoids and the stroma. (3)

40. The diagram given below shows stages in the light-independent reactions of photosynthesis. Answer the following

(i) At which stage NADPH is oxidised?

(ii) What are *A*, *B* and *C* ?

(iii) At what stages ATP is converted into ADP?

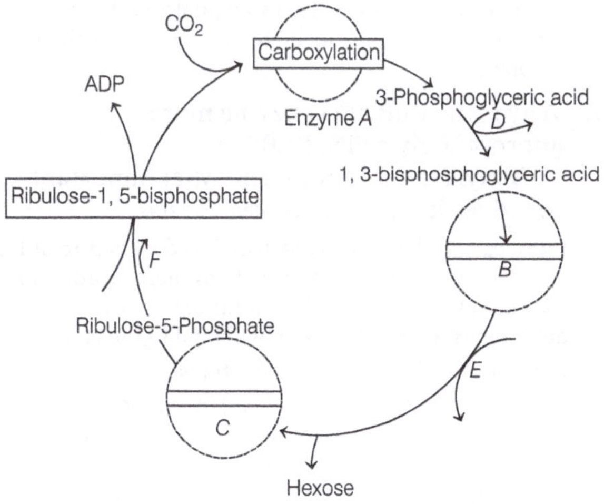

Ans (i) NADPH is oxidised at stage *E*.

(ii) *A*—RuBP Carboxylase Oxygenase (RuBisCO), *B*—Reduction, *C*—Regeneration

(iii) ATP is converted to ADP at stages *D* and *F*. (1×3)

41. Find out how Melvin Calvin worked out the complete biosynthetic pathway for synthesis of sugar.

Ans Melvin Calvin used *Chlorella* as an experimental material and discovered the first stable compound of photosynthesis, i.e. 3 phosphoglyceric acid, so as to trace the path of carbon by using a radioactive isotope of carbon (C^{14}) and autoradiography technique.

He then, compared the radioactive compounds on the chromatogram as a result of which he found and concluded that the PGA (Phosphoglyceric Acid), as the first stable product of photosynthesis and gradually the other sugars including hexoses, tetroses and pentoses etc. Thus, he derived the pathway of CO_2-fixation from these radioactive products (sugars) formed. (3)

42. Even though a very few cells in a C_4-plant carry out the biosynthetic Calvin pathway, yet they are highly productive. Can you discuss why? **NCERT**

Ans C_4-plants chemically fix carbon dioxide in the cells of the mesophyll by adding it to the Phosphoenol Pyruvate (PEP), This reaction is catalysed by an enzyme called PEP carboxylase. It creates the 4 carbon organic acid, oxaloacetic acid.

Oxaloacetic acid synthesised by this process is then translocated to specialised bundle sheath cells where the enzyme, RuBisCO and other Calvin cycle enzymes are located and where CO_2 released by decarboxylation of the 4 carbon acids is then fixed by RuBisCO enzyme to form 3-phosphoglyceric acid (3C).

The physical separation of RuBisCO from the oxygen driven light reactions inhibits photorespiration and increases CO_2-fixation. This way photosynthetic capacity of the C_4-plants increases many folds than C_3-plants. (3)

43. Why is the RuBisCO enzyme more appropriately called RuBP carboxylase-oxygenase and what important role does it play in photosynthesis?

Ans RuBP carboxylase and oxygenase has dual nature. It has affinity for both CO_2 and O_2 but has more affinity for CO_2 than O_2. Thus, the concentrations of two determines which of the two will bind to the enzyme.

Consider the following two situations

(i) In a normal condition when CO_2 and O_2 concentrations are normal, it acts as carboxylase and fix CO_2 by combining with ribulose bisphosphate and C_3-cycle operates normally, producing glucose molecule as first product of photosynthesis.

(ii) If O_2 concentration goes up and CO_2 goes down, it starts acting as an oxygenase enzyme and C_2-cycle (photorespiration) starts where RuBP binds with O_2 to from phosphoglycolate.

(iii) C_4-plants have mechanisms to increase the concentration of CO_2 at enzyme site, and increasing the intracellular concentration of CO_2. Thus, here RuBisCO acts as carboxylase, minimising the affect of oxygenase. (3)

Long Answer Type Questions

5 Marks

44. The entire process of photosynthesis consists of a number of reactions. Name the part of the cell where following reactions take place. **NCERT Exemplar**

(i) Synthesis of ATP and NADPH ....
(ii) Photolysis of water ....
(iii) Fixation of CO_2 ....
(iv) Synthesis of sugar molecule ....
(v) Synthesis of starch ....

Ans (i) Synthesis of ATP and NADPH in thylakoids.

(ii) Photolysis of water occurs in inner side of thylakoid membrane in PS-II (680 nm).

(iii) Fixation of CO_2 occurs in stroma of chloroplast.

(iv) Synthesis of sugar molecule occurs in chloroplast.

(v) Synthesis of starch occurs in cytoplasm. (1×5)

45. In the diagram shown below label *A*, *B* and *C*. What type of phosphorylation is possible in this? **NCERT Exemplar**

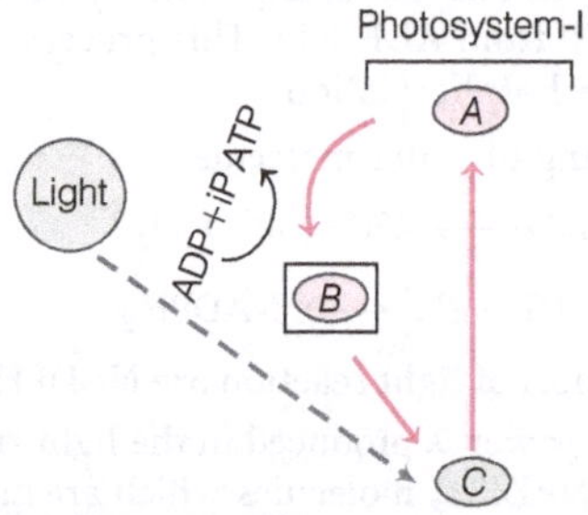

Ans The diagram is showing cyclic photophosphorylation. Here, *A* is electron acceptor, *B* is electron transport system and *C* is Photosystem-I (PS_{700}). In cyclic photophosphorylation, only PS-I is functional.

The electron is circulated within the photosystem and the phosphorylation occurs due to the cyclic flow of electrons. (3+2)

46. Give comparison between the cyclic and non-cyclic photophosphorylation **NCERT**

Ans Comparison between cyclic and non-cyclic photophosphorylation are

Cyclic Photophosphorylation	Non-cyclic Photophosphorylation
It occurs in photosystem-I in stromal or intergranal lamellae.	It is carried out by both PS-I and PS-II in the granal thylakoids.
It is not connected to photolysis of water, so no oxygen is evolved.	It is connected with photolysis of water, so oxygen is evolved in it.
It is activated by light of 700 nm wavelength.	It occurs in 680 nm as well as 700 nm wavelength.
It generates ATP only, there is no formation of $NADPH_2$.	It produces both ATP as well as $NADPH_2$.
Chlorophyll does not receive any electron from donor.	The source of electrons is photolysis of water.
The system does not take part in photosynthesis except in bacteria.	This system is connected with CO_2-fixation and is dominant in green plants.

(5)

47. Why is RuBisCO enzyme the most abundant enzyme in the world? **NCERT Exemplar**

Ans The enzyme Ribulose-1, 5-bisphosphate carboxylase/ oxygenase, most commonly known by the shorter name RuBisCO is used in the Calvin cycle of photosynthesis to catalyse the first major step of carbon-fixation.

RuBisCO is thought to be the most abundant protein in the world since it is present in every plant that performs photosynthesis.

It makes about 20-25% of the soluble protein in the leaves and is made on the earth at the rate of about 1000 kg/s. It is estimated that every person on earth is supported by about 44 kg of RuBisCO. (5)

48. Six turns of Calvin cycle are required to generate one mole of glucose. Explain. **NCERT Exemplar**

Ans Calvin cycle is a series of reactions that leads to the formation of glucose. The steps involve utilisation of 2 molecules of ATP for phosphorylation and 2 of NADPH for reduction per CO_2molecule fixed.

The fixation of six molecules of CO_2 and six turns of the cycle are required for the synthesis of one molecule of glucose through these reactions.

Hence, for every CO_2 molecule entering the Calvin cycle, 3 molecules of ATP and 2 of NADPH are required. It is probably to meet this difference in number of ATP and NADPH used in the dark reaction that the cyclic phosphorylation takes place. To make one molecule of glucose six turns of the cycle are required. (5)

TOPIC 03 Photorespiration and Factors Affecting Photosynthesis

C_4 Pathway

It was worked out by two Australian scientists Hatch and Slack (1966). Thus, this is also known as **Hatch** and **Slack pathway.** C_4-plants are special as they have a special type of leaf anatomy that can tolerate high temperatures and show a response to high light intensities. Inspite of having Oxaloacetic Acid (OAA) as their first CO_2-fixation product, they use C_3 pathway or the Calvin cycle as the main photosynthetic pathway. This cycle occurs mostly in monocots as maize, sugarcane and *Cyperus*, etc.

Only angiospermic (no gymnosperm, bryophytes and pteridophytes, etc.) plants show this process to fix CO_2.

The main aim of C_4-cycle is to fix very dilute solution of CO_2 (0.03% or 300 ppm) to concentrated CO_2 solution in bundle sheath cells and to produce Oxaloacetic Acid (OAA).

Kranz Anatomy

According to the structural leaf anatomy of C_3 and C_4- plants, the leaves of C_3-plants show only one type of cells called **mesophyll cells,** which contain only mesophyll chloroplast, while leaves of C_4-plants show two types of cells, i.e. outer mesophyll cells and inner spongy (which are large) cells around the vascular bundles called **bundle sheath cells** arranged in a circular manner. It refers to the presence of two types of the chloroplast in the leaves.

The mesophyll cells contain well-developed granal chloroplast. They actively participate in light reaction. These produce ATP and $NADPH_2$.

The rudimentary chloroplasts are present in the cells of bundle sheath. They are agranal. The bundle sheath cells are mainly meant to carry out C_3-cycle.

This does not require well-developed chloroplast, so they are rudimentary lamellar type.

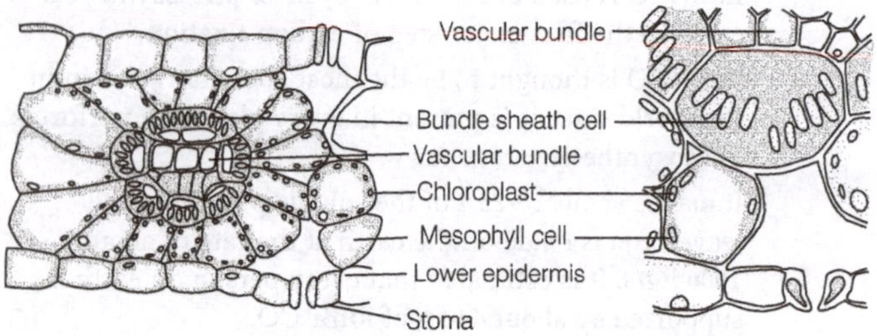

Fig. 14.11 TS of maize leaf showing Kranz anatomy

The bundle sheath cells tend to form several layers around the **vascular bundles.**

They possess several special features such as

- Have large number of chloroplast.
- Thick walls which are impervious to gaseous exchange.
- There are no intercellular spaces.

Mechanism of Hatch and Slack Pathway

The Hatch and Slack pathway is also a cyclic process, which occurs in the following steps

Step I In C_4-plants, the initial fixation of CO_2 occurs in mesophyll cells. The primary acceptor of CO_2 is **Phosphoenol Pyruvate** (PEP).

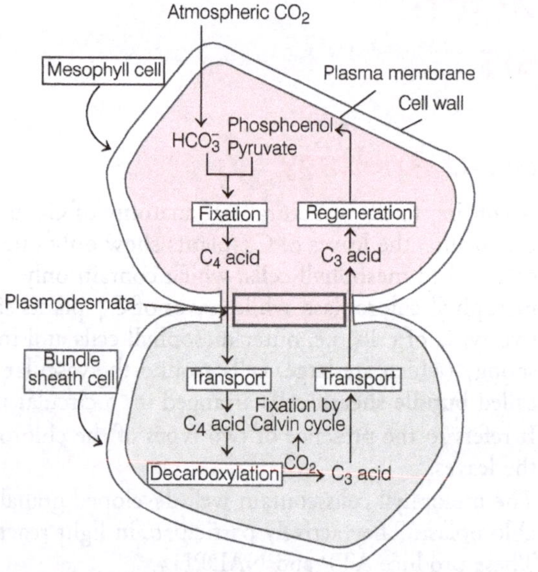

Fig. 14.12 Diagrammatic representation of Hatch and Slack pathway

Step II It combines with CO_2 in the presence of an enzyme **phosphoenol pyruvate carboxylase** or **PEP carboxylase** (PEPcase) to form the first stable (or a 4 carbon organic acid) product of C_4 pathway, i.e. the Oxaloacetic Acid (OAA).

Step III The compound (OAA) is transported to the bundle sheath cells where it is broken down, releasing CO_2 and a 3-carbon molecule.

Step IV The 3-carbon compound is again transported back to the mesophyll cells where regeneration of PEP takes place, thus, completing the cycle.

The CO_2 thus, released in the bundle sheath cells enters the C_3 or the Calvin cycle (common pathway to all plants).

Differences between C_3 and C_4 Pathway

C_3 Pathway	C_4 Pathway
The primary acceptor of CO_2 is RuBP, a 5 carbon compound.	The primary acceptor of CO_2 is PEP, a 3 carbon compound.
It operats under low concentration of CO_2 in mesophyll cells.	It can operate under very low CO_2 concentration in mesophyll cells.
CO_2 once fixed is not released back.	CO_2 once fixed is released back in bundle sheath cells.
Fixation of one molecule of CO_2 needs 3 ATP and 2 $NADPH_2$ molecules. It requires 18 ATP for the synthesis of one molecule of glucose.	C_4 pathway requires 30 ATP for the synthesis of one molecule of glucose.
C_3-cycle operates in all categories of plants.	It operates in only C_4-plants.

CAM (Crassulacean Acid Metabolism)

This pathway is mostly present in succulent xerophytes such as plants of family–Crassulaceae, Euphorbiaceae, Cactaceae, etc. The stomata in these plants remain closed during the day and open during the night for gaseous exchange. In this way, CO_2 is fixed during night and sugars are formed during day.

This is a desert adaptation that helps to check transpiration. This pathway is similar to C_4-pathway. However, there is no separation of initial PEP carboxylase fixation and final RuBisCO fixation of CO_2. These two steps occur in the same cell, but at different times.

Photorespiration

The process of photorespiration generally occurs in temperate plants such as beet, bean, cotton, rice, wheat, barley, etc., while the tropical grasses such as maize, sugarcane, *Sorghum,* etc. lack this process.

Photorespiration occurs when the CO_2 level inside a leaf becomes very low (~ 50 ppm). It is a light dependent cyclic process of oxygenation of RuBP and release of carbon dioxide by the photosynthetic organs of a plant. The site of photorespiration is chloroplast. Mitochondria and peroxisome are also required for completing the process. RuBP carboxylase, oxygenase is the main enzyme of dark reaction. It also catalyses another reactions that interferes with the functioning of Calvin cycle. It has active site for both, i.e. CO_2 and O_2.

The relative concentration of CO_2 and O_2 determines which of the two will bind to the enzyme.

Under the conditions, when O_2Concentration is more in atmosphere than CO_2, then in C_3-plants, RuBisCO acts as oxygenase enzyme and CO_2-fixation does not lead to PGA formation. Instead phosphoglycerate and phosphoglycolate are formed and photorespiration occurs.

Thus, the photorespiratory pathway is called a **wasteful process** due to two reasons

(i) There is no synthesis of sugar and ATP or NADPH.

(ii) The CO_2 is released with the utilisation of ATP.

On the other side, the process of photorespiration does not take place in C_4-plants, because through a certain mechanism the CO_2 concentration increases at the enzyme site.

This happens when the C_4acid, i.e. OAA from the mesophyll cells tends to be broken down in the bundle sheath cells releasing CO_2 thereby, increasing the intracellular concentration of CO_2. Hence, the RuBP Carboxylase enzyme (RuBisCO) functions more as carboxylase and minimising the role of oxygenase. As C_4-plants lack the process of photorespiration the productivity and yield in these plants are better than those in C_3-plants.

Differences between C_3 and C_4-Plants

Characteristics	C_3-Plants	C_4-Plants
Cell type in which the Calvin cycle takes place	Mesophyll	Bundle sheath
Cell type in which initial carboxylation takes place	Mesophyll	Mesophyll
How many types of cells does the leaf have that fix CO_2	1; mesophyll	2; mesophyll and bundle sheath
Number of carbon in primary CO_2 acceptor	5	3
Primary CO_2-fixation product	3 Phosphoglyceric Acid (PGA)	Oxaloacetic Acid (OAA)
Number of carbon in primary CO_2-fixation product	3	4
Presence of RuBisCO	Yes	Yes
Presence of PEP case	No	Yes
Cells having RuBisCO	Mesophyll	Bundle sheath
CO_2-fixation rate under high light conditions	No	Yes
Presence of photorespiration at low light intensities	No	No
Presence of photorespiration at high light intensities	Yes	No
Presence of photorespiration at low CO_2 concentration	Yes	No
Presence of photorespiration at high CO_2 concentration	No	No
Optimum temperature	20-25° C	30-40 ° C
Geographical location of plants	Present everywhere	In tropical climate
Examples	Mango and guava	Maize and sugarcane

Factors Affecting Photosynthesis

The rate of photosynthesis is essential in determining the plants yield including the crop plants. It is generally influenced by the number of factors including both external, i.e. environmental and internal (plant) factors. These are as follows

1. Internal Factors

The internal or plant factors greatly depend on the **genetic predisposition** and basically on the growth of the plant.

These include the number, size, age and orientation of leaves. These also include chlorophyll content, internal concentration of CO_2,

(i) **Chlorophyll content of leaves** The chlorophyll only acts as a biocatalyst. Hence, a small quantity of chlorophyll is enough to carry out photosynthesis.

(ii) **Accumulation of byproducts** The final product in the photosynthetic reaction is sugar. Accumulation of sugars in the cells slows down the process of photosynthesis.

(iii) **Internal structure of leaf** The thickness of the cuticle and epidermis of the leaf, the size and distribution of intercellular spaces and the stomata also affect the rate of photosynthesis.

2. External Factors

These factors generally include an environmental factor like availability of sunlight, temperature, concentration of CO_2 and water.

Factors available at sub-optimal levels help in determining the rate of photosynthesis at any point.

> **Concept of Limiting Factors**
>
> For a study of the above factors, it is essential to have knowledge of Blackman's law of limiting factors. Before 1905, early scientists attempted to determine the effect of individual factors on the photosynthetic rate in terms of minimum, optimum and maximum values which are known as **cardinal points**. The simultaneous effects of other factors, also has an importance in determining the rate of photosynthesis.

Blackman criticised the above said concept and stated law of limiting factors that, when a process is controlled by more than one factor then the rate of the process is limited by the factor, which is nearest to its **minimal value** (is limited by the pace of the slowest factor), i.e. it is the factor which will affect the rate if its quantity will be changed. For example, despite the presence of a green leaf and optimal light and CO_2 conditions, the plant may not photosynthesise till the moment the temperature is very low. But if the optimal temperature is provided again to this it will surely start photosynthesising.

Some of the factors that affect the photosynthetic rate are discussed ahead in detail.

i. Light

The light provides the energy for photosynthesis. Thus, it is one of the major factors, which affects the rate of photosynthesis. Three characteristics of light, i.e. the intensity, quality and duration generally influences the rate. So, discussing the light as a factor that affects photosynthesis, two conditions are observed.

(a) At **low light intensities**, the linear relationship between incident light and rate of CO_2-fixation occurs.

(b) While at **higher intensity of light**, the rate fails to show further increase as the other factors become limiting (saturation point).

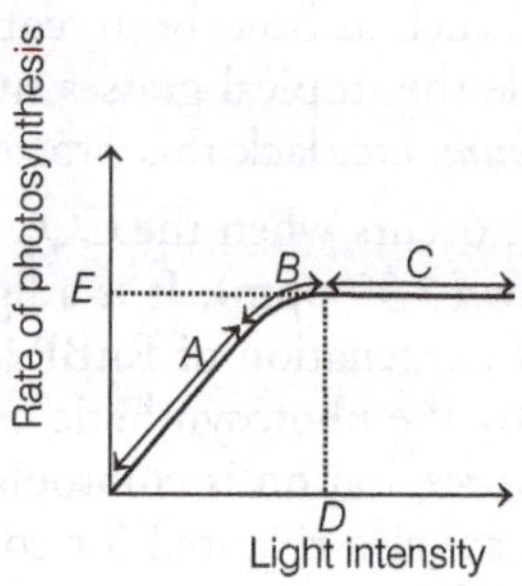

Fig. 14.13 Graph of light intensity on the rate of photosynthesis

At 10% of full sunlight, the saturation of light occurs. Thus, excepting the shade and the dense forests, the light is a limiting factor in a very rare conditions in nature. If an increase of light beyond a certain limit or point occurs it causes the breakdown of chlorophyll and decrease in the rate of photosynthesis.

Note

If low light conditions are prevailing, both C_3 and C_4-plants fail to respond to high CO_2 conditions, while at high light intensities both show increase in the photosynthetic rates but upto a certain limit.

ii. Carbon Dioxide Concentration

In C_4-plants also, the photosynthesis increases as the CO_2 concentration increases, but at much lower concentration of CO_2, these plants tend to attain saturation (around 360 μL^{-1}) while, the C_3-plant becomes saturated at much higher CO_2 level (around 450 μL^{-1}). Thus, it concludes that the current availability of CO_2 levels is a limiting factor to the C_3-plants.

It has been demonstrated by the scientists itself that the C_3-plants can grow much faster and lead to higher productivity due to the higher rate of photosynthesis.

Thus, in order to obtain higher yield some greenhouse crops like tomatoes, bell pepper, etc., are allowed to grow in atmosphere enriched with carbon dioxide.

iii. Temperature

Enzyme controlled dark reactions are affected by change in temperature. Photosynthesis occurs in a very wide range of temperature. The C_4-plants respond to a higher temperature showing higher rate of photosynthesis. On the other hand, the C_3-plants have much lower optimum temperature range.

When temperature is increased from minimum to optimum, the rate of photosynthesis doubles for every 10°C rise in the temperature. But when the temperature reaches above optimum range the rate of photosynthesis shows initial increase for a very short duration of time which later gets declined.

Different plants have different optimum temperature range for photosynthesis. It depends on their habitat. The tropical plants have higher temperature range for photosynthesis than the temperate plants.

iv. Water

The effect of water as a factor is more on the plant as a whole rather than directly on photosynthesis. In water stress conditions, the **stomata** become closed which reduces the availability of CO_2 to plants, thereby causing reduction in the rate of photosynthesis.

Besides this the decrease in water availability causes leaves to **wilt** thus, reducing the surface area of the leaves and ultimately reducing their **metabolic activity**.

Topic Practice 3

Multiple Choice Questions

1 Mark

1. PEP is primary CO_2 accepter in **NCERT Exemplar**
   (a) C_4 plants
   (b) C_3 plants
   (c) C_2 plants
   (d) Both (a) and (b) plants

Ans (a) C_4 plants have evolved PEP as primary acceptor of CO_2 to avoid the sensitivity of RuBP carboxylase-oxygenase to high concentration of oxygen, so that they can avoid photorespiratory loss of CO_2 occurring in them.

Other options (b), (c) and (d) are incorrect. PEP in not primary acceptor in them.

2. When CO_2 is added to PEP, the first stable product synthesised is **NCERT Exemplar**
   (a) pyruvate
   (b) glyceraldehyde-3-phosphate
   (c) phosphoglycerate
   (d) oxaloacetate

Ans (d) **Oxaloacetate** is a four carbon compound formed in C_4 cycle and is a first stable product, that is why such plants are called C_4 plants.

Rest of the options are incorrect as because

(a) Pyruvate is formed in glycolysis.

(b) Glyceraldehyde-3-phosphate is also an intermediate compound of glycolysis.

(c) Phosphoglycerate is also an intermediate compound of glycolysis.

3. Which of the following statements is false in case of (C_4-plant)?
   (a) CO_2 acceptor is RuBisCO in mesophyll cell
   (b) Carboxylation occurs in mesophyll cells
   (c) Leaves have two cell types
   (d) Mesophyll cells lack RuBisCO

Ans (a) C_4-plants have Kranz anatomy, which includes bundle sheath cells and mesophyll cells. In case of C_4- plants, the primary CO_2 acceptor is a 3 carbon molecule, i.e. phosphoenol pyruvate and is present in the mesophyll cells.

4. Find out the reason that creates an important difference between C_3 and C_4-plants.
   (a) Photorespiration (b) Calvin cycle
   (c) Glycolysis (d) Pressure of cuticle

Ans (a) In C_3-plants, photorespiration takes place, but this pathway is absent in C_4-plants.

5. In C_3-plant, when O_2 concentration is more, the O_2 binds to RuBisCO and RuBP gets changed to
   (a) 2 molecules of PGA
   (b) 2 molecules of phosphoglycerate
   (c) 2 molecules of phosphoglycolate
   (d) one molecule each of phosphoglycerate and phosphoglycolate

Ans (d) The site for photorespiration is chloroplast. RuBP carboxylase functions as oxygenase and instead of fixing carbon dioxide, it converts ribulose-1, 5-bisphosphate (RuBP) to phosphoglycerate and phosphoglycolate.

$$\text{RuBP} + O_2 \xrightarrow[\text{Oxygenase}]{\text{RuBP}} \text{PGA} + \text{Phosphoglycolate}$$

6. C_4-plant minimises the photorespiration because C_4-plants
   (a) use PEPcase to initiate CO_2-fixation
   (b) do not carry out the Calvin cycle in low CO_2 level
   (c) exclude Calvin cycle
   (d) show photorespiration

Ans (a) C_4-plants have very little photorespiration because its initial carbon fixation is done by PEP carboxylase not by RuBisCO.

7. Peroxisomes in photorespiration
   (a) help in the oxidation of glycolate
   (b) help in the oxygenation of vacuole
   (c) help in the synthesis of PGA
   (d) help in the reduction of glyoxylate

Ans (a) Glycolate is formed in chloroplast, which usually passes in the peroxisomes, where it is oxidised to glyoxylate. Glyoxylate is aminated and gives rise to amino acid glycine, which enters into the mitochondria.

8. Plant factors affecting photosynthesis include
(a) number, age, size and orientation of leaves, mesophyll cells and chloroplast, internal CO_2 concentration, the amount of chlorophyll
(b) nature of leaves, size of mesophyll cell and light
(c) mesophyll cells distribution and temperature
(d) quantity of chlorophyll, size of leaves and CO_2

Ans (a) The plant factors involve the number, size, age and orientation of leaves, mesophyll cells and chloroplast, internal CO_2 concentration and amount of chlorophyll.

9. If a chemical process is affected by more than one factor then its rate will be determined by
(a) two closely related factors
(b) only one factor, which is close to its minimal value
(c) only one factor, which is close to its maximum value
(d) only one factor, which is close to its appropriate value

Ans (b) Only one factor, which is close to the minimal value.

10. Light compensation point is the point where
(a) gaseous exchange occurs in photosynthesis
(b) gaseous exchange do not occur in photosynthesis
(c) gaseous exchange reduces in photosynthesis
(d) light intensity become appropriate for photosynthesis

Ans (b) There is a point in the light intensity, where there is no gaseous exchange in photosynthesis. It is called light compensation point.

11. Light is rarely a limiting factor in nature expect in
(a) maize
(b) sugarcane
(c) *Sorghum*
(d) plants in shade or in dense forests

Ans (d) Except for plants in shade or in dense forest, light is rarely a limiting factor in nature.

12. The optimum temperature for photosynthesis of different plants depends on
(a) CO_2 concentration (b) habitat
(c) light intensity (d) water

Ans (b) The temperature optimum for photosynthesis of different plants also depends on the habitat.

13. Which of the following would not be a limiting factor in photosynthesis?
(a) CO_2 (b) Oxygen
(c) Light (d) Chlorophyll

Ans (d) Chlorophyll would not act as a limiting factor in photosynthesis, e.g. sunloving plants contain less chlorophyll as compared to shadeloving plants, but the rate of photosynthesis in bright light is much higher in sunloving plants than is shadeloving plants.

Very Short Answer Type Questions

1 Mark

14. Why photosynthesis is an oxidation reduction process?

Ans Photosynthesis is an oxidation reduction process because water is oxidised to release oxygen and carbon is reduced to produce carbohydrate (glucose).

15. The enzyme, which is not found in C_3-plants.

Ans PEP carboxylase enzyme is not found in C_3-plants.

16. A type of anatomy of leaves possessed by C_4-plants is different from those of C_3-plants. Explain.

Ans C_4-plants possess a special anatomy of leaves called Kranz anatomy, which means the presence of two types of chloroplasts, agranal in bundle sheath cells and granal in mesophyll cells.

17. Succulents are known to keep their stomata closed during the day to check rate of transpiration. How do they meet their photosynthetic CO_2 requirements?
NCERT Exemplar

Ans Succulents (water storing) plants such as cacti, fix CO_2 into organic compound (malic acid) using PEP carboxylase at night, when the stomata are open.

18. Why photorespiration is called as C_2-cycle?

Ans Photorespiration is also called as C_2-cycle because of the formation 2-carbon intermediate compound named glycolic acid.

19. What would happen to the rate of photosynthesis in C_3-plants if CO_2 concentration level almost doubles from its present level in the atmosphere?

Ans If the CO_2 concentration in C_3-plants almost get doubles from its present level in the atmosphere, plants will grow much faster and lead to the higher productivity due to higher rate of photosynthesis.

Short Answer Type I Questions

2 Marks

20. What is the basis for designating C_3 and C_4 pathways of photosynthesis? **NCERT Exemplar**

Ans C_3 pathway or Calvin cycle represents phase-II, i.e. dark reaction of photosynthesis. In Calvin cycle, a 5C pentose sugar, Ribulose Bisphosphate (RuBP) acts as first acceptor of CO_2 whereas, the C_4 pathway is also called Hatch-Slack pathway in which, the first CO_2 acceptor is 3C Phosphoenol Pyruvate (PEP). (2)

21. By looking at a plant externally, can you tell whether it is C_3 or C_4? Why and how?

Ans The plants which are adapted to dry tropical regions have the C_4 pathway. However, the C_4-plants do not show any characteristic in external morphology. Therefore, it is difficult to say whether a plant is C_3 or C_4 by looking it only externally. (2)

22. A cyclic process is occurring in C_3-plants, which is light-dependent and needs CO_2. This process does not produce, but consumes energy.

(i) Can you name the given process?

(ii) Is it essential for survival? **NCERT Exemplar**

Ans (i) Photorespiration.

(ii) Yes, because by consuming oxygen at higher temperature, it protects the chlorophyll from photo-oxidation. (1+1)

23. Why does the rate of photosynthesis decrease at higher temperatures?

Ans Photosynthesis is an enzyme specific process. All enzymes act at an optimum temperature (i.e. 25-35°C). As temperature increases, enzyme get denatured, thus leading to fall in the rate of photosynthesis. (2)

24. How does water stress affect/decrease the rate of photosynthesis?

Ans Water stress causes closure of stomata and decreases the availability of CO_2 for photosynthesis. Water stress also causes wilting of leaves, thus reducing the surface area of leaves for metabolic functions. (2)

Short Answer Type II Questions

3 Marks

25. Name the two important enzymes of C_3 and C_4 pathways, respectively. What important role do they play in fixing CO_2? **NCERT Exemplar**

Ans The important enzymes of C_3-cycle is RuBisCO and that of C_4 pathway is PEP carboxylase. They help in the fixation of CO_2.

In C_3-cycle the CO_2 acceptor is Ribulose-1, 5 Biphosphate (RuBP) and the first stable product is Phosphoglyceric Acid (PGA). In C_4-cycle, the CO_2 acceptor is PEP carboxylase and the first stable product is Oxaloacetic Acid (OAA). (3)

26. Give comparison between the C_3 leaf anatomy and C_4 leaf anatomy.

Ans Comparison between C_3 and C_4-leaf anatomy

C_3 Leaf Anatomy	C_4 Leaf Anatomy
Only one type of chloroplast is present.	Kranz anatomy, each cell with its own type of chloroplast is present.
Less efficient in photosynthesis than C_4 leaves.	More efficent in photosynthesis than C_3 leaves.
Only mesophyll cells carryout photosynthesis.	Both mesophyll cells and bundle sheath cells carryout photosynthesis.

(3)

27. In what kind of plants do you come across Kranz anatomy? To which conditions are those plants better adapted? How are these plants better adapted than the plants, which lack this anatomy? **NCERT Exemplar**

Ans C_4-plants are better adapted to dry tropical regions. They have the following features (1)

(i) Can tolerate high temperatures.

(ii) Can perform photosynthesis in high light intensities.

(iii) Have overcome the problem of photorespiration and have greater productivity of biomass. (2)

28. Fill in the blanks at *A*, *B*, *C*, *D*, *E* and *F* and complete the C_4 pathway/Hatch-Slack pathway.

Atmospheric CO_2 enters (*A*)

↓

CO_2 is accepted by (*B*) and forms four carbon acid compound (*C*)

↓

C_4 acid enters into (*D*) and splits into CO_2 and (*E*)

↓

CO_2 enters Calvin cycle and 3C acid (*F*) is formed

Ans *A*–Mesophyll cell, *B*–Phosphoenol Pyruvate (PEP), *C*–Oxaloacetic Acid (OAA), *D*–Bundle sheath cells, *E*–Pyruvate, *F*–Phosphoglyceric Acid (PGA). (½ × 6)

29. **Observe the diagram and answer the following.**

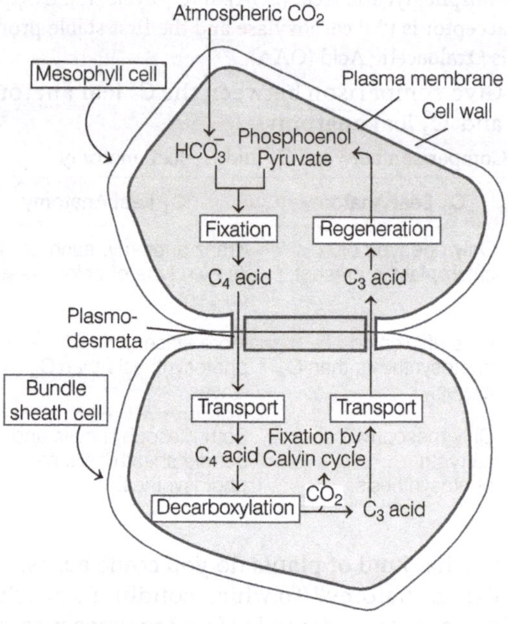

(i) Which group of plants exibit these two types of cells?
(ii) What is the first product of C_4- cycle?
(iii) Which enzyme is there in bundle sheath cells and mesophyll cells? **NCERT Exemplar**

Ans (i) Monocot plants belonging to Graminae/Poaceae family, e.g. sugarcane, maize, etc., possess these two types of cells, i.e. bundle sheath and mesophyll cell (in Kranz anatomy).

(ii) A 4-carbon compound oxaloacetic acid is the first product of C_4- cycle.

(iii) Mesophyll cells have PEP carboxylase to fix atmospheric CO_2 to form a 4-carbon compound oxalo acetic acid, whereas bundle sheath cells have RuBP carboxylase which fix CO_2 by this enzyme to form 3-carbon compound 3 PGA (3 phosphoglyceric acid). (3×1)

30. **What conditions enable RuBisCO to function as an oxygenase? Explain the ensuing process.** **NCERT Exemplar**

Ans Carboxylation is the most crucial step of the Calvin cycle, where CO_2 is utilised for the carboxylation of RuBP. This reaction is catalysed by the enzyme RuBP carboxylase, which results in the formation of two molecules of 3-PGA.

Since, this enzyme also has an oxygenation activity, it would be more correct to call it RuBP carboxylase oxygenase or RuBisCO. (3)

Under the conditions, when O_2 concentration is more in atmosphere than CO_2, then in C_3 plants, RuBisCO acts as oxygenase enzyme. Then, phosphoglycerate and phosphoglycolate are formed and photorespiration occurs.

31. **Why does not photorespiration take place in C_4 plants?** **NCERT Exemplar**

Ans Photorespiration is associated with C_3 cycle, where plant lose CO_2-fixation because of the increase in concentrate ion of O_2 and change the nature of activity of RuBP carboxylase-oxygenase.

C_4-plants have evolved a mechanism to avoid loss of CO_2. There is not a direct contact of RuBP carboxylase-oxygenase as C_3-cycle operates in bundle sheath cells (where both temperature and oxygen level are low). CO_2-fixation is done by another enzyme PEP carboxylase in mesophyll cells and oxaloacetate is formed which is converted to malic acid and transported to bundle sheath cells.

There, it gives off CO_2 which is used in Calvin cycle, operating in bundle sheath cells of C_4-plants. (3)

Long Answer Type Questions

5 Marks

32. **Some of these terms/chemicals are associated with the C_4-cycle. Explain.**

(i) Hatch-Slack pathway
(ii) Calvin cycle
(iii) PEP carboxylase
(iv) Bundle sheath cells **NCERT Exemplar**

Ans The terms associated with C_4-cycle are

(i) **Hatch-Slack Pathway** The process of synthesis of glucose in C_4-plants is different from C_3-plants which was discovered by two scientists **MD Hatch** and **CR Slack** (1977). Hence, named Hatch-Slack pathway.

(ii) **Calvin Cycle** This cycle operates in bundle sheath cells and fixes CO_2 to form glucose molecules.

(iii) **PEP Carboxylase** It is an enzyme present in mesophyll cells of C_4-plants. It fixes CO_2 to form 4-carbon compound, i.e. Oxalo Acetic Acid (OAA).

(iv) **Bundle Sheath Cells** These are specialised sclerenchymatous cells present around the vascular bundle, in the veins of monocot leaves. These have agranal chloroplast. C_3-cycle occurs in these cells to manufacture glucose in C_4-plants. (5)

33. **What special anatomical features are displayed by leaves of C_4-plants? How do they provide advantage over the structure of C_3-plants?** **NCERT Exemplar**

Ans The particularly large cells around the vascular bundles of the C_4-pathway plants are called bundle sheath cells and the leaves, which have such anatomy are said to have Kranz anatomy. Kranz means wreath and is a reflection of the arrangement of cells.

The bundle sheath cells may form several layers around the vascular bundles, they are characterised by having a large number of chloroplasts, thick walls impervious to gaseous exchange and no intercellular spaces.

C_4-plants can produce more sugar than C_3-plants in conditions of bright light and high temperature. Many important crop plants are C_4-plants, i.e. maize, *Sorghum*, sugarcane and millet. (5)

34. Under what conditions are C_4-plants superior to C_3? **NCERT Exemplar**

Ans. C_4-plants can produce more sugar than C_3-plants in conditions of bright light and high temperature. It is because of the following reasons

(i) They have a special type of leaf anatomy.

(ii) They can tolerate higher temperature.

(iii) They show response to high light intensities.

(iv) They lack a process called photorespiration.

(v) They have greater productivity of biomass. (1× 5)

Many important crop plants are C_4-plants including maize, *Sorghum*, sugarcane and millet.

35. Suppose *Euphorbia* and maize are grown in the tropical area.

(i) Which one of them do you think will be able to survive under such conditions?

(ii) Which one of them is more efficient in terms of photosynthetic activity?

(iii) What differences do you think are there in their leaf anatomy? **NCERT Exemplar**

Ans (i) *Euphorbia* will be able to survive under such conditions. (1)

(ii) Maize is more efficient in terms of photosynthetic activity. (1)

(iii) The maize is a C_4-plant having Kranz anatomy type of leaf anatomy. The bundle sheath cells are characterised by having a large number of chloroplasts, thick walls impervious to gaseous exchange and no intercellular spaces.

While, *Euphorbia*, which undergoes CAM (Crassulacean Acid Metabolism) both pathways occur in mesophyll cells only they do not have Kranz anatomy, and also their stomata remain closed during the day. (3)

36. RuBisCO is an enzyme that acts both as a carboxylase and oxygenase. Why do you think RuBisCO carries out more carboxylation in C_4-plants? **NCERT**

Ans RuBisCO has a much greater affinity for CO_2 than for O_2 under normal conditions. It is the relative concentration of O_2 and CO_2 that determines which of the two will bind to the enzyme.

In C_3-plants some O_2 does bind to RuBisCO and hence, CO_2-fixation is decreased. Here the RuBP instead of being converted to 2 molecules of PGA binds with O_2 to form one molecule of phosphoglycolate in a pathway called photorespiration.

In the photorespiratory pathway, there is neither synthesis of sugars, nor of ATP, rather it results in the release of CO_2 with the utilisation of ATP. In the photorespiratory pathway, there is no synthesis of ATP or NADPH. Therefore, photorespiration is a wasteful process.

In C_4-plants, photorespiration does not occur. This is because they have a mechanism that increases the concentration of CO_2 at the enzyme site.

This takes place when the C_4 acid from the mesophyll is broken down in the bundle cells to release CO_2, this results in increasing the intracellular concentration of CO_2.

In turn, this ensures that the RuBisCO functions as a carboxylase minimising the oxygenase activity. (5)

37. A cyclic process is occurring in C_3-plant, which is light dependent and needs O_2. This process does not produce energy rather it consumes energy.

(i) Can you name the given process?

(ii) Is it essential for survival of the plant?

(iii) What are the end products of this process?

(iv) Where does it occur?

(v) Does it occur in C_4-plants also?

Ans (i) Photorespiration.

(ii) No, it is not essential for survival of the plant.

(iii) Hydrogen peroxide.

(iv) The photorespiration occurs in chloroplast, peroxisomes and mitochondria.

(v) No, it does not occur in C_4-plants. (1×5)

SUMMARY

- **Photosynthesis** is the manufacturing of organic compounds, i.e. carbohydrates inside the chlorophyll containing cells from CO_2 by utilising light energy. It occurs in two phases-light reaction and dark reaction.
- **Chloroplasts** are the site of photosynthesis, which are present in mesophyll cells of leaves.
- **Photosynthetic pigments present** in the leaves are chlorophyll, carotenoids and xanthophylls.
- **Absorption spectrum** is a graph, which represents the amount of absorption of different wavelength of light by a particular pigment.
- **Action spectrum** represents the degree of different wavelengths, which affect the rate of photosynthesis.
- **Quantasomes** are the smallest number of pigment molecules required as a unit to carry out light reaction of photosynthesis. They are also called photosynthetic unit.
- **Light reaction** includes light absorption, water splitting, oxygen release and formation of high energy intermediates ATP and NADPH.
- **Photolysis** includes water splitting into H^+, O and electrons. It requires minerals such as Mn^{2+}, Cl^- and Ca^{2+}.
- **Photophosphorylation** is the light driven synthesis of ATP molecules, which can be cyclic or non- cyclic.
- **Non-cyclic photophosphorylation** includes non-cyclic transfer of electrons during ATP formation. The various electron carriers in the process are cytochrome-b_6, cytochrome-f, plastocyanin and plastoquinone.
- **Cyclic photophosphorylation** involves the formation of ATP from ADP and iP *via* a cyclic flow of electrons, i.e. donor and acceptor is same (P_{700}).
- **Chemiosmotic hypothesis** was proposed by Mitchell in 1961 and it explains the formation of ATP molecules in photosynthesis and respiration. Also, it states that ATP synthesis is linked to development of proton gradient across thylakoid membrane.
- **Products of light reaction** are ATP, $NADPH_2$ and O_2, which are used in dark reaction for reduction of CO_2 to carbohydrates.
- **Dark reaction** is independent of light and includes reduction of carbon dioxide to form carbohydrates by utilising ATP and $NADPH_2$ generated in light reaction.
- **Calvin cycle** takes place in majority of green plants. The first stable compound is PGA, which is a 3- carbon compound. So, it is also called C_3-pathway. It takes place in 3 stages-carboxylation of RuBP, reduction of CO_2, regeneration of RuBP.
- **C_4 pathway** was discovered by Hatch-Slack. Its first stable product is a C_4 compound (OAA), so its called C_4 pathway. It is observed in monocots and dicot plants. The major steps are-first CO_2 fixation in mesophyll cells, second CO_2 fixation in bundle sheath cells.
- **Photorespiration** involves loss of fixed carbon as CO_2 in the presence of light. It starts in chloroplasts, other cell organelles involved are peroxysomes and mitochondria. It is also called wasteful process because it does not produce ATP or NADPH.
- **Factors affecting photosynthesis** could be external such as light, CO_2 and temperature or internal such as chlorophyll content in leaves, structure of leaf and accumulation of byproducts in the leaf.
- When many factors affect the rate of biochemical process then rate will be determined by the factor which is nearest to its minimum value was stated by Blackman and termed as Blackman's law of limiting factor.

Chapter Practice

Multiple Choice Questions

1 Mark

1. The main purpose of photosynthesis is to
   (a) consume CO_2
   (b) produce ATP
   (c) convert light energy into chemical energy
   (d) produce starch

2. Which one of the following statements is false about chloroplast?
   (a) Usually chloroplast align themselves along the walls of mesophyll cells, so that they get optimum quantity of incident light
   (b) Within chloroplast there is a membranous system consisting of grana, stroma lamellae and stroma
   (c) There is division of labour
   (d) In grana CO_2 is fixed

3. Cyclic photophosphorylation occurs in
   (a) stroma lamellae
   (b) appressed part of grana lamellae
   (c) stroma cell wall
   (d) grana cell wall

4. ATP and NADPH produced in light reaction by the movement of electrons in ETC are used immediatly for
   (a) oxidation of carbohydrate
   (b) synthesis of sugar
   (c) reduction of carbon dioxide
   (d) Both (b) and (c)

5. The membranous system or grana is responsible for
   (a) trapping light energy, but not ATP and $NADPH_2$ formation
   (b) trapping light energy and also for fixation of CO_2
   (c) for ATP and $NADPH_2$ formation, but not for light trapping
   (d) for light capturing and also for $NADPH_2$ and ATP formation

6. $PEP + CO_2 + H_2O \xrightarrow{X} \text{Oxaloacetic acid} + H_3PO_4$.
   Identify *X*.
   (a) Ligase (b) Oxidoreductase
   (c) PEP carboxylase (d) Lyase

7. Malic acid or Aspartic acid and oxaloacetic acid both are found in
   (a) mesophyll cell (b) meristematic cell
   (c) bundle sheath cell (d) epidermal cell

8. In photorespiration pathway, there is release of CO_2 with utilisation of
   (a) NADPH (b) ATP
   (c) ADP (d) $NADP^+$

9. The internal factors that affect photosynthesis of plant depend on the
   (a) morphological pre-disposition
   (b) genetic pre-disposition
   (c) temperature
   (d) environmental pre-disposition

10. Under normal condition, which one of the following is a major limiting factor?
    (a) Light (b) CO_2
    (c) Temperature (d) Chlorophyll

Assertion-Reason Type Questions

1 Mark

Direction (Q. Nos. 11-19) *In each of the following questions, a statement of Assertion (A) is given followed by corresponding statement of Reason (R). Of the statements, mark the correct answer as*

(a) If both A and R are true and R is the correct explanation of A
(b) If both A and R are true, but R is not the correct explanation of A
(c) If A is true, but R is false
(d) If A is false, but R is true

11. **Assertion** (A) During photosynthesis, glucose is formed, but it is stored in the form of starch.
    Reason (R) Glucose is osmotically active, while starch is inactive.

12. **Assertion** (A) In thylakoid, Light Harvesting Complexe (LHC) broadens the range of light absorption.
Reason (R) They transfer electrons to reaction centre.

13. **Assertion** (A) Assimilatory power in photosynthesis is generated in ETS occurring in thylakoid membrane.
Reason (R) They are required for CO_2 reduction.

14. Given below is the non-cyclic photophosphorylation of flowering plants. It is carried out in the collaboration with both photosystems-I and II. Study the cycle and comment upon the appropriateness of the Assertion and Reason.

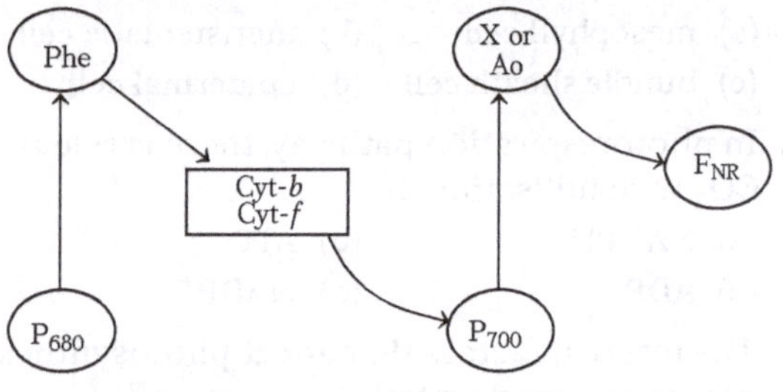

Assertion (A) Non-cyclic photophosphorylation occurs in the granum of chloroplasts.
Reason (R) There is cyclic flow of electrons in this process.

15. Given below is the graph showing the absorption spectrum of chlorophyll-*a* and *b*. Comment upon the appropriateness of both Assertion and Reason.

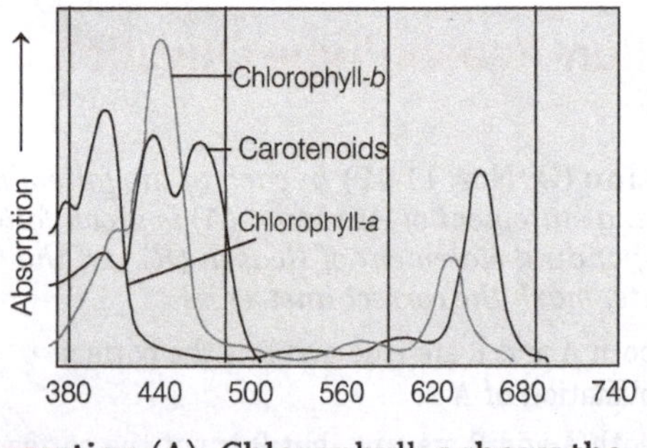

Assertion (A) Chlorophyll-*a* shows the maximum absorption peak at 450 nm and also shows another peak at 650 nm.
Reason (R) Absorption spectrum is constituted by the pigments like violet, blue, orange and red.

16. **Assertion** (A) In photosynthesis, dark reactions are temperature controlled processes.
Reason (R) Most of the reaction are enzymatic in nature.

17. **Assertion** (A) In C_4-plants, granal type of chloroplast is present in bundle sheath cells.
Reason (R) The bundle sheath cells are mainly meant to carryout C_4 cycle.

18. **Assertion** (A) In CAM plants, the dark acidification of cytoplasm takes place.
Reason (R) Organic acids are decarboxylated during night.

19. **Assertion** (A) PS-I and PS-II names are given on the basis of activity in the photosynthesis.
Reason (R) During non-cyclic photophosphorylation, PS-II works first and then PS-I.

Answers

1. (c)	2. (d)	3. (a)	4. (d)	5. (d)	6. (c)
7. (a)	8. (b)	9. (b)	10. (b)	11. (a)	12. (b)
13. (a)	14. (c)	15. (b)	16. (b)	17. (d)	18. (c)
19. (d)					

Very Short Answer Type Questions

1 Mark

20. Write the simplified equation of photosynthesis given by van Niel.
21. By which technique, the leaf pigments can be separated out?
22. On exposure of which colour of light, plants get starved?
23. What is the major function of chlorophyll in photosynthesis?
24. Mention the wavelength of two peaks at which the chlorophyll-*a* show maximum absorption of light.
25. Which photosystem will work if only longer wavelengths of light are given to a plant?
26. What is the role of chlorophyll-*a* molecule in light reaction?
27. Which is the primary CO_2 acceptor in C_3-plants?
28. Who proposed Z-scheme and suggested that two photosystems operate in series?
29. During dark phase of photosynthesis, which is oxidised and which is reduced.

30. Mention the number of carbon atoms in the primary carbon dioxide acceptor of
(i) C_3-plants
(ii) C_4-plants

31. What is the first stable product formed in C_4 cycle?

Short Answer Type I Questions

2 Marks

32. What is the advantage of having more than one pigment molecule in photosystem?

33. Explain about assimilatory power.

34. Bring out any four differences between cyclic and non-cyclic photophosphorylation.

35. What are the two components of ATPase complex? Where are these located and what are their functions?

36. Who proposed chemiosmotic hypothesis? Which molecule is synthesised by chemiosmosis?

37. Complete the following equation

$$3CO_2 + 6\ NADPH + H_2O \longrightarrow \underset{....}{?} + ADP + \underset{....}{?}$$

38. Mention the name of the enzyme that catalyses the carboxylation as well as oxygenation reaction. In which cell organelle is this enzyme found?

Short Answer Type II Questions

3 Marks

39. Why is the colour of a leaf kept in the dark, frequently becomes yellow or pale green? Which pigments do you think are more stable?

40. Mention the name and characteristics of various classes of pigments used in photosynthesis.

41. What are the roles played by antenna complex and photosystems in the process of photosynthesis?

42. Give a schematic representation of cyclic photophosphorylation?

43. Represent schematically the process of ATP synthesis through chemiosmosis in chloroplast.

Long Answer Type Questions

5 Marks

44. Describe the basic characteristics of a photosystem and explain how photosystem-I is different from photosystem-II?

45. Where does non-cyclic photophosphorylation take place? Describe this process. Why is this process called so?

46. Where does Calvin cycle take place in chloroplasts? Describe the three phases of Calvin cycle.

47. Make a flow chart of all the steps involved in photosynthesis initiating from light harvesting mechanism.

48. RuBisCO carries a dual role as carboxylase as well as oxygenase. Explain both the reactions. Under what conditions does this shift from one to other take place?

Case Based Questions

4/5 Marks

49. *Read the following passage and answer the questions that follows.*
A student is wondered to observe that the leaves of a green plants are found in many shades. So, he is trying to separate the leaf pigments of a green plant through paper chromatography. In this experiment, he found that the green leaf possess four different types of pigments. He asked about the types of pigment in plants to his biology teacher.
(i) What are the four different types of pigment?
(ii) Which pigment shows bright or blue-green patch in the chromatogram?
(iii) Which pigment is responsible for the yellow-orange colour of leaf?
(iv) Name the pigment which acts as antioxidants.
(v) Which of the chlorophyll is present in photosystem-II?

50. *Read the following passage and answer the questions that follows.*
Akshita who is a biology tutor was teaching photosystems to the students at her place. While explaining the topic light reaction, she said that, 'Two of the three products of light

reaction, ATP and NADPH are used to drive the reactions in the biosynthetic/dark phase.'
It has been verified by the fact that immediately after light becomes unavailable, the biosynthetic phase continues for some time and then stops; if light becomes available again, the process continues. Her brother, student of class XI was also listening the same and recalled that he had listened the same from his biology teacher also. He interrupted her sister and asked her to re-explain the whole process for a better understanding.

(i) What are the products of light reaction?
(ii) Can we say that calling the biosynthetic phase, as a dark reaction is a misnomer? Justify.
(iii) Name the first stable product of photosynthesis.
(iv) What product (s) is/are obtained at the end of Calvin cycle?

51. The graph below shows the absorption spectra of three photosynthetic pigments.

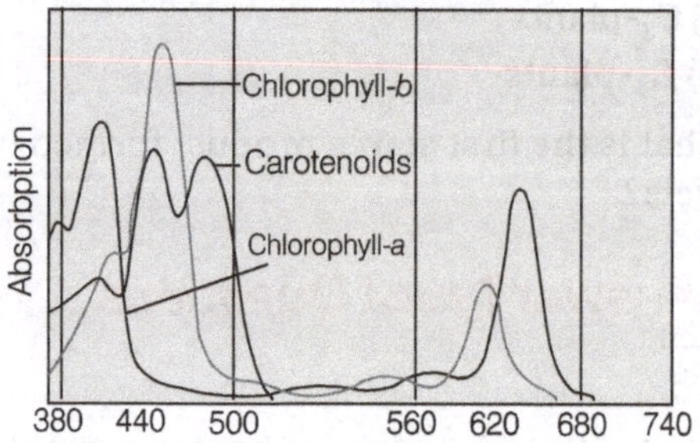

(i) Which out of the three are the main photosynthetic pigment?
(ii) Name the instrument used to study the phenomenon of absorption spectrum.
(iii) What does the absorption spectra of chlorophyll-*a* and *b* shows ?

Or

(iii) How does the pigment are often known ?

CHAPTER

15

Respiration in Plants

All living organisms require a continuous supply of energy for their survival. Energy is used to carry out various functions such as uptake of nutrients, absorption, growth, development, movement, reproduction and even breathing. About 50% of the energy produced by the cell is utilised by these cellular activities and rest of it is changed into heat and is lost into environment. Now, the question arises from where does this energy come to carry out all these processes of life. This chapter deals with basic concepts of energy producing biological process called **cellular respiration**.

TOPIC 01 Respiration : The Basics

We eat food in order to obtain energy. The food we eat in the form of **macromolecules** is oxidised to fulfil energy requirement of our body for carrying out all the basic life processes.

As we have already studied that only green plants and some bacteria can prepare their own food by the process called **photosynthesis**. They obtain their food by converting light energy into chemical energy, which thereby gets stored into the bonds of carbohydrate molecules such as glucose, sucrose, starch, etc.

But all cells, tissues and organs in plants do not photosynthesise instead, photosynthesis takes place in only some parts of plants, i.e. only cells that contain **chloroplasts**, i.e. green parts of the plants.

Hence, all other non-green parts of plant need food for oxidation to get energy. Thus, food has to be translocated from the green parts to the non-green parts for the oxidation processes to generate energy.

Respiratory Substrates

The compounds that are oxidised during the process of respiration are called respiratory substrates.

Carbohydrates are used as major respiratory substrates by most of the organisms to get energy, but under some conditions in some organisms proteins, fats and organic acids are also used as respiratory substrates.

Differences between Respiration and Combustion

Respiration	Combustion
It is the breakdown of complex compounds through oxidation within the cells, leading to release of considerable amount of energy.	Combustion is the complete burning of organic compounds which produces CO_2 and H_2O and yield energy in the form of heat and light.
It is a controlled stepwise biochemical process.	It is an uncontrolled physico-chemical process.
Many chemical bonds break simultaneously releasing large amount of energy.	Chemical bonds break one after another to release energy.
Enzymes are involved.	Enzymes are not involved.
A number of intermediates are formed for the synthesis of different organic compounds.	No intermediate products are produced in this case.

ATP : Energy Currency of the Cell

During the process of oxidation of food within a cell, all the energy contained in the respiratory substrates is not released free into the cell, or in a single step. Instead it is released in a series of **stepwise reactions** controlled by enzymes and is trapped as chemical energy in the form of **ATP**. Hence, the energy released in respiration by the process of oxidation is not used directly but is used in synthesising ATP (which is utilised whenever energy is needed).

Thus, it is said that ATP acts as the **energy currency of the cell**. The energy trapped in ATP is used in many energy requiring processes of the organisms, and the carbon skeleton produced during respiration is used as precursors for the biosynthesis of other molecules in a cell.

Exchange of Gases in Plants

For the process of respiration, plant takes O_2 and releases CO_2. Plants have stomata and lenticels for gaseous exchange instead of specialised organs that are present in animals for exchange of gases.

Following are the reasons which show, how plants can get along without respiratory organs

(i) Every part of the plant has the ability to take care of its own needs of gaseous exchange and also very little transport of gases occur from one part of the plant to another.

(ii) It is only during the process of photosynthesis that large volumes of gases are exchanged and each leaf of the plant has ability to take care of its own needs during these periods.

Thus, when cells photosynthesise, availability of O_2 is not a problem in these cells due to a continuous release of O_2 that takes place within the cell.

(iii) Gases may easily diffuse in large, bulky plants as distance for diffusion is not so great because living cells in a plant are located quite close to the surface of the plant.

In case of stems, which are thick and woody in nature, the organisation of living cells is in the form of thin layers, which are found inside and beneath the bark. Like leaves which have **stomata** for gaseous exchange, these stems also have openings called **lenticels**. Internal cells are dead and provide only mechanical support to the plant. This depicts that most cells of plant have atleast a part of their surface in contact with the air. The loose packing of **parenchyma cells** in leaves, stems and roots, provides an interconnected network of air spaces which help in facilitating this process.

Types of Respiration

We know that during the process of respiration, utilisation of O_2 takes place with the release of CO_2, water and energy as products.

Cellular respiration may be classified into two types as given below

1. Aerobic Respiration

This is the type of respiration in which organism utilise oxygen for the complete oxidation of organic food into CO_2, water and energy. It starts in cytoplasm and gets completed inside the **mitochondria**.

Note Aerobic respiration yields more energy as the respiratory substrate is completely oxidised in the presence of O_2.

2. Anaerobic Respiration

This is the type of respiration in which organic food is oxidised incompletely. It occurs in **cytoplasm** and releases small amount of energy.

It is believed that the first cells on this planet lived in a reducing environment when O_2 was not present in the atmosphere, i.e. they were **anaerobes**. Even among present day living organisms, several are adapted to anaerobic conditions.

Some of them are **facultative anaerobes** (organisms that have capability of switching from aerobic to anaerobic conditions according to the availability of oxygen) while others are **obligate anaerobes** (organisms that are killed by normal atmospheric concentration of oxygen of 21%).

Thus, in any case, all living organisms retain the enzymatic machinery for partial oxidation of glucose in the absence of oxygen. And this breakdown of glucose to pyruvic acid is called **glycolysis.** It occurs in **cytoplasm** of the living cell.

Topic Practice 1

Multiple Choice Questions

1 Mark

1. Choose the correct combination of *A* and *B*. All living organisms need ... *A*... for carrying out daily life activities and is obtained by ... *B* ... of macromolecules.
(a) *A*–oxygen; *B*–reduction
(b) *A*–energy; *B*–reduction
(c) *A*–energy; *B*–oxidation
(d) *A*–oxygen; *B*–oxidation

Ans (c) All living organisms need energy for carrying out daily life activities which is obtained by oxidation of macromolecules.

2. Release of energy by breaking down of C–C bond of various organic molecules by oxidation process for cellular use is known as
(a) respiration
(b) photorespiration
(c) oxidative phosphorylation
(d) combustion

Ans (a) Respiration is defined as breaking down of C-C bond of various organic molecules by oxidation process for cellular use.

3. Respiratory substrates are the organic substance, which are......during respiration to liberate energy.
(a) oxidised (b) reduced
(c) synthesised (d) Both (a) and (b)

Ans (a) In the process of respiration, the compound, i.e. glucose reacts with oxygen, which is called oxidation therefore, organic substance gets oxidised.

4. The released energy obtained by oxidation is stored as
(a) A concentration gradient across a membrane
(b) ADP
(c) ATP
(d) NAD^+

Ans (c) The energy released by oxidation in respiration is not directly used, but it is stored as ATP which is broken down whenever energy needs to be utilised.

5. Plant does not need specialised respiratory organ because
(a) each plant part takes care of its own gas exchange needs
(b) plants do not need great demands for gas exchange
(c) it has roots for respiration
(d) Both (a) and (b)

Ans (a) Plants can get along without respiratory organ because plant part takes care of its own gas exchange needs.

6. In plants, exchange of gases takes place through
(a) lenticels (b) stomata
(c) chlorophyll (d) Both (a) and (b)

Ans (d) Plant needs both lenticels and stomata for exchange of gases.

7. Steps of respiration are controlled by
(a) substrates (b) enzymes
(c) hormone (d) bile juice

Ans (b) Enzymes control the process of cellular respiration in a stepwise manner.

8. The complete combustion of glucose in respiration is represented by
(a) $C_6H_{12}O_6 + 6O_2 \rightarrow 6CO_2 + 6H_2O + \text{Energy}$
(b) $C_6H_{12}O_6 + 6CO_2 \rightarrow 6O_2 + 6H_2O + \text{Energy}$
(c) $C_6H_{12}O_6 + 6O_2 + 6CO_2 \rightarrow 6CO_2 + 6H_2O + \text{Energy}$
(d) $C_6H_{12}O_6 + 6O_2 + 6CO_2 + ATP \rightarrow 6CO_2 + 6H_2O + 6O_2 + \text{Energy}$

Ans (a) It is the fact that in respiration, glucose is broken down in oxidation within the cell and CO_2, water and energy is released. Therefore, the suitable equation is

$$C_6H_{12}O_6 + 6O_2 \rightarrow 6CO_2 + 6H_2O + \text{Energy}$$

9. In respiration, respiratory substances which can be used is /are
(a) carbohydrate (b) protein
(c) organic acid (d) All of these

Ans (d) Usually carbohydrates are oxidised to release energy, but proteins, fats and even organic acids can be used as respiratory substances in some plants, under certain condition.

10. Cell respiration is carried out by

(a) ribosome (b) mitochondria
(c) chloroplast (d) Golgi bodies

Ans (b) Mitochondria are the sites of cellular respiration, oxidative phosphorylation, synthesis of haemprotein, cytochrome, myoglobin, etc.

Very Short Answer Type Questions

1 Mark

11. Respiration requires O_2. How did the first cells on the earth manage to survive in an atmosphere with no oxygen present at that time?

Ans The first cells on the earth managed to survive in an atmosphere that lacked O_2 by the process of anaerobic respiration.

12. Name two openings in plants through which exchange of gases takes place?

Ans The two openings in plants through which exchange of gases takes place are stomata and lenticels.

13. Write the overall equation of respiration.

Ans $C_6H_{12}O_6 + 6O_2 \rightarrow 6CO_2 + 6H_2O + \text{Energy (ATP)}$

Short Answer Type I Questions

2 Marks

14. What are respiratory substrates? Name the most common respiratory substrate. **NCERT**

Ans The organic substances, which are catabolised in the living cells to release energy are called as respiratory substrates. Though any foodstuff-carbohydrate, fat or protein may act as a respiratory substrate, the common respiratory substrate is glucose. (2)

15. Differentiate between respiration and combustion. **NCERT**

Ans Refer to text on page no. 340.

16. We commonly call ATP as the energy currency of the cell, why? Can you think of some other energy carriers present in a cell? Give names of any two. **NCERT Exemplar**

Ans ATP is known as the energy currency of the cell because it acts as reservoir of energy and it releases energy. The other energy carriers present in a cell are ADP and AMP. (2)

17. Anaerobic respiration cannot continue for long in higher organisms. Why?

Ans Anaerobic respiration cannot continue for long in higher organisms because of

(i) low yield of energy.
(ii) decomposition of large amount of substrates, so that little is left for growth and repair.
(iii) toxic effect of end products in higher concentration.
(iv) inhibition of a number of physiological process linked with aerobic respiration. (½ × 4)

18. When does anaerobic respiration occur in man and yeast?

Ans Anaerobic respiration occurs in man in muscles at the time of excessive exercising as the blood supply does not meet the oxygen demand of the exercising body.

At that time in muscle, lactic acid is produced as a result of anaerobic respiration. In yeast also, anaerobic respiration occurs in the condition of absence of oxygen. (2)

Short Answer Type II Questions

3 Marks

19. What is the significance of stepwise release of energy in respiration? **NCERT**

Ans During oxidation within a cell, all the energy contained in respiratory substrates is not released free in a single step. It is released in a series of slow stepwise reactions controlled by enzymes and it is trapped as chemical energy in the form of ATP. The significance of this stepwise release of energy is that some energy is used to synthesise ATP. This ATP is stored for the later utilisation wherever, required. Hence, ATP acts as the energy currency of the cell. The energy stored in ATP can be utilised for the following

(i) In various energy requiring processes of organisms.
(ii) The carbon skeleton produced during respiration is used as precursors for the synthesis of other molecules. (2+1)

20. What are the two types of respiration? Differentiate between the two.

Ans The two types of respiration are aerobic and anaerobic respiration.

Differences between Aerobic and Anaerobic Respiration

Aerobic Respiration	Anaerobic Respiration
It occurs in the presence of O_2.	It occurs in the absence of O_2.
It is a permanent process and goes on throughout the life of plants.	It occurs for a temporary phase under anaerobic conditions in higher plants.
Energy released in larger amount in the form of ATP.	Energy released in lesser amount in the form of 2 moles of ATP.

(1+2)

Long Answer Type Question

5 Marks

21. Define the following
   (i) Respiration
   (ii) Respiratory substrate
   (iii) How does a tree trunk exchange gases with the environment although it lacks stomata?
   (iv) Which is the most important energy carrier? Is this compound mobile?
   (v) Name the major respiratory substrates used by most organisms.
   If it is unavailable at same time, what other substances can be used for respiration?

Ans (i) Enzymes controlled process of biological oxidation of various organic food materials in a living cell, producing CO_2 and H_2O, and releasing energy in the form of ATP, is called respiration.

(ii) The organic compounds catabolised in the living cells to release energy are called respiratory substrates.

(iii) A tree trunk can exchange gases due to the presence of lenticels in the periderm. It is connected internally to the network of parenchyma with outside world.

(iv) The most important energy carrier is ATP. This energy rich compound is mobile, but cannot pass from one cell to another.

(v) The major respiratory substrate used by most organisms is carbohydrates. In condition of its unavailability, proteins, fats and organic acids can be used. (1×5)

TOPIC 02 Cellular Respiration

It is the process of breaking of the C-C bonds of complex compounds through oxidation within the cells, leading to release of considerable amount of energy in the form of ATP. It is to be noted that site of breaking down of complex molecules to yield energy is **cytoplasm** and **mitochondria** of the living cell. Plant cells also carry out cellular respiration to get energy.

Mechanism of Respiration

Cellular respiration occurs in all living cells and proceeds with the help of enzymes. The first step in respiration (taking glucose as substrate) is the **glycolysis** (glucose is oxidised to pyruvic acid). After which the pyruvic acid may enter the **Krebs' cycle** (aerobic respiration) or undergo **fermentation** (anaerobic respiration).

Glycolysis

Glycolysis (Gr. *Glycos*–sugar; *lysis*–splitting), is a stepwise process by which one molecule of glucose (6C) breaks down into two molecules of pyruvic acid (3C).

The scheme of glycolysis was given by **Gustav Embden, Otto Meyerhof** and **J Parnas** and is often referred as the **EMP pathway.** It is a common pathway in both aerobic and anaerobic modes of respiration. But in case of anaerobic organisms, it is the only process of respiration.

Glycolysis occurs in the **cytoplasm** of the cell. During the process glucose gets partially oxidised. In plants, this glucose is derived from sucrose (end product of photosynthesis) or from storage carbohydrates.
During the course of process in plant this sucrose is first converted into glucose and fructose by the action of **invertase** enzyme, after this, these two monosaccharides enter the glycolytic pathway.

Steps Involved in Glycolysis

In glycolysis there is a chain of reactions. There reactions often occur under the control of different enzymes.

It involves the following steps

Step I **Phosphorylation** of glucose occurs under the action of an enzyme **hexokinase** and Mg^{2+} that gives rise to glucose-6-phosphate by the utilisation of ATP.

Step II **Isomerisation** of this phosphorylated glucose-6-phosphate takes place to form fructose-6-phosphate with the help of an enzyme **phosphohexose isomerase** (reversible reaction).

Step III This fructose-6-phosphate is again phosphorylated by ATP in order to form fructose 1, 6-bisphosphate in the presence of an enzyme **phosphofructokinase** and Mg^{2+}. The steps of phosphorylation of glucose to fructose 1, 6-bisphosphate (i.e. from step 1 to 3) activates the sugar thus, preventing it from getting out of the cell.

Step IV Splitting of fructose 1, 6-bisphosphate takes place into two triose phosphate molecules, i.e. dihydroxyacetone 3-phosphate and 3-phosphoglyceraldehyde (i.e. PGAL). This reaction is catalysed by an enzyme **aldolase.**

Step V Each molecule of PGAL removes two redox equivalents in the form of hydrogen atom and transfer them to a molecule of NAD^+ (This NAD^+ forms $NADH + H^+$) and accepts inorganic phosphate (Pi) from phosphoric acid. This reaction in turn leads to the conversion to PGAL (which gets oxidised) to 1, 3-bisphosphoglycerate (BPGA) (reversible reaction).

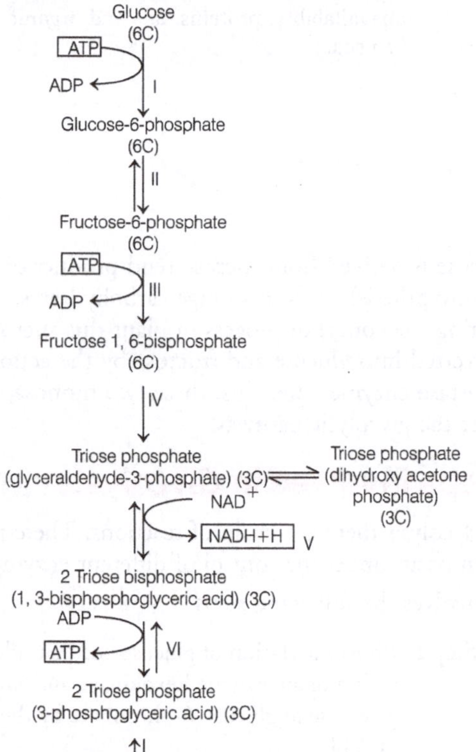

Fig 15.1 Steps of glycolysis

Step VI 1, 3-bisphosphoglycerate is converted to 3-phosphoglycerate with the formation of ATP. This reaction is catalysed by an enzyme **phosphoglycerate kinase.** It is also known as energy yielding process.

The formation of ATP directly from metabolites constitutes **substrate level phosphorylation** (reversible reaction).

Step VII In this step, 3-phosphoglycerate is subsequently isomerised to form 2-phosphoglycerate, catalysed by enzyme **phosphoglyceromutase** (reversible reaction).

Step VIII In the presence of enzyme **enolase** and Mg^{2+}, with the loss of a water molecule, 2-phosphoglycerate is converted to Phosphoenol Pyruvate (PEP) (reversible reaction).

Step IX High energy phosphate group of Phosphoenol Pyruvate (PEP) is transferred to a molecule of ADP, by the action of enzyme **pyruvate kinase** in the presence of Mg^{2+} and K^+. This turn produces two molecules of pyruvic acid (pyruvate) and a molecule of ATP by **substrate level phosphorylation.** The pyruvic acid, thus produced is the key product of glycolysis.

Metabolic Fate of Glycolysis

The overall reaction of glycolysis can be depicted as

- $\text{Glucose} + 2\text{Pi} + 2\text{ADP} + 2\text{NAD}^+ \rightarrow 2\text{ Pyruvate} + 2\text{ATP} + 2\text{NADH} + 2\text{H}^+$
- Two molecules of NADH on oxidation produce 6 molecules of ATP. Therefore, a net gain of **8 ATP molecules** occurs during glycolysis.
- The fate of glycolysis depends upon the availability of oxygen in the cell. In the presence of oxygen, pyruvic acid will enter the mitochondrion and undergo complete oxidation of glucose to CO_2 and H_2O in **aerobic respiration** (Krebs' cycle and ETC).
- On the other hand in the absence of oxygen, the pyruvic acid will undergo anaerobic respiration (lactic acid fermentation or alcoholic fermentation).

Knowledge Plus

Kostytcher (1902) coined the term anaerobic respiration.

Glycolysis has two phases, i.e. preparatory (glucose is broken down to glyceraldehyde-3-phosphate) and payoff phase (the GAL-3-PD4 is changed into pyruvate producing NADH and ATP).

Aerobic Respiration of Pyruvic Acid

Aerobic respiration is the next step (after glycolysis) that leads to complete oxidation of organic substances. It occurs in the presence of oxygen. The oxygen acts as a final acceptor of electron and protons are removed from the substrate.

The final product of glycolysis, i.e. pyruvic acid is transported from the cytoplasm mitochondria and thus, the second phase of respiration is initiated. The process of aerobic respiration involves two crucial events

(i) The complete oxidation of pyruvate occurs by the stepwise removal of all the hydrogen atoms, thereby, leaving three molecules of CO_2. This occurs in the **matrix of mitochondria**.

(ii) The electrons removed as part of the hydrogen atoms are then passed on to molecular O_2 with the simultaneous synthesis of ATP. This on the contrary takes place on the inner membrane of the mitochondria.

Oxidative Decarboxylation of Pyruvic Acid

In mitochondria, pyruvic acid (formed by the glycolytic catabolism of carbohydrates in cytosol) undergoes oxidative decarboxylation (i.e. removal of CO_2 in aerobic conditions) forming a key compound, i.e. acetyl Co-A by the action of **pyruvic acid dehydrogenase** (in mitochondrial matrix) through a series of reactions.

$$\text{Pyruvic acid} + \text{Co-A} + NAD^+ \xrightarrow[\text{Pyruvate dehydrogenase}]{Mg^{2+}} \text{Acetyl Co-A} + CO_2 + NADH + H^+$$

Thus, acetyl Co-A acts as a connecting link between glycolysis and citric acid cycle. During this process, two molecules of NADH are produced by breaking down of two molecules of pyruvic acid (produced from one glucose molecule during glycolysis).

Tricarboxylic Acid (TCA) Cycle or Krebs' Cycle

The acetyl Co-A then enters a cyclic pathway, Krebs' cycle (or Tricarboxylic Acid or TCA cycle) in mitochondrial matrix. Various coenzymes including NAD^+ and Co-A also participate in the reaction catalysed by **pyruvic acid dehydrogenase**. It was first elucidated by **Sir Hans Krebs**, a British Biochemist in 1940.

The whole cycle explains how pyruvate is broken down to CO_2 and water. Following are the steps of Krebs' cycle

(i) **Condensation** The Krebs' cycle starts with the condensation of acetyl group with oxaloacetic acid and water to yield citric acid, a 6C compound. This is the first stable product of the cycle.

This step is catalysed by an enzyme **citrate synthetase**. Co-A is liberated during this reaction.

(ii) Citric acid then undergoes reorganisation in two steps in the presence of an enzyme ***cis* acotinase.**

(iii) **Oxidative decarboxylation** Isocitrate is followed by two successive steps of oxidative decarboxylation, that leads to the formation of α-ketoglutaric acid, (a 5C compound in the presence of an enzyme **isocitrate dehydrogenase** and Mn^{2+}) and then succinyl Co-A, catalysed by α-complex.

The succinyl Co-A then splits into a 4C compound succinic acid and Co-A with the addition of water. During this conversion, a molecule of GTP (Guanosine Triphosphate) is synthesised (catalysed) by an enzyme **succinyl Co-A synthetase** (this occurs when coenzyme-A transfers its high energy to a phosphate group added to GDP to make GTP molecule).

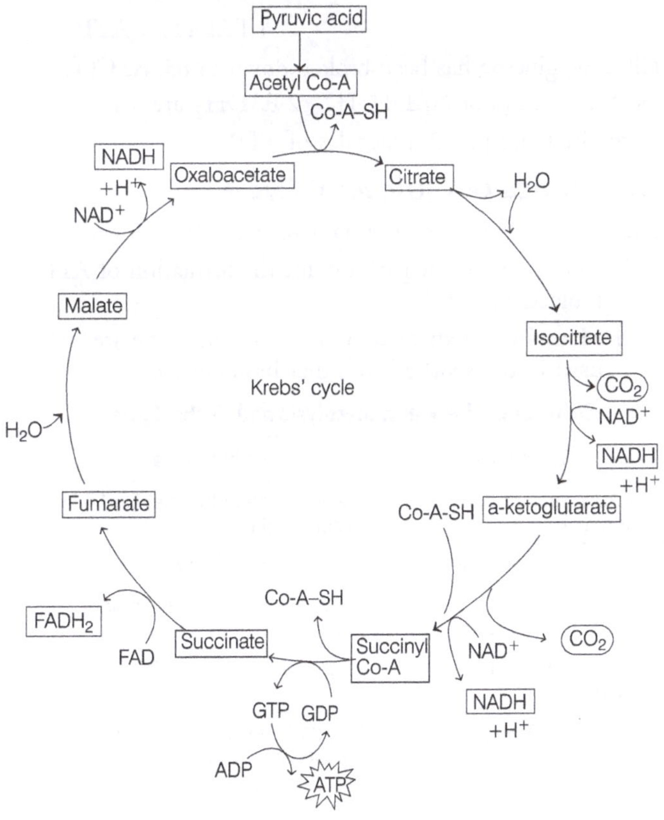

Fig 15.2 The citric acid cycle or Krebs' cycle

Note

(i) GTP is also an energy carrier like ATP. Thus, this is the only high energy phosphate produced in the Krebs' cycle.

(ii) In plants cells, this reaction also produces ATP from ADP.

In the remaining steps of Krebs' cycle, succinyl Co-A is oxidised to oxaloacetic acid, a 4C compound following the formation of fumaric acid and malic acid catalysed by enzymes **succinate dehydrogenase** and **fumarase**, respectively.

Output of Krebs' Cycle or Citric Acid Cycle

During this cycle of reactions, 3 molecules of NAD^+ are reduced to $NADH + H^+$ and one molecule of FAD^+ is reduced to $FADH_2$. And also one molecule of ATP is reduced directly from GTP (by substrate level phosphorylation). For continuous oxidation of acetyl Co-A, continued replenishment of oxaloacetic acid is necessary. In addition to this, regeneration of NAD^+ and FAD^+ from NADH and $FADH_2$, respectively are also required.

The summary equation for this phase of respiration is as follows

$$\text{Pyruvic acid} + 4NAD^+ + FAD + 2H_2O + ADP + Pi \xrightarrow{\text{Mitochondrial matrix}} 3CO_2 + 4NADH + 4H^+ + FADH_2 + ATP$$

Till now, glucose has been broken down to release CO_2 and 8 molecules of $NADH+H^+$, 2 $FADH_2$ are synthesised and just 2 molecules of ATP.

Importance of Citric Acid Cycle

The citric acid cycle is important in the following ways

(i) This is the major pathway for the formation of ATP molecules.

(ii) Many intermediate compounds of this cycle are used in the synthesis of other biomolecules.

Differences between Glycolysis and Krebs' Cycle

Glycolysis	Krebs' Cycle
It takes place in the cytoplasm.	It takes place in the matrix of mitochondria.
It is a linear pathway.	It is a cyclic pathway.
It occurs in aerobic as well as anaerobic respiration.	It occurs in aerobic respiration only.
It consumes 2 ATP molecules.	It does not consume ATP.
It yields 2 NADH per glucose molecule.	It yields 6 NADH molecules and 2 $FADH_2$ molecules from 2 acetyl coenzyme-A molecules.
It generates 2 ATP molecules net from 1 glucose molecule.	It generates 2 GTP/ATP molecules from 2 acetyl coenzyme-A molecules.
It oxidises glucose partly, producing pyruvate.	It completely oxidises acetyl coenzyme-A.
It does not produce CO_2.	It produces CO_2.
All enzymes catalysing glycolytic reactions are dissolved in cytosol.	Two enzymes of Krebs' cycle reactions are located in the inner mitochondrial membrane, all others are dissolved in matrix.

Factors Affecting Aerobic Cellular Respiration

The factors affecting respiration in plants are as follow

(i) Rate of aerobic respiration decreases, if the atmospheric oxygen concentration is below 5% for whole tissues.

(ii) CO_2 has a limited direct inhibitory effect on the respiration rate.

(iii) Under suitable light, the rate of photosynthesis is optimum, Thus, it supplies respiratory substrates at a moderate rate. Therefore the rate of respiration is increased.

(iv) Respiration increases as the temperature increases from 0°C and 30°C. Above 30°C, the respiration rate often increases more slowly and decreases at further higher temperatures, i.e. 40-50°C and above.

(v) The internal factors, which affect aerobic cellular respiration include water contents of the cell, kinds and age of tissue as well as the amount and the type of substrate available.

Topic Practice 2

Multiple Choice Questions

1 Mark

1. In which of the following reactions of glycolysis, oxidation takes place?

(a) Glucose-6-PO_4 to fructose-6-PO_4

(b) Glyceraldehyde-3-phosphate to 1, 3-diphosphoglycerate

(c) 1, 3-diphosphoglycerate to 3-phosphoglycerate

(d) 2-phosphoglycerate to phosphoglycerate

Ans (b) In glycolytic pathway, 3PGAL is converted into 1, 3-diphosphoglyceric acid by an oxidation and phosphorylation reaction, which occurs in the presence of H_3PO_4 and coenzyme NAD.

$$\text{3-phosphoglyceraldehyde} + H_3PO_4 \xrightarrow[\text{3-phosphoglyceraldehyde dehydrogenase}]{NAD^+ \rightarrow NADH} \text{1, 3-bisphosphoglyceric acid}$$

2. Link enzyme in cellular respiration is
(a) citrate synthetase
(b) pyruvate dehydrogenase
(c) isocitrate dehydrogenase
(d) succinyl thiokinase

Ans (b) Pyruvic acid synthesised in glycolysis must enter inside the mitochondrion where oxidative decarboxylation occurs in the presence of NAD^+, **pyruvic acid dehydrogenase complex** and coenzyme-A.

$$\text{Pyruvic acid} + \text{Co-A} + NAD^+ \xrightarrow{\text{Pyruvic dehydrogenase complex}} \text{Acetyl Co-A} + CO_2 + NADH + H^+$$

3. TCA cycle enzymes are present in
(a) cytoplasm
(b) intermembrane space of mitochondria
(c) mitochondrial matrix
(d) inner membrane of mitochondria

Ans (c) In eukaryotes, all the reactions of Tricarboxylic Acid (TCA) cycle or Krebs' cycle take place in the matrix of mitochondria because all enzymes of this cycle are found in the matrix of mitochondria except succinic dehydrogenase, which is located in the inner membrane of mitochondria.

In prokaryotes, Krebs' cycle occurs in cytoplasm.

4. Which one is not correct about Krebs' cycle?
(a) It is also called citric acid cycle
(b) The intermediate compound, which links glycolysis with Krebs' cycle is malic acid
(c) It occurs in mitochondria
(d) It starts with six carbon compound

Ans (b) Krebs' cycle or Citric acid cycle occurs in the matrix of mitochondria. It occurs in aerobic respiration. Acetyl Co-A is the connecting link between glycolysis and Krebs' cycle.

Pyruvic acid is oxidised into acetyl Co-A (6C), which is the first or initiating organic acid of Krebs' cycle.

5. In citric acid cycle, first step is
(a) acetyl Co-A combines with oxaloacetic acid
(b) acetyl Co-A combines with citric acid
(c) citric acid combines with oxaloacetic acid
(d) citric acid combines with malic acid

Ans (a) In the first reaction of citric acid cycle, one molecule of acetyl Co-A combines with 4 carbon Oxaloacetic Acid (OAA) to form 6 carbon citric acid and Co-A is released.

6. In which of the following, reduction of NAD does not occur?
(a) Isocitric acid $\rightarrow$ α- ketoglutaric acid
(b) Malic acid $\rightarrow$ Oxaloacetic acid
(c) Pyruvic acid $\rightarrow$ Acetyl Co-A
(d) Succinic acid $\rightarrow$ Fumaric acid

Ans (d) During the step of Krebs' cycle, where succinic acid undergoes oxidation or dehydrogenation to form fumaric acid, FAD is reduced to $FADH_2$ and enzyme involved in this step is succinic acid dehydrogenase.

Conversion of isocitric acid to α-ketoglutaric acid, malic acid to oxaloacetic acid and pyruvic acid to acetyl Co-A, all involve reduction of NAD to NADH + H^+.

7. FAD is electron acceptor during oxidation of which of the following?
(a) α- ketoglutarate $\rightarrow$ Succinyl Co-A
(b) Succinic acid $\rightarrow$ Fumaric acid
(c) Succinyl Co-A $\rightarrow$ Succinic acid
(d) Fumaric acid $\rightarrow$ Malic acid

Ans (b) In the Krebs' cycle, when succinic acid undergoes oxidation or dehydrogenation to form fumaric acid, two hydrogens are transferred to FAD. FAD is reduced to $FADH_2$ and enzyme involved in this step is succinic acid dehydrogenase.

8. α-ketoglutarate acid, an intermediary compound of Krebs' cycle is a
(a) 5 carbon compound (b) 6 carbon compound
(c) 4 carbon compound (d) 3 carbon compound

Ans (a) Oxalosuccinic acid - 6 C compound
Malate - 4C compound
α-ketoglutarate - 5C compound
Pyruvic acid - 3C compound

9. Which of the following biomolecules is common to respiration mediated breakdown of fats, carbohydrates and proteins?
(a) Glucose-6-phosphate
(b) Fructose 1, 6-bisphosphate
(c) Pyruvic acid
(d) Acetyl Co-A

Ans (d) Carbohydrates, fats and proteins, all can be used as a substrate in cellular respiration. All of them first get converted to acetyl Co-A to enter into Krebs' cycle of aerobic cellular respiration.
Thus, it is the common factor of respiration entering Krebs' cycle after breakdown of carbohydrates, fats and proteins.

10. In aerobic respiration, removal of 3 molecules of CO_2 occurs in
(a) matrix of the mitochondria
(b) inner membrane of the mitochondria
(c) anywhere in mitochondria
(d) Both (a) and (b)

Ans (a) With the complete oxidation of pyruvate by the stepwise removal of all the hydrogen atoms form 3 molecules of CO_2, which occurs in matrix of the mitochondria.

11. Sequence of events in Krebs' cycle is
(a) Acetyl Co-A→ Citrate → Pyruvate → Oxaloacetic acid → α-ketoglutarate → Succinate →Malate→Fumarate
(b) Acetyl Co-A→ Citric acid → α-ketoglutarate acid → Succinic acid → Fumaric acid → Malic acid → Oxaloacetic acid
(c) Acetyl Co-A→ Citric acid → Malic acid → Oxaloacetic acid → Oxaloacetic acid → Succinic acid → α-ketoglutaric acid
(d) None of the above

Ans (b)

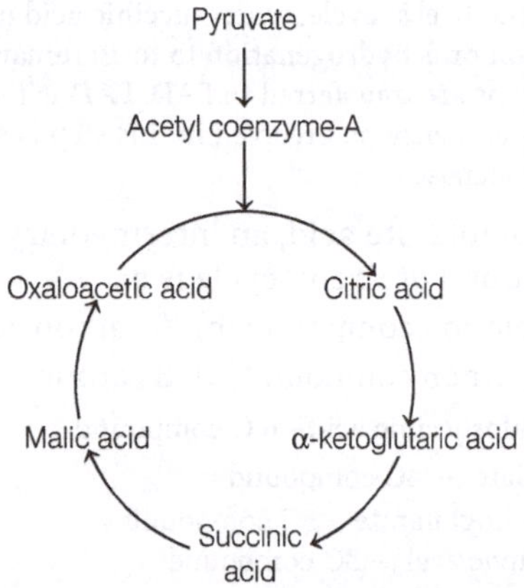

Very Short Answer Type Questions

(1 Mark)

12. Name the first step in cellular respiration.

Ans Glycolysis, which involves breaking down of sugar to pyruvic acid is the first step in cellular respiration.

13. Write the reaction where substrate level phosphorylation takes place in glycolysis.

Ans Substrate level phosphorylation takes place during the following reactions
(i) When 1, 3-bisphosphoglycerate is converted into 3-phosphoglycerate.
(ii) When phosphoenol pyruvate is converted into pyruvic acid.

14. Pyruvic acid, the key end product of glycolysis has many metabolic fats. What does it form under aerobic condition?

Ans Pyruvic acid forms carbon dioxide and water, with the release of energy under aerobic condition.

15. How many $NADH_2$ molecules are produced from one molecule of acetyl Co-A in TCA cycle?

Ans $3NADH_2$ molecules are produced from one molecule of acetyl Co-A in TCA cycle.

Short Answer Type I Questions

(2 Marks)

16. What are the main steps in aerobic respiration? Where does it take place? **NCERT**

Ans The main steps in aerobic respiration are as follows
(i) Glycolytic breakdown of glucose into pyruvic acid. It occurs in cytoplasm of the living cell.
(ii) Oxidative decarboxylation of pyruvic acid to acetyl Co-A (acetyl coenzyme-A).
(iii) Krebs' cycle.
(iv) Terminal oxidaiton and phosphorylation in respiratory chain. It occurs inside the mitochondrial matrix. (2)

17. Write two energy yielding reactions of glycolysis. **NCERT Exemplar**

Ans The conversion of BPGA to 3-phosphoglyceric acid (PGA), is an energy yielding process. This energy is trapped by the formation of an ATP. Another ATP is synthesised during the conversion of PEP to pyruvic acid. (2)

18. ATP produced during glycolysis is a result of substrate level phosphorylation. Explain. **NCERT Exemplar**

Ans Substrate level phosphorylation is a type of metabolism that results in the formation and creation of Adenosine Triphosphate (ATP) or Guanosine Triphosphate (GTP) by the direct transfer and donation of a phosphoryl (PO_3) group to Adenosine Diphosphate (ADP) or Guanosine Diphosphate (GDP) to form a phosphorylated reactive intermediate. (2)

19. What is the end product of glycolysis and where does this process occur?

Ans **End product of glycolysis** are

Glucose + 2ADP + 2Pi + 2NAD → 2 Pyruvic acid + 2ATP + $2NADH_2$

It occurs in cytoplasm, i.e. outside the mitochondria. (2)

20. Mention the step of citric acid cycle, which is not mediated by dehydrogenase enzyme.

Ans Conversion of oxaloacetic acid to citric acid is not mediated by dehydrogenase enzyme in citric acid cycle. (2)

21. Do you know any step in the TCA cycle, where there is substrate level phosphorylation? Which one? **NCERT Exemplar**

Ans In TCA cycle, during the conversion of succinyl Co-A to succinic acid, a molecule of GTP is synthesised. This is a substrate level phosphorylation.

In a coupled reaction, in which GTP is converted to GDP with the simultaneous synthesis of ATP from ADP. (2)

22. What is meant by the statement 'aerobic respiration is more efficient'? **NCERT Exemplar**

Ans The aerobic respiration is a high energy yielding process. During the process of aerobic respiration as many as 36 molecules of ATP are produced for every molecule of glucose that is utilised.

This shows that aerobic respiration produces much more energy than anaerobic respiration, which produces only 2 ATP molecules. (2)

23. Comment on the statement, 'Respiration is an energy producing process, but ATP is being used in some steps of the process'. **NCERT Exemplar**

Ans Respiration is a complex oxidative process in which there is formation of several intermediate molecules. In the end water molecule is produced and ATP molecules are released in cell.

Although ATP molecules are consumed in the glycolysis and Krebs' cycle, there is also production of more molecules of ATP, thus a positive balance of ATP molecules is obtained. (2)

24. Which amongst the following are 3 and 6 carbon compound? Oxaloacetate, phosphoglyceraldehyde, isocitrate, α-ketoglutarate.

Ans Phosphoglyceraldehyde → 3C, isocitrate → 6C. (2)

25. Differentiate between glycolysis and Krebs' cycle.

Ans Refer to text on page no. 346.

Short Answer Type II Questions

(3 Marks)

26. Glucose ...... *A* ...... 3-phosphoglyceric acid ...... *B* ...... pyruvic acid ...... $C + CO_2$.

Ans Glucose *A* – Glyceraldehyde-3-phosphate, *B* – Phosphoenol pyruvate, *C* – Ethanol. (1×3)

27. Name the end products of aerobic and anaerobic fate of glycolysis. List two ways by which molecules of ATP are produced in glycolysis during aerobic respiration in a cell.

Ans End product of aerobic glycolysis

$$\text{Pyruvic acid} \xrightarrow{O_2} CO_2 + \text{water}$$

End product of anaerobic glycolysis are CO_2 and ethanol or lactic acid.

Molecules of ATP are produced in two ways in glycolysis by

(i) direct transfer of phosphate to ADP.

(ii) oxidation of NADH produced during glycolysis to NAD^+. (2+1)

28. Name the site (s) of pyruvate synthesis. Also, write the chemical reaction, wherein pyruvic acid dehydrogenase acts as a catalyst. **NCERT Exemplar**

Ans Pyruvate synthesis takes place in cytoplasm by the process of glycolysis. (1)

The chemical reaction, wherein pyruvic acid dehydrogenase acts as a catalyst is as follows

The reactions catalysed by pyruvic dehydrogenase require the participation of several coenzymes, including NAD^+ and Co-A.

$$\text{Pyruvic acid} + \text{Co-A} + NAD^+ \xrightarrow[\text{Pyurvate dehydrogenase}]{Mg^{2+}} \text{Acetyl Co-A} + NADH + H^+$$ (2)

29. It is known that red muscle fibres in animals can work for longer periods of time continuously. How is this possible? **NCERT Exemplar**

Ans Red or Dark muscles store myoglobin and hence, oxygen for meeting the gap between supply and consumption during continuous activity. Therefore, these muscles can continuously work and respire aerobically for long periods.

High proportion of these muscles allow athletes to participate in long duration events like cycling, swimming and distance running, etc. (3)

30. Does pyruvic acid enter the Krebs' cycle directly?

Ans No, before pyruvic acid as such does not enter Krebs' cycle, pyruvate is first decarboxylated, and then oxidised by the enzyme pyruvate dehydrogenase to form acetyl Co-A. This molecule enters the mitochondria for further oxiation reaction. This is the connecting link between glycolysis and Krebs' cycle.

During the process, NAD^+ is reduced to $NADH + H^+$.

The summary of the reaction is given below

$$\text{Pyruvic acid} + \text{Co-A} + NAD^+ \xrightarrow[Mg^{2+}]{\text{Pyruvate dehydrogenase}} \text{Acetyl Co-A} + CO_2 + NADH + H^+$$

During this process, two molecules of NADH are produced (from the metabolism of two molecules of pyruvic acid produced during glycolysis), and thus, it results in a net gain of 6 ATP molecules (2 NADH × 3 = 6 ATP). (3)

Long Answer Type Questions

5 Marks

31. **Give the schematic representation of glycolysis.** **NCERT**

Ans Refer to text on page no. 343 and 344.

32. **Explain the major steps of Krebs' cycle. Where does this process occur in a cell ?**

Ans Refer to text on page no. 345 and 346.

33. **Describe output of TCA cycle in terms of its end products. Also, discuss its importance in the metabolism of living cell.**

Ans Refer to text on page no. 345-346.

TOPIC 03 Respiration : The Generation of Energy Currency

At the end of Krebs' cycle, the oxidation of glucose is completed as it has given out $6CO_2$ molecules. But the energy obtained till now is very less (i.e. 2ATPs in each glycolysis and Krebs' cycle).

Thus, the full amount of energy is yet to be obtained from substrate, i.e. **glucose**. This occurs through the following steps in the respiratory process and utilises the energy stored in the $NADH + H^+$ and $FADH_2$.

Electron Transport System (ETS)

It is the metabolic pathway through which the electron passes from one carrier to another. It occurs in the inner mitochondrial membrane.

The electron transport system consists of four enzyme complexes, which are arranged in a series on the inner membrane of the mitochondria.

(i) Electrons from NADH produced in citric acid cycle are oxidised by NADH dehydrogenase (complex I) and are transferred to ubiquinone located within the inner membrane of the mitochondria.

(ii) Reducing equivalents are also received by ubiquinone *via* $FADH_2$ (complex II), generated during the oxidation of succinate in the citric acid cycle. This reduced ubiquinone (ubiquinol) is then oxidised with the electron transfer to cytochrome-*c* (small protein attached to the outer surface of the inner membrane).

Now, *via* cytochrome-*b*, c_1 complex (complex III). Cytochrome-*c*, acts as a mobile carrier for transfer of electrons between complex III and IV.

(iii) The (complex IV), known as cytochrome-*c* oxidase complex contains cytochromes-*a*, a_3 and two copper centres.

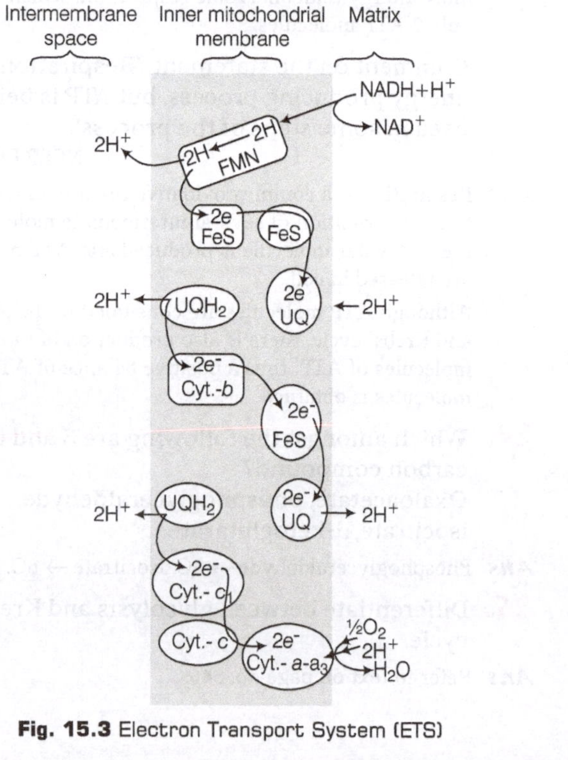

Fig. 15.3 Electron Transport System (ETS)

During the course of transfer, when electrons pass from one carrier molecule to another (*via* complex I to IV) in the electron transport chain, they get coupled to ATP synthase (i.e. complex V) for the production of ATP from ADP and inorganic phosphate. The number of ATP molecules synthesised depends on the nature of the electron donor.

One molecule of NADH on oxidation provides 3 molecules of ATP while one $FADH_2$ produces 2 molecules of ATP, because its redox potential is higher than NADH and thus, enters the ETS after bypassing the first site of phosphorylation. The electrons are finally accepted by **oxygen** having the highest redox potential in the series which along with H^+ ions forms water.

Aerobic process of respiration takes place only in the presence of O_2. The role of O_2 is limited at the terminal stage of the process. Yet, the presence of oxygen is vital because it drives the whole process by removing hydrogen from the system.

Oxidative Phosphorylation

It is the synthesis of energy rich ATP molecules with the help of energy liberated by oxidation of reduced coenzymes produced during respiration. Oxidative phosphorylation in mitochondria is catalysed by a multicomponent enzymatic complex called **ATP synthase** (complex V) or **coupling factor.** The ATP synthase complex consists of two major components

(i) **F_1-particle** The head piece is a peripheral membrane protein complex and contains the site for ATP synthesis from ADP and inorganic phosphate.

(ii) **F_0-particle** It is an integral membrane protein complex that forms the channel through which protons cross the inner membrane.

The passage of protons through the channel is coupled to the catalytic site of the F_1 component for the production of ATP. For every $2H^+$ that passes through F_0 from the intermembrane space to the matrix (down the electrochemical proton gradient), one ATP molecule is produced.

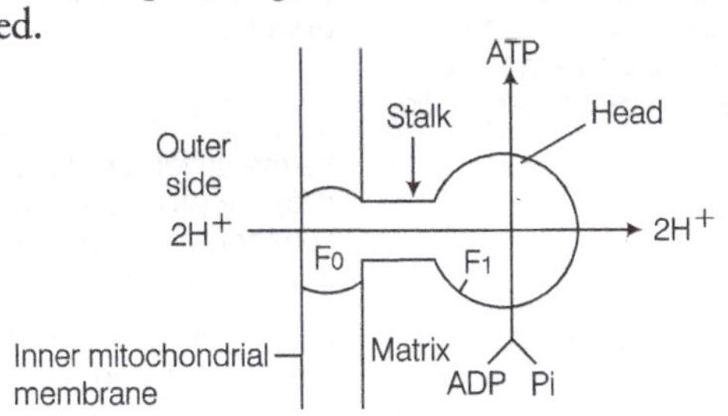

Fig. 15.4 Diagrammatic representation of ATP synthesis in mitochondria

Chemiosmotic Hypothesis

Peter Mitchel proposed this hypothesis in 1961. According to this hypothesis, the ATP molecule is synthesised during electron transport by the movement of hydrogen ions H^+ or protons across the mitochondrial membrane. The electron transfer *via* ETC pumps protons out of the mitochondrial matrix into intermitochondrial space. Thus, the pH of matrix becomes higher, while that of intermitochondrial space become lowered. Due to this movement of $H^+$and change in pH, an electrochemical gradient is generated.

This electrochemical gradient is responsible for the generation of a Proton Motive Force (PMF). Due to which, protons flow back to the matrix. During this flow, energy is released. This energy is used in the formation of ATP by ATP synthase.

The Respiratory Balance Sheet

The complete aerobic breakdown of one molecule of glucose results in the release of 2 molecules of NADH from glycolysis and 8 molecules of NADH and 2 molecules of $FADH_2$ within the mitochondrial matrix.

The calculation of the net gain of ATP for every glucose molecule oxidised can be made only on certain assumptions.

All pathways function in an orderly sequential manner with one substrate forming the next with glycolysis, TCA cycle and ETS pathway following one after another.

NADH synthesised during glycolysis is transferred into the mitochondria for oxidative phosphorylation.

None of the intermediates in the pathway are utilised to synthesise any other compound.

Only glucose is being respired, no other alternative substrates are entering in the pathway at any of the intermediary stages.

But this kind of assumptions are not exactly valid in a living system due to the following reasons

(i) All pathways do not take place one after another instead, they work simultaneously.

(ii) Substrates tend to enter and withdraw from the pathways whenever required.

(iii) Utilisation of ATP takes place at the time of need.

(iv) Rates of enzyme actions are controlled by multiple means.

Yet, inspite of all these reasons, it is necessary to do this exercise in order to appreciate the beauty and efficiency of the living system in extracting and storing of energy.

Net Gain of ATP

Due to all the criteria mentioned above, it is predicted that there can be net gain of 36 ATP molecules from one molecule of glucose during aerobic respiration as given below

Glycolysis	2 ATP directly	=	2 ATP
	2 molecules of NADH	=	6 ATP
Pyruvic acid to acetyl Co-A	2 molecules of NADH	=	6 ATP
Citric acid cycle	6 molecules of NADH	=	18 ATP
	2 molecules of FADH	=	4 ATP
	2 molecules of GTP	=	2 ATP
	Total	=	38 ATP

In eukaryotic cells, 2 molecules of ATP are spent for transporting 2 molecules of NADH formed during glycolysis (in the cytoplasm) to the mitochondria, hence the net gain is 36 molecules of ATP.

Fermentation

Various microorganisms, bacteria, animals and plants are known to catabolise pyruvic acid into various organic compounds depending upon the specific enzymes they possess.

Some of these types are as follows

(i) **During Alcoholic Fermentation,** in fungi (e.g. yeast), and some higher plants, the incomplete oxidation of glucose is achieved under anaerobic condition by a series of reactions in which pyruvic acid is converted to CO_2 and ethanol.

It is done under two steps

(a) **Pyruvic acid** is first decarboxylated to acetaldehyde formed in the presence of enzyme **pyruvic acid decarboxylase.**

$$CH_3COCOOH \rightarrow \underset{\text{(Acetaldehyde)}}{CH_3CHO} + CO_2$$

(b) This acetaldehyde is further reduced to **ethyl alcohol** or **ethanol** in the presence of enzyme, i.e. **alcohol dehydrogenase.**

$$CH_3CHO + NADH + H^+ \rightarrow \underset{\text{(Ethanol)}}{C_2H_5OH} + NAD^+$$

(ii) **During Lactic Acid Fermentation** which occurs in muscles, organisms like some bacteria produce lactic acid as an end product from pyruvic acid.

During the reduction, the pyruvic acid produced in glycolysis is reduced by $NADH_2$ to form lactic acid, CO_2 is not produced and $NADH_2$ is oxidised to NAD^+. This reaction is catalysed by **lactic acid dehydrogenase,** FMN proteins and Zn^{2+} ions.

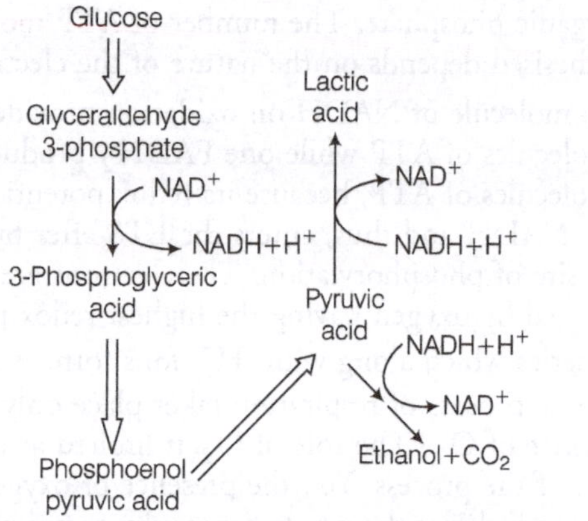

Fig 15.5 Major pathways of anaerobic respiration

Likewise, in case of animal cells also (such as muscles) during exercise, when there is inadequate amount of oxygen for cellular respiration, pyruvic acid is reduced to lactic acid in the presence of enzyme **lactate dehydrogenase.**

Thus, in both the processes oxidation of reducing $(NADH + H^+)$ agent takes place.

Energy Yield in Fermentation

In both alcoholic and lactic acid fermentation, the energy released is very less, i.e. not more than 7% of the energy is released from glucose and not all of it is trapped as high energy bonds of ATP. Also, the fermentation processes are proved to be hazardous in nature because either acid or alcohol is produced on oxidation.

Apart from this, yeasts may also poison themselves to death if the concentration of alcohol reaches about 13%.

Differences between Glycolysis and Fermentation

Glycolysis	Fermentation
It is the first step of respiration which occurs without requirement of oxygen and is common to both aerobic and anaerobic mode of respiration.	It is anaerobic respiration which does not require oxygen.
It produces pyruvic acid.	Fermentation produces different products. The common ones are ethanol (and CO_2) and lactic acid.
It produces two molecules of NADH per glucose molecule.	It generally utilises NADH produced during glycolysis.
Glycolysis forms 2ATP molecules per glucose molecule.	It does not produce ATP.

Comparison between Fermentation and Aerobic Respiration

Fermentation	Aerobic Respiration
It accounts for only a partial breakdown of glucose.	It accounts for complete degradation of glucose to CO_2 and H_2O.
There is net gain of only two molecules of ATP for each molecule of glucose degraded to pyruvic acid.	In this, many more molecules of ATP are generated (i.e. 38).
Electron transport is absent in this.	It involves electron transport system.

Knowledge Plus

ATP (Adenosine Triphosphate) is formed of an adenine, a ribose and a row of three phosphate radicals attached to ribose. ATP was discovered by Karl Lohman in 1929.

Fritz Lipmann (1941) discovered the functioning of ATP through build up and hydrolysis of high energy phosphate bond, Lipmann is called father of ATP cycle.

The conversion of ATP to ADP yields about 7.3 kcal/mol of energy. This is the energy source in a variety of biological processes occurring in both plants and animals.

Amphibolic Pathway

The term amphibolic is used to denote a biochemical pathway involving both catabolism and anabolism, e.g. the citric acid cycle, acts as a central metabolic pathway that completes the oxidative degradation of monosaccharides, fats and amino acids. Usually, glucose is the primary substrate for respiration for most of the organisms.

All carbohydrates are first converted into glucose before they are used for respiration. Different substrates like fats and proteins can also be respired, but they do not enter the respiratory pathway at the very first step.

If fats have to enter the pathway, they first have to be converted into fatty acids and glycerol. Fatty acids are then degraded into **acetyl Co-A,** which **enters the citric acid** cycle. Glycerol is first converted to 3-phosphoglyceraldehyde (PGAL), before entering the pathway. Likewise, the proteins (if acts as respiratory substrates) are degraded by **proteases** into individual amino acids which after deamination (removal of amine group from a molecule) enters the citric acid cycle either as pyruvate or acetyl Co-A.

Thus, it is clear from the above discussion that respiration involves breakdown of organic compounds. It has been considered as catabolic process and the respiratory pathway is called **catabolic pathway**.

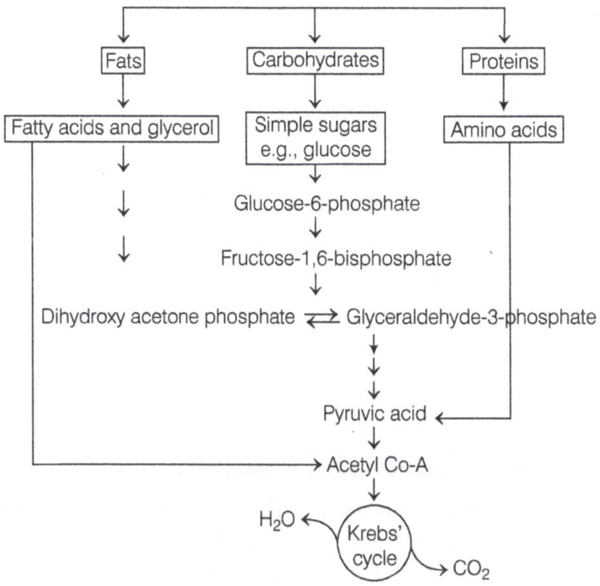

Fig. 15.6 Interrelationship among metabolic pathway showing respiration mediated breakdown of different organic molecules to CO_2 and H_2O

But at the same time certain intermediates of respiratory pathway are also withdrawn in order to synthesise other compounds, e.g. fatty acids would be broken down to acetyl Co-A, but when organisms need to synthesise fatty acids acetyl Co-A would be withdrawn from respiratory pathway. Hence, respiratory pathway comes into picture both during breakdown and synthesis. Breaking down processes within living organism is catabolism and synthesis is anabolism. Thus, it would be better to consider the respiratory pathway as an amphibolic pathway rather than as a catabolic one.

Respiratory Quotient (RQ)

It is the ratio of the volume of CO_2 evolved to the volume of O_2 consumed in respiration. It is also known as respiratory ratio.

$$RQ = \frac{\text{Volume of } CO_2 \text{ evolved}}{\text{Volume of } O_2 \text{ consumed}}$$

The respiratory quotient tend to vary with respiratory substrate used during respiration. This can be understood from following

(i) **Respiratory Quotient of Carbohydrates** When carbohydrates are used as substrate and are completely oxidised, the RQ is always 1 (because amount of CO_2 evolved is always equal to the amount of O_2 consumed.

$$C_6H_{12}O_6 + 6O_2 \longrightarrow 6CO_2 + 6H_2O + \text{Energy}$$

$$RQ = \frac{6CO_2}{6O_2} = 1.0$$

(ii) **Respiratory Quotient of Fats** If the respiratory substrate is fat, then RQ of the respiring cells will be less than 1, because the volume of CO_2 evolved is quite less in comparison to the volume of O_2 being consumed.

Calculations for a fatty acid, tripalmitin, if used as a substrate is shown below

$$\underset{\text{Tripalmitin}}{2(C_{51}H_{98}O_6)} + 145O_2 \longrightarrow 102CO_2 + 98H_2O + \text{Energy}$$

$$RQ = \frac{102CO_2}{145O_2} = 0.7$$

Note Fats always require more amount of O_2 for their oxidation as compared to the other substrates.

(iii) **Respiratory Quotient of Proteins** If the respiratory substrate is protein then the RQ is variable, i.e. it varies from 0.5-0.9 depending upon the oxygen content of the substrate.

Topic Practice 3

Multiple Choice Questions

1 Mark

1. Which one of following is complex V of the ETS of inner mitochondrial membrane?
(a) NADH dehydrogenase
(b) Cytochrome oxidase
(c) Ubiquinone
(d) ATP synthase

Ans (d) The complex V of ETS of mitochondrial membrane is ATP synthase, which has a head piece, stalk and a base piece.
Out of these, the head piece is identified as the coupling factor-1(F_1), stalk portion is necessary for binding F_1 to inner mitochondrial membrane and base piece is isolated as F_0 and present within the inner mitochondrial membrane.

2. The main purpose of electron transport chain is to
(a) cycle NADH+ H^+ back to NAD^+
(b) use the intermediate from TCA cycle
(c) breakdown pyruvic acid
(d) All of the above

Ans (a) In electron transport chain, respiratory processes are to release and utilise the energy stored in NADH + H^+ and $FADH_2$. This is accomplished when they are oxidised through the electron transport system and the electrons are passed on to O_2, resulting in the formation of H_2O.

3. Correct sequence of electron acceptor of ATP synthesis is
(a) cyt- a, a_3, b, c
(b) cyt-b, c, a, a_3
(c) cyt-b, c, a_3, a
(d) cyt-c, b, a, a_3

Ans (b) The electron acceptors of respiratory chains occur in linear sequences (cyt- b, c, a, a_3) and their enzymes are components of the inner mitochondrial membrane.

4. How many NADH + H^+ molecules are released from a single pyruvate in Krebs' cycle?
(a) 3 (b) 6 (c) 12 (d) 8

Ans (a) One molecule of pyruvic acid converted to acetyl Co-A for 3 molecules of NADH + H^+.

5. From one molecule of glucose during oxidative phosphorylation, the total gain of ATP is
(a) 40 (b) 38 (c) 34 (d) 30

Ans (c) 34 molecules of ATP (30 through NADH and 4 through $FADH_2$) are obtained as a result of oxidative phosphorylation. Rest 4 molecules are obtained as a result of direct phosphorylation.

6. Oxidative phosphorylation is
(a) formation of ATP by transfer of phosphate group from a substrate to ADP
(b) oxidation of phosphate group in ATP
(c) addition of phosphate to ATP
(d) formation of ATP by energy released from electron removed during substrate oxidation

Ans (a) Oxidative phosphorylation is the synthesis of energy rich ATP molecules with the help of energy liberated during oxidation of reduced coenzymes (NADH, $FADH_2$).

7. The three boxes in this diagram represent the three major biosynthetic pathways in aerobic respiration. Arrows represent net reactants or products

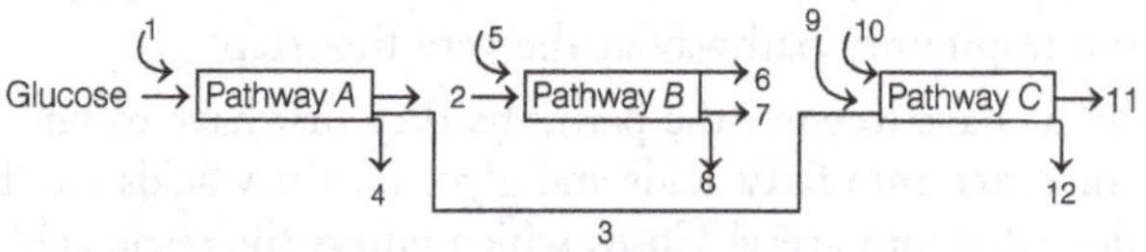

Arrows numbered 4, 8 and 12 can all be
(a) NADH
(b) ATP
(c) H_2O
(d) FAD^+ or $FADH_2$

Ans (b) Pathway *A* is glycolysis, pathway *B* is the Krebs' cycle and pathway *C* is oxidative phosphorylation.

Arrow 1	–	ADP or NAD^+
Arrow 2	–	Pyruvate
Arrow 3	–	NADH
Arrow 4	–	ATP
Arrow 5	–	ADP, NAD^+ or FAD
Arrow 6 and 7	–	$FADH_2$ and NADH

(either one can be 6 or 7)

Arrow 8	–	ATP or CO_2
Arrow 9 and 10 one	–	O_2 and ADP (either can be 9 or 10)
Arrow 11 and 12 one can	–	H_2O and ATP (either be 11 or 12)

8. Choose the correct combination of labelling of the molecules involved in the pathway of anaerobic respiration in yeast.

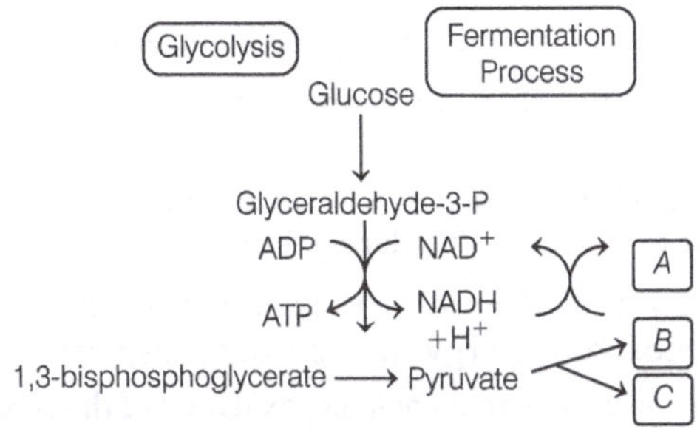

(a) *A*–Ethanol, *B*–CO_2, *C*–Acetaldehyde
(b) *A*–CO_2, *B*–Ethanol, *C*–Acetaldehyde
(c) *A*–Acetaldehyde, *B*–CO_2, *C*–Ethanol
(d) *A*–Ethanol, *B*–Acetaldehyde, *C*–CO_2

Ans (d) Alcoholic fermentation by yeast causes decarboxylation of pyruvate to acetaldehyde producing CO_2 as byproduct. Acetaldehyde accepts 2H atoms from $NADH_2$ to produce ethanol.

9. In which one of the following processes, CO_2 is not released ?
(a) Aerobic respiration in plants
(b) Aerobic respiration in animals
(c) Alcoholic fermentation
(d) Lactate fermentation

Ans (d) Lactic acid fermentation is a process by which glucose, fructose and sucrose are converted into energy and the metabolite lactate.
It is an anaerobic fermentation reaction which occurs in some bacteria and animal cells that allow glycolysis to continue by ensuring that NADH is returned to its oxidised state (NAD^+).

10. In alcoholic fermentation,
(a) there is no electron donor
(b) oxygen is the electron acceptor
(c) triose phosphate is the electron donor, while acetaldehyde is the electron acceptor
(d) triose phosphate is the electron donor, while pyruvic acid is the electron acceptor

Ans (d) In alcoholic fermentation, NADH (formed during conversion of triose-3-phosphate to 3-phosphoglycerate) is oxidised to NAD^+.
Electrons are accepted by acetaldehyde formed by decarboxylation of pyruvate.

11. Pyruvate $\longrightarrow C_2H_5OH + CO_2$
The above reaction needs two enzymes named as
(a) pyruvate decarboxylase and alcohol dehydrogenase
(b) pyruvate decarboxylase and enolase
(c) pyruvate decarboxylase and pyruvate kinase
(d) pyruvate carboxylase and aldolase

Ans (a) During fermentation, the pyruvic acid releases one molecule of CO_2 to produce acetaldehyde. The acetaldehyde, then reoxidises NADH and is itself reduced to ethanol. These reactions are catalysed by the enzyme, pyruvic acid decarboxylase and alcohol dehydrogenase.

12. Which of the following substrate can enter into the respiration?
(a) Glucose (b) Amino acid
(c) Fatty acid (d) All of these

Ans (d) Respiratory pathway is involved in both anabolism and catabolism, hence it is regarded as amphibolic pathway.
In respiratory pathway not only the glucose, but also amino acid and fatty acid can be used as intermediatory substances used as precursors for many biomolecules of cells.

13. The Respiratory Quotient (RQ) or Respiratory ratio is

(a) $RQ = \dfrac{\text{Volume of } O_2 \text{ evolved}}{\text{Volume of } CO_2 \text{ consumed}}$

(b) $RQ = \dfrac{\text{Volume of } O_2 \text{ consumed}}{\text{Volume of } CO_2 \text{ evolved}}$

(c) $RQ = \dfrac{\text{Volume of } CO_2 \text{ consumed}}{\text{Volume of } O_2 \text{ evolved}}$

(d) $RQ = \dfrac{\text{Volume of } CO_2 \text{ evolved}}{\text{Volume of } O_2 \text{ consumed}}$

Ans (d) RQ is the ratio of volume of carbon dioxide evolved and volume of oxygen consumed in the process of respiration.

14. The respiratory quotient during cellular respiration would depend on the
(a) nature of enzymes involved
(b) nature of the substrate
(c) amount of carbon dioxide released
(d) amount of oxygen utilised

Ans (b) RQ is the ratio of the volume of carbon dioxide released to the volume of oxygen taken in respiration. It depends on the nature of the substrate, which is oxidised. For carbohydrates RQ is one, for fats and proteins less than one but more than one for organic acids, etc.

15. **Refer the given equation.**

$$2(C_{51}H_{98}O_6) + 145\ O_2 \rightarrow 102\ CO_2 + 98\ H_2O + \text{Energy}$$

The respiratory quotient in this case is

(a) 1 (b) 0.7

(c) 1.45 (d) 1.62

Ans (b) The given compound ($C_{51}H_{98}O_6$) is tripalmitin (2 molecules) used as a substrate.

This substrate is used in respiration. The respiratory quotient is less than 1. The given below derivation explains it in a much clear way.

$$\text{Respiratory quotient} = \frac{\text{Evolved } CO_2}{\text{Consumed } O_2} = \frac{102\ CO_2}{145\ O_2} = 0.7$$

Very Short Answer Type Questions

1 Mark

16. **Why oxygen is an ultimate acceptor of electrons in ETS?**

Ans Oxygen is the ultimate acceptor of electrons in ETS because it is highly reactive and combines with protons to form metabolic water.

17. **What is the name given to the oxidation, found in aerobic respiration occurring towards the end of the catabolic process involving the passage of both electrons and protons of reduced coenzymes to oxygen.**

Ans The name given is terminal oxidation.

18. **At which step of respiration, hydrogen of $NADH_2$ is used?**

Ans The hydrogen atoms accepted by $NADH_2$ during glycolysis are introduced to route I of ETS. In this route, 3 ATP molecules are produced.

19. **F_0-F_1 particles participate in the synthesis of ....** **NCERT Exemplar**

Ans ATP (Adenosine Triphosphate), the energy currency of the cell.

20. **Name the haem protein present in the ETC.**

Ans Cytochrome is a small protein containing iron atom, so it is called haem protein.

21. **Mention the number of protons that passes through complex V for the synthesis of 2 molecules of ATP.**

Ans Two pairs of protons (i.e. 4) pass through complex V for the synthesis of 2 molecules of ATP from 2 ADP and 2 inorganic phosphate molecules.

22. **Mention the significance of F_0-F_1 combination in mitochondria.**

Ans It helps in maintaining proton gradient on the two sides of the membrane. It also helps in synthesis of ATP molecule.

23. **What is oxidative phosphorylation?** **NCERT**

Ans It refers to the formation of ATP in the mitochondria, utilising the energy obtained by the oxidation of organic molecules.

24. **Name the unit of oxidative phosphorylation.**

Ans The unit of oxidative phosphorylation is oxysomes.

25. **What makes dough spongy when it is kept over night?**

Ans Dough kept overnight in warm water becomes spongy due to release of CO_2 during fermentation.

26. **Why does anaerobic respiration/fermentation yields less energy than aerobic respiration?**

Ans It happens due to incomplete oxidation of the substrate.

27. **The product of aerobic glycolysis in skeletal muscle and anaerobic fermentation in yeast are respectively ...... and ....**

Ans The product of aerobic glycolysis in skeletal muscles is pyruvic acid while in anaerobic fermerntation in yeast ethanol and CO_2 are produced.

28. **What are the end products of alcoholic fermentation?**

Ans Ethyl alcohol and CO_2 are the end products of alcoholic fermentation.

29. **List two instances where lactic acid is formed by fermentation.**

Ans Instances where lactic acid is formed by fermentation are

(i) During fermentation by lactic acid bacteria.

(ii) During strenuous exercise, in the striated muscles in humans.

30. **What is the respiratory quotient when fats are used in respiration?**

Ans If the respiratory substrate is fat, then RQ of the respiring cells will be less than one because the volume of CO_2 evolved is quite less in comparison to the volume of O_2 being consumed.

31. **Which of the following will release more energy on oxidation ? Arrange them in ascending order.** **NCERT Exemplar**

(i) 1 gm of fat

(ii) 1 gm of protein

(iii) 1 gm of glucose

(iv) 0.5 gm of protein + 0.5 gm glucose

Ans The ascending order of substrate that will release more energy on oxidation will be as follows

1 gm protein < 0.5 gm in potein < 1 gm glucose < 1 gm fat + 0.5 gm glucose.

Short Answer Type I Questions

(2 Marks)

32. **If a person is feeling dizzy, glucose or fruit juice is given immediately, but not a cheese sandwich, which might have more energy. Explain.** **NCERT Exemplar**

Ans If a person is feeling dizzy, glucose or fruit juice is given immediately because, it is readily oxidised and oxidation of 1 g of glucose yields more energy than a cheese sandwich. (2)

33. **Oxygen is critical for aerobic respiration. Explain its role with respect to ETS.**

Ans Oxygen is critical for aerobic respiration due to following reasons

(i) It acts as the terminal acceptor of hydrogen.

(ii) It drives the whole process by removing hydrogen from the system. (1×2)

34. **Where is cytochrome-*c* located? What is its function?**

Ans Cytochrome-*c* is attached to the outer surface of the inner membrane of mitochondria.

It acts as a mobile carrier for transfer of electrons between complex III and complex IV. (1+1)

35. **(i) Where is the respiratory electron transport system located in a cell?**

(ii) What compound is the terminal electron acceptor in aerobic respiration?

Ans (i) The respiratory electron transport system is present in the membranes of mitochondria.

(ii) Oxygen. (2)

36. **What is fermentation? Name any two organic compounds produced in the process.**

Ans Anaerobic respiration is also called fermentation. It involves the production of energy from food nutrients in the absence of oxygen. Organic compounds produced in the process are

(i) Ethyl alcohol in yeast cell

(ii) Lactic acid in muscles. (1+1)

37. **What would be the RQ value of yeast if it were to respire glucose anaerobically?**

Ans The RQ will be infinity (∞) during anaerobic respiration. In anaerobic respiration, CO_2 is evolved, but oxygen is not used.

Therefore, RQ in such a case, will be infinite.

e.g. $C_6H_{12}O_6 \rightarrow 2C_2H_5OH + 2CO_2 + \text{Energy}$

$$RQ = \frac{2CO_2 \text{ (2 molecules)}}{O_2 \text{(zero molecules)}} = \text{Infinity.}$$ (2)

38. **Glucose, malic acid, oxalic acid and tartaric acid are oxidised to give energy in plant cell. Which of the mentioned acids will give RQ of value 4 and why?**

Ans The RQ of value 4 is expected from oxalic acid because it is an organic acid and whenever organic acids are oxidised, then RQ value is always greater than one. (2)

39. **When a substrate is being metabolised, why does not all the energy that is produced get released in one step? It is released in multiple steps. What is the advantage of stepwise release?** **NCERT Exemplar**

Ans The stepwise release of energy have advantage to the cell. Because if all the energy from the glucose would be released at once then most of it would be lost in the form of light and heat. This energy is trapped in ATP which is utilised in various energy requiring processes of the organisms and for the synthesis of other biomolecules in the cell. (2)

40. **When is RQ slightly more than unity?**

Ans RQ slightly more than unity is found when organic acids are broken down as respiratory substrates under aerobic conditions, e.g.

$$\underset{\text{Oxalic acid}}{2(COOH)_2} + O_2 \longrightarrow 4CO_2 + 2H_2O$$

$$RQ \frac{4CO_2}{1O_2} = 4.0$$

$$\underset{\text{Malic acid}}{C_4H_6O_5} + 3O_2 \longrightarrow 4CO_2 + 3H_2O$$

$$RQ = \frac{4CO_2}{3O_2} = 1.3$$ (1+1)

Short Answer Type II Questions

(3 Marks)

41. **Given below is a diagram showing ATP synthesis during aerobic respiration, replace the symbols *A, B, C, D* and *E* by appropriate terms as given below.**

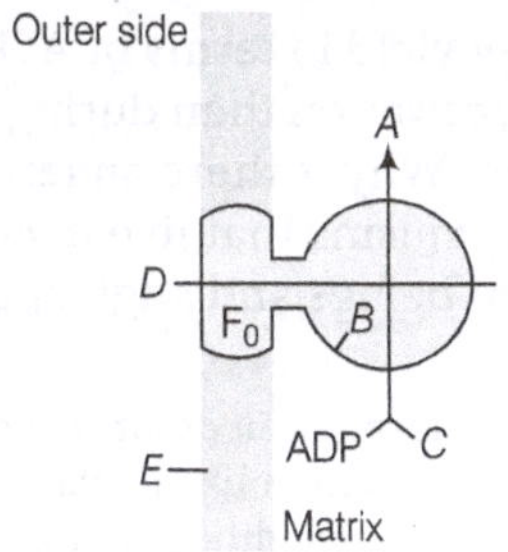

F_1-particle, formation of Pi, $2H^+$, inner mitochondrial membrane, ATP, F_0-particle, ADP. **NCERT Exemplar**

Ans Symbol *A, B, C, D* and *E* in the diagram represents

A — ATP *B* — F_1-particle *C* — Pi

D — $2H^+$ *E* — inner mitochondria membrane. (3)

42. **What are the assumptions made during the calculation of net gain of ATP?** **NCERT**

Ans The calculations of net gain of ATP can be made only on certain assumptions

(i) There is a sequential, orderly pathway functioning with one substrate forming the next and with glycolysis, TCA cycle and ETS pathway following one after another.

(ii) The NADH synthesised in glycolysis is transferred into the mitochondria and undergoes oxidative phosphorylation.

(iii) None of the intermediates in the pathway are utilised to synthesise any other compound.

(iv) Only glucose is being respired, no other alternative substrates are entering in the pathway at any of the intermediary stages. (3)

43. **Respiration is an energy releasing and enzymatically controlled catabolic process, which involves a stepwise oxidative breakdown of organic substances inside living cells. In this statement about respiration explain the meaning of (i) stepwise oxidative breakdown (ii) organic substances (used as substrates).** **NCERT Exemplar**

Ans (i) **Stepwise Oxidative Breakdown** Respiration is a stepwise oxidation of organic molecules in a cell involving main three steps

(i) Glycoysis, (ii) Krebs' cycle, (iii) Electron transport chain. Glucose passes through series of enzymatically controlled reactions and is finally converted into H_2O + ATP + CO_2.

(ii) **Organic Substances** (used as substrates) The organic substances, which are catabolised in the living cells to release energy are called as respirato/ry substrates. Though any food stuff, carbohydrate, fat or protein may act as a respiratory substrate, the common respiratory substrate is glucose because it can be oxidised easily and is present abundantly. (1+2)

44. **The energy yield in terms of ATP is higher in aerobic respiration than during anaerobic respiration. Why is there anaerobic respiration even in organisms that live in aerobic condition like human beings and angiosperms?** **NCERT Exemplar**

Ans The anaerobic respiration occurs even in organisms that live in aerobic condition like human beings and angiosperms under conditions of oxygen scarcity.

Under intense use, muscles demand too much energy (ATP) and consume much more oxygen to produce that energy. This high consumption leads to oxygen scarcity and the muscle cells begin to make lactic acid by anaerobic respiration trying to fulfill their energetic needs. Similarly, yeast cells under deficient conditions carry out anaerobic respiration. (3)

45. **RuBP carboxylase, PEPase, pyruvate dehydrogenase, ATPase, cytochrome oxidase, hexokinase, lactate dehydrogenase. Select/Choose enzymes from the list above which are involved in**
(i) photosynthesis
(ii) respiration. **NCERT Exemplar**

Ans (i) **Photosynthesis** RuBP carboxylase, hexokinase and cytochrome oxidase.

(ii) **Respiration** Pyruvate dehydrogenase, ATPase, lactate dehydrogenase and cytochrome oxidase. (1½ × 2)

46. **A process is occurring throughout the day in 'X' organism. Cells are participating in this process. During this process, ATP, CO_2 and water are formed. It is not a light dependent process.**
(i) Name the process.
(ii) It is a catabolic or an anabolic process.
(iii) What could be the raw material of this process? **NCERT Exemplar**

Ans (i) Cellular respiration.

(ii) It is an amphibolic pathway, which involves both anabolism and catabolism.

(iii) Carbohydrates, proteins, fats and organic acids can be the raw material; but glucose is the form that ultimately enters the pathway. (1×3)

47. **Discuss 'the respiratory pathway is an amphibolic pathway.'** **NCERT**

Ans Refer to text on page no. 353.

48. **Define respiratory quotient. What is its value for fats?** **NCERT**

Ans Refer to text on page no. 353-354.

Long Answer Type Questions

(5 Marks)

49. **Explain ETS.** **NCERT**

Ans Refer to text on page no. 350-351.

50. **How many ATP molecules are produced by complete aerobic and anaerobic respiration of the glucose molecule?**

Ans Refer to text on page no. 350-351.

51. **What is the significance of stepwise release of energy in respiration?** **NCERT**

Ans Complex organic food molecules such as sugars, fats and proteins are rich sources of energy for cells. The energy in these food molecules is stored in the form of chemical bonds. During the oxidation of each of these molecules in the presence of O_2, these bonds are broken down. It happens in the enzymatically controlled stepwise reactions.

So, at different steps, slowly energy is released in the form of ATP molecules as per the need of cells. (5)

SUMMARY

- **Respiration** is defined as the process of breaking of complex C—C bonds with the help of O_2 to release energy. The compounds oxidised during this process are called **respiratory substrates.** Respiration can be aerobic or anaerobic.
- **Aerobic respiration** occurs in the presence of oxygen and respiratory substrate is completely oxidised during this. Energy released is utilised for ATP synthesis. It takes place in two stages-glycolysis and breakdown of pyruvic acid, and the end products are CO_2, H_2O and energy.
- **Glycolysis** is an oxidative process in which glucose is converted into pyruvic acid and it is common in both aerobic and anaerobic respiration. Net gain in glycolysis is 8 ATP molecules.
- **Breakdown of pyruvic acid** involves three steps which are oxidative decarboxylation (formation of acetyl Co-A), Krebs' cycle (oxidation of acetyl Co-A into organic acids, CO_2 and H_2O), electron transport chain (generation of ATP molecules).
- **Oxidative phosphorylation** is the process of production of ATP *via* terminal oxidation of reduced coenzymes. Terminal oxidation refers to the acceptance of electrons at the end of respiratory chain.
- **External factors** affecting aerobic respiration are concentration of O_2, CO_2, light, temperature and minerals.
- **Internal factors** that affect aerobic respiration are water content of the cells, kind and age of tissue, amount and type of substrate available.
- **Anaerobic respiration** occurs in the absence of oxygen and respiratory substrate is partially oxidised and energy remains unutilised. The main process includes–alcoholic fermentation, lactic acid fermentation and acetic acid fermentation. Its end products are ethyl alcohol or lactic acid and CO_2.
- **Fermentation** is main process of anaerobic respiration. It takes places after glycolysis when oxygen is absent. It is dependent on type of organism and tissue.
- **Alcoholic fermentation** occurs in yeast with the help of zymase enzyme.
- **Lactic acid fermentation** occurs in lactic acid bacteria and our muscles with the help of enzyme lactate dehydrogenase.
- **Fermentation by microbes** is useful in various industries to produce substances which are useful for mankind, e.g. antibiotics, dairy products, etc.
- **Respiratory Quotient** (RQ) is the ratio of volume of CO_2 released to the volume of O_2 consumed in respiration. It is different for different substrate.
- **RQ** is unity (1) for carbohydrates, infinite for anaerobic respiration, zero(0) for xerophytes.

Chapter Practice

Multiple Choice Questions

1 Mark

1. Phosphorylation of glucose during glycolysis is catalysed by
   (a) phosphoglucomutase
   (b) phosphoglucoisomerase
   (c) hexokinase
   (d) phosphorylase

2. Pyruvic acid, the key product of glycolysis can have many metabolic fates. Under aerobic condition it forms
   (a) lactic acid
   (b) $CO_2 + H_2O$
   (c) acetyl Co-A + CO_2
   (d) enthanol + CO_2

3. The end product of oxidative phosphorylation is
   (a) NADH
   (b) Oxygen
   (c) ATP
   (d) ATP + H_2O

4. The ultimate electron acceptor of respiration in an aerobic organism is
   (a) cytochrome
   (b) oxygen
   (c) hydrogen
   (d) glucose

5. Match the following columns.

	Column I		Column II
A.	Molecular oxygen	1.	α-ketoglutaric acid
B.	Electron acceptor	2.	Hydrogen acceptor
C.	Pyruvate dehydrogenase	3.	Cytochrome-c
D.	Decarboxylation	4.	Acetyl Co-A

Codes

	A	B	C	D
(a)	2	3	4	1
(b)	3	4	2	1
(c)	2	1	3	4
(d)	4	3	1	2

6. Match the following columns.

	Column I		Column II
A.	Oxaloacetate	1.	6-C compound
B.	Phosphoglyceraldehyde	2.	5-C compound
C.	Isocitrate	3.	4-C compound
D.	α-ketoglutarate	4.	3-C compound
		5.	2-C compound

Codes

	A	B	C	D
(a)	4	5	2	3
(b)	3	4	1	2
(c)	3	5	1	2
(d)	2	4	1	5

Assertion-Reason Type Questions

1 Mark

Direction (Q. Nos. 7-15) *In each of the following questions, a statement of Assertion (A) is given followed by corresponding statement of Reason (R). Of the statements, mark the correct answer as*

(a) If both A and R are true and R is the correct explanation of A
(b) If both A and R are true, but R is not the correct explanation of A
(c) If A is true, but R is false
(d) If A is false, but R is true

7. **Assertion** (A) Glycolysis occurs in the cell's cytoplasm.
   Reason (R) Enzymes for glycolysis are found in the cytoplasm. It is common in aerobic/ anaerobic respiration.

8. **Assertion** (A) The conversion of glyceraldehyde-3-phosphate into 1,3-bisphosphoglycerate is an oxidation reaction.
   Reason (R) The reaction in which 1, 3-bisphosphoglycerate is formed from glyceraldehyde-3-phosphate utilises NAD^+.

9. **Assertion** (A) In glycolysis, 4 ATPs are produced.
   Reason (R) The net gain of ATP in glycolysis is 8 ATP.

10. **Assertion** (A) Carbohydrates are used first by most cells in respiration.

Reason (R) Lipids are never used in respiration.

11. **Assertion** (A) Aerobic respiration is bioenergetically more efficient than anaerobic glycolysis.

Reason (R) Aerobic respiration occurs in the presence of oxygen, while fermentation occurs in the absence of oxygen.

12. **Assertion** (A) Yeast cells show alcoholic fermentation.

Reason (R) Fermentation is an aerobic process.

13. **Assertion** (A) GTP is also an energy carrier like ATP.

Reason (R) GTP is the only high energy phosphate produced in the Krebs' cycle.

14. Given below is the metabolic breakdown of respiratory substrate under anerobic condition in living organisms. Study this reaction and comment upon the appropriateness of the Assertion and the Reason.

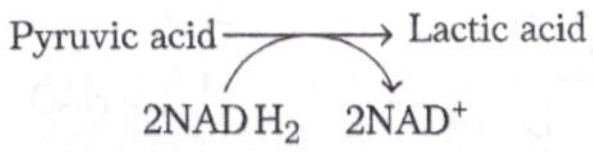

Assertion (A) The above reaction occurs when there is lack of oxygen in muscles leading to muscle cramps.

Reason (R) Accumulation of lactic acid from anaerobic respiration causes cramping in muscles.

15. Given below is the complex V of ETS, which is the actual site of ATP synthesis in mitochondria? Study the given diagrammatic representation and comment upon the appropriateness of the Assertion and the Reason.

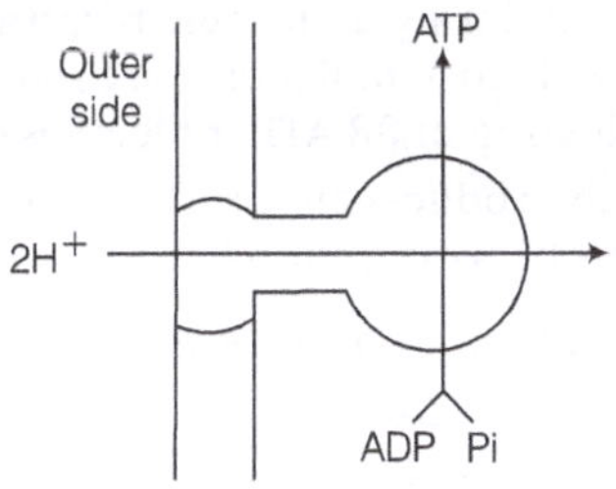

Assertion (A) It is ATP synthase having two parts; one called the F_1 is embedded in the mitochondrial membrane of thylakoid and the other portion is called F_0 that protrudes on the mitochondrial membrane towards the matrix.

Reason (R) The passage of protons through the channel F_0 is coupled to the catalytic site of F_1 component for the production of ATP.

Answers

1. (c)	2. (c)	3. (d)	4. (b)	5. (a)	6. (b)
7. (a)	8. (a)	9. (b)	10. (c)	11. (b)	12. (c)
13. (b)	14. (a)	15. (d)			

Very Short Answer Type Questions

1 Mark

16. What are the products formed by the splitting of fructose-1, 6-bisphosphate?

17. Where does the formation of acetyl Co-A take place in a cell ?

18. For what purpose is the energy from electron transfers used in electron transport chain?

19. Why is no distinction made between ATP and GTP in calculating energy yield in cell respiration ?

Short Answer Type I Questions

2 Marks

20. Why most of the living cells cannot survive without oxygen?

21. Energy is released during the oxidation of compounds in respiration. How is this energy stored and released as and when it is needed?

22. Respiration requires O_2. How did the first cells on the earth manage to survive in an atmosphere that lacked O_2?

23. In a way green plants and cyanobacteria have synthesised all the food on the earth. Comment.

Short Answer Type II Questions

3 Marks

24. Aerobic respiration occurs inside mitochondria in the presence of molecular oxygen. Glycolysis is also called EMP pathway. In glycolysis, net gain is 2 ATP molecules, 2 pyruvate and 2 $NADH_2$.

(i) Name two phases of glycolysis. Which of these two phases produce energy?

(ii) What is the fate of pyruvate after glycolysis?

25. Food is required to attain energy. Energy obtained by the oxidation of food is stored in the living cell in the form of ATP. In ATP, the last two phosphate radicals are attached by bonds of high transfer potential.
   (i) Expand ATP.
   (ii) Who discovered ATP and who is the father of ATP cycle?
   (iii) Why ATP is known as energy currency of the cell ?

26. Respiratory pathway is believed to be a catabolic pathway. However, nature of TCA cycle is amphibolic. Explain.

Long Answer Type Questions

5 Marks

27. Trace the fate of the products formed in glycolysis.

28. Draw a well-labelled diagrammatic representation of TCA cycle.

29. It is necessary to calculate and study the respiratory balance sheet occurring during respiration. Why ?
   What are the factors taken into account for this study?

Case Based Questions

4/5 Marks

30. *Read the following passage and answer the questions that follows.*
   There are three major ways in which different cells handle pyruvate (pyruvic acid) produced by glycolysis. These are lactic acid fermentation, alcoholic fermentation and aerobic respiration.
   Fermentation takes place under anaerobic conditions in many prokaryotes and unicellular eukaryotes for the complete oxidation of glucose to CO_2 and H_2O. However, organisms adopt Krebs' cycle which is also called as aerobic respiration. This required O_2 supply.
   In fermentation, the incomplete oxidation of glucose is achieved under anaerobic conditions by sets of reactions where pyruvate is converted to CO_2 and ethanol. Other organisms like bacteria produce lactic acid from pyruvic acid. In animal cells also, like muscles during exercise, when oxygen is inadequate for cellular respiration, pyruvic acid is reduced to lactic acid.
   In both lactic acid and alcohol fermentation, not much energy is released.
   (i) In which processes, CO_2 is not released?
   (ii) Which compound acts as reducing agent in lactic acid and alcoholic fermentation?
   (iii) Which products are formed by pyruvic acid under aerobic condition?
   (iv) How many ATP molecules are produced when a molecule of glucose undergoes fermentation?
   (v) At which concentration of alcohol, it is poisonous to yeast?

31. The flow chart given below depicts the major pathway of anaerobic respiration. Based on the figure answer the following questions.

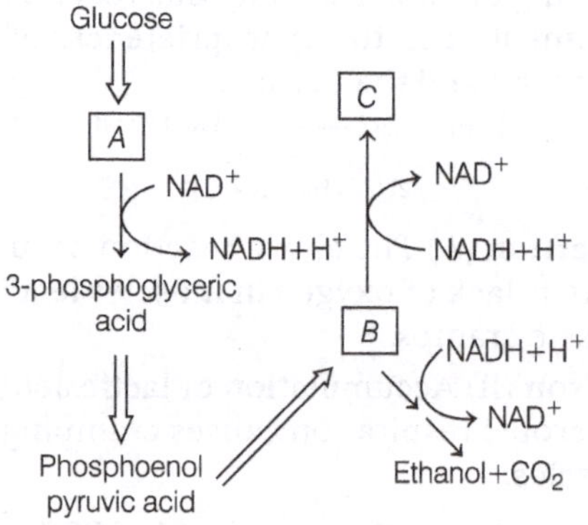

   (i) Identify the *A*, *B* and *C* in the figure given above.
   (ii) In the production of ethanol, pyruvic acid is first converted to acetaldehyde by which enzyme?
   (iii) In yeast during anaerobic respiration, how many glucose molecules are required for the production of 38 ATP molecules?
   (iv) Which products are produced by bacteria in anaerobic respiration?

32. *Read the following passage and answer the questions that follows.*
   The process of respiration in plants includes the utilisation of carbohydrates produced during photosynthesis to produce energy which in turn contributes to the growth of plants.

Respiration in plants occurs in two phases, i.e. light reactions and dark reactions. The first step of respiration is glycolysis in which glucose is oxidised to pyruvic acid. After this, the product of pyruvic acid enters the Krebs' cycle which provides the reducing power to generate many more ATP molecules in the next stage of aerobic respiration, i.e. the electron transport chain.

(i) Glucose-6-phosphate ⟶ Fructose-6-phosphate
Which enzyme is used in the above reaction?

(ii) How many molecules of pyruvic acid are formed in glycolysis?

(iii) What is the name of the 4C compound formed in Krebs' cycle?

(iv) Which is the final electron acceptor in the electron transport system?

(v) In which part of mitochondria does ATP synthesis occur?

33. The data given below shows the effect of exercise intensity on carbohydrate consumption (and lactate production).

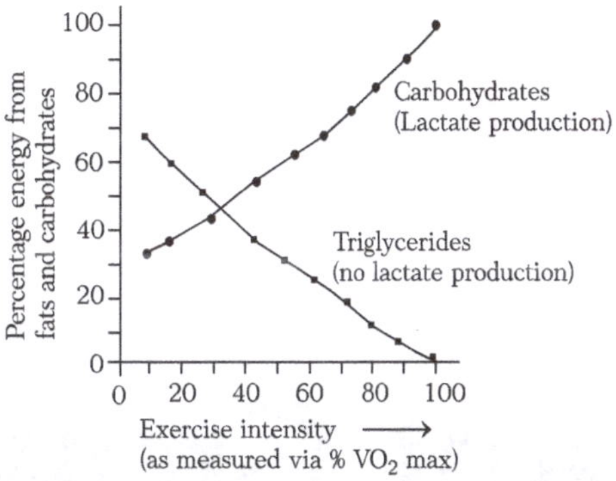

(i) With reference to the above graph what trend is seen for change in cellular respiration with increasing energy demand?

(ii) In our skeletal muscle undergoing anaerobic respiration, lactic acid is formed. What is formed in our muscles under normal aerobic conditions?

(iii) How are lactic acid fermentation and alcoholic fermentation similar? How are they different?

(iv) Name the enzyme involved in lactic acid fermentation.

CHAPTER 16

Plant Growth and Development

f961All plant organs are made up of various kinds of tissues which occupy specific locations within the plant body and perform specific designated functions. Thus, the development of a plant follows a very precise growth pattern. During this period complex body organisation is formed. It produces, roots, leaves, branches, flowers, fruits, seed and then ultimately dies.

TOPIC 01 Growth, Differentiation and Development

Growth

It is regarded as an essential, fundamental and one of the most conspicuous characteristics of a living being. Growth can be defined as a dynamic, irreversible permanent increase in size of an organ, its parts or even an individual cell.

The growth is generally accompanied by the metabolic processes, i.e. anabolic and catabolic reactions occurring in an organism (mainly protein synthesis). Thus, growth in living organism is an intrinsic phenomenon (unlike, non-living organisms in which growth is extrinsic).

Characteristic Feature of Plant Growth

Growth of plant is unique as they retain the capacity for unlimited growth throughout their life. In plants the growth is generally confined only to the meristematic tissues present at definite locations in the plant body. Meristems in the plant have certain cells that have the capacity of dividing and self-perpetuation.

The new cells produced by the division of meristematic cells, soon loose, the ability of dividing and make up the plant body.

The form of growth in which newly produced cells are always being added to the body of the plant by the activity of meristems is called **open form of growth.**

Some plant structures such as leaves, flowers and fruits may show **determinate** growth. These grow upto a size and then undergo death. The vegetative stem and roots show **indeterminate** or indefinite growth.

Regions of Growth

Apical, lateral and intercalary are the special regions, where growth is localised in plants.

At the apex of every root and shoot apical meristems are present which are responsible for the elongation of plant along their axis. This is known as **primary growth** of the plant. The lateral meristems, vascular cambium and cork cambium appear later in life in dicotyledonous plants and gymnosperms and are responsible for the increase in the girth of the stem. This increase in girth is known as **secondary growth** of the plant.

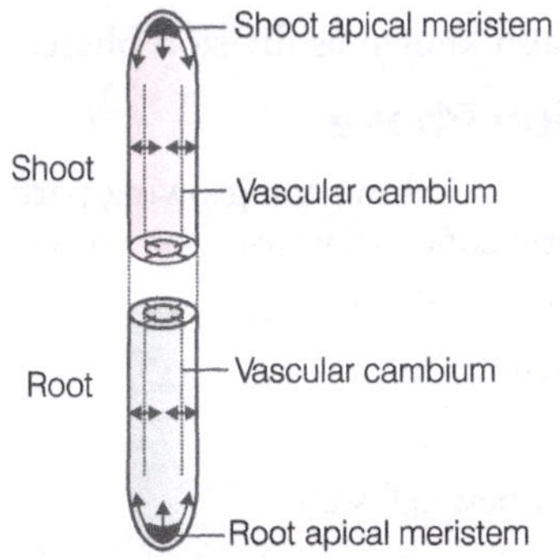

Fig. 16.1 Diagrammatic representation of locations of root apical meristem, shoot apical meristem and vascular cambium. Arrows exhibit the direction of growth of cells and organ.

Measurement of Growth

As stated that at cellular level, growth is the consequence of increase in the amount of protoplasm. It is difficult to measure the increase in the protoplasm directly, so it can generally be measured by measuring some quantity of it that is more or less proportional to it.

Hence, growth can be easily measured by a variety of parameters such as

(i) Dry weight
(ii) Fresh weight
(iii) Length
(iv) Area
(v) Volume
(vi) Cell number

Growth can be expressed in terms of **increase in the cell number**, e.g. single root apical meristem in maize which gives rise to more than 17500 new cells per hour.

It can also be expressed as an increase in the **size of the cell**, e.g. cells in watermelon increases about 350000 times per hour.

Growth can be measured in terms of **length,** of plant parts, e.g. pollen tube and can also be measured in terms of surface area, e.g. leaf surface area.

Various aids designed to measure the growth include horizontal microscope, auxanometer, crescograph (sensitive instrument giving magnification upto 10000 times), etc.

Direct Method

It is a method in which growth is measured using a scale at regular intervals. It is one of the simplest method of measuring growth.

Horizontal Microscope

This microscope is used to measure linear growth of the plant. Here, a horizontal microscope placed over a graduated vertical stand is focussed on a point marked near the growing tip of plant (shoot or root tip). At regular interval microscope is again refocussed to observe any change in the height of the plant by sliding it up (incase of shoot tip) or down (in case of root tip). The difference in the initial and final readings, shows the overall increase in the height of the plant.

Auxanometer

It is an instrument used to register the total growth rate of growth at specific time and overall pattern of growth.

(i) **Arc Auxanometer** It is the most simple type of auxanometer. It is used to measure vertical growth of the plant.

It consists of a small pulley to the axil of which is attached a long pointer sliding over a graduated arc. A thread, one end of which is tied to the stem tip and the other end to a weight passes over the pulley tightly.

As soon as the stem tip increases in length, the pulley moves and the pointer slides over the graduated arc.

By recording the movement of the pointer by angular degrees at particular intervals, the growth rate of the plant can be measured.

$$\text{One angular degree} = \frac{\pi}{180} = \frac{3.142}{180}$$

In linear measurement one angular degree

$$= \frac{3.142}{180} \times \text{radius of the arc (cm)}.$$

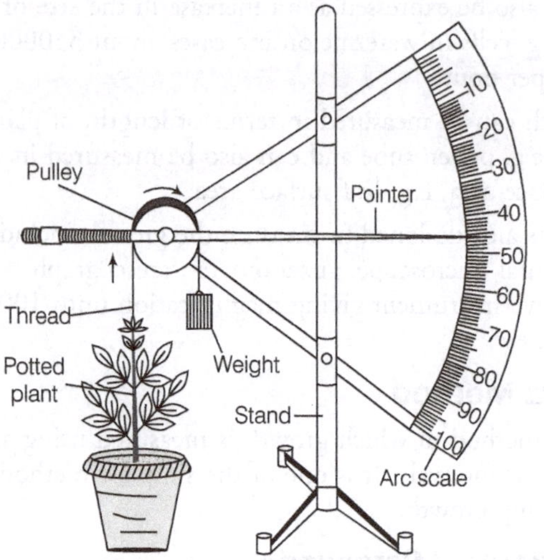

Fig. 16.2 An arc auxanometer

(ii) **Pfeffer's Auxanometer** It is a complex instrument that gives more detailed idea of growth rates in plants (both during day or night time).
It consists of a compound pulley with a small and a large wheel both having the same axil. A thread, one end of which is tied to the stem tip and the other end to a weight passes over the smaller wheel tightly. Another thread whose both ends are tied with weights tightly passes over the larger wheel. Near one end of this thread is attached a pointer which remains in touch with a rotating cylindrical drum covered by a smoked paper.

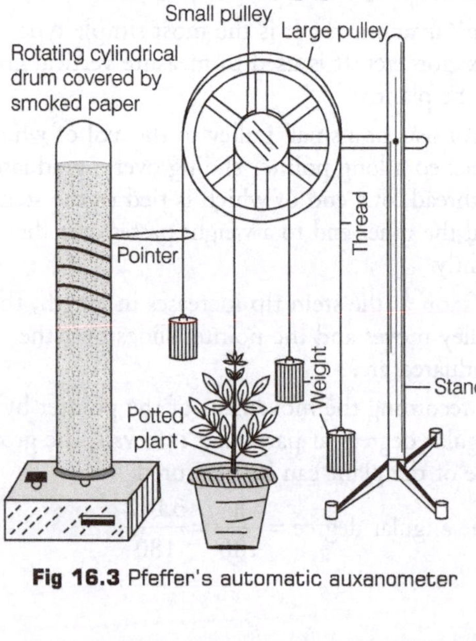

Fig 16.3 Pfeffer's automatic auxanometer

As soon as the stem tip increases in length, the wheels of the pulley move, so that the pointer also moves downward and traces a special white marking on the smoked paper which gives an idea of the growth in the stem tip. Actual increase in length of the stem can be calculated by knowing the radii of larger and smaller wheels and rate of rotation of the drum.

Phases of Growth

Under favourable conditions, growth of plant shows a characteristic course. The period of growth is generally divided into three phases.

1. Meristematic Phase

The cells that are constantly dividing, i.e. both at the apex of the root and shoot represent the meristematic phase of growth.

Features shown by the cells of this phase are

- rich in protoplasmic content.
- has large conspicuous nuclei.
- cell walls are primary in nature.
- cells have plasmodesmatal connections.

This phase is also known as **division phase**.

2. Elongation Phase

This phase lies just behind the growing parts, i.e. behind the meristematic zone away from the growing tip.

Features shown by this phase are

- increased vacuolation.
- enlargement of cell.
- deposition of new cell wall.

Enlargement of cell during this phase occurs in all directions. Maximum elongation is seen in **conductive tissues and fibres**.

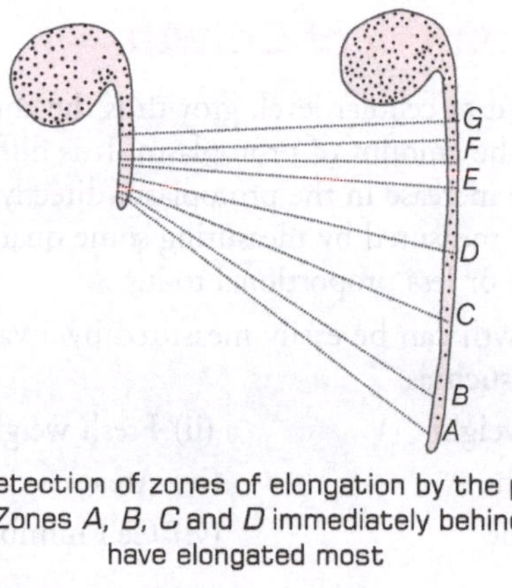

Fig. 16.4 Detection of zones of elongation by the parallel line technique. Zones *A*, *B*, *C* and *D* immediately behind the apex have elongated most

3. Maturation Phase

Just behind the phase of elongation, occurs a phase of maturation. It occurs further away from the apex, i.e. more proximal to the elongation phase.

Features shown by this phase are

- cells attain maximum thickening of their walls.
- protoplasmic modifications are maximum as per need of the cells.

Growth Rate

The growth rate is defined as the increased growth per unit time. Rate of growth can be expressed mathematically. It shows increase that may be arithmetic or geometric in nature.

1. Arithmetic Growth

Somatic cells increase in number due to mitosis. This type of growth occurs by mitotic cell division. Only one daughter cell continues to divide, while others follow differentiation and attain maturity.

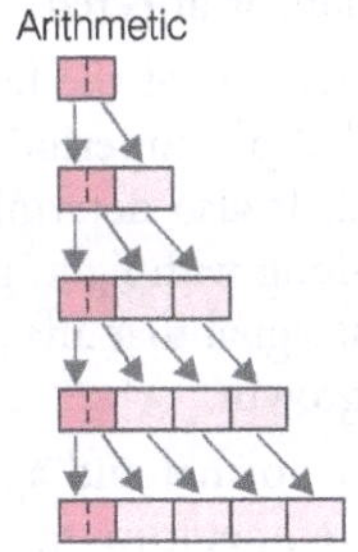

Fig. 16.5 Diagrammatic representation of arithmetic growth

Expression of arithmetic growth can be exemplified by a root elongating at a constant rate. A linear curve is obtained on plotting the length of root against time.

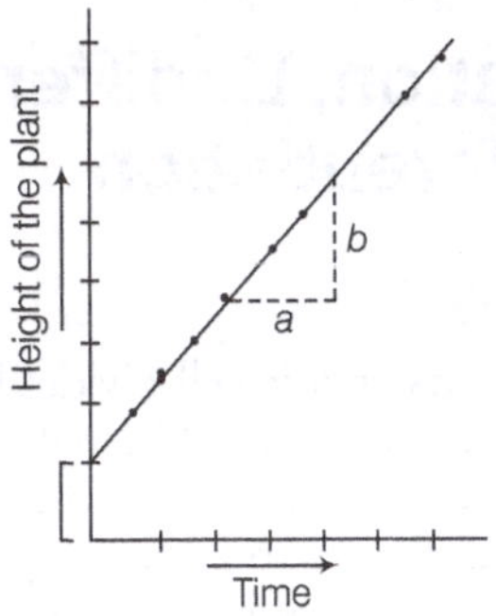

Fig. 16.6 Constant linear growth

$$L_t = L_0 + rt$$

where L_t = Length at time 't',

L_0 = Length at time 'zero'

and r = Growth rate/elongation per unit time.

2. Geometric Growth

In living organisms, during geometric type of growth rate, the pattern follows three important phases

(i) **Lag Phase** (Initial or The Beginning Phase) It is mainly characterised by very slow growth.

(ii) **Log Phase** (Exponential Phase) It is the middle phase of the system and is characterised by very fast and rapid growth of the plant body. After initiation of growth, it increases rapidly at an exponential rate.

During this phase, both progeny cells undergoing mitotic cell division retain the ability to divide and continue dividing till the next phase appears till the time nutrient supply is appropriate.

(iii) **Stationary Phase** (Steady Phase) This phase occurs when either the plant reaches maturity or the supply of nutrients becomes limited.

Due to the above mentioned factors, the growth of the plant slows down to come to a halt.

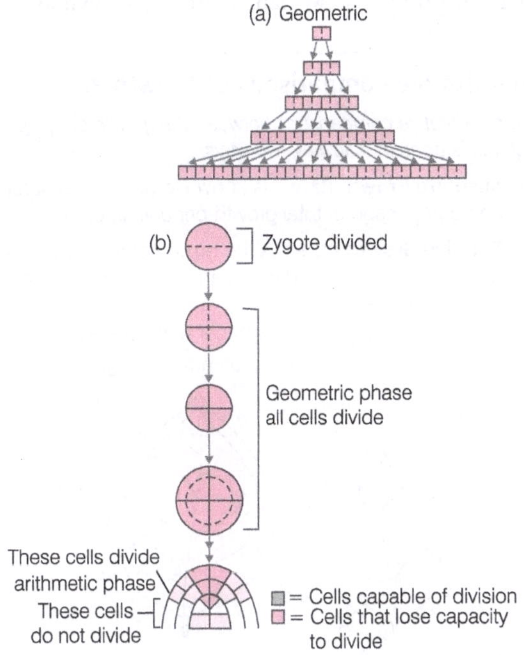

Fig. 16.7 Diagrammatic representation of (a) Geometric growth and (b) Stages during embryo development showing geometric and arithmetic phases

Under favourable conditions, the characteristic course of growth is observed. Thus, if we plot the parameter of growth rate against time, the typical **sigmoid curve** is observed.

It shows a characteristic feature of living organism growing in a natural environment. This curve is typical for all cells, tissues and organs of a plant.

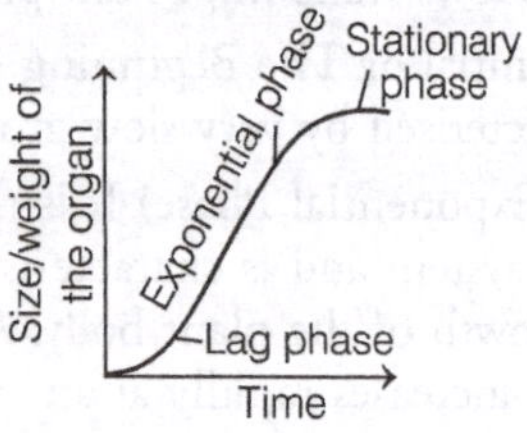

Fig. 16.8 An ideal sigmoid growth curve typical of cells in culture and many higher plants and plant organs

The exponential growth can be expressed as

$$W_1 = W_0 e^{rt}$$

where, W_1 = Final size (weight, height, number, etc.)

W_0 = Initial size at the beginning of the period

t = Time of growth

e = Base of natural logarithms

and, r = relative growth rate, that measures the ability of the plant to produce new plant material, known as **efficiency index.**

Quantitative Comparisons of Growth Rate

The quantitative comparisons between the growth of living systems is done in following two ways

i. **Absolute Growth Rate** It is known to be the measurement and comparison of total growth per unit time.

ii. **Relative Growth Rate** It is the growth of the given system per unit time expressed on a common basis, e.g. per unit initial parameter.

$$\text{Relative growth rate} = \frac{\text{Growth per unit time (AGR)}}{\text{Initial parameter (e.g. size)}}$$

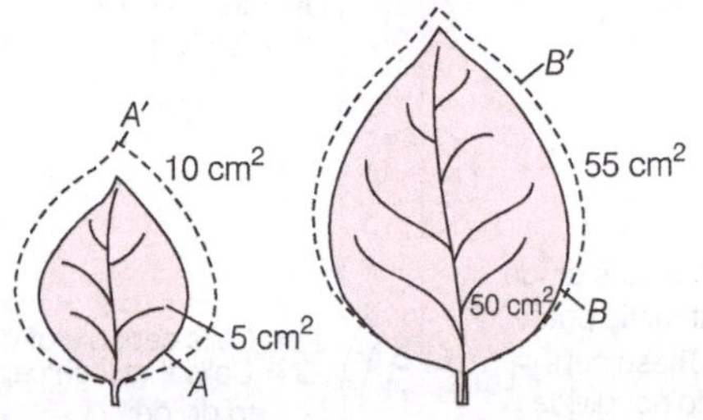

Fig. 16.9 Diagrammatic comparison of absolute and relative growth rate. Both leaves *A* and *B* have increased their area by 5 cm² in a given time to produce *A*′, *B*′ leaves.

Leaves *A* and *B* shown in the figure have grown 5 cm^2 in one day. Although their sizes are different, i.e. 5 cm^2 and 50 cm^2, respectively but both of them shows absolute increase in area in the given time to give leaves *A*′ and *B*′, i.e. 5 cm^2 in both cases. Out of these two, the relative growth rate is higher or faster in leaf *A*.

Conditions or Factors for Growth

The growth of a plant is influenced by a variety of external and internal factors. Growth of plant involves synthesis of protoplasm, cell division, cell enlargement and cell differentiation.

Some of the factors due to which growth of plants is influenced are mentioned below

(i) **Water** It is the first and the foremost requirement of the plants for the enlargement of cell, maintaining turgidity of growing cells, for extension of growth. It also acts as a medium for many enzymatic activities. In water stress conditions growth of the plants seems to get retarded.

(ii) **Oxygen** It helps in releasing metabolic energy essential for growth activities.

(iii) **Nutrients** These act as (macro and micro essential nutrients) major raw materials for protoplasmic synthesis and also acts as a source of energy. However, under nutrient deficient conditions the growth of the plant is affected.

(iv) **Light** The requirement of the light to the plants for its growth is called **photoperiodism.** It helps in synthesis of food. It also determines the root and shoot growth. Along with light, gravity also serves as an environmental signal that affects certain phases/stages of growth.

(v) **Temperature** For normal and appropriate growth of plant optimum temperature range is necessary, i.e. 25-30°C (this happens because enzymatic reactions are very fast at optimum temperature range).

(vi) **Genetic Factors** These are internal factors. They are involved in overall maintenance of a plant.

Differentiation, Dedifferentiation and Redifferentiation

Differentiation

During growth, meristematic cell divides by mitotic division to form daughter cells. The cells from root and shoot apical meristem, cambium or other meristems tend to differentiate and mature to perform specific functions. This act of differentiation of cells which leads to maturation of cells and organ to perform specific function is called **differentiation.** For example, cells tend to loose their protoplasm, in order to form tracheary element. These cells also develop a very strong, elastic, lignocellulosic secondary cell wall in order to carry water to long distance even under extreme conditions.

Dedifferentiation

The living differentiated cells also show another interesting phenomenon during which they regain the capacity to divide mitotically under certain conditions. The dedifferentiated cell can act as a meristem, e.g. formation of meristems-**interfasicular cambium** and **cork cambium** from fully differentiated parenchyma cells.

Redifferentiation

The product of dedifferentiated cells or tissue which when lose the capacity to divide, but mature to perform specific functions is known as redifferentiation, e.g. **secondary cortex** and **cork.**

It is so because cells/tissues that arise out of the single or same meristem show different structures after attaining maturity. Thus, the final structure at maturity of a cell/tissue arising from the same tissue is also determined by the location of the cells, e.g. cells positioned away from the root apical meristems differentiate as root cap cells, while those which are pushed to the periphery develop and mature as epidermis.

Development

It is the process that includes a series of changes that an organism goes through during its life cycle, i.e. from germination till senescence.

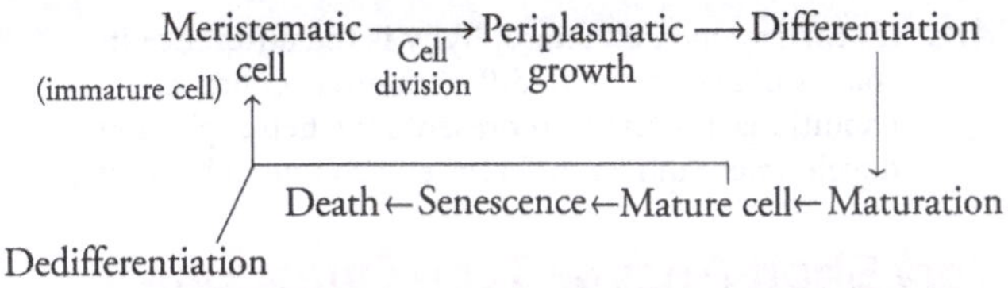

Fig. 16.10 Sequence of development of plant cell

In broad terms development is the sum total of both growth and differentiation in plants.

The developmental process of growth and differentiation is controlled by several intrinsic and extrinsic factors

(i) **Intrinsic factors** includes, both intracellular (genetic) or intercellular factors (such as plant growth regulators).

(ii) **Extrinsic factors** includes, light, temperature, water, oxygen, nutrition, etc.

Plasticity

Plasticity refers to a phenomenon in which plants follow different pathways in response to environment or phases of life forming different kinds of structures, e.g. heterophylly, the phenomenon in plants by which more than two types of leaves occur on the same plant. The heterophylly is common in cotton, coriander, larkspur and ivy. The environmental plasticity is best seen in emergent hydrophytes, e.g. *Ranunculus flabellaris* (buttercup). In this, the submerged leaves are highly dissected, while emerged leaves are broad and lobed.

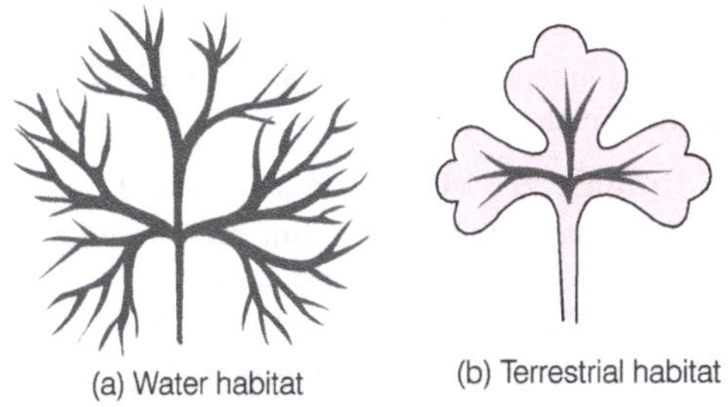

Fig. 16.11 Heterophylly in *Ranunculus flabellaris* (buttercup) (a) Submerged leaf, (b) Emerged leaf

Similarly as in larkspur the juvenile leaves are broadly lobed, while mature leaves become pinnately divided with lobes becoming linear in the region of flowers.

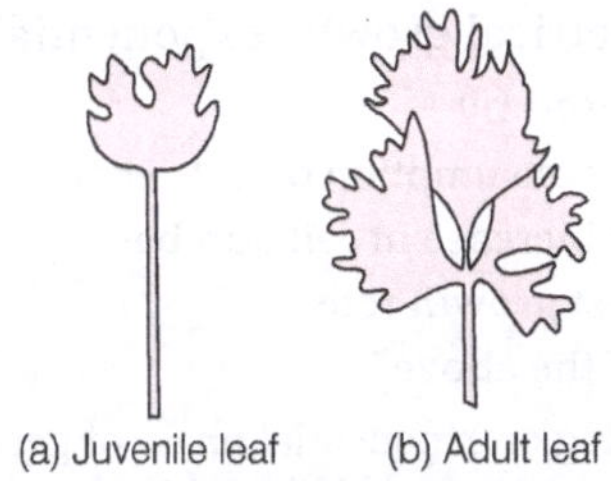

Fig. 16.12 Heterophylly in larkspur (a) Juvenile leaf, (b) Adult leaf

Topic Practice 1

Multiple Choice Questions

(1 Mark)

1. The tissues responsible for secondary growth in plants are
   (a) vascular cambium
   (b) cork cambium
   (c) root and shoot apical meristem
   (d) Both (a) and (b)

Ans (d) Secondary growth in plants is mainly increase in the girth of plants (organ), which takes place by vascular and cork cambium.

2. Growth at cellular level is the increase in the amount of
   (a) cell wall (b) cell membrane
   (c) protoplasm (d) All of these

Ans (c) Growth at cellular level is principally a consequence of increase in the amount of protoplasm.

3. Auxanometer is used to measure
   (a) growth in the length of plant organ
   (b) growth in the width of plant organ
   (c) population of the pest-attacking plants
   (d) Both (a) and (b)

Ans (a) Auxanometer is used to measure growth in the length of plant organ.

4. Arithmetic growth is linear because
   (a) one daughter cell remains meristematic and other differentiates and mature
   (b) both daughter cells remain meristematic
   (c) both daugther cells get matured
   (d) all of the above

Ans (a) Arithmetic growth is linear because in this type of growth, there is a sequential adding of the new cells. One daughter cell remains meristematic (dividing), while the other becomes mature and gets differentiated to perform special function.

5. In geometrical growth, exponential phase is represented by
   (a) rapid consumption of nutrients
   (b) rapid increase in cell number
   (c) highest growth rate
   (d) All of the above

Ans (d) In the log or exponential phase of geometrical growth there is a rapid increase in size, cell number and mass of an organism, due to the rapid consumption of nutrients. This leads to highest rate of growth at this stage.

6. In the expression, $W_1 = W_0 e^{rt}$ (geometrical growth), W_1, W_0, r and t represents

	W_0	W_1	r	t
(a)	Initial size	Final size	Growth rate	Time of growth
(b)	Final size	Initial size	Growth rate	Time of growth
(c)	Final size	Initial size	Growth rate	Time of single cell division
(d)	Initial size	Final size	Growth rate	Time of single cell division

Ans (a) The exponential growth can be expressed as
$W_1 = W_0 e^{rt}$, where
W_0 = Initial size at the beginning of the period
W_1 = Final size (weigth, height, number, etc.)
r = Growth rate
t = Time of growth
e = Base of natural logarithms

7. Measurement and comparison of total growth of a plant per unit time is called
   (a) absolute growth rate
   (b) qualitative growth rate
   (c) relative growth rate
   (d) exponential growth rate

Ans (a) Measurement and comparison of total growth of a plant per unit time is called absolute growth rate.

8. Which one is the example of dedifferentiation?
   (a) Procambium and vascular cambium
   (b) Cork cambium and interfascicular cambium
   (c) Cork cambium and vascular cambium
   (d) Procambium and cork cambium

Ans (b) Formation of cork cambium and interfascicular cambium is the example of dedifferentiation.

9. The ability of plants to follow different pathways to form different structures in response to environment is called
   (a) plasticity (b) elasticity
   (c) growth (d) development

Ans (a) Plants follow different pathways in response to environment or phases of life to form different kind of structures. This ability is called plasticity, e.g. heterophylly in cotton, coriander and larkspur.

10. Environmental heterophylly is seen in
   (a) cotton (b) coriander
   (c) larkspur (d) buttercup

Ans (d) Environmental heterophylly is the difference in shapes of leaves due to different environmental conditions. Buttercup represents the heterophyllous development due to different environmental conditions.

Very Short Answer Type Questions

1 Mark

11. Growth is one of the fundamental characteristics of all living organisms. Do unicellular organisms also grow? If so, what are the parameters? **NCERT Exemplar**

Ans Yes, unicellular organisms also grow. Their cell size increases upto a certain fixed dimension only and then they divide.
Their growth and reproduction is synchronised, i.e. it goes hand in hand.

12. Write the correct chronological sequence of developmental stages in plants?

Ans The correct chronological sequence of developmental stages in plants is
Germination → Vegetative growth → Flowering → Fruiting

13. **Mention any two symptoms that reflect the occurrence of growth.**

Ans The symptoms of growth are
(i) permanent increase in size (length and volume)
(ii) increase in fresh weight.

14. **Indicate the term for the formation of new protoplasm.**

Ans Formation of new protoplasm is known as real growth.

15. **Identify the actively dividing cells in plants.**

Ans Meristems are the actively dividing cells present in the higher plants such as gymnosperms and angiosperms.

16. **What happens if the meristematic cells ever cease to divide?**

Ans If meristematic cells cease to divide, the growth of the plant will be hindered and will undergo a period of dormancy depending upon the seasonal changes in the climate.

17. **In which type of growth, all daughter cells produced after mitotic cell division grow and divide?**

Ans In geometric growth, all daughter cells produced after mitotic cell division undergo cell division.

18. **Name two processes which are common to both plants and animals during growth and development.**

Ans Two processes common to both plants and animals are
(i) cell division (ii) cell differentiation.

19. **Mention the name of the internal factors that control development in plants.**

Ans Internal factors that control development in plants are
(i) Genetic factors (intracellular)
(ii) Plant growth regulators (intercellular).

20. **Name the plant in which dimorphic leaves are found.**

Ans *Ranunculus flabellaris.*

21. **Name the type of heterophylly shown by**
(i) cotton and
(ii) buttercup, respectively.

Ans (i) Developmental heterophylly.
(ii) Environmental heterophylly.

Short Answer Type I Questions

2 Marks

22. **Justify 'growth of plant is unique'.**

Ans Plant growth is unique, as plants retain the capacity to grow throughout their life. This ability is due to the presence of meristems.

The cells of meristematic tissue have the capacity to divide and self-perpetuate. This form of growth, where new cells are continuously added to the plant body by the activity of meristems, is called open form of growth. (2)

23. **Explain whether the growth in plants is definite or indefinite.**

Or

State what do we call a form of growth in which newly producing cells are always being added to the body of the plant.

Ans Growth in plants is indefinite because they have the capacity for unlimited growth throughout their life. This ability of the plants is due to the presence of meristems at certain locations.

This type of growth is exhibited by roots, stem and their branches and is called open form of growth. (2)

24. **In a slide showing different types of cells, can you identify which type of the cell may be meristematic and the one which is incapable of dividing and how?** **NCERT Exemplar**

Ans The meristematic cells can be identified of the basis of the following characteristics
(i) Cell have thin cellulose wall and dense cytoplasm with large nucleus.
(ii) Plasmodesmal connections are more numerous among meristematic cells.
(iii) Chromosomes of cells replicate and divide into two homologous chromatids.

Whereas, cells incapable of divinding show features such as
(i) attains particular shape, size and thickening.
(ii) Undergoes structural and physiological differentiation. (2)

25. **Which of them shows higher relative growth rate? Justify.**

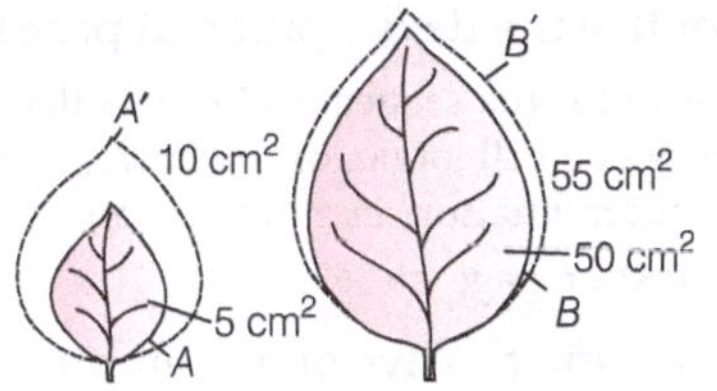

Ans Relative growth rate of $A = \frac{(10-5)}{x \times 5} = \frac{5}{5x}\text{cm}^2$

Relative growth rate of $B = \frac{(55-50)}{50 \times x} = \frac{5}{50x}\text{cm}^2$

Thus, A shows higher relative growth rate. (2)

26. **A primary root grows from 5-19 cm in a week. Calculate the absolute growth rate and relative growth rate over the period.** **NCERT Exemplar**

Ans Absolute growth rate = $\frac{(19-5)}{7} = 2$ cm/day

Relative growth rate = $\frac{(19-5)}{7 \times 5} = 0.4$ cm/day (2)

27. **Write few lines about growth curve.**

Ans The few lines about growth curve are as follows

(i) It is the graphic representation of the total growth against time.

(ii) The period of time in which growth takes place has been called grand period of growth by Sachs.

(iii) The rate of growth is not uniform during grand period of growth.

(iv) If total growth is plotted against time, a S-shaped or Sigmoid curve is obtained. It consists of four parts, i.e. lag phase, exponential phase (log phase), phase of diminishing growth and stationary phase. (2)

28. **In the figure of sigmoid growth curve below label segments *A*, *B* and *C*.** **NCERT Exemplar**

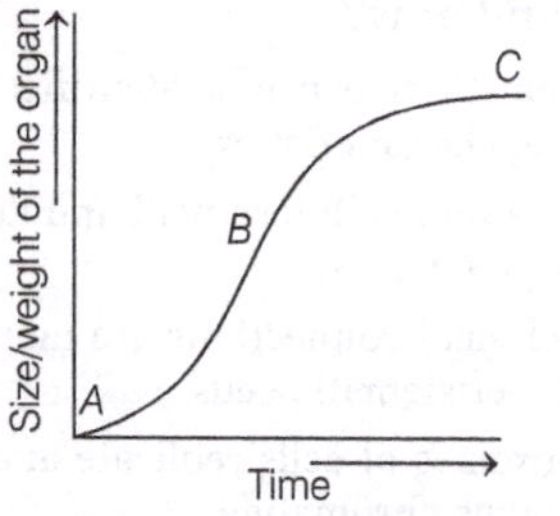

Ans (i) Lag phase – Growth is slow in the phase.

(ii) Exponential phase – Shows rapid growth and maintains maximum growth for some time.

(iii) Stationary phase – Growth diminishes and ultimately stops in this phase. (2)

29. **What do you understand by development in plants. Name the intrinsic and extrinsic factors that control the developmental process.**

Ans Development is the sequence of events that occur in the life history of a cell, organ or organism, which include growth, differentiation, maturation and senescence.

Refer to text on page no 369. (2)

30. **Define plasticity. Give one example.**

Ans Refer to text on page no. 369.

Short Answer Type II Questions

3 Marks

31. **Both growth and differentiation in higher plants are open. Comment.** **NCERT**

Ans Plant growth is open, i.e. they grow throughout their life due to following reasons

(i) This is due to the presence of meristems, where cells have the capacity to divide.

(ii) New cells are always added by the meristems and this form of growth is called open form of growth.

(iii) Development in plants is also open, because cells/tissues arising out of the same meristem from different structures at maturity.

(iv) The final structure at maturity of a cell/tissue is determined by the location of the cells within the plant body. (3)

32. **What are meristems? How does the primary growth differ from that of secondary growth?**

Ans Meristems are tissues present in the growing regions of plants.

Primary growth refers to the elongation (growth in length) of stems and roots. All plants exhibit primary growth. Root apical meristem and shoot apical meristem are responsible for the primary growth of the plants and principally contribute to the elongation of the plants along their axis.

The growth that makes plants thicker (growth in diameter) is called **secondary growth**. For example, in dicotyledonous plants and gymnosperms, the lateral meristems, vascular cambium and cork cambium appear later in life. These are the meristems. Their activity in plant helps these plants to grow in girth (diameter). (3)

33. **What are the structural characteristics of** **NCERT Exemplar**

(i) meristematic cells near root tip?

(ii) the cells in the elongation zone of the root?

Ans (i) Meristematic cells near root tip are in the process of active divisions, i.e. mitotic cell division. Each chromosome splits lengthwise into two homologous chromatids, which pass equally into daughter cells.

(ii) The cells in the elongation zone of the root have enlarged size due to vacuolation, i.e. by absorption of water. In these a large central vacuole is present, which push the cytoplasm to a thin boundary layer against the cell wall. The daughter cells formed after divisions have half the size of the parent cell.

$(1\frac{1}{2} \times 2)$

34. **Why is not that only one parameter is good enough to demonstrate growth throughout the life of a flowering plant?** **NCERT**

Ans Any one parameter is not good enough to demonstrate growth throughout the life of a flowering plant because the plants exhibit different types of growth during different stages of their life cycle. In the seedling stage, they are in state of active mitotic cell divisions, then they undergo active cell enlargement stage during growing stage. After the formation of various organs, they undergo cell differentiation or get matured. Finally in the reproductive or flowering stage of their life cycle, they exhibit reductional divisions. (3)

35. Describe briefly

(i) Arithmetic growth

(ii) Geometric growth

(iii) Sigmoid growth curve

(iv) Absolute and relative growth rate

Ans Refer to text on page no. 367 and 366.

36. Both animals and plants grow. Why do we say that growth and differentiation in plants is open and not so in animals? Does this statement hold true for sponges also? **NCERT Exemplar**

Ans Plant growth is a unique phenomenon because plants retain the capacity for unlimited growth throughout their life. This ability of the plants is due to the presence of meristems at certain locations in their body. The cells of meristems have the capacity to divide and self-perpetuate.

The cells thus produced, however, soon loses the capacity to divide and such cells make up the plant body.

This form of growth wherein new cells are always being added to the plant body by the activity of the meristem is called the open form of growth. Yes, this statement holds true for sponges also. (3)

Long Answer Type Questions

5 Marks

37. Describe use of auxanometer in measuring plant growth.

Ans Refer to text on page no. 365 and 366.

38. Define growth, differentiation, development, dedifferentiation, redifferentiation, determinate growth, meristem and growth rate. **NCERT**

Ans Refer to text on page no. 364-369.

39. Mention the phenomenon of growth in plants. Explain the phases of growth in detail.

Ans Growth is defined as a permanent or irreversible increase in dry weight, mass or volume of cell, organ or organism.

Plant growth takes place in three steps or phases–cell division (in meristematic cells), cell elongation (newly formed cells) and cell maturation.

For detail Refer to text on page no. 366 and 367. (5)

40. Describe the neccessary conditions for the occurrence of growth in detail.

Ans Refer to text on page no. 368.

41. Define differentiation? Also give details about how can you distinguish between dedifferentiation and redifferentiation?

Ans The cells which are derived from root apical meristem and shoot and other meristems undergo certain changes to attain maturity to perform specific functions. This process which leads to maturation of cells is termed as differentiation. During this, the cells undergo a few major structural changes both in their cell walls and protoplasm to perform some specific functions throughout their life. (2)

(i) In plants, some living differentiated cells, e.g. parenchyma can regain the capacity to divide mitotically under certain conditions. A dedifferentiated tissue can act as meristem, e.g. interfascicular vascular cambium, cork cambium and wound meristem.

(ii) The product of dedifferentiated cells or tissues which lose the ability to divide is called redifferentiated cells and the term is known as redifferentiation. Secondary xylem and secondary phloem from interfascicular vascular cambium, secondary cortex and cork are the examples of redifferentiated tissues. (3)

42. Describe the mechanism of plasticity in plants with suitable examples.

Ans Refer to text on page no. 369.

TOPIC 02 Plant Growth Regulators (PGRs), Seed Germination and Seed Dormancy

It has been suggested from sufficient evidences that the plants have certain chemical substances, which help to control the mechanism of growth.

Plant growth regulators are variously described as plant growth substances, plant hormones or phytohormones. These are the small, simple organic molecules of diverse chemical composition produced naturally in higher plants that control the growth and other physiological functions. These are required in a very small amount by the plant.

Classification of Plant Growth Regulators

The plant growth regulators fall under the following categories of chemical groups

(i) **Indole compounds,** e.g. Indole-3- Acetic Acid (IAA).

(ii) **Adenine derivatives,** e.g. -furfuryl amino purine, kinetin.

(iii) **Carotenoid derivatives,** e.g. Abscisic Acid (ABA).

(iv) **Terpenes,** e.g. Gibberellic Acid (mainly GA_3).

(v) **Gases,** e.g. Ethylene C_2H_4).

On the basis of functions they perform in a living plant body in broad terms, PGRs are divided into two groups

1. Plant Growth Promoters

PGRs that exhibit growth promoting activities such as cell division, cell enlargement, tropic growth, pattern formation, flowering, fruiting, seed formation, etc., are called **plant growth promoters**, e.g. auxins, gibberellins and cytokinins.

2. Plant Growth Inhibitors

These primarily function in response to wounds and stresses of biotic and abiotic origin. These are also involved in various growth inhibiting processes like dormancy and abscission, e.g. abscisic acid.

Note The gaseous form of PGR, (ethylene), can fit in either category and may function both as promoter and inhibitor. But largely it functions as an inhibitor of growth activities.

Discovery of Plant Growth Regulators

It is interesting to know that the discovery of all five major groups of plant growth regulators have been done accidentally. All these help in understanding the phenomenon of development and abnormal behaviour in plants.

1. Discovery of Auxin

This is the **first growth hormone** to be discovered. The knowledge of this hormone came into existence through the observation of **Charles Darwin** and his son **Francis Darwin.**

They observed that the coleoptiles of canary grass responded to unilateral source of light (phenomenon known as photoperiodism) by growing towards it.

After performing series of experiments they came to the conclusion that **coleoptile tip** was the site that has the property of transmittable influence due to which bending of complete coleoptile was caused. The first PGR, i.e. auxin was isolated by **FW Went** in 1928, from coleoptile tip of oat seedlings.

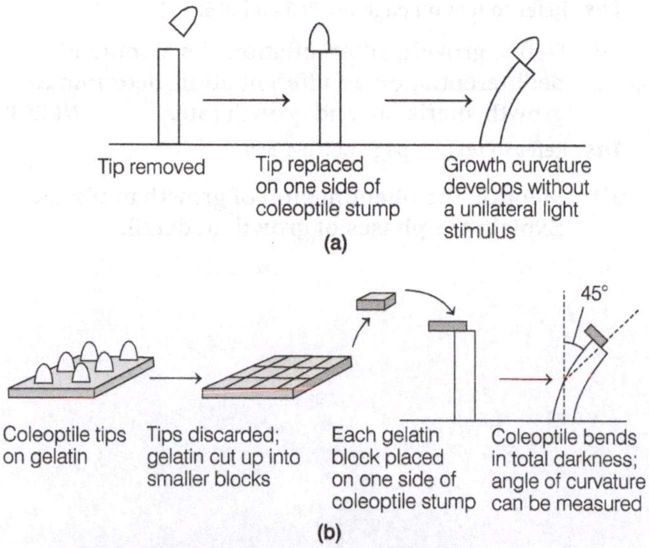

Fig. 16.13 (a-b) Discovery of auxins-experiments of FW Went-Avena curvature test

2. Discovery of Gibberellin

In early part of 20th century the **bakane** (foolish seedlings disease of rice), was reported to be caused by a fungal pathogen *Gibberella fujikuroi*. Symptoms shown by the infected plant were elongated stems, little or no production of grains and plants became weak. Thus, it was later identified that the active substance involved here was gibberellic acid. The Japanese plant pathologist **E Kurosawa**, reported the appearance of symptoms of the disease in uninfected rice seedlings when they were treated with **sterile filtrate** of the fungus.

3. Discovery of Cytokinin

F Skoog and his coworkers, studied the nutritional requirements of tissue culture. They made nutrient medium derived from the internodal segments of tobacco stems.

They observed that from that internodal segments, a **callus** (i.e. a mass of undifferentiated cells) proliferated, only when the nutrient medium containing auxin was supplemented with the extract of vascular tissues or yeast or coconut milk (water of endosperm of coconut).

It was later found that the active substance present in coconut milk is a modified form of adenine which was crystallised and identified as **kinetin**. Further the compounds that exhibited kinetin like properties were termed as **cytokinins**.

4. Discovery of Abscisic Acid

With the progression in the research on plant growth regulators, three independent researchers reported the purification and chemical characterisation of three different kinds of inhibitors (during mid 1960), i.e. **inhibitor B, abscission II** and **dormin.** Later, three were proved to be chemically identical in nature and were named as Abscisic Acid (ABA).

5. Discovery of Ethylene

Cousins (1910), confirmed the release of a volatile substance from ripened oranges that enhance the ripening of stored unripened bananas. This volatile substance was later identified to be a gaseous plant growth regulator, i.e. ethylene.

Physiological Role of Plant Growth Regulators

All five categories of plant growth regulators discussed above, have the following physiological effects on the growth of the plant

1. Auxins

Auxin (Gk. *auxein*–to grow) was initially isolated from the urine of human, but later on, their presence was also found in plants and was proved to be the first PGR ever known. The real plant auxin is chemically known as **Indole -3-Acetic Acid** (IAA).

The term is also applied to other natural and synthetic compounds having various growth regulating properties. Production of auxin generally takes place in the region of **growing apices** of the stems and roots from where they migrate to the site of their action.

Note

Auxins can move only through cell to cell by diffusion, i.e. they cannot move through vascular tissues.

Types of Auxins

There are generally two basic categories in which auxins are divided

(i) **Natural Auxins** It occurs naturally in plants and fungi, e.g. Indole Acetic Acid (IAA) and Indole Butyric Acid (IBA).

(ii) **Synthetic Auxins** These are prepared from synthetic compounds that cause several responses to IAA. They can easily move in all directions inside the plants, e.g. Naphthalene Acetic Acid (NAA), 2, 4-Dichlorophenoxyacetic acid (2, 4-D).
All these types of auxins are extensively been used in agricultural and horticultural practices.

Knowledge Plus

- The compounds, which can be converted into auxins, are called auxin precursors. e.g. IAA is synthesised from tryptophan amino acid hormone.
- **Antiauxin** They inhibit auxin activity, e.g. Tridobenzoic Acid (TIBA), P-chlorophenoxy Isobutyric Acid, etc.

Functions of Auxins

Auxins perform several functions, these are as follows

(i) **Apical Dominance** Presence of auxin in higher concentration (in higher plants) in shoot apex, promotes apical dominance. It is been seen commonly in many vascular plants, that presence of apical buds does not allow the lateral buds to grow. They only start developing into branches when the apical bud is removed.

Fig. 16.14 Apical dominance in plants (a) A plant with apical bud intact, (b) A plant with apical bud removed

(ii) **Initiation of Roots** In contrast to stem, higher concentration of auxin inhibits the elongation of shoots, but it initiates more lateral branches of roots.

(iii) **Inhibition of Abscission** It is the shedding of leaves, flowers and fruits from mature plants. These parts abscise in a region near the petiole of leaves. This region is called **abscission zone**. Abscission starts when an abscission layer is formed in this region. Natural auxins delay abscission of young fruits and leaves and also used to control pre-harvest fruit drop.

(iv) **Cell Elongation** Auxin stimulates the elongation of cells of shoots.

(v) **Promotes Flowering** Presence of auxin helps in promoting flowering in some plants, e.g. pineapple, litchi, etc.

(vi) **Parthenocarpy** Auxins are sprayed on to the unpollinated pistil and make them develop into parthenocarpic fruits, which carry a better market values.

(vii) **Metabolism** Application of auxin can enhance metabolism due to mobilisation of nutrients and growth promoting substances.

Applications of Auxins

As stated, use of synthetic auxins is widely accepted now-a-days in various agricultural and horticultural practices.

Following are the applications of auxins

(i) **Eradication of Weeds** Auxins are used as weedicides and herbicides. Application of 2, 4-Dichlorophenoxyacetic acid (2, 4-D) is widely done in order to kill dicotyledonous weeds. It does not affect mature, monocotyledonous plants.

(ii) **Helps in Cell Division** Besides cell elongation, auxin may also play an important role in cell division.

(iii) **Controls Xylem and Phloem Differentiation** Auxin controls differentiation of xylem and phloem is stems and roots. There are evidences that low concentration of auxin induces phloem differentiation while higher concentration of auxin is responsible for differentiation of both xylem and phloem tissues.

2. Gibberellins

These are another group of plant growth regulators, which are known to be weakly acidic growth hormones. There are more than 100 different gibberellins reported from widely different organisms like fungi and higher plants. All of them are known to be **acidic** in nature, thus, they are termed as **Gibberellic Acids** (i.e. and so on). However, GA_3 is the most important gibberellic acid which was first to be discovered. It is most extensively studied amongst all gibberellins.

Functions of Gibberellins

Gibberellins show various important physiological effects

(i) **Elongation of Internodes** It helps in elongation of the internodes, so as to increase the height of the plant. They cause an increase in length of axis and is also used in increasing length of grapes stalks.

(ii) **Elongation of Genetically Dwarf Plants** It has been seen that if gibberellins are administered to a dwarf plant (pea, maize, etc.), it may help in overcoming dwarfism. It also causes fruits to elongate and improve their shape, e.g. in apples, etc.

(iii) **Bolting** The gibberellins also help in promoting bolting (internode elongation) just prior to their reproductive phase or flowering. If gibberellin is sprayed on rosette plants like beet, cabbage, these plants show extensive internodal growth and profuse leaf development.

(iv) **Breaking Dormancy** It also helps in overcoming natural dormancy in buds, tubers, seeds, etc. and helps them to grow.

(v) **Flowering** This can also be induced in long day plants by the action of gibberellins.

Applications of Gibberellins

Gibberellins, apart from showing varied physiological effects, also have numerous applications. These are as follows

(i) **Delays Senescence** Gibberellins can delay the ripening of fruits such as *Citrus* fruits, apples, etc. This can also be used for safe and prolonged storage of the fruits.

(ii) **Malting Process** The process of malting in brewing industry can be speeded up by the use of GA_3.

(iii) **Sugar Yield** The carbohydrate is stored in the form of sugar in the stems of sugarcane. Thus, if crop of sugarcane is sprayed with gibberellins, it results in increased internodal length of the stem. This, enhances the increase in the yield of sugarcane as much as 20 tonnes per acre.

(iv) **Early Seed Production** Plants like *Cycas* and *Pinus,* when these juvenille conifers are sprayed with gibberellins, hastens the maturity period of them leading to early seed production.

3. Cytokinins

These are growth promoters that are **basic** in nature. They have specific effects on cytokinesis (division of cytoplasm) and were discovered as **kinetin** (a modified form of adenine, a purine).

Lethometal (1964), while searching for a substance with cytokinin like activity, isolated **zeatin** from corn kernels and coconut milk. Now presently, several naturally occurring cytokinins and some synthetic compounds having cell division promoting activities have been identified after the discovery of zeatin.

Region of Synthesis of Cytokinins

Natural cytokinins are known to be synthesised in the regions where rapid cell division takes place, e.g. root apex, developing shoot, buds, young fruits, etc., out of these roots are the major source of synthesis of cytokinins, from where, they move upwards through xylem.

Naturally Occurring Cytokinins

Coconut Milk Factor The liquid endosperm of coconut is known as coconut milk. This contains some factors, that show kinetin like activity and enhance, stimulate the growth in many plant tissues (*in vitro*). All these factors are collectively called as 'coconut milk factor'. These represent an example of naturally occurring cytokinins.

Zeatin It is also a naturally occurring cytokinin, isolated from maize grains. It is remarkably known to be more active than any other cytokinin.

Functions of Cytokinins

Cytokinins have following remarkable physiological effects

(i) **Promotes Cell Division** This is one of the most common and important biological effect of kinetin on plants, i.e. to induce cell division in the presence of sufficient amount of auxin (IAA).

(ii) **Reduces Apical Dominance** They promote the growth of lateral buds by breaking apical dominance.

(iii) **Morphogenesis** Differentiation or Morphogenesis of plant tissues/organs is seen to be in control, if ratio of cytokinins and auxins is proportionate.

(iv) **Resistance** They also increase resistance of plants to high or low temperature and diseases.

(v) **Delays Senescence** These also helps in delaying senescence (ageing) of leaves and other organs by controlling synthesis of protein and mobilisation of resources or nutrients. It is called as **Richmond-Lang effect.**

Applications of Cytokinins

(i) **Tissue Culture** Cytokinins are essential for tissue culture; apart from cell division they are also involved in **morphogenesis.**

(ii) **Shelf Life** Administration of cytokinins to harvest fruits and vegetables keeps them fresh for several days and **increase their shelf life.**

Note Shelf life of flowers and cut shoots can also be increased by dipping them in cytokinin solution.

4. Ethylene

It is a simple gaseous plant growth regulator, which is synthesised from the amino acid **methionine.** In plants, synthesis of ethylene takes place in almost every part of the plant, i.e. roots, leaves, flowers, seeds, fruits, etc.

Most important effect of ethylene is the promotion of **senescent changes** in the plant. Thus, it is synthesised by tissues in large amounts that undergo senescence and also by ripening fruits. Due to this property it is also known as **fruit ripening hormone.**

Functions of Ethylene

Ethylene shows various important physiological effects

(i) In dicot seedlings, ethylene influences the horizontal growth of seedling, swelling of the axis and formation of apical hook.

(ii) **Fruit Ripening** It is highly effective in fruit ripening. It also increases the rate of respiration. This rise in the respiration rate is called **respiratory climacteric.**

(iii) **Breaking Dormancy** Helps in breaking seed and bud dormancy.

(iv) **Seed Germination** Initiation of germination in peanut seeds and sprouting of potato tubers is also due to the production of ethylene in plants.

(v) **Transverse Growth** In deep water rice plants, ethylene promotes rapid **internode and petiole elongation.**

(vi) **Root Growth** It proves to be helpful in increasing absorption surface of plants by promoting growth of root and formation of root hairs.

(vii) **Flowering** It also stimulates flowering in fruits like pineapple, mango and other related plants.

Applications of Ethylene

As ethylene helps in regulating these many physiological processes in plants, it is known to be the most widely used PGR in agricultural field.

Ethephon It is the most widely used compound as a source of ethylene. This tends to absorb readily in an aqueous solution and transported within the plant. This slowly releases ethylene.

(i) **Ethephon** is known to control fruit ripening (in tomatoes and apples).

(ii) It also helps in **accelerating abscission** in flowers and fruits (causes thinning of fruits like cotton, cherry, walnut, etc).

(iii) Helps in **promoting formation of female flowers,** thus enhancing the yield of the fruits, e.g. cucumber.

5. Abscisic Acid (ABA)

It is slightly acidic growth hormone that functions as a **growth inhibitor** by counteracting with other mentioned growth hormones, i.e. auxins, gibberellins and cytokinins. Thus, like other PGR, abscisic acid also has a wide range of effects on growth and development of plants. Its production is stimulated under stress (unfavourable conditions such as drought, water lodging, excessive temperature, etc).

So, it is known as **stress hormone.** It acts antagonistically to gibberellic acid.

Note This hormone is transported to all parts of the plants through the process of diffusion by **conductive channels**.

Functions of Abscisic Acid

Abscisic acid shows various important physiological effects

(i) **Abscission and Dormancy** It has a primary role in regulating abscission and dormancy of buds and seeds. By inducing dormancy it helps the seeds to withstand the dessication and other factors related to unfavourable growth.

(ii) It acts as a general plant growth inhibitor and also inhibits metabolism of plants.

(iii) **Seed Germination** It has its role in inhibition of seed germination.

(iv) Also plays an important role in seed development and maturation.

(v) **Induces Stomatal Closure** Abscisic acid stimulates the closure of stomata.

The Mechanism of Stomatal Closing by ABA

ABA binds to receptors of the plasma membrane at the surface of the guard cells.

The receptors in turn activate several **interconnecting pathways,** which cause a rise in pH in the cytosol promoting the transfer of Ca^{2+} from the vacuole to the cytosol.

All this causes stomata to close, and opening of stomata occurs when conditions are just reverse to it.

Interaction between Growth Regulators

For the regulation of every phase of growth, i.e. for differentiation and developmental processes in plants, two or more phytohormones are intimately related to each other. These can either act **synergistically** or **antagonistically.**

Thus, every PGR has one or the other role to play. Likewise, there are also number of events in the life of a plant where more than one PGR is also involved to affect that particular event to take place. For example,

(i) Dormancy of seeds and buds is mostly due to abscisic acid, while it is broken down by gibberellins.

(ii) Auxins and cytokinins act antagonistically in controlling apical dominance, i.e. auxins cause apical dominance, while cytokinins help to overcome them.

(iii) Senescence is prevented by both auxins and cytokinins, while its stimulation is done by abscisic acid.

(iv) Auxins and cytokinins act synergistically in promoting cell division.

Seed Germination

The life of a plant initiates from a single cell called **zygote**. All the structures of plants such as roots, stems, leaves, flowers, fruits and seeds arise from seed on its germination. Seed itself developes from fertilised ovum present in the ovary in an orderly sequence of growth.

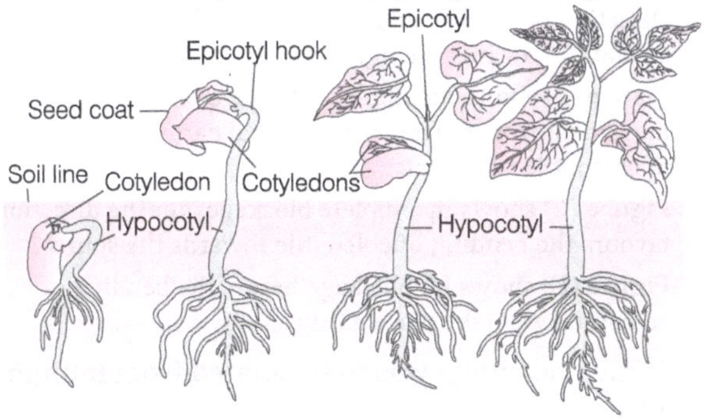

Fig. 16.15 Germination and seedling development in bean

Seed germinates by absorbing water through micropyle. The food present in seed gets mobilised by the activation of enzymes like amylase, lipase, proteinase and transported to embryo.

The radicle grows first, followed by growth of either epicotyl or hypocotyl. After that plumule grows.
Seed germination can be of following types

1. Epigeal Germination

In this type of germination the cotyledons are first pushed above the ground by the rapid elongation of hypocotyl. Cotyledons soon turn green and start photosynthesising, e.g. *Phaseolus, Ricinus* (castor), *Dolichos* (bean).

2. Hypogeal Germination

Here, the epicotyl elongates faster than hypocotyl at the time of seed germination. This keeps cotyledons inside the soil or may bring them just above the soil surface, e.g. pea, mango, coconut, maize, rice, etc.

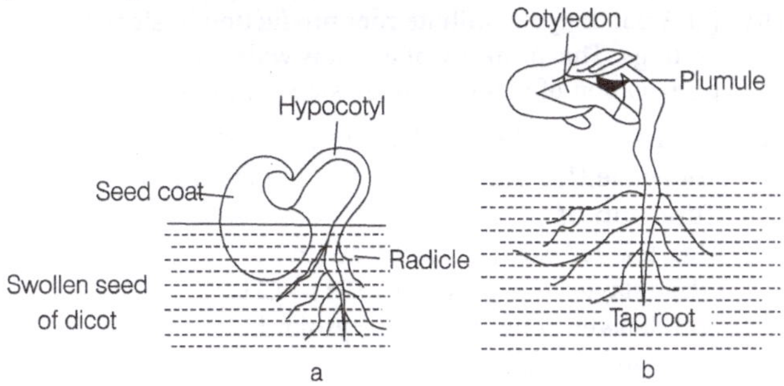

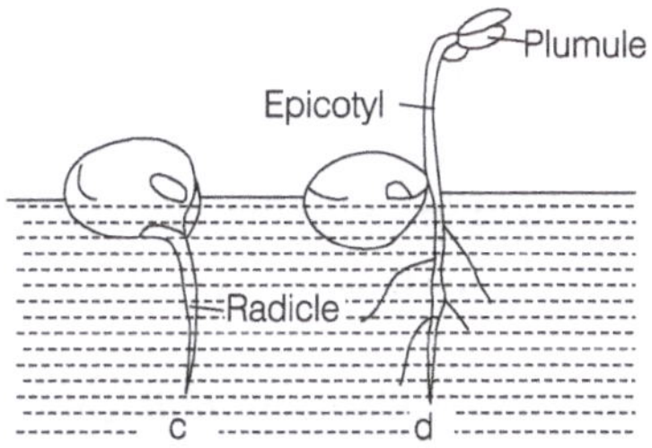

Fig. 16.16 (a,b) Epigeal germination, (c-d) Hypogeal germination

3. Viviparous Germination (Vivipary)

Germination of seeds inside the fruit, that is still attached to the parent tree is called vivipary, e.g. *Agave*.

Factors Affecting Seed Germination

Various external and internal factors influence seed germination. Internal factors can be seed viability, dormancy, enzymes, maturity of embryo, etc. On the other hand external factors can be water, light, oxygen temperature, etc.

Seed Dormancy

Dormancy is defined as the inactive state of a seed. During dormancy, growth of the embryo remains suspended and does not resume even in the presence of favourable conditions. It could be due to various factors like

1. **Hard Seed Coat** In many plants, impermeability of seed coat to water, (e.g. *Chenopodium, Trigonella, Meliotus*), oxygen (e.g. *Brassica alba, Pyrus malus* (apple), *Sinapis arvensis*) and chemicals (e.g. *Xanthium*) causes dormancy.
2. Seed coats can be mechanically resistant, e.g. *Capsella* and *Lepidium.*
3. **Germination Inhibitors** It may occur due to some chemical substances, such as abscisic acid, phenolic acids, short chain fatty acids, etc. These inhibit seed germination.
4. Dispersed seeds of wheat, barley, oat, etc., need an interval for ripening and gaining the ability to germinate.
5. **Immature Embryo** The embryo of some seeds are immature at the time of seed germination, e.g. *Ginkgo biloba* (gymnosperm), *Eranthis hyemalis.*
6. Some seeds, e.g. *Atriplex* contain high concentration of salt at the time of shedding.

Methods of Breaking Seed Dormancy

Various methods used for breaking seed dormancy are

(i) **Use of hydrolytic enzymes** such as pectinases, cellulose, etc.

(ii) **Destruction of germination inhibitors** using heat, light or oxidation.

(iii) **Breaking** of seed coats by microbial action.

(iv) **Use of growth hormones** like cytokinins, gibberellins and auxins.

(v) **By sacrification** which makes seed coat soft and weak. It is done by using acids, alcohols and knives.

(vi) **By stratification** which involves exposure of seeds to low temperature and O_2.

Biological Significance of Seed Dormancy

Dormancy allows storage of seeds in viable state for longer periods like in deserts. Dormant seeds are a means of survival. It also aids in seed dispersal over long distances.

Note Quiscence refers to the resting condition of the seed. It is a state of suspended growth of the embryo. It occurs when the required environmental conditions are not available for its germination.

Topic Practice 2

Multiple Choice Questions

1 Mark

1. Auxin was isolated by
   (a) Charles Darwin
   (b) Francis Darwin
   (c) FW Went
   (d) de Vries

Ans (c) Auxin was isolated by FW Went from the tips of coleoptiles of oat seedlings in 1928.

2. Four coleoptiles for experiment.

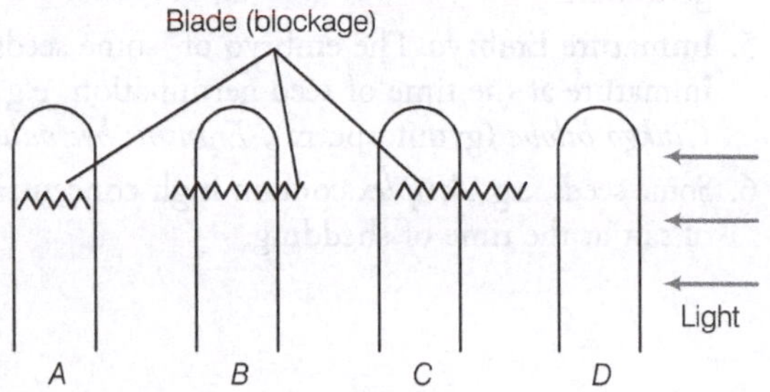

Which coleoptile will bend towards the light? Choose the correct option.
(a) A and B (b) C and D
(c) A and D (d) C and B

Ans (b) Coleoptile (plant organ) will bend towards the light due to auxin.

Figure (*A*) shows incomplete blockage of auxin. Direction of blockage does not favour the bending of coleoptile towards the light source.

Figure (*B*) shows incomplete blockage of auxin movement from apical part to lateral part. So, no bending of coleoptile will occur.

Figure (*C*) shows incomplete blockage, but the direction favours the bending of coleoptile towards the source.

Figure (*D*) shows no blockage hence, the bending of coleoptile will take place easily.

3. Which hormone was first isolated from human urine?
   (a) Auxin (b) ABA
   (c) Ethylene (d) Gibberellic acid

Ans (a) Auxin (derived from Greek word *auxein,* which means to grow) was first isolated from human urine. Kogl and Heagen Smith (1931) isolated three chemicals from human urine and named them as auxin.

4. Select the pair that consists of plant growth promoters only.
   (a) Auxins and cytokinins
   (b) Gibberellins and ABA
   (c) Ethylene and ABA
   (d) All of the above

Ans (a) Auxin, gibberellin and cytokinin are called plant growth promoters in which abscisic acid and ethylene are inhibitors as they inhibit growth in response to biotic and abiotic stress conditions.

5. If shoot cuttings are treated with auxin then
   (a) root production takes place
   (b) shoot elongation takes place
   (c) lateral dominance takes place
   (d) Both (a) and (b)

Ans (a) Auxin helps to initiate root production in stem cuttings. This property of auxin is widely used in the propagation of plants through stem cuttings.

6. Fruits can be left on the tree longer, so as to increase the market period. This is due to the function of
   (a) delayed senescence by auxin
   (b) delayed senescence by $CH_2—CH_2$
   (c) delayed senescence by cytokinin
   (d) delayed senescence by GA

Ans (d) Gibberellin delay senescence. Thus, the fruit can be left on tree longer, so as to extend the market period.

7. Gibberellin promote the production of
(a) male flowers (b) female flowers
(c) neutral flowers (d) abscission layer

Ans (a) Male flowers.

8. Difference between kinetin and zeatin is
(a) kinetin is active while zeatin is non-active
(b) zeatin is active while kinetin is non-active
(c) zeatin is synthetic while kinetin is natural
(d) zeatin is natural while kinetin is synthetic

Ans (d) The first cytokinin was discovered as kinetin (a modified form of adenine). Kinetin does not occur naturally. Search for natural substances with cytokinin like activity led to the isolation of zeatin from corn-kernels and coconut milk.

9. Richmond-Lang effect is concerned with
(a) delay in senescence
(b) breaking dormancy
(c) suppression of apical dominance
(d) cell elongation

Ans (a) Richmond and Lang (1967) observed that the degradation of proteins and chlorophyll was delayed in the detached leaves of *Xanthium* by the application of cytokinin. This effect of cytokinin (delaying the senescence) is called as Richmond-Lang effect.

10. In response to biotic and abiotic stress, growth inhibition activities are caused by
(a) ABA (b) CH_2—CH_2
(c) IAA (d) IBA

Ans (a) ABA (Abscisic Acid) was discovered for its role in regulating abscission and dormancy. It acts as the general plant growth inhibitor and an inhibitor of plant metabolism. ABA inhibits seed germination.

11. Choose the incorrect pair.
(a) Auxin – To grow
(b) Gibberellin – *Gibberella fujikuroi*
(c) Cytokinin – Herring sperm DNA
(d) ABA – Flowering hormone

Ans (d) ABA is a naturally occurring growth inhibitor. It acts as the stress hormone. It initiates flowering only in certain short day plant. But, ABA is called stress hormone. It is not a flowering hormone.

12. The term synergistic action of hormones refers to **NCERT Exemplar**
(a) when two hormones act together but bring about opposite effects
(b) when two hormones act together and contribute to the same function
(c) when one hormone affects more than one function
(d) when many hormones bring about any one function

Ans (b) Synergistic effect means when two hormones work together, they increase the effect or functioning of each other so, there will be enhanced effect of both the hormones.

Very Short Answer Type Questions

1 Mark

13. In which region of the plant, production of auxin in abundant amount occurs?

Ans In meristematic region of shoot, production of auxin in abundant amount occurs.

14. In most plants, the terminal bud suppresses the development of lateral buds into branches. What is this phenomenon called? Name one phytohormone that can promote this phenomenon.

Ans The phenomenon is called apical dominance. Auxin is the phytohormone involved in promoting this phenomenon.

15. Define parthenocarpy. Name the plant hormone used to induce parthenocarpy. **NCERT Exemplar**

Ans **Parthenocarpy** is the process where fruit develop without fertilisation and so, it does not contain seed. This can also be induced artificially by spraying auxin and gibberellins in certain plants like, grapes, papaya, etc.

16. While eating watermelons, all of us wish it was seedless. As a plant physiologist can you suggest any method by which this can be achieved. **NCERT Exemplar**

Ans The process of parthenocarpy produce the seedless fruits. This is a process in which fruits are developed without fertilisation so, seeds are not formed in the fruit. Artificially parthenocarpy can be induced by spraying auxin and gibberellin to produce seedless watermelons.

17. A gardener finds some broad-leaved dicot weeds growing in his lawns. What can be done to get rid of the weeds efficiently? **NCERT Exemplar**

Ans The broad leaved dicot weeds can be killed and eliminated by the spray of weedicide 2-4 D, (a kind of plant phytohormone auxin). This will make the lawn free of weeds and will help the gardener, to make the lawn weed free.

18. A farmer is using a substance called 2, 4-D in his field growing wheat crop. Mention the purpose of using this substance in the field.

Ans 2, 4-D is selective herbicide (weed killer). The spray of 2, 4-D is used to kill plants with broad leaved weeds.

19. **Name the plant hormone which causes internodal elongation in plants.**

Ans Gibberellin is the plant hormone related with internodal elongation. This phenomenon is called bolting.

20. **In some germinating seeds, enzymes mobilise nutrients present in the cotyledons. Name the phytohormone that stimulates the production of such enzymes.**

Ans Gibberellic acid is the phytohormone that induces production of hydrolytic enzymes (protease, amylase, lipase) in the endosperm of germinating seeds.

21. **What special ability is possessed by cytokinin as PGR?**

Ans Cytokinin has the ability to initiate morphogenesis in plant tissues and organs.

22. **Mention the name of the growth regulator, which was first isolated from endosperm of maize. Give its main biological activity.**

Ans Zeatin is the growth regulator isolated from endosperm. It controls cell division (cytokinesis) even in non-meristematic tissues.

23. **A student cultures a callus from the tobacco pith in a sterilised minimal nutritive medium, but adds more cytokinins than auxins. What would develop first from the callus, the shoot buds or the roots?**

Ans Callus will develop into shoot buds first.

24. **Due to the release of which plant hormone from over-ripened apple, can affect other apples in the basket?**

Ans Presence of ethylene hormone can affect other apples in the basket.

25. **Which hormone induces flowering in pineapple?**

Ans Ethylene induces flowering in pineapple.

26. **Why is abscisic acid also known as stress hormone?** **NCERT**

Ans Abscisic acid acts as a general plant growth inhibitor and an inhibitor of plant metabolism. ABA inhibits seed germination. ABA stimulates the closure of stomata in the epidermis and increases the tolerance of plants to various kinds of stresses. Therefore, it is also called the stress hormone.

27. **Discuss the various factors affecting seed germination.**

Ans Various factor affecting seed germination are

(a) **Internal Factors** Seed viability, dormancy, maturity of embryos, etc.

(b) **External Factors** Water, light, temperature, oxygen, etc.

28. **A situation occurs when seeds fail to germinate even if they are placed under favourable conditions for germination either due to internal factors or due to specific requirement for some internal factors. Identify the name of that situation.**

Ans This situation is known as dormancy of seeds.

29. **What is the biological significance of seed dormancy?**

Ans Seed dormancy allow storage of seeds in viable state for longer periods in adverse climatic conditions. Here, it is important means of survival.

30. **Explain different types of seed germination.** **NCERT**

Ans Refer to text on page no. 379.

Short Answer Type I Questions

(2 Marks)

31. **What is the mechanism underlying the phenomenon by which the terminal/apical bud suppresses the growth of lateral buds? Suggest measures to overcome this phenomenon.** **NCERT Exemplar**

Ans This phenomenon is known as apical dominance. It is the phenomenon of suppression of growth of lateral buds by the growth of terminal bud. Removal of apical bud causes the sprouting of lateral buds. However, a paste of auxin can stimulate the effect of apical bud. (2)

32. **Explain inhibitory effect of auxins with the help of one example.**

Ans Higher concentration of auxins inhibit growth of the plants. In normal course in nature, self produced auxin in plants inhibits the growth and development of lateral buds and as a result lateral bud remains dormant. (2)

33. **In botanical gardens and tea gardens, gardeners trim the plants regularly so that they remain bushy. Does this practice have any scientific explanation?** **NCERT Exemplar**

Ans The apical buds present in tea and other plants prevents the growth of lateral buds in them by releasing auxin hormone. This phenomenon is called apical dominance. Trimming of tea garden and botanical garden removes the apical bud and allowing the lateral buds to grow laterally and give plants a dense bushy appearance.

The scientific explanation for this trimming method is that apical bud is removed and thus it results in the removal of auxin and phenomenon of apical dominance is overcomed. (2)

34. How do IBA and 2, 4-D are used in agriculture?

Ans IBA and 2, 4-D are used to induce formation of roots on cuttings of many ornamental, horticultural and forest trees. 2, 4-D can also be used as a weedicide. (2)

35. Explain what is meant by the terms auxin precursors, anti-auxins, free auxins and bound auxins.

Ans The compounds, which can be converted into auxins, are called auxin precursors. The compounds, which inhibit the actions of auxins, are termed anti-auxins. The auxins, which can easily be extracted, are called free auxins and auxins, which are hard to extract and need the use of organic solvents, are referred to as bound auxins. ($\frac{1}{2} \times 4$)

36. Where are the following hormones synthesised in plants?

(i) IAA (ii) Gibberellin **NCERT Exemplar**

Ans (i) IAA is synthesised in tip of coleoptile.
(ii) Gibberellin is synthesised inside the plastids of immature seeds, young leaves or even roots. (1+1)

37. The rice seedlings infected with fungus *Gibberella fujikuroi* are called foolish seedlings? What was the reason behind it? **NCERT Exemplar**

Ans The rice seedlings infected with fungus *Gibberella fujikuroi* are called foolish seedlings because these seedlings grow foolishly so tall that they ultimately, fall on ground and result into death of plants. (2)

38. What conditions can induce the phenomenon of bolting naturally and how can it be induced artificially?

Ans Some plants require specific long day periods or specific cold treatments for flowering. Bolting can be induced artificially by the treatment with gibberellins. (1+1)

39. How does spraying of sugarcane plants with gibberellins increase the yield of sugar?

Ans Spraying of sugar plants with gibberellin can increase the yield of sugar. Spraying increases the length of internodes and increased or lengthy internodes will produce more sugar. (2)

40. What would be expected to happen if,

(i) GA_3 is applied to rice seedlings.
(ii) dividing cells stop differentiating.
(iii) a rotten fruit gets mixed with unripe fruits.
(iv) you forget to add cytokinin to the culture medium. **NCERT**

Ans (i) Rice seedlings will grow extremely tall.
(ii) An undifferentiated mass of cells is formed.
(iii) The unripe fruits will ripe quickly.
(iv) The callus will not develop shoot buds. ($\frac{1}{2} \times 4$)

41. In an experiment, the callus produced from internodal segments did not proliferate until coconut water was added. Given reason.

Ans Callus (i.e. undifferentiated mass of cells) proliferates only when nutrient medium containing auxin was supplemented with coconut milk because it contains kinetin (a cytokinin) which stimulates growth of plant tissues. (2)

42. Why do cut leaves dipped in cytokinins stay green for longer duration?

Ans The cut leaves dipped in cytokinins stay green for longer duration because cytokinins retard ageing of plant organs by promoting protein synthesis and mobilisation of nutrient resources. (2)

43. A farmer grows cucumber plants in his field. He wants to increase the number of female flowers in them. Which plant growth regulator can be applied to achieve this? **NCERT Exemplar**

Ans Ethylene is also responsible to play a major role in determining the sex of monoecious flowers and is associated with the promotion of femaleness in plants thus the farmer must spray ethylene hormone on cucumber crop to produce female flowers and to increase the yield (number of fruits produced). (2)

44. Plant growth substances (PGSs) have innumerable practical applications. Name the PGR you should use to

(i) increase yield of sugarcane
(ii) promote lateral shoot growth
(iii) cause sprouting of potato tuber
(iv) inhibit seed germination **NCERT Exemplar**

Ans (i) Gibberellin
(ii) Cytokinins
(iii) Gibberellin
(iv) Abscisic acid ($\frac{1}{2} \times 4$)

45. State the antagonistic effect of cytokinin and ABA.

Ans Cytokinin delays senescence, while ABA promotes senescence. (2)

46. Explain different type of seed germination.

Ans Refer to text on page no. 379

47. Which factors affect the germination of seed?

Ans Refer to text on page no. 380.

Short Answer Type II Questions

(3 Marks)

48. **List five main natural plant growth regulators. Write a note on discovery, physiological functions and agricultural /horticultural applications of any one of them.**

Ans Five main natural plant growth regulators are auxins, gibberellins, ethylene, cytokinins and ABA. (1/2)

Auxins

(i) **Discovery** Refer to text on page no. 374.

(ii) **Physiological Functions** Refer to text on page no. 375.

(iii) **Agricultural/Horticultural Applications** Refer to text on page no. 376. (2½)

49. **Which parts of the plants produce gibberellins? State two functions of this hormone and mention why it was named gibberellin.**

Ans The major sites of gibberellin production in plants are embryos, roots and young leaves near the shoot tip. (1)

For two functions of gibberllins Refer to text on page no. 376. (½ + ½)

It was named after the fungus, which is the source of it, i.e. *Gibberella fujikuroi*, they have a gibbane ring in their molecular structure. (1)

50. **How are gibberellins useful in agriculture to improve productivity. Give any three points in support of your answer.**

Ans Refer to text on page no. 377.

51. **Which plant hormone can transform genetically dwarf plants into tall plants ? State the mechanism involved with suitable example.**

Ans Cabbage and sugarbeet plants have rosette habit of leaves. The leaves in these plants are condensed because of shortening of internodal area of the stem. It is a genetic character, when we spray GA_3 solution on these plants, these became abnormally tall. It happens because of increase in internodal area. Thus, such genetically dwarf plant is made tall by GA_3. (3)

52. **The role of ethylene and abscisic acid is both positive and negative. Justify the statement.** **NCERT Exemplar**

Ans The role of ethylene and abscisic acid is both positive and negative. Ethylene is a simple gaseous PGR. It is synthesised in large amount by tissues undergoing senescence and ripening. It also promotes senescence and abscission of plant organs especially of leaves and flowers. This is its negative effect.

As it's positive effect, ethylene breaks seed and bud dormancy, initiates germination in peanut seeds, sprouting of potato tubers. It promotes internode/petiole elongation in deep water rice plants. It helps leaves/ inner parts of the shoot to remain above water. (1½ × 2)

Long Answer Type Questions

(5 Marks)

53. **What are plant growth regulators? Name any four different chemical nature of them with one example of each.**

Ans Plant growth regulators are small, simple molecules secreted in minute quantities, that influence various physiological functions in plants. They are of diverse chemical composition. (1)

(i) Indole compounds [such as- Indole-3- Acetic Acid (IAA)]

(ii) Adenine derivatives [such as kinetin, 6-furfuryl amino purine]

(iii) Derivatives of carotenoids [such as Abscisic Acid (ABA)]

(iv) Terpenes [such as gibberellic acids] (1× 4)

54. **Explain why ?**

(i) Exogenous application of auxin fails to enhance the growth of intact plants.

(ii) Vitamins are not considered as plant growth hormones.

(iii) Some plants, belonging to halophytes and growing in marshy lands, face great difficulty in seed germination.

(iv) Gibberellins do not enhance the growth of isolated plant parts.

Ans (i) Auxin fails to cause growth of intact plants because the required amount of auxin is already present in the apical region of such plants and only these parts grow.

(ii) Vitamins have no specific influence on growth of plants. They are essential dietary factors needed by an organism in small amounts. They influence on growth and metabolism through their indirect effect on metabolism because some vitamins are cofactors of many enzymes.

(iii) Plants belonging to halophytes and growing in marshy lands face a great difficulty in seed germination due to the presence of high concentration of salt in water. These plants solve this problem by vivipary.

(iv) Gibberellins require the presence of meristematic cells to cause elongation growth. Therefore, they do not enhance growth of isolated plant parts if meristematic cells are absent. (5)

55. **Name a hormone, which** **NCERT Exemplar**

(i) is gaseous in nature

(ii) is responsible for phototropism

(iii) induces femaleness in flowers of cucumber

(iv) is used for killing weeds (dicots)

(v) induces flowering in long day plants

Ans (i) Ethylene (ii) Auxin hormone

(iii) Ethylene hormone (iv) 2, 4-D (Auxin)

(v) Gibberellin hormone. (1×5)

56. What is ethylene? Give its functions.

Or Name the only gaseous natural plant growth regulator. Mention any two of its effects on plants in detail.

Ans Refer to text on page no. 377 and 378.

57. Write in detail about abscisic acid.

Ans Refer to text on page no. 378.

58. While experimentation, why do you think it is difficult to assign any effect seen to any single hormone? **NCERT Exemplar**

Ans Most of the hormones are synergistic to each other in their mode of action. Thus, during experimentation, we cannot judge whether, a particular effect is produced by a single hormone or is an additive effect of many hormones. For example, (2)

(i) Auxins help to initiate rooting in stem cuttings, (an application widely used for plant propagation.) Cytokinins also show the similar function of root formation. Auxins promote flowering, e.g. in pineapples.They also induce parthenocarpy, e.g. in tomatoes.

(ii) Both gibberellins and ethylene are synergistic to auxin in initiating flowering and for synchronising fruit set in pineapples.

(iii) Cytokinins and gibberellins help overcome the apical dominance and delay the process of leaf senescence.

(iv) On the other hand, ethylene promotes senescence and abscission of plant organs especially of leaves and flowers. This shows that all hormones are synergistic to each other in their mode of action in plants. (3)

59. Some time the growth of embryo remain suspended and does not resume even in the favourable condition what does this phenomenon called? And mention various factors responsible for it.

Ans Refer to text on page no. 379.

SUMMARY

- **Growth** is an irreversible change, increase in physiological parameters like length, height, weight, etc., of living beings. Determinate growth ends after attaining maturity while indeterminate growth is unending.
- **Phases of growth** are the series of events during growth. In **meristematic phase** active growth occurs, followed by **elongation phase** where size increases and **maturation phase** signifies structural and functional differentiation, i.e. cell develops into specialised tissues, e.g. xylem and phloem.
- **Arithmetic growth**, i.e. constant rate, i.e. 2, 4, 6 and 8, etc., expressed as

$$\boxed{Lt = L_o + rt}$$

- **Geometric growth** is the repeated division of each cell. It has a lag phase expotential and stationary phase and it is expressed as

$$\boxed{W_1 = W_0 e^{rt}}$$

- **Growth rate** is the increased growth per unit time.
- **Absolute growth rate** measures total growth per unit time while **relative rate** measures growth rate per unit time per unit of initial parameter.
- **Measurement of growth** is the measure of increase in length, surface area, volume, dry weight, etc. Auxanometer, crescograph and horizontal microscope are used for this measurement.
- **Conditions for growth** are light, temperature, water, salts, food and oxygen are external factors. Internal factors growth hormones, enzymes and genetics.
- **Differentiation, Dedifferntiation** and **Redifferentiation** A permanent localised qualitative change in size, biochemistry, function, etc., is differentiation. The attainment of dividing ability by differentiated cells is **dedifferentiation.**
- The process where dedifferentiated cells again loose ability to divide is **redifferentiation**.
- **Development** includes all changes an organism goes through during its life cycle.
- **Plasticity** is the ability of a plant to modify its development due to extrinsic and intrinsic factors.
- **Plant hormones** are the organic compounds, which regulates the growth and development in plants. Based on their functions they can be promoters, e.g. auxin, gibberellin and cytokinin and inhibitors, e.g. abscisic acid and ethylene.
- **Seed dormancy** is the inactive state of the seed, caused by impermeability of seed coat, chemicals and mechanical resistance, etc. Dormancy allow viable seed storage for long, effective dispersion, etc.

Chapter Practice

Multiple Choice Questions

1 Mark

1. Growth can be measured in various ways. Which of these can be used as parameters to measure growth?
   (a) Increase in cell number
   (b) Increase in cell size
   (c) Increase in length and weight
   (d) All of the above

2. Coconut water contains **NCERT Exemplar**
   (a) ABA (b) auxin (c) cytokinin (d) gibberellin

3. Ethylene is used for
   (a) retarding ripening of tomatoes
   (b) hastening of ripening of fruits
   (c) slowing down ripening of apples
   (d) Both (b) and (c)

4. ABA acts as antagonistic to
   (a) ethylene (b) cytokinin
   (c) gibberellic acid (d) IAA

5. Plasticity in plant growth means that
   (a) plant roots are extensible
   (b) plant development is dependent on the environment
   (c) stems can extend
   (d) None of the above

Assertion-Reason Type Questions

1 Mark

■ **Direction** (Q. Nos. 6-13) *In each of the following questions, a statement of Assertion (A) is given followed by corresponding statement of Reason (R). Of the statements, mark the correct answer as*

(a) If both A and R are true and R is the correct explanation of A
(b) If both A and R are true, but R is not the correct explanation of A
(c) If A is true, but R is false
(d) If A is false, but R is true

6. **Assertion** (A) Growth is invariably associated with differentiation.
   Reason (R) Growth and differentiation are permanent changes which occur in an organism's body.

7. A logistic growth curve is basically S-shaped and is used to represent the growth of living organisms in their natural environment. Considering the above statement, comment upon the appropriateness of the Assertion and the Reason.

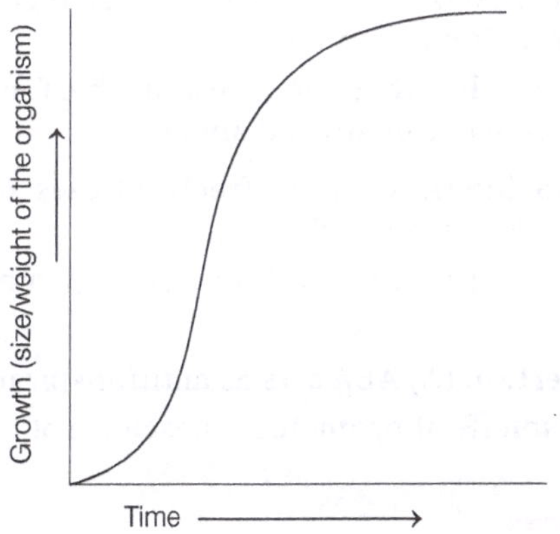

   Assertion (A) Sigmoid growth curve consists of three parts.
   Reason (R) Lag phase is also known as grand phase of growth.

8. **Assertion** (A) Hormones are also called growth regulators.
   Reason (R) These promote or inhibit plant growth.

9. **Assertion** (A) Plants have hormones called phytohormones.
   Reason (R) These increase the rate of reactions, thus always accelerate growth and other related changes.

10. Given below is a diagram showing the phenomenon of apical dominance wherein the shoot apex of a plant grows faster, thus, preventing the growth of lateral bud present at a lower position. Study the diagram and

comment upon the appropriateness of the Assertion and the Reason.

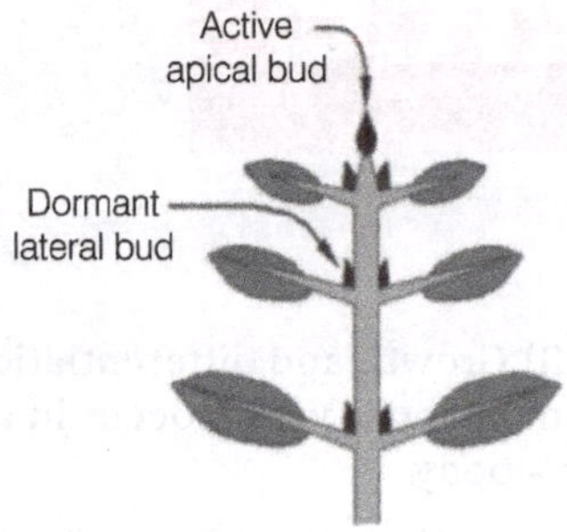

Assertion (A) Removal of shoot tip increases apical dominance.

Reason (R) Due to the accumulation of auxin in lateral parts, growth is enhanced.

11. **Assertion** (A) Gibberellin is useful in early seed production in conifers.

Reason (R) Ethephon is responsible for early ripening in tomato and apple.

12. **Assertion** (A) Ethylene freely diffuses across the membrane of plant cells.

Reason (R) It causes climacteric ripening of fruit.

13. **Assertion** (A) ABA acts as antitranspirant.

Reason (R) It promotes senescence of leaf.

Answers

1. (d) 2. (c) 3. (b) 4. (c) 5. (b) 6. (a)
7. (c) 8. (a) 9. (c) 10. (d) 11. (b) 12. (b)
13. (b)

Very Short Answer Type Questions

(1 Mark)

14. What do you mean by the term absolute growth rate?

15. Name the groups of growth regulating plant hormones, which stimulate the following
    (i) Cell division even in non-meristematic tissues.
    (ii) Elongation of stem and expansion of leaves.

16. Supply the scientific terms for the following
    (i) A period of suspended growth and even a period of rest is referred to as dormancy; usually occurs during the dry or cold season of the year.
    (ii) A growth promoting substance first isolated from maize kernels.

17. Define plasticity.

Short Answer Type I Questions

(2 Marks)

18. Differentiate between dedifferentiation and redifferentiation.

19. In most plants, the terminal bud suppresses the development of lateral buds. What is this phenomenon called? Name the phytohormone that can promote the phenomenon.

20. Which hormone breaks seed dormancy? State the mechanism involved.

Short Answer Type II Questions

(3 Marks)

21. What are important characterstics of plant growth?

22. Give one antagonistic functions of each of the following hormone pairs.
    (i) Gibberellins – Abscisic acid
    (ii) Cytokinin – Ethylene
    (iii) Ethylene – Auxin

23. What is the significance of seed dormancy?

Long Answers Type Questions

(5 Marks)

24. (i) Define plant growth.
    (ii) What is meaning of bakanae?
    (iii) Name the microorganism which yields gibberellins.

25. (i) Name the cytokinin-like substance isolated from corn kernels and coconut milk.
    (ii) How gibberellins are different from auxins in their chemical structure?

26. (i) What will you do to prevent leaf and fruit drop in plants? Support your answer with reason.
    (ii) Explain inhibitory effect of auxin with the help of an example.

Case Based Questions

(4/5 Marks)

27. The graph given below depicts the length of sugarcane before and after the application of Gibberellic acid (GA_3) in the sugarcane field.

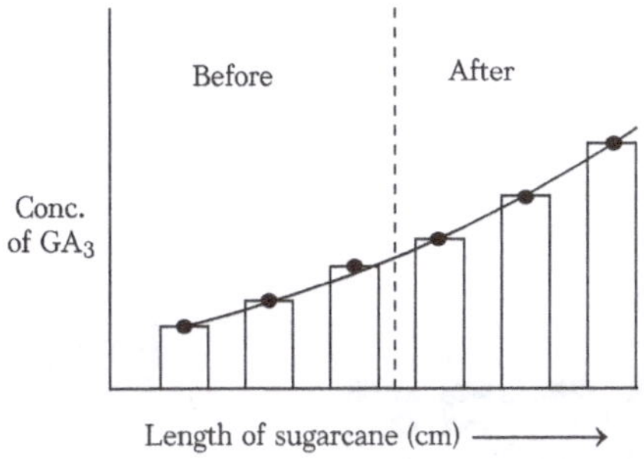

Consider the graph given above and answer the following questions.

(i) What conclusion can be drawn from the above graph ?

(ii) Application of gibberellins in the sugarcane field, tend to increase sugarcane yield upto 20 tonnes/acre. How ?

(iii) Comment upon the nature of gibberellins. How are gibberellins transported in the plants?

(iv) Gibberellins can be used to store fruits for a long time. Why ? Give two other applications of gibberellins.

28. *Read the following passage and answer the questions that follow.*

Phytohormones play vital roles in the growth and development of plants as well as in interactions of plants with microbes. These are naturally occurring small organic substances which are generally active at very low concentration and often, impose inhibitory effects if applied or present at higher concentration. The five classical phytohormones are auxins, cytokinins, gibberellins, abscisic acid and ethylene. These hormones produce various effects in plants like phototropism, bolting, dormancy, abscission, etc. They also have synergistic and antagonistic functions in various processes.

(i) Which hormone induces phototropism and geotropism in plants?

(ii) What is precursor of gibberellins?

(iii) In which part of plant, high concentration of auxin is present?

(iv) If a ripe banana is kept in a basket full of unriped ones, what will happen? Will the changes be morphological.

(v) Which hormone is used to speed up the malting process? Does the hormone find any other use in industry?

29. Plant growth regulators are the chemicals that controls the growth and development of the plants.
Two graphs given below represent two conditions (i) Before and (ii) After the application of a hormone.

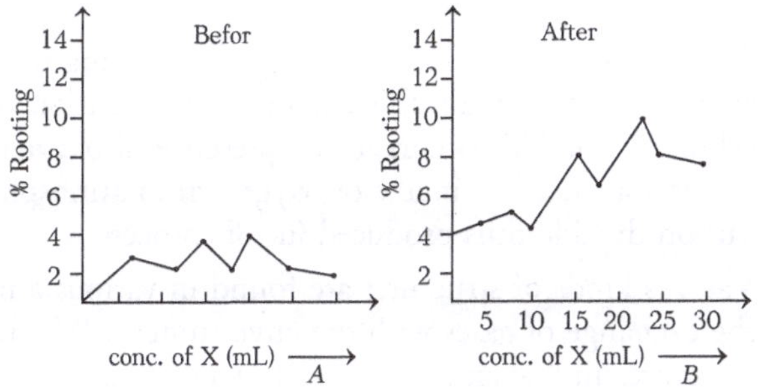

(i) Which hormone is referred to here ?

(ii) Why is there a difference in the percentage of rooting as visible from the graphs above? How does the hormone help in combating this?

Or

(ii) Does the increasing concentration of X always support root elongation? Is the case same with shoot elongation?

(iii) State two functions of the hormone identified in (i) above.

CHAPTER

17

Breathing and Exchange of Gases

All living organisms require energy for carrying out various cellular activities. They obtain this energy from oxidation of food material at cellular level. This occurs in the presence of oxygen. So, there is a continuous need of intake of oxygen from atmosphere and removal of carbon dioxide thus produced in this process.

Various kinds of structures are found in various animals which facilitate the exchange of gases with the environment. We shall study these structures in few animals in brief. The exchange of gases in human beings is given in this chapter.

TOPIC 01 Respiration : Types and Respiratory Organs

As we already know cellular respiration occurs in the presence or absence of oxygen. So, it is of the following types

1. Aerobic Respiration

When oxygen is used for respiration, its called **aerobic respiration**. The organisms undergoing the process are termed as **aerobes**.

2. Anaerobic Respiration

It occurs in the absence of molecular oxygen in the cytoplasm (also called as **fermentation**). It yields only about 5% of the food energy. The organisms undergoing the process are called **anaerobes**, e.g. yeasts oxidise glucose to ethanol and CO_2.

- Anaerobic respiration appeared first in primitive atmosphere due to the absence of oxygen there.
- Respiration is a catabolic process. It breaks organic molecules and releases their bond energy.

> **Knowledge Plus**
>
> The term breathing and respiration are not same. Breathing is the first step of respiration and is a physical process, while respiration is a biochemical process involving exchange of gases and oxidation of food. Inspiration is an active process of breathing while expiration is a passive process.

Respiratory Organs in Animals

Different animal groups have evolved different mechanism of breathing for the exchange of gases.

Lower animals like sponges, cnidarians, Platyhelminthes and free-living roundworms exhange O_2 by simple diffusion through body surface. Annelids like earthworms respire through skin and few forms exhibit gills to respire.

Arthropods have gills, trachea, book gills, book lungs for respiration. In several forms cutaneous exchange is also seen.

Special feather-like **gills,** pulmonary sac and body surface are used by most of the molluscs. In echinoderms papulae, cloacal respiratory tree, skin, gills, peristominal gills and even genital bursae are used as respiratory organs. The highly vascularised bags called **lungs** are used by the terrestrial forms for the exchange of gases, e.g. reptiles, birds and mammals. Amphibians (frog) respire through their skin as well as lungs.

Human Respiratory System

Human respiratory system may be divided into two major components, i.e. **conduction of gases** and **respiration** or **exchange of gases.**

Conduction of Gases

This component includes the passage for transportation of atmospheric air to the lung alveoli and return from lungs to the exterior. It clears air, humidifies it and bring it to body temperature. In this part, gaseous exchange does not take place. It is also called **dead air space**.

The various parts are as follows

(i) **External Nares** (Nostrils) There is a pair of slits at the lower end of the nose, which opens into the nasal chamber through the nasal passage.

(ii) **Nasal Chambers** Pair of passage located at the back of nostrils just above the mouth cavity. **Nasal septum** is a median partition that separate the two chambers.

Each chamber has three regions, i.e. **vestibular, respiratory** and **olfactory**. The chambers has special pseudostratified ciliated epithelium by which air is filtered (by hairs) and moistened (by mucus).

(iii) **Internal Nares** These are the posterior openings of the nasal chambers that lead into the nasopharynx.

(iv) **Nasopharynx** It is the upper part of pharynx, into which internal nares open.

(v) **Larynx** It is the upper part of trachea. Larynx is often called the **Adam's apple** and is more prominent in men than in women. It allows the air to pass into lungs. Nasopharynx opens through **glottis** of the larynx into trachea. Glottis is a slit-like aperture that remains open except during swallowing.

The glottis bears a leaf-like cartilaginous flap, the **epiglottis** at its anterior region. It closes the glottis to check the entry of food during swallowing. Larynx helps in sound production and hence, called the **sound box.**

The laryngeal skeleton consists of nine cartilages, i.e. three single (thyroid, cricoid and epiglottis) and three paired (arytenoid, corniculate and cuneiform). Thyroid cartilage is involved in formation of Adam's apple, cuneiform cartilage connects epiglottis with arytenoid cartilage.

Note Snoring during the sleep occurs due to the partial blockage of respiratory tract by the tongue.

(vi) **Trachea** It is a thin-walled tube, about 11cm long and 2.5 cm wide. It extends upto the mid-thoracic cavity. It passes the air to the alveoli.

(vii) **Primary and Secondary Bronchi** At the level of 5th thoracic vertebra, the trachea divides into two tubes, right and left primary bronchi.

Each bronchi further divides into **secondary bronchi**. The secondary bronchi subdivides into smaller **tertiary bronchi**, which is further divided into still smaller **bronchioles**. The small terminal bronchioles give off a number of thin, irregular walled, one cell thick, vascular bag-like structure called **lung alveoli.**

Wall of trachea, bronchi and bronchioles is composed of fibromuscular tissue and is lined by pseudostratified ciliated columnar epithelium rich in mucus secreting cells. Cartilaginous rings support the walls of the trachea and the bronchi to prevent their collapse. The branching network of bronchi, bronchioles and alveoli form the lungs.

Respiratory/Exchange of Gases

The **alveoli** and their **ducts** form this part of the respiratory system. It is the site of actual diffusion of O_2 and CO_2 between blood and atmospheric air. The branching network of bronchi, bronchioles and alveoli comprises the **lungs**, which provide the surface for exchange of gases in humans.

Lungs

Humans have two lungs one at right and other on left side in chest region. These are triangular bags that constitute the respiratory organ and are site for gaseous exchange (O_2 / CO_2).

They lie in the **thoracic cavity** on the sides of the heart. It is an anatomically airtight chamber. The thoracic cavity is enclosed dorsally by **thoracic vertebrae**, laterally by the **ribs**, ventrally by the **sternum** and closed below by a dome-shaped **diaphragm**. The arrangement of lungs is such that, any change in the volume of thoracic cavity will be manifested in the pulmonary cavity. This arrangement is necessary for breathing as the pulmonary volume cannot be altered directly.

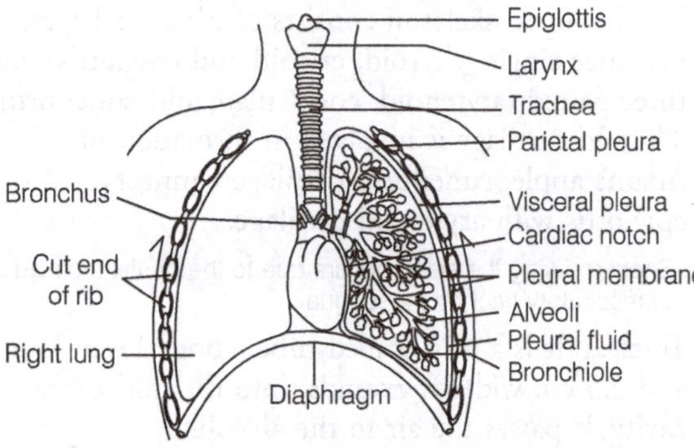

Fig. 17.1 Diagrammatic view of human respiratory system (sectional view on the left side)

Each lung is enclosed by two membranes called the **pleura** (layers of peritoneum of the thorax). The inner membrane, called the **visceral pleuron**, firmly bounds to the surface of lungs. The outer membrane, called the **parietal pleuron** is held to the thoracic wall and diaphragm by connective tissue. **Pleural cavity** is a very narrow space that exists between the two pleura. It contains the **pleural fluid** secreted by the pleura, for reducing friction on the lung surface.

External Features of Lungs

(i) The **left lung** has two lobes, i.e. superior lobe and inferior lobe separated by oblique fissure. It has a cardiac notch, a concave cavity where the heart lies. It is longer and narrower than right lung.

(ii) The **right lung** is bigger and has three lobes, i.e. superior lobe, middle lobe and inferior lobe separated by horizontal fissure and oblique fissure.

> **Knowledge Plus**
> - There are about 300 million alveoli in the two lungs with a combined surface area of about 70 m^2.
> - A film of lecithin lines the alveoli, that lowers the surface tension.
> - If the chest wall is pierced (e.g. by a stab wound), atmospheric air rushes into the pleural cavity, eliminating the pressure difference across lung walls causing the lungs to collapse. The condition is called pneumothorax, which is lethal.

Topic Practice 1

Multiple Choice Questions

1 Mark

1. Oxygen (O_2) is utilised by an organism to

(a) directly breakdown the nutrient molecules
(b) indirectly breakdown the nutrient molecules
(c) obtain nourishment from the food
(d) burn the organic compounds indirectly

Ans (b) Oxygen (O_2) is utilised by the living entities to indirectly breakdown the nutrients like glucose to derive energy for performing various activities, etc.

2. Tracheal respiration is a feature of

(a) cockroach (b) centipedes
(c) arachnids (d) Both (a) and (b)

Ans (a) Tracheal respiration is a mode of respiration in insects like cockroach, centipedes and millipedes. Arachnid like spiders and scorpion performs book lung respiration.

3. Correct sequence of the air passage in humans is

(a) Nose → Larynx → Pharynx → Bronchioles → Alveoli
(b) Nose → Pharynx → Larynx → Bronchioles → Bronchi
(c) Nose → Pharynx → Larynx → Bronchioles → Trachea
(d) External nostril → Nasal passage → Internal nostril → Pharynx → Larynx → Trachea → Bronchi → Bronchioles → Alveoli

Ans (d) The correct sequence of air passage in humans in given by option (d).

4. At which thoracic vertebra does trachea divide into right and left primary bronchi?

(a) 5 (b) 6 (c) 9 (d) 4

Ans (a) Trachea is a straight tube extending upto the mid-thoracic cavity, which divides at the level of 5th thoracic vertebra into the right and left bronchi.

5. Which of the following statement is incorrect about nasopharynx?
 (a) Internal nostrils opens into the nasopharynx
 (b) It is the common passage for air and food
 (c) It is a portion of pharynx
 (d) Nasopharynx opens through the glottis of the larynx region into the trachea

Ans (b) Nasopharynx is a portion of pharynx through which only air can pass. It opens through the glottis into the trachea.

6. Which portion of the human respiratory system is called sound box?
 (a) Larynx (b) Trachea
 (c) Nasopharynx (d) Glottis

Ans (a) Larynx is a cartilaginous box, which helps in sound production and hence called sound box.

7. Friction on the lungs surface is reduced by
 (a) double layered pleura
 (b) single layered pleura
 (c) epiglottis upto trachea
 (d) mucous membrane surrounding the lungs

Ans (a) Humans lungs are covered by a double membrane called pleura, with pleural fluid between them. Pleural fluid reduces the friction on the lung surface.

8. Conducting part of the respiratory system comprises
 (a) external nostrils upto the terminal bronchioles
 (b) internal nostrils upto trachea
 (c) epiglottis upto trachea
 (d) larynx upto bronchi

Ans (a) Human respiratory system comprises of

Conducting Portion	Respiratory Portion
The conducting portion provides a passage for the air. It consists of nasopharynx, larynx, trachea, bronchi, bronchioles and terminal bronchioles.	The respiratory portion consists of bronchioles, alveolar ducts and alveolar sacs. It serves to get rid the body of CO_2 and pick up oxygen.

9. Which of the following option correctly describe the function of given respiratory organs of human body?
 (a) Trachea–long tube supported by complete cartilaginous rings for conducting inspired air
 (b) Pleural membrane–surround ribs on both sides to provide cushion against rubbing
 (c) Alveoli–thin-walled vascular bag-like structures for exchange of gases
 (d) Lower end of lungs–diaphragm pulls it down during inspiration

Ans (c) Alveoli are thin-walled vascular bag-like structures for exchange of gases. Trachea is an air conducting tube through which transport of gases takes place.

Pleural membrane reduces friction on the lung surface. Diaphragm is involved in the inspiration and expiration process of breathing.

Very Short Answer Type Questions

(1 Mark)

10. What is the importance of oxygen in respiration?

Ans Majority of organisms respires aerobically as they use oxygen for the breakdown of the food molecules to liberate energy for their metabolic activities to sustain life.

11. Why do cells need a constant supply of oxygen?

Ans Cells continuously need oxygen for the metabolic reactions that releases energy from the molecules. This energy is used by cells for various functions of the body.

12. Give the name of the two phases of indirect respiration. Also name the preliminary phase preceding them.

Ans External respiration and internal respiration are the two phases of indirect respiration. Breathing or ventilation is the preliminary phase preceding them.

13. Name the factors on which mechanism of respiration depends.

Ans Mechanism of respiration varies depending mainly on animal's habitat and level of organisation.

14. What is the site of gaseous exchange in an insect? NCERT

Ans The actual site of gaseous exchange in an insect is tracheoles and tracheolar end cells.

15. Why is respiration in insect called direct?

Ans The insects have network of tubes (tracheal system). The cells of the tracheal system exchange O_2 / CO_2 directly with the air by the spiracles present in insect's body.

16. Name the structure that regulates the air passage during eating or drinking.

Ans During swallowing, the glottis is covered by the leaf like cartilaginous flap called epiglottis at its anterior region. It regulates the air passage during eating or drinking.

17. What causes snoring?

Ans Partial blocking of upper respiratory tract by tongue leading to turbulence of airflow which causes a rough rattling inspiratory noise is called snoring.

18. A fluid-filled double membranous layer surrounds the lungs. Name it. **NCERT Exemplar**

Ans A fluid-filled double membranous layer surrounding the lungs is called pleural membrane and pleural fluid is found in between the two.

19. Give the name of the site of actual diffusion of O_2 and CO_2.

Ans The name of the site of actual diffusion of O_2 and CO_2 is alveoli and their ducts.

Short Answer Type I Questions

2 Marks

20. Give the name of the organs of respiration in the following organisms.

(i) Flatworm (ii) Birds
(iii) Frog (iv) Cockroach

Ans (i) Body surface
(ii) Lungs
(iii) Skin, buccopharyngeal lining and lungs
(iv) Trachea. (½ × 4)

21. Complete the following sentences.

(i) Nasal chambers are separated from the oral cavity by ....
(ii) A film of .... lines the alveoli to lower the surface tension.
(iii) Sound is produced by vibration of .... located in the ....
(iv) Left lung has ..... lobes, while right lung has .... lobes.

Ans (i) palate
(ii) lecithin
(iii) vocal cords, larynx
(iv) two, three (½ × 4)

22. What is Adam's apple? Is it more prominent in males or females?

Ans Larynx is often called as Adam's apple. It is more prominent in males than females. (1+1)

23. What prevents the trachea and the bronchi from collapsing?

Ans Cartilaginous rings are incomplete from behind which supports the walls of the trachea and the bronchi to prevent them from collapsing. (2)

24. Name the epithelium and the cells present in the walls of trachea, bronchi and bronchioles.

Ans The walls of trachea, bronchi and bronchioles have pseudostratified ciliated columnar epithelium which is rich in mucus secreting cells. (1 × 2)

25. How the movement of lungs during breathing is protected from rubbing against visceral organs?

Ans A very narrow cavity called pleura exists between the two membranes enclosing the lungs, which bears the pleural fluid that reduces the friction on lung surface and protects it from mechanical jerks. (1 × 2)

Short Answer Type II Questions

3 Marks

26. Give two examples of each of the following

(i) Animals having internal gills.
(ii) Animal groups showing tracheal respiration.
(iii) Anaerobes.

Ans (i) Fishes and *Pila*, etc.
(ii) Insects, centipedes and millipedes, etc.
(iii) Certain bacteria, parasitic worms (e.g. *Ascaris* and tapeworm), etc. (1×3)

27. Draw a labelled diagram of the human respiratory system.

Ans Refer to fig. no. 17.1 on page no 392.

28. State the anatomical dissimilarities between the left and right lung.

Ans Refer to text on page no. 392 (External features of lungs).

29. A person dies in an accident in which his chest cavity was punctured, but no lung damage was there. Point out the cause of death.

Ans The movement of air into and out of the lungs is carried out by creating a pressure gradient between the lungs and the atmosphere.

The pressure within the lungs is less than the atmospheric pressure so, there is a negative pressure in the lungs with respect to atmospheric pressure. The puncture in the chest affects this pressure gradient maintained by the lungs and thus may cause cessation of breathing. (3)

Long Answer Type Questions

5 Marks

30. Describe the various air passages that the air has to cross, in order to reach alveoli.

Ans Refer to text on page no. 391.

31. Distinguish between

(i) Tracheoles and bronchioles
(ii) Right lung and left lung

Ans (i) Differences between tracheoles and bronchioles are

Tracheoles	Bronchioles
These are respiratory tubes of insects.	These are respiratory tubes of mammals.
They penetrate all parts of the body.	They occur only in the lungs.
They end blindly in tissue cell.	They give off alveolar ducts.

(2½)

(ii) Differences between right and left lungs are

Right Lung	Left Lung
It has three lobes and median border is entire.	It has two lobes with anteromedian border having cardiac notch.
It is larger and heavier.	It is smaller and lighter.
It is shorter, but broader than the left lung.	It is longer, but narrower than the right lung.

(2½)

32. **Describe the structure of lungs with suitable diagrams.**

Ans Refer to text on page no. 392.

TOPIC 02 Respiration Processes : Breathing and Gaseous Exchange

Mechanism of Respiration

The main mechanism of respiration is categorised into following three steps

(i) **Breathing** (pulmonary ventilation) is the inflow of atmospheric air and release (outflow) of CO_2 rich alveolar air.

(ii) **Exchange of gases** (O_2 and CO_2) across alveolar membrane as well as in tissues.

(iii) **Transport of gases** by the blood.

Breathing

It is an extracellular, energy consuming and physical process. It involves movement of thorax, expansion (inflation) and deflation of lungs and flow of air into and from the lungs by creating a pressure gradient between the lungs and the atmosphere. The movement of diaphragm and a specialised set of muscles (i.e. external and internal intercostals between the ribs) help in generation of such difference of pressure gradients between lungs and atmosphere. Breathing mainly involves two steps

1. Inspiration

It is an active process by which fresh air enters the lungs. It can occur if the pressure within the lungs (intrapulmonary pressure) is less than the atmospheric pressure, i.e. negative pressure in lungs with respect to atmospheric pressure.

Following muscles play an important role

(i) **Diaphragm** It is lowered by the contraction of its muscle fibres and becomes flat. This causes an increase in the volume of thoracic chamber in the antero-posterior axis.

(ii) **External Intercostal Muscles** They occur between the ribs (internal intercostal muscles are related to expiration). The external intercostal muscles contract and pull the **ribs** and the **sternum** upward and outward thus, increasing the volume of thoracic chamber in dorsoventral axis.

Thus, the overall increase in the volume of thoracic cavity causes an increase in pulmonary volume. As a result, there is a decrease in the intra-pulmonary pressure. The greater atmospheric pressure outside the body now causes air to flow rapidly into external nares, which sequentially leads to alveoli.

From the alveoli, O_2 passes into blood of the capillaries and CO_2 diffuses out from blood to alveoli's lumen.

2. Expiration

It is a passive process by which CO_2 is expelled out from the lungs. It takes place when the intra-pulmonary pressure is higher than the atmospheric pressure.

The movements of muscles involved in the breathing mechanism are as follows

(i) **Diaphragm** The muscle fibres of the diaphragm relax making it convex, decreasing volume of the thoracic cavity.

(ii) **Internal Intercostal Muscles** These muscles contract, thus, pulling the ribs downward and inward, decreasing the thoracic volume. The overall volume of the thoracic cavity, thus decreases thereby reducing the pulmonary volume. As a result, the intra-pulmonary pressure increases slightly above the atmospheric pressure.

This in turn causes the expulsion of the air from the lungs. The process of expiration is simpler than inspiration.

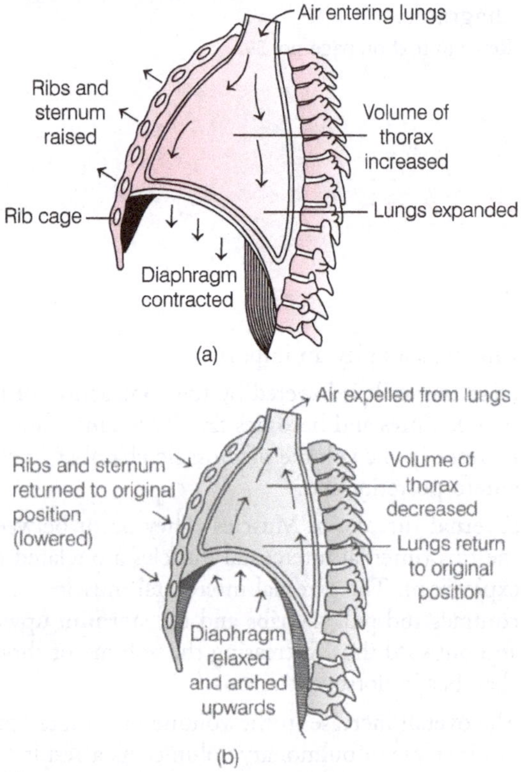

Fig. 17.2 Mechanism of breathing showing (a) Inspiration, (b) Expiration

Respiratory Volumes and Capacities

The quantity of air, the lungs can receive, hold or expel under different conditions are called **respiratory** (or pulmonary) **volumes.** Combination of two or more pulmonary volumes are called **respiratory** (pulmonary) **capacities.**

The different volumes and capacities are as follows

(i) **Tidal Volume** (TV) It is the volume of air inspired or expired during normal breathing in relaxed or resting position. It is about 500 mL. It consists of 150 mL of dead space volume and 350 mL of alveolar volume.

A healthy man can inspire or expire approximately 6000-8000 mL of air per minute.

(ii) **Inspiratory Reserve Volume** (IRV) It is the additional amount of air that can be inspired forcibly after a normal inspiration. It is about 2500-3000 mL of air.

(iii) **Expiratory Reserve Volume** (ERV) It is the additional volume of air that can be expired forcibly after a normal expiration. It is about 1000-1100 mL.

(iv) **Residual Volume** (RV) It is the volume of air remaining in the lungs even after a forcible expiration. It is about 1100-1200 mL. It cannot be measured by spirometry.

(v) **Anatomical Dead Space** The portion of respiratory passage, in which incoming and outgoing air is completely locked and this air is not used in gaseous exchange and is about 30% of tidal volume, i.e. 150 mL.

(vi) **Alveolar Ventilation** (minute volume) This is the volume of air that moves into and out of the alveoli per minute.

Alveolar ventilation = (TV− anatomical dead space) × Respiratory rate

$$= (500 - 150) \text{ mL} \times 15 \text{ times per minute}$$
$$= 5.25 \text{ litre per minute}$$

Various pulmonary capacities are derived from the above mentioned volumes. These help in the clinical diagnosis of functioning of lungs. These are as follows

(i) **Inspiratory Capacity** (IC) It is the total volume of air a person can inspire after a normal expiration. It is about 2500-3000 mL. It includes **tidal volume** and **inspiratory reserve volume.**

$$IC = TV + IRV$$

(ii) **Expiratory Capacity** (EC) It is the total volume of air a person can expire after a normal inspiration. It includes **tidal volume** and **expiratory reserve volume.**

$$EC = TV + ERV$$

(iii) **Functional Residual Capacity** (FRC) It is the volume of air that will remain in the lungs after a normal expiration. It includes **residual volume** and **expiratory reserve volume.**

$$FRC = RV + ERV$$

(iv) **Vital Capacity** (VC) It is the maximum volume of air a person can breathe in after a forced expiration or the maximum volume of air a person can breathe out after a forced inspiration.

This includes TV+ IRV+ ERV.

It varies from 3400-4800 mL depending upon age, sex and height of individual.

(v) **Total Lung Capacity** It is the total volume of air present in the lungs after a forced (maximum) inspiration.

It includes

RV+ ERV+ TV+ IRV or (VC+RV)

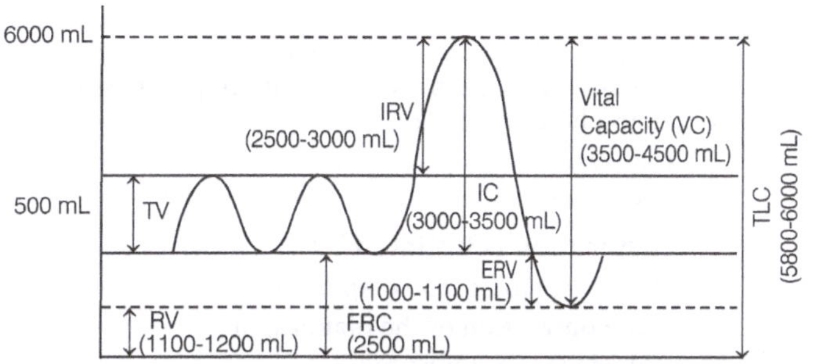

Fig. 17.3 Lung volumes and capacities

Knowledge Plus

- The vital capacity is higher in athletes, mountain dwellers than in plain dwellers, in men than women and in the young ones than in the old persons.
- All pulmonary volumes and capacities are about 20-25% less in women than in men and they are greater in tall persons and atheletes than in small and asthenic people.
- The volume of air involved in breathing movements can be estimated by using a spirometer. It is done in clinical assessment of pulmonary functions.
- Partial pressure of a gas is the pressure it exerts in a mixture of gases. It is equal to the total pressure of the mixture divided by percentage of that gas in the mixture.

Exchange of Gases

The primary sites for exchange of gases are the **alveoli** and **tissues.** It occurs by simple diffusion mainly based on pressure/concentration gradient. The factors that affect rate of diffusion are

(i) Thinness of the membrane.

(ii) Surface area of the membrane.

(iii) Permeability of the membrane.

(iv) Solubility of the gases.

(v) Partial pressure gradient (difference) of gases on the two sides of the diffusing surfaces of lung alveoli.

1. Exchange of Gases between Alveoli and Blood

The exchange of gases between lung alveoli and pulmonary capillaries is called **external respiration.** The alveolar wall is very thin with a rich network of blood capillaries.

It is also called as **respiratory membrane** (alveolar-capillary membrane).

(i) Alveolar epithelium

(ii) Epithelial basement membrane

(iii) Their interstitial space

(iv) Capillary basement membrane

(v) Capillary endothelium

All these form a membrane of about 0.2 mm thickness.

This membrane has a limit of gaseous exchange between alveoli and pulmonary blood. It is called **diffusing capacity.** It is the volume of gas that diffuses through membrane per minute for a pressure difference of 1 mm Hg.

At a particular pressure difference, the diffusion of CO_2 is 20-25 times faster than oxygen. Thus, the amount of that can diffuse through the membrane per unit difference in partial pressure is much higher as compared to oxygen.

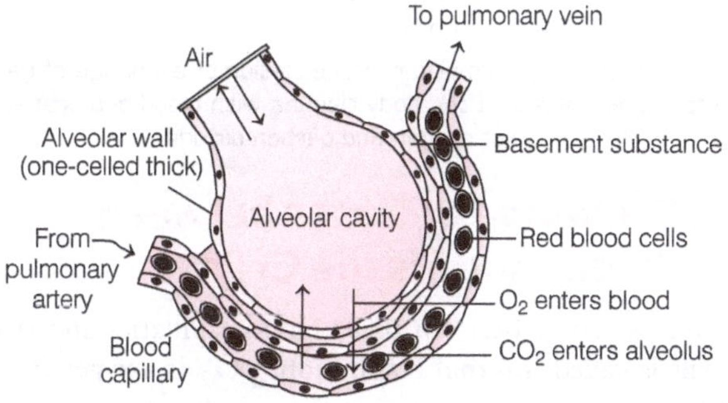

Fig. 17.4 A diagram of a section of an alveolus with the pulmonary capillary

Partial pressures (in mm Hg) of oxygen and carbon dioxide at different parts involved in diffusion in comparison to those in atmosphere are as follows

Respiratory Gas	Atmospheric Air (mm of Hg)	Alveoli (mm of Hg)	Blood (Deoxygenated) (mm of Hg)	Blood (Oxygenated) (mm of Hg)	Tissues (mm of Hg)
O_2	159	104	40	95	40
CO_2	0.3	40	45	40	45

As seen in the above table, pO_2 in the alveoli (104 mm Hg) is higher than that in the deoxygenated blood in the capillaries of pulmonary arteries (95 mm Hg). So, there is diffusion of O_2 from alveoli to the blood capillary. Also, pCO_2 is higher in deoxygenated blood (45 mm Hg) than in alveoli, therefore CO_2 diffuses from blood to the alveoli.

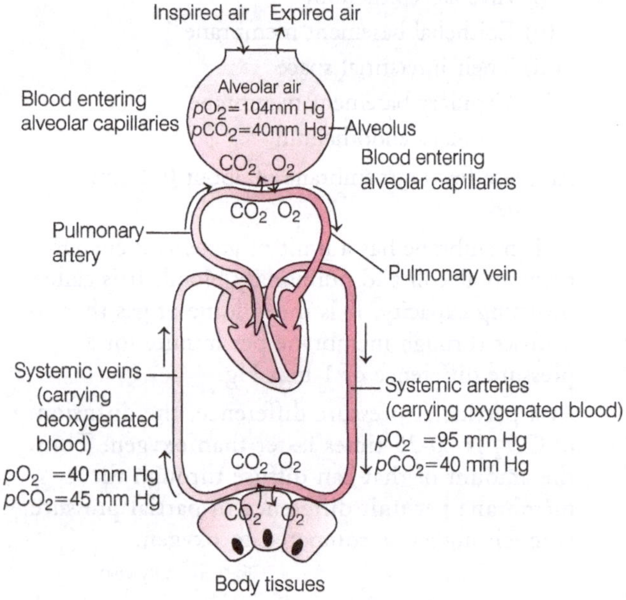

Fig. 17.5 Diagrammatic representation of exchange of gases at the alveolus and the body tissues with blood and transport of oxygen and carbon dioxide

2. Exchange of Gases between Blood and Tissue Cells

This exchange between tissue blood capillaries and tissue cells is called **internal respiration.** pO_2 in oxygenated blood (95 mm Hg) > pO_2 in body cells (40 mm Hg) and pCO_2 in oxygenated blood (40 mm Hg) < pCO_2 in body cells (45 mm Hg).

Due to this partial pressure differences, oxygen diffuses from the capillary blood to the body cells and CO_2 diffuses from the body cells to the capillary blood *via* tissue fluid. Now, the blood becomes deoxygenated, which is further carried to the heart by veins and finally it goes to lungs for purification.

Topic Practice 2

Multiple Choice Questions

(1 Mark)

1. Movement of the air into and out of the lungs is carried out by

(a) imbibition (b) pressure gradient
(c) osmosis (d) diffusion

Ans (b) The movement of the air into and out of the lungs is carried out by creating a pressure gradient between the lungs and the atmosphere. **Inspiration** occurs if negative pressure in the lungs with respect to the atmospheric pressure.

Expiration takes place when there is positive pressure in the lungs with respect to the atmospheric pressure.

2. Inspiration is initiated by

(a) extension of the diaphragm
(b) contraction of the diaphragm
(c) extension of the lungs
(d) contraction of the lungs

Ans (b) Inspiration is initiated by the contraction of diaphragm, which increases the volume of thoracic chamber in the antero-posterior axis. The contraction of the external intercostal muscles lifts up the ribs and the sternum causing an increase in the volume of thoracic chamber in the dorso-ventral axis. The overall increase in the thoracic volume causes a similar increase in the pulmonary volume.

3. During expiration, the diaphragm becomes

(a) normal (b) flattened
(c) dome-shaped (d) oblique

Ans (c) Expiration is the process by which CO_2 is expelled out from the lungs. During expiration, muscle fibres of the diaphragm gets relaxed, making it convex and dome-shaped, so as to decrease the volume of the thoracic cavity.

4. Additional muscles in the ..... impacts the ability of humans to increase the strength of inspiration and expiration.
Complete the given statement with an appropriate option.

(a) chest (b) diaphragm
(c) abdomen (d) lungs

Ans (c) We can voluntarily take deep breath by an effort. In the process of deep inspiration, chest distention is brought about by the external intercostal muscles and the abdominal muscles.

5. A spirometer cannot be used to measure

(a) IC (b) RV (c) ERV (d) IRV

Ans (b) Residual Volume (RV) remains in the lungs even after the forcible expiration. That is why, spirometer cannot measure the volume of residual volume.

6. Tidal volume is
(a) volume of air inspired or expired in normal breath
(b) additional volume of air, a person can inspire by a forcible inspiration
(c) additional volume of air, a person can expire by a forcible expiration
(d) remaining volume of air in the lungs even after a forcible expiration

Ans (a) **Tidal Volume** (TV) The volume of the air inspired or expired involuntarily in each normal breath. It is about 500 mL of air in average young adult man.

7. Total lung capacity is
(a) Total volume of air accommodated in lungs at the end of a forced inspiration
(b) RV + ERV + TU+ IRV
(c) vital capacity + residual volume
(d) All of the above

Ans (d) **Total lung capacity** is the total volume of the air accommodated in the lungs at the end of a forced inspiration. This includes RV, ERV, TV and IRV.

It is the sum of vital capacity and the residual volume.

8. Primary site of the gaseous exchange in humans is
(a) lungs (b) alveoli
(c) bronchus (d) diaphragm

Ans (b) Alveoli are the primary site of exchange of gases in humans. Exchange of gases also occur between the blood and tissue. O_2 and CO_2 are exchanged in these sites by simple in humans diffusion, mainly based on pressure/concentration gradient.

9. Factors affecting the rate of diffusion is/are
(a) pressure gradient
(b) solubility of gases
(c) thickness of membranes
(d) All of the above

Ans (d) Pressure/Concentration gradient, solubility of gases as well as the thickness of the membranes involved in diffusion are some important factors that affects the rate of diffusion.

10. Partial pressure of the gas is the pressure contributed by
(a) all gases in a mixture
(b) individual gas in a mixture
(c) pressure exerted by atmosphere on gases
(d) atmosphere on O_2 only

Ans (b) Pressure contributed by the individual gas in a mixture of gases is called partial pressure and is represented as pO_2 for oxygen and pCO_2 for carbon dioxide.

Very Short Answer Type Questions

(1 Mark)

11. Why is it advisable to do nasal breathing rather than mouth breathing?

Ans Nasal breathing is advisable because it is healthier as the air inhaled gets filtered through the hairs present inside the nose, so cleaner air reaches to the lungs.

12. Define pulmonary ventilation.

Ans Pulmonary ventilation is the inflow of atmospheric air and release (outflow) of CO_2 rich alveolar air.

13. What is the normal breathing rate?

Ans 12-16 times per minute in an adult human being is the normal breathing rate.

14. Which components of the respiratory system help in generation of pressure gradient for breathing? **NCERT Exemplar**

Ans The diaphragm and a specialised set of muscles called external and internal intercostals present in between the ribs help in generation of pressure gradient for breathing.

15. How is negative pressure breathing helpful for mammals?

Ans The negative pressure breathing allows the mammals to eat and breathe at the same time.

16. How is clinical assessment of pulmonary function done?

Ans The clinical assessment of pulmonary function is done with the special instrument called spirometer.

17. Define Residual Volume (RV). **NCERT Exemplar**

Or

State the volume of air remaining in the lungs after a normal breathing. **NCERT Exemplar**

Ans **Residual Volume** (RV) It is the volume of air remaining in the lungs even after a forcible expiration is done. It is about 1100-1200 mL.

18. Give the vital capacity of the lungs of a normal adult person.

Ans The vital capacity of the lungs of a normal adult preson is 3400-4800 mL.

19. Define alveolar ventilation.

Ans Alveolar ventilation is the volume of air that moves into and out of the alveoli per minute.

20. What is a dead air space?

Ans The conducting portion of the human respiratory system is called dead air space.

It starts with the external nostrils upto the terminal bronchioles.

21. **Give the name of the three major layers of diffusion membrane.**

Ans The name of the three major layers of diffusion membranes are

(i) Thin squamous epithelium of alveoli.

(ii) Endothelium of alveolar capillaries.

(iii) Basement substance in between.

22. **Compared to O_2, diffusion rate of CO_2 through the diffusion membrane per unit difference in partial pressure is much higher. Explain.**

Ans As, the solubility rate of CO_2 is 20-25 times higher than that of the O_2, the amount of CO_2 that can diffuse through the diffusion membrane per unit difference in partial pressure is much higher as compared to that of O_2.

Short Answer Type I Questions

2 Marks

23. **In normal breathing, which is the active process inspiration or expiration? Explain.**

Ans In normal breathing, inspiration is an active process as it is brought about by the contraction of diaphragm and external intercostal muscles, while expiration is a passive process as it simply involves relaxation of inspiratory muscles. (2)

24. **Give the condition of the following muscles during expiration.**
 (i) **Diaphragm muscles**
 (ii) **Internal intercostal muscles**

Ans During expiration

(i) The muscles of the diaphragm are in a relaxed position, making it convex.

(ii) The internal intercostal muscles are contracting thus, pulling the ribs downward and inward. (1 × 2)

25. **Fill in the blanks.**
 (i) **During normal quiet breathing, on an average, approximately .... mL of air is inspired or expired in each breathe, termed as ....**
 (ii) **Actually, only about .... mL of air enters the lung alveoli for the exchange of gases. The remaining fills the respiratory passage and is termed ....**
 (iii) **Diaphragm contracts to help in......while the contraction of abdominal muscles help in ..... .**
 (iv) **Alveolar pO_2 is .... than the venous pO_2 in lungs while arterial pO_2 is .... than the alveolar pO_2.**

Ans (i) 500 mL, tidal volume. (ii) 350 mL, dead space air
(iii) inspiration, forced expiration
(iv) higher, lower. (½ × 4)

26. **Arrange the following terms based on their volumes in an ascending order.**
 (i) **Tidal Volume (TV)**
 (ii) **Residual Volume (RV)**
 (iii) **Inspiratory Reserve Volume (IRV)**
 (iv) **Expiratory Capacity (EC)** **NCERT Exemplar**

Ans Tidal volume → Residual volume →
(500 mL) (1100-1200 mL)
Expiratory capacity → IRV
(1500-1600 mL) (2500-3000 mL) (½ × 4)

27. **Define vital capacity. What is its significance?** **NCERT**

Ans Vital capacity is the maximum amount of air a person can breathe in after a forced expiration or breathe out after a forced inspiration.

It represents the maximum amount of air one can breathe in the respiratory system during a single respiration. Thus, the greater the VC, more is the energy available to the body. (1+1)

Short Answer Type II Questions

3 Marks

28. **Write the role of diaphragm and intercostal muscles in the inspiratory process.**

Ans The diaphragm and intercostal muscles (external and internal) present between the ribs help in generation of a pressure gradient between the lungs and the atmosphere.

During inspiration diaphragm is lowered by contraction of its muscle fibres and becomes flat. The external intercostal muscles contract pulling the ribs and sternum upward and outward. This increases the volume of thoracic cavity and thus, decrease the intra-pulmonary pressure.

The greater atmospheric pressure outside the body now causes the air to flow rapidly into external nares, which sequentially leads to alveoli. Thus, causing inspiration. (3)

29. **Why is breathing of women regarded as thoracic, while that of male as abdominal? Also state who among the two has higher vital capacity.**

Ans In males, the lateral movement of thorax constitutes 25% of breathing, while the abdominal movement accounts for 75% breathing. Thus, it is regarded as abdominal breathing.

In women, particularly in pregnant women, the entire breathing is through lateral movement of thorax. Thus, breathing in women is regarded as thoracic. The VC is higher in men than in women and in the young ones than in the old persons. (2+1)

30. State the route of foul air from the lungs to outside. Also state whether TV increases or decreases during excitement and activity.

Ans The foul air follows the route given below

Alveoli → Alveolar ducts → Bronchioles → Bronchi → Trachea → Larynx → Glottis → Pharynx → Internal nares → Nasal chambers → External nares → Atmosphere.

The tidal volume increases 4-10 times during excitement and activity. (3)

31. Complete the missing terms.

(i) Inspiratory Capacity (IC) = ... + ...

(ii) .... = TV + ERV

(iii) Functional Residual Capacity (FRC) = ... + ...

Ans (i) Tidal Volume (TV) + Inspiratory Reserve Volume (IRV)

(ii) Expiratory Capacity (EC).

(iii) Residual Volume (RV) + Expiratory Reserve Volume (ERV). (3)

32. Distinguish between **NCERT Exemplar**

(i) IRV and ERV

(ii) Vital capacity and total lung capacity

Ans Refer to text on page no. 396-397.

33. State the factors that affect the rate of diffusion.

Ans Refer to text on page no. 397.

34. Diffusion of gases occurs in the alveolar region only and not in the other part of respiratory system. Why? **NCERT**

Ans For efficient exchange of gases, respiratory surface must have certain characteristics such as

(i) it must be thin, moist and permeable to respiratory gases.

(ii) it must be large.

(iii) it must be highly vascular.

Only alveolar region has these characteristics. Thus, diffusion of gases occurs in this region only. (1×3)

35. For completion of respiration process, write the given steps in sequential manner

(i) Diffusion of gases (O_2 and CO_2) acroses alveolar membrane.

(ii) Transport of gases by blood.

(iii) Utilisation of O_2 by the cells for catabolic reactions and resultant release of CO_2.

(iv) Pulmonary ventilation by which atmospheric air is drawn in and CO_2 rich alveolar air is released out.

(v) Diffusion of O_2 and CO_2 between blood and tissues. **NCERT Exemplar**

Ans Steps in the process of respiration are as follows

(i) Pulmonary ventilation by which atmospheric air is drawn in and CO_2 rich alveolar air is released out.

(ii) Diffusion of gases (O_2 and CO_2) across alveolar membrane.

(iii) Transport of gases by blood to the farthest tissues in body.

(iv) Diffusion of O_2 and CO_2 between blood and tissues.

(v) Utilisation of O_2 by the cell for catabolic reaction and resultant release of CO_2 and energy. (3)

Long Answer Type Questions

5 Marks

36. Explain the process of inspiration under normal conditions.

Ans Refer to text on page no. 395.

37. Describe the functioning of intercostal muscle in breathing.

Ans The internal intercostal muscle contracts to pull the ribs downward and inward, this decreases the thoracic volume and consequently the pulmonary volume. Thus, the resulted increased pulmonary pressure causes expiration.

Likewise, when the external intercostal muscles contract, they pull the ribs and sternum upwards and outwards which increases the thoracic volume and consequently the pulmonary volume. This results in decreased pulmonary pressure, which sequentially leads to flow of air into the lungs (inspiration). (5)

38. Explain the mechanism of breathing with neat labelled sketches.

Ans **Mechanism of Breathing** Breathing involves two stages, inspiration during which atmospheric air is drawn in and expiration by which the alveolar air is released out. The movement of air into and out of the lungs is carried out by creating a pressure gradient between the lungs and the atmosphere with the help of diaphragm and intercostal muscles.

Refer fig no. 17.2 on page no. 396 (5)

39. Explain the mechanism of expiration in humans. Also, give diagrams for the process of breathing.

Ans Refer to text on page no. 396.

40. What is tidal volume? Find out the tidal volume for a healthy human in an hour time?

Also, label the parts *A*, *B*, *C* and *D* in the given figure of alveolus.

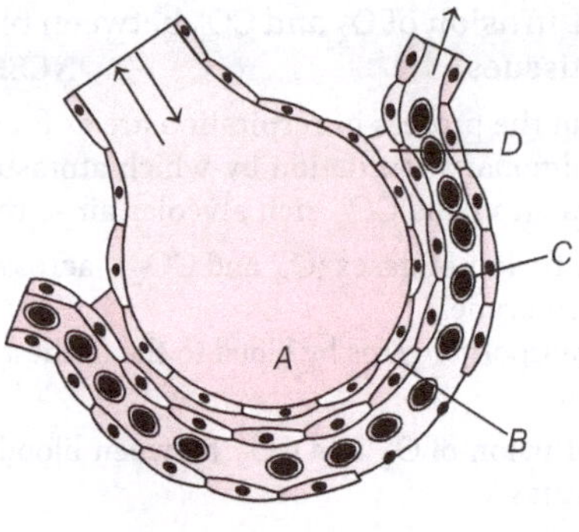

Ans Tidal volume is the volume of air inspired or expired during normal breathing in relaxed or resting position. Its volume is about 500 mL.

Amount of Tidal Volume (TV) in an hour

= Respiratory rate × TV × 60 min

= (12 – 16 breaths per minute) × 500 mL × 60

= 6 – 8 L × 60

TV = 360 – 480 L, *A* – Alveolar cavity

B – Alveolar wall, *C* – Red blood cells

D – Basement substance. (5)

41. Give diagrammatic representation of exchange of gases at the alveolus and the body tissues with transport of O_2 and CO_2. Also, explain how does exchange of gases occur between blood and tissue cells.

Ans Refer to text on page no. 397-398 and fig. no. 17.5.

TOPIC 03 Respiration : Gaseous Transport, Regulation and Disorders

Transport of Gases

Blood carries oxygen from the lungs to tissue cells for oxidation and carbon dioxide from the tissue cells to the respiratory surface for elimination. Transport of oxygen and carbon dioxide in detail is discussed below

Transport of Oxygen

It is done in the following manner

(i) **As Dissolved Gas** About 3% of oxygen in the blood is carried in a dissolved state through the plasma.

(ii) **As Oxyhaemoglobin** About 97% of O_2 is carried by RBCs in the blood.

Haemoglobin is a **red** coloured **iron** containing pigment present in RBCs to which O_2 can bind in a reversible manner to form **oxyhaemoglobin.** Four molecules of oxygen bind with one molecule of haemoglobin.

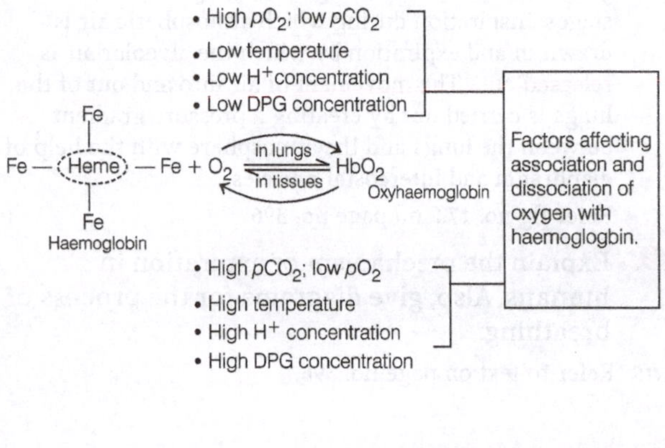

Where, Fe-Iron (have strong affinity for oxygen).

DPG-Diphosphoglyceraldehyde

Oxygen Dissociation Curve or Oxyhaemoglobin Dissociation Curve

It is the curve obtained on plotting percentage saturation of Hb with O_2 against pO_2. The curve thus, obtained is **sigmoid shaped** or **S-shaped,** under normal conditions.

(i) This curve is useful in studying the effect of factors like pCO_2, H^+ concentration and temperature, etc., on binding of O_2 with Hb.

(ii) The lower part of the curve indicates dissociation of oxygen from haemoglobin while, the upper part of the curve indicates the acceptance of O_2 by Hb.

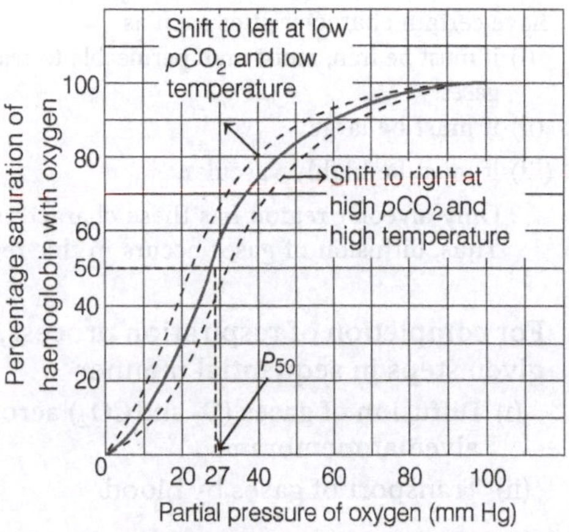

Fig. 17.6 Oxygen dissociation curve

(iii) The oxygen haemoglobin dissociation curve is shifted either to left or right by various factors.

Shift to left indicates association of O_2 by Hb. It occurs in the alveoli where there is low pCO_2, high pO_2, lesser H^+ concentration and low temperature.

Note In the foetal blood, there is a shift to left because foetal haemoglobin ($2\alpha, 2\gamma$) has more affinity for oxygen than the adult Hb ($2\alpha, 2\beta$).

(iv) **Shift to right** indicates dissociation of O_2 from Hb. It occurs in the tissues where there is low pO_2, high pCO_2, low pH (high H^+ concentration) and higher temperature.

(v) This clearly indicates that O_2 gets bound to Hb on the lung surface and gets dissociated at the tissue level.

(vi) Every 100 mL of oxygenated blood can deliver around 5 mL of O_2 to the tissues under normal physiological conditions.

People feel difficulty in breathing at hills because air pressure falls at hills. So, less oxygen is diffused to lung blood vessels.

Transport of Carbon Dioxide

CO_2 in gaseous form diffuses out of the cells into capillaries, where it is transported in following ways

(i) Transport in Dissolved Form

About 7% CO_2 is carried in dissolved form through the plasma because of its high solubility.

(ii) Transport as Bicarbonate

The largest fraction (about 70%) is carried in plasma as bicarbonate ions (HCO_3^-). At the tissues site, where pCO_2 is high due to catabolism, CO_2 diffuses into the blood (RBCs and plasma) and forms HCO_3^- and H^+.

$$\underset{\text{Carbon dioxide}}{CO_2} + H_2O \underset{\text{anhydrase}}{\overset{\text{Carbonic}}{\rightleftharpoons}} \underset{\text{Carbonic acid}}{H_2CO_3}$$

$$\underset{\text{anhydrase}}{\overset{\text{Carbonic}}{\rightleftharpoons}} \underset{\text{Bicarbonate ion}}{HCO_3^-} + \underset{\text{Hydrogen ion}}{H^+}$$

This reaction is faster in RBCs because they contain an enzyme **carbonic anhydrase.** Increased pH due to the hydrogen ion released during the reaction bind to Hb, triggering the **Bohr's effect.**

At the alveolar site, where pCO_2 is low, the reaction proceeds in opposite direction forming CO_2 and H_2O.

Thus, CO_2 is trapped as bicarbonate at tissue level and is transported to alveoli to be released as CO_2.

Hamburger's Phenomenon (Chloride Shift)

This is the phenomenon in which an exit of bicarbonate ions considerably changes ionic balance between the plasma and erythrocytes.

This ionic balance is restored by the diffusion of chloride ions from the plasma into the erythrocytes.

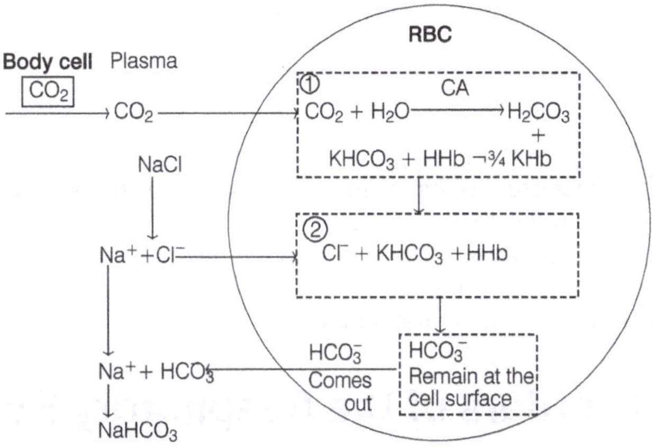

Fig. 17.7 Schematic representation showing the steps of chloride shift (CA = Carbonic Anhydrase)

(iii) Transport as Carbaminohaemoglobin

Nearly 20-25% CO_2 is carried by haemoglobin as carbaminohaemoglobin. CO_2 entering the blood combines with the NH_2 group of the reduced Hb.

$$HbO_2 + CO_2 \rightleftharpoons \underset{\text{(Carbaminohaemoglobin)}}{HbCO_2} + H^+ + O_2$$

The reaction releases oxygen from oxyhaemoglobin. Factors affecting the binding of CO_2 and Hb are

(i) Partial pressure of CO_2.

(ii) Partial pressure of O_2 (major factor).

In tissues, pCO_2 is high and pO_2 is low, more binding of CO_2 occurs while, in the alveoli, pCO_2 is low and pO_2 is high, dissociation of CO_2 from $HbCO_2$ takes place, i.e. CO_2, which is bound to Hb from the tissues is delivered at the alveoli.

Every 100 mL of deoxygenated blood delivers approximately 4 mL of CO_2 to the alveoli.

Haldane effect states that binding of oxygen with Hb tends to displace CO_2 from the blood. It is quantitatively more important in promoting CO_2 transport than the Bohr effect in promoting O_2 transport. Thus, Haldane effect and Bohr effect complement each other.

Regulation of Respiration

The respiratory rhythm can be maintained and moderated by human beings to suit the demands of the body tissues.

It is under dual control, i.e. nervous and chemical. This is explained below as

1. Neural Control

The **respiratory rhythm centre** is composed of a group of neurons located in the **medulla oblongata** and **pons varolii.** A chemosensitive area is located adjacent to rhythm centre that is highly sensitive to CO_2 and hydrogen ions.

They increase activity of this centre, which in turn signals the respiratory centre to make necessary changes in order to eliminate these substances. Oxygen does not have a significantly direct effect on the respiratory centre of the brain in controlling respiration.

The flow chart given below shows the neural control of breathing

Dorsal Respiratory Group (DRG) ← **Medulla Respiratory Centre** → **Ventral Respiratory Group** (VRG)

- **Dorsal Respiratory Group (DRG)**
  - Causes inspiration
  - Located in the dorsal portion of medulla
- **Ventral Respiratory Group (VRG)**
  - Causes expiration
  - Located in the ventrolateral portion of medulla

Pneumotaxic Centre ← **Pons Respiratory Centre** → **Apneustic Centre**

- **Pneumotaxic Centre**
  - Fuctions to limit inspiration
  - Located in dorsal part of pons varolii
- **Apneustic Centre**
  - Controls the depth of inspiration
  - Located in the lower part of pons varolii

2. Chemical Control

Large number of **chemoreceptors** are located in the carotid bodies, which lie bilaterally in the bifurcations of the common **carotid arteries.** Their afferent nerve fibres pass through **glossopharyngeal cranial nerve** and thus, to dorsal respiratory area of the medulla oblongata. Receptors of aortic arch and carotid artery recognise changes in CO_2 and H^+ concentration and send necessary signals to the rhythm centre for remedial actions.

Disorders of the Respiratory System

The respiratory system can be affected by a number of disorders as given in table below

Disorders of Respiratory System

Disorders	Causes	Symptoms	Preventions	Cure
Asthma (difficulty in breathing)	Allergens stimulate the release of histamine from the mast cells causing inflammation of bronchi and bronchioles.	Coughing, wheezing, excess amount of mucus clog the bronchi and bronchioles.	By avoiding exposure to allergens.	Antibiotic therapy to remove infection. Use of bronchodilator drugs and inhalers for relief.
Emphysema (inflation or distension of bronchioles or alveolar sacs)	Cigarette smoking and inhalation of other smoke or toxic substances over a period of time leads to damage of alveolar walls.	Due to the collapse of alveolar septa, surface area for gas exchange is reduced, lungs inflated, exhalation becomes difficult.	Cigarette smoking and exposure to air pollutants must be avoided.	It causes irreversible distortion. Hence, no permanent cure. Symptomatic treatment involves use of bronchodilators antibiotics and oxygen therapy.
Occupational respiratory disorders (it is due to occupation of individual especially those in grinding or stone breaking industry such as anthracosis (Pneumatoconiosis is of coal workers), silicosis, asbestosis, black lung, byssinosis, brown lung disease, chronic beryllium disease, etc).	Occur due to the chronic exposure of harmful substances as silica, aesbestos, etc., (silicosis, asbestosis). The defence mechanism of body fails to cope with the situation.	Proliferation of fibrous connective tissue (fibrosis) of upper part of lung causing inflammation.	Minimise use of harmful dust. Use of protective gears and clothing at work place. Regular health check up of workers.	No permanent cure. Patient is given symptomatic treatment such as bronchodilators and antibiotics for secondary infection.

Topic Practice 3

Multiple Choice Questions

1 Mark

1. Each haemoglobin molecule can carry maximum of
   (a) two molecules of O_2
   (b) three molecules of O_2
   (c) four molecules of O_2
   (d) one molecule of O_2

Ans (c) Each haemoglobin molecule can carry a maximum of four molecules of O_2.

$$Hb_4 + 4O_2 \longrightarrow Hb_4O_8$$

Binding of oxygen with haemoglobin is primarily related to the partial pressure of O_2, partial pressure of CO_2, hydrogen ion concentration and temperature.

2. What is Bohr's effect?
   (a) A rise in levels of pCO_2 or fall in pH decreases the oxygen affinity of haemoglobin
   (b) Decrease in levels of pCO_2 or fall in pH decreases the oxygen affinity of haemoglobin
   (c) A rise in levels of pCO_2 or increase in pH decreases the oxygen affinity of haemoglobin
   (d) Shifting of the oxygen-haemoglobin curve to left

Ans (a) Arise in pCO_2 or fall in pH decreases the oxygen affinity of haemoglobin, raising the P_{50} value and shifts the curve to the right. This is called Bohr's effect.

Conversely, a fall in pCO_2 and rise in the pH increases oxygen affinity of haemoglobin.

3. Which of the following equation is correct?
   (a) $KHbO_2 + H^+ \underset{RBC}{\rightleftharpoons} Hb + K + H_2O$
   (b) $Hb + O_2 \underset{\text{Dissociation in lungs}}{\xrightarrow{\text{Association in tissues}}} HbO_2$
   (c) $Na^+ + HCO_3^- \underset{\text{Erythrocyte}}{\rightleftharpoons} NaHCO_3$
   (d) $HbO_2 \underset{\text{Association in lungs}}{\xrightarrow{\text{Dissociation in tissues}}} Hb + O_2$

Ans (d) In tissues, dissociation of oxyhaemoglobin and the formation of carbamino-haemoglobin takes place.

In lungs, dissociation of carboxyamino-haemoglobin and the formation of haemoglobin takes place.

4. Under normal conditions, what amount of O_2 is delivered by 100 mL of the oxygenated blood?
   (a) 5 mL (b) 4 mL
   (c) 3 mL (d) 2 mL

Ans (a) Under the normal physiological conditions, 100 mL of the oxygenated blood can deliver around 5 mL O_2 to the body.

5. Which situation would result in the greatest degree of O_2 saturation for haemoglobin, if pO_2 remains constant?
   (a) Increased CO_2 level, decreased temperature
   (b) Decreased CO_2 level, decreased temperature
   (c) Increased CO_2 level, increased temperature
   (d) Decreased CO_2 level, increased temperature

Ans (b) Increased temperature dissociates the O_2 from oxyhaemoglobin and low temperature favours the binding of O_2 to haemoglobin. The decreased pCO_2 causes formation of oxyhaemoglobin.

6. Blood do not become acidic although it carries CO_2 because
   (a) CO_2 is continuously diffused through tissues
   (b) CO_2 combines with H_2O to form H_2CO_3
   (c) in CO_2 transport, buffers plays an important role
   (d) CO_2 is absorbed by WBC

Ans (c) Blood do not become acidic due to the buffering action of bicarbonates.

7. Pneumotaxic centre of the brain can
   (a) moderate the function of respiratory system
   (b) decrease the heart rate
   (c) increase the heart rate
   (d) increase the flow of blood

Ans (a) The pneumotaxic centre can present in the pons region of the brain moderate its functions of the respiratory rhythm centre. Neural signal from this centre can reduce the duration of inspiration and thereby, alter the respiratory rate.

8. Which of the following gas is quite insignificant for the regulation of respiration rhythm?
   (a) H^+ (b) CO_2
   (c) O_2 (d) None of these

Ans (c) CO_2, H^+, plays a very significant role in the respiration rhythms. The role of oxygen (O_2) in the regulation of respiratory rhythm is quite in significant.

9. Why do human beings face difficulty to breath in high elevations?
   (a) Lower % of O_2
   (b) Temperature lower
   (c) High pressure
   (d) Low pO_2

Ans (d) Inspiration takes place when there is negative pressure of O_2 inside the body than outside. In the mountains, there is less pressure of O_2 (negative) than inside, that is why, breathing is difficult in mountain regions.

10. Respiratory centre of the brain is stimulated by
(a) CO_2 content in venous blood
(b) CO_2 content in arterial blood
(c) O_2 content in arterial blood
(d) O_2 content in venous blood

Ans (b) Respiratory centre is stimulated when there is more CO_2 in the arterial blood. In normal conditions, there is less amount of CO_2 in the arterial blood.

Very Short Answer Type Questions

1 Mark

11. A major percentage of O_2 (97%) is transported by RBCs in the blood. How does the remaining 3% of O_2 transported? **NCERT Exemplar**

Ans The remaining 3% of O_2 is transported in dissolved state through plasma.

12. What is the amount of O_2 supplied to tissues through every 100 mL of oxygenated blood under normal physiological conditions? **NCERT Exemplar**

Ans Around 5 mL.

13. Why there is a shift towards left in the oxygen dissociation curve in foetus?

Ans In the foetus, there is a shift to left because structure of foetal haemoglobin (2α, 2γ) has more affinity for oxygen than adult Hb (2α, 2β).

14. What is the role of oxyhaemoglobin after releasing molecular oxygen in the tissues?

Ans Amino group of reduced haemoglobin combines with CO_2, forming carbaminohaemoglobin to transport CO_2.

15. What controls the respiratory rhythm in human beings?

Ans The respiratory rhythm in human beings is under dual control, i.e. nervous and chemical.

16. Give the name of some common respiratory disorders.

Ans The name of some common respiratory disorders are asthma, emphysema, occupational lung disorders (e.g. silicosis and asbestosis).

17. Cigarette smoking causes emphysema. Give reason. **NCERT Exemplar**

Ans Cigarette smoking causes damages to the alveolar walls and reduces elasticity of the lungs, which leads to decreased respiratory surface for exchange of gases. Thus, causing emphysema.

Short Answer Type I Questions

2 Marks

18. How does haemoglobin help in the transport of oxygen from lung to tissues?

Ans Haemoglobin combines with O_2 in a reversible manner to form oxyhaemoglobin. This oxygenated blood circulates in the body. When, it reaches the tissues having low pO_2, the oxygen is released into the tissues. (2)

19. State the factors affecting the oxygen haemoglobin binding.

Ans Factors that affect the oxygen haemoglobin binding are
(i) Partial pressure of oxygen
(ii) Partial pressure of carbon dioxide
(iii) Hydrogen ion concentration
(iv) Temperature (½ × 4)

20. What does the oxygen haemoglobin dissociation curve indicate?

Ans The lower part of the curve indicates dissociation of oxygen from haemoglobin while, the upper part of the curve indicates acceptance of oxygen by Hb. (2)

21. How is CO_2 transported in human body.

Ans CO_2 is transported in the human body in the following ways
(i) In dissolved form about 7%.
(ii) As bicarbonate ions about 70%.
(iii) As carbaminohaemoglobin about 20-25%. (2)

22. What is the role of carbonic anhydrase in humans?

Ans Nearly 70% of CO_2 enters the RBCs and reacts with water to form carbonic acid in the presence of enzyme carbonic anhydrase.
This dissociates to form bicarbonate ions, which are circulated by plasma. (2)

23. What is the effect of pCO_2 on oxygen transport? **NCERT**

Ans Increase in pCO_2 tension in blood brings rightward shift of the oxygen-dissociation curve of haemoglobin thereby decreasing the affinity of Hb for O_2. This effect is called Bohr's effect. It plays a crucial role in enhancing oxygenation of the blood in the lungs and in release of O_2 in the tissues. (2)

24. **Write about Haldane effect. How does Haldane effect and Bohr effect complement each other?**

Ans Haldane effect states that binding of oxygen with haemoglobin tends to displace CO_2 from the blood.

It is quantitatively more important in promoting CO_2 transport than the Bohr effect in O_2 transport. Thus, Haldane effect and Bohr effect complement each other. (2)

25. **What is Hamburger's phenomenon?**

Ans The movement of bicarbonate ions out from the erythrocytes into the plasma, changes the ionic balance between plasma and erythrocytes. In order to restore the ionic balance, the chloride ions diffuse from plasma to the erythrocytes. This phenomenon is called chloride shift or Hamburger's phenomenon. (2)

26. **Differentiate between oxyhaemoglobin and carbaminohaemoglobin.**

Ans Differences between oxyhaemoglobin and carbaminohaemoglobin are

Oxyhaemoglobin	Carbaminohaemoglobin
It is formed by the combination of oxygen with the Fe^{2+} part of haemoglobin.	It is formed by the combination of CO_2 with the amino group of haemoglobin.
Its formation occurs on the alveolar surface.	Its formation occurs in the tissues.

(1 × 2)

27. **What makes carbon monoxide more harmful to animals than carbon dioxide?**

Ans Haemoglobin consists of a protein globin and pigment haem. The four portions of iron in haem combine with molecule of oxygen. It is an easy reversible reaction to form oxyhaemoglobin

$$Hb + O_2 \rightleftharpoons HbO_2$$

Whereas, the complex formed by the reaction of carbon monoxide and haemoglobin is incredibly strong

$$\underset{\text{(Haemoglobin)}}{Hb + CO} \longrightarrow \underset{\text{(Carboxy haemoglobin)}}{HbCO}$$

As a result of this strong bonding between the haemoglobin and carbon monoxide, the haemoglobin looses its affinity to oxygen, thus may lead to choking or even death. (2)

28. **How marine mammals are able to make long underwater dives? Explain.**

Ans Marine mammals (e.g. seals and whales) can make long underwater dives as they have

(i) more blood per kg of body weight.
(ii) can store more oxygen in blood and muscles.
(iii) have a large spleen with blood.
(iv) can reduce O_2 consumption rate when underwater.

(½ × 4)

29. **What happens to the respiratory process in a man going up a hill?** **NCERT**

Ans At hills, the pressure of air falls and the person cannot get enough oxygen in the lungs for diffusion in blood. Due to the deficiency of oxygen, the person feels breathlessness, headache, dizziness, nausea, mental fatigue and a bluish colour on the skin, nails and lips. (2)

30. **Describe the role of pons in the process of breathing.**

Ans Refer to text on page no. 404.

Short Answer Type II Questions

(3 Marks)

31. **What will be the pO_2 and pCO_2 in the atmospheric air compared to those in the alveolar air?**

(i) pO_2 lesser and pCO_2 higher
(ii) pO_2 higher and pCO_2 lesser
(iii) pO_2 higher and pCO_2 higher
(iv) pO_2 lesser and pCO_2 lesser

Ans (i) In the alveolar tissues, where low pO_2, high pCO_2, high H^+ concentration, these conditions are favourable for dissociation of oxygen from the oxyhaemoglobin.

(ii) When there is high pO_2, low pCO_2, less H^+ concentration and lesser temperature, the factors are all favourable for formation of oxyhaemoglobin.

(iii) When pO_2 is high in the alveoli and pCO_2 is high in the tissues then the oxygen diffuses into the blood and combines with oxygen forming oxyhaemoglobin and CO_2 diffuses out.

(iv) When pO_2 is low in the alveoli and pCO_2 is low in the tissues then these conditions are favourable for dissociation of oxygen from the oxyhaemoglobin. (3)

32. **How the carbonic anhydrase help in transportation of carbon dioxide?**

Ans Refer to text (Transport of CO_2 as bicarbonate) on page no. 403.

33. **State the different modes of CO_2 transport in blood.**

Ans Carbon dioxide is carried by the blood in three forms

Refer to text on page no. 403.

34. **Why is it not advisable to sleep in closed rooms warmed with burning of coals continuously?**

Ans A person sleeping in such room gets carbon monoxide poisoning. CO combines with Hb more readily than oxygen forming carboxyhaemoglobin. This reduces the amount of free Hb available for carrying O_2.

Thus, the tissue is starved of O_2. This is the reason why it is not advisable to sleep in closed rooms warmed with coals. (3)

35. How is respiration regulated? **NCERT**

Ans A specialised centre present in the medulla region of the brain called respiratory rhythm centre is primarily responsible for the regulation of respiration.

Another centre present in the pons region of the brain called pneumotaxic centre can moderate the functions of the respiratory rhythm centre.

Neural signal from this centre can reduce the duration of inspiration and thereby, alter the respiratory rate. (3)

36. Which of the regulatory centre of respiration can reduce the inspiratory duration when it is stimulated?

Ans Respiratory process is regulated by certain specialised centres present in hindbrain. Amongst them, pneumotaxis centre is located in the dorsal part of pons varolii of the brain, can reduce the duration of inspiration and thus, alter the respiratory rate. (3)

37. Explain the role of neural system in regulation of respiration.

Ans Refer to text on page no. 404.

38. Explain chemical control of respiratory rhythm.

Ans Refer to text on page no. 404.

Long Answer Type Questions

5 Marks

39. Define oxygen dissociation curve. Can you suggest any reason for its sigmoidal pattern?

Ans Refer to text on page no. 402-403.

40. Give the transport of carbon dioxide as bicarbonate. Also explain chloride shift.

Ans For first part of Question refer to text on page no. 403. (2½)

Chloride shift is the phenomenon where exit of bicarbonate ions considerably changes ionic balance between the plasma and erythrocytes. This ionic balance is restored by the diffusion of chloride ions from the plasma into the erythrocytes.

This movement is called as chloride shift or Hamburger's phenomenon. (2½)

41. What are the major transport mechanisms for CO_2? Explain. **NCERT**

Ans Refer to text on page no. 403.

42. Give cause, symptoms, prevention and cure of the following disorders.

(i) Asthma (ii) Emphysema

(iii) Occupational respiratory disorder

Ans Refer to text on page no. 404.

SUMMARY

- **Respiration** is the process of oxidising nutrients to release energy, which is used in various body functions. Aerobic respiration occurs in the presence of oxygen releasing large number of ATPs per glucose molecule. Anaerobic respiration occurs in the absence of oxygen, releases less ATPs per glucose molecule.
- Different organisms use varying modes of organs for respiration, e.g. gills in fish, skin in earthworms, trachea in cockroaches, etc.
- **Human respiratory system** consists of a nose, larynx, trachea, bronchi and bronchioles, alveoli and lungs.
- External nostrils initiate the respiratory passage, used for breathing. Nasal passage has two chambers for respiratory and olfactory purpose.
- **Larynx**, is involved in sound production. Epiglottis is a leaf-shaped cartilaginous structure which prevents entry of food into larynx.
- **Trachea** is a non-collapsible air conducting tube (with C-shaped 16-17 rings).
- **Bronchi and Bronchioles** The first branching by which trachea enters the lungs are bronchi. Repeated divisions of bronchi form very thin terminal bronchioles.
- **Alveoli** are the functional units of lungs, richly supplied with blood cells.
- **Lungs** are the major respiratory organ of respiration present in thoracic cavity covered by a pleural membrane.
- **Breathing** is the process of exchange of oxygen rich air from the environment with carbon dioxide produced in cells of the body. It includes inspiration and expiration.
- **Inspiration** occurs when diaphragm contracts along with external intercostal muscles while abdominal muscles relaxes. The volume of thoracic cavity increases and air enters into the lungs.
- **Expiration** involves relaxation of the diaphragm and external intercostal muscles, this reduces thoracic volume which creates positive pressure leading to exhalation.
- **Lung volumes and capacities** help in mapping the functioning of lungs in living body. These include tidal volume, inspiratory reserve volume, inspiratory capacity, residual volume, expiratory reserve volume, functional residual capacity, vital capacity, total capacity and dead space.
- **Alveolar ventilation** is the volume of air moving in and out of alveoli per minute.
- **Spirometer** is the device used to measure lung capacities and volumes.
- **Regulation of breathing** The rate and depth of breathing can be adjusted according to bodily requirements.
- **Nervous regulation** occurs by respiratory centres present in medulla (dorsal) and pons (ventral).
- **Chemical regulation** occurs *via* chemoreceptors located in carotid, aortic bodies and in brain.
- **Exchange of gases** occurs in alveoli of lungs by simple diffusion based mainly on pressure gradients.
- **Diffusing capacity** is the limit of gaseous exchange between alveoli and pulmonary blood.
- **Transport of gases** like oxygen and CO_2 occurs in blood. These can be transported (a) in physical solution (b) as chemical compound. CO_2 can also be transported as bicarbonates and carbamino compounds.
- **Oxyhaemoglobin-dissociation curve** studies the relation between partial pressure of oxygen and amount of oxyhaemoglobin formed or dissociated.
  It can be affected by (a) CO (b) foetal Hb (c) myoglobin.
- **Disorders of respiratory system** occurs due to the impairement of respiratory organs and their functions. Major disorders include asthma, emphysema,

Chapter Practice

Multiple Choice Questions

1 Mark

1. Nasopharynx opens through the ...*A*... of the larynx region into the ...*B*... .

   Choose the correct option for *A* and *B* to complete the given statement.

   (a) *A*–trachea, *B*–lungs
   (b) *A*–trachea, *B*–glottis
   (c) *A*–glottis, *B*–lungs
   (d) *A*–glottis, *B*–trachea

2. Respiratory or Exchange part of the respiratory system comprises

   (a) lungs and pleural membrane
   (b) alveoli and their ducts
   (c) bronchus and their protecting covering
   (d) diaphragm and alveoli

3. Which of the following statement is false?

   (a) The conducting part of the respiratory system transports the atmospheric air to alveoli
   (b) Conducting part of the respiratory system clears the air from foreign particles, humidifies and brings it to the body temperature
   (c) Exchange part of the respiratory system is the actual site at which O_2 and CO_2 exchange takes place
   (d) None of the above

4. In humans, which of the following is not a step in respiration?

   (a) Alveolar diffusion of O_2 and CO_2
   (b) Transport of gases by blood
   (c) Diffusion of O_2 and CO_2 between blood and tissues
   (d) Utilisation of CO_2 by cells for catabolic reactions

5. Alveoli of the lungs are lined by

   (a) simple epithelium
   (b) squamous epithelium
   (c) cuboidal epithelium
   (d) ciliated epithelium

6. In humans, exchange of gases occurs

   (a) by diffusion
   (b) between blood and tissue
   (c) between alveoli and pulmonary blood capillary
   (d) All of the above

7. The partial pressure of O_2 is the highest in

   (a) alveoli (b) bronchi
   (c) trachea (d) tissues

8. Oxygen dissociation curve is a

   (a) sigmoid curve
   (b) J-shaped curve
   (c) exponential growth curve
   (d) hyperbolic curve

9. Which part of the brain is called respiratory rhythm centre?

   (a) Cerebellum region (b) Brain stem region
   (c) Medulla region (d) Temporal region

10. Name the chronic respiratory disorder caused mainly by cigarette smoking

    (a) asthma (b) respiratory acidosis
    (c) respiratory alkalosis (d) emphysema

Assertion-Reason Type Questions

1 Mark

Direction (Q. Nos. 11-17) *In each of the following questions, a statement of Assertion (A) is given followed by corresponding statement of Reason (R). Of the statements, mark the correct answer as*

(a) If both A and R are true and R is the correct explanation of A
(b) If both A and R are true, but R is not the correct explanation of A
(c) If A is true, but R is false
(d) If A is false, but R is true

11. **Assertion** (A) Trachea and bronchioles are supported by cartilaginous ring.

    Reason (R) Trachea can collapse during expiration.

12. **Assertion** (A) In normal breathing, inspiration is an active process.
Reason (R) Inspiration is facilitated by contraction of diaphragm and external intercostal muscles.

13. **Assertion** (A) Expiration is a passive process.
Reason (R) It occurs when the intrapulmonary pressure is higher than the atmospheric presssure.

14. **Assertion** (A) Mammals perform negative pressure breathing.
Reason (R) Using muscular movement, mammals create a pressure gradient, so that they can perform inspiration and expiration.

15. The pie chart given below is shows the amount of different gases present in the inhaled and exhaled air. Read the chart carefully and answer according to the appropriateness of the Assertion and Reason given below.

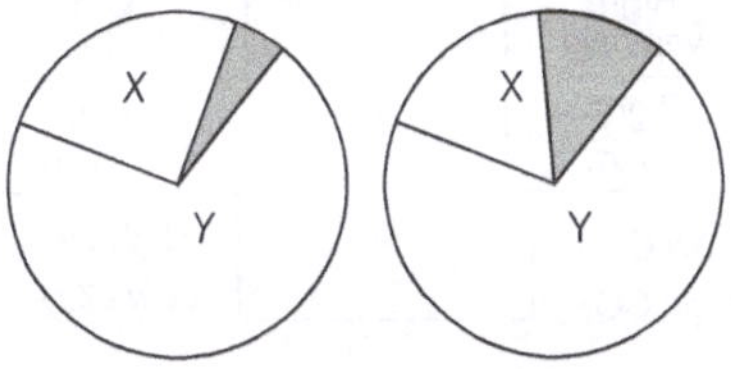

Inhaled air — Exhaled air

Assertion (A) The 97% of gas *X* is carried by RBC's in the blood as oxyhaemoglobin.
Reason (R) *X* gets bound to Hb on the lung surface and gets dissociated at the tissue level. They can perform inspiration and expiration.

16. **Assertion** (A) pO_2 is the highest in alveoli.
Reason (R) Partial pressure of a gas is the pressure contributed by individual gas in a mixture.

17. **Assertion** (A) The amount of CO_2 that can diffuse through diffusion membrane per unit difference in partial pressure is much higher as compared to O_2.
Reason (R) Solubility of CO_2 is 20-25 times higher than that of O_2.

Answers

1. (d)	2. (b)	3. (d)	4. (d)	5. (b)	6. (d)
7. (a)	8. (a)	9. (c)	10. (d)	11. (c)	12. (a)
13. (b)	14. (b)	15. (b)	16. (b)	17. (a)	

Very Short Answer Type Questions

1 Mark

18. How is respiration carried out in earthworm?
19. Which epithelium covers the nasal chamber?
20. Write the function of epiglottis.
21. Give the name of the structure that separate right from the left lung.
22. Name the compound present in the inner lining of lungs.
23. What do you understand by forceful expiration?.
24. What is (RV + ERV)?
25. Where is carbonic anhydrase found in human body?
26. What is the amount of CO_2 supplied to the alveoli through every 100 mL of deoxygenated blood?

Short Answer Type I Questions

2 Marks

27. Name the cartilages that support the larynx.
28. Mention the boundaries of the thoracic cavity.
29. What is meant by inspiration and expiration?
30. Distinguish between inspiratory capacity and expiratory capacity?
31. How is the inspired air conditioned in man?
32. What happens to oxyhaemoglobin, when the blood reaches the tissues?
33. What does the right and left shift of oxygen haemoglobin dissociation curve indicate?
34. What is the significance of Bohr's effect?

Short Answer Type II Questions

3 Marks

35. Enumerate the different types of respiration found in animals.
36. List the parts of respiratory tract. Describe the nasal chamber.
37. Write note on larynx.
38. Explain the different respiratory capacities.

39. How does exchange of gases take place in the alveoli of lungs?

40. What happens to the oxygen dissociation curve in
(i) Alveoli (ii) Tissues?

41. What is the crucial role of Bohr's effect?

Long Answer Type Questions

5 Marks

42. Explain human respiratory system.

43. Give an account of human respiratory tract with proper labelled diagrams.

44. How do gases (O_2 and CO_2) are transported in blood?

45. What are the major transport mechanism for gases in humans? Explain.

46. Explain various disorders of respiratory system.

Case Based Questions

4/5 Marks

47. Observe the diagram given below and answer the questions that follows.

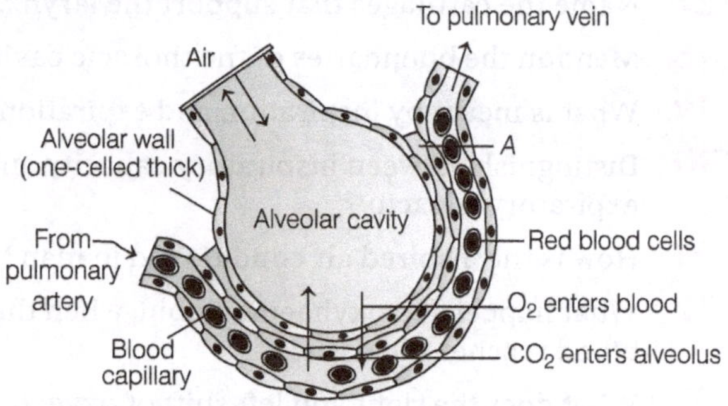

(i) What is being represented in the above diagram?
(ii) Which vein contains the oxygenated blood in humans?
(iii) How is oxygen carried from alveoli into the blood in pulmonary capillaries?
(iv) Which factors affect the rate of diffusion?
(v) Identify *A* and write its feature and/or function.

48. The figure given below represents the exchange of CO_2 and O_2 at the alveolus and the body tissues. Observe the figure and answer the questions that follows.

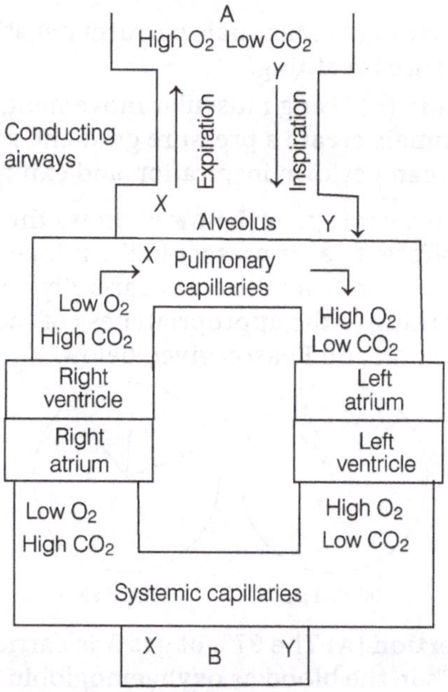

(i) At a particular pressure difference, among *X* and *Y*, which gas can diffuse faster.
(ii) With reference to the above figure, mention the partial pressure of gases *X* and *Y* at location *A* and *B*.
(iii) How will the decreased partial pressure of *X* affect the oxygen dissociation curve ?
(iv) How does the transport of *Y* takes place ?

CHAPTER
18

Body Fluids and Circulation

During metabolism, cell produces some useful and some waste products. Substances that are useful, need to be transported to other cells, while harmful or waste substances are to be removed from the body.

Circulatory system consists of a fluid medium that circulates throughout the body and helps in the distribution of useful products and elimination of waste products, from the various cells of the body.

TOPIC 01 Blood and Lymph

Simple organisms such as **sponges** and **coelenterates** have simple body organisation. These are in direct contact with atmosphere. Thus, they do not require any circulatory system. They instead circulate water from their surroundings into their body cavities. This facilitates the cells to exchange gases and excretory substances with immediate surroundings.

In more complex organisms, special fluids are used to transport these substances within the body. Blood and lymph are the two types of fluids that act as a carrier in the body. **Blood** is a **special connective tissue** comprising of a fluid matrix, plasma and formed elements. Plasma forms the fluid medium in which the blood cells (corpuscles) float and carry out different important functions.

Plasma

It is a straw coloured, viscous, slightly alkaline aqueous body fluid. It forms about 55% of the blood.

Composition of Plasma

It is composed of many organic and inorganic substances. It contains 90-92% water and 6-8% solutes in it.

The solutes found in plasma are various ions (like Na^+, Mg^{2+}, Ca^{2+}, HCO_3^-, etc.), glucose, traces of other sugars, plasma proteins, amino acids, hormones, cholesterol, other lipids, urea, other wastes and other organic acids.

Factors for clotting or coagulation of blood are also present actively in the plasma. Plasma without the blood clotting factors is called **serum**.

Plasma Proteins

Proteins found in plasma are important as they are responsible for providing **viscosity** to the plasma. The major proteins found in plasma are fibrinogen, globulins and albumins.

Functions of Plasma

It performs various functions in the blood, these are as follows

(i) Helps in transport and uniform distribution of heat all over the body.
(ii) Provides body immunity.
(iii) Maintenance of blood pH.
(iv) Helps in prevention of blood loss.
(v) Fibrinogen helps in blood clotting, globulin helps in defence mechanism, albumin maintains osmotic balance.

Formed Elements

The formed elements or blood corpuscles include erythrocytes, leucocytes and platelets. These constitute about 45% of the blood.

1. Erythrocytes (Red Blood Corpuscles)

These are the most abundant of all cells found in the blood. They are red in colour due to the presence of a pigment called **haemoglobin**, which acts as an oxygen carrier. The formation of RBCs takes place in the **red bone marrow** in adults.

Shape, Size and Structure

RBCs are biconcave, disc-shaped cells with the diameter of about 7-8 micron. The shape of RBC is slightly variable. As there are no cell organelles found in it, whole volume is filled with haemoglobin. A healthy individual has about 12-16 gm of haemoglobin in every 100 mL of blood.

Number

- In men, the average number of RBC is about 5-5.5 million per cubic millimeter (mm^3) of blood.
- In women, the average number is about 4-4.5 million per cubic mm^3 of blood.

Lifespan of RBC

Total lifespan of RBC is **120 days.** After which RBC becomes non-functional and gets destroyed in spleen. So, spleen is graveyard of RBCs.

> **Disintegration of RBC**
>
> The process of disintegration of RBC occurs in liver. The Kupffer's cells of liver help in complete disintegration process. The haemoglobin is disintegrated to release iron. Free iron is transported back to the bone marrow and the debris that remains, forms two toxic pigments, i.e. bilirubin and biliverdin (as studied in chapter 16). The remaining membrane of RBC known as ghost (i.e. without haemoglobin) is transported to spleen, where it gets destroyed completely.

2. Leucocytes (White Blood Cells)

These are known to be the most **active** and **motile** constituent of blood as well as lymph. They do not possess the red colour pigment (haemoglobin) in them, so they are **colourless** in nature.

These are nucleated and are generally short lived cells. The number of WBCs are relatively lesser in number, about 6000-8000 per mm^3 of blood. They move in an amoeboid fashion. These can squeeze through capillary wall and move to the site of action. This phenomenon is called **diapedesis.**

Leucocytes or White blood corpuscles are categorised into two main categories such as

i. Granulocytes

They contain granules in the cytoplasm and have regularly lobed nucleus. The granulocytes are further subdivided into three main types

(a) **Neutrophils** These are the most abundant cells (about 60-65%) of the total WBCs. They stain equally well with acidic as well as basic dyes, because they are neutral in nature. These are phagocytic cells that destroy foreign organisms entering the body.

(b) **Eosinophils** They are characterised by their bilobed nucleus. They are stained bright red in colour with acidic dye (due to the presence of numerous coarse granules in it) such as eosin.

They are about 2-3% of total WBCs. They resist infections and are also associated with all allergic reactions. They also help in dissolving blood clots. They help to destroy the toxic substances present in the body.

During allergic conditions, the number of eosinophils increases in the body.

(c) **Basophils** They contain fewer coarse granules than the eosinophils and can be stained with basic dyes such as, methylene blue. They are found least abundantly (0.5-1.0%) among WBCs. They secrete histamine, serotonin, heparin, etc., and are involved in inflammatory reactions.

ii. Agranulocytes

They lack granules in their cytoplasm and have rounded or oval nucleus. Agranulocytes are also further subdivided into two main types

(a) **Lymphocytes** These are smaller in size and have rounded nucleus. Lymphocytes are of further two types, i.e. B-cells and T-cells. Both of these (i.e. B and T-cells) are responsible for immune responses of the body.

(b) **Monocytes** These are largest of all types of WBCs, but are fewer in number. Mature monocytes are known as macrophages. They help to kill foreign particles. These are phagocytic in nature.

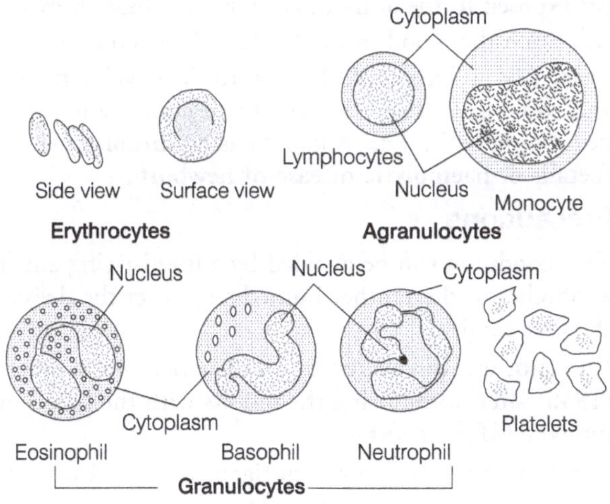

Fig. 18.1 Types of blood corpuscles

3. Blood Platelets (Thrombocytes)

These are cell fragments produced from **megakaryocytes** (i.e. the special cells found in the red bone marrow).

Structure

These are oval-shaped, disc-like cells found only in mammalian blood. These are devoid of nuclei.

Platelets contain mitochondria, Golgi bodies and some other structures such as granules, tubules, filaments of actin and myosin, ADP, etc.

Number

Blood normally contains 150000-350000 platelets per cubic meter (mm^3). A reduction in their number can lead to clotting disorders which will lead to excessive blood loss from the body if some one gets injured.

Lifespan

The lifespan of platelets is only about 7-12 **days.**

The formation of thrombocytes is called **thrombopoiesis.**

Function of Blood Platelets

Their main function in the body is to release factors most of which are involved in coagulation or clotting of blood.

Differences between Red Blood Cells and White Blood Cells

Red Blood Cells	White Blood Cells
These are smaller in size and more numerous in number, i.e. number of RBCs per cubic millimeter of blood is 5 million.	These are larger in size and fewer in number, i.e. number of WBCs per cubic millimeter of blood is only 8000.
These are non-nucleated, biconcave disc-like cells.	WBCs are nucleated and amoeboid cells and keep on changing their shape.
RBCs contain haemoglobin (respiratory pigment).	WBCs do not contain haemoglobin.
RBCs cannot diffuse out through capillary wall.	WBCs can diffuse out through capillary walls.
RBCs help in gaseous transport.	WBCs help in killing bacteria and foreign particles.
RBCs settle together to form rouleaux (i.e. stack over each other due to abnormal shape).	WBCs do not form rouleaux.

Blood Groups

The plasma membrane of RBCs contain certain glycoproteinaceous molecules known as **antigens**. These differ in different persons. Depending upon the nature of antigens two common types of blood grouping found in human beings are

1. ABO Grouping

It was reported by **Karl Landsteiner.** It is based on the presence or absence of antigen-A or antigen-B on the surface of RBCs.

People with blood group A have the antigen A on the surface of their RBCs and have antibodies against antigen B in their plasma. While in the people having blood group B, the case is just *vice-versa* to blood group-A.

Apart from both these blood groups (i.e. A and B) people with blood group AB have both antigen-A and B on their RBCs surface and no antibodies for either of the antigens in their plasma A. A, B and O blood groups were discovered by Landsteiner (1900). Blood group AB was discovered by de **Castello** and **Steini** (1902).

In people with blood group O, both antigen-A and B are not present on their RBCs but they have antibodies against the plasma. The distribution of antigens and antibodies is in the four blood groups (A, B, AB and O). Can be well-explained through the table given below

Blood Groups and Donor Compatibility

Blood Group	Antigens on RBCs	Antibodies in Plasma	Donor's Group
A	A	Anti-B	A, O
B	B	Anti-A	B, O
AB	A, B	Nil	AB, A, B, O
O	Nil	Anti-A, B	O

Blood Reactions

In humans, during **transfusion of blood,** the blood of a donor has to be carefully matched to the blood of a recipient before transfusing, so as to avoid the problem of **clumping** (destruction of RBC).

A person with blood group O can donate blood to persons with any of the other blood group (i.e. either A, B, AB and O). Hence, is called **universal donor**. Whereas, the persons with blood AB can accept blood from any blood group (i.e. AB as well as A, B and O). Hence, are called **universal recipients**.

During pregnancy, if an O type mother is carrying an A type/B type foetus then the mother will have anti-A and anti-B antibodies in her blood. The foetus will be having A/B antigen. The anti-A and anti-B antibodies of mother will reach the foetus by circulation. This will destroy foetus red blood cells. Thus, the child will suffer from anaemia and jaundice.

2. Rh Grouping

Apart from the antigens discussed in the previous section, another antigen, known as **Rh antigen** (similar to the one present in Rhesus monkey) is also found on the RBCs surface in majority of humans (nearly about 80%). Individuals having Rh antigen are called **Rh positive** (Rh^+) and those without the Rh antigen are called **Rh negative** (Rh^-). Rh group is mandatory to be matched before transfusion of blood is done. An Rh^- person if gets exposed to Rh^+ blood, it will form specific antibodies against the Rh antigens.

Rh Incompatibility During Pregnancy

A special case of **mismatching** of Rh group or **Rh incompatibility** has been observed between the Rh^- blood of a pregnant mother with Rh^+ blood of the foetus (the foetus of Rh^- woman and a Rh^+ man).

In such a case, mother becomes sensitive, while carrying an **Rh^+ baby** in her womb. The reason is that some of the RBCs from the developing foetus enter into the bloodstream of the mother during development. This causes the development of **anti-Rh antibodies** in mother's blood.

The Rh antigens of the foetus do not get exposed to the Rh^- blood of the mother in case of first pregnancy (because two blood remain separated by placenta). However, during delivery of the first child, there occurs a possibility that maternal blood may get exposed to small amounts of Rh^+ blood from the foetus. Hence, preparing antibodies against Rh antigens in her blood.

Thus, in case of her subsequent pregnancies, Rh^+ foetuses get exposed to the anti-Rh antibodies. These antibodies will reach the blood of the foetus (Rh^+) and destroy foetal RBCs. This could be fatal to the developing foetus and could cause severe **anaemia** and **jaundice** to the developing baby. This is known as **erythroblastosis foetalis** or **haemolytic disease of newborn.**

Precautions

This condition can be avoided by administering anti-Rh antibodies to the mother immediately after the delivery of the first child.

Rh-factor was discovered by **Landsteiner** and **Weiner** (1940) after immunising the rabbits with the blood of a monkey (*Macaca rhesus*).

There are 30 or so, known **antigens** on the surface of red blood cells that give rise to different blood groups, e.g. MN, etc.

During Blood Transfusion

The first transfusion betwen Rh^+ and Rh^- blood causes no harm because Rh^- person develops anti-Rh antibodies in his blood. But, in the second transfusion of Rh^+ blood to Rh^- blood the anti-Rh antibodies in the later's blood destroy the RBCs of the donor.

Coagulation of Blood or Clotting of Blood

When an injury is caused, the wound normally does not continue to bleed for a long time and the blood stops flowing after some time. It is the natural property exhibited by the blood to check the excessive loss of blood from an injury or trauma. Clotting of blood is a complex process that involves various enzymatically controlled steps for its completion.

> **Natural Anticoagulants**
>
> Inside an intact blood vessel, the blood does not coagulate because of the presence of an active anticoagulants, i.e. heparin or antiprothrombins. These procoagulants are present in the blood in their inactive forms.
>
> Haemophilia is a genetic disease, which is caused due to deficiency of prothrombin, fibrinogen and vitamin-K. In this condition, the blood does not clot. If there is any injury in such person, death of that person occurs due to excessive bleeding.

Formation of a Clot

An injury or trauma causes stimulation of platelets cells to release certain platelet factors. This in turn activates the mechanism of coagulation or clotting of blood at the site of injury. It occurs in following three steps

(i) **Thromboplastin,** helps in formation of an enzyme prothrombinase (which inactivates heparin) that converts the inactive plasma protein, i.e. **prothrombin** into its active form **thrombin.**

(ii) Thrombin thus, acts as a **proteolytic enzyme** to convert **fibrinogen** molecule (produced from the liver in the presence of vitamin-K) to form insoluble **fibrin** monomer.

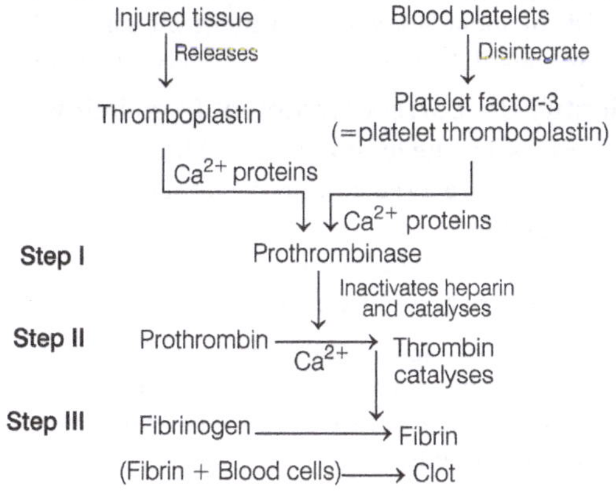

Role of thrombocytes in blood coagulation

This reaction required **thrombokinase** an enzyme complex, which is formed by a series of linked enzymatic reactions (with cascade effects) which involves a number of various factors present in the plasma in their inactive state. Both the changes mentioned above require Ca^{2+} ions for their reaction.

(iii) These fibrin monomers polymerise to long, sticky fibres. The fibrin threads forms a fine network of threads called **fibrins,** in which dead and damaged formed elements of blood are trapped. This finally leads to the formation of a **clot** or **coagulum,** which is a dark reddish brown **scum** formed over the surface of injury.

Functions of Blood

Blood performs the following important functions

(i) Helps in transportation of respiratory gases (i.e. O_2, CO_2, etc).
(ii) Helps in healing of wounds.
(iii) Maintains body pH, water and ionic balance.
(iv) Fight against infections by forming body immunity.
(v) Also helps in transportation of hormones from endocrine glands to target organs.
(vi) Coagulation of blood.
(vii) Helps in transportation of body wastes from different body parts to kidneys.
(viii) Maintains normal body temperature.

Lymph (Tissue Fluid)

It is another fluid connective tissue that floats inside specialised vessels known as lymph vessels.

Composition

It is a colourless fluid containing high concentration of WBCs (specialised lymphocytes). The overall composition of lymph is similar to blood with the exception of the absence of RBCs, platelets and some plasma proteins and in having less calcium and phosphorus than their levels in the blood. It also contains all the ions, present in the blood plasma.

Lymphatic System

It is an elaborate network of vessels, which collects the **interstitial fluid** (tissue fluid), along with some protein molecules and drains it back into the major veins. The lymphatic vessels are present in all tissues (except the central nervous system and cornea).

Lymphatic Capillaries

These capillaries are thin-walled, small and are composed of a single layer of endothelial cells. They lie close to the blood capillaries, but differ from them to the extent that they end blindly.

The lymphatic capillaries of intestinal regions,which absorb the digested fats are called lacteals.

Lymphatic Nodes

These are oval or bean-shaped structures located along the length of lymphatic vessels. They are 1-25 nm long. They are covered by a capsule of dense connective tissue. Lymph filters through the lymph nodes.

They contain phagocytic white blood corpuscles and macrophage, which eat harmful microorganisms and foreign particles from the lymph.

Formation of Lymph

As the blood passes through the capillaries of the arterial system into the tissues, some water along with many water soluble substances come out in the spaces between the cells of tissues.

But a very small amount of proteins come out from the capillary with the plasma (leaving the larger proteins and most of the formed elements in the blood vessel).

The fluid thus, released out is called **interstitial fluid** (tissue fluid) or **Extracellular Fluid** (ECF).

After entering the lymph vessel, the ECF becomes lymph.

Functions of Lymph

Lymph performes the following important functions

(i) It acts as an important carrier of nutrients, hormones, etc.

(ii) Absorption of fat also occurs through lymph in the **lacteals** present in the intestinal villi.

(iii) Also helps in the **renewal of ECF**.

(iv) Maturation of lymphocytes, i.e. B-cells and T-cells occur with the help of lymph nodes, releasing them into the lymph.

(v) Helps in keeping tissue cells moist.

The lymph first reaches the lymph nodes like thymus, tonsils, Peyer's patches, spleen, etc., in the body.

Differences between Blood and Lymph

Blood	Lymph
It is red in colour due to the presence of haemoglobin in red cells.	It is colourless as red blood cells are absent.
It consists of plasma, RBC, WBC and platelets.	It consists of plasma and very low number of WBC.
Glucose concentration is low.	Glucose concentration is higher than blood.
Clotting of blood is a fast process.	Clotting of lymph is comparatively slow.
It transports materials from one organ to other.	It transports materials from tissue cells into the blood.
Flow of blood is fast.	Lymph flows very slowly.
Its plasma has more proteins, calcium and phosphorus.	Its plasma has less protein, calcium and phosphorus.
It moves away from the heart and towards the heart.	It moves in one direction, i.e. from tissues to subclavians.

Topic Practice 1

Multiple Choice Questions

(1 Mark)

1. Plasma is a straw coloured viscous fluid constituting nearly ...*A*... % of the blood, ...*B*...% of the plasma is water and the protein constitutes ...*C*... % of it.
Choose the correct option for the blanks *A*, *B* and *C*.

(a) *A*–55, *B*–90-92, *C*–6-8
(b) *A*–45, *B*–70-80, *C*–6-8
(c) *A*–35, *B*–90-92, *C*–6-8
(d) *A*–45, *B*–90, 92, *C*–6-8

Ans (a) Plasma is a faint yellow, slightly alkaline viscous fluid. It consists of about 90% water, 1% inorganic salts, 6-8% proteins and it constitutes of about 55% of the blood.

2. Identify the correct statement from below.

(a) RBCs are the least abundant blood cells
(b) They have a red coloured, copper containing pigment
(c) RBCs are devoid of nucleus in most mammals
(d) They are biconvex in shape

Ans (c) RBCs are the most abundant blood cells which are biconcave in shape. They have a red coloured iron containing pigment called haemoglobin which imparts colour to these cells.

3. Your friend has gone for blood test and his haemoglobin count is 17 gm per 100 mL. What should he do?
(a) No need to worry
(b) Take rest
(c) Take rest and prescribed medicines
(d) Take rest and lots of leafy vegetables

Ans (a) If haemoglobin count is 17 gm per 100 mL, then there is no need to get worried as the normal haemoglobin count in human blood should be between 12-17 gm/mL.

4. Lymphocytes (20-25%) are of two major types, B and T forms. They are responsible for
(a) blood coagulation (b) thickness of blood
(c) immune responses (d) All of these

Ans (c) Lymphocytes (20-25%) are smaller with large rounded nucleus. They produce antibodies, which are the key cells of immune response.

5. Find out the incorrect match.

(a)	Eosinophils	—	Allergic response
(b)	Basophils	—	Secrete histamine and serotonin
(c)	Neutrophils	—	Phagocytic and destroy foreign organisms
(d)	Monocytes	—	Secrete heparin

Ans (d) Monocytes are the largest agranular leucocytes and are phagocytic, while mast cells of connective tissues continuously release, in blood plasma, a conjugated polysaccharide, named heparin.

6. Platelets are
(a) also called thrombocytes
(b) cell fragments
(c) produced from megakaryocytes
(d) All of the above

Ans (d) Blood platelets occur only in mammals. They are non-nucleated, round or oval biconvex and bud from megakaryocytes. They are much smaller than RBC. Blood platelets are the source of thromboplastin, necessary for blood clotting.

7. Which of the following option describes all the components of human blood?
(a) A and B blood group
(b) AB and O blood group
(c) Rh and ABO blood group
(d) Rh and AB blood group

Ans (c) More than 20 different blood group systems are recognised in medicine. Out of which, the best known are ABO system and Rh system. In 1900, Dr. Karl Landsteiner discovered the ABO blood groups and in 1940 Rh was found by Landsteiner and Weiner.

8. Grouping of ABO blood is based on the
(a) surface antigens present on RBCs
(b) surface lipids present on the cell membrane
(c) nature of all constituents
(d) nature of RBCs and WBCs

Ans (a) ABO blood grouping is based on the presence or absence of the surface antigens-A and B on RBCs.

9. Which of the given option is correct about blood groups and donor compatibility?

(a)
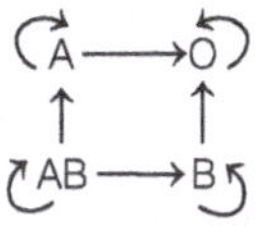

(b)
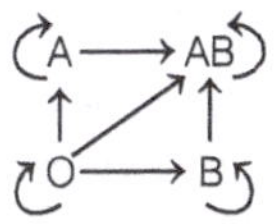

(c)
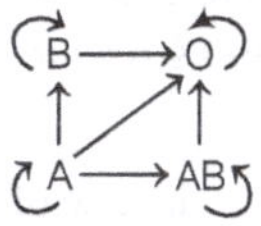

(d)
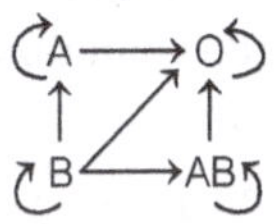

Ans (b) AB individuals can receive blood from all other blood groups.

Blood Group	Receive Blood	Donate Blood
O	O	O, A, B, AB
A	A, O	A, AB
B	B,O	B, AB
AB	O, A, B, AB	AB

10. Example of Rh incompatibility is
(a) mother Rh^- and father Rh^+
(b) father Rh^- and mother Rh^+
(c) Both mother and father are Rh^-
(d) Both mother and father are Rh^+

Ans (a) A special case of Rh incompatibility has been observed between Rh^- blood of pregnant mother with Rh^+ blood of foetus. During the delivery of the first child there is a possibility of exposure of the maternal blood to small amount of Rh^+ blood from foetus.

In such cases, the mother starts preparing antibodies against Rh antigen in her blood. In the case of her subsequent pregnancies, the Rh antibody from the mother can leak to blood of foetus and destroy foetal RBC. This could be fatal to foetus or could cause severe anaemia and jaundice to the foetus. This condition in called erythroblastosis foetalis.

11. What will happen if a Rh^- person donates blood to a Rh^+ person for the first time?
(a) Rh^- person will die
(b) Rh^+ person will die
(c) Nothing will happen to both
(d) Rh^- will live and Rh^+ would die

Ans (c) The blood of an Rh(-) person has no Rh antigen, therefore he can safely donate blood to people having Rh(-) as well as Rh(+) blood without the fear of antibody generation in the acceptor.

12. Clotting disorders occur mainly due to the reduction in the number of
(a) granulocytes (b) RBC
(c) WBC (d) platelets

Ans (d) Clotting disorders occurs mainly due to the reduction in the number of the platelets as platelets releases variety of substances which are involved in clotting.

13. When thromboplastin is released in humans?
(a) During hypertension
(b) By the traumatised cell at the place of injury
(c) In the condition of erythroblastosis foetalis
(d) During anaemia

Ans (b) Thromboplastin is released from the site of injury. It initiates the clotting mechanism.

14. Which system has a major role in defence against infection?
(a) Respiratory system (b) Circulatory system
(c) Lymphatic system (d) All of these

Ans (c) Lymph is a colourless fluid containing specialised lymphocytes (B and T-cells) which are responsible for the immune response of the body.

Very Short Answer Type Questions

1 Mark

15. Name the blood component which is viscous and straw coloured fluid. **NCERT Exemplar**

Ans Plasma is a straw coloured, viscous fluid constituting of nearly 55% of the blood, 90-92% of plasma is water and proteins contributes approximately 6-8%. The plasma proteins contains fibrinogen, globulins and albumins.

16. Blood is called river of life. Comment.

Ans Blood is called so, because blood which is a fluid connective tissue, helps in transportation of biologically important materials for life processes like nutrients, gases, wastes, hormones, etc., within the body, which is very essential for the survival of life.

17. It is seen that RBC count is more in the persons living at high altitudes. Indicate the reason behind this.

Ans It is due to the low concentration of O_2 in the air, which leads to less O_2 binding capacity of the haemoglobin. Thus, there is increase in the RBC count in persons living at high altitude.

18. Mention the total amount of normal leucocyte count in human.

Ans 6000-8000 per cubic mm is the normal leucocyte count in human.

19. What is the effect of dengue fever on the platelets of blood in humans?

Ans One of the major effect of dengue fever is the low platelet count. It leads to life threatening condition if left untreated.

20. A person has a blood group AB positive. What does it mean?

Ans AB positive means that a person has both A and B antigens and also has Rh-factor in his blood.

21. Why is blood group identification not needed for serum identification?

Ans The blood group identification is not needed for serum identification because serum does not have the coagulation/clotting factor.

Short Answer Type I Questions

2 Marks

22. What is the importance of plasma proteins? **NCERT**

Ans Fibrinogen, globulins and albumins are the major plasma proteins. Fibrinogens (present in insoluble form) are needed for clotting or coagulation of blood. Globulins primarily are involved in defence mechanisms of the body and the albumins help in osmotic balance to and from the body cells. (2)

23. Why do we consider blood as a connective tissue? **NCERT**

Ans Blood is a mobile connective tissue derived from mesoderm. It consists of fibre-free fluid matrix, plasma and other cells.
It is called so, as it regularly circulates in the body and takes part in transport of materials to end from the body cells. (2)

24. State the functions of the following in blood
(i) Fibrinogen
(ii) Globulin
(iii) Neutrophils
(iv) Lymphocytes **NCERT Exemplar**

Ans Functions of the following are
(i) Fibrinogens are needed for clotting or coagulation of blood at the site of injury to stop bleeding.
(ii) Globulins are primarily involved in immunity, i.e. defence mechanisms of the body (to fight infections).
(iii) Neutrophils and monocytes are phagocytic cells which destroy foreign organisms entering the body and then blood stream.
(iv) Lymphocytes provide immunity to the body. ($\frac{1}{2}\times 4$)

25. Differentiate between granulocytes and agranulocytes.

Ans Differences between granulocytes and agranulocytes are as follows

Granulocytes	Agranulocytes
They contain granules in the cytoplasm and have regularly lobed nucleus.	They lack granules in their cytoplasm and have rounded or oval nucleus.
Neutrophils, eosinophils and basophils are granulocytes.	Lymphocytes and monocytes are agranulocytes.

(2)

26. One of the ABO blood groups is sometimes called the universal donor. Which group do you think it is and why?

Ans Individuals with blood group O are called universal donors. These individuals do not have either A or B antigens on the surface of their RBCs, but their blood serum contains antibodies against both A and B antigens. Therefore, O group individuals can only receive blood from a group O individual, but they can donate blood to individuals of any ABO blood group (i.e. A, B, O or AB). (2)

Short Answer Type II Questions

(3 Marks)

27. Name the components of the formed elements in the blood and mention one major function of each of them. **NCERT**

Ans Refer to text on page no. 414.

28. An Rh^- woman is carrying an Rh^+ foetus for the second time. Describe the consequences of Rh^-incompatibility in this case?

Or Why is it necessary to check the Rh-factor of the blood in a pregnant woman?

Or What physiological circumstances lead to erythroblastosis foetalis? **NCERT Exemplar**

Ans Rh antigen is present on the surface of erythrocytes in about 80-85% of the human beings. The individuals, who possess this antigen are called Rh^+(Rh positive) and those, who do not have it are called Rh^-(Rh negative). A person when exposed to Rh^+ blood, develops anti Rh-antibodies. A pregnant women who is Rh^-, if bears an Rh^+ foetus, will develop anti-Rh-antibodies during the first delivery, when the foetal blood comes in contact with her blood. These antibodies linger in the blood for sufficiently longer periods.

If she carries a second foetus, that is Rh^+, the anti-Rh-antibodies in her blood enter the foetal circulation and cause damage to the foetal RBCs. This, could become fatal. This condition is called erythroblastosis foetalis. (3)

29. Explain the chemical events that take place to form a blood clot to seal the wound.

Ans Chemical events that take place to form a blood clot are as follows

(i) When blood comes out of a blood vessel in case of injury the platelets clump together, break and release platelet factors, thromboplastin.

(ii) The enzyme thrombokinase initiates the conversion of prothrombin into thrombin.

(iii) Thrombin thus, catalyses the conversion of fibrinogen into fibrin which forms a mesh/network in which blood cells get entangled.

(iv) Ca^{2+} ions are necessary for both the above steps. (3)

Long Answer Type Questions

(5 Marks)

30. What is the differences between blood and lymph? **NCERT**

Ans Refer to text on page no. 418.

31. Thrombocytes are essential for coagulation of blood. Comment. **NCERT Exemplar**

Ans Refer to text on page no. 417.

32. Explain different types of blood groups and donor compatibility by making a table. **NCERT Exemplar**

Ans Two groupings, i.e. the ABO and Rh are widely used all over the world. ABO grouping is based on the presence or absence of two surface antigens (chemicals that can induce immune response) on the RBCs, i.e. A and B. Similarly, the plasma of different individuals contain two natural antibodies (proteins produced in response to antigens). (2)

Blood Groups and Donor Compatibility

Blood Group	Antigen on RBCs	Antibody in Plasma	Donor's Group
A	A	Anti-B	A, O
B	B	Anti-A	B, O
AB	A, B	Nil	AB, A, B, O
O	Nil	Anti- A, B	O

From the above mentioned table it is evident that group 'O' blood can be donated to persons with any other blood group such individuals are called 'universal donors'. Persons with 'AB' group can accept blood from persons with AB as well as the other groups of blood. Therefore, such persons are called 'universal recipients'. Rh grouping is done on the basis of presence or absence of Rh antigen. The individuals having Rh antigens are known as Rh (+) whereas those who lack Rh antigen are known as Rh(-). Rh(-) individual can donate blood to both Rh (+) and Rh(-) individuals but can receive blood only from Rh(-) individuals. (3)

TOPIC 02 Circulatory System

As we know blood and lymph are the important fluids in the body that act as a carrier in transporting nutrients, hormones, and various other materials even to the farthest tissue in the body. Now, the question arises what makes this blood to circulate inside the body. So, the answer to this question lies in the fact that to circulate this blood throughout the body, a muscular pump is required which is known as **heart.**

Types of Circulatory System

Depending upon the circulatory patterns in higher organisms the circulatory system is of following two types

1. Open Circulatory System

In this type of circulatory system in which blood pumped by the heart is passed through a vessel into the spaces or body cavities known as **sinuses.** From there the blood is collected by large veins, which open into the heart.

In this type of system, the blood does not contain the respiratory pigment and if present, is dissolved in plasma. This type of system is found in **arthropods** and **molluscs.** There is no capillary system (i.e. interconnecting vessels) found in this type of circulatory system (i.e. open type).

2. Closed Circulatory System

In this type of circulatory system, the blood pumped by the heart is always circulated inside the vessels (i.e. it is never present in large spaces or sinuses). From evolutionary point of view, this pattern is considered to be most advantageous as it supplies blood to the **deepest tissues** of the body. It is found in **annelids** and **chordates.**

Differences between Open and Closed Circulatory System

Open Circulatory System	Closed Circulatory System
The blood is pumped by the heart into the blood vessels that open into blood spaces (sinuses).	The blood is pumped by the heart into closed blood vessels.
Blood is in direct contact with the tissue cells.	Blood does not come in direct contact with the tissue cells.
Exchange of respiratory gases, nutrients and waste products occurs directly between blood and tissues.	Exchange of respiratory gases, nutrients and waste products between tissues and blood occur via tissue fluid.
Blood returns to the heart slowly.	Blood returns to the heart rapidly.
The pressure of the blood is low.	The pressure of the blood is high.
Respiratory pigment, if present, is dissolved in blood plasma.	Respiratory pigment is present, and may be dissolved in plasma, but is usually held in red blood corpuscles.

Heart (The Pumping Organ)

All vertebrates possess a muscular chambered heart. Depending upon the different types of circulation in them, heart is of following three types

1. Two-Chambered Heart

This is found mostly in **fishes.** It is comprised of an atrium and a ventricle. During circulation of blood, the heart pumps out **deoxygenated** blood. This blood gets **oxygenated** by the gills and is then supplied to the body parts from where the deoxygenated blood is returned to the heart. Hence, the type of circulation is called **single circulation.**

2. Three-Chambered Heart

Amphibians and **reptiles** (except crocodiles) have a three-chambered heart. This type of heart comprises of two atria and a single ventricle. During the circulation of blood, the left atrium receives the oxygenated blood from the gills/lungs/skin and the right atrium receives the deoxygenated blood from the other body parts. The blood gets mixed up in the single ventricle which further pumps out the mixed blood. This type of circulation is called **incomplete double circulation.**

3. Four-Chambered Heart

Crocodiles, birds and **mammals** possess this type of heart. It comprises of two atria and two ventricles. During the course of circulation, the oxygenated and deoxygenated blood is received by the left and the right atria, respectively. The blood from each atria is passed on to the ventricles of the same sides (i.e. left and right ventricles). There is no mixing of oxygenated and deoxygenated blood and both flow simultaneously in heart chambers but separately, so it is called **double circulation.**

Human Circulatory System

Circulatory system in humans is also known as **blood vascular system.** It consists of a muscular chambered heart, a network of closed branching blood vessels and the fluid that is circulated, i.e. blood.

Human Heart

Heart is a **mesodermally derived organ**, situated in the thoracic cavity in between the two lungs. It appears to be slightly tilted towards the left side. It is a hollow, **fibromuscular organ,** slightly conical in shape of about 12 cm length and 9 cm breadth. The upper broad part is called the **base** and the lower narrow part is known as the **apex.** It has a size of a clenched fist.

Protective Covering

The heart is protected by a double-walled membranous sac or a bag called **pericardium.** The fluid present between two membrane is called **pericardial fluid.** This fluid helps in keeping the surface of the heart moist and also protects it from **shock** and **mechanical injuries.**

Structure of human heart can be studied under two heads for easy understanding, i.e. external and internal structure.

External Structure

Externally, the human heart is composed of four chambers, i.e. two relatively small upper chambers called **auricles** (sing. atria) and two larger lower chambers called **ventricles.** The right atrium is slightly larger than the left atrium. Both these atria are meant to receive blood from different body parts.

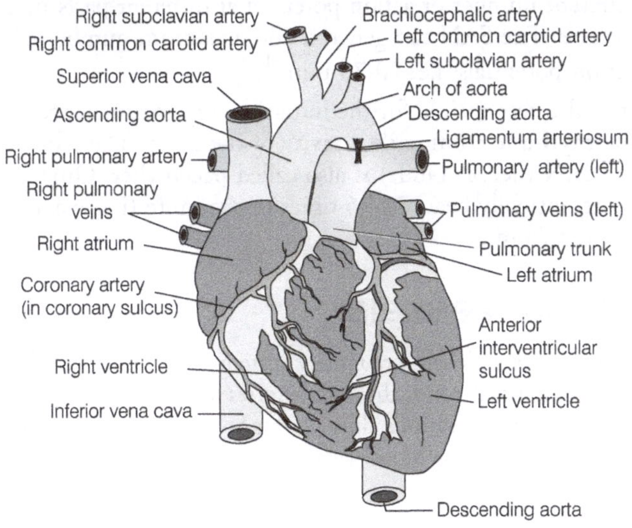

Fig 18.2 External structure of human heart

Internal Structure

Internally, the chambers of heart, i.e. two auricles (atria) and ventricles are separated by different septa and valves.

Auricles (Atria)

These are the upper two thin-walled and smaller chambers. They serve to receive the blood, therefore are called **receiving chambers** (right atrium and left atrium). Both the right and the left atria are separated by a thin, muscular wall, known as **interatrial septum.**

(i) **Right Atrium** This right chamber deals with only **impure** (deoxygenated) blood. It receives impure blood from various parts of the body, through two major veins, i.e. superior and inferior vena cava.

It also receives blood from the walls of the heart itself (through a coronary sinus).

(ii) **Left Atrium** This chamber is meant to deal with only **pure** (oxygenated) blood. It receives blood (pure) from lungs through two **pulmonary veins** (i.e. one from the each lung).

Ventricles

These are lower two chambers of the heart, that pumps the blood away from the heart. These functions as **pumping chambers.** Both the right and the left ventricles are separated by the **interventricular septum.**

The atrium and the ventricle of the same side are also separated by another septum, a thick fibrous tissue called **Atrio-Ventricular septum** (i.e. AV septum).

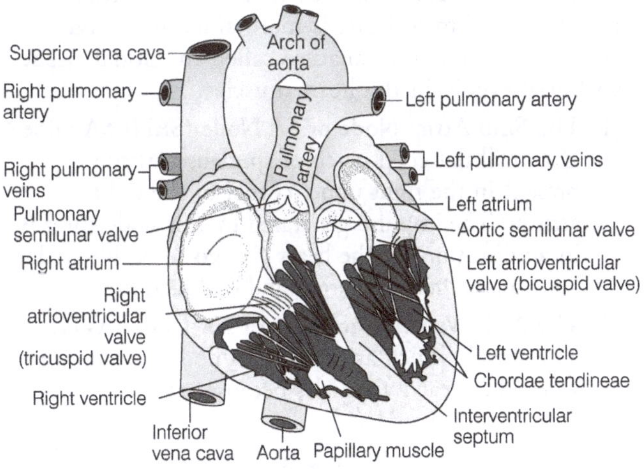

Fig. 18.3 Internal structure of human heart

(i) **Right Ventricle** It receives impure blood from right atrium and pumps blood into **pulmonary artery,** which further takes this blood to lungs for purification.

(ii) **Left Ventricle** It receives pure (oxygenated) blood from left attium and pumps its pure blood to aorta (largest attery in the pathway), which in turn takes this blood to whole body and organs.

Cardiac Valves

The valves are membranous door-like structure in the heart that serves to maintain the **unidirectional flow** of blood.

Different valves present in the heart are given below

(i) **Tricuspid Valve** It is formed by **three muscular flaps or cusps** to guard the opening between the right atrium and the right ventricle.

(ii) **Bicuspid Valve** (Mitral valve) It is the type of valve that guards the opening between the left atrium and the left ventricle.

(iii) **Semilunar Valve** The opening of the right and the left ventricles into the pulmonary artery and the aorta, respectively are provided with the semilunar valves.

Functions of Cardiac Valves

The valves in the heart allow the flow of blood only in one direction, i.e. from the atria to ventricles and from the ventricles to the pulmonary artery or aorta and prevent any backward flow of blood into four chambers.

Conducting System of Heart

The heart is made up of cardiac muscles. The ventricular walls are thicker than that of the atrial walls. The rhythm of heart is maintained by a highly specialised cardiac musculature called the **nodal tissue** distributed evenly in the heart muscles.

1. **The Sino-Atrial Node or SA Node** (SAN) SA node is a small flattened patch of specialised tissue present in the right upper corner of the right atrium. The impulse generated by this node spreads in all directions of the heart (i.e. go to both auricles and causes their relaxation and contraction).
2. **The Atrio-Ventricular Node or AV Node** (AVN) The signals which arise from SA node become weak when they reach ventricles because ventricles are far away from SA node.

   Thus, to strengthen these signals, another mass of tissue is seen in the lower left corner of the right atrium close to the **atrio-ventricular septum** (i.e. at the junction of ventricles and atrium) known as **AV node.** This is also known as **pacesetter.**
3. **Bundle of His** A bundle of **nodal fibres,** i.e. Atrio-Ventricular bundle (AV bundle) continues from the AV node, which passes through the Atrio-Ventricular septa to emerge on the top of the interventricular septum immediately dividing into a right and left bundle.

   This bundle gives rise to a network of minute fibres (which are myocardial in origin) throughout the ventricular musculature of the respective side known as **Purkinje fibres.**

   These fibres along with the right and left bundles are called **bundle of His.** The Purkinje fibres conduct impulses to all portions of ventricular walls of the heart.

Differences between SA Node and AV Node

SA Node	AV Node
It is located at the upper lateral wall of right auricle.	It is situated at the base of right auricle, near auriculo-vetricular junction.
It generates impulses to initiate heart beating.	Normally it does not generate impulse, but strengthen them.
SA node is also called pacemaker.	AV node is also called pacesetter.
It supplies signals directly to auricles.	It supplies signals to ventricles.
It is not associated with bundle of His and Purkinje fibres.	It is associated with bundle of His and Purkinje fibres.

Working of Nodal Tissue

The nodal musculature possesses the ability of generating action potentials without any external stimuli, i.e. it is **autoexcitable.** However, the nodal system generates different number of action potential at different parts in a minute. The SAN can generate the maximum number of action potentials, i.e. 70-75 min^{-1}.

It is also responsible for the initiation and maintenance of the **rhythmic contractile activity** of the heart. Therefore, the SAN (i.e. SA Node) is also called **pacemaker.** Our heart normally beats 70-75 times in a minute (i.e. average 72 beats/min).

Blood Vessels

As man has a closed circulatory system, the blood strictly flows in a fixed route through arteries and veins. It maintains a continuous flow throughout the body inside the closed tubes or blood vessels.

These tubes or vessels are mainly of two types

Arteries

These blood vessels carry blood from the heart to different body parts. All arteries carry pure or oxygenated blood, with the exception of **pulmonary artery** that carries the impure or deoxygenated blood (i.e. from heart to the lungs for purification). As the walls of arteries are thick and non-collapsible, the pressure inside them is very high.

Features of Arteries

(i) Valves are absent in arteries.

(ii) Arteries are divided into fine branches, known as **arterioles,** which are further divided to form finer branches, called **capillaries.**

Veins

These are another type of blood vessels that bring blood from different body parts to the heart, i.e. carry blood towards the heart. All veins are meant to carry impure blood except the pulmonary vein that carries pure blood, i.e. from lungs to the heart. Veins are provided with valves to prevent backward flow of blood.

Internal Structure of Blood Vessels

The wall of arteries and veins consists of the following layers from inside to outside.

(i) **Tunica Interna** (intima) It has inner endothelium of long, thin cells of squamous epithelium resting on a basement membrane along with an outer elastic membrane of yellow elastic tissue.

(ii) **Tunica Media** It has circular smooth muscles and elastic fibres.

(iii) **Tunica Externa** (tunica adventitia) It has loose connective tissues with longitudinally arranged white and yellow fibres.

Capillary walls are thin and composed of a single layer of endothelium only.

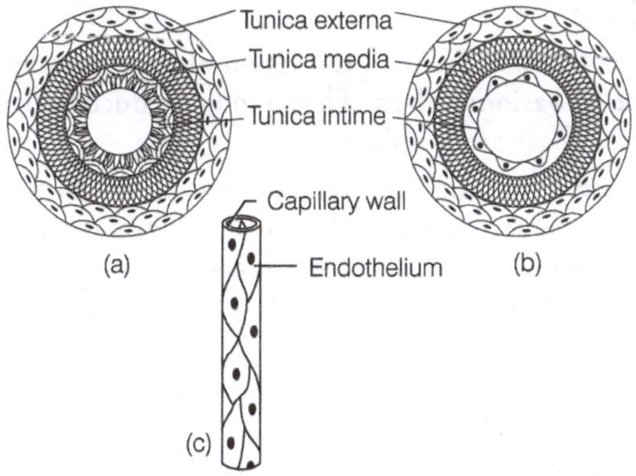

Fig 18. 4 Structure of blood vessels (a) an artery in transection, (b) a vein in transection, (c) part of a capillary in surface view

Differences between Arteries and Veins

Arteries	Veins
Arteries carry blood from the heart to the different parts of the body.	Veins bring back blood from different parts of the body to the heart.
The wall of arteries are thick and muscular.	The wall of the veins are thin and non-muscular.
They are usually deep seated.	They are situated superficially under skin.
The flow of the blood is fast as the blood in arteries is under great pressure.	The flow of blood in veins is not so fast because the blood in veins is under low pressure.
Except the pulmonary arteries, all the arteries carry oxygenated blood.	Except pulmonary veins all the veins carry deoxygenated blood.
Arteries have no valves.	Veins have valves to prevent backflow of the blood.

Cardiac Cycle

The heart pumps the blood to all parts of the body. The changes that take place in heart during one heartbeat, together constitute cardiac cycle.

The heart beats at an average rate of about 72 times/min. Thus, the total duration of a cardiac cycle is **0.8 s.** During a heartbeat, the contraction and relaxation of atria and ventricles take place. The phase of contraction is known as **systole,** while the relaxation phase is called the **diastole.** Thus, a single heartbeat consists of a systole and diastole of both the atria and the ventricles.

To begin with the cardiac cycle, all four chambers of heart are in a relaxed state, i.e. they are in **joint diastole,** during which, the blood flows from the **superior** and the **inferior venae cavae** into the atria and from there to the respective ventricles through **auriculo-ventricular valves.**

The complete cardiac cycle is comprised of following events that take place in a sequential manner

(i) **Atrial or Auricular Systole** A wave of contraction occurs from anterior to posterior side stimulated by the SA node. The blood flows from the pulmonary veins and vena cava into the left and right ventricles, respectively as the tricuspid and bicuspid valves are open.

During this time the blood does not return to the great veins (as blood is already present in them). The semilunar valves are closed. The atrial systole increases the flow of blood into the ventricles by about 30% (as 70% filling of ventricles occurs passively during relaxation of ventricles, before the atrial contraction).

(ii) **Atrial or Auricular Diastole** At the end of the atrial systole, there start **relaxation** of the atria (atrial diastole) and **contraction** of the ventricles (ventricular systole) simultaneously. The atrial systole occurs for 0.1s, while the atrial diastole on the other hand is of about 0.7s.

(iii) **Ventricular Systole** This step involves the **simultaneous relaxation** of atria (atrial diastole) and contraction of ventricles (ventricular systole).

As the contraction of the ventricles begins, the pressure of blood rises in them almost immediately (above the pressure in the atria). This rapidly **closes the atrio-ventricular valves,** in order to prevent the back flow of blood from ventricles to atria.

The conduction of action potential to the ventricular side occurs by the AV node and AV bundle from where the bundle of His transmits it through the entire ventricular musculature. The contraction of ventricles thereby, increases the ventricular pressure causing the closure of the tricuspid and bicuspid valves due to attempted backflow of blood into the atria.

Finally, due to this, the increase in the pressure occurs in the great arteries (i.e. pulmonary and aortic arches), so semilunar valves guarding the pulmonary artery (right side) and the aorta (left side) are forced open and blood enters through great arteries into ventricles.

(iv) **Ventricular Diastole** When ventricles relax (**ventricular diastole**), the ventricular pressure falls which causes the closure of semilunar valves preventing the backflow of blood into the ventricles.

A further decline in the ventricular pressure, opens the tricuspid and bicuspid valves by the pressure in the atria exerted by the blood, which was being emptied into them by the veins. This allows the blood to move freely to the ventricles once again.

(v) **Joint Diastole** The ventricles and atria are now again in a **relaxed state (joint diastole)** as earlier. Soon, the SAN generates a new action potential and the events described above sequencially repeated to continue the process (next cardiac cycle).

Beat and Pulse

The heart regularly and rhythmically contracts and relaxes at short intervals throughout life without pause and fatigue. This inherent activity of heart is called its heartbeat.

Each heartbeat has two phases, i.e. contraction phase or systole and relaxation phase or diastole.

The rate of throbbing felt in arteries due to pumping action of heart (left ventricle) is called **pulse** or atrial phase. The number of pulse is equal to number of heart beats. It can be felt in the radial artery near the wrist, in neck and ankles pulse rate is about 72 times per minute in men and about 80 times per minute in women.

Heart Rate and Cardiac Output

We have just studied that, our heartbeats for about 72 times per minute (on an average). This concludes that in a single minute, many cardiac cycles are performed. Thus, deducing that duration of each cardiac cycle is **0.8 s.**

During each cardiac cycle (i.e. in one beat) each ventricle pumps out about 70 mL of blood. This is known as **stroke volume.**

The volume of blood pumped out by each ventricle in one minute is called cardiac output.

We know that , in one minute heartbeats for 72 times. Thus, cardiac output will be 5040 mL or approximately. 5L in a normal individual.

Thus, Cardiac output = Stroke volume × Numbers of beats/min.

It is to be noted that the body has the ability to alter stroke volume as well as the heart rate and thereby, the cardiac output. Athlete has much higher cardiac output than the normal man.

Heart Sounds

During each cardiac cycle, two prominent sounds are produced which can be easily heard by a **stethoscope** (an instrument used for the amplification of sound). This allows to hear sounds and pulse of an individual.

The basic reason for the production of these sounds is the **closure of various valves.** The sounds produced during each heartbeat are as follows

(i) **LuBB** It is the first sound, being produced when inter auriculoventricular valves (tricuspid and bicuspid valve) are closed. This marks the end of the atrial systole and beginning of ventricular systole.

(ii) **DuPP** It is the second sound being produced when semilunar valves (of aorta and pulmonary artery) get closed. This marks the end of ventricular systole.

Arterial Blood Pressure

The pressure exerted by the flow of blood on the elastic wall of arteries is called **blood pressure.** It is greater during systole than during the diastole. In a normal person the **systolic pressure** is 120 mm Hg and **diastolic pressure** is 80 mm Hg. Blood pressure changes with age and health of the person. It is measured by sphygmomanometer.

Electrocardiograph (ECG)

It is a graphical representation of the electrical activity of the heart during a single cardiac cycle. The electrocardiogram is obtained by a machine known as electrocardiograph. The study or the process of recording of electrocardiogram is called **electrocardiography.**

Einthoven (1903) is known as 'father of electrocardiography'.

The impulse generated by the SA node causes contraction and relaxation of heart chambers. To obtain an ECG, a patient is connected to the machine with **three electrical leads** (i.e. one to each wrist and one to the left ankle), monitoring the activity of heart continuously and heart's functioning is evaluated by attaching multiple leads to the chest region.

Reading an ECG

An ECG consists of five peaks, identified with the letter P to T that corresponds to a specific electrical conductivity of the heart. These corresponds to a specific electrical activity of the heart as follows

(i) ***P*-Wave** It is the first and the foremost wave of low amplitude. It represents the **electrical excitation** or **depolarisation of the atria** which leads to contraction of both the atria.

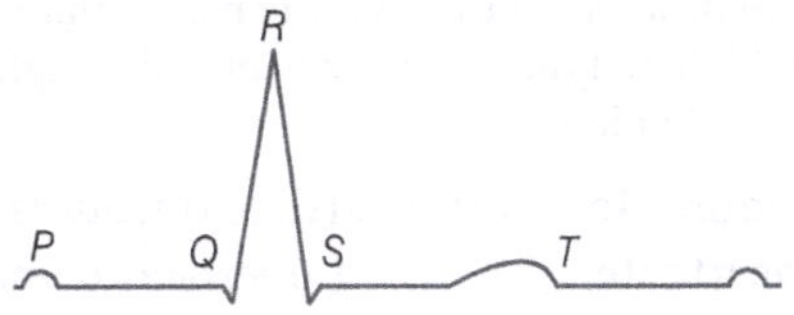

Fig. 18.5 Diagrammatic representation of a standard ECG

(ii) ***QRS*-Wave or Complex** The *Q*, *R* and S wave together forms the *QRS* complex. This represents the **depolarisation of the ventricles**, which initiates the ventricular contraction.

It marks the spread of impulse from AV node to ventricles, through bundle of His and Purkinje fibres. The contraction starts shortly after *Q* and marks the beginning of the systole.

(iii) ***T*-Wave** It is a broad and smoothly rounded deflection, which represents the return of the ventricles from excited to normal state (repolarisation). The end of *T*-wave marks the end of systole. It has been observed that, by counting the number of *QRS* complexes, that occur in a given time period, one can easily determine the rate of heartbeat of an individual.

However, the deviation in the ECG of any person from the normal shape ECG, indicates a possible abnormality or a disease.

Significance of ECG

ECG is proved to be of great clinical significance due to following reasons

(i) It gives accurate information about the normal functioning of atria and ventricles.

(ii) Indicates the functioning of valves.

(iii) Also helps in indicating any damage to local tissues of the heart in detection of overgrowth of cardiac/heart chambers.

Note

In electrocardiography, during a cardiac cycle, once an action potential is initiated, there is a period of time that a new action potential cannot be initiated. This is termed the **Effective Refractory Period** (ERP) of the tissue. This period is also termed the **Absolute Refractory Period** (ARP), it occurs due to calcium ion influx.

Topic Practice 2

Multiple Choice Questions

(1 Mark)

1. Open circulatory system is present in
   (a) arthropods and mammals
   (b) molluscs and aves
   (c) arthropods and molluscs
   (d) mammals and aves

Ans (c) Circulatory patterns are two types

Open Circulatory Pathways Present in arthropods and molluscs in which the blood pumped by the heart passes through the large vessels into the open spaces of body cavity called sinuses.

Closed Circulatory Pathways Annelids and chordates have closed circulatory system in which the blood pumped by the heart is always circulated through a closed network of blood vessels.

2. All reptiles have a three-chambered heart except
(a) snake (b) crocodile
(c) lizard (d) Both (b) and (c)

Ans (b) All reptiles have three-chambered heart containing two atrium (left and right) and one ventricle. There is a single ventricle and so mixing of oxygenated and deoxygenated blood occurs. But in crocodile, which is an exception have four-chambered heart.

3. Which of the following statement is incorrect?
(a) Heart is endodermal in origin
(b) Human heart is situated in between the two lungs slightly tilted to left
(c) Heart is a double walled membranous bag
(d) Human heart has two atria and two ventricles

Ans (a) Heart is mesodermal in origin not endodermal.

4. The valves, which allows the blood to flow from the ventricles into the pulmonary arteries and from right atrium to ventricle are
(a) AV valve and semilunar valve
(b) bicuspid and tricuspid valve
(c) semilunar and tricuspid valve
(d) aortic and mitral valve

Ans (c) Three semilunar valves are located at the base of the pulmonary trunk and aorta. Tricuspid valve guards the opening between the right atrium and right ventricle.

5. The branches of the nodal tissue, which give rise to minute fibres throughout the ventricular musculature of the respective sides are called
(a) sino-auricular node
(b) atrio-ventricular node
(c) Purkinje fibre
(d) bundle of His

Ans (c) SA node lies in the wall of right atrium near opening of superior vena cava and contract about 72 times per minute. Form SA node cardiac impulse travels to atrio-ventricular node (lies between right atrium and ventricle).

Then pass to AV bundle (also called bundle of His) and its branches reaches to the Purkinje fibres in ventricles. Bundle of His provides the only route for the transmission of wave of excitation from atria to ventricles. Purkinje fibres conducts the impulses five times more rapidly than surrounding cells. It forms a pathway for conduction of impulse that ensures that the heart muscle contracts in the most efficient manner.

6. A specialised cardiac musculature called ...*A*... tissue is also distributed in the heart. A patch of this tissue is present in the right upper corner of the right atrium called ...*B*... . Another mass of this tissue is seen in the lower left corner of the right atrium close to the atrio-ventricular septum called ...*C*... .

Choose the correct option for *A*, *B* and *C*.
(a) *A*–Nodal tissue, *B*–SA node, *C*–AV node
(b) *A*–Nodal tissue, *B*–AV node, *C*–SA node
(c) *A*–AV node, *B*–Nodal tissue, *C*–SA node
(d) *A*–SA node, *B*–AV node, *C*–Nodal tissue

Ans (a) *A*–Nodal tissue, *B*–SA node, *C*–AV node. The nodal musculature has the ability to generate action potential without any external stimuli.

7. 'Bundle of His' can be named as a muscular tissue which is found between
(a) ventricles
(b) interatrial groove
(c) atrium
(d) atrio-ventricular septum

Ans (a) Bundle of His is a network of muscle fibres found in between two ventricles.

8. Cardiac cycle is a cyclic event that occur in
(a) single heartbeat (b) double heartbeat
(c) atrium (d) ventricle

Ans (a) The cycle of events which occur in a single heartbeat is called cardiac cycle. It involves contraction and relaxation of the heart muscle.

Systole When blood is ejected from the heart contraction.

Diastole When chambers of the heart are filled with the blood. It is also called relaxation.

9. Atrial diastole takes place when
(a) right atrium is filled with blood
(b) left atrium is filled with blood
(c) Both atriums are filled with blood
(d) Both ventricles are filled with blood

Ans (c) Atrial diastole takes place when both the atria are filled with blood (having deoxygenated in right and oxygenated in left).

10. Determination of the cardiac output is done by
(a) heart rate (b) stroke volume
(c) blood flow (d) Both (a) and (b)

Ans (d) **Cardiac output** is the volume of the blood pumped by the ventricles per unit time.

Cardiac output = Stroke volume × Heart rate/Heartbeat

11. The first heart sound 'Lubb' occurs in which phase of the cardiac cycle?
(a) Isometric relaxation
(b) Atrial diastole
(c) Ventricular systole
(d) Ventricular diastole

Ans (c) **Ventricular Systole** When the contraction of the ventricles occurs immediately after atrial systole, the pressure in the ventricles rises and closes the atrio-ventricular valves, preventing blood from returning to the atria.

The closing of atrio-ventricular valves during ventricular systole produces the first heart sound lubb.

12. Choose the incorrect pair.
(a) Dupp → Opening of semilunar valve
(b) Lubb → Sharp closure of AV valve
(c) Initiation of heartbeat → AV nodel tissue of heartbeat
(d) Pulmonary artery → Deoxygenated blood artery

Ans (a) During ventricular systole, the closure of atrio-ventricular valve produces the first heart sound lubb and during ventricular diastole, the closure of semilunar valve produces the dupp sound.

13. Which wave of human heart out of *PQRST* is used for determining the heartbeat of an individual?
(a) *P* (b) *QRS*
(c) *T* (d) *RS*

Ans (b) By counting the numbers of *QRS* complexes that occur in a given time period, one can determine the heartbeat rate of an individual.

Very Short Answer Type Questions

1 Mark

14. Mitral valve is present between right atrium and right ventricle. State yes or no. If no explain why?

Ans No, mitral valve or bicuspid valve is the type of cardiac valve that guards the opening between left atrium and left ventricle of the heart.

15. Due to developmental abnormality, the wall of the left ventricle of an infant's heart is as thin as that of right ventricle. What would be its specific effect in circulation of blood?

Ans It may not be able to develop sufficient pressure to pump blood to all distant parts of the body.

16. Why are veins provided with valves along their length?

Ans Valves are present in the heart and veins to prevent the backward flow of blood.

17. It is said that arteries are more elastic and more contractile than veins. Comment.

Ans It is so, because tunica media of an artery is formed of smooth muscle fibres and elastic fibres.

18. Where does the cardiac impulse originate?

Ans The cardiac impulse originates in cardiac muscle fibres and is not brought to the heart by any nerve fibres. The origin of cardiac impulse is said to be myogenic.

19. Sino-atrial node is called the pacemaker of our heart. Why? **NCERT**

Ans Sino-atrial node of heart is responsible for initiating and maintaining the rhythmic activity, therefore it is known as pacemaker of the heart.

20. How many action potentials can be generated by the SA node in a minute.

Ans 70-75 number of action potentials can be generated by the SA node in a minute.

21. Given below is the diagrammatic representation of a standard ECG. Label its different peaks. **NCERT Exemplar**

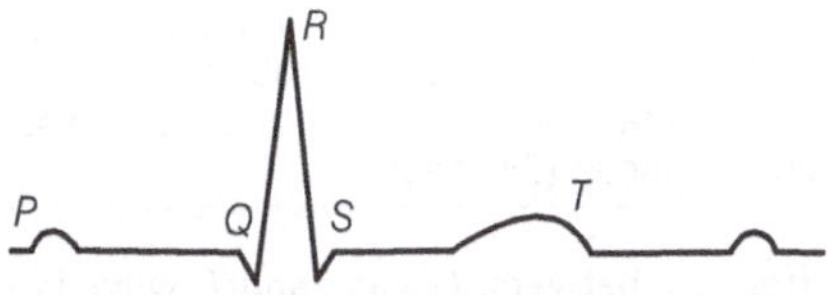

Ans The representation of a standard ECG diagram is as follows

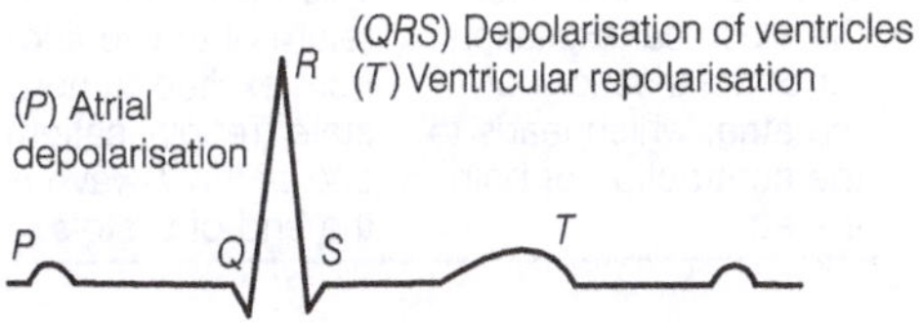

22. What does the *T*-wave in a normal electrocardiogram indicate?

Ans *T*-wave indicates the return of ventricles from excited to normal state (repolarisation).

23. A cardiologist observed an elevated *ST* segment in the ECG of a patient. What is it indicative of?

Ans An elevated *ST* segment in the ECG of a patient is indicative of acute myocardial infarction (heart attack).

Short Answer Type I Questions

2 Marks

24. Why is closed circulatory system more efficient than the open system?

Ans The closed circulatory system considerably enhances the speed, precision and efficiency of circulation. The blood flows far more rapidly, it takes less time to circulate through the closed system and return to the heart. This fastens the supply and removal of materials to and from the tissues by the blood. (2)

25. **A fish's heart pumps only deoxygenated blood, why?**

Ans A fish's heart pumps only deoxygenated blood as it is a two-chambered heart with an atrium and a ventricle.

The heart pumps out deoxygenated blood which is oxygenated by the gills and supplied to other body parts, from where deoxygenated blood is returned to the heart. (2)

26. Write the differences between
(i) Open and closed system of circulation
(ii) *P*-wave and *T*-wave **NCERT**

Ans (i) Differences between open and closed circulatory system is

Open Circulatory System	Closed Circulatory System
The blood is pumped by the heart into the blood vessels that open into biood spaces (Sinuses).	The blood is pumped by the heart into closed blood vessels.

(ii) Difference between *P*-wave and *T*-wave is

P-wave	*T*-wave
This wave represents the electrical excitation (or depolarisation) of the atria, which leads to the contraction of both the atria.	This wave represents the return of the ventricles from excited to normal state (repolarisation). The end of the *T*-wave marks the end of systole.

(1+1)

27. **Define the following terms and give their location.** **NCERT Exemplar**
(i) Purkinje fibre
(ii) Bundle of His

Ans (i) **Purkinje fibres** are the impulse conducting fibres which relay the contraction impulses from AV node into the walls of ventricles. (1)

(ii) **Bundle of His** are mass of specialised fibres that oringinates form the AV node. (1)

28. **Match the items listed in column I with appropriate items from column II.**

Column I	Column II
A. SA node	1. Fishes
B. Right AV aperture	2. Right auricle
C. Interstitial fluid	3. Tricuspid valve
D. Single circulation	4. Intercellular spaces

Ans A–2; B–3; C–4; D–1 (½ × 4)

29. **What happens to the mitral valve and the related blood flow during ventricular systole?**

Ans At the start of the ventricular systole, the mitral valve closes to prevent the flow of blood back into the atrium. As systole continues, blood from the right ventricle enters the pulmonary artery and blood from the left ventricle enters the aorta. (2)

30. **What is the significance of time gap in the passage of action potential from sino-atrial node to the ventricle?** **NCERT Exemplar**

Ans The time gap in the passage of action potential from sino-atrial node to the ventricles allows ventricles to relax. The ventricular pressure falls, causing the closure of semilunar valves, which prevents the backflow of blood into the ventricles. (2)

31. **What are the two heart sounds heard through stethoscope? How is each of these produced?**

Or

What are two heart sounds? When and how are these sounds produced?

Or

Explain heart sounds. **NCERT**

Ans We can hear with a stethoscope, the two main heart sounds (i.e. lubb and dupp), which repeat rhythmically. These sounds result from the closure of the heart valves. The first sound (lubb), which is of longer duration (0.16-0.90 s) and a louder one is created by the closure of the atrio-ventricular valves immediately after the start of the ventricular systole.

The second sound is of shorter duration (0.10 s) and is created by the closure of the semilunar valve at the end of the ventricular systole. (2)

32. **What is meant by *P-Q* interval and *S-T* interval in electrocardiography?**

Ans In electrocardiography, *P-Q* interval (also called *PR* interval) is the time taken by the impulse to travel through atria, AV node and the rest of the conducting tissues.

The normal *PR* interval lasts for about 0.16 s. The *S-T* interval is the representation of time between the end of the spread of impulse through ventricles and its repolarisation. (1+1)

33. **If a patient's ECG reveals an abnormally long delay between the *P*-wave and the *QRS* deflection, what does this suggest?**

Ans If a patient's ECG reveals an abnormally long delay between *P*-wave and the *QRS* deflection, it suggests that there is a delay of conduction from the atria to the ventricles. Hence, the stimulation from SA nodes are conducting stimuli to the ventricles very slowly. (2)

Short Answer Type II Questions

3 Marks

34. Answer the following

(i) Name the major site where RBCs are formed.

(ii) Which part of heart is responsible for initiating and maintaining its rhythmic activity?

(iii) What is specific in the heart of crocodiles among reptilians? **NCERT Exemplar**

Ans (i) Bone marrow.

(ii) Sino-Atrial node (SA node).

(iii) Reptiles have three-chambered heart except crocodile, which has four-chambered heart. (1×3)

35. Differentiate between right ventricle and left ventricle.

Ans Differences between right ventricle and left ventricle are

Right Ventricle	Left Ventricle
Right ventricle is smaller than the left ventricle.	Left ventricle is comparatively larger than right ventricle.
Moderator band is present.	Moderator band is lacking
Columnae carneae thicker, but less intricate.	Columnae carneae narrower, but more intricate.
Receives and pushes deoxygenated blood.	Receives and pumps oxygenated blood.
Crescent-shaped.	Biconvex in shape.
The wall of right ventricle is thinner than left ventricle.	The wall of left ventricle is thicker than right ventricle.

(½ × 6)

36. What is the significance of atrio-ventricular node and atrio-ventricular bundle in the functioning of heart? **NCERT**

Ans Refer to text on page no. 424.

37. How can we say that artificial pacemaker is a life saving instrument?

Ans Artificial pacemaker is an electronic device, which regularly sends a small amount of electrical charge for maintaining the rhythmicity of the heart. It is implanted subcutaneously in the upper thoracic region having a connection with the heart. (1)

The artificial pacemaker is called a life-saving instrument because, it stimulates the heart electrically at regular intervals to maintain its beats. Thus, it replaces the SA node as the originator of the cardiac impulse. It is to be noted that some pacemakers stimulate the heart at a fixed rate, others sense when the natural heart rate falls below a predetermined value and then stimulates the heart. (2)

38. Define a cardiac cycle and the cardiac output. **NCERT**

Ans Refer to text on page no. 425-426.

39. Write a short note on electrocardiograph (ECG).

Ans Refer to text on page no. 427.

Long Answer Type Questions

5 Marks

40. Describe the evolutionary change in the pattern of heart among the vertebrates. **NCERT**

Ans The heart among the vertebrates shows different patterns of evolution. Different groups of animals have evolved different methods for this transport. All vertebrates possess a muscular chambered heart. (2)

(i) Fishes have a two-chambered heart with an atrium and a ventricle. The heart pumps out deoxygenated blood which is oxygenated by the gills and supplied to the body parts from where deoxygenated blood is returned to the heart. (1)

(ii) Amphibians and the reptiles (except crocodiles) have a three-chambered heart with two atria and a single ventricle. The left atrium receives oxygenated blood from the gills/lungs/skin and the right atrium gets the deoxygenated blood from other body parts.

However, they get mixed up in the single ventricle which pumps out mixed blood. (1)

(iii) Crocodiles, birds and mammals possess a four-chambered heart with two atria and two ventricles.

Oxygenated and deoxygenated blood received by the left and right atria respectively passes on to the ventricles of the same sides.

The ventricles pump it out without any mixing up, i.e. two separate circulatory pathways are present in these organisms, hence, these animals have double circulation. (1)

41. Describe briefly the external structure of human heart with neat and labelled diagram.

Ans Refer to text on page no. 423, Refer to fig 18.2.

42. Describe briefly the internal structure of human heart with neat and labelled diagram.

Or Draw a diagram to show the internal structure of human heart. Label six parts in all including three valves.

Ans Refer to text on page no. 423-424 and Refer to fig. no. 18.3.

43. (i) What is cardiac output and how it is calculated.

(ii) Why is the left ventricular wall thicker than the right ventricular wall in the human heart?

(iii) Explain cardiac cycle in brief.

Ans (i) Refer to text on page no. 426. (1)

(ii) This is because the left ventricle is required to pump oxygenated blood all over the body, while the right ventricle needs to pump deoxygenated blood to the nearby lungs only. (1)

(iii) Refer to text on page no. 425. (3)

44. Draw a standard ECG and explain the different segments in it. **NCERT**

Ans Refer to text on page no. 427.

TOPIC 03 Circulatory System : The Circulation and Disorder

Double Circulation

The mammalian heart is four-chambered, undergoing the process of complete separate double circulation. This means that blood passes twice through the heart to supply the blood for once to the body. This transmission is neccessary, as it helps in oxygenation of blood.

The following processes constitute the double circulation

(i) **Pulmonary Circulation** In this system, blood completes its circulation from right ventricle to the left atria through the lungs. Here, the deoxygenated blood pumped by the right ventricle enters the **pulmonary artery** while, the left ventricle pumps blood into the **aorta.** The deoxygenated blood is passed on to the lungs from where, the oxygenated blood is carried out by the **pulmonary veins** into the left atrium of heart.

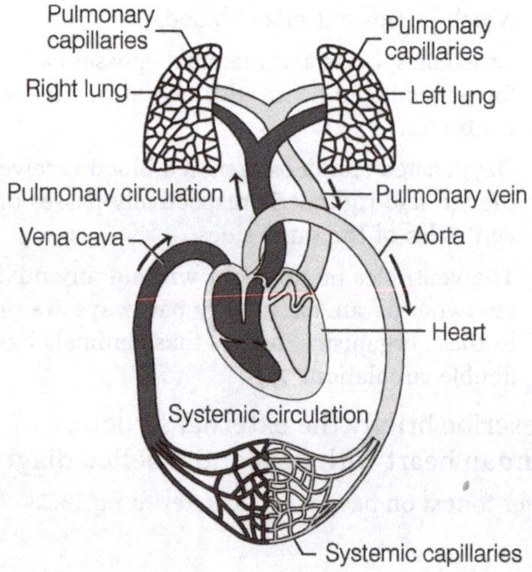

Fig 18.6 Systemic and pulmonary circulation

(ii) **Systemic Circulation** In this system, the pure blood is supplied to all parts of the body. During transport, the oxygenated (pure) blood entering the aorta is carried by a network of arteries, arterioles and capillaries to the tissues from where the deoxygenated (impure) blood is collected by a system of **venules, veins** and **vena cava,** thus, emptying it into the right atrium.

This system provides essential nutrients, O_2 and other essential substances to all the tissues of body and eventually takes away CO_2 and other harmful substances away from tissues for their elimination from body.

Differences between Pulmonary Circulation and Systemic Circulation

Pulmonary Circulation	Systemic Circulation
It is smaller circuit, which carries blood to the lungs and back to the heart.	It is a larger circuit, which supplies blood to the various parts of the body and back to the heart.
It carries deoxygenated blood to the lungs for oxygenation.	It supplies oxygenated blood to all parts of the body.
The blood is pumped by right ventricle and received by left atrium.	The blood is pumped by left ventricle and received by the right atrium.

Circulation through Special Regions

Apart from the pulmonary or systemic circulation, heart also possesses the following circulatory pathways

(i) **Hepatic Portal System** It is the type of portal system, which is universally present in all vertebrates. It is a unique vascular system that exists between the digestive tract and liver.

A vein called hepatic portal vein, carries blood from intestine to the liver (hepatic gland).

The liver finally opens into inferior vena cava through its own vein (i.e. hepatic vein) before delivering it to the systemic circulation.

(ii) **Hypophysical Portal System** Apart from hepatic portal system, another minor portal system called **hypophysical portal system** is also present which consists of two hypophysical portal veins which carry blood from the hypothalamus (brain) to the anterior lobe of pituitary gland.

Coronary Circulation

Although the heart is always filled with blood, it does not take its oxygen and nutrient supply from the blood present in its chamber. Thus, in order to supply oxygen and nutrients to the muscles of the heart, a coronary system is present. The **right** and **left coronary arteries** arise from the ascending aorta which supply oxygenated blood to the heart muscles. The coronary veins bring deoxygenated blood to coronary sinus. Thus, carries it to the right atrium.

> **Knowledge Plus**
>
> - The physiology of blood circulation was described by **William Harvey** in 1628.
> - Significance of double circulation is to check the mixing of oxygenated and deoxygenated blood.
> - Systemic circulation is also called the peripheral circulation because, it supplies to most of the tissues of the body.

Regulation of Cardiac Activity

The normal activities of the heart are intrinsically regulated, i.e. autoregulated by the specialised muscles (nodal tissue). Thus, the heart is known as **myogenic heart**. The neurogenic heartbeat is initiated by a nerve impulse, e.g. annelids and most arthropods. The rate of its formation and conduction is regulated by the following

1. Neural Regulation of Heartbeat

In medulla oblongata, a special neural centre is present, which can moderate, the cardiac function through the **Autonomic Nervous System** (ANS).

The neural signals through the **sympathetic nerves** (part of ANS) increase the rate of heartbeat by stimulating SA node, it also increases the strength of ventricular contraction and thereby, the cardiac output. Whereas, the neural signal through **parasympathetic nerves** (another component of ANS) can decrease the rate of heartbeat by inhibiting the SA node, speed of conduction of action potential, thereby decreasing the cardiac output.

2. Hormonal Regulation of Heartbeat

Adrenaline and **nor-adrenaline** hormones secreted by the medulla of adrenal gland have significant role in regulating heartbeat and thus increasing the cardiac output. The nor-adrenaline accelerates the heartbeat, while adrenaline does this function at the time of emergency.

Details about the functioning of each hormone will be discussed later in the 22nd chapter of the book.

Disorders of Circulatory System

Many diseases may affect the blood vessels and the normal functioning of the heart. Some of the common disorders are as follows

1. High Blood Pressure (Hypertension)

The pressure exerted by the flow of blood on the elastic walls of the arteries is known as blood pressure. **Hypertension** is the term used for blood pressure higher than the normal.

The normal blood pressure in humans is measured as **120/80 mm Hg** (millimetres of mercury pressure), in which 120 mm Hg is the **systolic pressure** (pumping pressure), while, the 80 mm Hg is the **diastolic pressure** (or resting pressure). Persistent increase in blood pressure above 140 mm Hg (systolic) and 90 mm Hg (diastolic) is termed as hypertension.

It is a mojor health problem. It has no symptoms. It is caused by nervous tension and emotional stress (fear, worry, anxiety, anger, excitement, physical stress, excessive joy) that leads to contraction of the arteries.

Condition of Hypertension

It may lead to many heart diseases and also affects vital organs of the body, like the brain and kidney.

2. Coronary Artery Disease (CAD)

It is the hardening of **arteries** and **arterioles** due to the thickening of the fibres tissue and the consequent loss of elasticity. It is often referred to as **atherosclerosis.** This mainly affects the vessels, which are mainly responsible for supplying blood to the heart muscle. It seems to occur due to deposition of calcium, fat, cholesterol and fibrous tissues, making the lumen of arteries narrower.

3. Angina (Angina Pectoris)

his tends to occur when enough oxygen does not reach the heart muscles. It occurs both in men and women of any age but seems to be more common among the middle-aged and elderly individual. A symptom of **acute chest pain** occurs in individual suffering from angina, which mainly occurs due to the conditions that affect the bloodflow.

4. Heart Failure

It is the condition of the heart when it fails to pump blood effectively to meet the needs of the body. The heart failure is sometimes called the congestive heart failure, as its main symptom is congestion of lungs.

5. Bradycardia and Tachycardia

Tachycardia is a term applied to a rapid heart or pulse rate (over 100/min). Bradycardia is the term indicating a slow heart or pulse rate (under 50/min).

Topic Practice 3

Multiple Choice Questions

1 Mark

1. Double circulation is
   (a) passage of blood twice in heart through the same way
   (b) passage of blood twice in heart through the unique way
   (c) passage of blood twice in heart through the separate way
   (d) None of the above

Ans (c) Double circulation is the passage of the blood twice in the heart through the separate pathways for completing one cycle.

It consists of two parts
(i) Pulmonary pathway
(ii) Systemic pathway

2. Pulmonary circulation is
   (a) Left auricle $\xrightarrow[\text{blood}]{\text{Oxygenated}}$ Lungs $\xrightarrow[\text{blood}]{\text{Deoxygenated}}$ Right ventricle
   (b) Left auricle $\xrightarrow[\text{blood}]{\text{Deoxygenated}}$ Lungs $\xrightarrow[\text{blood}]{\text{Oxygenated}}$ Right ventricle
   (c) Right ventricle $\xrightarrow[\text{blood}]{\text{Deoxygenated}}$ Lungs $\xrightarrow[\text{blood}]{\text{Oxygenated}}$ Left auricle
   (d) Right ventricle $\xrightarrow[\text{blood}]{\text{Oxygenated}}$ Lungs $\xrightarrow[\text{blood}]{\text{Deoxygenated}}$ Left auricle

Ans (c) **Pulmonary circulation** is the movement of blood take place from heart to lung and then from lung to heart.

3. Which of the following statement is incorrect?
   (a) The pulmonary trunk with left and right arteries are part of pulmonary circulation
   (b) The aorta is a part of systemic circulation
   (c) The aorta is located beneath the heart
   (d) The pulmonary artery is located directly beneath the aorta

Ans (c) The aorta is located above the heart.

4. Hepatic portal system is a
   (a) vascular connection between the digestive tract and liver
   (b) vascular connection between the liver and lungs
   (c) vascular connection between the spleen and liver
   (d) vascular connection between the digestive tract and spleen

Ans (a) A unique vascular connection exists between the digestive tract and liver called hepatic portal system. The hepatic portal vein carries the blood from the intestine to liver before it is delivered to systemic circulation.

5. In given diagram which one is vena cava?

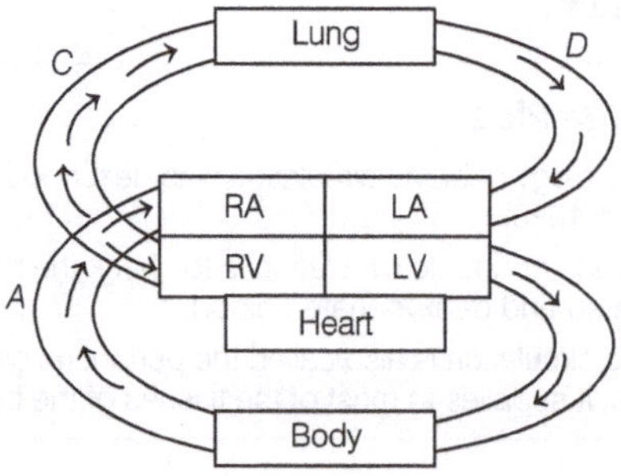

(a) A (b) B (c) C (d) D

Ans (a) Vena cava (great veins) are of two major types
(i) **Superior vena cava** which collects the deoxygenated blood from the cephalic head region of the body.
(ii) **Inferior vena cava** which collects the deoxygenated blood from the lower portion of the body. The vena cava drains deoxygenated blood to the right auricle.

6. Neural signals through the sympathetic nerves (ANS) can increase the rate of heartbeat by
   (a) increasing cardiac output
   (b) increasing the strength of ventricular contraction
   (c) Both (a) and (b)
   (d) increasing the contraction of atrium

Ans (c) Neural signals through the sympathetic nerves (part of ANS) can increase the rate of heartbeat by increasing the strength of the ventricular contraction and cardiac output.

7. Systolic pressure in a normal human is
(a) 70 mm of Hg (b) 80 mm of Hg
(c) 90 mm of Hg (d) 120 mm of Hg

Ans (d) **High Blood Pressure** (hypertension) is the term for blood pressure that is higher than normal (120/80). In this measurement 120 mm of Hg (millimeters of mercury pressure) is systolic or pumping, pressure and 80 mm of Hg is diastolic or resting pressure.

8. Which one indicates hypertension or high Blood Pressure (BP)?
(a) 120/80 (b) 110/70
(c) 130/80 (d) 140/90

Ans (d) If repeated checks of blood pressure of an individual is 140/90 (140 over 90) or higher, it shows hypertension. High blood pressure leads to heart diseases and also affects the vital organs like brain and kidney.

9. Coronary heart disease is due to the inadequate blood supply to
(a) heart ventricle (b) heart auricle
(c) heart volume (d) heart muscles

Ans (d) **Coronary Circulation** Circulation of the blood in the heart muscle is called coronary circulation. Coronary heart diseases occur due to the insufficient blood supply to the heart muscles.

Very Short Answer Type Questions

1 Mark

10. From where does the hepatic portal system brings the blood?

Ans Hepatic portal system brings blood from the alimentary canal, pancreas and spleen to the liver.

11. Indicate the blood vessel that transports hormones from the hypothalamus to the anterior pituitary.

Ans Hypophyseal portal vein.

12. Given below are the abnormal conditions related to blood circulation. Name the disorders.
(i) Acute chest pain due to failure of oxygen supply to heart muscles.
(ii) Increased systolic pressure. **NCERT Exemplar**

Ans (i) Angina
(ii) High blood pressure

13. Heart failure is called congestive heart failure. Why?

Ans The congestion of lungs is a symptom of heart failure. Thus, it is also called congestive heart failure.

Short Answer Type I Questions

2 Marks

14. Schematically represent double circulation.

Ans Flowchart of double circulation

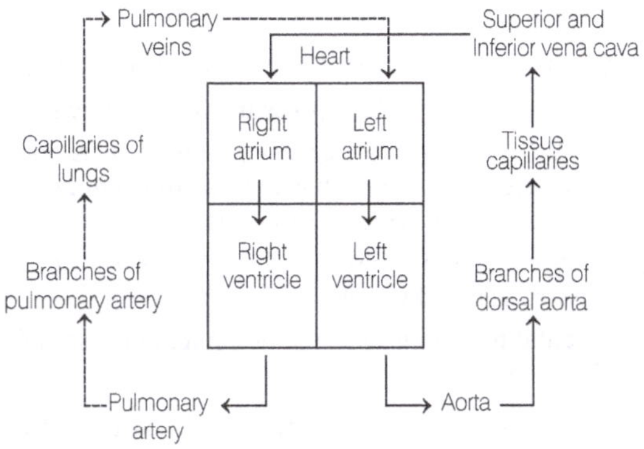

(2)

15. Differentiate between pulmonary and systemic circulation.

Ans Refer to text on page no. 432.

16. Name the unique vascular connection between digestive tract and the liver. What is its significance?

Ans Hepatic portal vein is the unique vascular connection between digestive tract and the liver.

Significance It brings blood from intestine to the liver, before it is delivered to the systemic circulation due to which the liver gets its nutrients. (1+1)

17. Differentiate between hepatic portal system and hypophysical portal system.

Ans The differences between hepatic portal system and hypophysical portal system are

Hepatic Portal System	Hypophysical Portal System
It is present in all chordates including humans.	It is present in higher vertebrates like amphibians reptiles, birds and mammals.
It is a special vascular connection existing between the different parts of the alimentary canal and liver.	It is a specialised portal system formed by a vein from hypothalamus, which breaks up into capillaries in pituitary gland.

18. Give the reason for reduced bloodflow to the heart muscles leading to their death.

Ans When the blood supply to myocardium of the heart is greatly reduced, then the cardiac muscle fibres die. This reduced blood supply can be due to the blockage of the coronary vessels by the thrombus (blood clot formed in the coronary artery). (2)

19. **Mention the phases of blood pressure, when are they seen?**

Ans Phases of blood pressure are

(i) **Systolic Blood Pressure** It is seen during the contraction of left ventricle.

(ii) **Diastolic Blood Pressure** It is seen during the relaxation of left ventricle. (1×2)

20. **Mention the causes of high blood pressure.**

Ans The causes of high blood pressure are as follows

(i) A diet full of oily and greasy products, increase cholesterol level, which can cause thickening of the arteries due to which BP may rise.

(ii) Tobacco smoking also speeds up the heart rate and contracts blood vessels.

(iii) Mental tension is also one of the main causes of hypertension. (2)

21. **Which coronary artery disease is caused due to narrowing of the lumen of arteries?**

NCERT Exemplar

Ans Atherosclerosis affects the vessels that supply blood to the heart muscle. It is caused by the deposits of calcium, fat, cholesterol and fibrous tissues, which makes the lumen of arteries narrower. (2)

Short Answer Type II Questions

3 Marks

22. **Explain the advantage of the complete partition of ventricle among birds and mammals and hence leading to double circulation.**

NCERT Exemplar

Ans The birds and mammals have evolutionary advancement as far as structure of heart is concerned. They need more oxygen to live in terrestrial habitat.

In these animals, the blood received by left and right auricles is oxygenated and deoxygenated, respectively. It passes towards the left and right ventricles and thus, no oxygenated and deoxygenated blood is mixed. The ventricles pump oxygenated and deoxygenated blood without mixing.

Thus, two separate circulatory pathways are found and this type of blood circulation is called as double circulation, which includes **systemic** and **pulmonary circulation.**

23. **What is the significance of hepatic portal system in the circulatory system?**

NCERT Exemplar

Ans A unique vascular connection exists between the digestive tract and liver called hepatic portal system. The hepatic portal vein carries blood from intestine to the liver before it is delivered to the systemic circulation. This ensures that the liver, which has the metabolic versatility to interconvert various organic molecules has first access to nutrients after the food is digested. (3)

24. **Why renal portal system is absent in mammals?**

Ans The mammals have no renal portal system due to the following facts

(i) It is an evolutionary trend that fishes and amphibians have well-developed renal portal system, while, in reptiles and birds this system gets reduced. Finally in mammals it ultimately disappears.

(ii) The heart of mammals is four-chambered, due to which there is a total separation of oxygenated and deoxygenated blood.

(iii) Posterior portion of the body gets oxygenated blood from the heart and after oxidation process, etc., the blood does not contain so much impurities that it should go to the kidneys for filtration. (1×3)

25. **Write a note on regulation of cardiac activity.**

Ans Refer to text on page no. 433.

26. **What is meant by coronary artery disease?**

Ans Refer to text on page no. 433.

Long Answer Type Questions

5 Marks

27. **Describe in detail the neural and hormonal regulation of heart functioning.**

Ans Refer to text on page no. 433.

28. **Briefly describe the followings**

(i) Anaemia (ii) Angina pectoris

(iii) Atherosclerosis (iv) Hypertension

(v) Heart failure

NCERT Exemplar

Ans (i) Anaemia is the decrease in the number of RBC than the normal value in blood. It may also be due to less quantity of haemoglobin than the normal value in blood.

(ii) to (v) Refer to text on page no. 433-434.

29. **Write short note on the following**

(i) Bradycardia and tachycardia

(ii) Coronary artery disease.

Ans Refer to text on page no. 433 and 434.

SUMMARY

- **Blood** is a specialised connective tissue containing fluid matrix, plasma and formed elements (i.e. RBC, WBC and plateles). On the basis of surface antigen on RBC's **blood groups** are classified as ABO and Rh. Rh incompatibility leads to erythroblastosis foetalis and transfusion reactions. **Coagulation** is a blood function facilitated by platelets and several clotting factors.
- **Lymph** a colourless or yellowish extracellular fluid. It is an important component of our body's defence system.
- **Human lymphatic system** contains lymph capillaries, vessels, lymphatic ducts and nodes. Tonsils, thymus gland, Peyer's patches, liver and spleens are other lymphoid organs which secretes lymph.
- **Circulatory system** facilitates circulation of substances *via* body fluids. **Open circulatory system** (invertebrates) allows direct contact between blood and tissue cells. In **closed circulatory system** there is no direct contact between blood and tissue cells. Also, blood flows through closed vessels.
- **Human heart** is present between the lungs in thoracic cavity, e.g. mediastinum slightly tilted to left. It is covered with pericardium.Human heart has two auricles separated by interatrial septum; two ventricles separated by interventricular septum. Auricles and ventricles are separated by an auriculo-ventricular septum.
- Major blood vessels associated with heart are systemic aorta, pulmonary arch, superior and inferior vena cava, pulmonary veins and coronary veins.
- Heart valves are tricuspid (between right atrium and ventricle), pulmonary, mitral (between left atrium and ventricle), aortic, eustachian and thebasian valve.
- **Conducting system of heart** consists of sino-atrial node (pacemaker), generates heartbeat impulses, atrio-ventricular node (pacesetter), bundle of His and Purkinje fibres which convey contraction impulse to bring ventricle contraction.
- **Blood vessels** are vessels carrying blood to and from the heart and body organs. They are arteries (heart to body), veins (body to heart) and capillaries (between arteries and veins).
- **Cardiac cycle** is the repeating pattern of the systole and diastole of the heart. Each cycle is of 0.8 second.
- **Heartbeat** is the regular and rhythmic contraction of the heart. Human heartbeats about 75 times/minute. It occurs in two phases systole (contraction) and diastole (relaxation).
- **Cardiac output** is the volume of blood ejected from left or right ventricle into aorta per minute. It is stroke volume × heart rate.
- **Heart sounds** are produced by beating of heart. **LuBB** (first sound) is produced when atrio-ventricular valves close. **DuPP** (second sound) is produced by closure of semilunar valves.
- **Blood pressure** is the pressure exerted by blood flow on arterial walls. Normal range is 120 mm Hg (systolic) and 80 mm Hg (diastolic). It can be measured by sphygmomanometre.
- **Electrocardiogram** is a graphical representation of the electrical activity of the heart during a cardiac cycle. It shows five consecutive waves.
- **Portal systems** are vascular arrangements where blood from capillaries of one organ is transported to capillaries of another organ. It can be hepatic (between parts of alimentary canal and liver), renal and hypophysial.
- **Abnormal conditions** related to circulatory system includes hypertension, arterio sclerosis and atherosclerosis.
- **Cardiovascular disease** occurring commonly in human are coronary artery disease (like myocardial infarction, angina pectoris) and heart failure.

Chapter Practice

Multiple Choice Questions

1 Mark

1. Organisms which circulate water from their surrounding through their body cavities to facilitate the cells to exchange the substances are
   (a) Porifera
   (b) Sponges
   (c) Both (a) and (b)
   (d) None of the above

2. RBCs have an average lifespan of
   (a) 90 days (b) 100 days
   (c) 120 days (d) 140 days

3. Leucocytes are colourless due to
   (a) lack of water
   (b) lack of haemoglobin
   (c) the presence of a white pigment
   (d) the presence of calcium ions

4. A certain road accident patient with unknown blood group needs immediate blood transfusion. His one doctor friend at once offers his blood. What was the blood group of the donor?
   (a) Blood group-B (b) Blood group-AB
   (c) Blood group-O (d) Blood group-A

5. Subsequent normal pregnancies of Rh^+ husband and Rh^- wife could be possible by
   (a) administrating anti Rh-antibody to the mother just after the delivery of 1st child
   (b) transfusion of blood to the 2nd baby just after the birth
   (c) living anti-Rh antibody to the 2nd baby just after the birth
   (d) All of the above

6. In living body coagulation of blood in blood vessels is prevented by
   (a) prothrombin
   (b) heparin
   (c) prothrombin and calcium together
   (d) plasminogen and calcium together

7. Advantage of closed circulatory system is that
   (a) exchange occurs more rapidly
   (b) flow of blood more precisely regulated
   (c) it can support high metabolic activity
   (d) All of the above

8. 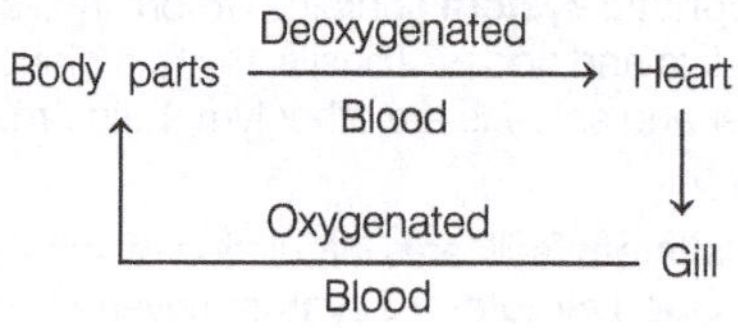

   Given diagram depicts the circulation in
   (a) fishes (b) mammals
   (c) reptiles (d) amphibians

9. SA node is called the pacemaker of heart because
   (a) it can change the contractile activity generated by AV node
   (b) it delays the transmission of impulse between the atria and ventricles
   (c) it gets stimulated when it receives neural signals
   (d) it initiates and maintains the rhythmic contractile activity of heart

10. Bicuspid and tricuspid valve opens when
    (a) blood from the pulmonary artery and vena cava flows into the left and right ventricles, respectively
    (b) blood from the pulmonary vein and vena cava flows into left and right ventricles, respectively
    (c) blood from the pulmonary vein and vena cava flows into left and right atrium, respectively
    (d) oxygen from the pulmonary vein and vena cava flows into left and right atrium, respectively

11. Duration of a cardiac cycle is
    (a) 0.6 second (b) 0.7 second
    (c) 0.8 second (d) 0.9 second

12. Cardiac output is
    (a) volume of the blood pumped out by each ventricle per minute
    (b) volume of the blood contained in the entire heart
    (c) volume of the oxygenated blood pumped by heart
    (d) volume of the deoxygenated blood pumped by heart

13. To obtain a standard ECG, the patient is connected to the machine with three electrical leads. These three electrical lead are connected as one each to the
(a) biceps and third one at the ankle
(b) triceps and third one at the ankle
(c) thigh and third one at the ankle
(d) wrist and third one at the ankle

14. Neural centre in medulla oblongata can moderate the cardiac function through
(a) ANS (Autonomic Nervous System)
(b) sympathetic nervous system
(c) parasympathetic nervous system
(d) somatic nervous system

15. Blood pressure is defined as the force with which blood
(a) comes out of the atrium
(b) is pushed from atrium to ventricle
(c) pushes against the wall of blood vessels
(d) comes out of the ventricle

16. Atherosclerosis is caused by deposition of
(a) calcium
(b) fat and cholesterol
(c) deposition of fibrous tissue
(d) All of the above

Assertion-Reason Type Questions

1 Mark

Direction (Q. Nos. 17-24) *In each of the following questions, a statement of Assertion (A) is given followed by corresponding statement of Reason (R). Of the statements, mark the correct answer as*
(a) If both A and R are true and R is the correct explanation of A
(b) If both A and R are true, but R is not the correct explanation of A
(c) If A is true, but R is false
(d) If A is false, but R is true

17. **Assertion** (A) Reduction in number of platelets can lead to excessive loss of blood from the body in case of injury.
Reason (R) Platelets help in the coagulation of blood.

18. **Assertion** (A) Thrombin is essential for blood clotting.
Reason (R) Ca^{2+} plays an important role in blood clotting.

19. **Assertion** (A) A person with blood group O is considered to be universal recipient.
Reason (R) O blood group has no antigens, but have anti-A and anti-B antibodies.

20. **Assertion** (A) In amphibians and reptiles, the double circulation is incomplete.
Reason (R) Unlike birds and mammals, in amphibians and reptiles, the left atrium receives oxygenated blood and right atrium receives deoxygenated blood.

21. **Assertion** (A) Bundle of His is a part of autoexcitable tissue.
Reason (R) This region comprises of cardiac tissue that can generate impulse on its own at a frequency less than SA node.

22. **Assertion (A)** The body has the ability to alter the stroke volume and the heart rate.
Reason (R) The metabolic needs of the body are met by these changes, but the duration of cardiac cycle remains same.

23. **Assertion** (A) The end of T-wave marks the end of ventricular systole.
Reason (R) T-wave represents the return of ventricles from excited to normal state which is repolarisation.

24. **Assertion** (A) Atherosclerosis affects the blood vessels which supply blood to the heart.
Reason (R) It is caused by the deposition of fats, calcium, cholesterol and fibrous tissue which makes the lumen narrower.

Answers

1. (c)	2. (c)	3. (b)	4. (c)	5. (a)	6. (b)
7. (d)	8. (a)	9. (d)	10. (c)	11. (c)	12. (a)
13. (d)	14. (a)	15. (c)	16. (d)	17. (a)	18. (b)
19. (d)	20. (c)	21. (a)	22. (d)	23. (a)	24. (a)

Very Short Answer Type Questions

(1 Mark)

25. Which term is used for destruction of RBCs?
26. Where does the destruction of RBCs take place in the body?
27. Write two forms of lymphocytes.
28. Where are semilunar valves present in the heart?
29. What do you mean by autoexcitability of SA node?
30. For what purpose, coronary circulation exists in humans?
31. How sympathetic nerves function in neural regulation?

Short Answer Type I Questions

(2 Marks)

32. What is amoeboid movement? Which blood cells show them?
33. Mention any two important functions of blood.
34. Why is circulation of lymphatic fluid is slow?
35. Write two functions of lymph.
36. How are the heart valves helpful in preventing back flow of blood?
37. Give differences between artery and vein (any two points).
38. Define a portal system. Explain the functions of such a vein in our digestive system.

Short Answer Type II Questions

(3 Marks)

39. Explain the basic functions of lymphatic system.
40. List the sequence of steps that occur in pumping action of heart during one cardiac cycle.
41. How will you calculate the cardiac output of heart?
42. What are the basis behind reading of an electrocardiogram?
43. What is hypertension? List its causative factors.
44. Write a short note on congestive heart failure.

Long Answer Type Questions

(5 Marks)

45. Write a short note on erythrocytes and leucocytes, including their types in detail.
46. Why blood transfusion is necessary in case of blood loss?
47. Describe briefly the conducting system of human heart.
48. Differentiate between SA node and AV node.
49. Describe step by step what happens in the different phases of cardiac cycle in human.
50. Give details about the pulmonary and systemic circulation.

Case Based Questions

(4/5 Marks)

51. In a biology lab, students were asked to make blood smear and observe different types of blood cells. Most of the students were able to see neutrophils while only two students observed monocytes.
    (i) Name the category of blood cells to which neutrophils and monocytes belong.
    (ii) How neutrophils appear under the microscope?
    (iii) Mention the shape and function of monocytes.
    (iv) How would you identify eosinophils in a blood smear?
    (v) Thrombocytes or platelets in our body range from 1,50,000 to 3,50,000 mm^{-3}. What consequences will person having platelet count less than 1,50,000 per mm^3 face?

52. Given below is a graphical representation of the two processes which constitute the double circulation. Conside the graph and answer the following questions.

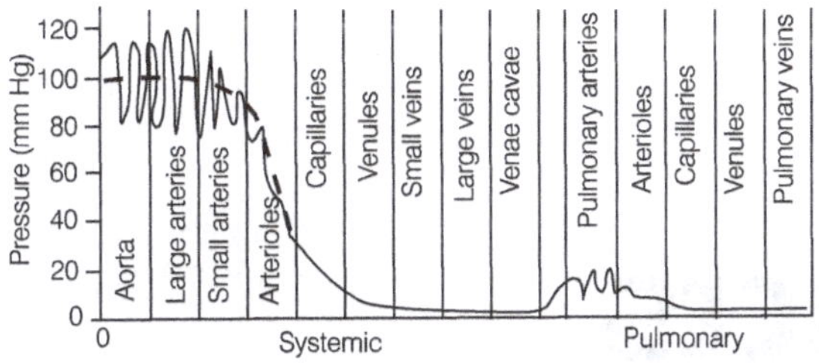

(i) On the basis of the blood pressure pattern in the above graph, what conclusion can you draw about the pressure difference in systemic and pulmonary circulation?

(ii) What will happen to the double circulation, if valves are absent in the circulatory system?

(iii) Why aorta has the highest blood pressure ? What will happen if its pressure increases?

Or (iii) How does the lumen of arteries turn out to be narrower than normal?

53. The graph below shows the events occurring in a cardiac cycle. Observe the graph carefully and answer the questions that follows.

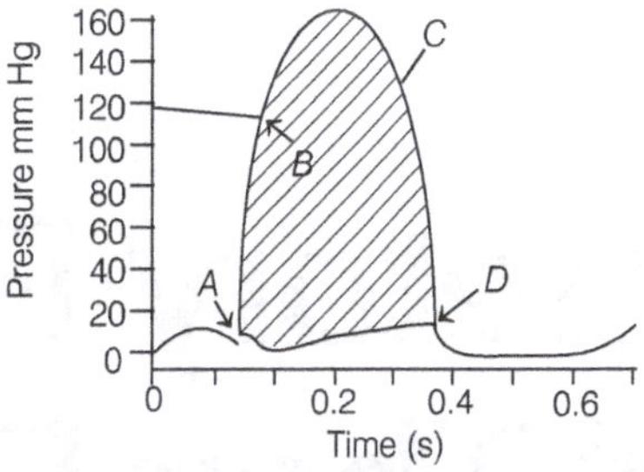

(i) Give the labelling of *A*, *B*, *C* and *D* with respect to the opening and closure of the valve.

(ii) Comment upon the event occurring in the shaded area of the above graph.

(iii) What will happen if the valve *A* and *B* get damaged?

CHAPTER 19

Excretory Products and Their Elimination

Excretion is a process of the removal of nitrogenous waste products and other metabolites from the body of the animal. It is also associated with the process of osmoregulation within the body.

Both **excretion** and **osmoregulation** are important for the maintenance of homeostasis of the body.

TOPIC 01 Excretion : Major Excretory Products, Human Excretory System and Uropoiesis

Ammonia, urea and uric acid are the major forms of nitrogenous wastes excreted by different animals as a result of their metabolic activities.

Forms of Nitrogen Excretion

Depending upon the nature of excretory product, animals exhibit different processes of nitrogenous excretion. These are described as follows

(i) **Ammonotelism** Ammonia is the most toxic form of nitrogenous waste, it requires large amount of water for its elimination. The organism that excrete ammonia are called **ammonotelic** and this process to eliminate ammonia is known as ammonotelism. Examples of ammonotelic animals are bony fishes, aquatic amphibians and aquatic insects. Ammonia, as it is readily soluble in water is generally excreted by diffusion across body surfaces or through **gill surfaces** (in fish) as ammonium ions. So, ammonotelism is found in aquatic animals.

(ii) **Ureotelism** The process of excreting urea is called ureotelism. Animals, which do not live in high abundance of water convert ammonia produced in the body into urea (in the liver) and release into the blood, which is filtered and excreted out as urine by the kidneys.

Examples of ureotelic animals are mammals, many terrestrial amphibians and marine fishes.

(iii) **Uricotelism** The process of excreting uric acid is called uricotelism. Uric acid, being the least toxic nitrogenous waste can be removed with a minimum loss of water from the animal body. Thus, it is excreted in the form of pellet or paste (i.e. semi-solid form). Normally, the animals which live in desert exhibit uricotelism. Examples of **uricotelic** animals are reptiles, birds, land snails and insects.

Other Excretory Products in Animals

(i) **Trimethylamine Oxide** (TMAO) A nitrogenous excretory product in some marine teleosts, crabs, etc.

(ii) **Guanine** It is secreted by birds as excretory product as it is less soluble than uric acid.

(iii) **Creatinine and Creatine** bile pigments, excess water and mineral salts are some other excretory products of animals.

Excretory Organs

Different animal groups have a variety of excretory structures (organs) to perform the process of excretion. In most of the invertebrates, these structures are simple tubular form, whereas, vertebrates have complex structured organs called **kidneys.** Some of these structures are mentioned below in the given table

Excretory Organs and Main Nitrogenous Wastes of Different Animal Groups

Animal Groups	Excretory Organs	Main Nitrogenous Waste
Protozoans (*Amoeba*), Poriferans (*Sycon*), Coelenterates (Cnidaria) (*Hydra*)	Plasma membrane, pellicle and general body surface	Ammonia
Ctenophora	Anal pores	Ammonia
Platyhelminthes (flatworms) e.g. *Planaria, Fasciola, Taenia*	Protonephridia with flame cells	Ammonia
Rotifers	Flame cells	Ammonia
Nemathelminthes (Aschelminthes) e.g. roundworms, *Ascaris*	Renette cells	Ammonia and urea
Annelida	Metanephridia (in *Nereis* and leech), Metanephridia and chloragogen cells (in earthworm)	Ammonia and urea
Arthropoda	Malpighian tubules (in cockroaches), coxal gland, green glands or antennary glands (in crustaceans)	Uric acid and ammonia
Mollusca	Renal gland or organ of Bojanus (in *Pila* and *Unio*) and Keber's organ (in *Unio*)	Ammonia in aquatic and uric acid in larva forms
Echinodermata	Tube feet (podia) and dermal branchiae (thin walls of gills)	Ammonia
Chordata	Protonephridia (in lancelets), neural gland (in *Herdmania*), pharyngeal nephridia and Hatschek's nephridium in cephalochordates (*Amphioxus*) a pair of kidneys in vertebrates	Ammonia, urea and uric acid

Human Excretory System

Human excretory system consists of a pair of kidneys, a pair of ureters, a urinary bladder and urethra, these are described below in detail

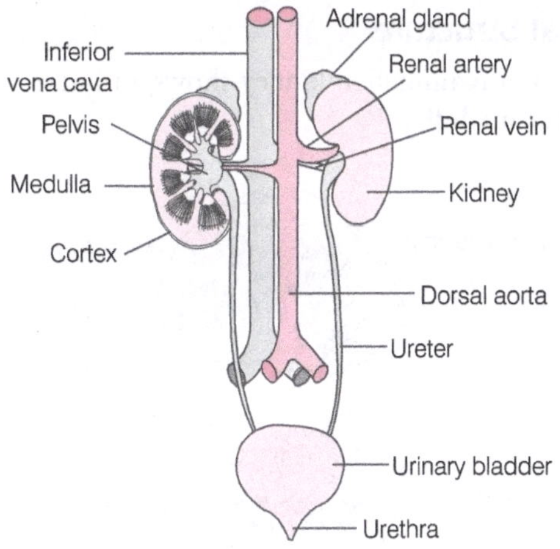

Fig. 19.1 Human excretory system

1. Kidneys

These are reddish brown, bean-shaped structures situated between the levels of last **thoracic** and third **lumbar** vertebra. These are close to the dorsal inner wall of the abdominal cavity. Each kidney of an adult human measures, 10-12 cm in length, 5-7 cm in width, 2-3 cm in thickness with an average weight of 120-170 gm (i.e. 150 gm in males and about 135 gm in females).

Kidneys are **mesodermal** in origin. They develop from mesodermal **nephrostomes** or **mesomeres** (ciliated structures, functional in embryonic conditions).

Position of Kidneys

The kidneys retroperitoneal, i.e. are located below the diaphragm on the left and right sides. The right kidney is lower and smaller than the left kidney because the liver takes up much space of the right side.

Structure of Kidney

Structure of kidney can be studied well under two heads, i.e. **external** as well as **internal** structure.

These are described below as

External Structure

The outer surface of each kidney is convex. Inner concave surface has a notch called **hilum**. The supply of blood occurs through hilum, i.e. renal artery and renal vein, pass in and out of the kidneys along with the ureter and the nerve supply of kidney.

If we look from outside to inside, three layers cover the kidneys, i.e. **renal fascia** (outermost), the **adipose layer** and then **renal capsule** (innermost layer). These coverings protect the kidneys from external shocks and injuries.

Internal Structure

The LS of a mammalian kidney shows an **outer cortex** and **inner medulla**.

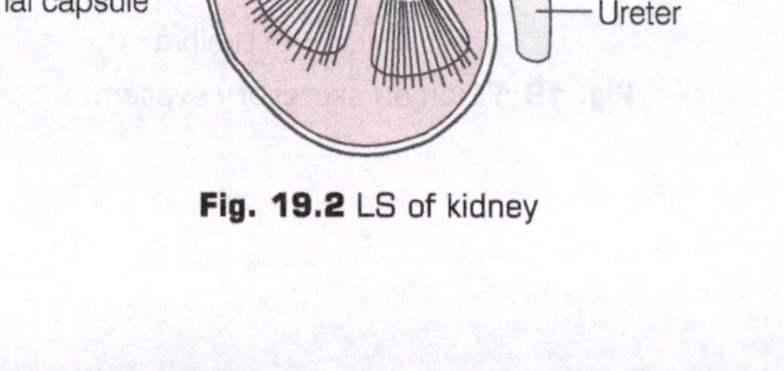

Fig. 19.2 LS of kidney

Inside the kidney, the ureter is expanded as a funnel-shaped cavity called pelvis. The free end of pelvis has number of cup-like cavities are called major calyces (sing. calyx) and minor calyces. Medulla projects into the calyces as conical processes, called renal pyramids or medullary pyramids. The tip of pyramids are called renal papillae. The cortex spreads in between medullary pyramids as renal columns called **columns of Bertini.**

Structure of Nephron or Uriniferous Tubule

Each kidney is composed of numerous (nearly one million) complex tubular structure called **nephrons.** These are the functional units of kidney.

Each nephron consists of two parts, i.e. the **Malpighian body** or renal corpuscle and the **renal tubule.**

(i) **Malpighian Body or Renal Corpuscle** Glomerulus along with Bowman's capsule is called the Malpighian body or renal corpuscle which filters out large solutes from the blood and delivers small solutes to the renal tubule for modification.

Glomerulus It is a tuft of thin-walled capillaries formed by the branching of afferent arteriole (a fine branch of renal artery). The **afferent arteriole** is short and wide that supplies blood to the glomerulus, while, the **efferent arteriole** is narrow and long carrying blood away from the glomerulus.

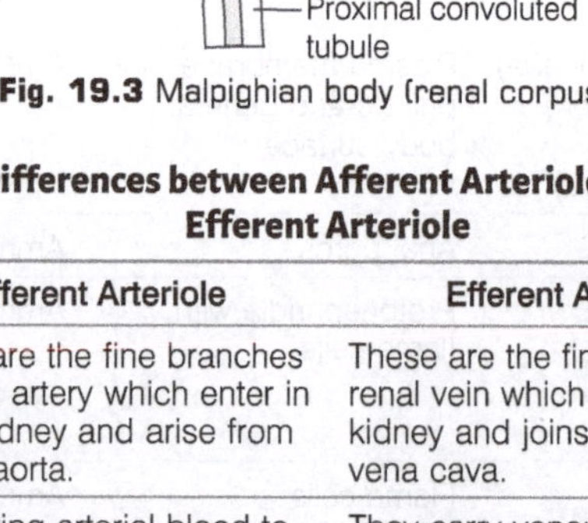

Fig. 19.3 Malpighian body (renal corpuscle)

Differences between Afferent Arteriole and Efferent Arteriole

Afferent Arteriole	Efferent Arteriole
These are the fine branches of renal artery which enter in each kidney and arise from dorsal aorta.	These are the fine branches of renal vein which leave the kidney and joins with inferior vena cava.
They bring arterial blood to the renal corpuscles.	They carry venous blood away from the renal corpuscles.
Its diameter is more.	Its diameter is comparatively less.
The blood flowing in it is rich in waste products.	The blood flowing in it is poor in waste products.

- **Bowman's Capsule** (Glomerular capsule) It is a double-walled, cup-like structure that surrounds the glomerulus. The **outer parietal wall** of glomerulus is composed of flattened (squamous) cells and the **inner visceral wall** is composed of a special type of less flattened cells, called **podocytes.**

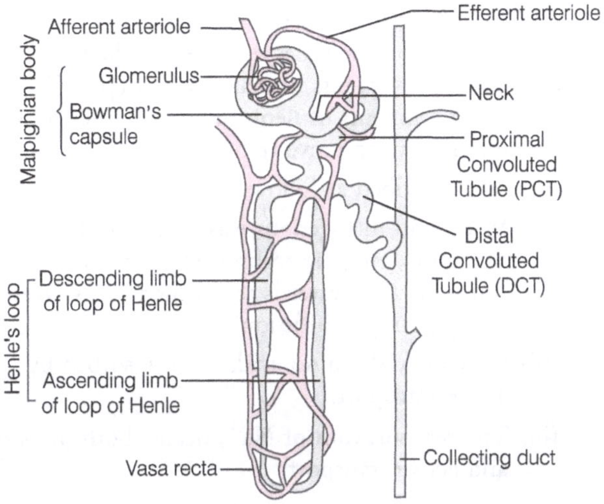

Fig. 19.4 Diagrammatic representation of a nephron

(ii) **Renal Tubules** Attached to each Bowman's capsule is a long, thin tubule with three distinct regions. These regions are described as follows

(a) **Proximal Convoluted Tubule** (PCT) Behind the neck, it makes few coils and is restricted to the cortical region of the kidney.

(b) **Henle's Loop** It is quite narrower and U-shaped (or hair pin-shaped) having a **descending limb** that ends into the medulla and an **ascending limb** that extends back from the medulla into the cortex.

Differences between Descending Limb and Ascending Limb of Henle's Loop

Descending Limb	Ascending Limb
It is very thin.	It is thick.
Direction of fluid flow is downward.	Direction of fluid flow is upward.
Permeable to water.	Impermeable to water.

(c) **Distal Convoluted Tubule** (DCT) is thicker and highly, coiled structure situated in the cortex like the proximal tubule. Coils of both convoluted tubules are intermingled.

(d) **Collecting Tubule** The last part of nephron is called **collecting** or **straight tubule,** which is lined by **cuboidal cells.**

Collecting tubules of many nephrons open into a large collecting duct. Several adjacent collecting tubules converge to open into a short and thick **duct of Bellini.** All ducts of Bellini, then open into the renal pelvis through medullary pyramids in the calyces.

Peritubular Capillary Network (PTCN) is formed when a minute vessel of peritubular capillaries runs parallel to the loop of Henle forming a U-shaped vasa recta.

All these capillaries join to form renal venules, which join to form a renal vein that opens into the inferior vena cava.

Types of Nephrons

Based on the location in the kidney, nephrons are of following two types

(i) **Cortical Nephrons** In majority of nephrons, the loop of Henle is too short and extends only very little into the medulla, i.e. lie in the renal cortex. Such nephrons are called cortical nephrons.

(ii) **Juxtamedullary Nephrons** In some of the nephrons, the loop of Henle is very long and runs deep into the medulla. These nephrons are called juxtamedullary nephrons.

Note The cortical nephron forms about 80% of the total nephron count while rest 20% are the juxtamedullary nephron.

Functions of Kidney

Following functions are served by kidney

(i) Regulation of water and electrolyte balance.

(ii) Regulation of arterial pressure.

(iii) Excretion of metabolic waste and foreign chemicals.

(iv) Secretion of hormones like renin.

2. Ureters

The pelvis of each kidney is continued as a ureter and emerges out at hilus. Ureter is a long and muscular tube. Ureters of both sides extend posteriorly and open into the urinary bladder.

3. Urinary Bladder

It is a thin-walled, pear-shaped, white transparent sac present in the pelvic cavity. It temporarily stores the urine.

4. Urethra

It is a membranous tube, which conducts urine to the exterior. The **urethral sphincters** keep the urethra closed except during voiding of urine.

Physiology of Urine Formation

The formation of urine is the result of the processes like glomerular filtration, reabsorption and secretion. These processes occur in different parts of nephrons. Details of these are as follows

1. Glomerular Filtration or Ultrafiltration

The first step of urine formation is the filtration of blood. It is carried out by the glomerulus. That is why this step is called **glomerular filtration.** Kidneys filter about 1100-1200 mL of blood per minute, which constitute roughly 1/5th of the blood pumped out by each ventricle of the heart in a minute. The glomerular capillary blood pressure causes filtration of blood through three layers, i.e.,

(i) the **endothelium** of glomerular blood vessels.
(ii) the **epithelium** of Bowman's capsule.
(iii) a **basement membrane** (present between the above mentioned two layers).

The podocytes (epithelial cells of Bowman's capsule) are arranged in such a manner, so that some minute spaces called **filtration slits** or **slit pores** occur between them. On account of the high pressure in the glomerular capillaries, the substances are filtered through these pores into the lumen of the Bowman's capsule (but the RBC, WBC and plasma proteins having high molecular weight are unable to pass out).

That's why this process of filtration through glomerular capillaries in the Bowman's capsule is known as ultra filtration and the filtrate is called **glomerular filtrate.**

It is hypotonic to urine that is actually excreted. Basic function of nephron is to clear out the plasma from unwanted substrates and also maintain the osmotic concentration of the blood plasma. Thus, the fluid coming out is known as **urine,** whose formation occurs inside the kidney.

Glomerular Filtration Rate

- The amount of the filtrate formed by the kidneys per minute is called Glomerular Filtration Rate (GFR). In a healthy person it was found approximately 125 mL /min, i.e. 180 L/day.
- GFR is regulated by one of the efficient mechanism carried out by Juxta Glomerular Apparatus (JGA).
- JGA is a special sensitive region formed by cellular modifications in the distal convoluted tubule and the afferent arteriole at the location of their contact.
  This apparatus includes
  (i) granular juxtaglomerular cells in the afferent arteriole.
  (ii) macula densa cells of DCT.
  (iii) agranular mesangial cells situated in between the above two.
- A fall in GFR can activate the JG cells to release renin, which can stimulate the glomerular blood flow and thereby, the GFR back to normal.

2. Selective Reabsorption

This is the second step in the formation of urine from filtrate. The urine released is 1.5 L as compared to the volume of the filtrate formed per day (180 L).

It suggests that as much as 99% of the material in the filtrate is reabsorbed by the renal tubules. Thus, the process is called **reabsorption.**

Depending upon the types of molecules being reabsorbed, movements into and out of epithelial cells in different segments of nephron occur either by passive transport or active transport.

These are described as follows

(i) Water and nitrogenous wastes like urea, ammonia, etc., are reabsorbed by passive transport (i.e. water is reabsorbed by osmosis and urea by simple diffusion).
(ii) **Glucose** and **amino acids** are reabsorbed by active transport.
(iii) The **reabsorption of Na^+**, occurs both by passive and active transport.

3. Tubular Secretion

It is also an important step in urine formation. Certain chemicals in the blood that are not removed by filtration from the glomerular capillaries are removed by this process of tubular secretion.

It helps in the maintenance of **ionic** and **acid-base balance** of body fluids by removing chemicals like foreign bodies, ions (K^+, H^+, NH_4^+) from the epithelial cells in exchange of Na^+ and molecules (medicines), etc., that are **toxic** at elevated levels.

Differences between Tubular Reabsorption and Tubular Secretion

Tubular Reabsorption	Tubular Secretion
It involves the absorption of water and useful solutes from the glomerular filtrate into the blood.	It refers to the passage of waste materials from blood into the filtrate or nephrons.
It occurs by back diffusion and active transport.	It takes place only by active transport.
It occurs mostly in PCT.	It occurs mostly in DCT.
It does not occur in animals that lack glomerulus (e.g. marine fish and desert animals).	It is the only mode of excretion in animals that lack glomerulus.

Functions of the Tubules

When the glomerular filtrate or primary urine passes through renal tubule, water and different materials of filtrate get reabsorbed at various places.

These are given below in the following manner

(i) **Proximal Convoluted Tubule (PCT)** The epithelial cells of the PCT have numerous **microvilli** (simple cuboidal brush-border epithelium) which increase the surface area available for reabsorption.

The process of reabsorption mostly (65%) takes place within PCT (i.e. nearly all of the essential nutrients, 70-80% of electrolytes and water). PCT also helps in the absorption of HCO_3^- from the filtrate.

Selective secretion of hydrogen ions, ammonia and potassium ions takes place here to maintain the pH and ionic balance of the body fluids. The filtrate is considered **isotonic** to blood plasma.

(ii) **Henle's Loop** Reabsorption in Henle's loop is minimum, besides this, it plays an important role in maintaining the high osmolarity of medullary interstitial fluid. Two portions of Henle's loop, play different role in osmoregulation. These are as follows

(a) **Descending Limb of Loop of Henle**
Water is reabsorbed here due to increasing osmolarity of interstitial fluid but, sodium and other electrolytes are not reabsorbed here. This concentrates the filtrate as it moves down.

(b) **Ascending Limb of Loop of Henle**
This segment is impermeable to water, but permeable to K^+, Cl^- and Na^+ and partially permeable to urea. Thus, in the thick ascending limb of the loop of Henle Na^+, K^+, Mg^{2+} and Cl^- are reabsorbed. Therefore, as the concentrated filtrate pass upward, it gets diluted due to the passing out of electrolytes to the medullary fluid of kidney. Thus, it contributes to high osmolarity of interstitial fluid.

(iii) **Distal Convoluted Tubule** (DCT) Active reabsorption of sodium ions from the filtrate takes place under the influence of aldosterone.

Water is also reabsorbed here.

With associated secretion of potassium (K^+), hydrogen (H^+) ions, NH_3, some Cl^- (chloride) ions and HCO_3^- are also reabsorbed here. It is necessary to maintain the **pH** and **sodium-potassium balance** in blood. This makes the filtrate isotonic to blood plasma.

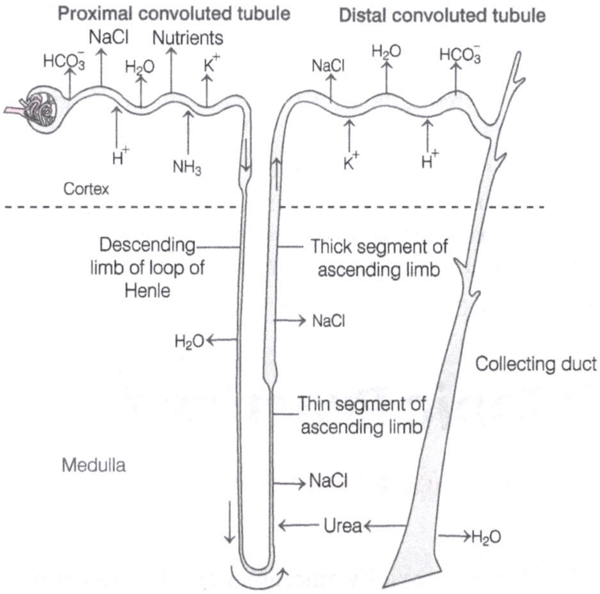

Fig. 19.5 Reabsorption and secretion of major substances at different parts of the nephron (arrows indicate direction of movement of materials)

(iv) **Collecting Duct** This duct extends from the cortex of the kidney to the inner parts of the medulla and is highly permeable to water. Thus, a considerable amount of water is reabsorbed here under the influence of ADH to produce concentrated filtrate.

Sodium ions are also reabsorbed here as release of aldosterone increases the permeability of wall of DCT for sodium ions.

CT (Collecting Tubule) allows passage of small amounts of urea into the **medullary interstitial** tissue to maintain the osmolarity. It also plays an important role in the maintenance of pH and ionic balance of the blood by the selective secretion of H^+ and K^+ ions.

Therefore, the filtrate is now becomes **urine.** Thus, urine is isotonic to medullary fluid and **hypertonic** to blood.

Note Concentrations of important ions and other substances in the blood are controlled by regulating levels of water in the blood.

Osmoregulation

It is the process of maintenance of salt and water (osmotic) balance across membranes within the body.

The composition of body fluids is influenced more by the output through the kidneys than by the intake *via* the gut. Therefore, the kidneys are important guardians of the internal environment.

By means of the regulated production of urine from the blood the nephrons carry out the dual process of excretion and osmoregulation. The two types of nephrons, differing both in their position in the kidney and in the length of the loop of Henle, play an important role in osmoregulation.

Cortical nephrons function most importantly when the water supply is normal to excessive. Juxtamedullary nephrons work when water is in short supply.

Note The term 'Osmoregulation' was first coined by **Hober** (1902).

Topic Practice 1

Multiple Choice Questions

1 Mark

1. Order of toxicity among ammonia, urea and uric acid (from lower to higher) is
   (a) uric acid < urea < ammonia
   (b) uric acid < ammonia < urea
   (c) urea < uric acid < ammonia
   (d) ammonia < urea < uric acid

Ans (a) Ammonia is most toxic form and requires large amount of water for its elimination whereas uric acid being the least toxic, can be removed with a minimum loss of water.

2. Why terrestrial organism excrete lesser toxic nitrogenous waste?
   (a) For conservation of water
   (b) For maintaing osmolarity
   (c) To fucilitate simple diffusion
   (d) It is easy to excrete less toxic substances

Ans (a) Terrestrial adaptation necessitated the production of lesser toxic nitrogenous waste like urea and uric acid for conservation of water.

3. Part of the kidney through which the ureter, blood vessels and nerves enters into it is
   (a) renal cortex (b) renal medulla
   (c) hilum (d) urethra

Ans (c) Towards the centre of the inner concave surface of the kidney, there is a notch called hilum through which ureter, blood vessels and nerves enter.

4. In juxtamedullary nephrons,
   (a) vasa recta is prominent
   (b) loop of Henle is long
   (c) loop of Henle runs deep into the medulla
   (d) All of the above

Ans (d) Juxtamedullary nephrones have following characteristics
(i) Vasa recta is prominant.
(ii) Loop of Henle is long.
(iii) Loop of Henle runs deep into the medulla.

5. Choose the correct statement.
   (a) The juxtamedullary nephrons have reduced Henle's loop
   (b) Vasa recta is well developed in cortical nephrone
   (c) The PCT and DCT are situated in the medulla of the kidney
   (d) The ascending limb of Henle's loop extends as the DCT

Ans (d) The ascending limb of the Henle's loop (the next part of renal tubule) continues as another highly coiled tubular region called DCT.

6. Ultrafiltrate generated by the glomerulus is having all the constituent of the blood plasma except
   (a) protein (b) RBC
   (c) WBC (d) All of these

Ans (a) Blood is filtered so finely through the these membranes (three layers) that almost all the constituents of the plasma except the proteins, pass into the lumen of the capsule.

7. Choose the false statement.
   (a) Tubular cells secrets H^+, K^+, ammonia to filtrate
   (b) Tubular cells helps to maintain the acid base balance of the body fluid
   (c) Tubular cells helps in ionic balance
   (d) Tubular secretion is not very important step in urine formation

Ans (d) During urine formation, the tubular cells secretes substances like H^+, K^+ and ammonia into the filtrate. It helps in acid base balance and electrolyte balance of the body.

8. Removal of proximal convoluted tubule from the nephron will result in
   (a) more diluted urine
   (b) more concentrated urine
   (c) no change in quality and quantity urine
   (d) No urine formation

Ans (a) Proximal convoluted tubule reabsorb most of water so if it is removed, more diluted urine will be formed.

9. The maximum amount of electrolytes and water (70-80%) from the glomerular filtrate is reabsorbed in which part of the nephron?
   (a) Ascending limb of loop of Henle
   (b) Distal convoluted tubule
   (c) Proximal convoluted tubule
   (d) Descending limb of loop of Henle

Ans (c) From the Bowman's capsule, the glomerular filtrate enters the Proximal Convoluted Tubule (PCT). PCT is surrounded by a network of peritubular capillaries and is the seat of reabsorption. About 75% of glomerular filtrate is normally reabsorbed in PCT before reaching the loop of Henle.

10. Choose the mismatched part of nephron with their function.
(a) Bowman's capsule–Glomerular filtration
(b) PCT–Reabsorption of Na^+ and K^+
(c) DCT–Reabsorption of glucose
(d) Loop of Henle–Urine concentration

Ans (c) **Distal Convoluted Tubule** (DCT) Conditional reabsorption of Na^+ and water takes place in this segment. DCT is also capable of reabsorption of HCO_3^- and selective secretion of hydrogen and potassium ions and NH_3 to maintain the pH and Na–K balance in blood.

Very Short Answer Type Questions
1 Mark

11. What is the excretory product from the kidney of reptiles? **NCERT Exemplar**

Ans Uric acid.

12. In which of the organisms antennary glands are found as excretory organ?

Ans Crustaceans.

13. Give the name of the reservoir of urine in the body.

Ans Urinary bladder.

14. In which part of excretory system of mammals you can first use the term urine?

Ans Collecting duct.

15. Give the name of vessel of peritubular capillaries that runs parallel to the loop of Henle.

Ans Vasa recta.

16. Define Glomerular Filtration Rate (GFR). **NCERT**

Ans Glomerular Filtration Rate (GFR) is the amount of the filtrate formed by the kidneys per minute. GFR in a healthy individual is approximately 125 mL/min, i.e. 180 L day.

17. What is meant by the term osmoregulation? **NCERT**

Ans It is the phenomenon of regulation of change in the concentration of body fluids according to the concentration of external environment. In most marine invertebrates, some freshwater invertebrates, hagfish, etc., it can be clearly seen but it is found in all animals.

18. Write the mode of excretion performed by *Xenopus*.

Ans Dual excretion (mainly ammonotelism and partly ureotelism).

19. Give the name of cells that are responsible for the formation of filtration slits or slit pores.

Ans Podocytes (epithelial cells present in inner wall of Bowman's capsule).

20. Give the name of the nitrogenous waste which is produced in birds. In what form is it eliminated from the body? What is the advantage of this type of excretion?

Ans Birds excrete uric acid in the form of pellet or paste (semi-solid form). It helps in conservation of water.

Short Answer Type I Questions
2 Marks

21. Give the name of the three common nitrogenous waste materials in vertebrates. Which of these is most toxic and which one is least toxic?

Ans Ammonia, urea and uric acid. Ammonia is most toxic, while uric acid is least toxic. (1+1)

22. Distinguish between ureotelism and uricotelism.

Ans Refer to text on page no. 442 and 443.

23. Give the name of the excretory organ present in the following animals.
(i) Rotifers
(ii) Cockroaches
(iii) Lancelets
(iv) *Amphioxus*

Ans
(i) Rotifers — Flame cells
(ii) Cockroaches — Malpighian tubules
(iii) Lancelets — Protonephridia
(iv) *Amphioxus* — Nephridium ($\frac{1}{2} \times 4$)

24. (a) Name the two components of nephron that together form Malpighian body or renal corpuscle.
(b) In between the two adjacent renal pyramids, __*A*___ is present. Identify A.

Ans (a) Glomerulus and Bowman's capsule.
(b) Colums of Bertini. (1+1)

25. What are the two main types of nephrons?

Ans Cortical nephrons and juxta medullary nephrons. (1+1)

26. Give the name of the two actively transported substances in glomerular filtrate. **NCERT Exemplar**

Ans Glucose and amino acids are actively transported substances in glomerular filtrate. (1+1)

27. Where does the selective reabsorption of glomerular filtrate take place?

Ans The selective reabsorption of glomerular filtrate takes place in Proximal Convoluted Tubules (PCT) and Distal Convoluted Tubules (DCT).

In PCT all essential elements nutrients, 70-80% of electrolytes and water is absorbed whereas, Distal Convoluted Tubule (DCT) is involved in conditional reabsorption of Na^+ and water. (2)

28. **Indicate whether the following statements are true or false.**

(i) ADH helps in water elimination, making the urine hypotonic.

(ii) Protein-free fluid is filtered from blood plasma into the Bowman's capsule.

(iii) Henle's loop plays an important role in concentrating the urine.

(iv) Glucose is actively reabsorbed in the proximal convoluted tubule. **NCERT Exemplar**

Ans (i) False (ii) True

(iii) True (iv) True ($\frac{1}{2} \times 4$)

Short Answer Type II Questions

3 Marks

29. **What is ureotelism? Describe the process of formation of urea.**

Ans The process of excreting urea is called ureotelism. Animals, which do not live in high abundance of water convert toxic ammonia produced in the body into urea by the liver and then release it into the blood. This in turn is filtered and excreted out by the kidneys. (1+2)

30. **Draw a simple diagram of a human kidney. Label any six parts.**

Ans Refer to fig. no. 19.2 and text on page no. 444.

31. **Show the structure of a renal corpuscle with the help of a diagram.** **NCERT Exemplar**

Ans Glomerulus along with Bowman's capsule is called the Malpighian body or renal corpuscle. (1)

For diagram Refer to fig. no. 19.3 and text on page 444. (2)

32. (a) **Where does the urine formation take place? Name the processes involved in the formation of urine.**

(b) **In which part of the nephron does the adjustments in sodium concentration?**

Ans (a) Urine formation occurs in the kidneys.

It involves three steps.

(i) Glomerular filtration

(ii) Selective reabsorption

(iii) Tubular secretion (2)

(b) Distal tubule (1)

33. **Where do ultrafiltration, reabsorption and secretion occur in a nephron?**

Ans (i) Ultrafiltration occurs in Bowman's capsule.

(ii) Reabsorption occurs in PCT, loop of Henle, DCT and collecting ducts.

(iii) Secretion occurs in PCT, loop of Henle and DCT. (1×3)

34. **Explain the autoregulatory mechanism of GFR.** **NCERT**

Ans Refer to text on page no. 446.

35. **Distinguish between tubular secretion and tubular reabsorption.**

Ans See table on page no. 446.

36. **Explain the condition in the collecting duct that makes the urine hypertonic.**

Ans Refer to text on page no. 447.

37. **Give the name of the layers through which the glomerular capillary blood pressure causes filtration.**

Ans The layers through which the glomerular capillary blood pressure causes filteration are

(i) The endothelium of glomerular blood vessels.

(ii) The epithelium of Bowman's capsule.

(iii) A basement membrane (present between these two above mentioned layers). (1×3)

38. (i) **Name the excretory organs found in Aschelminthes and leeches.**

(ii) **Name the arterioles through which blood enters and leaves the glomerulus.**

(iii) **Name the vessel of peritubular capillaries that runs parallel to the loop of Henle.**

Ans (i) Renette cells, metanephridia

(ii) Afferent arteriole and efferent arteriole

(iii) Vasa recta. (1×3)

Long Answer Type Questions

5 Marks

39. **Terrestrial animals are generally either ureotelic or uricotelic, not ammonotelic, why?** **NCERT**

Ans Terrestrial adaptation requires the production of less toxic nitrogenous wastes like urea and uric acid for the conservation of water. Aquatic animals excrete ammonia which requires large amount of water to dissolve. The huge quantity of water is easily available to such animals from surroundings. However, for terrestrial animals, such a huge quantity of water is not available, hence, they modify NH_3 to comparatively less toxic products like urea and uric acid which require less amount of water for their excretion. (5)

40. (i) Study the given structure carefully and label the parts given as *A*, *B*, *C*, *D* and *E*.

(ii) Give one major function of each of these.

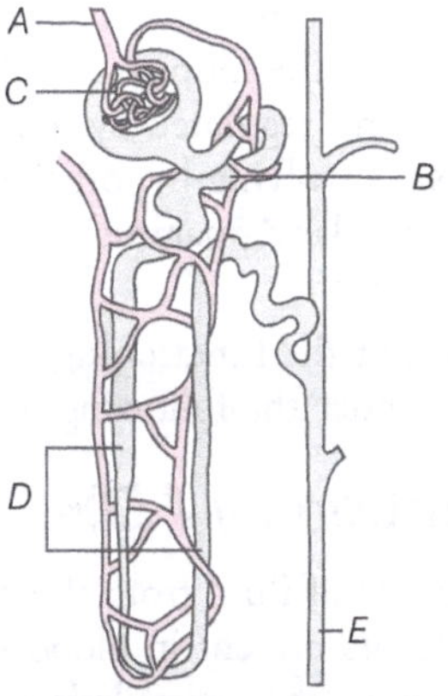

Ans (i) *A* – Afferent arteriole,

B – Proximal convoluted tubule,

C – Glomerulus,

D – Loop of Henle,

E – Collecting duct (2)

(ii) Following are the functions of each above mentioned part

A – Carry blood to glomerulus for ultrafiltration.

B – Selective reabsorption of useful substances.

C – Ultrafiltration of blood.

D – Maintenance of the high osmolarity of medullary interstitial fluid.

E – Reabsorption of water to form hypertonic urine. (3)

41. Describe the process of urine formation in the nephron through filtration, reabsorption and secretion.

Ans Refer to text on page no. 446.

TOPIC 02 Excretion : Various Controlling Mechanisms and Disorders

Counter-Current Mechanism

Kidney of higher vertebrates (such as mammals, birds and man) has the ability of absorbing more and more water from tubular filtrate to conserve water and make the urine more concentrated.

This can be achieved by a special mechanism known as counter-current mechanism. The basic concept and mechanism of this mechanism is as follows

Basic Concept

(i) **Henle's loop** and **vasa recta** (capillary loop) play an important role in this mechanism. The flow of filtrate in the limbs of Henle's loop is in opposite directions and thus, forms a **counter-current.**

The flow of blood within the two limbs of vasa recta also occurs in the counter-current pattern.

(ii) The osmolarity (i.e. number of osmols of solute per litre) of renal cortical interstitium is the same (300 mOsmol/ L) as in other tissues, but that of the interstitium of renal medulla is hypertonic with a gradient of hyperosmolarity from renal cortex to the tips of medullary papillae.

The hyperosmolarity of medullary interstitium near the tips of the papillae is as high as 1200-1450 mOsmol/L.

The Mechanism

The gradient of increasing hyperosmolarity of medullary interstitium is maintained by a counter-current mechanism and the proximity between the Henle's loop and vasa recta.

This gradient is mainly caused by the to and fro movements of **NaCl** and **urea**. The transport of these substances is facilitated by the special arrangement of Henle's loop and vasa recta.

There are two aspects of this mechanism

(i) **Counter-current multiplication** (by the Henle's loop).

(ii) **Counter-current exchange** (by the vasa recta).

NaCl is transported out by the ascending limb of Henle's loop from where they enter in the descending limb of vasa recta.

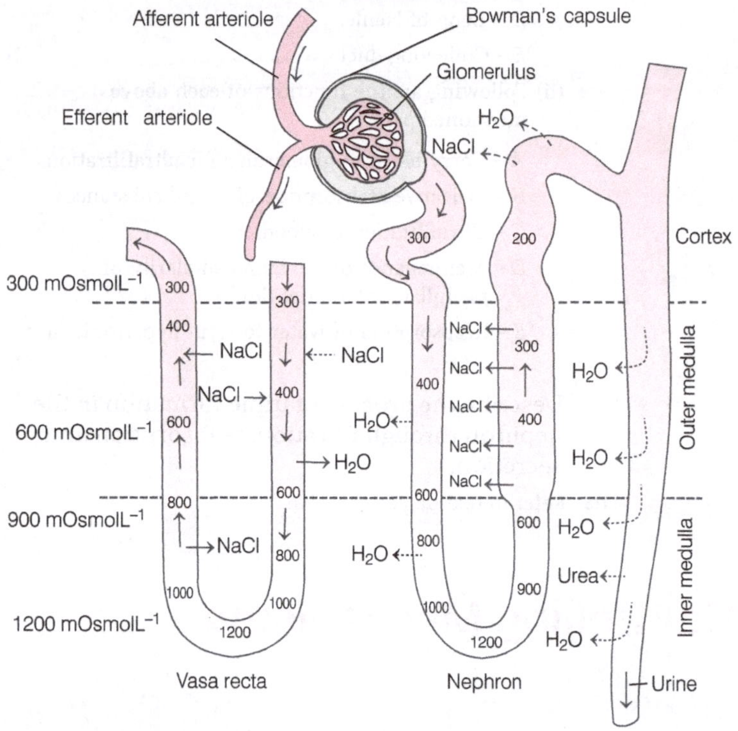

Fig. 19.6 Diagrammatic representation of a nephron and vasa recta showing counter-current mechanism

NaCl is returned to the medullary interstitium by the ascending part of vasa recta. But, contrarily, the water diffuses into the blood of ascending limb of vasa recta and is carried away into the general blood circulation.

Permeability to urea is found only in the deeper parts of thin ascending limb of Henle's loop and collecting ducts.

Urea diffuses out of the collecting ducts and enters into the thin ascending limb. A certain amount of urea recycled in this way is trapped in medullary interstitium by the collecting tubule. Thus, collecting tubule also plays a minor role in the process (as shown in the figure above). The counter-current mechanism helps in the maintenance of a concentration gradient in the medullary interstitium. Presence of such gradient helps in an easy passage of water from the collecting tubule resulting in the formation of concentrated urine (filtrate), i.e. nearly four times concentrated than the initial filtrate formed.

Regulation of Urine Formation

To maintain homeostasis, the regulation of water and solute contents of the body fluids is performed by the kidneys. The vertebrate kidney is very flexible in its functioning.

It excretes larger quantities of dilute urine when water is abundant in the body tissues and small amounts of concentrated urine when there is shortage of water.

Hormones act as an important signalling molecules in controlling the regulation of water content in blood with the help of kidneys. The functioning of the kidneys is efficiently monitored and regulated by **hormonal feedback mechanism** involving hypothalamus, JGA (Juxtaglomerular Apparatus) and to a certain extent, the heart.

Regulation of the functioning of kidneys can be discussed under the following headings

Regulation by ADH

Excessive loss of fluid from the body activates osmoreceptors present in blood vessels of hypothalamus, thus stimulating it to release ADH or vasopressin from the neurohypophysis. ADH release increases water reabsorption from DCT.

An increase in body fluid volume switches off the osmoreceptors and suppresses the ADH release to complete the feedback. ADH also causes constrictory effects on blood vessels of glomerulus thus, increasing pressure for faster filtration.

Regulation by Renin-Angiotensin

As blood pressure/glomerular blood flow /GFR decreases, the cells of the JGA release the enzyme renin.

Renin converts angiotensinogen in blood to Angiotensin I and Angiotensin II (active form). This mechanism is generally known as the **Renin-angiotensin mechanism.**

Angiotensin has following effects

(i) Raises blood pressure by constricting blood vessels (being a powerful vasaconstrictor) and thereby, GFR.

(ii) Activates the adrenal cortex to release aldosterone.

(iii) Aldosterone causes reabsorption of Na^+ and water from the distal parts of the tubule. This also leads to an increase in blood pressure and GFR.

Regulation by ANF

Atrial Natriuretic Factor (ANF) is produced by the atria of heart when blood volume decreases. This causes vasodilation (dilation of blood vessels) and thereby, decreases the blood pressure.

ANF also inhibits Na^+ and Cl^- ions reabsorption in DCT and increases concentration of urine.

> **Role of Erythropoietin**
>
> Erythropoietin (EPO) is a hormone produced by the kidney that promotes the formation of red blood cells by the bone marrow.
>
> The kidney cells that make erythropoietin are sensitive to low oxygen levels in the blood that travels through the kidney. These cells make and release erythropoietin when the oxygen level is too low. A low oxygen level may indicate diminished number of red blood cells (anaemia) or haemoglobin molecules that carry oxygen through the body.
>
> This hormone is now-a-days produced using recombinant DNA technology to treat various medical conditions. It is used in treating anaemia resulting from chronic kidney disease, chemotherapy induced anaemia in patients with cancer, etc.

Homeostasis

It is the mechanism used to maintain a stable, relatively constant internal environment in body.

The term homeostasis was coined by **Walter Cannon** in 1932. The internal environment of our body includes temperature, ionic concentration in blood, glucose level, etc., kept within physiological needs.

Biological systems are constantly tested to cross their equilibrium levels. Any disturbances in homeostasis, leads to sickness or ill health. The volume and composition of body fluids is an important aspect of homeostasis maintenance. Thus, for proper function of our body's systems, homeostasis is very essential.

Micturition

Urine is produced and drained continuously by the nephron into the renal pelvis, from here, it is carried down to the ureters and then into the urinary bladder.

The bladder serves to store the urine temporarily till a voluntary signal is given by the **Central Nervous System** (CNS). As urine collects, the muscular walls of the bladder distend to accommodate it.

The stretch receptors on the walls of the bladder send up reflexes to the CNS, by sensory nerve ending in the bladder.

The act of expulsion of urine involves the coordinated contraction (as CNS passes on motor messages) of the smooth muscle of the bladder wall and simultaneous relaxation of the **internal** and **external urethral sphincters**. The process of release of urine is called micturition and the neural mechanism causing it is called the **micturition reflex.**

Urine

An adult man normally passes about 1-1.5 L of urine per day.

Composition Urine normally contains, water 95%, salts 2%, urea 2.6%, uric acid 0.3%, traces of creatinine, creatine, ammonia, etc.

Colour Pale yellow, due to pigment **urochrome** produced by the breakdown of haemoglobin.

pH Ranges from 4.5-8.2, average pH 6.0 (i.e. slightly acidic).

Odour Unpleasant, if allowed to stand imparts strong smell like, ammonia.

Least concentration of urea is found in renal vein because urea is excreted through urine formed in kidney. On an average, 25-30 g of urea is excreted out per day. Highest concentration of urine is found in hepatic vein because urea is synthesised in liver.

Analysis of urine helps in clinical diagnosis of many metabolic disorders as well as malfunctioning of the kidney. For example, presence of glucose (glycosuria) and ketone bodies (ketonuria) in urine are indicative of diabetes mellitus and presence of protein, blood and pus in the urine is called **proteinuria, haematuria** and **pyuria,** respectively.

Role of Other Organs in Excretion

Other than the kidneys, there are some accessory excretory organs also that help in the elimination of excretory wastes. These are described as follows

1. Skin

The sweat glands and sebaceous glands in the skin can eliminate certain substances through their secretions.

(i) **Sweat Glands** The secretion of sweat glands (sweat) is an aqueous fluid containing NaCl, lactic acid, small amounts of urea, amino acids and glucose. Control of sweat lost is an example of homeostasis control, for regulating the body temperature (i.e. to facilitate a cooling effect on the body surface).

(ii) **Sebaceous Glands** Sebum from sebaceous glands eliminates sterols, fatty acids, waxes and hydrocarbons. This secretion is mainly meant for protective oily covering of the skin.

2. Liver

It changes the decomposed haemoglobin of the wornout red blood corpuscles into bile pigments, i.e. **bilirubin** and **biliverdin**. These pigments pass into the alimentary canal with the bile for elimination in the faeces. The liver also excretes cholesterol, steroid hormones, certain vitamins and drugs *via* bile. Liver deaminates the excess and unwanted amino acids, producing ammonia, which is quickly combined with CO_2 to form urea in **urea cycle** or **Ornithine cycle**, which is further removed by the kidneys.

3. Lungs

Carbon dioxide and water are the waste products formed in respiration. Lungs remove the CO_2 and some water as vapour in the expired air. About 18 L of CO_2 per hour and 400 mL of water per day are eliminated by human lungs.

4. Intestine

Epithelial cells of colon excrete excess salts of calcium, magnesium and iron along with faeces.

5. Salivary Glands

Heavy metals and drugs are excreted in the saliva.

Important Metabolic Wastes and Substances Excreted from the Body

Chemical	Source	Organ of Excretion
Ammonia	Deamination (removal of amine group) of amino acids in liver	Kidneys
Bile pigments	Haemoglobin breakdown in liver	Liver (into small intestine)
Carbon dioxide	Breakdown of glucose in cells	Lungs
Inorganic ions	Food and water	Kidneys and salivary glands
Urea	Derived from ammonia	Kidneys and skin
Uric acid	Nucleotide breakdown in liver	Kidneys
Urochrome	Haemoglobin breakdown in liver	Kidneys
Water	Food and water, breakdown of glucose	Kidneys, skin and lungs

Disorders of the Excretory System

Malfunctioning of kidneys can lead to several disorders of the excretory system. Some of these are as follows

(i) **Uremia** It is the presence of an excessive amount of urea in the blood. Urea is highly harmful as it poisons the cells at high concentration and may lead to kidney failure.

(ii) **Kidney Failure** (renal failure) Partial or total inability of kidneys to carry on excretory and salt-water regulatory functions is called **renal** or kidney failure.

(iii) **Renal Calculi** It is the formation of stone or insoluble mass of crystallised salts (calcium, magnesium, phosphates and oxalates, etc.), formed within the kidney.

(iv) **Glomerulonephritis** It is the inflammation of glomeruli of kidney.

(v) **Diabetes Insipidus** (DI) It is a condition characterised by excessive thirst and frequent micturition. The urine excreted is severely diluted. There are several different types of DI, each with a different cause. The most common type in human is central DI, caused by the deficiency of Arginine Vasopressin (AVP), also known as Anti Diuretic Hormone (ADH). The second common type of DI is nephrogenic diabetes insipidus, which is caused by an insensitivity of the kidney to ADH.

Artificial Kidney (Haemodialyser)

Artificial kidney is a machine that is used to filter the blood (to remove urea and other nitrogenous wastes) of a person, whose kidneys are damaged. The process is called **haemodialysis**.

The outline details of apparatus and the process are as follows

(i) It works on the principle of dialysis (i.e. diffusion of small solute molecules through a semipermeable membrane (cellophane).

(ii) Blood of the patient is pumped from one of the arteries into the dialysing unit (haemodialyser) after cooling it to 0°C and mixing with an **anticoagulant** (heparin).

(iii) Haemodialyser is a cellophane tube suspended in a dialysing fluid (salt-water solution) of the same composition as that of plasma except the nitrogenous wastes (urea).

(iv) Pores of the cellophane tube allow the passage of molecules based on concentration gradient. Nitrogenous wastes like urea, uric acid, creatinine, excess salts and excess H^+ ions easily get diffuse from the blood into the surrounding solution. Thus, the blood is cleared of nitrogenous waste products without loosing plasma proteins.

(v) The blood thus purified, is warmed to body temperature, checked to ensure that it is isotonic to the patients blood. Now, the blood is mixed with an **anti-heparin** to restore its normal clotting power and then pumped back to the body of patient through a vein, usually the radial vein.

Renal (Kidney) Transplantation

Grafting a kidney from a compatible donor to restore kidney functions in a recipient suffering from kidney failure is called renal or kidney transplantation. It is an ultimate method in the correction of acute renal failures. A living donor can be used in a kidney transplant. It may be an identical twin, a sibling or a close relative to minimise the chances of **rejection** by the immune system of the host. To prevent the rejection of transplanted kidney, special drugs are also used, which suppress the recipient's immune system.

Topic Practice 2

Multiple Choice Questions

1 Mark

1. The counter-current mechanism operates in nephron
   (a) in ascending and descending limb of vasa recta
   (b) in ascending limb of Henle's loop
   (c) in descending limb of Henle's loop
   (d) between the loop of Henle and vasa recta

Ans (d) The proximity between the Henle's loop and vasa recta as well as the counter-current in them helps in maintaining an increasing osmolarity toward the inner medullary interstitium.

2. Osmolarity in the cortex and inner medulla respectively are
   (a) 300 $mOsmolL^{-}1$, 1200 mOsmol L^{-1}
   (b) 200 $mOsmolL^{-1}$, 1300 mOsmol L^{-1}
   (c) 1200 $mOsmolL^{-1}$, 300 mOsmol L^{-1}
   (d) None of the above

Ans (a) The osmolarity is 300 $mOsmolL^{-1}$ in cortex and 1200 $mOsmolL^{-1}$ in inner medulla.

3. NaCl is transported by ascending limb of Henle's loop, which is exchanged with
   (a) DCT
   (b) PCT
   (c) ascending limb of vasa recta
   (d) descending limb of vasa recta

Ans (d) The gradient of medullary region is primarily by NaCl and urea. NaCl is transported by ascending limb of Henle's loop, which is exchanged with descending limb of vasa recta.

4. The renal fluid isotonic to the cortical fluid and blood is found in
   (a) collecting duct and ascending duct
   (b) distal convoluted tubule and ascending limb
   (c) the proximal convoluted tubule and distal convoluted tubule
   (d) the ascending limbs and descending limb

Ans (c) The process of filtration through glomerular capillaries in Bowman's capsule is known as glomerular filtration and the filtrate is called renal fluid. Renal fluid is isotonic to cortical fluid and blood in PCT.

5. Which of the following causes an increase in sodium reabsorption in the distal convoluted tubule?
   (a) Increase in aldosterone levels
   (b) Increase in antidiuretic hormone levels
   (c) Decrease in aldosterone levels
   (d) Decrease in antidiuretic hormone levels

Ans (a) Increase in aldosterone levels cause an increase in sodium reabsorption in DCT. It is secreted by outer layer of adrenal gland.

6. Angiotensin-II increases glomerular blood pressure and GFR as it is a
   (a) osmoregulator
   (b) vasoconstrictor
   (c) vasodilator
   (d) None of the above

Ans (b) Angiotensin-II is a powerful, vasoconstrictor thus increases glomerular blood pressure and thereby GFR.

7. Indication of diabetes mellitus is/are
   (a) the presence of glucose in urine
   (b) the presence of ketone bodies in urine
   (c) the presence of amino acid in urine
   (d) Both (a) and (b)

Ans (d) Analysis of urine helps in clinical diagnosis of many metabolic disorders as well as malfunctioning of the kidney.

For example, presence of glucose (glycosuria) and ketone bodies (ketonuria) in urine are indicative of diabetes mellitus.

8. Choose the correct statements.
(a) Sebaceous gland eliminate sterols, hydrocarbons, waxes
(b) Secretion of sebaceous gland provide oily protective covering of skin
(c) Small amount of nitrogenous wastes eliminated through saliva
(d) All of the above

Ans (d) Sebaceous glands eliminate certain substances like sterols, hydrocarbons and waxes through sebum.
This secretion provides a protective oily covering for the skin. Small amounts of nitrogenous wastes could be eliminated through saliva.

9. Renal calculi is
(a) soluble mass of crystallised salts in kidney
(b) soluble mass of protein in kidney
(c) insoluble mass of proteins in kidney
(d) insoluble mass of crystallised salts in kidney

Ans (d) Renal calculi is presence of stones or insoluble mass of crystallised salts (oxalates, etc.) formed with in the kidneys.

10. Which statement is correct regarding the haemodialysis procedure?
(a) Haemodialysis is the ultimate method in the correction of acute renal failure
(b) Blood is drained from a convenient artery and pumped into dialysing unit containing heparin
(c) The dialysing unit have a coiled parafine tube surrounded by dialysing fluid
(d) The composition of dialysing fluid is different from that of plasma

Ans (b) Haemodialysis is used in patient with uremia to remove urea collected in blood. The dialysing unit have a cellophane tube and composition of dialysing fluid is similar to that of plasma.

Very Short Answer Type Questions

1 Mark

11. By which part of the vasa recta NaCl is returned to the medullary interstitium?

Ans NaCl is returned to the medullary interstitium by the ascending part of the vasa recta by reabsorption mechanism.

12. What are the two substances responsible for causing the gradient for increasing hyperosmolarity of medullary interstitium?

Ans NaCl and urea.

13. What is the pH of urine? **NCERT Exemplar**

Ans It ranges from 4.5-8.2, average pH is 6.0.

14. Micturition is carried out by a reflex. Consider the statement as true or false. **NCERT**

Ans True.

15. What type of excretory products get excreted through saliva?

Ans Heavy metals and drugs are excreted in the saliva.

16. How do lungs help in excretion?

Ans Carbon dioxide and water are the waste products removed by the lungs in the expired air.

17. What is the ratio of the concentrated filtrate to that of the initial filtrate?

Ans The concentrated urine (filtrate) is nearly four times concentrated than the initial filtrate formed.

18. What will be the effect on the amount of urine released when water is abundant in the body tissues in case of vertebrates?

Ans Vertebrates excrete large quantities of dilute urine when water is abundant in the body tissues and *vice-versa*.

19. Give the name of the main components that play an important role in the counter-current mechanism.

Ans Henle's loop and vasa recta.

Short Answer Type I Questions

2 Marks

20. How does ADH regulate body fluid volume? Explain.

Ans Excessive loss of fluid from the body activates osmoreceptors, which stimulate the hypothalamus to release ADH from the neurohypophysis. ADH facilitates water reabsorption from posterior parts of tubule. This decreases osmolarity of blood. An increase in body fluid volume can switch off the osmoreceptors and suppress the ADH release to complete the feedback. ADH also causes constrictory effects on blood vessels. (2)

21. Describe the role of alcohol and caffeine in the concentration of urine.

Ans Alcohol inhibits the release of ADH and caffeine interferes with ADH action and sodium reabsorption. Thus, both of these artifically dilute the urine. Such compounds which dilute urine are called diuretic substances. (2)

22. Discuss the regulation of kidney function by the heart.

Ans Atrial Natriuretic Factor (ANF) is secreted by the atria of heart. It causes vasodilation (dilation of blood vessels) and thereby, decrease the blood pressure. ANF works antagonistically to RAAS. (2)

23. Explain the process of micturition. **NCERT**

Ans Refer to text on page no. 453.

24. **State the importance of counter-current systems in renal functioning.**

Ans Counter-current mechanism has been evolved in higher vertebrates (birds and mammals including man) to excrete hypertonic urine (urine is more concentrated than blood) for conserving body water so necessary for land life. (2)

25. **What will happen if the stretch receptors of the urinary bladder wall are totally removed? Explain.**

Ans As urine collects in the urinary bladder, the muscular walls of the bladder distend to accommodate it. The stretch receptors on the walls of the bladder send signals to the CNS by stimulating the sensory nerve ending in the bladder. It causes an urge to pass out urine. So, if the stretch receptors are totally removed from the bladder, urine will not be collected in the bladder and urination will keep continuing. (2)

Short Answer Type II Questions

3 Marks

26. **How is glomerular filtrate hypertonic and hypotonic in descending and ascending limb of loop of Henle, respectively? What is the effect of ADH on collecting tubules?**

Ans Counter-current system is found in two limbs of loop of Henle. The ascending limb transports Na^+ and some urea into surrounding medullary tissue. It is impermeable to water. So, it makes urine diluted or hypotonic. The walls of descending limbs are permeable to water and salt, so Na^+ and water from surrounding fluid are absorbed. So, the content of urine becomes hypertonic.

ADH (Antidiuretic Hormone) is secreted when the osmotic pressure of blood increases due to excess loss of water and body.

The hormone renders the walls of distal convoluted tubule, Collecting Tubule (CT) and collecting duct of a nephron permeable to water and increases the reabsorption of water into the surrounding tissues and particular capillaries. The urine becomes hyperosmotic and less in volume and water is conserved in the body.

$(1\frac{1}{2} + 1\frac{1}{2})$

27. **Give full form of ANF. Name the organ that secretes it. Under what condition of the body is it released? What is its role in regulating kidney function?**

Or

Write a brief note on atrial natriuretic factor.

Ans ANF is commonly known as Atrial Natriuretic Factor. (1)

ANF is a hormone produced by the walls of the atria of the heart in response to an increase in blood volume and pressure. It increases sodium excretion and decreases blood pressure. ANF inhibits release of renin from **Juxta Glomerular Apparatus** (JGA) and thereby, inhibits NaCl reabsorption by the collecting duct and reduces aldosterone release from the adrenal gland. (1)

Function The function of counter-current mechanism is to concentrate NaCl in the intestitial fluid and thereby cause water to diffuse out of the collecting tubules and ducts and concentrate the urine. (1)

28. **Describe the role of liver, lungs and skin in excretion.**

Ans Refer to text on page no. 453 and 454.

29. **Describe the disorders of excretory system.**

Ans Refer to text on page no. 454.

Long Answer Type Questions

5 Marks

30. **Give a brief account of the counter-current mechanism.** **NCERT**

Ans Refer to text on page no. 451 and 452.

31. **The glomerular filtrate in the loop of Henle gets concentrated in the descending and then gets diluted in the ascending limbs. Explain.** **NCERT Exemplar**

Ans. The gradient of increasing hyperosmolarity of medullary interstitium is maintained by a counter-current mechanism and the proximity between the Henle's loop and vasa recta.

This gradient is mainly caused by NaCl and urea. The transport of these substances facilitated by the special arrangement of Henle's loop and vasa recta is called the counter-current mechanism. NaCl is transported by the ascending limb of Henle's loop, which is exchanged with the descending limb of vasa recta. NaCl is returned to the medullary interstitium by the ascending part of vasa recta. But, contrarily, the water diffuses into the blood of ascending limb of vasa recta and is carried away into the general blood circulation.

Permeability to urea is found only in the deeper parts of thin ascending limbs of Henle's loops and collecting ducts. Urea diffuses out of the collecting ducts and enters into the thin ascending limb. A certain amount of urea recycled in this way is trapped in medullary interstitium by the collecting tubule. This mechanism helps in the maintenance of a concentration gradient in the medullary interstitium. Presence of such gradient helps in an easy passage of water from the collecting tubule, resulting in the formation of concentrated urine (filtrate), i.e. nearly four times concentrated than the initial filtrate formed. (5)

32. **Define haemodialyser. Describe the process of kidney transplantation.**

Ans Refer to text on page no. 454-455.

SUMMARY

- **Excretion** is the process of removal of waste material from the body.
- **Osmoregulation** is the process of maintaining osmotic and ionic concentration of body fluid.
- **Type of excretory products** depends on the habitat, feeding habits and metabolism of an organism. It can be ammonia (ammonotelism), urea (ureotelism) and uric acid (uricotelism).
- **Human excretory system** consists of two kidneys, two ureters, a urinary bladder and a urethra.
- **Human kidneys** are mesodermal in origin, with retroperitoneal arrangement (present outside coelomic cavity). Externally, they are reddish brown, bean-shaped. Right kidney is smaller and placed lower compared to left one.
- Internally, human kidneys contain three protective layer, renal capsule, adipose capsule and renal fascia. Kidney is divided into two zones, i.e. an outer **cortex** and an inner **medulla**.
- **Nephrons** are the structural and functional unit of kidneys. They consists of renal corpuscle or Malpighian body and renal tubules.
- **Renal corpuscles** consists of **Bowman's capsule**, i.e. a cup-shaped structure containing network of thin capillaries called **glomerulus**.
- **Renal tubules** are associated with process of reabsorption and secretion. It is formed of four parts, i.e. proximal convoluted tubule, Henle's loop (descending, ascending and a main loop), DCT and collecting duct.
- **Ureters** are muscular tubes conveying urine from kidneys to the bladder. **Urinary bladder**, pear-shaped structure where urine is stored. **Urethra** is present in mammals only, it is a canal extending from bladder to outside *via* external urethral orifice.
- **Urea** is main excretory product in humans, formed in the liver *via* **deamination** and **ornithine cycle**.
- **Urine** formation is called **uropoiesis** and occurs in three steps. These are ultrafiltration, selective reabsorption and tubular secretion.
- **Ultrafiltration** occurs when blood containing water and solutes enters the afferent arteriole in glomerulus. Glomerulus Filtration Rate (GFR) is the amount of filtrate formed by kidneys per minute (180 L/day).
- **Selective reabsorption** is the absorption of almost 99% of filtrate in renal tubules. 65% of filtrate reabsorbed in PCT (Na^+, K^+, glucose, amino acids, etc.) Reabsorption is minimum in Henle's loop, absorption of Na^+ occurs in DCT due to aldosterone. In collecting duct, water reabsorption occurs.
- **Counter-current mechanism** concentrates the urine produced in mammals in the loop of Henle.
- **Tubular secretion** is the phenomenon of secretion of metabolic wastes by tubular cells into the filtrate. It is an active process which occurs in PCT, DCT and collecting duct. It helps in maintenance of ionic and acid-base balance of body fluid.
- The blood supply to kidneys is maintained by the renal artery and renal veins.
- **Regulation of kidney functions** occurs *via*.
  - **Juxtaglomerular apparatus**, it works *via* Renin-Angiotensin Aldosterone System (RAAS).
  - **Antidiuretic Hormone** (ADH) or vasopressin secreted by neurohypophysis of pituitary gland. It is released when a change in blood volume, body fluid volume and ionic concentration by hypothalamus.
  - **Atrial Natriuretic Factor** (ANF) works opposite to RAAS.
- **Micturition** is the release of urine from bladder. It occurs due to contraction and relaxation of urinary bladder and urethral sphincter. The signal for micturition originates from a stretched bladder.
- **Urine** is pale yellow (due to urochrome pigment), slightly acidic (pH-6), normally transparent and faintly aromatic.
- **Accessory excretory organs** are skin (sweat), lungs (CO_2), liver (bile pigments), intestine (inorganic ions), saliva, etc.
- **Disorders of excretory system** occurs due to failure of kidneys or malfunctioning of renal components, e.g. renal stones, nephritis (inflammation of kidney), renal failure, anuria, uremia, etc.
- **Artificial kidney** or **Dialysis** is used when both kidneys get damaged.
- **Renal transplantation** is the ultimate cure for treating kidney failures.

Chapter Practice

Multiple Choice Questions

1 Mark

1. The following substances are the excretory products in animals. Choose the least toxic form among them.
   (a) Urea
   (b) Uric acid
   (c) Ammonia
   (d) CO_2

2. Which of the followmg pairs is wrong?
   (a) Uricotelic–Birds
   (b) Ureotelic–Insects
   (c) Ammonotelic–Tadpole
   (d) Ureotelic–Elephant

3. We can produce a concentrated/dilute urine. This is facilitated by a special mechanism. Identify the mechanism.
   (a) Reabsorption from PCT
   (b) Reabsorption from collecting duct
   (c) Reabsorption/secretion in DCT
   (d) Counter-current mechanism in Henle's loop/vasa recta

4. Which of the following statements is incorrect?
   (a) ADH helps in water elimination making urine hypotonic
   (b) Protein free-fluid is filtered from blood plasma into the Bowman's capsule
   (c) Glucose is actively reabsorbed in the proximal convoluted tubule
   (d) Henle's loop plays an important role in concentrating the urine

5. The pH of human urine is approximately
   (a) 6.5 (b) 7
   (c) 6 (d) 7.5

6. Dialysing unit (artificial kidney) contains a fluid which is almost same as plasma except that it has
   (a) high glucose
   (b) high urea
   (c) no urea
   (d) high uric acid

7. Match the following columns.

	Column I		Column II
A.	Hematuria	1.	Excess of protein level in urine.
B.	Ketonuria	2.	The presence of high ketone bodies in urine.
C.	Glycosuria	3.	The presence of blood cells in urine.
D.	Proteinuria	4.	The presence of glucose in urine.

Codes

	A	B	C	D
(a)	3	2	4	1
(b)	4	3	2	1
(c)	3	4	2	1
(d)	3	2	1	4

Assertion-Reason Type Questions

1 Mark

■ **Direction** (Q. Nos. 8-15) *In each of the following questions, a statement of Assertion (A) is given followed by corresponding statement of Reason (R). Of the statements, mark the correct answer as*

(a) If both A and R are true and R is the correct explanation of A
(b) If both A and R are true, but R is not the correct explanation of A
(c) If A is true, but R is false
(d) If A is false, but R is true

8. **Assertion** (A) RAAS gets activated in a person suffering from diarrhoea.
   Reason (R) Both loss of water and electrolytes takes place in such a patient.

9. **Assertion** (A) Haemodialysis is used to clean the excretory products generated from the blood.
   Reason (R) Dialysing fluid has same composition as that of plasma except, nitrogenous wastes.

10. **Assertion** (A) Dialytic fluid/solution is iso-osmotic to blood plasma.
    Reason (R) The fluid used during dialysis procedure contain glucose and ions.

11. **Assertion** (A) Some ureotelic organisms retain some amount of urea in their kidney matrix.
    Reason (R) The ureotelic organisms maintain desired osmolarity by retaining some urea.
12. **Assertion** (A) Malpighian tubules are excretory organs in most of the insects.
    Reason (R) These help in excretion of urea and creatinine.
13. **Assertion** (A) During urination, the back flow of urine into the ureters is prevented.
    Reason (R) Urethral sphincters relax during urination.
14. Given below is the diagrammatic representation of a nephron. Comment upon the appropriateness of both Assertion and Reason.

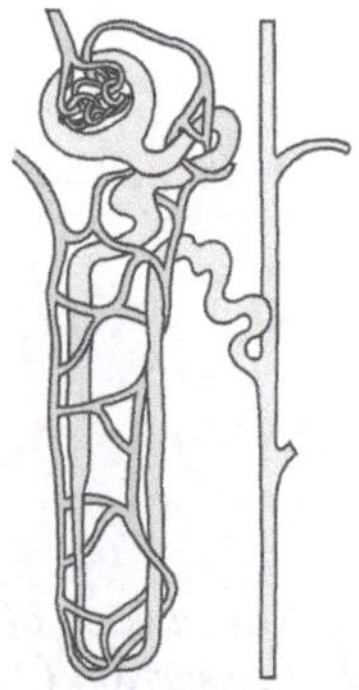

    Assertion (A) Tubular secretion is an important step in urine formation which occurs in nephron.
    Reason (R) It helps in the maintenance of ionic and acid base balance of body fluids.
15. **Assertion** (A) Women are more prone to urinary tract infections than man.
    Reason (R) In women, the urethra is short (4cm) as compared to men (20 cm). This makes it easier for the bacteria to get into the bladder.

Answers

1. (b)	2. (b)	3. (d)	4. (b)	5. (c)	6. (c)
7. (a)	8. (a)	9. (b)	10. (d)	11. (a)	12. (c)
13. (b)	14. (a)	15. (a)			

Very Short Answer Type Questions

(1 Mark)

16. Explain the function of vasa recta?
17. What difference is observed in the ascending and the descending limbs of Henle's loop regarding permeability to H_2O ?
18. Name the pigment that causes pale yellow colour of urine.
19. What is the composition of sweat produced by sweat gland?

Short Answer Type I Questions

(2 Marks)

20. What changes occur to the walls of Distal Convoluted Tubule (DCT) of a nephron when vasopressin is released by pituitary into the bloodstream?
21. The longer loop of Henle produces more hypertonic urine. Is this statement true or false? Explain it correctly.
22. Explain mechanism by which nephron adds some materials to the filtrate?
23. How is urea formed in the animal body?
24. What is an artificial kidney?

Short Answer Type II Questions

(3 Marks)

25. Describe some important metabolic wastes excreted from the human body.
26. How does the loop of Henle help in concentrating the urine in mammals of terrestrial adaptation?
27. How are the major excretory products eliminated from the body?
28. Where do ultrafiltration, reabsorption and secretion occur in a nephron?
29. Briefly describe the hormonal regulation of kidney function.
30. Write a brief note on diabetes insipidus.

Long Answer Type Questions

5 Marks

31. Describe the role of different organs in the process of excretion.
32. What is the filtration process? How is it performed?
33. Sketch and label the excretory system of man. Also give a brief account on the functions of kidney.

Case Based Questions

4/5 Marks

34. Study the given figure and answer the following questions.

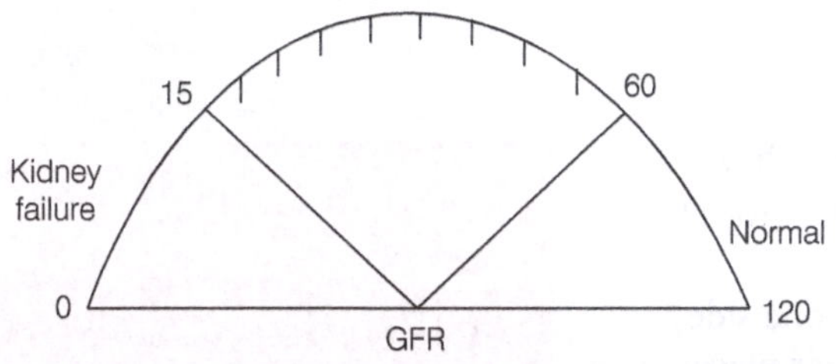

(i) What is the full form of GFR ?
(ii) What are some of the disorders of the excretory system ?
(iii) What is the use of GFR test?

Or

(iii) What could be the possible treatment in case of kidney failure?

35. Refer to the given graph answer the questions that follows.

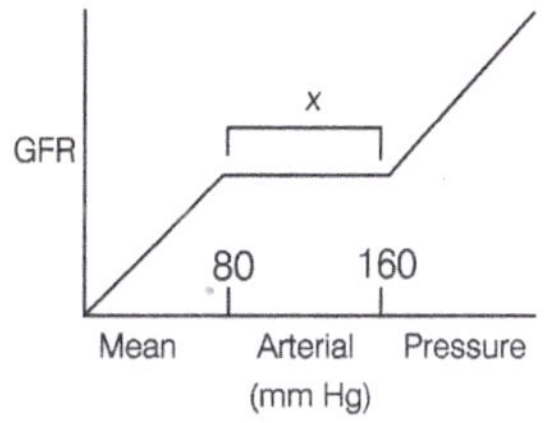

(i) What does '*X*' represents in the above graph?
(ii) Explain '*X*' in the above graph.
(iii) How neural control can over-ride renal autoregulation?

Or (iii) If the GRR is 125 mL/min and the renal plasma flow is 650 mL/min, then what will be their filtration fraction.

36. Observe the given diagram *A* and answer the questions that follows

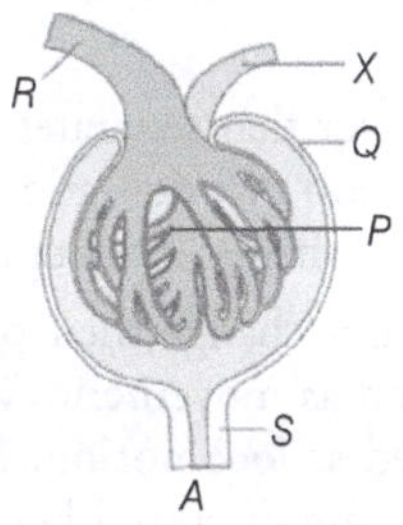

(i) What is the role of structure *A* shown above?
(ii) Give one point of differentiation between labels *R* and *X*.
(iii) Identify *X* and write any one of its feature.
(iv) Define podocytes.
(v) Where do we find label '*S*' in the kidney?

CHAPTER

20

Locomotion and Movement

The distinctive character that separates living from non-living is that, they can change their position or orientation. This is required for various purposes such as search of food, shelter, preying, mating, etc.

When organisms do not change their position and just orient from one side to an other, it is called as **movement**. When there is a change in their place or location, it is called as **locomotion**. Both may be voluntary or involuntary in nature. The details are discussed below.

TOPIC 01 Body Movements, Locomotion in Organisms and Muscle Structure

Movement

It is one of the most important characteristics of living organisms.

The movement of living things are **autonomic** (self-sustained) while, the movement of non-living objects is **induced** (due to external forces). Both animals and plants exhibit wide range of movements. Movement of animals can be **muscular** and **non-muscular**. Plants show **cellular** and often **organ** movement. The study of movement is called **Kinesiology.**

Types of Movement

Three main types of movement are exhibited by the cells of the human body. These are as follows

1. **Amoeboid** (Pseudopodial) **Movement** Movement with the help of finger-shaped protoplasmic extensions (i.e. **pseudopodia** or **false feet** as seen in *Amoeba*) is called **amoeboid movement.**

These types of movements are also found in leucocytes and macrophages of blood when they leave blood to move into tissues. Cytoskeletal elements, like microfilaments are also involved in this type of movement.

2. **Ciliary Movement** Movement in the cells or organs with the help of cilia is called **ciliary movements.** Cilia are short, fine, hair-like structures present all over the body surface in large numbers, which beat in succession in **coordinated manner** to help in movements. Removal of dust particles and foreign substances through the trachea, passage of ova through female reproductive tract occurs through cilia.

   This type of movement occurs in most of our internal tubular organs that are lined by ciliated epithelium.
3. **Flagellar Movement** This type of movement occurs in protozoans like *Trypanosoma, Euglena*, etc., along with sponges. In sponges, flagella of choanocyte cells maintain a regular current of water through the canal system. In case of human beings, the sperms swim in water or in female genital tract with the help of its flagellar movements only.
4. **Muscular Movement** Movement with the help of muscles is called muscular movement. These are brought about by the movement of myofilaments packed within the muscle fibres.

   The contractile property of muscles is used effectively to bring about the movement. This type of movement is found in majority of multicellular animals including humans.

Locomotion

It defined as the movement of an animal as a whole from one place to another. These are voluntary movements that result in change of place or location.

It requires a perfect coordinated activity of **muscular, skeletal** and **neural system.** Locomotion takes several forms such as walking, running, flying and swimming, etc.

Advantages of Locomotion

It helps the animal in search of food, shelter, mate, to escape from enemies/predators, to locate suitable areas for breeding or to disperse to new locations. Methods of locomotion in animals vary with their habitats and the demand of situation.

> **Locomotion Movement**
>
> It is very difficult to separate movement from locomotion because an animal cannot change its place (locomotion) without movement, e.g. **cilia** helps in movement of food inside cytopharynx and in locomotion in ***Paramecium***. **Tentacles** in ***Hydra*** are used for capturing prey and in locomotion.
>
> **Limbs** are used for change of body postures as well as for locomotion in **humans** and other animals.
>
> This suggests that movements and locomotion are interlinked thus, stating that all locomotions are movements, but all movements are not locomotions.

Muscles

These are made up of highly specialised thin and elongated cells called **muscle fibres.** Muscles arise from the **embryonic mesoderm.** It makes about 40-50% of a human body weight.

Muscles exhibit various special properties, some of them are given below

(i) **Contractibility** The cells of muscle can be shorten considerably and return to the original relaxed state.

(ii) **Excitability** It is due to the energy stored in the electrical potential difference across the plasma membrane.

(iii) **Muscles** also possess properties of extensibility and elasticity (because of proteins–actin and myosin).

> **Knowledge Plus**
>
> - Muscle tissue is the most abundant tissue in most animals.
> - Human body has some 639 separate muscles that bring about movement in its various body organs.
> - The study of muscle is called Myology.
> - The largest/biggest muscle in human body is gluteus maximus (hip muscle), the longest muscle is sartorius (back muscle), the strongest muscle is masseter (jaw muscles).
> - The longest smooth muscle is rectus abdomins and the shortest muscle is stapedial muscle.
> - Muscles of iris and ciliary body are ectodermal in origin.

Types of Muscles

Muscles have been classified using different criteria, i.e. **location**, **appearance** and **nature of regulation** of their activities. Based on their location, the muscles are of three types, i.e. skeletal, visceral and cardiac.

1. Skeletal or Striated Muscles

These muscles function in association with the skeleton of organism. Under the microscope, they show a striped appearance and hence are called **striated muscles.**

They are also known as **voluntary muscles** as their activities are under the voluntary control of the central nervous system. They are primarily involved in locomotory actions and change of body postures.

2. Visceral or Smooth Muscles

They are found in the inner walls of hollow visceral (internal) organs of body like alimentary canal, reproductive tract, etc.

They do not exhibit any striation, and are smooth in appearance and hence, are called **smooth muscles** (non-striated muscle). They are also known as **involuntary muscles** as they are not under the voluntary or direct control of the nervous system.

They assist in the transportation of materials, e.g. movement of food through the digestive tract and gametes through the genital tract.

3. Cardiac Muscles

It occurs in the wall of the heart and in walls of big veins (e.g. pulmonary veins and superior vena cava), where these veins enter the heart. These are **striated** and **involuntary** in nature. Presence of **oblique bands** and **intercalated** discs are their characteristic feature.

These assemble in a branching pattern to form a cardiac muscle. They never get fatigue.

Knowledge Plus

- Two types of muscles fibres are found in the body. Slow twitch (in muscles that require endurance) and fast twitch (in muscles that contract quickly).
- High intensity exercise causes an increase in muscle mass, while low intensity exercise, aerobic exercise, build mass, but do not burn calories.

On the basis of functions the skeletal muscles are classified as follows

Functional Classification of Skeletal Muscles

Types of Skeletal Muscles	Functions	Examples
Flexor	Muscles, which bend one part of the body over the other.	Biceps bending forearm towards upper arm.
Extensor	Muscles, which extend or straighten the limbs.	Triceps extending forearm and is antagonous to biceps.
Abductor	Muscles, which pull a limb away from the median line.	Deltoids of shoulder.
Adductor	Muscles, which bring a limb towards the median line of the body.	Latissimus dorsi, which draw the whole forelimb towards the body and is antagonous to deltoides.
Depressor	Muscles, which lower some part.	Depressor mandibularis lowers the lower jaw (similarly pectoralis major is the depressor muscle for the wings of birds).
Elevator	Antagonistic to depressors, as they raise a body part.	Masseter, which lifts the lower jaw (similarly pectoralis minor is the elevator muscle for the wings of birds).
Pronator	The muscle that turns the palm downward or backward.	Pronator teres in mammalian limbs.
Supinator	Antagonistic to pronator, i.e. turns the palm upward or forward.	Supinator in human forelimbs.
Sphinctor	Decrease the size of an opening and close it.	Pyloric sphincter of alimentary canal.
Dilator	The muscles around the openings, which increase their size and open them. Antagonistic to sphinctors.	Iris.
Rotator	Associated with rotatory movements of a body part.	Pyriformis, which raises and rotates the thigh.

Detailed Structure of a Skeletal Muscle

Skeletal muscle is made up of a number of **muscle bundles** or **fascicles** held together by **fascia** (collagenous connective tissue layer).

Composition of Muscle Bundle

Each muscle bundle contains a number of **muscle fibres** (muscle cells), bounded by **sarcolemma** (plasma membrane) and contains well-developed **endoplasmic reticulum** (sarcoplasmic reticulum), specialised for calcium storage in its sarcoplasm (cytoplasm).

Muscle fibre is a **syncitium** as its sarcoplasm contains many nuclei. There are large number of parallel arrangment of filaments called **myofilaments** or **myofibrils** (characteristic feature of muscle fibre).

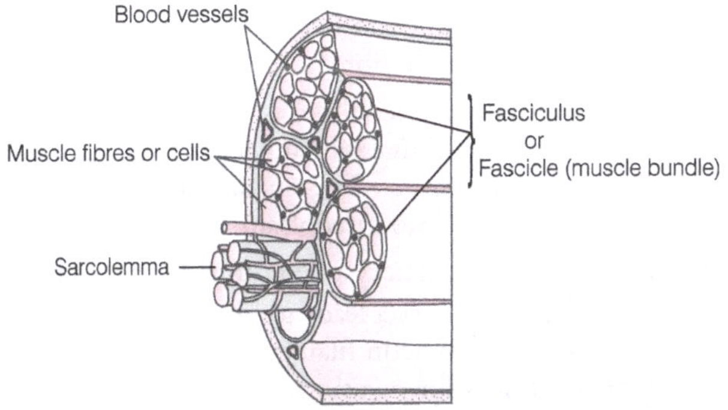

Fig. 20.1 Diagrammatic cross sectional view of a muscle showing muscle bundles and muscle fibres

Detailed Study of a Myofibril and Contractile Proteins

A myofibril has alternate **dark** and **light bands**. The dark bands are also called **Anisotropic band** or **A-band** which contains protein **myosin**. The light bands are called **Isotropic band** or **I-band** which contain protein **actin**.

The striated appearance of myofibril is due to the distribution pattern of the proteins **actin** and **myosin** in the muscle tissue. Both these proteins are arranged as rod-like structures, parallel to each other and also to the longitudinal axis of myofibrils. Actin filaments are thinner than myosin filaments.

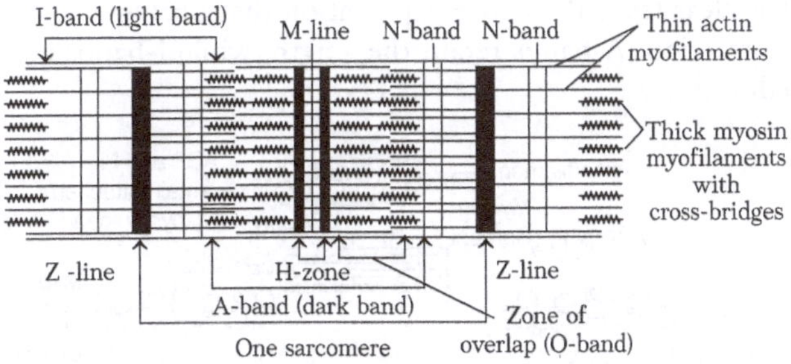

Fig. 20.2 Composition of sarcomere

Each I-band has its centre, a dark membrane called **Z-line** (an elastic fibre). It is also called **Z-disc** or **Krause's membrane** or **Dobie's line**. The part of the myofibril between two successive Z-lines is called a **sarcomere** (functional unit of muscle contraction). A sarcomere consists of the A-band and half of each adjacent I-band. A thin fibrous membrane called **M-line** present in the middle of A-band holds the thick filaments together.

The A and I-bands are arranged alternately throughout the length of myofibril. At the centre of A-band, a portion is present that is not overlapped by thin filaments. It is called the **H-zone** (Hensen zone).

In resting state, the edges of thin filaments on either side of thick filaments partially overlap each other leaving H-zone in the centre of thick filaments.

The thick myofilaments are formed by **myosin protein**. The thin myofilaments are formed by three types of proteins called **actin, tropomyosin** and **troponin**. These four proteins are collectively known as **contractile proteins.**

(i) **Myosin** Each myosin (thick) filament is a polymerised protein made up of many monomeric proteins called **meromyosins.** Each meromyosin has two important parts which are as follows

(a) **Globular Head** It has a short arm, called **Heavy Meromyosin** (HMM). The HMM components project outwards at regular distance and angle from each other, from surface of a polymerised myosin filament and known as **cross arm.**

The globular head is an **active ATPase enzyme,** which has binding sites for ATP and active sites for actin.

(b) **Tail** It is called the **Light Meromyosin** (LMM). The myosin molecule has two identical heavy chains and four light chains. The two heavy chains wrap spirally around each other to form a double helix. The light chains are the parts of the myosin heads and help in control the function of head during the contraction of muscle.

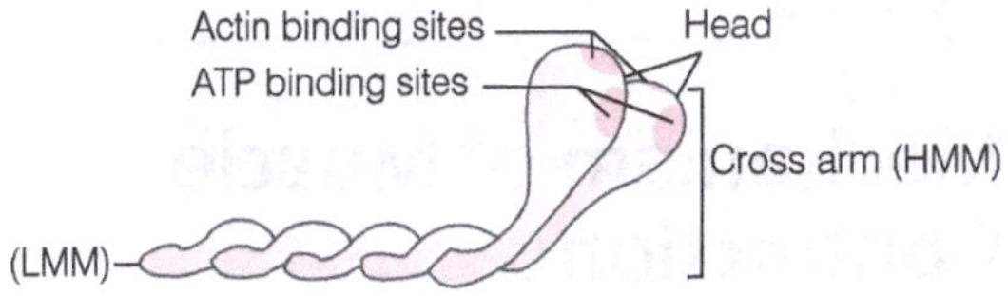

Fig. 20.3 Myosin monomer (meromyosin)

(ii) **Actin** It is a globular protein with low molecular weight. Each actin (thin) filament is made up of two 'F' (filamentous) actin helically wound to each other. Each **F-actin** is a polymer of monomeric **'G'** (globular) **actins.**

(iii) **Tropomyosin** Two filaments of this protein run close to the 'F' **actins** throughout its length.

(iv) **Troponin** It is a complex protein of three globular peptides (Troponin-T, Troponin-I and Troponin-C) distributed at regular intervals on tropomyosin.

In the resting stage of muscle fibre, a subunit of troponin masks the active sites for myosin on the actin filaments.

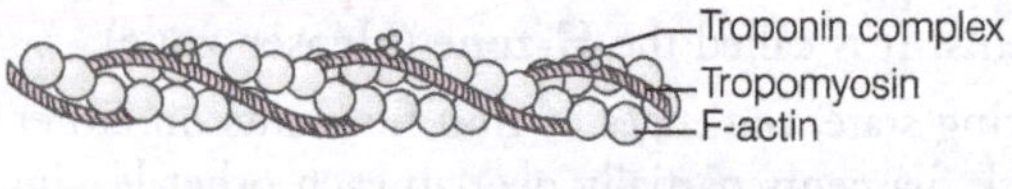

Fig. 20.4 An actin (thin) filament

> **Knowledge Plus**
> - Partial overlapping of primary myofilaments by the secondary myofilaments imparts dark appearance to the A-bands.
> - The strong affinity of the troponin for calcium ions is believed to initiate the contraction process.

Red and White Muscle Fibres

Birds and mammals have two kinds of striated muscle fibres, in their skeletal muscles, i.e. red (or slow) and white (or fast) muscle fibres.

Differences between Red and White Muscle Fibres

Red Muscle Fibres	White Muscle Fibres
They are dark red muscle fibres due to the presence of abundant myoglobin in them.	They are pale or whitish as they have less myoglobin.
Mitochondria are more in number, but they have less sarcoplasmic reticulum.	Mitochondria are few in number, but amount of sarcoplasmic reticulum is high.
They depend on aerobic process for energy.	They depend on anaerobic process for energy.
They have slow rate of contraction for long periods.	They have fast rate of contraction for short periods.
e.g. extensor muscle of the human back.	e.g. eyeball muscles.

Mechanism of Muscle Contraction
(Sliding Filament Theory)

The contraction of muscle is best explained by the **sliding filament theory**. It states that contraction of muscles takes place by the sliding of thin and thick filaments (that are placed over each other) with the help of **cross-bridge**. It reduces the length of the sarcomere.

This theory was proposed independently by **AF Huxley** and **R Niedergerke** and by **HE Huxley** and **Jean Hanson** in England in 1954. The sequence of events leading to contraction is initiated by a signal in the Central Nervous System (CNS), either from the **brain** (voluntary activity) or from **spinal cord** (reflex activity) *via* a motor neuron.

A **motor neuron** along with the muscle fibres connected to it, forms a motor unit and the action potential is conveyed to a **motor end plate** at neuromuscular junction, i.e. it is the junction between a motor neuron and sarcolemma of muscle fibre.

A **neurotransmitter** (acetylcholine) is released at the junction by the neural signal which generates an action potential in the sarcolemma. This spreads and causes the release of calcium ions into sarcoplasm.

Calcium plays a key regulatory role in muscle contraction. Increase in calcium ions level leads to binding of Ca^+ ions the troponin subunit on actin filament. This removes the masking of active sites for myosin.

Formation of Cross-Bridge

An ATP molecule joins the active site on myosin head of myosin myofilament. These heads contain an enzyme, **myosin ATPase** that along with Ca^{2+} and Mg^{2+} ions catalyses the breakdown of ATP.

$$\text{ATP} \xrightarrow[\text{Ca}^{2+},\,\text{Mg}^{2+}]{\text{Myosin ATPase}} \text{ADP} + \text{Pi} + \text{Energy.}$$

The energy is transferred to myosin head, which energises and straightens to join an active site on actin myofilament, forming a cross-bridge.

The energised cross-bridges move, causing the attached actin filaments to move towards the centre of A-band. The Z-line is also pulled inwards causing shortening of sarcomere, i.e. contraction.

It is clear from the above explanation that during contraction, A-bands retain the length, while I-bands get reduced.

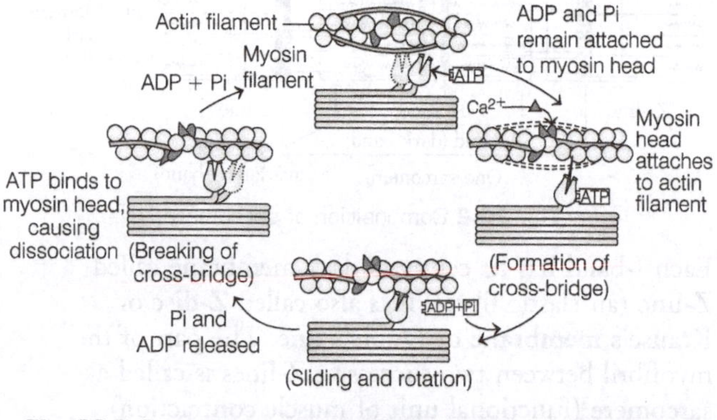

Fig. 20.5 Stages in cross-bridge formation, rotation of head and breaking of cross-bridge

The myosin head releases ADP and Pi, relaxes to its low energy state. The head detaches from actin myofilaments when new ATP joins it (cross-bridge broken).

In repeating cycle, the free head cleaves the new ATP. The cycles of cross-bridge formation and breakage is repeated causing further sliding.

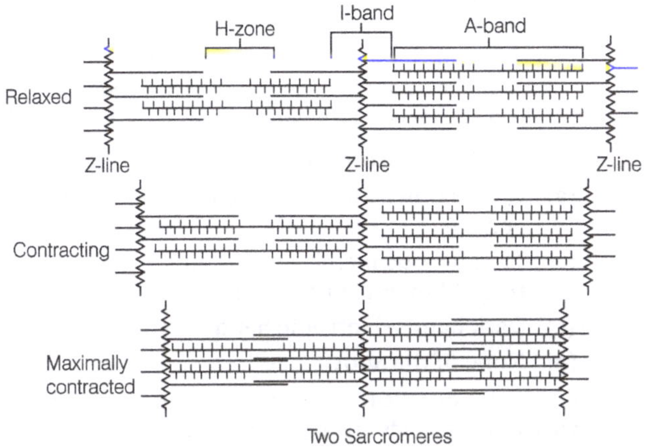

Fig. 20.6 Sliding filament theory of muscle contraction (movement of the thin filaments and the relative size of the I-band and H-zones)

Chemical Events during Muscle Contraction

All the chemical processes involved in the muscular contraction can be summarised as follows

1. The immediate source of energy is from the breakdown of ATP.
$$\text{ATP} \xrightarrow{\text{ATPase}} \text{ADP} + \text{Pi}$$
2. ATP is regenerated by the transfer of its high energy phosphate bond from creatine phosphate to ATP. However, this reaction is of limited scope and serves only the immediate needs.
$$\text{Creatine phosphate} + \text{ADP} \xrightarrow[\text{kinase}]{\text{Creatine}} \text{Creatine} + \text{ATP}$$
3. The next step is the metabolism of carbohydrate to yield pyruvate. The sources may be either glycogen in the muscle or glucose from the blood. These are converted into glucose 6-phosphate and finally into pyruvic acid and the process yields eight molecules of ATP for each glucose unit. In the lack of oxygen pyruvate is converted into lactate. The complete process is anaerobic.
4. Pyruvate and lactate are oxidised to carbon dioxide and water (citric acid cycle). One unit of glucose result in the formation of about 30 molecules of ATP.
5. Another source of energy for muscle contraction is the oxidation of fatty acids through the citric acid cycle.

Muscle Relaxation

After contraction, the calcium ions are pumped back to the sarcoplasmic cisternae, blocking the active sites on actin myofilaments. The Z-line returns to original position, i.e. relaxation of muscle fibre takes place.

Specialised Muscle Phenomenon

Certain specialised phenomena associated with muscles are as follows

All-or-None Law

It is also called **Bowditch's law**. This principle states that the response of a muscle or nerve to a stimulus is not proportionate to the intensity of stimulus instead a minimum (threshold) intensity is required. Above this intensity a muscle contracts always with its maximum strength. In other words, we can say a stimulus will either cause the muscle to contract or it will not.

Summation

If a skeletal muscle is stimulated and second stimulus is applied before relaxation is complete, a second contraction, which develops a greater tension, is fused to the first contraction. One possible reason may be that calcium (Ca^{2+}) ions remaining from the previous contraction and together with additional Ca^{2+} ions from second stimulus constitutes more activator Ca^{2+} ions than would be available if relaxation had been incomplete.

Muscle Fatigue

Muscle fatigue is the decrease in the force of contraction of a muscle after prolonged stimulation. A muscle is able to contract for a short time in the absence of oxygen. But it soon gets fatigued. The metabolic products of glycolysis mainly lactic acid accumulates around it. This accumulation leads to muscle fatigue. Normally, pain is experienced in the fatigued muscle. The site of fatigue is the **neuromuscular junction.**

Rigor Mortis

Just few hours after death, muscles stiffen and become hard. This condition is called rigor mortis. It first appears in lower jaw and then appears in all body muscles. It occurs due to permanent irreversible contraction between actin and myosin, which in turn occurs due to exhaustion of ATP from the blood.

Tetanus

A prolonged contraction without relaxation and which results from repeating stimulation before the muscle has a chance to relax at all. It is known as tetanus.

Topic Practice 1

Multiple Choice Questions

1 Mark

1. Movement of our limbs, jaws, tongue, etc., requires
   (a) ciliary movement
   (b) amoeboid movement
   (c) muscular movement
   (d) flagellar movement

Ans (c) The contractile property of the muscles is effectively used for locomotion and other movements by human beings and majority of multicellular organisms.

2. Choose the incorrect statement about muscles.
   (a) Muscles are specialised tissues of mesodermal origin
   (b) About 40-50% of the body weight is contributed by muscles
   (c) Muscles have special properties like excitability, conductivity and extensibility
   (d) None of the above

Ans (d) Muscle is a specialised tissue of mesodermal origin. About 40-50% of body weight of human adult is contributed by muscles. They have special properties like excitability, contractibility, conductivity, extensibility and elasticity.

3. In the centre of each I-band there is an elastic fibre called
   (a) I-line (b) Z-line
   (c) A-line (d) H-zone

Ans (b)

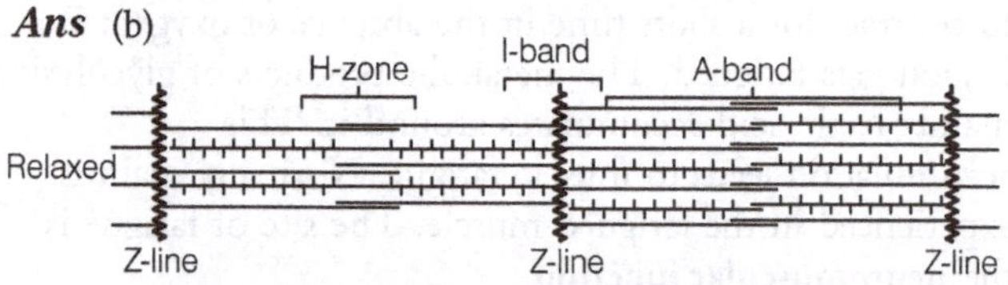

Sarcomere in relaxed state

4. The H-zone in the skeletal muscle fibre is due to
   (a) the absence of myofibrils in the central portion of A-band
   (b) the central gap between myosin filaments in the A-band
   (c) the central gap between actin filaments extending through myosin filaments in the A-band
   (d) extension of myosin filaments in the central portion of the A-band

Ans (c) H-zone in skeletal muscle is the central gap between actin filaments extending through myosin filaments in the A-band.

Alternate arrangement of dark and light bands gives the striated appearance to a skeletal muscle. At the centre of A-band, a comparatively less dark zone called H-zone is present. In the centre of H-zone, M-line formed by the threads that connect the myofilaments.

5. Choose the incorrect pair.
   (a) Globular head of meromyosin – Active ATPase enzyme
   (b) Thin fibrous membrane holding thick filaments in A-band – M-line
   (c) Dark bands–Isotropic band
   (d) None of the above

Ans (c) Dark bands called 'A' bands are anisotropic bands whereas light bands are isotropic or I-bands.

6. F-actin is a polymer of
   (a) G (molecular)-actin (b) G (globular)-actin
   (c) G (meromyosin)-actin (d) All of these

Ans (b) Each actin (thin) filament is made up of two F-(filamentous) actins, which are helically wound to each other. Each F-actin is a polymer of monomeric G (globular)-actins.

7. Cross arms of the myosin monomer consists of
   (a) outward projection of G-actin filament
   (b) outward projection of the head region of meromyosin
   (c) outward projection of the tail region of meromyosin
   (d) Both (b) and (c)

Ans (b) Outward projection of head region of meromyosin. The HMM component, i.e. the head and short arm projects outwards at regular distance and angle from each other from the surface of polymerised myosin filament and is called cross arm.

8. Actin binding sites are located on
   (a) troponin (b) tropomyosin
   (c) meromyosin (d) Both (a) and (c)

Ans (c) The globular head, i.e. HMM is an active ATPase enzyme and has binding sites for ATP and active sites for actin.

9. Neuromuscular junction is a junction between
   (a) two neurons and muscles
   (b) sensory neurons and muscles
   (c) motor neurons and sarcolemma of muscles
   (d) sensory neurons and sarcolemma of muscles

Ans (c) The junction between a motor neuron and the sarcolemma of the muscle fibre is called the neuromuscular junction or motor end-plate.

10. For how long, contraction of the muscles continues in sliding filament theory?

(a) Till ATP binds to myosin head

(b) Till ADP binds to myosin head

(c) Till Ca^{2+} present in sarcoplasm

(d) Till polymerisation of myosin head is going on

Ans (c) Sliding of actin and myosin filaments continues till the Ca^{2+} ions are pumped back to the sarcoplasmic cisternae, resulting in masking the actin filaments. This causes the return of Z-lines back to their original position, i.e. relaxation.

Very Short Answer Type Questions

(1 Mark)

11. Give reason for variation in methods of locomotion.

Ans Methods of locomotion vary with animal's habitat and demand of situation.

12. Give the name of the cells/tissues in human body which

(i) exhibit amoeboid movement.

(ii) exhibit ciliary movement. **NCERT Exemplar**

Ans (i) Macrophages.

(ii) Ciliated epithelium of trachea.

13. Which property of muscles is used effectively in muscular movement?

Ans Contractile property of muscles.

14. Label the different components of actin filament in the diagram given below. **NCERT Exemplar**

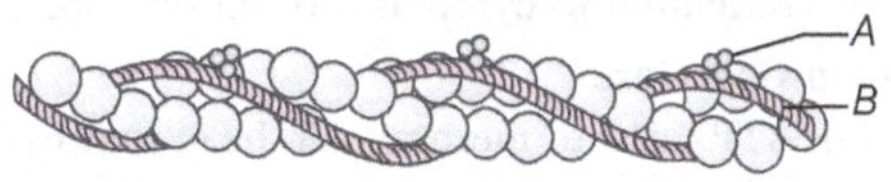

Ans *A*–Troponin *B*–Tropomyosin

15. Fill in the blanks

(i) Thin filament of myofibril contains two F actins and two other proteins namely ...... and ....

(ii) In a muscle fibre Ca^{2+} is stored in........ **[NCERT]**

Ans (i) Troponin and tropomyosin.

(ii) Sarcoplasm.

16. Give the name of oxygen carrying pigment present in skeletal muscle.

Ans Myoglobin or Muscle haemoglobin.

17. Give an example of red muscle fibre.

Ans Extensor muscle of human back.

18. Which compound provides energy for muscle contraction?

Ans ATP

19. Which energy is converted to mechanical energy during contraction ?

Ans Chemical energy.

20. State all or none law ?

Ans **All-or-None Law** States that a muscle either responds to a stimulus maximally or it does not responds at all. Skeletal muscles do not follow this rule. This law is also called Bowditch's law.

21. What causes muscle fatigue ?

Ans Accumulation of lactic acid.

22. What is rigor mortis ?

Ans Rigor mortis is the permanent stiffening of muscles after death. It occurs due to exhaustion of ATP from blood.

Short Answer Type I Questions

(2 Marks)

23. Name the type of movement found in majority of multicellular animals. Explain.

Ans Muscular movement is the type of movement found in majority of multicellular organisms.

This occurs with the help of muscles. These are brought about by movement of myofilaments present within the muscle fibre. (1+1)

24. Sarcolemma, sarcoplasm and sarcoplasmic reticulum refer to a particular type of cell in our body. Which is this cell and to what parts of that cell do these names refer to? **[NCERT Exemplar]**

Ans The cell is muscle.

These names refer to the following parts

Sarcolemma–Plasma membrane

Sarcoplasm–Cytoplasm

Sarcoplasmic reticulum–Endoplasmic reticulum (2)

25. Why is muscle fibre a syncitium? How are myofilaments arranged in it?

Ans Muscle fibre is a syncitium as the sarcoplasm contains many nuclei.

Myofilaments are parallelly arranged and are present in large number in muscle fibre. (1+1)

26. Write true or false. Correct each false statement to make it true.

(i) Actin is present in thin filament.

(ii) H-zone of striated muscle fibre represents both thick and thin filaments.

(iii) In a muscle fibre, Ca^{2+} is stored in nucleus.

(iv) Thin filaments of myofibrils contain 2-F actins. **NCERT**

Ans (i) True.

(ii) False, H-zone of striated muscle fibre represents only thick filaments.

(iii) False, in a muscle fibre, Ca^{2+} is stored in sarcoplasmic reticulum.

(iv) True. ($\frac{1}{2} \times 4$)

27. Name the two important parts of meromyosin.

Ans Two important parts of meromyosin are

(i) Globular head with short arm, called Heavy Meromyosin (HMM).

(ii) Tail, called the Light Meromyosin (LMM). (1×2)

28. What kind of muscle fibres are richly found in the extensor muscles of the back? What characteristics enable these fibres to serve their purpose?

Ans Red striated muscle fibres. (1)

Their abundant myoglobin and mitochondria enable them to serve their purpose. (1)

29. Give differences between red and white muscle fibres, other than colour. **NCERT**

Ans Refer to text on page no. 466.

30. What is the role of calcium in muscle contraction?

Ans. Calcium plays a key regulatory role in muscle contraction. The increase in Ca^{2+} level leads to their binding to troponin subunit.

Thus, exposing active sites on F-actin leading to cross-bridge formation. (2)

Short Answer Type II Questions

3 Marks

31. What are the different types of movements exhibited by the cells of human body? **NCERT**

Ans Refer to text on page no. 462 and 463.

32. Mention and explain the special properties of muscle.

Ans Refer to text on page no. 463.

33. Give a brief account of visceral muscles. Mention their function.

Ans Refer to text on page no. 464.

34. How do you distinguish between a skeletal muscle and a cardiac muscle? **NCERT**

Ans Differences between skeletal muscle and cardiac muscle are

Skeletal Muscle	Cardiac Muscle
It is found in limbs, tongue, all parts in association with the skeleton of organism.	It is found in the walls of heart and large veins.
Fibres are unbranched.	Fibres are branched.
It is multinucleate.	It is uninucleate.
No oblique bridge and intercalated discs.	Oblique bridges and intercalated discs are present.
It gets fatigued soon.	It never gets fatigued.
It is voluntary in nature.	It is involuntary.

($\frac{1}{2} \times 6$)

35. Draw the diagram of a sarcomere of skeletal muscle showing different regions. **NCERT**

Ans Refer to fig. no. 20.2.

36. Describe the important steps in muscle contraction. **NCERT**

Ans Summary of steps in skeletal muscle contraction

(i) **Stimulation**

(a) Nerve impulse arrives at neuromuscular junction and release of acetylcholine takes place.

(b) Spreading of action potential through muscle fibre.

(c) The release of Ca^{2+} from sarcoplasmic reticulum to cytoplasm of muscle fibre.

(ii) **Contraction**

(a) ATP joins to meromyosin head that hydrolyses into ADP and Pi releasing energy, which in turn raises the head to high energy state (the head joins active site on actin, forming cross-bridge).

(b) ADP and Pi are released. And head returns to low energy state.

(c) Actin filament is thus, pulled towards centre of sarcomere. And a new ATP joins head, detaching it from actin filament.

(d) Above mentioned steps are thus, repeated many times during one contraction to draw the thin myofilaments further inward. ($1\frac{1}{2} \times 2$)

37. Explain the formation of a cross-bridge during muscle contraction.

Ans Refer to text on page no. 466 and 467.

38. Radha was running on a treadmill at a great speed for 15 minutes continuously. She stopped the treadmill and abruptly came out. For the next few minutes, she was breathing heavily/fast. Answer the following questions.

(i) What happened to her muscles when she strenously exercised?

(ii) How did her breathing rate change?

NCERT Exemplar

Ans (i) By strenous exercise, the metabolism of the muscle increases, which leads to increased consumption of oxygen and ATP. To meet this demand, blood supply of muscle is also enhanced.

(ii) Increased consumption of oxygen and increased production of CO_2 stimulates the respiratory centres, which causes the change of breathing rate.

(1½ × 2)

39. Why are muscles rigidly locked in whatever position they are after death? What is the phenomenon known as?

Ans Muscles require ATP to relax as well as to contract. On animal's death, its muscles soon exhaust ATP and lose the ability to contract or relax. They become rigidly locked in whatever position they were when ATP gets completely used up. This phenomenon is known as rigor mortis. It is used in determining the time of death.

(2+1)

Long Answer Type Questions

5 Marks

40. Differentiate between

(i) Actin and myosin filament

(ii) A-band and I-band.

(iii) Non-muscular and muscular movements

Ans (i) Differences between actin and myosin filaments are

Actin Filaments	Myosin Filaments
These are found in I-band.	These are found in A-band.
These are thin.	These are thick.
Cross-bridges (heads) are absent.	Cross-bridges (heads) are present.
It is a globular protein with low molecular weight.	It is a heavy molecular weight polymerised protein.

(2)

(ii) Differences between A-band and I-band are

A-Band	I-Band
It is formed of myosin filaments.	It is formed of only actin filaments.
It gives dark appearance.	It gives light appearance.
It has a light H-zone, in the centre.	It has dark Krause's membrane, in the centre.
It is anisotropic band which possesses two type of proteins.	It is isotropic band which possesses only one type of proteins.

(2)

(iii) Differences between non-muscular and muscular movements are

Non-muscular Movement	Muscular Movement
These movements include pseudopodial and ciliary movements.	These movements are brought about by movement of myofilaments within muscle firbres.
They persist in the animals in some of their cells.	These are found in majority of animals.

(1)

41. Explain sliding filament theory of muscle contraction with neat sketches. **NCERT Exemplar**

Ans Refer to text on page no. 466 and 467.

42. (i) How does a muscle return to its original form during relaxation? Also draw a diagram showing relaxation of muscle.

(ii) What causes muscle fatigue?

Ans (i) The calcium ions after contraction are quickly pumped back to the sarcoplasmic cisternae. This leads to blocking of active sites on actin. The Z-line returns to the original position. Causing muscles to return to its original position, i.e. relaxation form.

(2)

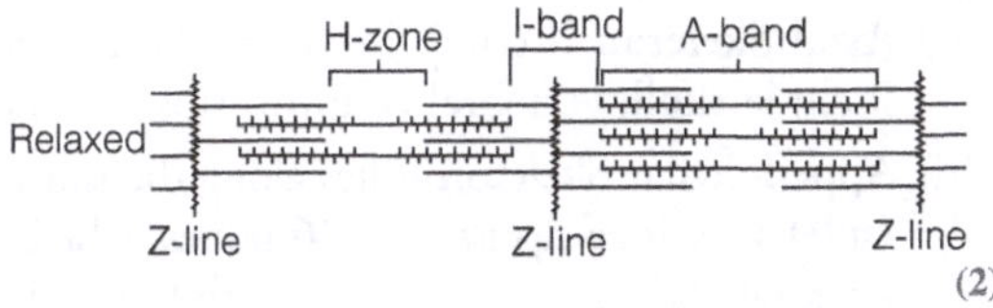

(2)

(ii) Repeated activation of the muscles leads to accumulation of lactic acid due to anaerobic breakdown of glycogen in them which causes fatigue.

(1)

TOPIC 02 Human Skeletal System : Structure, Functions and Disorders

Skeleton (Skeletal System)

The framework of bones and few cartilage constitute the skeletal system or skeleton. It is present inside the human body, so it is called **endoskeleton.** Bone and cartilage both are **specialised connective tissues.**

Bone has a very hard matrix due to **calcium salts** and made up of a protein called **ossein.**

Cartilage has slightly pliable matrix due to **chondroitin salts.** It is made up of a protein called **chondrin.**

Functions of Skeleton

Skeleton serves to perform following functions

(i) **Support** It gives support to softer body parts.

(ii) **Protection** It protects the delicate internal organs like brain, heart, lungs, etc.

(iii) **Muscle Attachment** Provide surface for attachment of muscles.

(iv) **Movement Bones** Help in bringing about movements also.

(v) **Blood Cell Formation** To manufacture blood corpuscles in bone marrow.

(vi) **Helps in Breathing and Hearing** Tracheal rings, sternum and ribs are helpful in breathing, while ear bones (middle ear) transmit sound vibrations.

Human Skeleton

The skeleton in human body is made up of **206 bones** and few cartilages. On the basis of the position of the skeletal structures in the human body, the endoskeleton is divisible into two parts

(i) **Axial Skeleton** It comprises of **80 bones,** which include skull, vertebral column, ribs and sternum.

(ii) **Appendicular Skeleton** It lies along the transverse (side) axis. It comprises of **126 bones,** which include pectoral and pelvic girdles and limb bones, i.e. bones of arms and legs.

Knowledge Plus

- Smallest bone is **stapes**.
- Longest and strongest bone is **femur**.
- Funny bone is **olecranon** present on top of the ulna.
- There are remarkable differences in the skull of male and female, thus together with the pelvis it is used for identification of sex.

The details of axial skeleton system are as follows

Skull

It is the bony framework of the head. It is composed of two sets of bones (cranial and facial) that form total of 22 bones [bones of middle ear (6 bones) and hyoid bone (1) are also included in bones of skull].

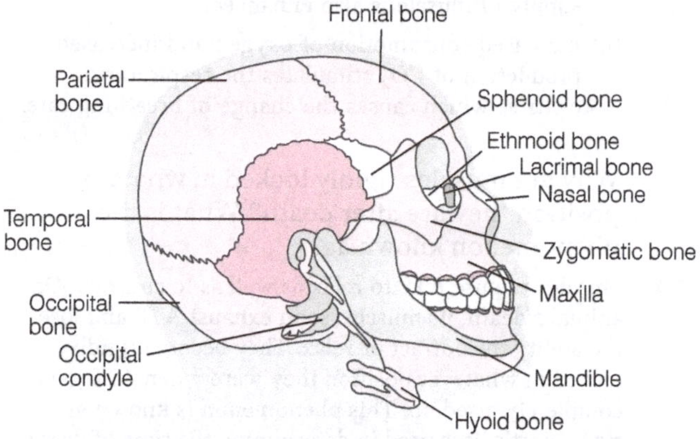

Fig. 20.7 Diagrammatic view of human skull

Bones of skull are as follows

(i) **Cranium** (8) includes frontal (1), parietal (2), temporal (2), occipital (1), sphenoid (1), ethmoid (1).
They form the hard protective outer covering (cranium) for the brain.

(ii) **Facial bones** (14) includes maxillae (2), palatine (2), mandible (1), vomer (1), nasal (2), zygomatic (2), lacrimal (2), inferior turbinate (2).
They form the front part of the skull.

(iii) **Ear ossicles** (6) includes 2 malleus, 2 incus, 2 stapes.
These three tiny bones belong to the middle ear.

(iv) **Hyoid** A U-shaped bone present at the base of buccal cavity. It is the only bone which is not in contact with any other bone. This is also callezd **tongue bone.**
Human skull is **dicondylic,** the skull region articulates with vertebral column with the help of two **occipital condyles.**

Vertebral Column

It is also called **backbone** or **spine.** It is dorsally placed, extending from the base of the skull and constitutes the main framework of the trunk.

It is made of 33 serially arranged units called **vertebrae.** It includes cervical (7), thoracic (12), lumbar (5), sacral (5-fused) and coccygeal (4-fused). The vertebral formula for humans is $C_7, T_{12}, L_5, S_5, C_{(4)}$.

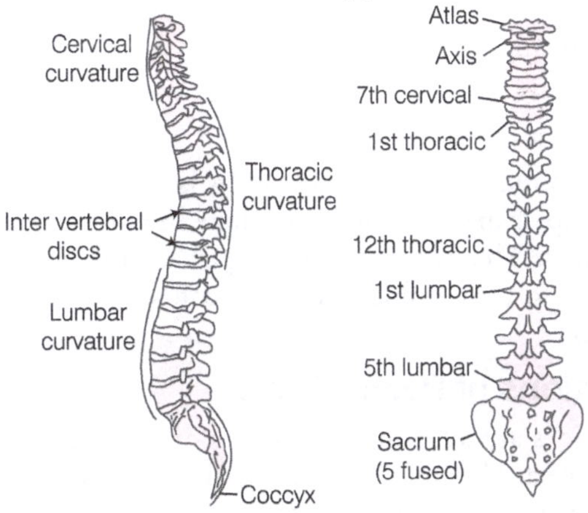

Fig. 20.8 Vertebral column (human)

> **Knowledge Plus**
> - Altas is the first vertebra and it articulates with the occipital condyles of skull.
> - Lumbar is the largest and the strongest in the vertebral column of mammals.

Functions of Vertebral Column

Vertebral column performed following functions

(i) Provides protection to the spinal cord.

(ii) Supports the head.

(iii) Allows flexion and bending of the back and body.

(iv) Also serves as point of attachment for the ribs.

Sternum

It is a flat daggar-shaped bone located on the ventral midline of thorax.

Ribs

These are the thin, flat curved bones that form a protective cage around the organs of upper body.

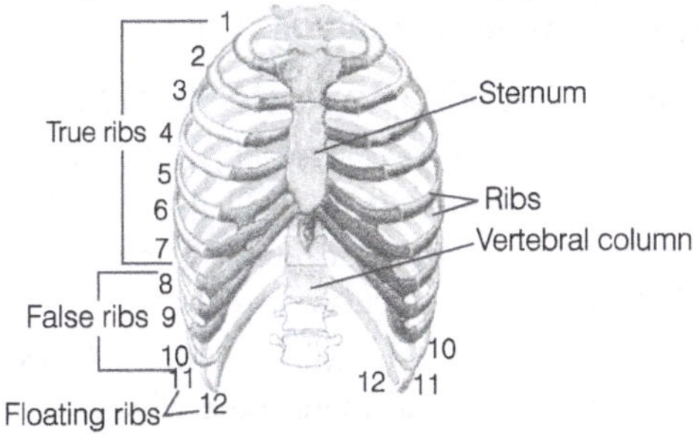

Fig. 20.9 Ribs and rib cage

The ribs are composed of **24 bones** arranged in **12 pairs,** connected dorsally to thoracic vertebrae and ventrally to sternum by **hyaline cartilage**. It has two articulation surfaces on its dorsal end and hence called **bicephalic.**

Ribs are mainly categorised into following types

(i) **True Ribs** The first seven pairs are attached directly with the sternum and are called true ribs.

(ii) **False Ribs** The 8th, 9th and 10th pairs of ribs join the seventh rib with the help of hyaline cartilage. They do not articulate directly with sternum. Hence, are called **vertebrochondral** (false) **ribs.**

(iii) **Floating Ribs** The last two (11th and 12th) pairs of ribs are not attached to the sternum at all and remain free anteriorly, hence called floating ribs.

Functions of Ribs

Ribs serve following functions

(i) They protect the heart, large blood vessels and lungs.

(ii) Bear respiratory muscles.

(iii) Also lower two pairs of ribs also protect the kidneys.

(iv) Ribs along with sternum and thoracic vertebrae form the rib cage.

The appendicular skeleton includes bones of limbs and pelvic and pectoral girdles. These are as follows

Limbs

The bones of the limbs alongwith girdles constitute the appendicular skeleton. Each limb is made of **30 bones.**

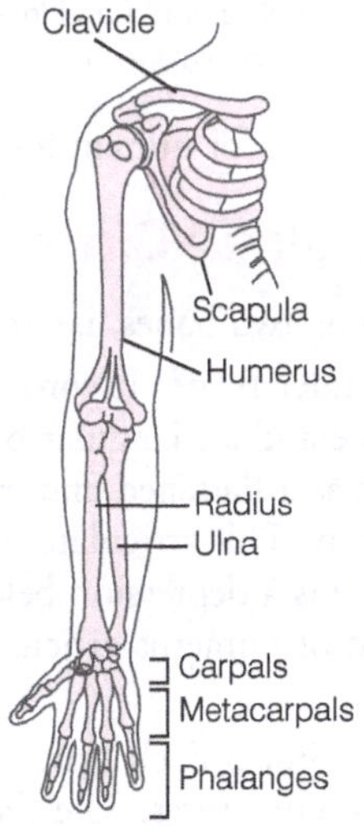

Fig. 20.10 Right pectoral girdle and upper arm (frontal view)

Forelimb

The bones of the hand (forelimb) constitute–**humerus** (1), **radius** (1), **ulna** (1), **carpals**/wrist bones (8), **metacarpals**/palm bones (5) and **phalanges**/digits (14).

The humerus and ulna together make up the elbow. The ulna is longer than the radius and connects more firmly to the humerus.

The radius contributes to the movement of the wrist.

The **phalangeal formula** for human hand is 2, 3, 3, 3, 3.

Hindlimb

The bones of the leg (hindlimb) constitute–**femur** (1), **tibia** (1), **fibula** (1), **tarsals** (7), **metatarsals** (5) and **phalanges** (14).

A cup-shaped bone called **patella** covers knee ventrally. It is a seasmoid bone (bone embedded within a tendon). Femur, tibia and fibula bones together support the **shank** of leg. Tarsals form the ankle, metatarsals form the sole and phalanges form the **digits** of the foot.

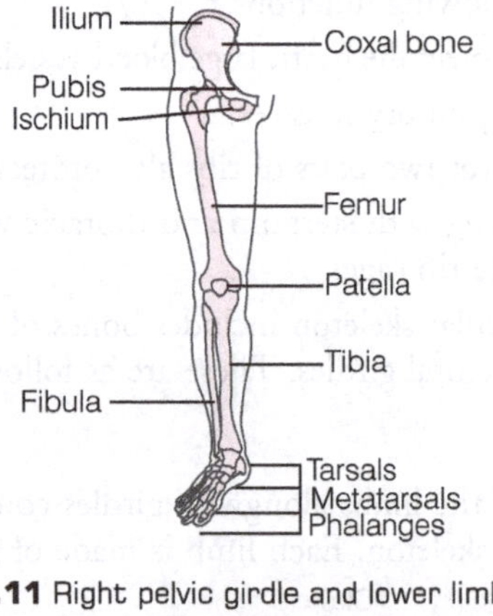

Fig. 20.11 Right pelvic girdle and lower limb bones (frontal view)

The **phalangeal formula** for human foot is 2, 3, 3, 3, 3.

Pectoral (Shoulder) Girdle

It consists of following two bones, i.e. scapula and clavicle.

(i) **Scapula** (Shoulder Blade) It consists of a sharp ridge-the **spine** and a triangular bone. The end of spine projects as a flattened and expanded portion called **acromion.** This articulates with the clavicle. **Glenoid cavity** is a depression below the acromian to which head of humerus articulates forming shoulder joint.

(ii) **Clavicle** (Collar Bone) Each clavicle is a long slender bone with two curvatures. The clavicle helps in articulation of the upper limb with axial skeleton.

Functions of Pectoral Girdle

This provides an attachment point for numerous muscles that allows shoulder and elbow joints to move.

Pelvic (Hip) Girdle

It is located in the lower part of the trunk. It consists of **two coxal** (hip) bones. Each coxal is also known as **ossa coxae** or **innominate bone.** This is formed by fusion of the following three bones

(i) Upper ilium (ii) Lower ischium

(iii) Inner pubis

The innominate at the middle of its lateral surface has a deep, cup-shaped **acetabulum,** where head of femur articulates. The two halves of the pelvic girdle meet ventrally to form **pubic symphysis** containing fibrous cartilage.

Functions of Pelvic Girdle

It provides articulation to the bones of the leg, supports and protects abdominal viscera. It also provides attachment to certain leg muscles.

Joints

The place of articulation between two or more bones or between a bone and a cartilage is called a **joint.** The study of joints is known as **arthrology.**

Classification of Joints

Classified as three major structural forms, i.e. fibrous, cartilaginous and synovial. The description of these joints are as follows

1. Fibrous (Immovable Joints)

The bones are held firmly by bundles of dense white fibrous tissue. So, these joints do not allow any movement of bones, e.g. the **sutures** (joints between the bones of skull) and **syndesmosis** (joint between tibia and fibula).

2. Cartilaginous (Slightly Movable Joints)

The bones making a joint are joined together by cartilage. So, slight movement of bones is possible, e.g. pubic symphysis of pubis, the joints between the adjacent vertebrae in the vertebral column.

3. Synovial (Freely Movable Joints)

A considerable movement is allowed at all synovial joints. It is because there is present fluid-filled synovial cavity between articulating surface of bones. These are also surrounded by tubular articular capsule.

The capsule consists of two layers, i.e. **outer fibrous capsule** and **inner synovial membrane** which 'secretes synovial fluid' that lubricates and is responsible for providing nourishment to articular cartilage.

Note In old age, stiffness of joints is due to decrease in synovial fluid in the synovial cavity.

Types of Synovial Joints

According to shape of bones and types of movement, the synovial joints are of follwoing six types

(i) **Ball and Socket Joint** In this type, a ball-like structure on one bone fits into a socket like structure in another bone, e.g. shoulder joint (between pectoral girdle and head of humerus) and hip joint (between acetabulum and head of femur).

(ii) **Hinge** (Knee) **Joint** This joint allows the movement in one plane only, e.g. elbow, knee, ankle and interphalangeal joints.

(iii) **Pivot Joint** This joint is responsible for providing movement in one plane, e.g. joint between atlas and axis and radioulnal joint (between radius and ulna).

(iv) **Gliding Joint** This joint allows limited movement in all direction as the bones are closely packed together or held in place by ligaments, e.g. joints between the carpal bones and between the tarsal bones.

(v) **Saddle Joint** This type of joint is like ball and socket joint, but not developed fully, e.g. joint between carpal of hand and metacarpal of thumb.

(vi) **Condyloid or Ellipsoid Joint** This allows movement in two planes (i.e. back-forth and side-side), e.g. joint between metacarpals and phalanges (metacarpophalangeal joint) of the fingers.

Some Common Injuries of the Joints

Sprain	Partially or Completely torn ligament.
Dislocation	Occurs when bones are forced out of a joint, often accompanied by sprains, inflammation and joint immobilisation.
Cartilage tears	Cartilage may tear when joints are twisted or when pressure is applied to them.

Functions of Joints

Joints serve following functions in human body

(i) These are essential for all types of movement.

(ii) Force generated by muscles is used to carry out movement through joints, where joints act as a fulcrum.

(iii) The joints make body flexible.

(iv) Some joints allow the growth of the structures that they connect to.

Disorders of Muscular and Skeletal System

(i) **Myasthenia Gravis** It is a chronic, **autoimmune, neuromuscular** disease characterised by varying degrees of weakness in the skeletal muscles of body. It leads to fatigue and ultimately to paralysis of skeletal muscles.

(ii) **Muscular Dystrophy** It is an inborn (genetic) disorder of muscles associated with dysfunction and ultimately with deterioration. The patient is unable to walk after the age of 12, and is dead usually by the age of 20.

(iii) **Tetany** It is an **abnormal condition characterised** by **periodic painful muscular spasms** (wild contractions) and tremors. It is caused by low calcium levels in body fluid and associated with diminished function of parathyroid gland.

(iv) **Arthritis** It is caused by inflammation of the **joints.** It is of several types, some of them are as follows

(a) **Rheumatoid Arthritis** It is an inflammation of the synovial membrane in synovial joints, and can occur at any age.

(b) **Osteoarthritis/Degenerative Joint Disease** It is characterised by progressive erosion of articular cartilage at synovial joint.

(c) **Infectious Arthritis** It is a form of joint inflammation caused by a microorganism (such as bacterium, virus or a fungus).

(d) **Gout/Gouty Arthritis** It is the type of arthritis that occurs mainly due to defect or accumulation of uric acid crystals in the joints.

Knowledge Plus

- **Still's disease** (juvenile rheumatoid arthritis) is another kind of rheumatoid arthritis that occurs in younger people.
- There is no cure for this type of arthritis. However, pain relieving (analgesic) drugs are available to give comfort.

(v) **Osteoporosis** In this, a reduction in bone tissue mass occurs. It results in weakness of skeletal muscles. It is caused due to excessive reabsorption of calcium and phosphorus from the bone. The decreased level of oestrogen is a common cause for this.

(a) It is an age-related disorder that is more common in women than in men.

(b) It leads to increased chances of fractures.

Topic Practice 2

Multiple Choice Questions

1 Mark

1. Hardness of the bones is due to
   (a) hard matrix made up of calcium salts
   (b) hard matrix made up of phosphates
   (c) hard matrix made up of sodium salts
   (d) hard matrix made up of chelates

Ans (a) Bone and cartilage are specialised connective tissues. The former has a very hard matrix due to calcium salts in it.

2. First vertebrae in humans is called
   (a) axis (b) atlas (c) lumbar (d) cervical

Ans (b) The first vertebra is the atlas and it articulates with the occipital condyles. It is articulated to the skull.

3. Select the correct function of vertebral column in humans.
   (a) Protects the spinal cord
   (b) Supports the head
   (c) Provides surface as an attachment for ribs and musculature of back
   (d) All of the above

Ans (d) The vertebral column protects the spinal cord, supports the head and serve as a point of attachment for ribs and musculature of back. Sternum is a flat bone on the vertebral midline of thorax.

4. Number of tarsals, metatarsals and phalanges in human skeleton is
   (a) 7, 5, 14 (b) 8, 5, 14
   (c) 9, 5, 14 (d) 5, 6, 7

Ans (a) Hindlimbs leg bones. Each lower limb has 30 bones, e.g. femur (1), tibia (1), fibula (1), tarsals (7), metatarsals (5), phalanges (14), patella (1).

5. Glenoid cavity articulates
   (a) clavicle with acromion
   (b) scapula with acromion
   (c) clavicle with scapula
   (d) humerus with scapula

Ans (d) Glenoid cavity articulates humerus with scapula. It is a feature on the scapula (shoulder blade or shoulder bone). It is slightly concave from above.

It is shallow and a site of attachment of glenoid labrum (glenoid ligament), which forms fibrocartilaginous rim around the glenoid cavity.

It is important because it has the effect of deepending the socket into which head of humerous bone rests, forming the shoulder joint. It represents a type of synovial, ball and socket joint.

6. The joint of humerus with pectoral girdle is
   (a) hinge joint
   (b) pivot joint
   (c) non-movable joint
   (d) ball and socket joint

Ans (d) In ball and socket joint, the one bone fits into a cup-like depression of other bone, so that the former is freely movable in all directions, e.g. shoulder joint and hip joint.

7. Cavity called acetabulum is formed by
   (a) ilium and incus
   (b) ilium and ischium
   (c) incus and ischium
   (d) ilium, ischium and pubis

Ans (d) Acetabulum is the fusion of ilium, ischium and pubis. The two halves of pelvic girdle meets ventrally to form the pubic symphysis containing fibrous cartilage.

8. Choose the incorrect pair.
   (a) Facial bones – Made up of 14 skeletal elements
   (b) Sacral vertebrae – 2 fused
   (c) Vertebrochondral ribs – False ribs (8th, 9th, 10th)
   (d) Pivot joint – Between atlas and axis

Ans (b) Sacral vertebrae (1 fused)

9. Lack of relaxation between successive stimuli in sustained muscle contraction is known as
   (a) fatigue
   (b) tetanus
   (c) tonus
   (d) spasm

Ans (b) Sustained muscle contraction due to repeated stimulus is known as tetanus. This leads to muscle fatigue.

10. Select the correct statement regarding the specific disorder of muscular or skeletal system.
    (a) Muscular dystrophy –Age related shortening of muscles
    (b) Osteoporosis –Decrease in bone mass and higher chances of fractures with advancing age
    (c) Myasthenia gravis –Autoimmune disorder which inhibits sliding of myosin filaments
    (d) Gout–Inflammation of joints due to extra deposition of calcium

Ans (b) Osteoporosis is age related disease in which bones loose minerals and fibres from the matrix causing decreased bone mass and higher chances of fractures with advancing age.

Very Short Answer Type Questions

1 Mark

11. What is the difference between the matrix of bone and cartilage? **NCERT Exemplar**

Ans The matrix of bone is hard due to calcium salts, whereas, the cartilage has slightly pliable matrix due to chondroitin salts.

12. How many total bones are there in human body? Name the largest and strongest bone.

Ans Human body contains 206 bones. Femur is the largest and strongest bone of human body.

13. The axial skeleton comprises of ...*A*... . It includes ...*B*..., ...*C*... ribs and ...*D*....

Ans *A*– 80 bones, *B*– Skull, *C*– Vertebral column and *D*– Sternum

14. Give the name of the funny bone.

Ans Olecranon process on top of the ulna is called the funny bone.

15. The three tiny bones present in middle ear are called ear ossicles. Write them in correct sequence beginning from ear drum. **NCERT Exemplar**

Ans Malleus, incus and stapes.

16. Give the name of the cavity in the girdle to which head of femur articulates.

Ans Acetabulum.

17. Give an example of cartilaginous joints.

Ans The joint between the adjacent vertebrae of vertebral column.

18. What substance is responsible for lubricating the freely movable joint at the shoulder?

Ans Synovial fluid.

19. Give the location of ball and socket joint in a human body. **NCERT Exemplar**

Ans Shoulder joint (between pectoral girdle and head of humerus).

20. What is Still's disease?

Ans Still's disease is a kind of rheumatoid arthritis that occurs in younger people.

Short Answer Type I Questions

2 Marks

21. The human endoskeleton consists of two parts. Name them with number of bones in each.

Ans Two parts of human endoskeleton are as follows
(i) Axial skeleton, it comprises of 80 bones.
(ii) Appendicular skeleton, it comprises of 126 bones.
(1×2)

22. Fill in the blank spaces. **NCERT**
(i) All mammals (except a few) have .... cervical vertebrae.
(ii) The number of phalanges in each limb of human is ....
(iii) ...... and ..... pairs of ribs are called floating ribs.
(iv) The human cranium is made of ...... bones.

Ans (i) seven (ii) fourteen
(iii) 11th and 12th (iv) eight ($\frac{1}{2}\times 4$)

23. (i) What do you mean by ear ossicles?
(ii) How many vertebrae are there in general in neck region of mammals ?

Ans (i) The bones found in middle ear are called ear ossicles (malleus, incus and stapes)
(ii) Mammals in general has seven cervical vertebrae in neck region. (1+1)

24. What are the points of articulation for pelvic and pectoral girdles? **NCERT Exemplar**

Ans Pelvic girdle articulates with femur through its acetabulum. Pectoral girdle by its glenoid cavity articulates with head of humerus. (2)

25. Name the joint, present between the vertebrae in the vertebral column. Also write in brief about the joint.

Ans Cartilaginous joint is present in between the vertebrae. It allows slight movement because of the elastic pads of fibrocartilage present between the ends of bones taking part in the joints. (1+1)

26. Which tissue is affected by Myasthenia gravis? What is the underlying cause? **NCERT Exemplar**

Ans Myasthenia gravis affects the skeletal muscles of the body. (1)
It is caused due to chronic autoimmune neuromuscular disease characterised by varying degree of weakness in the skeletal muscles. (1)

27. Why is osteoarthritis common in old people ?

Ans Old people generally develop osteoarthritis because the secretion of synovial fluid in the joints decreases with age. (2)

Short Answer Type II Questions

3 Marks

28. (i) Which bones of the skull are movable?
(ii) How many vertebrae are there in vertebral column?
(iii) Why is atlas vertebra called yes bone ?

Ans (i) Mandible and ear ossicles are the movable joints.
(ii) There are 33 vertebrae in vertebral column.
(iii) The atlas and the occipital bone form the atlanto-occipital joint, which allows neck flexion.

When you nod your head as if to say 'yes' that is neck flexion. This is the reason why atlas vertebrae also called **yes bone**. (1+1+1)

29. The following parts in our body has specific names in osteology. Write the name for each.

(i) Knee cap (ii) Collar bone
(iii) Skull (iv) Spine
(v) Shoulder bone (vi) Coxal bone

Ans (i) Patella (ii) Clavicle
(iii) Cranium (iv) Vertebral column
(v) Scapula (vi) Innominate ($\frac{1}{2} \times 6$)

30. What are joints? Write their function. What is its study called as?

Ans Refer to text on page no. 474 and 475.

31. What makes the synovial joint (freely movable)? List the various types of synovial joints.

Ans Refer to text on page no. 474 and 475.

32. In old age, people often suffer from stiff and inflammed joints. What is this condition called? What are the possible reasons for these symptoms? **NCERT Exemplar**

Ans This condition is called as arthritis. (1)

The possible reasons can be
(i) inflammation of the synovial membrane,
(ii) progressive erosion of articular cartilage,
(iii) infection by a microorganism,
(iv) due to metabolic defect causing excess of uric acid and urate crystals. ($\frac{1}{2} \times 4$)

33. Write a few lines about gout. **NCERT Exemplar**

Ans When metabolic waste like uric acid and urate crystals are present in excess in blood, they get accumulated in the joints causing gout or gouty arthritis. It is very painful, particularly at night and makes movement difficult. (3)

Long Answer Type Questions

5 Marks

34. Give answer for the following.

(i) Female pelvis is larger and has a broader front than male pelvis. Why ?
(ii) Name the different curves of vertebral column.
(iii) What is a seasmoid bone? Name it.
(iv) Which bones have become modified to form ear ossicles?

Ans (i) Female pelvis is larger and has a broader front. This is an adaptation for childbirth. (1)

(ii) Vertebral column forms four curves, i.e. cervical, thoracic, lumbar and sacral located in the neck, thorax, abdomen and pelvis, respectively. (1½)

(iii) A bone embedded within a tendon is called a seasmoid bone's patella which cover the knee ventrally. (1)

(iv) Articular bone of lower jaw modifies to be malleus. Quadrate bone of upper jaw becomes incus and hyomandibular gets modified to become stapes. (1½)

35. Name the type of joint between the following. **NCERT**

(i) Atlas/Axis
(ii) Carpal/Metacarpal of thumb
(iii) Between phalanges
(iv) Femur/acetabulum
(v) Between cranial bones
(vi) Between pubic bones in the pelvic girdle.

Ans. (i) Pivot joint (ii) Saddle joint
(iii) Hinge joint (iv) Ball and socket joint
(v) Suture (vi) Fibrous joint (5)

36. Differentiate between pectoral and pelvic girdle. **NCERT Exemplar**

Ans Differences between pectoral and pelvic girdle are as follows

<table>
<tr><th>Pectoral Girdle</th><th>Pelvic Girdle</th></tr>
<tr><td>It occurs in the shoulder region, hence also called as shoulder girdle.</td><td>It occurs in the hip region, hence also called as hip girdle.</td></tr>
<tr><td>Pectoral girdles are divided into two parts, i.e. one clavicle and one scapula.
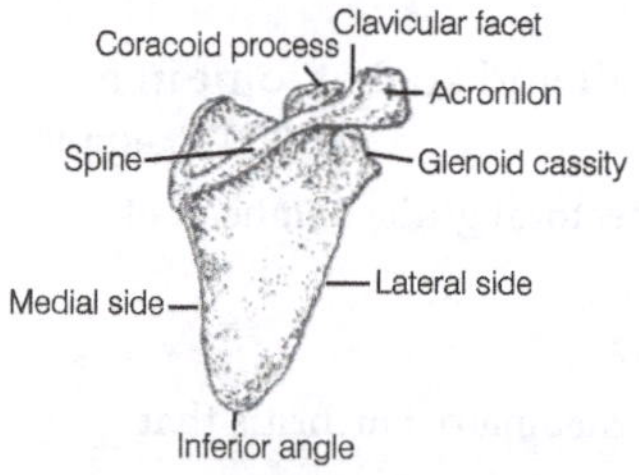

Scapula
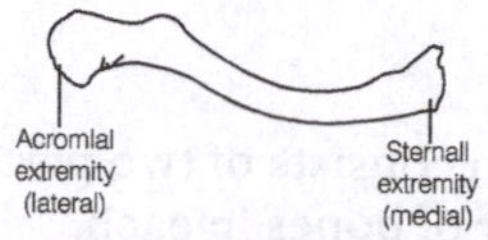

Clavicle</td><td>There is one pelvic girdle, which is formed by two, innominate bones. Each bone consist of three parts, i.e. ilium, ischium and pubis.
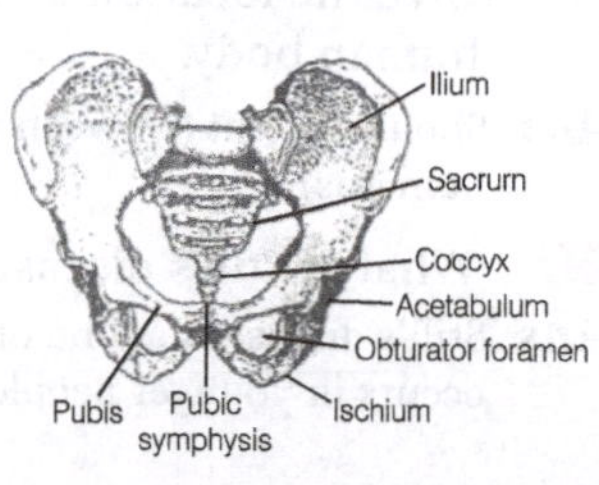

Human pelvis from anterior aspect</td></tr>
</table>

For more detail refer to text on page no. 474. (5)

SUMMARY

- **Movement** refers to any change in body position. It is a fundamental characteristic of living beings.
- **Locomotion** is the movement of body parts that leads to change of place.
- The movement in an organism's body can be of two types, i.e. non-muscular and muscular movements.
- Muscular tissue consists of muscles that are mesodermal in origin. These show properties such as excitability, contractibility, extensibility and elasticity.
- On the basis of location, muscles can be of three types of muscles : **visceral** (smooth and involuntary), **cardiac** muscles (muscles of heart, striated, branched and involuntary), **skeletal** muscles (striated and voluntary).
- According to the type of movement the body muscles are named flexors, extensors, abductors, adductors, depressors, elevators, rotators, pronators, suprinators, sphincters and dilators.
- **Skeletal muscle** is composed of elongated muscle fibres that remain covered by sarcolemma. Each muscle fibre encloses watery fluid sarcoplasm in which sarcoplasmic reticulum (ER of muscles) are present.
- Each muscle fibre is composed of units called **myofibrils** that are consists of alternating dark (A) and light (I) bands. At the centre of A-band, H-zone is present that is bisected by M-line. The I-band is bisected by Z-line. The portion between two succesive Z-lines is **sarcomere** which is the unit of contraction.
- At molecular level, myofibrils are composed of myofilaments that are made up of **myosin**, **actin**, **tropomyosin** and **troponin**. Myofilaments can be thick or thin.
- **Thin myofilaments** are composed of actin, tropomyosin and troponin. **Actin** is a globular protein that occurs in two forms, i.e. G-actin and F-actin. These form cross-bridges with myosin during muscle contraction. **Tropomyosin** prevents the muscle contraction by preventing exposure of actin binding site on myosin. **Troponin** is a trimeric protein that is responsible for keeping tropomyosin in place when muscle is relaxed. It has three components, i.e. troponin-I, troponin-T (bind to tropomyosin) and troponin-C (binds with calcium).
- Muscle fibres are of two types, i.e. **red muscle fibres** (thinner fibres with myoglobin) and **white muscle fibre** (thicker fibres with less or no myoglobin).
- **Muscle contracts** when a signal reaches neuromuscular junction *via* motor neurons. It causes the generation of action potential that leads to release of Ca^{2+}. These events cause ATPase myosin to catalyse conversion of ATP into ADP+ Pi. This leads to formation of myosin-actin cross-bridges causing shortening of sarcomere.
- **During relaxation of muscles**, acetylcholinesterase, causes breakdown of acetylcholine, thus action potential is retarded and cross-bridges are not formed.
- **All-or-none law** states that a muscle either respond to a stimulus maximally or it does not respond at all. Skeletal muscles do not follow this rule. This law was proposed by Bowditch's law.
- **Muscle fatigue** is the decrease in the force of contraction of a muscle after prolonged stimulation.
- **Rigor mortis** is the permanent stiffening of muscles after death. It occurs due to exhaustion of ATP from blood.
- The skeletal system of humans is divided into two parts, i.e. axial skeleton (80 bones) and appendicular skeleton (126 bones).
- Axial skeleton includes skull, vertebral column, ribs and sternum.
- Skull consist of cranium having 8 bones, ear ossicles with 6 bones (2 malleus, 2 incus and 2 stapes), single hyoid bone and 14 bones that constitute facial bones.
- Vertebral column consists of 33 vertebrae of which five are fused to form sacrum, while other four are fused to form one coccyx.
- Sternum, is a flat bone with 7 bony segments.
- There are total 24 ribs arranged in 12 pairs. First seven pairs are **true ribs**, VIII, IX and X pairs ribs are called **false ribs**. The last two pairs of ribs are called **floating ribs**.
- Appendicular skeleton includes forelimbs, hindlimbs, pectoral girdle and pelvic girdle.
- Pectoral girdle consists of triangular bone scapula and S-shaped clavicle.
- Forelimbs consists of 30 bones *viz.*, humerus, radius and ulna, carpals, metacarpals and phalanges.
- **Pelvic girdle** consists of three bones ilium, ischium and pubis.
- Hindlimb has 30 bones *viz.*, femur which is the longest bone of thigh, knee cap (patella) is triangular, tibia and fibula, tarsals, metatarsals and phalanges.
- Joints are points of contact between bones or between bones and cartilage joints are of three types, i.e. **fibrous joint**, **cartilaginous joint** and **synovial joint**.
- Myasthenia gravis is an autoimmune neuromuscular disorder leading to fluctuating muscle weakness and fatiguability.
- **Tetany** causes muscle to undergo a smooth sustained contraction as relaxation cannot occur between successive contractions.
- **Muscular dystrophy** is a genetic disorder characterised by progressive skeletal muscle weakness, defects in muscle protein, etc.
- **Arthritis** is the inflammation of joints that is common in old age people. It includes pain and stiffness in joints.
- **Gout** is an inherited disorder of purine metabolism that occurs especially in men.
- **Osteoporosis** is the reduction in bone tissue mass that causes weakness in skeletal strength.

Chapter Practice

Multiple Choice Questions

(1 Mark)

1. Macrophages and leucocytes exhibit **NCERT Exemplar**
   (a) ciliary movement
   (b) flagellar movement
   (c) amoeboid movement
   (d) gliding movement
2. Muscles with characteristic striations and involuntary are **NCERT Exemplar**
   (a) muscles in the wall of alimentary canal
   (b) muscles of the heart
   (c) muscles assisting locomotion
   (d) muscles of the eyelids
3. ATPase of the muscle is located in
   (a) actinin (b) troponin (c) myosin (d) actin
4. Which one of the following is showing the correct sequential order of vertebrae in the vertebral column of human beings ? **NCERT Exemplar**
   (a) Cervical – Lumbar – Thoracic – Sacral – Coccygeal
   (b) Cervical – Thoracic – Sacral – Lumbar – Coccygeal
   (c) Cervical – Sacral – Thoracic – Lumbar – Coccygeal
   (d) Cervical – Thoracic – Lumbar – Sacral – Coccygeal
5. What is the type of movable joint present between the atlas and axis?
   (a) Pivot (b) Saddle
   (c) Hinge (d) Gliding
6. Which one of the following pair is incorrect? **NCERT Exemplar**
   (a) Hinge joint – between humerus and pectoral girdle
   (b) Pivot joint – between atlas, axis and occipital condyle
   (c) Gliding joint – between the carpals
   (d) Saddle joint – between carpals and metacarpals of thumb

Assertion-Reason Type Questions

(1 Mark)

■ **Direction** (Q. Nos. 7-14) *In each of the following questions, a statement of Assertion (A) is given followed by corresponding statement of Reason (R). Of the statements, mark the correct answer as*

(a) If both A and R are true and R is the correct explanation of A
(b) If both A and R are true, but R is not the correct explanation of A
(c) If A is true, but R is false
(d) If A is false, but R is true

7. **Assertion** (A) The myosin rich zone called A-band maintains its length during sarcomere contraction.
   Reason (R) The length of I-band remains the same during muscle contraction.
8. **Assertion** (A) On stimulation, a muscle cell releases calcium ions (Ca^{2+}) from sarcoplasmic reticulum.
   Reason (R) By reacting with a protein complex, Ca^{2+} uncover active sites on the actin filaments.
9. **Assertion** (A) Calcium is required for skeletal muscle contraction.
   Reason (R) Calcium influx releases acetylcholine at neuromuscular junction.
10. **Assertion** (A) The most abundant joints in human body are synovial joints.
    Reason (R) Gliding joints offer movement in all the three planes/axis.
11. **Assertion** (A) The cranium and carpals are the part of axial skeleton.
    Reason (R) Both carpals and cranium have 8 bones each.
12. **Assertion** (A) Human skull is dicondylic.
    Reason (R) It is attached to vertebral column through two occipital condyles.
13. **Assertion** (A) The contraction of muscle is best explained by the sliding filament theory.

Reason (R) It states that contraction of muscles take place by the sliding of thin and thick filaments with the help of cross-bridge.

14. Consider the following diagram of cross-bridge formation. Comment upon the appropriateness of Assertion and Reason.

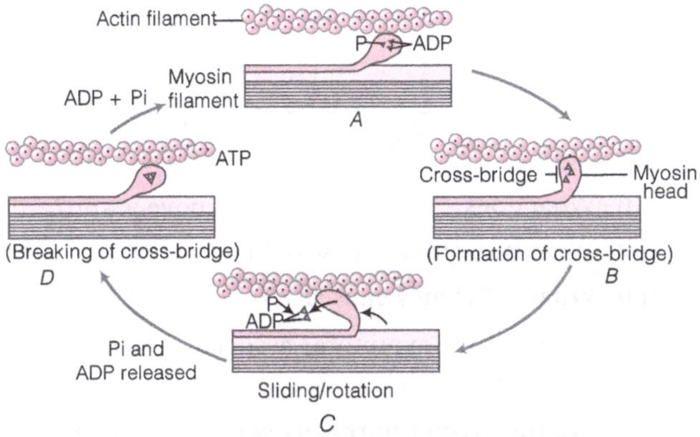

Assertion (A) Energy from ATP hydrolysis moves the myosin actin cross bridges.

Reason (R) It cause thick myofilaments to slide along the thin myofilament.

Answers

1. (c) 2. (b) 3. (c) 4. (d) 5. (a) 6. (a)
7. (c) 8. (a) 9. (b) 10. (b) 11. (d) 12. (a)
13. (a) 14. (c)

Very Short Answer Type Questions

(1 Mark)

15. Name the pigment concerned with storage of oxygen in vertebrate muscles.
16. Name the protein present in cartilage.
17. Which bones help in hearing? Where are they found?
18. Name one animal that has seven cervical vertebrae.
19. Where is acromion found ?
20. Which type of movable joint makes the hip joint?

Short Answer Type I Questions

(2 Marks)

21. How can a red muscle fibre work for prolonged period?
22. Why do muscles fatigue ?
23. Give functions of sternum.
24. What are floating ribs ? How many of them are there in human body?
25. What is the function of girdles?
26. What is gout arthritis ?

Short Answer Type II Questions

(3 Marks)

27. Describe the structure of smooth and cardiac muscles.
28. Explain the initiation of muscle contraction.
29. How many bones are present in each human limb? Name these in different parts of a forelimb.

Long Answer Type Questions

(5 Marks)

30. Write down the biochemical events in the mechanism of muscle contraction.
31. What is skeleton? Describe basic functions of human skeleton.
32. Give classification of joints. Also give an example of each type. Explain the functions of joints.
33. Write short note on
    (i) Myosthenia Gravis
    (ii) Meromyosin

Case Based Questions

(4/5 Marks)

34. *Read the following passage and answer the questions that follows.*

Abhay, a police officer, discovered a human pelvis from the jungle. After checking the reports of missing people, he found that a couple had been missing from that area since a month. Abhay was confused as to whom the pelvis belonged to and therefore, took it to the forensic investigator. The forensic expert reported it to be a female pelvis. Afterwards, the DNA from the missing female's mother and pelvis was matched. Since, both the DNA matched. It confirmed that out of the couple, the lady had died.

(i) How did the investigator opened it to be a female pelvis?
(ii) What other bones of human can be used for sex identification?
(iii) Give a possible reason for the change in female pelvis.
(iv) What is the function of pelvic girdle?
(v) Coxal is also known as.

35. Refer to the figure given below and answer the following questions.

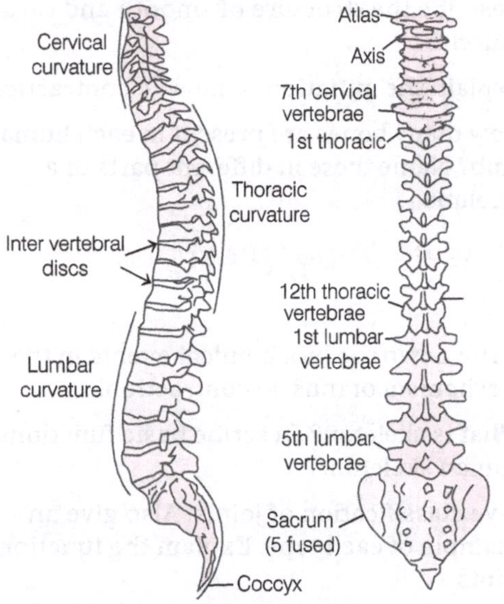

(i) What are the functions of vertebral column?
(ii) Based on the figure, can you draw the vertebral formula for humans?
(iii) In humans, which group of vertebrae are considered as vestigial?
(iv) Which is the first vertebra that articulates with the occipital condyles of skull.

36. Refer to the given graph answer the following questions.

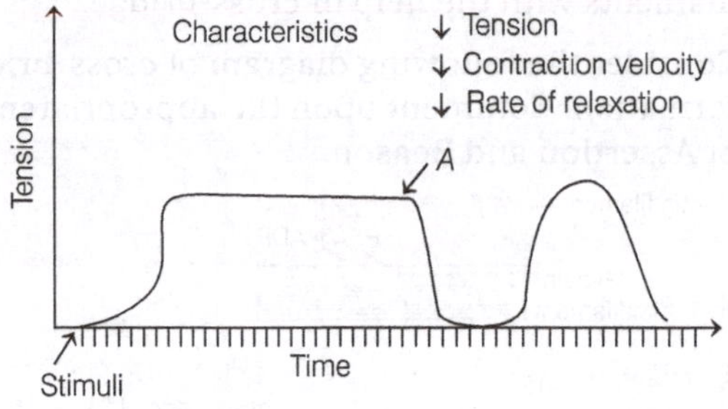

(i) What does *A* represents in the above graph?
(ii) What is the main cause of '*A*'?
(iii) What deficiency causes '*A*'?

Or (iii) What are the symptoms associated with labelled '*A*'

37. Refer to the given figure, answer the following questions.

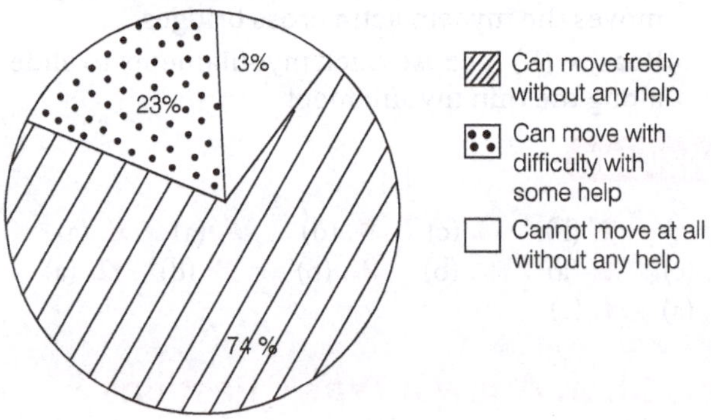

(i) What does the above figure represents.
(ii) What are the problems of locomotor disability ?
(iii) What causes locomotive syndrome?

Or (iii) What are the preventive measures of locomotor disability ?

CHAPTER

21

Neural Control and Coordination

An essential feature of living things is their ability to detect changes in their environment. They also exhibit responsiveness to the external stimuli. This becomes possible only due to the presence of well-organised network of neural system. It provides point to point connections for quick coordination for receiving and responding to stimuli.

The nervous system in human beings is the most advanced in terms of evolution. The detailed structural and functional components have been discussed in this chapter with properly labelled figures.

TOPIC 01 Nervous System : An Overview

Coordination is the process through which two or more organs of the body interact and complement the functions of each other. On the other hand, **integration** is a process, which makes two or more organs to work as a functional unit in harmony to carry out some vital functions of the body.

For instance, when we do exercise, we observe significant increase in the rate of respiration, heartbeat, bloodflow, sweating, etc., to meet enhanced need of nutrients and energy for increased activities of lungs, heart, muscles and many other body organs. When we stop exercising, we witness that the increased activities of lungs, heart, nerves, kidneys, muscles, etc., gradually return to normal. Thus, during exercise, functions of various organs of the body are coordinated and integrated.

In higher animals (including human), two types of system have been developed for the control, coordination and integration, i.e. **nervous system** and **endocrine system**. The nervous system provides an organised network of neurons spread throughout the body of animal. The endocrine system provides chemical coordination of organs and organ systems through which hormones act as chemical messenger.

Neural System

The neural system is the control system of the body, which consists of highly specialised cells called **neurons.** The sensory neurons detect and receive information from different sense organs (receptors) in the form of stimuli and transmit the stimuli to the **Central Neural System** (CNS) through sensory nerve fibres. In CNS, the processing of information is done and a conclusion is drawn. The conclusion message is sent to different organs (effectors) through motor nerves to act accordingly.

The nervous system is present in most of the multicellular animals. Its complexity increases from lower to higher animals. The nervous system in *Hydra* is composed of only a network of neurons. In insects, the nervous system is present along with the ganglia and neural tissue. Invertebrates have relatively simpler nervous system than the vertebrates.

Human Nervous System

The whole nervous system of human being is derived from **embryonic ectoderm.**

The human nervous system can be categorised into

(i) Central Nervous System (CNS)
(ii) Peripheral Nervous System (PNS)

Central Nervous System (CNS)

It is the integrating and command centre of the nervous system, which consists of the **brain** and **spinal cord.**

Brain

The brain is the central information processing organ of our body and acts as the '**command and control system**' of all body activities.

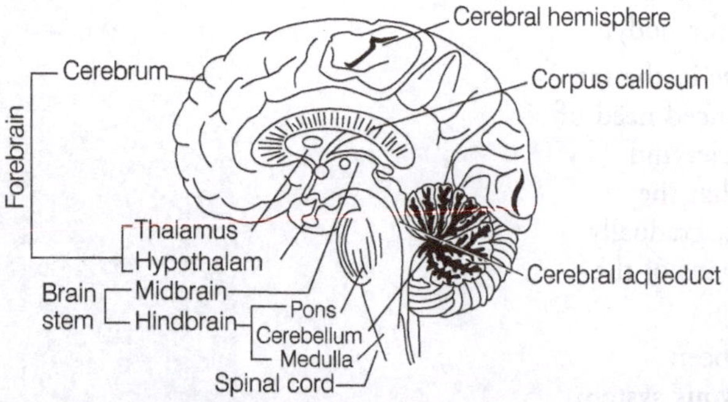

Fig. 21.1 Diagram showing sagital section of the human brain

It controls the following activities

(i) The voluntary movements and balance of the body.
(ii) Functioning of vital involuntary organs, e.g. lungs, heart, kidneys, etc.
(iii) Thermoregulation, hunger and thirst.
(iv) Circardian (24 hrs) rhythms of our body.
(v) Activities of several endocrine glands and human behaviour.
(vi) It is also the site for processing of vision, hearing, speech, memory, intelligence, emotions and thoughts.

Location

The brain is the anterior most part of the central neural system, which is located in the **cranium** (cranial cavity) of the skull.

Protective Coverings of the Brain

It is covered by three membranes or meninges (cranial meninges) present in the cranial region of the skull. These membranes are as follows

(i) The outermost membrane, the **duramater** is the tough fibrous membrane adhering close to the inner side of the skull.
(ii) The middle membrane, is very thin layer called **arachnoid membrane** (arachnoid mater).
(iii) The innermost membrane, the **piamater** is thin, very delicate, which is in contact with the brain tissue.

Note The human brain weighs from 1200-1400 g. Brain alone has about 2 billion neurons and trillions of interneuron connections.

Structure

The human brain is divisible into three main parts

(i) Forebrain (ii) Midbrain (iii) Hindbrain

i. Forebrain

It is the largest part of the human brain and forms most of the anterior region. The forebrain consists of

(a) **Olfactory Lobes** The anterior part of the brain is formed by a pair of short club-shaped structures, the olfactory lobes. These are **concerned with the sense of smell.**
(b) **Cerebrum** It is the largest and most complex of all the parts of the human brain. A deep cleft divides the cerebrum longitudinally into two equal halves. These are termed as the left and right **cerebral hemispheres.** These hemispheres are connected by a large band of myelinated fibres, the **corpus callosum.**

The outer cover of cerebral hemisphere is called **cerebral cortex.** The cerebral cortex is referred to as the grey matter due to its greyish appearance (as neuron cell bodies are concentrated here).

The cerebral cortex is greatly folded. The upward folds, **gyri**, alternate with the downward grooves or **sulci**. Beneath the grey matter, there are millions of myelinated nerve fibers, which constitute the inner part of the cerebral hemisphere.

The large concentration of medullated nerve fibres gives this tissue an opaque white appearance. Hence, it is called the **white matter.**

(c) **Lobes** Each cerebral hemisphere of the cerebrum is divided into four lobes, i.e. frontal, parietal, temporal and occipital lobes. In each cerebral hemisphere, there are three types of functional areas

- **Sensory Areas** It receives impulses from the receptors and **motor areas** and transmit impulses to the effectors.
- **Association Areas** These are large regions that are neither clearly sensory nor motor in function. They interpret the input, store the input and initiate a response in light of similar past experience. Thus, these areas are responsible for complex functions like memory, learning, reasoning and other intersensory associations.

(d) **Diencephalon** is the posterio-ventral part of the forebrain. Its main parts are as follows

- **Epithalamus** is a thin membrane of non-nervous tissue. It is the posterior segment of the diencephalon.
- The cerebrum wraps around a structure called **thalamus**, which is a major coordinating centre for sensory and motor signalling.
  The hypothalamus that lies at the base of the **thalamus** contains a number of centres, which control body temperature, urge for eating and drinking.
  It also contains several groups of neurosecretory cells, which secrete hormones called **hypothalamic hormones.**
- The inner parts of cerebral hemispheres and a group of deeply associated structures like amygdala, hippocampus, etc., form a complex structure (limbic lobe or limbic system) that are involved in the regulation of sexual behaviour, expression of emotional reactions, e.g. excitement, pleasure, rage and fear and motivation.

ii. Midbrain

The midbrain is located between the thalamus, hypothalamus of the forebrain and pons of the hindbrain. A canal called the **cerebral aqueduct** passes through the midbrain. The dorsal portion of the midbrain mainly consists of two pairs (i.e. four) of rounded swellings (lobes) called **corpora quadrigemina.**

iii. Hindbrain

The hindbrain consists of

(a) **Pons** consists of fibre tracts that interconnect different regions of the brain.

(b) **Cerebellum** is the second largest part of the human brain (means first being the cerebrum). It has very convoluted surface in order to provide the additional space for many more neurons.

(c) **Medulla oblongata** is connected to the spinal cord and contains centres, which control respiratory rhythm, cardiovascular reflexes, gastric secretions and the postural gestures of the body (vertigo).

Knowledge Plus

- Midbrain and hindbrain form the **brain stem.** It is the posterior part of the brain that continues with the spinal cord.
- Out of the twelve pairs of cranial nerves (in higher vertebrates), ten pairs come from the brain stem.

Cavities or Ventricles of Brain

The cavities of brain are called ventricles. Human brain contains following four ventricles

Cerebral Ventricles and their Locations

Ventricle	Also known as	Location
Ventricle I	Paracoel or Lateral ventricle	Right cerebral hemisphere
Ventricle II	Paracoel or Lateral ventricle	Left cerebral hemisphere
Ventricle III	Diocoel	Diencephalon
Ventricle IV	Metacoel	Between brain stem and cerebellum

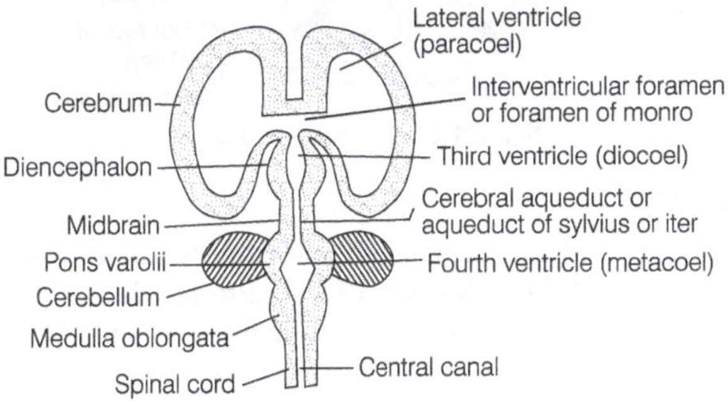

Fig. 21.2 LS of brain showing its ventricles

Cerebrospinal Fluid (CSF)

The fluid present in and around brain and spinal cord is called cerebrospinal fluid. It is secreted by modified ependymal cells of brain, which form plexus of cells called **choroid plexus.**

It is a colourless fluid similar to the plasma. Its volume is about 80-150 mL and pH is about 7.33 in an adult.

The main functions of CSF are as follows

(i) It absorbs shock or jerk to protect brain and spinal cord.

(ii) It serves as medium for exchange of nutrients and waste products between blood and nervous tissue.

(iii) It serves as endocrine medium for transport of hormones.

Spinal Cord

(i) It forms the posterior part of the CNS, running mid-dorsally in the neural canal of the vertebral column. In an adult, the spinal cord is about 42-45 cm long. Its diameter varies at different stages of growth.

(ii) The spinal cord is formed of two types of nervous tissue, i.e. grey matter and white matter.

(iii) The grey matter is surrounded by white matter. It consists of groups of myelinated axons.

(iv) The spinal nerve tracts are divisible into two, **ascending** (conducting sensory impulses towards brain) and **descending** (conducting motor impulses from brain).

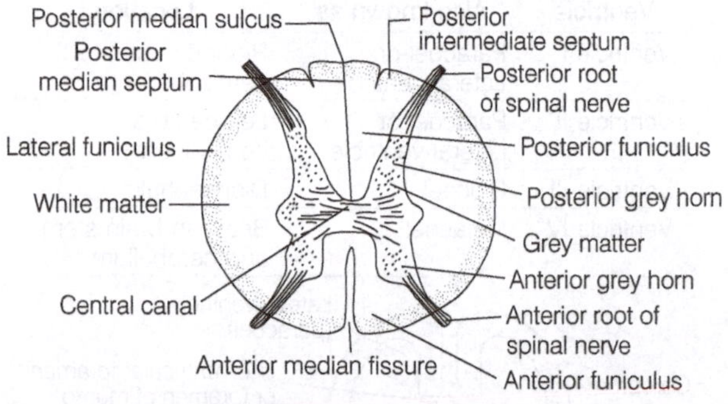

Fig. 21.3 TS of spinal cord

Function

Spinal cord conducts impulses to and from the brain and controls most of the reflex activities. It also provides a means of communication between spinal nerves and the brain.

Peripheral Nervous System (PNS)

The Peripheral Nervous System (PNS) transmits information to and from the CNS. The peripheral nervous system consists of

1. Somatic Nervous System (SNS)
2. Autonomic Nervous System (ANS)

1. Somatic Nervous System

It contains nerves, which relay impulses from the CNS to skeletal muscles. These can be further categorised into **cranial** (from brain) and **spinal** nerves on the basis of their origin.

i. Cranial Nerves

12 pairs of cranial nerves emerge specifically from the forebrain and brain stem.

Knowledge Plus

- Trochlear nerve is the smallest and thinnest nerve and controls movement of eyeball.
- Trigeminal nerve is also called **dentist nerve.** It is the largest cranial nerve. At its origin it is associated with 'Gasserian ganglion'.
- Facial nerve is associated with geniculate ganglion at its origin.

ii. Spinal Nerves

The spinal nerves originate in the spinal cord and extend to the parts of body below the head.

All spinal nerves are mixed, having sensory and motor fibres in approximately equal numbers. In humans, 31 pairs of spinal nerves are present as cervical (8 pairs), thoracic (12 pairs), lumber (5 pairs), sacral (5 pairs) and coccygeal (1 pair).

Based on the presence or absence of myelin sheath, the nerve fibres are divided into two groups, i.e. myelinated fibres and non-myelinated fibres. In myelinated nerve fibres, Schwann cells form myelin sheath around the axon. The gaps between two adjacent myelin sheaths are called **nodes of Ranvier.** Myelinated nerve fibres are found in cranial and spinal nerves and white matter of brain.

In non-myelinated nerve fibres, Schwann cells do not form myelin shealth around the axon and are without nodes of Ranvier. They are commonly found in autonomic and somatic neural systems.

Based on their functions, the nerve fibres of PNS are divided into two groups, i.e. afferent fibres and efferent fibres.

The afferent nerve fibres transmit sensory impulses from tissues/organs to the CNS and form the sensory or afferent pathways. The efferent nerve fibres transmit motor impulses from CNS to the concerned tissues/organs and form the motor or efferent pathways.

2. The Autonomic/Visceral Nervous System (ANS)

The ANS regulates the internal environment of the body.

The ANS is also known as visceral nervous system as it innervates the visceral organs like lungs, stomach, etc., blood vessels and glands. It consists of the sympathetic and parasympathetic nervous system. The former is called **thoracolumber outflow** and the latter is called **craniosacral outflow** depending upon their origin.

(i) Sympathetic Nervous System

It is related to the arousal and energy generation, i.e. the fight or flight responses. The ganglion in sympathetic system are intercepted to form a sympathetic trunk which is situated near the CNS. Hence, here preganglionic fibres are small and postganglionic fibres are large.

(ii) Parasympathetic Nervous System

It is related to opposite response that promotes calming and return to self-maintenance functions. The ganglion in this system are situated away from the CNS. Hence, here preganglionic fibres are large as compared to postganglionic fibres.

Their functions in comparative manner in a nut shell are given below

Functions of Sympathetic Nervous System	Functions of Parasympathetic Nervous System
Vasoconstriction in general and vasodilation (brain, heart, lungs and skeletal muscles).	Vasodilation of coronary vessel.
Dilates pupil	Constricts pupil
Increases lacrimal glands secretion.	Inhibits lacrimal glands secretion.
Inhibits salivary glands and digestive glands.	Stimulates secretion of salivary and digestive glands.
Accelerates heartbeat.	Retards heartbeat.
Dilates trachea, bronchi and lungs.	Constricts trachea, bronchi and lungs.
Inhibits gut peristalsis.	Stimulates gut peristalsis.
Contracts anal sphincter.	Relaxes anal sphincter.
Relaxes urinary bladder.	Contracts and relaxes.
Increases adrenal secretion.	Inhibits adrenal secretion.
Blood sugar increases (glucagon).	Blood sugar inhibits (insulin).
Semen ejaculation increases.	Increases external genitalia and sex.
Increases sweat secretion.	Inhibits sweat secretion.
Contracts arrector pili.	Relaxes arrector pili.

Generation and Conduction of Nerve Impulse

Nerve impulse is a wave of bioelectric/electrochemical disturbance that passes along a neuron during conduction of an excitation.

Impulse conduction depends upon

(i) Permeability of axon membrane (axolemma).

(ii) Osmotic equilibrium (electrical equivalence) between the axoplasm and Extracellular Fluid (ECF) present outside the axon.

The generation of a nerve impulse is the temporary reversal of the resting potential in the neuron.

It occurs in the following three steps

Polarisation (Resting Potential)

In a resting nerve fibre (a nerve fibre that is not conducting an impulse), the axoplasm (neuroplasm of axon) inside the axon contains high concentration of K^+ and negatively charged proteins and low concentration of Na^+.

(i) In contrast, the fluid outside axon contains a low concentration of K^+ and a high concentration of Na^+ and thus, forms a concentration gradient.

(ii) These ionic gradients across the resting membrane are maintained by the active transport of ions by the **sodium-potassium pump**, which transports $3Na^+$ outwards and $2K^+$ inwards (into the cell).

(iii) As a result, the outer surface of the axonal membrane possesses a positive charge, while its inner surface becomes negatively charged and therefore, is polarised.

(iv) The electrical potential difference across the resting plasma membrane is called as the **resting potential**. The state of the resting membrane is called **polarised state**.

Depolarisation (Action Potential)

When a stimulus of adequate strength (threshold stimulus) is applied to a polarised membrane, the permeability of the membrane to Na^+ ions is greatly increased at the point of stimulation (site A).

(i) This leads to a rapid influx of Na^+ followed by the reversal of the polarity at that site, i.e. the outer surface of the membrane becomes negatively charged and the inner side becomes positively charged.

The polarity of the membrane at the site *A* is thus, reversed and neuron at that point is said to be **depolarised.**

(ii) The electrical potential difference across the plasma membrane at the site *A* is called the **action potential** (another name of **nerve impulse**).

(iii) At adjacent sites, e.g. site *B*, the membrane (axon) has positive charge (still polarised) on the outer surface and a negative charge on its inner surface.

(iv) The stimulated negatively charged point on the outside of the membrane sends out an electrical current to the positive point next to it. As a result, a current flows on the outer surface from site *B* to site *A*, while on the inner surface current flows from site *A* to site *B*.

This process (reversal) repeats itself over and over again and a **nerve impulse** is conducted through the length of the neuron.

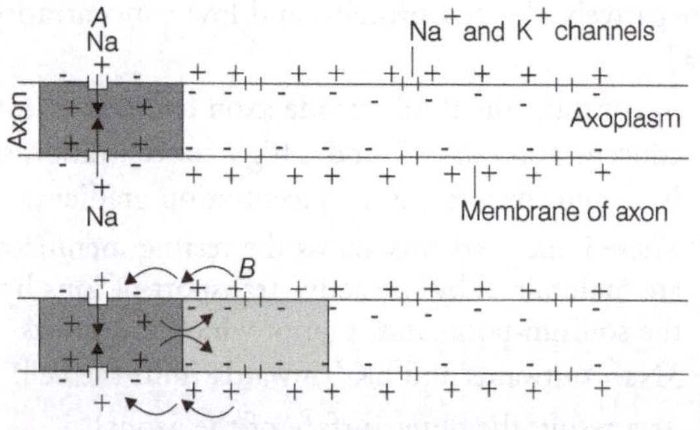

Fig. 21.4 Diagrammatic representation of impulse conduction through an axon

Repolarisation

(i) The rise in the stimulus-induced permeability to Na^+ is extremely short lived. It is quickly followed by a rise in membrane permeability to K^+.

(ii) Within a fraction of a second, Na^+ influx stops and K^+ outflow begins until the original resting state of ionic concentration is achieved.

Thus, resting potential is restored at the site of excitation, which is called **repolarisation** of the membrane. This makes the fibre once more responsive to further stimulation.

(iii) In fact, until repolarisation occurs, neuron cannot conduct another impulse. The time taken for this restoration is called **refractory period.**

Knowledge Plus

- When an impulse travels along a myelinated neuron, depolarisation occurs only at the **nodes of Ranvier**. It leaps over the myelin sheath from one node to the next. This process, is called **saltatory conduction**.
- This process accounts for the greater speed of an impulse travelling along a myelinated neuron than along a non-myelinated one. It is upto 50 times faster than the non-myelinated nerve fibre.

Transmission of Impulses

(Through Junctions)

A nerve impulse is transmitted from one neuron to another through junctions called **synapses.** It is formed by the membranes of a presynaptic neuron and a postsynaptic neuron. There are mainly two types of synapses

I. Electrical Synapses

(i) The membranes of pre and postsynaptic neurons are in very close proximity (i.e. in continuity). The continuity is provided by the **gap junction** between the two neurons.

(ii) In electrical synapse, there is minimal synaptic delay because of the **direct flow** of electrical current from one neuron into the other across these synapses. Thus, impulse transmission across an electrical synapses is always faster than that across a chemical synapse. In such synapses, transmission of impulse is very similar to impulse conduction along a single axon.

(iii) Electrical synapses are found in cardiac muscle fibres, smooth muscle fibres of intestine and the epithelial cells of lens.

II. Chemical Synapses

The membranes of pre and postsynaptic neurons are separated by a fluid-filled space called **synaptic cleft.**

A brief description of the mechanism of synaptic transmission is given below

(i) When an impulse (action potential) arrives at a presynaptic knob, calcium ions from the synaptic cleft enter the cytoplasm of the presynaptic knob.

(ii) The calcium ions cause the movement of the synaptic vesicles to the surface of the knob.

The synaptic vesicles are fused with the presynaptic plasma membrane and get ruptured (exocytosis) to discharge their contents (neurotransmitter) into the synaptic cleft.

(iii) The neurotransmitter of the synaptic cleft binds with specific protein receptor molecules, present on the postsynaptic membrane.

(iv) This binding action changes the membrane potential of the postsynaptic membrane, opening channels in the neurolemma and sodium ions to enter the cell. This causes the **depolarisation** and generation of **action potential** in the postsynaptic membrane. Thus, the impulse is transferred to the next neuron.

(v) The new potential developed may be either excitatory or inhibitory.

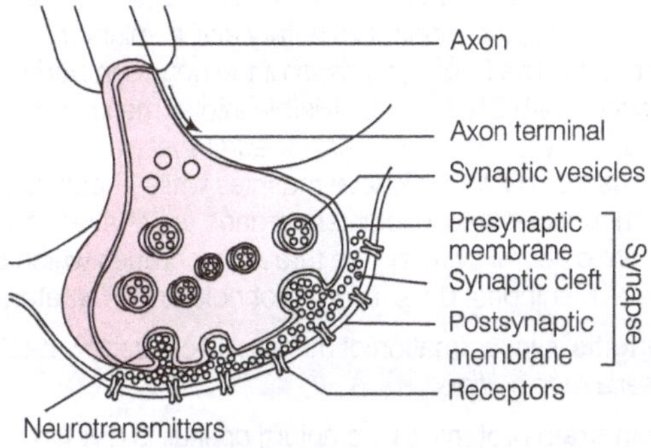

Fig. 21.5 Axon terminal and synapse

SUMMARY

- **Nervous system** provides an organised network of point to point connections for quick neural coordination and fastest means of communication.
- The nervous system of all animals is composed of structural and functional units called neurons which can detect, receive and transmit different types of stimuli.
- **Human neural system** is divided into-Central Nervous System (CNS), Peripheral Nervous System (PNS) and Autonomic Nervous System (ANS).
- **Central Nervous system** (CNS) includes brain and spinal cord. They together control voluntary and involuntary movements. The PNS comprises of the nerves in body associated with CNS and is divisible into somatic and autonomic systems. The somatic neural system conducts impluses from CNS to skeletal muscles while impulses from smooth muscles and involuntary organs are relayed to CNS by autonomic neural system. The three membranes which cover CNS are Meninges, durameter Arachnoid and Piamater.
- **Meningitis** is inflammation of meningitis caused by bacterium *Neisseria meningitidis*.
- **Human brain** protected by cranium or skull is divided into Forebrain, Midbrain and Hindbrain. The cavities of brain are known as ventricles which are four in number.
- **Forebrain** is the largest and highly developed part of brain divisible into two cerebral hemispheres by a tract of nerve fibres called corpus callosum (mammalian feature). Anterior part of corpus callosum is called genu while splenium is the posterior part. The different lobes of cerebrum are named after the skull bones.
- **Cerebral cortex** is greatly convoluted into gyri and sulci. Two thirds of surface of the cortex is hidden in these and their presence triples the area of cerebral cortex. While matter seen is due to the presence of myelin sheath on the axons of neurons.
- **Diencepholon** of forebrain comprises of epithalamous (non-nervous part whose anterior region is fused with to form anterior choroid plexus that forms (CSF), thalamus (that works as a relay centre) and hypothalamus which is centre for hunger, thirst satiety and temperature control.
- **Autonomic Nervous System** (ANS) includes sympathetic and parasympathetic nervous system. It is generally involuntary and control smooth and cardiac muscles. Organs of digestive system CV, excretory and endocrine system.
- **Parasympathetic fibres** do not travel in the dorsal and ventral nerve of spinal nerve. No parasympathetic innervation is received by skin, sweat glands and arrector pili muscles.
- **Nerve impulse** takes place through a nerve fibre is an electrochemical process which involves two phases-resting potential and action potential.
- **Initiation of impulse** is due to opening of voltage gated vein channels clustered in trigges zone (Axon hillock).
- **Conduction of impulse** occurs as the local current created becomes the stimulus and causes depolarisation of adjoining region of axon by opening of voltage-gated Na^+ channels.
- **Transmission of impulse** from one fibre to another is done through specialised junction called synapse. These can be electrical or chemical.
- Calcium stimulates fusion of synaptic vesicles with pre-synaptic membrane and release of neuro transmitter by exocytosis into synaptic cleft.
- **Neurotransmitters** are the chemical messengers for transmitting impulses to the next neuron. Acetylcholine being most common one.

Chapter Practice

Multiple Choice Questions

1 Mark

1. The neural system is composed of highly specialised cells called neurons that can

(a) detect stimuli (b) receive stimuli
(c) transmit stimuli (d) All of these

Ans (d) The plasma membrane of neuron is polarised due to difference in the concentration of positive ions across it. Any deflection in this condition is detected by plasma membrane and is further transmitted to other neurons. Thus, neurons can detect, receive and transmit stimuli.

2. Brain controls the

(a) voluntary movements
(b) balance of the body
(c) functioning of vital involuntary organs
(d) All of the above

Ans (d) Brain acts as the command and control system and it controls the voluntary movements, balance of the body, functioning of vital involuntary organs (e.g. lungs, heart, kidneys, etc.), thermoregulation, hunger and thrist, circadian (24-hours) rhythms of our body, activities of several endocrine glands and human behaviour.

It is the site for processing of vision, hearing, speech, memory, intelligence, emotions and thoughts.

3. Inside the skull, the brain is covered by

(a) arachnoid (b) cranial meninges
(c) piamater (d) duramater

Ans (b) The human brain is well-protected by the skull. Inside the skull, the brain is covered by **cranial meninges**, consisting of an outer layer called duramater, a very thin middle layer called arachnoid and an inner layer called piamater.

4. The forebrain consists of

(a) cerebrum (b) thalamus
(c) hypothalamus (d) All of these

Ans (d) The forebrain consists of cerebrum, thalamus and hypothalamus. Cerebrum forms the major part of the brain. It is divided longitudinally into two halves, which are termed as right and left **cerebral hemispheres**. The cerebrum wraps around a structure, which is called **thalamus** and is a major centre for coordinating sensory and motor signalling. Hypothalamus is a very important part of the brain, which lies at the base of the thalamus.

5. Association areas of the brain are

(a) always sensory areas
(b) always motor areas
(c) Both sensory and motor areas
(d) None of the above

Ans (c) The cerebral cortex contains motor areas, sensory areas and large regions that are neither clearly sensory nor motor in function. These regions are called as the association areas. These are responsible for complex functions like intersensory associations, memory and communication.

6. Injury localised to the hypothalamus would most likely to disrupt

(a) short term memory
(b) coordination during locomotion
(c) executive function, such as decision making
(d) regulation of body temperature

Ans (d) The hypothalamus performs many functions which are important for the survival and enjoyment of life. It serves as a link between 'mind' and 'body' and between the nervous and endocrine system. The hypothalamus is responsible for hormone production.

The hormone produced by this area govern body temperature thirst, hunger, sleep, circulation rhythm, mood sex drive, etc. This area of the brain also controls the functioning of pituitary gland. Thus, if any injury localised to the hypothalamus, will disrupt the complete regulation of body temperature and other activities.

7. The inner parts of cerebral hemispheres and a group of associated deep structures like amygdala, hippocampus, etc., form a complex structure called

(a) arbor vitae
(b) limbic lobe/limbic system
(c) corpora quadrigemina
(d) reticular system

Ans (b) The inner parts of cerebral hemispheres and a group of associated deep structures like amygdala, hippocampus, etc. form a complex structure called the **limbic lobe** or **limbic system** along with hypothalamus. It is involved in the regulation of sexual behaviour expression of emotional reactions (excitement, pleasure, rage and fear) and motivation.

8. Which of the following regions of the brain is incorrectly paired with its function?
(a) Medulla oblongata–Homeostatic control
(b) Cerebellum–Language comprehension
(c) Corpus callosum–Communication between the left and right cerebral cortices
(d) Cerebrun–Calculation and contemplation

Ans (b) Language comprehension includes understanding of speech and written words. It requires input of sensory information (from hearing and vision), processing of the information in different centres of cerebral cortex and the coordination of motor output.

9. Brain stem is formed by
(a) midbrain and forebrain
(b) forebrain and hindbrain
(c) midbrain and hindbrain
(d) All of the above

Ans (c) The midbrain is located between the thalamus/hypothalamus of the forebrain and pons of the hindbrain. The hindbrain comprises pons, cerebellum and medulla. Midbrain and hindbrain forms the brain stem.

10. The medulla contains centres, which control
(a) respiration
(b) cardiovascular reflexes
(c) gastric secretions
(d) All of the above

Ans (d) The medulla is also called as the medulla oblongata. The medulla contains centres, which control respiration, cardiovascular reflexes and gastric secretions.

11. The PNS includes
(a) central nervous system and sympathetic nervous system
(b) somatic nervous system and autonomic nervous system
(c) only sympathetic nervous system
(d) only somatic nervous system

Ans (b) The PNS includes somatic nervous system and autonomic nervous system.

12. Non-myelinated nerve fibres, that do not form a myelin sheath around the axon are commonly found in ...*A*... and the ...*B*... neural systems. Fill in the blanks (*A* and *B*) with correct options.
(a) *A*–central; *B*–peripheral
(b) *A*–autonomous; *B*–central
(c) *A*–somatic; *B*–peripheral
(d) *A*–autonomous; *B*–somatic

Ans (d) Non-myelinated nerve fibre, that do not form a myelin sheath around the axon, are commonly found in autonomous and the somatic neural systems.

13. The afferent nerve fibres transmit impulses
(a) from tissues/organs to the CNS
(b) from the CNS to the concerned peripheral tissues/organs
(c) from the CNS to skeletal muscles
(d) from the CNS to the involuntary organs

Ans (a) The afferent nerve fibres transmit impulses from tissues/organs to the CNS and it is the efferent nerve fibres that transmits regulatory impulses from the CNS to the concerned peripheral tissue/organs.

14. A wave of action potential is termed as
(a) sensory impulse (b) nerve impulse
(c) activation impulse (d) motor impulse

Ans (b) A wave of action potential is termed as a nerve impulse.

When a nerve fibre receives stimulus inside the cell, plasma membrane become positively charged with respect to outside. The change in polarity across the plasma membrane is known as an action potential.

The membrane with this reversed polarity across it is said to be depolarised.

15. In resting stage, the axonal membrane is comparatively more permeable to ...*A*... ions and nearly impermeable to ...*B*... ions. Fill in the blanks (*A* and *B*) with correct options.
(a) *A*–sodium; *B*–potassium
(b) *A*–sodium; *B*–calcium
(c) *A*–potassium; *B*–sodium
(d) *A*–potassium; *B*–calcium

Ans (c) In resting stage, the axonal membrane is comparatively more permeable to potassium ions and nearly impermeable to sodium ions.

16. Stimulation of a muscle fibre by a motor neuron occurs at
(a) the neuromuscular junction
(b) the transverse tubules
(c) the myofibril
(d) the sarcoplasmic reticulum

Ans (a) Stimulation of a muscle fibre by a motor neuron occurs at the neuromuscular junction. The area of contact between a nerve and muscle fibre is called motor end plate.

At neuromuscular junction a neuron activates the muscle to contract. Acetyl choline is a neurotransmitter that is involved in the transmission of impulse at the neuromuscular junction.

17. A synapse is formed by the membrane of
(a) presynaptic neuron and a postsynaptic neuron
(b) presynaptic dendrite and postsynaptic axon
(c) presynaptic dendrite and postsynaptic dendrite
(d) None of the above

Ans (a) One nerve fibre is attached to another nerve fibre *via* a junction called synapse. A synapse is formed by the membrane of a presynaptic neuron and postsynaptic neuron.

18. Synapses are of two types namely ...*A*... synapses and ...*B*... synapses. Here *A* and *B* refers to
(a) neuron-neuron, chemical
(b) electrical, chemical
(c) neuron-neuron, electrical
(d) electrochemical, neuron

Ans (b) Synapsis are of two types, i.e. electrical synapses and chemical synapses. Electrical synapses is mediated by electrical impulse. It is very fast but rare. On the other hand, chemical synapses is mediated by chemicals such as neurotransmitter.

19. On postsynaptic membrane, the new potential developed is
(a) always inhibitory
(b) always excitatory
(c) may be excitatory or inhibitory
(d) neither excitatory nor inhibitory

Ans (c) The kind of action potential to be developed on the membrane of postsynaptic neuron depends upon the action of neurotransmitter. It is summarised as follows

(i) Neurotransmitter → Excitatory receptor → Open channels of Na^+ ions or both for Na^+ and K^+ → Depolarising of plasma membrane of postsynaptic neuron → Action potential.

(ii) Neurotransmitters → Inhibitory receptor → Opens K^+ or Cl^- channels → Hyperpolarisation of plasma membrane of postsynaptic neuron → No action potential. So, the new potential developed may be either excitatory or inhibitory.

Assertion-Reason Type Questions

(1 Mark)

■ **Direction** (Q. Nos. 20-27) *In each of the following questions, a statement of Assertion (A) is given followed by corresponding statement of Reason (R). Of the statements, mark the correct answer as*

(a) If both A and R are true and R is the correct explanation of A
(b) If both A and R are true, but R is not the correct explanation of A
(c) If A is true, but R is false
(d) If A is false, but R is true

20. Given below is the diagrammatic representation of impulse conduction through an axon (At points *A* and *B*). Study the diagram and comment upon the appropriateness of the Assertion and the Reason.

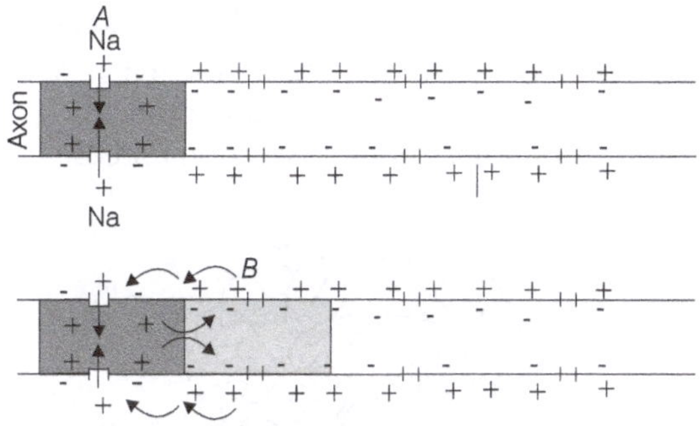

Assertion (A) A nerve impulse is an electrochemical event.

Reason (R) A current flows on the inner surface from site *A* to site *B* and on the outer surface, current flows from site B to site *A* to complete the circuit of current flow.

Ans (b)

21. **Assertion** (A) The imbalance in concentration of Na^+, K^+ and proteins generate resting potential.

Reason (R) To maintain the unequal distribution of Na^+ and K^+, the neurons use electrical energy.

Ans (d)

22. **Assertion** (A) Arrival of an impulse at the axon terminal, stimulates the release of neurotransmitters in the synaptic cleft.

Reason (R) These neurotransmitters are responsible for the opening of ion channels.

Ans (b)

23. **Assertion** (A) The membrane of a neuron remains in polarised state.

Reason (R) Ion channels on the neural membrane are selectively permeable to different ions.

Ans (a)

24. **Assertion** (A) The axoplasm inside the axon contains high concentration of K^+ and negatively charged proteins.

Reason (R) The axonal membrane is impermeable to Na^+ and negatively charged proteins.

Ans (c)

25. **Assertion** (A) The pre-synaptic neuron transmits an impulse (action potential) across the synaptic cleft to the post-synaptic neuron.
Reason (R) For the transmission of impulses at synapses, chemicals called neurotransmitters are responsible.

Ans (a)

26. Given below is the diagram showing sagittal of the human brain with a part labelled as *X*. Study the diagram and comment upon the appropriateness of the Assertion and the Reason.

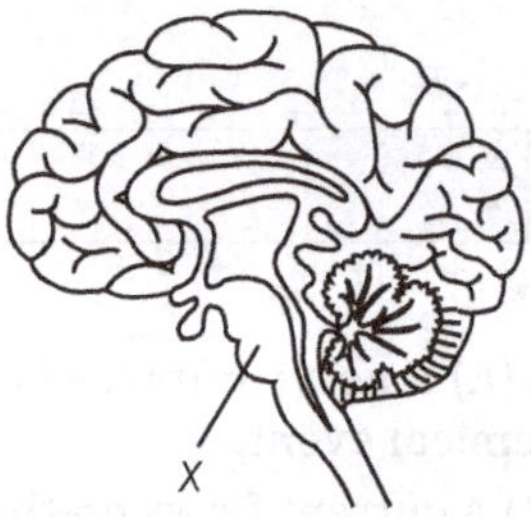

Assertion (A) The part *X* is pons.
Reason (R) In brain stem, pons is called, pneumotaxic centre with the ability to moderate the function of the 'respiratory rhythm' centre.

Ans (b)

27. **Assertion** (A) Midbrain is located above the thalamus and hypothalamus.
Reason (R) Cerebral aqueduct passes through midbrain.

Ans (d)

Very Short Answer Type Questions

1 Mark

28. Give the name of the part of human neural system that lies along the main axis of the body.

Ans Central neural (nervous) system, lies along the main central axis of the body.

29. Give the name of the central information processing organ of our body.

Ans Brain.

30. Name the structure, which contains and protects the brain in vertebrate animals.

Ans Cranium.

31. Name the canal that passes through the midbrain.

Ans Cerebral aqueduct.

32. What do grey and white matter in the brain represent?

Ans Grey matter is a major component of CNS consisting of cell bodies of neurons, dendrite, non-myelinated glial cells and capillaries. White matter is also a component of CNS and consists mostly of glial cells and myelinated axons.

33. Which is the largest and most complex of all the parts of the human brain?

Ans Forebrain, which mainly includes cerebrum.

34. How do the efferent fibres work?

Ans The efferent nerve fibres transmit motor impulses from the CNS to the concerned tissues/organs and form the motor or efferent pathway.

35. How does the somatic nervous system work?

Ans The somatic nervous system controls the movements of the body by acting on the skeletal muscles (i.e. relays voluntary impulses from the CNS to skeletal muscles).

36. What is the term used for the stimulus of adequate strength?

Ans Threshold stimulus. It fires the signals in the neuron.

37. Name the small tubular gap structures between the two neurons.

Ans Gap junctions.

38. What is the nature of nerve impulse?

Ans Bioelectric/electrochemical disturbance (change).

39. Give the name of the chemicals, which are released at the synaptic junction.

NCERT Exemplar

Ans Neurotransmitters are the chemicals, which are released at synaptic junctions.

40. The autonomic nervous system is considered as involuntary nervous system. Why?

Ans This system transmits impulses from the CNS to the involuntary organs and smooth muscles of the body. So, it is also called involuntary nervous system.

Short Answer Type I Questions

2 Marks

41. Write a short note on neural coordination.

NCERT

Ans The organised network of point-to-point connection for quick coordination provided by neural system is called neural coordination.

The mechanism of neural coordination involves transmission of nerve impulse, impulse conduction across a synapse and the physiology of reflex action. (2)

42. Name the main division of nervous system in human.

Ans Central nervous (neural) system and peripheral nervous (neural) system. (2)

43. Answer the following

(i) Which part of the human brain is most developed?

(ii) Which part of the central nervous system acts as biological clock? **NCERT**

Ans (i) Cerebrum (ii) Pineal body of the brain (1+1)

44. Which nerve tract connects the right and left hemispheres of the cerebrum? Name the four lobes of hemisphere of brain?

Ans Right and left hemispheres of the cerebrum are connected by corpus callosum. Each hemisphere is divided into frontal lobe, temporal lobe, parietal lobe and occipital lobe. (2)

45. Describe the functions of limbic system?

Ans It is involved in the regulation of sexual behaviour, expression of emotional reactions, e.g. pleasure, excitement, rage and fear and motivation. (2)

46. Differentiate between myelinated and non-myelinated axons. **NCERT**

Ans Differences between myelinated and non-myelinated axons are

Myelinated Axon	Non-myelinated Axon
These nerve fibres are enveloped with Schwann cells, which form a myelin sheath around the axon.	These nerve fibres are enclosed by a Schwann cell that does not form a myelin sheath around the axon.
Myelinated nerve fibres are found in spinal and cranial nerves.	These are commonly found in autonomous and the somatic nervous systems.

(2)

47. Complete the statement by choosing appropriate match among the following. **NCERT Exemplar**

A.	Resting potential	1.	Chemicals involved in the transmission of impulses at synapses.
B.	Nerve impulse	2.	Gap between the presynaptic and postsynaptic neurons.
C.	Synaptic cleft	3.	Electrical potential difference across the resting neural membrane.
D.	Neurotransmitters	4.	An electrical wave-like response of a neuron to a stimulation.

Ans A-3, B-4, C-2, D-1. (2)

48. How do the ionic gradients across the resting membrane can be maintained?

Ans The ionic gradients across the resting membrane are maintained by the active transport of ions by the sodium-potassium pump. (2)

49. State the role of sodium-potassium pump in the maintenance of ionic gradients.

Ans The sodium-potassium pump helps in the active transport of ions, 3 Na^+ are transported outwards and $2K^+$ inwards through the neurolemma of neurons. (2)

50. Compare the following
Resting potential and action potential. **NCERT**

Ans **Resting potential** The electrical potential difference across the plasma membrane is called the resting potential.

Action potential The action potential is an electrical signal that travels along an axon. It is another name of nerve impulse. (2)

51. Explain the factors on which the impulse conduction depends.

Ans Impulse conduction depends upon

(i) permeability of axolemma (axon membrane)

(ii) osmotic equilibrium between the axoplasm and extracellular fluid present outside the axon. (2)

52. Explain the significance of saltatory conduction.

Ans This process accounts for the greater speed of an impulse travelling along a myelinated neuron than along a non-myelinated one. It is upto 50 times faster than the non-myelinated nerve fibre. (2)

53. Why does synapse act as a one-way valve?

Ans Synapse acts as a one-way valve because neurotransmitter is secreted at the terminal knobs of axon only. The dendrite membrane (postsynaptic membrane) has the specific protein receptor molecules to break this neurotransmitter. (2)

54. Compare Central Nervous System (CNS) and Peripheral Nervous System (PNS) **NCERT**

Ans The CNS includes the brain and the spinal cord and is the site of information processing and control. The PNS comprises of all the nerves of the body associated with the CNS (brain and spinal cord). (2)

55. Nervous system and computers share certain common features. Comment in five lines. (Hint : CPU, input-output devices). **NCERT Exemplar**

Ans The brain might be compared to a computer as its memory banks. The spinal cord to the conducting cable for the computer's input and output and the nerves to a circuit supplying input information to the cable and transmitting the output to muscles and organs. The most important of these components is the Central Processing Unit (CPU) or microprocessor, which acts as the 'brain' of your computer. (2)

56. If someone receives a blow on the back of neck, what would be the effect on the person's CNS? **NCERT Exemplar**

Ans If a person receives a blow on the back, it results in an impairment of cognitive abilities or physical functioning. It can also result in the disturbance of behavioural or emotional functioning. Cervical injuries often result in quadriplegia (tetraplegia). (2)

Short Answer Type II Questions

3 Marks

57. Describe the protective coverings of the brain.

Ans Refer to text on page no. 484.

58. Discuss the functional areas of the cerebrum.

Ans Refer to text on page no. 484 and 485.

59. Briefly describe the structure of the brain. **NCERT**

Ans Refer to text on page no. 484.

60. Differentiate between thalamus and hypothalamus. **NCERT**

Ans Differences between thalamus and hypothalamus are

Thalamus	Hypothalamus
The cerebrum wraps around a structural part of brain called thalamus.	It lies at the base of the thalamus.
All types of sensory input passes synapses to the thalamus.	It contains neurosecretory cells that secrete hypothalamus hormones.
It controls emotional and memory functions.	It regulates, sexual behaviour expression of emotional reactions and motivation.

(1×3)

61. Differentiate between cerebrum and cerebellum. **NCERT**

Ans Differences between cerebrum and cerebellum are

Cerebrum	Cerebellum
It is the most developed part in brain.	It is the second developed part of brain also called as little cerebrum
A deep cleft divides cerebrum into two cerebral hemispheres.	Externally the whole surface contains gyri and sulci.
Its functions are intelligence, learning, memory, speech, etc.	It contains centres for coordination and error checking during motor and cognition.

(1×3)

62. The major parts of the human neural system is depicted below. Fill in the empty boxes with appropriate words.

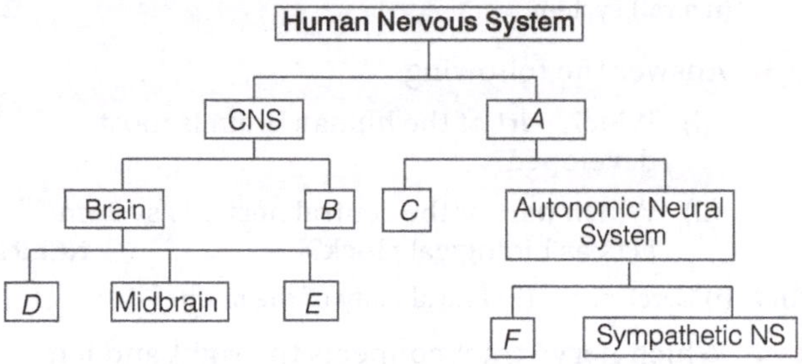

Ans

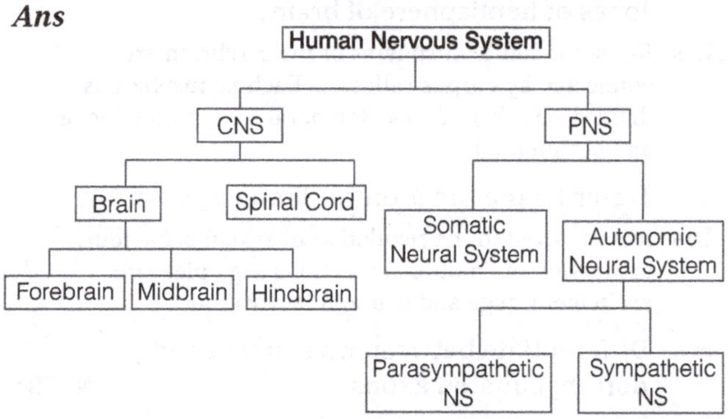

(3)

63. Distinguish between cranial nerve and spinal nerve in human. **NCERT**

Ans Differences between cranial nerve and spinal nerve in human are

Cranial Nerve	Spinal Nerve
The cranial nerves originate in the brain and terminate mostly in organs of head and upper body.	The spinal nerves originate in the spinal cord and extend to parts of the body below the head.
There are 12 pairs of cranial nerves.	There are 31 pairs of spinal nerves.
Most of the cranial nerves contain axon and both sensory and motor neurons.	All of the spinal nerves contain axons of both sensory and motor neurons.

(1×3)

64. Define nerve impulse. Explain the factors on which impulse conduction depends.

Ans Refer to text on page no. 487-488.

65. Explain the role of Na^+ in the generation of action potential. **NCERT**

Ans When a stimulus is applied to a nerve, the membrane of the nerve becomes freely permeable to Na^+.

This leads to a rapid influx of Na^+ followed by the reversal of the polarity at that site, i.e. the outer surface of the membrane becomes negatively charged and the inner side becomes positively charged.

The electrical potential difference across the plasma membrane at the membrane is called the action potential, which is in fact termed as a nerve impulse. Thus, this shows that Na^+ ions play an important role in the conduction of nerve impulse. (3)

66. Write a short note on synapse. **NCERT**

Ans Refer to text on page no. 488.

Long Answer Type Questions

5 Marks

67. What is brain? Also describe the components of CNS with their functions.

Ans Refer to text on page no. 484-486.

68. Write short notes on the following

(i) Forebrain

(ii) Midbrain

(iii) Hindbrain **NCERT**

Ans Refer to text on page no. 484-485.

69. During resting potential, the axonal membrane is polarised. Explain the movement of positive and negative ions leading to polarisation. **NCERT Exemplar**

Ans Refer to text on page no. 487.

70. Give a brief account on the mechanism of synaptic transmission. **NCERT**

Ans Refer to text on page no. 488-489.

71. What is the difference between electrical transmission and chemical transmission? **NCERT Exemplar**

Ans Refer to text on page no. 488-489.

72. Explain the following processes

(i) Polarisation of the membrane of a nerve fibre

(ii) Depolarisation of the membrane of a nerve fibre

(iii) Conduction of a nerve impulse along a nerve fibre

(iv) Transmission of a nerve impulse across a chemical synapse **NCERT**

Ans (i) Refer to text on page no. 487.

(ii) Refer to text on page no. 487-488.

(iii) Refer to text on page no. 487 and 488

(iv) Refer to text on page no. 488-489.

Case Based Questions

4/5 Marks

73. *Read the following passage and answer the questions that follows.*

Raju has recently joined the gym. The first day, while doing exercise, he felt increased rate of respiration, heartbeat, sweating, etc. He got worried as he experienced the sudden changes in his body. He discussed it with his brother who is a biology student. His brother smiled and explained him that these are the normal activities of the organs/organ systems that occur during exercise for the maintenance of normal physiology of the human body.

(i) Name the processes that are necessary for maintaining normal physiology of the human body.

(ii) Define coordination and integration.

(iii) Explain how does the various organs of the body are coordinated and integrated during exercise.

(iv) Name the two main parts of the human neural system.

Ans (i) Coordination and integration of body organs is done by neural system, which regulate normal physiology of human body. (1)

(ii) Coordination is the process through which two or more organs interact and complement the functions of one another. On the other hand, integration is a process, which makes two or more organs to work as a functional unit in harmony. (1)

(iii) When we do exercise, we observe significant increase in the rate of respiration, heartbeat, bloodflow, sweating, etc., to meet enhanced needs of nutrients and energy for increased activities of lungs, hearts, muscles and many other body organs. When we stop exercising, we witness that the increased activities of lungs, heart, nerves, kidneys, muscles, etc., gradually return to normal. Thus, during exercise, functions of various organs of the body are coordinated and integrated. (2)

(iv) Human neural system is divided into the Central Neural System (CNS) and Peripheral Neural System (PNS). (1)

74. The data below shows the working of various part of a student's brain during a three hours long exam.

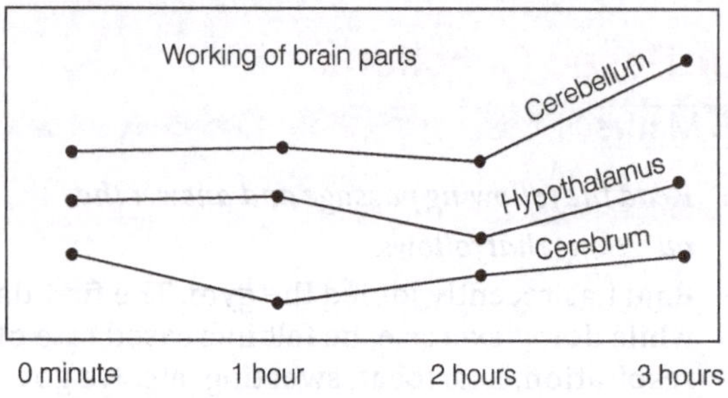

(i) With reference of the above graph explain which part of the brain is the most active during the examination?

(ii) What is the location and function of hypothalamus?

(iii) Cerebellum is the least active among the three brain parts shown in the graph. What is its role in the body?

(iv) Human brain is divided into three main regions-forebrain, midbrain and hindbrain. Categorise the parts of the brain given in the graph into their respective region.

Ans (i) The cerebrum is the most active region during the examination because it is the site for controlling thought, learning, intelligence, intellectual activities, translating perception and memories into plan actions, reasoning, decision-making, etc. (1)

(ii) Hypothalamus lies at the base of the thalamus. It contains a number of centres which control the body temperature, urge for eating and drinking. It also contains several groups of neurosecretory cells, which secrete hormones called hypothalamic hormones. (2)

(iii) The function of the cerebellum is to maintain body posture, muscle toning, coordination and equilibrium of the body.

(iv) Cerebrum and hypothalamus belongs to forebrain. Cerebellum is a part of hindbrain.

75. The graph given below shows the change in voltage for a non-myelinated neuron sending impulses.

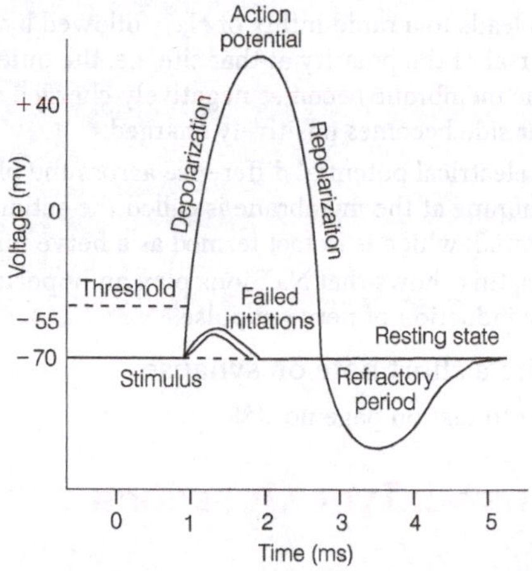

(i) With reference to the above graph explain along what structure does the impulse travel?

(ii) Where would sodium channels open and where would potassium channels open?

(iii) During propagation of a nerve impulse, the action potential results from movement of which ions from extracellular fluid to intracellular fluid?

Or

(iii) If this axon were myelinated, what advantage would it have?

Ans (i) Nerve impulse also called as action potential travels along the membrane of neuron. It is an electrical charge that can be generated when a neurons membrane potential is changed by chemical signals from a nearby cell. (1)

(ii) In neurons, the rapid rise in potential, depolarisation, is initiated by the opening of sodium ion channels within the plasma membrane. The subsequent return to resting potential, depolarisation, is mediated by the opening of potassium ion channels. (1 + 1)

(iii) Na^+ ions move from extracellular fluid to intracellular fluid. (1)

Or (iii) The speed of transmission of nerve impulses is more in myelinated axons than in non-myelinated axons. This is due to the reason that myelinated axons have nodes of Ranvier. Nerve impulse can jump node to node in myelinated axons which favours a faster transmission speed. (1)

CHAPTER

22

Chemical Coordination and Integration

In the previous chapter, you have already learnt that the nervous system in the body, provides point-to-point connection through nerve fibres and coordination amongst the organs. The neural coordination is rapid, but short lived in nature. However, the nerve cells do not reach to each and every cell of the body. So, a special kind of coordination and integration is provided to each cell for its continuous cellular functions. This special function is performed by hormones.

Thus, the nervous system and endocrine system are intimately related to each other forming neuroendocrine system together that jointly coordinate to regulate the physiological functions of the body.

- Endocrinology : Major Glands and their Hormones
  - Endocrine Glands and hormones
  - Human Endocrine System
  - Structure and Functions of Major Endocrine Glands
- Endocrinology : Various Tissues, Hormones and Mechanism of Hormone Action
  - Mechanism of Hormone Action

TOPIC 01 Endocrinology : Major Glands and their Hormones

Endocrine Glands and Hormones

The endocrine glands are **ductless glands**, i.e. lack ducts. They pour their secretions into the surrounding blood for transport to the site of action or distantly located target organ. Their secretions are called **hormones** or **internal secretion**.

Hormones

These are non-nutrient chemicals, which are produced in trace amounts and act as **intercellular messengers**. These are responsible for regulating the biological processes in the body. The organised endocrine glands also secrete a number of other molecules in addition to the hormones.

Vertebrates have large number of chemicals acting as hormones that provide coordination, while invertebrates possess very simple endocrine system with few hormones.

Note

- The first hormone was discovered by **William M Bayliss** and **Ernest H Starling** in 1903.
- **Endocrinology** is the study of endocrine glands and hormones secreted by them.

Hypo and Hyperactivity of Hormones

When hormones are secreted in deficiency, the role of the hormones decreases which leads to hypoactivity of the hormones. On the other hand, excess secretion of the hormones increases hormone action which is called hyperactivity of the hormones.

The hypoactivity or hyperactivity of hormones can cause disorders. For example, deficiency of insulin causes diabetes mellitus. Likewise excess of growth hormone from early age causes gigantism.

Chemical Nature of Hormones

Hormones are derived from different building-block molecules. Their chemical nature depends on these molecules.

The molecules and hormones derived from them are

1. **Amino Acids** Thyroxine secreted from thyroid gland is an iodinated thyronine.
2. **Amines** These are amino acid derivatives. Melatonin (from pineal gland) and catecholamines, adrenaline and nor-adrenaline (from tyrosine in adrenal medulla) are derived from amino acids.
3. **Peptides** Hypothalamic hormones, such as TRH, GRH, GIH, MSH, hormones of posterior lobes of pituitary, i.e. ADH, oxytocin, ACTH of anterior pituitary and calcitonin of thyroid belong to this category.
4. **Proteins** Insulin, glucagon (hormones of pancreas), hormones of gastrointestinal tract, PTH (parathyroid hormone), female hormones-like relaxin and hCG are protein in nature.
5. **Steroids** The steroid hormones derived from cholesterol are aldosterone, cortisol, sex corticoids (adrenal cortex), testosterone, oestrogen, progesterone (gonadal hormones).

Human Endocrine System

The endocrine system in humans constitutes the **endocrine glands** and **hormone** producing diffused tissues/cells located in different parts of our body. In endocrine system, the hormone from one gland may stimulate or inhibit another endocrine gland. These can also vary in structure.

Types of Human Endocrine Glands

The endocrine glands are of following two types in humans

i. Pure Endocrine Glands

These work entirely for the secretion of hormones. They include the hypothalamus, pituitary, pineal, thyroid, adrenal, pancreas, parathyroid, thymus glands and gonads (i.e. testes in males and ovaries in females).

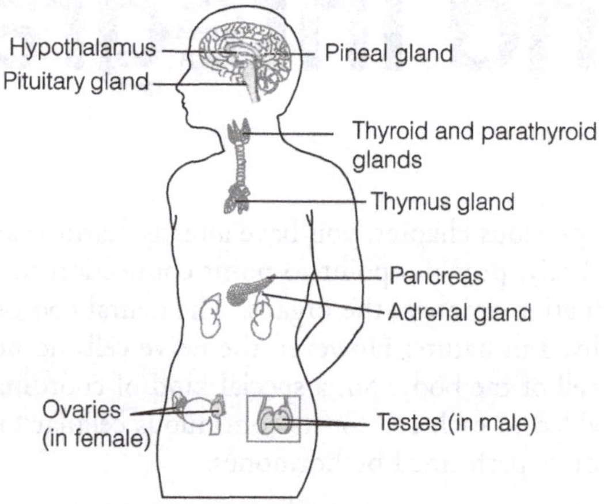

Fig 22.1 Location of different endocrine glands

ii. Partial Endocrine Glands

These are partly endocrine and partly exocrine in function. They include kidneys, gastrointestinal tract, heart, placenta, etc.

Structure and Functions of Major Endocrine Glands

Hypothalamus

In humans, the complete endocrine system works more or less under the influence of hypothalamus.

Origin

It develops from the ectoderm of embryo like other parts of brain.

Location

Hypothalamus is located in the basal part of diencephalon (forebrain) and it regulates a wide spectrum of functions in the body.

Structure

It is composed of **nervous tissues.** It connects with the anterior lobe of pituitary by **hypophyseal portal** blood vessels and to the posterior lobe of pituitary by the **axons** of its neurons.

Hormones

Hypothalamus contains several groups of **neurosecretory cells,** known as nuclei, which produce hormones. The function of these hormones is to regulate the synthesis and secretion of pituitary hormones. Hormones produced by hypothalamus are of following two types

(i) **Releasing Hormones** These are the hormones that stimulate the secretion of pituitary hormones, e.g. **Gonadotropin Releasing Hormone** (GnRH), which stimulates the gonadotroph cells of anterior pituitary gland to release gonadotropins.

(ii) **Inhibiting Hormone** These are the hormones that inhibit the release of pituitary hormones, e.g. **somatostatin,** which inhibits the secretion of growth hormone from anterior lobe of pituitary gland. All these hormones originating in the hypothalamic neurons, pass through the axons and are released from their nerve endings.

These hormones finally reach the pituitary gland through a **portal circulatory system** (hypophyseal portal system) thereby, regulating the functions of anterior pituitary.

The posterior pituitary however, functions under the direct regulation of the hypothalamus.

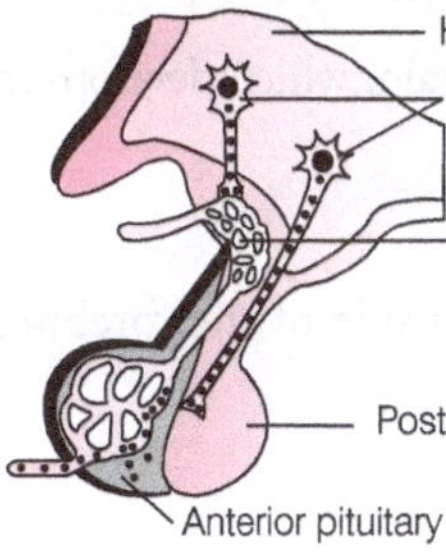

Fig 22.2 Diagrammatic representation of pituitary and its relationship with hypothalamus

Pituitary Gland (Hypophysis)

It is the smallest endocrine gland, but serves very important role in the human endocrine system. It directly or indirectly controls almost all other endocrine glands of the body. It is also known as **master gland.**

Origin

It originates from the ectoderm of the embryonic germ layers.

Location and Structure

It is **reddish grey** in colour and is roughly oval in shape. It is about a size of a pea seed. The pituitary gland is located in a small bony cavity of the brain called **sella tursica.**

Anatomy

The pituitary gland has three major lobes, i.e. anterior, intermediate and posterior lobe.

It is anatomically divided into two major portions

1. Adenohypophysis

It is the glandular anterior portion of the pituitary gland. It further consists of two parts, i.e. pars distalis and pars intermedia. These two parts represent the anterior and intermediate lobes of pituitary.

(i) **Pars Distalis** It is also called as anterior pituitary. It produces different hormones. These hormones are given below with their functions

- **Growth Hormone** (GH) stimulates the somatotroph cells of anterior lobe of pituitary gland to release growth hormone or somatotropin. It stimulates body growth, protein, fat and carbohydrate metabolism.
- **Prolactin** (PRL) The prolactin releasing hormone stimulates **lactotroph cells** of the anterior lobe of pituitary gland to secrete prolactin. PRL regulates the growth of mammary glands and formation of milk in them.
- **Thyroid Stimulating Hormone** (TSH) Thyroid releasing hormone stimulates **thyrotroph cells** of the anterior lobe of pituitary to secrete its thyroid Stimulating Hormone, i.e. TSH or thyrotropin. This TSH stimulates the synthesis and secretion of thyroid hormones from the thyroid gland.
- **Adrenocorticotropic Hormone** (ACTH) This is secreted when Adrenocorticotropin Releasing Hormone (ACRH) stimulates the **corticotroph cells** of anterior lobe of pituitary. This stimulates the synthesis and secretion of steroid hormones called **glucocorticoids** from the adrenal cortex.
- **Gonadotropin Hormone** It is the **gonadotroph cells** of anterior lobe of the pituitary gland, which secrete, Luteinizing Hormone (LH) and Follicle Stimulating Hormone (FSH). Both of these hormones stimulate the gonadal activity hence, called gonadotrophin.

- **Luteinizing Hormone** (LH) In males, it stimulates the synthesis and secretion of hormones called androgens from testis. While, in females, it induces ovulation of fully mature follicles (Graafian follicles) and also helps in maintaining the corpus luteum formed from the remnants of the Graafian follicles after ovulation.
- **Follicle Stimulating Hormone** (FSH) In males, the FSH and androgens together regulate spermatogenesis. In females, this hormone stimulates the growth and development of ovarian follicles.

(ii) **Pars Intermedia or Intermediate Lobe** This portion of adenohypophysis secretes only one hormone, i.e.

- **Melanocyte Stimulating Hormone** (MSH) or **Melanotropin** The melanocyte releasing hormone or hypothalamus stimulates the intermediate lobe of pituitary gland to secrete its Melanocyte Stimulating Hormone. MSH acts on **melanocytes** (melanin containing cells) and regulates the pigmentation of the skin.

2. Neurohypophysis

It is a collection of axonal projections from the hypothalamus, which terminate behind the anterior pituitary gland. It is **pars nervosa** of the neurohypophysis that forms the posterior lobe of pituitary gland. The posterior pituitary stores and releases two hormones which are given below

(i) **Oxytocin** It is a short peptide of nine amino acids, also known as **pitocin.** It acts on the smooth muscles of our body and stimulates a vigorous contraction of uterus at the time of child birth. It also plays role in ejection of milk from the mammary glands in females.

(ii) **Vasopressin** It is a small peptide hormone, also known as **Antidiuretic Hormone** (ADH) or **pitressin.** This hormone acts mainly at the kidney, stimulating the reabsorption of water and electrolysis by the distal tubules. Thereby reducing the loss of water through urine (diuresis).

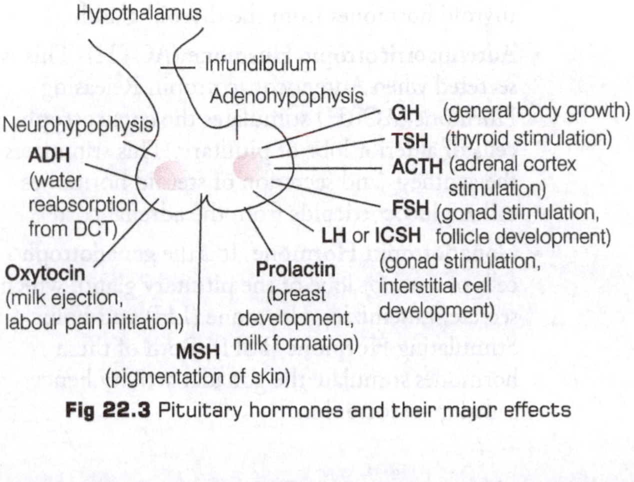

Fig 22.3 Pituitary hormones and their major effects

Disorders

The disorders caused by the malfunctioning of pituitary gland are as follows

(i) **Hyperactivity** The disorders caused by the hyperactivity of pituitary hormones are

Acromegaly (*Acro*-extremity, *megaly*-large) It is caused by the hypersecretion of growth hormone after adulthood is reached. It is characterised by disproportionate increase in size of bones of face, hands and feet.

Gigantism It is caused by the hypersecretion of growth hormone from early stage. It is characterised by large and well proportioned body.

(ii) **Hypoactivity** The disorders caused by the hypoactivity of pituitary hormones are **pituitary dwarfism.** It is caused by the deficiency of growth hormone from childhood. It is characterised by small but well proportioned body and sexual immaturity.

Diabetes insipidus It is caused by the hyposecretion of ADH. It is characterised by excessive dilute urine (diuresis). It leads to a condition of reduced water absorption.

> **Knowledge Plus**
>
> - During the time of parturition (delivery time) in mother, the secretion of oxytocin hormone is at its maximum. This hormone causes labour pain at the time of birth. Thus, because of its role, it is called **birth hormone** and **milk ejecting hormone**.
> - LH is also called ICSH (Interstitial Cell Stimulating Hormone) in males, as it affects the interstitial cells or cells of Leydig of testes.

Pineal Gland (Epiphysis)

It is a small gland in the brain, which develops from the embryonic ectoderm.

Location

It is located on the dorsal side of the forebrain between the cerebral hemispheres.

Structure

Pineal is a very small gland, reddish grey in colour, vascular conical in shape and has solid body. It is composed of pineal cells and supporting glial cells.

Hormones

It secretes a hormone called **melatonin** that plays a very important role in the regulation of a 24 hrs (diurnal) rhythm of our body. Melatonin also helps in maintaining the normal rhythms of sleep-wake cycle, body temperature, Metabolism, pigmentation, menstrual cycle as well as our defence capability is also influenced by this hormone.

Thyroid Gland

The thyroid gland is known to be the largest endocrine gland.

Origin

It is endodermal in origin, i.e. it originates from the endoderm of the embryo. The thyroid gland is bilobed, highly vascular organ.

Location and Structure

It surrounds the front of the **larynx** and is composed of two lobes. Each of its lobe is located on either side of the trachea in the neck interconnected with each other through a thin flap of connective tissue, called **isthmus**.

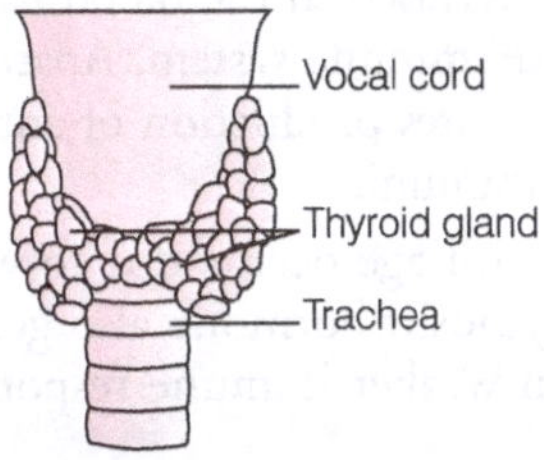

Fig 22.4 Diagrammatic view of the position of thyroid gland (ventral side)

It is composed of **follicles** (round in shape) held together by loose connective tissue called **stromal tissues.** Each thyroid follicle is composed of follicular cells, enclosing a cavity.

Hormones

The follicular cells synthesise following two hormones

(i) Tetraiodothyronine or thyroxine (T_4) hormone

(ii) Triiodothyronine (T_3) hormone.

Both these hormones are iodinated forms of the amino acid, tyrosine. They are stored in the colloid that fills the follicles and are released to the blood when needed. Iodine (in diet) is essential for the synthesis of hormone at normal rate in thyroid.

Disorders

(i) **Hypothyroidism** It occurs due to the deficiency of iodine in our diet. It can cause following disorders

Simple goitre It is caused by deficiency of iodine in diet because iodine is needed for the synthesis of thyroid hormone. It causes thyroid enlargement. Addition of iodine to the table salt prevents this disease.

Cretinism This disorder is caused by deficiency of thyroid hormone in infants. A cretin has slow body growth and mental development of reduced metabolic rate. Its other symptoms are slow heartbeat, lower blood pressure, decrease in temperature, stunted growth, etc.

(ii) **Hyperthyroidism** It is the condition during which, rate of synthesis and secretion of thyroid hormones is increased to abnormal high levels. It may occur due to the cancer of the thyroid gland or due to development of nodules of the thyroid gland. It adversly affects the body physiology of an organism.

- **Exophthalmic Goitre** (Grave's disease) In this enlargement of thyroid gland takes place. Thus, thyroid secretion increases. It leads to protrusion of the eyeballs, increased basal metabolic rate and weight loss.

Knowledge Plus

- **Hashimoto's disease** is an autoimmune disorder in which the thyroid gland is destroyed by autoimmunity. All the functions of thyroid gland gets impaired during this disease.
- **Myxoedema** is caused by the deficiency of thyroid hormones in adults. It is more common in women and is characterised by puffy appearance due to accumulation of fat in subcutaneous tissue because of low metabolic rate and retarded oxidation.

Functions of Thyroid Hormones

Thyroid hormones serve several functions in the body, such as

(i) These hormones regulate and maintain the **Basal Metabolic Rate** (BMR), i.e. both T_3 and T_4 hormone increase the overall metabolic rate of the body.

(ii) They support the process of formation of red blood cells. They also help in controlling the metabolism of carbohydrates, proteins and fats.

(iii) They influence the maintenance of water and electrolyte in our body.

Apart from the hormone T_3 and T_4, thyroid gland also secretes a protein hormone called **Thyrocalcitonin** (TCT). Its main function is to regulate the level of calcium in blood.

Parathyroid Gland

These are small glands in the human neck that produce parathyroid hormone.

Origin

It is endodermal in origin.

Location

These glands are situated on the **posterior side** of the thyroid gland.

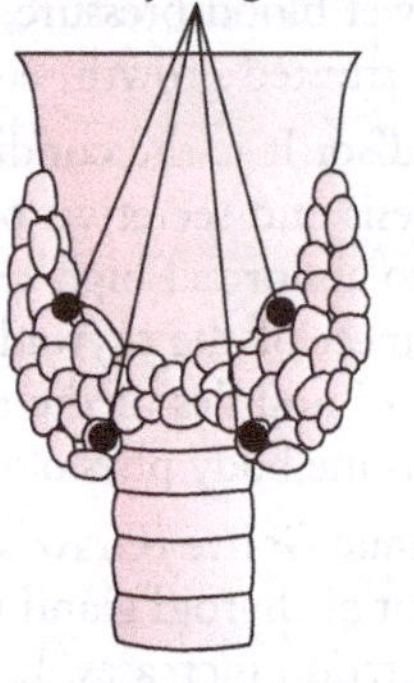

Fig 22.5 Diagrammatic view of the position of parathyroid gland (dorsal side)

Structure

Parathyroid glands are **four** in number, i.e. each pair is situated in the two lobes of the thyroid gland on its either side. These are small, flat and oval glands.

Hormones

Parathyroid glands secrete a single hormone known as **parathormone** or **Parathyroid Hormone** (PTH) (functions opposite to the thyrocalcitonin hormone). The secretion of PTH is regulated by the circulating level of calcium ions in the blood.

Functions of Parathyroid Hormone

Parathyroid hormone serves several functions in the body, such as

(i) It increases the level of Ca^{2+} in the blood.

(ii) It stimulates the process of bone reabsorption (i.e. dissolution/demineralisation) by acting on bones.

(iii) It also stimulates reabsorption of Ca^{2+} by the renal tubules and absorption of Ca^{2+} from the digested food.

By the above mentioned functions of parathyroid hormone, it is clear that PTH acts as a **hypercalcaemic hormone** (increases the level of Ca^{2+} in the blood). Parathyroids are under the feedback control of blood calcium level. A fall in Ca^{2+} in blood stimulates them to secrete PTH.

Thus, both the hormones (TCT and PTH) play a significant role to control and regulate the concentration of Ca^{2+} and phosphorus.

Thymus

It is a lymphoid gland that plays an important role in the development of immune system.

Origin

It arises from the endoderm of the embryo.

Structure and Location

The thymus gland is a lobular structure situated on the dorsal side of the heart and the aorta (in the upper part of thorax near the heart). It is a soft, pinkish, bilobed mass of lymphoid tissue and is a prominent gland that gets degenerated with age.

Hormones

The thymus gland secretes peptide hormone called **thymosin**, which plays a major role in the differentiation of T-lymphocytes, which provide cell-mediated immunity. Thymosins, when released in the blood has a stimulating effect on the entire immune system. Apart from this, thymosin also promotes production of antibodies to provide humoral immunity.

Its degeneration with age occurs due to which production of thymosin hormone also gets decreased. Thus, resulting in weaker immune response in old people.

Adrenal Gland (Suprarenals)

Location

Our body has a pair of adrenal glands. Each located at the anterior part of each kidney.

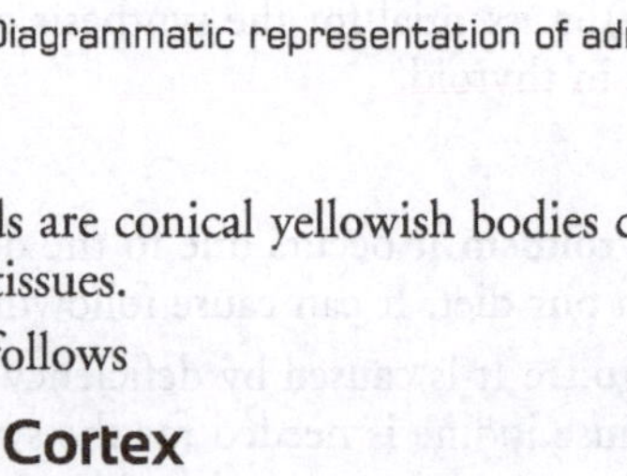

Fig 22.6 Diagrammatic representation of adrenal gland

Structure

Adrenal glands are conical yellowish bodies composed of two types of tissues.

These are as follows

1. Adrenal Cortex

It is an external firm, pale yellowish tissue derived from mesoderm of embryo.

It is further divided into three concentric layers

(a) **Zona Reticularis** It is the inner layer of the cortex where cells are arranged in the net-like fashion.

(b) **Zona Fasciculata** It is the middle layer of the cortex. It is the widest of all three layers.

(c) **Zona Glomerulosa** It is the outermost layer. It is composed of five layers of compactly arranged cells.

Hormones secreted by these three layers of adrenal cortex are collectively known as **corticoids**.

Three groups of steroid hormones are secreted by adrenal cortex, such as

(i) Mineralocorticoids (Aldosterone)

They regulate the balance of water and electrolytes in our body. **Aldosterone** is the major mineralocorticoid found in our body. It mainly acts on renal tubules stimulating the reabsorption of Na^+ and water. It also stimulates the excretion of K^+ and phosphate ions from the body.

Functions of Mineralocorticoids

Its main function is to maintain electrolytes, body fluid volume, osmotic pressure and blood pressure of the body.

(ii) Glucocorticoids (Cortisol)

These are the hormones, which regulate the metabolism of carbohydrates, proteins and fats. **Cortisol** is the main glucocorticoid found in our body.

Functions of Glucocorticoids

(i) Cortisol stimulates the liver for the synthesis of carbohydrates from non-carbohydrate sources (like amino acids and glycerol). This process is known as **gluconeogenesis**. Hence, glucocorticoids stimulate gluconeogenesis, lipolysis and proteolysis.

(ii) Inhibition of cellular uptake and utilisation of amino acids.

(iii) Cortisol is involved in the maintenance of cardiovascular system and in proper functioning of kidneys.

(iv) Cortisol produces anti-inflammatory reactions and also functions in suppression of immune response.

(v) It stimulates the production of RBC.

(iii) Sexocorticoids (Androgens)

Adrenal cortex also produces a small quantity of androgenic steroids, i.e. **sex hormone** (androgens) both in males and females.

These hormones are secreted as **DHEA** (Dehydroxy Epiandrosterone), which act as a precursor of both testosterone and oestrogen.

Functions of Sexocorticoids

(i) It plays a major role in the growth of axial, pubic and facial hair during puberty in humans.

(ii) Development of acne is also due to these hormones in young girls.

(iii) It also plays an important role in the development of embryo (foetus).

> **Knowledge Plus**
>
> - **Addison's disease** is caused by the deficiency of mineralocorticoids.
> - **Cushing's syndrome** is due to excess of cortisol, while an excess of aldosterone leads to aldosteronism.
> - **Adrenal virilism** is caused by excess of sex corticoids in a female. In this there is development of male secondary sexual characters such as beard, moustaches, etc., in females.

2. Adrenal Medulla

The adrenal medulla lies in the centre of the adrenal gland. It is an internal soft, dark reddish brown tissue derived from the ectoderm.

The adrenal medulla secretes two hormones

(i) Adrenaline (epinephrine)

(ii) Nor-adrenaline (nor-epinephrine)

Activation of Adrenaline and Nor-adrenaline

Both hormones belong to the category of compounds known as **catecholamines** and are secreted in response to any kind of stress, danger and during emergency situations and increase respiratory rate, heartbeat, etc.

The CNS at the time of stress or danger stimulates the adrenal medulla to release both these hormones. These are also known as **emergency hormones** or **hormones of fight** or **flight**.

Functions of Adrenaline and Nor-adrenaline

These hormones serve following purposes

(i) Increase alertness.

(ii) Dilation of pupil.

(iii) Piloerection (raising of hairs of hands and legs).

(iv) Increase in heartbeat and rate of respiration.

(v) They also stimulate the breakdown of glycogen due to which the concentration of glucose increases in the blood.

(vi) Stimulate breakdown of lipids and proteins.

Pancreas

It is a composite gland that acts as both exocrine and endocrine gland. Such glands are also called **heterocrine gland.**

Origin

It originates from the endoderm of the embryonic germ layers.

Location

It lies below the stomach, in the loop of duodenum.

Structure

It is an elongated yellowish gland that consists of large number of acini and ducts. Besides these, pancreas consists of 1-2 millions of small group of specialised cells, called **islets of Langerhans** (after the name of their discoverer Paul Langerhans in 1869).

In normal human pancreas, these cells represent only 1-2% of the pancreatic tissue.

Each islet consists of major two types of cells as

(i) **α-cells** (about 25%) They secrete a peptide hormone called **glucagon.**

(ii) **β-cells** (about 60%) They secrete another peptide hormone called **insulin.**

Note Apart from α and β-cells, islets of Langerhans consist of two or more types of cells called **delta cells** or **D-cells** (about 10%) which secrete somatostatin hormone and **PP-cells** or **F-cells** which secrete Pancreatic Polypeptide-PP hormone.

Hormones

Glucagon and insulin have antagonistic effect on blood glucose level. This can be cleared from their functioning given below

(i) Glucagon

This peptide hormone plays an important role in maintaining the normal blood glucose level. It brings about change of liver glycogen to blood glucose.

Functions of Glucagon

(a) It acts mainly on liver cells (hepatocytes) and stimulates glycogenolysis, which results in an increased blood sugar known as **hyperglycaemia.**

(b) Apart from this, glucagon also stimulates the process of gluconeogenesis which also contributes to hyperglycaemia.

Glucagon is known as hyperglycaemic hormone because it reduces the cellular glucose uptake and utilisation.

(c) It reduces glycogenesis and also enhances lipolysis.

Note Glucagon also stimulates the secretion of insulin from β-cells by its paracrine effect.

(ii) Insulin

This peptide hormone plays a major role in regulation of glucose level in the blood. It mainly acts on **hepatocytes** and **adipocytes** (cells of adipose tissue), increasing the cellular glucose uptake and utilisation.

As a result, the movement of glucose takes place rapidly from blood to liver cells and cells of adipose tissues, decreasing the blood glucose level (hypoglycaemia).

Deficiency Disorder of Insulin

Diabetes mellitus is the common complex disorder caused due to prolonged hyperglycaemia.

This is associated with the loss of glucose (when complete glucose cannot be reabsorbed by the kidneys) in the urine as pancreas fails to release adequate amount of insulin to lower the level of glucose in the body.

During this disorder, cells fail to utilise glucose and other carbohydrate for production of energy instead start utilising proteins and fats for it (due to which person becomes weak). Diabetic patients are successfully treated with insulin therapy.

Functions of Insulin

(a) Insulin stimulates the conversion of glucose to glycogen (glycogenesis) in the target cells.

(b) Decreases gluconeogenesis.

(c) Decreases glycogenolysis.

(d) Also reduces the catabolism of proteins and fats.

(e) Increases synthesis of fat in the adipose tissue from fatty acids.

Gonads

These are the primary reproductive organs in human, i.e. the testes in males and the ovaries in females. These organs are responsible for producing the sperm and ova, but they also secrete hormones and are considered to be endocrine glands.

Testes

Location

A pair of testes is located in the **scrotal sac** (outside abdomen) of male individuals.

Structure

A testis is composed of many **seminiferous tubules** which are lined by germinal epithelium and stromal or interstitial tissues. This epithelium consists of three types of cells

(i) **Follicular cells** give rise to sperms.

(ii) **Interstitial cells** or **Leydig cells** secrete group of hormones called **androgens** mainly testosterone.

(iii) **Sertoli cells** provide nourishment to sperms and also secrete hormone (inhibin).

Hormone

Interstitial cells present in the intertubular spaces produce a group of hormones, i.e. androgens. These include testosterone, dihydrotestosterone and androstenedione, but mainly secrete testosterone.

Functions

Androgen (mainly testosterone) performs a variety of functions given below

(a) It regulates the development, maturation and functions of **male accessory sex organs** like epididymis, vas deferens, seminal vesicles, prostate gland, urethra, etc.

(b) These hormones also stimulate changes associated with **puberty in males**, i.e. muscular growth, growth of facial and axillary hair, aggressiveness, low pitch of voice, etc.

(c) Also stimulates the process of **spermatogenesis**, i.e. formation of spermatozoa.

(d) Promotes the growth of body tissues such as bones and muscles and helps in the formation of musculine body.

(e) Also have **anabolic effects** (synthetic effects) on the metabolism of protein and carbohydrate.

> **Inhibin Hormone**
>
> Beside testosterone, another hormone is also secreted by the Sertoli cells, of testes known as inhibin. Its main function is to check and regulate the overactivity of testosterone by inhibiting its secretion.

Ovaries

These are the **primary sex organ** in females that serve to produce ova (female gametes) and female sex hormones.

Location

A pair of ovaries is located in the pelvic cavity (in the abdomen).

Structure

It is an almond-shaped structure. Internally it is composed of **ovarian follicles** and **stromal tissues.**

Hormones

Ovary produces two groups of steroid hormones, i.e. **oestrogen** and **progesterone.** Oestrogens are secreted by granulosa cells of Graafian follicle.

After ovulation, the ruptured follicle is converted to another structure called **corpus luteum**, responsible for the secretion of progesterone. Both oestrogen and progesterone play a vital role in various processes in females.

Oestrogen

(i) It helps in the growth of uterine endometrium layer during each menstrual cycle.

(ii) It directly influences the development of mammary glands.

(iii) Regulates female sexual behaviour and stimulates growth and activities of female secondary sex organs.

(iv) Plays a role in the development of growing ovarian follicles.

(v) Appearance of female secondary sex characters (deposition of fat on thigh and hip region, high pitch etc).

Progesterone

(i) It is secreted in very high amount continuously during pregnancy. It supports pregnancy by forming placenta and preventing contractions in uterine wall.

(ii) It also acts on mammary glands and stimulates the formation of alveoli (sac-like structures that store milk) and **milk secretion.**

(iii) It also helps in forming a mucus plug at cervix.

Note

Relaxin is another hormone secreted by ovary in the later stages of pregnancy. Its main role is in softening ligament, widening pelvic cavity. It also affects other ligaments such as of foot, etc., due to which women may experience increase in their foot size during pregnancy.

Topic Practice 1

Multiple Choice Questions

1 Mark

1. When hormones are secreted is excess amount, it is known as ....A.... of hormones. Choose the correct option for A.

(a) hypoactivity
(b) hyperactivity
(c) hypo and hyperactivity
(d) None of the above

Ans (b) When hormones are secreted in excess amount, it is known as hyperactivity of hormones.

2. Which is the incorrect statement from the following?

(a) Hypothalamus is a basal part of mesencephalon
(b) It regulates wide spectrum of body functions
(c) Neurosecretory cells of hypothalamus secrete hormones
(d) Hormones of hypothalamus regulate the synthesis of pituitary hormones

Ans (a) Hypothalamus is the basal part of diencephalon, i.e. forebrain.

3. Hypothalamus releases two types of hormones mainly

(a) stimulating hormones; releasing hormones
(b) stimulating hormones; inhibiting hormones
(c) exocrine hormones; inhibiting hormones
(d) exocrine hormones; stimulating hormones

Ans (b)

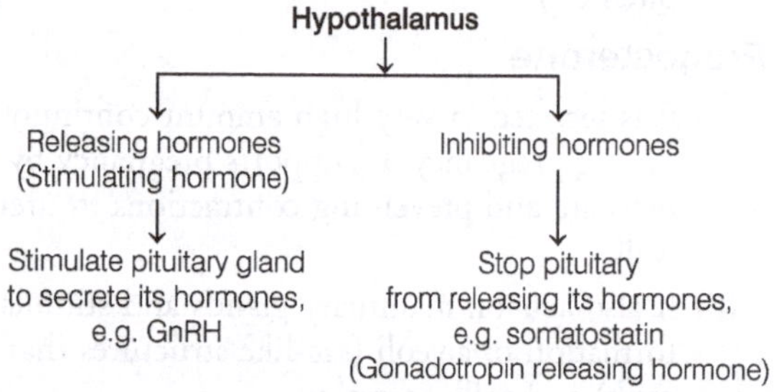

4. Functions of oxytocin is/are

(a) smooth muscle contraction
(b) contraction of uterus
(c) milk ejection
(d) All of the above

Ans (d) Oxytocin acts on the smooth muscles of our body and stimulates their contraction. In females, it stimulates a vigorous contraction of uterus at the time of childbirth and milk ejection from the mammary gland.

5. GnRH (Gonadotropin Releasing Hormone) stimulates the

(a) pituitary to release the gonadotropin
(b) pituitary for synthesis and release of gonadotropin
(c) testis to release the gonadotropin
(d) hypothalamus to release the gonadotropin

Ans (b) GnRH (Gonadotropin Releasing Hormone) from hypothalamus stimulates the pituitary to synthesise and release of gonadotropin. On the other hand, somatostatin from hypothalamus inhibits the release of growth hormone from pituitary.

6. Gigantism and dwarfism are the diseases related to

(a) prolactin hormone of mammary gland
(b) growth hormone of adenohypophysis
(c) luteinizing hormone of pituitary gland
(d) thyroid stimulating hormone of thyroid

Ans (b) Oversecretion of GH (Growth Hormone) stimulates abnormal growth of the body leading to gigantism and low secretion of GH results in stunted growth resulting in dwarfism.

7. Pineal gland is located on the

(a) ventral side of forebrain
(b) lateral side of forebrain
(c) dorsal side of forebrain
(d) back side of forebrain

Ans (c) The pineal gland is located on the dorsal side of the forebrain. Pineal gland secretes a hormone called melatonin. Melatonin plays a very important role in regulating of 24 hrs (diurnal) rhythm of our body.

8. The thyroid gland is composed of

(a) follicles (b) stromal tissue
(c) trachea (d) Both (a) and (b)

Ans (d) The thyroid gland is composed of follicles and stromal tissues. Each thyroid follicle is composed of follicular cells enclosing a cavity. These follicle cells synthesise two hormones tetraiodothyronine or thyroxine (T_4) and triiodothyronine (T_3).

9. Cretinism, mental retardation, low intelligence quotient, abnormal skin, deaf-mutism, etc., are the results of

(a) hyperthyroidism (b) goitre
(c) hypothyroidism (d) Both (b) and (c)

Ans (c) Hypothyroidism during pregnancy causes defective development and maturation of the growing baby leading to stunted growth (cretinism), mental retardation, low intelligence quotient, abnormal skin, deaf-mutism, etc. In adult women, hypothyroidism may cause irregular menstrual cycle.

10. Secretion of PTH is regulated by the circulating levels of .... in blood.

(a) Na^+ (b) I^- (c) Ca^{2+} (d) Fe^{2+}

Ans (c) The parathyroid gland secretes a peptide hormone called Parathyroid Hormone (PTH). The secretion of PTH is regulated by the circulating levels of calcium ions (Ca^{2+}) in the blood.

11. Hormone that increases the blood calcium (Ca^{2+}) and decreases the excretion of $Ca^{2+}$by reabsorption is

(a) calcitonin (b) parathormone
(c) insulin (d) ACTH

Ans (b) Parathormone, secreted by parathyroid gland, regulates the calcium and phosphate balance between blood and other tissues.

It increases the plasma Ca^{2+}, represses plasma phosphate and decreases Ca^{2+} excretion by the kidney.

12. Adrenal gland is present at the

(a) lateral side of each kidney
(b) dorsal side of each kidney
(c) posterior side of each kidney
(d) anterior side of each kidney

Ans (d) Our body has one pair of adrenal glands, one at the anterior part of each kidney. The gland is composed of two types of tissues. The centrally located tissue is called adrenal medulla and outside this lies the adrenal cortex.

13. Cortisol is involved in

(a) maintaining cardiovascular system
(b) kidney functions
(c) RBCs production
(d) All of the above

Ans (d) Cortisol is involved in maintaining the cardiovascular system as well as kidney functions. Glucocorticoids, particularly cortisol, produces anti-inflammatory reactions and suppresses the immune response. Cortisol stimulates the RBCs production.

14. Correct characteristics of insulin includes

(a) hypoglycemic hormone
(b) decreases the blood sugar
(c) act on adipose tissue and hepatocytes
(d) All of the above

Ans (d) Insulin is a peptide hormone which plays a major role in the regulation of glucose homeostasis. Insulin acts mainly on hepatocytes and adipocytes (cells of adipose tissue) and enhances cellular glucose uptake and utilisation. As a result there is a rapid movement of glucose from blood to hepatocytes and adipocytes resulting in decreased blood glucose level (hypoglycemia). Insulin also stimulates conversion of glucose to glycogen (glycogenesis) in target cells.

15. Oestrogen

(a) stimulate the growth of ovarian follicle
(b) stimulate the appearance of secondary sex characters
(c) stimulate the growth of mammary glands
(d) All of the above

Ans (d) Oestrogen produces wide ranging actions such as stimulation of growth and activities of female secondary sex organs, development of growing ovarian follicle, appearance of female secondary sex characters (e.g. high pitch voice, etc.), mammary glands development.

Oestrogen also regulates the female sexual behaviour.

16. Progesterone

(a) supports the pregnancy
(b) acts on the mammary gland and stimulates the formation of alveoli
(c) Both (a) and (b)
(d) controls secondary sexual characters in females

Ans (c) Progesterone supports pregnancy. Progesterone also acts on the mammary glands and stimulates the formation of alveoli (sac-like structures which store milk) and milk secretion.

Very Short Answer Type Questions

1 Mark

17. Identify the neurohormone that has its functioning in inhibiting the secretion of growth hormone from anterior lobe of pituitary.

Ans Somatostatin inhibits the secretion of growth hormone from anterior lobe of pituitary gland.

18. Name the only hormone secreted by pars intermedia of pituitary gland. **NCERT Exemplar**

Ans Melanocyte Stimulating Hormone (MSH).

19. Acromegaly is caused by the hypersecretion of which hormone?

Ans Acromegaly is caused by the hypersecretion of growth hormone by the pituitary gland.

20. State the reason for the occurrence of diabetes insipidus in an individual.

Ans Deficiency in the secretion of vasopressin (ADH) leads to the disorder known as diabetes insipidus.

21. Mention the name of the largest and the smallest endocrine gland found in man.

Ans Thyroid gland is the largest endocrine gland and pituitary gland is the smallest endocrine gland.

22. **Which of the two adrenocortical layers, zona glomerulosa and zona reticularis lies outside enveloping the other?** **NCERT Exemplar**

Ans Zona glomerulosa (outer layer) envelops zona reticularis (inner layer) from the outside.

23. **The outermost layer of adrenal cortex is responsible for secretion of which hormone? Identify.**

Ans Mineralocorticoids.

24. **Locate the hormone that controls Na^+ and K^+ metabolism in the body.**

Ans Aldosterone is responsible for controlling Na^+ and K^+ metabolism in the body.

25. **Name the hormone which can suppress immune response. What is its chemical nature?**

Ans Cortisol is responsible for the suppression of immune response. Chemically it is a steroid.

26. **A patient complains of constant thirst, excessive passing of urine and low blood pressure. When the doctor checked the patient's blood glucose and blood insulin level, the level were normal or slightly low. The doctor diagnosed the condition as diabetes insipidus. But he decides to measure one more hormone in patient's blood. Which hormone does the doctor intend to measure?** **NCERT Exemplar**

Ans Glucagon.

27. **Give the name of the disorder that is marked by the increased output of sugar in urine.**

Ans Diabetes mellitus.

28. **There are many endocrine glands in human body. Name the gland, which is absent in male and the one absent in female.** **NCERT Exemplar**

Ans The glands, which are absent in males are ovaries and which are absent in females are testes.

29. **Mention the name of the hormone that is responsible for the urge of sex in males.**

Ans Testosterone hormone is responsible for the urge of sex in males.

30. **Name the hormone and its source, which produces change in secondary sex organs in human female to prepare for anticipated pregnancy?**

Ans Oestrogen secreted by granulosa cells of developing ovarian follicle.

Short Answer Type I Questions

(2 Marks)

31. **Why is chemical and hormonal coordination necessary?**

Ans As the nerve fibres do not innervate all the cells of the body and cellular functions need to be regulated in a continuous manner. So, to regulate this coordination, endocrine system (chemical and hormonal coordination) is necessary. (2)

32. **Comment 'hormones are called informational molecules.'**

Ans Hormones are known as informational molecules because their synthesis takes place in one part of the body, i.e. the endocrine cells and are carried by the blood to another part of the body, i.e. target organ or tissues. They stimulate or inhibit the specific physiological processes according to the need of the body. (2)

33. **How are the hypothalamic hormones transported to target organs?**

Ans The hypothalamic hormones secreted by the neurosecretory cells called nuclei are transported through their axons and released from their nerve endings and mixed with blood of hypophyseal portal vein.

These are then transported to anterior pituitary. The posterior pituitary hormones pass through the axons that reach the posterior pituitary and remain stored in the axon terminals, till they are stimulated for release. (2)

34. **Which hormone is responsible for the maintenance of diurnal rhythm of our body? Mention its source.**

Ans The hormone responsible for diurnal rhythm of our body is melatonin. The source of its secretion is pineal gland. (2)

35. **When does the secretion of adrenocorticotropin take place in the body? What is the purpose of its secretion?**

Ans Adrenocorticotropin is secreted when Adrenocorticotropin Releasing Hormone (ACRH) stimulates the corticotroph cells of the anterior lobe of pituitary gland. (1)

It is released because its stimulation is responsible for the synthesis and secretion of glucocorticoid steroid hormone from the adrenal cortex of adrenal gland. (1)

36. **In countries where dietary intake of iodine is low, goitre, i.e. enlargement of the thyroid are common. What would you say about the chain of events leading to the formation of goitre?**

Ans In the absence of iodine, neither **thyroxine** or **triiodothyronine** hormone is produced, due to which their concentration in the blood decreases. To compensate this, the anterior pituitary secretes large amount of TSH, which stimulates the growth of thyroid gland, sometimes to gigantic proportions, leading to the formation of goitre.

However, enlargement of the gland cannot increase production of the hormones, because of the deficiency of its main ingredient, i.e. iodine. (2)

37. Inflammatory responses can be controlled by a certain steroid. Name the steroid, its source and also its other important functions. **NCERT Exemplar**

Ans Inflammatory responses are controlled by steroid hormones called glucocorticoids, which are secreted by adrenal cortex.

Its other functions are to stimulate gluconeogenesis, lipolysis and proteolysis and inhibit cellular uptake and utilisation of amino acids. (2)

38. What are the effects of hypothyroidism (observed during pregnancy) on the development and maturation of a growing baby? **NCERT Exemplar**

Ans Hypothyroidism during pregnancy causes defective development and maturation of the growing baby leading to stunted growth (cretinism), mental retardation, low intelligence, abnormal skin, deaf-mutism, etc. (2)

39. Mention the difference between hypothyroidism and hyperthyroidism. **NCERT Exemplar**

Ans Hypothyroidism is low secretion of thyroxine hormone. Hyperthyroidism is oversecretion of thyroid hormones. It occurs due to low or hyper activity of the thyroid gland. (1+1)

40. Give the name of the endocrine gland that produces calcitonin and also mention the role played by this hormone.

Ans Calcitonin (CT) or Thyrocalcitonin hormone is produced by thyroid glands. (1)

It is hypocalcaemic and hypophosphatemic peptide hormone, which checks excess plasma Ca^{2+} and phosphate by decreasing mobilisation from bones. (1)

41. Describe the endocrine functions of thymus. (Any four)

Ans Functions of thymus are as follows

(i) It secretes thymosin, a peptide hormone that plays an important role in differentiation of T-lymphocytes.

(ii) Release of thymosin provides cell-mediated immunity.

(iii) It is also responsible for creating antibodies for the immune system during childhood.

(iv) It gets degenerated with age due to which production of thymosin gets decreased. ($\frac{1}{2} \times 4$)

42. Old people have weak immune system. What could be the reason? **NCERT Exemplar**

Ans Thymus is degenerated in old individuals resulting in a decreased production of thymosin.

Due to which the immune responses of old persons become weak. (2)

43. Differentiate between hyperglycaemia and hypoglycaemia.

Ans Differences between hyperglycaemia and hypoglycaemia are

Hyperglycaemia	Hypoglycaemia
It results from hyposecretion of insulin.	It results from hypersecretion of insulin.
Its symptoms include high blood glucose level, breakdown of muscles tissues, loss of weight and tiredness.	Its symptoms include low blood glucose level, hunger, sweating, irritability, double vision.

(1 × 2)

44. Briefly mention the mechanism of action of FSH. **NCERT**

Ans In males, FSH and androgens regulate spermatogenesis. In females, FSH stimulates growth and development of the ovarian follicles. It stimulates the secretion of oestrogen in ovaries. (2)

45. A milkman was very upset one morning as his cow refusesed to give any milk. The milkman's wife gets the calf from the shed. On fondling by the calf, the cow gave sufficient milk. Describe the role of endocrine gland and pathway associated with this response. **NCERT Exemplar**

Ans The fondling by the calf stimulates the release of oxytocin from the posterior pituitary.

Oxytocin brings about contractions of the smooth muscles of the mammary glands that causes ejection of milk. (2)

46. Match the following columns.

	Column I		Column II
A.	T_4	1.	Hypothalamus
B.	PTH	2.	Thyroid
C.	GnRH	3.	Pituitary
D.	LH	4.	Parathyroid

NCERT

Ans A–2, B–4, C–1, D–3. ($\frac{1}{2} \times 4$)

47. State whether true or false.

(i) Gastrointestinal tract, kidney and heart also produce hormone.

(ii) Pars distalis produces six trophic hormones.

(iii) B-lymphocytes provide cell-mediated immunity.

(iv) Insulin resistance results in a disease called diabetes mellitus. **NCERT Exemplar**

Ans (i) True (ii) True (iii) False (iv) True ($\frac{1}{2} \times 4$)

48. Correct the following statements by replacing the term underlined.

(i) Insulin is a <u>steroid</u> hormone.

(ii) TSH is secreted from the <u>corpus luteum</u>.

(iii) <u>Tetraiodothyronine</u> is an emergency hormone.

(iv) The pineal gland is located on the <u>anterior part</u> of the kidney. **NCERT Exemplar**

Ans (i) Insulin is a proteinaceous hormone.

(ii) TSH is secreted from the thyroid gland.

(iii) Adrenaline is an emergency hormone.

(iv) The pineal gland is located on the dorsal side of the forebrain. ($\frac{1}{2} \times 4$)

Short Answer Type II Questions

3 Marks

49. Mention the major classes of hormones in humans. Give examples of each.

Ans Although hormones are chemically diverse, they generally belong to one of the four different chemical groups.

(i) **Steroid Hormones** These hormones are manufactured by endocrine cells from cholesterol, an important type of lipid in the human body. Examples include cortisol, aldosterone, oestrogen, progesterone and testosterone.

(ii) **Amino Acid Derivatives** The thyroid hormones (T_3 and T_4) are synthesised from the amino acid tyrosine and iodide, respectively.

Adrenaline (also known as epinephrine) and nor-adrenaline (also known as nor-epinephrine) are produced by the medulla of the adrenal gland, are also derived from tyrosine. Melatonin is synthesised from the amino acid tryptophan.

(iii) **Protein Hormones** These hormones are long, folded chains of amino acids. Included among these hormones are insulin, glucagons, parathyroid hormone, growth hormone, prolactin, etc.

(iv) **Peptide Hormones** Hormones such as oxytocin and antidiuretic hormone are smaller than protein hormone. They are made up of a short chain of amino acids. (3)

50. Define the following

(i) Exocrine gland (ii) Endocrine gland

(iii) Hormones **NCERT**

Ans (i) **Exocrine gland** is a gland that pours its secretions on the surface or into a particular region by means of ducts for performing a metabolic activity, e.g. sebaceous glands, sweat glands, salivary glands, etc.

(ii) **Endocrine gland** is a gland that pours its secretion into blood or lymph for reaching the target organ because the gland is not connected with the target organ by any duct. It is also known as ductless gland.

(iii) **Hormones** are non-nutrient chemicals which act as intercellular messengers and are produced in trace amount. (1×3)

51. Distinguish between endocrine and exocrine glands.

Ans Differences between endocrine and exocrine glands are

Endocrine Glands	Exocrine Glands
They do not have ducts.	They have ducts.
They secrete hormones directly into the blood.	They secrete their secretions into the ducts.
e.g. thyroid, hypothalamus, pituitary, etc.	e.g. sweat and oil glands (of skin), liver and salivary glands.

(1×3)

52. Diagrammatically indicate the location of the various endocrine glands in our body. **NCERT**

Ans Refer to fig. no. 22.1. (3)

53. Which hormones are secreted by the posterior pituitary gland? What function does each serve? Where are these hormones actually produced? How are these hormones transported to the region from where they are released?

Ans Oxytocin and vasopressin are secreted by the posterior pituitary gland. (1)

(i) **Oxytocin** is released into the blood when hypothalamic neurons are stimulated by the widening of uterus at the time of delivery or by the sucking of breasts by an infant. It induces contraction of smooth muscles of the uterus during the birth of a youngone and myoepithelial cells of mammary glands to cause release of milk during sucking by an infant. Therefore, it is also known as 'birth hormone'. (1)

(ii) **Vasopressin** is also called Antidiuretic Hormone (ADH). It decreases the loss of water in urine by increasing reabsorption of water in distal convoluted tubules, collecting tubules and collecting ducts of kidneys. (1)

54. How do you justify the statement that hormones of adrenal medulla are emergency hormones?

Ans Hormones of adrenal medulla, i.e. adrenaline and nor-adrenaline (belong to the category of compounds called catecholamines) are secreted in response to any kind of stress, danger and during emergency situations like fall in blood pressure or sugar, increase respiratory rate and heartbeat.

CNS at the time of stress or danger stimulates adrenal medulla to release these hormones. All these conditions need more energy for their action. Thus, because these hormones prepare the body to face stress or danger hence, are called emergency hormones. (3)

55. On an educational trip to Uttarakhand, Ketki and her friends observed that many local people were having swollen necks. Please help Ketki and her friends to find out the solutions to the following questions

(i) Which probable disease are these people suffering from?

(ii) How is it caused?

(iii) What effects does this condition have on pregnancy? **NCERT Exemplar**

Ans (i) The people are suffering from the goitre disease.

(ii) Goitre is caused by the deficiency of iodine which leads to the hypothyroidism.

(iii) It leads to defective development of foetus and birth of child with cretinism. (1×3)

56. Write short notes on the functions of the following hormones

(i) Parathyroid Hormone (PTH)

(ii) Thyroid Hormones

(iii) Thymosins **NCERT**

Ans Refer to text on page no. 503 and 504. (1 × 3)

57. Write short notes on the following

(i) Androgens

(ii) Oestrogen

(iii) Glucagon and insulin **NCERT**

Ans Refer to text on page no. 505-507. (1 × 3)

58. George comes on a vacation to India from US. The long journey disturbs his biological clock and he suffers from jet lag. What is the cause of his discomfort?

Ans Jet lag is caused by the disruption of the body clock as it is out of synchronisation with the unfamiliar time zone of the two different parts of the world. The body experiences different patterns of light and dark than it is normally used to which disrupts the natural sleep-wake cycle. Melatonin is a hormone that plays a key role in body rhythms and jet lag.

After the Sun sets, the eyes perceive darkness and alert the hypothalamus to begin releasing melatonin, which promotes sleep.

Conversely, when the eyes perceive sunlight, they tell the hypothalamus to with-hold melatonin production. However, the hypothalamus cannot read just its schedule instantly, it takes several days. (3)

59. Give examples of

(i) hyperglycaemic hormone and hypoglycaemic hormone

(ii) hypercalcaemic hormone

(iii) gonadotropic hormone

(iv) progestational hormone

(v) blood pressure lowering hormone **NCERT**

(vi) androgens and oestrogens

Ans (i) glucagon and insulin, respectively

(ii) Parathyroid hormone

(iii) Follicle Stimulating Hormone (FSH) and Luteinizing Hormone (LH)

(iv) Progesterone

(v) Atrial Natriuretic Factor (ANF)

(vi) Androgens are mainly testosterone and oestrogens include oestriol, oestradiol and oestrone. ($\frac{1}{2}$ × 6)

60. Which hormonal deficiency is responsible for the following?

(i) Diabetes mellitus

(ii) Goitre

(iii) Cretinism **NCERT**

Ans (i) Diabetes mellitus is due to deficiency of insulin.

(ii) Goitre is due to the deficiency of thyroxine (T_4) and triiodothyronine (T_3).

(iii) Cretinism is due to deficiency of thyroxine hormone. It mainly occurs in children. (1 × 3)

Long Answer Type Questions

5 Marks

61. Hypothalamus is a super master endocrine gland. Elaborate. **NCERT Exemplar**

Ans Hypothalamus regulates a wide spectrum of body functions. It contains several groups of neurosecretory cells called nuclei, which produce hormones. These hormones regulate the synthesis and secretion of pituitary hormones.

However, the hormones produced by hypothalamus are of two types, the releasing hormones (which stimulate secretion of pituitary hormones) and the inhibiting hormones (which inhibit secretions of pituitary hormones).

The hormones reach the pituitary gland through a portal circulatory system and regulate the functions of the anterior pituitary. The posterior pituitary is under the direct regulation of hypothalamus.

The oxytocin and vasopressin are the two hormones synthesised by hypothalamus that are transported to posterior pituitary. (5)

62. **Explain the following by giving scientific reasons**

(i) **Hypothalamus and pituitary function as an integrated and coordinated system.**

(ii) **Body growth is greatly accelerated at puberty in males.**

Ans (i) The hypothalamus and pituitary function as an integrated and coordinated system because both of them are connected at the base of the brain. They interact to each other in the following two ways

(a) By the hypophyseal portal system, which is a system of blood vessels that connects part of hypothalamus to the anterior lobe of pituitary gland. Hypothalamus secretes hormones into this portal system and the hormones act on the anterior pituitary, triggering the synthesis/ secretion of pituitary hormone.

(b) The other is that they have direct anatomical connection between the hypothalamus and the posterior lobe of pituitary (posterior pituitary is actually an extension of hypothalamus). Thus, it is said that hormones released through posterior pituitary are actually released from the hypothalamus. (3)

(ii) Puberty is the phenomenon of physical changes by which child's body matures into an adult male, capable of sexual reproduction to enable fertilisation. It is initiated by the hormonal signals from the brain to the gonads, i.e. testes in a male.

In response to the signals, gonads produce hormones that in turn stimulate libido and the growth, function and transformation of the brain, muscles, blood, hair, sexual organs, etc. An androgen called as testosterone in males, functions as principal sex hormone, producing all changes in male related to growth and development at puberty. (2)

63. **Calcium plays a very important role in the formation of bones. Write about the role of endocrine glands and hormones responsible for maintaining calcium homeostasis.**

NCERT Exemplar

Ans The secretion of Parathyroid Hormone (PTH) regulates the concentration of calcium ions (Ca^{2+}). (1)

Parathyroid hormone increases the Ca^{2+} levels in the blood. It acts on bones and stimulates the process of bone resorption (dissolution/ demineralisation).

It also stimulates reabsorption of Ca^{2+} by the renal tubules and increases Ca^{2+} absorption from the digested food.

It is, thus, clear that PTH is a hypercalcaemic hormone, i.e. it increases the blood Ca^{2+} levels. Along with TCT, it plays a significant role in calcium balance in the body. (4)

64. **Give scientific reasons of the following statements.**

(i) **Adrenals are called glands of emergency.**

(ii) **Parathormone is also called Collip's hormone.**

(iii) **The hormones released by the posterior lobe of pituitary are not its own products.**

(iv) **Endocrine glands directly release their products into the blood.**

Ans (i) It is called so, because hormones of adrenal medulla increase the metabolism for preparing the animal to face physical, emotional stress as well as emergencies which could be life threatening.

(ii) It is called so, because a Canadian Endocrinologist James B Collip discovered parathormone in 1925.

(iii) The hormones released by posterior lobe of pituitary gland are, in fact, synthesised by the neurons in the hypothalamus and sent to the former *via* axons for release.

(iv) Endocrine glands are ductless glands and their products act at a distant organ or tissue. (5)

65. **Explain the structure of pancreas and also mention the roles of the hormone secreted by it.**

Ans Refer to text on page no. 506-507.

66. **A sample of urine was diagnosed to contain high content of glucose and ketone bodies. Based on this observation, answer the following.**

NCERT Exemplar

(i) **Which endocrine gland and hormone is related to this condition?**

(ii) **Name the cells on which this hormone acts.**

(iii) **What is the condition called and how can it be rectified?**

Ans (i) Pancreas gland and insulin hormone is related to this condition. (2)

(ii) Insulin hormone acts on hepatocytes and adipocytes. Thus increaces the cellular glucose uptake and utilisation. (1)

(iii) Prolonged hyperglycaemia leads to a complex disorder, called diabetes mellitus, which is associated with loss of glucose through urine and formation of harmful compounds known as ketone bodies. Diabetic patients are successfully treated with insulin therapy. (2)

67. Fill in the blanks.

Hormones	Target gland
(i) Hypothalamic hormones	....
(ii) Thyrotropin (TSH)	....
(iii) Corticotropin (ACTH)	....
(iv) Gonadotropins (LH and FSH)	....
(v) Melanotropin (MSH)	....

NCERT

Ans (i) Pituitary gland
(ii) Thyroid gland
(iii) Adrenal gland
(iv) Testes and ovaries
(v) Melanocytes. (1×5)

68. List the hormones secreted by the following
(i) Hypothalamus (ii) Pituitary
(iii) Thyroid (iv) Parathyroid
(v) Adrenal (vi) Pancreas **NCERT**

Ans Hormones secreted by the following glands are as follows

(i) Hypothalamus secretes thyrotropin releasing hormone, adrenocorticotropin releasing hormone, gonadotropin releasing hormone, somatotropin releasing hormone, prolactin releasing hormone, Melanocyte stimulating hormone.

(ii) (a) Pars distalis part of pituitary (anterior pituitary) secretes Growth Hormone (GH), Prolactin (PRL), Thyroid Stimulating Hormone (TSH), Adrenocorticotropic Hormone (ACTH), Luteinizing Hormone (LH), Follicle Stimulating Hormone (FSH).
(b) Pars intermedia secretes Melanocyte Stimulating Hormone (MSH).
(c) Pars nervosa secretes oxytocin, vasopressin.

(iii) Thyroid secretes thyroxine (T_4) and triiodothyronine (T_3).

(iv) Parathyroid secretes Parathyroid Hormone (PTH).

(v) Adrenal
(a) secrets adrenaline, nor-adrenaline from adrenal medulla
(b) also secretes corticoids (glucocorticoid and mineralocorticoid) and sexocorticoids from adrenal cortex.

(vi) Pancreas' α-cells secrete glucagon, while its β-cells secrete insulin. The delta (δ) cells secrete somatostatins. (5)

TOPIC 02 Endocrinology : Various Tissues, Hormones and Mechanism of Hormone Action

We have studied about various endocrine glands of the body and hormones secreted by them till now. However, certain endocrine tissues are not organised to form compact endocrine gland, but are present isolated in the body, i.e. hormones are also secreted by some tissues. Some examples of hormones secreted by various tissues are as follows

Hormones of Heart

A very important peptide hormone known as **Atrial Natriuretic Factor** (ANF) is secreted by the atrial walls of our heart, when blood pressure is increased. Its secretion causes dilation of blood vessels thereby reducing the blood pressure.

Hormones of Kidney

A peptide hormone called **erythropoietin** is produced by the juxtaglomerular cells of kidney. This hormone stimulates formation of RBCs, i.e. erythropoiesis. It is done by activating increased erythropoiesis in haemopoietic tissues.

Hormones of Gastrointestinal Tract

GI tract develops from the endoderm of the embryo. Endocrine cells that are present in different parts of this tract secrete four major **peptide hormones.**

These are as follows

(i) **Gastrin**, which acts on the gastric glands and stimulates the secretion of hydrochloric acid and pepsinogen.
(ii) **Secretin**, which acts on the exocrine portion of pancreas (remember pancreas is a mixed gland, performing both exocrine and endocrine roles), stimulating secretion of water and bicarbonate ions.
(iii) **Cholecystokinin-Pancreozymin** (CCK-PZ) This hormone acts on both pancreas and gall bladder stimulating secretion of pancreatic enzymes and bile juice, respectively.
(iv) **Gastric Inhibitory Peptide** (GIP), which is secreted by intestinal mucosa. Its function is to stop or inhibit the secretion of gastric juice and its motility into stomach.

Apart from all these hormones, several other non-endocrine tissues secrete hormones known as **growth factors.** These factors are essential for normal growth, repair and regeneration of tissues.

Hormones Secreted by Placenta

Placenta is the intimate connection between the foetus and the uterine wall of the mother to exchange materials. It is a temporary endocrine gland.

It secretes some hormones like oestrogens, progesterone, human Chorionic Gonadotropin (hCG), human Chorionic Somatomammotropin (hCS), chorionic thyrotropin, chorionic corticotropin and relaxin. Placental progesteron checks contraction of uterine muscles and thus helps to maintain pregnancy. hCG stimulates progesterone release from the corpus luteum and maintains it.

Mechanism of Hormone Action

Hormones are released from their respective gland in very small amount. They carry out widespread effects in the body of an individual. Their response is very specific and accurate.

Their effects are produced on target tissues by binding to the specific proteins known as **hormone receptors,** located in the target tissues only.

Types of Hormones

On the basis of the chemical nature, hormones are divided into following four groups

(i) **Peptide, polypeptide, protein hormones** (e.g. insulin, glucagon, pituitary hormones, hypothalamic hormones, etc).

(ii) **Steroids** (e.g. cortisol, testosterone, oestradiol and progesterone).

(iii) **Iodothyronines** (e.g. thyroid hormones).

(iv) **Amino acid derivatives** (e.g. epinephrine).

Types of Hormone Receptors

Hormone receptors are of following two types

(i) **Membrane Bound Receptors** Hormone receptors present on the cell membrane of the target cells.

(ii) **Intracellular Receptors** Hormone receptors present inside the target cell, e.g. nuclear receptor (present in the nucleus of a cell).

Hormone Receptor Complex

Binding of a hormone to receptor leads to the formation of a hormone receptor complex. Formation of this complex leads to certain biochemical reactions or changes in the respective target tissue. Metabolism of target tissue and their physiological function are thus, regulated by hormones.

Action of Hormone Through Extracellular Receptor

Hormones that interact with the membrane bound receptors do not enter their target cell in normal condition, but generate secondary messengers such as cyclic AMP (*c*AMP), IP_3, Ca^{2+} etc., which regulate cellular metabolism of the body, e.g. protein or peptide hormone.

Note Hormones do not participate in a metabolic reaction themselves, they instead act as messengers only, i.e. mainly primary messengers.

Functioning of Peptide Hormone

Protein hormone is water soluble in nature, binds to the extrinsic receptors (present on cell surface) to form the **hormone receptor complex.**

The formation of this complex causes the release of enzyme **adenyl cyclase.** This activated enzyme, thus leads to the formation of *c*AMP (i.e. cyclic adenosine monophosphate) from ATP in the cell from the receptor site.

$$\text{ATP} \xrightarrow[\text{adenyl cyclase } + \text{Mg}^{2+}]{\text{Activated}} c\text{AMP} + \text{PPi}$$

The hormone receptor complex changes the permeability of the cell membrane to facilitate the passage of materials through it (and thereby, regulates cellular activities of the cell causing specific response to occur).

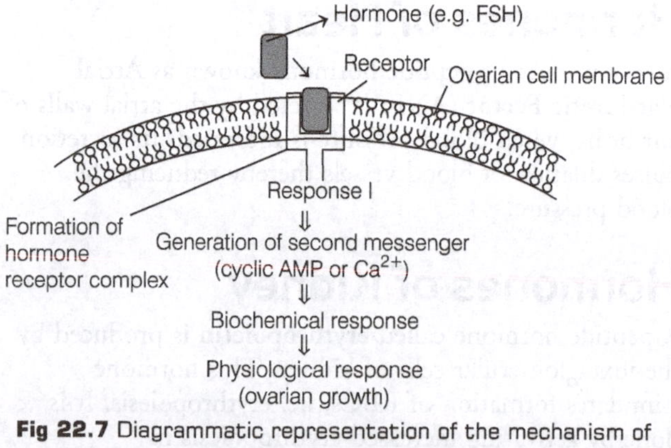

Fig 22.7 Diagrammatic representation of the mechanism of hormone action of peptide or protein hormone

Action of Hormone Through Intracellular Receptors

Hormones that interact with intracellular receptors are mostly involved in the regulation of gene expression or chromosome function by interaction of hormone receptor complex with the genome, e.g. steroid hormone, iodothyronines, etc.

Functioning of Steroid Hormone

Steroid hormones are lipid soluble in nature, so they can easily diffuse through the cell membrane and bind to receptor molecules present in the cytoplasm to form a hormone receptor complex that enters the nucleus.

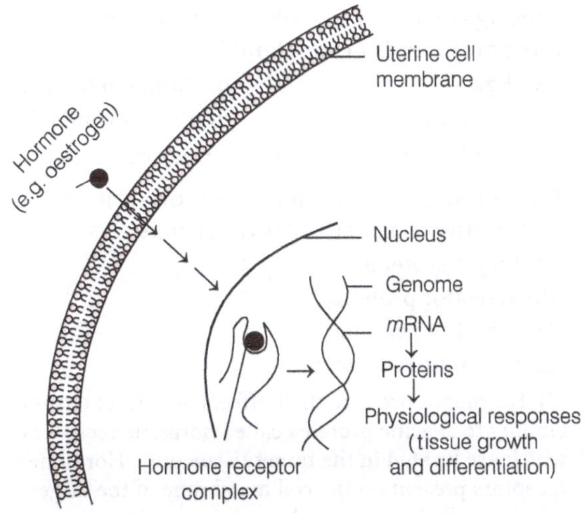

Fig 22.8 Mechanism of hormone action : Steroid hormone

Control of Hormone Action

Both hypo and hyperactivity of an endocrine gland produces structural or functional abnormalities called diseases. Hence, the normal functioning of endocrine glands and the level of hormones in the body needs to be regulated. This is possible by feedback mechanisms. The feedback mechanism may be positive or negative and may operate in following ways

Feedback Control by Hormones

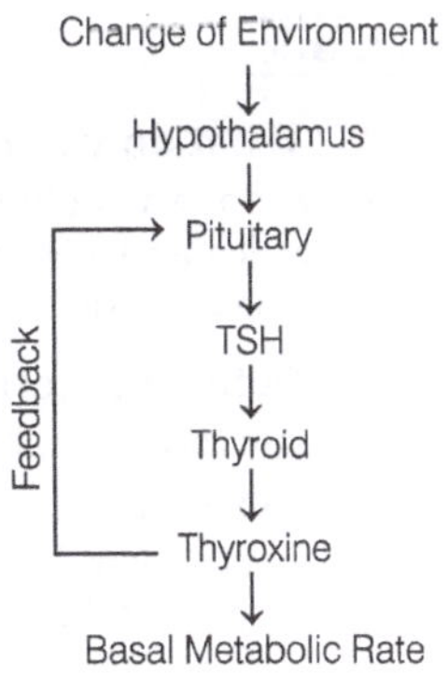

Hypothalamus is stimulated by some external stimulus and produces a releasing hormone. This stimulates anterior pituitary to secrete a specific hormone called Thyrotropic Hormone (TH) or Thyroid Stimulating Hormone (TSH). TSH stimulates thyroid gland to produce hormone thyroxine.

If the level of thyroxine in blood is high, it exerts a negative feedback effect on hypothalamus and anterior pituitary. Hypothalamus secretes less thyroxine releasing hormone and in turn less thyroid hormone, respectively. If the level of thyroxine is less than normal, it stimulates hypothalamus to produce more Thyroid Stimulating Hormone-Releasing Factor (TSH-RF). This causes to release more TSH by the anterior pituitary lobe.

In turn, TSH will stimulate thyroid to produce more thyroxine to raise its level in blood. This type of mechanism is called positive feedback mechanism.

> **Antagonistic and Synergistic Interactions of Hormones**
>
> Hormones can show both antagonistic and synergistic interactions with each other. In antagonistic interactions effects of two hormones are opposite to each other on the target cells, e.g. **insulin** and **glucagon** hormones, act antagonistically on blood glucose level.
>
> In synergistic interaction, two or more hormones tend to complement each other for their effect on target cells, e.g. oestrogen, progesterone, oxytocin, prolactin all act synergistically for the secretion, production and ejection of milk from mammary glands.

Topic Practice 2

Multiple Choice Questions

(1 Mark)

1. 'Atrial Natriuretic Factor' (ANF) is secreted by
   (a) antrum Graafian follicle
   (b) atrial wall of heart
   (c) Both (a) and (b)
   (d) None of the above

Ans (b) The atrial wall of our heart secretes a very important peptide hormone called Atrial Natriuretic Factor (ANF), which is peptide in nature.

ANF decreases blood pressure. When blood pressure is increased, ANF is secreted which causes dilation of the blood vessels. This reduces the blood pressure.

2. ANF has exactly opposite function to which of the following hormones?
   (a) PTH (b) Oestrogen
   (c) Aldosterone (d) Androgen

Ans (c) Aldosterone is a steroid hormone (mineralocorticoid family) produced by the outer section (zona glomerulosa) of the adrenal cortex in the adrenal gland. It plays a central role in the regulation of blood pressure mainly by acting on the distal tubules and collecting ducts of the nephron, increasing reabsorption of ions and water in the kidney.

Thus causes the conservation of sodium, secretion of potassium and increased water retention as well as and increases blood pressure.

When disregulated, aldosterone is pathogenic and contributes to the development and progression of cardiovascular and renal disease. Aldosterone has exactly the opposite function of the atrial natriuretic hormone secreted by the heart.

3. JGC (Juxtaglomerular Cell) secretes
   (a) ANF (b) erythropoietin
   (c) renin (d) Both (b) and (c)

Ans (d) The juxtaglomerular cells of kidney produce a peptide hormone called renin, which increases blood pressure through angiotension-II and erythropoietin which stimulates erythropoiesis.

4. Erythropoietin
   (a) stimulates erythropoiesis
   (b) inhibits erythropoiesis
   (c) inhibits platelets formation
   (d) stimulates platelets formation

Ans (a) Erythropoietin (EPO) is a glycoprotein hormone that controls erythropoiesis or red blood cell production. It is a cytokine (protein signaling molecule) for erythrocyte (red blood cell) precursors in the bone marrow.

5. Which hormone acts on the exocrine part of pancreas and stimulates secretion of water and bicarbonate ions?
   (a) Gastric (b) Secretin
   (c) CCK (d) GIP

Ans (b) **Secretin**, a digestive hormone secreted by the wall of the upper part of the small intestine (the duodenum) acts on the exocrine pancreas and stimulates secretion of water and carbonate ion. Secretin is a polypeptide made up of 27 amino acids. It was discovered in 1902 by British physiologists Sir William M Bayliss and Ernest H Starling.

6. Cholecystokinin (CCK) acts on
   (a) pancreas (b) gall bladder
   (c) Both (a) and (b) (d) liver

Ans (c) Cholecystokinin is a peptide hormone of the gastrointestinal tract which is responsible for stimulating the digestion of fat and protein.

Cholecystokinin, previously called pancreozymin, is synthesised by I-cells in the mucosal epithelium of the small intestine and is secreted in the duodenum, the first segment of the small intestine and causes the release of digestive enzymes and bile from the pancreas and gall bladder, respectively.

7. Gastric Inhibitory Peptide (GIP)
   (a) inhibits the gastric secretion and motility
   (b) inhibits the gastric secretion
   (c) activate the gastric secretion and motility
   (d) activate the gastric secretion

Ans (a) **Gastric Inhibitory Polypeptide** (GIP), also known as the glucose-dependent insulinotropic peptide is a member of the secretin family of hormones. It has traditionally been called gastrointestinal inhibitory peptide or gastric inhibitory peptide and was believed to neutralise stomach acid to protect the small intestine from acid damage, reduce the rate at which food is transferred through the stomach and inhibit the GI motility and secretion of acid.

8. Among the following which one acts as a temporary endocrine gland?
   (a) Egg (b) Graafian follicle
   (c) Placenta (d) Both (a) and (c)

Ans (c) Placenta works as a temporary endocrine gland.

9. Hormones produce their effect on target tissue by binding to specific proteins called as
   (a) target proteins
   (b) activator proteins
   (c) inhibitor proteins
   (d) hormone receptors

Ans (d) Hormones produce their effects on target tissues by binding to specific proteins called hormone receptors, which are located in the target tissue only. Hormone receptors present on the cell membrane of the target cells are called membrane bound receptors and receptors present inside the target cell are called intracellular receptors.

Intracellular receptors are mostly nuclear receptors (present in the nucleus).

10. Which one of the following is not a second messenger in hormone action?
    (a) Calcium (b) Sodium (c) cAMP (d) cGMP

Ans (a) Sodium, cAMP and cGMP are secondary messengers.

Very Short Answer Type Questions

1 Mark

11. What do you understand by the term ANF?

Ans Atrial wall of human heart secretes a peptide hormone called Atrial Natriuretic Factor (ANF) which decreases blood pressure by dilation of the blood vessels.

12. Define the term erythropoiesis. Also name the hormone that stimulates it. **NCERT Exemplar**

Ans Erythropoiesis is the process of formation of RBCs. The juxtaglomerular cells of kidney produce a peptide hormone called erythropoietin which stimulates it.

13. Name any two hormones secreted by the placenta. **NCERT Exemplar**

Ans (i) human Chorionic Gonadotropin (hCG).
(ii) Relaxin.

14. Mention the name given to the hormones produced by some non-endocrine tissues.

Ans Hormones produced by some non-endocrine tissues are called growth factors.

15. Mention the role of second messenger in the mechanism of protein hormone action.

Ans Second messenger regulates the metabolism of a cell, which results in many physiological effects.

16. What act as the secondary messengers in hormone action?

Ans cAMP, DG and IP_3 act as secondary messengers in hormone action.

17. Give an example of intracellular hormone receptor.

Ans Nuclear receptor (present inside the nucleus of a cell) acts as intracellular hormone receptor.

18. Which two hormones are steroids chemically?

Ans Cortisol and testosterone are chemically steroid in nature.

Short Answer Type I Questions

(2 Marks)

19. Which hormone is secreted by heart? Mention its role.

Ans Heart produces Atrial Natriuretic Factor (ANF) which promotes renal sodium excretion and lowers blood pressure. (1+1)

20. Write short note on
(i) Atrial natriuretic factor
(ii) Erythropoietin

Ans Refer to text on page no. 515.

21. Rearrange the following hormones in column I so as to match with their chemical nature in column II. **NCERT Exemplar**

	Column I		Column II
A.	Oxytocin	1.	Amino acid derivative
B.	Epinephrine	2.	Steroid
C.	Progesterone	3.	Protein
D.	Growth hormone	4.	Peptide

Ans A–4, B–1, C–2, D–3. ($\frac{1}{2} \times 4$)

22. What is the role of second messenger in protein hormone action? **NCERT Exemplar**

Ans Hormones which do not enter the target cells, interact with specific receptors located on the surface of the target cell membranes, generate second messengers (e.g. cAMP) on the inner side of the plasma membrane.
The second messenger in turn carries out all the hormonal functions. (2)

23. Explain amplification of a signal in hormone action? What is its role?

Ans Although hormones are present in very small amounts, they effectively regulate many physiological processes. This is the result of signal amplification, i.e. an increase in signal strength. For example, a single hormone receptor complex can stimulate the production of many cAMP molecules. In turn, each cAMP can activate a protein kinase that phosphorylates many protein molecules. In this way, a single hormone molecule can activate many proteins. (2)

24. What is meant by 'synergistic effect'? Explain with an example.

Ans It is a type of hormonal interaction, where two or more hormones complement each other's actions and both are needed for full expression of the hormone effects , e.g. the production, secretion and ejection of milk by mammary glands require the synergistic effects of oestrogens, progesterone, prolactin and oxytocin. (2)

Short Answer Type II Questions

(3 Marks)

25. Mention about the role of all four peptide hormones secreted by gastrointestinal tract.

Ans Refer to text on page no. 515.

26. Write a note on hormone receptors.

Ans Refer to text on page no. 516.

27. Explain the mechanism of steroid hormone action.

Ans Refer to text on page no. 516.

28. (i) What is termed as first messenger and second messenger in the target cells?
(ii) How do protein hormones act on target cells?

Ans (i) Hormone is called first messenger and cAMP is called second messenger. (1)

(ii) Protein hormone is water soluble, it binds to the extrinsic receptors present on the cell surface of the plasma membrane. Hormones when bind to them activate a membrane bound enzyme, adenyl cyclase, which catalyses the conversion of ATP to cAMP. The cAMP then activates one more enzyme known as protein kinases. After phosphorylation of protein, alteration of its function occurs which thereby, leads to some metabolic effect. (2)

29. **What is meant by antagonistic effect? Illustrate your answer with an example.**

Ans It refers to the effect of a hormone that are countered by an antagonistic (opposing) signal, often another hormone. For example, the sympathetic and parasympathetic nervous systems achieve antagonistic effect on heartbeat.

This mechanism involves the use of more than one second messengers. In heart cells cyclic form of adenosine monophosphate (*c*AMP) serves as a second messenger, speeding up muscle cell contraction in response to adrenaline, while cyclic Guanosine Monophosphate (*c*GMP) serves as another second messenger, slowing muscle contraction in response to acetylcholine. (3)

Long Answer Type Questions

5 Marks

30. **(i) Give a diagrammatic representation of the mechanism of protein hormone (e.g. FSH) action.**

(ii) Illustrate the differences between the mechanism of action of a protein and a steroid hormone. **NCERT Exemplar**

Ans (i) Refer to fig. no. 22.7. (2)

(ii) Differences between mechanism of action of a protein and a steroid hormone

Protein Hormone	Steroid Hormone
Protein hormones interact with membrane bound receptors.	They interact with intracellular receptors.
They generate second messengers (cyclic AMP, IP_3, Ca^{2+}, etc).	They regulate gene expression or chromosome function by the interaction of hormone receptor complex with the genome.
The second messengers regulate cellular metabolism.	Cumulative biochemical action of hormone receptor complex results in physiological and developmentel effects.

(1×3)

SUMMARY

- **Endocrine system** is needed to regulate the cellular functions continuously as the nerve fibres do not innervate all cells of the body, which is done with the help of special chemical messengers called **hormones**.
- **Hormones** are the non-nutrient chemicals messengers produced in trace amounts by ductless glands called endocrine glands. These hormones act as intracellular messengers. In addition to endocrine glands. GI tract, liver and kidney also produce hormones.
- Chemically hormones are derived form lodothyronines, amines, peptides, proteins and steroids and the chemical nature of the molecule depends on them.
- Human endocrine system consist of various glands present in our body separated with each other with no anatomical links.
- **Hypothalamus** is made up of neuro secretory cells which produce hormones that regulate the synthesis and secretion of pituitary gland hormones. They produce releasing hormones and inhibiting hormones. Most hormones originating in the hypothalamic neurons, pass through axons and reach anterior pituitary through hypophysial portal circulation. Posterior pituitary is under direct neural regulation of hypothalamus.
- **Pituitary gland** also called master gland is the regulating unit of hormonal system. It is formed of pars dorsalis and pars intermedia (adenohypophysis) and pars nervosa (neurohypophysis) and is safely harboured in sella turcica. While adenohypophysis secretes and hormones, no hormone is secretes formed by neurohypophysis. The hormones secreted by anterior pituitary are growth hormone, gonadotropic hormones, prolactin, ACTH, melanin adrenocorticotropic hormone, thyroid stimulating hormone and lipotropin. Posterior pituitary releases the hormones (ADH oxytocin secreted by hypothalamus) in the time of need.
- **Thyroid gland** is the largest endocrine gland made up of two lobes connected to each other by isthmus. It is composed of follicles and stromal tissues which is made up cuboidal epithelium. The hormones synthesised by these follicles are thyroxine (T_4), triiodothyronine (T_3) and calcitonin.
- Thyrocalcitonin (TCT) is antagonistic to parathormone (PTH) from parathyroid glands and play a role in calcium metabolism. It is a proteinaceous, non-iodised hormone secreted by thyroid gland.
- **Parathyroid glands** are developed from epithelial buds and consist of two types of cell-chief cells and oxyphil cells. The hormone secreted by parathyroid is parathormone (PTH) or Collip's hormone. PTH is hypercalcemic and it does so by promoting bone demineralisation and increases absorption from gut.
- **Adrenal glands** are composed by adrenal cortex and adrenal medulla, adrenal cortex is responsible for secretion of steroid hormones called corticoids. These are mineralocorticoids, glucocorticoids and sexocorticoids on the other hand , adrenal medulla produce adrenaline and epinephrine. Catecholamines released from adrenal medulla are responsible for the 3F 'fight', 'flight' and 'fright' during stressful condition, they are lipolytic, proteolytic and also promote glycogenolysis.
- **Pancreas** is a heterocrine gland. Its endocrine part consist of cells called islets of Langerhans, which is further composed of α, β and γ-cells they secrete glucagon, insulin and somatostatin respectively.
- **Thymus** is an endocrine gland present as a lobular structure between pericardium and sternum that mainly secretes thymosin hormone, which is involved in proliferation and maturation of T-lymphocytes.It also promotes antibody production. Degeneration of thymus in adults is responsible for their weaker immune system.
- **Pineal gland** is small rounded, reddish brown gland that secretes melatonin (targets melanophore cells of skin), serotonin (acts as vasoconstrictor) and adrenoglomerulotropin (stimulates adrenal cortex to secrete aldosterone).
- **Gonads** are mixed glands that secretes sex hormones. In males testis is present that secretes androgens mainly testosterone which stimulates spermatogenesis, while in females ovaries are present that secretes female sex hormones, i.e. oestrogen, progesterone, relaxin, human chorionic gonadotropin, etc.
- Apart from the above mentioned glands, **heart, kidney** and **Gastrointestinal Tract** (GIT) also secretes hormones for example, heart secretes atrial natriuretic factor that decreases blood pressure, kidney produces erythropoietin that promotes RBCs production, GI secretes enterogastrone and choleocystokinin that aid indigestion.
- **Local hormones** are secreted by cells which act locally on their neighbouring cells or on the same cells. These includes histamines (part of inflammatory process), prostaglandins (modify cellular response to other stimuli), pheromones (used for communication amongst organisms) cytokines, etc.
- The mechanism of hormone action is different for peptide, i.e. water soluble hormones and steroid, i.e. water insoluble hormones.
- **Peptide hormones** bind to surface receptors of target cells and a hormone receptor complex is formed that activate cAMP which in turn causes ATP to convert into AMP and thus accelerating the metabolic reaction in cell, e.g. insulin.
- **Steroid hormones** are lipid soluble thus, they can cross the cell membrane of target cells and bind to cytoplasmic receptors. The hormone receptor complex directly changes the gene expression by entering into the nucleus, e.g. cortisol.
- Hormones maintains homeostasis by integrated action and **feedback control**.

Chapter Practice

Multiple Choice Questions

1 Mark

1. Which of the following statement is incorrect?
   (a) Neural septum provides point to point rapid coordination among organs
   (b) Neural coordination is slow and long lived
   (c) Nerve fibre do not innervate all cells of the body
   (d) None of the above

2. Hormones provide coordination in
   (a) vertebrates
   (b) invertebrates
   (c) Both (a) and (b)
   (d) None of the above

3. The pituitary gland is located in a bony cavity called ...*A*... and is attached to ...*B*... by a stalk.
   Identify *A* and *B* to complete the given statement.
   (a) A- sella tursica; B-midbrain
   (b) A- sella tursica; B-forebrain
   (c) A- sella tursica; B-hypothalamus
   (d) A- sella tursica; B-pineal

4. In females, the ...*A*.. induces the ovulation of fully mature follicle called ...*B*... and maintain the ...*C*... formed from remnants of the Graafian follicle after ovulation. Select the correct combination in reference to the above given statement.
   (a) A-LH, B-Graafian follicle, C-pregnancy
   (b) A-FSH, B-Graafian follicle, C-corpus luteum
   (c) A-FSH, B-Graafian follicle, C-pregnancy
   (d) A-LH, B-Graafian follicle, C-corpus luteum

5. Select the incorrect option.
   (a) Thyroid gland is the largest endocrine gland in humans
   (b) Thyroid secretes T_3 and T_4
   (c) Thyroid gland is composed of follicle and stromal tissues
   (d) Thyroid consists of four lobes

6. Small amount of ...*A*... steroids are also secreted by adrenal ...*B*... which play a role in the growth of axia hair, pubic hair and facial hair during puberty.
   Choose the correct combination for *A* and *B*.
   (a) A-glucocorticoids; B-cortex
   (b) A-androgenic; B-cortex
   (c) A-mineralocorticoids; B-medulla
   (d) A-cortisol; B-medulla

7. The Leydig cells or ...*A*... cells, which are present in ...*B*... spaces produce a group of hormones called androgens and mainly ...*C*... .
   Choose the correct option for *A*, *B* and *C*.
   (a) A-interstitial cells, B-intratubular, C-cortisol
   (b) A-intrastitial cells, B-intertubular, C-testosterons
   (c) A-intrastitial cells, B-intratubular, C-LH
   (d) A-interstitial cells, B-intertubular, C-testosterone

8. The oestrogen is synthesised and secreted mainly by growing ...*A*... . After ovulation the ruptured follicle is converted to a structure called ...*B*..., which secretes ...*C*... .
   Choose the correct option for *A*, *B* and *C*.
   (a) A-corpus luteum, B-corpus callosum, C-progesterone
   (b) A-Graafian follicle, B-corpus luteum, C-progesterone
   (c) A-corpus callosum, B-corpus luteum, C-oestrogen
   (d) A-Graafian follicle, B-corpus luteum, C-oestrogen

Assertion-Reason Type Questions

(1 Mark)

■ **Direction** (Q. Nos. 9-17) *In each of the following questions, a statement of Assertion (A) is given followed by corresponding statement of Reason (R). Of the statements, mark the correct answer as*

(a) If both A and R are true and R is the correct explanation of A

(b) If both A and R are true, but R is not the correct explanation of A

(c) If A is true, but R is false

(d) If A is false, but R is true

9. Given below is the structure of an endocrine gland. Study the figure and comment upon the correctness of both Assertion and Reason.

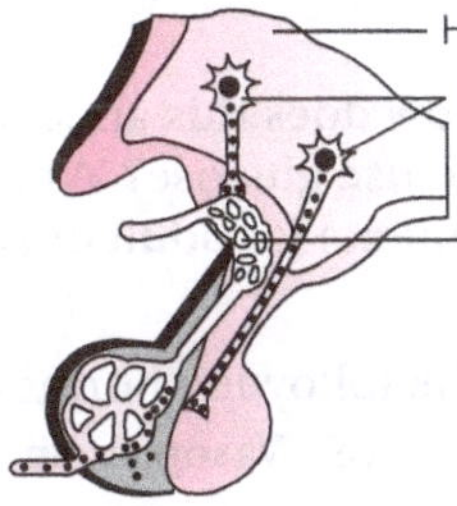

Assertion (A) This gland releases oxytocin and vasopressin which are synthesised by the hypothalamus.

Reason (R) This gland is located in the sella turcica.

10. **Assertion** (A) Hormone calcitonin has antagonistic effect to that of parathormone.

Reason (R) Calcitonin decreases blood Ca^{2+} level while parathormone increases blood Ca^{2+} level.

11. **Assertion** (A) ADH increases the volume of urine by increasing the reabsorption of water from the urine.

Reason (R) Failure of secretion of ADH causes diabetes insipidus.

12. **Assertion** (A) Mineralocorticoids regulate the balance of water and electrolytes in our body.

Reason (R) Cortisol is the main mineralocorticoid.

13. **Assertion** (A) Our body secretes adrenaline in intense cold.

Reason (R) Adrenaline raises metabolic rate.

14. **Assertion** (A) Graves's disease is due to the enlarged adrenal gland.

Reason (R) Graves's disease leads to protrusion of the eyeballs, increased basal metabolic rate and weight loss.

15. **Assertion** (A) Insulin and glucagon hormones are antagonistic to each other.

Reason (R) Insulin increases the blood glucose level whereas glucagon decreases the blood glucose level.

16. **Assertion** (A) Hormones are also secreted by some tissues which are not organised to form compact endocrine gland.

Reason (R) Heart, kidney, GIT and placenta also secrete hormones.

17. **Assertion** (A) Hormones interacting with membrane bound receptors normally do not enter the target cells.

Reason (R) They generate second messengers like cyclic AMP, IP_3 and Ca^{2+}.

Answers

1. (b)	2. (c)	3. (c)	4. (d)	5. (d)	6. (b)
7. (d)	8. (b)	9. (b)	10. (a)	11. (d)	12. (c)
13. (a)	14. (d)	15. (c)	16. (a)	17. (a)	

Very Short Answer Type Questions

(1 Mark)

18. How do hypo and hyperactivity of hormones cause disorders.

19. Name two categories of hormones released by hypothalamus.

20. Expand the term PRL, TSH, FSH and ACTH.

21. Give two hormones secreted by the follicular cells of thyroid.

22. What happens to the glycogen concentration in the liver cells, when the concentration of adrenaline in the bloodstream increases?

23. Why are catecholamines called emergency hormones?

24. Mention the pancreatic hormone that maintains glucose homeostasis.

25. 'Glucagon is hyperglycemic hormone'. Justify.

26. Mention the role of cholecystokinin hormone.

27. Why is growth factor essential in humans?

28. Placenta works as a temporary endocrine gland. Comment.

29. Write one function of gastrin.

30. Expand terms CCK and GIP.

31. List two types of hormone receptors found in an individual.

32. Give an example of antagonistic interaction of hormones.

Short Answer Type I Questions

(2 Marks)

33. What do you know about endocrine systems? Mention its components.

34. Name the disease in which there is a reduced renal absorption of water with a consequent elimination of a large volume of very dilute urine. What is its cause?

35. Differentiate between diabetes insipidus and diabetes mellitus.

36. What are the four major activities that oestrogen hormones regulate?

37. On what basis hormone receptors are classified?

38. Mention different categories of hormones on the basis of their chemical structures.

39. Write an explanatory note on the second messenger. How does it leads to metabolic effect?

Short Answer Type II Questions

(3 Marks)

40. Give the functions of any five hormones of pituitary.

41. Name the T_3 and T_4 components of thyroid hormones. Explain their specification.

42. Old people have weak immune system. State the reason behind this.

43. Give the role of testosterone in males. Mention its source also.

44. How does the formation of hormone receptor complex take place?

45. Diagrammatically represent the mechanism of steroid hormone action.

46. Why the functioning of steroid hormone does not require second messengers ?

Long Answer Type Questions

(5 Marks)

47. What do you know about effects of hormones produced on target tissues? How are such specific effects is produced?

48. Write differences between hormones and enzymes.

49. Describe mode of action of protein and polypeptide hormones.

50. Briefly describe the structure of the parathyroid gland and also list the effects of parathyroid hormone.

51. How do thymus and thymosin hormone play a vital functioning in the development of immunity? Explain.

52. What is diabetes? How does this affect an individual's ability to use glucose? What are some possible treatments for adult onset diabetes?

53. Write functions of the following hormones
    (i) Androgen (ii) Vasopressin

Case Based Questions

(4/5 Marks)

54. *Read the following passage and answer the questions that follows.*

Radha's father who is a diabetic patient does not avoid food items doctor has told him in diet. He also feels lazy to go for a walk. One day, his glucose level was checked by his doctor. The doctor advised him to take injections regularly, as he was not able to control his diabetes with diet and medication. He came home and while telling the things to Radha's mother, Radha (biology student) heard them and interrupted in between. She explained that doctor has given insulin injections to control his blood glucose level. This may be discontinued, if he will take precautions in his daily routine.

(i) Which endocrine gland and its part is involved in the secretion of insulin?

(ii) Which hormone stimulates the secretion of insulin from beta cells by paracrine effect?

(iii) Why doctor preferred him to take insulin injections and what is the role of insulin in controlling level of glucose in blood?

(iv) What effect does insulin show on glycogenesis?

(v) What precaution he should take to protect himself from such disorder?

55.

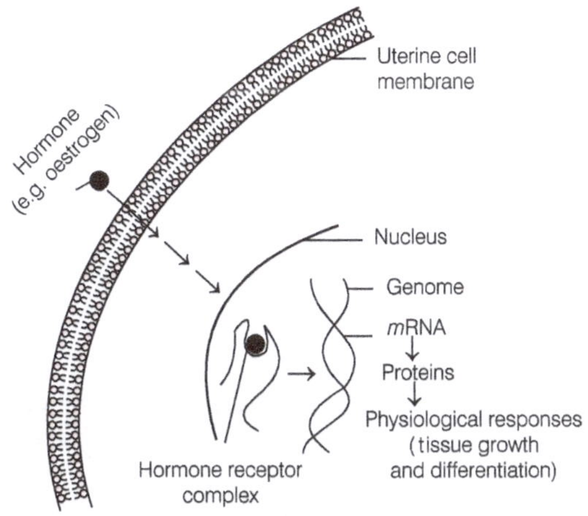

Mechanism of hormone action is depicted in the above diagram. Study the diagram and answer the questions that follows.

(i) Which type of hormone can be taken up by the cell membrane?

(ii) What do you understand by hormone receptor complex?

(iii) State the physiological response brought about by this kind of hormone actions.

(iv) Hormones interacting with membrane bound receptors play an indirect role in regulating cellular metabolism of the body. Justify.

56. The data below shows the levels of thyroid hormone production rate which can cause hypothyroidism and hyperthyroidism in the human.

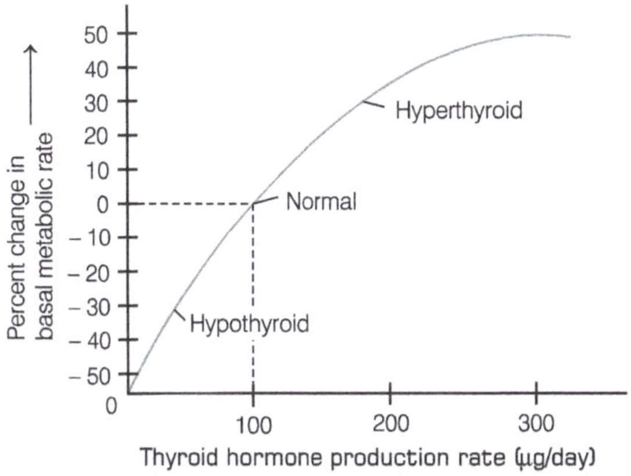

(i) With reference to the above graph what could be one of the reason behind hypothyroidism in the body?

(ii) What symptoms can be seen if hypothyroidism occurs during pregnancy?

(iii) Give two important function of thyroid hormone.

(iv) Thyroid gland produces another hormone called thyrocalcitonin, what is its role in our body?

SAMPLE QUESTION PAPERS (1-3)

SAMPLE QUESTION PAPER 1

A Highly Simulated Sample Question Paper for ISC Class XI

BIOLOGY (Unsolved)

Time : 3 hours **Max. Marks : 70**

GENERAL INSTRUCTIONS

1. This paper is divided into four sections-A, B, C and D. Answer all questions.
2. **Section-A** consists of one question having sub-parts of one mark/two marks each.
3. **Section-B** consists of seven questions of two marks each.
4. **Section-C** consists of seven questions of three marks each.
5. **Section-D** consists of three questions of five marks each.
6. Internal choices have been provided in one question each in Section-B, Section-C and Section-D.
7. The intended marks for questions or parts of questions are given in brackets[].

Section-A

(20 Marks)

1. Answer the following questions briefly and to the point.

(i) Give example of protistan having flagellar locomotion. • *Recall* [1]

(ii) Name the point where two sister chromatids are held together. • *Recall* [1]

(iii) In eukaryotes, where does TCA and ETS takes place? • *Recall* [1]

(iv) The lawn grass needs to be mowed frequently to prevent its overgrowth. Which tissue is responsible for its rapid growth? • *Understanding* [1]

(v) What does the symbols ⊕ and % indicate? • *Recall* [1]

(vi) Define vital capacity. • *Recall* [1]

(vii) Observe the diagram given below carefully and state one of its characteristic features. • *Analysis & Recall* [1]

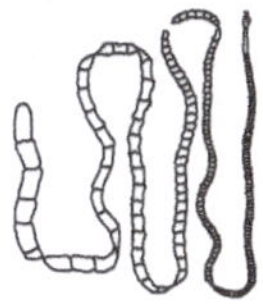

(viii) Observe the relation between first two words and then fill the fourth word.

Bolting: Gibberellins:: Stomata closure: .... • *Analysis* [1]

(ix) The pyrimidines of DNA are represented by • *Recall* [1]

(a) adenine and guanine

(b) uracil and guanine

(c) cytosine and adenine

(d) thymine and cytosine

(x) The hormone that initiate flowering and synchronism fruit set in pineapple. • *Recall* [1]

(a) Cytokinin (b) Ethylene

(c) ABA (d) Gibberellins

(xi) **Assertion** (A) PS-I and PS-II names are given on the basis of activity in the photosynthesis.

Reason (R) During non-cyclic photophosphorylation, PS-II works first and then PS-I. • *Analysis* [1]

(a) Both A and R are true and R is the correct explanation of A

(b) Both A and R are true, but R is not the correct explanation of A

(c) A is true, but R is false

(d) A is false, but R is true

(xii) **Assertion** (A) Prolonged hyperglycemia leads to complex disorder called diabetes mellitus.

Reason (R) Diabetes mellitus is associated with the loss of glucose through urine and formation of ketone bodies. • *Analysis* [1]

(a) Both A and R are true and R is the correct explanation of A

(b) Both A and R are true, but R is not the correct explanation of A

(c) A is true, but R is false

(d) A is false, but R is true

(xiii) Many bacteria contain a circular DNA 'X' other than the chromosomal or genomic DNA. Identify X and write its unique character. • *Recall* [1]

(xiv) What are the factors that results in decline of rate of photosynthesis under water stress? • *Recall* [1]

(xv) Answer the following questions.

(a) Expand the abbreviation DCT. • *Recall*

(b) Name the scientist who explained that cells are formed from the pre-existing cells. • *Recall* [2]

(xvi) Name a chronic respiratory disease in which alveolar walls are damaged. Also, mention the major cause of this disease. • *Analysis* [1]

(xvii) Observe the graph given below and answer how can you determine the heart beat rate of an individual from it.

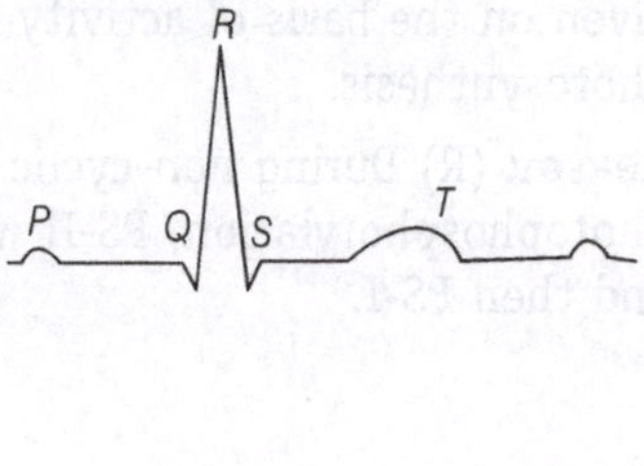

• *Analysis* [1]

(xviii) Give a reason for each of the following.

(a) The given organism is not included in the plant kingdom.

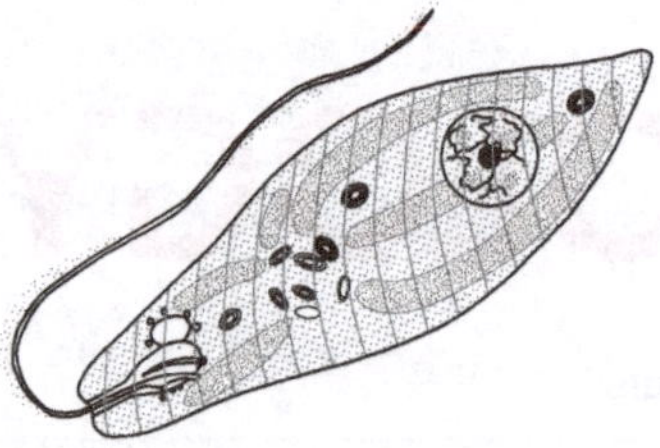

(b) The heart of fishes is commonly called 'venous heart'. • *Application* [2]

Section-B (14 Marks)

2. The slide given below was observed to visualise the stages of the cell division from an onion root tip. Observe it carefully and identify the stage observed in the image and state its characteristics. Will the chromosome number in the daughter cells in this case be the same or reduced by half? • *Understanding* [2]

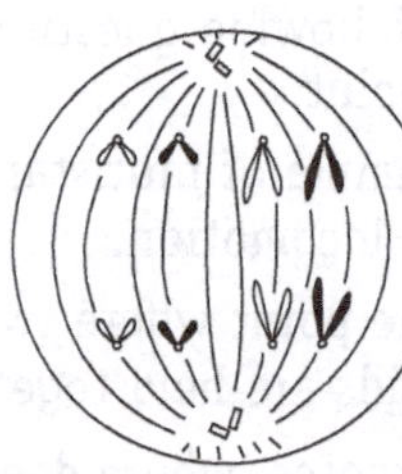

Or Given below are the features of stage A and stage B. Study them carefully and answer the question that follows.

Stage A	Stage B
Chromatin condenses into visible chromosomes, the nuclear envelope begins to breakdown and spindle fibres start forming.	Chromosomes align at the equatorial plane of the cell, spindle fibres attach to the centromeres, ensuring equal distribution of genetic material.

Identify stage A and stage B based on the phases of mitosis. Explain the importance of the events occurring in stage B for accurate cell division. • *Analysis & Understanding* [2]

UNSOLVED

3. Sunflower is not a flower. Explain.
• *Analysis* [2]

4. Read the passage given below carefully and answer the questions that follows.
During a visit to a pond in the monsoon season, Raj observed several frogs of different colours. He noticed that frogs near the green grass were green, while those near the water were yellow. The frogs seemed to blend into their surroundings, making it difficult to spot them. However, when Raj returned to the same pond in the winter season, he noticed fewer frogs. Although he could still spot a few near the water, they were much less active and stayed very still.
(i) How does camouflage help the frog in the given scenario? • *Evaluate*
(ii) Why were the frogs less active during the winter season? • *Understanding* [1+1]

5. What happens to an enzyme's activity if
(i) a non-competitive inhibitor is present in the same environment?
• *Understanding*
(ii) the non-competitive inhibitor is removed from the environment?
• *Understanding* [1+1]

6. Rahul went to visit his doctor. He suggested him an ECG test. While reading Rahul's ECG report the doctor observe an abnormally long delay between the *P*-wave and the *QRS* deflection. What does this suggest?
• *Application & Analysis* [2]

7. Where in the chloroplast is the NADP reductase enzyme located? State its role in the proton gradient development.
• *Evaluate* [2]

8. The diagram given below represents the changes in the number of chromosomes during several processes that occur in an animal cell.

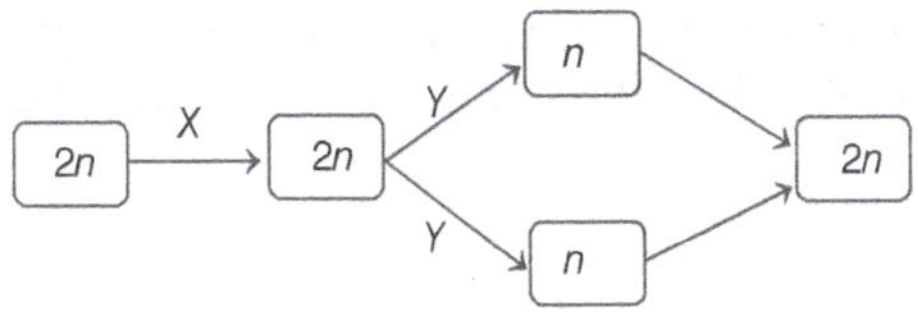

(i) Name the process of cell division occurring at *X* and *Y*. • *Recall*
(ii) State two differences in the behaviour of chromosomes between *X* and *Y*.
• *Recall* [1+1]

Section-C (21 Marks)

9. (i) What are ETS and RQ? • *Recall* [1½]
(ii) What is oxidative decarboxylation? What happens to pyruvate immediately after this reaction? • *Evaluate* [1½]

10. Explain the role of Na^+ in the generation of action potential. • *Understanding* [3]
Or Describe the significance of Ca^{2+} ions in the contraction of muscles. • *Understanding* [3]

11. (i) Draw a labelled diagram of the human respiratory system. • *Recall* [1½]
(ii) Draw a well-labelled diagram of a section of alveolus with pulmonary capillary. • *Recall* [1½]

12. The human body contains various types of connective tissues that play vital roles in supporting, protecting and facilitating movement of different organs and structures. Among these tissues, cartilage and bones are two crucial components that serve distinct but essential functions.
(i) List out the important features of hyaline cartilage. • *Recall* [1½]
(ii) What is yellow bone marrow? What is its function and location?
• *Recall & Understanding* [1½]

13. What is the function of hypothalamus and name the hormones secreted by it? • *Recall* [3]

14. A farmer noticed slower growth in his tomato plants during the dry season. To improve growth, he applied a plant hormone that promotes cell elongation and root development, along with another hormone that encourages stem elongation and flowering. After several weeks, the treated plants grew taller, produced more flowers, and set fruit earlier than the untreated plants.

UNSOLVED

(i) Name the two plant hormones used by the farmer in the given situation. • *Understanding* [1½]

(ii) Mention the functions of these hormones apart from the one given above. • *Understanding* [1½]

15. The term amphibolic is used to denote a biochemical pathway involving both catabolism and anabolism. [1×3]

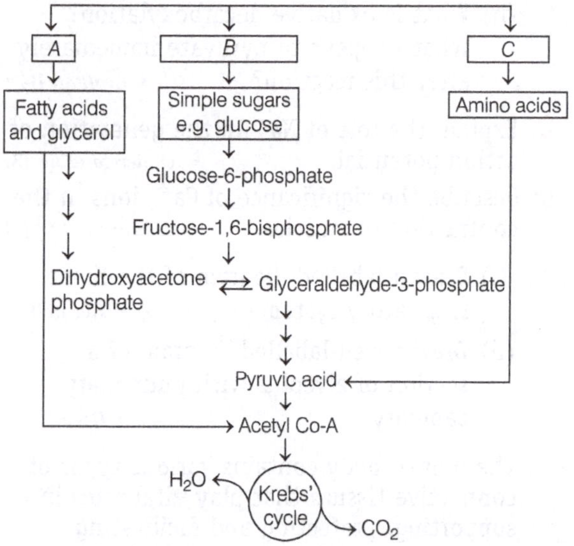

Answer the following questions.

(i) Identify *A*, *B* and *C*. • *Analysis*

(ii) State the importance of Krebs' cycle in the amphibolic pathway. • *Understanding*

(iii) Pyruvic acid the key product of glycolysis has many metabolic fates. What does it form under aerobic conditions? • *Evaluate*

Section-D (15 Marks)

16. Answer the following questions.

(i) Meiosis is advantageous than mitosis as it produces variations. So it plays important role in evolution. What are the stages during which chances of recombination of genes are increased during meiosis? Explain these events. • *Evaluate*

(ii) How meiosis leads to variation in the daughter cells genetically? • *Understanding* [2½+2½]

Or

(i) Explain why a pair of homologous chromosomes is genetically different, but a pair of sister chromatids is genetically identical before crossing over in meiosis? • *Application* [2½]

(ii) What is chiasmata? Mention its significance also. • *Recall* [1+1½]

17. The following figure shows the effect of light on the rate of photosynthesis. Based on the graph, answer the following questions.

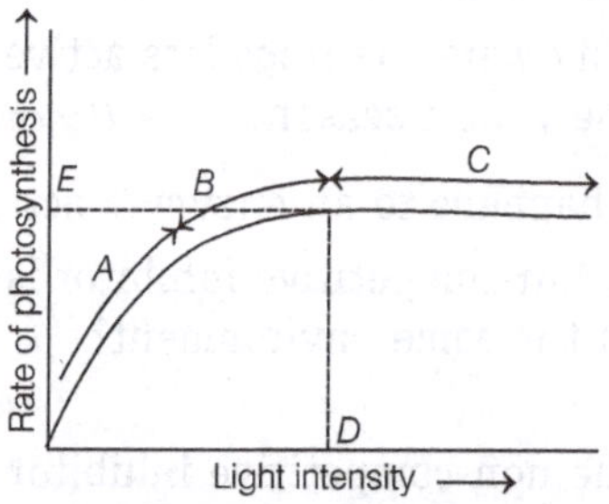

(i) At which point in the curve, light acts as a limiting factor? What are characteristics of light which affect the rate of photosynthesis? • *Analysis* [2½]

(ii) At which condition linear relationship between incident light and rate of CO_2-fixation is observed? What is the effect of green light in plants? • *Application* [2½]

18. The process of respiration in plants includes the utilisation of carbohydrates produced during photosynthesis to produce energy which inturn contributes to the growth of plants. Respiration in plants occurs in two phases, i.e. light reactions and dark reactions.

The first step of respiration is glycolysis in which glucose is oxidised to pyruvic acid.

UNSOLVED

After this, the product of pyruvic acid enters the Krebs' cycle which provides the reducing power to generate many more ATP molecules in the next stage of aerobic respiration, i.e. the electron transport chain. [1×5]

(i) Glucose-6-phosphate → Fructose-6-phosphate

Which enzyme is used in the above reaction? • *Evaluate*

(ii) How many molecules of pyruvic acid are formed in glycolysis? • *Recall*

(iii) What is the name of the 4C compound formed in Krebs' cycle? • *Understanding*

(iv) Which is the final electron acceptor in the electron transport system? • *Understanding + Recall*

(v) In which part of mitochondria does ATP synthesis occur? • *Understanding*

Answers

1. (ix) (d) (x) (b) (xi) (d) (xii) (a)

SAMPLE QUESTION PAPER 2

A Highly Simulated Sample Question Paper for ISC Class XI

BIOLOGY (Unsolved)

Time : 3 hours **Max. Marks : 70**

GENERAL INSTRUCTIONS

1. This paper is divided into four sections-A, B, C and D. Answer all questions.
2. **Section-A** consists of one question having sub-parts of one mark/two marks each.
3. **Section-B** consists of seven questions of two marks each.
4. **Section-C** consists of seven questions of three marks each.
5. **Section-D** consists of three questions of five marks each.
6. Internal choices have been provided in one question each in Section-B, Section-C and Section-D.
7. The intended marks for questions or parts of questions are given in brackets[].

UNSOLVED

Section-A

(20 Marks)

1. Answer the following questions briefly and to the point.

(i) Name any two cellular structures absent in kingdom-Animalia and present in kingdom-Protista. • *Understanding* [1]

(ii) Explain how denaturing an enzyme may affect its efficiency as a catalyst? • *Understanding* [1]

(iii) What are the end products of alcoholic fermentation? • *Recall* [1]

(iv) Identify *A* in the following reaction.

Triglycerides $\xrightarrow{A}$ Fatty acids + Glycerol • *Analysis* [1]

(v) Which type of movement is exhibited by macrophage and leucocytes in blood? • *Recall* [1]

(vi) Why are veins provided with valves along their length? • *Analysis* [1]

(vii) In the diagram given below, X represents one of the formed elements in the blood. Identify *X*. • *Recall [1]*

X

(viii) Observe the relation between the first two words and then fill in the fourth word.

Auxin : IAA:: Gibberellic acid : .... • *Analysis [1]*

(ix) All eukaryotic unicellular organisms belong to • *Recall [1]*

(a) Monera (b) Protista
(c) Fungi (d) Animalia

(x) In epigynous flowers, ovary is situated below the • *Recall [1]*

(a) thalamus (b) androecium
(c) receptacle (d) None of these

(xi) **Assertion** (A) Arrival of an impulse at the axon terminal, stimulates the release of neurotransmitters in the synaptic cleft.

Reason (R) These neurotransmitters are responsible for the opening of ion channels. • *Analysis* [1]

(a) Both A and R are true and R is the correct explanation of A
(b) Both A and R are true, but R is not the correct explanation of A
(c) A is true, but R is false
(d) A is false, but R is true

(xii) **Assertion** (A) The S-phase is the stage in the cell cycle where DNA replication occurs.

Reason (R) The purpose of the S-phase is to ensure that each daughter cell receives an exact copy of the genome during mitosis. • *Analysis* [1]

(a) Both A and R are true and R is the correct explanation of A
(b) Both A and R are true, but R is not the correct explanation of A
(c) A is true, but R is false
(d) A is false, but R is true

(xiii) What waste product is primarily excreted by humans through urine? • *Recall* [1]

(xiv) In a patient with a damaged liver, the production of certain proteins is affected. Based on your understanding of cellular structure, which organelle is most likely compromised in this case. • *Understanding & Analysis* [1]

(xv) Answer the following questions. [2]

(a) Expand the abbreviation 2,4 D. • *Recall*

(b) Identify the scientist whose extensive research on plant tissues and vascular structures greatly advanced our understanding of plant anatomy. • *Recall*

(xvi) Give reason for each of the following. • *Analysis* [2]

(a) Urochordates are called as tunicates.
(b) Pneumatic bones are present in birds.

(xvii) What distinguishes pteridophytes from bryophytes despite both being non-flowering plants? • *Understanding* [2]

(xviii) The organism given in the diagram below, migrates to the freshwater at a specific period of their lifespan. Identify the organism. • *Analysis* [1]

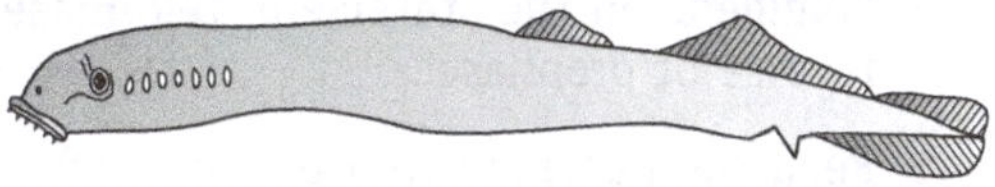

Section-B (14 Marks)

2. During the cell cycle, the cell passes through different phases, each with its own specific function. Observe the cell cycle diagram given below and describe the function of the phases marked as *A* and *B*. • *Analysis & Understanding*

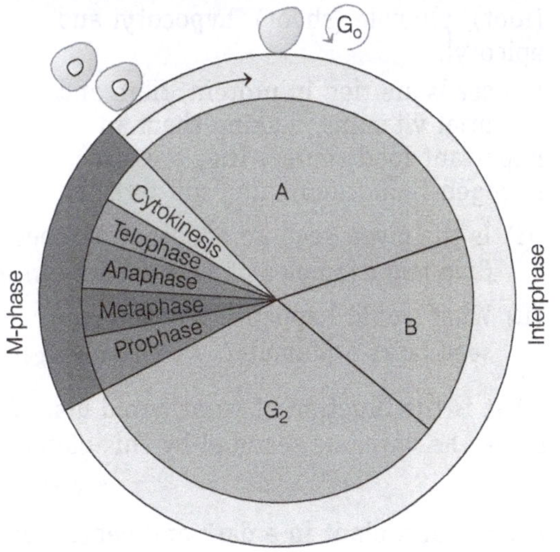

[2]

Or

(ii) Given below are the features of structure A and structure B. Study them carefully and answer the question that follows.

Structures	Features
Stage A	Network of tubules with ribosomes attached, involved in protein synthesis and transport. Often found near the nucleus.
Stage B	Smooth network of tubules without ribosomes, associated with lipid synthesis, detoxification, and calcium storage.

Identify structure A and structure B. one example of a function for each structure. • *Understanding* [2]

3. Comment on the statement 'telophase is reverse of prophase'. • *Understanding* [2]

4. Read the passage given below carefully and answer the questions that follows.

A pea seed (*Pisum sativum*) is the reproductive unit of the pea plant, which belongs to the Leguminosae family. It consists of several key parts, the seed coat (testa), which protects the seed; the cotyledons, which store nutrients like starch and protein for the growing embryo; and the embryo, which includes the radicle (root), plumule (shoot), hypocotyl and epicotyl.

Pea seeds are rich in protein, fibre and essential vitamins, making them an important food source. They are also nitrogen-fixing, enriching soil fertility.

(i) Is the given seed an endospermic seed? Give two examples of such seed. • *Recall*

(ii) What would happen if a developing seed lacks a plumule? • *Understanding* [1+1]

5. What is the function of parathyroid gland? Name the hormone secreted by this gland. • *Recall* [2]

6. Ashok put a plant in a dark and ventilated place for two days. After two days, he observe that the colour of a leaf kept in the dark frequently becomes yellow or pale green. Why is it so? Also mention the pigment is more stable in this conditions and why? • *Application* [2]

UNSOLVED

7. Name the components of the formed elements in the blood and mention one major function of each of them. • *Understanding* [2]

8. Answer the following questions based upon the given figure.

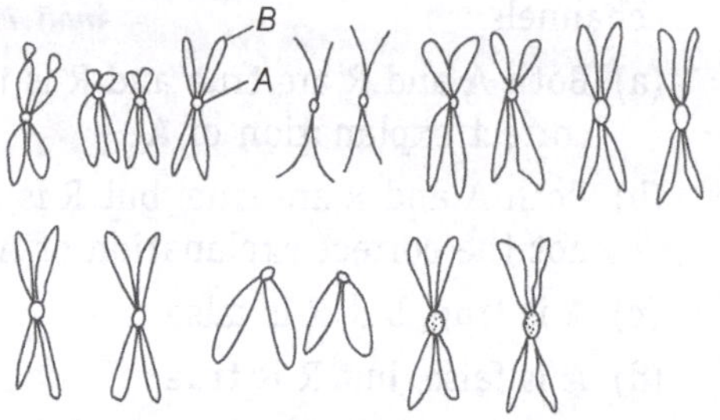

(i) What type of division is this? Whether meiotic or/and mitotic and which stage? • *Evaluate* [1]

(ii) What are *A* and *B*? • *Analysis* [1]

Section-C (21 Marks)

9. List out three disorders of circulatory system. • *Recall* [3]

10. Describe the important steps in muscle contraction. • *Understanding* [3]

Or

Mechanism of hormone action is depicted in the below diagram. Study the diagram and answer the questions that follows [1×3]

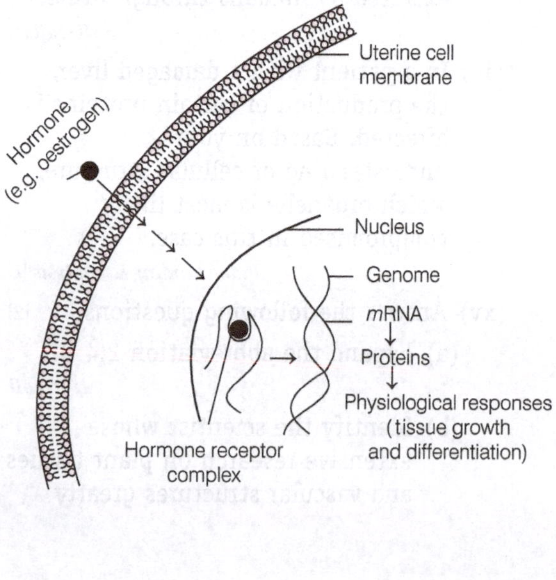

(i) Which type of hormone can be taken up the cell membrane? • *Understanding*

(ii) What do you understand by hormone receptor complex? • *Application*

(iii) State the physiological response brought about by this kind of hormone actions. • *Analysis*

11. Draw a well-labelled diagram of human kidney. • *Application* [3]

12. (i) Name the sheath covering the plumule in maize grain. • *Recall* [1½]

(ii) Which structures form gynoecium? How is placenta related to gynoecium? • *Understanding* [1½]

13. During an intense physical activity, such as sprinting, Rahul feels a burning sensation in his muscles after a short period of running. His muscles begin to fatigue quickly, and he notices that his breathing rate increases.

(i) Identify and define the type of respiration taking place in his muscle cells. • *Evaluate* [1½]

(ii) How many ATP molecules are produced during this process? • *Recall* [1½]

14. Study the two animals (fishes), A and B in the pictures given below and answer the following questions.

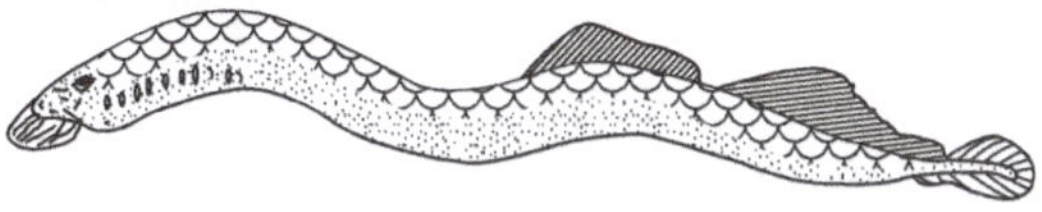

(A)

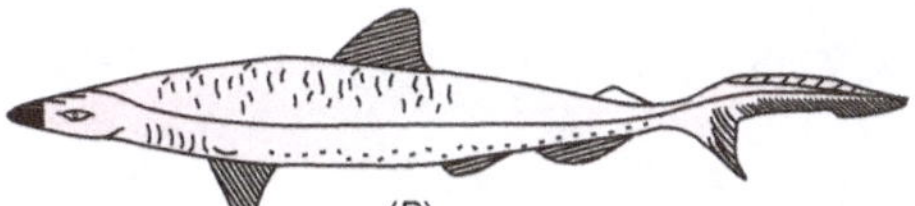

(B)

(i) Identify the class, which each of them belongs to. • *Recall* [1½]

(ii) Write two differences between the two. • *Analysis* [1½]

15. The vertebral column (spine) is a bony structure that runs from the skull to the pelvis, made up of 33 vertebrae. The vertebral column supports the body, protects the spinal cord, allows movement, and serves as an attachment point for muscles. It also helps maintain body posture and balance. Answer the following questions. [1×3]

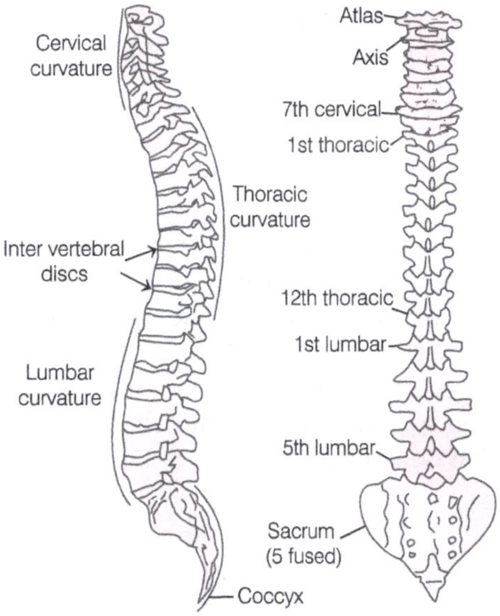

(i) What are the functions of vertebral column? • *Understanding*

(ii) Based on the figure, can you draw the vertebral formula for humans? • *Analysis*

(iii) In humans, which group of vertebrae are considered as vestigial? • *Recall*

Section-D (15 Marks)

16. Discuss the types of enzyme cofactors that are required for the efficient activity of enzymes. • *Understanding* [5]

17. Answer the following questions.

(i) Where does Krebs' cycle take place? How many CO_2 molecules are released during one Krebs' cycle? • *Recall* [2½]

(ii) Name any two enzymes involved in Krebs' cycle. Mention any one importance of Krebs' cycle. • *Understanding* [2½]

Or

(i) What is the use of carbide and what chemical reaction occurs when carbide powder is placed with raw mangoes? • *Application* [2½]

(ii) Which gas is released by carbide powder that helps in the ripening process of fruits? Suggest a safer method for ripening fruits naturally. • *Analysis* [2½]

18. Rama conducted an experiment on two types of gymnosperm species, species A and species B.

She removed both species from their original habitats and placed them in a nitrogen-deficient environment. After a period of one month, she made the following observations.

Species A developed specialised roots near the soil surface and flourished in the new environment.

Species B exhibited no such adaptations and showed signs of stress and struggles to survive.

Based on the given information, answer the following questions.

(i) Why was species A able to survive in the nitrogen-deficient environment? • *Evaluate* [1½]

(ii) State one characteristic of gymnosperms that distinguishes them from other plant groups. • *Recall* [1½]

(iii) What is the term for these specialised roots? Also, give an example of a gymnosperm that possesses such roots. • *Understanding* [2]

Answers

1. (ix) (b) (x) (a) (xi) (a) (xii) (b)

SAMPLE QUESTION PAPER 3

A Highly Simulated Sample Question Paper for ISC Class XI

BIOLOGY (Unsolved)

UNSOLVED

Time : 3 hours **Max. Marks : 70**

GENERAL INSTRUCTIONS

1. This paper is divided into four sections-A, B ,C and D. Answer all questions.
2. **Section-A** consists of one question having sub-parts of one mark/two marks each.
3. **Section-B** consists of seven questions of two marks each.
4. **Section-C** consists of seven questions of three marks each.
5. **Section -D** consists of three questions of five marks each.
6. Internal choices have been provided in one question each in Section-B, Section-C and Section-D.
7. The intended marks for questions or parts of questions are given in brackets[].

Section-A

(20 Marks)

1. Answer the following questions in briefly and to the point.

(i) What is a taxon? • *Recall* [1]

(ii) Name the organism which is extensively used in biochemical and genetic work. • *Recall* [1]

(iii) Identify the name and phylum of the given organism. • *Analysis* [1]

(iv) How is diversity in living world related to taxonomy? • *Understanding* [1]

(v) What is emphysema? • *Recall* [1]

(vi) Define G_0-phase of cell division. • *Recall* [1]

(vii) Observe the relation between first two words and then fill the fourth word.

Thylakoid : Chloroplast :: Crista : .... • *Analysis* [1]

(viii) Define Rh-factor. • *Recall* [1]

(ix) The image given below represents the pteridophyte. Give its scientific name and name the kind of spores formed in them. • *Analysis* [1]

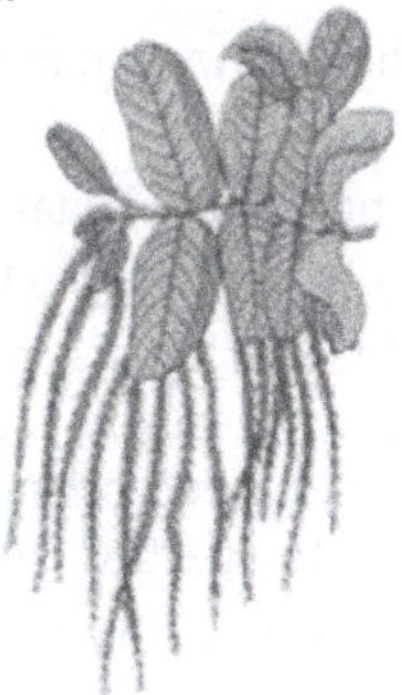

(x) **Assertion** (A) Zinc is an apoenzyme for carboxypeptidase.

Reason (R) A complete catalytically active enzyme together with its group is called apoenzyme. • *Analysis* [1]

(a) Both A and R are true and R is the correct explanation of A
(b) Both A and R are true, but R is not the correct explanation of A
(c) A is true, but R is false
(d) A is false, but R is true

(xi) **Assertion** (A) Diakinesis is the final stage of prophase-I.

Reason (R) Terminalisation of chiasmata occurs in diakinesis. • *Analysis* [1]

(a) Both A and R are true and R is the correct explanation of A
(b) Both A and R are true, but R is not the correct explanation of A
(c) A is true, but R is false
(d) A is false, but R is true

(xii) Which of the following is the parasitic fungi on mustard? • *Recall* [1]

(a) *Rhizopus* (b) *Penicillium*
(c) *Albugo* (d) *Mucor*

(xiii) What happens to the rate of photosynthesis if a plant is exposed to temperature higher than its optimal range? • *Analysis* [1]

(xiv) Give a term for the arrangement of veins and veinlets in the leaf lamina. • *Recall* [1]

(xv) Answer the following questions. • *Recall* [2]

(a) Expand the abbreviation RuBP
(b) Name the scientist who described the first action spectrum of photosynthesis by using *Cladophora* and prism for splitting light into spectral components.

(xvi) Give reason for each of the following. • *Analysis* [2]

(a) The decrease in the synthesis of the given gland leads to the cretinism.

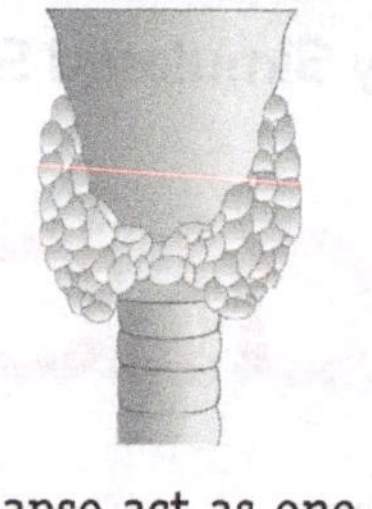

(b) Synapse act as one way valve.

(xvii) Name the scientist that is known for discovering the path of carbon during the process of photosynthesis. • *Recall* [1]

(xviii) Which compound is meant for donating hydrogen to carbohydrate in Calvin cycle? • *Recall* [2]

Section-B (14 Marks)

2. (i) A cell is the basic structural and functional unit of life, capable of carrying out all the essential processes for an organism's growth, reproduction, and maintenance. Cells can be unicellular, like bacteria, or multicellular. Observe the image given below and describe the function of organelles marked as A and B. • *Analysis* [2]

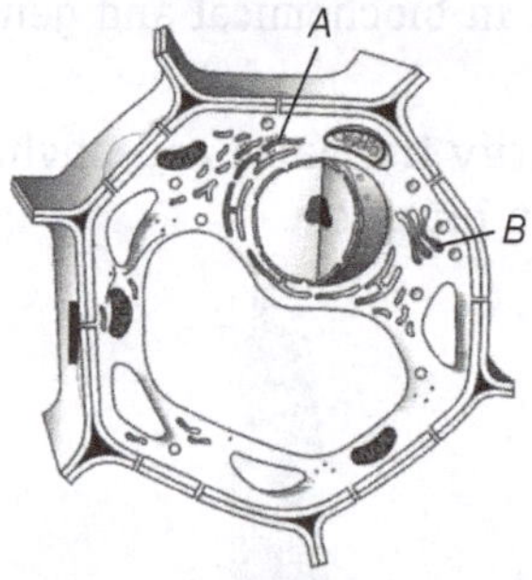

Or (ii) Given below are the features of cell A and cell B. Study them carefully and answer the question that follows.

Cell A	Cell B
Presence of naked genetic material and small circular DNA outside the genomic DNA.	Presence of extensive compartmentalisation of cytoplasm.

Identify the type of cell A and cell B. Cite one example of each of cell A and cell B. • *Understanding* [2]

3. Given below is a floral formula of a family. Based on your understanding identify the type of ovary present in it and the type of symmetry possesed by the plant. • *Analysis & Understanding* [2]

$\oplus$ ⚥ $K_{(5)}\ \overset{\frown}{C_{(5)}\ A_{(5)}}\ \underline{G}_{(2)}$

4. The anatomy of a frog is well-adapted for both aquatic and terrestrial life. Frogs have a streamlined body with powerful hindlimbs for jumping and swimming and webbed feet for better propulsion in water. They breathe through their lungs and skin, with the skin also serving to keep them hydrated.

(i) Mention the location and function of the cloaca in the given organism. • *Recall*

(ii) What type of reproductive system do these organisms have, and how is it different from other animals? • *Understanding* [1+1]

5. Discuss the role of meiotic cell division in sexually reproducing animals. • *Understanding* [2]

6. A student of class XI appeared for his practicle exam. Where he observe the slides and based on his observation he has to differentiate between the meristematic and non-meristematic cells. Write down some characteristic feature of meristematic cells which he should look for to correctly identify the cell. • *Analysis & Understanding* [2]

7. Write a short note on CAD. • *Recall* [2]

8. Observe the figure given below and answer the questions that follows. [1+1]

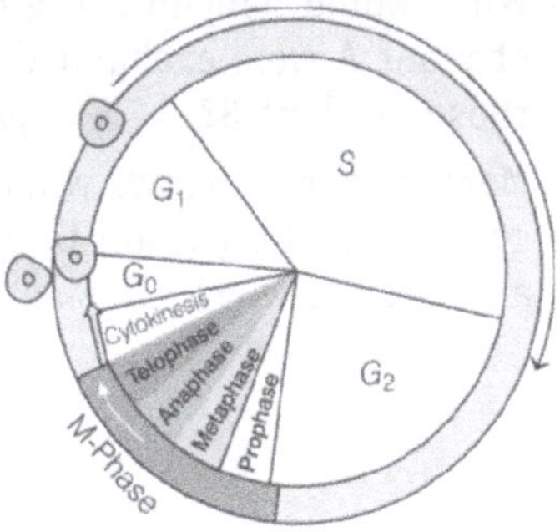

(i) A cell has entered the G_0-phase of cell cycle. How will its growth and multiplication affected in this phase? • *Analysis*

(ii) How would the daughter cell at the end of complete mitosis and cytokinesis compare with their parents when they entered G_1-phase of the cell cycle? • *Understanding*

Section-C (21 Marks)

9. Describe the different kinds of placentation found in ovary of flowering plants. • *Recall* [3]

10. How can we say that artificial pacemaker is a life saving instrument? • *Application* [3]

Or

Refer to below diagram and answer the following questions. [1×3]

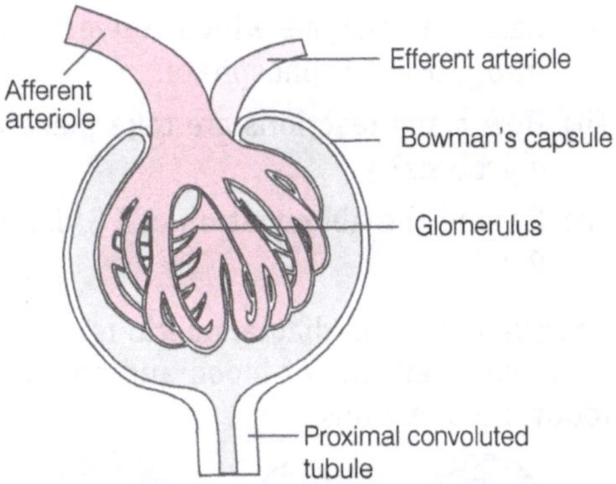

(i) What is the role of the structure shown above? • *Analysis*

(ii) Give one point of difference between afferent arteriole and efferent arteriole. • *Understanding*

(iii) Indicate the function performed by glomerulus as a part of nephron. • *Understanding*

11. Illustrate Electron Transport Chain (ETC) that occurs in inner mitochondrial membrane. • *Understanding* [3]

12. Draw a well labelled diagram of structure of neuron. • *Recall* [3]

UNSOLVED

Or

Draw a well-labelled diagram showing axon terminal and synapse. • *Recall* [3]

13. Laura is hiking up a steep mountain trail with a group of friends. The hike is physically demanding due to the incline, but she maintains a steady pace, taking breaks when needed. She is prepared with enough water and snacks to stay hydrated and fueled.

(i) What type of respiration is taking place in Laura's muscles as she hikes up the steep mountain trail? • *Application* [1½]

(ii) Where does this type of respiration primarily occur in Laura's muscle cells? • *Recall* [1½]

14. A student was reading the pathways of glycolysis. In this process, glucose undergoes partial oxidation to form two molecules of pyruvic acid. His sister talked about the process of glycolysis and asked some questions. [1×3]

(i) Name the enzyme which convert glucose into glucose-6-phosphate. • *Recall*

(ii) How many reactions are take place in glycolysis? • *Recall*

(iii) Expand the abbreviation of PGAL and BPGA. • *Recall*

15. Observe the given diagrammetic representation of formed elements of blood and answer the following questions. [3]

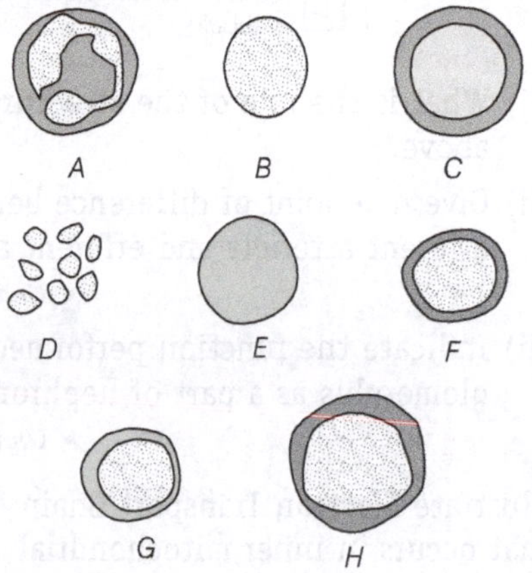

(i) Name the category of blood cells to which *A* and *H* belong. • *Understanding*

(ii) How does *A* appears under the microscope? • *Recall*

(iii) Mention the shape and function of *H*. • *Recall*

(iv) Among the given formed elements of blood which of the following constitute 2-3% of blood volume? • *Recall*

(v) What is the approximate number of erythrocytes, leucocytes and thrombocytes in human blood? • *Recall*

Section-D (15 Marks)

16. Answer the following questions.

(i) Name the excretory organs found in Aschelminthes and leeches. • *Recall*

(ii) Explain the structure of renal tubules. • *Understanding* [2½+2½]

Or (i) Name the arterioles through which blood enters and leaves the glomerulus. • *Recall*

(ii) Explain the process of ultrafiltration occur in a nephron. • *Analysis* [2½+2½]

17. Two groups (A and B) of bean plants of similar size and same leaf area were placed in identical conditions. Group A was exposed to light of wavelength of 400-450 nm and group B to light of wavelength of 500-550nm.

(i) Compare the photosynthetic rate of the two groups giving reason. • *Analysis* [2]

(ii) What would happen if the conditions of plant A were exchanged with those of plant B? • *Application* [1½]

(iii) Mention the structure where only cyclic phosphorylation takes place and explain why? • *Understanding* [1½]

UNSOLVED

18. Akshita who is a biology tutor was teaching photosystems to the students at her place. While explaining the topic light reaction said that, "Two or the three products of light reaction, ATP and NADPH are used to drive the reactions in the biosynthetic/dark phase."

It has been verified by the fact that immediately after light becomes unavailable, the biosynthetic phase continues for sometime and then stops; if light becomes available again, the process continues.

Her brother, student of class XI was also listening the same and was remembering that he had listened the same from his biology teacher also. He interrupted her sister and asked her to re-explain the whole process for the better understanding.

(i) What are the products of light reaction? Can we say that calling the biosynthetic phase, dark reaction is a misnomer? Justify. • *Evaluate* [2½]

(ii) Name the first stable product of photosynthesis. Why is proton gradient is important in photosynthesis? • *Understanding* [2½]

Answers

1. (x) (d) (xi) (a) (xii) (c)